MW01089914

THE ORIGINS OF GRAMMAR

Language in the Light of Evolution II

Language in the Light of Evolution

This work consists of two closely linked but self-contained volumes in which James Hurford explores the biological evolution of language and communication and considers what this reveals about language and the language faculty. In the first book the author looks at the evolutionary origins of meaning ending at the point where humanity's distant ancestors were about to acquire modern language. In the second he considers how humans first began to communicate propositions to each other and how the grammars developed that enable communication and underlie all languages.

Volume I
The Origins of Meaning

Volume II
The Origins of Grammar

THE ORIGINS OF GRAMMAR

James R. Hurford

OXFORD

UNIVERSITY PRESS

OXFORD
UNIVERSITY PRESS

Great Clarendon Street, Oxford OX2 6DP

Oxford University Press is a department of the University of Oxford.
It furthers the University's objective of excellence in research, scholarship,
and education by publishing worldwide in

Oxford New York

Auckland Cape Town Dar es Salaam Hong Kong Karachi
Kuala Lumpur Madrid Melbourne Mexico City Nairobi
New Delhi Shanghai Taipei Toronto

With offices in

Argentina Austria Brazil Chile Czech Republic France Greece
Guatemala Hungary Italy Japan Poland Portugal Singapore
South Korea Switzerland Thailand Turkey Ukraine Vietnam

Oxford is a registered trade mark of Oxford University Press
in the UK and in certain other countries

Published in the United States
by Oxford University Press Inc., New York

British Library Cataloguing in Publication Data
Data available

Library of Congress Cataloging in Publication Data
Data available

Typeset by SPI Publisher Services, Pondicherry, India
Printed in Great Britain
on acid-free paper by
CPI Antony Rowe, Chippenham, Wiltshire

ISBN 978–0–19–920787–9

1 3 5 7 9 10 8 6 4 2

Contents

Detailed Contents

Part Two   What Evolved

Part Three   What Happened

Preface

This book takes up the thread of a previous book, *The Origins of Meaning*. That was the easy bit. That book traced the basic precursors in animal behaviour of the kinds of meanings conveyed in human language. The first half of that book explored animals' private conceptual representations of the world around them; I argued for a form of prelinguistic representation that can be called **proto-propositions**. The second half of the book explored the beginnings of communication among animals. Animal communication starts with them merely **doing things to each other** dyadically, for example threatening and submitting. In some animal behaviour we also see the evolutionary seeds of triadically **referring** to other things, in joint attention to objects in the world. In the light of evolutionary theory, I also explored the social and cognitive conditions that were necessary to get a public signalling system up and running. Thus, at the point where this book begins, some of the deepest foundations of modern human language have been laid down.

The earlier book left off at a stage where our non-human animal ancestors were on the brink of a capacity for fully modern human language. Stepping over that brink took our species into a dramatic cascade of consequences that gave us our present extraordinarily developed abilities. We modern humans have a capacity for learning many thousands of arbitrary connections between forms and meanings (i.e. words and constructions); for expressing a virtually unlimited range of propositions about the real world; for conjuring up abstract, imaginary, and fictitious worlds in language; and for conveying many layers of subtle nuance and degrees of irony about what we say. All of these feats are performed and interpreted at breakneck speed, and there are thousands of different roughly equivalent ways of achieving this (i.e. different languages) which any normal human child can acquire in little over half a dozen years. Simplifying massively for this preface, the core of the starting discussion here will be about what must have been the earliest stages of humans communicating propositions to each other using **learned arbitrary symbols**, and beginning to put these symbols into **structured sequences**. These are the **origins of grammar**.

The later evolution of grammar into the fantastically convoluted structures seen in modern languages follows on from this core. In tracking the possible sequence of these rapid and enormous evolutionary developments as discussed here, it will not be necessary to know the earlier book to take up the thread of the story in this book. The essential background will be sketched wherever necessary.

It was convenient to organize the present book in three parts. The whole book does tell a cohesive story, but each part is nevertheless to some degree self-contained. Depending on the depth and breadth of your interests in language evolution, it could be sufficient to read just one part.

Part I, *Pre-Grammar*, explores one possible and one necessary basis for human linguistic syntax. Chapter 1 surveys syntactically structured, but semantically non-compositional, communicative behaviour in non-human animals, such as birds and whales, suggesting even at this point some methodological conclusions about how to approach human syntax. Chapter 2 discusses the likely routes by which shared vocabularies of learned symbols could have evolved, and the effects on human thought.

Part II, *What Evolved*, gets down to real grammar. Following the now accepted wisdom that 'evolution of language' is an ambiguous expression, meaning either the biological evolution of the language faculty or the cultural evolution of particular languages, two chapters in this part flesh out respectively what seems to be the nature of the human language faculty (Chapter 4) and the nature of human languages (Chapter 5). Before this, in Chapter 3, a theoretical background is developed, informed by evolutionary considerations, trying to chart a reasonable path through the jungle of controversy that has surrounded syntactic theorizing over the last half-century. This part contains much material that will be familiar to linguists, even though they may not agree with my take on it. So Part II, I believe, can serve a useful tutorial function for non-linguists interested in language evolution (many of whom need to know more about the details of language).

Finally, Part III, *What Happened*, tells a story of how it is likely that the human language faculty and human languages evolved from simple beginnings, such as those surveyed in Part I, to their present complex state. The emphases developed in Part II provide a springboard for this story, but it should be possible to follow the story without reading that previous part. If you feel that some assumptions in the story of Part III need bolstering, you should find the necessary bolsters in Part II.

In all three parts, linguists can obviously skip the more 'tutorial' passages throughout, except where they feel impelled to disagree. But I hope they will withhold disagreement until they have seen the whole broad picture.

Years ago I conceived of a relatively short book which would discuss the whole sweep of language structure, from phonetics to pragmatics, in the light of evolution, with each chapter dealing with one 'component': pragmatics, semantics, syntax, phonology, and phonetics. I still teach a very condensed course like that, on the origins and evolution of language. The book project 'just growed'. The time has passed for simple potted versions. I managed to say something about the evolution of semantics and pragmatics in *The Origins of Meaning*, and this book, *The Origins of Grammar* takes a hefty stab at the evolution of syntax. That leaves the origins of speech—phonetics and phonology. I have some ideas about that, but it's clear that a third book would take too long for patient publishers to commit to now. Besides, (1) there is already a lot of solid and interesting material out there,[1] and (2) the field is probably maturing to the point where original contributions belong in journal articles rather than big books. So don't hold your breath for a trilogy. I'm also aware that I may have given morphology short shrift in this book; see Carstairs-McCarthy (2010) for some stimulating ideas about that.

The content and style of this book are born of a marriage of conviction and doubt. I am convinced of the continuity and gradualness of evolutionary change, and have been able to see these properties where discreteness and abruptness were assumed before. On the empirical facts needed to sustain a detailed story of continuity and gradualness, my insecurity in the disciplines involved has compelled me always to interrogate these disciplines for backup for any factual generalizations I make. This is a thousandfold easier than in the past, because of the instant availability of online primary sources. There can now be far fewer excuses for not knowing about some relevant counterexample or counterargument to one's own ideas. So this book, like the last, brings together a broad range of other people's work. I have quoted many authors verbatim, because I see no reason to paraphrase them and perhaps traduce them. Only a tiny fraction of the primary research described is mine, but the broad synthesis is mine. I hope you like the broad synthesis.

While you read, remember this, of course: we never know it all, whatever it is. Human knowledge is vast in its range and impressive in its detail and accuracy. Modern knowledge has pushed into regions undreamt of before. But all knowledge expressed in language is still idealization and simplification. Science proceeds by exploring the limits of idealizations accepted for the convenience of an era. The language of the science of language is especially reflexive, and evolves, like language. What seemed yesterday to be The Truth turns out to have been a simplification useful for seeing beyond it. There is progress, with

---

[1] For example Lieberman (1984); de Boer (2001); Oudeyer (2006); Lieberman (2007); MacNeilage (2008); Fitch (2010).

thesis, antithesis and synthesis. As we start to label and talk about what we glimpse beyond today's simplifications and idealizations, we move onward to the next level of idealizations and simplifications. The evolution of language and the evolution of knowledge run in the same direction. We know more and know it more accurately, but, as public knowledge is couched in language, we will never know 'it' all or know 'it' exactly right.

Acknowledgements

I have wobbled on the shoulders of many giants. Naming and not naming are both invidious, but I risk mentioning these among the living: Bernd Heine, Bill Croft, Chuck Fillmore, Derek Bickerton, Dick Hudson, Haj Ross, Joan Bybee, Mike Tomasello, Peter Culicover, Pieter Seuren, Ray Jackendoff, Talmy Givón, Terry Deacon. They in their turn have built upon, or reacted against, the thinking of older giants. More generally, I am appreciative of the hard work of linguists of all persuasions, and of the biologists and psychologists, of all sub-branches, who made this subject. Geoff Sampson, Maggie Tallerman, and Bernard Comrie read the whole book and made recommendations which I was (mostly) glad to follow. They saved me from many inaccuracies and confusions. I am grateful for their impressive dedication.

And, lastly, all of the following have also been of substantial help in one way or another in building this book, and I thank them heartily: Adele Abrahamsen, Giorgos Argyropoulos, Kate Arnold, the ghost of Liz Bates, Christina Behme, Erin Brown, Andrew Carstairs-McCarthy, Chris Collins, Karen Corrigan, Sue N. Davis, Dan Dediu, Jan Terje Faarlund, Nicolas Fay, Julia Fischer, Simon Fisher, Tecumseh Fitch, Bruno Galantucci, Tim Gentner, David Gil, Nik Gisborne, Patricia Greenfield, Susan Goldin-Meadow, Tao Gong, Stefan Hoefler, David Houston, Melissa Hughes, Eve, Rosie, and Sue Hurford, Simon Kirby, Karola Kreitmair, Albertine Leitão, Stefan Leitner, Anthony Leonardo, Gary Marcus, Anna Martowicz, Miriam Meyerhoff, Lisa Mikesell, Katie Overy, Katie Pollard, Ljiljana Progovac, Geoff Pullum, Frank Quinn, Andrew Ranicki, Katharina Riebel, Graham Ritchie, Constance Scharff, Tom Schoenemann, John Schumann, Peter Slater, Andrew Smith, Kenny Smith, Mark Steedman, Eörs Szathmáry, Omri Tal, Mónica Tamariz, Carrie Theisen, Dietmar Todt, Hartmut Traunmüller, Graeme Trousdale, Robert Truswell, Neal Wallace, Stephanie White, Jelle Zuidema. Blame me, not them, for the flaws.

PART ONE: PRE-GRAMMAR

Introduction to Part I: Twin Evolutionary Platforms—Animal Song and Human Symbols

Before complex expressions with symbolic meaning could get off the ground, there had to be some facility for producing the complex expressions themselves, even if these were not yet semantically interpreted. Birds sing in combinations of notes, but the individual notes don't mean anything. A very complex series of notes, such as a nightingale's, only conveys a message of sexual attractiveness or a threat to rival male birds. So birdsong has syntax, but no compositional semantics. It is the same with complex whale songs. Despite this major difference from human language, we can learn some good lessons from closer study of birds' and whales' songs. They show a control of phrasal structure, often quite complex. The songs also suggest that quantitative constraints on the length and phrasal complexity of songs cannot be naturally separated from their structure. This foreshadows a conclusion about how the human language faculty evolved as a composite of permanent mental structure and inherent limits on its use in real-time performance.

Also before complex expressions with symbolic meaning could get off the ground, there had to be some facility for learning and using simple symbols, arbitrary pairings of form and meaning. I argue, contrary to views often expressed, for some continuity between ape cries and human vocalized words. There was a transition from innate involuntary vocalizations to learned voluntary ones. This was a biological development to greater behavioural plasticity in response to a changing environment. The biological change in the make-up of individuals was accompanied by the development in social groups of shared conventions relating signals to their meanings. One pathway by which this growth of shared social norms happened capitalized on sound symbolism and synaesthesia. Later, initially iconic form-meaning mappings became stylized to arbitrary conventions by processes which it is possible to investigate with modern experiments. With the growth of a learned lexicon, the meanings denoted by the developed symbols were sharpened, and previously unthinkable thoughts became accessible.

Thus, the two chapters in this part survey the situation before any semblance of modern grammar was present, exploring the possibility of non-human antecedents for control of complex syntax and of unitary symbols, proto-words. These two chapters deal respectively with pre-human semantically uninterpreted syntax and early human pre-syntactic use of symbols.

CHAPTER I

Animal Syntax? Implications for Language as Behaviour

The chapter heading poses a question, and I will answer it mostly negatively. Some wild communicative behaviour is reasonably described as having syntactic organization. But only some wild animal syntax provides a possible evolutionary basis for complex human syntax, and then only by analogy rather than homology. That is, we can find some hierarchical phrase-like syntactic organization in species distantly related to humans (e.g. birds), but not in our closer relatives (e.g. apes). The chapter is not, however, a wild goose chase. It serves (I hope) a positive end by clarifying the object of our search. Non-linguists find linguists' discourse about syntax quite impenetrable, and the chapter tries to explain some theoretical points that cannot be ignored when considering any evolutionary story of the origins of human syntax. Using a survey of animal syntactic abilities as a vehicle, it will introduce and discuss some basic analytic tools applicable to both human and non-human capacities. These include such topics as semantic compositionality (as opposed to mere combinatorial structure), the competence/performance distinction, the hierarchical structuring of behaviour and the relation of overt behaviour to neural mechanisms. A special tool originating in linguistics, Formal Language Theory (FLT), will come in for particular scrutiny. This body of theory is one of the most disciplined and mathematical areas of syntactic theorizing. FLT is on firmer formal ground than descriptive syntactic theories, giving an accumulation of solid results which will stand the test of time. These are formal, not empirical, results, in effect mathematical proofs. Some may question the empirical applicability of Formal Language Theory to human language. It does give us a precise yardstick by which to compare the syntax of animal songs and human language. It will become clear to what extent any syntactic ability at all can be attributed to songbirds and some whales.

The first section below will, after a survey of candidates among animals, reinforce the point that animals in the wild indeed do not have any significant semantically interpreted syntax. The second and third sections will examine how much, or how little, the non-semantic syntactic abilities of animals can tell us. I will illustrate with facts about the songs of birds and whales,[1] fascinating in themselves. To make the proper comparison between these songs and human syntax, it is necessary to introduce some key concepts underlying the analysis of syntax in humans. Discussing these key concepts in a context away from the common presuppositions of linguistics allows us to reconsider their appropriateness to human language, and to suggest some re-orientation of them. So some of this chapter is theoretical and terminological ground-clearing, spiced up with interesting data from animals.

Syntax, at its most basic, is putting things together. Of course, 'putting things together' is a metaphor, but a significantly insightful one. Syntactic spoken language is not *literally* a putting together in the sense in which bricks are put together to make a wall, or fruit and sugar are put together to make jam. Speech is serial behaviour, but serial behaviours differ in the complexity of control of putting things together. Breathing is basic and can be described as putting certain routines of muscular contraction together in a prolonged sequence. Walking is a bit more complex, and the way strides are put together involves more volition and sensory feedback from the surroundings. All animals put actions together in serial behaviour. Indeed that is a defining characteristic of animals, who seem to have some 'anima',[2] dictating the order of their movements. In all animals many action sequences are instinctive, somehow programmed into the genome, without any shaping by the environment in the individual's lifetime. Quite a lot of animals also learn motor sequences, used for practical purposes of survival. With most sequences of actions carried out by animals, the environment provides constant feedback about the state reached and prompts the animal for its next step. For example a gorilla picks, packages, and eats nettles in a somewhat complex way (Byrne and Byrne 1991; Byrne 1995). All through this systematic behaviour the animal is getting feedback in

---

[1] Birdsong and whale songs are typical enough to make my general points, and space prohibits discussion of gibbons and other singing species.

[2] The etymology of *animal* reflects a narrowing of Aristotle's concept of anima or ψ υ χ η, which he saw as the essence of all living things, including plants. Aristotle's *anima* is often translated as *soul*, but he did not regard it as a non-physical substance.

the form of the current state of the nettles, whether they are (1) still growing undisturbed in the earth, (2) with stalk held tightly in the gorilla's right hand, (3) stripped of their leaves, held in the left hand, or (4) leaves folded into a package and ready to pop into the mouth. There are millions of such examples, wherever an animal is dealing systematically with its environment. Much rarer are learned routines of serial behaviour not scaffolded throughout the sequence by feedback from the environment. During the singing of a nightingale's song, there are no external landmarks guiding it to its next note. All the landmarks are within, held in the animal's memorized plan of the whole complex routine. Most, and maybe all, such complex 'unguided' routines are communicative, giving information to conspecifics. Although all complex serial behaviour has a kind of 'syntax' or 'grammar', I will restrict the term 'syntax' in the rest of this work to complex, unguided communicative routines. No doubt, a specialized facility for syntax in this narrow sense evolved out of a facility for serial behaviour more generally.

A fancier term for 'putting things together' is **combinatorial**. Music has combinatorial syntax, because it involves putting notes together in strictly defined ways. Different musical traditions are roughly like different languages, in the sense that they define different rules for combining their elementary constituents—notes for music, and words for language. Dances, the tango, the waltz, the Scottish country dance Strip-the-Willow, each have their own syntax: ways of putting the elementary moves together into an approved sequence. The syntax of such human activities tends to be normative, hence the use of 'approved' here. But behaviour can be syntactically organized without the influence of any norms made explicit in the social group, as we will see in this chapter when discussing the structured songs of birds and whales. (This does not, of course, mean that syntactic organization cannot be influenced by the behaviour of others, through learning.)

Peter Marler (1998) distinguishes between **phonological syntax** and **lexical syntax**. In its broad sense of putting things together, syntax applies to phonology. Phonology puts phonemes together to make structured syllables. Each language has its own phonological syntax, or sound pattern. The units put together in phonology don't mean anything. The English /p/ phoneme, on its own, carries no meaning. Nor does any other phoneme. And it follows that the syllables put together out of phonemes can't mean anything that is any function of the meanings of the phonemes, because they have no meanings. *Cat* does not mean what it means because of any meanings inherent in its three phonemes /k/, /a/, and /t/. Phonological syntax is the systematic putting of meaningless things together into larger units. Birdsong, whale song and gibbon song all exhibit phonological syntax, and I will discuss two of these in the third section below. It is possible that some phonological syntactic ability developed in our species independent of meaning, which is why I devote space to these complex non-human songs.

Lexical syntax, or lexicoding, as Marler calls it, is the kind of putting things together where the elements mean something, and the whole assembly means something which is a reflection of the meanings of the parts. This is **compositionality**. Complex meanings are expressed by putting together smaller meaningful units. As Marler summarizes it, 'Natural lexicoding appears to be a purely human phenomenon. The only animals that do anything remotely similar have been tutored by humans' (Marler 1998, p. 11). In order to be clear that this is indeed the case, the first section of this chapter will look at some challenges to Marler's assertion that have surfaced since he wrote. With some tiny reservations, Marler's assertion stands. (Marler mentioned animals tutored by humans. We will come to them in a later chapter.)

I will weave into the second and third sections of this chapter an introduction to Formal Language Theory. On its own, such an introduction might seem both dry and unmotivated. But the Formal Language Theory approach to repertoires of complex meaningless songs[3] turns out to give a useful way of classifying the overt characteristics of song repertoires. The approach also draws out some differences and similarities between these animal songs and human languages that push us to question some of our common assumptions about human language.

1.1 Wild animals have no semantically compositional syntax

This section describes some non-starters as candidates for evolutionary analogues or homologues of human semantically compositional syntax. In brief, no close analogues or homologues are to be found in wild animal communication systems. But surveying cases that show, or might appear to show, some compositionality can clarify what exactly we are looking for.

1.1.1 Bees and ants evolve simple innate compositional systems

Insects are only very distantly related to humans. But even some insects put elements together in a semantically composed signal. Parts of the signal are

---

[3] The songs are not wholly meaningless, of course, or the animals would not sing them. I mean that the songs do not convey referential meanings by combining the meanings of their elementary parts. One way of putting this is to say that the songs have pragmatic, but not semantic, significance.

combined to express a message which is a function of the meanings of the parts. These communication systems are (1) extremely simple, comprising only two meaningful elements, (2) extremely limited in the domain to which they apply—location of food or a good hive site, and (3) innate. These simple systems are adaptive, enhancing the survival chances of the animals. How far can nature go in engineering a genetically fixed semantically compositional system? The insect systems seem to be the limit. There are no more complex innate systems in nature. Without **learning**, a semantically compositional system cannot evolve beyond the narrowest limits we see in a few insects. So we have an important conclusion here already. Highly complex semantically compositional systems need to be learned. Now I'll briefly survey what we know about the unlearned insect systems. In their way, they are impressive, but impressive in a totally different way from the wonders of human language, which has evidently taken a different evolutionary course.

The honeybee, *Apis mellifera*, provides a well known example of animal communication. Surprisingly, for an animal genetically so far distant from us, bees use a simple, but arguably semantically compositional, system.[4] They signal the location of food relative to the hive by a vector with two components, a distance component and a direction component. Distance is signalled in analogue fashion by the duration of the 'waggle' dance—the longer the dance, the farther away is the food. And direction is signalled by the angle to the vertical of the waggle dance: this corresponds to the angle relative to the sun's position in which the food lies. Thus a fairly precise location is described in terms of two components and each component is signalled by a separate aspect of the overall signal. The receiving bees may possibly be said in some sense to 'compose' the location from its elements, direction and distance.

The question arises, however, whether this description is our own anthropomorphic account of their behaviour. The bee observing the dance no doubt registers somehow the two components of the signal, and responds systematically to both, by flying a certain distance in a certain direction. And then, of course, it gets to roughly the right place. But it does not follow that the bee has in its brain any representation of the place it is going to before it actually gets there. If I give you precise latitude and longitude specifications of a place, you can consult a map and know what place I am talking about.

---

[4] The summary of bee communication given here is basic and omits many fascinating details of the variety between species, and the scope of their responses to different environmental conditions. For a highly informative and readable account, see Lindauer (1961). Other significant works are von Frisch (1923a, 1923b, 1967, 1974); Riley et al. (2005).

Or, more familiarly, if I say 'You know, the pub two hundred yards south of here', you will identify what I mean, and we can talk about it, without either of us necessarily flying off there. There is some evidence that bees can do this as well.[5] Gould (1986) showed that bees could find their way directly to a feeder station when released at a novel site away from the hive, and construed this as evidence that the bees were computing the new route by reference to a cognitive map. The term 'cognitive map' requires some unpacking. For Gould, it was consistent with 'landmark map', and his bees could be taken to be finding their way by reference to familiar landmarks. It is accepted that bees use landmarks in their navigation. On the basis of more carefully controlled experiments, Dyer (1991) argues, however, that the bees acquire 'route-based memories' but not cognitive maps. Dyer released his experimental bees in a site, a quarry, from where they could not see landmarks visible from the hive. On release from the quarry, they tended to fly off on a compass bearing close to that on which they would have flown from the hive, that is in a wrong direction. Dyer concludes that his 'results suggest that honey bees do not have the "mental maps" posited by Gould (1986), or any other mechanism to compute novel short cuts between familiar sites that are not in view of each other' (p. 245). Nevertheless, it is clear that signalling bees do base their performances on a computation of several factors. 'Fully experienced bees orient their dances on cloudy days by drawing upon an accurate memory of the sun's entire course relative to familiar features of the terrain' (Dyer and Dickinson 1994, p. 4471). More recently, and using hi-tech radar equipment, Menzel et al. (2005) were able to track the entire flights of bees. They concluded:

Several operations must be at the disposal of the animal: (i) associations of headings and distance measures toward the hive with a large number of landmarks all around the hive that are recognized from different directions; (ii) shift of motivation (flight to hive or feeder); (iii) reference to the outbound vector components of the route from hive to feeder; and (iv) addition and subtraction of the heading and distance components for at least two conditions, those that would lead directly back to the hive and those that lead from the hive to the feeder. It is difficult to imagine that these operations can be done without reference to vectors that relate locations to each other and, thus, make up a map.
(Menzel et al. 2005, p. 3045)

---

[5] Reznikova (2007) cites Dyer (1991): 'In the experiments of Dyer (1991), bees left the hive when the returning scout indicated that the food was beside a lake. However they did not leave the hive when they were informed that food was near the middle of the lake. Thus, honey bees appear to interpret the meaning of the dance—possibly by identifying the potential location of food, and then decide whether it is worth making the journey'. Unfortunately, this passage is not actually to be found in the cited article by Dyer, so the lake story must have come from somewhere else.

All these navigational experiments involve observing the flights taken by bees, and are not directly about what is signalled in the honeybee waggle dance. Thus the compositional nature of the dance signal itself is not directly investigated. But the evidence for quite rich navigational abilities makes it seem unlikely that the response to the dance by bees already familiar with the landscape is entirely robot-like, following two instructions simultaneously, flying for a certain distance in a certain direction. On the other hand, inexperienced bees, who have not become familiar with the local topology, can do nothing but follow the two components of the message conveyed by the waggle dance, insofar as the landscape allows them. On the evidence, the processing of the signal by experienced bees seems likely to be somewhat analogous to what happens when a human understands a phrase such as *two hundred yards south-west of here*, even when a straight-line walk to that location is not possible, because of the street layout. The human, if he already knows the locality, can make a mental journey by putting the two elements of meaning together, and perhaps never take the actual physical journey. The bee is almost as clever (in this very limited domain), but not quite. Von Frisch (1967) reviews experiments in which bees had to go around an obstacle such as a large ridge to get to their food, thus making a two-leg trip with an angle in it. On returning, their dance signalled the real compass direction of the food (which was not a direction of either leg of their flight) and the actual distance flown, around the obstacle. This shows impressive ability to integrate two flown angles, and the distances flown at those angles, into a single angle. But the location signalled was technically false, being further away from the hive (in a straight line) than the actual food source. One can see this as a simple evolutionary solution to the problem of signalling location over a restricted communication channel. The bee receiving the signal goes in the direction signalled, as best she can, for the distance signalled. Signalling a complex two-leg journey would be more of a challenge.[6] This is a case where the bees' private computational capacity, allowing them to do complex path integration, outstrips what they can communicate publicly. The given message is a simple synopsis of their more complex experience.

In later experiments, it was found that bees could be tricked into believing that they had flown longer distances than they actually had. Srinivasan et al. (2000) trained bees to fly, on either their outward or their inward flight, through a tube painted with many closely-packed colours. After flying through

---

[6] Even humans asking for directions in a strange town find it hard to remember oral instructions with more than about three legs.

such a tube, bees signalled distances much longer than the actual distances flown. Following this up, De Marco and Menzel (2005) made bees take a 90° detour through a painted tube to get to their food. Once these bees had arrived at the food source they took a diagonal shortcut back to the hive, presumably relying on landmarks. The experimenters watched the signalling behaviour of the returning bees. They found that the bees signalled the direction of the shortcut route to the food, figured out from their return journey, but the perceived long distance flown through the tube on their outward journey. On this evidence, bees can separate out two factors of their experience, the length (sometimes misperceived) of their outward flight, and the direction of their return flight. And they code these separate aspects of their experience into the waggle dance. This is compositional coding, but of course in an extremely limited domain, and is not learned behaviour.

Bees have an accurate sense of time and anticipate the movement of the sun across the sky as the day proceeds (Lindauer 1961; Dyer and Dickinson 1996; Dickinson and Dyer 1996). Bees who have received a message in the morning about the direction of food can be kept in the hive for a few hours, and when they are released later in the afternoon they compensate for the movement of the sun during the time they were cooped up. For example, if the waggle dance at noon signals due south, and the bees are released immediately, they fly off directly towards the sun;[7] but if after receiving that same signal at noon they are not released until 3.00 p.m., they don't fly directly towards the sun, but about 45° to the left of it. Thus the code is interpreted with some contextual 'pragmatic' input, namely the time elapsed since reception of the message. This is a lesson that simply having a code is not enough for practical communication. The information conveyed in a code is supplemented, even in such a simple system as honeybee dancing, by contextual information.[8] (Fascinatingly, Lindauer also reports experiments in which bees who had been accustomed to the movement of the sun in one global hemisphere (i.e. left-to-right in the northern and right-to-left in the southern) were shifted overnight to the other hemisphere. The originally transported bees did not adapt, but their descendants, after 43 days, did make the correct new adjustment, interpreting the direction aspect of the dance in the new appropriate way. See Lindauer (1961, pp. 116–26) and Kalmus (1956).

[7] in the northern hemisphere.
[8] Humans who leave a message on a door saying 'Back in an hour' seem oblivious of the importance to the receiver of such contextual information about when the message was written.

Some species of ants, socially organized like honeybees, also show evidence of semantically compositional signalling (Reznikova and Ryabko 1986; Reznikova 2007). It seems that ants communicate by contact with each other with their antennae. In controlled experiments, scout ants reported the location of food to teams of forager ants, who reliably followed the directions given by the scout through a series of T-junctions in a maze. There was individual variation: not all ants were very good at transmitting such information. In the case of the effective ant signallers, the evidence for compositional signalling is indirect. That is, the research has not 'decoded' the signals given by the ants into their component meaningful parts, as von Frisch did with the honeybees. Rather, the experimenters carefully controlled the **amount** of information, measured in bits as defined by Information Theory (Shannon and Weaver 1963). Each turn taken at a T-junction in the maze counted as one bit of information. In complex cases, it was possible for the food to be located at a point six turns into the maze from the entrance. Not surprisingly, a correlation was found between the complexity of the message in bits (i.e. number of turns in the maze), and the time taken by ants to convey it.[9] More significantly, where there were regular patterns in the message to be conveyed, such as a succession of turns in the same direction (e.g. Right-Right-Right-Right-Right, or Left-Left-Left-Left-Left), the time taken to convey such messages was shorter than in the case of less regularly structured messages, such as Right-Left-Left-Right-Left. This, as the authors point out, is evidence of data compression.

One way in which data compression can be achieved is with some kind of compositional coding, where one element of the code systematically denotes the way in which the data is to be compressed. For example, we can imagine (although we don't know exactly) that a message such as Right-Right-Right-Right-Right was compressed by the signalling ant into the equivalent of 'All-Right' or 'Only-Right'. A less regularly structured message could not be compressed in this way, assuming obvious intuitions about what is 'regular structuring'. We must remember that the natural environment of ants in the wild is unlikely to present them with routes so neatly defined as a series of T-junctions in a lab maze. But the correlation between regularity in the message, measured in information bits, and duration of the signalling episode needs some explanation. The data raise the possibility that these ants have a semantically compositional (albeit very simple) code.

---

[9] Three species of ant showed such behaviour in these experiments, *Formica pratensis, F. sanguinea* and *F. rufa*. (There are over 11,000 species of ant.)

However, the data also support another interpretation, which is that the ant signals are entirely holophrastic. That is, the ants may just have the equivalent of a lexicon, a lookup table in which each separate mapping from a meaning to a form is stored, with no general rules for constructing the signals from meaningful subparts. (This presupposes that the number of conveyable messages is finite, and presumably small.) The observed correlation between short signals and repetitively structured messages (e.g. Right-Right-Right-Right-Right) may come about through some tendency to associate such meanings with short signals, holophrastically. Information Theory tells us that more efficient communication is achieved if the most frequent messages are coded as the shortest signals. This fact is illustrated by several well-known phenomena, including Zipf's Law inversely correlating word frequency with word length, and Morse Code, in which the commonest English letter, E, is signalled by the shortest possible dot-dash sequence, namely a single dot. The messages to be conveyed by the ants in these experiments did not vary significantly in frequency, so Information Theoretic efficiency of coding is probably not a driving force here. But there might be something salient about such repetitively structured meanings to ant brains which makes them assign them shorter signals. The fact of signal compression in itself does not necessarily imply compositionality in the code. Morse Code, for example, is not semantically compositional in its mappings from dots and dashes to letters: the letters of the alphabet are not treated as bundles of features, with each feature signalled by something in the code. Incidentally, humans find it easier to remember sequences of digits, such as telephone numbers, if they contain repetitions; 666 1000 is much easier to remember than 657 3925.

These several species of bees and ants may have converged in their evolution on a common principle for efficient information transmission, applying it in very limited ways, and in very narrow domains. These insect encoding and decoding systems are probably wholly innate. (This is not to deny that bees, at least, can learn to apply the messages of the signals appropriately in the context of their local landscape.) We are interested in syntactic systems with a much more significant element of learning and with much wider expressive range.

1.1.2 Combining territorial and sexual messages

Birds' songs typically express either a courtship or a territorial message—'Welcome, ladies', or 'Keep away, gents'. Can these two messages be combined into a single composite song? If so, could this ability to compose songs be a remote beginning of more complex semantically compositional syntax?

Chaffinches, unlike ants and bees, learn their songs to some extent. The characteristic chaffinch song is quite complex, as we will see later. It can be divided into two main parts, an initial 'trill' and a final 'flourish'. The whole signal serves a dual function, acting both as a territorial challenge to other males and a way of attracting females. Using experimentally manipulated playback calls in the field, Leitão and Riebel (2003, p. 164) found that 'Males showed the closest approach to songs with a relatively short flourish. . . . These were the songs found less attractive by females tested previously (Riebel and Slater 1998) with the same stimuli'. In other words, if the flourish part of the song is short, males will tend to come a lot closer to other males than if the song has a longer flourish. It would be an oversimplification to say that the trill is a territorial challenge to rival males while the flourish functions to attract females, but undoubtedly the two parts of the song do tend somewhat to emphasize these respective functions.

Dual function calls that serve both a territorial and a courtship function are common in nature. But it is not so common that different features of the call can be teased apart and analysed as serving the different functions. Another example is the coqui frog, named after the two parts of its simple call, a low note followed by a higher note (the reverse of a cuckoo call, and higher pitched overall). Here again, it seems that a separate meaning can be assigned to each separate part of the call, each serving a different function. 'Acoustic playback experiments with calling males in their natural habitat and two-choice orientation experiments with females indicate that males and females of the neotropical tree frog *Eleutherodactylus coqui* respond to different notes in the two-note call of the male' (Narins and Capranica 1976, p. 378). 'In the Puerto Rican "Co Qui" treefrog, *Eleutherodactylus coqui*, the duration of the first note "Co", is critical in eliciting male territorial behavior, while the spectral content of the second note, "Qui", is crucial in eliciting positive phonotaxic responses from females' (Feng et al. 1990). The low 'Co' part of the call tends to serve a territorial function, while the higher 'Qui' part of the call tends to serve a courtship function.

Are these chaffinch and frog calls candidates for semantic compositionality, with the meaning of the whole call being formed by a combination of the meanings of its parts? No. The two meanings, territorial challenge and courtship invitation, are incompatible, and directed at different receivers. In the coqui frog, in fact, the male and female brains are tuned differently to be sensitive to the different parts of the call (Narins and Capranica 1976), so it is possible that neither male nor female actually hears the whole call, let alone puts its parts together. The parts of the chaffinch call cannot be combined in the way that distance and direction, for example, can be combined to yield location. The closest to a compositional interpretation would be that the whole call conveys a conjunction of the meanings of the components.

1.1.3 *Combinatorial, but not compositional, monkey and bird calls*

Monkeys are more closely related to us than the insects, birds, and frogs that we have considered so far. Can we see any signs of semantically composed messages in monkeys? Klaus Zuberbühler is a leading investigator of this question. My conclusion from his work, surveyed below, is that some monkey communication is at the margins of semantic compositionality, expressing nothing even as complex as *hit Bill*. Likewise, there is no firm evidence of semantic compositionality in bird calls.

Arnold and Zuberbühler (2006) describe a call system used by putty-nosed monkeys in which different call elements are strung together. These monkeys only have two elementary (i.e. unitary) signals in their repertoire, labelled 'pyow' and 'hack'. They also have the ability to combine the elementary 'pyow' and 'hack' signals into longer sequences. This combinatorial power gives ways of expressing more than two meanings. So 'pyow' roughly means LEOPARD, 'hack' roughly means EAGLE, and 'pyow-hack' seems to mean LET'S GO, and so on. Note that the meaning LET'S GO is not a function, in any natural sense, of LEOPARD and EAGLE. This, then, is a (very small) **combinatorial** system, but it is not obviously semantically **compositional**, because in the case of the 'pyow-hack' the meaning of the whole is not a function of the meanings of the parts.

Arnold and Zuberbühler write, very carefully, 'Our findings indicate that non-human primates can combine calls into higher-order sequences that have a particular meaning'. There are two ways to interpret the data. One interpretation is that the internally represented meaning of 'pyow-hack' in the receiving monkey's mind has nothing to do with eagles or leopards, and that it invokes instead some separate notion of imminent travel. In this case the 'particular meaning' that the researchers mention is not a function of the meanings of the basic calls combined, and so the 'pyow-hack' call of the putty-nosed monkeys is not semantically compositional. This would be a case of animals overcoming the limits of their repertoire of individual calls by combining them, but not in any way reflecting the composition of the meanings expressed.

The other interpretation of the data, perhaps more plausible, is that 'pyow-hack' conjures up in the receiver's mind both concepts, EAGLE and LEOPARD, and the monkey takes appropriate action. In this case, the call is, in the simplest sense, compositional, expressing a **conjunction** of the meanings of its parts, that is EAGLE & LEOPARD. In a later paper (Arnold and Zuberbühler 2008), somewhat extended data is described, with responses to longer series of pyows and hacks. Series combining pyows and hacks again elicited travel. Here the authors use the title 'Meaningful call combinations in a non-human primate'. This is again careful: the call combinations are meaningful, but whether they are interpreted compositionally remains an open question.[10]

A similar point can be made about another case carefully observed, and carefully discussed, by Klaus Zuberbühler (2002). This is more problematic, because part of the story involves the responses of one species, Diana monkeys, to the alarm calls of another species, Campbell's monkeys. Campbell's monkeys have specific alarm calls for leopards and eagles, and Diana monkeys respond to these by giving their own different alarm calls for these predators. There is some interest in first discussing the significance of the calls to the Campbell's monkeys alone. Zuberbühler writes 'In addition to the two alarm calls, male Campbell's monkeys possess another type of loud call, a brief and low-pitched "boom" vocalization.... This call type is given in pairs separated by some seconds of silence and typically precedes an alarm call series by about 25 s. Boom-introduced alarm call series are given to a number of disturbances, such as a falling tree or large breaking branch, the far-away alarm calls of a neighbouring group, or a distant predator. Common to these contexts is the lack of direct threat in each, unlike when callers are surprised by a close predator' (2002, p. 294). The responses of Campbell's monkeys to these boom-introduced calls are not described, but if they are like the responses of the Diana monkeys (to the Campbell's calls), the Campbell's monkeys show little or no alarm on hearing a pair of booms followed about 25 seconds later by what sounds like a regular alarm call. The booms could be interpreted as in some sense negating, or qualifying, the normal meaning of the alarm call, just as the English expressions *maybe* or *not-to-worry-about* might modify a shout of 'Police coming!' This is the strongest interpretation one can put on the facts. The 20-second delay between the booms and the alarm call is problematic, as it does not suggest composition of a unitary message. One would expect a unitary communicative utterance consisting of several parts to be produced with little or no delay between the parts (unlike the slow stately progress of whale songs.) The contexts in which the boom-introduced calls occur, as Zuberbühler describes them, can possibly be thought of as semantically composite, for example something like THREAT + DISTANT, but

---

[10] Another interesting fact is that in these studies female receiving monkeys only responded to the calls of 'their own' males, so this is not a case of a group-wide code. Also, Anderson (2008a, p. 800) has an identical take to mine on the 'pyow-hack' data.

the do-nothing responses cannot be seen as any obvious function of the panic reactions induced by the plain alarm calls.[11]

More recently, a team including Zuberbühler (Ouattara et al. 2009) have found more complex behaviour among wild Campbell's monkeys. Besides the 'boom' (B) call, they distinguished five different types of 'hack', which they labelled 'krak' (K), 'hok' (H), 'krak-oo' (K_+), 'hok-oo' (H_+) and 'wak-oo' (W_+). Their observations are worth reporting at length as they are the most complex yet seen in wild primates, and have some syntax, though it is not semantically compositional.

The different call sequences were not randomly assembled but ordered in specific ways, with entire sequences serving as units to build more complicated sequences. As mentioned, pairs of booms alone instigate group movements toward the calling male, while K_+ series functioned as general alarm calls. If combined, the resulting sequence carried an entirely different meaning, by referring to falling wood. In all cases, the booms preceded the K_+ series. We also found that another sequence, the H_+ series, could be added to boom-K_+ sequences, something that callers did when detecting a neighboring group. H_+ series were never given by themselves. ...

These call combinations were not random, but the product of a number of principles, which governed how semantic content was obtained. We found five main principles that governed these relationships. First, callers produced sequences composed of calls that already carried narrow meanings (e.g., K = leopard; H = crowned eagle). In these instances, sequence and call meanings were identical. Second, callers produced meaningful sequences, but used calls with unspecific meanings (e.g., K_+ = predator). Third, callers combined two meaningful sequences into a more complex one with a different meaning (e.g., B + K_+ = falling wood). Fourth, callers added meaningless calls to an already meaningful sequence and, in doing so, changed its meaning (e.g., B + K_+ + H_+ = neighbors). Fifth, callers added meaningful calls to an already meaningful sequence and, in doing so, refined its meaning (e.g. K + K_+ = leopard; W + K_+ = crowned eagle). We also found regularities in terms of call order. Boom calls, indicative of a nonpredation context, always preceded any other call types. H' and K calls, indicators of crowned eagles or leopards, were always produced early in the sequence and were relatively more numerous if the level of threat was high.

(Ouattara et al. 2009, p. 22029)

These monkeys do produce systematically formed call-sequences, so, like birds, they have some combinatorial syntax. The sequences are meaningful, apparently referential, but the meanings of the sequences are not functions of the

---

[11] For sure, one can always think of **some** function getting from one concept to another, but it won't necessarily be a very natural function. This assumes, of course (what else can we assume?) that what is a 'natural' function for a monkey is also at least somewhat natural for us human investigators.

meanings of the parts, so the syntax is not semantically compositional. What could be happening here is that there is a felt need to express more meanings than can (for some reason) be expressed by an inventory of four one-unit calls 'boom', 'krak', 'hok', and 'wak'. The monkeys cannot produce any further one-unit distinct calls, so they resort to making new signals by concatenating what they have. The meanings expressed are all of the same level of concreteness— LEOPARD, EAGLE, NEIGHBOURS, TREE-FALLING—and not in any hierarchical relation with each other, so a compositional system would not be appropriate. This is pure speculation, and not very convincing, at that, but maybe other similar examples will be found that shed some light on this case. It seems unlikely that Campbell's monkeys are the only species with such behaviour. We need more empirical field research.

Moving on to birds, the dominant consensus in the birdsong literature is that songs are meaningful in the sense that they function to attract mates or defend territory. The great variety in some birdsong repertoires is interpreted as impressive display, or versatile echoing of rival songs. Very few authors claim any compositional semantics for birdsong. Exceptions to this general trend are Hailman et al. (1985), writing about the black-capped chickadee, and Smith (1972), on its close relative, the Carolina chickadee.

These preliminary discoveries of S. T. Smith obviously do not specify referents of note-types completely, but they do suggest that the locomotory signals have something to do with such acts as take-off, landing, flight, perching, and change of direction.
(Hailman et al. 1985, p. 221)

S. T. Smith (1972) went on to make preliminary identification of note-types with specific 'messages' about locomotion, and noted that the combination of these notes in calls encoded a combination of their separate messages. She also pointed out that note-types are commonly repeated within a call, which suggests that the repetitions encode intensive aspects of the basic message of note-types.   (Hailman et al. 1985, p. 191)

Hailman et al. have no hesitation in writing about the 'referents' of the various note-types, of which there are just four in the black-capped chickadee. The last quotation above is a clear statement of compositionality, but it has not, to my knowledge, resurfaced in the literature. At most, the kind of compositionality involved expresses a conjunction of the meanings of the basic notes. For example, if note 'A' signals something to do with take-off, and 'B' signals something to do with change of direction, then the sequence **AB** might signal something to do with take-off and with change of direction. This is like the well-known child example 'Mommy sock', meaning something to do with Mummy and with a sock. It is the simplest form of compositionality. As Hailman et al. (1985) concede: 'Unlike written words made recombinantly from their component letters, calls strung into bouts have no evident higher level of structure such as the grammar of human sentences' (p. 221).

In sum, there is no compelling evidence for any semantically compositional learned signalling in wild animals. Even if the problematic cases that have been mentioned are held to be strictly compositional, they are of limited scope, and provide only a slight platform upon which the impressive human capacity for compositionality might have evolved.

1.2 Non-compositional syntax in animals: its possible relevance

Some wild animals do produce syntactically complex behaviour, in semantically uninterpreted 'songs'. In such songs, although they are structurally somewhat complex, the meaning of a whole signal is not in any way composed as a function of the meanings of its elementary parts. How might signals which don't express any complex meaning be relevant to the evolution of human language? A number of writers, dating back several centuries, have seen in this behaviour the beginnings of human syntax. For these authors, the link lies in the sheer syntactic complexity of the songs. In this section and the next I survey these animal systems, and extract some general lessons about how to conceive of such pure syntactic abilities within biological organisms.

One evolutionary possibility is that after the chimp/human split the ancestors of humans developed somewhat syntactically complex songs like birds or gibbons, initially with no systematic combining of the meanings of the elements to convey some perhaps complex message (even if the elements had some meanings, which they might not have had). This is in fact a venerable idea. Rousseau and Darwin believed it, and so did Otto Jespersen, a renowned early twentieth-century linguist. These all saw music, in some form, as a pre-existing kind of syntactically complex expressive behaviour from which referentially meaningful language later evolved. The function of such complex songs was purely for display, to attract sex partners, they suggested (Darwin 1871; Jespersen 1922). The idea was of a separate syntactic ability, used for composing seductively complex songs—that is songs which were seductive purely by virtue of their complexity, and not by virtue of any semantic content, because they had none (apart from 'come mate with me'). For birdsong,

The evidence from the laboratory data is highly consistent and shows that, when females are exposed to large repertoires, they display higher levels of sexual arousal than when they hear small repertoires (e.g. Catchpole et al. 1986; Lampe and Saetre 1995; Searcy and Marler 1981) Field data however are not as straightforward. ... [However] in the great reed warbler *Acrocephalus arundinaceus*...cuckolded males had smaller song repertoires than their cuckolders (Hasselquist, Bensch, and T. von Schantz, 1996).   (Gil and Slater 2000, p. 319)

The hypothesis of an early-evolved syntactic, specifically musical, ability, predating the exaptation of syntactically structured songs for propositional semantic purposes by humans, is explicitly argued by Fitch (2005, p. 16). 'The many similarities between music and language mean that, as an evolutionary intermediate, music really would be halfway to language, and would provide a suitable intermediate scaffold for the evolution of intentionally meaningful speech'.[12] Mithen (2005, 2009) has argued for a closely related view, involving coevolution of the human musical and linguistic capacities; see also Molnar-Szakacs and Overy (2006) who emphasize a common neural substrate for music and language, and similar hierarchical structure. Fitch points out that the function of such song need not be for sexual attraction, but could also have a role in promoting group cohesion, or could be used by mothers to calm their young. Cross and Woodruff (2009, pp. 77–8) also stress the functions of music in 'the management of social relationships, particularly in situations of social uncertainty'. For birds with extremely large repertoires, such as the nightingale, it has been pointed out that sexual attraction is an implausible function, as females are unlikely to spend time listening to over a hundred songs, just to be impressed by the male's versatility. In this case, a territory-marking function may be more likely, but the question remains whether rival males need to be told in so many different ways to get lost.

Music has complex syntax, but the meaning of a whole tune is not put together from the elementary meanings of each note or phrase; and music certainly does not refer to outside objects or events (though it may iconically evoke them). It is possible that some purely syntactic capacity, possibly used for display, or to enhance group cohesion, or to claim territory, evolved in parallel with private, somewhat complex, conceptual mental representations. (Here 'syntactic' simply means 'exploiting combinatorial possibilities, given a set of elementary forms'.) Then, according to this hypothesis, at some later stage the conceptual and syntactic abilities got combined to give complex semantically compositional syntax. The syntax-from-song hypothesis has been seriously argued by serious people, so I will give it a fair hearing in this chapter. I do not think that pre-existing complex song can be the whole story of how

---

[12] See also an essay by Fitch at http://languagelog.ldc.upenn.edu/nll/?p=1136.

humans got complex syntax. But it may be some part of the story. How large that part is cannot be argued, given present evidence.

Command of a range of different complex songs may have served a mnemonic function when they finally began to carry some semantic content. Sometimes you have to repeat a sentence to yourself before you really understand what it means. The ability to repeat it before fully understanding it involves some capacity for holding a (somewhat) meaningless, but nevertheless structured, string in your head.

One intriguing similarity between the songs of many bird species and human utterances in conversation is that they are of roughly the same duration, between two and about ten seconds. A bird will sing one song from its repertoire, lasting, say, about five seconds, and then wait for a similar period, during which a territorial rival may sing its responding song, often identical or similar (Todt and Hultsch 1998, p. 488). Thus a kind of discourse exists with the same temporal dimensions as human casual conversation. (But whalesong is an entirely different matter, with individual songs lasting up to half an hour; this conceivably is connected to the greater distances over which songs transmitted through water can carry.)

A striking difference between bird repertoires and human languages illustrates the unproductivity of bird syntax: 'The composition of vocal repertoires reveals a basic principle in most songbirds: The sizes of element-type repertoires are larger than the sizes of their song-type repertoires' (Hultsch et al. 1999, p. 91). This assertion is surprising to a linguist if one equates element-types with words and song-types with sentences. This fact is also stated by Todt (2004, p. 202) and Bhattacharya et al. (2007, p. 2), and is borne out by the examples I will discuss here. Podos et al. (1992) devised a method to put identification of song-types, and hence song repertoire sizes, on a firmer objective footing. They introduced a concept of 'minimal unit of production', MUP for short. An MUP is typically an individual note, but can be a sequence of notes if these notes always occur together in the same order. Then one can count the MUP repertoire size and the song repertoire size of any bird. Using this method, Peters et al. (2000) quantified the MUP repertoire and song repertoire sizes of five geographically separate groups of song sparrows. In all cases the MUP repertoire sizes were greater than the song repertoire sizes, by factors of about six or seven.

Much depends, of course, on how you count song-types. Hailman et al. (1985) studied chickadee (*Parus atricapillus*) 'calls' (most of which more recent researchers would classify as 'songs'). They counted 362 different 'call-types' composed from a basic vocabulary of four notes. This includes one-note, that is non-combinatorial, calls, and calls with different numbers of repetitions of the component notes, which other researchers would classify as belonging to the same song-type. Counting only songs in which notes are combined and counting repetitions of the same note as one, the number of distinct songs comprising over 99 per cent of the repertoire comes, by my reckoning, to just four, the same as the basic vocabulary. A spectacular example of a bird's failure to exploit syntactic combinatorial possibilities is provided by the brown thrasher (*Toxostoma rufum*). This bird is reported as being at the extreme of vocal virtuosity, having 'a repertoire of several thousand different types of song' (Brenowitz and Kroodsma 1996, p. 287). The original students of this bird's repertoire (Kroodsma and Parker 1977) report that each distinct song type is in fact a repetition of a distinct syllable type. There is not, apparently, any combination of one syllable type with another in the same song. So this bird has an estimated vocabulary in the thousands, and its song repertoire is in fact no larger than its vocabulary. This extreme example illustrates a general point that whatever syntax can be found in bird repertoires, they do not take advantage of its combinatorial possibilities. An analogy from English orthography would be a repertoire of, say, five words which happen to use all 26 letters of the alphabet. Given so many letters, and some possibility of combining them, why restrict the combinations to less than the number of letters? Why not make up and use more words? In human languages, the inventory of phonemes is always orders of magnitude smaller than the vocabulary size; and the vocabulary size is always orders of magnitude smaller than the number of possible sentences. Birdsong is thus strikingly different in this respect.

Conceivably, an ability for complex song provided an evolutionary basis for human **phonological syntax**, but no basis, or only a slight basis, for the semantically interpreted syntax of whole sentences. '[P]honology (sound structure), the rules for ordering sounds, and perhaps the prosody (in the sense that it involves control of frequency, timing, and amplitude) are the levels at which birdsong can be most usefully compared with language' (Doupe and Kuhl 1999, p. 573). MacNeilage (2008, pp. 303–8) also finds suggestive parallels between the serial organization of birdsong and human phonological syntax. A complementary part of the story, and perhaps the whole story, of how we got complex semantically compositional syntax is that it evolved on a platform of complex conceptual representations, plus some natural principles of the communication of information. These last complementary ideas are not for now but for later chapters.[13]

---

[13] The evolutionary contribution of pre-existing song-like syntax to modern semantically interpreted syntax is bound up with a debate between advocates of two different possible routes to modern syntax, an 'analytic' route and a 'synthetic' route. This debate will be the topic of a later chapter.

Pure uninterpreted syntax is not found in communication systems in the recent human lineage. The closest species to us displaying such asemantic song are gibbons. The absence of any complex songlike behaviour in great apes is not necessarily a problem. Complex song occurs many times in nature, in subsets of classes and families. Many, but not all, bird species have complex song. Among oscine birds, chaffinches have complex songs, but crows do not. Some hummingbirds have complex song (Ficken et al. 2000), while others don't. Among whales and dolphins, humpback whales have the most complex song. Among primates, only gibbons have complex songs. Complex song, it appears has evolved separately several times. So it could have evolved separately in humans after the chimp/human split.

Learned vocal behaviour also cross-cuts phylogenetic classifications, and so has probably also evolved independently several times. There is a close correlation between complexity of song and the degree to which the song is learned. If we can class human speech with song, humans have 'songs' that are both complex and learned. Despite the great genetic distance between songbirds and humans, and despite the large differences in their brain structure (e.g. birds do not have a many-layered cortex like mammals), there are significant similarities in the neural circuitry used for the production and learning of vocalizations. Jarvis (2004a, 2004b, 2007) argues for a hypothesis that 'vocal learning birds—songbirds, parrots, and hummingbirds—and humans have comparable specialized forebrain regions that are not found in their close vocal non-learning relatives' Jarvis (2007, p. 35). To argue this, Jarvis has to depend on a number of hypothesized functional equivalences of parts among the anatomically different brains involved (of parrots, songbirds, hummingbirds, and humans). He gives a long list of evidence that lesions in equivalent places in these brains produce functionally similar deficits in the respective species (2007). In similar vein, Doupe and Kuhl (1999, p. 567) summarize a broad survey thus: 'Although some features of birdsong and speech are clearly not analogous, such as the capacity of language for meaning, abstraction, and flexible associations, there are striking similarities in how sensory experience is internalized and used to shape vocal outputs, and how learning is enhanced during a critical period of development. Similar neural mechanisms may therefore be involved'. They also cite lesion and stimulation studies which bring out the similarities among learners, and their differences from non-learners. The relevant areas are areas of higher control:

Both songbirds and humans have high-level forebrain areas that control the preexisting hierarchical pathways for vocal motor control..., whereas nonlearners do not. There are no neocortical sites in monkeys from which vocalization can be elicited by stimulation nor whose ablation affects calls (Ploog 1981). In striking contrast, in humans the entire perisylvian cortical area as well as posterior parieto-temporal cortex is critical for speech production, as shown by both stimulation and lesion studies.

(Doupe and Kuhl 1999, p. 599)

This again suggests convergent evolution by somewhat different kinds of brain onto a common working solution to the problem of vocal learning.

Complex signals of wild animals are only partly learned, or not at all; in all species, there is a very hefty innate component. Without assigning percentages to innate and learned components, it is clear that the parallel between human language and animal songs is not strong on this point. Commitment to a nativist and syntactocentric view of language can lead to an emphasis on parallels between birdsong and language:

Certainly, little or no overlap occurs in the details of the development of speech in children and of song in birds. Equally obvious, however, is the remarkable similarity of these two processes at only a modest level of abstraction. ... We should have little hesitation in seeing both processes as essentially similar, as the working out of a species' developmental program in biologically guided maturation. In other words, nestlings and babies both grow up in a specific way, determined in its essence by the fact that they are birds and humans, respectively.   (Anderson 2004, p. 165)

What this view underemphasizes is the massive functional (semantic) difference between birdsong and language, accompanied by an equally great difference in structural complexity, differences that Anderson elsewhere acknowledges. Additionally, a remarkable difference between nestlings and babies growing up and learning their language is the fact that birds do not learn their song incrementally through a process of discourse with their parents (or other group members). Birds store the patterns they hear as nestlings, and then only later, sometimes as much as eight months later, start to produce their own songs.[14]

In birdsong, there is also some evidence of voluntary control. 'We found that chaffinches (*Fringilla coelebs*) in noisier areas (i.e., close to waterfalls and torrents) sang longer bouts of the same song type before switching to a new type, suggesting that they use increased serial redundancy to get the message across in noisy conditions' (Brumm and Slater 2006a, p. 475). In another study, Brumm and Slater (2006b) found that zebra finches sang louder when the receiving female was further away, and draw a superficial parallel with humans raising their voices. However, they suggest that 'this behaviour can be

---

[14] See Fehér et al. (2009) for an interesting recent study in which zebra finches developed a wild song type, over three or four generations, by iterated learning starting from birds who had had no model to imitate.

accounted for by simple proximate mechanisms rather than by the cognitive abilities that have been thought necessary in humans' (p. 699).

To recap, it is worth looking at complex song in species not closely related to humans because of the possibility of a parallel independent evolution adapting to similar functions, and involving similar brain mechanisms. If this happened, then some time after the human/chimp split, our ancestors developed a capacity for complex musical or song-like behaviour that was later recruited for the expression of complex meanings. Perhaps it did happen. Some empirical light could be shed on this question by testing the susceptibility of apes and monkeys to various sequences with music-like structure.

1.3 Formal Language Theory for the birds, and matters arising

So far, I have only mentioned that birdsong and whalesong can be syntactically 'complex'. But how complex is 'complex'? In the rest of this chapter, we get to grips with a way of comparing meaningless syntax across species. It will emerge that despite big quantitative differences between animal song and human language, the more complex animal songs do have some similarities with language. Apart from the obvious lack of compositional, and referential, semantics, these songs are not qualitatively, but only quantitatively, different in their basic combinatorial structure.[15]

If we are seriously to compare human syntax and the complex songs of animals, we need some common scale by which to measure each of them. Formal Language Theory provides a scale which is in some ways suitable. The cross-disciplinary exercise of applying this body of theory to animal songs will reveal some of the serious theoretical issues that arise when applying the tools of one trade to data from another. One conclusion will be that applying this scale shows that human languages are not just head and shoulders above animal songs in syntactic complexity, but (to continue the metaphor) head, shoulders, trunk, and legs above them. The familiar assertion of a huge gap between humans and non-humans is thus reinforced. But it is good to have a non-impressionistic way of justifying this common assertion, and Formal Language Theory provides a tool for this. The other main conclusion to arise from this exercise is that certain issues which have been contentious in theorizing about

---

[15] This is not to deny that certain semantico-syntactic, or pragmatico-syntactic features of human language are absent from animal song (see Chapters 3 and 4). I assume that these features were superimposed on any basic syntactic structure if and when it was recruited for expressing complex meanings.

human language start to arise even when considering much simpler systems, leading me to suggest some modifications of common theoretical distinctions. In this way, many of the concepts introduced here will also be useful in later chapters of the book. So bear with me in this section while I give you an introduction to Formal Language Theory.

In the 1950s and early 1960s, Chomsky, in a number of highly ingenious and original technical papers,[16] set out the skeleton of a subject that became known as 'Formal Language Theory'. At the heart of this theory is a hierarchy of possible language types, now known, especially among linguists, as the 'Chomsky Hierarchy'. Although Chomsky's early work, such as *Syntactic Structures* (1957), argued largely from premises established within the framework of this theory, his later work moved away from it, reflecting a growing recognition of its irrelevance to a theory of human languages. It is said that Chomsky never personally approved of the label 'Chomsky Hierarchy', and out of respect for this, and to emphasize its content rather than its personal associations, I will refer to it as the 'Formal Language Hierarchy'.

In computer science, as opposed to linguistics, the Formal Language Hierarchy became very important as a way of classifying computer languages. The hierarchy defines a ranking of classes of languages paired with the kinds of machine that could automatically process the languages of each class, given a relevant program, or 'grammar'. Outside computer science, the only area of theoretical linguistics that has maintained any common reference to this hierarchy is learnability theory, which is also a highly formal, highly idealized and technical branch of linguistics, dealing in theorems and proofs. Mainstream syntactic theory is not completely devoid of theorems and proofs; the Formal Language Hierarchy remains part of a syntactician's basic training, but it does not typically figure in the focus of theoretical attention for working syntacticians.

For those interested in the evolution of language, the Formal Language Hierarchy holds out the promise of a kind of easily definable *scala naturae* in terms of which it might be possible to classify the communication systems of various animals. The motivating idea is that human language makes computational demands on the mind of a qualitative type unattainable by other creatures. And it might be possible to peg the communication systems of other species

---

[16] See Chomsky (1956a, 1956b, 1956c, 1958, 1959a, 1959b, 1962a, 1963); Chomsky and Miller (1958); Chomsky and Schutzenberger (1963). Chomsky's formulations did not, of course, spring from nowhere. As noted by Scholz and Pullum (2007, p. 718), it was Emil Post (1943) who invented rewriting systems of the kind assumed in Formal Language Theory, and also did the first work on the generative power of such systems.

at various lower levels on the hierarchy. Then the evolutionary story would be of an ascent up the Formal Language Hierarchy from the syntactic abilities of various non-humans to the present impressive syntactic abilities of humans. Some recent experiments with tamarin monkeys and starlings have appeared to take this idea seriously, in that they have expressed their conclusions literally in terms of the Formal Language Hierarchy. We will come to those studies later. The *scala naturae* analogy is not totally crazy, although, as we will see, many serious reservations must be expressed about it. Even the most complex of animal songs seem to occupy lower places on the Formal Language Hierarchy than human languages. Something about the hierarchy expresses some truth about animal songs, but it is too idealized in its conception to tell the whole story about the factors affecting real biological systems. In this section I will explain the central ideas of the Formal Language Hierarchy, especially its lower end. In the ensuing subsections I will consider its application to animal songs, and discuss those animal studies which have used the hierarchy as a frame of reference.

Two theoretical distinctions made by linguists are crucial to thinking about human languages in terms of the Formal Language Hierarchy. These are the distinctions (1) between the **weak** and **strong generative capacity** of descriptions (or grammars), and (2) between **competence** and **performance**. I will explain these concepts, but first here is why they are relevant. Linguists have tended to think of animal songs only in terms of weak generative capacity and performance. I will argue that animal songs, like human languages, are sensibly considered in terms of strong generative capacity and competence. Thus animal song and human language, despite huge differences between them, can be thought of using the same conceptual tools. In its original basic conception, the Formal Language Hierarchy is also resolutely **non-numerical**. I will also argue for numerical augmentation of the animal song grammars. These arguments will be woven into a basic exposition of what the Formal Language Hierarchy is.

Within the theory of the Formal Language Hierarchy, a 'language' is taken to be nothing more than a set of strings of elements, a 'stringset'. (We will later have reason to move on from this idealized view of what a language is, but it will be helpful to stay with the simple stringset idea for the moment.) Applied to a human language, think of a language as a set of sentences, say the set of well-formed sentences in French. In relation to Formal Language Theory, it is assumed that this is an infinite set. Sets can be infinite, like the set of natural numbers. Postulating infinite languages conveniently eliminates any awkward question of constraints on the length of sentences and on the memory mechanisms involved in processing them. Also, the theory makes the idealization that there is a clear-cut distinction between the grammatical expressions in a language and strings of elements which are not grammatical. That is, the assumption is that there are no unclear or borderline cases. Let that pass for now. A formal grammar is a set of precise statements (usually called 'rules') which specifies the whole set of grammatical sentences in a language, and nothing but those sentences. The usual formulation is that a grammar 'generates' **all and only** the well-formed expressions in the language. The elements constitute the ('terminal') vocabulary of the language, and the grammar defines, or generates, all and only the well-formed strings of these elements. The elements are the smallest observed parts of the signals. I don't call the elements 'symbols' because that could carry the implication that the elements in the vocabulary are treated as if they mean something. Formal Language Theory doesn't deal with the meanings of the vocabulary elements in languages, nor with the meanings of the strings of these elements which belong in the language.

The avoidance of any issue of meaning is actually an advantage when dealing with animal communication systems such as birdsong or whale or gibbon songs, because the elements of these songs are not put together by the animals in such a way that the whole song conveys some complex message assembled from the meanings of the parts. Animal songs have no semantically compositional syntax. For human languages, however, treating them as merely sets of uninterpreted strings of uninterpreted elements is clearly wrong. Human languages are not **merely** sets of sentences. But it does not follow that Formal Language Theory has nothing to contribute about the ways in which human languages syntactically construct their sentences. That is, knowing that human sentences convey meaning is not enough in itself to tell us how the grammar of a language will construct its meaningful sentences. Just to say 'put the meaningful elements together in any way that makes the whole string express a complex meaning' only describes a recipe for 'semantic soup', as Anderson (2004) calls it. It is not an adequate description of any language,[17] except a pidgin 'language'. Pidgin languages are not fully-fledged human languages. Pidgins are arguably semantically compositional, in the simplest possible way, but have no syntactic organization. The songs of birds, whales, and gibbons, by complete contrast, have somewhat complex syntax, but no hint of semantic compositionality linked to this syntactic organization.

---

[17] This statement is true, but we will see in Chapter 5 that some languages get nearer than others to a semantic soup state. See also discussion of protolanguage in Chapter 6.

The **weak generative capacity** of a grammar is its capacity to generate a **set of strings** of elements, no matter whether this seems naturally to capture the way in which we as insightful humans intuitively feel the system works. Imagine a simple system with a vocabulary of a thousand nouns and a thousand verbs, and a single grammatical rule forming two-element sentences by putting any noun first and any verb second; only two-element strings exist in this language. This 'language', then, has just a million sentences, and hence is finite. So the language could be specified with a long list. But this would obviously be to miss something about the organization of the language. As far as weak generative capacity is concerned, a million-long list is as good as the more elegant and sensible description in terms of a combinatory rule which I just used to describe the language. The strict Formal Language Hierarchy is based on considerations of weak generative capacity. If a language is technically finite, it belongs at the bottom of the hierarchy. So, in terms of weak generative capacity, our hypothetical language, with a systematic way of combining its thousand nouns and its thousand verbs, and, crucially, a two-element limit to sentence length, sits in the same broad rank in this hierarchy as the call of the cuckoo and the hiss and rattle of the rattlesnake.

A finite language can be described as a finite list of all the possible expressions in it. Mere lists are boring, of little theoretical interest. A finite language can be learned by rote by anybody with enough memory; the whole language can literally be memorized. Where learning is not involved, a short finite list of communicative signals can be coded into the genes. The finite repertoires of non-combinatorial calls of many animals, such as the various coos and warbles of ravens, the alarm calls and social grunts of vervet monkeys and all the calls of wild chimpanzees are presumably at this level. These systems have no apparent syntax. Only syntax raises a system from finiteness to a potentially infinite number of signals. Human languages are, at least potentially, infinite;[18] one cannot put a principled limit on the length of a sentence, because one can always in principle extend any sentence by conjoining some further clause. For example, in English one can always in principle lengthen any sentence by

---

[18] Pullum and Scholz (2010b) point out that it is not an empirical fact about languages that they are infinite. How could it be? One cannot observe an infinite number of sentences. Rather, the 'infinitude' claim about human languages is a consequence of one's basic theoretical assumptions. It will do no harm here to stick with assumptions that entail infinitude for languages, where appropriate. Much of the pure mathematical fascination of Formal Language Theory lies with proofs that there are different classes of infinite languages, each successive class containing the class below it, and each class making successively stronger demands on the computing machinery that is needed to process its sentences.

adding *I said that* . . . to the front of it. A sentence with a number of *I said that*s at the beginning may be tediously redundant and stylistically awful, but it is still a sentence of English. You can in principle go on adding *I said that*s as long as you like. This kind of example is what gives rise to the claim that the sentences of a language, such as English, are infinite in number. Just as there is no highest number (every number has a successor), there is no longest sentence, the way sentences are conceived within the Formal Language Theory approach to natural languages.

In computer science also, finite languages are of little interest, as any useful computer language should not stipulate an artificial upper bound on the length of well-formed expressions in it. Some computer programmers like to write extremely intricate 'hairy' code, with many embedded and conjoined conditions. Designers of computer languages and the compiling algorithms that translate them into nuts-and-bolts machine code are constrained by finiteness, but they always allow for more memory than any competent programmer is likely to need. When a computer actually runs out of memory, this is usually a result of bad programming or error. Different computers have different memory limits, but the same programming language will run on them.

When we come to ask whether bird- and whalesong repertoires can be regarded as infinite in the same way as human languages, we are on stickier ground, because we have no privileged insight into these systems. We can only observe finite sets of data, but it might strike us that something about the way a system works seems to project an infinite number of examples similar to those we have observed. As speakers of English we know that we can always add a clause onto the end of any sentence, but there is also a practical limit to the length of sentences. Could we say the same of a bird's, or a whale's, repertoire if it contains many instances of repetition of some unit? As all animals are subject to constraints of the flesh, it can seem reasonable to distinguish between the idealized system that guides an animal's behaviour, and the limits on actual products of this system. Although native speakers of human languages may be credited with a tacit 'knowledge' of what the well-formed sentences of their language are, they obviously sometimes make errors in speaking, because of tiredness, running out of memory, being interrupted, and so on. You might observe an English speaker literally say 'of of the of' in the middle of an utterance, but would put this down to hesitancy or distraction, rather than admitting that *of of the of* can be part of a well-formed English sentence. Many linguists (and I am one of them) find it sensible to distinguish between two factors affecting what we actually say when we speak: (1) a set of canonical target expressions, or knowledge of the 'right' way to say something,[19] and (2) factors of a different type, which affect not only speech but other kinds of activity as well, such as getting dressed, cooking, and driving. These factors are **competence** and **performance**, respectively.

There is evidence that adult birds have tacit target canonical songs, built more or less closely, depending on the species, upon innate templates. For various reasons, the birds sometimes produce these canonical songs imperfectly, or with some unprogrammed variation. MacNeilage (2008, p. 305) mentions work of Thorpe and Hall-Craggs (1976) on birdsong errors: in their research notes, they used such phrases as 'Bird getting in a muddle'. Mooney (2004, p. 476) refers to birds 'using auditory feedback to match their own song to a memorized tutor model'. On a long ontogenetic timescale, 'Male swamp sparrows reared in the laboratory and exposed to taped songs during infancy produce accurate imitations of the material following an 8-month interval with no rehearsal' (Marler and Peters 1981, p. 780). When they do start to sing, and before they eventually home in on the adult song, these sparrows produce a range of relatively imperfect 'subsong' and 'subplastic' song. This indicates storage of a canonical target song as an auditory template guiding the gradual perfection of performance. Stored learned templates can be maintained intact without feedback for impressively long periods, sometimes over a year (Konishi 1965), but tend to deteriorate if they are not refreshed by feedback from the bird's own singing (Nordeen and Nordeen 1992). Todt and Hultsch (1998) describe training nightingales on artificially modified variants of typical nightingale songs, and report a kind of gravitation by the learning birds back to song types more typical of the species. They conclude 'Taken together, these findings suggest that the birds have access to a "concept" of a species-typical song' (p. 492). Adret (2004, p. 321) warns that 'templates (innate or acquired) represent [researchers'] constructs, rather than [actual neural] mechanisms. . . . Despite the many issues outstanding, the template concept will continue to be a heuristically useful model of the song-learning process'. These wise words apply equally well to the linguist's quest for the mechanisms underlying human language. In the brain, of course, there are no symbolic templates or descriptions, only activation potentials and synaptic plasticity. But in the absence of detailed results on the neural mechanisms of language, the concept of a speaker's competence, her tacit knowledge of her language, which we

---

[19] I am not referring here to schoolbook prescriptions, or conventions of politeness or etiquette, but to whatever it is in speakers' heads that causes them to conform, quite unconsciously, to complex regularities when they speak.

researchers describe symbolically, will continue to be a heuristically useful model.

It is possible that the bird's representation of the canonical form projects an infinite set of possible songs in its repertoire. If this were the case, the infinite set would reflect the bird's competence, and the actual observed finite subset of this, influenced by other factors, such as tiredness and distraction, would reflect its performance. Such a view would attribute to the bird something like a characteristically human kind of declarative knowledge about its potential behaviours. Competence is often defined as a speaker's tacit knowledge of her language. Linguists tap this knowledge by asking whether presented examples are intuited by native speakers to be grammatical. You can't ask birds questions like that. All you can do is watch their behaviour. But arguably the behaviour of birds that learn their songs involves what can be called declarative knowledge ('knowing that', rather than just procedural knowledge 'knowing how'). This is because their performance during song acquisition slowly approximates, through stages of subsong (like human infant babbling), to a target characteristic adult form that was laid down in their brain many months earlier, and not subsequently reinforced by external models.

Undoubtedly humans are often reflective about their language, and in the case of normative prescriptive rules, they will tailor their behaviour to the rules. It is indeed this kind of reflection that leads to acquiescence in the proposition that languages are infinite sets, because, on reflection, a human cannot identify the longest sentence in a language. It is clearly impossible to put a precise number on it. There is a marked distaste in formal linguistics for describing competence in terms of numbers. For understandable reasons, one rarely, if at all, finds statements like 'language X allows sentences of up to about 50 words in length, but no more', or 'language Y allows a maximum of three adjectives modifying a noun', or 'language Z only permits centre-embedding of clauses within clauses to a depth of two'.[20] In the next subsections I will revisit these issues in the light of specific examples of animal song. I will maintain the usefulness of a distinction between competence and performance, but will suggest a renegotiation of the division of labour between them, and a rethinking of the relationship between them in the light of behaviour in biological organisms generally.

Competence resides in individuals, and only indirectly in the social group, as a result of all members sharing (roughly) the same individual competences.

---

[20] See Chapter 3, section 7 for discussion of such points.

Competence is not essentially social, even though some of it may be acquired through social processes, by learning. For this reason, the descriptions I will consider will only be of the repertoires of individual animals, rather than trying to make generalizations over the varied 'dialects' of social groups. This is not to deny the relevance of group dynamics in the historically evolving patterns of animal songs and human languages. But the focus of this chapter is on the extent to which any individual non-human exhibits human-like syntactic behaviour.

The **strong generative capacity** of a system of rules (or equivalent diagrams) is a more intuitive notion than weak generative capacity. It appeals to the naturalness with which a system can be described. When dealing with human languages, such considerations of naturalness can involve semantics as well. A natural description provides an efficient way of carving up a string so that the parts are meaningful substrings which are re-used with the same meaning in other examples.[21] For instance, a purely sequential description of *The cat sat on the mat*—first say 'the', then say 'cat', then say 'sat', and so on, in a purely beginning-to-end way—misses the fact that *the cat* and *the mat* carry meaning in similar ways, referring to specific objects, and show up as meaningful chunks in other sentences. With animal songs, semantics is not relevant, but there could be non-semantic aspects of naturalness, to do with the economy or simplicity of a description, and with re-use of the same substrings in different examples. To return to the case of the thousand nouns combining in two-word sentences with a thousand verbs, a description with two thousand-long lists and a simple combinatory rule is more economical than one million-long list with no rule. Put crudely, it takes five hundred times more paper to write out the million-long list of examples than to write out the alternative. There are no perfect objective numerical criteria capturing such intuitions of naturalness.[22] Nevertheless, there is much agreement among linguists about a core body of examples.

---

[21] In computational linguistics, especially in parsing theory, the goal of strong generative capacity is often associated with assigning the correct tree structures to parsed strings, rather than just judging them as well-formed or not. Syntactic tree structures for sentences are largely semantically motivated, and serve as a convenient proxy for real semantic representations in computational linguistics.

[22] But numerical techniques do exist for measuring the data-compression that grammars achieve, roughly capturing the degree to which a language is susceptible to description by generalizing statements. See the end of Chapter 5, section 3 for some discussion of these 'bit-counting' methods, including Kolmogorov complexity and Minimal Description Length (MDL) (Rissanen 1978, 1989).

In Chomsky's seminal *Syntactic Structures* (Chomsky 1957), he set out three successively more powerful[23] ways of describing languages: in my terms State Chain descriptions, Phrase Structure descriptions, and a 'Transformational' descriptive method that is even more powerful than Phrase Structure descriptions. (I will define the first two of these very soon.) Appealing just to weak generative capacity, he showed that English and other languages simply cannot be described by State Chain descriptions. There are sets of strings in human languages which cannot be generated by State Chain descriptions. We shall see that no such sets of strings are to be found in animal song repertoires, and so State Chain descriptions are all that we need, at the very most, to describe, in terms of weak generative capacity, what these animals do. Chomsky's next step was to argue that Phrase Structure grammars are themselves unsatisfactory as descriptions of human languages, but here he could not argue from the more objective basis of weak generative capacity. At that time, no parts of any language had been found whose strings could strictly not be generated by Phrase Structure rules, though these might be ungainly and repetitive.[24] Chomsky's argument for the inadequacy of Phrase Structure grammars for human languages was based on strong generative capacity, that is the capacity of grammars to provide intuitively natural descriptions. The intuitions of naturalness involve both meaning (semantics) and economy or simplicity of the overall description.

In approaching animal song we face several decisions about our goals. One decision to be made is whether to be concerned with weak or strong generative capacity. Should we always prefer the weakest form of grammar that permits a description of a repertoire—that is, be concerned only with weak generative capacity? Or should we try to decribe the repertoires in terms that reflect intuitions about their structure—that is be concerned with strong generative capacity? If possible, this latter approach should be backed up by evidence from outside the bare facts of the repertoire, for example from neuroscience and from observations of the animals' learning processes. On a weak capacity approach, we will see below that from this perspective, almost all birdsong repertoires can be captured by the least powerful type of description. But we will also see that classifying repertoires at the lowest possible level of the Formal Language Hierarchy hides facts about the underlying mechanisms,

---

[23] Remember that to adopt a more powerful way of describing some domain is in fact to make a weaker claim about it. Power should be used sparingly.

[24] Later on, linguists discovered a few languages which had 'cross-serial dependencies', giving a more objective way to demonstrate the inadequacy of Phrase Structure grammars, but here semantic relations also play a role in the argument.

leading me to prefer the approach in terms of strong generative capacity. This is consistent with standard generative theorizing: 'The study of weak generative capacity is of rather marginal linguistic interest' (Chomsky 1965, p. 60). This applies no less to animal songs.

Another decision regards what to do about numerical constraints on repertoires. The numerical information relevant to animal songs mostly involves how many times an element or phrase is likely to be repeated. To avoid giving numerical information, one can simply postulate that any number of repetitions is possible, idealizing the object of description to an infinite set. This decision, though simplifying, is not objective. An alternative approach is to augment a description of the animal's competence with numerical information about the typical limits of the songs. Where possible, I will add this numerical information. An idealized form of competence can still be regarded as non-numerical. But I will be concerned with what I will call **competence-plus** (where using this neologism is not too tedious). Competence-plus has two kinds of component, 'algebraic' rules for generating song repertoires, and numerical statements of the typical lengths of parts of a song or whole songs. In later chapters, when we come to human language, such numerical constraints will be applied also to the depth of embedding of phrases and clauses within each other.

1.3.1 Simplest syntax: birdsong examples

Based on considerations of weak generative capacity, it is often envisaged that complex animal songs belong at the bottom end of the Formal Language Hierarchy, while human languages belong in the higher ranks. The bottom end of the Formal Language Hierarchy, in slightly more detail than linguists usually consider, looks like this.[25]

		Linear		Finite State		Context Free
(Finite)	⊂	Strictly 2-Local	⊂	Regular	⊂	**Phrase Structure**
		First-order Markov		**State Chain**		

Here, after every term, read 'languages', for example 'State Chain languages' or 'Phrase Structure languages'. There is some variation in terminology. The terms in each column here are equivalent to each other. The boldfaced terms are my own preferences for three of the classes of languages. My preferred terms are more transparent to an interdisciplinary audience. With some terminological variability, both Strictly 2-Local and State Chain languages are

---

[25] '⊂' means 'is a subset of'.

associated with 'Markov processes' or 'Markov models', named after the Russian mathematician Andrei Markov (1856–1922). I use the term 'State Chain', rather than the more normal 'Finite State', in order to avoid any possibility of confusion between these languages and merely finite languages. A State Chain language (usually called a Finite State language) is not necessarily finite, because of the possibility of indefinite iterative looping behaviour, to be illustrated shortly. In this discussion, where a finite song repertoire clearly involves putting things together (i.e. some syntax), I will not locate it at the very bottom 'Finite' end of the Formal Language Hierarchy. For reasons of strong generative capacity, it is desirable to represent how songs are put together, even if there are only a finite number of them.

The successive classes of languages are each more inclusive of the classes lower in the hierarchy.[26] Thus all First-order Markov (or Strictly 2-Local) languages can also be described, if one wishes, as State Chain languages or as Phrase Structure languages; and all State Chain languages can also be described, according to one's theoretical motivation, as Phrase Structure languages. But the converses do not necessarily hold. A Phrase Structure language might be too complex, in a well-defined sense, to be describable at all as a State Chain language. So there exist Phrase Structure languages which are not State Chain languages. Similarly, not all State Chain languages are First-order Markov languages. (In fact we will see later that the Bengalese finch repertoire is a State Chain language, but not a First-order Markov language.) So the classes of languages higher up the hierarchy are successively less restrictive. The set of First-order Markov languages is a proper subset of the set of State Chain languages, which in turn is a proper subset of the set of Phrase Structure languages, even though each **class** of languages contains infinitely many languages. The following analogy might be helpful.

(All prime numbers   all prime   all odd numbers   all natural
below 1000)   ⊂   numbers   ⊂   and 2   ⊂   numbers

I will start to illustrate the formal devices used to describe particular languages, or song repertoires, by considering the call of a particular bird, the blue-black grassquit, a native of South and Central America. On the face of things, this bird has a simple and boring repertoire, a single note without pauses,[27] each

---

[26] To understand this paragraph, it is essential to remember the definition of a 'language' as a set (possibly infinite) of sentences, where a sentence is a finite string of elements.

[27] There is some variability in the birdsong literature in the use of the term 'note'. For some (e.g. Fandiño-Mariño and Vielliard 2004; Williams 2004) a note is any sequence of sound uninterrupted by silence; inside a note, there may be 'elements' delineated by

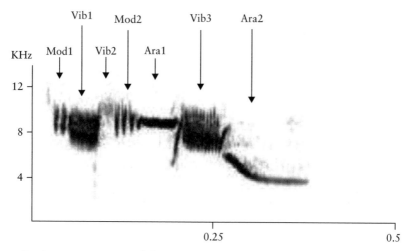

Fig. 1.1 Basic song structure of the blue-black grassquit *Volatinia jacarina* showing its single note compacted into a 'window' between 2 and 13 kHz and rarely occupying more than half a second.

Note: The labels above the spectrogram are my abbreviations for the seven different identifiable parts of the song.

Source: From Fandiño-Mariño and Vielliard (2004).

call 'rarely occupying more than half a second' (Fandiño-Mariño and Vielliard 2004, p. 327). To a human ear, such a short call sounds like nothing more than a simple chirp or squeak. And this bird's repertoire is definitely finite. In fact it could be described by a simple list with one member, give or take some aberrations. But a case can be made that even this simple call has some clear syntactic organization, in the basic sense where syntax is 'putting things together'. Have a look at Figure 1.1, a spectrogram of a call lasting no more than four-tenths of a second. All the bird's chirps are like this. Fandiño-Mariño and Vielliard (2004) analyse the call as a sequence of seven 'blocks' of three different types which they classify as 'Isolated modulations', 'Vibrations' and 'Arabesques'. Clearly the bird has a program defining the sequence of parts in its chirp. Even though the sequence is always the same, any description of the call needs to reflect the nature of this motor program.

The song of the blue-black grassquit can be adequately described by a First-order Markov model, or Strictly 2-Local stringset description, without any mention of internal states of the organism, as below: the list below specifies all the possible transitions in the bird's repertoire, which happens in this case to be a single call.

---

abrupt transitions to spectrally different sound structures. For others (e.g. Leonardo 2002), these are the definitions assumed for a 'syllable' and a 'note' respectively; in this case a syllable may consist of several notes.

START ⌢ Mod1
Mod1 ⌢ Vib1
Vib1 ⌢ Vib2
Vib2 ⌢ Mod2
Mod2 ⌢ Ara1
Ara1 ⌢ Vib3
Vib3 ⌢ Ara2
Ara2 ⌢ END

The symbol ⌢ means 'may be followed by'. This First-order Markov, or Strictly 2-Local, description captures the bird's repertoire adequately.

Definition of First-order Markov languages: A First-order Markov language is one that can be completely described by a list of pair-wise transitions between elements of the language (e.g. notes of a bird's song or words in a human language). The only 'abstract' items in the description are START and END. At least one (possibly more) of the pair-wise transitions must begin with START, and at least one transition must have END as its second term. The set of transitions must provide at least one 'route' from START to END. There is no further restriction on the pair-wise transitions between elements that may be listed as belonging in the language concerned.

A First-order Markov language is not necessarily finite. To cite a human example, inclusion of the transition *very⌢very* beside possible transitions from *very* to other elements, will generate an infinite language. Strings in this language could have indefinitely long sequences of *very*s in them. The song repertoire of the blue-black grassquit is, however, finite, consisting of a single call. Representing this extremely simple repertoire by a First-order Markov description, rather than as a holistic chirp, does justice to its somewhat complex internal structure.

A First-order Markov, or Strictly 2-local, model specifies the set of possible sequences of actions, or sequences of elements in a string, by a transition table which shows, for each element in the system, what element may immediately follow it.[28] Sometimes the pairs in the transition list are augmented by probabilities. For instance, a First-order Markov model approximation to English would calculate from a large corpus of English texts the probabilities with which each English word in the corpus is followed immediately by the other

---

[28] Sometimes, just to add to the confusion, such a model is called a 'Second-order' model, and in such cases all the other orders are promoted by 1. We won't be concerned with higher-order Markov models.

words. The model would manage to generate an extremely crude approximation to English text by simply moving from the production of one word to
production of the next, according to the probabilities in the transition table.
Here is an example of a 20-word string generated by such a First-order Markov
process: *sun was nice dormitory is I like chocolate cake but I think that book is
he wants to school there.*[29] By sheer chance here, some sequences of more than
two words are decent English, but the model only guarantees 'legal' transitions
between one word and the next.

An interesting demonstration that birds can learn somewhat complex songs
on the basis only of First-order transitions (as above) is given by Rose et al.
(2004). The white-crowned sparrow (*Zonotrichia leucophrys*) song is typically
up to five phrases[30] in a stereotyped order, call it **ABCDE**. The authors isolated
white-crowned sparrow nestlings and tutored them with only pairs of phrases,
such as **AB, BC,** and **DE.** They never heard an entire song. Nevertheless,
when the birds' songs crystallized, several months later, they had learned to
produce the whole intact song **ABCDE.** By contrast, birds who only ever heard
single phrases in isolation did not eventually produce a typical white-crowned
sparrow song. These researchers also gave other birds just pairs of phrases
in reverse of normal order, for example **ED, DC,** and **BA.** In this case, the
birds eventually sang a typical white-crowned sparrow song backwards. (Other
work on the same species demonstrates, however, that the order of phrases
is not solely a product of learning, but to some degree a matter of innate
biases. Soha and Marler (2001) exposed white-crowned sparrows just to single
phrases at a time, but the birds ended up singing songs with more than one
phrase, and in a species-typical order.)

The example of the blue-black grassquit was a simple start, showing serial
structure in what might seem to the human ear to be a unitary, atomic signal.
The white-crowned sparrow study showed the adequacy, for this bird at least,
of a simple First-order transition model for song-learning. In general, First-
order Markov descriptions are adequate to capture the bare observable facts
of wild birdsong repertoires. That is, in terms of weak generative capacity,
the natural songs do not even require the slight extra power of State Chain
descriptions (which I will describe immediately). For even such a versatile bird
as the nightingale, 'the performance of his repertoire can be described as a
Markov process of first (or some times second) order' (Dietmar Todt, personal
communication).

[29] From Miller and Selfridge (1950, p. 184).
[30] Each phrase consists only of a note of a single type, sometimes repeated several
times, so these are rather low-level 'phrases'.

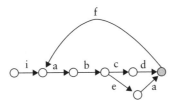

Fig. 1.2 State Chain diagram of a simple Bengalese finch song.

Note: The START state is the left-hand circle. The filled circle is the END state, where it is possible to finish the song. Note the appearance in two different places of the note 'a'. First-order transitions after this note are: to 'b', but only if the 'a' was preceded by 'i' or 'f'; and to 'f', but only if the 'a' was preceded by 'e'. Thus a First-order Markov transition table could not accurately describe this song pattern.

Source: From Katahira et al. (2007).

An interesting exception is the case of Bengalese finches, bred in captivity for about 240 years (Okanoya 2004). These birds have developed a song requiring a State Chain description (or a higher-order Markov description, taking into account more than just a single preceding element). Katahira et al. (2007, p. 441) give a succinct summary of the issue: 'Bengalese finch songs consist of discrete sound elements, called *notes*, particular combinations of which are sung sequentially. These combinations are called *chunks*. The same notes are included in different chunks; therefore, which note comes next depends on not only the immediately previous note but also the previous few notes'. A simple example is described by the State Chain diagram given in Figure 1.2. In this example, it is crucial that the note identified as 'a' in both places is in fact the same note. If it is actually a slightly different note, the song possibilities can be captured by a First-order Markov description. Also crucial to the analysis in terms of Formal Language Theory is a decision as to what the basic units of the song are. In this example, if the sequences 'ab' and 'ea' were treated as single units, then the song possibilities could also be captured by a First-order Markov description. In fact there is widespread agreement among bird researchers as to what the basic units are, based on (the potential for) brief periods of silence during the song, data from learning patterns, and neuroscientific probing. In the case of Bengalese finches, it is uncontroversial that the basic units are as shown in Figure 1.2. Thus this bird's song repertoire should be classified as a State Chain language.

Definition of a State Chain language: A State Chain language is one which can be fully described by a State Chain diagram. A State Chain diagram represents a set of 'states' (typically as small circles in the diagram), with transitions between them represented as one-directional arrows. On each arrow is a single element (e.g. word or note) of the language described. One particular state is designated as START, and one is designated as END. A sentence or song generated by such a diagram is any string of elements passed through while following the transition arrows, beginning at the START state and finishing at the END state. The transition arrows must provide at least one route from START to END.[31] There is no other restriction on the transitions between states that may be specified as contibutory to generation of the language concerned.

A State Chain language is not necessarily finite, because of the possibility of a transition arrow looping back to a previously passed state, thus generating an indefinite number of possible passages through a certain portion of the diagram.

State Chain languages make only very simple demands on computational machinery, such as keeping no memory of earlier parts of the sentence (or string of characters input to a computer). The instructions needed to generate a sentence of a State Chain language basically say only 'given the state you have got yourself in, here is what to do next'. For instance, at the start of the utterance there is a limited choice of designated first elements to be uttered—pick one of them and utter it. Once some first element has been chosen and uttered, that leads the organism into some particular 'state', from which the next choice of designated elements can be listed. Having chosen and uttered this second element of the signal, the organism is now in a (possibly new) state, and given a choice of next (in this case third) elements of the signal. And so on, until an 'END!' choice is given. For State Chain languages, the structure is inexorably linear, from beginning to end of the signal. Do the first thing, then do the next thing, then do the next thing, . . . , then stop. The specification of a State Chain language recognizes no higher-level units such as phrases. Applied to a human language, this would be like attempting to describe the structure of grammatical sentences without ever mentioning higher-level units such as phrases or clauses—obviously inappropriate. But as we will see later, some phrase-like hierarchical structure can be easily captured in a State Chain description.

A more complex example of Bengalese finch song is given by Honda and Okanoya (1999), in which a note labelled 'b' immediately follows, depending on the place in the song, any of four other notes. This certainly motivates a State Chain description, but it is notable that even in this case, according to

---

[31] If there is only one route in a diagram from START to END, there would in fact be no need to use a State Chain description, because a weaker First-order Markov description would suffice.

their diagram, just six transitions need the State Chain mechanism, whereas 26 other transitions can be accounted for in First-order Markov terms. Thus even this somewhat complex song does not exploit State Chain machinery very comprehensively. Based on a statistical analysis of chickadee songs, Hailman et al. (1985, p. 205) conclude that 'transitional frequencies do not occur strictly according to [a] first-order analysis...; small, but possibly important, effects occur over greater distances within a call than simply adjacent notes'.

These last examples demonstrate that there exist State Chain languages, the simple Bengalese finch repertoire and possibly that of the chickadee, that are not First-order Markov languages. Rogers and Pullum (2007) mention another example (infinite, as it happens) of a State Chain language that is not a First-order Markov language. This is a set of strings that they call 'Some-B', made up from any combination of As and Bs, with the sole proviso that each well-formed string must contain at least one B (but not necessarily any As). It is not possible to devise a First-order Markov transition table for Some-B, capturing **all and only** the 'legal' strings of this stringset, but a State Chain description can be given for it. The example of the Bengalese finch showed a possible, and very rare, case from birdsong where a First-order transition model is not adequate, and a State Chain description is necessary.

There is an alternative, and entirely equivalent, way of representing the information in a State Chain diagram, in terms of a very constrained type of rewrite rules. The rules below are equivalent to the diagram in Figure 1.2. You can match each of these rewrite rules to one arc in the State Chain diagram in Figure 1.2.

$$S_{START} \rightarrow \mathbf{i}\, S_1$$
$$S_1 \rightarrow \mathbf{a}\, S_2$$
$$S_2 \rightarrow \mathbf{b}\, S_3$$
$$S_3 \rightarrow \mathbf{c}\, S_4$$
$$S_3 \rightarrow \mathbf{e}\, S_5$$
$$S_4 \rightarrow \mathbf{d}\, S_{END}$$
$$S_5 \rightarrow \mathbf{a}\, S_{END}$$
$$S_{END} \rightarrow \mathbf{f}\, S_1$$

Here the terms $S_1, S_2, \ldots, S_5$ correspond to the circles in the diagram notation; they denote internal states of the machine or organism. And each boldface small letter denotes an actual note of the song. A rule in this format (e.g. the second rule) can be paraphrased as 'When in state S_1, emit the element $\mathbf{a}$ and get into state S_2'. The rewrite rules for State Chain systems may only take the above form, with a single internal-state symbol before the arrow, then a terminal symbol after the arrow, that is an actual observable element of the system, followed optionally by another internal-state symbol, leading to the next action (rule) in the system; where no next-state symbol occurs, this is the end of the utterance. Although the format of rewrite rules does not make the form of songs as obvious to the eye as the diagram format, the rewrite rule format has the advantage of being closely comparable with the format in which the more powerful, less constrained, Phrase Structure grammars are presented. Phrase Structure grammars are defined and illustrated in a later section.

Notice the reference to **states** of the organism or machine in the characterization of State Chain languages. A description of a language in State Chain terms thus postulates abstract entities, the states through which the machine or organism is running, in addition to the actual elements of the language, so-called terminal symbols.[32] The action that is to be performed next, or the elementary sound unit that is to be emitted next, depends on the state that the system is currently in, and not directly on the action that it has just previously performed or the sound that it has just previously uttered. This distinguishes State Chain languages from weaker systems such as First-order Markov models.

As State Chain machinery is clearly inadequate for human languages, linguists pay little attention to classes of languages of this lowly rank on the Formal Language Hierarchy. In terms of weak generative capacity, almost all birdsong repertoires belong down here, even below the State Chain languages. It is in fact possible to define a richly textured sub-hierarchy of languages below the level of State Chain languages, and characterizations of these classes of languages can be given purely in terms of the terminal elements of the languages. Rogers and Pullum (2007) describe a 'Subregular Hierarchy', which subdivides the space of languages below the State Chain (or Regular) languages in the Formal Language Hierarchy. Only one of these classes of languages has concerned us here, a class that Rogers and Pullum call the 'Strictly Local' stringsets. The members (strings or 'sentences') in a Strictly Local stringset are defined, as the label suggests, just by the local preceding neighbours of each word. The Strictly Local (SL) stringsets are in fact themselves an infinite set (of classes of language), one for each natural number from 2 up. The number associated with each level of Strictly Local stringset indicates

---

[32] In fact, appeal to abstract states is not necessary to describe a State Chain, or 'Regular', language, as it can also be done by Boolean combinations of expressions consisting of only the elements of the language, so-called 'regular expressions'. But in this case, the regular expressions themselves can be indefinitely large, and such a description is no more conspicuously insightful than a State Chain description.

how many elements figure in a string defining what element may come next. For example, a SL_2 stringset description of a language is just a list of the pairs of successive elements that occur in strings of the language. Thus a SL_2 stringset description of a language is equivalent to a (non-probabilistic) First-order Markov model of the language. As Rogers and Pullum (2007, p. 2) note, in the context of some attempts to apply the Formal Language Hierarchy to animal behaviour, 'the CH [the Formal Language Hierarchy] seems to lack resolution'. As far as linguists are typically concerned, the bottom is the level of State Chain languages, and even these are only mentioned as a way of quickly dismissing non-human behaviours as far less complex than human languages. The message is well taken, and this subsection has shown that, on a narrow approach, many animal song repertoires can be described by devices even less powerful than State Chain descriptions, namely First-order Markov descriptions.

Let's take a moment (three paragraphs, actually) to reflect on the spirit of the enterprise that is our background here. One way of conceiving a central goal of linguistics is that we are interested in finding the strongest justifiable hypotheses about what can be, and what cannot be, a human language. 'This general theory can therefore be regarded as a definition of the notion "natural language" ' (Chomsky 1962b, p. 537). At the level of weak generative capacity, we can also use the Formal Language Hierarchy to arrive at the definition of 'possible bird song'. This approach has the simplifying attraction that it brings with it a pre-conceived broad hypothesis space, and the goal becomes to eliminate wrong hypotheses. Further, the Popperian imperative to make more readily falsifiable, and therefore stronger, conjectures pushes theorists to constrain the class of languages that they claim are possible human languages. On this approach, to claim, for example, that all human languages are State Chain languages is to make a more falsifiable claim than claiming that all human languages are Phrase Structure languages. Chomsky's early work convincingly demonstrated that human languages are not State Chain languages, leaving us with the less falsifiable hypothesis that they occupy a rank higher on the Formal Language Hierarchy than State Chain languages. So humans have evolved brain mechanisms allowing them to control a larger class of languages than State Chain languages. Among birds, only the captive human-bred Bengalese finch apparently has a song complex enough to require a State Chain description. All other songs, as far as weak generative capacity is concerned, are of the simplest type, namely First-order Markov systems.

In the history of this branch of linguistics, the problem became where to stop on the Formal Language Hierarchy without going all the way to the top. The very top, which I have not included in the scheme above, is the class of **all abstractly conceivable** languages.[33] It is empirically uninteresting, in fact tautologous, to equate the class of human languages with the class of all abstractly conceivable languages. It says nothing more than that human languages are languages. This became a problem in the 1970s, when Peters and Ritchie (1973) proved that the formalisms current at the time were capable of describing any conceivable language, and were therefore strictly empirically vacuous.

To briefly step aside from linguistics, biologists do not consider the central goal of their discipline to be the characterization of the set of theoretically possible life forms. Even more outlandishly, social anthropology students are not taught that the main point of their subject is to delineate the set of theoretically possible human societies. In both cases, the 'theoretically possible X' goal is not obviously incoherent, but within life sciences, including human sciences, only linguistics (and only one branch of it) has taken it seriously as a central goal. In non-life sciences, many subjects, for example chemistry or astronomy, have set out basic principles, for example the periodic table of elements or Einsteinian laws, which do in fact set limits on possible systems. An implicit understanding has been reached in these subjects of what systems there could possibly be, based on 'known' principles of how things are. In life sciences, such as neuroscience or genetics, however, although obviously many basic principles are known, the ongoing quest to discover more and further principles in these subjects is so vital and consuming that ultimate objectives such as 'theoretically possible functioning nervous system' or 'theoretically possible viable genome' are impractical distractions from the central research effort. It is a mark of the ambition of early Chomskyan linguistics that it articulated a goal so closely resembling what had been implicitly approximated in chemistry or astronomy, but not in neuroscience or genetics. This ambition seemed more realistic to the extent that the study of language was detached from such considerations as **viability** or **function**. These considerations bring in complications from outside the domain of immediate concern, such as how individuals manage to get along in primate society, and what kinds of message it would be advantageous be able to communicate and understand. But it seems very likely that the language faculty and individual languages got to be the way they are largely under the constraints and pressures of viability and function. These thoughts echo Culicover and Nowak (2003, pp. 6–12), writing 'Linguists have, either consciously or unconsciously, modelled their

[33] More technically put, an organism that could manage any of the abstractly conceivable languages would have the power of a universal Turing machine, i.e. it could generate any member of the class of recursively enumerable languages.

ideas of what a linguistic theory should look like on physics. ... [Language] is a social and psychological phenomenon, and has its roots in biology, not physics. ... [Linguistics] has historically not aggressively sought unification [with other subjects], while physics has'.[34]

1.3.2 *Iteration, competence, performance, and numbers*

I turn now to two birds with slightly fancier repertoires, the much-studied zebra finch and the chaffinch. These provide good examples for making a point about iterative re-use of the same elements in a variety of somewhat different songs.

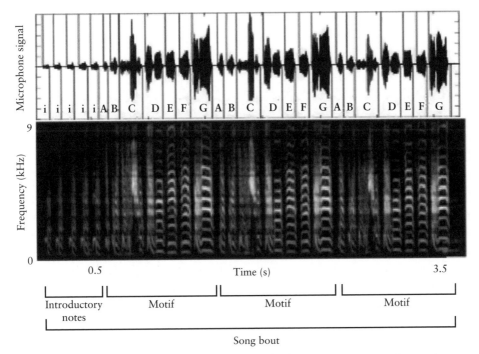

Fig. 1.3 The normal structure of adult zebra finch song. Top trace shows the raw microphone signal, parsed into discrete bursts of sound (syllable). Bottom trace shows the time-frequency spectrogram of the song. After some introductory notes, syllables are produced in a repeated sequence called a motif. During a bout of singing, a motif is repeated a variable number of times.

Source: From Leonardo (2002).

[34] See Newmeyer's 2005 book *Possible and Probable Languages* for extensive discussion of the idea of possible languages, relating it to the competence–performance distinction.

Leonardo (2002, p. 30) gives a spectrogram of normal adult zebra finch song, reproduced in Figure 1.3. Leonardo gives a parse of a typical songbout as:[35]

i i i i i A B C D E F G A B C D E F G A B C D E F G

This song pattern is economically described by the First-order Markov transition table below.

START ⌢ i
i ⌢ i
i ⌢ A
A ⌢ B
B ⌢ C
C ⌢ D
D ⌢ E
E ⌢ F
F ⌢ G
G ⌢ A
G ⌢ END

In some cases there is more than one possible transition. These account for the optional iteration of initial 'i's, and the option of going round the **A B C D E F G** cycle again after a **G**, or just ending the song.

The zebra finch repertoire is varied, in several ways. (1) The motif may be repeated a variable number of times, and (2) within a motif there can be slight variations, although apparently not enough to make it a different motif. I will discuss the variable repetitions of single notes or whole motifs later. Now, we'll address the within-motif variation, which has only been described recently. 'In his landmark study, Immelmann (1969) indicated that individual zebra finches sing the notes in their song motifs in a stereotyped order. One assumes Immelmann to mean that males sing notes of unvarying form in a fixed order in each motif.' (Sturdy et al. 1999, p. 195). Sturdy et al.'s own research showed that this is not strictly true. There is some variability in the song, but nothing that cannot be handled (on a narrow approach) by a First-order Markov model. 'The predominant motif accounted for an average proportion of only .66 of all the motifs sung by 20 zebra finches recorded. ... How do zebra finches deviate from their predominant note order? About half the deviations result from

---

[35] Researchers vary somewhat in their classification of the basic units of the zebra finch song, but not enough to affect the discussion here. Whereas Leonardo recognized seven distinct notes, A to G, the classification of Sturdy et al. (1999) identified six notes, labelled 'Introductory', 'Short slide', 'Flat', 'Slide', 'Combination', and 'High'. One of these is the vocabulary of the zebra finch repertoire; we'll use Leonardo's analysis. The classification by Zann (1993) was finer, identifying 14 different units. Nothing rests on these differences here.

skipped notes and the other half from added and repeated notes' (*ibid.*, p. 201). Skipped steps and repetitions of the immediately preceding note can be incorporated into a First-order Markov description (but at the cost of projecting an infinite set of potential songs). A First-order Markov description of zebra finch song breaks the song down into a number of elements and shows how these are linearly combined. 'The probabilistic sequencing of syllables by the bird on a particular day can be fully characterized as a Markov chain..., in which the likelihood of singing a particular syllable depended only on the occurrence of the last syllable produced, and not on any prior syllables'[36] (Leonardo 2002, p. 36).

Zebra finches, then, have a stereotyped song, which can be varied by occasional skips, repeats, and additions of notes. This actually raises an issue much discussed in connection with human language, the distinction between **competence** and **performance**. Without using these specific terms, Sturdy et al. suggest an explanation of this kind for the variability in zebra finch motifs. 'One explanation for why zebra finches sing more than one note order is that intact, normally reared males intend to produce a stereotyped motif but memory and other constraints interfere' (1999, p. 202). The use of 'intend' here may shock some. Who can know what a finch intends? Nevertheless, it seems plausible that the finch's behaviour is determined by two distinct kinds of factor: (1) a learned motor routine, requiring ideal conditions for its smooth execution, and (2) the natural shocks that flesh is heir to. Sturdy et al. (1999) mention some evidence for this competence/performance distinction affecting variability in zebra finch song—lesioned or deprived finches produce more variable songs (Scharff and Nottebohm 1991; Volman and Khanna 1995).

Linguists tend strongly to compartmentalize competence and performance. Syntactic theorists only study competence,[37] native speakers' intuitions of the well-formedness of strings of words in their language. The study of performance, for example relative difficulty in parsing sentences, speech errors by normal speakers, and aphasic language, typically assumes certain canonical target forms as a baseline for study. That is, it is assumed that performance factors can disrupt the output of an idealized competence. The sentence blueprint (competence) defines a perfect product; execution of this blueprint in real time and space introduces imperfections. Certainly, this happens. But it

---

[36] That is, in the terms I have used, a First-order Markov transition table, with probabilities associated with each transition. Leonardo's assertion is probably not strictly true in that assigning probabilities at the micro-level to transitions between notes will not capture the observed distribution of numbers of repetitions of a higher-level motif.

[37] At least in their capacity as syntactic theorists. Some individual researchers can switch roles.

is seldom admitted that the causality can also go the other way, that is that performance factors can affect the shape of competence. We will discuss this in greater detail in several later chapters, but for now, it is interesting to note an insightful comment on zebra finch variability by Sturdy et al.:

It is possible to accept the hypothesis that an intact brain and normal experience work together to make the note order in individual birds' songs more consistent without accepting the idea that the goal of this consistency is highly stereotyped songs. According to this explanation, zebra finches strike a balance, singing more than one note order to create variation to avoid habituation effects on females without increasing variation in note order so much that it hinders mate recognition.

(Sturdy et al. 1999, p. 203)

Metaphorically, what they are suggesting is that zebra finches allow themselves a certain amount of deviation from their canonical target motif, and that this may have adaptive value. This is putting it too anthropomorphically. A more acceptable formulation is that evolution has engineered an adaptive compromise between absolutely faultless control of the stereotype song and a certain level of disruptibility. This seems to be a particular case of a very general property of evolution, that it tolerates, and even tends toward, a certain level of 'error-friendliness'—see von Weizsäcker and von Weizsäcker (1998). If such a thing worked in human language, this would mean, translated into linguists' terms, an evolutionary interaction between performance factors and what determines competence. I think this does work for human language, especially when thinking about how languages evolve over time; the theme will be taken up in later chapters. For now, note that the issue arises even in a species as remote from us as zebra finches.

Some hummingbird song is complex in a similar way to the zebra finch's repetition of motifs. The longest song that Ficken et al. (2000, p. 122) reported from a blue-throated hummingbird was ABCDEBCDEBCDEABCDE. On a narrow approach, this repertoire is also economically described by a First-order Markov transition table.

Chaffinch songs are quite complexly structured too, for a bird. Here is a description by an expert:

Each bird has 1–4 song types, rarely 5 or 6. The sequence of syllable types within a song type is absolutely fixed, though numbers of each may vary. Every song has a trill, of 2–4 phrases, rarely 1 or 5, followed by a flourish of unrepeated elements. The occasional brief unrepeated element may occur between phrases in the middle of a song (we call these 'transitional elements'). The same phrase syllable or flourish type may occur in more than one song type in an area or in the repertoire of an individual bird but, unless

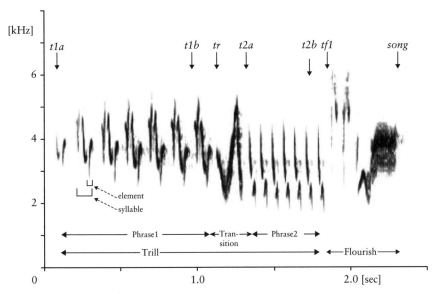

Fig. 1.4 A typical chaffinch song.

Note its clear structure into discrete parts. The initial 'Phrase1' consists of a number of iterated 'syllables'; this is followed by a single 'transition', after which comes 'Phrase2' also consisting of a number of iterated 'syllables' of a different type; the song ends with a single distinctive 'Flourish'. (I have used scare quote marks here because the use of terms like 'phrase' and 'syllable' in linguistics is different.)

Source: From Riebel & Slater (2003).

this happens, hearing the start of a bird's song will tell you exactly what the rest of it will be.   (Peter Slater, personal communication)

Figure 1.4 is an example a typical chaffinch song, from Riebel and Slater (2003). 'The transitions between different syllable types are fixed, but the number of same type syllable repetitions within phrases varies substantially between different renditions of the same song type (Slater and Ince 1982)' (Riebel and Slater 2003, p. 272). A First-order Markov description of this particular chaffinch song type is given below, in seven transition statements.

START ⌢ syllable1
syllable1 ⌢ syllable1
syllable1 ⌢ transition
transition ⌢ syllable2
syllable2 ⌢ syllable2
syllable2 ⌢ Flourish
Flourish ⌢ END

Here the transitions from one element to the same element describe iteration. Iteration must be carefully distinguished from recursion. Purely repetitive behaviour usually does not involve recursion. Iteration is doing the
same thing over and over again. Walking somewhere is achieved by iterated striding. Dogs scratch iteratively. In doing something iteratively, the
main consideration is when to stop, usually when some goal or satisfactory (or exhausted!) state has been reached. With iteration, no memory for the number of times the repeated action has been performed is
necessary. Iteration is simply about sequence; recursion entails hierarchical
organization.

Recursion involves keeping track of the steps that have been gone
through. Recursion is defined as performing an operation of a particular
type while simultaneously performing the same type of operation at a
'higher' level. For example, in the sentence *John said that Mary had left*,
the sentence *Mary had left* is embedded inside the larger sentence. English
allows this kind of recursive embedding quite extensively, as in *I know
that Bill wondered whether Harry believed that Jane said that Mary had left*.
In this example, the successive underlinings indicate the successive recursive
embeddings of a sentence within a sentence. To correctly grasp the meaning
of the whole large sentence, it is necessary to keep track of exactly what is
embedded in what, for example what was the object of Harry's belief, or of
Bill's wondering.

Recursion is a special subcase of hierarchical procedural organization.
Depending on one's analysis, not every hierarchically organized activity
involves doing an action of type X while doing the same type of action at a
'higher' level. For forty years, until recently, linguists have defined recursion
in terms of the phrasal labels assigned to parts of a sentence's structure. So a
noun phrase (NP) inside a larger NP, as in *the house at the corner*, or a sentence
inside another larger sentence, as in *Mary said she was tired*, counts as a case of
recursion. But a sentence can have quite complex structure, with phrases inside
other, different kinds of, phrases, and this would not have been counted as
recursion. For instance, the sentence *Yesterday Mary might have bought some
very good shoes on the High Street* is hierarchically structured, but linguists
would not have given it as an example of grammatical recursion, because here
there is no embedding of a phrase of one type inside a phrase of the same type.
But if one considers the overall goal of **parsing** such a phrase, then arguably
recursion is involved in even such a simple expression as *very good shoes*
because one has to parse the constituent *very good* and store (keep track of)
its analysis as a subtask of the parsing of the whole phrase. There is parsing of

parts within parsing of the whole. This new interpretation of recursion, quite reasonably based more on procedures of use than, as hitherto, on grammatical labels, has crept rather surreptitiously into the recent literature. Essentially the same idea seems to be what Nevins et al. (2009a) have in mind when they write 'if Pirahã really were a language whose fundamental rule is a nonrecursive variant of Merge, no sentence in Pirahã could contain more than two words' (p. 679). It is a pity, and confusing, that in their previous paper in the same debate (Nevins et al. 2009b), they constantly referred to 'iterative Merge'. If a Merge operation can be applied to its own output, as it definitely can, this is recursion. (The Pirahã language and recursion will be discussed more fully in Chapter 5, section 4.) This suggestion does not weaken the concept of recursion to vacuity. There remains a crucial difference between iteration and recursion. A dog scratching, for instance, does not keep track of the individual 'strokes' in its scratching routine. Nor does the production of the chaffinch song involve recursion. The chaffinch song is a hierarchical arrangement of subparts 'Phrase1' and 'Phrase2', each of which consists of iterated syllables. But the song is not a case of recursion, as far as can be seen, principally because there are no meanings of subparts of the song whose contribution to the meaning of the whole needs to be kept track of. The First-order Markov description I have given for a typical chaffinch song, while adequate in weak generative capacity, does not explicitly recognize the hierarchical organization into phrases, which would be intuitively desirable from a standpoint of strong generative capacity. I will return in a later section to how neuroscientific evidence can shed some light on a bird's neural representation (subconscious of course) of hierarchical 'phrasal' structure in its song.

Iteration can be captured in a First-order Markov description by a transition from one element to itself. And as we saw with the zebra finch and blue-throated hummingbird songs, iterated sequences of longer 'phrases' or motifs can also (on a narrow approach) be handled by First-order Markov descriptions. (The champion syllable iterator among birds is the canary. Stefan Leitner (personal communication) tells me he has observed a canary 'tour', in which a syllable is iterated 137 times; and he has sent me the sonogram to prove it!) The closest we get in English to this kind of iteration is with the childish string *very, very, very, very,*... repeated until the child gets tired. Extensive iteration is indeed rare in human language, but at least one language is reported as using it with, interestingly, a similar numerical distribution of iterations as found for the chaffinch syllables. The Hixkaryana language of northern Brazil had, in the 1970s, about 350 speakers remaining. Derbyshire (1979a), in a careful description of this language, writes 'The ideophone is a noninflected onomatopoeic word...The ideophone may be a single morpheme...or a

sequence of reduplicated forms (e.g. *sih sih sih sih sih* "action of walking";
in the latter case the number of repeats of the form may be from two to ten or
more, but it is usually not more than six' (p. 82).

In the above Markov description of chaffinch song, I have not built in any
upper or lower limit to the number of times the bird may go around the several
iterative loops. According to this transition table, the bird might repeat the
syllable in the first phrase of the trill perhaps a hundred times, perhaps not
repeat it at all, choosing not to go around the loop. This fails to capture a
typical feature of the song. In real chaffinch song, some phrase types may
involve between four and eleven iterations, with a median of seven (Riebel
and Slater 2003); other phrase types may involve somewhat fewer iterations.
So the transition table does not do justice to the numerical range of iterations
in the chaffinch song. No doubt, the number of iterations is conditioned by
such factors as the bird's current state of health, how long it has been singing
in the current bout, and the phrase type. But it also seems reasonable to assume
that the median number of seven iterations is part of the bird's canonical
target. There is also a negative correlation between the length of the initial Trill
component and the final Flourish component; '. . . the two song parts must be
traded off against each other as either long trills or long flourishes can only
be achieved by shortening the other part of the song' (Riebel and Slater 2003,
p. 283). The authors suggest the idea of a 'time window' for the whole song.
It is tempting to attribute this to the bird's need to finish the whole call on the
same out-breath, but in fact we cannot assume that the whole call is achieved
in a single breath. Franz and Goller (2002) found that zebra finch syllables
within the same call are separated by in-breaths. Hartley and Suthers (1989)
show that canaries take 'mini-breaths' in the pauses between syllables of their
songs.

A natural description of the chaffinch song recognizes it as a complex motor
program, organized into a sequence of subroutines. These subroutines may
loop iteratively through certain defined gestures, a particular gesture being
appropriate for each separate subroutine type. The whole motor program for
the song is constrained by certain limits on length, so that the whole program
has to be got through in a certain number of seconds. Here again, we see
something analogous to an interaction between competence and performance,
as linguists would perceive it. Evolution seems to have engineered the chaffinch
song so that it is constructed in phrases, with the possibility of iteration of
syllables inside each phrase. First-order Markov descriptions are not inherently designed for expressing numerical limits on iteration or on the overall
length of whole signals. And indeed no type of grammar as defined by the
basic Formal Language Hierarchy is designed to express such quantitative

facts. A defining assumption is that the classes of grammars and languages specified are not subject to any numerical constraints. In the typical division of labour used in describing human languages, issues to do with number of repetitions (e.g. of adjectives or prepositional phrases) or of sentence length are the province of stylistics or performance and not of grammar or competence. From the perspective of human language, chaffinch song is designed to be both syntactically somewhat complex and attractively stylish. The sequential structure with apparent 'phrases' gives it a certain complexity, and the numerical limitations on iterations and overall length mould this to a style attractive to female chaffinches. But for the chaffinch, its syntax and its style are all one indissoluble package. I have suggested the term 'competence-plus' to describe such a package of 'algebraic' and numerical information.

For human language, the distinction between grammaticality and good style is, for most linguists and for most cases, clear. But there are definitely borderline cases where it's not clear whether a problem with a sentence is grammatical or stylistic. Here is a notorious example, involving self-centre-embedding, a contentious issue since the beginnings of generative grammar.

Where is the book that the students the professor I met taught studied?

The orthodox view in generative linguistics is that such examples are perfectly grammatical English, but stylistically poor, because they are hard to parse.[38] If some degree of control over complex syntax evolved in humans independent of any semantic function, as suggested by Darwin and Jespersen, it was probably also constrained by the kind of factors I have, from my human viewpoint, identified as 'stylistic' in chaffinch song. If the Darwin/Jespersen scenario has any truth in it, then possibly as we humans later began to endow our signals with complex referential content, rather than just to impress mates with their form, numerical constraints on style or form were relegated to a lesser role compared to the more pressing need for conveying complex meanings. But there is no reason to suppose that numerical constraints were eliminated completely from the factors determining syntactic competence. This highlights a very general problem with a purely formal approach to natural biological systems, both human and non-human. Nowhere are numerical constraints on memory taken into account. Yet biological organisms, including humans, are constrained by memory and processing limitations. Grammars are good tools for describing idealized **potential** behaviour. A full account of **actual** behaviour, in humans and non-humans alike, needs to marry the regular non-numerical

---

[38] The topic of centre-embedding will come up again in a later subsection, and in Chapter 3.

grammar-like properties of the behaviour with the constraints of memory and processing. This is not to abandon the idea of competence, but rather to envisage a description with two kinds of component, grammar rules and numerical constraints, 'competence-plus'. I will revisit this issue in Chapter 3, on human syntax. For the moment, in the context of chaffinch song, the canonical target song can be described by the First-order Markov transitions given earlier, but now significantly augmented by numerical statements of the approximate numerical constraints, as follows.

START ⌒ syllable1
syllable1 ⌒ syllable1 $4 \leq x \leq 11$
syllable1 ⌒ transition
transition ⌒ syllable2
syllable2 ⌒ syllable2 $4 \leq y \leq 11$
syllable2 ⌒ Flourish
Flourish ⌒ END $x + y \approx 14$

This says that there can be between 4 and 11 iterations of 'syllable1', and between 4 and 11 iterations of 'syllable2', and that the total of the two iterative batches should be approximately 14. This conforms to Riebel and Slater's (2003) description, and gives a much more accurate picture of the possible range of chaffinch songs. Augmenting the transition table with numbers like this actually makes it no longer a First-order Markov model, because it implies a counting mechanism that must remember more than just the previous syllable, in fact maybe as many as the ten previous syllables.[39] Thus adding the numbers implies a significant increase in the power of the processing mechanism. I will not delve into the implications for the place of such numerically augmented models in relation to the Formal Language Hierarchy. Very likely, the incorporation of numerical information fatally undermines a central pillar of the Formal Language Hierarchy.

The description given is of one particular song type. An individual chaffinch may have several (typically two to four) different song types. The structural pattern of all song types is very similar: from one to four 'phrases' each consisting of a number of iterated identical syllables, all followed by a 'flourish' marking the end of the song. The First-order Markov description of one song type above is easily expanded to accommodate the whole repertoire of an individual. For each different song type in the repertoire, the transition from

---

[39] Specifying probabilities for the individual First-order transitions would not give the desired frequency distribution with about 7 as the most common number of iterations.

START is to a different initial syllable; after the prescribed number of iterations of this syllable constituting the initial phrase, the next significant transition is to a syllable characterizing the second phrase in that song; and so on.[40]

Chaffinch songs are highly stereotyped, the birds being genetically disposed to singing from a narrow range of songs, summarized by Peter Slater's description: 'Every song has a trill, of 2–4 phrases, rarely 1 or 5, followed by a flourish of unrepeated elements' (see above, p. 48). A description of the innate template, then, should also incorporate numerical information about the number of phrases that the learned songs may contain, as well as the range and central tendency of the repetitions of notes.

As with iterations of chaffinch syllables, a numerical qualifier can be added to the First-order Markov description of zebra finch songs to account for the variable number of repetitions of its motif. A linguist might object, if he were bothered about birdsong, 'How messy!'. Well, yes, biological facts are messy. We shall see later to what extent such ideas can be applied to the syntax of human languages. It must be acknowledged here that allowing the augmentation of a First-order Markov description with such numerical qualifiers introduces a new class of descriptions whose place on the Formal Language Hierarchy is not made clear. Indeed the introduction of numerical information seriously affects the pristine categorical approach to classes of languages. It is not my business here to try to develop a numerically sensitive alternative to the Formal Language Hierarchy.

One more point about the competence/performance distinction is in order. Performance factors are often portrayed as whatever is accidental or temporary, factors such as distraction, interruption or drunkenness while speaking. Another emphasis links performance to a distinction between what applies only to the language system (e.g. syntactic principles) and factors applying to other activities, factors such as short-term memory and processing speed, with performance factors being the latter. Note that these latter factors, such as short-term memory limits, are relatively permanent properties of organisms. Short-term memory, for example, does not fluctuate significantly in an adult (until dementia), whereas happenings like interruption by loud noises, distraction by other tasks, or medical emergencies are genuinely accidental and beyond prediction. A description of an organism's typical behaviour cannot be responsible for these accidental factors. But relatively constant factors, such as processing speed and memory limitations, can be incorporated into

---

[40] For quite thorough exemplification of a range of chaffinch song types, and how they change over time, within the basic structural pattern, see Ince et al. (1980).

a description of communicative behaviour, once one has made the *a priori* decision to be responsible for them. In fact, a comprehensive account of the growth of linguistic competence in an individual, or of the learning of its song by a songbird, cannot ignore such factors. No organism learns or acquires competence immune from the quantitative constraints of its body.

This last point about quantitative physical constraints contributing to the form of competence echoes a connection made in *The Origins of Meaning* (pp. 90–6). There, a robust quantitative constraint on the number of arguments that a predicate[41] can take was attributed to a deep-rooted constraint on the number of separate objects the visual system can track. When linguists describe the argument structure of verbs, their valency is drawn from a very small range of possibilities, either 1 or 2 or 3 (some may argue for 4). Newmeyer (2005, p. 5) lists 'No language allows more than four arguments per verb' as a 'Seemingly universal feature of language', citing Pesetsky (2005). A few languages, including Bantu languages, have 'causative' and/or 'applicative' constructions which add an extra argument to a verb, but even in these languages the number of arguments explicitly used rarely exceeds three. The number of arguments that a predicate can take is central to human language, and the same general numerical constraints on semantic structure apply, though they are seldom explicitly stated, in the grammars of all languages.

1.3.3 Hierarchically structured behaviour

This subsection is mainly descriptive, giving well-attested examples of the hierarchical organization of singing behaviour in some species. We have already seen hierarchical structure in the chaffinch song. There are more spectacular examples. The species most notable are nightingales and humpback whales, very distantly related. In the case of whales' songs, while accepting their clear hierarchical organization, I will dispute the claims of some authors that they reveal previously unsuspected complexity going beyond what has become familiar in birdsong.

In all the birdsong literature, there is a convergence on the concept of a song as a central unit of the birds' performance, very much like the concept of a sentence in human syntax. A distinction is made between songs and mere calls, with calls being very short and having no complex internal structure. 'Although

---

[41] It is vital to certain arguments in this book to make a distinction between predicates in a semantic, logical sense, and the Predicate element of a grammatical sentence. I will always (except when quoting) use lowercase 'predicate' or small caps PREDICATE for the semantic/logical notion, and an initial capital letter for 'Predicate' in the grammatical sense.

the differences between songs and calls are occasionally blurred, most of the time they are clear and unequivocal. First, calls are usually structurally much simpler than songs, often monosyllabic.... Singing is always a more formal affair.... Calling behavior is much more erratic and opportunistic' (Marler 2004, p. 32).

... the linkage between a given social context and a particular signal pattern is quite fixed in calls, but astoundingly flexible in songs. In other words, during an episode of singing, most bird species perform different song patterns without any evidence that the social context has changed.... In contrast to calls, songs are learned and generated by vocal imitation of individually experienced signals.

(Bhattacharya et al. 2007, pp. 1–2)

Bird songs are roughly the same length as typical spoken human sentences, between one and ten seconds, and have some internal structure of syllables and notes. 'In most species, songs have a length of a few seconds and the pauses separating songs usually have a similar duration. This patterning allows birds to switch between singing and listening, and suggests that songs are significant units of vocal interactions. A song is long enough to convey a distinct message and, at the same time, short enough to allow a sensory check for signals of conspecifics or to reply to a neighbor' (Todt and Hultsch 1998, p. 488). In looking for bird behaviour possibly related to human sentential syntax, it is natural to focus mainly on the song as the unit of interest.

The birdsong literature is generally confident in stating how many songs a species has in its typical repertoire, within some range. This assumes that song-types are categorially distinct, and can be counted. It is also of great interest, of course, to know whether the distinct categories are valid for the birds, rather than just for the human researchers. Searcy et al. (1995) describe the results of habituation tests suggesting that 'in the perception of male song sparrows, different song types are more distinct than are different variants of a single type' (p. 1219). Consistent with this, Stoddard et al. (1992) found that 'song sparrows readily generalize from one exemplar of a song type to other variations of that song type' (p. 274). Most bird researchers, working with a variety of species, assume the psychological reality of categorially distinct song-types, and the size of repertoires of song-types can be reliably quantified.

The champion combinatorial songster is the nightingale '(*Luscinia megarhynchos*), a species that performs more than 200 different types of songs (strophen), or more than 1000 phonetically different elements composing the songs' (Todt and Hultsch 1998, p. 487).[42] A nightingale's song repertoire is quite complex in itself, but still technically describable by First-order Markov transitions. This bird's behaviour is also interesting because it can clearly be analysed into several units larger than the individual song, just as human discourse can be analysed into units larger than the sentence, for example paragraphs and chapters in written language. We will discuss this higher-level structuring of nightingale behaviour shortly, after a brief survey of the internal structure of the songs of this versatile bird.

A nightingale song typically contains sections (phrases) of four types, which the main researchers of this bird, Dietmar Todt and Henrike Hultsch, label *Alpha, Beta, Gamma,* and *Omega.*

Alpha sections are low in volume, whereas Beta sections consist of louder element complexes or motifs. Gamma sections are made up by element repetitions that results in a rhythmical structure of this song part (trill), whereas Omega sections contain only one unrepeated element.   (Todt and Hultsch 1998, p. 489)

The sections always occur in this order, barring the odd accident. Figure 1.5 reproduces Todt and Hultsch's flowchart of element-types composing the nightingale songs. The flowchart makes it clear that the repertoire can be captured by a First-order Markov transition table, as given partially below, equivalent to Todt and Hultsch's incomplete flowchart.

START ⌒ $1a,b$	$1_{a,b}$ ⌒ $2_{a,b}$	$2_{a,b}$ ⌒ $3_{a,b}$
($2_{a,b}$ ⌒ other notes)	$3_{a,b}$ ⌒ $4_{a,b}$	$4_{a,b}$ ⌒ $5_{a,b}$
$5_{a,b}$ ⌒ $6_{a,b}$	($5_{a,b}$ ⌒ other notes)	$6_{a,b}$ ⌒ $7a$
$6_{a,b}$ ⌒ $7b$	($6_{a,b}$ ⌒ another note)	$7a$ ⌒ $7a$
$7a$ ⌒ $8a$	$8a$ ⌒ $9a$	$9a$ ⌒ $10a$
$10a$ ⌒ $9a$	$10a$ ⌒ $11a$	$11a$ ⌒ END
$7b$ ⌒ $7b$	$7b$ ⌒ $8b$	$8b$ ⌒ $9b$
$9b$ ⌒ $10b$	$10b$ ⌒ $9b$	$10b$ ⌒ $11b$
$11b$ ⌒ END		

To confirm the applicability of a First-order Markov model to nightingale song, I asked Dietmar Todt, the main expert on this bird, 'Is the end of one part

---

[42] The assertion of over 1000 different elements is at odds with Anderson's (2004, p. 151) assertion that 'The nightingale's many songs are built up from a basic repertoire of about forty distinct notes'. I take Todt and Hultsch (1998) to be the experts. 1000 notes, rather than 40, is consistent with the interesting generalization which Hultsch et al. (1999) make about all birdsong having smaller repertoires of songs than of notes, thus failing to exploit combinatoriality to advantage. A smaller vocabulary used for composing a larger song repertoire is in line with a linguist's expectations, but apparently not the way birds do it.

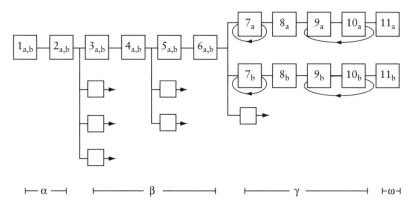

Fig. 1.5 Flowchart of a typical nightingale repertoire.

Note: The numbers with subscript letters in the boxes represent distinct song elements. The empty boxes represent the beginning notes of sequences left unspecified in this incomplete flowchart. The Greek letters below the chart label the Alpha, Beta, Gamma, and Omega sections of the song. It is clear that this flowchart can be converted into an equivalent set of First-order Markov transition statements.

Source: From Todt and Hultsch (1998, p. 489).

(e.g. alpha) identifiable as a distinct end note/syllable of that part, so that the transition to a following part (e.g. some beta part) can be predicted just from the last note of the previous part?' He replied 'Yes, but with stochastic transitional probabilities' (D. Todt, personal communication). That is, where there is more than one transition from a particular element, some information on the probability of the respective transitions needs to be given. A corroborative piece of evidence that the repertoire does not technically require a more powerful form of description, such as a State Chain diagram, is this statement: 'Particular types of elements assessed in the singing of an individual bird occur at one particular song position only' (Todt and Hultsch 1998, p. 488). In human grammar this would be like a particular word being confined to a single position in a sentence. There is perhaps an ambiguity in the authors' statement. Does it apply to all element-types, or just to a 'particular' subset of element-types? It is consistent with the rest of their descriptions of nightingale song, in this paper and others, that the statement applies to all element-types. In this case, every note in a song occupies its own unique characteristic slot in the sequence of notes. This is still compatible with there being several possible transitions from one note to the next. It also makes it clear how 200 songs are composed from a vocabulary of a thousand different notes. An analogy is with different journeys radiating outward from the same point of origin, with different routes often diverging but never reconverging (what Todt and Hultsch call 'diffluent flow'). A given route may make short, one-or-two-place loops back to the same place, later in the journey/song. Many journeys are possible, the places visited are a predictable distance from the origin, and never revisited, apart from the short iterative loops, and more places are visited than there are journeys. These facts show nightingale song to be strikingly different from human grammar.

Nightingale song-types are typically collected into higher-level units called 'packages'. 'Each package was a temporally consistent group of acquired song types which could be traced back to a coherent succession of, usually, three to five (max. seven) model song types' (Hultsch and Todt 1989, p. 197). In other words, depending on the order in which the young nightingale had experienced song-types in infancy, it reproduced this order in its adult performance, up to a maximum sequence of seven song-types. If it heard the song-type sequence **A B C D** frequently enough (about twenty times) as a youngster, then its characteristic song would also have these song-types contiguous in a long session of song. The particular packages have no clear structural features. That is, you can't say, given a large set of song-types, which ones most naturally go together to form a package. The formation of packages results from each individual bird's learning experience, and different birds have different packages. Isolated nightingales, who hear no model songs, do not form packages of song-types (Wistel-Wozniak and Hultsch 1992). So it seems that nightingales memorize whole sequences of song-types, analogous to a human child memorizing a whole bed-time story, except **without the meaning.**

The final notes of song-types are distinctive of the song-types, so memory for a transition between the last note of one song and the beginning of the next would be possible. But this is not how the birds keep their packages together. '[M]ost song types within a package were connected to each other by multidirectional sequential relationships, in contrast to the unidirectionality of transitions in the tutored string' (Hultsch and Todt 1989, p. 201). Thus it seems unlikely that packages are maintained through memorization of one-way transitions between song-types or notes. This is clear evidence of higher-level hierarchical structuring. Hultsch and Todt (1989) assume a battery of submemories, each responsible for a package. They justify this analysis by pointing out that nightingales can learn sequences of up to sixty song-types with as much ease as sequences of twenty, and this most probably involves some chunking process. They also point out that songs that are presented during learning as not part of any frequently experienced package tend to be the songs that the birds fail to acquire.

In the wild, a bird's choice of what song to sing depends on many factors, including responding to singing from rivals. In competitive singing, the patterns are harder to discern. Todt and Hultsch (1996) studied the simpler case of solo singing by nightingales. Song sequencing here shows a remarkable fact. With a repertoire of 200 songs

...on average about 60–80 songs of other types are used before a given song type recurs. The recurrence number of 60–80 is not a mere function of repertoire size of an individual but varies with the frequency of use of a given song type: rare song types, for example, normally recur after a sequence that is two, three, or even four times as long as the average intersong string (i.e. after 120, 180 or 240 songs).

(Todt and Hultsch 1996, p. 82)

The different frequency of songs is a complicating factor, but there is an analogy here with the familiar statistical 'birthday problem'. How many people need to be in a room for there to be a 50–50 chance of some two of them having the same birthday? The answer is 23. If there were only 200 days in a year, the answer would be much lower.[43] So if a nightingale chooses its songs randomly and with equal frequency from a repertoire of 200, how many songs does it need to sing for there to be a 50–50 chance that the next song will be one that it has sung before? The answer is much lower than 23. Even with the different frequency of songs (like there being some days of the year on which more people are born than others), the figure of 60–80 is significant. As humans, we would find it hard to keep track of items from a vocabulary of 200, making an effort not to repeat any item too soon after its previous use. The obvious trick to achieve this is to recite the vocabulary in a fixed order. Then we can be certain that each item will occur only once every 200 words. It is clear that nightingale song sequences are rather strictly fixed. Todt and Hultsch conclude, 'Because the periodic recurrence of a song type is not a consequence of a rigid sequence of song type delivery, the periodic recurrence has to be distinguished as a separate rule of song delivery' (p. 82). But they give no statistical reasoning. I am not so sure that the periodicity of the songs is not a consequence of their somewhat fixed order. If it is a separate rule of song delivery, it attributes an impressive memory feat to the nightingale. Memorizing a fixed sequence is one memory feat. Not memorizing a fixed sequence, but having the ability to remember what items have occurred in the last 60–80 events (like poker players remembering what cards have already appeared on the table) is a different kind of feat, certainly rarer in humans than the ability to memorize passages by rote.

The hierarchical behaviour of nightingales goes further than packages. Todt and Hultsch (1996) report a 'context effect'. Two different tutors (humans using tape-players) exposed young nightingales to different sequences of master

---

[43] Geoff Sampson tells me he believes the answer, for a 200-day year, would be 17, based on calculations at http://en.wikipedia.org/wiki/Birthday_problem.

songs. The birds learned these song sequences, but kept them separate as 'subrepertoires'. They tended not to mix packages, or songs, from one context of learning with packages or songs from another context. This reminds one of the behaviour of children growing up bilingually. If they get one language from their mother and another from their father, they will mostly keep the two languages separate, apart from occasional mid-sentence code-switching.

Overall, the authors propose a deep hierarchical organization of nightingale song:

notes (elements) < phrases (or motifs) < songs < packages < context groups

As argued above, the song is the most natural correlate in bird vocalization of the human sentence. Birdsong (or at least nightingale song) has structured behaviour both above and below the level of the song. Similarly, human language has discourse structure above the level of the sentence and grammatical and phonological structure below that level. But there the similarities peter out. Even such a versatile performer as the nightingale achieves the complexity of its act very largely by drawing on memorized sequences. There is very little of the flexibility and productivity characteristic of human language.

At this point, still guided by the overall framework of the Formal Language Hierarchy, we leave the birds in their trees or lab cages and take a dive into the depths of the ocean, where whales and other cetaceans sing their songs. Recent studies have spawned some badly exaggerated reports in the popular science press and websites: for example, 'fresh mathematical analysis shows there are complex grammatical rules. Using syntax, the whales combine sounds into phrases, which they further weave into hours-long melodies packed with information' (Carey 2006). On the contrary, I will show that the rules are very simple, and the songs are far from being packed with information. And as previous examples from birdsong show, whalesong is not the only natural song with hierarchical organization. Don't believe articles by credulous pop science reporters!

Not all whale 'song' is structured in the same way. Sperm whales, for example, have distinctive calls and regional dialects, all based on a vocabulary of one! The one unit is a click; clicks can be emitted in groups of various sizes, and with various time spacings between the groups. The distinctive calls are known as 'codas'. 'Codas can be classified into types according to the number and temporal pattern of the clicks they contain. For example, "2+3" is a coda containing two regularly spaced clicks followed by a longer gap before three more clicks while "5R" is a coda with five regularly spaced clicks' (Rendell and Whitehead 2004, p. 866). This is a lesson in itself. Communicative signals can be based on a vocabulary of one, and rhythm and temporal spacing used to distinguish calls. This is not how human language works. We won't consider sperm whale codas further.

It has been claimed that humpback whale songs are in a clear sense more complex than anything we have seen so far. The most data have been collected from humpback whales, mainly by Payne and McVay (1971). Complete humpback whale songs may last as long as half an hour, and they string these songs together into sessions which can last several hours. In a single song session, the whale cycles around the same song over and over again, usually without a break between the end of one instance and the beginning of the next. The longest song session recorded by Winn and Winn (1978) lasted twenty-two hours! Each individual whale has a characteristic song, which changes somewhat from one year to the next. 'There seem to be several song types around which whales construct their songs, but individual variations are pronounced (there is only a very rough species-specific song pattern)' (Payne and McVay 1971, p. 597). It is not known whether both sexes or only one sex sings. In any given season, an individual whale sings just one song, over and over. Other whales in the same group sing distinct but similar songs. Across seasons, whale songs change. The 'dialect' changing over the years is reminiscent of chaffinch dialects changing.

Payne and McVay (1971) published a detailed description of recordings of humpback whale songs, in which they detected many instances of repeated 'phrases' and 'themes'. They attributed a hierarchical structure of considerable depth to the songs, with different-sized constituents nested inside each other as follows: subunit < unit < phrase < theme < song < song session (p. 591). Their figure illustrating this structure is reproduced in Figure 1.6.

The great regularity of the songs is captured in the following quotations:

...phrases in most themes are repeated several times before the whale moves on to the next theme. ...we find it true of all song types in our sample that, although the number of phrases in a theme is not constant, the sequence of themes is. (For example, the ordering of themes is A,B,C,D,E...and not A,B,D,C,E...). We have no samples in which a theme is not represented by at least one phrase in every song, although in rare cases a phrase may be uttered incompletely or in highly modified form.

(Payne and McVay 1971, p. 592)

In our sample, the sequence of themes is invariable, and no new themes are introduced or familiar ones dropped during a song session. Except for the precise configuration of some units and the number of phrases in a theme, there is relatively little variation in successive renditions of any individual humpback's song.

(Payne and McVay 1971, p. 591)

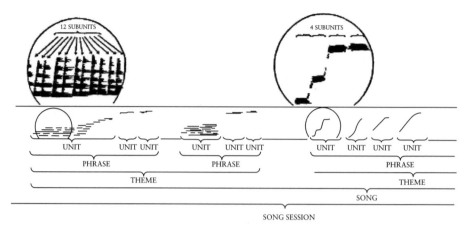

Fig. 1.6 Hierarchical structuring of humpback whale songs.

Note: The circled areas are spectrograms enlarged to show the substructure of sounds which, unless slowed down, are not readily detected by the human ear. Note the six-tier hierarchical organization: subunit < unit < phrase < theme < song < song session.

Source: From Payne and McVay (1971, p. 586).

'A series of units is called a "phrase." An unbroken sequence of similar phrases is a "theme," and several distinct themes combine to form a "song"'.

(Payne and McVay 1971, p. 591)

From the spectrograms the authors give on p. 591 of repeated phrases within a theme, it can be seen that the phrases morph gradually with each repetition. Each repeated phrase is very similar to the next, but after a large number of repetitions similarity between the first phrase and the last phrase of the cycle is much more tenuous. In these examples, the lowest number of repeated phrases with a theme is nine, and the highest number is forty-one. Figure 1.7 shows the same theme, sung twice by the same whale, once with nine repetitions of its characteristic phrase and once with eleven repetitions.

A human analogue of this behaviour is musical variations on a theme. It is unlike anything required by the structure of any language, although poets can reproduce such an effect, given the resources that a language provides. The difference between the first and last instances of the phrase in the same theme is so great that, given these two spectrograms, a birdsong researcher would almost certainly classify them as different units.

For the birdsong examples, researchers typically rely on an intuitive 'eye-balling' method to spot repetitions of phrases. *iiABCDEABCDEABCDE* obviously contains three repetitions of *ABCDE*, which we might decide to call a 'phrase'. Payne and McVay (1971) relied on similar impressionistic methods for the humpback whale song, albeit backed up by very careful and detailed

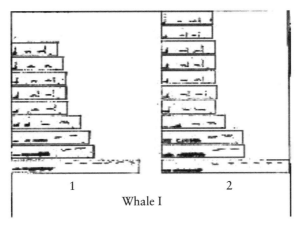

1   2

Whale I

Fig. 1.7 The same theme sung by the same whale in two separate songs.

Note the broad similarity between the two instances of the theme. But note also that the term *repetition* for the phrases is not strictly accurate, as each successive 'repetition' changes the phrase slightly, so that the first and last instances are hardly the same at all.

Source: From Payne and McVay (1971, p. 591).

examination of their recordings. Technically, a repeated sequence in a series illustrates a case of **autocorrelation,** that is the correlation of a portion sliced out of a series of events with other portions earlier in the series. If the portions in question are identical, there is a perfect correlation, but less-than-perfect matches can still be significantly correlated. Suzuki et al. (2006) took Payne and McVay's recordings and subjected them to close mathematical analysis, based on information theory. They discovered two layers of autocorrelation, confirming an important feature of the analysis of the earlier researchers. Their analysis demonstrated that: '(1) There is a strong structural constraint, or syntax, in the generation of the songs, and (2) the structural constraints exhibit periodicities with periods of 6–8 and 180–400 units' (p. 1849). They continue with the strong claim that 'This implies that no empirical Markov model is capable of representing the songs' structure' (*ibid.*). Note the position of the apostrophe (*songs'*) in this latter claim, meaning that a Markov model is incapable of accounting for patterns across songs from many whales in different seasons. It will also be clear that there is a crucial difference between what Payne and McVay called a 'song' and the use of 'song' by Suzuki et al.

What we have with whales goes one step (but only one step) further than the zebra finch and chaffinch songs. Both birds repeat elements of their song at one specific level in its hierarchical organization. Chaffinches repeat low-level syllables within a phrase; the very same low-level unit is iterated, like a child's *very, very, very, very,* .... The repetitions in zebra finch song are of higher-level elements, namely whole motifs, consisting of several syllables, more like a repeated multi-word mantra. The humpback whale song has repetitions at two levels, of 'phrases' and of 'themes'. The repeated themes are not identical, as the phrases are (allowing for the significant morphing of a phrase during a theme). But themes are nevertheless identifiable as repeated structural types, in that each theme consists of a repetition-with-morphing of a single phrase. The repetitions are nested inside each other. The 'phrase' tier of this two-level layered organization is reflected in the shorter (6–8 units) of the two periodicities detected by Suzuki et al.'s autocorrelation analysis. They write of 'a strong oscillation with a period of about 6, corresponding to the typical phrase length of Payne et al. (1983)' (p. 1861).

The longer of the two autocorrelations, with a phase of between 180 and 400 units, is most likely to come about because a whale sings the same song over and over again, without pausing between versions. Payne and McVay (1971) are clear on this point. 'The gap between spectrographs of songs 1 and 2 is designed to make the individual songs clear and is not indicative of any gap in time' (p. 586). 'At the end of the second song, whale II stopped singing— one of our few examples of the end of a song' (p. 588). '[H]umpback songs are repeated without a significant pause or break in the rhythm of singing' (p. 590).

Following the last phrase of the final theme in either song type A or B, the whale starts the first sound in the next song... without any noticeable break in the rhythm of singing. The pause between any two phrases of the last theme is, if anything, longer than the pause between the last phrase of one song and the first phrase of the succeeding song. ...

It is clear, however, that, regardless of where a song may begin, the whale continues the sequence of themes in the same irreversible order (that is, 3, 4, 5, 6, 1, 2, 3, 4, 5 ...).

(Payne and McVay 1971, p. 595)

The article by Suzuki et al. uses the term 'song' in a crucially different way. They took sixteen of Payne and McVay's recordings, each containing several part or whole songs, and referred to these recordings as 'songs'. For consistency with the earlier paper, they should have expressed their results in terms of **recordings**, not 'songs'. Suzuki et al.'s longest recording lasted forty-five minutes and contained 1,103 units of song; the shortest recording was twenty minutes long and contained 380 units. Payne and McVay's longest recorded song lasted thirty minutes and the shortest lasted seven minutes. At an 'average singing rate of 2.5 s/unit' (Suzuki et al. 2006, p. 1855) the longest, thirty-minute, song would have had about 720 units, and the shortest, seven-minute, song would have had about 168 units. The average length in song units of Suzuki et al.'s recordings was 794 units, longer than the likely length of Payne

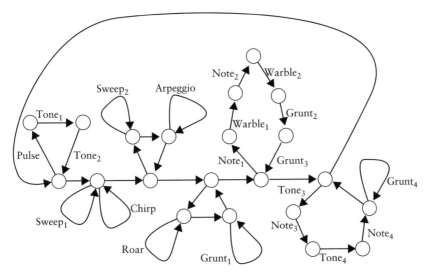

Fig. 1.8 State Chain diagram for humpback whale song.

Note: Subscripts are mine, to distinguish between elements of the same type, e.g. different grunts. Note the six repeatable (looping) themes, the A, B, C, D, E, ... mentioned in the text. Note also the transition from the end of the song back to the beginning, without a break. The unlabelled transition arrows are a convenience in diagramming, with no theoretical implications. (The typical number of repetitions of phrases is not specified here. The diagram also makes no provision for the morphing of phrases within a theme; in fact such continuous, rather than discrete, variation is outside the scope of Formal Language Theory.)

Source: This is my diagram based on Payne and McVay's detailed but informal prose description of one particular song type, and using their descriptive terms.

and McVay's longest song.[44] The range of song lengths, in units, that is 168–720, is comparable to the range of the longer periodicity, 180–400, detected by Suzuki et al. This mathematically detected higher layer of organization very probably comes about because of a whale's habit of singing one same song over and over again without pausing.

Given that a phrase can be repeated an unspecified number of times, the distance between the units the next level up, the themes, is also unspecified, but nevertheless the whale remembers where it has got to in its sequence of themes. Suzuki et al. (2006) write: 'The correlation data demonstrate that the songs possess strong long-distance dependencies of the sort discussed in Hauser et al. (2002) as a hallmark of phrase structure grammar' (p. 1864). This is a serious overestimate of the humpback's sophistication. The whale's song is a rigorously uniform sequence of themes, A B C D E F, never in any other order, with each theme repeating (and morphing) its characteristic phrase many times. Such a song can be adequately described by a State Chain diagram, as in Figure 1.8.

---

[44] In one of Payne and McVay's recordings, not one used by Suzuki et al., there were seven successive songs.

The figure gives an idea of the complexity of the whale's habitual song, even though it is describable by a State Chain description.

It is even just possible that an individual humpback's song, at any given time in a given season, can technically be described by a First-order Markov model. It depends whether the units such as those labelled 'grunts', 'tones', 'sweeps', and so on in Figure 1.8 are the same units wherever they occur in the song, or are somewhat different, depending on their place in the song. If exactly the same 'grunt', for example, is used in four different places, with different transitions before or after it, this calls for a State Chain description. But if the grunts, notes, sweeps, etc., are actually different at each place in the song, then a First-order Markov transition model would be adequate. Judging from the various descriptions in the literature, it seems likely that at least some of these units are re-used 'verbatim' at several different places, so a State Chain description is called for.

I attribute less complex capacity to the humpback whale than Suzuki et al., but we are concerned with different things. In line with a linguist's approach, where competence is the property of an individual, I am interested in the repertoire of a single animal. Social behaviour begins with and develops out of (and finally reciprocally affects) the behaviour of individuals. Suzuki et al. were trying to generalize over all sixteen recordings, from different whales, over two seasons. At one point they write 'the humpback songs contain a temporal structure that partially depends on the immediately previous unit within a song' (p. 1860). So even across a population there is some scope for First-order Markov description. This is followed up by 'the Markov model failed to capture all of the structure embodied by the majority of the humpback songs we analyzed, and that the humpback songs contain temporal structure spanning over the range beyond immediately adjacent units' (p. 1860). But this last conclusion was reached on the basis of only nine out of the 16 recordings. The other seven recordings were discounted because they 'were recorded in a one week period in early February 1978. Since they are likely to be quite similar, those data points may not be statistically independent' (p. 1860). This is fair enough, if one is trying to find structure across a broad population, but our interest is in the singing capabilities of individual whales. So for the seven discounted recordings, taken within a one-week period, it is not the case that a Markov model failed to capture the structure of the song. Further, the 'majority of the humpback songs' referred to is nine out of 16 recordings— not an impressive majority, and certainly not a statistically significant one.

It is not necessary to invoke any power greater than that of a State Chain model to describe humpback whalesong. A certain level of hierarchical organization can be accommodated with State Chain descriptions. A more powerful type of description, Phrase Structure grammar (to be defined in section 1.3.4) is designed to accommodate phrasal structure of a certain complex kind, which is most obviously associated with its **semantic interpretation**. Of whalesong, we have only the recorded behaviour, with no evidence that the song is informed by any compositional semantic principles. Simply equating hierarchical organization with Phrase Structure grammar is incorrect, despite the naturalness of describing some of the constituents of a song as 'phrases'. The extraordinary structural rigidity of the whale's song is easily captured by a State Chain diagram. As for long-distance dependencies, mentioned by Suzuki et al. (2006), this is a matter of terminology. Generally when linguists talk of dependencies between elements in a sentence, the criteria are at least partly semantic. An item is said to be dependent on another if their two meanings interact to contribute to the meaning of the sentence. A standard linguistic example of a long-distance dependency occurs in a sentence-type such as *If X, then Y*, where the clause instantiating *X* can be of any length; thus the distance separating the mutually dependent items *if* and *then* is unpredictable. Another kind of long-distance dependency, often purely syntactically motivated, involves agreement, as between a subject and its verb in English. Such a dependency requires there to be some choice of a feature, say between singular and plural, or between genders, where choice of a feature at one point in the sentence requires a matching choice to be made some distance away. But there is nothing like this in humpback song. Note that many of the long-distance dependencies mentioned by linguists are of a kind that Suzuki et al.'s heuristic methods could not possibly detect, because they involve empty or null items, not physically present in the sentence, but inferred to be 'present' for purposes of semantic interpretation. An example would be *Who did Mary think John was asking Bill to try to find?*, where an understood 'gap' after *find* is taken to be in a dependency relation with the *Who* at the beginning of the sentence. By contrast, consider the hypothetical case of a pathological person whose performance consists solely of reciting the alphabet over and over again, sometimes repeating a particular letter several times, but never deviating from strict alphabetical order, apart from these repetitions. Here, it would be true, strictly speaking, that occurrence of, say, M, depended on prior occurrence of B, and of F, and of K, and at unpredictable distances, because of the unpredictability of the individual letter repetitions. In this sense, and only in this very limited sense, there are in this case, essentially like the humpback whale's song, long-distance dependencies. They are not the kind of long-distance dependencies that require Phrase Structure grammar to describe them.

My arguments here directly counter the following conclusions of Suzuki et al:

The hierarchical structure proposed by Payne and McVay (1971) for humpback whale song challenges these conjectures on the uniquely human nature of long-distance hierarchical relations, and potentially on the uniquely human property of recursion and discrete infinity. Hierarchical grammars may be efficiently represented using recursion, although recursion is not necessarily implied by hierarchy. (2006, p. 1863)

The long-distance hierarchical relations in humpback whalesong are of an entirely simpler nature than those in human language. The mention of recursion is gratuitous; nothing in whalesong suggests the capacity to keep track of an element of one type while simultaneously processing an element of the same type 'inside' it, which is what recursion involves. There is no sense in which the humpback embeds one song inside a bigger song. There is certainly hierarchical structure, embedding **phrases** inside a **song**, but that is another matter. The authors continue to speculate on 'the possibility that humpback whales can, in theory, create an infinite number of valid songs from the finite set of discrete units' (p. 1863). This is in stark contrast to the fact that a single humpback, at any one time in its life, only sings **one** song (over and over).[45] Over the course of many seasons, observing many whales, many different songs would be observed. A 'theory' that extrapolated an infinite number of songs from such observations would need some justification. We don't need to leap from cyclical repetitive behaviour all the way to human-like (e.g. Phrase Structure) grammars for humpback song. And humpback whalesong is by no means unique among animal songs in showing autocorrelation. Many of the bird species discussed above exhibit quite strict autocorrelation: the zebra finch song in Figure 1.3 is a very clear example. Humpback whalesong may be unique in showing autocorrelation at two different levels, but it is likely that this can also be found in nightingale song, if one looks for it.

The autocorrelations discovered by Suzuki et al. are not characteristic of normal human use of language. Mark Liberman, in another perceptive online comment[46] has amusingly noted the lack of autocorrelation in ordinary prose by doing an autocorrelation analysis of Suzuki et al.'s own Discussion section, finding no autocorrelation. Liberman also mentions the autocorrelations that can be found in particularly repetitive songs. A hymn with many verses sung to

---

[45] Two performances of a song with different numbers of repetitions of a phrase still count as one song. This is the common practice with birdsong researchers, and is also assumed by these writers on humpback whalesong.

[46] This could be found at http://158.130.17.5/~myl/languagelog/archives/002954. html. This website was active as of 9 June 2008.

the same tune is an example of autocorrelation in the musical tune. Somewhat weaker types of autocorrelation are typical of many artistic forms, especially rhymed verse. Here is Robert Louis Stevenson's epitaph:[47]

> Under the wide and starry sky
> Dig the grave and let me lie.
> Glad did I live, and gladly die,
> And I laid me down with a will.
>
> This be the verse you grave for me:
> "Here he lies where he longed to be.
> Home is the sailor, home from the sea,
> And the hunter home from the hill."

There are two levels of autocorrelation here, the short-distance *sky/lie/die* and *me/be/sea* rhymes, and the longer-distance *will/hill* rhyme. Within the third line of each stanza, there are further local autocorrelations, *glad...gladly* and *home...home*. The level of autocorrelation here is weaker than it is in the whale's song, because the poet does not repeat whole portions of the work over and over again. This degree of repetitiveness would be uninformative. Though some repetitive patterning is appreciated in poetry, it should also be informative. The artist strikes a balance. But notice that if this *Requiem* poem were the only song you ever sing, always producing it word-for-word in this order, sometime stutteringly repeating a word, and you were otherwise mute, your vocal behaviour could be described by a Second-order Markov model. A First-order model would be almost adequate, but not quite, because such frequent words as *and*, *the*, *me*, and *he* are immediately followed or preceded by different other words. But the previous two words are enough to predict the next word in all cases. This is just about the situation with humpback whale song. The only variation is in the number of phrases repeated in each theme.[48]

Suzuki et al. (2006) also calculated the amount of information carried by humpback song. Given the variable number of repetitions of a phrase, the next unit in a song is not always entirely predictable, so the song is capable of carrying some information. They calculated that 'the amount of information carried by the sequence of the units in the song is less than 1 bit per unit' (p. 1864). Compare this with ...... anything that could finish this sentence! The number of possible next words in a typical human conversational sentence

---

[47] Stevenson actually wrote 'home from sea', which scans better, in the seventh line, but the carvers of his gravestone thought they knew better.

[48] For an extremely ingenious demonstration relating to human perception of autocorrelation in ordinary language, see Cutler (1994).

is immense. Sometimes people say predictable, so strictly uninformative, things, but most of the time they don't. The extreme redundancy of humpback songs, and indeed birdsong too, means that they are easier to remember. Despite a certain level of complexity, they don't carry much information. It can be argued that the lack of any detailed semantic plugging-in to the circumstances of the animal's life is what limits the complexity of these songs. If the songs systematically carried any propositional information about who is doing what to whom, or where is a good place to look for food, they would conceivably gain in complexity. This is a possibility to be taken up in later chapters.

1.3.4 *Overt behaviour and neural mechanisms*

I have defined and explained two lower ranks on the Formal Language Hierarchy, namely First-order Markov models and State Chain models. In terms of weak generative capacity, almost all animal song belongs at the lowest end of this hierarchy. First-order Markov descriptions are adequate to describe even the most complex wild animal songs, if one dismisses intuitive judgements that they exhibit phrasing. A more powerful model of grammar, Phrase Structure grammar, explicitly reflects phrasing in human language. So the question arises whether any further evidence can be found justifying a Phrase Structure approach to at least some animal songs. This follows the theme of recommending that considerations of strong generative capacity be applied to animal songs, no less than in analysis of human language. I will put a case that neuroscientific findings may be used to justify a Phrase Structure analysis of some complex bird songs.

As we have seen, the internal structure of songs is often described by bird and whale researchers in terms of middle-sized units, with labels such as 'phrase', 'motif', 'theme', 'trill', and 'flourish'. A very low-level component of songs is the syllable. A syllable itself can sometimes be somewhat complex, as with the chaffinch flourish, but researchers concur in labelling it a syllable. Adopting the least powerful descriptive devices available, we have seen that it is possible to describe songs by First-order Markov transitions between syllables, and occasionally, as in the case of the Bengalese finch, by a State Chain diagram. None of these descriptive methods refer to units bigger than the syllable, such as phrases, trills, or motifs.

Students of zebra finch, chaffinch, and many other species' songs usually analyse them into phrases, as implied above. And this seems right. The First-order Markov descriptions given earlier for zebra finch and chaffinch songs do not recognize any hierarchical structure. A description of chaffinch song more fitting the bird researcher's natural-seeming description would be the Phrase Structure grammar[49] below.

SONG → TRILL FLOURISH
TRILL → PHRASE1 transition PHRASE2
PHRASE1 → syllable1*
PHRASE2 → syllable2*

Read the arrow here as 'consists of', so that the first rule can be paraphrased as 'A SONG consists of a TRILL followed by a FLOURISH'. Read the other rules in the same way. The superscript stars in the 3rd and 4th rules indicate optional iteration. For example, the grammar states that a phrase of type 'PHRASE1' can consist of any number of instances of syllables of type 'syllable1'. Likewise the star in the 4th rule allows indefinite iteration of syllables of type 'syllable2', constituting a phrase of type 'PHRASE2'. For some added clarity here (although this is not a general convention of such grammars), the capitalized terms are abstract labels for particular types of recurring stretches of the song (non-terminal symbols), and the lower-case terms are all actual notes of the song ('terminal symbols').

Phrase Structure grammar is the third and last rank in the Formal Language Hierarchy that I will describe and define.

Definition of Phrase Structure grammars: A Phrase Structure language is one that can be fully described by a Phrase Structure grammar. A Phrase Structure grammar consists of a finite set of 'rewrite rules', each with one abstract, or nonterminal, element on the left-hand side of the arrow, and with any sequence of symbols on the right of the arrow. These latter symbols may be either actual 'terminal' elements of the language described (e.g. notes or words), or abstract 'nonterminal' symbols labelling phrasal constituents of the language. Such nonterminal symbols are further defined by other rules of the grammar, in which they appear on the left-hand side of the arrow. One nonterminal symbol is designated as the START symbol. In the case of grammars for human languages, this starting symbol can be taken as standing for 'sentence', since the grammar operationally defines the set of possible sentences in the language. In the case of birdsong the start symbol can be taken to stand for 'song'. A string of words or notes is well-formed according to such a grammar if it can be produced by strictly following the rewrite rules all the way to a string

---

[49] Recall that I depart from the normal terminology of the Formal Language Hierarchy. What I will call 'Phrase Structure grammars' here are usually called 'Context Free grammars', not a label that brings out their natural way of working.

of terminal elements. Here, following the rewrite rules can be envisaged as starting with the designated start symbol, then rewriting that as whatever string of symbols can be found in a rewrite rule with that symbol on its left-hand side, and then rewriting that string in turn as another string, replacing each nonterminal symbol in it by a string of symbols found on the left-hand side of some rule defining it. The process stops when a string containing only terminal symbols (actual words of the language or notes of the song) is reached. As a convenient shorthand, the rewrite rules may also use an asterisk (a so-called Kleene star) to indicate that a particular symbol may be rewritten an indefinite number of times. Use of the Kleene star does not affect the weak generative power of Phrase Structure grammars.

Note that the format of Phrase Structure grammars, in terms of what symbols may occur on the right-hand side of a rewrite rule, is more liberal than that for the rewrite format of State Chain languages. This is what makes Phrase Structure grammar more powerful than State Chain grammar. There exist Phrase Structure languages that are not State Chain languages. This result of Formal Language Theory depends on the postulation of infinite languages. Any finite language requires no grammar other than a list of its sentences, in terms of weak generative capacity.

In terms of weak generative capacity, the little Phrase Structure grammar above describes the stereotypical chaffinch song just as well, and just as badly, as the First-order Markov transition table. They both generate the same infinite set of potential songs, so both are observationally adequate. (Neither description captures the numerical range of the iterations inside the two phrases, as discussed earlier, but for simplicity we'll overlook that point here.) Is there any reason to prefer the Phrase Structure grammar, which may appeal to an undesirably powerful type of mechanism, over the simple transition table, which attributes a less powerful type of mechanism to the bird? I will argue that certain neuroscientific facts can be interpreted in such a way as to justify a Phrase Structure description as 'psychologically real' for the birds in question.

The intuitions of bird researchers about song structure are obviously valuable, and the strategy of rigorously adopting the least powerful descriptive device may deprive us of insights into the bases of behaviour. This conclusion applies very generally to a wide range of animal behaviour. Fentress and Stillwell (1973), for example, studying self-grooming behaviour by mice, found that while the sequences of actions could be somewhat adequately described in a totally linear (First-order Markov) way, a hierarchically organized description was more satisfactory. 'Even in animals there are sequential rules embedded among other sequential rules' (Fentress 1992, p. 1533). The limitations of the most economical description of behaviour are echoed, with a different emphasis, in Stephen Anderson's statement, that 'We cannot assume that the tools we have are sufficient to support a science of the object we wish to study in linguistics' (Anderson 2008b, p. 75). The most economical description of surface behaviour may not reflect the mechanisms underlying that behaviour. For both birdsong and language, sources of extra evidence include studies of the acquisition (of song or language) and neurological studies of brain activity (while singing or speaking).

Williams and Staples (1992) studied the learning of songs by young zebra finches from older 'tutors' finding that the learning is structured by chunks. 'Copied chunks had boundaries that fell at consistent locations within the tutor's song, ... Young males also tended to break their songs off at the boundaries of the chunks they had copied. Chunks appear to be an intermediate level of hierarchy in song organization and to have both perceptual (syllables were learned as part of a chunk) and motor (song delivery was broken almost exclusively at chunk boundaries) aspects' (Williams and Staples 1992, p. 278). Cynx (1990, p. 3) found structuring into lower-level units (syllables) in experiments in which the birds were artificially distracted by bursts of strobe light while singing: 'Ongoing zebra finch song can be interrupted, interruptions occur at discrete locations in song, and the locations almost always fall between song syllables'. In this latter case, the units are likely to be influenced by the bird's brief in-breaths during song (Suthers and Margoliash 2002; Franz and Goller 2002).

The neuroscience of birdsong is well developed, and reports ample evidence of hierarchically organized management of song production. In a neurological study of birdsong generally, Margoliash (1997, p. 671) writes that 'neurons in the descending motor pathway (HVc and RA) are organized in a hierarchical arrangement of temporal units of song production, with HVc neurons representing syllables and RA neurons representing notes. The nuclei Uva and NIf, which are afferent to HVC, may help organize syllables into larger units of vocalization'. 'HVc' (sometimes HVC) stands for 'higher vocal centre', and RA neurons are 'downstream' neurons more directly involved in motor output to the syrinx and respiratory system.[50] Both syllables and notes are low-level

---

[50] Both HVc and RA are premotor forebrain nuclei. More exactly, HVc is in a telencephalic nucleus in the neostriatum. See Brenowitz et al. (1997, p. 499) for the historic morphing of the referent of HVC or HVc from 'hyperstriatum ventrale, pars caudale' to 'higher vocal centre'. 'RA' stands for 'robustus archistriatum', and 'RA is a sexually dimorphic, spherical-to-oval, semi-encapsulated nucleus in the medial part of the arcopallium' (Wild 2004, p. 443). NIf is the neostriatal nucleus interfacialis. Uva is a thalamic nucleus.

units in the hierarchical organization of song. A motif, as in zebra finch song, is a higher-level unit. A study by Fee et al. (2004) associates HVc with control of motifs, and RA with control of syllables. Either way, from syllables to notes or from motifs to syllables, there is hierarchical neural control of the song.

How does hierarchically organized brain control of song relate to the hierarchical assumptions built into such high-level descriptive terms as 'phrase' and 'motif'? Can bird neuroscience resolve an issue of whether a First-order Markov transition description for zebra finch song, such as I gave on p. 46, is less faithful to the neurological facts than a Phrase Structure description as below?

SONG → INTRO MOTIF*
INTRO → i*
MOTIF → A B C D E F G

Here, the superscript star notation represents iteration, paraphraseable as 'one or more repetitions of'. Both the First-order Markov transition table and the little Phrase Structure grammar capture the facts of zebra finch song. Doesn't the neuroscience discovery of separate control of motifs (by HVc) and syllables **i, A, B, C, D, E, F, G** (by RA neurons) clinch the matter in favour of the Phrase Structure description? After all, the Phrase Structure description identifies a unit, MOTIF, which corresponds to a segment of the song controlled by a particular brain structure, HVc. Well, with some caution, and definite reservations about the extent of the parallelism claimed, yes, the neural facts seem to support the Phrase Structure version. My claim is based on a study by Fee et al. (2004), following up on an earlier study by the same research team (Hahnloser et al. 2002). The details are fascinating and instructive of how neural research may possibly inform some linguistic descriptions.

Fee and colleagues compared two hypotheses about the role of HVc and RA neurons in the control of zebra finch song. These hypotheses correspond nicely with our two kinds of description, First-order Markov versus Phrase Structure. One hypothesis was labelled 'Intrinsic dynamics in RA'. According to this, HVc sends a signal to the particular RA neurons responsible for producing the first note of the motif, 'A'. After that, all the action is between groups of RA neurons, and HVc is not involved until the next motif. Within a motif, according to this hypothesis, the production of 'A' by its RA neurons triggers activation of other RA neurons responsible for producing the next note, 'B'. And production of 'B' triggers production, all still within RA, of 'C'; and so on until the last note of the motif. This is strikingly analogous to the idea of a First-order Markov transition table. One thing leads to another, and no higher control is involved, except to kick off the beginning of the motif. This is a familiar type of mechanism in neuroscience, famously criticized by Lashley (1951) as 'associative chaining', and appearing in a new guise as 'synfire chains' (Abeles 1991) as one way of explaining serial behaviour. Despite Lashley's critique, the idea has not gone away.

The alternative hypothesis was labelled 'Feedforward activation from HVC'. According to this, putting it informally, HVC (or HVc) has a plan for the serial activation, at 10-millisecond intervals, of all the notes in the motif. An instruction for each separate note is sent from HVC to RA, in sequence. This is analogous to the Phrase Structure rule above defining MOTIF:

MOTIF → A B C D E F G

If the Feedforward activation from HVC hypothesis is correct, it should be possible to detect firings in HVC timed in lockstep, with a small latency, with the various firings in RA producing each of the notes in a motif. And, in brief, this is what the researchers found. No need here to go into such feathery and intricate details as the insertion of probes into sleeping birds or the statistical tests used to verify that the HVC firings were genuinely in lockstep with the RA firings. '... the simplest explanation is that burst sequences in RA, during sleep and singing, are driven by direct feedforward input from HVC' (p. 163).[51] The separate functions of RA (individual syllables) and HVC (sequencing of syllables) is also borne out by a study of song learning; Helekar et al. (2003) showed a dissociation between the learning of these two aspects of the zebra finch song.

So it seems that the higher vocal centre stores information spelling out the sequence of notes in a specific motif. This conveniently static way of putting it, in terms of stored information, still hides a neural puzzle. What makes the HVC send out the sequence of timed bursts to RA? In their concluding paragraph (2004, p. 168), Fee et al. accept that this question naturally arises, and propose using a similar methodology to investigate the control of HVC by nuclei that project to HVC, such as the nucleus Interface (NIf) or nucleus Uvaeformis (Uva). But isn't this just a repeated process of shifting the problem ever upstream to a higher brain centre, first from RA to HVC, then from HVC to NIf and/or Uva? In one account, NIf sends auditory input to the HVC (Wild 2004, p. 451) and is thus plausibly involved in monitoring

---

[51] Glaze and Troyer (2006) take the 'clock-like bursting' in HVC to imply 'nonhierarchical' organization of the song. I can't see that it does. The correlation of hierarchical song patterning with corresponding hierarchical brain control is otherwise generally accepted (see, e.g. Yu and Margoliash 1996). The hierarchicality lies in the undisputed relationship between HVC and RA, not in matters of timing.

the song through feedback. In another account (Fiete and Seung 2009, p. 3),
'...auditory feedback is not important for sequence generation. Also, lesion
studies indicate that input from the higher nucleus NIf to HVC is not necessary
for singing in zebra finches'. What is true for zebra finches is apparently not
true for Bengalese finches, which have a more complex song. Okanoya (2004,
pp. 730–1) reports lesion studies on this species. Unilateral lesions of NIf did
not affect the complexity of their song. However, for two birds with complex
song, bilateral lesions of NIf reduced the complex song to a much simpler
song. A third bilaterally lesioned bird had a rather simple song in the first
place, as apparently some Bengalese finches do, and its song was not affected
by the lesions. Okanoya concludes that the 'NIf is responsible for phrase-to-
phrase transitions' (p. 730). The phrase-to-phrase transitions are what makes
the Bengalese finch's song more complex than that of its wild relative, the
white-rumped munia.

For relatively simple birdsongs, such as that of the zebra finch, the neu-
roscientist's consensus formulation is that HVC is the main organizer of
the song: 'HVC generates the spatiotemporal premotor drive for sequential
motor activation in the form of sequential neural activity. The HVC activity
is "abstract", in the sense that it encodes only temporal ordering, rather than
song features' (Fiete and Seung 2009, p. 2). This way of putting it is somewhat
misleading; how can you specify a temporal ordering of elements without
somehow referring to what those elements are? But certainly the information
that HVC sends to RA about the detailed features of the notes that it orders is
coded in a sparse form. The triggers from HVC to RA can perhaps be thought
of as 'abstract' concise labels for notes: on receiving a particular 'label', RA
starts to fill in all the appropriate detailed articulatory information to be sent to
the syringeal and respiratory muscles. An earlier study (Vu et al. 1994) showed
that electrical stimulation of RA in zebra finches distorted individual syllables
but did not change the order or timing of syllables, but stimulating HVC did
alter the overall song pattern. At the higher 'abstract' level of HVC, it remains
a possibility that the timed sequence of instructions is implemented by a synfire
chain.

The coding of information about particular song types in HVC is sparse.
That is, the instructions sent to RA ultimately causing particular notes to be
sung are provided by ensembles of rather few specialized neurons; and each
ensemble responsible for sending a particular instruction to RA for a particular
note is only active for a small proportion of the total duration of the song. Fee
et al. (2004) suggest that this sparse coding could have advantages for song-
learning. The ensembles of HVC-to-RA neurons correspond in my linguist's
interpretation with the symbols after the arrow in a Phrase Structure rule

defining the sequence of notes in a motif. During learning, when the bird is struggling to match its behaviour with a song template acquired months earlier, individual mismatches between behaviour and template at any point in the sequence can be fixed more easily if the responsible ensembles are relatively isolated from each other by being sparsely coded. This is putting it very informally, but I hope it helps non-neuroscientists (like me) to get some grip on the advantage of what Fiete and Seung (2009), above, called the 'abstract' nature of the song representation in HVC. The key point is that an animal that learns its song, rather than just having it completely innately specified, needs much more complex upstream structuring in its neural apparatus. If the song is wholly innate, there need be no connection between hearing and production. The animal just sings. For learning, there has, of course, to be machinery for comparing stimuli, or the templates acquired from stimuli, with feedback from the animal's own faltering attempts to get it right, plus machinery for gradually adjusting these faltering steps in the right direction. This kind of advantage of more powerful grammar types for learning is seldom discussed in the formal language literature.

If a bird has several motifs in its repertoire, details of each of these are presumably stored in its HVC. Female canaries and zebra finches have little or no song repertoire, and females have markedly smaller vocal control centres, HVC, RA, and 'Area X', than males (Nottebohm and Arnold 1976). In species whose females are not so mute, typically from tropical regions, there is also less sexual dimorphism in the vocal control centres (Brenowitz et al. 1985; Brenowitz and Arnold 1986). Besides this striking sexual dimorphism correlated with singing behaviour, there is a correlation across songbird species. Fee et al. report that 'across many species of songbirds, total repertoire size is correlated with HVC volume' (2004, pp. 167–8). This is corroborated by DeVoogd (2004, p. 778): 'Across a group of 41 very diverse species, the relative volume of HVC was positively correlated with the number of different songs typically produced by males in the species'. Pfaff et al. (2007) established a three-way correlation between size of song repertoire, volume of HVC and body quality, as measured by various physiological and genetic properties, in song sparrows. Finally, Airey and DeVoogd (2000) found a correlation between the typical length of a phrase in a song and HVC volume in zebra finches. All this is consistent with the idea of HVC as a store for abstract song templates.

So far, I have only mentioned the machinery involved in song production. A central tenet of generative linguistics is that the object of interest is a speaker's tacit knowledge of his language, the declarative store of information upon which performance in speaking and interpreting speech is based. A linguist's formal description of a language aims to be neutral with respect to production or perception, just as a geographical map is neutral with respect to eastward or westward travel—the information in the map can be used to go in either direction. A linguist's Phrase Structure rule is not relevant only to production, but also to perception. In birdsong neuroscience, a well-established finding is that individual neurons in HVC respond selectively to playback of a bird's own song. See, for example, Theunissen and Doupe (1998) and Mooney (2000), studying zebra finches. A zebra finch only has a repertoire of one song. In species with more than one song, there is evidence that HVC is also a centre where different individual neurons are responsive to different songs played back from a bird's repertoire. Mooney et al. (2001) investigated swamp sparrows by playing back recordings of their songs to them. Swamp sparrows have small repertoires of between two and five song types. The main finding was that 'single HVc relay neurons often generate action potentials to playback of only a single song type' (p. 12778). This indicates a role for HVC in song perception as well as song production. This work was followed up by Prather et al. (2008), still working with swamp sparrows. These researchers discovered a vocal-auditory analogue of mirror neurons, as found in the macaque brain (Rizzolatti et al. 2001; Gallese et al. 1996). Mirror neurons have been widely regarded as providing a basis for imitative action. In the swamp sparrows, neurons projecting from HVC to Area X responded robustly to specific song playback.

In a substantial proportion of responsive HVC_X neurons (16 of 21 cells), auditory activity was selectively evoked by acoustic presentation of only one song type in the bird's repertoire, defined as the 'primary song type', and not by other swamp sparrow songs chosen at random. The primary song type varied among cells from the same bird, as expected given that each bird produces several song types.

(Prather et al. 2008, p. 305)

The same neurons fired when hearing a song as did when singing that song. Interestingly, this HVC_X response was switched off while the bird was actively singing, so the bird does not confuse feedback of its own song with song from other birds (or experimenters' loudspeakers). 'HVC_X cells are gated to exist in purely auditory or motor states' (Prather et al. 2008, p. 308). These versatile cells, then, can be taken as part of a declarative system that represents particular song types in the swamp sparrow's brain, usable as the occasion demands for either production or recognition of a song.[52]

---

[52] Tchernichovski and Wallman (2008) provide a less technical summary of these findings.

We need to beware of naive localization. Of course, HVC is not the only place in a bird's brain where it can be said that song is represented. 'HVC by itelf does not learn or produce a song. It is part of sensory and motor circuits that contain many brain regions, and it is the connectivity and interaction between these components that determines outcome' (DeVoogd 2004, p. 778).

While the evidence about HVC and RA neurons indicates something parallel to a Phrase Structure rule, it would be wrong to think of the bird brain as storing a truly generative grammar of its repertoire. The essence of generative syntax is the capacity to 'make infinite use of finite means', by taking advantage of many combinatorial possibilities. In a generative grammar, this is typically achieved by each type of constituent (e.g. a noun phrase) being defined just once, and the definition being re-used in the many different contexts in which it is called by other rules of the grammar. In this way, many thousands (perhaps even an infinite number) of sentences can be generated by a set of only tens of rules.[53] In humans, it is in the lexicon that storage matches data, taking little or no advantage of combinatorial possibilities. The lexicon (passing over some complexities) is basically memorized item by item. The correlation between repertoire size and HVC volume in birds indicates that they memorize each item, even though it seems appropriate to describe their production in terms of Phrase Structure rules. Birds whose songs are naturally analysed into phrases store sets of unconnected Phrase Structure rules. In this sense, the bird's store of motifs is like a list of simple constructions, each defined by a particular Phrase Structure rule. We shall see in a later chapter that a recent grammatical theory, Construction Grammar, claims that human knowledge of grammar also takes the form of a store of constructions, described, in essence, by complex Phrase-Structure-like rules. Human constructions are far more complex than bird phrases, and combine with each other in far more productive ways, but the parallel is noteworthy. Complex birdsong is hierarchically organized in ways parallel to human composition of simple phrases, and thus shows signs of human-like syntax. But the full combinatorial possibilities of Phrase Structure grammar are definitely not exploited by birds. In fact, though most constructions in human languages are quite well described by Phrase Structure grammars or their equivalent, the full range of theoretically possible Phrase Structure grammars is also not exploited by humans. One can write fanciful descriptions of made-up languages using Phrase Structure rules alone, but

---

[53] This is a Mickey-Mouse example. No one knows how many grammatical rules human speakers have in their heads. But the principle stands, that whatever they store in their heads generates, through use of combinatoriality, vastly more diverse data than they could possibly memorize explicitly.

nothing like these languages is found in real human populations. We will see an example in the next subsection.

I interpreted the function of HVC to store a sequence of instructions to RA as parallel to the Phrase Structure rule MOTIF → A B C D E F G. As mentioned above, two other nuclei, Uva and NIf are afferent to HVC (or HVc), and may help organize units larger than that organized in HVC. Here the interpretation of brain structure and activity as Phrase Structure rules becomes problematic. Are we to expect that for each successive higher layer in a hierarchical description there will be a separate higher brain nucleus, sending signals downstream to lower-level nuclei? This is certainly the implication of Okanoya (2004), reporting on the responsibility of NIf for higher-level phrase-to-phrase transitions in Bengalese finches. Maybe the lack of much depth to the hierarchical structure of birdsong can be accounted for by the lack of higher-level nuclei, ultimately attributable to lack of sufficient brain space. Human phrase structure can get very deep, with many layers of structure, from words, through various types of phrases, then via subordinate clauses to the level of the main clause, the whole sentence. There is no evidence for hierarchical stacks of nuclei in the human cortex, or elsewhere, corresponding to the various levels of phrase structure.

It is implausible that the phrase structure of human sentences is implemented in the same way (*mutatis mutandis*) as the zebra finch brain implements the structure of motifs as series of notes. At least one fatal objection is that the bird's HVC-to-RA instruction is associated with very specific timing, in milliseconds. 'Remarkably, during directed singing, syllable duration is regulated to around 1 ms or a variation of <1%' (Suthers and Margoliash 2002, p. 687).[54] Such precise timing is not a feature of human sentential syntax. One can speak fast or slowly, one may hesitate in mid-phrase and still pick up the thread. Precisely timed serial behaviour is more typical of human phonetics and phonology. In a recent paper, examining perception rather than production, Pulvermüller and Shtyrov (2009, p. 79) 'found that acoustic signals perceived as speech elicited a well-defined [precisely timed] spatiotemporal pattern of sequential activation of superiortemporal and inferiorfrontal cortex'; this work, however, related to the perception of a single, low-level unit, a [t] sound. It is possible that a repertoire of syllables, or other small phonotactic units, in a language is stored as a set of phonological constructions each represented in a way parallel to a Phrase Structure rule. Pulvermüller (2002, pp. 150–4) discusses the possibility of synfire chains underlying phonological

---

[54] Glaze and Troyer (2006) confirmed this impressively precise timing, but found slight but significant variations in the global tempo of the song related to time of day and the arousal state of the bird.

behaviour, such as the organization of syllables into sequences of phonemes, whose relative timing is more narrowly constrained than the timing of phrases in a sentence. However, even here, Pulvermüller admits the problem of fast and slow speech. He also, in a following section, sets out clearly 'at least five reasons' why such chain mechanisms are inappropriate as direct explanations of the production of higher-order sequences of meaningful units, morphemes, and words (2002, pp. 154–6).

The zebra finch's HVC fires off a sequence of instructions, A B C D E, at precisely timed intervals, dictating the shape and timing of a motif. Not all repeated items in bird and whale songs are as tightly time-controlled as the elements in a zebra finch motif. For example, the trill part of a chaffinch song varies in length, so the instruction to execute the following flourish part cannot be a constant time after the instruction to execute the trill. In nightingale song, the Alpha, Beta, Gamma, and Omega parts are always in this order, so there is likely to be something in its brain determining this sequence, analogous to a Phrase Structure rule. But these song-parts are of variable length, especially the Gamma part, due to optional repetitions of some notes or pairs of notes. Here again, the bird's mental rule determining the sequencing is at least somewhat free from strict timing. The best such example is in humpback whalesong. As we have seen, a whale's song consists of a fixed sequence of themes, always A B C D E F, each of which is internally complex and of variable length, due to optional repetitions. The whale's brain must have a mechanism for specifying the serial order relatively free from timing information. All these animals have evolved ways of representing the serial order of elements in a higher-level component of their song, relatively free of precise timing information. We don't know how they achieve this trick,[55] but it is a significant step toward the much fuller syntactic competence of humans. Consistent serial order of subparts of a construction is a hallmark of human syntax; without it syntax as we know it is inconceivable. Our ancestors achieved the same trick of controlling serial order unconstrained by tight timing as the whales and nightingales, either before or in parallel with the systematic assignment of meanings to the ordered elements.

This discussion brings out a feature of the Formal Language Hierarchy that is possibly disguised by formulating it as a hierarchy of systems for generating successively inclusive sets of languages. It is possible to be led to believe that if a stringset cannot be generated by State Chain diagram, then no chain-like mechanism at all can be involved in generating it. This is an error. The crucial difference in descriptive devices, as one proceeds up the hierarchy, is in

---

[55] Imagine doing neuroscience on live whales!

degree of abstraction. First-order Markov transition tables describe languages in terms of chains of their terminal elements; and State Chain diagrams describe languages in terms of chains of slightly more abstract entities, the internal states of the organism or machine. A State Chain diagram is a single transition network connecting states, with terminal elements of the language emitted (or accepted) in the transitions between states. It is possible to have not just one, but a **set** of such basic networks, with a higher-level network connecting them, that is a network of networks, or a chain of subchains. This step up in abstraction corresponds to a generating (or accepting) device known as a Recursive Transition Network (Woods 1970). Recursive[56] Transition Networks (RTNs) were proved, in the early literature of the Formal Language Hierarchy, to be capable of generating (or accepting) exactly the class of Phrase Structure languages.

A 'natural' description of an animal song recognizes hierarchical phrasal organization where it seems to exist, even though a description in terms of a less powerful grammar type (e.g. State Chain or First-order Markov table) may be strictly possible. The more complex animal songs are naturally described by Phrase Structure grammars, equivalently by RTNs. But no animal song, not even a humpback whale's, has hierarchical structure with a depth greater than 2. An animal with a large repertoire, such as a nightingale, may have (the neural equivalent of) a large number of separate RTNs stored, one for each song, but none are of a greater depth than 2. Also, no natural description of any animal song requires an RTN (or Phrase Structure grammar) incorporating genuine recursion, that is reference to a subnet labelled 'X' within a subnet labelled 'X'.

The job of accounting for a bird species' song capacity involves more than just production and recognition. An RTN is not a model of how the song repertoire is acquired. The focus of the Formal Language Hierarchy is on mechanisms for producing and recognizing strings from specified stringsets, assuming they have somehow been acquired. Whatever level of the hierarchy turns out to be appropriate to generate sentences of human languages, the architecture of models at that level does not give any direct insight into the crucial question of how the grammar of the language was learned. If all human

---

[56] Beware the slippery word 'recursive'. It is used in a loose variety of senses in the literature. The systems known as Recursive Transition Networks can implement 'true' recursion (embedding a procedure of type X within a procedure of type X), but do not necessarily do so. It is possible that a bird's brain implements something like a simple Recursive Transition Network, but highly unlikely that the bird has any capacity for recursion in the strict sense of using one procedure while simultaneously using another instantiation of that same procedure 'inside itself'. No proper recursion is evident in birdsong or whalesong.

languages can be generated with Phrase Structure rules, the bare theory of Phrase Structure is not in itself a model of the human language capacity, because it does not address the question of how Phrase Structure grammars can be acquired on exposure to relevant experience. Tunable devices, such as connectionist neural nets, can be trained to accept languages at certain levels of the Formal Language Hierarchy. There is, however, no well-developed theory of the different neural net architectures necessary for acquiring languages of different degrees of complexity.

In many cases, a straightforward correlation holds between rank on the formal language hierarchy and processing effort or complexity. For example, parsing strings that can only be generated by a Phrase Structure grammar typically requires more computational effort than parsing strings generated by a State Chain process. There are exceptions to this correlation, however. A language with indefinitely many 'cross-serial dependencies' occupies a yet higher rank in the Formal Language Hierarchy than Phrase Structure languages. I will not discuss these cases, except to note that Gibson (1998) shows 'the lower complexity of cross-serial dependencies relative to center-embedded dependencies' (p. 1). Gibson is here referring to complexity of processing, as measured by reasonable criteria of load on memory. Languages with cross-serial dependencies (of indefinite length) cannot be generated by a Phrase Structure grammar, whereas languages with centre-embedded dependencies can be. Centre-embedded dependencies are in fact also harder for the real human parser to process. This is an area in which rank on the formal language hierarchy does not neatly correlate with processing complexity, undermining its potential usefulness in theorizing about classes of grammars that humans, or any animals, can manage. See Chapter 3 for further discussion.

1.3.5 Training animals on syntactic 'languages'

A study by two eminent primate researchers (Fitch and Hauser 2004) certainly did take the Formal Language Hierarchy seriously. They claimed to show, in the spirit of the *scala naturae* that I have linked to the hierarchy, that tamarin monkeys lack the computational capacity to process languages at the Phrase Structure level, while they are capable of processing lower-level State Chain languages. Humans, in contrast, and unsurprisingly, were shown to be able to process languages of both classes. The experiments involve two specific 'languages' well known in the literature of the Formal Language Hierarchy, called $A^n B^n$ and $(AB)^n$.

In the original literature, both $A^n B^n$ and $(AB)^n$ are **infinite** languages (stringsets). $A^n B^n$ is the name given to a language whose sentences consist of any number of 'A's, followed by exactly the same number of 'B's. Thus, sentences of this language include *AB, AABB, AAABBB*, a sequence of a trillion 'A's followed by exactly a trillion 'B's, and so on. There is no longest sentence in this language. Strings such as *ABBB* or *AAAB* are not members of this language, since they have different numbers of 'A's and 'B's. And *BA* and *BBBBAAAA* are also not members of this language. It is mathematically provable that this infinite language cannot be generated by a State Chain description, but can be generated by a Phrase Structure description. The crux is that the number of iterations on 'A' must be counted, remembered, and matched exactly by the the number of iterations on 'B', and State Chain descriptions provide no way of keeping track in this way. Phrase Structure descriptions do assume a counting mechanism.[57] But note that any **finite** version of this language, say putting a cap on sentence length at a billion elements, could be described, albeit extremely inelegantly, by a State Chain diagram; it would just need half a billion separate routes through the State Chain diagram.

By contrast, the infinite language called *(AB)^n* can be simply generated by a State Chain description. The sentences of this language are composed by iterations of the sequence 'AB'. There is no longest sentence in this language, either. Its members include *AB, ABAB, ABABABABAB* and so on ad infinitum. In this language, there is no need for controlled counting of the number of iterations; any number of iterations of 'AB' is OK.

This classic formal contrast between two classes of languages was Fitch and Hauser's starting point. It was an attempt to make a connection between animal learning research and formal language theory.

Rule systems capable of generating an infinite set of outputs ('grammars') vary in generative power. The weakest possess only local organizational principles, with regularities limited to neighboring units. We used a familiarization/discrimination paradigm to demonstrate that monkeys can spontaneously master such grammars. However, human language entails more sophisticated grammars, incorporating hierarchical structure. Monkeys tested with the same methods, syllables, and sequence lengths were unable to master a grammar at this higher, 'phrase structure grammar' level.

(Fitch and Hauser 2004, p. 377)

Note that Fitch and Hauser start with a (correct) statement about infinite sets of outputs, that is languages. They attempted to train tamarin monkeys to recognize example sentences from both classes of language. Corresponding to 'A' they used syllables drawn from a small set spoken by a female voice,

---

[57] The counting mechanism can be implemented by a 'push-down stack memory'.

and corresponding to 'B' they used syllables drawn from a different small set spoken by a male voice. (This experimental choice of stimuli is itself problematic, as a sequence of such 'A's and 'B's might naturally be taken as a discourse between two different speakers, rather than a sentence spoken by one speaker. But this is not the major problem with this study.) Necessarily, of course, the example sets were finite, and in fact very small. For a strict comparison, the stimuli from the A^nB^n language had to be matched for length with the stimuli from the $(AB)^n$ language. Thus one half of the tamarin subjects heard repeated instances of either $ABAB$ or $ABABAB$—that's all! And the other tamarins heard repeated instances of either $AABB$ or $AAABBB$—again, that's all! Having been exposed to stimuli consistently drawn from one set (of two examples) the tamarins were tested to see if they noticed when exposed to examples from the other set. Or putting it another way, the monkeys were exposed to one set of regularities and tested to see if they noticed deviations from those regularities. 'Noticing' was tested by seeing whether the monkey's attention was unusually drawn to the loudspeaker; this was all done with immaculate experimental care. Perhaps not surprisingly, the monkeys trained on $ABAB$ and $ABABAB$, representative of a State Chain language, did notice deviations from the implicit regularity. It was concluded that they had mastered a State Chain grammar, or equivalent, for this limited set of examples. On the other hand, the monkeys trained on $AABB$ and $AAABBB$, representative of a Phrase Structure language, failed to notice deviations from the regularity they had been trained on. It was concluded that they had not mastered a Phrase Structure grammar. Human subjects trained on the same sets of stimuli easily managed to spot violations of the regularities in both sets of data.

This study comparing humans and tamarins was followed up by Gentner et al. (2006), working with starlings. They used the same two formal languages, but more naturally instantiated, with parts of real starling songs, a 'rattle' motif standing for an 'A' element, and a 'warble' motif standing for a 'B' element. Thus a stimulus 'rattle-rattle-warble-warble' was an example from the A^nB^n language, but not from the $(AB)^n$ language. For the basic training sessions, the n of the languages was restricted to 2, so birds heard only $AABB$ or $ABAB$. One set of starlings was trained positively (by food reward) on $AABB$ and negatively (by dimming of the lab lights) on $ABAB$; the other birds were trained in the reverse way. The stimuli were varied, as more than one type of rattle motif could be an A, and more than one kind of warble motif could be a B. They were then tested to see if they had generalized to stimuli that had not been included in the basic training sets. Some of the testing stimuli went beyond the limit of n to 2, with birds being asked to respond, for example, to longer strings such as $AAAABBBB$ or $ABABABAB$ (where $n = 4$). Nine out of eleven birds learned the appropriate 'languages', after prolonged training. The fastest learner took 9,400 trials, the slowest successful learner took 56,200 trials. After successful learning, the birds quickly transferred what they had learnt to novel stimuli. The authors conducted a number of careful 'probe' tests attempting to ensure that birds that seemed to have learned the A^nB^n language were not faking it by approximating to the goal Phrase Structure grammar with an equivalent State Chain grammar. Overall, the study claimed that the starlings who learned the A^nB^n language had narrowed down their recognition procedures to something closely equivalent to a Phrase Structure grammar. Now, assuming, crucially, that the starlings had indeed internalized a Phrase Structure grammar, the particular grammar required to generate this language has the property of **recursion**; a structure of one type, *AB*, is embedded in the middle of a structure of the same type, giving *AABB*. Part of the theoretical context of the study was the claim by Hauser et al. (2002) that a capacity for recursion is unique to humans and distinctive of language. (Gentner et al. 2006, p. 1204) put an opposing conclusion: '[T]he capacity to classify sequences from recursive, centre-embedded[58] grammars is not uniquely human. This finding opens a new range of complex syntactic processing mechanisms to physiological investigation'.

What does all this tell us? These studies have attracted criticism, much of it justified.[59] In a crisp reply to the Gentner study, three linguists and a philosopher note that

It is not clear that the starlings learned a recursive rule. Becoming habituated to a pattern like AAABBB does not necessarily imply grasping recursively center-embedded structures like A(A(A(...)B)B)B. This pattern could equally be detected by comparing the number of A's and B's, given that some birds such as pigeons can subitize numbers up to 4 or more (Dehaene S, The Number Sense, Oxford University Press, 1997).

(Jackendoff et al. 2006)

This is right.

In another attack on this strand of work, Perruchet and Rey (2005) claim to see a logical inconsistency in Fitch and Hauser's reasoning.

---

[58] Gentner et al. classify the A^nB^n sentences as centre-embedded, but in fact a distinction needs to be made between centre-embedding, or better centre-self-embedding, and nesting of structures. It is not possible, without any semantics, to tell whether A^nB^n sentences involve centre-self-embedding or mere nesting. This issue will be taken up shortly below.

[59] Mark Liberman has written perceptive online commentary on these studies, to which I am indebted. See http://158.130.17.5/%7Emyl/languagelog/archives/000355.html, and http://158.130.17.5/-myl/languagelog/archives/001399.html. These websites were active as of May 2008.

Regarding their demonstration that students are able to master a PSG, [Fitch and Hauser] remained cautious, noting that 'limited output from a PSG can always be approximated by a more complicated FSG' (p. 378). But they continued, 'however, failure to master a grammar (as demonstrated by a failure to distinguish grammatical from ungrammatical strings) can be empirically confirmed' (p. 378). It is notable that there is a logical contradiction between these two statements. If it is not possible to demonstrate that achievement in a specific task *t* implies the mastery of a grammar *g*, how could it be possible to conclude that failure in *t* attests that *g* cannot be mastered?

(Perruchet and Rey 2005, p. 308)

In fact it is Perruchet and Rey who have their logic wrong. The propositions involved can be reduced to simple formulae. Let T be 'subjects achieve task *t*' and let G be 'subjects master grammar *g*'. Then logically

'subjects achieving task *t* does not imply that subjects master grammar *g*'
is $\neg(T \rightarrow G)$

and

'subjects not achieving task *t* implies that subjects do not master grammar *g*'
is $\neg T \rightarrow \neg G$.

These two complex propositions are not logically contradictory. Think, in parallel, of

$\neg\,(\text{COLOURED}(x) \rightarrow \text{RED}(x)\,)$ and $\neg\,\text{COLOURED}(x) \rightarrow \neg\,\text{RED}(x)$
If something is coloured,   and   *If something is not coloured,*
it's not necessarily red   *it's not red*

So Fitch and Hauser's claim that the tamarins didn't master the grammar, in fact **any** grammar or mnemonic trick, for $A^n B^n$ is valid.

The Phrase Structure language $A^n B^n$ tested on tamarins is not like anything found in a natural language. No language insists for purely syntactic reasons on the same number of elements in one part of a sentence being matched by exactly the same number of elements in another part of the sentence. In experimental conditions, such as Fitch and Hauser's, humans can learn a language like this, up to a certain small number of matched elements, but no language of a human community ever works this way. So even if it were the case that all human languages are Phrase Structure languages, the converse does not hold: it is not the case that all Phrase Structure languages (for example $A^n B^n$) are, or even could be, naturally occurring human languages. In fact there are 'languages' (stringsets) at all levels of the Formal Language Hierarchy, including the lowest, that could not be learned by any human.[60] Even a First-order Markov language could be unlearnable in practice if its vocabulary, or its list of transitions, were too big for a human to manage. The $A^n B^n$ language is a classically cited case in the formal language literature, used to make the basic point about asymmetry between classes of languages, that is that one class of languages properly includes another. (It is ironic that numerical constraints are countenanced in the 'data' (hypothetical stringsets) of formal language theory, but not in the definitions of the basic grammar types, and of the processing automata that correspond to them.)

As noted, Gentner et al. (2006) say that the $A^n B^n$ stringset, if analysed in terms of Phrase Structure grammar (a crucial assumption), involves centre-embedding. Apart from the centre-embedding of the arithmetical counting type, which does not occur in languages, it is necessary to distinguish between **nesting** and **centre-self-embedding**. Consider an English sentence like *Either the song finches sing is innate or it is learned*. Here, three of the first four words set up expectations which are met later in the sentence. *Either* sets up the expectation of a subsequent *or*; *song* sets up the expectation of a singular verb, which is fulfilled by the subsequent *is* (*are* would be wrong here); and *finches* sets up the expectation of a plural verb, fulfilled by *sing* (not *sings*). There is a **dependency** between the earlier expectation-setting item and the later expectation-fulfilling item. These dependencies can be shown in a diagram, as follows.

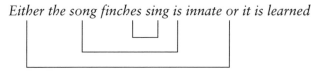

These dependencies are **nested** in an obvious sense. The example is short, for convenience. Only six words separate the *Either* from its dependent *or*. But there is no principled limit to the distance between such interdependent items. Consider the example *Either the language European children acquire from their primary caregivers at home is the same as the official language of instruction at school or it is not*. Here there are 22 words between the *Either* and its *or*. Nothing in the grammar of English limits this distance. The same can be said for the other dependencies in the example. There is no maximum distance separating a verb from the subject with which it agrees. But obviously

---

[60] This states more generally a point made by Pullum and Scholz (2010a).

factors of memory and style affect the likelihood of the distance between dependent items getting too long in actual behaviour.

By contrast, consider the two examples below:

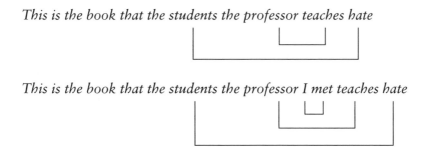

This is the book that the students the professor teaches hate

This is the book that the students the professor I met teaches hate

Let us call these examples 'centre-self-embedded', because they involve attempts to embed a clause (e.g. *I met*) inside another (e.g. *the professor teaches*). The second example here has the same level of embedding of dependencies as the earlier example, *Either the song finches sing is innate or it is not* but it is clearly harder to process. Jackendoff et al. (2006) note that even a four-word example of centre-self-embedding, *People people cheat cheat*, is hard to process, and ask rhetorically 'Are starlings outperforming humans syntactically?'.

The kind of centre-embedding found in human languages cannot be processed by mere counting. Perruchet and Rey (2005) took up the difference between mere counting centre-embedding and centre-self-embedding with grammatical dependencies between distant elements. Using stimuli very similar to Fitch and Hauser's, they constructed artificial languages with centre-embedding, with dependencies between earlier and later syllables. For example an early *ba* set up the expectation of a later *gu*, an early *la* predicted a later *do*, and an early *no* primed for a later *sa*. These dependencies were embedded as Figure 1.9, an example from their training strings. In this example, the depth of centre-embedding is 3. In one set of training data, all the 'earlier' elements,

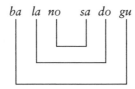

ba la no   sa do gu

Fig. 1.9 One of Perruchet and Rey's examples of grammatical dependencies between nonsense syllables nested at depth 3.
Source: From Perruchet and Rey (2005).

that is the first half of each string, were spoken by a (synthesized) high-pitched voice, and the later, dependent, elements were pronounced by a lower-pitched voice, as in Fitch and Hauser's study. In most ways not crucial to this new experiment, details were kept as close as possible to those of Fitch and Hauser's study. Human subjects were exposed to 32 such examples, half of depth 2 and half of depth 3. Then they were given test examples and asked whether the test examples were consistent with the training data or not. The test examples could violate the pattern of the training data in either of two ways. In an acoustic violation, the all-high-pitched followed by all-low-pitched pattern was violated, but the 'grammatical' dependencies between the syllables may or may not have been consistent with the training data. In a 'grammatical' violation, the high-pitch/low-pitch relationships may or may not have been preserved, but the syllable dependencies were violated. The subjects easily spotted the acoustic violations, but performed no better than chance on the 'grammatical' violations. So these human subjects had not learned the nested grammatical dependencies between syllables. This result certainly upsets Fitch and Hauser's conclusions, that humans can easily learn Phrase Structure grammars, and does so with a type of Phrase Structure grammar more like that found in human languages. But this leaves a problem for anyone who believes, along with the great majority of linguists, that Phrase Structure grammars, rather than State Chain descriptions, are appropriate for human languages.

Perruchet and Rey express a radical position with regard to humans' abilities to use Phrase Structure grammars: '...is it still worthwhile to pursue experimental investigations about tamarins' abilities to master PSG grammars? A positive response would entail that such grammars are (1) commonly mastered by humans and (2) actually crucial for describing human language structures. We believe that neither of these conditions is met' (2005, p. 311). Perruchet and Rey argue that it has not been shown that humans use Phrase Structure grammars. But their conclusion is over-general, and does not distinguish between different types of Phrase Structure. They appeal to the well-known difficulty that humans have with centre-self-embedded sentences with embedding of depth greater than 3. Along with most linguists, they appear to prefer qualitative statements about the human language capacity, such as 'humans don't use Phrase Structure grammars', over quantitive statements, such as 'humans use Phrase Structure grammars with centre-self-embedding up to a depth of about 3'.

Perruchet and Rey's subjects were equally bad at spotting violations in examples of depths 2 and 3. An example at depth 2 is given in Figure 1.10. The dependencies here correspond to those in easy English sentences such as *The song finches sing is innate* or *Either they sing or they don't*. So how come

Fig. 1.10 One of Perruchet and Rey's examples of grammatical dependencies between nonsense syllables embedded at depth 2.
Source: From Perruchet and Rey (2005).

the experimental subjects performed so badly? The answer staring us in the face is that the stimuli in all these studies **have no semantics**. The humans, tamarins, and starlings were asked to respond to abstract patterns in meaningless strings, in the spirit of the basic Formal Language Hierarchy. Nine out of eleven of the poor old starlings managed Gentner et al.'s Phrase Grammar task, but only after very laborious training. Probably humans could manage Perruchet and Rey's centre-embedding task after equally gruelling exposure, if they had some incentive for staying with the experiment that long. But the facts of **meaningful** sentences in any language show that children can easily learn structures with nested dependencies as in these experimental stimuli.

All of the studies mentioned here are interesting, because there are lessons to be gained from them, in the context of attempts to forge interdisciplinary links between theories of learning and a seminal formal linguistic theory from the 1950s. It was good to try to make these links, and those who have carried out these studies have contributed by throwing the problems into sharp relief. A substantial population of scholars who have from the beginning maintained a healthy scepticism about the Formal Language Hierarchy, and formal, syntactocentric approaches to language in general, might clamour 'I told you so'. They would especially emphasize the problem of discussing language with no appeal to meaning. At its most extreme, this dissenting view would hold that the phrase 'meaningless language' embodies a contradiction, like 'square circle'. But let's not throw out the baby with the bathwater. Yes, semantics is crucial to the structure of language, but there is some structure in human sentences that is not directly derivable from the meanings they express. Human sentences are meaningful, and are processed with a view to retrieving meaning. It still makes sense to ask whether this processing is done in a purely local way, incrementally from the first word to the last, in the spirit of a State Chain model, or in a way that recognizes higher-level units such as phrases, in the spirit of Phrase Structure grammar.

There is no well-developed equivalent of the Formal Language Hierarchy that deals with languages as sets of meaning–form pairings, rather than with meaningless stringsets. This historical fact is largely due to the success of the

Formal Language Hierarchy and early works associated with it appealing to strong generative capacity. It is simply taken for granted by most theorists in language processing that a Phrase Structure model (sometimes slightly augmented in various ways) is the appropriate way to describe the meaning–form pairings in human languages. I believe this assumption is correct. Obviously, parsing an actual sentence in real time proceeds incrementally, word by word from first word to last. But the knowledge of the relevant language that is applied during such processing is not merely knowledge about local transitions between words. In both applied computational linguistics and psycholinguistics, the most common models of sentence processing involve building up higher-level phrasal structures on the basis of knowledge about such structures which the computer, or the human processor, has stored in long-term memory. The phrasal structures are associated in long-term memory with particular semantic interpretation rules. The lack, or at least the extreme paucity, of Phrase Structure organization in animal songs is very probably attributable to the fact that animal syntax, such as it is, is semantically uninterpreted. So a lesson to be taken from these attempts to train animals on various stringsets is that useful comparison with humans must deal with languages whose sentences are systematically related, via their structure, to meanings.

A second lesson to be learned, already mentioned in an earlier section, is that we need to overcome our reluctance to include some numerical, quantitive information in descriptions of particular languages and the human language faculty. There is much good sense in what Gentner et al. have to say about the experiments surveyed here, including their own with the starlings.

Although uniquely human syntactic processing capabilities, if any, may reflect more complex context-free grammars or higher levels in the Chomsky grammatical hierarchy, it may prove more useful to consider species differences as quantitative rather than qualitative distinctions in cognitive mechanisms. Such mechanisms (for example, memory capacity) need not map precisely onto strict formal grammars and automata theories. There might be no single property or processing capacity that marks the many ways in which the complexity and detail of human language differs from non-human communication systems. (Gentner et al. 2006, p. 1206)

Where does all this leave the Formal Language Hierarchy? Is it really 'strictly for the birds'?[61] In principle, the hierarchy is applicable to the repertoire of any animal, including birds, whales, and humans. Humans' languages are their

---

[61] In case you don't know this mainly American idiom, *(strictly) for the birds* means 'Trivial; worthless; only of interest to gullible people'. I included it in the heading of this whole section as a wry comment. I hate to explain a joke, but this was too good to miss, and it turns out that some people don't know the idiom.

repertoires. The emphasis on stringsets allows a comparison between animal repertoires and the purely syntactic properties of human languages. This is not to deny the importance of human semantics, but it helps us to separate semantic properties of languages from purely syntactic properties, such as major word order, agreement, and some long-distance dependencies. That said, there are two principal ways in which the Formal Language Hierarchy is a hindrance in our search for the mechanisms underlying human and animal competences.

First, the focus on potentially infinite stringsets, together with the imperative always to prefer the weakest possible way of describing a repertoire, masks the real complexities, such as they are, of animal repertoires. All animal repertoires are finite,[62] so should simply be relegated to the lowest level of the Formal Language Hierarchy, the rank of finite stringsets. But this misses even the gross difference between calls and songs, and the finer differences in complexity among songs—compare the chaffinch to the humpback whale. Secondly, the Formal Language Hierarchy, being a theory of devices for describing observable (and potentially observable) overt behaviour, makes only one-directional claims about underlying mechanisms. If a stringset requires a powerful type of grammar to describe it, the machine or organism that uses it must have resources of at least a certain power. But the implication does not go the other way. It is quite possible that a stringset formally requiring only a weak grammar type to describe it is actually produced, and/or recognized, by mechanisms of a more powerful type. For example, the zebra finch song's motif appears to be neurally controlled by a mechanism analogous to a Phrase Structure rule; yet the zebra finch's repertoire is finite. Grammars of a more powerful type may be more learnable than grammars of a weaker type on the Formal Language Hierarchy, as suggested above in connection with the sparse coding of motif information in the zebra finch HVC.

So is the Formal Language Hierarchy worthless for our purposes? Not quite. The skeleton it provides outlines a range of possible ways to describe the syntactic aspects of languages and animal repertoires, paired exactly with a matching range of types of processing device. The hierarchy of processing devices is a useful frame of reference when investigating what goes on inside human and animal brains as they build their messages. The theoretical, idealized concept of a processing device assumes infinite memory resources. If we realistically modify this idealized conception to admit quantitative, numerical constraints on memory, we can be on the road to seeing more clearly how human language

---

[62] Remember we are concerned with the competences of individual animals, not whole populations.

processing differs from the ways animals manage complex songs. There will be some overlap, for sure. Animals' syntactic processing mechanisms are, it is safe to assume, a proper subset of human mechanisms. Thus, for example, where a zebra finch has room in its brain (to put it informally!) for the equivalent of one Phrase Structure rule, and a nightingale has more room, both birds fail to exploit the depth of hierarchical organization that the full theory of Phrase Structure grammar provides. A reasonable hypothesis about humans is that they can exploit Phrase Structure grammar to greater depths, even including some recursive embedding of structures. But, as is well known, even human processing collapses at certain depths of embedding. For centre-embedding, the critical depth is even quite shallow. Other possible numerical constraints on Phrase Structure grammars reflecting the difference between humans and non-humans include the number of different types of nonterminal unit (e.g. phrases, motifs, themes) admitted, the length of phrases, and the preferred direction of branching (i.e. whether phrases tend to be nested inside other phrases at their beginnings or at their ends).

1.4 Summary, and the way forward

The main conclusions that have been argued for in this rather long chapter can be briefly expressed in these points.

- No non-human has any semantically compositional syntax, where the form of the syntactic combination determines how the meanings of the parts combine to make the meaning of the whole. There may be some very rare instances of juxtaposed items conveying a vague conjunction of their meanings.

- Natural birdsong and whalesong is minimally combinatorial. The size of the 'vocabulary' always exceeds the number of songs. Whales and birds, even those with large repertoires, such as the nightingale, use holistically memorized sequences. The song is highly stereotyped.

- The information content of bird- and whalesong is very low.

- The lack of compositional semantics in bird- and whalesong is consistent with its low information content and its serious underexploitation of combinatoriality.

- Bird- and whalesong often involves repetitions of the same note or phrase. Variability in the number of repetitions is a major source of variety in songs.

- The more complex animal songs contain sequences of up to about seven distinct constituents, such as zebra finch motifs, chaffinch phrases, and humpback whale themes. In birdsong, the constituents of such sequences are always iterations of basic notes, so the hierarchical structure of the song is only two layers deep. Humpback whalesong is only slightly more complex, with themes consisting of iterated short sequences of basic units.

- On a narrow approach ignoring numerical information, the overt patterns of natural bird- and whalesong can mostly be adequately described by First-order Markov transition tables. Some unusual exceptions require State Chain descriptions. But Phrase Structure grammar is never required, in terms of weak generative capacity, to capture the overt patterns.

- Just as with human language, analysis in terms only of weak generative capacity does not capture the structure of the more complex animal songs.

- Despite serious underexploitation of combinatoriality, when considered in terms of strong generative capacity, whalesong and much birdsong exhibit a hierarchically layered structure formally similar to the hierarchical structure of human syntax.

- Many unrelated species have evolved a capacity for serial ordering of items in songs, relatively unconstrained by precise timing. That is, the consistently ordered items are not necessarily separated by the same distance in time. In the case of humpback whalesong, ordered items occur at two different hierarchical levels.

- Bird neuroscience shows a higher vocal centre (HVC) responsible for representing many of the sequences of elements in birdsong, analogous to a phrase structure rule, or rules. But this phrase-structure-like organization does not exploit the full generative power of Phrase Structure grammars.

- The 'abstract' sparse coding of sequential information in HVC is particularly adaptive for song learning.

- Birds store templates of their song repertoires, analogous to human linguistic competence. These templates constitute declarative knowledge, because learning birds slowly approximate their singing behaviour to these targets stored months earlier. The ideal products of this competence are affected by accidental performance factors such as distraction and injury.

- The size of HVC and other song centres in birds is positively correlated with the size of the species repertoire. This reinforces the idea of these centres as the repository of birdsong competence.

- Constant, non-accidental, and quantitative properties of brain organization, such as permanent limits on short-term memory, influence the template. It is argued that competence is causally affected by such permanent factors, in birds and humans.

- Thus, stored representations, 'templates' of ideal song should specify the numerical limits and ranges characteristic of the song. This is a departure from the typical assumptions of Formal Language Theory, which has no place for numerical, quantitative constraints. I have introduced the term 'competence-plus' for the package consisting of both grammatical specifications and numerical constraints on their application.

- A key difference between human syntax and bird- and whalesong is better expressed as a quantitative difference in the degree to which Phrase Structure capacity is exploited than as a qualitative difference between different levels of the Formal Language Hierarchy.

- Experiments training animals on 'languages' at different levels of the Formal Language Hierarchy focus unduly on these qualitative differences, rather than on quantitative differences.

I suggest that nightingales and humpback whales have evolved about as far as they can go in complexity with song that carries no referential meaning and is semantically non-compositional. Remembering such large repertoires as nightingales have, or such a complex single song as a humpback whale's, makes great demands on memory. To evolve further, I suggest, one vital step was necessary—the incorporation of complex descriptive **meaning** into the songs, relating different songs to different possible experiences in the creature's life. Meaningful strings, that is strings that map systematically onto a creature's wide and general experience of the world, are easier to remember than strings of the same length but whose parts contribute nothing to the meaning of the whole. Which of the following strings are easiest to remember?

Kingdom phylum class order family genus species
Kids playing chicken on freeways get smashed
Mercury Venus Earth Mars Jupiter Saturn Uranus Neptune
Men very easily make jugs serve useful needs

The grammatical English sentences here are much easier to remember than the mere lists of words. This is why these odd sentences are taught, as mnemonics for the harder-to-remember sequences. The moral is that strings with whole complex compositional meaning are easier to take in and store, **because they mean something**. The addition of meaning, or information, to a pre-existing system of meaningless strings would have made the existing strings easier to remember, and would have paved the way for expanding the system to further, more complex, reaches of syntactic organization. In short, complex syntax is easier to manage if it is **meaningful**.

Fig. 1.11 How syntax and semantics might have evolved separately at first, and then combined to give semantically compositional syntax.

Part Three of the book will explore the routes by which syntactically complex meaningful language could have evolved. To the extent that pre-humans had some prior capacity for learning to control serial order in somewhat complex ways, the route to semantically interpreted complex serial behaviour would have been facilitated. Figure 1.11[63] shows a schema by which separate strands of syntactic and semantic evolution could have combined to yield semantically compositional syntax.

This chapter has discussed how far pure syntax has evolved in several different taxa of non-human animals. The earlier book, *The Origin of Meaning*, discussed the origins of human semantics and pragmatics in non-human animals. Vocal learning has also been mentioned here, and Chapter 2 will start the theme of some continuity between the innate involuntary vocalizations of animals and the learned, referentially meaningful, vocalizations of humans under voluntary (neocortical) control.

[63] The diagram is borrowed from Kazuo Okanoya.

CHAPTER 2

First Shared Lexicon

You can't have grammar without a lexicon, a set of unitary items to arrange according to the rules or principles of the grammar. The lexicon of a language is a shared reservoir of mappings between phonic (or gestural) forms and their 'meanings'. Any plausible account of the evolution of language postulates that there would have been single units of communication before they got strung together into longer sequences, or (as a theoretical alternative) analysed into meaningful subparts. This has been a solid theme throughout all speculation on language origins; it was advocated in the nineteenth century by Müller (1864) and Schleicher (1863), among others. In the twenty-first century, Givón (2002, p. 157) calls 'lexicon before grammar' one of his 'safe bets as evolutionary trends', and Paivio (2007, p. 283) glosses the same idea as 'In the beginning was the word' (with a completely different intention from St John). In between, at the beginning of the twentieth century, MacColl (1909, p. 114) summed up the persistent idea clearly: '...his [prehistoric man's] language consisted of simple, independent, unrelated elementary sounds, each a complete statement in itself (a subject and predicate, as it were, rolled into one) and conveying its own separate information'. 'Lexicon before grammar' has been a consistently self-evident evolutionary assumption, even for those who, like Müller and MacColl, could not bring themselves to take the next step and admit any degree of continuity between the calls of apes and prehistoric unitary human signs. (For Müller, at least, it was divine intervention that gave humans their first words.)

Beyond the conceptual necessity of lexicon-before-syntax, I should say here that evolving a simple symbolic lexicon was probably a more crucial step in the evolution of language as a whole than the later evolution of syntactic ways of combining the lexical items. This is broadly in line with Terry Deacon's thinking in *The Symbolic Species* (Deacon 1997). In this chapter I do what I can to explain the evolution of a symbolic lexicon, but as the focus of the book is on syntax, I will not claim to have full answers for how and why symbolic lexicons evolved.

Health warning: in this chapter, the term 'word' will occasionally be used because it is familiar and simple. In this chapter, there is no mention of the evolution of any combinatorial system forming words into sentences. If one's definition of a word is that it is always part of a sentence, then the term 'word' is misused here. I use it in the natural and familiar sense in which human babies' first utterances are counted as 'words', even though at that holophrastic stage, babies don't form sentences. I thought that this was preferable to some more cumbersome term such as 'proto-word'. Really, we are talking about the entries in a learned and conventionally shared lexicon.

2.1 Continuity from primate calls

It is sometimes argued (e.g. by Burling 2005, pp. 50–8) that human word-like symbols did not emerge by a continuous evolution from animal calls. 'An alarm call is more like a scream than a word' (Burling 2005, p. 53). This echoes an influential nineteenth-century view: 'no process of natural selection will ever distil significant words out of the notes of birds or the cries of beasts' (Müller 1864, p. 340). Such views leave a gaping hole. They suggest no alternative evolutionary source for modern spoken words. Human language evolved somehow out of earlier primate behaviour. In this section I will try to see by what steps this evolutionary journey could have been made.

2.1.1 Referentiality and glimmerings of learning

Animals in the wild don't have shared learned vocabularies. Some do have quite meagre shared, and largely innate, vocabularies. The alarm calls of vervet monkeys are a well-known example, and many other species of mammals and birds have similar small sets of alarm calls and food calls which they do not seem to learn to produce, although they sometimes learn to refine their meanings (the class of stimuli that trigger them) to some degree. The alarm calls are probably not totally involuntary, in that there are audience effects— calls tend to be made when there is a conspecific, or a close relative, nearby to receive them. In the small element of learning involved in such largely innate calls, and in the audience effects, one can see the beginnings of a possible transition from involuntary behaviour encoded in the genes, and not subject to environmental influence, to voluntary behaviour learned from the existing members of the group.

Many species of monkeys have predator alarm calls, and some (e.g. rhesus macaques and tufted capuchins) have food calls. Distinct alarm calls for different predators have not been observed in apes, more closely related to humans than monkeys are. This might be taken to be an obstacle to the idea of continuity between primate calls and human words. The absence of such calls in apes is probably due to their not being vulnerable to predators as much as monkeys (until humans came along!). But chimpanzees are well known to vocalize in the presence of food (Leavens and Hopkins 2005). '[C]aptive chimpanzees produce acoustically distinct rough grunts to different types of high-preference food' (Slocombe and Zuberbühler 2006, p. 997). Further, 'In a naturalistic playback experiment, a focal subject was able to use the information conveyed by these calls produced by several group mates to guide his search for food, demonstrating that the different grunt types were meaningful to him. This study provides experimental evidence that our closest living relatives can produce and understand functionally referential calls as part of their natural communication' (Slocombe and Zuberbühler 2005b, p. 1779). And Crockford and Boesch (2003) also found distinct wild chimpanzee barks specific to the contexts of hunting and snakes, respectively. (Interestingly, the context-specificity of these barks was enhanced when they were combined with drumming on the buttresses of trees.) Clay and Zuberbühler (2009) found five acoustically distinct calls given by bonobos in response to finding food; the facts here are complex as the calls are embedded in longer sequences which apparently have some structure, but the precise nature of any sequential coding is as yet unclear. Brumm et al. (2005) describe calls produced by Barbary apes (which are actually monkeys) which seem to 'comment on' the interactions of other conspecifics: '... such calls might not be directed towards the agents of the commented situation, but towards other group members. The vocal comments may signal the caller's awareness of the observed interaction and possibly attract the attention of others to the situation' (Brumm et al. 2005, p. 141). This can be interpreted as referential behaviour, referring to the social events concerned. (And it also reminds one of Dunbar's 1996b hypothesis that an early function of language was gossip.)

Researchers are usually careful to distinguish functional referentiality, a relatively strong property, from context-specificity, a weaker property. The context-specificity of a behaviour is a prerequisite for its functional referentiality. The difference lies in the response of others to the behaviour. An animal may consistently behave in specific ways in particular contexts, but if that behaviour is not interpreted by another animal as indicating something in the environment, it is not functionally referential. In a very thorough study of Carolina chickadees (*Parus carolinensis*), Smith carefully emphasized the 'message' of a display (vocal or non-vocal) as 'that information about the displaying individual that the recipient of the display would know in the theoretical event in which he received only the display, unaccompanied by information from contextual sources' (1972, p. 119). Smith identified twenty vocal displays as bearing such messages. But these messages always encoded information about the next likely behaviour of the displayer, not about any third event or object. So these messages are not referential in the sense of drawing attention to some object or event other than the sender or receiver of the display. Context-specificity is easier to observe and test than functional referentiality. There is general agreement that the alarm calls of vervets are functionally referential, because of the results of playback experiments. If context-specificity of some behaviour has been reported, without testing for functional referentiality, we cannot yet be sure whether the behaviour is also functionally referential.

The only study with evidence [in chimps] of context-specific calls showed that a long-distance chimpanzee call, the pant hoot, had three acoustic variants, produced in three contexts: travel, food and encountering within-community conspecifics (Uhlenbroek 1996). Another study, however, with a different chimpanzee population of the same subspecies, *Pan troglodytes schweinfurthii* (Marler and Hobbett 1975; Mitani et al. 1992; Mitani 1994), found no evidence of context specificity in pant hoots (Mitani 1994). (Crockford and Boesch 2003, p. 116)

It is well documented that different chimpanzee populations have different conventional behaviours, presumably learned and culturally transmitted. The mismatch between the two populations mentioned here may reflect a cultural difference between them. If this is the case, then learned, culturally transmitted and potentially referential vocal calls are not absent in our closest relatives, the chimpanzees, in the wild.

The transition envisaged here is from largely innate symbols to learned ones. In Chapter 7 I will consider the possibility that relaxation of functional constraints on the pre-human genome permitted control of calls to be offloaded from genetic control to learned voluntary control, along the lines suggested by Deacon (2010). **Symbols** are defined as linking a meaning to a form in an arbitrary way. That is, there is no obvious causal connection, or physical similarity, between the form and the meaning of a symbol. There is nothing inherently leopardy about a vervet's bark (its alarm call for a leopard), just as there is nothing inherently leopardy in our English word *leopard*. By contrast, agonistic calls, expressing emotions such as fright and anger, have an iconic nature. The more fright you feel, the louder or higher-pitched is your call; the degree of anger or fear expressed is scaled to acoustic features of the cry. Moreover, interestingly, the human brain responds to agonistic calls by rhesus

monkeys in the same location (orbitofrontal cortex) as to human affective
vocalizations 'supporting claims of shared emotional systems across species'
(Belin et al. 2007, p. 473).

2.1.2 Monkey–ape–human brain data

Significant evidence for continuity between monkey calls and human speech
now comes from studies revealing monkeys' preferential left hemisphere
processing of conspecifics' vocalizations. Ghazanfar and Hauser (2001) summarize some of this evidence:

> [B]ehavioural experiments under laboratory and field conditions reveal that at least
> two Old World monkey species exhibit asymmetries in their perception of conspecific
> vocalizations. Psychophysical studies of coo calls in Japanese macaques reveal a right
> ear advantage (Zoloth et al. 1979; Heffner and Heffner 1986). Field playback studies
> of rhesus macaques demonstrate a right ear orienting bias in response to conspecific
> vocalizations (Hauser and Andersson 1994; Ghazanfar et al. 2001). Finally, recent
> psychophysical experiments with rhesus macaques show a right-ear advantage when
> discriminating between species-specific 'scream' vocalizations (Le Prell et al. 2002).
>
> (Ghazanfar and Hauser 2001, p. 714)

(Input to the right ear is processed in the left hemisphere, of course.) Petersen
et al. (1978) presented field-recorded Japanese macaque vocalizations to the
left and right ears of five Japanese macaques and five Old World monkeys of
other species. They tested the animals' abilities to discriminate communicatively relevant aspects of these vocalizations, and concluded that 'Japanese
macaques engage left-hemisphere processors for the analysis of communicatively significant sounds that are analogous to the lateralized mechanisms used
by humans listening to speech' (Petersen et al. 1978, p. 324). Heffner and
Heffner (1984) showed, by cutting out various parts of macaque brains and
then trying to train them to discriminate between two forms of macaque 'coo'
vocalizations, that the left temporal cortex plays a predominant role in the
perception of species-specific vocalizations by these monkeys. More recently,
taking advantage of new brain-scanning technology, Poremba et al. (2004) did
PET scans of rhesus monkeys while the monkeys listened to six different kinds
of auditory stimulus. They found two kinds of hemispheric specialization. A
relevant part of the right hemisphere was used for processing a whole variety
of different sounds, while '[t]he second type of lateralization, represented in the
dorsal temporal pole—a late station in the putative ventral auditory pathway—
apparently reflects left-hemisphere specialization for processing monkey calls
specifically' (Poremba et al. 2004, p. 450). They speculate that this area 'could

be a precursor for an acoustic language area in humans' (p. 450). Petkov et al. (2008) also found significant similarities between macaque and human voice recognition regions in the brain. Left-lateralized perception of conspecific calls is likely to be of very ancient origin, as it is also found in sea-lions (Böye et al. 2005).

There is evidence that the left-hemisphere advantage in chimpanzees is connected not just to recognizing that a sound comes from a conspecific, but also to meaningful symbols generated by members of other species. Experimenting with symbol-trained chimpanzees, Hopkins et al. (1992) measured the differences between reaction times to stimuli presented in different visual fields (right versus left), and between lexigram stimuli on which the animals had been trained and other merely familiar stimuli (meaningful versus familiar). They found a left-hemisphere advantage for the meaningful symbols, concluding, with due reservations about the size of the data sample, 'Collectively, the data suggest that the manner in which these chimpanzees perceive symbols that have acquired functional meaning may be similar to that observed in human subjects in the processing of words' (p. 581). Human lateralization of language, and of vocabulary in particular, to the left hemisphere, in the great majority of the population, is well known, of course. It is also known that language lateralization increases as a function of age in normal children (Ressel et al. 2008).

Left-hemisphere specialization for auditory attention to conspecific calls links monkeys and humans in a thread of continuous evolution. Furthermore, there is evidence that when macaques hear the calls of other macaques, the brain areas activated include those for processing visual stimuli, as involved in recognizing objects and types of motion (da Costa et al. 2004). This suggests that the calls evoke something like conceptual representations in the macaque's brain. The idea of pre-existing conceptual representations in animals as a basis for the evolution of human expressions was argued at length in *The Origins of Meaning*. Maggie Tallerman (2009a, p. 185), in sympathy with this view, argues that 'A proto-lexicon evolved by building on pre-existing conceptual categories likely shared by other anthropoids'. But necessarily complicating this picture, Tallerman also assumes, like Ray Jackendoff in several books, a distinction in humans between 'raw' conceptual categories and the lexical representations that plug into language. From a neuroscientific viewpoint, Martin (1998) argues that pre-existing perceptual representations are a basis for, but subtly distinct from, lexical semantic representations. We will return to the question of how language modifies pre-existing concepts in section 5 of this chapter. The linkage of communicative calls to proto-conceptual representations is a further sign of possible continuity between ape calls and human words. A significant way in which humans have changed is in the degree to which our speech is under voluntary control, and uses many thousands of learned, rather than innate, mappings between forms and meanings.

It is widely accepted that there are no neocortical sites in monkeys controlling vocal production of calls (Aitken 1981; Kirzinger and Jürgens 1982; Robinson 1967; Sutton et al. 1974), whereas 'in humans the neocortex is involved in the voluntary control of speech' (Lieberman, 1991, p. 21). Jürgens (2002) noted some inhibitory activity in the medial cortex in monkeys suppressing vocalizations, but this is different from mechanisms actively producing calls. Such facts go against a straightforward continuity account of evolution of speech from primate calls, as far as production as is concerned. But there is some rather old evidence for the connection of laryngeal muscles to the motor cortex in macaques (Hast et al. 1974). There is also now evidence of neocortical activity during vocalization in macaques intensively trained to produce calls when prompted (Gemba et al. 1999, 2002). Gemba et al. (1997) found field potentials in the cortex of macaques, including the homologue of Broca's area, just prior to the animals making a vocalization. They summarize the implications of their work thus: 'These facts suggest that the neocortical area homologous to the human speech area takes part in the generation and control of monkey vocalization together with the cerebellum possibly through cerebro-cerebellar interactions. This is against ideas so far proposed on non-human primate vocalization, that is, it is generally considered that animal vocalization differs fundamentally from human speech' (p. 96). Hihara et al. (2003) also trained a Japanese macaque to vocalize when requesting either food or a tool. They 'found that the monkey spontaneously differentiated [its] coo-calls to ask for either food or tool during the course of this training. This process might involve a change from emotional vocalizations into intentionally controlled ones by associating them with consciously planned tool use. We thus established a novel hypothesis about the origin of voluntary vocal control' (p. 383). Coudé et al. (2007) observed similar trained vocalizations in macaques and found correlated activation in F5, the cortical area homologous with human Broca's area. Pointing in roughly the same evolutionary direction, a study by Sherwood et al. (2004) found significant differences between Old World monkeys, on the one hand, and great apes and humans in their cortical representation of facial movements.

Compared to Old World monkeys, the orofacial representation of area 4 in great apes and humans was characterized by an increased relative thickness of layer III and overall lower cell volume densities, providing more neuropil space for interconnections. These phylogenetic differences in microstructure might provide an anatomical substrate for the evolution of greater volitional fine motor control of facial expressions in great apes and humans.   (Sherwood et al. 2004, p. 61)

Another independent line of research has suggested how there could have been an evolutionary transition from involuntary emotionally based vocal calls to voluntarily controlled speech. Schulz et al. (2005) compared normally voiced speech with whispered speech, in humans. The key fact underlying this comparison is that whispered speech is almost exactly the same as normal voiced speech in all gestures of the articulators (tongue, jaw, velum, etc.) except for the vibration of the vocal folds in the larynx, that is voicing. Voicing is common to human speech and non-human primate calls. What the non-humans lack is fine control of articulation, which is present in both normal and whispered human speech. Thus whispered speech is simply, to a significant extent, evolved human speech minus the primitive component. The experimenters hypothesized that normal voiced speech would involve all the brain areas involved in whispered speech, and more, in particular the non-cortical regions associated with emotionally based calls. This is in fact what they found.

Taken together, our results suggest that human vocalization is not exclusively regulated by neocortical or visceromotor mechanisms, but by a combination of both. That the PAG[1] and paramedian cortices—elements of the species-specific call system that regulates vocal production in lower species—are selectively activated during vocalization in humans, may represent the process of 'exaptation' (Gould, 1999), whereby features previously designed for one function (species specific vocalizations that may convey information about emotional state) are co-opted for a different purpose (linguistic and paralinguistic use of voice during propositional speech) in the course of evolution.
    The greater degree of voluntary control that humans have over phonation can be explained by neocortical regulation of these visceromotor structures.
                                        (Schulz et al. 2005, p. 1845)

Lieberman (1991) sums up the continuity argument well 'The voluntary control of vocalization in human beings appears to be another example of evolutionary "add-ons" and concurrent modifications of older coordinate structures' (p. 21). That is, rather than having evolved quite independently of the mechanisms underlying animal cries, human vocalization evolved **on top of** these mechanisms, and remained interconnected with them. A conceptual issue about continuity needs to be clarified here. A reader of a draft, intending to argue against my version of continuity in this section, writes 'I see our vocalizations as an add-on, and not a development from, our primate calls'. Certainly our learned voluntary vocalizations are an add-on, but this is consistent with

---

[1] PAG is periacqueductal grey matter [JRH].

continuity. An add-on presupposes some related pre-existing organ or function to which the new development is added. Much continuous evolution proceeds by some kind of adding on. Consider an analogy with the evolution of the eye. Eyes with lenses evolved out of 'pit-eyes', light-sensitive cup-shaped depressions without lenses. The lenses were an evolutionary add-on. But it seems reasonable to say that eyes with lenses developed from eyes without lenses. It may be objected that this analogy fails because the species that developed eyes with lenses did not retain (somewhere else in their bodies) primitive pit-eyes. A more general and perhaps better analogy is with the effects of gene duplication. When some portion of the genome is duplicated, the genome at first carries redundant information. The next step can be a divergence of the two copies of genetic material, with one developing specialized functions not seen in the other. The newly duplicated material and its phenotypic effects are an add-on, but clearly are also a development from the pre-duplication material and its phenotypic effects. I do not suggest that the evolution of learned voluntary vocalizations involved genetic duplication (though it might have). But the modern human vocal tract serves a double communicative function: an ancestral but nonetheless still adaptive function is the production of relatively involuntary emotive aspects of vocalization. The human vocal tract is under greater voluntary control, and its movable parts have more degrees of freedom, than the corresponding anatomical structures in apes. The flexibility of the human vocal apparatus, especially above the larynx, is a recent evolutionary development, since the chimp–human split, probably co-evolving with more elaborate linguistic coding capacity.[2] This new capacity for control is an evolutionary add-on. It is not, of course, an add-on to (for example) the patterning of body hair, or bipedal gait, or omnivorous diet. The only reasonable candidate for what it was added to was the pre-existing vocalization system, which split into voluntary and relatively involuntary sectors after the addition. It is a reasonable surmise that if there had been no pre-existing involuntary calls, then voluntary vocalization would not have evolved. It is in this sense that I advocate continuity with primate calls.

Humans have not abandoned iconic affective signalling; a human utterance simultaneously conveys some aspects of meaning by arbitrary symbolic connections and other aspects of meaning (e.g. degree of arousal) by iconic means, the two mechanisms (somewhat identified with different hemispheres) both

---

[2] Also probably co-evolving was phonological segmentation of human meaningful utterances into re-usable units, phonemes. I don't go into the evolution of phonological structure here.

being active together. For example, intonation, the manipulation of the musical pitch of the voice, serves both affective and more arbitrary symbolic types of communication. In a study of Russian intonation, Chernigovskaya et al. (2000, p. 142) found that 'statistical analysis of latent periods and errors made by the test subjects demonstrated a significant preference of the *right* hemisphere in perceiving emotional intonations and complete/incomplete sentences; sentences with different logical stress were perceived mainly by the *left* hemisphere'. The correlation of symbolic language processing with the left hemisphere, and of emotional/affective processing with the right hemisphere, is the simple picture, holding true in outline. Inevitably, the brain facts are more complex, but the symbolic:left/emotional:right story is a consistent strand in conclusions of studies. In a survey of this topic, Baum and Pell (1999) write:

[R]esearch has provided consistent support for the functional lateralization hypothesis (Van Lancker 1980) at the phonemic and lexical levels. The left hemisphere has been shown to be active in the production and comprehension of tonal contrasts and lexical stress, with minimal evidence of right hemisphere involvement. . . . Few would argue that the right hemisphere is not implicated in the processing of emotion in general—be it language-based or otherwise. . . . However, the question of whether emotional prosody, in particular, is lateralized to the right hemisphere has not yet been resolved.

(Baum and Pell 1999, pp. 602–3)

More recently, Belin et al. (2007, p. 473) write 'An increasing number of neuroimaging studies suggest that processing vocal affective information involves brain regions different from those involved in speech perception'.[3] In the production of calls by marmosets, primates only distantly related to humans, a similar division of labour between the hemispheres has been found. Calls indicating negative emotions such as fear are controlled from the right hemisphere, and more deliberately communicative social contact calls are controlled from the left hemisphere (Hook-Costigan and Rogers 1998).

Left-hemisphere control of call production or perception is quite general in a range of species, including frogs (Bauer 1993), songbirds (Nottebohm 1977), mice (Ehret 1987), and rats (Fitch et al. 1993). The brain mechanisms underlying production of non-iconic referential calls, such as vervet alarm calls, are not known.[4] It seems likely that these too are generated from the left hemisphere. If this can be shown, then continuous evolution from such calls to human

---

[3] They cite Sander and Scheich (2001), Fecteau et al. (2005, 2007); Grandjean et al. (2005); Schirmer and Kotz (2006).

[4] It is much easier to study perception than production, in both humans and nonhumans, because we can control the stimuli an experimental subject receives, whereas

words is yet more plausible, the significant change being in the growing degree to which the form–meaning linkages are learned rather than genetically determined. This significant change involves a growing separation and reorganization of functions within the left hemisphere, distinguishing between the new functions of processing and storing learned symbols, and the older functions of largely unlearned conspecific call production and recognition.

A clue to the specific neural change that occurred in humans is found in comparative studies of the arcuate fasciculus, the white matter fibre tract approximately connecting Broca's area to Wernicke's area.[5] 'An obvious place to look for human/non-human differences would be in the connection between these two areas' (Schoenemann 2005, p. 54). In humans, 'lesions to this pathway result in conduction aphasia, in which, among other defects, patients can comprehend speech, but cannot repeat what was said' (Ghazanfar 2008, p. 383).[6] Recent advances in imaging technology (e.g. diffusion tensor imaging, DTI) have made it possible to explore connectivity and the flow of information between brain regions. Rilling et al. (2008) compared the arcuate fasciculi of humans, chimpanzees, and macaques, concluding 'our results indicate that the organization and cortical terminations of the arcuate fasciculus were strongly modified in human evolution. Notably, in humans, but not chimps or macaques, frontal cortex of the left hemisphere was strongly connected via the arcuate fasciculus with the left MTG and ITG, ventral and anterior to the cortex usually included in Wernicke's area' (p. 428). The pictures in (Ghazanfar, 2008) show chimpanzees as intermediate between macaques and humans in the density and elaboration of the connections between frontal and temporal areas. In humans, there is very considerable, almost extreme, asymmetry in the various strands of the arcuate fasciculus, strongly favouring the left hemisphere—see Nucifora et al. (2005) and references in Catani and Mesulam (2008). The role in vocal imitation played by the arcuate fasciculus and other pathways linking Broca's and Wernicke's areas is discussed by Iacoboni, Kaplan, and Wilson (2007).

---

we cannot easily control the circumstances triggering the production of a meaningful signal.

[5] The arcuate fasciculus is not the only connection between Broca's and Wernicke's areas. Catani et al. (2005) found another, indirect pathway, passing via inferior parietal cortex. See (MacNeilage 2008, pp. 189–96) for a discussion of the functions of these various pathways in speech imitation and production.

[6] Brown (1975) expresses an older, contrary, view. A history of discoveries around the arcuate fasciculus and an up-to-date survey of its anatomy and function is given in Catani and Mesulam (2008).

The significant change just mentioned involves vocal learning, in which there is a **discontinuity** between humans and our ape-like ancestors, as discussed earlier in Chapter 1, section 2. There is no inconsistency in arguing for (1) continuity in production of simple calls and auditory attention to the calls of conspecifics, and (2) discontinuity in vocal learning and in production of complex signals. As noted earlier, vocal learning and complex signals (songs) have evolved independently in several distantly related species, sometimes without more closely related species going along in this evolutionary shift. It seems likely that this is what happened in the human case. Jarvis (2007) emphasizes **similarities** among the brains of vocal learning species (songbirds, parrots, hummingbirds, humans) corresponding to **differences** between the brains of these species and their close relatives (e.g. comparing songbirds to chickens, or humans to apes). But Jarvis also emphasizes a relevant ancient continuity across all mammals, birds, and reptiles:

Given that the auditory pathways in avian, mammalian, and reptilian species are similar, whether or not a given species is a vocal learner, this suggests that the auditory pathway in vocal learning birds and in humans was inherited from their common stem-amniote ancestor, thought to have lived ~320 million years ago (Evans, 2000). Having a cerebral auditory pathway would explain why nonhuman mammals, including dogs, exhibit auditory learning, including learning to understand the meaning of human speech, although with less facility than a human.   (Jarvis 2007, p. 41)

Note the important distinction between auditory learning (which dogs and chimpanzees can do, and they don't talk back) and vocal learning, which involves learning to perform as one hears. The new vocal learning mechanisms are 'higher' than the existing lower vocal motor areas, which they evolved to control.

Apes and monkeys are not capable of vocal learning. Largely this is due to their vocal anatomy, and their (lack of) control of it, not being up to the job. However, research on mirror neurons has shown brain activity in macaques which is consistent with an imitation-like motor response to observation of a facial gesture which could produce a heard vocal sound.

Another category of mirror neurons called 'communicative mouth mirror neurons' (Ferrari [et al.] 2003...) are specifically activated by the observation of mouth-communicative gestures belonging to the monkey repertoire, such as lip-smacking, lip protrusion, or tongue protrusion. Interestingly enough, all acts found to be effective in triggering the visual response of these neurons are affiliative acts—that is, friendly gestures with low emotional content—and not threatening or aggressive gestures.
                    (Fogassi and Ferrari 2007, pp. 138–9)

Thus some basis for vocal-imitative learning seems to be in place before the animals concerned are able actually to perform it, in particular before they are able to imitate sounds.

In captivity, apes can learn several hundreds of vocabulary items taught them by humans. They use them in comprehension of the utterances of their trainers, and to make requests for food and pleasurable treatment, such as tickling. Mostly, unlike humans, they don't volunteer information for no immediate advantage to themselves. So I start from the assumption that apes have a disposition to learn small vocabularies, given the right social setup. But their natural social setup in the wild does not foster the growth of any shared learned vocabulary. Humans have an instinctive trust of others, and a disposition to share in the activities of others, nourished of course by generally trusting and cooperative social environments. This high degree of widespread mutual trust and cooperation is lacking in non-human apes. Tomasello et al. (2005) attribute this to 'shared intentionality', which only humans have a capacity for—a sharp qualitative difference, in their view. Their idea is encapsulated thus:

In general, it is almost unimaginable that two chimpanzees might spontaneously do something as simple as carry something together or help each other make a tool, that is, do something with a commitment to do it together and to help each other with their role if needed. ...Nor does ape communication seem to be collaborative in the same way as human communication. Most basically, there is very little communication about third entities (topics), and there are no signals serving a declarative or informative motive.   (Tomasello et al. 2005, p. 685)

In fact, the difference between humans and chimpanzees may not be as stark as this quotation suggests. In Lock and Colombo (1996, pp. 623–4) there is a series of photographs showing an episode very aptly described by the caption 'Three chimpanzees collaborate in setting a pole ladder against a tree to avoid electrified wires. Note how one animal holds the base of the ladder while another climbs. (From Menzel (1972))'. Later research by some of the same researchers expressing the 'almost unimaginable' view above gives a different impression.

[W]e report experimental evidence that chimpanzees perform basic forms of helping in the absence of rewards spontaneously and repeatedly toward humans and conspecifics. In two comparative studies, semifree ranging chimpanzees helped an unfamiliar human to the same degree as did human infants, irrespective of being rewarded (experiment 1) or whether the helping was costly (experiment 2). In a third study, chimpanzees helped an unrelated conspecific gain access to food in a novel situation that required subjects to use a newly acquired skill on behalf of another individual. These results indicate that chimpanzees share crucial aspects of altruism with humans, suggesting that the roots of human altruism may go deeper than previous experimental evidence suggested. (Warneken et al. 2007)

It seems reasonable that the difference between humans and chimpanzees in shared intentionality is a matter of degree, like other chimp/human differences. The occasions when chimpanzees spontaneously help each other with a tool (such as a pole ladder) are much rarer than similar instances among humans. Postulating shared intentionality (and other aspects of cooperation and social learning) as the catalysts which led to language may, as Derek Bickerton (personal communication) puts it, 'replace one puzzle with another puzzle; where did shared intentionality come from?' Well, all theories beg certain questions, or postulate certain unexplained premises. I argued in *The Origins of Meaning* that it was possible to have shared intentionality without language, but not possible to have language without shared intentionality. Given the emergence, somehow, of such trusting and cooperative social arrangements, the ancestors of modern humans found themselves in an environment where learned meaningful signals were advantageous, and there would have been pressure for the shared vocabularies to grow culturally, which in turn would have exerted pressure for a capacity to learn larger vocabularies to evolve by biological natural selection. These are the assumptions on which this chapter is founded.

Along with the growth of symbol-learning comes an increase in voluntary control over the use of symbols. Humans can choose when and where to use a word with enormously greater apparent freedom than vervets have when making their calls. Partly, this increased freedom is a concomitant of the increased trust between individuals mentioned earlier. Despite the philosophical problems with the concept VOLUNTARY, ethologists do not hesitate to describe some primate social actions as voluntary. Whether to attack a rival, whether to join in the monkey hunt, whether to woo a certain female, whether to join in rough-and-tumble play—it is reasonable, and comparable to usage about humans, to describe all these as 'decisions' taken 'voluntarily' by apes. With increased symbolic exchange of information coming from increased mutual trust and shared intentionality, acts of giving meaningful information join this list of relatively voluntary actions.

Voluntary control is not completely absent from agonistic cries, such as threat or distress calls. There is evidence that chimpanzees being attacked exaggerate their screams when there is a potential rescuer nearby, in contrast to when there is no potential rescuer present (Slocombe and Zuberbühler, 2008b,

2008a) (see also Slocombe and Zuberbühler, 2005a). This seems to indicate a degree of calculated control over the scream.

2.1.3 *Manual gesture and lateralization*

Much of language is lateralized to the left hemisphere in a large majority of humans. A large majority of humans are also right-handed, controlling manual gestures from the left hemisphere. Apes are less lateralized, but do show some asymmetry in behaviour and cerebral organization. This broadly encourages the idea of some continuity between pre-human ape communication and modern human language, crucially via the gestural medium. Here below, I look at the evidence in more detail.

Undoubtedly, ape manual gestures are under far greater voluntary control than their vocalizations. A famous report by Jane Goodall tells of a chimpanzee finding food and trying to suppress his instinctive food-finding vocal call by holding his hand over his mouth. Wild chimpanzees use a variety of communicative gestures, and these can vary from one population to another, so there is evidence that they are learned and culturally transmitted. In captivity, chimpanzee communicative gestures do not become group-wide codes. '[Y]oungsters were not imitatively learning their communicatory gestures from conspecifics, but rather that they were individually conventionalizing them with each other' (Tomasello et al. 1994, p. 137). Wild chimpanzees do not use gestures in any referential way, drawing the attention of receivers to other things in the environment. The chimp communicative gestures are of the dyadic doing-things-to-each-other kind, for such purposes as attracting attention (to oneself), display, play, and threat. '... we have much evidence that non-human primates use their gestures much more flexibly than their vocal signals. But we still have very little evidence that they use their gestures symbolically or referentially' (Pika et al. 2005, pp. 47–8). Captive chimpanzees, however, when making begging gestures to humans for food placed out of reach, are a different story. 'Overall, significantly more chimpanzees, especially females and adults, gestured with their right than with their left hand. Foods begs were more lateralized to the right hand than pointing, and a greater prevalence of right-hand gesturing was found in subjects who simultaneously vocalized than those who did not. Taken together, these data suggest that referential, intentional communicative behaviors, in the form of gestures, are lateralized to the left hemisphere in chimpanzees' (Hopkins and Leavens 1998, p. 95).

In humans, one-handed communicative gestures are mostly right-handed, as most of the population is right-handed. For most people, control of both speech and (one-handed) gestures emanates from the left hemisphere, where (broadly) the calls of conspecifics are also processed. A plausible way-stage in the transition from ape communication was a gestural protolanguage, which gradually gave way to a spoken protolanguage. The gestural origins of language have been advocated extensively, and there is a growing appreciation of the plausibility of the idea.[7] Manual gestures lend themselves more readily to iconic signalling of actions, shapes, and sizes, and thus could plausibly bootstrap a conventional shared vocabulary (see the next section). Pollick and de Waal (2007) studied two captive bonobo groups and two captive chimpanzee groups, all animals untrained and presumed to be behaving naturally. 'It was found that homologous facial/vocal displays were used very similarly by both ape species, yet the same did not apply to gestures. Both within and between species gesture usage varied enormously. Moreover, bonobos showed greater flexibility in this regard than chimpanzees and were also the only species in which multimodal communication (i.e. combinations of gestures and facial/vocal signals) added to behavioral impact on the recipient' (p. 8184). The authors speculate that, although bonobos and chimpanzees are evolutionarily equidistant from humans, bonobos offer a better model for steps toward human language. Humans, like the bonobos, integrate vocal and manual communication, as McNeill et al. (2008), among many others, have noted.

Deacon (1997, pp. 309–18) argues that the human biases toward right-handedness and left-lateralization of language probably co-evolved in the recent human lineage, each reinforcing the other. But the pre-existing left-lateralization of processing of conspecific calls in other primates would have been a factor predisposing this language/handedness co-evolution toward the left hemisphere. There is weak population-level[8] right-handedness in great apes, both wild and captive.[9]

Such handedness preferences in chimpanzees have until recently been hard to correlate with brain asymmetries. The problem appears to be that for simple tasks, such as reaching for a peanut and hand-to-mouth feeding, chimps are fairly ambidextrous. Hopkins and Cantalupo (2004) tested 66 chimps on a more complex, bi-manual task, where the animal had to stick its finger inside a PVC tube to extract peanut butter, while holding the tube with its other hand. The significant population-level right-handed bias that they found, replicating

[7] See, for example Hewes (1973); Armstrong et al. (1995); Corballis, (2002, 2003); Bonvillian et al. (1997).

[8] About 2:1 in chimpanzees

[9] Bradshaw and Rogers (1993); Byrne and Byrne (1991); Byrne and Corp (2004b); Hopkins and Cantalupo (2005); McGrew and Marchant (1997); Ward and Hopkins (1993).

earlier work, was correlated with three separate asymmetries in the chimp brains, as measured by MRI scanning.[10]

But the relationship between weak right-handedness in chimpanzees and human language is not straightforward.

[T]he collective results of this study indicate that individual variation in the handedness of chimpanzees is associated with variation in primary motor regions of the brain rather than areas typically defined as 'language' regions in the human brain. This pattern of results suggests that the neurobiological basis for handedness evolved as early as 5 million years ago and emerged independent of systems associated with language and speech, as some have proposed (see Bradshaw and Rogers, 1993; Corballis, 1991; Rogers and Andrew, 2002).   Hopkins and Cantalupo (2004, p. 1182)

Corballis (2003) also notes that different left hemisphere areas in non-human primates control vocalization and manual movements. The monkey homologue of Broca's area does not control vocalizations, but contains the mirror neurons that correlate observation of manual gestures with production of the same gestures. In humans, Corballis suggests, Broca's area took over vocal expression of communicative gestures. Xu et al. (2009) used functional MRI scans to investigate whether symbolic manual gestures and spoken words are processed by the same system in the human brain. They found that:

both classes of stimuli activate a common, left-lateralized network of inferior frontal and posterior temporal regions in which symbolic gestures and spoken words may be mapped onto common, corresponding conceptual representations. We suggest that these anterior and posterior perisylvian areas, identified since the mid-19th century as the core of the brain's language system, are not in fact committed to language processing, but may function as a modality-independent semiotic system that plays a broader role in human communication, linking meaning with symbols whether these are words, gestures, images, sounds, or objects.   (Xu et al. 2009, p. 20664)

Consistent with this, Grèzes et al. (1998) had also found activation in Brodmann areas 44 and 45 on viewing meaningful manual gestures, and other researchers have got similar results (Decety et al. 1997; Hamzei et al. 2003; Johnson-Frey et al. 2003). Gentilucci (2003) got subjects to speak the syllables *ba* or *ga* while watching an experimenter grasp either a large or a small object. Gentilucci found that subjects' lip apertures and the loudness of their voice were significantly greater when watching the larger object being grasped. This suggests a vestigial link between manual gestures and speech. Three years later,

---

[10] The asymmetries were detected by MRI scans on anaesthetized animals at a separate time from when they were performing the diagnostic handedness task.

workers from the same lab (Bernardis and Gentilucci 2006) observed reciprocal effects of speaking on simultaneous gesturing, and vice-versa, concluding, somewhat sweepingly 'These results suggest that spoken word and symbolic gesture are coded as single signal by a unique communication system' (p. 178). Arbib (2005) also argues for an evolutionary transition from gestures to speech, invoking mirror neurons.[11]

2.1.4 *Fitness out of the here and now*

Another component of the human voluntary control of words is our freedom to think about things in their absence. Non-human behaviour is driven to a far greater degree than ours by basic urges such as hunger, the need for sleep, and desire for sex. This immediacy relates to the selectional pressures driving evolution. Bickerton (2008b), in keeping with his tendency to see abrupt changes in language evolution, identifies a key difference between human and non-human communication, and a key question for language evolution, as yet not satisfactorily answered. 'Another crucial new feature was a departure from the direct linkage with evolutionary fitness that characterized all other communication systems. The communication system of each species...comprises just those signals that relate directly to the fitness of species members, and excludes any that don't contribute to such fitness. In language, no units in and of themselves relate in any way to evolutionary fitness' (p. 170). Humans have a greater aptitude for contemplating and talking about a wide range of other things, with, mostly, ample leisure to do so. Humans can suppress their instinctive behaviour more successfully than non-humans, which frees up our minds for communication about things other than immediate goals relating to survival or reproduction. Bickerton does not see how there can be a gradual progression from the immediate here-and-now communication of animals to the human state of Olympian detachment.

But regardless of how gradually language evolved, there must have been specific times at which communicational novelties appeared. Displacement, for instance—the capacity to refer to objects or events not physically present—is an all-or-nothing category, like marriage or imprisonment; you're either married or not, in jail or out of it, and signals either refer exclusively to the here and now or can go beyond it.

(Bickerton 2008b, p. 170)

---

[11] The main sources for mirror neurons, especially in relation to language, are Gallese et al. (1996); Gallese (2003a 2003c, 2003b, 2004); Rizzolatti et al. (1996); Rizzolatti and Arbib (1998).

But HERE and NOW are relative, not absolute concepts, unlike the concepts of marriage and jail, possibly.[12] How long is 'now'? How far does 'here' extend? *Here* can be used to pinpoint a flyspeck on a window, or to locate an event in a particular room, or city, or country, or even in this universe as opposed to some parallel universe. *Now* is similarly stretchable. Context tells you how to interpret it on a given occasion. I argued in *The Origins of Meaning* that the seeds of displaced reference can be found in animals, in their (limited) ability to hold in mind objects or events that are not present to the senses. A dog can remember for about five minutes that a juicy bone was hidden behind a particular screen (without smelling it). Scrub jays, famously, can remember what they cached, and where and when. Here too, a gradualist, non-saltational course of events is easy to envisage. Obviously it benefits an animal to be aware of a predator present to its senses. But it would also benefit an animal to recall the presence of a predator a few seconds, or a few minutes, or a few hours, or even a few days ago. We can imagine communication stretching its reference gradually to what was here a few seconds ago, then to minutes ago, then to hours or days ago. Likewise with spatial location. It is obviously beneficial to be aware of food right under your nose. Depending on your mobility and your memory, it's also useful to be aware of, and communicate about, food a mile or two away. Bees do it.

I will speculate that this gradual stretching of the here and now, both in awareness and in what is communicated, is at least partly also a product of mutual trust and cooperation. If you can rely on other group members, some of the time, to 'put food on the table', and they, similarly, some of the time, can rely on you, then each of you now has some spare time for concentrating on something else, maybe recalling a past episode, or roughly planning some future action. It would be adaptive, in some circumstances, to be able to mull over non-present situations in this way, as we humans can. What do gorillas think about while sitting around munching plants? Brain activity is energetically costly, so there has to be some adaptive benefit to active thinking about the non-here-and-now.[13] Maybe the gorillas' environment is (or was!) so stable that there is no great adaptive advantage to thinking about hypothetical alternative circumstances (assuming that they don't, much). For humans, however, it is widely held that our evolution owes a lot to adapting to

---

[12] Common law marriage is an intermediate kind of marriage, between formal marriage and non-marriage. And house arrest is a kind of imprisonment short of jail. So Bickerton's examples of (other) all-or-nothing categories are not well chosen.

[13] 'In effect, all animals are under stringent selection pressure to be as stupid as they can get away with' (Richerson and Boyd 2005, p. 135).

a new and less predictable environment, with the change from the forest to the savannah. Here is one example of this claim:

> Over the last fourteen million years..., increases in climatic variability are mirrored by increases in brain ratio. This combination of evidence, alongside the formal theory that independently implicates environmental variation with increases in social learning abilities, suggests that human cultural capacities may be a hypertrophied subset of a larger class of learning abilities that have evolved in many species.
>
> (Henrich and McElreath 2003, p. 125)

Richerson and Boyd (2005, pp. 131–5) devote a substantial section to arguing that 'Social learning may be an adaptation to Pleistocene climate fluctuations'. A plausible hypothesis is that early hominins[14] evolved some limited capacity for 'voluntary' thinking out of the tight box of the here-and-now, and for voluntary control over expression of their thoughts using simple symbols, due to the joint effects of social cooperation, social learning, and a fluctuating environment. This is all speculative, of course, but it seems to be coherent. (In *The Origins of Meaning*, there is lengthy discussion of the extent to which the evolutionary seeds of mental representations not directly tied to the here-and-now can be found in non-human animals.)

To summarize this section, the following are the factors which indicate that the substantial gap between non-human primate signals and proto-human unitary 'words' is not quite as unbridgeable as has sometimes been supposed:

1. general primate left-hemisphere bias for perception of conspecific calls;
2. left-hemisphere preference in symbol-trained chimpanzees for visual attention to meaningful symbols;
3. widespread (amphibians, birds, mammals) left-hemisphere bias for production of communicative calls;
4. some slight learning of 'innate' referential (alarm and food) vocal calls, as in vervets and capuchins;
5. some small degree of voluntary control over emotional/affective vocal calls in chimpanzees;
6. the existence of communicative mouth mirror neurons in macaques;

---

[14] Throughout this book, I use 'hominin' for humans and all their ancestors and close relatives, going back only as far as *Australopithecus*, thus including Neanderthals, *Homo erectus* and *Homo habilis*. 'Hominid' is now a broader term, including extant great apes. 'Hominid' has recently changed its usage, with 'hominin' taking over some of its previous range. See http://www.madsci.org/posts/archives/2003-04/1050350684.Ev.r.html for a note reflecting the terminological confusion in this area.

7. considerable flexibility and voluntary control of manual gestures in chimpanzees;

8. the widespread use of gestures for interpersonal, but not referential purposes, by chimpanzees;

9. a small number of context-specific vocal calls, probably learned and culturally transmitted, in at least one population of chimpanzees;

10. weak population-level righthandedness for gestures in chimpanzees.

11. continuing substantial involvement of manual gestures in modern human
spoken language.

Nevertheless, there is a gap between non-human primate calls and human
learned vocal signals. We now have a good idea of at least one of the ways
in which human-specific evolution bridged that gap. Along with, and no doubt
parallel to, the evolution of the vocal tract, there was substantial growth in the
frontal-parietal-temporal pathways facilitating vocal imitation and learning.

Hombert (2008) also argues for continuity between the communication
system of non-human primates and humans. And he also sees gestures as a
likely stepping stone in the transition. But his aphoristic summary is too simple.
It goes:

Non-human primate vocalizations > 'non-linguistic' human vocalizations
Non-human primate communicative gestures > articulated human language.

(Hombert 2008, p. 441)

This leaves unmentioned the vocal nature of articulated human language. The
primate left hemisphere was ready for the processing of vocal calls, whether
merely interpersonal or referential. Voluntary control of one-handed meaningful gestures was also from the left hemisphere in a majority of our ape
ancestors. In human ontogeny, gestures are a stepping stone to the first words.
'[T]he emergence of single words is predicted by (1) earlier reorganizations
in gestural communication (e.g. pointing, giving, showing), (2) the age of
emergence of tool use and means–end relations..., (3) the concomitant emergence of "gestural naming", i.e. recognitory gestures with familiar objects (e.g.
drinking from an empty cup, putting a shoe to one's foot' (Bates et al. 1988,
p. 28. See also Bates et al. 1977).

We know hardly anything about how hominins got their first learned
'words'. But thinking of how it **could possibly** have happened is a useful
exercise. Among other things, this exercise reveals facts which are interesting
in themselves, about such topics as lateralization of brain function, ape vocalizations, and climate change. Taken together, such empirical facts contribute
to a coherent story (with other bits left unfilled-in, to be sure) of a continuous

thread from primate calls, quite possibly via gestures, to the first proto-human 'words'. The relevant parallel transitions were from innate to learned, and from involuntary to voluntary signals. Given these transitions, the scene was set for an expansion of the size of the inventories of symbols used by our early ancestors.

2.2 Sound symbolism, synaesthesia, and arbitrariness

The vast majority of mappings from meanings to sounds in modern languages are arbitrary. Shakespeare's Juliet knew this: 'What's in a name? That which we call a rose / By any other name would smell as sweet'. Karl Marx agreed with Juliet: 'The name of a thing is entirely external to its nature' (Marx 1867, p. 195). Plato, surprisingly to us now, thought that there was an issue here. His *Kratylos* is a dialogue between an advocate of the position that the sounds of words have a natural necessary connection to their meanings, and an opponent who takes the essentially modern view that mappings between meanings and forms are arbitrary. We shall see that, for some people at least, maybe the word *rose* does have a certain smell to it, and we may wonder whether Plato, being a few millennia closer to the origins of language than we are, with a less cluttered mind, was onto an issue that is not so cut-and-dried as we think.

There is no natural connection at all between middle-sized furry canine quadrupeds and the words *dog* (English), *chien* (French), *kalb* (Arabic), *kutya* (Hungarian), *inu* (Japanese), or *perro* (Spanish). These mappings, being 'unnatural', now have to be learned by children from the usage of the previous generation. But how did the very first words in the evolution of language arise, when there was nobody to learn from? Conceivably, some hominin ancestor made a random noise while attempting to convey some idea; the hearers were able to make a good guess from the context what idea was meant, and the random noise became arbitrarily associated with that idea. It may well have happened like that in many cases. Modern languages vary in the extent to which their vocabulary contains iconic items. Vietnamese, for example, has more onomatopeic words ('ideophones') than typical European languages (Durand 1961). But across all languages now, relatively few meanings are apparently **naturally** connected to the acoustic shapes of the words which express them. This is **sound symbolism**. It is possible that in some cases, these natural connections were felt and exploited by the earliest speakers. Below, I review a small sample of studies of sound symbolism. A more complete survey would only otiosely reinforce the point that this is a natural phenomenon in languages, however marginal it might be. Many authors of such studies relate the phenomenon to the evolution of language, even when writing at times when this topic was not generally approved of.

Discussion of sound symbolism has not been in high fashion in linguistics for the past few decades. Diffloth (1994, p. 107) even writes, too harshly, 'the study of sound symbolism has a tarnished reputation in current linguistics'. It is clear that the phenomenon exists, while being admittedly marginal in languages. The preface of a recent central work resurrecting the topic (Hinton et al. 1995) states that 'sound symbolism plays a far more significant role in language than scholarship has hitherto recognised'.

2.2.1 Synaesthetic sound symbolism

One type of sound symbolism is related to synaesthesia. This is a condition in which stimuli in one modality evoke sensations in another modality. For example, some people with synaesthesia ('synaesthetes') regularly associate a particular number with a particular colour, or a vowel sound with a colour. Ward and Simner (2003) describe a case 'in which speech sounds induce an involuntary sensation of taste that is subjectively located in the mouth' (p. 237). There are many different types of synaesthesia, some connecting natural perceptual modalities, like vision and sound, and others associating cultural objects such as names and letters with perceptual modalities such as taste and smell. Synaesthesia also comes in various strengths, and is sometimes a permanent condition and sometimes sporadic. Some synaesthetes think of their condition as a beautiful gift (Savage-Rumbaugh 1999, pp. 121–4). The condition can reach pathological dimensions in some unfortunate people, such as Luria's (1968) patient S and Baron-Cohen's (1996) patient JR. To some extent many people share these cross-modal associations. This is why musicians can talk about 'bright' sounds and 'sharp' and 'flat' notes. Phoneticians call a velarized lateral approximant, as in English *eel* (in most accents) a 'dark L' and the nonvelarized counterpart, as in *Lee* (in most accents) a 'clear L'. Some examples are given below of apparently synaesthetic sound symbolism surfacing in languages.

Traunmüller (2000) summarizes one of the most prominent cases:

It is well known that we associate high front vowels like [i] with qualities like 'small', 'weak', 'light', 'thin', etc., while we associate back and low vowels with qualities like 'large', 'strong', 'heavy', and 'thick'. Such a result has been obtained quite consistently in experiments in which speakers of various languages had been asked to attribute selected qualities to speech sounds and nonsense words (Sapir 1929; Fónagy 1963; Ertel 1969; Fischer-Jorgensen 1978).   (Traunmüller 2000, p. 216)

Woodworth (1991) cites a large number of discussions of sound symbolism, almost all from the middle two quarters of the twentieth century.[15] Jespersen (1922, ch. XX) devoted a 16-page chapter to sound symbolism. Sapir (1929) did an early experimental study. Roger Brown et al. (1955), while remarking on the 'unpopularity' of the topic, concluded:

Three separate investigations, using three lists of English words and six foreign languages, have shown superior to chance agreement and accuracy in the translation of unfamiliar tongues. . . . The accuracy can be explained by the assumption of some universal phonetic symbolism in which speech may have originated or toward which speech may be evolving. For the present we prefer to interpret our results as indicative of a primitive phonetic symbolism deriving from the origin of speech in some kind of imitative or physiognomic linkage of sounds and meanings.

(Brown et al. 1955, p. 393)

Cases of sound symbolism, though still rare, are more common than is often realized. The best known examples are onomatopeic words like *cuckoo*, *meow*, and *cockadoodledoo*. It would have been natural for our ancestors, seeking an effective way to convey the sound made by a cat, or perhaps the cat itself, to utter a syllable like *meow*. As languages emerged, with their own conventional constraints on pronunciation, the likeness with the original sound became distorted. Thus English *purr*, German *knurren*, and French *ronronnement* are still all recognizably onomatopeic on the noise made by a contented cat, yet conform to the special speech patterns of those languages. Only a tiny minority of words in modern language are onomatopeic.

In signed languages of the deaf, a visual version of onomatopeia, and a similar subsequent squeezing into the constraints of the language, occurs. Thus in British Sign Language (BSL), the original expression for a tape recorder involved pointing downwards with both index fingers extended, and making a clockwise circular motion with both hands, simulating the movement of the reels in a reel-to-reel machine. Moving both hands clockwise is not as easy as rotating them in opposite directions, the left clockwise and the right anticlockwise, and the BSL sign later became conventionalized in this latter way. Here is a microcosm of how some of the earliest 'words' may have been

---

[15] 'More recent discussions of sound symbolism concentrate on language-specific examples, exploring both structured and unstructured word lists (de Reuse 1986; Haas 1978; Jespersen 1922; Langdon 1970; Newman 1933; Sapir 1911), experimental work with nonce-words and/or non-native words (Bentley and Varon 1933; Chastaing 1965; Eberhardt 1940; Newman 1933; Sapir 1949), general discussions of the phenomenon (Brown 1958; Jakobson 1978; Jakobson and Waugh 1979; Jespersen 1922; Malkiel 1987; Nuckolls 1999; Orr 1944; Wescott 1980), and a cross-linguistic study (Ultan 1984)' (Woodworth 1991, pp. 273–4).

invented and soon conventionalized in an easy-to-use form. In the next section, we shall see some modern experiments in which this process of invention and conventionalization is re-created. For the moment, we return to show how sound symbolism is somewhat more common than is usually thought.

Some of the most pragmatically central expressions in languages, namely demonstratives such as English *this* and *that*, and 1st and 2nd person pronouns, such as French *je/me/moi* and *tu/te/toi*, have been shown to use the same classes of sounds, across languages, with far greater than chance probability.

Woodworth (1991) tested the hypothesis that

[g]iven a series of forms either deictic pronouns ('this', 'that', 'that one over there'), place adverbs ('here', 'there', 'yonder'), or directional affixes (toward/away from speaker) which have differing vowel qualities, there is a relation between the pitch (that is, the value of the second formant) of the vowel qualities such that the pitch of the vowel associated with the form indicating proximal meaning is higher than that of the vowel associated with the form indicating distal meaning.   (Woodworth 1991, p. 277)

('Pitch' is not the best way of describing this phenomenon, as 'pitch' usually refers to the fundamental frequency of a sound—the musical note. Higher values of second formant are characteristic of vowels produced relatively high and front in the mouth, as in English *bee, bit, bet*. Lower second formant values are characteristic of vowels made low and back in the mouth, as in English *far, four*.) From a sample of 26 languages (24 maximally genetically[16] distant, one creole, and one isolate), Woodworth found the following results:

	CON-FIRMING	DIS-CONFIRMING	(NEUTRAL OR NOT APPLICABLE)	BINOMIAL PROBABILITY
deictic pronouns	13	2	(11)	0.0037
place adverbs	9	1	(16)	0.0107

This demonstrates that in these pragmatically important domains, the relation between sound and meaning tends significantly not to be arbitrary. Traunmüller (2000) did a similar study, on a different sample of 37 languages in which the deictics were etymologically unrelated, and found '32 in support of [the same] hypothesis and only 4 counterexamples. The binomial probability of observing no more than 4 counterexamples among 36 cases is 10^{-7}' (p. 220).

---

[16] In the context of historical linguistics the term 'genetic' does not denote any biological relationship. Keep this in mind below.

High values of second formant, characteristic of the [i] vowel, are also significantly correlated with female proper names in English. Cutler et al. (1990), comparing 884 male names with 783 female names, and a control set of common nouns, found that 'the female set contains a much higher proportion of [i] than the other two sets, and a lower proportion of vowels towards the other end of the brightness continuum. On χ^2 tests there was a significant difference between the female names and the male names... The male names did not differ significantly from the nouns' (p. 479). These authors also found that female names contain significantly more syllables than male names, and that male names begin significantly more often with a strong syllable[17] than female names. Wright et al. (2005) found that 'male names are significantly more likely to begin with voiced obstruents than female names' (p. 541) and that 'monosyllabic female names are significantly more likely than male names to contain long vowels' (p. 542). See also Slater and Feinman (1985) for similar results.

Berlin (1994) paired up randomly chosen names for fish and birds from Huambisa, a language of north central Peru. Each pair had one fish name and one bird name, in a random order. Then he presented lists of these word-pairs to English speakers who had no knowledge of Huambisa, and asked them to guess which was the fish name and which was the bird name. They did surprisingly well, much better than chance ($p = 0.005$). Analysing his results, Berlin selected 29 pairs on which subjects had tended to guess accurately (one pair was even guessed right 98 percent of the time). 'Almost 3/4 (or 72 percent) of the bird names recognized with greater than chance accuracy include the high front vowel [i] in one or more syllables. The contrasting fish names in these pairs differ markedly. Less than half of them (44%) show syllables with vowel [i]' (p. 78). Then, looking at his sample of the bird and fish vocabulary of Huambisa as a whole, Berlin found that 'in comparison with fish, bird names favor [i] as a first syllable (33% of the full inventory) while names for fish appear to actively avoid this vowel as an initial syllabic (fewer than 8% of fish names are formed with first syllable [i]). By contrast, 54% of fish names exhibit the central vowel [a] as their first syllabic' (p. 79). He also found some interesting correlations with consonants.

(It strikes me impressionistically that it may also be possible to find similar statistical sound-symbolic correlations cross-linguistically in the words for urine (e.g. *piss*, *pee*) and excrement (e.g. *kaka*, *poo*), with a tendency for the

---

[17] They define a strong syllable as one with primary or secondary stress, as opposed to unstressed.

former to use high front vowels significantly more often than the latter. I got an undergraduate to do a project on this, and her results are suggestive of a correlation, but a more controlled study with more data needs to be done.)

Recently Ramachandran and Hubbard (2001) have discussed a possible genetic basis for synaesthesia, and speculated on its relation to the origin of language. They discuss a striking example in which the great majority of people share an unlearned association between visual shapes and spoken words.

Consider stimuli like those shown [in my Figure 2.1], originally developed by Köhler (1929, 1947) and further explored by Werner (1934, 1957); Werner and Wapner (1952). If you show [Figure 2.1] (left and right) to people and say 'In Martian language, one of these two figures is a "bouba" and the other is a "kiki", try to guess which is which', 95% of people pick the left as kiki and the right as bouba, even though they have never seen these stimuli before. ... (In his original experiments Köhler (1929) called the stimuli *takete* and *baluma*. He later renamed the *baluma* stimulus *maluma* (Köhler, 1947). However, the results were essentially unchanged and 'most people answer[ed] without hesitation' (p. 133))   (Ramachandran and Hubbard 2001, p. 19)

Considering the vowels in these stimuli, a correlation (counterintuitive to me) is suggested between jagged shape and smallness, weakness, and female gender, and between rounded shape and large size, strength and male gender. Think of the stereotypically female names *Fifi* and *Mimi*.

My student David Houston suggested that the association of the jagged shape with *kiki* might be due to the jagged shape of the letter 'k' in the Roman alphabet. So the experiment needs to be done with illiterates or people using other writing systems, or somehow controlling against orthographic effects. This has been followed up by Cuskley et al. (2009) who concluded that indeed while their 'experiments indicate overwhelming orthographic interference in the traditional *bouba/kiki* paradigm, this should not detract from a cross-modally based theory of protolanguage'. They mention 'a wealth of work in cross-modality more generally which supports the existence of regular cross-modal associations (see Marks 1978 for a review)'.

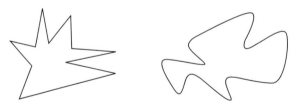

Fig. 2.1 Which of these shapes is *bouba* and which is *kiki*?
Source: From Ramachandran and Hubbard (2001).

Following up on the *kiki/bouba* studies, David Houston did an interesting experiment showing a natural association between different musical keys and *kiki* and *bouba*. The next two short paragraphs are David's description of his experiment.

There are two melodies (written and played by David on classical guitar), each of identical length (28 seconds), articulation, and dynamics. If written out in music notation, they would look identical except for the key signature (D minor versus D major). So the only difference here is the tonality (major or minor).

D minor—D E F G A B$_{flat}$ C D
D major—D E F$_{sharp}$ G A B C$_{sharp}$ D

As you can see, there is only a difference in tonality of 3 notes (half steps). The tonal centre of D remains constant in both of them.

Participants heard the two melodies once each consecutively and were told that one of them is called *Kiki* and the other *Bouba*. Overwhelmingly (18 of 20 subjects), and without hesitation, participants chose *Kiki* for D major and *Bouba* for D minor. They usually used words like 'brighter' and 'darker' to describe why they made this choice. Of the few that chose otherwise, they did so for non-phonetic reasons, claiming that *Bouba* sounds more childish and corresponds with the major melody which to them also sounds more childish (as compared with the darker and sadder quality of the minor melody).

What have sound symbolism and synaesthesia to do with the evolution of language? They seem good candidates to solve the problem of how an early population managed to 'invent', and subsequently 'agree upon' apparently **arbitrary** connections between meanings and sounds. Some slight element of naturalness in connections between meanings and sounds could have been the bootstrap needed to get such a system up and running. According to this idea, the very first learned meaningful expressions would have been sound-symbolically, or synaesthetically, connected to their meanings, facilitating their learning and diffusion through the community. (This idea only works to the extent that synaesthetic links were shared across individuals. Many modern synaesthetes have idiosyncratic links not shared by others. But this is probably what singles these people out as in some way unusual—their synaesthetic associations are not the usual ones found in most individuals.) Later developments would have stylized and conventionalized the forms of these expressions, in ways that we will see experimentally replicated in the next section (and in a similar way to the ontogenetic ritualization of the 'nursing poke' discussed in *The Origins of Meaning*).

Ramachandran and Hubbard (2001, pp. 18–23) correctly identify the significance of synaesthesia for language evolution, and also mention the bootstrapping idea, but some of their discussion tends to confuse two different issues. One issue (the one we are concerned with here) is the emergence of the arbitrary relation between meanings and sounds, and another, distinct, issue is the coordination of neural motor information with sensory information, as happens with mirror neurons. The discovery of mirror neurons, about which Ramachandran is enthusiastic, does not in itself provide a ready explanation for our ability to map acoustic forms to arbitrary meanings. This is argued in detail by Hurford (2004); see Arbib (2004) for a partly agreeing, and partly disagreeing, response.

It has been suggested that babies are particularly synaesthetic for the first few months after birth (Maurer 1993; Maurer and Mondlach 2005). If our ancestors around the era when the first lexicons were emerging were also more synaesthetic than modern adult humans, this might have facilitated the emergence of form–meaning correspondences. An extreme form of synaesthesia yielding only buzzing blooming confusion would not be adaptive, but some slight disposition to associate distinct vocal sounds with certain classes of referent could have helped. It would be interesting to know whether non-human primates show any evidence of synaesthesia; I have not been able to find any report of such evidence. Only the synaesthetic type of sound symbolism offers a potential solution to the problem of how the earliest learned arbitrary symbols may have arisen by bootstrapping from naturally occurring sound-symbolic forms.

2.2.2 Conventional sound symbolism

The most common other type is called 'conventional sound symbolism' by Hinton et al. (1994) in their typology of sound symbolism. English examples of conventional sound symbolism are the [sn] cluster at the beginning of words like *sneak*, *snigger*, *snide*, *snot*, and *snarl*, which all have connotations of unpleasantness or underhandedness; the [ʌmp] rhyme in *lump*, *hump*, *bump*, *rump*, *clump*, and *stump*, all denoting some kind of small protrusion. These vary from language to language[18] and creative coining of new words based on them uses examples already learned. Such associations as these cannot

---

[18] Kita (2008) discusses the extensive set of sound-symbolic words in Japanese, relating them to protolanguage. It is not clear to me to what extent synaesthetic dispositions, as opposed to language-specific conventions, underlie these Japanese examples.

be attributed to the universal weak innate synaesthetic dispositions which, I hypothesize, were present in early humans.

Conventional sound symbolism, while based on learned patterns, unlike synaesthetic sound symbolism, does have some evolutionary relevance. It is adaptive. If the meaning or grammatical categorization of a word is somewhat predictable from its phonetic shape, this eases the tasks of speech perception and parsing. The correlation between phonological and semantic information across the whole lexicon has been quantified in a novel, ingenious, and power-ful way by Tamariz (2004), following up an idea of Simon Kirby's. She calcu-lated, for two large subsets of the Spanish lexicon (CVCV and CVCCV words), both the phonological similarity between all pairs of words, and the semantic similarity between all pairs of words. Both measures were relatively crude, but this did not bias the results. Phonological similarity between two words was measured by the number of aspects of word-form that were identical in both words. These aspects were: the initial, middle, and last consonants; all the consonants; the first and final vowels; all vowels; stressed syllable; and stressed vowel in the same syllable. Each of these aspects was assigned a value accord-ing to its rating in a psycholinguistic study of their relative impact of word similarity judgements. So for instance *mesa* and *mano* share the first consonant (value = 0.07) and the stress position (first syllable, value = 0.12), so for this word pair the similarity value is 0.19. This similarity was calculated between all pairs of words. In parallel, an attempt was made to calculate the semantic similarity between all pairs of words. The best available approximation to semantic similarity between words used cooccurrence-based lexical statistics, a technique that clusters words according to their frequency of collocation in a large corpus. Thus if *mesa* and *mano* tend to occur very frequently in the same text they get a high semantic similarity score, that is they are close to each other in semantic space. The 'semantic similarity' between words that rarely occur in the same text is correspondingly low. Given these two measures of similarity in two spaces, phonological and semantic, is it possible to see whether there is any correlation between the two spaces? The question is: do phonologically similar (close) words tend, with some statistical significance, also to be semantically similar (close)? And conversely, do semantically dissimilar (distant) words tend also to be phonologically dissimilar (distant)? The answer is Yes. Tamariz was able to measure 'a small but statistically significant degree of systematicity between the phonological and the cooccurrence-based levels of the lexicon' (2004, p. 221), thus demonstrating in a completely new way a slight but significant tendency to sound symbolism across the whole lexicon. She argues for the adaptivity of this correlation between sounds and meanings, as it facilitates both speech recognition and language acquisition.

In many languages there is a correlation between phonetic form and grammatical category. Monaghan and Christiansen (2006) analysed the 1,000 most
frequent words from large corpora of child-directed speech in English, Dutch,
French, and Japanese. For each language, they assessed approximately 50 cues
that measured phonological features across each word. For all four languages,
they found that there were phonological cues that significantly distinguished
function words from content words[19] and nouns from verbs. The number of
statistically significant phonological cues they found distinguishing function
words from content words was 17 (for English), 14 (for Dutch), 16 (for
French), and 8 (for Japanese). The number of statistically significant phonological cues they found distinguishing nouns from verbs was 7 (for English),
16 (for Dutch), 16 (for French), and 17 (for Japanese). For each language,
they combined all the cues and found that, combined, they made the relevant
discrimination with greater that 61 percent success, and in one case with
success as high as 74 percent. For these authors, the correlation between
phonological cues and grammatical categories confirms their 'phonological-
distributional coherence hypothesis', also explored in Monaghan et al. (2005).

In a similar study, Sereno (1994) found 'The phonological analysis of nouns
and verbs in the Brown Corpus [Francis and Kučera (1982)] revealed a systematic, skewed distribution....A greater number of high-frequency nouns
have back vowels, while high-frequency verbs have a greater number of front
vowels' (p. 265). Such correlations are important because they make the job of
the child language-learner easier, a point made in several publications by M. H.
Kelly (1996, 1992, 1988). To the extent that the language-learning task of the
child is facilitated by such correspondences, the need to postulate an innate
grammar learning mechanism is diminished. Sereno found that her correlation
is exploited by English speakers in categorizing words as nouns and verbs.
She showed subjects words on a screen and required them to press one of
two buttons labelled 'Noun' or 'Verb' to classify the word. She measured their
reaction times at this task. 'Nouns with back vowels (716 ms) were categorized
significantly faster than nouns with front vowels (777 ms), and verbs with
front vowels (776 ms) faster than verbs with back vowels (783 ms)' (p. 271).
Hinton et al. (1994) interpret this result of Sereno's, and the presence of sound
symbolism in general, in evolutionary terms. 'In terms of evolution, the value of
a sound-symbolic basis to communication is fairly obvious, as it allows greater

---

[19] Function words are those which belong to very small closed classes typically
indicating some grammatical function, such as conjunctions, determiners, and auxiliary
verbs; content words are all the rest, including nouns, verbs, and adjectives.

ease of communication. . . . It is the evolutionary value of arbitrariness, then, that must be explained' (p. 11).

This last challenge has been taken up by Gasser (2004). He points out the difficulty of arranging a large vocabulary in accordance with close sound-symbolic relationships. He experimentally trained an artificial neural network to learn vocabularies of four types: arbitrary small, arbitrary large, iconic small, and iconic large. He found that 'iconic languages have an early advantage because of the correlations that back-propagation can easily discover. For the small languages, this advantage holds throughout training. For the large languages, however, the network learning the arbitrary language eventually overtakes the one learning the iconic language, apparently because of the proximity of some of the form–meaning pairs to one another and the resulting confusion in the presence of noise' (p. 436).

To envisage the problem informally, imagine trying to compose a large vocabulary, naming a few thousand familiar classes of objects in such a way that, for example, all the names for fruit are phonologically similar, all the names for cities are phonologically similar in a different way, all the names for animals are similar in another way, all the names for virtues are similar in yet another way, and so on. There has long been a fascination for such schemes. In 1668, John Wilkins published *An Essay towards a Real Character and a Philosophical Language* in which he set up an ambitious and complex hierarchical ontology. Each category of thing in the world was to be named according to its place in this semantic hierarchy. You could tell the meaning of some term by inference from its initial, second, and third letters, and so on. It was a hopelessly flawed idea. Cross-classification presents one problem. If all edible things must have phonologically similar names, distinct from inedible things, this cross-cuts the fruit/animal distinction, and different kinds of phonological cues have to be used. Obviously, as a mind-game, this is challenging, and with ingenuity can be taken quite a long way. But as the vocabulary size and degree of cross-category relatedness increase, the number of possible phonological cues must also increase, and this adds to the overall phonological complexity of each word, which has to carry markers for all the various categories to which its meaning belongs. If one were designing a large vocabulary, covering a diverse range of meanings, it would soon be better to cut the Gordian knot and just settle for arbitrary meaning–form correspondences.

So far, this is not a properly expressed evolutionary argument. Couching it in evolutionary terms, one would presumably assume there is some advantage to individuals in a group in having a large vocabulary.[20] Acquiring a large

---

[20] See the end of section 2.4 for discussion of what might seem to be a problem here.

vocabulary unconstrained by iconicity is easier for an individual learner, as Gasser's experiments show. As more words were invented ad hoc by individuals, initially as nonce-words, they would progressively become harder to assimilate into existing learners' lexicons if they still conformed to constraints of iconicity. If on the other hand they were only arbitrarily connected to their meanings, and the learner had already acquired a large store of meaning–form correspondences, the new mappings would be more easily acquired. This is not a case of the learning organisms evolving. It is assumed that the learning organisms can in principle acquire both iconic and arbitrary form–meaning pairings, but that the inherent geometry of the multidimensional spaces of phonological form and semantic content ultimately makes an arbitrary vocabulary more likely to be the one readily learned by an individual, and hence passed on to successive generations. In short, this is a case of a feature of **language evolving**, rather than of its carrier organisms (proto-humans) evolving. Of course, all linguistic evolution happens within a biological envelope, and none of this could happen without the organisms having evolved the necessary memory and learning dispositions.

The challenge two paragraphs back was to compose a thoroughly sound-symbolic basic vocabulary without cheating by using compounding. The semantically meaningful subparts of words may not be separately pronounceable. Thus, the English consonant cluster /sn/ is not pronounceable on its own. However, at a level above the atomic word or morpheme, most language is in a sense sound-symbolic. As a simple example, think of two-word sequences formed by any English colour word followed by any English common noun, for example *green tea, green man, green book, red tea, red man, red book, blue tea, blue man, blue book*, and so on. Barring idiomatic cases, all sequences starting with the same colour word will have something semantic in common, and all sequences ending with the same noun will have some other semantic feature in common. What this shows is that it is almost a tautology that the basic vocabulary of a language will not be sound-symbolic, because if 'words' could be decomposed into meaningful subparts, then the 'words' would not themselves be members of the **basic** vocabulary; here 'basic' means 'not decomposable into meaningful subparts'. The 'almost' caveat here is necessary because some subparts of a word may not be separately pronounceable, due to the phonological constraints in a language. The possibility of sound-symbolism arises only where the relevant subparts of a word are not separately pronounceable. If the subparts are separately pronounceable, then the combination is a compound expression whose elementary parts are themselves arbitrarily meaningful symbols.

To summarize this section, there is ample evidence that modern human language has not entirely embraced 'the arbitrariness of the sign'. Synaesthetic sound symbolism offers a clue as to how the learning and propagation of the first learned symbols may have been facilitated by existing natural, in some sense innate, linkages between meanings and sounds. And the existence of conventional sound symbolism is also facilitatory in modern language, so there is some small but significant tendency for languages to evolve in such a way as to preserve some traces of sound-symbolism. Beside this, there is an evident tendency, given the mathematical problems of maintaining consistent iconic meaning–form relationships, for larger vocabularies to become increasingly arbitrary. Note that traces of sound symbolism discovered in the studies cited above all involved relatively high-frequency words, or binary distinctions between grammatical categories.

2.3 Or monogenesis?

There are some sound–meaning correspondences that recur frequently in language and that may not be explicable by any theory of synaesthesia or sound-symbolism. The most prominent cases are those of the 1st and 2nd person pronouns and words for MOTHER and FATHER.

Traunmüller (2000) collected data on 1st and 2nd person personal pronouns in 25 different language families (e.g. Indo-Hittite, Uralic-Yukagir, Algonkian, Niger-Congo). Within each family these personal pronouns are very uniform in phonetic shape. One complex hypothesis investigated was that 1st person pronouns tend to contain (usually as initial consonant) a voiced nasal stop (e.g. [m, n]), while 2nd person pronouns tend significantly to contain an oral stop, usually voiceless (e.g. [p, t, k]). Traunmüller found 16 language families in support of this hypothesis and only 3 against it. He calculated the binomial probability of this result as 0.0022, and concludes 'we can be confident that the consonants used in the first and second pronouns tend to be chosen on the basis of sound symbolism in agreement with [this] hypothesis' (p. 228). (The consonant sounds that Traunmüller found to be frequent in 1st person pronouns are those associated with the rounded shape by synaesthesia, and those that he found to be frequent in 2nd person pronouns are those associated by synaesthesia with the angular shape. I am rounded, you are jagged, this seems to tell us!)

Nichols (1992) also notes a correlation between consonants and personal pronouns.

Specifically, personal pronoun systems the world over are symbolically identified by a high frequency of nasals in their roots, a strong tendency for nasality and labiality to cooccur in the same person form, and a tendency to counterpose this form to one containing a dental. In the Old World, the labial and nasal elements favor the first person; in the New World, they favor the second person. The Pacific is intermediate, with a distribution of dentals like that of the Old World and nasals as in the New World.   (Nichols 1992, pp. 261–2)

Ruhlen (2005, pp. 348–58) discusses these pronoun correspondences in a way clearly illustrating the starkness of the controversy over how to explain them and other correspondences. The existence of some pronoun correspondences is a noteworthy statistical fact. Ruhlen's version, like Nichols' and unlike Traunmüller's, distinguishes between Old World and New World patterns. He discusses 'the prevalence of N/M "I/thou" pronominal pattern in the Americas, and a different pronominal pattern, M/T "I/thou" in northern Eurasia' (p. 348). This description is not exactly consistent in detail with Nichols' brief characterization, but I take it that some broad generalization about pronoun forms can be worked out. The world geographical distribution of both N/M and M/T patterns over samples of 230 languages can now be seen in two chapters of the World Atlas of Language Structures online (Nichols and Peterson 2008a, 2008b). As Ruhlen notes, the widespread correspondences had been seen and discussed by several eminent linguists in the early twentieth century, including Trombetti (1905) and Meillet (1921).

Edward Sapir a decade later [than Trombetti] noted the presence of both first-person N and second-person M throughout the Americas and wrote, in a personal letter, 'How in the Hell are you going to explain the general American *n-* "I" except genetically?' (quoted in Greenberg 1987). Franz Boas was also aware of the widespread American pattern, but opposed the genetic explanation given by Trombetti and Sapir: 'the frequent occurrence of similar sounds for expressing related ideas (like the personal pronouns) may be due to obscure psychological causes, rather than to genetic relationship' (quoted in Haas 1966).   (Ruhlen 2005, p. 351)

There you have the clear alternative explanations, deep historical common origins ('genetic') versus 'obscure psychological causes' such as, presumably, synaesthesia as discussed above. In the pronoun case, since the Old World and New World patterns are different, the historical account stops short of monogenesis, that is the idea that there was a single common ancestor for all the world's forms. The difference between Old World and New World correspondences also probably rules out an explanation in terms of synaesthesia, as the biology of synaesthesia seems unlikely to differ across these populations. To Ruhlen, the explanation is clearly historical: 'a single population entered the Americas with the N/M pronoun pattern, spread rapidly throughout North and South America around 11,000[21] years ago' (Ruhlen 2005, p. 358). For the other side of the Bering Straits, Bancel and Matthey de l'Etang (2008) also favour a historical explanation, arguing for 'the millennial persistence of Indo-European and Eurasiatic pronouns'. These authors side with Ruhlen in the starkly drawn controversy over historical 'super-families' of languages (such as Eurasiatic and Amerind) and ultimately over monogenesis for at least some vocabulary items—the 'Proto-World' hypothesis (Ruhlen 1994).

Approaching the topic with a very different scientific methodology, Mark Pagel (2000b) has capitalized on the long-standing assumption that some words change faster than others and some are resistant to change. Using quite complex mathematical models, he postulates 'half-lives' for particular words. 'A word with a half-life of 21,000 years has a 22 per cent chance of not changing in 50,000 years' (p. 205). This follows from Pagel's definition, and is not a claim that any particular word does have such a long half-life. Pronouns, along with low-valued numerals, basic kinship terms and names for body parts, are linguistically conservative, tending to resist phonetic change more than other forms.[22] Pagel estimates the half-lives of seven slowly evolving Indo-European words (for I, WE, WHO, TWO, THREE, FOUR, FIVE) at 166,000 years, but warns that 'these figures...should not be taken too literally, and most certainly do not imply time-depths of 166,000 years or even 15,000 years for the Indo-European data' (p. 205). These last numbers differ so wildly that it is hard to know what to believe. What is reinforced, as Pagel says, is that some words, including pronouns, are especially resistant to change. This gives some more plausibility to the idea that, just possibly, the current patterns reveal something of the words that were first brought out of Africa. I will go no further than that.

A further well-known cross-linguistic correlation between meanings and sounds is seen in words for MOTHER and FATHER. Murdock (1959) looked at vocabularies from 565 societies, collecting 531 terms for MOTHER and 541 for FATHER. Scrupulously, '[i]n order to rule out borrowings from European languages due to recent missionary and other influences, forms resembling mama and papa were excluded unless comparative data on related languages clearly demonstrated their indigenous origin. This perhaps biases the test

---

[21] In general, Ruhlen's estimated dates are more recent than those of most other writers on language evolution. As a strategy, he needs to keep his estimated time-depths as low as possible in order to minimize the possible effects of language change.

[22] Of course, as this is a statistical generalization, counterexamples may exist in some languages.

slightly against confirmation of the hypothesis' (p. 1). Murdock compressed
the phonetic data from these vocabularies into large classes. 'Significantly, the
terms falling into the Ma and Na classes are preponderantly those for mother,
while those in the Pa and Ta classes overwhelmingly designate the father.
Among the sound classes of intermediate frequency, the Me, Mo, Ne, and No
terms denote mother, and the Po and To terms denote father, by a ratio greater
than two to one' (p. 2). Note that the typical consonants in MOTHER words
here are also those typical of 1st person pronouns, and the typical consonants
from FATHER words here are those typical of 2nd person pronouns, according
to Traunmüller's findings, cited above.

Jakobson (1960) proposed an explanation for the *mama*/MOTHER correlation, namely that a slight nasal murmur while suckling becomes associated
with the breast and the its owner. This may work for *mama* but not for
papa/FATHER. Jakobson also noted that *ma* syllable is the first, or one of the
first, made by a baby. The reduplication to *mama* is typical of early child speech
and in speech to children.[23] A child's mother is the first significant person
she interacts with, which may be enough to strengthen the *mama*/MOTHER
connection across generations. Even if the baby's first *mama* is in no way
intended by the baby as referring to anyone, it may be natural for a mother to
assume that this first word-like utterance is indeed referential ('there's my clever
baby!'), and this form–meaning pairing gets subsequentially reinforced by the
mother using it. Such accounts still leave many gaps to be filled, regarding
the detailed mechanisms. They are not in themselves inconsistent with an
explanation from monogenesis.

Pierre Bancel and Alain Matthey de l'Etang have collected an even greater
body of data conforming to the correlation between nasals and MOTHER and
oral stops and FATHER. The 29 July 2004 issue of *New Scientist* first reported
some of their factual findings: 'the word "papa" is present in almost 700 of the
1000 languages for which they have complete data on words for close family
members. ... Those languages come from all the 14 or so major language
families. And the meaning of "papa" is remarkably consistent: in 71 per cent
of cases it means father or a male relative on the father's side'. These authors
mostly publish in the *Mother Tongue* journal, not widely accessible.[24] They are
advocates of the possibility of global etymologies, following Merritt Ruhlen,

---

[23] Describing his own son's development, Darwin (1877, p. 293) wrote 'At exactly
the age of a year, he made the great step of inventing a word for food, namely, *mum*,
but what led him to it I did not discover'.

[24] See Matthey de l'Etang and Bancel (2002, 2005, 2008); Bancel and Matthey de
l'Etang (2002, 2005). Four of these papers can be found on the Nostratica website
(Global Comparisons section) at http://www.nostratic.ru/index.php?page=books .

and hence of monogenesis for at least some lexical forms. They do not deny, however, the relevance of factors tending to keep the phonetic forms of some words relatively constant. Indeed the existence of such factors is essential to their hypothesis.

Most words do not survive in a recognizable ancestral form in a significant number of languages. Language change stirs the pot, moving the paddle in many directions. If you stir a pot for tens of thousands of years, you break up any original patterning in the original contents of the pot, **unless** there are other factors tending to keep things together. Universal slight synaesthesia or the link suggested by Jakobson may be enough to prevent the forms for MOTHER and FATHER from changing much over the millennia. (The Jakobsonian explanation works for *mama* but not for *papa*.)

In the most naive approach to language evolution, there is a tendency to ignore the crucial distinction between biological and cultural evolution, leading to unanswerable questions such as 'Which was the first language?' The *mama*/MOTHER and *papa*/FATHER correlations **are** relevant to questions of language evolution, because they may give us a clue about how the very first hominins to use learned symbols could have bootstrapped their way to sound–meaning correlations that lacked the apparent naturalness of sound-symbolic correspondences.

2.4 Social convergence on conventionalized common symbols

At the start of this section, I take a leap over a major gap in our knowledge. I assume that, somehow, we have an evolved species capable of sporadic invention (by individuals) of sounds or gestures with non-deictic referential content, and capable of learning these form-to-meaning pairings on observing them in use by others. Exactly how the first steps in this process were taken is still a mystery. Perhaps there was bootstrapping from synaesthetic sound sym-bolism, as suggested above. The later stages of the process, by which a whole social group comes to share the same learned forms-to-meanings pairings, are actually quite well understood. This is largely due to a wave of computer simulations, and experiments with human subjects. The question that such studies ask is typically: 'How can a socially coordinated code, accepted and used by a whole community, evolve in a population starting from scratch, with no such common code at all?'

The challenge is very ancient, and has appealed to scientifically minded monarchs for millennia. Herodotus reported that, in the seventh century BC, in a quest to determine what 'the first language' was, King Psammetichus of Egypt locked up two children and deprived them of all linguistic input, to see what language they would speak. After two years, they apparently involuntarily uttered *bekos*, the Phrygian word for BREAD, and Psammetichus granted that, although Egyptian power was dominant, the Phrygians had the most ancient language. The argument behind this experiment is flawed of course, revealing even stronger nativist assumptions about language than we find among nativist linguists today; but the decision to use two children, rather than just one, was a nod in the direction of a social factor in language genesis. King James IV of Scotland conducted a similar experiment on Inchkeith, an island a few miles from where I write, and the experimental child victims this time apparently spoke 'guid Hebrew'. The modern scientific question is not 'what was the first language?' but 'what are the processes by which a communication system can arise from scratch, on the basis of no prior linguistic input to the people concerned, and what does such a pristine communication system look like?'

In answering such questions, modern studies typically help themselves to several more or less generous assumptions about the initial conditions, summarized below:

- A population of individuals capable of internal mental representations of the meanings to be expressed, i.e. prelinguistic concepts, from some given set; these are typically assumed to be concepts of concrete kinds and properties in the world, such as FOOD, TASTY, TRIANGLE, or RED.

- An assumed willingness to express these concepts, using signals from a predetermined repertoire, to other members of the population; initially, of course, these signals are not assigned to any particular meanings.

- An ability to infer at least parts of meanings expressed by others from an assumed context of use.

- An ability to learn meaning-to-form mappings on the basis of observation of their use by others.

Given the assumptions listed above, it turns out to be a straightforward matter to get a population of simulated individuals ('agents', as they are called) to coordinate their signals with each other, ending up with a situation in which all agents use the same signal to express a given meaning, and conversely interpret this signal as expressing that meaning. In a simulation, agents are prompted to express random concepts from the available set. In the beginning, they have learned no connection between any concept and any particular signal, and in this situation of ignorance, they simply utter a signal chosen at random from their repertoire. Thus, at the beginning of a simulation, the agents' collective behaviour is not coordinated. But agents learn from observing the signals which other agents use to express particular meanings. After learning, they themselves express a particular meaning by a signal that they have observed used by another to express that meaning. The whole population gradually starts to use a single standardized set of signal-to-concept mappings. With larger simulated populations, of course, the standardization process is slower, but populations always converge on a shared two-way (*signal* ⇔ CONCEPT) lexicon. And the convergence on a shared lexicon is also slower with larger given sets of possible meanings and possible signals, as is to be expected. Examples of work in this vein are Hurford (1989); Oliphant (1999); Steels (1999); Smith (2004), approximately implementing the suggestions of an early philosophical study on the origins of convention by Lewis (1969).

This is a process of **self-organization**.[25] No single individual in the population envisages or organizes the end result. By the repeated interaction of many individuals, a social pattern emerges which is adhered to by everyone. This is the 'Invisible Hand' of Adam Smith, the eighteenth-century theorist of capitalism (Smith 1786), the 'spontaneous order' of Friedrich Hayek, his twentieth-century successor (Hayek 1944, 1988) and a 'phenomenon of the third kind' as Keller (1994) puts it. Phenomena of the first kind are natural phenomena, like stars, trees, and weather; phenomena of the second kind are human artifacts, like pots, pans, houses, and telescopes; a phenomenon of the third kind is neither natural nor artificial, but the 'unintended consequence of individual actions which are not directed towards the generation of this structure' (Keller 1989, p. 118). The shared lexicon of a social group is a phenomenon of the third kind, like the paths beaten across fields by many separate people just deciding to take the shortest route from corner to corner. Many other features of languages are phenomena of the third kind, but we will not pursue this thought further here.

Computer simulations of such processes of lexicon-building are of course very simple, and might be criticized for failing to correspond to real situations in which proto-humans might have developed a shared inventory of learned symbols. The first possible objection is that agents are assumed to be predisposed to play this kind of cooperative signalling game with each other. Any explanation of the emergence of human language must make this assumption, as language is a cooperative business. The survey of evolutionary theories of honest signalling in *The Origins of Meaning* (ch. 8) admitted that this is an

---

[25] Self-organization is compatible with, and complementary to, natural selection. Self-organization narrows the search space within which natural selection operates. See Oudeyer (2006) for a good discussion of the relation between self-organization and natural selection.

issue to be resolved. The models reviewed there gave enough indications that an evolutionary route can be envisaged for the remarkable step taken by humans to their cooperative use of shared signal-to-meaning codes.

Another criticism of such simulations is that they typically treat meanings as purely internal to the simulated agents, with no grounding in objects or events in any kind of real world. For instance, an agent might be prompted (at random by the process running the simulation) to express the meaning SQUARE; this meaning item is simply selected at random from a list within the computer, and assumed to be 'known' to the simulated agents. If the agent has already observed this meaning being expressed by another agent, say as the syllable sequence *wabaku*, the agent will present its simulated interlocutor with the meaning–form pair (SQUARE ⇔ *wabaku*). This interlocutor will in turn learn that specific meaning–form pairing from this simulated experience. The lack of grounding in anything resembling real experience of the world is a convenient short cut, and in fact there is no fudge in taking this short cut. It is simply assumed that agents, like real animals, have similar internal representations of the things in the real world that they talk about. But in case anyone is not satisfied with this assurance, some researchers have taken the trouble to ground their simulations in real objects. The best example is by Luc Steels (1999).[26]

In Steels' 'Talking Heads' experiment, a number of pairs of robotic cameras were set up, in several labs around the world. These cameras faced a whiteboard on which were a variety of coloured shapes, such as a red square, a green triangle, a yellow star, or a blue triangle. The cameras were able to focus on specific shapes, and they 'knew where they were looking'. They had visual recognition software enabling them to classify perceived shapes and colours, and so arrive at internal categorial representations of the things they were looking at. From then on this simulation proceeded pretty much as the others described above. If the software agent in the camera at the time already had a 'word' for the thing it was looking at, it transmitted this word (electronically) to another agent in a camera beside it. If this second agent had already associated a particular category (e.g. a shape, or a colour, or a shape–colour pair) with this 'word', it pointed to what it thought the 'referent' was, using a laser pointer aimed at the whiteboard. The first camera would then either confirm or disconfirm that the object pointed to was the object it had 'intended'. There was thus a feedback mechanism helping the population of agents to converge on a shared vocabulary for the objects, and their features, on the whiteboard. The use of the laser pointer and feedback corresponds

[26] See http://talking-heads.csl.sony.fr/ for an online description of this experiment.

to the joint attention of two creatures (here robots) to a third object in the outside world. If the agents had had no prior experience (as at the outset of the experiment) of the names of the objects on the whiteboard, they either made them up at random, or were given them by outside intervention (see below). It worked. The experiment ended up with a single standardized vocabulary for the items in its little whiteboard world. The important innovation in this experiment was to get the meanings from the outside world, rather than simply providing a list of items internal to the computer purporting to be the concepts available to the agents. This experiment had several other features designed to capture the popular imagination, such as the possibility for members of the public to 'launch a software agent' of their own to temporarily inhabit one of the cameras, and to give it arbitrary words for the things it was looking at. But most of the time, the software agents in the cameras were busy chatting to each other in the simulated naming game.

The inclusion in Steels' Talking Heads experiment of a feedback feature, by which agents were told whether they had guessed a meaning correctly, is unrealistic. Human children manage to infer the meanings of the words they hear mostly without any such explicit pedagogic help. Many of the other simulations in this field also manage successfully to get populations of agents to converge on a common vocabulary without any such feedback mechanism.

A further criticism of some such models of vocabulary evolution is that the simultaneous presentation, by the 'speaking' agent to the learner, of a **pair** consisting of a meaning and a form (e.g. (SQUARE ⇔ *wabaku*)) would imply that the use of the form itself is redundant. If a meaning can simply be 'given' to an interlocutor, as if by telepathy, there is no need for any lexical code translating that meaning into publicly observable syllables. Why talk, with arbitrary symbols, if you can telepathize thoughts directly? Steels' Talking Heads model avoids this problem by not presenting the hearer/learner with the meaning, but by coordinating the 'attention' of the robots with the laser pointer. The laser pointer does not point unambiguously. For example, if, on hearing the signal *wabaku*, the second agent guesses that it means RED, it may point at a red square in the top left of the whiteboard. Now if the first agent had intended to convey SQUARE, this would, wrongly, be interpreted as a successful communication. By successive exposures to different examples, the robotic agents can narrow down the intended meanings. For example, on receiving *wabaku* on a later occasion, if the second agent still 'erroneously' interprets it as RED, it might this time point to a red circle, and be given feedback indicating failure.

This is a version of Cross-Situational Learning (Siskind 1996; Hurford 1999; Akhtar and Montague 1999; Smith 2005a; Vogt and Smith 2005). In Cross-Situational Learning, the vocabulary learner is not given the entire meaning for a word, but is, realistically, aware of features of the context in which it is spoken. It is assumed that the intended meaning is some part of this context. From exposure to many different contexts in which the word is appropriately used, the learner distils out the common core of meaning which the word must have, or at least does this far enough to be able to communicate successfully using the word. This emphasizes the role of inference in vocabulary learning, rather than relying on a naive behaviouristic mechanism of simultaneous pre-sentation of the word and 'its meaning'. I put this last phrase in quotation marks because of Quine's (1960, pp. 51–3) famous *Gavagai* problem—in the limit, we can never know whether two people have exactly the same meaning for a word. Smith (2005b) has developed an inferential model of word-learning and communication which 'allows the development of communication between individuals who do not necessarily share exactly the same internal representa-tions of meaning' (p. 373).

Another criticism (e.g. by Quinn 2001) of such simulations of the emergence of shared lexicons is that they presume a pre-existing set of signals. At the beginning of a simulation none of these signals means anything; but it is nevertheless assumed that they are destined to mean something. Before there is any conventional pairing of some vocalization or gesture with a conventional meaning, how can an animal know to look for a meaning in it? Why does the observer not assume that the observed gesture or vocalization is just some random inexplicable movement or noise?[27] I believe that is where Tomasello et al.'s (2005) appeal to shared intentionality is particularly useful. If an animal really wants to tell another something, and makes insistent gestures of some kind (perhaps somewhat iconic) above and beyond the range of normal non-communicative behaviour, the recipient of this attention, given a disposition to shared intentionality, can reason 'She's trying to tell me something'. It is important here that the signal-to-be not be too closely iconic, otherwise it could be interpreted as simply non-communicative. For example, to try to convey the idea of running away by actually running away would defeat the purpose. Or to try to convey the idea of eating something by actually eating something in a completely normal way would run the serious risk of not being interpreted as an attempt at communication. This is an advantage of the vocal channel. We use our hands and limbs for a variety of practical purposes. Is that man just scratching himself or trying to tell me something? Almost the only function, nowadays, of noises made by the vocal tract is communication. Snoring, coughs, and belches are the exceptions, and it is significant that snores,

---

[27] Bickerton (1981, p. 264) identifies this key problem.

coughs, and belches are **not** incorporated into the phonological system of any language. Speaking carries the message 'this is communicative'.

Thom Scott-Phillips has coined a neat phrase, 'signalling signalhood', to express the step that must have been taken to distinguish communicative signals from ordinary actions. He has discussed the significance of this step and its relationship to evolutionary theory and linguistic pragmatics in several publications. (See Scott-Phillips et al. 2009; Scott-Phillips 2010.)

Greg Urban speculates on the rise of signals specifically marked as communicative.

As an example of metasignaling, consider the stylized or ritualized forms of lamentation found in many cultures around the world. Such laments involve the use of the vocal apparatus to produce sounds that remind the listener of crying. And these laments are deployed as part of strategic communicative interactions and are presumably neocortically induced, rather than innately controlled. (Urban 2002, p. 233)

To create a new signal, . . . like stylized crying, one differentiates the new signal shape from the old one. If the new signal is to be readily interpreted by others, it must have two important formal properties. First, the new signal must look (or sound or taste, etc.) sufficiently like the old one that the meaning of the old one can serve as a basis for guessing the meaning of the new one. However, second, the new signal must be obviously and unmistakably distinct from the old one, so that it is recognized as new and, hence, as requiring reasoning to figure out its meaning. (Urban 2002, p. 241)

Laakso (1993) makes a similar point to Urban and discusses the step from Gricean 'Natural Meaning' to 'Non-Natural Meaning'.

These remarks explain the adaptiveness of a move from closely iconic signals to less iconic, highly stylized signals. There are some very interesting modern experiments showing the rapid shift to highly stylized conventional signals in humans who are required, in a lab, to invent their own signalling systems from scratch. I will mention two such experiments (Fay et al. 2010; Galantucci 2005). Both studies used a graphical medium, rather than speech.

Galantucci (2005) conducted three games, of increasing complexity, in which two players, isolated from each other in different places, each had access to a map on a computer screen of a four-room (or nine- or sixteen-room) square space. These virtual rooms were uniquely identified by distinctive shape-labels. This might be taken as indicating that the experiment actually provided something like a proper name for each room—quite inappropriately for a study relating to the evolution of language. But the identification of the rooms could be interpreted more realistically as just providing unique properties, visible to their occupants, such 'The room with a star in it' or 'The room with a hexagon in it'. The map on the screen had nothing to do with the actual layout of the lab, but each player was fictitiously 'located' in an on-screen room. On the screen, a player could only see her own room. For example, one player knew that she was in the 'hexagon' room, but had no idea where the other player was. In the simplest, four-room game, the players' goal was simply to make at most one move each so that both ended up in the same room. Without any communication between the players, they had no more than chance probability of success. They were allowed to communicate by means of an ingenious graphic device, a moving pad that preserved horizontal motion across it but nullified vertical motion up and down it; a vertical line could be produced by holding the pen still and letting the pad move beneath it. In this way, the players were prevented from writing messages to each other or drawing diagrams. Only a limited range of relatively simple lines, dots, and squiggles was in practice available. The players had established no prior communication protocols. Nevertheless, most pairs of players managed to solve the problem of this simple game, mutually developing 'agreed' signals, either indicating their own location, or giving an instruction to the other player to move. They did this on the basis of trial and error, being penalized for failure to meet and rewarded for success. The fastest pair (of ten pairs) solved the problem in under 20 minutes, and the slowest pair took almost three hours. Interestingly, one pair of players simply never got the hang of the task, and had to be eliminated from the study—is this a parallel with natural selection eliminating animals who can't figure out how to communicate?

The successful pairs from Galantucci's first game were taken on to more complex games, with more virtual rooms, and more difficult tasks. The second task was to cooperate in 'catching' a prey in a room of a virtual nine-room space. This necessitated both players being in the same virtual room as the prey at the same time. On success, the players were rewarded, but the prey disappeared and relocated, and the players had to start over again, figuring out where it was and how to coordinate catching it again. Game 3 was even more complex, in a sixteen-room space, with an even more difficult coordination task. Some pairs of players quit in frustration, but most solved the problems by developing ad hoc communication protocols for coordinating their movements. And all this happened with the experimental subjects only able to communicate via the very restrictive channel of the moving pad device, and with no previously established conventions for communication. But of course, the subjects were modern humans, and already knew about the principle of communication.

Galantucci observed a kind of historical inertia, in that players who had established mutual conventions in earlier games were often constrained, even hampered, by these conventions in later games. That is, once a system adequate for a simple game had been converged on, the pair that used it always tried to build on it in subsequent, more complex games, even though a fresh start might have been a better way of proceeding.

For example, in Games 2 and 3 many pairs did not use the signs for locations as a way to avoid bumping into each other. This happened because the signs for location had acquired, in the course of Game 2, a duplex semantic role, meaning not only locations on the map but also, roughly, 'Hey, come here, I found the prey'. Once this duplex role for a sign was established, the location sign could not be used without causing costly false alarms.   (Galantucci 2005, p. 760)

The actual communication protocols developed were of various types, but almost all were iconic in some way, either relating to the shape symbol naming a room, or to its location in the overall virtual space. Galantucci observed two generalizations about the emerging signals:

a. The forms that best facilitate convergence on a sign are easy to distinguish percep- tually and yet are produced by simple motor sequences.
b. The forms that best facilitate convergence on a sign are tolerant of individual variations.   (Galantucci 2005, p. 760)

Galantucci accounts for the convergence of his subjects on successful commu- nication systems in terms of **shared cognition**, accomplished during the course of an experiment through a continuous feedback between individuals **learning by observing** and **learning by using**.

Galantucci has also experimented with variation on the nature of the signals used by his subjects. The moving pad device can be fixed so that the trace left by the pen either fades rapidly or fades slowly. When the signal fades rapidly (as is the case with human speech), he found a significant tendency for combinatorial systems to develop, in which different features of the signals given by subjects corresponded to different aspects of the intended meaning (such as vertical versus horizontal location) (Galantucci 2006). This was in contrast to the non-combinatorial (i.e. holophrastic) complexity of the evolved signals, which tended to correlate with slow fading of signals. For further details of this work, see Galantucci (2009).

A second experiment, by Fay et al. (2010) makes a similar point, but here the task and the graphical medium were quite different. The experimenters got undergraduate student subjects to play a game like 'Pictionary'. This game is a graphical version of Charades. Instead of miming some idea, players have to draw it; they are not allowed to speak to each other or to use any miming gestures. In the experiment, subjects played this game in pairs, and there was a pre-specified set of 16 possible target meanings. These were designed to contain concepts that are graphically confusable (THEATRE, ART GALLERY,

MUSEUM, PARLIAMENT, BRAD PITT, ARNOLD SCHWARZENEGGER, RUSSELL CROWE, DRAMA, SOAP OPERA, CARTOON, TELEVISION, COMPUTER MONITOR, MICROWAVE, LOUD, HOMESICK, POVERTY). Players interacted remotely by computer, completely non-verbally, by drawing with a mouse on a computer screen. One player was nominated the 'director', charged with conveying a given concept to the other player, the 'matcher'. They were allowed to see and modify each other's drawings, until the matcher thought he had identified the concept the director was trying to convey. Although the game was played in pairs, the subjects played with successive partners. 'In the community condition participants were organized into one of four 8-person communities created via the one-to-one interactions of pairs drawn from the same pool. Participants played six consecutive games with their partner, before switching partners and playing a further six games with their new partner. Partner switching continued in this manner until each participant had interacted with each of the other seven community members'. In this way, for a total group of eight players, a 'community-wide' set of standard conventions for expressing the required meanings started to evolve within the group. Early in the experiment players drew elaborate, quite iconic drawings to convey the ideas. By the end of the experiment the 'communities' had settled on much simpler, usually arbitrary symbols to convey the meanings. Tests indicated the emergence of a conventional referring scheme at Round 4. Tests show a large jump in drawing convergence from Rounds 1 to 4 and a smaller, marginally significant, increase in graphical convergence from Rounds 4 to 7. Naturally, the accuracy with which players identified the drawings also increased very quickly to near-perfect. Figure 2.2 shows two attempts from the first round, and two instances of the emergent symbol from the seventh round. This is typical of the results of the experiment.

Although the diagram was 'agreed', remember that there was no verbal or gestural negotiation of any sort during the games. On the other hand, in some examples, including possibly this one, the players resorted to prior

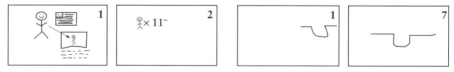

Fig. 2.2 Evolving a symbolic convention to represent the concept BRAD PITT over 6 games.

Note: The two left-hand pictures are by subjects 1 and 2 in the first round of the game. The two right hand drawings are by subjects 1 and 7 at the end of the game, after 6 rounds of pairwise non-verbal negotiations between partners. A simple arbitrary symbol, used by the whole group, has emerged.

Source: From Fay et al. (2010).

knowledge of language, as the emerging symbol for BRAD PITT could be a simple diagram of a pit. Such punning solutions were not common in the results of the experiment, however.

These two experiments, while very suggestive, have their limitations, as far as relevance to language evolution is concerned. Both involve fully modern humans, who are given explicit instructions about the nature of the game to be played, and the small set of conveyable meanings is clearly established for all players in advance. Nevertheless, they do shed some light on the kinds of stylization and conventionalization processes that could have led our ancestors from relatively iconic expressions to 'agreed' easy-to-produce, easy-to-recognize arbitrary expressions.

One further 'natural experiment' should be mentioned. This is the case of Nicaraguan Sign Language (Idioma de Señas de Nicaragua), a sign language that evolved spontaneously among a population of deaf children at a deaf school in Nicaragua. The birth of this new language has been extensively documented. (See Senghas 1995a, 1995b, 2001, 2003; Kegl and Iwata 1989; Kegl et al. 1999; Kegl 2002 for a representative sample of this work.) What is most striking about this language is the fact that deaf children, within the space of about a decade, created a full-blown sign language with its own syntax. What concerns us here, which is implicit in the first fact but less remarkable, is that the children also spontaneously developed their own common vocabulary of lexical signs. A similar case of the spontaneous creation, within three generations, of a new sign language, complete with a vocabulary and complex syntax standardized across the social group, is Al-Sayyid Bedouin Sign Language, described by Sandler et al. (2005). Clearly for modern humans, given the right social conditions, and a population of young people, the spontaneous emergence of a shared lexicon from scratch is possible and, we may even say, straightforward. At some era in the past, our ancestors had evolved to a stage where such vocabulary-creation became possible. No doubt at first the capacities of the creatures were more limited than ours. Given the utility of vocabulary, it is reasonable to suppose that an increasing capacity for vocabulary acquisition co-evolved with the cultural creation by social groups of ever larger communal vocabularies. (These new sign languages are discussed further in Chapter 5.)

At this point, we need to take stock of the extent to which the simulation and experimental studies described here capture the essence of modern human vocabulary acquisition. It is easy, and misleading, to think of a vocabulary as simply a list of unrelated (CONCEPT ⇔ *signal*) entries. The simulation and experimental studies have demonstrated that getting a community to converge on such a list is relatively straightforward. But such studies are missing two factors which make it easier for individuals to acquire, and for a population to converge on, a vocabulary. One factor is the significance of the concepts in the daily lives of the animals concerned; there is more motivation to learn a symbol for TASTY FOOD than for RED TRIANGLE. Following the argument of *The Origins of Meaning*, it is probably the case that the first symbols were not even referential, involving an entity other than the signaller and the receiver of the signal. In ape life in the wild, such signals are largely innately determined, but there is a degree of learning of socially significant signals. The first small core of an evolving learned vocabulary could well have consisted mostly of non-referential symbols, with conventional illocutionary force. It is also likely that the first referential acts were closely associated with specific behaviours connected with the entity referred to. For example, a signal whose referent might be glossed simply as ENEMY could also be most frequently associated with a ritual gathering of the males to fight some neighbour. Thus the purely referential gloss misses some of the interpersonal significance of the symbol. Modern human life is so varied and humans so versatile that very few referential words are now so closely associated with a particular social routine. An example might be the word *dinner-time*. Although it can be used dispassionately to describe a time of the day, as in *Dinner-time is at 7.00*, the utterance of this word on its own, with no previous context, usually signals the beginning of a particular social ritual.

The other factor typically missing from the simulations and experiments cited above is the relatedness of lexical entries to each other, via the relatedness of their conceptual significata. In most of the studies, for example, the meanings were either simply specified in the computers, or by the experimenters, by lists of unrelated items.

The nature of the capacities provided by learning arbitrary associations has important implications for debates on symbol acquisition in animals, since symbols, by definition, are arbitrarily connected with the referent they represent. Although it is clear that apes can acquire and use symbols effectively, it remains unclear whether those symbols have the same connotations that they have for humans. Unlike apes, human beings have an uncanny ability for quickly making sense of and learning arbitrary connections.

(Call 2006, pp. 230–1)

In the early days of language experiments with chimpanzees, the discipline of controlled experimentation dictated that the task of learning arbitrary form–meaning pairings be as isolated as possible from potentially confounding factors. Thus the training that some animals received focused solely on this learning task; the only nod to the animals' normal lives was the use of normal rewards, such as food. Deacon (1997, pp. 69–100) surveys experiments carried out by Savage-Rumbaugh et al. (1978, 1980) and Savage-Rumbaugh (1986) in which three chimpanzees, Lana, Sherman, and Austin, were trained on various sorting and labelling tasks. What emerges from these studies, insightfully analysed by Deacon, is that an animal strictly trained to associate certain objects with certain labels, and whose training involves only exposure to those stimulus–response pairs, ends up with only a knowledge of these specific pairings, and with no ability to extrapolate in any way from them. Sherman and Austin were first trained to request food or drink using two-term combinations of lexigrams such as *give banana*. This training was strictly limited to pairing the 'correct' sequences with the appropriate rewards. There were two 'verb' terms, *pour* and *give* for liquid or solid food, two solid food 'nouns' and two liquid food 'nouns'. Though Sherman and Austin learned these associations, they learned nothing more. Specifically, when given the whole vocabulary to choose from, they came up with random incorrect sequences such as *banana juice give*. They had not learned the exclusion relationships between terms, for example that *banana* is incompatible with *juice*. This is not to say, of course, that they could not tell juice from a banana; of course they could. They had not transferred this conceptual relationship to the labels they were learning. Next, Sherman and Austin were very laboriously trained on what specific sequences of terms would **not** be rewarded, using the same strictly controlled techniques. Of course, now they got it—but it was hard work for all concerned. And, having explicitly been given information about the whole set of positive and negative response-eliciting sequences of terms, Sherman and Austin were now able to make certain extrapolations they had not been capable of before. They were given new food items, paired with new lexigrams, and they rapidly incorporated these new terms into their system, without making the kinds of random errors they had made before the phase of negative training. In Deacon's words,

[w]hat the animals had learned was not only a set of specific associations between lexigrams and objects or events. They had also learned a set of logical relationships *between the lexigrams*, relationships of exclusion and inclusion. More importantly, these lexigram–lexigram relationships formed a complete system in which each allowable or forbidden co-occurrence of lexigrams in the same string (and therefore each allowable or forbidden substitution of one lexigram for another) was defined. They had discovered that the relationship that a lexigram has to an object *is a function of* the relationship it has to other lexigrams, not just a function of the correlated appearance of both lexigram and object. (Deacon 1997, p. 86)

This conclusion is reinforced by a comparison of Sherman and Austin, who had been given this extensive and complex training, with Lana, another chimp, who had earlier been trained on a large set of object–lexigram correspondences, but had received no further training designed to produce lexigram–lexigram relationships. All three chimps learned to sort food from tools. Then they were taught general terms (lexigrams) for the two classes, tools and food. All managed this. Next they were shown new food or tool items and asked to label them with the new terms. Sherman and Austin readily made the generalization, but Lana did not.

Although it typically took hundreds, even thousands of trials for the chimps to acquire a new rote association, once a systemic relationship was established, new items could be added essentially without any trial and error. This difference translated into more than a hundredfold increase in learning efficiency and supplies a key to understanding the apparent leap in human intelligence as compared to other species. Increased intelligence does not produce symbols; instead, symbols increase effective intelligence.

(Deacon 1996, p. 130)

These experiments do not primarily tell us about any significant difference between humans and chimpanzees. Rather, they tell us that there is more to vocabulary learning than just acquiring an unrelated list of meaning–form pairs. This 'list' approach often seems to be assumed in computer simulations of the emergence of a shared vocabulary in a population, in experiments with humans required to 'invent' some common set of signs, and in the early strictly controlled experiments with training apes with lexigrams. The controlled training given to chimpanzees such as Lana artificially divorced form–meaning correspondences from the rest of her life. The training that Sherman and Austin received was equally artificial. The strict discipline of psychological experimentation requires that all possible confounding factors be excluded from the experimental situation, or at least controlled for. Simply training an animal to respond to a certain stimulus by touching a certain lexigram manages to exclude the essential feature of communicative signals, namely that they **are communicative** and can be relevant to normal lives outside the experimental situation. This point is strongly argued by Savage-Rumbaugh and Brakke (1996). Kanzi, who learned his form–meaning correspondences in a much more naturalistic situation, never showed any sign of not knowing that the lexigram for a banana is incompatible with a lexigram for juice. When he wanted a banana he asked for one clearly, and when he wanted juice, he asked for juice.[28] In similar vein, Pepperberg (2000, ch. 14), based on her experiments with grey parrots, stresses 'The Need for Reference, Functionality, and Social Interaction If Exceptional Learning Is to Occur' (p. 268), where

---

[28] Surely, we are justified in claiming we know what he wanted when he signalled these things.

'exceptional learning' means learning human-like tasks that are not normal for parrots in their natural ecological niche.

The experiments with Sherman and Austin involved concatenating pairs of lexigrams, thus introducing an elementary form of syntax. Syntactic collocation in real language gives many clues to the meanings of words. This would not be possible without reliance on knowledge of a coherent network of relationships between words and other words, between words and things, and between things and things. Quoting Deacon again, 'symbols cannot be understood as an unstructured collection of tokens that map to a collection of referents because symbols don't just represent things in the world, they also represent each other' (Deacon 1997, p. 99).[29]

A basic semantic distinction is taught to all beginning linguistics students, between an expression's **reference** and its **sense**. The ideas date from Frege (1892). The idea of the reference of a term is easily grasped; it is the thing, or set of things, out there in the world, that the expression corresponds to. The idea of the sense of an expression is less easily grasped, and linguists and philosophers treat it differently. For many linguists, for example Lyons (1977), the sense of a word is its place in a network of **sense relations**. Sense relations are relations such as antonymy (e.g. *up/down, good/bad, male/female*) and hyponymy (e.g. *tulip/flower, gun/weapon, elephant/animal*). Sense relations between linguistic expressions generally relate systematically to relations between items in the world. Thus, for instance, the hyponymy relation between *elephant* and *animal* is matched by the fact that the set of elephants is included in the set of animals. Knowledge of relations in the world fits the sense relations between linguistic expressions. An animal that has prelinguistic concepts (such as BANANA, GRAPE, and FOOD) and knows the relationships between them is well on the way to knowing the structured sense-relations between the linguistic labels for them, *banana, grape,* and *food*. Learning a vocabulary involves learning both the reference and the sense of the lexical items.

In fact, there is an attested weak bias in children's learning of vocabulary against acquiring hyponym-superordinate pairs such as *banana-food* or *pigeon-bird*. Markman's (1992) Mutual Exclusivity bias expresses this fact. A child in the early stages of vocabulary-learning will have some difficulty assigning the labels *bird* and *pigeon* to the same object. I have even heard a child say 'That's not a bird, it's a pigeon'. Macnamara (1982) tells of a child

---

[29] I have complained elsewhere (Hurford 1998) about Deacon's unorthodox (to linguists and philosophers) use of terms such as *symbolic* and *represent*; it is worth going along with his usage, in spite of qualms from one's own discipline, to grasp his important message.

who could not accept that a toy train could be called both *train* and *toy*. Smith (2005b) has developed a computational model in which this Mutual Exclusivity bias helps in developing a vocabulary providing better communicative success than a model without this bias. He offers an evolutionary explanation: 'Biases such as mutual exclusivity, therefore, might have evolved because they allow communicative systems based on the inference of meaning to be shared between individuals with different conceptual structures' (p. 388). But this bias may not be limited to humans.

Pepperberg and Wilcox (2000) have argued that trained parrots show mutual exclusivity, as they readily learn labels for objects, but then find it difficult to learn colour labels for them.[30] More work needs to be done on this. Some evidence suggests that apes are not constrained by a mutual exclusivity bias in vocabulary learning, but that dogs are. A test commonly used with human toddlers (Kagan 1981; Markman and Wachtel 1988) is to show them two objects, one very familiar, such as a banana, which the child already knows how to name, and another, unfamiliar object, such as a whisk, for which the child has no name as yet. Then the experimenter asks the child 'Show me the fendle', using a plausible non-word. If the child shows the experimenter the whisk, as they usually do, it is reasoned that she is assuming that the word *fendle* cannot apply to the banana, because that already has a name, and the child assumes that things normally aren't called by two different names, that is she follows the Mutual Exclusivity bias. The child might simply follow this bias instinctively, or there might be some more elaborate Gricean reasoning involved, leading to the implicature that *fendle* must mean WHISK, because if the experimenter had wanted the banana, she would have said *banana*. Whichever is the actual mechanism is not my concern here;[31] it is sufficient that young children act as if they are following the Mutual Exclusivity bias. Apes, as far as we can see, do not behave in the same way. Even after exposure to the new names of some new objects, Kanzi and Panbanisha (bonobos) would often present old familiar objects in response to requests using the new names, thus showing that they did not seem to mind the idea of the old familiar objects having several names (Lyn and Savage-Rumbaugh 2000). Apes lack a constraint on vocabulary learning found in children. By contrast, Rico, the star border collie who has learned over 200 words, does appear to apply a principle such as Mutual Exclusivity.

---

[30] I thank Cyprian Laskowski for alerting me to this.
[31] There was a protracted debate in *Journal of Child Language* on whether a similar constraint, Eve Clark's Contrast principle, could be explained in Gricean pragmatic terms or not. See Clark (1988); Gathercole (1989); Clark (1990).

Apparently, Rico's extensive experience with acquiring the names of objects allowed him to establish the rule that things can have names. Consequently, he was able to deduce the referent of a new word on the basis of the principle of exclusion when presented with a novel item along with a set of familiar items.

(Kaminski et al. 2004, p. 1683)

Rico, moreover, learns words very fast, in very few exposures, sometimes just one. His accuracy in recalling words one month after learning them is compa-rable to that of a three-year old toddler. Here again we have an example of a domesticated species with abilities closer to those of humans than chimpanzees and bonobos, which are not domesticated species.

Finally in this section, a note about what may appear to be a puzzle con-cerning the very first occurrences of new lexical items in an evolving species. 'If no one else was around with the skills to understand, what could the first speaker have hoped to accomplish with her first words?' (Burling 2005, p. 20). This is only a puzzle if one clings to a pure language-as-code idea, with no role for inferring meanings from context. With a pure language-as-code model, both sender and receiver need to share the same form–meaning mappings for communication to succeed. If a sender sends a signal for which the receiver has no entry in its code look-up table, then, without using inference, the receiver cannot interpret the signal. Without a capacity for inference of meaning beyond conventional form–meaning mappings, it is impossible to see how a commu-nication system could be initiated. 'The puzzle dissolves as soon as we recog-nize that communication does not begin when someone makes a meaningful vocalization or gesture, but when someone interprets another's behavior as meaningful' (Burling 2005, p. 20). People's passive interpretive ability in a language always exceeds their active productive capacity. One can get the gist of utterances in a foreign language that one could not possibly have composed oneself. Having got the gist of some message from a stream of foreign speech, one may perhaps remember some small stretch of that utterance and be able, next time, to use it productively. This is how it presumably was with the rise of the first elementary lexicon (and much later, the first elementary syntax).

2.5 The objective pull: public use affects private concepts

So far, I have treated the development of a shared system of conventionalized symbols as if it was merely a matter of attaching public labels to hitherto pri-vate concepts. For some (though not for most researchers in animal behaviour) the idea that there can be private pre-linguistic concepts is even a contradiction.

I toured a few corners of this intellectual battlefield in *The Origins of Meaning*, when discussing the possibility of non-linguistic creatures having concepts. For William James (1890), the infant's world was a 'buzzing, blooming confusion'. Saussure was adamantly of the same view:

Psychologically our thought—apart from its expression in words—is only a shapeless and indistinct mass. Philosophers and linguists have always agreed in recognizing that without the help of signs we would be unable to make a clear-cut, consistent distinction between two ideas. Without language, thought is a vague, uncharted nebula. There are no pre-existing ideas, and nothing is distinct before the appearance of language.

(Saussure 1959, pp. 111–12)

Needless to say, I disagree; the prelinguistic mind is not so messy, and does carve the world into categories. But those who deny that animals can have full concepts do have a point, and the issue is to some extent merely terminological. There **is** a difference between pre-linguistic concepts, or proto-concepts, such as I have freely postulated in the earlier book, and fully-fledged human concepts associated with words in a public human language. What is this difference? Gillett (2003) expresses it well:

True concepts and mature conceptions of objects are tied to truth conditions by the normative uses of natural language so that there is a concurrence of semantic content between co-linguistic speakers. Thus, early in language learning I might think that a dog is a big black furry thing that bounds around the neighbourhood but later I discover that dogs include chihuahuas and poodles. Such convergence in categorisation with other competent language users occurs by conversational correction within a co-linguistic human group. By noticing this fact, we can, without denying the continuity between human thought and that of higher animals, bring out a point of difference which increases the power of human epistemic activity and in which language plays a central role.   (Gillett 2003, p. 292)

In describing the effect of public labelling as 'normative', I mean the term as I believe Gillett does, in the following 'nonevaluative' way, described by Ruth Millikan:

By 'normative' philosophers typically have meant something prescriptive or evaluative, but there are other kinds of norms as well. ... I argue that the central norms applying to language are nonevaluative. They are much like the norms of function and behavior that account for the survival and proliferation of biological species. ... Specific linguistic forms survive and are reproduced together with cooperative hearer responses because often enough these patterns of production and response benefit both speakers and hearers.   (Millikan 2005, p. vi)

It is worth mentioning the positions taken by two more venerable philosophers, Frege and Quine, on the private/public divide. Frege (1892) distinguished between private subjective **Ideen**, ideas, and public 'objective' **Gedanken**, thoughts. He was seeking the appropriate **senses** of linguistic expressions, as opposed to their referents.

> The idea is subjective: one man's idea is not that of another. There result, as a matter of course, a variety of differences in the ideas associated with the same sense. A painter, a horseman and a zoologist will probably connect different ideas with the name 'Bucephalus'. This constitutes an essential distinction between the idea and the sign's sense, which may be the common property of many and therefore is not part of or a mode of the individual mind. For one can hardly deny that mankind has a common store of thoughts which is transmitted from one generation to another.
>
> (Frege 1892, p. 59)

A modern reader is prompted to ask where mankind keeps this common store of thoughts which gets transmitted from one generation to another, and by what mechanism the transmission happens. Those were not Frege's concerns. But he had the same basic intuition as expressed by Gillett that the meanings of public expressions are not merely the private concepts of individuals. In his avoidance of psychologizing, Frege went too far and held that the 'sign's sense' is 'not a part of or a mode of the individual mind'. We need to capture the essential insight without losing the connection between the meaning of words and individual minds. After all, it is individual minds that make use of the meanings of words. It has to be noted that something extra happens to private concepts in the process of going public.

In a later generation, Quine (1960) articulated, albeit informally, this influence of social usage on an individual's representation of the meaning of a word. Section 2, titled 'The objective pull; or e pluribus unum' of his first chapter is a gem. I will quote just a little bit of it: 'The uniformity that unites us in communication and belief is a uniformity of resultant patterns overlying a chaotic subjective diversity of connections between words and experience' (p. 8). And later on the same page he writes of 'different persons growing up in the same language', an image well worth pondering. Here, in these well-expressed insights of Gillett, Frege, and Quine,[32] is one of the main differences between the proto-concepts of language-less creatures and the concepts of humans. In realizing that communication, or 'growing up in a language' modifies the private representations available only from direct experience of

---

[32] For sure, many others have had the same insight.

the world, we can see a gap, and a bridge over it, between animals' mental lives and our own.

So far, these have been only philosophical pronouncements. Can they be empirically confirmed? Yes, they can. There is now a wealth of experimental evidence, from children and adults, showing that attaching labels to things enhances, sharpens, or even helps to create, distinct categories. I will mention a few examples.

Babies can be tested for possession of some categorical distinction by seeing whether they gaze for longer when an instance of a new category is presented to them. For instance, if, after being shown a picture of a rabbit, they are shown a picture of a pig, and they don't look significantly longer at the pig picture, it is concluded that they haven't noticed the difference between the two pictures. If, on the other hand, they take a good long look at the second picture, this is taken as evidence that they have noticed a (categorical) difference. Balaban and Waxman (1992) found that speaking a word-label as the baby is exposed to a picture enhances their capacity to make such categorical distinctions. This was in contrast to a control condition with a mechanical tone sounding while the baby was looking at the picture, which made no difference to the baby's apparent judgement. The babies in this experiment were nine months old. Xu (2002, p. 227) interprets this as follows: 'Perhaps knowing the words for these objects is a means of establishing that they belong to different kinds which in turn allowed the infants to succeed in the object individuation task'.

Xu (2002) followed up Balaban and Waxman's (1992) experiment with another one, also using looking time as a criterion, and working again with nine-month-olds. In a baseline condition, a screen was removed to reveal one or two objects (e.g. a toy duck or a toy ball, or both). Not surprisingly, babies looked longer when there were two objects there. In the test conditions, two distinct objects were shown moving from behind a screen and then back behind the screen. While an object was in view, the experimenter said, for example, 'Look, a duck' or 'Look, a ball', or, for both objects 'Look, a toy'. Thus the baby subject was exposed to labels for the objects, but in one condition the labels were different (*duck/ball*), while in the other condition, the labels were the same (*toy*) for both objects. In the two-label case, the babies looked for significantly longer if the removal of the screen revealed, surprisingly, only one object. For the one-label case, the results were similar to the baseline condition. What seems to be happening here is that the explicitly different labelling of two objects leads the baby to expect two objects to be behind the screen, whereas labelling them both the same, as *toy*, does not produce this expectation. The application of explicit labels to objects changes the baby's categorizations of objects in the world. After a valuable discussion of her results in the context of others, on humans and on animals, Xu concludes that

[a]lthough language might not be the only mechanism for acquiring sortal/kind concepts and non-human primates may have at least some ability to represent kinds, it is nonetheless of interest that different aspects of language learning may shape children's conceptual representations in important ways. The current findings suggest a role of language in the acquisition of sortal/object kind concepts in infancy: words in the form of labeling may serve as 'essence placeholders'. (Xu 2002, p. 247)

The idea of an 'essence placeholder' is that categories should be different in some important way, and the explicit linguistic labels alert the child to the expectation that the objects shown will differ in an important way, so the child places them in different mental categories; fuller information about the different categories may come along later.

The two studies mentioned above are the tip of a large iceberg of research on the effect of labelling on categorization by children. Booth and Waxman (2002) is another study showing that 'names can facilitate categorization for 14-month-olds' (p. 948). In an early study Katz (1963) showed children four different geometrical shapes. With one group of children, each separate shape was identified by its own nonsense syllable; with the other group, only two syllables were used, each syllable to a specific pair of shapes. After this training, the children were tested on whether two presented shapes were the same or different. The children who had received only two arbitrary syllables tended more often than the other children to judge two shapes identified with the same syllable as the same shape. In later studies, Goldstone (1994, 1998) showed, more subtly, that the **dimensions** along which objects had been categorized in training (e.g. shape, colour) also had an effect on subsequent similarity judgements. He concludes: 'In sum, there is evidence for three influences of categories on perception: (a) category-relevant dimensions are sensitized, (b) irrelevant variation is deemphasized, and (c) relevant dimensions are selectively sensitized at the category boundary' (Goldstone 1998, p. 590).

Several interpretations of such results are possible. One which stresses the socially **normative** effects of labelling or categorization, has been called 'Strategic Judgement Bias' by Goldstone et al. (2001). By this account, subjects making same/different judgements are trying to conform socially to the categorizations implicit in the labels they have been trained with. An alternative account, called 'Altered Object Description' by the same authors, stresses the internal psychological restructuring of the representations of the categories. Goldstone et al. (2001) tried an experiment to distinguish between these alternatives. Before training, subjects were asked to make same/different judgements between faces. Then they were trained to classify a subset of these face stimuli into various categories. Some of the original stimuli were omitted from this training, and kept as 'neutral', uncategorized stimuli for post-training testing. In this testing, subjects were asked to make similarity judgements between categorized faces and neutral, uncategorized faces. In comparison to their pre-training judgements, they now tended more to judge faces from the same category as uniformly similar to, or different from, a neutral face. In other words, if A and B have been categorized as the same, they will now more often than before be judged either **both** similar to some neutral face X, or **both** different from X. The important point is that in the post-training testing, one of each pair presented for similarity judgement had not been categorized (or labelled) during training. Thus subjects could not be responding, the authors argue, to a pressure to judge two objects as similar because they belong to the same category, as instilled by training. It seems possible, however, to maintain a Strategic Bias account, if one assumes that subjects have some memory of their previous judgements and are concerned to behave consistently, reasoning somewhat as follows: 'I said earlier that A was similar to X, and now I'm asked about B and X; I know A and B belong to the same category, so I'd better also say that B is similar to X'. Goldstone et al. (2001, p. 27) conclude eclectically: 'The results indicate both strategic biases based on category labels and genuine representational change, with the strategic bias affecting mostly objects belonging to different categories and the representational change affecting mostly objects belonging to the same category'. Both accounts, however, are grounded in the effects of labelling.

Labelle (2005, p. 444) writes, 'One recurrent observation in the language acquisition literature is that formal [i.e. grammatical, JRH] distinctions orient the child toward discovering the semantic relations they encode, rather than cognitive distinctions orienting the child towards finding the formal way to express them [Bowerman and Choi (2001); Slobin (2001)]'. Note that this does not deny that cognitive distinctions exist before children express them. Sometimes a pre-existing proto-concept can just be lost, or at least not mature into a fully lexicalized concept, because the language being learned doesn't have a word for it. This is neatly shown by McDonough et al. (2003) in an experiment with nine- to fourteen-month old babies and English-speaking and Korean-speaking adults. English only has one word for 'containment', namely *in*, whereas Korean distinguishes two different types of containment, tight (Korean *kkita*), and loose (*nehta*). In Korean, these are verbs, meaning roughly *put in*; *kkita* would be used for putting a peg tightly into a hole, whereas *nehta* would be used for putting a knife in a drawer. By watching how the babies switched attention between different scenes presented on video, the experimenters were able to tell what differences between scenes were salient for the babies. The babies distinguished between scenes with tight insertion and those with loose insertion. Adult Korean and English speakers were tested in the same way. Adult English speakers did not respond differently to scenes of tight insertion or loose insertion, whereas adult Korean speakers did. The Korean language has enabled the Korean speakers to keep a proto-conceptual distinction which they had as babies, and which the English speakers have lost. Of course, English speakers can distinguish between tight insertion and loose insertion, but this distinction is not reflected in their habitual fast categorization of observed scenes. There is a growing consensus that although the Sapir–Whorf hypothesis does not hold in its strong form, vocabulary and other features of particular languages can influence the habitual mental processes of their speakers.[33]

These studies on human subjects have been backed up by computer modelling of category-learning by artificial neural nets; work of this kind can explore some of the formal factors that may be at work in the phenomenon. Lupyan (2005) trained a neural network to recognize sets of exemplars as categories. His network represented exemplars as sequences of ones and zeroes in an input layer, and the particular categories to which the exemplars were supposed to belong were similarly coded in an output layer. In between the input and output layers were two hidden layers. The way these nets work is that activation flows through weighted connections from nodes in the input layer, through nodes in the intermediate ('hidden') layers, to nodes in the output layer. An untrained network will, on activation of a representation of an exemplar in its input layer, feed the activations through to the output layer, where it will almost certainly 'light up' the wrong nodes, interpreted as an incorrect categorization. At this point correction is applied to the weights of connections between nodes through the network, in such a way that in future the net will tend not to repeat that early mistake, and, instead activation will flow through the net tending toward a correct categorization of exemplars, as represented in the output layer. It's all about 'learning' by gradually changing the connection weights so that a desired pattern of input–output correlations is replicated, so far as possible, by the network. It is well known that artificial neural nets of this sort can be trained to recognize different categories of input, their success

---

[33] For papers contributing to this consensus, see Boroditsky (2001, 2003); Bowerman and Choi (2001); Gentner and Boroditsky (2001); Gumperz and Levinson (1996); Hunt and Agnoli (1991); Levinson (1996); Lucy (1992); Pederson et al. (1998); Slobin (1996); Gilbert et al. (2006). Li and Gleitman (2002) have disagreed with some of the arguments and conclusions. The Sapir–Whorf hypothesis is too big a topic to be broached systematically in this book.

depending, among other things, on the homogeneity or otherwise of the sets of inputs.

Lupyan simulated the categorization of two kinds of categories, low-variability categories and high-variability categories. His examples are apples and strawberries for low-variability categories, and tables and chairs for high-variability categories. All apples are pretty similar to each other; strawberries, too, are pretty much alike. Tables and chairs, however, vary a lot, and there are even chair-like tables and table-like chairs. He simulated high variability by training the net to respond uniformly to relatively diverse inputs, and low variability by training it to respond uniformly to narrow ranges of inputs. He measured the net's success at this categorization task. So far, no labelling is involved. Next, he added four binary digits of extra information to the net's output, corresponding to labels, thus giving the network extra clues for the categorization task, and an extra source of feedback in the net's training or correction procedure. He found that the addition of these labels improved the network's performance on the high-variability categories, but not on the low-variability categories. The moral is that the addition of labels helps to sharpen up the boundaries of categories for which the environment provides only very diffuse and heterogeneous cues; but where the environment neatly separates kinds of objects from each other fairly clearly (there is no fruit which is half apple, half strawberry), the addition of labels does not significantly affect the representations of this artificial learning device. It seems plausible that this holds true for natural learning devices, such as humans and other animals, too. A human baby needs little help to distinguish the category of fellow-humans from that of domestic cats; the exemplars come neatly separated. But colours don't come neatly separated at all, and the child's acquired categories depend heavily on the labels it receives from adults.

A degree of sharpening up of innate categories can be seen in vervet monkeys. Young vervets inappropriately give alarm signals to harmless objects, like falling leaves or warthogs (Seyfarth and Cheney 1982). As they grow up, the range of things for which the specific alarm calls are given narrows down considerably. Probably the young vervets are sharpening up their largely innate predator categories, guided by the alarm calls of adults, tantamount to labels.

It needs to be emphasized, contra Saussure as quoted above, that labels are not the only source of categories in animal minds. Animals display categorical perception without training. Categorical perception occurs when an objectively continuous range of stimuli is not perceived as continuous but is broken up into discrete categories. A difference between objects within one such category tends not to be noticed, whereas the same objectively measured difference across a category boundary is readily perceived. A well known example is Kuhl and Miller's (1978) work on chinchillas, who were found to have categorical perception of speech sounds along a continuum of voicedness, making a distinction not unlike those made by humans in many languages. The chinchillas were not trained to make this categorical distinction.

Categorical distinctions can be innate or learned. Learned categorical distinctions can be learned either by individual learning, what Cangelosi and Harnad (2000)[34] call 'sensorimotor toil', or by social learning from other members of a group, which they call 'symbolic theft'. The terms are humorous, but they emphasize an important difference. 'Toil' brings out the hard trial-and-error work of learning to make important categorical distinctions on one's own, with no benefit from the experience of preceding generations; this is learning the hard way. 'Symbolic theft' brings out the relative ease with which categories can be learned if the learner accepts the categorization implicit in another person's labelling of the relevant exemplars. Symbolic theft, alias social learning, is clearly adaptive. On the basis of a simulation of individuals foraging for food and learning both ways (individual sensorimotor 'toil' and social symbolic 'theft') about the edible and inedible objects in the simulated environment, Cangelosi and Harnad (2000) conclude that ' "warping" of similarity space that occurs when categories are acquired by sensorimotor Toil is transferred and further warped when categories are acquired by Theft. Categorical perception induced by language can thus be seen as an instance of the Whorfian Hypothesis (Whorf 1956), according to which our language influences the way the world looks to us' (p. 122).

The term 'symbolic theft' emphasizes the social dependence of learners on other group members. To end this section where we began, with philosophers, Putnam (1975) has put forward a 'Hypothesis of the Universality of the Division of Linguistic Labor'. His example is the word *gold*, and he points out that very few people know exactly how to test whether some metal is gold or not. This is taken as showing that some people, expert metallurgists, know more about the meaning of the word *gold* than the rest of the English-speaking population, who just rely on the experts whenever it becomes really necessary to know whether something is gold or not. This is not to do with the warping of proto-concepts by labelling, but brings out the important fact that a population can effectively establish a communication system even when not all members share the same internal representations. Individual variation of concepts is not necessarily a barrier to communication (Smith 2005a, 2006). So, although, Quine's 'objective pull' does affect individuals' internal meaning

---

[34] See also Cangelosi et al. (2000).

representations, as we have seen from the psychological experiments and simulations, the effect is not draconian, and individuals remain free to vary within the rough boundaries of the envelope provided by society's common labellings. Communication can be successful despite the fact that to some extent we don't know exactly, and don't even always agree on, what we're talking about. Thus, when I ask an expert metallurgist whether my ring is gold, he 'knows what I mean', even though he has a richer internal representation of the meaning of *gold* than I do. Putnam asks an evolutionary question in relation to his Hypothesis of the Universality of the Division of Linguistic Labor:

> It would be of interest, in particular, to discover if extremely primitive peoples were sometimes exceptions to this hypothesis (which would indicate that the division of linguistic labor is a product of social evolution), or if even they exhibit it. In the latter case, one might conjecture that division of labor, including linguistic labor, is a fundamental trait of our species.   (Putnam 1975, p. 229)

It's a good question, but in answering it one needs to somehow specify where the cutoff between children and adults lies. Clearly children know less of the meanings of words in their language than adults, and rely on adults as the experts to explain the meanings of some words to them. So to the extent that any social learning of meanings happens, a division of linguistic labour necessarily exists.[35] Whether this division of labour universally persists into adult relationships is a more specific question. But what can we make of Putnam's idea that, conceivably, the division of linguistic labour is 'a fundamental trait of our species'? In the context of the *gold* example, it would seem to mean that, **innately** in some sense, some concepts are more fully fleshed out in some individuals than in others. Since we are talking about innate properties, this has to be about the nature of pre-existing categories, before they get labelled with words, or else about innate differences in responsiveness to such labelling. We should put pathological cases aside, because what Putnam had in mind was the functional division of labour in a smoothly running society. What instances might there be of such an innate division of linguistic/conceptual labour? It is hard to think of examples, but a possible candidate might be different conceptual sensitivities in men and women. Perhaps, because of physical differences between the sexes, the internal representations of the concept PENIS,

---

[35] It's not surprising that Hilary Putnam, an old political leftwinger, should be interested in the relation between language and labour. Another work on language evolution emphasizing the centrality of human labour is Beaken (1996), by a (former?) Marxist.

for example, that women and men can attain are 'innately' destined to be different. But this is not an example like *gold*. In any society where body-parts can be freely discussed, men and women can communicate effectively about penises; there is no need to ask the expert. In a species with innate sexual division of labour (e.g. only females care for the young), some of the mental representations of the sexes may well differ, but that is not a matter of the **linguistic** division of labour. In many species there is a communicative division of labour. For example, in many bird species only males sing, and the females respond non-vocally to the song. But what is distinctive of humans is how the communicative labour is more or less equally shared across the sexes. It seems most likely that Putnam's division of linguistic labour is indeed a product of social evolution, but of course the ability to make complex and subtle distinctions, including social distinctions, is innate in us.

Summarizing this section, learning a basic vocabulary involves attaching public labels to pre-available proto-concepts, with the result that the full concepts arising are modified in various ways from the pre-available proto-concepts. They can be extended to more examples, narrowed to fewer examples, shifted to different protypical examples, and associated in inferential networks with other lexicalized concepts.[36]

2.6 Public labels as tools helping thought

In the last section, we saw how going public could trim and transform previously private proto-concepts. It is also apparent that having public labels for things also enables animals, humans included, to perform mental calculations that were previously beyond their reach. The literature on the relation between language and thought is enormous, and I will only dip into it. One hefty limitation here will be that I will only consider **pre-syntactic** communication—principally the effects of having learned a set of publicly available (CONCEPT ⇔ *signal*) pairs, a lexicon. It might be thought that it is syntax alone that works the central magic of transforming limited animal thought into the vastly more

---

[36] Martin (1998) and Tallerman (2009a) also relate to these ideas and are supportive of a 'pre-existing concepts' hypothesis, and emphasize a difference between proto-concepts and lexicalized concepts. This also fits with the distinction made by Ray Jackendoff, in several publications, between 'conceptual', and 'lexical' or 'semantic', representations. Also, from a developmental viewpoint, see Clark (2004) and Mandler (2004).

powerful normal human adult capacity for thought.[37] The addition of syntax to a lexicon does indeed allow us to entertain thoughts that we couldn't entertain without syntax. But linguistic syntax couldn't do its thought-expanding work without the step that has already been described, namely going public, or external, with originally private, internal mental representations, at the basic level of single lexical items.

Note in passing that the private animal representations that I have proposed do have a syntax (well-formedness constraints) of their own, though of an extremely elementary kind. The box notation developed in *The Origins of Meaning* allows boxes within boxes, but boxes may not partially overlap. Thus Figure 2.3 is not a well-formed mental representation:

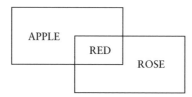

Fig. 2.3 A schematic diagram of an impossible mental representation of a scene. Properties of objects are bound to individual objects independently. It would take a second-order judgement to tell that two perceived objects (e.g. an apple and a rose) 'share' a property.

Figure 2.3 represents, I claim, an unthinkable thought, by any mammal or bird.[38] Perceiving the same property in two distinct objects involves perceiving it twice and binding it twice, to the separate objects. Evidence was given in *The Origins of Meaning* (ch. 4.3) that binding of properties to objects is a serial (not parallel) operation in the brain (Treisman and Gelade 1980). Other well-formedness constraints on prelinguistic semantic representations come in the form of selectional restrictions on how many inner boxes may be combined with particular global predicates (in an outer box). Thus a scene of a CHASE event requires two participant objects, and a GIVE event requires three. So the internal representations that I have proposed for animals close to *Homo* already do have an elementary syntax, and their thoughts are more limited

---

[37] It is common to say that human thought is 'limitless'. How would we know? 'Wovon man nicht sprechen kann, darüber muss man schweigen'. And obviously memory and computing capacity, being housed in a finite brain, are not limitless. Adding some hedge like 'limitless in principle' doesn't illuminate matters at all.

[38] This is not to suggest, of course, that some other animals can think thoughts unavailable to mammals or birds. Some less complex animals (I don't how far 'down' we need to go for this) may not even have distinct local and global attention, so even the simple boxes-within-boxes notation would represent thoughts unavailable to them.

than human thought. Thus the mere fact of having **some** syntax (i.e. well-formedness constraints, or structure) in prelinguistic mental representations is not sufficient to give access to the whole range of human thoughts. Certainly, the development of public syntactic schemes, that is the syntaxes of natural languages, augmented our thinking capacity. For the moment, we will see how, even without any further augmentation of their elementary syntactic form, the fact of going public with previously internal concepts (learning labels for them) can extend the reach of thinking.

Chimpanzees can be trained to judge relations between relations. This is quite abstract. An animal is required to make two SAME/DIFFERENT judgements, and then report whether the two judgements gave the same (or different) result. For example,

In this problem a chimpanzee or child is correct if they match a pair of shoes with a pair of apples, rather than to a paired eraser and padlock. Likewise, they are correct if they match the latter nonidentical pair with a paired cup and paperweight.

(Thompson and Oden 1998, p. 270)

But it is essential to note that the chimpanzees could only do this if they had previously been trained with 'abstract' symbols, plastic coloured shapes, for the more basic, first-order, concepts SAME and DIFFERENT.

The implication then is that experience with external symbol structures and experience using them transforms the shape of the computational spaces that must be negotiated in order to solve certain kinds of abstract problems.

(Thompson and Oden 1998, p. 270)

(See also Thompson et al. 1997 for a related study.) It is appropriate to use Quine's (1960 sec. 56) term 'semantic ascent' here. Quine used it for cases when we move from talking about things to talking about words, as if they are things. The plastic tokens used by the chimpanzees are not words in any human language, but they share the publicness, and are apparently used by the chimpanzees to augment their thought. Putting it anthropomorphically, what may go through the chimp's mind, confronted with two pairs of objects, is something like: 'I could tag this stimulus [a pair of objects] with my symbol *red-triangle*; that other stimulus [another pair] is also *red-triangle*; both stimuli are *red-triangle*—they are the same'. The public intermediate representation *red-triangle* has helped the animal get to this higher-order judgement.

Another demonstration of the effect of verbal labels on mental calculations is given in an early study by Glucksberg and Weisberg (1966). Subjects had to solve a problem with a number of everyday objects provided. The objects were a candle, a shallow open box containing tacks, and a book of matches.

The practical problem was to attach the lighted candle to a vertical board in such a way that the wax would not drip onto the table. The problem could be solved by using the box, tacked to the board, to support the candle and catch the wax—that is, its function of holding tacks was not relevant to the solution of the problem. Subjects solved the problem faster in a condition where the label *box* was explicitly provided. Where the box had a label *TACKS* on it, but there was no use of the word *box*, subjects were slower. 'Providing *S* with the verbal label of a functionally fixed object makes that object available for use, just as providing *S* with the label of another object leads him to use that object' (Glucksberg and Weisberg 1966, p. 663). This study shows that verbal labels are one method of directing a person's problem-solving thinking along a particular track. In an even earlier classic study, Duncker (1945) showed how non-linguistic factors can also direct problem-solving thought. Presenting a set of objects in a box, as opposed to spreading them out on a table with the box, tended to make subjects ignore the fact that the box itself could be used as a solution to the problem.

It seems very likely that the English words taught to Alex the parrot also helped him to get to his higher-order judgements—for example red is a colour, and square is a shape (Pepperberg 2000). Imagine trying to teach a child the meaning of the English word *colour* **without** ever teaching her any of the specific colour terms, *red*, *blue*, *green*, etc. For our purposes here, doggedly putting syntax aside, you are allowed to imagine teaching the child with one-word holophrastic utterances, and using deictic pointing. But even allowing some syntax to creep in, it is hard to see how it could be done. The accessible concepts RED, BLUE, GREEN, etc. can be named fairly immediately,[39] but if forbidden to use them, you would have to simply point to a variety of coloured objects, saying 'coloured'. There aren't many colourless things (water is one), so the task of the child would be somehow to extract this feature from all the others apparent in the objects pointed to. I'm not saying it can't be done. But it is clear that it is a lot easier if you are allowed to used the **words** *red, green, blue*, etc.

For Clark and Thornton (1997), learning the meaning of the word *colour* from a bunch of coloured exemplars, all of which have many other properties, would be a problem of 'type-2' difficulty. Learning the meaning of *red* would be a problem of type-1, a tractable problem. In a very general discussion of computing problems, they illustrate the utility of prior 'achieved representational

---

[39] Subject, of course, to the community's sharpening up of the boundaries around them, as discussed in the last section.

states' in reducing type-2 problems to type-1 problems. From my examples above, the chimpanzee's association of a plastic token with the concept SAME and the child's knowledge of the meaning of *red*, *green*, and *blue* are prior achieved representational states. 'Achieved representational states act as a kind of filter or feature detector allowing a system to re-code an input corpus in ways which alter the nature of the statistical problem it presents to the learning device. Thus are type-2 tigers reduced to type-1 kittens' (p. 66). Considering 'our...baffling facility at uncovering deeply buried regularities', Clark and Thornton suggest that 'the underlying trick is always the same; to maximise the role of achieved representation, and thus minimise the space of subsequent search' (p. 66).

One more example may be helpful. 'Chunking' is a well-known psychological move for tackling some complex memory task. Here is a random sequence of binary digits:

011100011001011100110

Your task is to memorize this sequence, and any others that I ask you to commit to memory. This is pretty difficult. There are 21 ones and zeroes in the sequence, well beyond the limits of normal working memory. But there is a trick you can use. Teach yourself a set of names for three-digit sequences of ones and zeroes, like this:

000 = *A*	001 = *B*	010 = *C*	011 = *D*
100 = *E*	101 = *F*	110 = *G*	111 = *H*

There are eight names to learn, easy for humans, chimps, dogs, and parrots. Now when you see the sequence above, you can mentally translate it into the sequence

D E D B D E G

This is a sequence of seven symbols, within normal working memory limits. I know a psycholinguist who has taught himself this trick, and impresses first-year students with his ability to repeat back verbatim arbitrary strings of ones and zeroes, up to a length of about twenty. (Then he lets them into the secret, as a way of introducing the topic of chunking.) The vocabulary of letters *A*,...*H* is a set of prior achieved representations, in Clark and Thornton's (1997) terms.

The efficacy of chunking is clear in the psychology of language processing, and much of the syntactic and phonological structure of language can be attributed to the utility of chunking. Our concern here is not with the utility of achieved representations in acquiring control of syntactically complex structures. Here, we are concerned with the question of whether knowing the meanings of some elementary single words can make possible mental computational tasks that would be impossible, or very difficult, without them. Acquiring an abstract concept, such as that of a relation between relations, or a property of properties, from exemplars drawn from a complexly structured world, would be an example of such a difficult mental computational task.

Chomsky has frequently written that a plausible function of language is internal computation as an aid to thought (as opposed to communication), but he has never amplified how this might actually work. The 'prior achieved representations' suggestion of Clark and Thornton's (1997) is a possible way. The important question is whether such representations need to be public. This question can be split into several separate questions. One question is this: does a prior achieved representation, now, on any occasion of use in some complex computation, **need** to be external, publicly expressed? The answer to this is 'No', as talking to oneself privately can be useful in solving problems, as Chomsky reminds us: 'Suppose that in the quiet of my study I think about a problem, using language' (Chomsky 1980b, p. 130).

The next question is an evolutionary one: could prior achieved representations have become available in the first place without some public expression? It is indeed possible that an animal could privately solve some simple problem, remember the solution, and apply this learned knowledge later in solving some more complex task, all without any public communication. Experimental demonstrations of such 'insight' are surprisingly rare, however.

A famous case was reported by Köhler (1925), whose chimpanzee Sultan knew how to use a stick to rake in some food just out of reach. One day, some food was put beyond reach of a single stick, but within reach of two sticks joined together, and Sultan, after several hours, realized he could solve the problem by joining two sticks together (they were hollow bamboo sticks, and one could easily be inserted in the end of the other). This observation is anecdotal, and commentators have seriously doubted whether Sultan really thought this out, or just happened to be playing with two sticks and joined them together, and then realized that he could get the food with the now single, longer stick. But if he did genuinely figure out how to make a longer stick, it seems certain that he would not have put his mind to this if he had not had prior learned knowledge of how to get food with a single short stick. Whatever went on in Sultan's mind, it did not involve problem solving using any public system of language-like expressions.

Another possible demonstration of an animal using prior learned knowledge to solve a new and (slightly) more complex problem is by Epstein et al. (1984). Pigeons were trained to push a box toward a spot on a wall. Quite independently, they were trained to hop on a box to peck at a picture over it.

They were rewarded for both these tasks with food grains. Next they were put in a space with the picture on the wall too high to reach, and with the box a some distance from it. The pigeons thought about it for a few minutes, and then pushed the box toward the picture on the wall, hopped on the box, and pecked at the picture.

So animals can (just about) apply prior knowledge to the solution of more complex problems, in unnatural laboratory conditions. A rather more natural and convincing case, still in a laboratory, involves New Caledonian crows, studied by Weir et al. (2002). One crow, a female, was impressively clever at bending pieces of wire to make hooks to get food out of a deep pipe.

In the wild, New Caledonian crows make at least two sorts of hook tools using distinct techniques, but the method used by our female crow is different from those previously reported and would be unlikely to be effective with natural materials. She had little exposure to and no prior training with pliant material, and we have never observed her to perform similar actions with either pliant or nonpliant objects. The behavior probably has a developmental history that includes experience with objects in their environment (just as infant humans learn about everyday physics from their manipulative experience), but she had no model to imitate and, to our knowledge, no opportunity for hook-making to emerge by chance shaping or reinforcement of randomly generated behavior. She had seen and used supplied wire hooks before but had not seen the process of bending. (Weir et al. 2002, p. 981)

This is a striking and rare result, but it shows the **possibility** of animals applying prior knowledge to solve a somewhat complex problem. It is also striking that the result is found in a bird, showing it to be at least as clever as our close primate cousins.

So, in answer to our question about whether the prior achieved representations applied in the solution of some complex task could be acquired privately, not by the use of any public symbol or token, we conclude that it **is possible** but evidently rare. Humans, of course, are great problem solvers, far beyond the abilities of any animals. How do we do it?

When Chomsky thinks about a problem in the quiet of his study, he uses language, he tells us. Where, in his case, do the prior achieved representations come from? Chomsky energetically argues that it is not clear that the essential function of language is communication, and that another plausible function for it is private problem solving. In that case, we can imagine him having somehow acquired a private language of thought from private experiences, and computing solutions to complex problems using these private representations (like the New Caledonian crow, only with loftier problems). Now the private 'talking to onself' part of this scenario is quite plausible; surely we all do this. But what is not plausible is that the prior achieved representations could have been acquired entirely privately. When we 'think in language', we usually rehearse sentences in our own particular language, using the learned words for the things we are thinking about. The words we use in private thought are taken from public use. It seems very likely that the impressive human problem-solving abilities are due to having learned a language, containing a repertoire of public tokens for complex concepts, accumulated over many previous generations. These meaning–form connections were **communicated** to us. The private thought function of language could not exist to the impressive degree that it does without this communicative function. Jackendoff sets out how language can enhance thought:

… imaged language in the head gives us something new to pay attention to, something unavailable to the apes—a new kind of index to track. And by paying attention to imaged language, we gain the usual benefit: increased power and resolution of processing. This increase in power extends not only to the phonological level, but to everything to which the phonology is bound, in particular the meaning. As a result,

Hypothesis 5 Being able to attend to phonological structure enhances the power of thought.   (Jackendoff 2007, p. 105)

Jackendoff also succinctly puts the case for the evolutionary priority of the communicative function of language over its problem-solving function.

[I]nner speech and its capability for enhancing thought would have been automatic consequences of the emergence of language as a communicative system. In contrast, the reverse would not have been the case: enhancement of thought would not automatically lead to a communication system. In other words, if anything was a 'spandrel' here, it was the enhancement of thought, built on the pillars of an overt communication system.
                                                                                  (Jackendoff 2007, p. 108)

The view that language enhances thought is hardly controversial. My argument with Chomsky is that this does not downgrade, let alone eliminate, communication as a function of language. Rather, transmission, via communication, of the basic tools (words paired with abstract concepts) with which to conduct linguistic thought is a major factor in humans' impressive problem-solving abilities. If we did not learn about such abstract concepts (like COLOUR and ever more abstract concepts) through verbal interaction, we would not be where we are today.

The contribution of learned symbols to non-linguistic cognition is documented.

Language-trained chimps exhibit 'enhanced' abilities over other chimps; for example, analogical reasoning and some forms of conservation. Thus, their abilities are, in a sense, not chimpanzee abilities, but consequences of the cognitive technology made available to them via the particular forms of social relationships and cultural patterns their training histories have established between them and humans.

(Lock and Peters 1996, p. 386)

The difference that language-training makes is not as well documented as some reports suggest. Gillan et al. (1981) showed some impressive analogical reasoning by Sarah, a symbol-trained chimpanzee, but made no comparisons with non-symbol-trained animals. Language-training is not a necessity for all kinds of reasoning in chimpanzees, as Gillan (1981) found, investigating their abilities in transitive inference.[40] Nevertheless, there are a number of studies of children and animals supporting the view that possession, or current awareness, of language facilitates the performance of non-linguistic tasks.

Loewenstein and Gentner (2005) got children to find a hidden object in a place analogous to one they had been shown. In one condition, the showing was accompanied by a spatial word such as *top*, *middle*, or *bottom*; in the other condition, no such verbal clue was given. Although the non-verbal demonstration was in fact informative enough to direct the child to the right location, the use of a spatial word along with the demonstration improved the children's performance. They conclude 'If indeed relational language generally invites noticing and using relations, then the acquisition of relational language is instrumental in the development of abstract thought' (p. 348).

Hermer-Vazquez et al. (2001) found that children who knew the meanings of the words *left* and *right* performed better than children who didn't know these meanings in searching tasks where no explicit verbal direction with these words was involved. They put their findings in an evolutionary context, suggesting that human adult abilities are significantly enhanced by the possession of words.

These are some of the scraps of evidence that have been gleaned under strict experimental conditions for a proposition that many would regard as self-evident, that language significantly facilitates thought. Human thinking is so far ahead of non-human thinking that these studies do not even glimpse the heights of accessible human thought. But in their humble experimental way, they show the beginning of the upward slope from the 'near-sea-level' of non-human thinking where our ancestors began. The evolutionary scaling of the heights[41] involved a feedback loop between the conventional languages that

---

[40] I argued in *The Origins of Meaning* that transitive inference is one of a suite of cognitive abilities available to apes and some other species before language.

[41] Poor metaphor, implying there is a top, a limit that we have reached.

human groups developed and their ability to use this powerful instrument to mental advantage.

Sapir was evidently thinking about such a feedback loop in human evolution when he wrote:

We must not imagine that a highly developed system of speech symbols worked itself out before the genesis of distinct concepts and thinking, the handling of concepts. We must rather imagine that thought processes set in, as a kind of psychic overflow, almost at the beginning of linguistic expression; further, that the concept, once defined, necessarily reacted on the life of its linguistic symbol, encouraging further linguistic growth. ... The instrument makes possible the product, the product refines the instrument. The birth of a new concept is invariably foreshadowed by a more or less strained or extended use of old linguistic material; the concept does not attain to individual and independent life until it has found a distinctive linguistic embodiment.

(Sapir 1921, p. 17)

In this chapter, we have traced a possible path, albeit still with gaps, from pre-human meaningful gestures and vocal calls, through the first learned connections between signals and pre-linguistic (proto-)concepts, through the emergence of a conventional inventory of form–meaning connections across a whole community, finally to the effects on individuals' concepts and thinking powers of these beginnings of a human-like communicative code, a lexicon. I will have more to say about the contents of human lexicons in later chapters. Meanwhile, remember, during our travels through the emergence of grammar, where we started this chapter, with 'You can't have grammar without a lexicon'. And remember the significant effect on individual thought that possession of publicly shared symbols can have, even as yet without any syntax to combine them.

This part of the book has set the stage for the evolution of grammar as we know it in humans. A shared lexicon of unitary learned symbols necessarily evolved before they could be put together in meaningful expressions with grammatical shape. And between the chimp–human split and the emergence of *Homo sapiens*, some ability to control patterned sequences, not entirely determined by their intended meanings, also arose. The next part of the book will also be stage-setting. First, it shows the way through a jungle of controversy over how to approach human grammar at all, granting some sense and rationale to all but the most extreme views, and showing how they are compatible. Then the basic facts about what aspects of grammar evolved, in the biological and cultural spheres, are set out.

Introduction to Part II: Some Linguistics—How to Study Syntax, and What Evolved

This part of the book, in three chapters, aims to answer the question: 'Human Syntax: what evolved?' As we all now know, the term 'evolution of language' has two distinct senses, (1) biological evolution of the human language faculty, and (2) cultural evolution of individual languages, such as Aramaic and Zulu. It is less often emphasized that the term 'language universals' has an exactly parallel ambiguity. There are the evolved traits of individual humans who acquire languages, traits biologically transmitted. And there are the culturally evolved properties of the particular languages they acquire, some of which may be common to all languages because the same basic pressures apply to the growth of languages in all societies. These latter pressures are only indirectly biological in nature, as all cultural development takes place within a biological envelope. In ordinary talk, for people innocent of linguistic theory, 'universals of language' naturally means features that are found in every language. In the generative tradition in linguistics, the term 'universals' is not about what features languages have or don't have. It is about what features of languages **human beings**, universally, can learn. Anderson (2008b, p. 795) avoids the term 'universal grammar', which he says 'tends to set off rioting in some quarters'. Claims about human syntax rouse a lot of heated debate, and it is necessary to clarify some basic methodological issues before we start. Chapter 3 will discuss how to approach the properties of humans in relation to their use and cognitive command of language. The next chapter, 4, will set out central facts that need to be explained about the human capacity for language. These facts implicitly characterize an upper bound on how **complex** languages can be, a bound set by human limitations. This follows the emphasis in the generative literature during most of the second half of the twentieth century, in emphasizing the complexity of language phenomena, and relating it in theory to a hypothesized innate 'universal grammar' (UG). Particular languages can get to be impressively complex, but not (obviously) without limit. The languages of communities do not always exploit the full innate capacities of their individual members. Some languages are simpler than others. Chapter 5 will discuss basic issues arising from the fact that individual languages evolve historically, through cultural transmission. This chapter explores how **simple** languages can be, and implicitly characterizes a lower bound on simplicity, a bound set by the need for effective communication among members of a cohesive community. Thus chapters 4 and 5 are complementary. My overall aim in these three chapters is to clear the pre-theoretical decks, to set out the basic explananda for an account of the origins of grammar. I will build up a picture of the central kinds of linguistic fact that biological and cultural evolution have given rise to.

CHAPTER 3

Syntax in the Light of Evolution

3.1 Preamble: the syntax can of worms

Now for the harder bit. This book is more controversial than *The Origins of Meaning*, because it gets further into linguistics proper, in particular into syntactic theory. In probing the origins of meaning, it was possible to draw connections between basic semantic and pragmatic concepts and well attested phenomena in animal life. Thus, deictic reference, displaced reference and illocutionary force, for example, were related to attention, the permanence of objects and animals doing things to each other, respectively. But in syntax, the basic concepts are more abstract,[1] including such notions as subject of a sentence (as opposed to the more concrete semantic notion of the actor in an event), noun (as opposed to physical object), hierarchical structure, and, depending on your theory, abstract 'movement' rules. Grammatical language, being unique to humans, cannot be rooted so directly in experiences that we share with animals. Humans have evolved a unique type of complex system for expressing their thoughts. (And their thoughts have become more complex as a result.)

Both the uniqueness of grammatical language and the arbitrary convention-ality of the connections between grammar and concrete moment-to-moment, life-or-death situations make syntactic theory a place where alternative views can be held more freely, without danger of relatively immediate challenge

---

[1] Distractingly, I can't resist mentioning a memorable student exam howler here. She wrote, explaining the distinction between syntax and semantics 'Syntax is the study of language using meaningless words'. I know what she meant, but can't help feeling some sympathy with what she actually wrote.

from empirical facts. Over the last fifty years, syntactic theory has been a maelstrom of argument and counterargument. Halfway through that period, Jim McCawley (1982), a central participant in syntactic theorizing, wrote a book called *Thirty Million Theories of Grammar*. In a review of that book, Pieter Seuren (1983, p. 326), another central figure, wrote 'one can't help smiling at the thought of those old debates, which for the most part have led to so surprisingly little'. Many would say that the second half of the post-1950s period has been similarly frustrating, even though, of course, the main players continue to argue that their contributions are advances. Another central figure, Jackendoff (2007, p. 25) writes that 'by the 1990s, linguistics was arguably far on the periphery of the action in cognitive science' and refers to 'linguistics' loss of prestige'. Certainly much has been learned along the way. But the intriguing fact is that we have not yet agreed which particular theory about human grammatical capacity is right, or even approaches rightness more than the others. The path of syntactic theorizing since the 1950s is strewn with the bodies (sometimes still twitching) of a bewildering host of challengers to the prevailing orthodoxies of the time, such as Generative Semantics, Arc-Pair Grammar, Relational Grammar, Role and Reference Grammar, to name just a few. And the prevailing orthodoxy has also mutated along the way, as theories should, if they are to develop and expand. Grammatical theorists now have vastly more experience and knowledge of the power and limitations of formal systems than was conceivable in the 1950s. To some extent there has been a fascination with formalism itself, so that part of the game of theorizing consists in showing that one theory is a notational equivalent of another, or is more powerful than another, regardless of whether such power is demanded by the facts to be explained. Formalism does indeed have its fascination, like pure mathematics, but it is not in itself an empirical domain.

Steedman and Baldridge, in a section titled 'The Crisis in Syntactic Theory' write,

[W]hy are there so many theories of grammar around these days? It is usual in science to react to the existence of multiple theories by devising a crucial experiment that will eliminate all but one of them. However, this tactic does not seem to be applicable to these proliferating syntactic theories. For one thing, in some respects they are all rather similar.   (Steedman and Baldridge, in press)

Steedman and Baldridge distinguish between areas of syntax where virtually all extant theories have provably equivalent accounts, and genuinely controversial areas, typically involving phonetically empty elements and movement rules, where incompatibilities remain. I will make no contribution to syntactic theory itself, except in the general sense that I take a certain class of syntactic theories, Construction Grammar, to be more compatible with evolutionary considerations. But I do hope to have built upon an emerging consensus to (1) reduce the bewilderment of non-linguists in the face of all the apparently competing theories and formalisms, and (2) use this consensus as the target of an evolutionary story. Much of this part of the book thus has a pedagogical function for non-linguists, to help non-linguists who theorize about language evolution to get to closer grips with what has proved to be of lasting validity in syntactic theory (in my view, of course). I will also cover some areas of syntactic theory which have been over-naively adopted as gospel by non-linguists, showing their limitations.

We have learned massively more about the complexity of the grammatical systems of many more languages than was ever dreamed of before the 1950s. And each syntactic school of thought may have its own theoretical proposal for some particular complexity. But, to date, there typically remains controversy among syntacticians about how to account for some of the most striking complexities that languages present. For example, should we posit any 'empty categories', elements of syntactic structure that have no concrete (i.e. phonetic) counterparts? The alternative to positing empty categories is to insist that all the computation that humans do when processing sentences involves elements, such as words and morphemes, that we can actually pronounce and hear. Another example is the question of whether there are syntactic 'movement rules' which claim a psychologically real (in some sense) underlying serial order of the elements in a sentence which is different from the observed order.

Formal systems give us the freedom to postulate empty categories and unobserved sequences of elements. Even the simplest model of grammar discussed by linguists, Finite State grammars, often taken to be the epitome of Behaviourist approaches to syntax, actually postulated unobservable 'states' of the processing organism or machine. Linguists have not been as cautious as they should have been in exercising the freedom to postulate unseen entities. Especially in the early days of generative theory, there was an exciting feeling that syntactic theory would allow us to **discover** facts beneath the observable surface of language. Formal analysis of complex surface patterns, it was hoped, would lead the way to underlying, but unobservable mechanisms, working on unobservable elements, economically projecting the true organizational principles of grammar. Berwick (1997, p. 233) captures the spirit of it: 'We might compare the formal computations of generative grammar to Mendel's Laws as understood around 1900—abstract computations whose physical bases were but dimly understood, yet clearly tied to biology'. The parallel with Freudian psychoanalysis, probing the depths of the subconscious, also lurked in the theoretical background. More self-awarely, theoretical linguists sailed with the wind of the Cognitive Revolution of the second half of the twentieth century, with its prospect of discovering inner mental processes and states. Another, more empirical, kind of parallel was also applicable, such as the astronomer's feat of deducing the existence of an unobserved planet beyond Neptune from observable aberrations in the orbits of the known planets. In a well-known paper, Ross (1970b), for example, argued for the existence of an underlying, but unobserved, main clause of the form *I tell you that...* for all English declarative sentences. This was argued not from semantic or pragmatic grounds, but from the idiosyncratic distribution of a number of actually observable elements, including the reflexive pronouns in examples like *The paper was written by Ann and myself* and *Linguists like myself were never too happy with deep structure*. Since, generally, a reflexive pronoun has to have an antecedent, the instances of *myself* in these examples were argued to have an invisible antecedent in an invisible (but indirectly inferrable) level of 'deep structure'.[2] More recent and prominent examples of extreme bold postulation of unobservable aspects of syntactic structure are found in works by Richard Kayne (1994, 2005). The title of his 2005 book, *Movement and Silence*, reveals the theme. Kayne holds that in underlying structure the basic word order of all languages is the same, resulting in the need for some massive movement rules to obtain the actual observed spoken order. He also postulates a large number of unobservable elements, such as an element HOURS in English *It is six* (meaning *it is six o'clock*), since in other languages such an element is made explicit, for example French *Il est six heures*. It is fair to say that this extreme theoretical stance is not appreciated outside of the school of linguists to which Kayne belongs, while supporters maintain that it is based on **empirical** evidence, notably comparative data from different languages. The balance between capturing the nature of the human language faculty, reflected in data from any language, and remaining true to the obvious facts of particular languages, is not an agreed matter among theorists.

Of course we should not be too shy of postulating unobservable elements and mechanisms to explain observable patterns, if this gives us an economical account of a wide range of facts. But the field is split on the issue of how much is gained by the various formal manoeuvres that have been explored. I have often asked syntacticians, in situations where their defensive guard was down, how much syntactic theory has succeeded in discovering the true organizational

---

[2] The examples that Ross invoked are all genuinely factual. It may be wrong to postulate invisible syntactic elements to account for the facts, but his examples raise important questions about the relationship between syntax and pragmatics that must be addressed.Ross (1975) is a valuable discussion of such issues.

principles of grammar. The answer I have often got is that, with hindsight, it seems that the correct theory is critically underdetermined by the data. Of course, in some sense, all theories are underdetermined by their data; there are always alternative ways of casting a theory to account for any given set of facts. But in many other fields, considerations of coverage and simplicity, problematic as those are, typically serve to forge a general consensus about which theory seems for now most likely to approach truth. Not so in syntactic theory. This pessimistic conclusion was admitted by Stephen Anderson, known as a generative linguist, in his Presidential Address to the Linguistic Society of America in 2008: 'We cannot assume that the tools we have are sufficient to support a science of the object we wish to study in linguistics' (Anderson 2008b, p. 75). The tools Anderson was referring to are the traditional tools of the linguist, arguments from the poverty of the stimulus and cross-linguistic universals. These are discipline-internal tools, taught to generations of students in Linguistics departments. Linguists must look outside the traditional narrow confines of their discipline for extra tools to shed light on the nature of language. A similar judgement is expressed by Sag et al. (2003). At the end of an appendix reviewing grammatical theories, they write:

[O]ne thing we can say with certainty about the field of linguistics, at least over the last half century, is that theories of grammar have come and gone quite quickly. And this is likely to continue until the field evolves to a point where the convergent results of diverse kinds of psycholinguistic experiments and computational modelling converge with, and are generally taken to have direct bearing on, the construction of analytic hypotheses. Until that day, any survey of this sort is bound to be both incomplete and rapidly obsolescent.   (Sag et al. 2003, p. 542)

Most linguists pay lip service, at the very least, to the idea that formal analysis is a way of getting insight into the psychological, ultimately neurological, organization of language in the brain. Up until now, there has been no realistic way of exploring real brain activity in any way which can help to resolve the theoretical disputes between syntacticians. Syntacticians are not about to start doing brain imaging. Brain imaging so far gives only very broad temporal and spatial resolutions of brain activity, and in any case we have barely any idea how to relate whatever brain activity we observe to the abstract postulates of syntactic theory. Nevertheless, future discoveries in neuroscience impose a constraint on our theories of grammatical behaviour; the easier it is to find neural correlates of the grammatical structures and processes that we hypothesize, the more plausible they will be.

Stephen Anderson's pessimistic admission above is followed by 'But on the other hand, we should also not assume that the inadequacy of those tools is evidence for the non-existence of the object on which we hope to shed light'. This object is the human language faculty, and the specific part of it discussed in this book is its syntactic component. The human capacity for syntax evolved. Another constraint, then, on syntactic hypotheses is **evolvability**; there has to be a plausible evolutionary route by which the human syntactic faculty has reached its present impressive state. Plausible evolutionary accounts should conform to general evolutionary theory, and this consideration tends strongly to recommend a gradual trajectory. Other things being equal, saltations to syntax are less plausible than gradualistic accounts. Correspondingly, our theory of syntax should be one that lends itself to a gradualistic account. I have settled on a particular class of syntactic theories, known as Construction Grammar, precisely for the reason that this view of syntax makes it much easier to see a gradual trajectory by which the language faculty, and individual languages, could have (co-)evolved. For a concerted argument for the relevance of evolutionary considerations to choice of syntactic theory (incidentally concluding against Minimalism on evolutionary grounds), see Parker (2006) and Kinsella (2009).

Considering the possible evolutionary paths by which modern syntax could have arisen is thus an extra tool, so far scarcely used, that can narrow down the field of hypotheses about the nature of the human syntactic capacity. Stephen Anderson's excellent book *Doctor Dolittle's Delusion* (2004) carefully sets out the ways in which anything that might pass for 'animal syntax' is very far away from human syntax. What Anderson does not discuss is how humans might have evolved to have that impressive capacity. It is one thing to point out differences. The evolutionary task is to try to see a route from non-language to language, using whatever evidence we can. Building on the foundations set out in this and the previous part, Part III of this book will, finally, sketch an evolutionary route from non-syntax to modern human syntax.

3.2 Language in its discourse context

Some aspects of syntax can be studied without reference to the discourse context in which sentences are used. And indeed some syntacticians rarely, if ever, refer to the discourse context of sentences. On the other hand, a full account of the interaction of syntactic structure with semantics, and especially pragmatics, typically requires reference to discourse structure. Most syntacticians implicitly or explicitly acknowledge this, and where necessary they have made the appropriate connections. The totality of the syntactic structure of a language is neither wholly derivative of semantics and pragmatics nor wholly autonomous from discourse. To some extent, the syntactic structure of a language has 'a life of its own', but it is hard to conceive how this could have come about without the use of sentences in discourse. The last chapter of the book (Chapter 9) will spell out the discourse motivation for the evolution of the most basic of syntactic structures. In the meantime, the present section will show in some detail the essential interwovenness of syntax and discourse factors.

Universally, healthy humans brought up in a language community can by their tenth year learn to participate fully in conversations in their group's language. In non-literate groups, universally again, the turns of healthy ten-year-olds in these conversations can be as complex as the conversational language of adults. 'Looking at a transcript of the speech of a typical six-year-old..., we will find that indeed it is not very different from informal unplanned adult discourse' (Dąbrowska 1997, p. 736). This is well known to all parents who are not unduly hung up on literary standards for conversational speech. When people speak, it is normally in dialogues with other people. In real life, sentences are seldom uttered in a vacuum, out of any communicative context. An exception is when a solitary person thinks aloud, as sometimes happens. But when people do talk to themselves in this way, they use the conventional grammar and vocabulary of their own social group, as if they were communicating with another person from that group. I take it that talking to oneself is derivative of talking to other people. Talking to other people evolved first, and it is this form of communicative, dialogic speech, that we have to explain.

The most formal approaches to syntax (e.g. Formal Language Theory, as noted in Chapter 1) treat a language simply as a set of sentences. English is seen as a set of sentences, Swahili is a different set of sentences, and so on. In this view, each sentence is an independent object, considered without concern for any possible context in which it might occur. The goal of research in this vein is to provide a grammar (e.g. of English or Swahili) that characterizes just the members of the set. The grammar will achieve economy by making gener-alizations over different members of the set, thus capturing systemic relations between the various alternative types of sentences and the phrases and other constituents that they are made up from. While an approach of this sort will refer to structural relations between parts of sentences, it will not mention or appeal to any such relations between a sentence and its surrounding discourse, the most extreme implicit assumption being that the surrounding discourse does not influence the form of a sentence. It is generally realized that this is a highly idealized and simplified view of what a language is, although much of the practice of syntacticians involves analysis of sentences considered out of any discourse context. Givón (2002) is one of many critics of this approach when he writes 'there is something decidely bizarre about a theory of language (or grammar) that draws the bulk of its data from . . . out-of-context clauses constructed reflectively by native speakers' (pp. 74–5). There are two separate criticisms here: the (1) sidelining of dialogue or discourse context, and (2) the reflective construction of examples. I'll first discuss the issue of sentences in context versus sentences considered without regard to any possible context. (Lest you object at this point that language really isn't organized in terms of 'sentences', wait until Section 3.3, where I defend the view that language is structured in sentence-like units.)

Most syntactic papers make no mention of the possible discourse context of their examples. In most cases, this is defensible on the grounds that the examples in question have the properties ascribed to them **in any conceivable context**. Take a classic example, the distribution of reflexive pronouns (e.g. *myself, yourself, herself*) in English. There is no question that, in most dialects of English, *She shot himself* is ungrammatical, whereas *She shot herself* is grammatical. Context doesn't come into it. You can't find, or even construct, a plausible discourse context in which these facts do not hold. Likewise in standard French *Sa femme est morte* is grammatical in any context, whereas *Sa femme est mort* in which the predicative adjective does not agree with its feminine subject, is ungrammatical in any context. When syntacticians discuss examples out of context, much of the time, their examples would not be affected by context, even if it were considered. This is true of most of the examples I will later give. What this shows about universal linguistic dispositions of humans is that they are capable of getting to know some patterns of well-formedness in their language which hold regardless of discourse context. Any healthy human baby, born wherever in the world, raised by English speakers, will get to know that there is something wrong with *The woman shot himself* in any situation in which one tries to use it communicatively.[3] Likewise, any healthy French-raised baby will get to know the discourse-free gender-agreement facts about cases such as *Sa femme est morte*. What proportion of grammatical facts in a language are independent of discourse context in this way? Typically, more complex examples tend to be more dependent on discourse context. Perhaps even a majority of examples that syntacticians analyse really need to be considered in relation to a range of possible discourse contexts. My case is that **some** grammatical facts hold independent of

---

[3] Rather than a situation in which such an example is merely **mentioned** as an example in a discussion about grammar.

discourse context. And these facts are of a basic type most likely to be relevant to evolutionary questions about the human capacity to learn grammatical facts.

In another class of cases, syntacticians do implicitly consider a certain kind of context, namely what a putative utterer of a sentence might mean by it. By far the most common consideration of this sort is whether two expressions in a sentence can be used to refer to the same entity. The best known example again involves pronouns. English *John shot him* is only acceptable on the understanding that *John* and *him* do not refer to the same person. By contrast, in *John was afraid that Mary would shoot him*, the same two words can, but need not, refer to the same person. Any normal human raised in the right circumstances can easily pick up facts like this. These are not erudite facts, only learned through explicit schooling.

The criticism that syntacticians ignore discourse context is not well-aimed. Sometimes, as I argued above, they don't need to, because discourse context is not relevant to the grammatical properties of some examples. But where discourse is relevant, it is mentioned. One example among many is from Andrew Radford, who indefatigably tracks each new wave of generativist theory with a new textbook. He bases a structural point on the fact that *Are trying to help you* is not an appropriate response to the question *What are you doing?*, whereas *We are trying to help you* is appropriate in that discourse context (Radford 2004, p. 72). Another pair of renowned professional syntactic theorists, Culicover and Jackendoff (2005) spend many pages discussing 'elliptical'[4] examples like *Yeah, with Ozzie* or *In a minute, ok?* or *What kind?* Anyone who could not use expressions like this in the right discourse context would not be a fully competent speaker of English. Culicover and Jackendoff (2005) argue that, obviously, competence to use such expressions involves command of the appropriate semantics and pragmatics, that is the meanings of the words used in the discourse, and the socially appropriate ways to respond to utterances. They also point out that the grammatical properties of preceding utterances can partly determine the well-formedness of such incomplete sentences. An example given by Merchant (2004) is from German, where different verbs arbitrarily, that is without semantic motivation, impose different cases on their objects. The object of the verb *folgen* 'follow' must be in the dative case, for example have the article *dem*, whereas the object of the verb *suchen* 'seek'

---

[4] I use the term 'elliptical' provisionally for convenience. It does not necessarily imply that anything has been 'elided' from some possibly fuller form of a sentence in a speaker's mind.

must be in the accusative case, for example have the article *den*. Merchant's examples are:[5]

	Q:	*Wem*	*folgt*	*Hans?*
		who.DAT	follows	Hans
		Who is Hans following?		
a.	A:	*Dem*	*Lehrer.*	
		the.DAT	teacher	
b.	A:	**Den*	*Lehrer.*	
		the.ACC	teacher	
	Q:	*Wen*	*sucht*	*Hans?*
		who.ACC	seeks	Hans
		Who is Hans looking for?		
a.	A:	**Dem*	*Lehrer.*	
		the.DAT	teacher	
b.	A:	*Den*	*Lehrer.*	
		the.ACC	teacher	

Merchant also gives parallel examples from Greek, Korean, English, Hebrew, Russian, and Urdu. The point is that some of the grammatical relationships found within sentences also stretch over to relationships between sentences in a discourse. The grammaticality of a two-word, one-phrase answer by one speaker depends on which verb was used in the preceding question, by another speaker. Universally, any healthy human can learn such discourse-related syntactic facts. '[C]onversation partners become virtual co-authors of what the other is saying' (Bråten 2009, p. 246). Certainly, a conversational discourse is a joint product of several people working together, but the contribution of each person springs in part from his own individual command of the grammatical facts of the language concerned. Analogously, any musician who aspires to play in ensembles with other musicians must first acquire an individual competence on his own instrument in the tunes concerned.

The effect of discourse on choice of syntactic structure is seen in the phenomenon of syntactic priming. The grammar of a language often provides several alternative ways of saying the same thing, that is paraphrases. Examples are these pairs:

---

[5] The asterisks in these examples indicate inappropriate answers to the respective questions.

John gave Mary a book	*John gave a book to Mary*
Fred sent Joan a letter	*Fred sent a letter to Joan*
The catcher threw the pitcher	*The catcher threw the ball to*
the ball	*the pitcher*

While the words are different, all the left-hand examples here have one syntactic structure, called a 'Double-Object' (DO) construction, while all the right-hand structures have another syntactic structure, called a prepositional object (PO) structure. Many such lists can be compiled with different pairs of alternative structures, for example Active–Passive pairs. I will illustrate with DO/PO pairs. Branigan et al. (2000) set up an experimental discourse game in which two players had to describe scenes on cards to each other. One player was an accomplice of the experimenters and produced a range of carefully controlled sentences; the other player was a genuine experimental subject. After the accomplice had used a sentence with one structure (say DO), the subject tended significantly, describing a different scene, to use a sentence of the same structure. The subject echoed the syntactic structure, but not the actual words, of the accomplice. This shows an effect of discourse on choice of syntactic structure. But this is not an example of discourse actually determining the set of structures from which a choice can be made. Each speaker independently has a store of syntactic structures, a similar store, in fact. Speakers select items from their grammatical stores to compose their contributions to a discourse. The phenomenon of syntactic priming is now well established: other relevant studies are Corley and Scheepers (2002); Pickering and Branigan (1998); Smith and Wheeldon (2001). Savage et al. (2003) have shown that priming for abstract grammatical patterns, such as the passive construction, works for six-year-olds, but not for younger children.

Going back as far as the early days of generative grammar, syntacticians have occasionally used discourse evidence in syntactic argumentation. For example, an early central textbook (Jacobs and Rosenbaum 1968, p. 154) argues for a particular sentence structure by appealing to what are appropriate conversational answers to questions. For sure, not all syntacticians delve into these kinds of facts, because not all of the syntactic properties of expressions are influenced by discourse factors. Chomsky, for example, has not to my knowledge researched these kinds of cases, and might consider them less interesting than examples involving purely intra-sentential relations. To each his own research emphasis. In parallel, specialists in discourse analysis, who focus, for instance, on the overall coherence of long texts, are not concerned much with intra-sentential structure, such as gender agreement between a French noun and a modifying adjective. But I do not know of any hardline grammarian arguing that the proper study of syntax has no business considering discourse factors where relevant. If any such characters exist, they are a small minority.

Merchant's case of *dem Lehrer* versus **den Lehrer* as an appropriate answer to *Wem folgt Hans?* follows from a purely syntactic fact about German, which manifests itself in discourse as well as intra-sententially. The verb *folgen* requires an object in the Dative case. In the history of syntactic theory, however, certain classes of facts that have for decades been held to be such purely syntactic facts can now be plausibly argued to be intra-sentential reflections of principles of discourse. The most prominent case is that of Island Constraints. One of the most widely respected 'results' of the generative enterprise was John Ross's (1967) discovery that so-called 'movement rules', such as the rule that puts an English *Wh*-question word at the beginning of a sentence, are subject to very specific grammatical restrictions. For example, the echo question, with incredulous intonation, *John saw WHO and Bill?* is OK, but you can't move the *Wh*-question word to the front to give **WHO did John see and Bill?*. For almost three decades after Ross's thesis, such facts were cited as one of the significant discoveries of generative grammar. They are indeed facts, and on the face of things rather puzzling facts. Their apparent arbitrariness fed the belief that the syntactic systems of languages are substantially autonomous, with their own purely syntactic principles, not motivated by non-syntactic factors such as discourse function. As early as 1975, however, Morgan (1975) observed some overlaps between such facts and discourse facts. He pointed out that similar grammatical environments are involved in describing appropriate answers to questions in discourse as are involved in so-called 'movement' rules in sentential syntax. As Morgan's examples require a lot of background explanation, I will not go into them here; the topic of Island Constraints will be taken up later, in Chapter 4. The message to be taken now is that the interpenetration of syntax and discourse/pragmatics works in both directions. Some genuinely pure syntactic facts, like the German Dative case-assignment by *folgen*, can reach outward from sentences into discourse practice. On the other hand, as will be argued more specifically later, some principles of discourse reach inward into details of sentence structure. This should not be surprising, as the natural habitat of sentences is in utterances embedded in discourse.

A large proportion of the most interesting data in syntax derives from the communicative use of sentences between people. The three major sentence types, declarative, interrogative, and imperative, exist as formally distinct because people need to make it clear when they are giving information, requesting information, or issuing orders. Different syntactic constructions are associated with different direct pragmatic effects. For example, the English interrogative main clause pattern with Subject–Auxiliary inversion as in *Have you had your tea?* is linked with the pragmatic function of a **direct** question. I emphasize that it is the direct pragmatic functions that are associated with constructions, because, as is well known, an utterance with a certain direct pragmatic force may have a different indirect force. On the face of it, *Is the Pope Catholic?* is a direct request for information. But for reasons having nothing to do with the syntax–pragmatics linkage, such a question is taken as a 'rhetorical' question, not requesting information, but jokingly implying that some other fact in the conversational context is (or should be) obvious. Such pragmatic effects, rather than negating any systematic linkage between syntax and pragmatics, are in fact only possible because of that linkage.

Sentences, beside representing propositions in a speaker's mind, are also tailored to be interpreted by hearers who may not share the same knowledge of what is being talked about. (Indeed if it were always the case that a speaker and hearer knew exactly the same facts about the world, and were currently attending to the same portion of the world, there would be no point in saying anything. Under such conditions, language as we know it would not have evolved.) Syntactic phenomena that have attracted a great share of interest among generative syntacticians over the years are just those where sentences deviate from bland neutral structure. The first sentence below has such a bland neutral form; the rest express the same proposition but in syntactically more interesting ways. (Emphatic stress is indicated by capital letters).[6]

1. *John gave Mary a BOOK*
2. *John gave MARY a book*
3. *John GAVE Mary a book*
4. *JOHN gave Mary a book*
5. *It was JOHN who gave Mary a book*
6. *It was a BOOK that John gave Mary*
7. *It was MARY that John gave a book (to)*
8. *As for JOHN, he gave Mary a book*
9. *As for MARY, John gave her a book*
10. *JOHN, he gave Mary a book*

---

[6] 'Emphatic stress' is a woefully simple label for a range of different effects that can be achieved by intonation in English. It will have to do for our purposes here.

11. *MARY, John gave her a book*

12. *A BOOK, John gave Mary/her* (OK in some dialects but not all)

13. *What John gave Mary was a BOOK*

14. *The one who gave Mary a book was JOHN*

15. *The one who John gave a book (to) was MARY*

16. *Mary was given a book (by John)*

17. *A book was given to Mary (by John)*

And there are more permutations of 'stress', word order and grammatical elements than I have listed here. Without such permutations, what would syntacticians theorize about?—Much less. Creider (1979, p. 3) makes the same point: 'discourse factors are probably the major force responsible for the existence and shape of the [syntactic] rules'. Notice some restrictions already in the English data above, for instance that a verb cannot be focused on by the *It*-cleft construction: you can't say **It was GAVE that John Mary a book*. Also, *As for* cannot introduce an indefinite phrase, such as *a book*. And inclusion of the preposition *to* interacts in a complex way with the patterns illustrated. English has this wealth of structures for discourse purposes. Other languages can have a similar range of possibilities, all peculiar to them in various ways.

The discourse concepts involved in such examples are **Topic** and **Focus**. This whole area is dreadfully complex and slippery. I will give simple explanations of common uses of these terms, and steer clear of controversy and problems. The key background ideas are **shared knowledge** and **attention**. Here is an illustrative case. The speaker assumes that the hearer knows some, but not all of the elements of the proposition involved—for example, the hearer may be assumed to know that John gave Mary something, but not to know what he gave her. In this case, sentences (1) (with extra oomph on the stressed word), (6), and (13) would be appropriate. Alternatively, these very same three sentences could be used when the hearer is assumed to know what John gave Mary, but the speaker pro-actively directs the hearer's attention to the salience of the type of object given—for example it was book, not a hat. Here a book is the Focus. The non-Focus remainder of the information expressed may be called a **presupposition**. In general, the Topic and Focus of a sentence do not coincide. The Topic is often defined unsatisfactorily as 'that which the sentence is **about**'. But this won't do, as surely all the above sentences are 'about' all of John, Mary, and a book. Topic is better defined as the part of a proposition that is 'old' information, assumed to be known to both speaker and hearer. In sentences (1), (6), and (13) above, then, the Topic is the assumed fact that John gave Mary something. Conversely the Focus is that part of a proposition that is presumed not to be shared, or to which the speaker wants to draw special attention, that is here, that a book is the object in question. The term 'Topic' is often paired with 'Comment', as in 'Topic/Comment structure'. To a first approximation, at least, Focus and Comment can be equated.

There are dedicated Focus constructions and dedicated Topic constructions. In English, intonation is also specially useful in indicating Focus. As can be seen, English variously uses intonational and word-order devices to signal Focus. In the examples above, the 'It-cleft' (5, 6, 7) and *What*-cleft constructions (13, 14, 15) are focusing constructions. The focusing construction and the intonation have to be compatible. You must stress the element that comes after *was* in sentence (6), hence *It was a book that John gave MARY* is weird at best. You can get double Focus, either with intonation alone, or using one of the focusing constructions along with compatible intonation, as in *What JOHN gave Mary was a BOOK.*[7] The great versatility of intonation in English, lacking in many other languages, allows focused elements sometimes to come at positions other than the end of a sentence. In languages where intonation is not such a flexible tool, the focused element tends to be signalled by a position closer to the end of the sentence than in a bland 'focus-neutral' sentence. In verb-final languages, this marked focus position may be just before the verb, rather than at the very end of the sentence. Kidwai (1999) shows the variety and complexity of focus marking in two Indian languages (Hindi-Urdu and Malayalam, thus from different language families) and two Chadic languages (Western Bade and Tangale); focus may be marked by syntactic position, by intonation or by special morphology. There can be dedicated Focus constructions, like the English *It*-cleft construction, in which the Focus is quite early in the sentence. Famously, in Hungarian, Focus is signalled by a position immediately before the verb, a prime example of the interweaving of discourse and syntax.

The *As for* construction (examples 8, 9) and the 'left-dislocation' examples (10, 11, 12) are topicalizing constructions. Notice the restriction here that the fronted or stressed element must be definite in the *As for* construction (or if indefinite, then generic, as in *As for tigers, they're really scary*), and definiteness is preferred in the left-dislocation construction. This is consistent with the fact that the stressed element is assumed to be known to the hearer. If your hearer doesn't know who John is, you can't use *As for JOHN, he gave Mary a book.* But the hearer is not assumed to know anything more about John; this sentence

---

[7] An exercise for the reader is to note the subtly different intonation contours on the two 'stressed' elements here, and to specify exactly what the speaker assumes the hearer knows.

is appropriate even if the hearer does not know that anyone had received anything from anybody. Here John is the Topic of the sentence, and the rest, that he gave Mary a book, is the Focus, or Comment. One function of the English Passive construction is to make a non-Agent the Topic of a sentence, as in *Mary was given a book*. Topicalizing constructions in languages generally put the topicalized element at or near the front of the sentence. 'Although the preference to place topics preverbally seems to be universal, there is language-specific variation in the exact position before the verb that the topic takes' (Van Bergen and de Hoop 2009, p. 173). In English there are other stylistic possibilities. *That fellow, he's crazy* and *He's crazy, that fellow* both have the fellow as Topic. Things get more complicated when a Focus construction, such as *It*-cleft, combines with a Topic construction, such as Passive, as in *It was MARY that was given a book*. I will not delve into such complications, apart from noting that sometimes a choice of which constructions to use is not wholly dictated by the shared knowledge of speaker and hearer. In this last example, the choice of Passive may be due to syntactic priming by a Passive construction used just earlier by another speaker.

This ends the mini-tutorial on Topic and Focus. The take-away lesson is that many facts of central interest to syntacticians exist for discourse reasons, because of the communicative purposes to which language is put, in settings where the interlocutors have differing knowledge and may seek to steer the discourse in chosen directions. As an end-note here, to foreshadow a later theme, the importance of pragmatic and contextual motivation for syntax also means that a good syntactic theory should be well-tailored to stating the pragmatic import of grammatical constructions. A set of ideas under the banner of 'Construction Grammar' seems to meet this requirement: 'Constructional approaches to grammar have shown that the interpretation of linguistic utterances can involve an interaction of grammar and context which vastly exceeds in complexity, formal structure and wealth of interpretive content the data discussed in the standard linguistic and philosophical literature on indexicals' (Kay 2004, p. 675). A more detailed exposition of Construction Grammar approaches, and their aptness for seeing syntax in an evolutionary light will be given in section 7 of the next chapter.

3.3 Speech evolved first

Speech is the primary modality of human language; we are not concerned here with the more elaborate standards of written languages. Nobody, except a few deaf people, learns to write before they learn to speak. Some of the erudite constructions special to written language will rarely occur, if at all, in spontaneous, natural, informal speech—for example constructions as in the following:

John and Bill are married to Mary and Sue, respectively.
My best efforts notwithstanding, I failed.

More widely, take any sentence from an academic book, like this one, and try to imagine it spoken in a conversation. It will generally sound too stilted. But this is largely a matter of the unusual length of written sentences, much longer than typical spoken sentences. Most written sentences are formed from the same basic constructions as spoken ones—they just do more conjoining and embedding of these constructions, producing longer sentences. A prominent writer on the differences between spoken and written language takes the view that the basic kinds of constructions that syntacticians consider, for example relative clauses and other forms of subordination, do occur in unplanned spoken language (Miller 2005a, 2005b).

Spoken language evolved at least tens of millennia before writing appeared about 5,000 years ago. So the first target of an evolutionary account should be the grammar of spoken language, a point made forcibly by John Schumann (2007) and Talmy Givón (2002). Further, we must not take the utterances of educated people in formal situations as our central model of spoken language. Accomplished performers, such as one hears interviewed on radio and TV, can spin out impressively long sentences, perhaps lasting up to a minute, with well-formed parenthesized asides, several levels of embedding, and many conjoined clauses and phrases, ending in a perfect intonational period. It is fun (for a grammarian at least) to try to track the course of utterances like this. At the beginning of an aside, marked by an intonational break, and an apparent break in the expected straightforward continuation of the words before, one wonders 'Will he manage to get back to his main sentence?' And as often as not, the politician or cultural commentator accomplishes this grammatical gymnastic feat flawlessly. Elected politicians who perform less ably are pilloried by satirists. The fact that even some prominent politicians have trouble with long sentences indicates that an ability to acquire command of long or very complex sentences is not a universal feature of human language capacity. This echoes the idea of quantitative constraints on competence, already mentioned in Chapter 1, and to be taken up again below.

Hesitation markers, variously spelled as *uhm* or *er* and the like, are characteristic of speech, and are usually thought of as not participating in the formal structure of a language. Hesitation markers are nevertheless conventionalized. People with different accents hesitate differently. In Scottish English, the hesitation marker is a long mid-front vowel, as in *bed*, whereas a speaker with a London accent uses a mid-central 'schwa' vowel, as in the second syllable of *sofa*. At the margins of linguistic structure, there can be rules for the integration of hesitation markers. An example is the vowel in the English definite article *the* when it precedes a hesitation marker. This word is pronounced two ways, depending on the following sound, with a 'schwa' sound [ə], as in *the man* [ðəmæn], or with a [i] vowel, as in *the egg* [ðiɛg]. Interestingly, this rule also applies before a hesitation marker, which begins with a vowel, so people hesitate with [ðiəːm], *the uhm*. This is a phonological rule. There are no syntactic rules applying to hesitation markers, although there are certain statistical tendencies relating to the structural positions where they may occur.

A few of the constructions, and combinations of constructions, around which theoretical syntactic debate has swirled, especially in the early days of generative grammar, are quite unnatural as spoken language. Here are some examples:

They proved that insufficient in itself to yield the result. (Postal 1974, p. 196)
That Harry is a Greek is believed by Lucy. (Grinder 1972, p. 89)
The shooting of an elephant by a hunter occurred frequently (Fraser 1970, p. 95)

In the exuberance of early syntactic theorizing in the late 1960s and early 1970s, examples like these were more common than they are now in theoretical debate. My impression is that Chomsky typically avoided particularly artificial examples. Any sampling of the example sentences in a syntax textbook or treatise from the last forty years quickly shows that the great majority of examples on which theoretical arguments are based are perfectly simple ordinary everyday constructions. It is true that one can find unnaturally artificial examples in papers on syntactic theory, and these tend to be picked upon by people sceptical of the generative approach. Dąbrowska (1997), for example, aimed 'to show that the ability to process complex syntactic structures of the kind that one encounters in the [generative] literature is far from universal, and depends to a large degree on the amount of schooling that one has had' (pp. 737–8). Such criticisms of the generative approach tend to come from scholars advocating a 'more empirical', less intuition-based methodology. But, taken as an empirical hypothesis about the generative linguistic literature, Dąbrowska's sampling method is informal. Any such hypothesis needs to characterize 'structures of the kind that one encounters in the generative literature' fairly. One of her experimental examples was *The mayor who Julie warned after learning the ex-prisoner wanted to interrogate managed to get away*, and the subjects were asked such questions as 'Who wanted to interrogate someone?', 'Who was supposed to have been interrogated?', and 'Who managed to get away?' I'm sure I'd do badly on such an example. Dąbrowska writes: 'All test sentences were based on examples drawn from *Linguistic Inquiry*' (p. 739). Yes, but **how** 'drawn from'? Were the test sentences really **typical** of the data on which generative argumentation is based? The argument needs a rigorously unbiased sampling of the data cited in *Linguistic Inquiry*.[8] Sometimes, to alleviate monotony, a linguist will use an example with somewhat exotic vocabulary, as in Chomsky's: *It is unimaginable for there to be a unicorn in the garden.* This is indeed stilted, but the vocabulary masks the fact that the syntactic construction in question is quite ordinary, being the same as in *It's unusual for there to be a Greek in my class.*

The case against a typical syntactician's approach is put by John Schumann thus:

A linguist, in trying to understand the human ability to produce and comprehend embedded relative clauses, might construct the following set of sentences:

(1) The professor published a book in 2005.

(2) The visiting professor published a book in 2005.

(3) The visiting professor that Bob knew as an undergraduate published a book in 2005.

(4) The visiting professor that Bob knew as an undergraduate and who recently received a travel fellowship published a book in 2005.

On the basis of the research reviewed earlier in this article, we know that as soon as we get to sentence (3), we are no longer dealing with utterances that are characteristic of oral language. We know that with training (schooling), English speakers can produce and comprehend sentences such as (3) and (4), but we have to ask whether studying the structure of such sentences tells us anything about the basic human capacity for language that must have developed millennia before the advent of literacy and formal education. (Schumann 2007, p. 285)

In relation to arguments and examples such as this, we need to ask whether the difference between spoken and written language, and between informal speech and trained formal speech, is a **qualitative** difference or a difference of **degree**. The main problem with examples (3) and (4) above is length, not unusual or difficult structure. Modifiers like *visiting*, *travel*, and *recently* and adjunct

---

[8] Dąbrowska's experimental setup was also quite artificial, with subjects being asked to judge sentences out of any discourse context relevant to their lives. Her results are important, as they tell us about individual variation in linguistic competence, a topic to which I will return in section 3.5.

phrases like *in 2005* and *as an undergraduate* fill out the length of sentence (4), placing a burden on processing not usually tolerated in informal dialogue. The *and* in sentence (4) is also a mark of formality, which might help to clarify the meaning of the sentence out of a conversational context. Strip these away, and replace the rather formal *received* with *got* and you get

The professor that Bob knew who got a fellowship published a book.

This is not so implausible in a conversation; and it would be even more typical of everyday language if we used exactly the same structure in a message about a less academic topic, not involving a professor, a fellowship and publication of a book, as in

A chap I know who smokes a pipe has cancer.
A guy that Bob knew who bought a Ferrari left his wife.

What is atypical about Schumann's example (4) is not its structure, but its length, and the degree to which it has piled basic grammatical patterns together in a single sentence. Each separate structural pattern is simple and easy to produce or interpret. There is nothing structurally exotic about any individual structural device used. It is just that people in normal conversation do not combine so many structural elements in the same sentence. As a rough analogy, laying one brick on another on firm ground is unproblematic, and we can even make a stable stack up to about four or five bricks high, but after that the tower is increasingly unstable. A more cognitive analogy, closer to language, is the number of moves ahead that a chess player can foresee; the rules for possible moves don't vary, but all players have some numerical limit on how far they can plan ahead.

Schumann's critique is typical of many who voice exasperation with syntactic theory. There is a danger of throwing out the baby with the bathwater. Tomasello (2003, p. 3) writes, in a slogan-like section heading, 'Spoken language does not work like written language'.[9] While recognizing the primacy of speech, and a certain artificiality in written language, spoken and written language obviously have much in common. There is empirical psycholinguistic evidence that writing and speech make use of the same representations of syntactic constructions. Cleland and Pickering (2006) report 'three experiments that use syntactic priming to investigate whether writing and speaking use the

---

[9] I agree with almost all the detailed points of Tomasello's article, but judge that he overrates the paradigm shift to 'Cognitive-Functional (Usage-Based) Linguistics'. When the dust settles, a combination of usage-based approaches and traditional, even generative, methods will be seen to be useful, as I hope much in this chapter will show.

same mechanisms to construct syntactic form. People tended to repeat syntactic form between modality (from writing to speaking and speaking to writing) to the same extent that they did within either modality. The results suggest that the processor employs the same mechanism for syntactic encoding in written and spoken production, and that use of a syntactic form primes structural features concerned with syntactic encoding that are perceptually independent' (p. 185). There is also evidence from pathological studies that spoken and written comprehension are equally impaired in some conditions regardless of the modality:

[T]he comprehension problems of children with Landau-Kleffner syndrome[10] are not restricted to the auditory modality, but are also found when written or signed presentation is used. Grammatical structure of a sentence has a strong effect on comprehension of sentences, whereas the modality in which the sentence is presented has no effect.

(Bishop 1982, p. 14)

Several individual pathological cases suggest that in some respects speech and writing have different grammatical representations. 'We describe an individual who exhibits greater difficulties in speaking nouns than verbs and greater difficulties in writing verbs than nouns across a range of both single word and sentence production tasks' (Rapp and Caramazza 2002, p. 373). Three other individual cases are reported in Caramazza and Hillis (1991) and Rapp and Caramazza (1998). These last authors (2002) list seven other pathological case studies indicating dissociations between grammatical representation (or processing) of speech and writing. I conclude that in normal functioning and in some pathologies speech and writing share the same representations, but some types of brain damage, not common, can disrupt the sharing arrangements (an admittedly vague formulation).

Certainly, some constructions are overwhelmingly found in written language. An example is the English 'Gapping' construction,[11] as in *John ate an apple and Mary a peach*, where an implicit *ate* is omitted from the second clause, understood as *Mary ate a peach*. Tao and Meyer (2006) found, after an extensive search of corpora, that 'gapping is confined to writing rather than speech'. In the Elia Kazan movie *The Last Tycoon*, a powerful film director rejects a scene in which a French actress is given the line 'Nor I you', on the grounds that this is unnatural speech. But his colleague, with earthier instincts,

---

[10] Landau-Kleffner syndrome is a childhood language disorder associated with epilepsy (Landau and Kleffner 1957).

[11] For convenience in the next few paragraphs, I will continue to refer to 'the gapping construction' as if it were a unitary phenomenon, a matter of some dispute.

comments on this line with 'Those foreign women really have class'.[12] This
rings true. The gapping construction is classy, and restricted to quite elevated
registers, though it is not lacking entirely from spoken English.

   For the origins of grammar, we are not primarily interested in such constructions as gapping, which probably arose late in the history of languages,
predominantly in their written forms, and only in some languages. This is
absolutely not to deny the value of studies of the gapping construction and their
relevance to the wider study of language.[13] Once mentioned, sentences with the
gapping construction can be readily interpreted. You surely had no problem
with interpreting the example above, while simultaneously being aware of its
stilted bookish character. And though the construction is limited almost exclusively to written texts, educated people have no trouble applying consistent
judgements to examples presented auditorily. Carlson (2002) experimented
with undergraduates at the University of Massachusetts, and got consistent
results from them when they heard gapped sentences with various intonation
contours. The patterns of grammaticality discussed by linguists are almost
unfailingly consistent with educated native speakers' intuitive judgements. For
example Culicover and Jackendoff (2005, p. 276) mention the fact that in
reply to the question *Who plays what instrument?*, an acceptable answer is
Katie the kazoo, and Robin the rebec, while just **Katie the kazoo* is not
acceptable. This example is a microcosm of a theoretical divide in syntax,
showing a tension between good intentions and old habits. On the one hand,
Culicover and Jackendoff laudably consider evidence from spoken dialogue.
However, what may be offputting to those unsympathetic to typical syntactic
theorizing is the contrived nature of the example, with its *Katie/kazoo* and
Robin/rebec alliteration; and whoever has heard of a rebec?—not me. I guess
syntacticians use faintly humorous examples like this to relieve the hard work
of analysing language, and to revel in its productivity. But don't let such trivial
considerations lead you to believe that there are not solid linguistic facts here.
Next time you are with a party in a restaurant trying to coordinate who wants
what to eat, persist with the *Who wants what?* question, and I bet you'll sooner

---

   [12] The movie was based on an unfinished novel by F. Scott Fitzgerald. A young
Robert de Niro played the powerful director Monroe Stahr, Robert Mitchum his earthy
colleague Pat Brady, and Jeanne Moreau the classy sexy Frenchwoman Didi. (How
much trouble did you have with the gapping in that sentence?)
   [13] Examples of the large productive literature on the gapping construction include
Carlson et al. (2005); Coppock (2001); Johnson (2000); McCawley (1993); Ross
(1970a); Siegel (1984) . John Ross (1970a) classically showed certain regular correlations across languages between word order and gapping constructions.

or later get an answer like *Dave tacos and Anna enchiladas*, but you are much less likely to get just *Dave tacos*.

In places later in this book, I will use examples drawn from *The Newcastle Electronic Corpus of Tyneside English (NECTE)*, a corpus of dialect speech from Tyneside in north-east England.[14] The informants for this corpus all spoke with Geordie accents, were listed as working class or lower middle class, and had no university or college education. Often they were reminiscing about the old days, or commenting on contemporary life in the 1990s. I use this corpus for somewhat complex examples to avoid the risk of artificiality or fabrication for features that I claim are natural and spontaneous. It is clear from the corpus that some quite complex syntactic structures can be attested in the spontaneous spoken language of relatively uneducated speakers. For simpler examples, I will, uncontroversially I hope, keep to the linguist's practice of rolling my own.

3.4 Message packaging--sentence-like units

Syntax is defined as a level of linguistic analysis based on a unit larger than a word and smaller than a discourse. There is no serious doubting that units of this intermediate size are psychologically real, that is used by people in packaging their thoughts for communication. Though the cases are different in many ways, recall nightingale song (Chapter 1, especially p. 62) with a level defined by a single song, intermediate between smaller notes and larger 'song-packages' and still larger context groups.

The common currency of spoken linguistic dialogue is not traditional whole sentences, but small sentence-like units, or clauses, with propositional content. Brief note on linguists' terminology: those last five words (beginning with *Brief*) weren't technically a sentence, because there wasn't a verb. Putting *Here's a* at the beginning would have made it a sentence, with the same meaning. It is common in speech to use elliptical sentences like this, with parts omitted, sometimes even the verb. The simplest (non-elliptical) sentence is also a **clause**. More complex sentences are built up by combining clauses, just as this sentence is. A complex sentence has a main clause, and one or more subordinate clauses, which come in various kinds. One kind is a relative clause, as in the underlined parts of *Jack knew the kid who shot Kennedy*. They can be

---

[14] The corpus website is http://www.ncl.ac.uk/necte/. The format is not easy, but not impossible, to use.

piled up as in *Jack's the guy who shot the kid who killed Kennedy*. Sometimes in speech you'll even hear a stack of relative clauses like this. Another kind of subordinate clause is a complement clause, attached to a noun or a verb. Examples of complement clauses are the underlined parts of these sentences: *The idea that parents know best is old-fashioned* or *You know that I'm right*. A little word such as *that* introducing complement clauses is called a 'complementizer'. One more common kind of subordinate clause is an adverbial clause, often stating when, how, why, or if something happened, as in the underlined parts of these sentences: *If John comes, I'm leaving*, or *He left because he felt ill*. None of the examples just given was particularly exotic, and they could all easily have occurred in conversational speech. All were, in a technical sense, complex sentences, because they contained subordinate clauses.

Miller and Weinert (1998) argue, quite plausibly, that the clause is a more fitting unit for the grammatical analysis of speech than the sentence. A lot of psycholinguistic literature on speech production also reinforces the view that the planning of spoken utterances involves units at a clausal level (Ford and Holmes 1978; Meyer 1996). In speech, people are not too careful about signalling the way one clause is inserted into another, which may be left unclear. In speech there is no equivalent of the capital letter or the full stop or period, although intonation contours play a very similar role in marking the ends of clauses. Miller and Weinert give this example transcribed from spontaneous speech, with the pauses marked by '+' signs.

I used to light up a cigarette + you see because that was a very quiet way to go + now when I lit up my cigarette I used to find myself at Churchill + and the quickest way to get back from Churchill was to walk along long down Clinton Road + along + along Blackford something or other it's actually an extension of Dick Place but it's called Blackford something or other it shouldn't be it's miles away from Blackford Hill + but it's called Blackford Road I think + uhm then along to Lauder Road and down Lauder Road...   (Miller and Weinert 1998, p. 29)

Hearing this rambling narrative, with its intonation, would make it easier to understand (and knowing the geography of Edinburgh also helps). But although the overall structural marking here is very informal, there is nevertheless a lot of quite complex syntax apparent in it, including several subordinate clauses of different kinds. There are many clear cases of simple clause, with subject, verb, sometimes an object, and sometimes various modifiers, all distributed in the normal English manner. The speaker is obviously a competent native English speaker; he doesn't make foreign-like or child-like errors.

In conversation, people often leave their sentences unfinished, or one person's incomplete sentence is finished by someone else, or people speak in noun phrases or short clauses, or even isolated words. The following are typical meaningful bits of English dialogue, in some context or other.

Two o'clock, then.
There!
Mary.
Coming, ready or not.
Away with you!
Who, me?

No language, however, consists only of such expressions as these. Normal adult speakers of any language are also capable of expressing the same thoughts, if the occasion demands, in full sentences, like this:

I'll see you at two o'clock, then.
Look there!
It was Mary.
I'm coming, whether you're ready or not.
Get away with you!
Who do you mean? Do you mean me?

Some people are not often in situations where such complete explicitness is appropriate, but even teenagers, even those we like to caricature as least articulate, are capable of expressing themselves in sentences and quite often do. Eavesdrop objectively on the casual chat of strangers. True, you will hear interruptions, hesitations, false starts and muddled sentences whose ends don't quite fit their beginnnings. But you will also hear a lot of perfectly well-formed clauses, and even quite a few fluent whole sentences. Remember, of course, that the speakers may not speak a standard variety of their language, and that different dialects have different rules. Sentences liberally peppered with *like* and *y'know* have rules, believe it or not, for where these little particles can occur, and how they contribute to the overall meaning conveyed (Schourup 1985; Siegel 2002). Pawley and Syder (1975, 1976) have proposed a 'one clause at a time' constraint on speech production. Reporting their work, Wray and Grace (2007, p. 560) write 'Pawley and Syder (2000), based on the patterns in spontaneous speech, conclude that processing constraints prevent us from constructing anything beyond the scope of a simple clause of six words or so without dysfluency'. This may be true, but people nevertheless produce much longer syntactically coherent strings (albeit with a few pauses and slowdowns) in spontaneous conversational speech. Despite some dysfluency, speakers are able to keep track of their grammatical commitments over much longer stretches. See many examples in the next chapter, collected from a corpus of spoken English.

At the start of this section I used the metaphor of the 'currency' of spoken linguistic dialogue. That metaphor can be pushed a bit further, to resolve a possible point of contention. Here goes with pushing the metaphor. The currency of trade in the USA is US dollars. If you owe someone a dollar, you can pay them in any appropriate combination of cents, nickels, dimes, and quarters, or with a dollar bill. The coins you use to make the payment are a way of **packaging** the currency unit that you owe. Obviously, the different ways of making the payment can be more or less convenient to you or the payee, but any way you repay the dollar meets at least one social obligation. The **semantic** currency of spoken dialogue is sentence-like units with propositional content, as the currency of the USA is the dollar. On the other hand, the discourse/phonological 'coinage' of spoken dialogue may package the currency in different ways, using units of different types, such as intonational units and conversational turns. The currency/coinage analogy is not perfect, of course, but may illuminate some comparative facts about languages that we will see in Chapter 5. The Pirahã language of Amazonia can express the complex of propositions implicit in *John's brother's house*, but not in the same concise package as English, with embedded possessives. Early forms of Nicaraguan Sign Language package the proposition(s) in *The man pushed the woman* as what appears to be a sequence of clauses, MAN PUSH WOMAN FALL. (More on such examples in Chapter 5.)

George Grace (1987) has written a thought-provoking book in which he challenges many of the standard assumptions of mainstream linguistics. His title, *The Linguistic Construction of Reality*,[15] is enough to hint at his direction. It is noteworthy, however, that he accepts that human language is packaged into sentence-like units. 'The sentence is the linguistic unit whose function it is to serve as the vehicle of speech acts' (p. 28). Indeed, the very fact that we package our message into discrete units is the start of the 'linguistic construction of reality'. The real world is not neatly packaged. Grace assumes the validity of 'conceptual events', which are the semantic packages expressed by sentence-like units. His most basic example of a conceptual event is what we assume to be the common shared mental representation of a dog biting a man. I should better say 'a stereotypical dog stereotypically biting a stereotypical

---

[15] Long before, Nietzsche (1873) articulated the profoundly challenging implications of our linguistic construction of reality.

man'. Grace's title is a bit of a come-on. He doesn't deny the existence of some external reality, which we don't construct. His point is rather that we humans are disposed to carve up this reality differently from other organisms with other sensory kit and other life-goals.

There is some human-universality in how we carve up actions and events into manageable packages. Schleidt and Kien (1997) analysed film of 'the behavior of 444 people (women, men, and children) of five cultures (European, Yanomami Indians, Trobriand Islanders, Himbara, Kalahari Bushmen)' (p. 7). Based on careful definitions and cross-checking by independent analysts, they found that 'human action units are organized within a narrow and well-definable time span of only a few seconds. Though varying from 0.3 seconds up to 12 seconds or more, most of the action units fall within the range of 1–4 seconds' (pp. 80–1). These are results about the production of action; not surprisingly, similar timing applies also to our perception of events. Much work by Ernst Pöppel and others[16] has shown a period lasting about 3 seconds as packaging our perceptions of events. See also p. 96 of *The Origins of Meaning*. When it comes to describing events as our action-production and event-perception mechanisms deliver them, we humans carve up this external reality in somewhat different ways depending on the words and sentence structures that our languages make available. Well-known cases include the difference between the preferred English *He swam across the river* and the preferred Spanish *Cruzó el río a nado*. Another example is Arabic verb roots, which often convey either an action or the resulting state, depending on the inflection. Thus for instance English *put on* (of clothes) and *wear* are both translated by the same Arabic verb, with an *l-b-s* root. Note that these examples involve differences in what information is coded into verbs. Gentner (1981) makes a perceptive observation about how different languages may package information. She calls it her principle of 'differential compositional latitude'.

In a given perceptual scene, different languages tend to agree in the way in which they conflate perceptual information into concrete objects, which are then lexicalized as nouns. There is more variation in the way in which languages conflate relational components into the meanings of verbs and other predicates. To put it another way, verb conflations are less tightly constrained by the perceptual world than concrete noun conflations. Loosely speaking, noun meanings are given to us by the world; verb meanings are more free to vary across languages.[17]   (Gentner 1981, p. 169)

---

[16] For example, Woodrow (1951); Borsellino et al. (1972); Pöppel (1978, 1997); Ditzinger and Haken (1989); Pöppel and Wittmann (1999).

[17] I will say more about syntactic categories such as Noun and Verb in Ch.4, sec.4, including more on psychological differences between nouns and verbs.

I would gloss Grace's theme, less provocatively, as 'The Linguistic **Selection** of Reality'. Humans' selection of what is a 'sayable thing' (Grace's nice phrase) is partly determined by their language. 'Grammatical structure with its concomitant complexity is not a straightforward tool for the communication of pre-existing messages; rather to a large degree, our grammars actually define the messages that we end up communicating to one another' (Gil 2009, p. 32).[18] But when humans select what to say, they all package their messages into units that are reasonably described as sentence-like, or better clause-like. The grammatical packages may be of somewhat different typical sizes in different languages. We saw some examples at the end of the last paragraph, and we shall see some more in Chapter 5.

There is a solid psychological limit on the number of entities that can be involved in a simple proposition. The limit is 'the magical number 4', argued by Hurford (2007, pp. 90–6) to be 'derived from the limits of our ancient visual attention system, which only allows us to keep track of a maximum of four separate objects in a given scene'. Respecting this limit avoids some of the circularity in the definitions of propositions and simple sentences (clauses). I hold that sentence/clause-like units, across languages, fall within a narrow size-range, and moreover, fall within a narrow range of possible form–meaning structural correspondences. This is unfortunately vague, as I have little idea how quantitatively to compare the actual range with the the logically conceivable space of possible clause-sizes. In theoretical predicate logic, no upper bound is placed on the number of arguments that a logical predicate may take. Logicians not concerned with the empirical limits of human psychology admit the theoretical possibility of a million-place predicate. However, in practice their examples are comfortingly down-to-earth and of language-like sizes, with the number of arguments rarely exceeding three. Pawley (1987) chooses to take a more pessimistic view of the prospects for making any very informative statement about human message-packaging. Based on a comparison of English and Kalam, a New Guinea Highlands language, he concludes 'there is no universal set of episodic conceptual events. Indeed, it seems that languages may vary enormously in the kind of resources they have for the characterization of episodes and other complex events' (Pawley 1987, p. 351). Asking for a universal set of anything in language is asking too much. More profitable is to try to discern the probabilistic distributions of linguistic phenomena within some theoretically conceivable space. And Pawley's 'enormously' is a subjective judgement, of course. He does concede some overlap between English and Kalam.

---

[18] Slobin's (1996) ideas about 'Thinking for Speaking' relate closely to the same idea.

Kalam and English do share a body of more or less isomorphic conceptual events and situations, namely *those which both languages may express by a single clause.* This common core presumably reflects certain characteristics of the external world and human experience that are salient for people everywhere. But it is a *fairly small core*, in relation to the total set which English can reduce to a single clause expression.

(Pawley 1987, p. 356)

Givón (1991) has an insightful discussion of how to define 'clause', 'proposition', and 'conceptual event' in a non-circular way. He opposes Pawley's extreme position, and proposes an empirical approach to the issue, bringing phonology, specifically intonation and pauses, into the picture. There is a rough correspondence between single intonation contours and clauses. Think of the typical way of intoning the nursery rhyme *This is the farmer—sowing his corn—that kept the cock—that crowed in the morn....* (We shall see this whole rhyme again later.) Humans are like other mammals in the approximate size of their action and perception packages:

We have shown that structuring a movement into segments of around 1 to 5 seconds appears to be a mammalian characteristic....In humans, this time segmentation is found in perception as well as in action. It is also found in highly conscious and intentional behavior, like speech, work, communication and ritual, as well as in behavior we are less aware of. (Schleidt and Kien 1997, pp. 101–2)

Not surprisingly, the typical size of a basic grammatical package for expressing a conceptual event coincides with a single intonation 'tune'. Fenk-Oczlon and Fenk (2002) point out the coincidence in size of action units, perceived events, intonation units,and basic clauses. This illustrates well the interdependence of levels in language structure. Semantic, grammatical,and phonological factors cohere.

Conversational analysis (CA) has taken phonology, and specifically pauses, as a clue to the basic unit of conversation. Syntax and conversational analysis are different, but neighbouring, research domains, with complementary methodologies. They are not rival theories of language. Both have their part to play in a larger account. A lasting focus of CA is the nature of the conversational turn. Schegloff (1996) uses the term *turn-constructional unit* instead of *unit-type* used earlier by Sacks et al. (1974). The intersection of syntax and CA is seen in this statement by Sacks et al. (1974, p. 702): 'Unit-types for English include sentential, clausal, phrasal, and lexical constructions'. Two decades later, the same theme of the links between syntax and CA is still a focus: 'We propose to explore the role of syntax, intonation, and conversational pragmatics in the construction of the interactionally validated units of talk known as turns.... Indeed, we assume that they work together and interact in complex ways' (Ford and Thompson 1996, pp. 136–7). It is not the business of syntax to describe or define conversational turns; and it is not the business of conversational analysis to decribe or define types of grammatical unit such as sentence, clause, or phrase. Synchronically, there is an asymmetric relationship between syntax and CA, in that CA may find grammatical notions useful in defining conversational turns, but syntax does not (synchronically) need to appeal to any notions defined within CA. Diachronically, the situation is probably somewhat different. The typical length of a sentence in a culturally evolved language can be partly explained by the typical length of a conversational turn, itself no doubt influenced by limitations on working memory.

To say that the **semantic** currency of dialogue in language is sentence-like units with propositional content is not to say very much. By 'propositional content', I mean that utterances **say something about some thing** (which can be some quite abstract 'thing' or 'things'). 'There must be something to talk about and something must be said about this subject of discourse once it is selected. This distinction is of such fundamental importance that the vast majority of languages have emphasized it by creating some sort of formal barrier between the two terms of the proposition' (Sapir 1921, p. 119). The idea of a propositional basis for language is not peculiar to generative linguists, so is not part of any possible formalist bias. A critic of generative approaches, Givón (1990, p. 896) writes that something like 'a mental proposition, under whatever guise, is the basic unit of mental information storage'. The idea is common to most psycholinguistic approaches that need to assume basic units of communication in language. If the examples above were uttered in a plausible real-life situation, they would all be understood as predicating some property or relation of one or more entities. The hearer of 'Look there!', for example, understands that she, the hearer, is to look somewhere; looking is predicated, in some desired state of affairs, of the addressee. Even if one just says 'Mary', this is not an act of pure reference—the hearer will know from the context what is being said about Mary, or if she doesn't, she will probably ask 'What about Mary?' and get a fuller, more sentence-like, answer. This may stretch the usual sense of 'predication', which is sometimes taken necessarily to involve an assertion, that is to have a truth value. Only declaratives may be true or false; imperative and interrogative sentences can't be literally true or false. But obviously questions and commands, just as much as statements, are about things. In order to accommodate interrogative and imperative sentences (questions and commands) as well as declaratives (statements), it is most profitable to speak of all these sentence types as having **propositional content**. So the propositional content of the imperative *Look there!* is the same as that of the declarative *You will look there*. The difference in meaning is a matter, not of what property is predicated of what person, but of the illocutionary force with which the sentence is normally used. The standard analysis (Searle 1979; Vanderveken 1990) is that interrogative, imperative,and declarative sentences all have propositional content, in which something is predicated of something. The difference is the pragmatic use to which these sentences are put, to try to make the world comply with the proposition involved, in the case of imperatives, or to ask a hearer to comment on the truth of a proposition, as in the case of a *Yes/No* question, like *Are you coming?*

I have a terminological quibble with Culicover and Jackendoff (2005) over the term 'sentence'. Under the heading 'Nonsentential utterance types', they list examples such as the following (pp. 236–7):

Off with his head!
A good talker, your friend Bill
Seatbelts fastened!
What, me worry?
One more beer and I'm leaving
The Red Sox four, the Yankees three.

In this connection, they argue (and I agree with them, except on a detail of terminology) against 'the idea that underlying every elliptical utterance has to be a Sentence, that is a tensed clause' (p. 236). They equate 'Sentence' with an abstract, apparently pre-theoretical concept of 'the category S' (p. 237). This is a curious hangover from earlier generative grammar. 'The category S' is not an empirically given entity; in much generative grammar this theoretical construct is essentially tied to a node in a tree marking tense (e.g. Past or Present). But on a wider view of languages, and what people generally mean by 'sentence', we cannot insist on a necessary connection between sentences and tense markers. Many languages have no markers of tense; Chinese is the best known example. A linguistic expression lacking tense, but expressing a proposition, can at least be said to be 'sentence-like'. All the examples just listed have propositional content, embedded in expressions with varying illocutionary force, such as ordering (for *Off with his head!*), or questioning (for *What me, worry?*) or asserting (for *A good talker, your friend*). I will continue to call such expressions 'sentence-like'.

A tiny minority of expressions in any language do not express any proposition, that is have no descriptive or predicative content, but just have illocutionary force, that is just carry out socially significant acts. English examples are *Hello, Ouch!, Blimey!* and *Damn!* These have little or no syntax and are conventionalized evolutionary relics of animal cries, now vastly overshadowed in all human groups by syntactic language expressing propositions. I put

Culicover and Jackendoff's examples *Hey, Phil!* and *Yoohoo, Mrs Goldberg!* in this category of expressions with purely illocutionary meaning, that is with no predicative content, although the proper names in them are referring expressions. From an evolutionary perspective, these can be seen as primitive, merely combining an attention-getting marker with a referring expression. Languages exhibit **layering**. Some expressions are of a more ancient, primitive type than others. Culicover and Jackendoff's example *How about a cup of coffee?* is also apparently a somewhat transitional case. It certainly has descriptive content, it is about a cup of coffee, but it is not very clear what, if anything, is being said about a cup of coffee. Another of Culicover and Jackendoff's examples is *Damn/Fuck syntactic theory!*. Clearly, anyone uttering this is saying something about syntactic theory but nothing is strictly predicated of syntactic theory. Less strictly, the angry affective meaning expressed by *Damn!* or *Fuck!* is in some sense applied to syntactic theory. I see this as suggestive of a primitive kind of syntactic expression, recruiting a pre-existing expression with predominantly illocutionary meaning for a predicate-like purpose.

Even when the real purpose of conversation is not to pass on information, humans seem addicted to using propositional sentence-like units. A well-known example is desultory talk between strangers in places like waiting rooms and bus stops. You see someone, who might be a neighbour, you don't know them very well, but you want to be friendly. There are many possible ways of being friendly. The safe way is to exchange propositional information about some neutral topic like the weather, or the constant roadworks by the council, or the stranger's dog. Among humans, initial chatting up is done in sentence-like units; only later, if the chatting up is successful, do other communicative modalities take over.

To bring this back to the question of language universals, humans are unique in being able to master communicative systems which express an enormous range of propositions about the actual world, and about fictitious or abstract worlds that they construct. All humans, with the slight reservations to be expressed in a later section (on individual differences) are capable of this, hence the aptness of the term 'universal'. They do this in sentence-like units. The vast majority of human utterances, no matter how truncated or elliptical, are understood as conveying propositions in which properties and relations are predicated of things. Universally, given motivation and the right social environment, humans can also master complex systems in which propositions are made more fully explicit by a range of devices including grammatical markers, function words, conventional word-order, intonation, and inflections on words.

3.5 Competence-plus

3.5.1 *Regular production*

Humans using language behave in strikingly regular and complex ways. The observed regularities are the product of internalized programme channelling overt behaviour. French speakers keep their verbal inflections in all tenses consistent from day to day, and in line with those produced by other speakers. German speakers chatting are consistent, with themselves and with each other, about the complex interaction between the genders of nouns (Masculine, Feminine, Neuter) and the grammatical cases (Nominative, Accusative, Genitive, Dative) that these nouns take in sentences. This regular behaviour happens because speakers have acquired an internalized **competence** in the rules of their respective languages. It is true that people occasionally make mistakes, and deviate from normal patterns, but these are exceptions which we notice precisely as showing the existence of underlying rules.

Competence is often defined as a speaker's tacit knowledge of her language, thus emphasizing an intuitive, introspective element, and playing down the strong regularizing effect of competence on speakers' overt behaviour. There is much philosophical discussion of the appropriateness of the term 'knowledge' in defining linguistic competence. I will barely go into the issue. For a philosophical discussion of Chomsky's use of the term, and a view that I am broadly in sympathy with, see Matthews (2006). Both Matthews and Chomsky are clear that the term 'knowledge of language' should not be taken to imply that there is some external object independent of the knower, that the knower knows. This is characterized as an **intentional** view of competence, because the knowledge is **about** something other than the knowledge itself. The alternative is a view that competence is **constitutive of** the internal state that we informally describe as 'knowing a language'. This internal state is different from any use that it may be put to in processing bits of language. The internal state is an enduring memory store, present in the mind even when we are asleep. An unfortunate confusion can arise about the relationship between 'static' and 'dynamic' aspects of language. In arguing that 'the distinction between competence and performance has outlived its usefulness', Bickerton (2009b) writes that '[a]ny evolutionary account surely demands that we treat language as an acquired behavior rather than a static body of knowledge' (p. 12). We behave in predictable ways, but we are not always behaving. Linguistic competence accounts for the regularities in potential behaviour. Competence is embodied in relatively permanent brain potentials that only fire when performance calls them up.[19] I will continue to use the commonsense expression 'knowledge of language', but let it be clear that this is constitutive of (part of) a speaker's linguistic capacity, and not about some external object, the language, wherever that may live.

Non-human animals behave in regular ways, determined by patterns of activation potentials in their brains. Thus songbirds can be credited with one aspect of competence, a template which is the basis for their complex regular singing behaviour. We saw reasons in Chapter 1 for believing that this template is laid down in songbirds months before they actually start to sing to it. But songbirds lack the other aspect of competence, namely an introspective access to their own potential outpourings. You can't ask a nightingale whether a particular song is in its repertoire or not. You just have to listen to the bird for some time to see if it sings the song you are interested in. This is practical with songbirds, because their repertoires are finite and stereotyped.

Not all regularities in nature justify postulating internal mechanisms. The regular movements of celestial bodies are not due to the bodies themselves having internalized any rules. But creatures with brains are different. Brains produce regular behaviour that cannot be completely predicted from the mass and velocity of the bodies housing them. Certainly, bodies with brains are constrained by physical laws, but the interesting topic in animal behaviour is the ways in which animals manage very complex movements which are not the result of external forces. A rock only moves if some external force acts on it; an animal can move itself.[20] Something inside the animal structures its behaviour. The internal structuring programme can profitably be analysed as containing **information**. This information may develop in ways mostly determined by the genes, but may also be subject to substantial influence from the environment, depending on which organism we are dealing with.

3.5.2 Intuition

Among animals, humans are absolutely unique in being able to obtain a high degree of contemplative insight into their own actions. They are able to reflect on their own potential behaviour and say with some (not complete) accuracy whether a particular behaviour pattern is characteristic of them. Nowhere is

---

[19] In this passage Bickerton also expresses a hope that the proliferation of complexity arising in successive theories of grammar will be avoided by focusing on neural processes. Focusing on neural processes will reveal more, not fewer, complexities, and no load will be shifted away from the structure of the language that a linguist describes.

[20] The distinction between animate and inanimate matter is a convenient idealization. Life evolved out of non-life, and there are borderline cases (such as viruses).

this more apparent than in the case of language, probably due to the strong socially normative nature of language behaviour. Schoolroom prescriptions, for example 'Don't start a sentence with *and*' or 'Don't end a sentence with a preposition', are the extreme counterproductive end of this normative nature. In everyday life, people with nonstandard grammar are noticed as different and assigned different status accordingly. They may be imitated, as with a child adopting the nonstandard usage of a peer group (e.g. saying *We was…* or *them things* instead of *We were…* or *those things*). Or a social sanction may be applied, as when a job interviewee with nonstandard grammar is judged not to be a good person to employ in a position dealing with the public. In language especially, humans are instinctively disposed to grow up conforming to the regular behaviour of their group. This regular behaviour becomes second nature to each individual. And humans are to some degree capable of making judgements about what grammatical behaviour is normal in their social group. All dialects have their own grammar; the standard dialect of a language is just a privileged variety among many.

It was never the case that speakers were assumed to have intuitive access to the actual rules or principles that constitute competence. Discovering these rules or principles is the business of the working linguist, who takes as data the intuitive judgements of native speakers, and tries to find the most economical system producing these judgements. The intuitive judgements taken as reliable data are about particular expressions, for example that *The girl washed himself* or *Joan is probable to go* are ungrammatical, while *The girl washed herself* or *Joan is likely to go* are grammatical. Linguists have been at pains to dissociate themselves from schoolroom prescriptivism, which is out of touch with everyday usage. As Churchill probably didn't say, 'That is something up with which I will not put!'[21] But the normative element in regular grammatical behaviour is seldom acknowledged. Linguists sometimes hear non-linguists say 'Oh, I don't know any grammar', whereupon the brave linguist will try to explain the difference between knowing a grammar tacitly, which anyone who speaks a language must, and knowing explicit grammatical generalizations about it. To this day, I have not quite figured out how to describe the exact distribution of the definite article *the* in standard written English, yet I know an aberrant *the*, or an aberrant omission of *the*, when I see one, as I often do when reading drafts by non-native speakers. This illustrates the difference between tacit and **metalinguistic** knowledge.[22]

---

[21] On the likely misattribution of this example to Churchill, see http://158.130.17.5/ -myl/languagelog/archives/001715.html.

[22] I use 'metalinguistic knowledge' equivalently to 'metalinguistic awareness', though I know (am aware) that some people make a distinction.

Metalinguistic knowledge consistent with a linguist's analysis can be teased out (not falsely) even from young children. Ferreira and Morrison (1994) investigated the metalinguistic knowledge of five-year-old children by getting them to repeat the subject noun phrase of a sentence that was played to them. The children were not, of course, asked in explicit grammatical terms, like 'What is the subject of this sentence?'. Instead they were given several examples of an adult hearing a sentence and then repeating the subject noun phrase. The authors concluded:

[C]hildren are quite accurate at identifying and repeating the subject of a sentence, even before they have had any formal schooling. In the name and determiner-noun conditions, even the youngest and least educated children could repeat the subject of a sentence over 80% of the time and generally performed better with the subject than with a nonconstituent such as the subject plus verb. It appears that even 5-year-old unschooled children have some metalinguistic knowledge of the syntactic subject of a sentence and can manipulate structural units such as subjects more easily than nonstructural sequences.   (Ferreira and Morrison 1994, p. 674)

These authors also found that children had a specific difficulty identifying subjects when the subject was a pronoun, and their performance improved with age, but not in correlation with extent of schooling. By contrast, schooling did have an effect on children's ability to identify subjects that were rather long (in number of words). This effect of schooling was attributed not to any growth in tacit linguistic knowledge, but to a stretching of 'immediate memory strategies (such as rehearsal)' (p. 676). (These authors assume here a 'classical' theory of the relationship between working memory and linguistic competence. In a later section, in connection with experiments by Ngoni Chipere, I will argue for a different relationship, which is still consistent with Ferreira and Morrison's results cited here.)

Critics of generative syntacticians' approach to data have described their examples as 'sanitized', 'composed' (Schumann 2007), or 'fabricated' (Mikesell 2009).[23] Givón (1979a), in a wide-ranging attack on this and related practices of generative linguists, writes of the 'sanitization', and even the 'gutting' of the data. I agree that these terms, except 'gutting', are appropriate to describe what syntacticians do, but I also hold that the use of intuitive judgements is defensible, if not taken to extremes.

The terms 'intuitive data' and 'introspective data' are not necessarily irreconcilable with scientific empiricism. I shall not go into the various nuances

---

[23] Mikesell's chapter in this co-authored book is entitled 'The implications of interaction for the nature of language', in Lee et al. 2009 (pp. 55–107).

of difference that may be posited between intuition and introspection. For some, introspection is a less rational and reflective process than intuition, but I will use the terms interchangeably. The basic premiss of syntacticians is that if you **know** an expression is grammatical,[24] you don't have to go looking for it in a corpus—you don't have to observe someone actually using the expression. This strategy is obviously open to abuse, and requires high standards of intellectual honesty. In the least problematic case, knowledge that an expression is grammatical comes from a native speaker's intuition about **potential** events.

Given a hypothesis about sentence structure, a syntactician can compose an example predicted by the hypothesis, to test it. The example may or may not turn out to be grammatical, and this is a kind of falsifying of data that cannot be easily obtained except by relying on linguistic intuitions. Finding that certain strings of words are ungrammatical is a valuable tool. One first notices a generalization: for example the long-distance relationship between a *Wh-* question word and a structural position later in a sentence, as in *Who do you believe that John saw?*, corresponding to the incredulous echo question *You believe that John saw WHO?*[25] Prompted by such examples, a syntactician tries to test the generalization further. Hence, given that *You believe the claim that John saw WHO?* is OK, it is reasonable to ask whether **Who do you believe the claim that John saw?* is OK, and it isn't, as indicated by the asterisk. The intuition-based methodology gives one a way of distinguishing language from non-language. This last asterisked sentence is not just rare; it is ungrammatical,[26] a fact which we wouldn't have discovered without making it up as a theoretical exercise.

The statement 'X is grammatical' can be taken to mean 'I might well say X in appropriate circumstances, and I would not feel that I had made any error, or needed to correct myself'. There is psycholinguistic evidence for an internalized standard by which speakers control their own language output.

Self-repairing of speech errors demonstrates that speakers possess a monitoring device with which they verify the correctness of the speech flow. There is substantial evidence that this speech monitor not only comprises an auditory component (i.e., hearing one's own speech), but also an internal part: inspection of the speech program prior to its motoric execution. Errors thus may be detected before they are actually articulated.

(Postma and Kolk 1993, p. 472)

---

[24] The term 'grammatical' is also a battleground, and I will come back to it.
[25] Pronounce this *WHO?* with a strong rising intonation.
[26] See the discussion near the end of the next chapter on whether such examples are ungrammatical or just unacceptable for discourse-related reasons.

Even in disfluent speech, characterized by repairs, when speakers do correct themselves they tend to do so in whole grammatical chunks. 'The segment that follows the site of repair initiation is always syntactically coherent in our data, that is, it forms a syntactic constituent' (Fox and Jasperson 1996, p. 108).

Aphasic patients, whose language production and comprehension is impaired, can typically nevertheless give normal intuitive judgements about the grammaticality of sentences they are presented with. This argues for a intuitive knowledge component of linguistic capacity separate from the production and reception mechanisms. Vicky Fromkin summarizes the situation:

> The nature of the deficit was further complicated by findings[27] that agrammatic patients who show the 'telegraphic' output typical of agrammatic aphasia and also demonstrate impaired comprehension in which interpretation depends on syntactic structure are still able to make grammaticality judgments with a high rate of accuracy. At the very least this argued for preserved syntactic competence in these patients and to a greater extent shifted inquiry back toward a processing account.
>
> (Fromkin 1995, pp. 2–3)

A double dissociation between intuitive metalinguistic judgements of grammatical gender and actual performance can be inferred from two separate studies. Scarnà and Ellis (2002) studied an Italian patient who could not accurately report the gender of Italian nouns, but who used them with correct agreement in a task involving translation of English noun phrases into Italian. Conversely, Bates et al. (2001) describe a group of 'Italian-speaking aphasic patients [who] retain detailed knowledge of grammatical gender, but this knowledge seems to have no effect on real-time lexical access'.

Linguistic intuitions are about competence, and competence resides in individuals. Thus, in principle, the facts are facts about each individual's own idiolect. It could happen that a person has quirkily internalized some idiosyncratic grammatical fact, uniquely in his linguistic group. In principle, though not in practice, such a grammatical fact is a legitimate object of study. How can we trust the reports of a person that don't correspond to those of anyone else? So in practice, a linguist must find facts consistent with the intuitive judgements of many native speakers. Syntactic arguments based on judgements peculiar to one individual are not taken seriously. This is consistent with the goal of characterizing the common linguistic dispositions of human children exposed to typical language data. A speaker with an idiolect significantly different from

---

[27] Here Fromkin cites the following: Friederici (1982); Grossman and Haberman (1982); Linebarger et al. (1983); Linebarger (1989, 1990); Lukatela et al. (1988); Shankweiler et al. (1989).

others in the same community has either had significantly different input or has inherited different language-acquisition dispositions. It might be possible to check the language input in such a case, for example for early deprivation. In this instance, the case would be abnormal, and hence for the present out of the scope of a theory of normal language. Given our present knowledge, it would not be possible to investigate the possibility of idiosyncratic inherited (e.g. mutant) language-acquisition dispositions in relation to clausal or phrasal structure.

In one special case, the idiosyncratic judgements of a single speaker are taken seriously. This is the case of the last available speaker of a dying language. Fieldworkers in such cases typically collect as much spontaneously uttered data as they can, but will then ask the informant to judge the acceptability of various expressions of the researcher's own fabrication, testing hypotheses formed on the basis of the observed data. Informants generally give fairly clear responses to such questions—equivalent to either 'Yes, that's OK' or 'No, one would not say that'. Depending on the sophistication of the informant, one may get further information about the kinds of contexts in which an expression could occur, its social register, or perhaps some correction of the expression in question—'No you wouldn't say X, but you could say Y', where Y and X differ by some detail. Data gathered from very few informants, even if they are mutually consistent, naturally carry less weight in theoretical argumentation. (For this reason it is vital to collect extensive data on as many languages as possible now, while they are still with us. It is projected that about half the world's languages will die out in the next 100 years.) It is wise to take any report of wildly outlying facts from languages with very few speakers, or languages researched by only one or two linguists, with a grain of salt. Here is a salutary tale from Dan Everett's experience of trying to elicit grammaticality judgements from his Pirahã informants over a span of many years.

I could get some to repeat the phrase in 51 after me, but most would not. Struggling in a monolingual situation and believing in NPs with multiple modifiers, I assumed that 51 was grammatical. During the years, however, I noticed that nouns followed or preceded by multiple modifiers are not found in natural conversations or texts. When I asked someone years later why they didn't utter sequences like 51, they said 'Pirahãs do not say that'. I replied 'You said I could say that.' I was answered: 'You can say that. You are not Pirahã.' A perfectly reasonable attempt to get examples of modification backfired because of my naivete and the challenges of a monolingual field experience and misled me for years. But this is just not that uncommon in field research. (Everett 2009, p. 422)

We just don't know whether the 'someone' that Everett asked years later was caught on a bad day, or didn't see Everett as bound by the conventions governing behaviour within the tribe, including linguistic conventions. Or possibly the problem was a semantic one with the particular example 51, which had (by Everett's latest account) two words both denoting a kind of size. We can't be certain of the facts until more researchers spend much more time with the Pirahã on the banks of the Maici river.

Human languages provide such an enormous range of possible expressions, used with such a skewed probability distribution, that expressions on which there is a substantial intuitive consensus are often unlikely to be found even in a very large corpus. This is the central argument for the use of intuition. If we were restricted to just the expressions that have been observed, this would be somewhat analogous to a physicist studying only the electromagnetic radiation in the observable visible spectrum. (No analogy is perfect.) Consider the very practical business that goes on in a second-language classroom. The teacher's goal is to get her pupils to be able to say **anything they want to** correctly in the target language. It would be absurd to restrict pupils only to examples that had actually been attested in corpora. The teacher has intuitions about what is sayable and what is not in the target language, and the purpose of the exercise is to get the pupils to the same level of competence, being able creatively to express meanings that had never been used as examples in class.

A host of problems stem from the use of intuitive judgements. These problems are real, but not crucial enough to justify abandoning intuitive data altogether. There are some quirky facts involving semantic interpretation. I will give examples of two types of these. Consider the sentence *More people drink Guinness than I do* or *More students are flunking than you are*. Most English speakers, when they hear such examples,[28] immediately respond that they are grammatical sentences, and then do a double-take and say 'But what on earth does it mean?' Geoff Pullum[29] writes that neither he nor his colleagues can find any explanation for this phenomenon, noting that 'more people have tried to find one than we have'.

Mark Liberman insightfully calls these curious cases 'Escher sentences'. He comments

---

[28] For somewhat technical reasons, the examples I have given here are better than the usually cited *More people have been to Russia than I have*. Ask me about it, if you're wondering.

[29] At http://itre.cis.upenn.edu/-myl/languagelog/archives/000860.html . (Website still active at 17 September 2008.)

Like Escher stairways and Shepard tones, these sentences are telling us something about the nature of perception. Whether we're seeing a scene, hearing a sound or assimilating a sentence, there are automatic processes that happen effortlessly whenever we come across the right kind of stuff, and then there are kinds of analysis that involve more effort and more explicit scrutiny. This is probably not a qualitative distinction between perception and interpretation, but rather a gradation of processes from those that are faster, more automatic and less accessible to consciousness, towards those that are slower, more effortful, more conscious and more optional. (http://itre.cis.upenn.edu/-myl/languagelog/archives/000862.html. Website active on 25 March 2009.)

Escher sentences are extremely rare. One or two examples have circulated in the linguistics blogs, with minor lexical mutations, but no one has come up with an example culled from text or even from spontaneous spoken conversation. The example does show a consensus about clashing intuitions, syntactic and semantic, among English speakers. Liberman's comment makes a wise and crucial general point about our linguistic judgements. Unlike Escher sentences, most expressions do not cause such a clash between immediate and more reflective judgements. The important question arises, however, as to which kind of judgement, the immediate or the reflective, is the proper kind of data for syntactic theory. I will pick up this question later in connection with the **virtuosity** of professional linguists. Note for now that any account of the evolution of syntactic intuitions that attempts some integration with biology ought to focus first on the faster, more automatic judgements that speakers make, rather than the more reflective ones.

Distinguishing between fast automatic and slower reflective judgements is not easy, and leads me to the tip of a massive philosophical iceberg, into which I will not dig, except to throw out some provocative suggestions. Brace yourself! Kant (1781) distinguished along two dimensions, on one dimension between **a priori** and **a posteriori** knowledge, and on another dimension between **analytic** and **synthetic** judgements, or sentences. A priori knowledge comes innately, and includes pure intuitions of time and space, which one doesn't learn from experience. A posteriori knowledge is gained from experience, such as the knowledge that there is an oak tree in Brighton Park. Analytic sentences express necessary truths, true simply by virtue of the meanings of their parts, and the way these are combined, such as *Oaks are trees*; synthetic sentences may or not may be true depending on the state of the world, for example *There is an oak in Brighton Park*. Kant thought that these two dimensions were distinct. Many people, however, have been puzzled by the distinction between a priori truths and what is expressed by analytic sentences. Kant maintained that there are some synthetic, but a priori truths. His example was the truths of arithmetic, such as $5 + 7 = 12$. This extends to all such arithmetical propositions, including for example, $3299 \times 47 = 155053$. Is this last formula true? The answer surely isn't immediately obvious to your intuition. It could take you more than a minute to work it out according to rules that you have learned (or trust a calculator). Judgements about impossibly complex sentences claimed to be grammatical, such as multiply centre-embedded sentences, are analogous to Kant's synthetic a priori truths. You can ascertain their grammaticality or otherwise by pen-and-paper calculation. You may even be able to do the calculation in your head, but the exercise does not come naturally. Miller and Chomsky (1963, p. 467) draw the same analogy between grammar and arithmetic: 'it is perfectly possible that M [a model of the language user] will not contain enough computing space to allow it to understand all sentences in the manner of the device G [a grammar] whose instructions it stores. This is no more surprising than the fact that a person who knows the rules of arithmetic perfectly may not be able to perform many computations correctly in his head'.

This common analogy between grammatical intuitions and synthetic a priori truths of arithmetic is flawed in a way that I suggest is critical. Propositions of arithmetic can be checked in two ways which are found to be consistent. One way to check $3299 \times 47 = 155053$ is to follow taught pen-and-paper procedures for multiplication, using a conventional notation, such as decimal. The other way is painstakingly to assemble 47 separate collections of 3299 distinct objects, throw them all together, and then to count the objects.[30] If you are careful, the answer from both methods will be the same. We put our trust in pen-and-paper procedures of arithmetic because they have been shown over the generations to apply with complete generality across all calculations, to our great practical advantage. We know that the answer we get from using taught shortcut multiplication procedures **must** be the same as the answer we would get by using the painstaking method of assembling collections and then counting their union. Assembling collections and counting their union is a possible experience. Numbers are **about** things in the world that we can count.[31] Arithmetic works. Thus, reason, as embodied in the taught multiplication procedure, is in harmony with possible experience. And these possible experiences can be shared publicly, so they have an objective nature.

The claim that overly complex sentences are definitely grammatical comes from applying a parallel logic to grammatical sentences. We know that some

---

[30] Of course you must take care not to choose objects at risk of blending together, like drops of water.

[31] There are more Platonic views of what numbers are, with which I don't agree. See Hurford (1987).

grammatical sentences can be formed by the procedure of embedding one clause into another and, so the assumption goes, **any** sentence formed by this same procedure **must** also be grammatical, no matter what the depth of embedding. Facts of grammaticality, however, are arbitrary, and the grammaticality of overly complex sentences cannot be independently verified by any external method in the domain of possible experiences. Unlike numbers, the grammaticality of a sentence is not **about** anything in the world, except itself or some acquired normative system. The grammaticality of a sentence, for example *The cat the dog chased escaped*, is just a self-standing fact. Furthermore, in the grammar case, unlike the arithmetic case, there is no practical advantage in assuming the validity of the generalization to complex examples that we can't understand. What shared, that is objective, knowledge there is of overly complex sentences is that they are judged as unacceptable. In Kantian terms, the grammarian who insists on the grammaticality of complex centre-embedded sentences is applying pure reason beyond the limits of possible experience. 'It is possible experience alone that can impart reality to our concepts; without this, a concept is only an idea without truth, and without any reference to an object' (Kant 1781, p. 489). The possible experiences can be indirect indications of the concepts whose reality we are interested in, as with instrument readings in particle physics. The strict Kantian philosophy of mathematics is rejected by modern pure mathematicians, who are concerned with constructing rigorously consistent edifices based on intuitive definitions, and these edifices are valued for their inherent beauty and interest as 'objects'. Nevertheless, as pointed out in a classic essay 'The unreasonable effectiveness of mathematics in the natural sciences' (Vigner 1960), such edifices often eventually prove indispensable to empirical physicists in calculating the predictions of physical theories. But the concept of grammaticality beyond normal processing limits as projected by a generative grammar cannot ever be detected by any method, direct or indirect. The grammaticality or otherwise of some excessively complex string is 'only an idea without truth'. This is true despite protestations of adopting a 'Galilean style' (Chomsky 1980b, pp. 8–9). Kant argued in similar terms against postulating such entities as souls independent of bodies. This puts some practising syntacticians dangerously close to the metaphysicians and cosmologists whom Kant criticized.[32] I start from the position of trying to account for human language as involving immediately accessible intuitions that

---

[32] Chomsky's main pre-twentieth-century guru is Descartes, and he less often refers to Kant, for whose innate intuitions he would have some sympathy. Maybe we can now see why Chomsky has tended to steer pretty clear of Kant.

have become second nature through natural language acquisition, intuitions that are backed up by observation of regular usage.

Another problematic fact for linguistic intuition, less quirky and more common than Escher sentences, involves examples like this—imagine it seen as a notice in a hospital:[33]

No head injury is too trivial to be ignored

Here again, there is a clash between immediate and more reflective judgements. At first blush, especially since the sentence is seen in a hospital, the message seems to be 'Don't ignore any head injury'. Some people can never be talked out of this interpretation. It was almost certainly what the writer of the message meant, so leave it at that, they say. But with a bit of thought you can (I hope) see that what the writer almost certainly meant is not what the **sentence**, if analysed, actually means. Let's take a simpler example: *This is too important to ignore*. OK? No problem with interpretation there. This, whatever it is, is so important that we shouldn't ignore it. But *important* and *trivial* are antonyms, opposites in meaning. So *too trivial to ignore* must imply paradoxically that we should ignore the important things and pay attention to the trivial things. If you think about it, this paradox is embedded in the sentence from the hospital notice. I think the problem here arises from the conspiracy between how one feels one ought to interpret notices in a hospital and the overloading of the sentence with explicit or implicit negatives, *No*, *trivial*, and *ignore*. I have a hard time with double negatives, let alone triple negatives. In this case, the sentence seems to be of a degree of complexity that an intuitive judgement (as to its actual meaning, as opposed to what the writer meant) is untrustworthy. The problem sentence is interpreted by a 'Semantic Soup' strategy. There is no problem with its grammaticality, however.

The *too trivial to ignore* case is the tip of a large iceberg, showing that hearers and readers often arrive at incorrect interpretations of even quite simple sentences. Two publications by Fernanda Ferreira and colleagues (Ferreira et al. 2002; Ferreira and Patson 2007) give excellent brief surveys of the experimental evidence that listeners and readers apply a 'Good Enough' strategy in sentence comprehension. The 'Good Enough' strategy is more sophisticated than a crude 'Semantic Soup' approach, in that it does take syntactic cues, such as word order, into account, but the idea is very similar. Comprehension does

---

[33] This example was discussed as a 'verbal illusion' by Wason and Reich (1979). I'm happy to read that Geoff Pullum has the same problem with implicit multiple negatives in examples like this as I do (Liberman and Pullum 2006, p. 108).

not always strive (indeed normally does not) to arrive at a complete semantic representation of a sentence's meaning compatible with its syntactic structure.

Some nice examples involve 'Garden Path' sentences, such as *While Anna dressed the baby played in the crib* (crucially presented in written form without a comma). To get the real meaning of this sentence, you have to backtrack over an interpretation that at first seemed likely, namely that Anna was dressing the baby. After backtracking, you realize that Anna was dressing **herself**, and not the baby. But Christianson et al. (2001) found by questioning subjects who had been given this sentence that they still maintained a lingering impression that Anna did dress the baby, even while being sure that Anna dressed herself. The short substring *dressed the baby* is having a local effect here, which does not entirely go away. Young children go through a stage of applying a Good Enough strategy to any sentence. 'Children of 3 and 4 systematically follow a word order strategy when interpreting passives. When told to act out "The car is hit by the truck" they regularly assume it means "The car hits the truck"' (Tager-Flusberg 2005, p. 175).

Another example of the Good Enough strategy involves the question *How many of each type of animal did Moses take on the ark?* Erickson and Mattson (1981) found that people asked this question overlooked, or did not notice, the semantic anomaly in it. It was Noah, not Moses who took animals on the ark. Similarly, the anomaly in the question *Where should the authorities bury the survivors?* is often overlooked (Barton and Sanford 1993). The latter authors call the phenomenon 'shallow parsing'.

The evidence for shallow parsing and a Good Enough comprehension strategy is convincing. What is also notable in all these studies is that the authors and the experimenters all unequivocally describe their subjects as making errors. That is, the existence of norms of correct interpretation is never called into question, despite the fact that experimental subjects often fail to respond in accord with these norms. Indeed this area of study is **defined** by a mismatch between subjects' performance and the norms assumed by the experimenters. This presents an evolutionary problem. How can it come about that the 'correct' design of the language is such that its users often get it wrong? I suggest that several factors contribute to the observed effects. One argument is that to some extent the effects are artefacts of the experiments. But this argument is not strong enough to invalidate the case for Good Enough comprehension altogether. The Good Enough idea actually fits in with some pervasive traits of many complex evolved systems.

Recall the earlier example: *While Anna dressed the baby played in the crib*, presented in written form without a comma. The effects are not observed when a comma is provided. In speech, of course, the sentence would be produced with an intonational break after *dressed*, and again there is no Garden Path problem. The majority of experiments in this area was carried out on written examples, presented out of any natural communicative context.[34] Given a suitable natural context and natural intonation, many of the errors in comprehension would not occur. (Ferreira et al., 2002, p. 13) concur:

First, as the earliest work in cognitive psychology revealed, the structure built by the language processor is fragile and decays rapidly (Sachs 1967). The representation needs almost immediate support from context or from schemas (i.e., general frameworks used to organize details on the basis of previous experience). In other words, given (10) [the anomalous passive *The dog was bitten by the man*], syntactic mechanisms deliver the proper interpretation that the dog is the patient and the man is the agent; but the problem is that the delicate syntactic structure needs reinforcement. Schemas in long-term memory cannot provide that support, and so the source of corroboration must be context. Quite likely, then, sentences like this would be correctly understood in normal conversation, because the overall communicative context would support the interpretation. The important concept is that the linguistic representation itself is not robust, so that if it is not reinforced, a merely good-enough interpretation may result.

                                                    (Ferreira et al. 2002, p. 13)

Command of syntax alone is not enough to enable the comprehension of sentences. All natural comprehension leans heavily on support from context and everyday expectations of what is a likely meaning. Imaging experiments by Caplan et al. (2008) also support a mixed strategy of sentence interpretation, calling on both structural syntactic information from an input sentence and plausibility in terms of general semantic knowledge.[35]

But even given suitable sentences with natural intonation spoken in a genuine communicative context, shallow Good Enough parsing happens, especially with somewhat complex examples like *No head injury is too trivial to ignore*. It seems reasonable to surmise that an early pre-syntactic precursor of language was rather like a pidgin, in which utterances are interpreted by a Semantic Soup strategy. Complex systems evolve on top of simpler systems, and vestiges of the simpler systems remain. This is an example of **layering**, a

---

[34] This is symptomatic of a problem with a great deal of psycholinguistic work on human parsing. Much of this work uses written stimuli, a trend encouraged by the availability of good eye-tracking equipment. But the human parser evolved to deal with speech, not writing. There is no close equivalent in auditory processing to glancing back along a line of printed text, as happens when people process printed Garden Path sentences.

[35] These authors measured a blood oxygenation level dependent (BOLD) signal in subjects interpreting sentences with systematically varied syntactic properties (subject- vs. object-relativizing) and semantic content more or less predictable on the basis of real-world knowledge.

phenomenon found generally across evolved systems. Older systems linger. An example in language is syntactically unintegrated interjections *Ouch, damn,* and several conventional vocal gestures for which there is no accepted spelling, such as intakes of breath indicating shocked surprise, sighs indicating controlled frustration, and so on. We shall see more of such layering in later chapters. The human parser is an eclectic evolved mix, including a cheap and fast Good Enough mechanism, and more computationally elaborate mechanisms sensitive to richer grammatical structure (but still limited by working memory). The more recently evolved elaborate mechanisms are not always called into play, when simpler procedures are good enough.

The basis of the 'Good Enough' parsing strategy is broadly similar to Townsend and Bever's (2001) Late Assignment of Syntax Theory (LAST). This theory has a memorable catch phrase—'You understand everything twice'. What this means is that a simple first-pass processor identifies such basic structural components as function words, content word-classes, and phrase boundaries. They call this stage in comprehension 'pseudo-syntax'. This process works very fast. A second stage delivers a fuller syntactic analysis.

What goes for comprehension probably also goes for production. In tight situations of various kinds, or with familiar partners, a more telegraphic form of language can be used in lieu of fully syntactic forms. Telegrams, newpaper headlines, warning notices (*DANGER Solvents*), commands to soldiers (*At ease!*), surgeons' requests for instruments (*Scalpel!*) and jokey forms such as *No can do* are examples.

One common problem with intuitive judgements is interference between dialects and languages. An expression may exist in one dialect but not in a neighbouring dialect. And then, through contact, people become bi-dialectal. While syntactic theory is most likely to attribute two separate compartmentalized competences to bilinguals, there is no clear position on what to do about bi-dialectal speakers. And in any somewhat mobile society, all speakers are at least somewhat multi-dialectal. In some clear cases, before complete dialect mixing has occurred, one can still identify one construction with one dialect and an alternative construction with another dialect. For example *Do you want it wrapping?* is a clear Northern English[36] alternative to Southern British English *Do you want it wrapped?* It used to be the case that *Do you have...* was distinctively American, whereas *Have you got...* was distinctively British, but I'm not sure any more. People's intuitions about facts such as these can be quite unreliable. They may claim that they never use a particular expression,

---

[36] But not Scottish.

but you can catch them at it. '[T]he speakers of local dialects may assess all possible syntactic variants, that is dialect, standard, and emerging intermediate variants to their local dialect. Subsequently, clear-cut judgements between the local dialect and the standard variety are not attainable at all' (Cornips 2006, p. 86). Such cases are seldom central to syntactic theorizing, and the uncertainty of intuitions about some expressions is not a fatal objection to the fact that there are many clear cases where speaker intuitions are clear and consistent.

Another problem with the use of intuitive data is the 'I just don't know any more' syndrome. Considering an expression afresh for the first time, a speaker can usually make a clear judgement about it. In somewhat uncertain cases, however, after tossing the expression around in theoretical debate for some time, a linguist will often lose her confident feel for the grammaticality or otherwise of the expression. In such a case, the judgement becomes hostage to a tradition in theoretical debate. There is a possibility that a 'fact' becomes accepted by all parties to a debate, with no one bothering to check its factual status. At worst, the debate comes to be based on dodgy data. In such a case, corpus studies can come to the rescue. An example of this is the analysis of English *each other*. Chomsky (1986, p. 164) classes *each other* as a 'pure anaphor' along with reflexive pronouns (e.g. *himself, myself, yourself*), and argues that special principles apply to this class of words. He judges *They expected that each other would win* as ungrammatical (p. 168), by the same principle that excludes **John expected that himself would win*. After Chomsky wrote this, the status of *each other* as a pure anaphor just like reflexive pronouns was accepted by many in theoretical debate. Fisher (1988, p. 25), for example, argues on the basis that *They believed that each other is innocent* in ungrammatical. (Sag et al. 2003, pp. 205, 221, 452) also class *each other* along with reflexives (using different but equivalent terminology for the class). And Pollard and Sag (1994, p. 239), presenting an alternative framework to Chomsky's, accept his facts about *each other*, classing it with reflexives as a pure anaphor. Thus, to some extent, the debaters have been content to accept the same basic linguistic 'facts' **for the sake of the argument**. Syntacticians love an argument. The 'facts' became institutionalized for the sake of argument, at least for some. I was never quite sure about the sameness of *each other* and reflexives, and I have certainly now observed many instances of *each other* used as the subject of a tensed subordinate clause, contrary to the institutionalized 'facts'. Uchuimi (2006) gives several examples collected from texts, and reports on a survey in which a majority of speakers accepted *John and Bill expect that each other will be wrong* as grammatical. Now Newmeyer (2005, p. 55) reports finding such a sentence not as bad as **John thinks that himself will* *win*. In every science there are cases where certain facts get widely assumed on the basis of inadequate evidence. But such cases do not invalidate the general method of data gathering. Syntax is no exception. Constant vigilance is necessary. But throwing out intuitive data altogether would be a counterproductive overreaction.

3.5.3 Gradience

Grammar is prone to fuzziness; there are often degrees of acceptability. Many syntacticians deal in terms of binary judgements. Either an expression is grammatical, or it is ungrammatical, in which case they put an asterisk on it. There is no third value. This is unrealistic, and can falsify the data. There are some quite simple expressions about which native speakers have genuine uncertainty. In my own case, if I want to describe the house that Sue and I jointly own, I am not sure whether *?My and Sue's house* is OK or not. Something about it feels odd to me, but it can be readily understood, and no more compact way exists to express its clear meaning. This uncertainty is itself a fact of grammar.

The practice of most theoretical syntacticians has not caught up with such facts of gradient acceptability. Ad hoc impressionistic schemes with various combinations of asterisks and question marks (e.g. *?, or ??*) are sometimes used. Belletti and Rizzi (1988), for example, implicitly use a seven-point scale of such markings. But among mainstream syntacticians there is no overall system of such notations, or agreement on how to relate them systematically to data. It is not that the gradience of data is unrecognized. Chomsky (1975a, p. 131) writes that 'an adequate linguistic theory will have to recognize degrees of grammaticalness' acknowledging that 'there is little doubt that speakers can fairly consistently order new utterances, never previously heard, with respect to their degree of "belongingness" to the language' (p. 132). Still, the most prominent syntactic theorists have not proposed ways of describing or accounting for this gradience.[37]

A small population of researchers has made significant inroads into empirical methods for measuring and describing gradience, and the classification of different types of gradience. The originally most extensive works are by Schütze (1996) and Cowart (1997), with the revealing titles *Experimental Syntax: Applying Objective Methods to Sentence Judgments* and *The Empirical Base of Linguistics: Grammaticality Judgments and Linguistic Methodology*. Bard et al. (1996) have developed an empirical technique for

---

[37] For discussions of gradience, mostly within a generative framework, see Aarts (2007); Fanselow et al. (2006).

eliciting relative degrees of acceptability from speakers. The technique, called 'Magnitude Estimation', is not widely known, let alone adopted, by syntactic theorists, although its use in psychophysics has been around for over 30 years (Stevens 1975). Sorace and Keller (2005), also investigating gradience, distinguish between hard and soft constraints on acceptability. Hard constraints give rise to strong categorical judgements of grammaticality or ungrammaticality. English examples such I have mentioned above involving pronouns, *John shot him, John shot himself,* and **The woman shot himself* are the product of hard constraints. A soft constraint can be illustrated by the following examples, which were found by a systematic survey to be decreasingly acceptable.

(a.) *Which friend has Thomas painted a picture of?*
(b.) *?Which friend has Thomas painted the picture of?*
(c.) *?Which friend has Thomas torn up a picture of?*
(d.) *?How many friends has Thomas painted a picture of?*

(Sorace and Keller 2005, p. 1506)

Hard constraints determine categorical grammatical facts, while soft constraints, which typically give rise to gradient judgements, usually involve interactions between grammatical structure and non-grammatical factors such as semantics and processing complexity. Soft constraints are also often correlated with frequency of use, with the intuitively least acceptable expressions also being found least frequently (if at all) in corpora.

A hard constraint or categorical fact in one language may correspond to a soft constraint or non-categorical fact in another language. Givón (1979a) mentions a well known example. 'In many of the world's languages, probably in most, the subject of declarative clauses cannot be referential-indefinite'[38] (p. 26). Thus in (Egyptian Colloquial) Arabic, for example, **raagil figgineena* 'A man [is] in the garden' is not a grammatical sentence, whereas *irraagil figgineena* 'The man [is] in the garden' is grammatical. The difference is in the definiteness of the subject noun phrase. These languages don't allow indefinite subjects. As Givón goes on to point out, 'In a relatively small number of the world's languages, most of them languages with a long tradition of literacy, referential-indefinite nouns may appear as subjects' (p. 27). Thus in English *A man is in the garden* is not felt to be strictly ungrammatical, although we may feel somewhat uneasy about it, and prefer *There's a man in the garden.* Givón further notes that such examples with definite subjects are used with

---

[38] A referential-indefinite expression is one that refers to some entity not previously present in the discourse context. Other, non-referential, indefinites include generic expressions like *Any fool* as in *Any fool can tell you that,* or *whoever.*

low frequency in the languages that do allow them. Examples like this, where a hard categorical grammatical fact in one language is matched by a gradable fact in another language, are widespread and now very familiar to linguists. Pithily, 'Soft constraints mirror hard constraints' (Bresnan et al. 2001). More explicitly, '[T]he patterns of preference that one finds in performance in languages possessing several structures of a given type (different word orders, relative clauses, etc.) look increasingly like the patterns found in the fixed conventions of grammars in languages with fewer structures of the same type' (Hawkins 2009, p. 55). Hawkins labels this the 'Performance-Grammar Correspondence Hypothesis', though it is hardly a hypothesis any more.[39] Such correspondences are compelling evidence for the evolutionary process of **grammaticalization**, the topic of Chapter 9. A gradient of acceptability is often a sign of ongoing evolution or past change in the language. Givón (1979a) argues (with great rhetorical force) that such correspondences between a categorical fact of grammar in one language and a scale of acceptability in another are counterevidence to the idea of competence, a native speaker's intuitive knowledge of her language.

In some languages (Krio, etc.) this communicative tendency is expressed at the *categorial* level of 100%. In other languages (English, etc.) the very same communicative tendency is expressed 'only' at the *noncategorial* level of 90%. And a transformational-generative linguist will be forced to count this fact as competence in Krio and performance in English....it seems to me, the distinction between performance and competence or grammar and behavior tends to collapse under the impact of these data.

(Givón 1979a, p. 28)

Note the hedging 'tends to'; does it collapse or not? Later in the same book, however, Givón finds a distinction between competence and performance useful: 'a language may change the restriction on referential-indefinites under negation over a period of time, from a restriction at the competence level (as in Hungarian, Bemba, and Rwanda) to a restriction at the performance or text-count level (as in English and Israeli Hebrew)' (p. 100). Remember that this was written before 1979. Mainstream linguistics was still in thrall to the exclusive Saussurean-Chomskyan dominance of synchronic description, and by extension synchronic explanation. Givón himself was well ahead of the general trend when, still later in the same book, he expounded a diachronic process of 'syntacticization', by which grammatical facts come into existence

---

[39] See Schmidtke-Bode (in press) for a recent survey of the methodological issues involved in filling out the details of the Performance-Grammar Correspondence Hypothesis. Some of my own work, dating quite far back, argues for this hypothesis without giving it that particular name. See, for example, Hurford (1987, 1991b).

in languages. This was a very early move in the modern renaissance of the idea of grammaticalization, to which I will return in Chapter 9.

Givón's rhetoric on intuitive judgements is let down by his consistent practice. In this 1979 book, Givón cites data from many languages, acknowledging his indebtedness to informants, who presumably just reported their own intuitive judgements. Further, when citing English data, he follows the same practice as the generative grammarians that he criticizes, and simply presents the examples as if their status is obvious, implicitly relying on his and our intuitions.[40] Speaker intuitions are not all categorical black-or-white judgements; as we have seen, speakers can grade some expressions as more acceptable than others.

Early generative grammar focused on categorical grammatical facts. Such facts became, in the minds of some critics, criterial to the notion of competence. We see this in the above quotation from Givón. With more recent attention to gradient phenomena, the idea arises that competence may be probabilistic. Bod et al. (2003b) advocate that competence is wholly probabilistic.

Language displays all the hallmarks of a probabilistic system. Categories and well-formedness are gradient, and frequency effects are everywhere. We believe all evidence points to a probabilistic language faculty. Knowledge of language should be understood not as a minimal set of categorical rules or constraints, but as a (possibly redundant) set of gradient rules, which may be characterized by a statistical distribution.

(Bod et al. 2003a, p. 10)

A wholly probabilistic theory of competence seems to deny the possibility that there are **any** all-or-nothing categorical grammatical facts. 'Categories are central to linguistic theory, but membership in these categories need not be categorical. Probabilistic linguistics conceptualizes categories as distributions. Membership in categories is gradient' (Bod et al. 2003a, p. 4). As a perhaps pernickety point, in general, any assertion that **everything** in some domain is 'probabilistic' is flawed. Probability distributions themselves are expressed in terms of all-or-nothing categories. A scatterplot of height against age assumes that height is height, not weight or girth, and that age is age, not maturity or health, notwithstanding that height and age are continuously varying categories. As an example nearer to syntactic home, a probability distribution of verbs appearing in particular subcategorization frames still assumes that each verb is a categorical entity (e.g. it either is or is not the verb *consider*) and each

---

[40] Newmeyer (1998, pp. 40–1) finds the same flaws in this argument of Givón's as I do.

subcategorization frame is a categorical entity (e.g. it either is or is not a frame with a *to*-infinitive complement).

Frequency effects are indeed very pervasive; people do store some knowledge of the relative frequencies of words and bigger constructions. Nevertheless, there are still clear cases of all-or-nothing categorical facts in syntax, such as the grammaticality of *The man shot himself* and *We are here*, as opposed to **The man shot herself* and **We is here*.[41] Individual speakers have instinctively acquired sets of private conventional norms which constrain much of their language. Norms, whether public or private, are discrete, and not necessarily accessible to awareness. Of course, multi-authored corpora or whole language communities may exhibit behaviour that is best described in probabilistic terms, but that is another matter. What we are concerned with is the biologically evolved capacities of individual humans to acquire syntactic competence in a language. A person's private norms may change over time or occasionally be flouted. Manning (2003), while (and despite) arguing for probabilistic syntax, gives a beautifully clear example of a changing individual norm.

As a recent example, the term *e-mail* started as a mass noun like *mail* (*I get too much junk e-mail*). However, it is moving to be a count noun (filling the role of the non-existent **e-letter*): *I just got an interesting email about that.* This change happened in the last decade: I still remember when this last sentence sounded completely wrong (and ignorant (!)). It then became commonplace, but still didn't quite sound right to me. Then I started noticing myself using it.   (Manning 2003, p. 313)

Here Manning reports a categorical intuitive reaction—'sounded completely wrong'—and is happy to describe the phenomenon in terms of the categories mass noun and count noun. For myself, I am happy to concede that at the tipping point between the usage not sounding quite right and his beginning to use it, there might have been a brief interval during which his private norm for this form had a non-categorical nature.

Newmeyer (1998, pp. 165–223) mounts a very detailed defence of the classical view that syntactic categories are discrete, while not denying frequency and gradience effects. (Bod and his co-authors do not mention Newmeyer's defence of discrete categories.) What is needed is a theory that allows both categorical and probabilistic facts within the same model of competence. In the domain of phonology, a procedure for the formation of competence, Boersma and Hayes's (2001) Gradual Learning Algorithm, assuming an Optimality Theory model of competence, achieves this. 'A paradoxical aspect of the Gradual Learning

---

[41] In the competence of a speaker of what happens to be a standard dialect of English.

Algorithm is that, even though it is statistical and gradient in character, most of the constraint rankings it learns are (for all practical purposes) categorical. These categorical rankings emerge as the limit of gradual learning' (Boersma and Hayes 2001, p. 46). Boersma's model has so far only been applied to phonology, and not to the learning of syntactic competence.

The use of the term 'probabilistic' in relation to competence should not be taken to imply that particular sentences are to be assigned specific probabilities, that is particular numbers between 0 and 1. This would be a completely unrealistic goal for syntactic theory. We can talk of greater and lesser probabilities without using actual numbers. Given a choice between several constructions to express a particular meaning, a probabilistic grammar can state a **ranking** among them, indicating which is the preferred, and which the least preferred expression. The framework known as Optimality Theory (Prince and Smolensky 2004) is well suited to generating rankings among expressions. Optimality Theory has been mostly applied to phonology; to date, there is little work on syntax in this vein. Papers in Legendre et al. (2001) and Sells (2001) are a start in this direction.

Now, as promised, a note about the term 'grammaticality', contrasted with 'acceptability'. I have used them somewhat interchangeably up to now. A reasonable distinction reserves 'grammatical' for categorical facts, those determined by hard constraints. Thus *She saw herself* is grammatical, and **She saw himself* is ungrammatical. On the other hand, the examples cited above from Sorace and Keller (2005), illustrative of soft constraints, are all grammatical, but decreasingly **acceptable**. Acceptability is a much less specific phenomenon than grammaticality, and may arise from the interaction of grammar with a variety of factors, including semantics, depth of embedding, unusual word order, and context of situation. Acceptability is a gradient property of grammatical sentences. But all ungrammatical expressions are also unacceptable.[42] This distinction between grammaticality and acceptability, as I have so far drawn it here, is fairly consistent with generative usage, as in Chomsky (1965), for example. In later sections below, in connection with sentences which are impossible to process, my concept of grammaticality will be seen to diverge from the standard generative view.

This relationship between all-or-nothing grammaticality and gradient acceptability among actually grammatical examples (in a particular language)

---

[42] Remember that we are dealing with facts of a single, possibly nonstandard, dialect here. To any English speaker, *He ain't done nothin* is easily comprehensible. For those dialects in which it is ungrammatical, I would also say it is unacceptable. In nonstandard dialects, it is both grammatical and perfectly acceptable.

is borne out by a neuro-imaging study. Friederici et al. (2006b) compared the responses of German-speaking subjects to four kinds of sentence, illustrated below. (All these sentences are intended to express the same meaning, in different stylistic variations. Abbreviations are: S = subject, IO = indirect object, DO = direct object, and V = verb.)

Canonical (S-IO-DO-V) (o permuted objects)
Heute hat der Opa dem Jungen den Lutscher geschenkt.
'Today has the grandfather (Nominative) the boy (Dative) the lollipop (Accusative) given'

Medium complexity (IO-S-DO-V) (1 permuted object)
Heute hat dem Jungen der Opa den Lutscher geschenkt.
'Today has the boy the grandfather the lollipop given'

High complexity (IO-DO-S-V) (2 permuted objects)
Heute hat dem Jungen den Lutscher der Opa geschenkt.
'Today has the boy the lollipop the grandfather given'

Ungrammatical (S-V-IO-DO)
Heute hat der Opa *geschenkt dem Jungen den Lutscher.
'Today has the grandfather given the boy the lollipop'

(after Friederici et al. 2006b, p. 1710)

The first three kinds of sentence are grammatical in German, and of increasing complexity or acceptability; the fourth sentence is ungrammatical. Thus the difference between the first three sentences and the fourth illustrates a categorical difference in grammaticality; the differences among the first three sentences illustrate a gradient of acceptability. Investigating such sentences, Friederici et al. (2006b) found

a functional–neuroanatomical distinction between brain areas involved in the processing of ungrammaticality and brain areas engaging in the comprehension of sentences that are well formed but differ in linguistic complexity.

...the observation that different neural networks engage in the processing of complex and ungrammatical sentences appears most striking in view of the fact that it also implicates distinct neural bases for the most complex grammatical condition as compared with the ungrammatical condition in the present experiment.

(Friederici et al. 2006b, pp. 1715–16)

I will not go into the anatomical details of which different brain areas were involved in these distinctions.

Pure intuitive judgements are often not fine-grained enough to reveal small psycholinguistic differences in complexity. The following two sentences are, to me at least, grammatical (of course) and equally acceptable.

The reporter who attacked the senator admitted the error
The reporter who the senator attacked admitted the error

The second sentence here involves 'object extraction', that is the phrase *the reporter* is understood as the object of the verb *attacked*. By contrast in the first sentence, this same phrase is understood as the subject of *attacked*, so that is a case of 'subject extraction'. To my intuition at least these sentences are equally acceptable, not differing noticeably in complexity. Gibson (1998) cites a mass of evidence that these types of sentences involving relative clauses do in fact differ in complexity.

The object extraction is more complex by a number of measures including phoneme-monitoring, on-line lexical decision, reading times, and response-accuracy to probe questions (Holmes 1973; Hakes et al. 1976; Wanner and Maratsos 1978; King and Just 1991). In addition, the volume of blood flow in the brain is greater in language areas for object-extractions than for subject-extractions (Just et al. 1996; Stromswold et al. 1996), and aphasic stroke patients cannot reliably answer comprehension questions about object-extracted RCs, although they perform well on subject-extracted RCs (Caramazza and Zurif 1976; Caplan and Futter 1986; Grodzinsky 1989a; Hickok et al. 1993).   (Gibson 1998, p. 2)

One can now add two further studies (Caplan et al. 2008; Traxler et al. 2002), stacking up the covert evidence that object-extraction in relative clauses involves more work than subject-extraction. Only greater differences in acceptability than those detected by these technological methods are evident to intuition. Gordon et al. (2001) have discovered a further wrinkle in the processing difference between object-extraction and subject-extraction.

The poorer language comprehension performance typically observed for object-extracted compared with subject-extracted forms was found to depend strongly on the mixture of types of NPs (descriptions, indexical pronouns, and names) in a sentence. Having two NPs of the same type led to a larger performance difference than having two NPs of a different type. The findings support a conception of working memory in which similarity-based interference plays an important role in sentence complexity effects.   (Gordon et al. 2001, p. 1411)

From the early days of generative grammar, there has been a persistent strain of scepticism, by critics of the approach, about the idea of grammaticality as distinct from any more obviously functional property of expressions. Newmeyer (1998) dubs this position 'extreme functionalism'. He mentions García (1979); Diver (1995), and Kalmár (1979) as examples. 'Advocates of this approach believe that *all* of grammar can be derived from semantic and discourse factors—the only "arbitrariness" in language exists in the lexicon....very few linguists of any theoretical stripe consider such an approach to be tenable' (Newmeyer 1998, pp. 17–18). Purely grammatical facts are on the face of things arbitrary, and lack any obvious **direct** functional motivation. Hard grammatical constraints are not, for instance, directly motivated by semantic coherence. One clear example involves the synonyms *likely* and *probable*. The sentences *It is likely that John will leave* and *It is probable that John will leave* are paraphrases of each other. But *John is likely to leave* is grammatical, whereas **John is probable to leave* is ungrammatical. We would understand this latter sentence if a non-native speaker said it (demonstrating its semantic acceptability), but we would be tempted to helpfully correct his English (demonstrating its ungrammaticality). There are many such examples of raw arbitrary conventionality[43] in languages. And any healthy human exposed to enough of a language exhibiting such facts can readily pick them up. Humans are disposed to acquire systems of grammatical rules orthogonal to other systems impinging on the form of language, such as systems of semantic relations between words ('sense relations') and systems of information structure (e.g. Topic–Comment structure). (The modern syntactic difference between *likely* and *probable* may be explainable historically, as one has a Germanic root and the other a Romance root. It is not uncommon for groups of words with different historical origins to exhibit synchronic differences in distribution.)

Although the most stereotypical facts of grammar (as opposed to facts of meaning or information-presentation) are arbitrary, at least some grammatical patterns can be explained in terms of their function. Such functional explanation relies on slight pressures operating on speakers, hearers, and learners over many generations in the history of a language. We will discuss such explanations in a later chapter, under the heading of grammaticalization. Suffice it here to say that grammaticalization is a historical process whereby grammatical facts in a language come into existence. Thus the idea of grammaticalization logically presupposes the idea of a grammatical (as opposed to semantic or discoursal) fact.

Grammaticality is a separate dimension from semantic acceptability, as shown by Chomsky's classic example *Colorless green ideas sleep furiously*,

---

[43] I once put the *likely/probable* example to Ron Langacker, defending the idea of grammaticality in languages. He replied that he didn't doubt the existence of some 'raw conventionality' in languages, but didn't want to use the term 'grammaticality' for some reason. His reasons are set out in slightly more detail in Langacker (1987, p. 66). It is unfortunate that individual terms connote, for some, so much associated theoretical baggage.

which is grammatical but semantically nonsensical.[44] The distinction between semantic anomaly and syntactic anomaly (ungrammaticalness) is backed up by neuroscientific evidence. Without going into details, electrodes placed on the scalp can detect two sorts of waves in brain activity, negative-going waves and positive-going waves. The time between the peak of such a wave and the stimulus producing it can be measured in milliseconds. A negative-going wave happening 400ms post-stimulus is called an N400; a positive-going wave 600ms post-stimulus is a P600. Kutas and Hillyard (1984) reported a consistent N400 effect when a semantically anomalous word was encountered, as in *John buttered his bread with socks*. About a decade later Osterhout and Holcomb (1992, 1993) discovered a P600 effect when a syntactic rule was violated, as in **John hoped the man to leave*. These results have broadly stood the test of time (e.g. Friederici et al. 1999), and have been used to shed light on interesting semantico-syntactic differences in processing (e.g. Hammer et al. 2008). While the results do reinforce a distinction between raw syntactic facts and semantic facts, other experimental results in both linguistic and non-linguistic domains are intriguing, and point to mechanisms that are not restricted to the domain of language. Dietl et al. (2005) measured such event-related potentials in subjects while showing them pictures of famous or unfamiliar faces. 'The faces evoked N400-like potentials (anterior medial temporal lobe N400, AMTL-N400) in the rhinal cortex and P600-like potentials in the hippocampus' (p. 401). Guillem et al. (1995) also found N400 and P600 responses to pictures. They suggest that these responses are involved in memory retrieval across a range of different cognitive systems. Nevertheless the semantics-N400 and syntax-P600 results seem to indicate a difference between access to grammatical knowledge and access to semantic knowledge. (Furthermore, and problematically for certain theories of sentence interpretation, the results indicate some access to semantic information before access to syntactic information. This is a problem for any theory claiming that a complete syntactic parse is the route by which hearers gain access to the meaning of a sentence.)

There is also neuroscientific evidence for the separation of inferences based on grammatical structure and inferences based on logical particles such as *not, or* and *if... then*. Monti et al. (2009) found that tasks involving these inferences activated different brain areas.

---

[44] Geoff Pullum, uncharacteristically, gets it wrong when he writes ' "A, or B, and both" is neither grammatical nor clearly interpretable' (Liberman and Pullum 2006, p. 105). It **is** grammatical, but not semantically coherent.

3.5.4 Working memory

Another example of different mechanisms interacting is the relationship between grammatical knowledge and working memory. Here is one experimental example among many:

Fourteen adolescents, 7 of whom stuttered, and 7 of whom were normally fluent, ages 10–18 years, participated in a sentence imitation task in which stimuli were divided into three classes of grammatical complexity. Results indicated that for both groups of speakers, normal disfluencies and errors in repetition accuracy increased as syntactic complexity increased. (Silverman and Ratner 1997, p. 95)

These results can naturally be explained by an appeal to working memory limitations. The classic, widely accepted account of the relationship between working memory and linguistic competence is by Chomsky and Miller (1963, p. 286f). They discuss example (3):

(3) The rat the cat the dog chased killed ate the malt.

This sentence, they write,

is surely confusing and improbable but it is perfectly grammatical and has a clear and unambiguous meaning. To illustrate more fully the complexities that must in principle be accounted for by a real grammar of a natural language, consider [(4)], a perfectly well-formed sentence with a clear and unambiguous meaning, and a grammar of English must be able to account for it if the grammar is to have any psychological relevance[:]

(4) Anyone who feels that if so-many more students whom we haven't actually admitted are sitting in on the course than ones we have that the room had to be changed, then probably auditors will have to be excluded, is likely to agree that the curriculum needs revision. (Chomsky and Miller 1963, p. 286f)

According to this account, the problem with the centre-embedded example (3) and the horrendously convoluted example (4) is the same, a problem not of linguistic knowledge itself, but of working memory. In this context, there are two ways to take the idea of working memory. It is either a general mental resource not specific to the language faculty, or there is a specifically linguistic mechanism of working memory that operates during langage processing. These alternative views of working memory are not often enough distinguished in debates about excessively complex sentences.

If working memory is taken as a general resource not specific to language, then Chomsky and Miller's argument means that difficulties in parsing complex, allegedly grammatical examples arise for reasons having nothing to do specifically with linguistic structure. One standard general measure of working memory involves getting a subject to repeat an unstructured list of numbers, letters or names, with no obvious relationships between them, apart from their linear order in the list. Most adults can keep up to about seven items in mind and repeat them faithfully. There is a massive literature on working memory, which I will not go into here. The key point to note is the **unstructured** nature of the test material; it is mainly the **length** of the string that matters. But any property measured in this simple way cannot be responsible for the distribution of difficulties that people have with sentences. The reason is that some very short sentences are hard to parse, and some much longer sentences are very easy to comprehend. Here are two seven-word centre-embedded sentences:

Actors women men like idolize get rich
Drugs chemists physicists trained make are better

It cannot be just the length of these sentences that poses the difficulty, because many much longer sentences, like the current one, are easy to process. It seems that the difficulty is related to the particular grammatical structure of the examples,[45] and not to their raw length. The processing resource involved is not independent of linguistic structure, but relates to the ways parts of sentences are hierarchically nested in relation to each other: 'self-embedding seems to impose a greater burden than an equivalent amount of nesting without self-embedding' (Miller and Chomsky 1963, p. 475). Beyond this remark, Miller and Chomsky go into very little detail about the specific kind of working memory involved in sentence processing, but their discussion does consider the task of keeping track of levels of hierarchical nesting in a complex sentence. It is the hierarchical nature of sentence structure, and its compositional meaningfulness, that makes it easy to process sentences far longer than any unstructured list that can be recalled by a typical subject. The kind of working memory that deals with hierarchically structured sequences, then, seems likely to be of a kind specifically applied to sentence processing.

The hypothesis of a kind of working memory specific to language processing has been substantially consolidated in later research. Caplan and Waters (1999) surveyed evidence for sentence comprehension not involving the same general working memory resource as is used in non-linguistic tasks, and they provided further evidence from their own experiments. 'All these results are consistent with the view that the resources that are used in syntactic processing in sentence comprehension are not reduced in patients with reduced verbal

---

[45] A structure that we can possibly work out after much staring and brain-racking, but that certainly does not come automatically to mind.

working memory capacity, and are not shared by the digit-span task' (p. 92). In other words, the kind of memory used in sentence processing is not what you use to keep a new telephone number in mind while you dial it (simple digit span). Gibson (1998) has developed a detailed theory of two separate burdens incurred in sentence processing. To take a familiar kind of example, consider question sentences beginning with a *Wh-* word, such as *What did John think Mary expected him to do?* To interpret this sentence, you have to hold the question word *What* in mind while taking in eight other words, and then integrate it semantically with the *do* at the end of the sentence. There is a memory cost and an integration cost, according to Gibson's theory, which works well to predict degrees of difficulty of a range of sentences. This theory

provides a unified theory of a large array of disparate processing phenomena, including the following:

1. On-line reading times of subject- and object-extracted relative clauses
2. The complexity of doubly-nested relative clause constructions
3. The greater complexity of embedding a sentential complement within a relative clause than the reverse embedding
4. The lack of complexity of multiply embedded structures with pronouns in the most embedded subject position
5. The high complexity of certain two-clause constructions
6. The greater complexity of nesting clauses with more arguments in Japanese
7. The lack of complexity of two-clause sentences with five initial NPs in Japanese
8. Heaviness effects
9. The greater complexity of center-embedded constructions as compared with cross-serial constructions
10. Ambiguity effects: (a) Gap-positing preference effects; (b) Syntactic complexity effects independent of plausibility and frequency.   (Gibson 1998, p. 68)

Note how linguistically specific these phenomena are, involving types of entity peculiar to syntactic structure—subjects, objects, relative clauses, sentential complements, pronouns, NPs, centre-embeddings, cross-serial constructions. You don't find these kinds of things outside syntactic structure. Nor do you find any everyday non-linguistic tasks demanding such quick processing, involving such intricate stacking of subtasks, and calling on such enormous stores in long-term memory (vocabulary) as is found in sentence processing.

It is clear that computational resources including working memory, of a kind specifically tailored to syntactic structure, largely explain parsing difficulties, even in some quite short sentences. The specifically linguistic nature of the computational resources makes it less plausible to claim that such difficult sentences are difficult 'for non-linguistic reasons'. As long as the working memory involved seemed not to be specifically linguistic, such a claim may have been tenable. But evidence such as Caplan and Waters' (1999) and Gibson's (1998) indicates a close link between competence and processing mechanisms; they deal in the same kind of stuff, found only in language.

From an evolutionary point of view, it is sensible to consider a speaker's knowledge of his language and his ability to process sentences as a single complex package. The innate capacity to acquire the knowledge and the innate ability to process what this knowledge generates are likely to have co-evolved. Tacitly knowing that clauses can be recursively embedded in other clauses would be useless without some ability to process at least some of the nested structures generated. Conversely, an ability to process nested structures would be useless in the absence of an internalized grammar specifying exactly which kinds of nestings are grammatical and which are not. The human parser evaluates an input string of words[46] by relating it to a known body of rules or principles defining the structures of the language. The most plausible evolutionary story is that humans gradually evolved larger long-term memory storage capacity for languages, and in parallel evolved an enhanced capacity for rapidly producing and interpreting combinations of the stored items. These two capacities, though theoretically separable, are interdependent in practice.

In early life, a child has some limited language processing capacity, but as yet no internalized grammar of the particular language she is acquiring. From initial simple trigger experiences, including both the heard speech and the child's own basic grasp of the communicative context, the child is first able to apply her inborn processor to extrapolate the first basic grammatical facts about the ambient language. In early stages the processor may be quite rudimentary, but enough to get the child on the road to understanding more sentences and registering the rules of their assembly for her own future use in speaking and listening. All this happens completely unconsciously, of course. Language acquisition is sometimes discussed as if it is divorced from language understanding. Here is Chomsky's famous diagram of the 'logical problem of language acquisition':

Experience → ⎢Language Acquisition Device⎢ → Internalized Grammar

---

[46] For simplicity, let's assume that phonological processing delivers words.

Put simply, given some input data, the learning device (the child) figures out the rules which (putting aside errors, disfluencies, etc.) produced the data. Undoubtedly, the feat performed by the child is impressive, and there is some usefulness in this extremely bare formal statement of what the child achieves. But this presentation of the problem ignores, as much generative theorizing does, the function and motivation of language acquisition. The child **tries to understand** what is being said around her. So sentence processing for understanding is at the heart of the language acquisition device from the outset. Language acquisition theory has emphasized the child's acquisition of a body of tacit declarative knowledge. This is undoubtedly part of the story. But as Mazuka (1998, p. 6) notes 'it is paradoxical to assume that children are able to parse a sentence in order to acquire grammar, whereas for adults it is assumed that grammar is required to parse a sentence'. In addition, as another theorist has emphasized 'the task of acquiring a language includes the acquisition of the *procedural skills* needed for the processing of the language' (Pienemann 2005, p. 2).

Working memory constraints are present in the child acquiring language, just as much as in the adult who has already acquired it.[47] So working memory limitations are in force during the process of building competence in a language. The Language Acquisition Device is not a conscious reflective process, but operates automatically. Normal children, exposed to the right data, just absorb a competence in their language. The 'right data' cannot include anything that a limited working memory cannot handle. A child hypothetically given a centre-embedded sentence like one of those above would be as confused by it as anyone else, if not more so. A child hypothetically attempting to apply a general recursive embedding rule to produce such a sentence would lose her way just as adults do. The result is that an ability to produce and interpret such sentences would not be formed. On this account, mature ability in a language has a probabilistic quantitative component. The language learner ends up with an ability to produce and interpret a wide range of grammatical sentences, including an indefinite number that she has never experienced before, but only such sentences as her working memory, at any time in her life, is able to cope with. Some sentences can be judged as clearly grammatical or ungrammatical, while other more complex ones are simply judged as too complex for any judgement to be made. In between, there are marginal cases of various degrees of acceptability, depending how complex they

---

[47] This contrast between the child and the adult is a convenient simplification. Adults learn too, but not as well or as fast as children.

are. Thus, in this view, a four-valued logic applies to the question of whether any particular expression is grammatical; the answers can be 'Yes definitely', 'No definitely', 'Yes but it's somewhat weird', and 'I can't tell'. Examples that are judged to be 'somewhat weird' are acceptable to varying degrees, with factors of various kinds, including complexity, semantic coherence, and pragmatic coherence, applying. Examples of the 'I can't tell' variety are above some critical approximate threshold for complexity; they are unacceptable and of unknown grammaticality.

This argument follows up the those made in Chapter 1 for **competence-plus**, a package consisting of the familiar recursive statements of grammatical rules, plus a set of numerical constraints on the products of those rules. It may turn out, indeed it would be desirable, that the 'set of numerical constraints' can be replaced by a theory of processing complexity such as Gibson's. In a later section, some evidence in favour of this modified, quantitatively limited view of competence-plus will be given.

The claim that memory constraints apply during acquisition is broadly consistent with a generative theory of acquisition. David Lightfoot (1989)[48] distinguishes between **language data** and the child's **trigger experience**.

> The trigger is something less than the total experience... The child might even be exposed to significant quantities of linguistic material that does not act as a trigger. ...
> This means that children sometimes hear a form which does not trigger some grammatical device for incorporating this form in their grammar. Thus, even though they have been exposed to the form, it does not occur in mature speech.
> (Lightfoot 1989, pp. 324–5)

Lightfoot does not mention memory or processing limitations as filters on the input to learning. His account of the filter is all in terms of what can be made sense of by a presumed UG of vintage *circa* 1989. Lightfoot states baldly that 'UG filters experience' (p. 321). This could be paradoxical, in the following way. The trigger experience is what is said to be **input** to UG, **after** the filter has operated, so how can UG itself be responsible for filtering what goes into it? Grodzinsky's commentary on Lightfoot's article (Grodzinsky 1989b) asks 'Given that it [the trigger experience] constitutes only a subset of the linguistic material the learner hears, how does he identify it and avoid the rest?' (p. 342). Grodzinsky says that finding the answer to this question will be hard, but doesn't consider limitations of memory and processing as a possibility.

---

[48] In a nicely waspish comment on this article and strong nativist approaches generally, Haider (1989, p. 343) writes 'I feel tempted to ask, as an *advocatus diaboli*, whether it is true that the difference between English and the flu is just the length of the incubation period'.

The 'UG filters experience' paradox can be avoided if one re-conceptualizes the acquisition device, call it now 'UG+', as having two interdependent parts, (1) a mechanism for making sense of (i.e. understanding) the input data, subject to computational constraints operating in the child at the time, and (2) a mechanism for responding to the understood input by internalizing rules or constraints for generating similar data in the future, typically for purposes of communication. The output of UG+, after adequate exposure to a language, is **competence-plus** in the language, a capacity for versatile production and comprehension of a vast number of expressions, subject to constraints on computation. The language acquisition capacity loses considerable plasticity some time around puberty, but plasticity is not lost altogether in adulthood. So the adult state retains the two aspects originally in UG+ and now made more specific to a particular language in competence-plus, namely mutually supportive and interdependent 'knowledge' and computational components. Of course it is theoretically possible to disentangle the 'knowledge' component of competence-plus from its computational component. Educated adults develop refined metalinguistic awareness which allows them to discuss idealized products of linguistic 'knowledge' dissociated from computational considerations. It may even be possible in pathological cases to show a dissociation between the two components. But in normal people in everyday conversation or giving spontaneous intuitive judgements the knowledge and the computational constraints act seamlessly together. It is the uniquely human capacity to acquire this kind of complex seamless behaviour that should be the target of an evolutionary explanation.

The idea that working memory filters the input to the child does not entail that a child can get **nothing** out of a complex input expression. There may be some parts of a complex expression that a child can take in, while not being able to parse the whole thing. Simon Kirby (1999a) makes this point and gives an example: 'If a structure contains an embedded constituent that is hard to parse, this does not necessarily mean that the branching direction of the superordinate structure cannot be adduced' (p. 88). The working memory filter on competence-forming is also not, obviously, a barrier to all generalizing from the trigger experience to previously non-experienced structures. A child whose only experience of relative clauses is of relative clauses modifying nouns in the subject position of a main clause may well tacitly assume that there is no reason not to apply relative clauses to nouns in object position. This is a kind of combinatorial promiscuity distinctive of humans. The limitations come when the promiscuity ventures into more complex structures that are hard to parse. Structures formed by valid combinatorial promiscuity that are somewhat hard, but not impossible, to parse online in rapid conversation will enter into the learner's competence, and be judged intuitively as grammatical but of problematic acceptability.

The competence/performance distinction is sometimes explained using the analogy of a geographical map, contrasted with actual routes travelled. A map specifies all possible routes between all locations. This is analogous to competence, which specifies a range of possible sentences that a speaker may use, even though in fact he may never happen to use some of them. The sentences that actually get uttered, the linguistic performance, are analogous to the routes actually travelled. This is not a bad analogy, but let me suggest a modification, at the serious risk of mixing my metaphors. All maps are limited by their resolution. A map of Europe in my atlas won't guide you from my house to the bus stop. Linguistic competence indeed provides a specification of possible sentences, but its resolution is limited. You can't keep zooming in (or zooming out, depending on how you take this map analogy) forever to give you an infinite number of possible journeys. Sentences of problematic acceptability are analogous to routes that you can only discern with difficulty on a map, due to its limited resolution. This analogy is not an argument in favour of the idea, of course, nor empirical evidence, but may help to clarify the kind of thing I am suggesting. Analogies are useful in science.

Limitations of working memory have been proposed as an explanation of how grammatical competence is acquired at all. In other words, working memory limitations are not just a noisy hindrance to making judgements about complex examples, but a necessary component of the incremental grammar learning process itself. In an influential paper, Elman (1993) describes a connectionist (artificial neural net) model of acquisition of a grammatical system from presented examples in which the 'window' of what the learner can attend to at one time starts small and gradually expands. In early stages of acquisition the learner can, in this model, only attend to strings that are three words long. This is sufficient for the learner to acquire some rules of local scope relating closely neighbouring elements, but not enough to allow learning of more long-distance grammatical relationships. The initially acquired knowledge of very local relationships is necessary, however, for the learner to progress to more complex structures involving more long-distance relationships, once the memory limitation is gradually relaxed through maturation. Without the initial quite severe constraint on working memory, or attention span, Elman showed, nothing gets acquired. He appropriately dubbed this effect 'the importance of starting small.'[49] Elman's implementation of working memory was very simple, and Elman himself may be quite opposed to the idea of the language-domain-specific computational constraints that I have appealed to (and cited evidence for) here. What we have in common is the absolutely critical role that computational constraints (whether specific to language or not) play in language acquisition and adult behaviour.

The proposal here for competence-plus is motivated by the same kind of considerations that gave rise, in another field, to Herb Simon's concept of **bounded rationality**. 'The term "bounded rationality" is used to designate rational choice that takes into account the cognitive limitations of the decision maker—limitations of both knowledge and computational capacity' (Simon 1997, p. 291). My vision of competence-plus is similar to this conclusion of Givón's:

One may suggest, lastly, that 'competence' can be re-interpreted as *the level of 'performance' obtained at the highest level of generativity and automaticity*. Such a level of performance indeed comes closest to mimicking some of the salient characteristics of Chomsky's 'competence'. But its domain is now shifted, radically—from the idealized realm of Plato's *eidon* to the rough-and-dirty domain of biological information processing.   (Givón 2002, p. 121)

There is not much sign among mainstream syntacticians that they are beginning to take seriously a quantitative theory of the gradation of examples. For our purposes here, all we can be interested in is a very broad picture of the kind of syntactic capacity that has evolved in humans. To this end, it is enough to point out that, universally, healthy humans exposed to a complex language produce quite complex and regular sentence-like expressions and make quite consistent intuitive judgements about their potential behaviour. Speakers use regular complex clause combinations, around a statistical norm of one or two clauses, with occasional excursions into more complex combinations. They are also capable of intuiting many clear cases of grammaticality, many clear cases of ungrammaticality, and, universally again, may still be uncertain about some, perhaps many, cases. In the cases of uncertainty, they are often able to rank one expression as more acceptable than another similar one. This productivity in performance and these intuitive judgements, both absolute and graded, are the raw data of syntax. The gradience or fuzziness of syntactic judgements does not undermine the core idea of linguistic competence, a speaker's intuitive

---

[49] An obvious example of the necessity of starting small is the fact that grammar acquisition depends on some earlier acquired vocabulary.

knowledge of the facts of her language. In Chapter 4 I will list a small number of the most interesting (and agreed upon) syntactic patterns about which there is substantial consistency in intuitive judgement across languages. These patterns are representative of the data that an account of the origins of human grammatical competence must have something to say about.

3.6 Individual differences in competence-plus

In any language, people vary in their production and comprehension abilities, just as they vary in other abilities. It would be amazing if there were complete uniformity in achieved language competence across a whole community; and there isn't. A noted generative linguist acknowledges an aspect of this: 'In fact, perception of ambiguity is a sophisticated skill which develops late and not uniformly' (Lightfoot 1989, p. 322). Chomsky also (maybe to some people's surprise) recognizes this, and puts it more generally:

I would be inclined to think, even without any investigation, that there would be a correlation between linguistic performance and intelligence; people who are intelligent use language much better than other people most of the time. They may even know more about language; thus when we speak about a fixed steady state, which is of course idealized, it may well be (and there is in fact some evidence) that the steady state attained is rather different among people of different educational level... it is entirely conceivable that some complex structures just aren't developed by a large number of people, perhaps because the degree of stimulation in their external environment isn't sufficient for them to develop.   (Chomsky 1980a, pp. 175–6)

It is important to note that Chomsky here mentions individual differences both in linguistic performance (first sentence of quotation) and in competence ('the steady state attained is rather different'). Let us first focus on the issue of possible differences in competence, the attained steady state of tacit knowledge of one's language. In particular, let's examine the premises of the last sentence in the quotation, about a possible relation between lack of knowledge of some complex structures and lack of sufficient stimulation from the external environment.

The first thing to note is that this is an implicit denial of any strong version of the Poverty of the Stimulus (PoS) argument. PoS is the pro-nativist argument that the linguistic experience of a normal child is insufficient to explain the rich knowledge of language that the grown adult ends up with, so the knowledge must come from somewhere other than experience, that is it must be innate. In the quotation above, Chomsky is sensibly conceding that sometimes the acquired competence may be incomplete **because** the child's experience is incomplete. In other words, in these cases of below-average competence, poverty in the stimulus explains it. If the stimulus is too poor, the acquired state may be less complete than that of other speakers. And evidently we are not here considering pathological cases, or cases of extreme deprivation. This is all sensible and shows an awareness of a statistical distribution in knowledge of language correlated, at least in part, with a statistical distribution of degree of exposure to the appropriate data in childhood. The practice of syntacticians in analysing sentences idealizes away from this variation. This idealization could be justified on the grounds that there is plenty of interesting analytical work to do on the tacit knowledge of **typical** speakers of a language. In fact practising syntacticians tend to analyse the tacit knowledge of the more accomplished speakers in a population because (a) the extra complexity is more interesting, and (b) professional syntacticians live and work among highly educated people. Even fieldworkers working with informants with little education try to find 'good' informants, who will report subtle judgements.

Now let's turn to another aspect of the claim that 'it is entirely conceivable that some complex structures just aren't developed by a large number of people, perhaps because the degree of stimulation in their external environment isn't sufficient for them to develop'. This was Chomsky speaking in the late 1970s. At that time Chomskyan generative linguistics did actually assume that complex syntactic structures exist in language. And, further, the quotation implies that you need to have sufficient exposure to these structures, individually, to be able to acquire them all. The orthodox Minimalist view now, thirty years later, is that complexity is only apparent and results from the interaction of a small number of simple syntactic operations, such as Merge. These simple operations are part of the normal child's innate linguistic capacity, and the language acquirer's task is to learn the inventory of lexical items on which the operations work. That is the core of the Minimalist Program (MP), but in fact it seems that such a simple elegant view of syntax cannot be maintained, and syntacticians who label themselves as Minimalists end up positing complexities well beyond the tiny set of basic operations. '[I]n its origins the leanest and most elegant expression of generative grammar...[Minimalism] has become a jungle of arcane technicalities' (Bickerton 2009b, p. 13). Fritz Newmeyer's (1998, p. 13) 'one sentence critique of the MP is that it gains elegance in the derivational component of the grammar only at the expense of a vast overcomplication of other components, in particular the lexicon and the morphology'.[50] These are not ultimately damning criticisms. Language **is**

---

[50] For other severe critiques of the Minimalist Program, see Seuren (2004); Lappin et al. (2000).

complex. It is debatable where the complexity mostly lies, in purely syntactic operations, or in the lexicon or morphology, or distributed somewhat evenly among these components. Although the Minimalist Program is for sociological reasons perhaps aptly labelled 'orthodox', it's not clear any more that it is 'mainstream', as a smaller proportion of practising syntacticians subscribe to it than subscribed to the earlier generative models. One of the rivals is Construction Grammar, which sees a language as an inventory of constructions. These constructions vary from simple lexical items to quite abstract and complex grammatical structures. This view of language is more consistent with the idea 'that some complex structures just aren't developed by a large number of people, perhaps because the degree of stimulation in their external environment isn't sufficient for them to develop'.

As Chomsky surmises in the quotation above, no doubt much of the individual variation in competence stems from differing environmental conditions. For example, Sampson et al. (2008) tracked over 2,000 African-American children aged between 6 and 12, in a longitudinal study for up to seven years. Their findings 'indicate that living in a severely disadvantaged neighborhood reduces the later verbal ability of black children on average by ~4 points, a magnitude that rivals missing a year or more of schooling' (Sampson et al. 2008, p. 845). The verbal ability measured here was in standard tests of vocabulary and reading. Experiments by Dąbrowska (1997) confirmed Chomsky's surmise about a correlation between education and linguistic competence.[51] At the University of Glasgow, she tested university lecturers, students, and janitors and cleaners on some quite complex sentences. She found a correlation between their sentence comprehension and their level of education, not surprisingly.

Moving from environmental effects, such as education, to biologically heritable effects on language, it is widely assumed in the linguistics literature that the innate **potential** for language is uniform. 'To a very good first approximation, individuals are indistinguishable (apart from gross deficits and abnormalities) in their ability to acquire a grammar' (Chomsky 1975b, p. 144). The mention of gross deficits and abnormalities reminds us that there are deficits and abnormalities that are not quite so gross, and some which, though reasonably called deficits or abnormalities, are relatively minor. In other words, there is a statistical distribution of innate language capacity. In fact it is likely that there are many different distributions, for different aspects of the language

---

[51] Confirming a surmise of Chomsky's is not how Dąbrowska herself would have seen her work. Chomsky and other generative linguists are well aware of the idealization in their theorizing.

capacity, such as segmental phonology, intonation, inflectional morphology, vocabulary, and so on.[52] These distributions may be mainly symmetrical bell-shaped curves, but it seems likely that they have a longer tail at the 'negative' end. This would be consistent with what is known about the effect of genes on cognitive development more generally. 'In fact, more than 100 single-gene mutations are known to impair cognitive development. Normal cognitive functioning, on the other hand, is almost certainly orchestrated by many subtly acting genes working together, rather than by single genes operating in isolation. These collaborative genes are thought to affect cognition in a probabilistic rather than a deterministic manner' (Plomin and DeFries 1998, p. 192). The probabilistic effect of collaborative genes yields a non-uniform distribution of unimpaired cognitive functioning. See also Keller and Miller (2006) for relevant discussion.

Stromswold (2001) surveyed a large range of individual variation in language influenced by genetic factors, including performance on morphosyntactic tasks. This is her summary on morphosyntax:

Despite the relative paucity of large-scale twin studies of morphological and syntactic abilities and the impossibility of obtaining an overall heritability estimate for morphosyntax, the results of existing studies suggest that genetic factors play a role in children's comprehension and production of syntax and morphology. The MZ correlation was greater than the DZ correlation for 33 of 36 morphosyntactic measures ($p < .0001$ by sign test). (Stromswold 2001, p. 680)

MZ twins are genetically identical, whereas DZ twins are not; thus genetically identical twins were more similar to each other in their morphosyntactic abilities than genetically different twins.

If language ability did not vary across individuals, it could not provide the raw material for natural selection. Of course, some people, including Chomsky, do not believe that syntactic ability arose by natural selection. But if one does believe that enhanced syntactic ability was naturally selected, then individual variability in this trait is to be expected. The claim in favour of natural selection needs to be backed up by specifying the selective mechanism—what exactly is better syntax good for? Note for now that the question in turn presupposes a view of what exactly constitutes the evolved syntactic abilities that humans have, the theme of this chapter.

---

[52] In parallel, note that there is not just one critical (or sensitive) period for language acquisition, but several. Acquiring vocabulary continues through life, whereas acquiring a native-like accent is near impossible after about ten years of age.

In the extreme tail of the statistical distribution of human syntactic abilities
are individuals who do not acquire language at all, like people with extreme
autism or extreme ataxia. Possibly the absence of language acquisition in
such cases is not due to any factor specific to language. For instance, Helen
Keller, blind and deaf from a very young age, might well have been dismissed
as incapable of language had not her teacher Anne Sullivan found a way to
discover her abilities, which were well within the normal range. There is some
evidence for a genetically-based dissociation of specifically linguistic abilities
and non-verbal cognition at two years of age. Dale et al. (2000) compared
non-verbal cognitive ability as measured by a test called PARCA with language
ability in two-year-olds. They summarize their findings thus: 'The modest
genetic correlations between PARCA and both language scales and the high
residual variances suggest that language development is relatively independent
of non-verbal cognitive development at this early age' (p. 636). Bishop et al.
(2006) studied 173 six-year-old twin pairs in terms of their phonological short-
term memory and score on (English) verbal inflection tests. In the latter tests
children were required to produce regular past tense and present-tense third
person singular inflections on known verbs. Their 'analysis showed that impairments on both tasks were significantly heritable. However, there was minimal
phenotypic and etiological overlap between the two deficits, suggesting that
different genes are implicated in causing these two kinds of language difficulty.
From an evolutionary perspective, these data are consistent with the view that
language is a complex function that depends on multiple underlying skills with
distinct genetic origins' (p. 158). Bishop (2003) summarizes the genetic and
environmental factors known as of 2003 in the condition broadly labelled SLI
(Specific Language Impairment), indicating a very mixed and complex picture.
Kovas and Plomin (2006) emphasize the strong correlations that exist between
verbal and non-verbal deficits.[53] A recent study (Rice et al. 2009b) gets more
specific about the genetic correlates of language disorders.

The results of the linkage and association analyses indicate that it is highly likely that
loci exist in the candidate regions that influence language ability...

In sum, this investigation replicated previous reports of linkages of SSD [Speech
Sound Disorder] and RD [Reading Disability] to QTLs [quantitative trait loci] on

[53] Further, recent studies with between-family, within-family, and twin designs show
correlations of 0.2–0.3 between aspects of brain volume and standard measures of
IQ (Gignac et al. 2003; Posthuma et al. 2002). This latter paper concludes that the
association between brain volume and intelligence is of genetic origin. The indirect link
thus provided between brain volume and language reinforces a connection between the
rapid evolutionary increase in brain size and the human language capacity.

chromosomes 1, 3, 6, 7, and 15. We identified new suggestive linkages to SLI diagnostic phenotypes, as well, and identified new and promising indications of association of SNPs on chromosome 6 to language impairment, SSD and RD.... The outcomes add to the growing evidence of the likelihood of multiple gene effects on language and related abilities.

(Rice et al. 2009b)

It is becoming increasingly clear that the condition broadly (and paradoxically) labelled 'Specific Language Impairment' (SLI) is in fact a family of related disabilities. In some cases, poor command of grammar is accompanied by processing deficits, such as inability to distinguish closely adjacent sounds (Tallal et al. 1993; Wright et al. 1997). In a subset of cases, labelled 'grammatical SLI' (G-SLI), there is no such association. Children with this more specific condition exhibit grammatical deficits, especially in control of long-distance dependencies, that do not involve weakly stressed words (van der Lely and Battell 2003; van der Lely 2005).

At present there is no evidence for any language-specific deficit so drastic that sufferers fail to acquire any syntactic competence at all. As far as specifically linguistic innate abilities are concerned, the extreme tail of the distribution in human populations may still include individuals who are capable of acquiring some syntactic competence.

A line of argument that is often taken in the face of apparent individual differences in linguistic competence is that the differences are differences in working memory, and not in speakers' tacit declarative knowledge of their language. In other words, these are not **linguistic** differences between speakers, but other psychological differences. In itself this formulation need not be puzzling, if we think of linguistic competence as just one cognitive module among many interacting modules of the mind. In the previous section I suggested an alternative view of the relationship between language competence and working memory. In this view, working memory limitations are in play from early infancy onwards, including the whole period over which competence-plus is acquired. Consequently, working memory indeed explains the difficulty of judging complex examples, but the interaction happens not **after** competence has been formed, but **while** competence is being formed, resulting in a competence limited by probabilistic working memory constraints, what I have labelled 'competence-plus'.

Experiments by Chipere (2003, 2009) provide evidence for the view that competence is not only affected by working memory after it has been formed (i.e. in adulthood), but during the formation of competence (i.e. in childhood). Chipere assessed competence in individuals in tests of sentence comprehension, like the following:

Tom knows that the fact that flying planes low is dangerous excites the pilot.

What does Tom know?—the fact that flying planes low is dangerous excites the pilot.

What excites the pilot?—the fact that flying planes low is dangerous.

(Chipere 2009, p. 189)

Here the first sentence is a sentence given to the subjects, the italicized questions were then put to the subjects, and the correct expected answers are those following the italicized questions.

The tests showed that competence, as measured by success in sentence comprehension, is variable across individuals, and correlated with academic achievement, consistent with Chomsky's view quoted earlier. Language-independent tests of working memory also showed a distribution of differences between individuals matching the distribution of individual differences in sentence comprehension. Now, if the theory that difficulty in processing somewhat complex sentences is due to working memory limitations at the time when the comprehension judgement is required, it should be possible to enhance people's competence by giving them training in working memory. This is roughly analogous to taking weights off a person's feet to see if his 'jumping competence' improves. Chipere tried this. He trained the poorer-performing group with exercises to boost their working memory capacity. This was successful, and the subjects with originally poorer working memory achieved, after training, levels of working memory performance like the originally better group. So memory training works to improve memory, not surprisingly. But the memory training did not work to improve sentence comprehension, interpreted as a sign of competence. 'Results showed that memory training had no effect on comprehension scores, which remained approximately the same as those that the group had obtained prior to training' (Chipere 2009, p. 189). Conversely, Chipere trained the poorer-performing group explicitly on sentence comprehension, and found, again not surprisingly, that training on sentence comprehension improves sentence comprehension. And training on sentence comprehension did improve this group's language-independent working memory capacity, as measured by recall tasks. These results are consistent with the view that I advanced earlier, that limitations on working memory act during the formation of the adult capacity, yielding competence-plus, that is competence augmented by numerical, quantitative constraints. This view predicts that working memory training **after** the acquisition of competence in childhood would not affect the acquired competence. This prediction is confirmed by Chipere's results. The results are not consistent with the classical view that competence is knowledge of sentences of indefinite complexity, access to which is hindered by working memory limitations. The classical account, in which working memory constraints do not affect the acquisition process, but do affect the judgements accessible in adulthood, predicts that working memory training should enhance the accessibility of competence judgements. This prediction is falsified by Chipere's experiment.

Chipere's results and conclusions are consistent with the results obtained by Ferreira and Morrison (1994), mentioned earlier, but not with a detail of their incidental conclusions. These authors assume an indirect effect of schooling on language, via working memory. Schooling enhances memory, and enhanced memory, they assume, works at the time of linguistic testing to help children perform better with longer grammatical subjects of sentences. The alternative, simpler, view that schooling enhances language competence directly is consistent with their experimental results. This is a more attractive view because schooling is generally targeted at improving language ability rather than at pure memory capacity. Chipere's results, that language training enhances working memory capacity, but not vice-versa, are also consistent with the results of Morrison et al. (1995) on the effect of schooling on memory.

It might be objected that answering questions on sentence comprehension is just another kind of performance, and so sentence comprehension tests do not reveal details of competence. But such an objection would isolate competence from any kind of empirical access whatsoever. For sure, like Descartes, we have intuitions that we know things, but any publicly replicable science of the knowledge in individual heads must depend on operational methods of access to that knowledge. If it be insisted that there are aspects of the linguistic competence of individuals that cannot be publicly tested, then we have to shut up about them.[54] Science is limited by what can be publicly observed, with or without the use of instruments which extend our senses. Of course, the theoretical entities postulated by science, such as physical forces, are not themselves observable, but the **data** used to confirm or falsify theories must be observable.

So far, the individual differences I have discussed have all been quantitative differences on a single dimension, a capacity to interpret complex sentences. Bates et al. (1988) showed, in a sophisticated and detailed study, that children also have different individual **styles** of first language learning. Children differ, at various stages, in the degree to which they rely on **storage** or **computation**.[55] Storage emphasizes the rote-learning of whole forms, without any analysis into parts, and with concomitant lesser productive versatility. A computational strategy emphasizes analysis of wholes into interchangeable parts, what I

---

[54] 'Wovon man nicht sprechen kann, darüber muss man schweigen'—We must be silent about things that we cannot talk about. This tautology, which people should respect more often, is the culminating aphorism of Wittgenstein's *Tractatus LogicoPhilosophicus* (Wittgenstein 1922).

[55] These are not Bates et al.'s terms.

have labelled 'combinatorial promiscuity'. One interesting correlation between language-learning style and a non-linguistic measure was this: 'There was a modest relationship with temperament in the expected direction: a link between sociability and rote production, suggesting that some children use forms they do not yet understand because they want to be with and sound like other people' (p. 267). The authors also found that the same child used different strategies for learning two different languages, English and Italian, in somewhat different social circumstances. Along with their fascinating observations of individual differences in the learning styles of children, the 'punchline' that Bates et al. (1988) offer for their whole study is illuminating and supportive of the theme of this chapter, that one can meaningfully speak of universals in human language capacity. They conclude:

The strands of dissociable variance observed in early child development reflect the differential operation of universal processing mechanisms that every normal child must have in order to acquire a natural language. For a variety of internal or external reasons, children may rely more on one of these mechanisms, resulting in qualitatively different profiles of development. But all the mechanisms are necessary to complete language learning.   (Bates et al. 1988, pp. 267–8)

Putting it informally, learning a language requires a toolkit of several complementary skills, and some children use one tool rather more than another. But all eventually get the language learning job done.

We will come back to the topic of storage versus computation in a later chapter; here I will just make a brief point. Since both a storage-biased strategy and a computation-biased strategy are adequate to get a child to a level of competence within the normal adult range, the same externally verifiable level of competence may correspond to somewhat different internal representations in the adult speaker's mind. We can have an 'external' characterization of competence in terms of a speaker's productions and intuitive judgements, but the psychological or neural characterization of that competence is not entailed by our description.

Individual differences in sentence comprehension can be created artificially. Blaubergs and Braine (1974) trained subjects on sentences with multiple levels of self-embedding, and found that with practice subjects could manage to interpret sentences with up to five levels of self-embedding. Chipere (2009) comments on this result: 'Presumably, the training procedure that they provided was able to push subjects beyond structure-specificity and enable them to grasp an abstract notion of recursion that could be generalized to an arbitrary degree of complexity. This study shows that subjects do have the potential to grasp the concept of recursion as an abstract generative device' (p. 184). It is important to note that the experimental subjects were still not able to perform in comprehending sentences 'to an arbitrary degree of complexity'; five levels of embedding was the limit, even though they may fairly be credited with 'the concept of recursion as an abstract generative device'.

Syntacticians are extraordinary individuals. They are virtuoso performers, better at unravelling complex syntax than most other people. Typically, they have developed a virtuosity in making up hypothetical examples deliberately designed to test hypotheses about sentence structure. They can think about the possible interpretations of complex sentences out of context. They are ace spotters of ambiguity. They are exemplars of what the human syntactic capacity can achieve in the limit. No doubt, a facility with written language, and constant thought about syntax, has helped them to get to this state. They are at one end of the statistical distribution of language competence. But for the most part, especially more recently, the examples that syntactic theorists typically use are not in the far reaches of competence.

'People are different' is the underlying message behind most studies of individual differences, and the implied moral is that generalizing across the species is counter to the facts. The picture of uniform innate syntactic potential across all individuals is an idealization, but it is a practically useful idealization in the current state of our knowledge. The syntactic abilities of humans, even those with relatively poor syntactic ability, are so strikingly different from anything that apes can be made to show, that the most obvious target for an evolutionary explanation is what we can call a species-typical level of syntactic capacity, somewhere in the middle of the statistical distribution. In this sense, it is completely practical to go along with Chomsky's 'first approximation' strategy, quoted above. In Chapter 4, I will set out a list of structural properties of sentences that all humans in a broad range in the centre of the statistical distribution can learn to command, given suitable input in a normal social environment.

3.7 Numerical constraints on competence-plus

Arguments for augmenting the theoretical construct of competence with quantitative, numerical information have already been put in several places earlier in this book. The mainstream generative view of competence does not admit of any quantitative or probabilistic component of linguistic competence. Against this strong trend, I know of just two claims by formal syntacticians that for certain constructions in certain languages, there are **competence**, not performance, limitations involving structures with embedding beyond a depth of 2.

Both papers infer from the depth limitations a preference for some particular model of grammar, in which the depth limitation can be naturally stated. The two articles are independent of each other and argued on different grounds, using different data. Neither paper makes a **general** claim that all competence is limited by depth factors, arguing only about specific constructions in particular languages.

One of the papers has a data problem. Langendoen (1998, p. 235) claims that in English 'the depth of coordinate-structure embedding does not have to exceed 2. This limitation on coordinate-structure embedding must be dealt with by the grammars of natural languages; it is not simply a performance limitation'. He argues that this limitation is captured by adopting an Optimality Theory approach to syntax. I find Langendoen's data problematic, and he has (personal communication) accepted a counterexample to his basic claim of a depth limitation on coordinate-structure embedding. My counterexample, with bracketing to show the embedding implied by the semantics, is:

[shortbread and [neat whisky or [whisky and [water or [7-up and lemon]]]]]

Here the most deeply embedded coordinate structure, *7-up and lemon* is embedded at a depth of 4. I don't find this ungrammatical. It can be said with appropriate intonation and slight pauses to get the meaning across. Admittedly, it is not highly acceptable, because of its length and the depth of embedding, but this is not a matter of competence, as Langendoen claimed. Many similarly plausible counterexamples could be constructed, if not easily found in corpora. (Wagner (2005, p. 54) also disagrees with Langendoen's data, on similar grounds.)

The other claim for a numerical limit on competence, for certain constructions, is by Joshi et al. (2000). They argue on the basis of 'scrambling' (fairly radical re-ordering of phrases) in certain complex German sentences. They do not rely on intuitions of grammaticality for the problem cases, implying rather marginal acceptability: 'Sentences involving scrambling from more than two levels of embedding are indeed difficult to interpret and native speakers show reluctance in accepting these sentences' (p. 173). They show how, in a particular grammar formalism, Lexicalized Tree-Adjoining Grammar (LTAG), it is impossible to generate sentences with the semantically appropriate structure involving scrambling from more than two levels of embedding. Thus, the argument goes, if we adopt that particular formalism (which I agree is probably well-motivated on other grounds), we can be content to classify the difficulty of the problematic sentences as a matter of grammatical competence, rather than as a matter of performance. In other words, they appeal to a tactic known from early in generative studies as 'let the grammar decide'. But letting the grammar decide puts the theoretical cart before the empirical horse. It is like saying that the precession of the perihelion of Mercury **can't** be anomalous because Newton's equations say so.

Neither Langendoen nor Joshi et al. provide a general solution, within a theory of competence, for limitations on depth of embedding. Langendoen's proposal applies only to English co-ordinate constructions. If we accepted Joshi et al.'s LTAG as a model for describing a range of sentence-types other than those involving German-like scrambling, there would still be sentences that the model could generate which are well beyond the limits of acceptability.

My coinage 'competence-plus' respects the widely-held non-numerical nature of competence itself. In this view competence is a set of unbounded combinatorial rules or principles, and the '-plus' factor represents the normally respected numerical limits on the productivity of these rules. The -plus factor is not just another label for all kinds of performance effects, including false starts and errors due to interruption or drunkenness or ill health. The -plus of competence-plus reflects the computational limitations operating in normal healthy language users in conditions of good alertness and lack of distraction or stress. A full specification of the precise content of this -plus could well begin with the kind of memory and integration costs described by Gibson (1998), mentioned earlier.

The very term 'competence' is quite vexed in the literature. Its politicized connotations are seen in an impressive paper by Christiansen and Chater (1999). They built a connectionist model of human performance in processing recursive structures, trained on simple artificial languages.

We find that the qualitative performance profile of the model matches human behavior, both on the relative difficulty of center-embedding and cross-dependency, and between the processing of these complex recursive structures and right-branching recursive constructions. ... we show how a network trained to process recursive structures can also generate such structures in a probabilistic fashion. This work suggests a novel explanation of people's limited recursive performance, without assuming the existence of **a mentally represented competence grammar allowing unbounded recursion.**

(Christiansen and Chater 1999, p. 157, boldface added, JRH)

Here the boldfaced last phrase collocates *competence* with *allowing unbounded recursion*. Christiansen and Chater are not against mental representations; their paper speaks of the internal representations in their model. The regularities observed in language behaviour, together with spontaneous (not reflective) intuitions about possible sentences and their meanings, lead inevitably to the fact that there is quite extensive hierarchical nesting of structure, including recursion. The traditional notion of competence captures this. But in allowing that language does not show unbounded depth of embedding or recursion, we must not veer to the other extreme conclusion that there is no embedding or recursion at all. My construct of competence-plus keeps the advantages of postulating competence, while maintaining that in the normal functioning organism it is indissolubly wrapped up with computational constraints which keep its products from being unbounded. Competence-plus is (the syntactic aspect of) the integrated capacity in a human that is applied in the production and interpretation of grammatical expressions, and in making spontaneous intuitive judgements about potential expressions. Human productions and intuitions are not unbounded. I agree with Christansen and Chater that it is not useful that the integrated human language capacity be credited with allowing unbounded recursion.

Fred Karlsson (2007) studied the real numerical constraints on grammatical productivity. He arrived at numbers for the maximum depth of embedding of clauses at various positions in their superordinate clauses. His data was almost exclusively from written language, from seven European languages with well-developed literary traditions. An estimate of the limits of productivity in spoken language should assume embedding-depth numbers less than those he arrived at for written language. The limits Karlsson found were asymmetric. Some syntactic positions permit greater depths of embedding than others.

'The typical center-embedded clause is a relative clause' (p. 374). One firm constraint is 'Double relativization of objects (*The rat the cat the dog chased killed ate the malt*) does not occur' (p. 365). An example of a centre-embedded clause (underlined here) at depth 2 (C^2 in Karlsson's notation) is *She thought that he <u>who had been so kind</u> would understand*. This is centre-embedded because there is material from its superordinate clause before it (*he*) and after it (*would understand*). It is at depth 2 because all this material is further (right-)embedded in *He thought that*.... In Karlsson's corpus he found 132 C^2s and thirteen C^3s. 'All thirteen C^3s are from written language. Of 132 C^2s only three...are from spoken language. Multiple center-embeddings are extremely rare in genuine speech' (p. 373). Extrapolating from the statistics of his corpus, Karlsson predicted

one C^3 in 2,300,000 sentences and 42,000,000 words. This suggests that there could be ten C^3s in the Bank of English, whose present size is 500,000,000 words. ...

...The thirteen instances of C^3 come from the ensemble of Western writing and philological scholarship through the ages. Given this enormous universe, the incidence of C^3 is close to zero in spoken language. But the existence of C^3s cannot be denied; also note that Hagège (1976) reports C^3s in the Niger-Congo language Mbum. No genuine C^4s have ever been adduced. ...

C^3 does not occur in speech.   (Karlsson 2007, pp. 375)

There are much less stringent constraints on multiple right-embedded clauses, as in this famous nursery rhyme, given in full here for light relief from grammatical theory.

> *This is the farmer sowing his corn*
> > *that kept the cock*
> > > *that crowed in the morn*
> > > *that waked the priest all shaven and shorn*
> > > > *that married the man all tattered and torn*
> > > > > *that kissed the maiden all forlorn*
> > > > > > *that milked the cow with the crumpled horn*
> > > > > > > *that tossed the dog*
> > > > > > > > *that worried the cat*
> > > > > > > > > *that killed the rat*
> > > > > > > > > > *that ate the malt*
> > > > > > > > > > > *that lay in the house*
> > > > > > > > > > > > *that Jack built!*

In Karlsson's notation, this is an F^{11} ('F' for final embedding).[56] An intuitive judgement here tells us quickly that this is a fully grammatical sentence, unlike typical responses to the impossible shallow centre-embeddings theorized about by syntacticians. The nursery rhyme is certainly a linguistic curiosity. Genuinely communicative examples with this depth are not found in spontaneous discourse. It can be easily memorized, partly because of its rhythm and rhyme. Once memorized, questions about its content can be reliably answered. For instance, What worried the cat? Answer: the dog. But from any such deeply embedded sentence uttered in real life (even if that could happen), especially without this rhythm and rhyme, it would be impossible to reliably extract 100 percent of its semantic content. The hearer would protest 'Wait a minute—who did what to whom?' The quick intuitive grammaticality judgement is possible because all the grammatical dependencies are very local. Each occurrence of *that* is interpreted as the subject of the immediately following word, its verb. As soon as the expectation that a *that* requires a role-assigning verb is discharged (which it is immediately), the parser is free to move on to the rest of the sentence unburdened by any need to keep that expectation in memory. The sentence could be cut short before any occurrence of *that* without any loss of grammaticality. A parser going through this sentence could stop at

---

[56] Karlsson calls this rhyme an F^{12}, maybe not having noticed that two of the relative clauses, namely *that crowed in the morn* and *that waked the priest...* are at the same depth, both modifying *the cock*.

any of the line breaks above and be satisfied that it had heard a complete sentence. Semantically, the sentence is hierarchically nested, because the whole damned lot just gives us more and more specific information about the farmer of the first line. But despite the hierarchical semantic structure, the first-pass parser responsible for quick intuitive grammaticality judgements can just process the sentence linearly from beginning to end with no great burden on memory.

I take grammatical competence to be the mental resource used both in the production of speech and in spontaneous intuitive judgements of grammaticality and acceptability. In native speakers, this resource is formed in childhood, the acquisition process being constrained by the externally presented data and internal limitations on memory and attention. Data such as Karlsson's confirm the numerically constrained nature of this resource. I suggest an asymmetric relation between data found in a corpus and spontaneous intuitive judgements. Spontaneous intuition trumps corpus data. The absence of an expression type, even from massive corpora, is not sufficient to exclude it from what is within a speaker's competence, if the speaker, when confronted with an example, spontaneously accepts it as grammatical. The kinds of examples that Karlsson failed to find in his massive corpus are all so complex as to be judged impossible to comprehend in normal conversational time.

A caveat about data such as Karlsson's must be expressed. Karlsson collected his data from developed European languages. The speakers and writers who produced the data had been exposed to a certain level of complexity in their social environments. They were conforming to the established rhetorical traditions of their languages. The human language capacity only reveals itself to its fullest if the language-acquirer is given a suitable linguistic experience. Recall the experiments of Blaubergs and Braine (1974), who trained subjects to be able to process sentences with up to five levels of centre-embedding. A modern European linguistic environment doesn't present such challenges. Karlsson mentions two rhetorical traditions, '[Ciceronian] Latin and older variants of German, both well known for having reached heights of syntactic complexity' (Karlsson 2007, p. 366). These were traditions of written style, but every social group also has its own tradition of spoken style. Educated modern Germans, at least as represented by a couple of my students, can manage greater depths of centre-embedding than can be managed by educated English speakers, even linguistics students. Here is one example that a student tells me is not particularly difficult to interpret: *Ich weiss dass der Kaiser den Eltern den Kindern Fussball spielen lehren helfen soll*. This ends with a string of four verbs, each with a subject or object some way distant earlier in the sentence. The best English translation of this is *I know that the Kaiser should help the parents teach the children to play football*. A schematic representation of the centre-embedding is given below:

Ich weiss,
    dass der Kaiser   *soll.*
        den Eltern   *helfen*
            den Kindern   *lehren*
                Fussball spielen

German speakers are not innately different in their language-learning capacity from English speakers. The difference is a product of the German language environment, a tradition of spoken style, probably facilitated by the verb-final structure of German subordinate clauses. Here is another example, which my German students say is easy to understand, though complex: *Entweder die Sprache, die Kinder von ihren, sich an den Haaren zerrenden Eltern lernen, ist Deutsch, oder sie sind dumm*. Translation: *Either the language that children learn from their hair-tearing parents is German, or they are stupid*. Schematic representation:

Entweder   *oder sie sind dumm*
    die Sprache   *ist Deutsch*
       die Kinder   *lernen*
          von ihren   *Eltern*
             sich an den Haaren zerrenden

These examples arose during a discussion of centre-embedding, and cannot be called spontaneous counterexamples to Karlsson's claims. But they do show a difference between educated German-speaking competence-plus and educated English-speaking competence-plus. This difference is widely acknowledged by people familiar with both languages. Pulvermüller (2002, p. 129) gives a similar German centre-embedded example, with the comment that this example 'might be considered much less irritating by many native speakers of German than its translation [into English] is by native speakers of English'. Pulvermüller is a native German speaker working in an English-speaking environment. In any language, educated subgroups tend to use more complex language than less educated subgroups. Any numerical statement of the typical constraints on grammatical competence can only be provisional, and related to the most developed tradition that is likely to be sustained naturally in a community. In this way, two 'universals' topics intertwine, universals of the human language capacity and universals of languages, the latter being the topic of Chapter 5.

Humans are universally capable of acquiring spoken languages containing large numbers of different patterns or constructions, each individually simple, and productively combinable with each other. There are rubbery quantitative limits to this combinatorial capacity. No human can learn a billion words or constructions. And no human can learn to combine constructions beyond certain relatively low limits. Nevertheless, despite these limits, the multiplicative power given by the capacity to combine constructions yields practically uncountable[57] numbers of different potential spoken sentences.

[57] not strictly uncountable in the mathematical sense, of course.

CHAPTER 4

What Evolved: Language Learning Capacity

The goal of this chapter is to set out (at last!) central universal properties of humans in relation to grammar acquisition. Given the state of the field, it was necessary in the previous chapter, before getting down to solid facts, to discuss the methodological status of their claimed solidity. My position preserves the generative construct of competence, while arguing from an evolutionary point of view that competence is indissolubly associated with quantitative constraints based in performance. Spontaneous (as opposed to reflective) intuitive grammaticality judgements, combined with observation of regular production, give solid evidence, especially when shared across individuals.

This chapter gives what I take to be a necessary tutorial about syntactic structure for non-linguists. All too often, writing by non-linguists on the evolution of language neglects the complexity of the command of grammar that normal speakers have in their heads. It is possible to dismiss theorizing by syntacticians as theology-like wrangling. While some disputes in syntax are not much more than terminological, there is a wealth of complex data out there that syntacticians have uncovered over the last half-century. We truly didn't understand just how complex syntax and its connections to semantics and pragmatics were. The theories that have emerged have been aimed at making sense of this complexity in a natural and economical way. You can't understand the evolution of grammar without grasping something of the real complexity of grammar. This is tough talk, but I have tried to make the overview in this chapter as palatable as possible to those without training in linguistics.

Thousands of naturally occurring 'experiments' have shown that any normal human child, born no matter where and to whichever parents, can acquire any human language, spoken anywhere in the world. Adopt a baby from deepest

Papua New Guinea, and bring it up in a loving family in Glasgow, and it will grow up speaking fluent Glaswegian English. Children of a linguist from Illinois, with him in the deepest Amazon rainforest and playing for long enough with the local children, will learn their tribal language well. Until recently, there have been no well-founded claims that any population anywhere differs in its basic language capacity from other populations in the rest of the world.[1] The developmental capacity to acquire a complex language, shared by all humans, is coded in our genes and evolved biologically.

So language universals in this sense are those features that are universally acquirable by a healthy newborn child, if its linguistic community provides it with a sufficient model. What do we know about language universals in this sense? Here below, in successive sections, is a shopping list. It sets out the most striking properties that linguists have identified as coming easily to language acquirers. I have attempted to describe features of language on which there is growing theoretical convergence, despite apparent differences, sometimes not much more than terminological, among theorists. Hence this shopping list may be seen as eclectic, which it is. The features of language are described quite informally, mostly as a kind of tutorial for non-linguists, aiming to give a glimpse of the formidable complexity of the systems that humans can acquire. Any such list of universally learnable features can be debated, and you may want to nominate a few other candidates or to delete some, but this list is ample and representative. The list I will give is not restricted to what has been called the 'faculty of language in the narrow sense' (FLN) (Hauser et al. 2002), allegedly consisting only of recursion. The faculty of language in the broad sense (FLB) may include many traits that are shared with non-linguistic activities, but in most cases there is a very significant difference in the degree to which these shared abilities are exploited by humans and non-humans.

Some linguists like to make bold claims. The 'recursion only' claim of Hauser et al. is one example. For several of the items on the shopping list in this chapter, different groups of linguists have made self-avowedly 'radical' proposals that the item in question is not part of a speaker's knowledge of her language. While acknowledging an element of truth in these claims, by contrast with commonplace views often complacently propagated, I will dispute their extreme versions. Thus I am with Culicover and Jackendoff (2005) when they

---

[1] A recent exception is a claim by Dediu and Ladd (2007) that people with certain genetic variants are very slightly more disposed to learning tone languages. This claim is based on a statistical correlation between genetic variants and the tone or non-tone types of language. If the claim is right, which it may not be, the effect on individual language learners is still extremely small.

write 'In a real sense, every theory has been right, but every one has gone too far in some respect' (p. 153).

This chapter's list of learnable features of languages focuses exclusively on language structure, rather than on language processing. This is in keeping with linguists' typical object of attention. For every structural property identified, it must be added that humans can learn to handle them at amazing speeds. Fast processing of all the items on my 'shopping list' is to be taken as read. Not only the potential complexity of languages, but also the processing mechanisms, are part and parcel of the human language faculty, UG+, as I have called it.

And, one more thing, I don't promise to provide evolutionary explanations for all the phenomena on the list. For some phenomena listed here, I will be restricted to hopeful handwaving in later chapters. But for other facts listed here I will claim that an evolutionary explanation can be identified, which I will sketch out later in the book. For all the phenomena listed here I do claim that these are the salient data that any account of the evolution of language has to try to explain. Here goes.

4.1 Massive storage

Syntacticians used to take the lexicon for granted as merely a rote-memorized repository, hence theoretically uninteresting. We know enormous numbers of individual words, idioms, and stock phrases. These are the basic building blocks that syntax combines. They must be stored because their meanings are not predictable from their forms. Who is to say which is the more impressive, the versatile combinatorial ability of humans, that is syntax, or the huge stores of individual items that the syntax combines? Both capacities are unique to humans. No other animal gets close to human vocabulary size, not even intensively trained apes. For a given language, estimates of vocabulary size vary. For English speakers, Goulden et al. (1990) give a very low estimate: 'These estimates suggest that well-educated adult native speakers of English have a vocabulary of around 17,000 base words' (p. 321). In contrast, Diller (1978) tested high school teenagers on a sample of words from *Webster's Third New International Dictionary*, and found that on average they knew about 48 percent of the sampled words. As that dictionary contains an estimated 450,000 words, he calculated that the teenagers knew on average about 216,000 words. Impressionistically, this seems high. The large discrepancies among estimates of English vocabulary size can be attributed to 'the assumptions made by researchers as to what constitutes a word and the issue of what it means to know a word' (Cooper 1997, p. 96), and also to whether one is measuring active or passive vocabulary. I have estimated my own passive vocabulary size by a method similar to Diller's. The *COBUILD* dictionary[2] (Sinclair 1987, an excellent practical dictionary) has 70,000 entries. I inspected each 100th page of this dictionary, 17 pages in all, and found that I knew every word or expression listed on each sampled page, and all the basic meanings and nuances of each listed form. I also found that some technical but not too obscure words that I know (e.g. *cerebellum, morpheme, subjacency*) were not in that dictionary. It seems fair to conclude that my brain stores at least 70,000 different form–meaning pairings. I'm not unusual.

We have to say that a particular known form–meaning pairing is mentally stored if there are no rules predicting that pairing from more basic facts. A majority of such pairings involve single word stems of a familiar part of speech (Noun, Verb, Adjective, etc.) which can be combined with very high productivity by the syntax of the language. This combinability of words with other words is constrained by factors which are independent of both form and meaning, namely specifically syntactic information. '[A] typically lexically stored word is a long term memory association of a piece of phonology, a piece of syntax, and a piece of semantics' (Culicover and Jackendoff 2005, p. 158).[3] Just how much specifically syntactic information needs to be given is a matter of debate. 'Should *all* syntactic structure be slashed away? Our goal, a theory of syntax with the minimal structure necessary to map between phonology and meaning, leaves open the possibility that there is *no* syntax at all. . . . we think it is unlikely' (Culicover and Jackendoff, 2005, p. 22). The 'how much syntax is there?' issue starts in the lexicon. I side with Culicover and Jackendoff in believing that humans can (and often do) internalize specifically syntactic categorial information, such as N(oun), V(erb) and A(djective), associated with the form–meaning pairings in the lexicon. More on this in the following sections.

A substantial minority of the known form–meaning pairings are not of this basic single-word sort. In some cases, a dictionary entry consists of several words, whose meaning is not wholly predictable from the meanings of the individual words, for example idioms or semi-idioms. Examples are: *knocking on*, meaning getting old; *by all means*, said to assure someone that what

---

[2] It was particularly relevant to use a dictionary such as *COBUILD* because it is solidly based on current usage, with data drawn from an extensive contemporary corpus. Using the *OED*, for instance, would have been beside the point, as the *OED* contains many archaic words and word-senses which nobody claims are part of modern English.

[3] A fourth kind of information, on the relative frequency in use of each item, is also stored.

they have suggested is acceptable; *old guard*, meaning a clique of conservative people in an organization; *old master*, meaning a famous painter or sculptor of the past; *tear off*, meaning to go away in a hurry; and so on—examples are easy to find. Compound nouns are mostly idiosyncratic in this way. If you only knew the meanings of *memory* and *stick*, how could you guess what a memory stick is, without having seen one or heard about them somehow? *Flash drive*, which denotes the same thing, is even more opaque. Likewise *carbon paper* (paper made from carbon?), *bus shelter* (for sheltering from buses?), *time trial*, *keyboard*, and so on. Competent English speakers know these idiosyncratic expressions as well as the more basic vocabulary of non-idiomatic forms. We are amused when non-native speakers get them slightly wrong. I have heard *I made him pay out of his nose* instead of . . . *through the nose*, and *back to base 1* instead of *back to square 1*.[4] Wray (2002b) emphasizes the formulaic nature of language, with ready-made familiar expressions stored as wholes. Her examples include *burst onto the stage, otherwise forgotten, stands on its head, proof of the pudding*, and *see the light of day*.

A simplistic view of syntax is that there are entities of just two sorts, basic **lexical items** with no internal (non-phonological) structure, and productive combinatorial **rules** that form sentences from the basic lexical items. It has long been recognized that this simple view cannot be upheld. Even in 1977, Kay wrote 'whatever contemporary linguists believe as a group, any clear notion dividing lexicon from "structure" is not part of this consensus. . . . It is no longer possible to contrast lexical variation and structural variation as if lexical items were unrelated units that are simply plugged into a grammatical structure' (Kay 1977, pp. 23–4). The inclusion of whole complex phrases in the lexicon was suggested by generativists quite early (Di Sciullo and Williams 1987). It is sensible to treat many lexical entries as having structure and parts, as in the examples of the previous paragraph. Having taken this step, several questions arise.

One issue is how richly structured the rote-learnt items stored in the lexicon can be. We can certainly store items as large as whole sentences, as in memorized proverbs and quotations, such as *A bird in the hand is worth two in the bush* and *If music be the food of love, play on*. It is worth considering whether such whole-sentence expressions are stored in the same lexicon where words and idioms are stored.

---

[4] Google finds about 672,000 instances of *back to square one*, but only about 26,000 cases of *back to base one*. I submit that these latter derive from speakers who have mislearned the original idiom. Of course, in their variety of English, the new version has probably become part of the language.

First, although whole-sentence stored expressions are meaningful, it might be argued that they do not embody the same kind of form–meaning pairing, between a word and a concept, as do words and idioms. Most words in the lexicon, all except a handful of grammatical 'function words', denote logical predicates that can be applied to some argument. This is as true for abstract words, like *esoteric*, as it is for concrete words like *vinegar*. Phrasal idioms also denote predicates, or predicate–argument combinations forming partial propositions. Thus *kick the bucket* entails DIE(x), a 1-place predicate taking a single argument to be supplied by the referent of the grammatical subject of this intransitive verb idiom. So *John kicked the bucket* implies that John died. The very use of the idiom carries a bit more meaning—let's call it jocularity. *Spill the beans* is a bit more complex, meaning DIVULGE(x, y) & SECRET(y), in which the agentive argument x is likewise to be supplied by the referent of the grammatical subject of the idiom. So *Mary spilled the beans* implies that Mary divulged some secret.

Note that *spill the beans* shows that some idioms are partly compositional, in their idiosyncratic way. Within the scope of this idiom, *spill* maps onto DIVULGE and *beans* maps onto SECRET. You can say, for example, 'No, it wasn't THOSE beans that she spilled', meaning that she disclosed some secret other than the one the hearer has in mind.[5] The real identity of the secret (e.g. who stole the coffee money) is supplied pragmatically from the shared knowledge of the speaker and hearer. Again, the use of the idiom carries an implication of jocularity. The partial compositionality of some idioms is also shown by cross-linguistic correspondences. English *make a mountain out of a molehill* corresponds to an idiom in Finnish literally translatable as 'turn a fly into a bull' (Penttilä et al. 1998), and to German and Dutch idioms translatable as 'make an elephant out of a fly'.

At least some whole-sentence stored expressions do map onto meanings in the same way as idiosyncratically partly compositional idioms like *spill the beans*. The difference is in how much remains to be supplied pragmatically from context. When the proverb *A bird in the hand is worth two in the bush* is used meaningfully in a conversation, the speaker and hearer have a good idea what *a bird in the hand* and *two in the bush* stand for. In a given context, for example, they might stand for a concrete job offer and the hope of other possibly better job offers, respectively. Roughly stating this in logical terms, the meaning of the whole proverb is something like WORTH-MORE-THAN(x, y) & AVAILABLE(x) & ¬AVAILABLE(y). In any given context the proverb has some

---

[5] This, with many other valuable insights about idioms, is pointed out by Nunberg et al. (1994).

propositional content, the core of which is the predicate WORTH-MORE-THAN, and which the speaker asserts. Such an argument can be mounted for at least some, but probably not all, whole-sentence stored expressions.

Next, since syntax is the study of how sentence-like units are formed by combination of smaller units, it might be argued that there is nothing to say in syntactic terms about whole-sentence stored expressions, at least so far as they don't give rise to any interesting combinatorial sentence-formation processes. However, this argument is vitiated to the extent that whole-sentence stored expressions can be productively used as templates for parallel expressions, like perhaps *A grand in the bank is worth two in the stock market* or *If Money Be the Food of Love, Play On.*[6] To the extent that stored whole-sentence expressions allow productive substitution of their subparts, they can be seen as a kind of construction with variable slots, as represented schematically below:

A NOUN *in the* NOUN *is worth two in the* NOUN.
If NOUN *be the* NOUN *of* NOUN, IMPERATIVE.

Some idioms don't allow any productive substitution. Goldberg (2006, p. 5) calls them 'filled idioms', with *going great guns* and *give the Devil his due* as examples. Other idioms, which allow some substitution of their parts, are called 'partially filled';[7] Goldberg's examples are *jog <someone's> memory*, and *send <someone> to the cleaners.*[8] Some well known whole-sentence quotations have taken on a life of their own as at least semi-productive constructions, or partially filled idioms. For example, parallel to Gertrude Stein's *Rose is a rose is a rose,*[9] Google finds *War is war is war*, *Money is money is money*, *A cauliflower is a cauliflower is a cauliflower*, *Eggs are eggs are eggs are eggs* and *Boys will be boys will be boys*. Honestly, these five were the first five that I searched for, and Google didn't disappoint. There must be hundreds of other such coinages, so it's reasonable to suppose that many English speakers have stored, not just the historically original expression with *a rose*, and maybe not even that one, but rather a template construction into which any noun phrase (NP) can be inserted, subject to the repetition condition

---

[6] This was the title of an episode in a British TV series. Google also finds *If politics be the path to profit, play on*, *If politics be the dope of all, then play on*, *If meat be the food of love, then grill on*, *If football be the music of life, play on*, and *If sex be the food of love, fuck on*, among others.

[7] Croft's (2001) alternative terms are 'substantive' for filled idioms, and 'schematic' for partially filled idioms.

[8] In my dialect, *send to the cleaners* is not idiomatic but interpreted literally, whereas *take to the cleaners* is an idiom roughly meaning *trick out of all one's money*.

[9] *Sic.* This was, apparently, Ms Stein's original formulation.

inherent in this construction. The NP$_i$ *be* NP$_i$ *be* NP$_i$ construction[10] carries its own conventional meaning, being used as a somewhat fatalistic reminder of life's necessary conditions. The NP can in principle be somewhat complex. I find *A man with a gun is a man with a gun is a man with a gun* is acceptable and serves the right rhetorical purpose. But on the whole, longer NPs in this construction detract from its stylistic pithiness. Note also the flexibility of the verb *be* in this template, allowing at least *is*, *are*, and *will be*. The historical generalization process from a memorable particular expression, with all words specified, to a template with variable slots, is one route by which constructions come to exist. For it to happen, humans must have the gift to make the early modifications and to store the somewhat abstract templates.[11]

The examples of the last paragraph and its footnote are all examples of 'snowclones'. The term arose from an appeal by Geoff Pullum: 'What's needed is a convenient one-word name for this kind of reusable customizable easily-recognized twisted variant of a familiar but non-literary quoted or misquoted saying. . . . "Cliché" isn't narrow enough—these things are certainly clichés, but a very special type of cliché. And "literary allusion" won't do: these things don't by any means have to be literary'.[12] Google 'snowclone' and you will find a flurry of collectors' items from several gaggles of ardent clonespotters. Snowclonespotters playfully exchange examples as curiosities. They don't draw any serious conclusion from the pervasive fecundity of the phenomenon. They are missing something important. Snowclones are examples of **intertextuality** (Kristeva 1986), a concept at the heart of a profoundly different view of language from that taken in (what I dare to call) mainstream linguistics. 'Any text is constructed as a mosaic of quotations; any text is the absorption and transformation of another. The notion of *intertextuality* replaces that of intersubjectivity, and poetic language is read as at least *double*' (Kristeva 1986, p. 37). I don't fully understand the second sentence of this quotation, but the reason may be explicable by this fundamentally different view of

---

[10] The subscript i is my relatively informal way of indicating that the NPs chosen must be identical. This is what gives this construction its rhetorical force. And the formula should actually be more complex with some possibility of more than one repetition, for speakers such as the one who produced *Eggs are eggs are eggs are eggs*.

[11] Reinforcing this argument about the productivity of at least some whole-sentence expressions, and for fun, the indefatigable Google attests *A cow in the field is worth two in the EU*, *A truffle in the mouth is worth two in the bush*, *A bag in the hand is worth two in the store*, *A beer in the hand is worth two in the Busch*, *Push in the bush is worth two in the hand* (lewd, apparently), *A spectrometer in the hand is worth two in the lab*, *One in the eye is worth two in the ear*, *A pistol in the hand is worth two in the glove box*, *An hour in the morning is worth two in the evening*, *A loser in love is worth two in the spotlight*, and so on.

[12] http://itre.cis.upenn.edu/-myl/languagelog/archives/000061.html.

language, based on a historical fabric of texts, rather than on grammars in individual heads. In this view full understanding of a sentence, to the extent that this is ever attainable, requires knowledge of the whole corpus of prior texts which this sentence echoes or transforms. 'Mainstream' linguistics works with the idealization of a competence grammar, a bounded inventory in an individual's head; creativity comes from recursively combining items from this inventory. Kristeva is not concerned with grammatical detail, or with grammatical generalizations, for that matter. She is a semiotic theorist, in the tradition of Bakhtin, who emphasized the essentially **dialogic** nature of language. She is concerned with verbal culture. Linguists like to draw a line between the grammar of a language and the verbal culture of a community. Diametrically opposed though Franco-Russian semiotic theory and Anglo-American structural linguistics may seem, the latter can benefit from some ideas developed by the former. A fully competent speaker of a language knows, and can productively exploit, a huge inventory of intertextual ('snowclone') patterns. An individual speaker's knowledge of her language includes a rich inventory of culturally inherited patterns of some complexity, not just words. And just as individual speakers can keep learning new words throughout their lifetime, they can expand their mastery of the verbal culture of their community by remembering and adapting exemplars from it. Call them 'snowclones' if you like.

The significance of the far-reaching exploitation of existing expressions was foreseen in a prescient article by Pawley and Syder (1983). Their work preceded the growth of work in Construction Grammar, and hence their terminology is different. What Pawley and Syder call 'sentence stems' can be equated with the constructions of Construction Grammar theorists such as Fillmore et al. (2003); Goldberg (1995, 2006). Some of the sentence-stems that they suggest are stored in their entirety are the following:

NP be-TENSE sorry to keep-TENSE you waiting
NP tell-TENSE the truth
Why do-TENSE n't NP$_i$ pick on someone PRO$_i$-gen own size
Who (the-EXPLET) do-PRES NP$_i$ think PRO$_i$ be-PRES!

A second issue arising from treating stored lexical entries as having structure and parts concerns the degree of overlap between the structures of complex lexical items and those of productively generated combinations. For example the idiom *have a chip on one's shoulder* is not directly semantically compositional; what it means is nothing to do with chips or shoulders. But this expression has a structure apparently identical to productively generated expressions like *have milk in one's tea*, *have milk in one's larder*, or *have a mouse in one's larder*, or

even *have a mouse in one's tea*. The surprise you may have felt at this last
example shows that it really is semantically compositional. Psycholinguistic
evidence (to be described more fully in the next section) indicates that speakers
store the shared structure of an idiom as a rote-learnt form, even though
they also store the rules which construct this structure. Some redundancy in
mental representations seems inevitable. Such a result has also been arrived
at in a computational simulation of language emergence in which simulated
learners were experimentally only weakly (25 percent) disposed to generalize
from their experience. 'The individuals in this experiment all internalised many
nongeneral rules, rote-learnt facts about particular meaning–form pairs. But
these holistically memorised meaning–form pairs all conformed to the general
constituent-ordering rules which had become established in the community as
a result of a quite weak (25 percent) tendency to generalise from observation'
(Hurford 2000b, p. 342).

Stored syntactically complex items, such as idioms, are to varying degrees
open to internal manipulation by productive rules. With simple English verbs,
the tense marker attaches to the end of the word, as in *kick/kicked*. But the past
tense of the idiom *kick the bucket* is not **kick the bucketed*, in which the tense
marker is attached to the whole item. The lexical representation of this idiom
must have a variable slot inside it allowing for the insertion of a tense marker
on *kick*, which itself must be identifiable as a verb, an appropriate recipient of
a tense marker.

A third issue arising from the possibility of structured lexical items is how far
the body of productive syntactic rules can be reduced. This is the question of
the correct division of labour between storage and computation. Several recent
syntactic theories converge significantly on this, reducing the combinatorial
rules to just one or two, and locating everything else that must be learnt about
the syntax of a language in the lexicon. The theory of Tree Adjoining Grammar[13] has lexical items which are pre-formed elementary tree structures and
just two syntactic rules, Substitution and Adjunction. Similarly, the Minimalist
Program (Chomsky 1995b) recognizes just two syntactic combinatorial rules,
Merge and Move.[14] In an essay on the Minimalist Program, in his section
enticingly called 'The End of Syntax', Marantz (1995, p. 380) summarizes:
'The syntactic engine itself . . . has begun to fade into the background. Syntax

---

[13] See Joshi et al. (1975); Joshi (1987); Vijay-Shanker et al. (1987); Abeillé and
Rambow (2000).

[14] By what seems to be some sleight of terms, movement is sometimes claimed to be
just a special 'internal' subcase of the Merge operation (e.g. Rizzi 2009). The retention
of movement operations in the Minimalist Program is an instance of non-convergence
with other theories.

reduces to a simple description of how constituents drawn from the lexicon can be combined and how movement is possible'. The theory of Word Grammar (Hudson 1984) also places an inventory of stored form–meaning linkages at the core of syntactic structure, rather than a large set of productive combinatorial rules. And Mark Steedman's version of Categorial Grammar (Steedman 2000, 1993) assumes a massive lexicon for each language, with only two productive syntactico-semantic operations, called Composition and Type-Raising. These theories thus converge in claiming a massive linguistic storage capacity for humans, although otherwise their central concerns vary. The most extreme claims for massive storage come from Bod (1998), in whose framework a speaker is credited with storing **all** the examples she has ever experienced, with their structural analyses and information about frequency of occurrence. Needless to say, this store is vast and redundant, as Bod recognizes. In Bod's approach, as in the others mentioned here, no language-particular combinatorial rules are stored; there is a single composition operation for producing new utterances for which no exact exemplars have been stored. The message behind this rehearsal of a number of named 'capital letter' theories of syntax is that there is actually some substantial convergence among them.

Syntactic theories tend to propose single monolithic answers to the question of storage versus computation, as if all speakers of a language internalize their knowledge of it in the same way. As noted earlier, Bates et al. (1988) detected different emphases in different children learning language, some biased toward rote-learnt storage, and others more biased toward productive combination of elements. Psychologically, it is unrealistic to suppose that there can be a one-size-suits-all fact of the matter concerning the roles of storage and computation. Furthermore, it is wrong to assume for any speaker an economical partition of labour between storage and computation. Some individually stored items may also be computable in their entirety from general rules also represented, an instance of redundancy. 'Very typically, a fully general linguistic pattern is instantiated by a few instances that are highly conventional. In such a case, it is clear that both generalizations and instances are stored' (Goldberg 2006, p. 55).[15]

Complementing the developments in linguists' theoretical models, Bates and Goodman (1997) argue from a range of empirical psycholinguistic data. They

---

[15] Goldberg's chapter entitled 'Item-specific knowledge and generalizations' is an excellent summary account of this basic issue on which linguists have tended to opt for elegant, non-redundant descriptions, contrary to the emerging psycholinguistic evidence.

review 'findings from language development, language breakdown and real-time processing, [and] conclude that the case for a modular distinction between grammar and the lexicon has been overstated, and that the evidence to date is compatible with a unified lexicalist account' (p. 507). Their title, significantly, is 'On the inseparability of grammar and the lexicon'. Also from the perspective of language acquisition, Wray and Grace (2007, p. 561) summarize a similar view: '[Children] apply a pattern-recognition procedure to linguistic input, but are not naturally predisposed to select a consistent unit size (Peters 1983). They home in on phonological forms associated with effects that they need to achieve, . . . The units in their lexicons are, thus, variously, what the formal linguist would characterise as morpheme-, word-, phrase-, clause-, and text-sized (Wray 2002b)'.

This convergence on a reduced inventory of syntactic rules, with concomitant expansion of the lexicon, is very striking. It significantly enhances the place of massive storage in any answer to the question 'What is remarkable about the human capacity for syntax?' In all these approaches, a very small number of combinatorial rules or operations are common to all languages, and so are plausibly innate in the human language capacity. Innate, too, is a capacity for storage of an enormous number of structures, some of which can be quite complex. Also part of the universal human syntactic capacity, in these accounts, are narrow constraints on possible stored structures; some theories are more specific on this latter point than others. We will revisit this theme of massive, somewhat redundant storage. The storage focused on in this section has been storage of symbolic meaning–form linkages, that is a semantic aspect of what speakers have learned. In later sections, storage of more specifically syntactic facts will be illustrated. The storage theme should be kept in mind while we go through the rest of the shopping list of the properties of languages that universally come easily to language acquirers, given appropriate experience.

4.2 Hierarchical structure

Non-linguists' eyes may glaze over when they meet a tree diagram of the structure of a sentence, just as non-mathematicians may cringe when they come to a complex mathematical formula. In the case of sentence structure, it's not that difficult, as I will try to assure non-linguists below. Stick with it, and I hope you'll see what linguists are talking about. The first subsection below is perhaps a bit philosophical, asking the basic question about what sentence structure **is**. The second subsection below gives examples, showing

how sentence structure often reflects meaning (semantics), and how complex
even sentences in ordinary conversation by less educated people can be.

4.2.1 What is sentence structure?

What does it mean to say that a sentence has a hierarchical structure? Syntax
is typically taught and studied by analysing sentences cold, like anatomy
practised on an etherized or dead patient.[16] In introductory linguistics classes,
students are given exercises in which they must draw tree structures over
given sentences. The instructor believes that there are correct answers, often
paraphrased as 'the way sentences are put together'. Mostly, intuitions concur; there is definitely something right about this exercise. But there is also
something quite misleading, in that sentences are treated in a way parallel to
solid manufactured objects. I plead guilty to this myself. I have often used the
analogy of dismantling a bicycle into its component major parts (e.g. frame,
wheels, saddle, handlebars), then the parts of the parts (e.g. spokes, tyres, inner
tubes of the wheels, brakes and grips from the handlebars) and so on, down
to the ultimate 'atoms' of the bike. A bicycle is hierarchically assembled and
dismantled.

   Hierarchical organization in the above sense is **meronomic**. 'Meronomic'
structure means part–whole structure, which can get indefinitely complex, with
parts having subparts, and subparts having sub-subparts, and so on. And each
entity in the meronomic hierarchy is a whole thing, not discontinuous in any
way. Here the analogy is with phrases and clauses, continuous substrings of a
sentence, known to linguists as the **constituents** of a sentence. There is another
sense in which complex objects can have a hierarchical structure. Pushing
the bike analogy to its limit, some parts, for example the gear levers, are
functionally connected to distant parts, for example the sprocket wheels, and
these parts are further connected to others, for example the pedals. Thus there
is a chain (not a bicycle chain!) of connections between parts which are not in
any sense in part–whole relationships. Here the analogy is with **dependency
relations** in sentences, such as the agreement between the two underlined
parts of *The man that I heard is French*, or between a reflexive pronoun
and its antecedent subject, as in *He was talking to himself*. For most of the
examples that I will discuss, analysis in terms of dependencies or constituents
is not crucially different. '[D]espite their difference—which may turn out to
be more a matter of style than of substance—Phrase Structure Grammars and

---

[16] The issue of analysing sentences out of their discourse context was discussed
earlier, in Ch. 3. That is not the issue here.

Dependency Grammars appear to share many of their essential tenets' (Ninio 2006, p. 15). In the most salient cases of hierarchical sentence organization, the phrasal, part–whole structure and the dependency structure coincide and reinforce each other. That is, there are continuous parts of a sentence, inside which the subparts have dependency relationships. For instance, in the phrase *quickly ran home* there are dependency relations (e.g. modification) between words which sit right next to each other. Such are the cases that I will start with for illustration. But first we need to see what is wrong with the bike analogy.

The analogy falls down in one significant way. A bike is a tangible object, whereas a sentence is not. The written representation of a sentence is not the real sentence, but only our handy tool for talking and theorizing about some class of potential mental events. An utterance is a real physical event, located in space and time, involving movement of the speech organs and vibrations in air. When we utter a sentence, behind the scenes there are mental acts of sentence-assembly going on. A copious literature on sentence production attests to the hierarchical nature of sentence-assembly in real time in the brain.[17] And when we hear a sentence uttered, corresponding acts of dis-assembly, that is parsing, take place in our heads. The goal of parsing by people in the real use of language is to arrive at a conception of what the sentence means, and ultimately to figure out what the speaker intended by uttering it. We will only be concerned here with the process of getting from an input string of words or morphemes to a representation of the meaning of the expression uttered.[18] Assuming that speaker and hearer speak exactly the same language, the hearer achieves the goal of understanding a sentence in part by reconstructing how the speaker 'put the sentence together'.

Speakers do put sentences together in hierarchical ways, and hearers decode uttered sentences in hierarchical ways. The grammatical objects put together by productive combinatorial processes are ephemeral, unlike bikes or houses. In this way they are like musical tunes. There are natural breaking or pausing points in tunes, too; it is unnatural to cut off a tune in the middle of a phrase. It is a moot point in what sense the hierarchical structure of a complex novel sentence exists in the mind of its speaker. It is not the case that the entire structure of the sentence (analogous to the whole tree diagram, if that's your

---

[17] See, for example, Garrett (1975, 1982); Dell et al. (1997); Levelt (1989, 1992); Smith and Wheeldon (1999).

[18] This is a very considerable simplification. Simplifying, I will assume that segmentation of the auditory stream of an utterance into words or morphemes is complete when the grammatical parsing process starts. Also simplifying here (but see later), I will assume that the analysis of a string of words into the meaning of the expression is completed before the pragmatic process of inferring the speaker's intention starts.

way of showing structure) is simultaneously present at any given time. As the utterance of a complex sentence unfolds in time, the early words have been chosen, ordered, lumped into larger units (e.g. phrases), and perhaps already sent to the speech apparatus, while the later words are still being chosen and shuffled into their eventual order and groupings. Smith and Wheeldon (1999) report the results of experiments in which subjects are prompted to produce sentences describing scenes seen on a screen: 'the data from the five experiments demonstrate repeatedly that grammatical encoding is not completed for the whole of a sentence prior to speech onset' (p. 239). The choice, ordering and grouping of the later words is partly determined by the original intended meaning and partly by the grammatical commitments made by the earlier part of the uttered sentence. Often this goes flawlessly. But sometimes a speaker gets in a muddle and can't finish a sentence in a way fitting the way he started off, or fitting his intended meaning. You can talk yourself into a corner in less than a single sentence. That's one reason why false starts happen. Likewise when a hearer decodes a somewhat complex sentence, the intended meaning (or a set of possible meanings) of some early phrase in the sentence may be arrived at, and the structure of that phrase discarded while the rest of the sentence is still coming in.[19]

So the whole grammatical structure of a sentence, especially of a somewhat complex novel sentence, is probably not something that is ever present in the mind all at once. But this does not mean that grammatical structure plays no part in the active use of sentences. During English sentence interpretation, when a reader encounters a *Wh-* word, such as *who* or *which*, there is evidence that an expectation is built and kept in short-term memory, actively searching for a 'gap' (or gaps) later in the sentence. For instance, in the following sentence, there are two gaps grammatically dependent on the initial *Who*.

Who did you meet _____ at the museum and give your umbrella to _____ ?

The 'gaps' here are a linguist's way of recognizing that, for example *Who* is understood as the object of *meet*, as in the equivalent 'echo question' *You met WHO?*, and the indirect object of *give*, as in *You gave your umbrella to WHO?* In the 'gappy' sentence beginning with *Who*, when an appropriate filler for the gap is found, reading time speeds up, unless there is evidence, signalled

---

[19] This sequential parsing motivates a pattern in which the informational **Topic** of a sentence, which identifies a referent presumed to be already known to the hearer, usually comes first in the sentence. If the whole sentence were taken in and stored in a buffer, and parsing did not attack it sequentially 'from left to right', there would be no motivation for putting the Topic first. Topic/Comment structure in sentences will be taken up again in a later chapter.

here by *and* that a further gap is to be expected (Wagers and Phillips 2009). Thus during reading, structural clues such as *wh-* words provide expectations relating to something about the overall structure of the sentence being read. 'Parsing decisions strongly rely on constraints found in the grammar' (Wagers and Phillips 2009, p. 427). Likewise, when a speaker utters a sentence beginning with a *wh-* word, he enters into a mental commitment to follow it with a string with a certain structural property, namely having a gap, typically a verb without an explicit object.

The grammatical structure of a sentence is a route followed with a purpose, a phonetic goal for a speaker, and a semantic goal for a hearer. Humans have a unique capacity to go very rapidly through the complex hierarchically organized processes involved in speech production and perception. When syntacticians draw structure on sentences they are adopting a convenient and appropriate shorthand for these processes. A linguist's account of the structure of a sentence is an abstract summary of a series of overlapping snapshots of what is common to the processes of producing and interpreting the sentence.

This view of grammatical structure is consistent with work in a theory known as 'Dynamic Syntax' (DS) (Kempson et al. 2001; Cann et al. 2005),[20] but has a quite different emphasis. DS theorists have made some strong statements implying that grammatical structure as reflected, for example, in tree diagrams or dependency diagrams is some kind of theory-dependent illusion. While agreeing with them on the central function of any structure in sentences, in the next few paragraphs I will defend the usefulness of the traditional representations. DS focuses on the semantic (logical) contribution of words and phrases to the process of arriving at a formula representing the meaning of a whole sentence. As each new word is processed, in a left-to-right passage through a sentence, it makes some contribution to an incrementally growing semantic representation, typically in the shape of a tree. In other words, while listening to a sentence, the hearer is step-by-step building up a 'picture' of what the speaker intends. Writing of Dynamic Syntax, Cann et al. (2004, p. 20) state 'There is no characterization of some independent structure that . . . strings are supposed to have, no projection of primitive syntactic categories and no encapsulation of constituency as something apart from the establishment of meaningful semantic units'.[21]

---

[20] *Dynamical Grammar* is also the title of a book by Culicover and Nowak (2003). This book has little detailed connection with the Dynamic Syntax theory discussed here.

[21] See also Wedgwood (2003, p. 28 and 2005, pp. 57–62) for an equally forthright assertion of this radically untraditional tenet of Dynamic Syntax.

So the DS theory is radical in explicitly eschewing any concept of sentence structure other than what may be implicit in the left-to-right parsing process. I agree with DS that a central function of complex syntactic structure is the expression of complex meanings. Much, admittedly not all, of the hierarchical organization of syntax transparently reflects the systematic build-up of complex semantic representations.[22] I take it that much of the hierarchical structure as traditionally conceived will actually turn out to be implicit in, and recoverable from, the formal statements about lexical items that DS postulates. Kempson et al. (2001, p. 3) write 'The only concept of structure is the sequence of partial logical forms' and later on the same page 'Language processing as a task of establishing interpretation involves manipulating incomplete objects at every stage except at the very end'. But in fact, during the course of a DS account of a sentence, the partial logical forms successively built up vary in their (in)completeness. At the beginning or in the middle of a phrase, the provisional representations of the meaning of a sentence contain more semantic variables waiting to be instantiated than the representations reached at the end of a phrase. With the end of each phrase, there is a kind of consolidation in the specific hypothesis which is being built up about the eventual meaning of the sentence. Noun phrases exist in the sense that (and insofar as) they are substrings of a sentence that typically map onto referent objects. And verb phrases exist in the sense that (and insofar as) they are substrings of sentences that typically identify complex predicates. DS could not work without taking advantage of the dependency relations between parts of a sentence. Expositions of DS still invoke traditional hierarchical (e.g. phrasal) categories, such as NP, and even sometimes refer to their 'internal structure'. There is much psycholinguistic evidence for the importance of phrases in sentence processing, though nobody doubts that the function of processing sentences in phrasal chunks is semantically motivated. Dynamic Syntax emphasizes the **process** of parsing, to the virtual exclusion of any other consideration.[23] Traditional phrasal descriptions are not necessarily incompatible with DS; they just focus on the **resources** that must be in any competent user's mind, 'statically' even when the user is not actually using language, for example when asleep. The lexicon is as yet a rather undeveloped aspect of DS. Presumably the lexicon in a DS framework contains lexical entries. It is hard to see how these entries are not themselves static, although of course expressing the potential of words to enter into dynamic relations with other words during processing of sentences.

---

[22] Some adherents of DS deny this, being also radical in rejecting any hint of semantic compositionality in the surface strings of sentences (Wedgwood 2005, pp. 21–37).

[23] Seuren (2004, pp. 85–6) attacks DS for its 'one-sided' focus on parsing.

Mark Steedman's (2000) theory of Combinatorial Categorial Grammar is motivated by the same concern as DS, 'in claiming that syntactic structure is merely the characterization of the process of constructing a logical form, rather than a representational level of structure that actually needs to be built' (p. xi). Steedman is careful to add that 'dynamic accounts always are declarativizable.... The dynamic aspects of the present proposals should not be taken as standing in opposition to declarative approaches to the theory of grammar, much less as calling into question the autonomy of grammar itself' (p. xiii).

The DS programme was foreshadowed in a prescient paper by Steve Pulman (1985). Pulman showed the possibility of designing a parser that reconciled incremental parsing with hierarchical structure. As he put it:

> As a sentence is parsed, its interpretation is built up word by word: there is little or no delay in interpreting it. In particular, we do not wait until all syntactic constituents have been completed before beginning to integrate them into some non-syntactic representation. Ample intuitive and experimental evidence supports this uncontroversial observation.   (Pulman, 1985, p.128)

> My aim was to develop a parser and interpreter which was compatible with [Hierarchical Structure and Incremental Parsing], resolving the apparent conflicts between them, and which also incorporated in a fairly concrete form the assumption that grammars have some status, independently of parsers, as mental objects. That is to say, it was assumed that what linguists say about natural language in the form of a grammar (including semantic interpretation rules) is available to the parser-interpreter as some kind of data structure having roughly the form that the linguist's pencil and paper description would suggest.   (Pulman, 1985, p.132)

Pulman's proof of concept was successful. A similar conclusion, that incremental parsing is compatible with a hierarchical view of grammatical competence, was demonstrated by Stabler (1991).

When parsing a sentence, the hearer is guided by pragmatic, semantic, and syntactic premises. If a language were pure semantic/pragmatic soup, there would be absolutely no syntactic clues to the overall meaning of a sentence other than the meanings of the words themselves. To the extent that a language is not pure semantic/pragmatic soup, it gives syntactic clues in the form of the order and grouping of words and/or morphological markings on the words. This is syntactic structure. Introductory linguistics books give the impression that no part of a sentence in any language is soup-like, that is that every word has every detail of its place and form dictated by morphosyntactic rules of the language. This is unduly obsessive. Even in the most grammatically regulated languages, there is a degree of free-floating, at least for some of the parts of a sentence. A traditional distinction between 'complements' and 'adjuncts' recognizes that the latter are less strictly bound into the form of a sentence. Common sentence-level adjuncts are adverbial phrases, like English *obviously*, *in my opinion*, *with a sigh*, *Susan having gone*, *having nothing better to do*, *sick at heart*, and *though basically a happy guy*, examples from Jackendoff (2002, p. 256). Jackendoff writes 'The use of these expressions is governed only by rudimentary syntactic principles. As long as the semantics is all right, a phrase of any syntactic category can go in any of the major breakpoints of the sentence: the front, the end, or the break between the subject and the predicate' (p. 256). A very different language from English, Warlpiri, has words marked by a 'goal' or 'result' suffix, *-karda*. For our simple purposes here, we can very loosely equate this with the English suffix *-ness*. Warlpiri has sentences that can be glossed as 'Tobacco lie dryness', 'Bullocks grass eat fatness', and 'Caterpillars leaves eat defoliatedness' (Falk 2006, p. 188). In these sentences, the '*-ness*' words apply semantically to the tobacco, the bullocks, and an unmentioned tree, respectively. Given the radically free word order of Warlpiri, these words could go almost anywhere in a sentence. Falk concludes that 'Warlpiri resultatives are anaphorically controlled adjuncts'. In other words, it is just the semantics of these words that contributes to sentence interpretation. But even these words are marked by the suffix *-karda*, which possibly notifies the hearer of this freedom. For such adjuncts, and to a limited degree, the DS claim that there is no 'independent structure that...strings are supposed to have' is admissible. Not every part of every sentence is bound in tight by firm syntactic structure. From an evolutionary viewpoint, it seems right to assume that the degree of tight syntactic management in languages has increased over the millennia since the very first systems that put words together.

There is a curious rhetoric involved in promoting 'dynamic' syntax over 'static' representations of structure. The path of an arrow through the air is undoubtedly dynamic. But it does no violence to the facts to represent its trajectory by a static graph on paper. Each point on the curve represents the position of the arrow at some point in time. Imagine the study of ballistics without diagrams of parabolas. Force diagrams are static representations of dynamic forces. A chemical diagram of a catalytic cycle is a static representation of a continuous dynamic process of chemical reaction. In phonetics, 'gestural scores' are static diagrams representing the complex dynamic orchestration of parts of the vocal tract. Analysis of static representations of dynamic sequences of events is useful and revealing.[24] Syntactic theory is no exception.

---

[24] Of course, everybody must be wary of inappropriate reliance on reification.

4.2.2 *Sentence structure and meaning—examples*

One of the oftenest-repeated arguments for hierarchical structuring involves child learners' 'structure dependent' response to the utterances they hear. The argument was first made by Chomsky (1975b). The key facts are these. English-learning children soon discover that a general way to form questions corresponding to statements is to use a form with an auxiliary verb at the front of the sentence, rather than in the post-subject-NP position that it occupies in declarative sentences. For example, the sentences on the right below are questions corresponding to those on the left.

John can swim	*Can John swim?*
Mary has been taking yoga lessons	*Has Mary been taking yoga lessons?*
The girl we had met earlier was	*Was the girl we had met earlier*
singing	*singing?*

Notice that in the last example the auxiliary at the front of the question sentence is not the first auxiliary in the corresponding statement (*had*), but the second (*was*). No child has been reported as getting this wrong. It is certainly a very rare kind of error for a child to ask a question with something like **Had the girl we met earlier was singing?* Sampson (2005, p. 87) reports hearing an adult say *Am what I doing is worthwhile?*, agreeing that this is a 'very unusual phenomenon'. You might say that this is because such utterances don't make any sense, and you would be right, but your correct analysis has been very oddly missed by generations of linguists who have rehearsed this line of argument. Anderson (2008a, p. 801) is typical. He succinctly sets out two possible rules that the child might internalize, as below:

String-based: To form an interrogative, locate the leftmost auxiliary verb in the corresponding declarative and prepose it to the front of the sentence.

Structure-based: To form an interrogative, locate the nominal phrase that constitutes the subject of the corresponding declarative and the highest auxiliary verb within the predicate of that sentence, and invert them.

Here, the child is portrayed as being only concerned with syntax, and not, as children surely must be, with making communicative utterances. When a child asks a question about something, she usually has a referent in mind that she is interested in finding out about. That's why she asks the question. *Is Daddy home yet?* is a question about Daddy. The natural thing for a child learning how to ask questions in English is to realize that you put an expression for the person or thing you are asking about just after the appropriate auxiliary at the start of the sentence. So imagine a child wants to know whether the girl we had met earlier was singing. She doesn't know the girl's name, so refers to her with the expression *the girl we had met earlier*, and puts this just after the question-signalling auxiliary at the beginning of the sentence. So of course, the question comes out, correctly, as *Was the girl we had met earlier singing?* What the child surely does is act according to a third possible rule, which Anderson's syntax-focused account doesn't mention, namely:

Meaning-based: To ask a question about something, signal the questioning intent with an appropriate auxiliary, then use an expression for the thing you are asking about. (This expression may or may not contain another auxiliary, but that doesn't distract you.)

My argument is not against the existence of hierarchical structuring or children's intuitive grasp of it. The point is that the hierarchical structure is **semantically motivated.**[25]

There are indeed cases where a referring expression is actually broken up, as in *The girl was singing that we had met earlier*. Such breaking up of semantically motivated hierarchical structure occurs for a variety of reasons, including pragmatic focusing of salient information and ease of producing right-branching structures. But the basic point of a connection between hierarchical syntactic structure and the structure of the situations or events one is talking about is not undermined.

We have already seen many examples of hierarchical structuring. We even saw some hierarchical organization in bird and whale songs in Chapter 1. The depth of hierarchical organization in language can be much greater, subject to the numerical limits mentioned earlier. For the benefit of non-linguists I will give a brief survey of the main kinds of hierarchical structure found in English. The survey is for illustrative purposes only, and is far from exhaustive. For the first couple of examples, I will give conventional tree diagrams. The particular diagramming convention that I will use at first here is a stripped-down version of the one most commonly encountered in textbooks, similar to the 'Bare Phrase Structure' suggestions in (Chomsky 1995a, 1995b). I will also give some equivalent diagrams in an alternative theory which emphasizes the dependency relations between words, rather than phrases. But in either case, whatever the diagramming convention, the existence of hierarchical organization of sentence structure is not in doubt.

For most languages, by far the most common chunk larger than a word and smaller than a sentence is a so-called noun phrase (NP). An NP has a 'head' noun and may have various types of modifiers with several levels of embedding,

---

[25] Tom Schoenemann (2005, pp. 63–4) independently makes the same point about examples like this.

involving further NPs with further modifiers. Consider the following sentence from the *NECTE* corpus:

I got on a bus to go to Throckley with the handbag with the threepence in my purse for my half-return to Throckley.

The simplest noun phrases here are the two instances of the proper noun *Throckley*, the name of a village. This word can stand on its own as an answer to a question such as *Where did you go?* Notice that several other nouns in the sentence, *bus, handbag, purse,* and *half-return* cannot stand on their own as answers to questions. Being singular common nouns, English requires that they be preceded by some 'determiner' such as *a, the,* or *my. A bus* or *the handbag* or *my purse* could all stand on their own as answers to appropriate questions. This is one linguistic piece of evidence that speakers treat these two-word sequences as chunks. Noun phrases commonly occur after prepositions, such as *on, with, in,* and *for.* The three-word sequences *on a bus, with the handbag, in my purse,* and *for my half-return,* along with the two-word sequence *to Throckley* would be grammatical answers to appropriate questions. So a preposition followed by a noun phrase also makes a self-standing chunk in English, a so-called **constituent.** These last-mentioned constituents are called 'prepositional phrases', because they are each headed by a preposition. Finally, a noun phrase may be followed by a prepositional phrase, as in *my threepence in my purse* and *my half-return to Throckley.* This much structure (but not the structure of the whole sentence) is shown in Figure 4.1. The justification for assigning this degree of nested structure to the example is semantico-pragmatic. That is, we understand this sentence as if it had been spoken to us just as it was to its real hearer (someone on Tyneside in the 1990s, as it happens), and glean the intended meaning because our English is close to that of the speaker. A particular real event from the speaker's childhood is described, in which she, a bus, the village of Throckley, her handbag, her threepence and her purse were all involved as participants, in a particular objective relationship to each other; this is part of the semantics of the sentence. The speaker has chosen to present this event in a certain way, with presumably less important participants (the threepence and the purse) mentioned nearer the end; this is part of the pragmatics of the sentence. It is also part of the pragmatics of this sentence that the speaker chose to give all this information in a single package, one sentence. She could have spread the information over several sentences. As fellow English speakers, we understand all this. Given this degree of understanding of the language, we know that the final phrase *to Throckley* modifies the preceding noun *half-return.* That is, *to Throckley* gives us more specific information about the half-return (a kind of bus ticket). By convention, the modification

I got on a bus to go to Throckley with the handbag with my threepence in my purse for my half-return to Throckley

Fig. 4.1 Hierarchically arranged constituents, headed by nouns and prepositions, in a conversational utterance (from the *NECTE* corpus). To identify a complete phrase in this diagram, pick any 'node' where lines meet; the whole string reached by following all lines downward from this node is a complete phrase. Clearly in this analysis, there are phrases within phrases. The sentence structure is only partly specified here, to avoid information overload.

relationship between an item and its modifier is shown by both items being co-daughters of a higher node in the tree, which represents the larger chunk (typically a phrase) to which they both belong. And we further know that *in my purse* and the larger phrase *for my half-return to Throckley* both directly modify the phrase *my threepence*. Because we understand the language, we are justified in inferring that the speaker added *in my purse* and *for my half-return to Throckley* to tell her hearer two further specific facts about her threepence. These last two prepositional phrases could just as well have been spoken in the opposite order, still both modifying *my threeence*, as in *my threepence for my half-return to Throckley in my purse*. For this reason they are drawn as 'sisters', rather than with one nested inside the other. And the even larger phrase *with my threepence in my purse for my half-return to Throckley* tells the hearer (and us fifteen years later) something about how she got on a bus to go to Throckley. 'Our intuitions about basic constituency [hierarchical] relations in sentences are almost entirely based on semantics' (Croft 2001, p. 186).

   The phrases mentioned here are of two types. One type has a noun as its main informative word, for example *my purse, my half-return to Throckley*. An English speaker observes regular rules for forming phrases of this type, and grammarians call it an NP, for 'noun phrase', to distinguish it from other phrasal types that speakers use. The other phrasal type mentioned here is one whose first element is drawn from a small class of words (*on, in, to, for,* etc.) known as prepositions. Accordingly phrases of this type are labelled PP, for 'prepositional phrase'. When uttering a complex sentence such as this, the labels NP and PP do not, of course, pass explicitly through a speaker's mind, any more than the labels Noun and Preposition do. But English speakers regularly use many thousands of sentences in which phrases of these recognizably distinct types recur. This justifies us, as analysts, in deciding that these two phrase-types are distinct entities in the English speaker's repertoire. Analysts have traditionally referred to these distinct phrase types with the labels NP and PP. Whether any such labels are necessary in a model of a speaker's tacit knowledge of her language is a moot point to which we will return in the next section. Using this terminology for expository convenience here, Figure 4.1 also shows the hierarchical arrangement of NPs within prepositional phrases (PPs). A PP is formed from a preposition (e.g. *on*, *with*, *to*) followed by an NP. Thus PPs have NPs inside them, and NP's themselves can be internally modified by PPs, as in this example, giving rise to a structure with a recursive nature—NPs within NPs, and PPs within PPs.[26] The speaker of the sentence in Figure 4.1 was able to give all this information about her trip to Throckley in a single sentence because of the availability in her language of simple rules nesting PPs within NPs and NPs in their turn within PPs, and of course because of her human capacity for handling this degree of recursive embedding. The recursive hierarchical embedding here, of both PPs and NPs, is to a depth of 3. For these constructions, this is well within normal conversational limits. Remember that we will question the necessity of all these grammatical labels in the next section. What is not in question is the hierarchical formal grouping of words and phrases.

Note that some of the branching in Figure 4.1 has three lines descending from a single node. This is typically the case where a head word is modified by one modifier in front and another modifier behind, as in *my threepence in my purse*. Here *threepence* is the head noun, modified in front by the possessive determiner *my* and behind by the prepositional phrase *in my purse*. There is often no reason to see one modifier as 'higher' than the other, and they are drawn as both modifying their head 'at the same level'.[27] This is actually an item of contention in syntactic theory, with Kayne (1994) insisting that all syntactic structure is binary branching,[28] and Culicover and Jackendoff (2005), among others, arguing that sometimes 'flat' structure (i.e. branching more than into two parts) is justifiable. Without argument here, I side with Culicover and Jackendoff, in favour of occasional more-than-binary branching.

---

[26] For convenience in this chapter I have presupposed an older, more restrictive definition of recursion in terms of phrasal types (e.g. NP, PP, etc.). More recent thinking suggests a view in which any semantically compositional combination of three elements or more is recursive. I mentioned this in Chapter 1, and will come again to it in Chapter 5.

[27] The fact that a determiner is obligatory before a Common noun, whereas modification by a prepositional phrase is optional, may somehow be adduced as an argument for binary branching in this case. The premises for such an argument are likely to be quite theory-specific.

[28] Guimarães (2008) shows that Kayne gets his own formalism wrong; technically, it does not block ternary branching.

His Dad's brother's friend

Fig. 4.2 Recursively nested phrases in a possessive construction in a conversational utterance.
Source: From the *NECTE* corpus.

Another example of recursive embedding in English involves possessive constructions, as in *his Dad's brother's friend* shown in Figure 4.2, with its structure assigned. Again, the motivation for this structure is semantico-pragmatic. The three noun phrases in this larger phrase are all referring expressions. The substring *his Dad* refers to a particular person, as does the larger substring *his Dad's brother* to a related person; and the whole expression refers to yet another person, a friend of his Dad's brother. The hearer would have been able to figure out the referent of the whole expression by first identifying the referent of *his Dad*, then identifying that Dad's brother, and finally knowing that the person referred to is a friend of the latter. None of this mental computation need be at the level of the hearer's awareness. Indeed, if the hearer was not paying much attention at the time, she may not even have done the computation, even subconsciously, just nodding and saying 'mmm', as we often do. But there can be little doubt that the speaker arranged his utterance this way so that the referent of the whole could be retrieved, if the hearer wanted to keep close track of the story being told. And in general, wherever English is spoken, this recursively structured phrase works this way, as do many thousands of others with different words substituted.

Note also that this English possessive structure uses a sub-word unit, 'apostrophe-S'. This is not problematic. The way a string of meaningful elements is sliced up into pronounceable units in English ('words') is not a matter of syntax. Syntax hands on a structured string of elements to downstream parts of the sentence factory (phonology, phonetics), which sometimes squeeze elements together for the sake of pronounceability. (As a technical note here, this amounts to treating inflectional morphology as just a part of syntax that happens to involve bound morphemes.)

Recursion is a special case of hierarchical structuring. Recursion of clauses, minimal sentence-like units, to a depth of three or four clauses, can be found in informal conversation, as in the next examples, also from the *NECTE* corpus.

. . . must remember your cheque number because you didn't half get a good clip if you forgot that.

and then your father'd give you a good tanning and all for being brought in by the police because you were in the wrong place to start with

because what the farmers used to do was ehm if they wanted a letter posted they used to put a little ehm envelope in a window you know because in the deep snow it saved the postman walking right up to the house you know

because I can remember my poor little mother who was less than five foot standing in the kitchen trying to turn the handle of a wringer to get the sheets through and she sort of practically came off her feet

An abbreviated tree diagram for the first of these examples, showing only the recursive embedding of clauses, is given in Figure 4.3.

The next example, also from spontaneous speech, is more complex.

I can remember being taken into Princess Mary's eh not allowed to go in of course that was definitely no it was forbidden eh being hoisted up on my uncle's shoulder to look over the window that was half painted to see a little bundle that was obviously my brother being held up by my Dad.

Here the speaker inserts a parenthetical digression of fourteen words, between the '*eh*'s, and resumes seamlessly without a pause where she had left off, producing a sentence with seven subordinate clauses, embedded to a depth of 3. An abbreviated tree diagram for this example is given in Figure 4.4. As before, the motivation for claiming all this hierarchical embedding is semantico-pragmatic. For instance, in the last example, *that was half painted* gives more information about the window. The clauses *that was obviously my brother* and *being held up by my Dad* give more information about the little bundle. These parts of the sentence are counted as clauses because each contains a single verb; for English

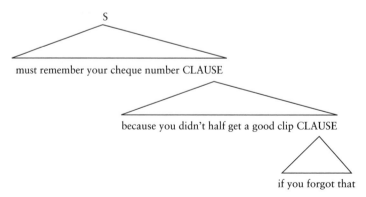

Fig. 4.3 Embedding of clauses, to a depth of 2.
Source: From the *NECTE* corpus.

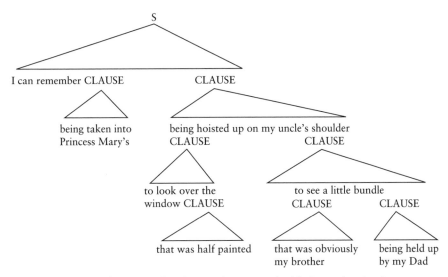

Fig. 4.4 Sentence with seven subordinate clauses, embedded to a depth of 3.

Note: The attachment of some of the CLAUSE triangles here is squashed to the left to fit them all onto the page. Read in a 'depth-first' way, with any two-line text between the triangles as a single run-on line.

Source: From the *NECTE* corpus.

at least, the rule of thumb 'one (non-auxiliary) verb–one clause' holds. A clause is a sentence-like unit that may take a different form from a simple sentence due to its being embedded. In the last example there are couple of infinitive clauses with a *to* before the verb and no tense marking on the verb, something that you don't find in a simple English sentence standing on its own. And there are also three so-called 'participial' clauses, with an *-ing* form of the verb (all passive, with *being*, as it happens).

Notice that in these last examples, the embedding happens predominantly toward the end of the sentence, giving mostly what is called a right-branching structure. This preference for right-branching sentence structures is widespread, not only in English, but across languages. It is a statistical fact about the syntax of languages. In principle, embedding toward the front of the sentence, giving left-branching structure, is usually also possible, but extensive left-branching ('front-loading') typically yields less acceptable sentences than the same amount of right-branching. Some languages, for example Japanese, permit much higher degrees of left-branching than others.

Semantically motivated structuring means that, with some exceptions, each chunk that a sentence can be analysed into corresponds to some whole semantic entity, such as a particular object, or a particular event or situation. The most obvious correlation is between noun phrases (NPs) and the objects they refer to.

To be sure, not all NPs are referring expressions, but a significant proportion of them are, and I take reference to specific entities to be a prototypical function of NPs. Linguists' tree diagrams reflect the semantically motivated meronomic (part–whole) aspect of the hierarchical structure of sentences. The lines in the tree diagrams are sufficient to represent this grouping of parts and subparts. All words falling under lines which join at a particular 'node' in the tree form a **constituent**.[29] Thus in Figure 4.2, *his Dad*, and *his Dad's* are two of the constituents of that expression. And in Figure 4.4 all the substrings under triangles labelled CLAUSE are constituents of that sentence.

While part–subpart syntactic structure is largely semantically motivated, it is not absolutely determined by semantics. Compare these two sentences, which are equivalent in propositional meaning:

The bullet hit John's shoulder
The bullet hit John in the shoulder

In the first sentence *John* and *shoulder* belong to the same noun phrase; in the second they don't. A speaker can choose to report the same event in different ways, to highlight or downplay the involvement of one participant. In the actual world, John's shoulder is a recognizable whole object. By grammatically separating John from his shoulder, as in the second sentence, the sentence conveys more clearly that it was John who took the bullet, and information about the particular bodypart is downgraded. A dispassionate doctor might be more likely to use the first sentence (or even just *The bullet hit the shoulder*), while a concerned relative of John's would be more likely to use the second sentence (and perhaps even omit *in the shoulder*).

Ability to manipulate such complex grammatical structure, where it exists in a language, is a solid fact about the human language faculty. Recall that this chapter is about universals of the human language faculty, so this is not a claim about all languages. Languages exploit stacking of parts around subparts and sub-subparts to different degrees. Languages which exhibit very little hierarchical grouping are known as 'nonconfigurational'. In these languages, much hierarchical organization is of a different nature, exploiting dependencies between distant words more than relying on formal grouping. Long-distance dependencies are discussed in a later section. Properties of actual languages, rather than what learners are universally capable of, given the chance, will be discussed in Chapter 5. A significant degree of hierarchically nested word/phrase/clause/sentence structure is no problem for a typical

[29] Or 'formal grouping', to use Bill Croft's preferred term.

healthy language learner. Remember also that the static diagrams I have used for illustration are a linguist's notation for representing what is mostly a dynamic process, either of producing a sentence as a speaker or interpreting one as a hearer. Novel sentences are built up by regular processes from smaller bits, typically the elementary words, and interpreted accordingly.

But not everything in fluent discourse is novel. Hierarchical structure is apparent both in some of the idiosyncratic items stored in the lexicon, and in what can be generated by combining these items by syntactic operations. This can be illustrated by underlining the successive parts and subparts of formulaic expressions and idioms[30] as in *once in a blue moon* and *not on your life*. Exactly parallel nested structures are reflected in the way novel expressions are put together, like *never at the northern beach* and *only at his office*. Thus hierarchical structure is reflected in two facets of human syntactic capacity, storage and computation. We can store hierarchically structured items, and we can compute novel ones. Most of the stored items have a structure that could also be generated by the productive rules that generate the vast numbers of novel expressions. This is an example of **redundancy** in grammatical storage. To capture the fact that *once in a blue moon* is stored as a unit, a structured item in the lexicon, as in Figure 4.5 (overleaf) is postulated. The idiom *once in a blue moon* is totally composed of items that occur elsewhere in the language. Only its semantics is irregular and at least somewhat unpredictable. Its pragmatic effect is to add an informal romantic or whimsical tone to the basic meaning 'extremely rarely'. By using completely familiar words and phrasal structures, this idiom is easier to keep in memory than if it had used words which occur only in this idiom. Thus the redundancy is actually functional.

Experimental evidence points to 'hybrid' representations of non-compositional idioms and fixed expressions. That is, the individual members of a fixed expression (i.e. the words) are stored, and the whole idiomatic expression using these words is also stored, with links between the idiom and the component words. Using priming techniques, Sprenger et al. (2006) showed that

during the planning of an idiomatic phrase the single words that make up the utterance are accessed separately. Both idiomatic and literal phrases can be primed successfully by means of priming one of their content words. This effect supports the compositional[31] nature of idiomatic expressions. . . . Moreover, the effect of Priming is stronger in the case of idioms. This is in favor of our hypothesis that the different components of

---

30 Also called 'fixed expressions'.
31 This is a non-semantic use of *compositional*; it is not implied that the meaning of the whole idiom is a function of the meanings of the words in it. [JRH]

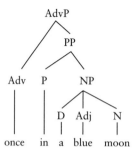

Fig. 4.5 A complex entry in the mental lexicon. It is composed completely of vocabulary and phrasal elements that occur elsewhere in the language. This is what Sprenger et al. (2006) call a 'superlemma', i.e. a complex lexical entry that cross-refers to simpler lemmas (lexical entries), also stored. The use of independently stored items presumably keeps this idiom from degenerating by phonetic erosion (slurring in speech).

Note: The traditional labels AdvP, PP, NP, etc. used in this figure are provisional, for convenience only; their status will be discussed below.

an idiom are bound together by one common entry in the mental lexicon. Priming one of an idiom's elements results in spreading activation from the element to all the remaining elements via a common idiom representation, resulting in faster availability of these elements. For literal items, no such common representation exists.

(Sprenger et al. 2006, p. 167)

These conclusions are consistent with other psycholinguistic accounts of the production of idioms (e.g. Cutting and Bock 1997) and the comprehension of idioms (e.g. Cacciari and Tabossi 1988). For reception of fixed expressions, Hillert and Swinney (2001, p. 117) conclude from a study of idiomatic German compound words, based on reaction times and priming effects, that 'The research presented here, combined with prior work in the literature, ... support a 'multiple-form-driven-access' version of such models (all meanings—both idiom and literal—are accessed)'. For instance, a German compound noun *Lackaffe*, meaning someone who shows off, but literally *lacquer monkey*, was found to prime **both** meanings related to the idiomatic meaning, such as VAIN, **and** meanings related to the meaning of the head noun *Lack*, such as VELVET.

The hybrid representation of idioms, which stores both the whole idiomatic expression and its components, would tend to shield the component words from phonetic erosion, or slurring in speech. For example, if *spill the beans* is stored with clear connections to its component words as used in non-idiomatic expressions (e.g. *spill my coffee* or *growing beans*) the parts of the idiom would not be susceptible to erosion in fast speech any more than the same words in non-idiomatic uses. Phonetic erosion does happen in extremely frequent fixed expressions (e.g. *going to* → *gonna*, and *want to* → *wanna*, *could have* → *coulda*, *why don't you* → *whyncha*). Very stereotyped expressions such as *you know what I mean*, or *I don't know*, or *thank you* can often become phonetically eroded in fast colloquial speech to something like *naamee* with nasality in the second syllable, or *dou*, again nasalized, or *kyu*. The drastic reduction of *don't* in frequent expressions like *I don't know*, but not in less frequent expressions, has been documented by Bybee and Scheibman (1999).[32] In these cases the connection between the holistically stored expression and separately stored component words has been weakened or lost. With brain damage, typically left hemisphere, there is often selective sparing of formulaic expressions. 'Although selectively preserved formulaic expressions produced by persons with severe propositional language deficits arising from stroke or traumatic brain injury are usually short (1–3 words), . . . longer sequences, such as proverbs, idioms, and Shakespearean quotes, have also been described' (Van Lancker Sidtis and Postman 2006, p. 412).[33]

Whole structures stored in the lexicon only very rarely use words which are not used elsewhere in the language. One example is *kith and kin*, which provides the only context in which the word *kith* is found. A few odd holistically stored expressions may resist analysis by the more regular rules of the language. One example is English *by and large*, in which we can recognize the words, but not any structure otherwise permitted in English. (**From and small?* **of and red?*, **with or nice?*—Naaah!) Such examples are rare.

In addition to the meronomic, part–whole, aspect of the hierarchical organization, I have mentioned another kind of grammatical structuring which is also hierarchically organized. In the Dependency Grammar[34] framework, the significant relationships between parts of a sentence are **dependencies**. Some words are dependent on others, in the sense of semantically modifying them or being grammatically licensed to occur with them. A simple example is given in Figure 4.6 (overleaf).[35] There can be long chains of such dependencies between

---

[32] My PhD thesis *The Speech of One Family* (Hurford 1967) also recorded many such examples of frequency-related phonetic reduction.

[33] The authors cite Whitaker (1976); Van Lancker (1988); Van Lancker Sidtis (2001); Critchley (1970); Peña Casanova et al. (2002). It is an old observation that taboo words are often also spared in aphasia: 'Patients who have been in the habit of swearing preserve their fluency in that division of their vocabulary' (Mallery 1881, p. 277).

[34] The classic work in Dependency Grammar is by Lucien Tesnière (1959). The principle was explored by Igor' Mel'chuk (1979, 1988). A modern version has been developed by Dick Hudson, under the banner of Word Grammar. See Hudson (1984, 1990, 2007).

[35] In this dependency diagram and several later ones, I have made a determiner, such as *my* or *the*, dependent on a head noun. Dependency grammarians differ on this, with Hudson taking the determiner to be the head of a dependent noun, and By (2004) and

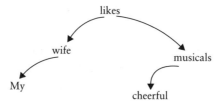

Fig. 4.6 A Dependency Grammar diagram.

Note: Hierarchical structure is shown in a different way, by dependencies between contiguous words. The sentence diagrammed here is *My wife likes cheerful musicals*. The hierarchical structure is apparent here in the fact that, for example, *My* is dependent on *wife*, which is in turn dependent on *likes*. The dependencies here involve adjacent (strings of) words. The two-dimensional arrangement in this figure preserves the left-to-right order of the words while suggesting the parallels between phrase structure and dependency structure.

words. Phrases are given a less basic status than words in this approach to grammar. A phrase can be defined derivatively as a word plus all the words that are dependent on it and adjacent to it, and all the words that are dependent on them and adjacent to them, and so on. Thus in the structure shown in Figure 4.6, the strings *My wife* and *cheerful musicals* are significant hierarchical chunks. The hierarchical structure of a couple of earlier examples is shown in Figures 4.7 and 4.8 'translated' into the conventions of Dependency Grammar.

Figures 4.1, 4.2, 4.7, and 4.8 illustrate the intertranslatability, in some cases, of phrase structure diagrams and dependency diagrams.[36] These are cases where the dependencies relate items within the same contiguous phrase. Dependency analysis has the advantage that it can represent grammatical and semantic relationships between words that are separated from each other, a topic to be taken up under the heading of 'long-distance dependencies' in a later section. The hierarchical analysis of sentences in Dependency Grammar is mostly the same as in frameworks giving more salience to phrases. One difference in their analysis of English is that most versions of Dependency Grammar do not recognize the hierarchical constituent VP (verb phrase). This is a detail that will not concern us. In more developed versions of Dependency Grammar, labels appear on the arcs, not for such chunks as phrases and clauses, but

---

Dikovsky (2004), for example, taking the determiner to be dependent on a head noun, as I have done here. Nothing in the text here hinges on this issue.

[36] See Osborne (2005) for a recent comparison of constituency-based and dependency-based analysis, emphasizing the usefulness of the idea of chains of dependencies.

I got on a bus to go to Throckley with the handbag with my threepence in my purse for my half-return to Throckley

Fig. 4.7 Dependency relations between nouns, determiners and prepositions, in a conversational utterance.

Note: The information about hierarchical organization is exactly the same as in the earlier diagram (Fig. 4.1). For example, by recursively following all the arrows that lead **from** (not into) *half-return*, we reach the words *my half-return to Throckley*, a phrase. Similarly, the larger phrase *with my threepence in my purse for my half-return to Throckley* can be retrieved by starting at the second *with* and following all the arrows.

Source: From the *NECTE* corpus.

His Dad's brother's friend

Fig. 4.8 Dependency relations between nouns and the possessive marker *'s* in a possessive construction in a conversational utterance.

Note: Following all the arrows from the first *'s* gets you the phrase *his Dad's*. Following all the arrows from *brother* gets the larger outer phrase *his Dad's brother*, and so on.

Source: From the *NECTE* corpus.

rather for the specific kinds of dependency **relations** that hold between words in a sentence, relations such as 'subject-of', 'object-of', and 'modifier-of'. The information in such labels, of all kinds, will be discussed below.

4.3 Word-internal structure

Linguists use the term *morphology* in a specialized sense, to refer specifically to the structure of **words**. The kind of hierarchical structure discussed above can involve not only relationships between words but also relationships **inside** words. We have seen one example already, with the English possessive marker 'apostrophe -s', as in *John's* and *brother's*. The same kind of dependency relationship exists between the suffix -s and the noun *John* as exists between the preposition *of* and *John* in a phrase such as *a friend of John*. English is not rich in morphology, but we can see some hierarchical structure with words in examples like *comings* and *goings*. *Comings* has three meaningful elements ('morphemes'), the stem *come*, the 'nominalizing' suffix *-ing* which makes *coming* in this context a noun, and the plural suffix *-s*. Plainly, the pluralization

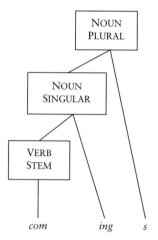

Fig. 4.9 Hierarchical structure within a word; *comings* shown as a tree.

applies to a form which has 'already' been converted into a noun, from a verb, by affixing *-ing*. Shown as a tree, the word has the structure in Figure 4.9.

Other languages have more complex morphology. The extreme case is that of **agglutinating** languages, in which up to about half a dozen (sometimes even more) meaningful elements can be stacked around a stem to form a single (long!) word. Well-known examples of agglutinating languages are Turkish and Inuit. Here is an example from Shona, the main language of Zimbabwe. The word *handíchaténgesá* means 'I will not sell'. Shona uses a single word where the English translation uses four. The Shona word is actually made up of six elements strung together, as shown below:

ha	*ndí*	*cha*	*téng*	*es*	*á*
Neg	I	Fut	buy	Cause	FinalVowel

This is not a particularly complex example. More extreme examples, often drawn from Inuit, can involve 'one-word-sentences' comprising up to a dozen morphemes all glued together. In agglutinating languages generally, although the meaningful elements may seem to lie together in sequence like beads on a string, there are reasons to ascribe hierarchical structure to words formed by agglutination. I will not go into the details, but the arguments are similar to those for hierarchical structure of phrases and sentences, as discussed earlier. Agglutination is simple in the sense that typically, given a transcription, it is not too hard to pick out the individual morphemes. They don't change very much from one word to another. On the other hand, acquiring fluent mastery of these complex word forms, in speaking and listening, is no easy matter.

In languages with complex morphology, much of the complexity is due to irregularity. Learning irregular verb forms is a right pain for second language learners. Irregularity comes in several guises. A language may separate its nouns and verbs into a variety of different patterns ('declensions' and 'conjugations'), none of which behave in quite the same way. In Latin, for example, verbs behave according to four different conjugations, each of which must be learnt to some extent separately; and nouns similarly separate out into at least four different declensions, each with its own partially different pattern to learn.

Another contributor to morphological complexity is the **fusion** of morphemes. Rather than each morpheme, suffix or prefix, making a single identifiable semantic contribution, as tends to be the case with agglutinating languages, in some languages several meanings are rolled into a single 'portmanteau' morpheme. The English verb suffix -s, as in *walks* and *teaches*, carries three pieces of information, namely PRESENT-TENSE, SINGULAR, and 3RD-PERSON. The French historic past suffix -*âmes* as in *nous allâmes* conflates the information PAST, PLURAL, and 1ST-PERSON.

Then there are variants of words which follow no patterns at all, and have to be learned individually. These are cases of **suppletion**, as with the English past tense of *go*, namely *went*. Synchronically, there is no rhyme or reason for the *go/went* alternation.[37] It is just something that has to be learned as a special case. An imaginary designer of a rationally organized language wouldn't allow any such irregularity. Everything would be neat, tidy, and predictable. But human children are not fazed, and take all such chaos in their stride. By the age of ten or sooner they manage to learn whatever morphological irregularities a language throws at them.

I have mentioned the similarity in hierarchical internal structure between words and sentences. Why is morphology regarded as a different kind of structure from syntax? In what circumstances do several meaningful elements belong so closely together that they make a single word, or when should they be regarded as short independent words strung together in a phrase? It's a good question, with very practical consequences. In the twentieth century, much work was put into developing orthographies for previously unwritten (but widely spoken) languages. In Shona, for instance, the example given above is now written in the standardized spelling system as a single word

---

[37] Diachronically, one can see how the *go/went* alternation came about. *Went* is the past tense of archaic *wend*, meaning (roughly) 'go', and fits in with other verbs such as *send/sent*, *bend/bent*, *lend/lent*, and *rend/rent*.

handíchaténgesá

When the basic research was being done to establish the principles for the new orthography,[38] there were alternatives. The 'conjunctive method of word-division', as above, was adopted. But another real possibility, used by early missionaries (e.g. Biehler 1913) was the 'disjunctive' method, according to which the above example would have been written with spaces, something like

ha ndí cha téng es á

The matter was resolved to accord with gut intuitions about what worked best for native speakers. Shona speakers responded intuitively to examples like *handíchaténgesá* as if they were to be read and written as single units of some sort. In some loose sense, the separate meaningful elements making up such forms were below the radar of speakers using the language fluently in everyday situations. Shona speakers intuitively know the difference between a single word, even if it is divisible into further elements, and a string of several words. The main clue, in Shona as in many other languages, is the placement of stress.

> Doke believed that Bantu languages were provided with a word marker in the form of penultimate stress and that all one had to do to arrive at a correct system of word division was to divide speech into different pieces, each with a stress on the last syllable but one.
>
> (Fortune 1969, p. 58)

The distinction between morphology and syntax rests on the concept of a **word**. In some sense it is obvious that words are not the basic building blocks of a language like English, and even less so for morphologically more complex languages. The most basic building blocks are the stems and affixes making up words—**morphemes**, as linguists call them. So why not stretch syntax down to the level of these basic elements? What is it about word-sized units that makes them special, a kind of boundary between two combinatorial systems? The answer is in phonology. Words are 'bite-sized' pronounceable units. The rule that Doke saw in Shona, 'one stress–one word', applies more or less straightforwardly to many languages. It gets more complicated and for some languages one needs to make a distinction between primary stress and secondary stresses. English has a few problem examples, like *seventeen* and *Tennessee* which have two potentially primary-stressed syllables, depending

---

[38] Doke (1931a, 1931b).

on the phonological context. Compare *TENnessee WILliams* with *CENtral TennesSEE* (with capital letters indicating primary stress). This phenomenon is known as 'iambic reversal' (Liberman and Prince 1977). Overall, a phonological criterion, such as stress, nothing to do with any kind of semantic unity, determines what a language treats as a word. In some languages, for example Turkish and Hungarian, there is another phonological clue, called 'vowel harmony', to whether a string of meaningful elements is a single word or not. In a language with vowel harmony, all the vowels in a single words must agree in some phonetic parameter, such as being all articulated at the front (or back) of the mouth, or all being pronounced with lip rounding (or with unrounded lips). In Turkish, for example, if you hear a succession of syllables with front vowels, and then suddenly you hear a syllable with a back vowel, this is a clue that you have crossed a boundary into a new word.

Morphology is more limited in scope than syntax, even though both systems involve putting things together. In some languages, the morphological structure is quite complex. In other languages (e.g. Mandarin, Vietnamese) there is little or no word-internal structure at all. Such languages, known as **isolating** (or **analytic**) langages, have hardly any morphology. But every language has some syntax, typically quite complex. Morphology is more limited in its structural possibilities. The order of morphemes within a word is almost always completely fixed, with no scope for variation. For example, the word *dramatizations* has four morphemes—roughly *drama + tize + ation + s*. It is unthinkable that these morphemes could be in any other order—try it! Another limitation of morphology, as opposed to syntax, is its boundedness. You can keep adding new clauses to a sentence, up to a point of exhaustion, and in principle after that you can see how the sentence could be even further extended by adding more clauses. Morphology is not like that. There is no longest sentence in English, but there is a longest word. A reader has suggested that this is not strictly true, because of examples like *re-read, re-re-read* and so on. Pretty obviously, any further iteration of prefixes like this would only be useful for word-play. It couldn't be interpreted according to the rule affecting single occurrences of the prefix. You wouldn't expect a listener quickly to recognize, for example, that *re-re-re-re-re-read* means *read for the sixth time*, although this could be worked out with pencil and paper. (See the other discussions of competence-plus in this book.) (For fun, look up 'longest word in English' in Wikipedia, and make your own mental comparison with the issue of 'longest sentence'.) It follows that within a word, the structural dependencies are never unbounded in linear distance, as they can be in syntax. In English syntax, for example, there is no principled limit to the distance between a verb and the subject with which it must agree. There are no such unbounded long-distance dependencies in morphology.

The boundary between syntax and morphology is blurred in languages which allow a lot of 'compound words'. Compound words are structures of independent words (i.e. not just stems, which always need some affix) juxtaposed. Simple English examples are *tractor driver* and *skyscraper*, both compound nouns, *pistol whip* and *drip-dry*, compound verbs, and *God awful* and *piss poor*, compound adjectives. Compound nouns especially can be of great length, as in *student welfare office reception desk* and even longer by several words. Notice from the above examples that spelling, with or without spaces or hyphens is not a consistent signal of a compound word. Compound words can be fairly productively formed, and the longer examples can have a hierarchical semantic structure, which makes them like examples of syntax. Also, the longer ones have more than one primarily stressed syllable, unlike non-compound words, again making them more like syntactic phrases. Traditionally, many of them, especially those spelled without a space, have been regarded as words, and included in dictionaries, as is *skyscraper*. The idiosyncratic meanings of compounds, often not predictable from the meanings of their parts (e.g. *memory stick* and *flash drive* as noted earlier), mean that such items must be mentally stored, like words, rather than like (non-idiomatic) phrases or sentences. The alleged great productivity of German compounding only stands out because of the lack of spacing in the orthography, as in *Donauschifffahrtsgesellschaft*, translatable as the English compound *Danube ship travel company*, or *Jugendgemeinschaftdienst*, translatable as *youth community service*. Jackendoff (2002) sees compound expressions formed by mere juxtaposition as an early evolutionary precursor of more complex syntax, a position with I agree, as discussed later in Chapter 5.

Human children learn to put meaningful elements together. Above the level of the word, that is defined as syntax; within words, putting meaningful elements together is defined as morphology. The dividing line between syntax and morphology is based on largely phonological criteria. Children can easily learn to assimilate the morphology/syntax divide into their production behaviour, putting some bits together into sequences defined by factors such as stress and vowel harmony, and productively putting these word-sized units together into longer expressions. The psycholinguistics of the morphology/syntax divide is not well explored. It may involve integration of whole-sentence output with stored motor routines regulating the typical shape and rhythm of words. (My speculative hypothesis—no evidence offered.)

4.4 Syntactic categories

Humans can learn where to put different kinds of words in a sentence. How many different kinds of words are there in a language? Languages differ in this. As we are concerned here with the upper limits on what humans can learn, it will be OK to keep the discussion to English. Several of the tree diagrams given so far have been examples of 'bare phrase structure', without any labels classifying the parts and subparts of the structures diagrammed. Most, indeed possibly all, standard textbooks on syntactic theory add labels such as CLAUSE, NP, PP, Pos, N, and P to tree diagrams. These are labels of so-called **syntactic categories**, some of which (e.g. N(oun), V(erb), P(reposition), A(djective)) correspond to the 'parts of speech' of schoolbook grammars. N(oun), V(erb), A(djective), and so on are word classes. The label Noun, for instance, applies to individual words. Other traditional syntactic category labels are for higher-level units, typically phrases, such as NP (noun phrase), VP (verb phrase), and AP (adjective phrase). These, obviously, are phrase classes. Categories at even higher levels, such as CLAUSE, can also be counted as phrase classes. I will discuss the informativeness (and hence the usefulness in a grammatical theory) of word classes and phrase classes separately. The question is: do people who have learned a language represent anything in their minds corresponding to these categories? Does the human capacity for language include a capacity for acquiring linguistic knowledge specifically in terms of such categories? The alternative is that people only acquire knowledge of the distributions of individual words, without generalizing to whole categories of words.

If syntactic structure were a completely faithful reflection of semantic structure, specifically syntactic categories would not exist. By including such syntactic category information in tree diagrams, a claim is made that at least some of the grammatical structure of sentences does not follow from their meanings. Sometimes the same meaning is expressed by forms with different parts of speech and different kinds of phrase. Consider the two sentences *John owns this car* and *John is the owner of this car*. English gives you a choice between expressing the relationship between John and his car either as a verb, *owns*, or with a nominal ('nouny') construction, *is the owner of ...*[39] Another example

---

[39] These two sentences are true in exactly the same set of circumstances. There is no state of affairs in which John owns the car but is not the owner of it, and no state of affairs in which John is the owner of the car but doesn't own it. We have an intuitive feeling that any two different expressions **must** differ at least somewhat in meaning, but in cases like this one can't put one's finger on any real difference between the two sentences, apart from the grammatical difference. In a conversation, the use of a nouny

is the pair *I am afraid of snakes* and *I fear snakes*, which are pretty much equivalent in meaning, as least as far as indicating my emotional response to snakes. But this relationship can be expressed with an adjectival expression, *be afraid of . . .*, or by the verb *fear*. This is an aspect of the partial 'autonomy of syntax',[40] the idea that a speaker's knowledge of the grammar of her language is at least to some extent independent of both semantics and phonology, while forming a bridge between the two.

The broad-brush labels in tree diagrams, V, N, etc. have been used by syntacticians to express generalizations about the specifically syntactic choices that are made in putting sentences together. This traditional rather simple view of a small number of syntactic categories in a language has never been adopted by computational linguists working on practical applications. Among more theoretical studies, the simple analysis has recently been critically re-examined. The emerging picture[41] is this:

- A speaker of a language like English (typical in this regard) has learned a very large number of different word classes, far more than the usual familiar small set of traditional parts of speech. Some individual words are completely *sui generis*, forming a singleton word class. The word classes of a language are particular to that language.[42]

- For any language, speakers have learned large numbers of different constructions, and the word classes that they know are defined by their distribution in the entire set of constructions in the language.

- The language-specific word classes that a speaker knows are each semantically homogeneous. Words in the same class have very similar meanings. This is not to say that the word classes that a speaker knows are absolutely

---

expression (e.g. *is the owner of*) may prime further use of the same kind of expression, but that is not a matter of meaning.

[40] The phrase 'autonomy of syntax' raises hackles. I use it here in the sense that syntax is not wholly reducible to semantics. My position is the same as that of John Anderson (2005), in an article entitled 'The Non-autonomy of syntax'. This article discusses some extreme positions on the autonomy of syntax in a valuable long-term historical perspective, and reveals confusion on this matter in claims that theorists have made about their historical antecedents.

[41] For a succinct and concise summary tallying with mine, see David Kemmerer's supplemental commentary on Arbib (2005) online at http://www.bbsonline.org/Preprints/Arbib-05012002/Supplemental/Kemmerer.html.

[42] Properly speaking, the word classes that a speaker has acquired are particular to that speaker's idiolect, since competence resides in individuals. As speakers in the same community behave very similarly, the statement in terms of 'a language' is not unduly harmful.

determined by semantics. Languages carve up a human–universal conceptual space in different ways.

• The messy picture of hundreds, possibly thousands, of tiny word classes is alleviated by certain mechanisms which allow a degree of generalization across subcategories, specifically the mechanisms of **multiple default inheritance hierarchies**.

Across languages, the gross categories of N(oun), V(erb), and A(djective) fit into the grammars of different languages in different ways. There is a quite good correspondence between nouns in one language and nouns in another, but it is seldom perfect. This is putting it rather loosely. Unpacking this a bit, it means that almost all members of the class of words in one language that typically denote physical objects can be translated into words in another language that belong to a class whose members also typically denote physical objects. For example, the English word *week*, though it does not denote a physical object itself, belongs to a class of words that fit grammatically into sentences in the same way, a class including *door, rock, chair, tree, dog,* and so forth. *Week* translates into French as *semaine*, a word distributed in French in the same way as *porte, rocher, siège, arbre, chien,* and so on. And these last French words, of course, denote physical objects. Likewise for verbs. And as one gets away from these central parts of speech, the correspondences across languages diminish. Across languages, 'there are typological prototypes which should be called noun, verb, and adjective' (Croft 2001, p. 63). Languages deviate in their own idiosyncratic ways from the semantic prototypes. French has no adjective corresponding to English *hungry* and *thirsty*.[43] French has no adjective corresponding to *wrong* as in English *He shot the wrong woman*; you have to say something like *He made a mistake in shooting the woman*. And here, the English Verb+Noun expression *make a mistake* translates into a single reflexive verb in French, *se tromper*. French has no single verbs translatable as *kick* or *punch*. And so on. 'The mismatches [between syntax and semantics] are then evidence of language-particular routinisations...imposed on a syntax based on [semantic] groundedness' (Anderson 2005, p. 242).

4.4.1 Distributional criteria and the proliferation of categories

We are all familiar with a very traditional schoolbook taxonomy in which there are exactly eight 'parts of speech', verbs, nouns, pronouns, adjectives, adverbs, prepositions, conjunctions, and interjections. The flaws in the traditional

---

43 *Affamé* and *assoiffé* describe more extreme conditions than *hungry* and *thirsty*.

semantic definitions of these classes of words (e.g. a noun is the name of a person, place or thing, a verb describes an action, and so on) are obvious and well known. Instead, linguists advocate **distributional** definitions, whereby all words that can occur in the same range of grammatical contexts are lumped together in the same class.

To account for the grammatical distribution of words controlled by a speaker of a single language, probably hundreds of different word classes need to be postulated. The case has been comprehensively argued by Culicover (1999) and Croft (2001). They grasp a nettle which recent syntactic theorists have almost invariably swept under the carpet (to mix metaphors!).

[W]hile there may be a universal conceptual structure core to the basic syntactic categories **Noun** and **Verb**, the set of possible syntactic categories found in natural language is limited only by the range of possible semantic and formal properties that may in principle be relevant to the categorization process. We thus predict not only the existence of the major categories **Noun** and **Verb** in all of the world's languages, but the existence of idiosyncratic and arbitrary minor categories that contain very few members, quite possibly only one member, categories that are defined by a specific combination of properties for a single language.   (Culicover 1999, p. 41)

In a typical introductory syntax course, the **distributional method** for deciding word classes is taught. One introductory syntax text expresses the core of the idea as: 'a particular form class has a unique range of morphosyntactc environments in which it can occur' (Van Valin 2001, p. 110). Here is a typical instance from another syntax textbook. Brown and Miller (1991, p. 31), in a chapter on 'Form classes', give the following definitions of the classes VI (intransitive verb) and VT (transitive verb).

VI occurs in the environment NP _____ #
VT occurs in the environment NP _____ NP

Note here the reliance on the category, NP, and the # marker denoting the boundary of another category, VP, assumed to be already established. In yet another introductory syntax text Carnie (2002, pp. 54–5), in explaining 'how to scientifically [*sic*] determine what part of speech (or word class or syntactic category) a word is' (in English), lists six distributional tests each for nouns and verbs, five for adjectives and four for adverbs. An intelligent student asks why these particular frames have been selected as criteria. Croft has a term for what is going on here, 'methodological opportunism'. 'Methodological opportunism selects distributional tests at the whim of the analyst, and ignores the evidence from other distributional tests that do not match the analyst's expectations, or else treats them as superficial or peripheral' (Croft 2001, p. 45). Croft cites a pioneer of American Structuralism, which took the distributional method as central to its approach, and a 1970s study critical of Transformational Grammar, which in this respect accepted the same methodological principle.

[I]n many cases the complete adherence to morpheme-distribution classes would lead to a relatively large number of different classes.   (Harris 1946, p. 177)

If we seek to form classes of morphemes such that all the morphemes in a particular class will have identical distributions, we will frequently achieve little success. It will often be found that few morphemes occur in precisely all the environments in which some other morphemes occur, and in no other environments.   (Harris 1951, p. 244)

In a very large grammar of French developed by Maurice Gross and colleagues, containing 600 rules covering 12,000 lexical items, no two lexical items had exactly the same distribution, and no two rules had exactly the same domain of application (Gross 1979, 859–60).   (Croft 2001, p. 36)

Most theoretical syntacticians, unlike Gross, are not concerned with broad coverage of a language. Practical computational linguists, however, developing tools aimed at processing as much of a language as possible, have to face up to the serious problem of large numbers of distributionally distinct word classes. Briscoe and Carroll (1997) 'describe a new system capable of distinguishing 160 verbal subcategorization classes. ... The classes also incorporate information about control of predicative arguments and alternations such as particle movement and extraposition' (p. 357).

Geoff Sampson (1995) came up with a list of 329 different word classes for English.[44] Some items in these classes are orthographically several words, like *as long as* and *provided that*; these belong in the same class as the single words *although* and *whereas*. Some of Sampson's word classes are singleton sets, for example *not* and existential *there*. You can't find any other words with the same distribution as *not* or existential *there*. Some of the subclassification is due to the distribution of words in quite specialized contexts. Thus names of weekdays, for example *Sunday* are distinct from names of months, for example *October*. This reflects a native speaker's knowledge that *Sunday the fifth of October* is grammatical, whereas *October the fifth of Sunday* is not grammatical. Several objections might be raised to this level of detail.

---

[44] By my count, and not including punctuation marks.

In connection with the month/weekday distinction, it might be objected that the problem with *October the fifth of Sunday* is not syntactic but a matter of semantics, like the famous *Colorless green ideas sleep furiously*. Certainly these word classes are semantically homogeneous. But their grammatical distribution does not follow completely from their meanings. One of the two English date constructions, exemplified by *the fifth of November*, is more versatile than the other, allowing not only proper names of months, but also any expression denoting a month, as in *the fifth of each month* and *the fifth of the month in which your birthday occurs*. But the other date construction, exemplified by *November the fifth*, is restricted to just the proper month names. *Each month the fifth* and *The month of your birthday the fifth* are ungrammatical. Thus the first construction has a slot for a truly semantically defined class of items, namely any month-denoting expression. But the second construction imposes a semantically unmotivated restriction to just the proper names for months. It might be argued that the restriction here is to **single-word** expressions denoting months, so that the restriction is part semantic and part morphological, but does not involve a truly **syntactic** class. It is hard to see how this is not equivalent to positing a class of (single) words, defined by their syntactic distribution. Adult learners of English, who already know about months and weekdays, and how they are related, nevertheless have to learn how to express dates in English. English dialects differ grammatically in date constructions; *April third* is grammatical in American English but not in British English, which requires a *the*. A Frenchman simply converting *le douze octobre* word-for-word into English would get the English grammar wrong. These are grammatical facts pertaining to a specific class of words, a class which is also semantically homogeneous. It is an arbitrary fact about English that it treats month names with special syntactic rules. We can imagine a language in which the hours of the day are expressed by the same constructions, as for example hypothetically in *the sixth of Monday*, meaning the sixth hour of a Monday. But English doesn't work this way. So the month names are a syntactically identifiable class, beside being a semantically identifiable class. Similar arguments apply to many word classes.

A second objection to postulating such narrow grammatical categories as MONTH-NAME might be that such facts are marginal to English. No one has proposed a criterion for deciding which grammatical facts are marginal and which are 'core'. The danger is of fitting the target facts to what some preconceived theory can handle. A theoretical stance opposed to linguistic knowledge including massive storage of a range of constructions, including those for expressing dates, might dispose one to dismiss such data. But why not instead reconsider the theoretical stance?[45] A few of Sampson's classifications relate to orthographic conventions of written English, and so it might be claimed that his list could be shortened a bit for spoken English. But conversely there are conventions in spoken language that do not find their way into the printed texts which Sampson's work was aimed at. And within some of his word classes, I can find differences. For example, he puts *albeit* and *although* in the same class, his 'CS'. But for me, *albeit* cannot be used to introduce a fully tensed subordinate clause, as in **Albeit he wasn't invited, he came anyway*. So overall, a figure of about 329 different word classes is not likely to overestimate the complexity of an English speaker's tacit knowledge of her language. Anyone who has learned English as a native speaker has at least this much detailed knowledge of lexical categories, alias word classes.

Beth Levin (1993), dealing only with English verbs, studied the argument syntax of 3,100 verbs, and grouped them into 193 different verb classes. As an example of her criteria, consider the differences and similarities among the four verbs *spray, load, butter,* and *fill.*

We sprayed paint onto the wall
We sprayed the wall with paint
We loaded hay into the wagon
We loaded the wagon with hay
*We filled water into the jug
We filled the jug with water
*We buttered butter onto the toast
?We buttered the toast with butter

On the basis of this and other patterns of alternation, Levin classifies *spray* and *load* together in one class, *fill* in a different class, and *butter* in yet another class. The judgements in such cases may be subtle, but they are real, and can distinguish native speakers from non-native speakers. There is a 'syntax or semantics' issue here, which remains open. I have tentatively taken the position that an English speaker has learned the fine-grained differences in syntactic distribution among verbs such as *spray, load, fill,* and *butter.* On this view, a learner first learns some syntactic facts, namely what constructions tolerate which verbs inside them, and then can extrapolate something of the meanings of the verbs themselves from their occurrence in these constructions.

---

[45] When it was suggested after a popular uprising in the Democratic Republic of Germany that the people had forfeited the confidence of the government, Bertolt Brecht acidly commented that the government should dissolve the people and elect another.

An alternative view is that the learner first learns fine-grained differences in the meanings of the verbs, and then it follows naturally from the semantics which constructions will allow these verbs inside them. Is 'verb meaning ... a key to verb behavior', as Levin (1993, p. 4) advocates, or is verb behaviour, sometimes at least, a key to verb meaning? The question should be put in terms of language acquisition. There may be no one-size-fits-all answer to this question. Some learners may adopt a syntactic strategy and extrapolate subtle details of word meaning from exemplars of the constructions they have learned. For such learners, it would be valid to say they have acquired (first) a very fine-grained set of syntactic subcategories, distinguished according to the constructions they are distributed in. Other learners may adopt a semantic strategy and figure out all the subtle details of the meanings of words first, and thenceforth only use them in appropriate constructions. The issue could resolved by finding a pair of words with **identical** meaning, differently allowed in various syntactic environments (constructions). I suggest the pairs *likely/probable* as a possible candidate; *John is likely to come* versus **John is probable to come*. Difficulties are (1) that such pairs are uncommon, and (2), relatedly, that syntactic differences may give rise quickly in the development of a language to assumptions that the words concerned must have different meanings just because they are used in different environments. Arbitrary or accidental syntactic/lexical differences can get re-interpreted as principled semantic/lexical differences. Humans seek meaning in arbitrary differences. I will briefly revisit this issue in section 4.6.

4.4.2 *Categories are primitive, too—contra radicalism*

These examples with *spray, load, fill,* and *butter* show how verbs vary in their distribution across constructions. But Levin still concludes that **there are categories** of verbs, albeit quite narrow ones. Here is where I, and probably most other linguists, part company with Croft's radicalism. In a brief passage which is the key to his whole framework, he writes,

I propose that we discard the assumption that syntactic structures are made up of atomic primitives [including syntactic categories, JRH]. CONSTRUCTIONS, NOT CAT-EGORIES AND RELATIONS, ARE THE BASIC PRIMITIVE UNITS OF SYNTACTIC REPRESEN-TATION.[46] The categories and relations found in constructions are derivative—just as the distributional method implies. This is Radical Construction Grammar.... At worst, theories of categories, etc. are theories of nothing at all, if the analyst does not apply his/her constructional tests consistently.   (Croft 2001, pp. 45–6)

---

[46] Croft uses small capitals for emphasis.

I take it that to reject syntactic categories as primitives is to reject classes of words as primitives. Thus Croft is espousing a modern synchronic version of a slogan used by nineteenth-century 'wave theorists' in historical linguistics, namely 'chaque mot a son histoire'[47] (Schuchardt 1868; Schmidt 1872). It would be good to eliminate as many theoretical primitives as possible, but it seems either that Croft is ultimately equivocal in his radicalism or that I have not grasped some profound point here. After much brain-racking, I settle for the former conclusion, that we cannot get rid of syntactic categories as part of a speaker's knowledge of his language. In a few paragraphs, here's why.

Speakers do indeed know a wide range of constructions. How is that knowledge stored? The representation of a particular construction gives, besides its semantics, its shape, the arrangement of its elements. Some of these elements are individual words or morphemes. The existential *there* construction, for example, refers specifically to the word *there*. But it also must have a way of referring to any of four finite 3rd-person forms of the verb *be*, the participle *been*, and the bare form *be* itself. We find *there is...*, *there are...*, *there was...*, *there were*, *there have been*, and *there might be*, for example.[48] These forms constitute a small abstract category, call it BE. Speakers' fluent productive use of different forms of the existential *there* construction makes it likely that they store it with the abstract BE category. This abstract BE category is a component of at least three other constructions. It is the 'copula' used with noun phrases and adjective phrases, as in *This is/was/might be a problem, They are/were/have been smokers, We are/were/won't be very happy* and so on. The category BE is also a component of the progressive aspect construction (*am writing, is writing, were writing*), and passive construction (*was killed, were killed, are killed*). The category BE is known independently of the constructions in which it figures. It is a building block of several constructions, and it is not derivative of these constructions. You might want to argue that BE is not a category, but a single word. But if *am, is, was,* and *were* are single words, how can BE be other than a superordinate category? This possible line of objection is even less applicable to some of other the examples I have mentioned.

---

[47] Each word has its own history.

[48] Interestingly, we don't find a progressive form of BE in the existential construction, as in *There are being mice in our attic*. I put this down to a general restriction blocking the progressive from stative sentences, as in *This book is weighing two pounds*. Also, the fact that the existential *there* construction can take several other verbs beside BE (*There remain a few problems, There appeared a ghost*) does not affect the point being made about BE.

The category BE is admittedly not a very big category, but that is not the point. The radical argument is not that categories are smaller than previously thought, but that they don't exist, except in a derivative sense. Croft very aptly invokes the common distinction between 'lumpers' and 'splitters'. '"Lumping" analyses of parts of speech succeed only by ignoring distributional patterns. . . . The empirical facts appear to favor the "splitters". But the "splitters" have their own problem. There is no way to stop splitting' (p. 78). But in almost all the examples that Croft discusses he does stop splitting somewhere short of individual words, usefully writing, as just one instance among many detailed analyses of grammatical phenomena in many languages, of 'two classes of property words and one class of action words' (p. 78) in Lango. So it seems that the radicality is a matter of degree and not absolute. The traditional categories that linguists have invoked are not finely textured enough.

Perhaps Croft's proposal is not as radical as I have taken it to be, and his attack is only on such very traditional broad categories as Noun and Verb. Within the family of Construction Grammarians, radical or otherwise, there is common cause against a shadowy view, seldom made explicit by generativists, that N(oun) and V(erb) are 'irreducible grammatical primitives without corresponding meanings or functions' and 'atomic, purely syntactic, universal categories' (Goldberg 2006, p. 221). A claim conjoining so many terms is more easily falsified than a claim for any one of the conjuncts on its own. The closest I have found in a generativist making such a strong conjunctive claim is 'I shall assume that these elements [syntactic categories, JRH] too are selected from a fixed universal vocabulary' (Chomsky 1965, pp. 65–6). That was influential. Goldberg also seems here to equate 'irreducible' with 'primitive'. Croft himself carefully distinguishes 'atomic' from 'primitive', helpfully clarifying his position.

But 'atomic' and 'primitive' are logically independent concepts. ATOMIC units are those that cannot be broken down into smaller parts in the theory. PRIMITIVE units are those whose structure and behavior cannot be defined in terms of other units in the theory. Primitive elements need not be atomic.   (Croft 2001, p. 47)

For Croft, whole constructions are primitive, but not atomic.

Theories in which the primitive theoretical constructs are complex [like Construction Grammar, JRH] are NONREDUCTIONIST theories. A nonreductionist theory begins with the largest units and defines the smaller ones in terms of their relation to the larger units. The paradigm example of a nonreductionist theory is the theory of perception proposed by Gestalt psychology (Koffka 1935; Köhler 1929; Wertheimer 1950). In Gestalt psychology, evidence is presented to the effect that the perception of features is influenced by the perceptual whole in which the feature is found.   (Croft 2001, p. 47)

The parallel with Gestalt psychology is too simple. Perception involves a to-and-fro negotiation between bottom-up data from the sensory organs and top-down expectations generated by a mind containing existing categories. Further, Croft's statement about the relations between constructions and categories involves **definitions**, whereas perception is not a matter involving definitions, but probabilistic interacting top-down and bottom-up activations. I suggest that a person's knowledge of his language has both constructions (e.g. the existential *there* construction) and categories (e.g. the category BE) as primitives, which mutually interdefine each other. This echoes the conclusion from psycholinguistic evidence for redundant storage of both whole idioms and their constituent words. Croft is elsewhere sympathetic to 'redundant representation of grammatical information in the taxonomic hierarchy' (p. 28). So, neither constructions nor categories are atomic (except perhaps single-word categories like *not*); constructions have parts, and categories have members.

I will briefly take on the other members of Goldberg's 'atomic, purely syntactic, universal' constellation of things which N(oun) and V(erb) are not, starting with 'universal'. Not mentioned is any hint of innateness, but I suspect this is what she had in mind. Obviously humans are biologically equipped to learn complex systems aptly described using such terms as 'noun', 'verb', 'adjective', and so on. But this does not entail that biology in any sense codes for, or hardwires, these particular syntactic categories. A possible contrast here is with the logical categories of true and false; arguably humans are hardwired to think in strictly binary yes/no, true/false terms about propositions. To be or not to be—no half measures. I'm not actually arguing that this is so, but it seems much more likely to be so than that humans are genetically bound to learn languages with two main word classes, one typically denoting physical objects and the other typically denoting actions.[49] Humans can learn systems making finer distinctions among syntactic categories, but there are variability of, and limits to, the granularity of syntactic categorization that humans in a normal lifetime find useful and manageable. I will argue (in Chapter 9) that **languages**, being culturally transmitted systems used for communication, evolve in such a way that categories like noun and verb inevitably emerge in developed languages. Humans are biologically equipped to learn systems incorporating such categories, but are not narrowly biased to learn just these specific categories. By analogy, human builders are not biologically biased to conceive of buildings as necessarily having lintels and arches. Human builders **can conceive** of lintels

---

[49] See section 4.4.7 of this chapter for discussion of possible brain correlates of nouns and verbs.

and arches, and the practical problems of making substantial and impressive shelters lead them to use these structural types repeatedly in their buildings. So in the sense of an innate universal grammar, UG, I agree with Goldberg that the categories N(oun) and V(erb) are not 'universal'. In a section discussing the possible existence of 'substantive universals', Chomsky (1965, pp. 27–30) attributes the view that Noun and Verb are universal categories to 'traditional universal grammar', but himself goes no further than to suggest that his modern brand of universal grammar 'might assert that each language will contain terms that designate persons or lexical items referring to specific kinds of objects, feelings, behavior, and so on' (p. 28). This choice of possibilities is interestingly functional.

Goldberg also attacks the idea that N(oun) and V(erb) are categories 'without corresponding meanings or functions' and thus 'purely syntactic'. If a language is useful for anything, even just for helping introspective thought, let alone for communication, it would be surprising if any part of it had no corresponding function at all. We should not necessarily expect a category to have one single function. The category BE has several functions. The English passive construction has several functions. There are no single functions of the broad categories N(oun) and V(erb), but within all the diverse constructions in which they appear, they do have some function, for example in aid of reference or predication. Among the best candidates for purely syntactic phenomena are the arbitrary classification of nouns in some languages into non-natural 'genders', for example into 'Masculine', 'Feminine', and 'Neuter' in German, and rules of agreement between features. Arguably, agreement rules add some redundancy to a signal, making it easier to interpret. It is harder to think of a real function for non-natural gender phenomena. These could be purely syntactic, just something you have to do to get your grammar right, because the community has adopted these arbitrary norms. In a footnote mentioning 'brute syntactic facts', Goldberg concedes the idea: 'While I do accept the existence of occasional instances of synchronically unmotivated syntactic facts (normally motivated by diachronic developments), these appear to be the exception rather than the rule' (Goldberg 2006, p. 167). I agree. If brute syntactic facts are salient enough, humans can learn to follow the relevant rules and maintain them in the language. But the lack of functional motivation for them means that either they will tend to drop out of the language, or else recruit some new meaning. Humans like things to be meaningful.

Accounts of Construction Grammar which are formally more explicit than Croft (2001) or Goldberg (2006) define constructions in terms of the categories of which they are built. In fact this is axiomatic in the approach called Sign-Based Construction Grammar (Michaelis, in press; Sag, 2007).

In this framework, the syntactic information about a construction (or 'sign') obligatorily includes a 'CAT' feature, whose values are typically the familiar syntactic categories, for example preposition, count noun, etc.

4.4.3 Multiple default inheritance hierarchies

So far, all I have argued about word-class syntactic categories is, contra Croft, that they are primitive elements (but not the only primitive elements) in what a speaker knows about her language, and that they can be highly specific, with very small numbers of members, like the categories BE, MONTH-NAME, WEEKDAY-NAME. This does not leave the traditional major categories such as N(oun) and (Verb) out in the cold. The structure of what a speaker can learn about syntactic categories is actually more complex, with categories at various levels of generality arranged in **multiple default inheritance hierarchies**. There are three concepts to unpack here, and I will start with the simplest, namely inheritance.[50]

April and *September* are nouns, no doubt about it. They share certain very general properties of all nouns, such as that they can be the dependent arguments of verbs, either as subject or object in sentences, for example *April is the cruellest month* or *I love September*, or dependent on a preposition, as in *before April* or *in September*. Also at this most general level, these words share with other nouns the property of being modifiable by an adjective, as in *last September* or *early April*. At a slightly more specific level, month names part company with some other nouns, being 'Proper' nouns, with a similar distribution to *Henry* and *London*, not needing any determiner/article, for example *in April, for Henry, to London*. This separates Proper nouns from Common nouns like *dog* and *house*, which require an article or determiner before they can be used as an argument in a sentence. Contrast *July was pleasant* with **dog was fierce*. At the most specific level, month names part company with other Proper nouns. Specific to the MONTH-NAMEs is information about what prepositions they can be dependent on. *In January, by February,* and *during March* are OK, but you can't use **at April* or **on April* as prepositional phrases,[51] even though you can say *on Monday*. And of course, quite specific rules apply to the MONTH-NAMEs in the specialized date constructions like *November the fifth* and *the fifth of November*. (*November the fifth* and

---

[50] Early arguments for inheritance hierarchies in grammatical representations are found in Daelemans et al. (1992) and Fraser and Hudson (1992).

[51] In examples like *We can look at April* or *We decided on April*, the words *at* and *on* are parts of the 'phrasal verbs' *look at* and *decide on*.

Henry the Fifth are instances of different constructions, as their semantics clearly differ.) An English speaker has learned all this. It seems reasonable to assume that the knowledge is represented somewhat economically, so that the information that applies to all nouns is not stored over and over again for each individual noun. By appealing to the idea of an inheritance hierarchy, simply saying that, for example, *November* is a noun has the effect that this word inherits all the grammatical properties associated with that most general category. Likewise, saying that *February* is a Proper noun means that it inherits the somewhat more specific properties that apply to Proper nouns. Down at the bottom level, there are certain very specific generalizations that apply just to words of the category MONTH-NAME, and the twelve words that belong in this category inherit the distributional properties spelled out by those specific generalizations. At the bottom of an inheritance hierarchy (in the default case), words accumulate all the properties, from very general to most specific, associated with the categories above them in the hierarchy, but none of the properties associated with categories on separate branches.

Staying briefly with the category of month names, when the French revolutionaries introduced a new calendar with twelve thirty day months, all with new names, no one apparently had any trouble assuming that the new names, *Brumaire, Frimaire, Nivôse*, etc., fitted into the date-naming constructions in exactly the same way as the old month names. We find *le douze Thermidor, le quinze Germinal* and probably all the other possible combinations. The existing French category MONTH-NAME acquired twelve new members, and was combined in the old way with the also-existing category CARDINAL-NUMBER in an existing date-naming construction. This across-the-board instant generalization to new cases (new words) reinforces the idea that a speaker's knowledge is represented in terms, not just of the individual words, but higher-level syntactic categories.

An inheritance hierarchy can be conveniently diagrammed as a tree, so the information in the above English example can be shown as in Figure 4.10.

A word of general caution. The term 'hierarchy' has many related senses. Hierarchies of many sorts can be represented as tree diagrams. The sense of 'hierarchy' in 'inheritance hierarchy' is different from the sense in which sentence structure was said to be hierarchical in the previous section. The relations between nodes in a tree diagram over a sentence (e.g. Figures 4.1 and 4.2) are not the same as the relations between nodes in an inheritance hierarchy diagram (e.g. Figure 4.10).

As a further example of an inheritance hierarchy, consider English verbs. Among their most general properties is that they take a dependent subject argument in (declarative and interrogative) sentences, and that they agree with

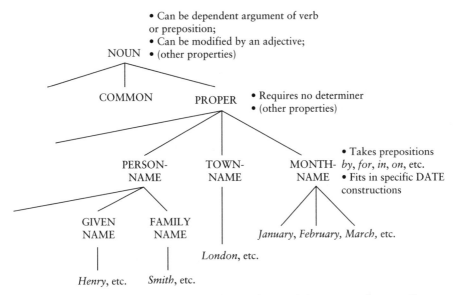

Fig. 4.10 Partial inheritance hierarchy diagram for English nouns. This just illustrates the idea. Obviously, there is much more information that an English speaker knows about the category of nouns and all its subclasses, sub-subclasses, and sub-sub-subclasses.

that subject in number and person (e.g. *You are going, Are you going?, You go, He goes* versus ungrammatical *are going, *goes (the latter considered as whole sentences). At a slightly less general level, English verbs split into two subcategories, Auxiliaries (e.g. HAVE, BE, and MODAL) and Main verbs. The category Auxiliary is associated with the properties of inverting with the subject argument in questions (*Has he gone? Can you swim?*), and preceding the negative particle *not* or *n't* in negative sentences. All actual Auxiliary verbs (e.g. *has, can, were*) inherit these properties from the Auxiliary category (*He hasn't gone, Can't you swim?, Why weren't you here?*). Main verbs, being on a separate branch of the verb inheritance hierarchy, do not inherit these properties. Within the Main verb category, words split three ways (at least) according to the number of non-subject dependent arguments that they take. Intransitive verbs take no further arguments (*China sleeps, Jesus wept*); 'monotransitive' verbs take one further argument, a direct object (*Philosophy baffles Simon, Irises fascinate me*); and 'ditransitive' verbs take two further arguments, a direct and an indirect object (*The Pope sent Henry an envoy, Mary gave Bill a kiss*). Each of these branches of the verb inheritance hierarchy subdivides further, according to more specific distributional properties. For instance ditransitive verbs subdivide into those whose direct object argument is omissible, as in

John smokes or *Fred drinks*, where an implicit object argument is understood, and those whose direct object arguments may not be thus omitted, as in **Mary omitted* or **Sam took*. Even further down the verb inheritance hierarchy are the small categories of verbs such as Levin identified according to very specific distributional criteria (mentioned above) . The sketch given here is a simplified tiny fragment of what an English speaker has learned about how to deploy verbs in sentences.

Now we add the idea of **default** to that of an inheritance hierarchy. A pure inheritance hierarchy allows the economical transmission of more or less specific exceptionless generalizations from categories to subcategories, and on 'down' ultimately to individual words. But languages are messy, and exhibit occasional exceptions to otherwise valid generalizations. So inheritance has to be qualified by 'unless otherwise stated'. The statement of exceptions can be located at any level, except the top, of an inheritance hierarchy, although exceptions typically occur at the lower, more specific, levels, that is to smaller subcategories. I will illustrate with English prepositions.

The word *ago* behaves in most, but not all, respects like a preposition. Like *to*, *for*, *by*, and *in*, *ago* takes a dependent noun, as in *two years ago*, parallel to *in two years* and *for two years*. Of course, the main difference is that *ago* is placed after its dependent noun, whereas normal prepositions are placed before their dependent noun. A convenient way of stating this is to associate the information 'prenominal' with the category P(reposition) in the inheritance hierarchy. Members of this class include *to*, *for*, *by*, *in*, and *ago*, so these individual words are lower down the hierarchy than the node for P(reposition), and they inherit the information 'prenominal', from the P(reposition) category. A special non-default statement is attached to the word *ago* stating that it, in particular, is 'postnominal', contradicting the inherited information. This more specific information overrides the default information that otherwise trickles down the inheritance hierarchy. Of course, much more information, not mentioned here, is associated with each node in the hierarchy, including the nodes for the individual words. The exceptional position of *ago* is one of the unusual cases where a specific statement about a particular element overrides the inherited default information. This example is a simplification of more complex facts, for illustrative purposes. Culicover (1999, pp. 1–74) discusses *ago* in more detail.

Another example of a non-default stipulation overriding an inherited property can be seen with the English word *enough*. *Enough* (in one of its uses) belongs to a category that we'll call INTENSIFIERs, which also contains *too*, *very, somewhat, rather,* and *quite.*[52] These modify adjectives, on which they are dependent, for example *too fat, rather nice, good enough.* One property of all of these words is that there can only be one of them (perhaps repeated) modifying any given adjective in a sentence. So we don't get **very good enough, *somewhat rather pleasant,* or **too very fat.* As you have noticed, they all, except *enough,* precede their adjective. It is economical to associate a general property 'pre-adjectival' with the category INTENSIFIER, which all its members normally inherit, and to let a special 'post-adjectival' statement associated only with *enough* override this default word order. Again, this is a simplified description, to illustrate the principle of the default-overriding mechanism. There are other uses of *enough* modifying nouns and verbs.

To complicate the picture further, there can be **mixed** or **multiple** inheritance. A word can belong to several different inheritance hierarchies. I will cite a couple of examples from Hudson (2007). One example involves *much* and *many.* Here is Hudson's case for the multiple inheritance of these words.

- Like adjectives, but not nouns, they may be modified by degree adverbs such as *very* and *surprisingly: very many* (but **very quantity*), *surprisingly much* (but: **surprisingly quantity*).

- Like some adjectives, but unlike all nouns, they may be modified by *not: not *(many) people came.*[53]

- Like adjectives, but not nouns, they have comparative and superlative inflections: *more, most.*

- Like nouns, but not adjectives, they may occur, without a following noun, wherever a dependent noun is possible, e.g. as object of any transitive verb or preposition: *I didn't find many/*numerous, We didn't talk about much.*

- Like determiners (which are nouns), but not adjectives, *much* excludes any other determiner: **the much beer, *his much money;* and *many* is very selective in its choice of accompanying determiners (e.g. *his many friends* but not **those many friends*).   (Hudson 2007, p. 168)

Hudson's other example of multiple inheritance involves gerunds, which have some noun-like properties and some verb-like properties. He devotes a whole

---

[52] Some of these words have other senses and other distributions, too, so we should rather include these other cases in other syntactic categories (as this sentence illustrates).

[53] This notation means that omission of the parenthesized word results in ungrammaticality—**not people came.*

chapter to arguing this case.[54] I will just cite a few suggestive examples
(not his).

My smoking a pipe bothers her.—*Smoking* is modified by a possessive, like a noun, but
has a dependent object, *a pipe*, like a verb.
Not having a TV is a blessing.—*Having* is modified by *not*, like a verb, but is the head
of the subject of the whole sentence, like a noun.

Multiple default inheritance hierarchies present serious technical problems
for computational approaches using conventional sequential computers. They
allow contradictions. A default property is contradicted by an overriding
property further down the hierarchy. And with multiple inheritance, how can
mutually contradictory properties from different hierarchies be prevented or
reconciled? I will not go into possible solutions to these problems here. Workers
in computational linguistics have been attracted enough by the general idea
to persevere with finding ways to programme computers to get around these
difficulties.[55] The human brain is not a sequential computer, and manages to
reconcile contradictory information in other spheres of life, so why not in our
representation of the organization of our languages?

4.4.4 *Features*

Beside categories like N(oun), V(erb), and A(djective), similar information
about words (and possibly phrases) is held in what are commonly called
grammatical **features**. Actually there is no very significant difference between
grammatical features and grammatical categories; both identify classes of
words. Features have been used to cross-classify words in different inheritance
hierarchies, as just discussed above.

For example, in English both the noun *children* and the verb *are* have the
feature Plural. This information is necessary to guarantee the grammaticality
of sentences like *The children are here*. Typically, grammatical features can be
associated with several different parts of speech. The most commonly found
classes of features are **Number, 'Gender', Person**, and **Case**. Features of the
Number class are Singular, Plural, and in some languages Dual or even Trial.
The term 'Gender' is misleading, being associated with biological sex. A better

---

[54] This being healthy linguistics, Hudson's multiple inheritance analysis of gerunds
has been challenged, by Aarts (2008). I find Hudson's analysis more attractive, despite
the problem of appealing to such a powerful mechanism. See also Hudson (2002).

[55] See, for example, Russell et al. (1991); Briscoe et al. (2003); Lascarides and
Copestake (1999); Finkel and Stump (2007). In 1992, two issues of the journal *Computational Linguistics*, 18(2) & 18(3), were devoted to inheritance hierarchies.

term is 'Noun-class'. Noun-class features have been given various names by grammarians working on different language families. In languages with Noun-class systems, each noun belongs inherently to a particular subclass of nouns. In German, for instance, a given noun is either 'Masculine', 'Feminine', or 'Neuter'. The false link to sex is shown by the fact that the German words for *girl* and *woman*, *Mädchen* and *Weib* (pejorative) are grammatically 'Neuter', while the word for *thing*, *Sache* is grammatically 'Feminine'. In some languages, there is a more systematic, but never perfect, link between the semantics of nouns and their grammatical class feature. In languages of the large Bantu family, widespread across sub-Saharan Africa, there can be as many as ten different noun-classes, with the classification of each noun only loosely related to its meaning. The noun-classes play a significant role in the grammar of these languages, for instance in determining agreement on verbs. Broadly speaking, the main role that Number and Noun-class features play in the grammar of languages that have them is in determining agreement with other words in a sentence, which may be quite distant, and are typically not themselves nouns. For example, in (Egyptian) Arabic, the Feminine Singular noun *bint* 'girl' determines Feminine Singular agreement on both an attributive adjective and a verb in the sentence *il bint ittawiila darasit* 'The tall girl studied'. By contrast, the Masculine Singular noun *walad* 'boy' determines (unmarked) Masculine Singular agreement on the adjective and the verb, as in *il walad ittawiil daras* 'the tall boy studied'. (In Arabic, as in French or Italian, adjectives follow the noun they modify.)

Person features are 1st, 2nd, and 3rd, and is marked on pronouns and verbs, with non-pronominal noun phrases being typically assigned 3rd person by default. English *you* translates into Arabic *inta* (2nd Masculine Singular), *inti* (2nd Feminine Singular), or *intu* (2nd Plural).[56] *He* translates as *huwwa* (3rd Masculine Singular) and *she* as *hiyya* (3rd Feminine Singular). All these features may trigger agreement in other parts of speech. Thus, *You studied*, addressed to a man, is *inta darast*; addressed to a woman, it is *inti darasti*; and addressed to several people, it is *intu darastu*.

Members of the Case class of features have varied functions. The most central function of Case features is in signalling the grammatical role of the main noun phrases in a sentence. In German, for example, the subject of a sentence is in the 'Nominative' case, the direct object of a verb is (mostly) in the 'Accusative' case, with the 'Dative' case reserved for indirect objects and the objects of certain prepositions. The link between grammatical Case and semantics is tenuous. 'Nominative', alias subject of a sentence, does not

---

[56] These forms should also be marked for 'Nominative' case, to be discussed below.

systematically correlate with the 'doer of an action', as the referent of the
subject of a passive sentence is not the doer, but more typically on the receiving
end of an action. In languages with more extensive 'Case' systems, such as
Hungarian or Finnish, a range of other different Case features, up to as
many as a dozen, are more semantically transparent, often being translatable
with prepositions into English. For example, Hungarian *Budapesten* has a
'Superessive' Case marker *-en* on the end of the place name *Budapest* and
translates as *in Budapest*. Another common function of a Case feature usually
called 'Genitive' is to express possession, but in most languages with a so-called
Genitive case, the feature also serves a big variety of other semantic functions
as well. Case is marked on noun phrases and often triggers agreement in words
modifying nouns such as adjectives and numerals.

To native speakers of relatively non-inflected languages, the widespread use
of features like these in the languages that have them presents a considerable
challenge to second-language learners. How on earth, I ask myself, does a
German child effortlessly manage to learn the genders of thousands of individual nouns, information that is often arbitrary and unpredictable from the
form of the noun itself? The interaction of features can present considerable
computational challenges, with the need to identify sometimes unpredictable
forms for combinations of features, and then often to get them to agree with
other forms quite distant in the sentence. Human children manage to acquire
these complexities with impressive ease, although there clearly are limits to the
complexity of feature systems, reflecting the challenges they pose for storage
and computation.

Linguists represent grammatical features on words in the same way as
information about major word classes such as Noun and Verb. I give some
example 'treelets' below.

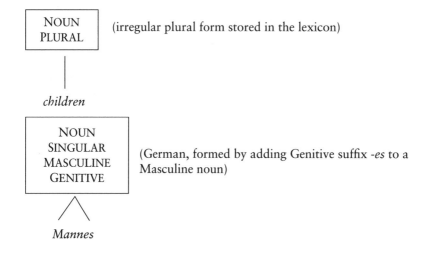

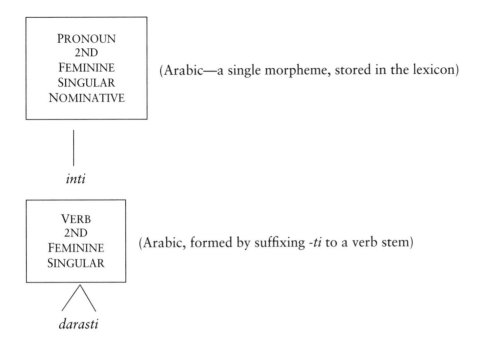

PRONOUN
2ND
FEMININE
SINGULAR
NOMINATIVE

(Arabic—a single morpheme, stored in the lexicon)

inti

VERB
2ND
FEMININE
SINGULAR

(Arabic, formed by suffixing *-ti* to a verb stem)

darasti

These figures represent the **symbolic link** between a word's phonological form and (some of) the grammatical information needed to ensure it fits appropriately into grammatical sentences. In a complete grammar, information about a form's semantic meaning and pragmatic use would also be linked to it. Such figures can be thought of as little bits of structure, some stored in a speaker's lexicon, and some the result of productive combining of elements, in this case of stems and affixes. The features on these structures give necessary information about how they may be inserted into larger structures, such as sentences. (The box notation I have used, though fairly conventional, is deliberately reminiscent of the semantic notation used for (simple) concepts in Hurford (2007). It is desirable, if possible, to seek common ways of representing semantic and syntactic information.)

In the previous subsection, in the context of inheritance hierarchies, various properties of grammatical categories were mentioned. These properties, which were informally expressed, have to do with the possible distributions of more or less specific categories and subcategories of words. For example, it was mentioned that *dog* belongs to the category of English 'Common' nouns, whose distributional characteristic is that they **must** be accompanied by a 'Determiner', a word such as *the* or *a*. Since this is essentially what *Common* means, the distributional information can be expressed directly as a feature, without need for the extra term *Common*. The (partial) lexical entry for *dog* would look like this:

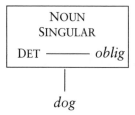

dog

This says, pretty transparently, that the word can only occur in the context of a Determiner. The long underline symbol '_____' is the 'slot' where the word itself will fit, and this lexical entry says that this slot follows a Determiner.[57] This information meshes with other lexical entries, for Determiners themselves, such as

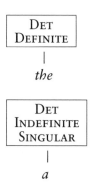

Distributional information about subclasses of verbs can likewise be expressed as features, as in the following sketchy examples (still pretty informal by the standards of the technical literature):

This gives the information, inherited by all English verbs, that *sleep* takes a nominal subject.[58] A transitive verb such as *take*, whose object noun phrase is not omissible, has a lexical entry as sketched below.

---

[57] For brevity, information about the relative placing of other noun modifers, such as adjectives, is not given.

[58] So probably, the specification 'VERB' is redundant here. The bare mention of the SUBJECT role also hides a multitude of issues that I will not go into.

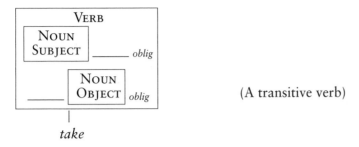

(A transitive verb)

take

In the last few examples, the obligatory co-ocurrence of items (e.g. of *dog* with a determiner, or of *take* with an object noun) can be shown in an alternative and equivalent notation, to be mentioned in a later section. This shallow foray into formal notation is as technical as I will get. A full description of all the distributional properties of English words and how they interact requires much more complex apparatus. The lesson to take from this is emphatically **not** that linguists like to work with formalism for its own sake, but that what a speaker of English has mastered is extremely complex. Amazingly, any healthy child can get it. The notation is just an analyst's way of describing what any English speaker has learned to do effortlessly and unconsciously. The notation is not, of course, to be found in the brain, any more than the chemical formula NaCl is to be found in a salt molecule.

4.4.5 *Are phrasal categories primitives?*

A few of the tree diagrams given so far (e.g. Figure 4.5) have included higher phrasal labels, such as NP, PP, and AdvP. This has become traditional, especially in introductory textbooks, but the matter needs to be reconsidered. Phrase classes are obviously derivative of corresponding word classes. A two-word phrase containing a N(oun) (e.g. *the boy*), is automatically a noun phrase (NP); likewise for verb phrases, headed by a verb (e.g. *took the money*), adjective phrases headed by an adjective (e.g. *as warm as toast*), and prepositional phrases headed by a preposition (e.g. *at the bus stop*). In a sense, these traditional tree diagrams give more information than is needed; some of the labels are unnecessary.

Various descriptive frameworks for syntax propose different ways of eliminating some or all of the labels from tree diagrams. A framework known as Categorial Grammar[59] assumes a very small set of primitive syntactic

---

[59] The originator of Categorial Grammar was Kazimierz Ajdukiewicz (1935). A modern version of it has been developed by Mark Steedman. See Steedman (1993, 2000); Steedman and Baldridge, in press.

categories, for examples S and NP, as basic, and uses a combinatorial notation
to refer to other categories derived from these. For example, the sentence-
chunk traditionally labelled VP (for verb phrase) is simply called an S\NP,
paraphraseable as 'something that combines with an NP to its left to form an
S'. Building on this, a transitive V(erb) is nothing more than something which
combines with an NP to its right to form an S\NP (i.e. what is traditionally
called a VP); the notation for this is the somewhat hairy (S\NP)/NP. A practical
(though theoretically trivial) problem with this kind of notation is that the
names for categories get more and more complex, hairier and hairier with
brackets and slashes, as more and more complex constructions are described.
But the labels do capture something about the ways in which parts of structure
can be combined. In Figure 4.11 two simple tree diagrams are given, comparing
Categorial Grammar notation with the more traditional notation.

I will not go into further details of the Categorial Grammar framework.
The main concern here is to recognize that, although frameworks agree considerably on the hierarchical structure attributed to sentences, the independent
categorical status of the higher nodes (phrasal entities) is in question. To what
extent are phrasal categories such as NP, VP, PP, etc. merely derivative of the
words they contain? The question does not arise in Dependency Grammar,
which does not even recognize phrases, but only dependencies between words.
And there is now increasing argument within the more phrase-oriented frameworks that phrasal categories have no separate primitive status. This is a move
in the direction of simplification of what a native speaker is claimed to have in
her head guiding her syntactic behaviour.

It might be easy to dismiss linguists' debates over whether the nodes in
tree structures should have underived labels. To an outsider, the question
might sound theological. Actually this issue marks an important paradigm

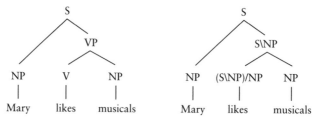

Fig. 4.11 A Combinatorial Categorial Grammar tree (on the right) compared with a
traditional phrase Structure tree (left). The two make equivalent claims about hierarchical structure. Categorial Grammar defines syntactic categories in terms of how they
combine basic categories (here NP and S) to form other categories. Thus, for example,
S\NP is equivalent to VP because it is something that takes an NP on its left to make
an S.

shift within syntactic theory, and is vital to our conception of how humans represent their grammars. In the 1930s, the most influential American linguist wrote in his most influential book 'The lexicon is really an appendix of the grammar, a list of basic irregularities' (Bloomfield 1933, p. 274). That view did not change with the advent of generative grammar, in which syntactic rules 'call the shots' and lexical items go where they are told. A bit more formally, syntactic rules (such as phrase structure rules) are the central informational engine of a grammar, defining abstract structures, such as NP, VP, and PP. Then lexical items are located at addresses in the space of abstract structures defined by the syntactic rules. Thus grammars conceived as rewriting systems, like the grammars ranked by Formal Language Theory, start by spelling out rules combining relatively abstract syntactic entities, and end by spelling out how individual words fit into these entities. This is a top-down view of grammar, beginning with the designated 'initial' symbol S, for (the intention to generate a) sentence, and with sentence structure growing 'downwards' toward the final more concrete entities, strings of words, significantly called the 'terminal symbols' of the grammar. In a new view, on which there is substantial convergence, the central informational engine of a grammar is the lexicon, and syntactic structures are just those combinations that entries stored there permit. This is a bottom-up view of grammar.

Putting this in a big-picture context, consider the top-down versus bottom-up nature of a grammar in the light of a comparison between birdsong repertoires and human languages. For a bird, the whole song is meaningful (courtship, territory marking), but its parts, the notes, have no meaning. For the bird the whole song is the target action. Press the 'song' button and out pours the stereotyped song. A top-down procedure is effective. The bird's song is not **about** anything. A bird's song, and a humpback whale's, is as far as we know essentially **syntactically motivated**. The goal is to get some specific type of complex song out there in the environment, where it will do its work of courtship, identification of an individual, or whatever. By contrast, when a human utters a sentence, she has a proposition that she wants to convey, already composed of concepts for which she has words (or larger stored chunks); she also wants to convey her attitude to this proposition. Sentence production involves first retrieving the right words for the job, and **then** combining them in a grammatical sequence. Human sentence structure is **semantically** and **pragmatically motivated**.

The new, bottom-up view is well expressed in Chomsky's (1995) formulation of what he calls the **Inclusiveness Condition** (though I'm sure nothing so functional as sentence production, or so non-human as birdsong was in his mind).

No new information can be introduced in the course of the syntactic computation.

Given the inclusiveness condition, minimal and maximal projections are not identified
by any special marking, so they must be determined from the structure in which they
appear. ... There are no such entities as XP (X^{max}) or X^{min} in the structures formed by
C_{HL}, though I continue to use the informal notations for expository purposes.

(Chomsky 1995b, p. 242)

Glossary:

A **maximal projection** of a category (such as Noun or Verb) is a full phrase
headed by a word of the category concerned. Thus *dog* is not a maximal
projection, but *this dog* is a maximal projection (a Noun phrase, NP), of a
Noun *dog*. Likewise, *between* is not a maximal projection, but *between the
table and the wall* is a maximal projection (a prepositional phrase, PP) of
the preposition *between*.

XP stands for any kind of traditional phrasal label, such as NP, VP, or PP.

X^{max} is a alternative notation for XP, i.e. a maximal projection of a
category X.

C_{HL} is a quaintly grandiose notation for 'the computational system, human
language'. Culicover and Jackendoff (2005, p. 91) gloss C_{HL} simply as
'syntax'.

The Inclusiveness Condition is a hypothesis. Much of what it seeks to eliminate is theoretical baggage inherited from pre-Chomskyan syntax, but which
was not seriously challenged within Chomskyan linguistics until the 1990s.
Dependency Grammar never did subscribe to NPs, VPs, PPs, and the like. The
empirical question is whether a completely radical bottom-up description of
the grammar of a language, in which any information about phrasal strings is
purely derivative of the words they contain, is feasible. Putting it another way,
the question is whether the distribution of what are traditionally called phrases
can only be stated in terms of some essential 'phrasehood' that they possess, or
whether it is always possible to state their distribution in terms of properties of
the words they contain. I will illustrate with a simple German example.

Take the two words *den* and *Mann*, whose partial lexical entries are given
on the left in Figure 4.12. The information they contain means that *Mann*
must be combined with a preceding determiner, and *den* is a determiner (which
happens also to carry the feature DEFINITE). Shown as a tree structure, the
sequence they form is on the right in Figure 4.12. This example shows that a
structure combining two elements can sometimes project features from both of
its members. The information that the whole phrase *den Mann* is Masculine

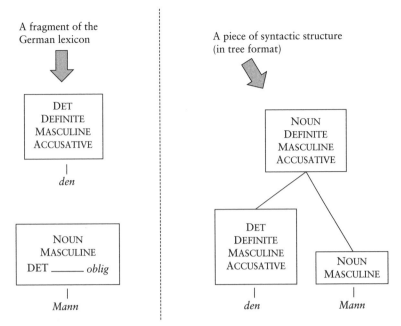

Fig. 4.12 Right: structure (shown as a tree) formed by combination of the lexical items *den* and *Mann*, as permitted (in this case indeed required) by their lexical entries, on the left. None of the information on the upper node is new; it is all 'projected' from one or the other of the two lexical entries. Note that none of the information expresses the idea of a phrase.

and nouny comes from *Mann*, and the information that it is accusative and definite comes from *den*. Both lots of information are necessary to account for the possible distribution of *den Mann* in sentences. The agreement on the MASCULINE feature permits this combination. Obviously, the *den Mann* sequence, being nouny, can occur as a dependent argument of a verb, as in *Ich sehe den Mann*. The ACCUSATIVE information from *den* allows this sequence to be an argument of this particular verb *sehen*, whose object is required to be in the Accusative case. (I have not given the lexical entry for *sehen*.) The DEFINITE information from *den*, projected onto the sequence *den Mann*, accounts for some subtle ordering possibilities of definite versus indefinite NPs in German (Hopp 2004; Weber and Müller 2004; Pappert et al. 2007).

An observant reader will have noticed that one piece of information from a lexical entry is actually **lost** (or suppressed) on combination with the other lexical entry. This is the syntactic category information DET in the entry for *den*. Once it has done its job of combining with a noun, as in *den Mann*, the information in DET is, to adopt a biological metaphor, 'recessive', not 'dominant', and plays no further part in determining the distribution of the

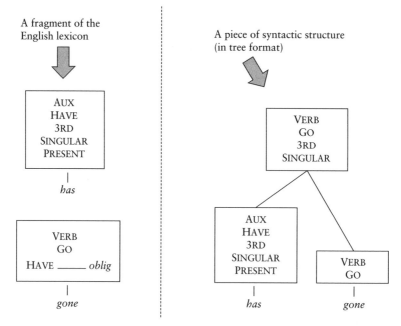

Fig. 4.13 Right: structure (shown as a tree) formed by combination of the lexical items *has* and *gone*, as required by their lexical entries, on the left. Again, none of the information on the upper node is new, being all projected from one or the other of the two lexical entries.

larger expression. It is necessary to ensure that such a larger expression as *den Mann* is never itself taken to be a DET, resulting in the possibility of recursive re-combination to give such ungrammatical forms as *den Mann Mann. The technical solution widely adopted is that only certain specified features on lexical items, known as 'Head Features' are taken on by the larger combination of items.[60] The relevant features to be taken on by *den Mann* from its component words are: DEFINITE and ACCUSATIVE, but not DET, from *den*. From *Mann*, both NOUN and MASCULINE are taken up by the larger phrase; there is no need to keep the contextual feature DET _____ *oblig*. The agreeing feature MASCULINE present on both words allows them to combine grammatically.

To reinforce the basic idea, Figure 4.13 presents another example, of the English string *has gone*. The word *gone* is the past participle form of the verb *go*. The past participle information is represented in the feature HAVE _____ *oblig*, meaning that such a form must be accompanied by a form of the auxiliary

---

[60] This is the Head Feature Principle of HPSG (Pollard and Sag 1987, p. 58), taken over from a parent theory, Generalized Phrase Structure Grammar (Gazdar et al. 1985).

have. Being a form of *go*, *gone* inherits the distributional features of *go*, such as being intransitive, and this information is projected onto the sequence *has gone*. *Gone* itself has no features agreeing in number (e.g. SINGULAR) and person (e.g. 3RD); these features are carried by the auxiliary *has*, and they are projected onto the sequence *has gone* for purposes of ultimately matching with the subject of the sentence in which this string occurs. *Has* carries the feature AUX (= auxiliary verb) to indicate that it has such distributional properties as occurring before its subject in questions, and being immediately followed by *not* in negative sentences. As in the previous example, certain information from one lexical entry, here AUX and HAVE, which are not Head Features, is actually lost or suppressed from the string formed by combination with another lexical item.

As is common in the literature, we'll refer generally to two elements combined into a syntactic unit as elements α and β. Citko (2008) gives examples of all possible projections of information from α and β onto the larger structure, namely only from α, or only from β, or from both, or neither. Collins (2002) mounts a radical argument against the inclusion of any labelling information on higher nodes in syntactic trees, with the necessary information about the properties of formal subgroups of words always being retrievable from the properties of the words themselves, given careful limitation of how deeply embedded the words are. Thus *a cat among the pigeons* is indefinite (from *a*) and singular (from *cat*), rather than definite and plural (from *the pigeons*). Citko argues in favour of labels, on the grounds that labels on higher nodes do not in themselves violate the Inclusiveness Condition, provided of course that the labels are only derived from the combined elements.

I will not pursue this further, but note a growing convergence on the view that no information is represented in hierarchical syntactic structures other than what can be derived from the order of assembly or dependency and the words themselves. Minimalism, Dependency Grammar, Radical Construction Grammar, and Categorial Grammar converge on a target of eliminating such extra information in grammatical structures. (Maggie Tallerman's (2009) is a voice arguing, against this trend, that reference to phrasal categories is necessary for a parsimonious generalization over the structures that trigger a particular consonantal mutation in Welsh.) The mere fact of being combined into a larger expression may add no categorial grammatical information. Independent or primitive phrasal categories are not, so the arguments go, among those which a language learner needs to learn. This conclusion is not inconsistent with the existence of phrases. Phrases are groupings of contiguous words all dependent on a common head word, with such groupings typically showing a certain robustness in hanging together in different sentential positions. Perhaps another way to express the non-necessity of phrasal categories is to say that phrases are no more than the sum of their parts. As a rough analogy, think of a group of people who habitually go around together, but the group has no institutional status conferred on it.

4.4.6 *Functional categories—grammatical words*

Humans can store thousands of contentful words such as *sky*, *blue*, and *shine* or larger chunks such as *shoot the breeze* or *make hay while the sun shines*. In addition, every speaker of a developed language[61] knows a small and diverse set of words whose semantic content is hard, or even impossible, to pin down. The meanings of *star* or *twinkle* can be demonstrated ostensively or paraphrased with other words. But what are the 'meanings' of *of*, *the*, *are*, *what*, and *but*? You understood this question, so those words must help to convey meaning in some way, but their specific contributions cannot be pointed to (e.g. with a finger) or easily paraphrased. Such words are variously dubbed **functional items, function words, closed class items,** or **grammatical items.**[62] Their contributions to understanding are as signals either of the pragmatic purpose of the sentence being used or of how a somewhat complex meaning is being grammatically encoded (or both). The grammatical distribution of such words is closely tied in with particular types of hierarchical structure. I'll give some specific examples, from English.

What (in one of its incarnations—there are actually several *what*s) serves the pragmatic purpose of signalling that a question is being asked, of a type that cannot be answered by *Yes* or *No*. For example *What time is it?*, *What are you doing?*, *What's that noise?* In this use, *what* occurs at the front of the sentence,[63] and the rest of the sentence has several traits characteristic of the *Wh*-question construction. These traits include (1) having its subject noun phrase after an auxiliary verb instead of before it (e.g. *are you* instead of *you are*, or *is that noise* instead of *that noise is*); and (2) the rest of the sentence being somehow incomplete in relation to a corresponding non-question sentence

---

[61] i.e, any language except a pidgin.

[62] See Muysken (2008) for a broad and thorough monograph on functional categories, and Cann (2001) for a formal syntactician's commentary on the implications of the function/content word distinction. In antiquity, Aristotle recognized the need for a class roughly like what we mean by function words, with his 'syndesmoi', distinct from nouns 'onomata' and verbs 'rhemata'. Aristotle's syndesmoi included conjunctions, prepositions, pronouns, and the article.

[63] The frontal position of *what* can be superseded or preempted by other elements competing for first place, such as topicalized phrases, as in *Those men, what were they doing?*

(e.g. *it is [what-o'clock not specified]* or *that noise is [WHAT?]*). Compare the rather edgy-toned *Your name is?* on a slightly rising pitch, with the more conventional *What is your name?* The former, in which the incompleteness is manifest, is deliberately more blunt, containing fewer grammatical signals as to its meaning—no *what*, and no unusual order of subject and auxiliary.

An even blunter way of asking for a person's name is to say 'Your name?' with the right intonation, and probably the right quizzical facial expression. This omits another function word, some form of the verb *be*, the so called copula. Non-colloquial English insists that every main clause have a verb. The main function of *is* in *My name is Sarah* is to satisfy this peculiar nicety of English. Many other languages (e.g. Russian, Arabic) don't do this, allowing simple juxtaposition of two noun phrases to express what requires a copula in English. The English copula doesn't have a single meaning, and corresponds to a number of semantic relations, including identity (*Clark Kent is Superman*) and class membership (*Socrates is a man*). A form of the verb *be* signals progressive aspect in English, obligatorily used with an *-ing* form of a main verb, as in *We are waiting*. Thus, the verb *be* is a component of a larger specific pattern, the progressive *be + V-ing* construction. This versatile little verb also signals passive voice, obligatorily taking a 'past participle' form of a main verb, as in *They were forgotten* or *We were robbed*. Again, the function of *be* is as a signal of a particular structural pattern. 'Short clauses', such as *Problem solved!* and *Me, a grandfather!*, which omit the copula, reflect a less 'grammaticalized' form of English, with less reliance on grammatical signals of structure, such as the copula. In general, simplified forms of language, as in telegrams (remember them?) and newspaper headlines, omit function words. Today's *Los Angeles Times* has *Death sentence upheld in killing of officer* and *Services set for officer in crash* with *is/are* and other function words missing.

Articles, such as English *the* and *a/an* are also function words. Their function is mostly pragmatic, signalling whether the speaker assumes the hearer knows what entity is being referred to. Roughly, this is what linguists call **definiteness**. If I say 'I met a man', I assume you don't know which man I'm talking about; if I say 'I met the man', I assume we both have some particular man in mind. These words have other less central uses, such as a generic use, as in *The Siberian tiger is an endangered species* and *A hat is a necessity here*. Grammatically, English articles are very reliable signals of the beginning of a noun phrase. Their central distribution is as the initial elements in noun phrases, thus giving a very useful structural clue for hearers decoding a sentence.

As one final example of a function word, consider *of* in its many uses. Actually it is rather seldom used to express possession. *The pen of my aunt* is notoriously stilted. *Of* is a general-purpose signal of some connection between a couple of noun phrases, as in this very sentence! Its grammatical distribution is reliably pre-NP. When you hear an *of*, you can be pretty sure that a noun phrase is immediately upcoming, and that the upcoming NP is semantically a hierarchical subpart of the whole phrase introduced by the preceding words, as in *a box of chocolates*. Sometimes, but less often, the larger phrase is not an NP, but a phrase of another type, as in *fond of chocolates* (an adjective phrase) or *approves of chocolates* (a verb phrase). Other classes of function words in English include modal verbs (*can, could, may, might, must, shall, should, will, would*), personal pronouns (*I, you, she, he, it, we, they*), relative pronouns (*that, which, who*). I will not go into further detail.

Three traits distinguish function words from content words. First the central uses of function words are to signal pragmatic force and aspects of grammatical structure, whereas content words, as the label implies, contribute mainly to the propositional content of a sentence. Secondly, the classes of function words are very small sets, unlike the classes of content words, for example sets of nouns or verbs, which are practically open-ended. Thirdly, function words are phonetically reduced in many ways. Shi (1996) and Shi et al. (1998) measured phonetic differences between function words and content words in the language spoken to children in three very different languages, English, Turkish, and Mandarin. The results are summarized thus:

Input to preverbal infants did indeed exhibit shorter vowel duration and weaker amplitude for function words than for content words. Function words were found to consist of fewer syllables than content words; in fact they tended to be monosyllabic. The syllabic structure of function words contained fewer segmental materials than that of content words in the onset, nucleus and coda positions. ...For function words, the syllable onset and coda tended to be reduced toward nullness, and the nucleus was rarely found to contain diphthongs in languages that have a repertoire of diphthongs.

(Shi 2005, p. 487)

As a specific example from this book, when reading the Stevenson poem quoted on page 71 aloud, you automatically know where to put the stresses, so that each line has the metrically correct number of stressed syllables. The words that don't receive stress are all function words, *the, and, me, did, I, with, a, he, where, to, is,* and *from*.

Some word classes sit on the borderline between content words and function words. English prepositions are an example. Prepositions such as *in, on, under, above*, and *between* make a definite contribution to propositional meaning, and yet, like other classes of function words, form a very small set. There are fewer than thirty prepositions in English, and new ones are not readily coined, unlike new nouns and new verbs.

Productive inflectional affixes, such as the *-ing* ending on English verbs, and case-marking affixes in languages with case systems, behave in many ways like function words. They are clearly structural signals, making little or no contribution to propositional content, but making crucial differences to the grammaticality or otherwise of sentences. Functional items that are single words in English sometimes translate into affixes in other languages. The English definite article *the* translates into Romanian as a suffix *-ul* on the relevant noun, as in *calul* (*cal + ul*), *the horse*. In Swedish, *the* also translates as different suffixes on nouns, depending on their gender (noun-class); thus *the hand* is *handen* (*hand + en*), and *the child* is *barnet* (*barn + et*).

A major part of learning a language is learning how to use its function words and grammatical inflections. They are vital keys to grammatical structure. Languages differ in the degree to which they exploit function words and grammatical inflections. But humans are universally capable of learning the richest systems that languages have developed to throw at them. (Of course, since humans are the loci of language development.)

4.4.7 *Neural correlates of syntactic categories*

Animals behave in regular ways because they have internal programmes that guide, and sometimes even determine, what they do in all the circumstances they are likely to meet in life. A human's regular language behaviour is guided by his internalized competence-plus, a rich store of neural potentials in a complex architecture. Thus we expect there to be underlying neural correlates of features of the observed regularities. Syntacticians don't do neuroscience or psycholinguistic experiments. By observing languages 'at the surface', they come up with descriptions incorporating structural features of the kind surveyed in this chapter. The linguist delivers a grammar, a description of a whole system with parts laid out in specific relationships with each other and with the system's phonetic and semantic/pragmatic interfaces with the world. Information about systematic aspects of grammar is taken up by psycho- and neurolinguistic researchers. They ask 'Can we find evidence of those particular system-parts and system-relationships beyond what motivated the linguist's description?' They look for evidence of the linguist's abstractions in brain activity and in experimental conditions where the particular features of interest can be isolated and controlled.

In the natural flow of speech, or in intuitive judgements about sentences, you cannot separate a word's meaning from its syntactic category or from its phonological properties, such as length. In the neuroscience or psychology lab, you can devise experiments which isolate and control the features of interest. Many researchers have, sensibly, started with the most basic and obvious of what linguists deliver, for instance the syntactic category distinction between nouns and verbs, or the distinction between content words and function words. The first question that can be asked is 'Have the linguists got it right?' In the case of the noun/verb distinction and the content/function word distinction, there can be no question, as the linguistic facts are so obvious. So the hunt narrows to looking for specific brain locations and/or mechanisms corresponding to the linguist's postulates. In general, the hunt is difficult, requiring very careful experimental design and often expensive technical kit. Continued failure would indicate that the linguists have somehow got it wrong, hardly conceivable in the case of the noun/verb and content/function word distinctions. Sometimes nature takes a hand and provides pathological cases, typically with brain damage, revealing deficits corresponding to some part(s) of the linguist's description of the system. The classic case is agrammatism or Broca's aphasia, in which patients produce utterances with no (or few) function words and morphological inflections. This indicates that the linguist's isolation of this specific category of words is on target. Nature is seldom clean, however, and often such natural experiments, at least when taken individually, are equivocal. They can be particularly problematic when it comes to localization. For instance the link between Broca's aphasia, diagnosed by standard tests, and Broca's area, is not at all reliable. Dronkers (2000) mentions that 'only 50 to 60% of our patients with lesions including Broca's area have persistent Broca's aphasia' (p. 31), and '15% of our right-handed chronic stroke patients with single, left hemisphere lesions and Broca's aphasia do not have lesions in Broca's area at all' (p. 31). And sometimes, the pathological cases show up parts of the linguistic system that linguists, especially syntacticians, have paid no particular attention to. A case in point is one where a patient had a category-specific deficit for naming fruit and vegetables, but no problem with naming animals and artefacts (Samson and Pillon 2003).[64] The fruit–vegetable case is a matter of semantics, not syntax, so need not have been particularly surprising for syntacticians. Other cases involve deficits in one modality, for example speech or writing, while the other is relatively intact—see Rapp and Caramazza (2002) and references therein.

When independent neuroscientific or psycholinguistic findings make sense in terms of the linguist's carving up of the language system, this is not evidence in favour of claims that the categories involved are innately hard-wired into the brain's developmental programme. Such confirmation can be taken as

---

[64] This article cites a number of other cases of category-specific deficits.

support for a weak kind of nativist claim, amounting to no more than that the human brain is genetically programmed to be capable of acquiring these particular categories or distinctions (which is obvious anyway). On the other hand, repeated findings of a specific brain area processing a particular linguistic category or distinction, and doing no other work, would provide support for a stronger version of language-domain-specific nativism. No such brain area has been identified. 'For language, as for most other cognitive functions, the notion of function-to-structure mapping as being one-area-one-function is almost certainly incorrect' (Hagoort 2009, p. 280).

There is evidence of neural noun/verb distinction, and separately of a content/function word distinction, but it has not come without a struggle. I will outline some of the more interesting studies.

In a very perceptive paper, Gentner (1981) summarizes some 'interesting differences between verbs and nouns', which I will briefly repeat, just showing the tip of her arguments and evidence.

Memory: Memory for verbs is poorer than memory for nouns ...

Acquisition: It takes children longer to acquire verb meanings than noun meanings, and this acquisition order appears to hold cross-linguistically ...

Breadth of Meaning: Common verbs have greater breadth of meaning than common nouns. One rough measure of this difference is the number of word senses per dictionary entry ...

Mutability under Paraphrase: ... we asked people to write paraphrases of sentences [in which] the noun and verb did not fit well together (e.g. 'The lizard worshipped'). When our subjects had to adjust the normal meanings of the words to produce a plausible sentence interpretation, they changed the meanings of the verbs more than those of the nouns ...

Cross-Linguistic Variability: ... a good case can be made that the meanings of verbs and other relational terms vary more cross-linguistically than simple nouns ...

Translatability: ... I have contrasted nouns and verbs in a double translation task. A bilingual speaker is given an English text to translate into another language, and then another bilingual speaker translates the text back to English. When the new English version is compared with the original English text, more of the original nouns than verbs appear in the final version.   (Gentner 1981, pp. 162–7)

Gentner states these differences as differences between syntactic categories. But she is clear that the real cause of the differences lies in semantics, not syntax: 'the correlation between syntax and semantics, although not perfect, is strong enough, at least for concepts at the perceptual level, for the form classes of noun and verb to have psychologically powerful semantic categories associated with them (p. 161). The key difference between the semantics of verbs and nouns is that verbs tend strongly to denote relationships between entities, whereas nouns tend strongly to denote entities. Computational operations with verbs are therefore expected to be more complex and offer more scope for variation.

Gentner's good sense has not thoroughly permeated the neuroscience population investigating alleged 'noun/verb' differences. Much of the neural noun/verb literature is plagued by a failure to distinguish syntax from semantics. There is frequent confusion between the syntactic categories of verb and noun and the semantic categories of action and object. While **prototypical** nouns denote physical objects, not all do; some obvious non-physical-object English nouns are *alphabet, day, entropy, example, fate, grammar, heat, idea, instant, month, problem, space, song, temperature, texture, time,* and *week*. Similarly, although prototypical verbs denote actions, there are many verbs which do not, such as English *believe, belong, comprise, consist, contain, differ, hate, hear, hope, know, love, own, resemble, see, seem, sleep, think, wait,* and *want*. One example of this syntax/semantics confusion, among many, is seen in 'The materials consisted of 72 black-and-white line drawings half representing an action and half an object. The subject was instructed to name the verb pictures in present participle, while nouns were named in citation form' (Hernández et al. 2008, p. 71). Very similarly, Daniele et al. (1994) claimed to investigate brain-damaged patients' control of nouns and verbs by showing them pictures of objects and actions. Pictures cannot reliably distinguish specifically grammatical categories. Preissl et al. (1995) claim, after a study eliciting electrophysiological scalp readings while subjects decided whether a presented string of letters was a word or not, that 'Evoked potentials distinguish between nouns and verbs' (p. 81). But the genuine words presented, half verbs and half nouns, were all semantically prototypical of their grammatical class. The verbs chosen referred to motor actions and the nouns were concrete. So this study only tells us about a difference between action-denoting words and object-denoting words. Another study, after consistently using the 'noun/verb' terminology, confesses that it might actually have been a study of representations of objects and actions. 'The tests used in our study, like most tests reported in the literature, cannot distinguish between the semantic (objects versus actions) and syntactic (nouns versus verbs) categories. Our results could, therefore, be interpreted as a selective deficit in naming and comprehension of actions rather than in that of verbs' (Bak et al. 2001, p. 15). I could go on, and on.

A useful survey of the neural noun/verb literature, as of 2002 (Cappa and Perani 2002), shows that this semantics/syntax confusion is endemic (although the authors of the survey themselves are clearly aware of the distinction). There is definite evidence for a double dissociation between action naming and object naming. It is well established that the semantic concepts of actions and physical objects activate different parts of the brain (Damasio and Tranel 1993; Fiez and Tranel 1996; Tranel et al. 1997, 1998). This kind of semantic distinction can in some cases be seen to be more specific, as with a dissociation between naming of man-made objects (e.g. tools) and naming of animals (Damasio et al. 1996; Saffran and Schwartz 1994). To complicate the neuro-semantic picture, some pictures of tools (objects), not so surprisingly, evoke brain areas activated by imagined hand movements (actions) (Martin et al. 1996). None of this is evidence for a dissociation between verb-processing and noun-processing.

Pulvermüller et al. (1999) directly addressed the problem of whether differences in brain activity reflect semantic or syntactic differences. They compared responses to different kind of German nouns, some strongly associated with actions, and others denoting physical objects. They summarize: 'words from different lexico-syntactic classes and words from the same class (nouns) were distinguished by similar topographical patterns of brain activity. On the other hand, action-related nouns and verbs did not produce reliable differences. This argues that word class-specific brain activity depends on word meaning, rather than on lexico-syntactic properties' (p. 84). Bak et al. (2006) reach a similar conclusion after a study using related materials.

Tyler et al. (2001) carefully controlled for the semantics/syntax problem. Their experimental stimuli, presented visually, were concrete nouns (e.g. *sand*), concrete verbs (e.g. *spill*), abstract nouns (e.g. *duty*), and abstract verbs (e.g. *lend*).[65] Subjects were also given an equal number of non-words, such as **hicton* and **blape*. While their brains were being scanned, subjects had to decide whether a presented word was a genuine word or a non-word. A significant reaction time difference was found between nouns and verbs, with nouns being recognized as genuine words faster than verbs ($P < 0.001$). The brain imaging results found no noun/verb difference. 'There is no evidence for cortical regions specific to the processing of nouns or verbs, or to abstract or concrete words. This was the case in spite of the behavioural data which showed a response time advantage for nouns over verbs, a result which is consistent with other behavioural experiments' (p. 1623). In a second experiment, subjects were given three semantically similar words (e.g. *bucket, basket, bin*) and asked whether a fourth word was semantically similar (e.g. *tub*) or different (e.g. *sun*). In all foursomes, words were of the same syntactic class, either all verbs or all nouns. As before, the stimuli were rigorously matched for frequency and

---

[65] Of course, *sand* can be used as a verb and *spill* can be used as a noun. Tyler et al. controlled for such problems by choosing words whose corpus frequency was overwhelmingly in one category or the other. Thus *sand* is used as a noun about 25 times more frequently than it is as a verb.

length. Again, reaction times were faster for decisions involving nouns than for decisions involving verbs ($P < 0.01$), but again imaging produced no significant localization differences. As for regional activation, 'there are no reliable effects of word class across both experiments' (p. 1629). The reaction time advantage for nouns is entirely compatible with Gentner's ideas about the key semantic difference between verbs and nouns. Verbs, being mostly relational in their meaning, involve more computation than nouns. They take longer to think about, even subconsciously.

There are many semantic and conceptual dimensions that interact with the grammatical noun/verb distinction. We have seen the object/action dimension, which many studies fail to disentangle from the noun/verb distinction. Another dimension is **imageability**, defined as the ease with which a subjective sensory impression can be associated with a word. *Anger* and *cow* are highly imageable, while *augur* and *low* are less imageable.[66] Statistically, nouns are more imageable than verbs. Bird et al. (2003) studied aphasic patients who exhibited poorer performance with verbs than nouns on a naming task, and found that 'when imageability was controlled, however, no dissociation was shown' (p. 113). Responding to this implicit challenge, Berndt et al. (2002) studied five aphasic patients who performed better with nouns than verbs on both a picture naming task and a sentence completion task. They did indeed find an imageability effect, but were able to separate this from the grammatical class effect. 'Inspection of the individual patient data indicated that either grammatical class, or imageability, or both variables may affect patient performance, but that their effects are independent of one another' (p. 353). So, with hard work, a deficit specific to a grammatical category can be reliably detected in some aphasic patients. Berndt et al. conclude their paper with 'the fact that words with different syntactic functions encode systematically different meanings does not imply that grammatical class and semantic category are equivalent. It is clear, however, that new and creative methods need to be devised for investigating the independence as well as the interaction of these variables' (p. 368).

For humans the meaning of a word is overwhelmingly dominant over its other properties. Doing experiments that try to get behind the meaning of a word to some other less salient property is like trying to get a chimpanzee to do SAME/DIFFERENT tasks with tasty morsels of food. The chimp would much rather eat the morsels than think about abstract relations between them. Humans' interest in words is primarily in their meanings, and it is hard to

---

[66] The University of Bristol has a publicly available set of ratings for imageability of a large set of words. See http://language.psy.bris.ac.uk/bristol_norms.html.

distract them to attend to other properties. Only careful experiments and cunning statistics can probe the non-semantic, specifically grammatical properties of words.

I move on now to the other main distinction among grammatical categories, the distinction between content words and function words. There is a very large literature on this topic and I will give a few representative examples. The most obvious neurolinguistic evidence is the existence of Broca's aphasia, a deficit in which sufferers prototypically produce 'agrammatic' speech lacking in function words and inflectional morphemes, but with content words intact. In research unrelated to aphasia, the neural and psycholinguistic correlates of the function/content word distinction are somewhat easier to dig out than for noun/verb differences. Imageability and concreteness are still confounding factors. Function words are less imageable and less concrete than content words. Two other confounding factors are length and text-frequency; function words are typically very short, and they are very frequent in texts.

As with the noun/verb research, there are studies showing that what appears to be a function/content word difference actually reflects a separate but correlated difference, such as a difference in word-length or imageability. For example, Osterhout et al. (2002) took ERP readings from normal subjects while reading texts, and found a significant difference between responses to function words and content words. They conclude, however, that this difference could also be a systematic response to word-length, as function words are statistically much shorter than content words. Also negatively, Bird et al. (2002) compared content words with function words in five aphasic patients. 'No true grammatical class effects were shown in this study: apparent effects were shown to be the result of semantic, and not syntactic, differences between words, and none of these semantic differences are sufficient to provide a clear delineation between syntactic categories' (p. 233). When imageability was controlled for, no significant difference was found between nouns and function words.

On the positive side, there are many studies showing a function/content word difference, with confounding factors controlled for, or not relevant to the experimental situation. A careful and striking study by Shillcock and Bard (1993) took as its background a classic article by Swinney (1979) on priming effects between words. Swinney had found that a phonological word with different senses primed words with senses related to **all** of the senses of the original word. His experiments show, for example, that on hearing a sentence like *They all rose*, both the *rose*/FLOWER and the *rose*/MOVED-UP senses are activated briefly in a hearer's mind, even though only one of these senses is relevant to the interpretation of the sentence. The sentence processor briefly entertains all possible senses of an input word before winnowing out the inappropriate senses, guided by grammatical form. For this winnowing to happen, some clue about the grammatical form of the incoming sentence must be available to the hearer, so that it can be applied to weed out the inappropriate word senses. Function words provide clues to grammatical form. Shillcock and Bard tested to see whether the priming effects that Swinney had discovered for content words (like *rose*) also apply to function words. The question is whether, for instance, *would* primes words like *timber* (because of its association with homophonous *wood*), and whether *by* primes *purchase* (because of its association with homophonous *buy*). In brief, Shillcock and Bard found that in this respect, function words behave differently from content words. The function word *would*, in an appropriate sentence context, does not call to mind, however briefly, any ideas associated with wood. Likewise, *by* does not prime any semantic associates of *buy*.

Friederici (1985) did an experiment in which normal subjects were shown a 'target' word and then listened to a recording of a sentence in which the word occurred. The subjects' task was to press a button as soon as they heard the target word in the spoken sentence. This is known as a word-monitoring task. Her results showed that during the comprehension of a sentence, function words are recognized faster than content words. This is consistent with their key function as signposts to the grammatical structure of a sentence.

Bradley (1978) gave subjects lists of words and nonwords. Subjects had to decide whether a particular example was a word or a nonword. The actual words were distractors, and the items of interest were all nonwords, of two types. One type incorporated a genuine content word, for example *thinage*; the other type incorporated a genuine function word, for example *thanage*. Subjects rejected nonwords incorporating function words faster than nonwords incorporating content words. This nonword interference effect of Bradley's was replicated by Kolk and Blomert (1985) and by Matthei and Kean (1989).

More recently, a special issue of *Journal of Neurolinguistics* 15(3–5) (2002) was dedicated to the question of the neurolinguistics correlates of grammatical categories. See the articles in that issue, and the copious citations of other relevant works. The principal distinctions of syntactic category, noun/verb, and function/content word, are now very well linked to neuro- and psycholinguistic evidence. This is what one would expect.

4.5 Grammatical relations

Noun phrases in a language like English can simultaneously carry out three different kinds of functions, pragmatic, semantic, and purely syntactic. Take the sentence *As for me, am I being met by Jeeves?* I have picked this sentence, which is grammatically somewhat complex, because only with a certain degree of complexity do the separate functions stand out as different from each other. Pragmatically, this sentence asks a question about a particular proposition in such a way that the identity of one of the participants, the speaker, is highlighted as the **Topic** of the communication. The word *me* is placed in a special position reserved for Topics by English grammar (the front), and marked by the special topicalization particle *As for*. In this sentence, *me* is the Topic phrase (a bare pronoun as it happens). Pragmatics is about how information is presented, not about what the information is. The information about (a future state of) the world described in this sentence could have been presented in other ways, like *Jeeves will meet me*, if the speaker was already sure what would happen, or as a less complex question, *Is Jeeves to meet me?*, if the conversational context did not call for emphatic topicalization. However it is presented, in the imagined state of the world described, Jeeves and the speaker have constant roles, Jeeves as the meeter, or **Agent** of the meeting event, and the speaker as the **Patient** of the meeting event. Semantics is about how the world (perhaps an imaginary world) is. So far, so functional. Being able to distinguish who does what to whom (semantics) is obviously useful. On top of that, being able to modulate semantic information by presenting it in different ways, according to context (pragmatics) is also useful. If a language has particular markers signalling such pragmatic functions as the Topic of an utterance, and such semantic roles as the Agent and Patient in a described event, child language learners easily pick them up.

Beside these obviously functional roles played by phrases or the entities they denote, parts of sentences can play different kinds of role, sometimes also, confusingly, called grammatical 'functions'. The main grammatical functions that languages express are **Subject** and **(Direct) Object**. It is essential not to accept the schoolroom fallacy that 'the Subject of a sentence is the doer of the action'. This is false. In our example, it is Jeeves, not the speaker, who is doing the meeting. Jeeves is the doer of this particular action. But *Jeeves* is not the Subject of this sentence. The word *I* is the Subject of this particular sentence. Although the words *I* and *me* refer to the same person, it is not a person or thing in the world that functions as the Subject of a sentence; it is some word or phrase, here the pronoun *I*. English grammar has developed special constraints that insist on certain correspondences within (non-imperative) sentences. There has to be some noun phrase (which can be a bare pronoun) that the sentence's verb agrees with in number (singular/plural). Hence *am*, not *is* or *are*. And it is this same noun phrase which gets inverted with an auxiliary in an interrogative (question) sentence. Hence *am I* in our example sentence. This grammatically designated noun phrase, if it happens to be a pronoun, must also take the specific form reserved for this subject 'function', for example *I* rather than *me*. If English did not insist on these rules about the Subject of a sentence, the same message as in our example sentence might be expressed as **As for me, me be being met by Jeeves?*, with no *I/me* distinction, no inversion of the Subject round the auxiliary, and no agreeing form of the verb BE. We could say that English, like many other languages, is fussy over and above the functional demands of pragmatics and semantics, in the way grammatical sentences are formed. It is analogous to a formal dress code. Being functionally dressed, enough to keep warm and cover nudity, is not enough. You have to do it with the right jacket and tie. That's the way it is. Following the Subject rules is a convention routinely observed by English speakers, without a squeak of protest at the formal requirement. Children easily master such formalities.

The roles of grammatical Subject and Object, and others, can be signalled in various ways. Some languages, like Latin, put suffixes onto nouns to indicate 'Case', 'Nominative' case for subject nouns, and 'Accusative' case for object nouns. Just as in English, a Latin noun that happens to be in Nominative case, that is, the subject of the sentence, is not necessarily the 'doer of the action'. In *Adonis ab apro occiditur* 'Adonis is killed by a boar', the doer of the action is the boar, but *Adonis* is the Subject of the sentence, as indicated by the Nominative ending *-is*.

My initial example *As for me, am I being met by Jeeves?*, was unusually complex, chosen so that the pragmatic, semantic, and grammatical 'functions', Topic, Agent, and Subject, respectively, could be teased apart. In simpler sentences, the roles often coincide. So in *The boar killed Adonis*, the boar is the Topic and the Agent, and the phrase *the boar* is also the grammatical Subject. One difference between Topic and Subject is that the Subject of a sentence is understood as bound into the argument structure of the verb. For example, in English you can say *Those houses, the council have replaced all the windows*. Here the Topic phrase *Those houses* is not in any direct semantic relationship with the verb *replace*; the council is the Agent of the replacing, and the windows are the Patient of the replacing. The Topic phrase just serves to get the hearer's attention into the right general ball-park. Some other languages are freer than English in allowing such 'unbound' Topics. For a clear and thorough explanation of the difference between Subject and Topic, see Li and Thompson (1976). The difference is more accentuated in some languages than in others. Li and Thompson distinguish between 'Subject-prominent' languages and 'Topic-prominent' languages. (We will see in Chapter 8 that there is a diachronic relationship between Topics and Subjects.)

It must also be said that these distinctions are not always respected so cleanly by languages. Sometimes a particular marker simultaneously signals both a semantic and a grammatical 'function'. For instance the Latin 'Ablative' case ending on a noun (as in *ab apro* 'by a boar') can signal both that its referent is the doer of some action, an Agent, and that the noun is not functioning as the grammatical subject of the sentence. In German, the 'Dative' form of a pronoun, for example *mir* or *dir*, is usually reserved simultaneously for grammatical Indirect Objects and for semantic Recipients of actions. Here the grammatical marker is a relatively faithful signal of the semantic relationship. But in some cases, with particular predicates, the same Dative form can be used to indicate a relationship which neither obviously grammatical Indirect Object nor semantic Recipient of an action, as in *Mir ist kalt* 'I am cold'. Notice that in the interrogative *Ist dir kalt?* 'Are you cold?', the pronoun *dir* is inverted with the auxiliary *ist*, normally in German a clue to grammatical Subjecthood. But the verb does not agree in person (1st/2nd/3rd) with the understood Subject *du/dir*. Children readily learn as many of such eccentricities as their native language throws at them. They don't necessarily learn very abstract rules, but just store classes of relevant exemplars.

4.6 Long-range dependencies

I have mentioned dependencies between words. There are various kinds of grammatical dependency. They all involve either the meaning or the form of a word depending on the meaning or form of some other word in the same sentence. For convenience here, I will take a broad view of dependency. When I write of 'the meaning of a word' I include the way it is interpreted in relation to other concepts mentioned in the sentence.

Agreement is a common kind of dependency, and it can apply at some distance. Here are examples (from *NECTE*) of agreement across intervals of up to nine words; the agreeing words are underlined and the number of words across which they agree is given in parentheses.

The only <u>one</u> that went to war <u>was</u> my uncle John (4)
The <u>year</u> that I was at North Heaton <u>was</u> nineteen forty seven (6)
The last <u>person</u> that was ever hanged at Gallowgate <u>was</u> eh buried in there (6)
The <u>thing</u> that really seems to annoy me <u>is</u> that . . . (6)
They had these big clothes <u>horses</u> you used to pull out of the wall which <u>were</u> heated (9)

Longer intervals than this between agreeing items are not common in conversation, but one can make up intuitively grammatical examples with much longer intervals, such as

The <u>shop</u> that sold us the sheets that we picked up from the laundry yesterday morning <u>is</u> closed now (14)

There is no principled reason to suppose that this sentence could not occur in normal English conversation. It is readily understandable, posing no great processing problems. On the other hand, it must be said that speakers, in many languages, do make errors of agreement across longer intervals. The longer the interval, the more likely an error is to occur. In some cases, a language has conventionalized agreement to connect with the nearest related word, despite what might be thought to be the 'logical' pattern. An example is seen by comparing *I've seen one too many accidents* versus *I've seen one accident too many*; here a singular noun would seem odd after *many* as would a plural noun after *one*. And sometimes in conversation, speakers use constructions which avoid the problem of long-distance agreement, as in this example from *NECTE*, where an additional *they* is used just before a verb whose subject, *those*, is six words earlier.

Those that they sent to pioneer corps they weren't backward

These examples with agreement are actually facilitated by hierarchical structuring. The verbs shown agree, not just with an earlier word, but with the whole phrase (e.g. *The last person that was ever hanged at Gallowgate*) that the earlier word is the grammatical head of. But many other instances of long-distance dependencies happen in ways that languages allow to **disrupt** hierarchical structure (of the phrasal meronomic kind). Languages depart from phrasal hierarchical structuring to various degrees. Sometimes elements that belong together semantically are not grouped adjacently. A classic example, first mentioned in the syntax literature by Ross (1967, p. 74) is from a Latin poem, Horace's *Pyrrha Ode* (*Carmina* (Odes) 1, 5). The poet ruefully addresses a jealous question to Pyrrha, his former mistress. The corresponding English words in the same order are given beneath.

Quis multā gracilis te puer in rosā perfusus liquidis urget odoribus grato, Pyrrha, sub antro?
What many slender you boy in roses sprinkled liquid courts scents pleasant, Pyrrha, in grotto?

Here, almost everything is semantically scrambled. What it means is

What slender boy, sprinkled with liquid scents, courts you, Pyrrha, in many roses in a pleasant grotto?

A grammatical dependency diagram, showing what words are linked together in this scrambled sentence is given in Figure 4.14. Horace's sentence is highly rhetorical poetry, and normal Latin was not so scrambled as this. The sentence can be decoded, not via the adjacent grouping of the words, but by inflections that the Latin words share. In brief, a Latin speaker knows that *quis*, *gracilis*, and *puer* belong together, despite their linear separation, because they share the same 'Nominative' case marking. Similarly, the pairs {*multa rosa*}, {*liquidis odoribus*}, and {*grato antro*} are clearly signalled as belonging together by other shared inflectional markings. The availability of such linked inflections allowed the Latin poet to have a kind of semantic soup, for the sake of metre and poetic effect, while not losing meaning conveyed by grammatical markers. With scarcely any such rich inflectional marking, English cannot get away with such freedom in its word order.

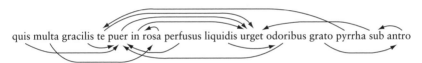

quis multa gracilis te puer in rosa perfusus liquidis urget odoribus grato pyrrha sub antro

Fig. 4.14 Dependency diagram showing what words belong together semantically in the scrambled sentence from Horace.

Source: This diagram is from Bird and Liberman (2001, p. 44). Unfortunately, their arrows show dependencies the other way round from my dependency diagrams, with the arrows pointing towards the grammatical head elements.

There is a correlation across languages between rich inflection, especially on nouns, and relative freedom of word order. A typological distinction has been proposed between 'non-configurational' (or relatively free word-order) languages and 'configurational' (or relatively fixed word-order) languages (Chomsky 1981). The best known example of a non-configurational language is Warlpiri, an aboriginal language of Central Australia. Hale (1983, p. 6) gives the following example, illustrating how two words which belong together semantically need not be adjacent, to form a phrase; the Warlpiri sentence is about 'that kangaroo', but contains no contiguous phrase with that meaning.

wawirri   kapi-rna panti -rni   yalumpu
kangaroo AUX   *spear* NON-PAST *that*
'I will spear that kangaroo'

Several other orderings of these words are possible, and equivalent in meaning. Warlpiri speakers manage to keep track of who did what to whom because the language is a case-marking language, and elements which belong together semantically are linked by inflections (or by common lack of inflections in the above example) and not necessarily by linear grouping. But even Warlpiri doesn't allow absolutely any word order; the AUX element must go in second position in a sentence. Non-configurational structures, in which parts that belong together semantically are not grouped together, require more use of short-term memory during parsing.

What such examples show is that humans are able to learn systems demanding a certain degree of online memory during processing of a sentence. Putting it informally, when a word is heard, the processor is able to store certain grammatical properties of that word in a temporary 'buffer' and wait until another word comes along later in the sentence with properties marking it as likely to fit semantically with the stored word. Here is another example from Guugu Yimidhirr, an Australian language of north-eastern Queensland (Haviland 1979).

Yarraga-aga-mu-n   *gudaa*   *gunda-y*   *biiba-ngun*
boy-GEN-mu-ERG   *dog*+ABS   *hit*-PAST   *father*-ERG
'The boy's father hit the dog'

Here ERG is a case marker indicating that the words for *boy* and *father* both help to describe the agent of the hitting act, despite these words being far apart in the sentence.

Online storage of words for later fitting into the overall semantics of a sentence does not necessarily depend on overt inflectional marking on words. Given a knowledge of the system, speakers of non-inflected languages can match an early word in a sentence with meanings that are spelled out much later in the sentence. We have already seen a good example of this in an English sentence repeated below.

I can remember being taken into Princess Mary's [fourteen-word digression] *being hoisted up on my uncle's shoulder to look over the window that was half painted to see a little bundle that was obviously my brother being held up by my Dad.*

Now, in this sentence, who is understood as 'being taken' and 'being hoisted'? And who is understood as the Subject of 'to look' and 'to see'? It's all the speaker herself, but she is not mentioned explicitly. In other words, we don't have *I can remember ME being taken...* or *... ME being hoisted.* And we don't have... *FOR ME to look over the window* or... *FOR ME to see a little bundle*. Normal users of a language take these things in their stride, and easily interpret the participants in the event described. But consider the feat. The verb *look* is taken to have *I* (i.e. the speaker) as its Subject, even though the only clue is at the very beginning of the sentence, sixteen words earlier. (And this is putting aside the intervening fourteen-word digression omitted here for convenience.) Even more impressive, the verb *see*, twenty-five words after the 'antecedent' *I*, is interpreted in the same way. If the original sentence had started with *JOHN can remember*..., then the understood looker and see-er would have been John. The interpretation of the subjects of these embedded verbs depends on an antecedent much earlier in the sentence. These are examples of one kind of long distance dependency. The rule for interpretation involves the hearer catching the fact that a verb is expressed in the infinitive form (preceded by *to*) and lacks an overt Subject (i.e we don't have *for John to look* or *for John to see*). Catching this, a hearer who is a fluent user of English has learned to 'supply the missing subject' and interpret these verbs as having the antecedent *I* as their understood Subject. And one last point: why don't you understand *my uncle* to be the missing Subject here, as it is much closer? The answer is in details of the grammatical structure of the sentence, which speakers and hearers have learned to manipulate with almost no effort and at great speed. The speaker of the above sentence had learned to use these truncated (i.e. formally Subjectless) clauses *to look*... and *to see*... with apparently effortless control, in full confidence that the hearer would know who she was talking about. Some of the work of interpretation here is undoubtedly done by fulfilling semantic expectations—we recognize the hospital scenario. But the grammatical structure is also doing some of the work.

The example just discussed shows only one of several types of long distance dependency involving a 'missing' element. A similar type in English involves *Wh-* words such as *what*, *where*, and *which*. In several different but related constructions these words come at the front of a clause, and are understood as fulfilling a semantic function usually fulfilled by a phrase at a position later in the clause. Here are some examples (from the *NECTE* corpus) in which these long distance semantic relationships are shown by an underlined word and an underlined gap later in the sentence.

Sam Smith's <u>which</u> we used to call _____ Ringtons's

A proper toilet seat with a lid <u>which</u> you never ever got _____ anywhere else

A hearer of the first example here understands that we used to call Sam Smith's Ringtons's. The job done by the *which* here is to link the phrase before it, *Sam Smith's*, to a position in the following clause in which it is to be understood, that is as the Object of the verb *call*. Likewise in the second example, a hearer understands that you never ever got a proper toilet seat with a lid anywhere else. Here the *which* does the same job of linking the preceding phrase *A proper toilet seat with a lid* with the position after the verb *got* in the following clause. These examples are of relative clauses where the relative pronoun, *which*, links to an Object role in the following clause. The word *that* can also play the same role of relative pronoun linking a previous phrase to a role usually played by a phrase in a later position, as in these examples (also from *NECTE*):

Now that was the game that everybody played _____

We understand that everybody played the game.

I can remember my first one that my mother got _____ *me*

We understand that the speaker's mother got her her first one.

   Now in Figure 4.15 are two examples of a different English construction, called a *What*-cleft construction. The sentences are

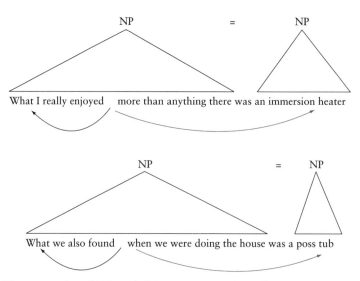

Fig. 4.15 Two examples of *What*-cleft constructions. In such a construction, two noun phrases (NPs) are equated. The first sentence expresses the same proposition as *I really enjoyed an immersion heater more than anything there*. But the pragmatic force, or information structure, of the two sentences is quite different. Likewise, the second sentence expresses the same propositional meaning as *We also found a poss tub when we were doing the house*, but presents this information with a quite different emphasis. The arrows in this figure are an informal way of suggesting the dependency relationships between parts of these sentences.

Source: From the *NECTE* corpus.

What I really enjoyed more than anything there was an immersion heater
What we also found when we were doing the house was a poss tub

Something a bit more complex is going on here. The same propositional meaning could have been expressed with a simpler sentence, with for example *I really enjoyed an immersion heater*. But the speaker, for conversational effect, has chosen to present the information by dispersing the core parts of the simpler sentence to non-adjacent positions in a more complex sentence. These constructions are a subclass of so-called 'equative' sentences. In each case, the expression beginning with *What* defines a certain thing by relating it to a clause in which it is understood to play a role. Thus in the first example, *What* anticipates a position after the verb *enjoyed*; another way to put this is that *What* is understood as if it were the Object of *enjoyed*. In the second example, *What* anticipates a position after the verb *found* (or, equivalently, is interpreted as if it were the Object of *found*). Note that both of these verbs would normally be expected to take a Direct Object NP after them, so that, for example, *I really enjoyed* seems incomplete. Enjoyed **what**? Likewise, *we also found* seems incomplete without an Object. Found **what**? These quite complex constructions are plainly motivated by pragmatic concerns. The speaker wants to save the climactic information (the immersion heater or the poss tub[67] until last. This involves quite a lot of switching around of the structure of the basic proposition, signalled by the initial *what*. These constructions are not exotic, appearing, as we have seen, in informal conversation by people without higher education. Humans born into an English-speaking community learn to manage the complex interaction of long-range dependencies with the hierarchical structures involved quite effortlessly.

I have been careful above not to commit to a view of these sentences which postulates that a phonetically empty, or null, element is actually present in their structure. This is a controversial issue. One school of thought has it that the expression *the game that everybody played*, for example, has a psychologically **real**, but phonetically contentless or silent element in the Object position after *played*. The grammatical theories toward which I lean deny the existence of such empty elements. They are a device for expressing the facts about the relationships between the non-empty elements (actual words) in the expression, and how they are understood. Notice that this is a matter of the relationship between syntax and semantics. The

---

[67] A poss tub is (or was) a tub in which washing was manually swirled around with a special long-handled tool, called a *posser*. The terms are characteristic of the north-east of England.

syntactic fact is that a verb which in other circumstances takes an Object is without one in expressions such as this. The parallel semantic fact is that the antecedent relative pronoun signals that the noun phrase just before it is understood as the Object of the verb.

Ordinary English conversation is rife with sentences illustrating such long-distance dependencies. Another class of constructions illustrating them is the class of 'embedded questions'. In such structures, the existence of something or someone is presupposed, and either is not mentioned explicitly at all or is only partly specified. I give some examples below, from the *NECTE* corpus, each with a partial paraphrase showing informally how the presupposed SOME-THING would be mentioned in a more canonical relationship between the parts of the sentence.

. . . can not remember what house I was in
        . . . I was in SOME *house*

Then it all came out about how what an awful life she'd led with this [man]
        . . . she'd led SOME *awful life with this [man]*

Do you know what they do with the tower now?
        . . . they do SOMETHING *with the tower . . .*

Do you remember what they called Deuchar's beer?
        . . . they called Deuchar's beer SOMETHING

. . . just to see these women of ill repute you know just to see what they look like
        . . . they look like SOMETHING

Such sentences are not exotic or contrived. It is not claimed that the informal paraphrases given have any psychological prior status in the minds of their speakers. But the paraphrases do show relationships between these sentences and other ways of expressing very similar meanings. These relationships must be tacitly known by the speakers, and also by us English-speaking readers, in order for them to be able to express, and for us to be able to comprehend, their meanings so easily. I give a few more examples below, without detailed comment on their grammatical structure. I hope it will be plain that they involve complex combinations of structures all of which involve some kind of long-distance dependency between linearly separated parts of the sentence. Again, the examples are all from the *NECTE* corpus.

The best thing I found at the school was a pound note that was like full of mud.

Anything that any elder said you did without question

This had a teeny weenie little coat hanger in it which I thought was absolutely wonderful

All the legs are falling off the table which had happened to some of the tables in father's house

Neville was a delivery boy with his bike you know with the the eh basket in the front which you never see these days

Finally, here are some more such English data, not from a corpus, of a type extensively discussed by Chomsky (1986), among many others:

	Understood Subject of *talk to*	Understood Object of *talk to*
John is too stubborn to talk to	Someone/anyone	John
John is too stubborn to talk to him	John	Some other male person
John wants someone to talk to	John	Someone
John wants someone to talk to him	Someone	John

Note two facts, in particular. (1) The simple addition of a pronoun *him* clearly switches the understood meaning in both pairs of sentences; and (2) the difference in the way the first pair is understood is the reverse of the difference in the way the second pair is understood. Most adult native speakers of English readily agree that these are the normal understood meanings of these sentences. This is not to say that contexts cannot be constructed in which the reverse meanings might come more naturally. Not all dialects of English show this pattern, and in dialects that do, these understandings are acquired rather late by children. Nevertheless, the people who do acquire these understandings of such sentences are not geniuses, but are just normal humans who have grown up in an environment where these sentences have been spoken often enough with these implicit meanings. These facts are obviously particular to a specific language. But they are universally acquirable by any normally healthy person brought up in a culture where such patterns occur often enough in the ambient usage. Examples like this are not isolated. Many such examples can be found in many languages, and to the extent that they are similar from one language to another, they reinforce the point that ability to master long-range dependencies is a universal of the human language acquisition capacity.

4.7 Constructions, complex items with variables

Up to here, I have made implicit and informal appeal to the concept of a **construction**. In this section I flesh out the idea of constructions, as they are seen in a growing body of theoretical work under the label of 'Construction Grammar'. There are several different versions of Construction Grammar,[68] and my account will not differentiate between them, but will describe, quite informally, what they have in common. The common idea is that a speaker's knowledge of his language consists of a very large inventory of constructions, where a construction is understood to be of any size and abstractness, from a single word to some grammatical aspect of a sentence, such as its Subject–Predicate structure. Construction Grammar emphasizes that there is a 'lexicon-syntax continuum', contrary to traditional views in which the lexicon and the syntactic rules are held to be separate components of a grammar. The central motive of Construction Grammar theorists is to account for the extraordinary productivity of human languages, while at the same time recognizing the huge amount of idiosyncratic grammatical data that humans acquire and store. 'The constructionist approach to grammar offers a way out of the lumper/splitter dilemma' (Goldberg 2006, p. 45). The key point is that storage of idiosyncratic facts is compatible with deploying these facts productively to generate novel expressions. In this sense, Construction Grammar is no less generative than theories in a more direct line of descent from Chomsky's early work.

The great combinatorial promiscuity of human grammars stems from the use of **variables**. Any productive construction incorporates one or more variables. We have already seen this, in many examples, one of which I repeat here, with the variables shown in capital letters.[69]

a NOUN *in the* NOUN *is worth two in the* NOUN.

---

[68] Some central references for Construction Grammar and sympathetic approaches are Fillmore and Kay (1993); Fillmore et al. (2003); Croft (2001); Goldberg (1995, 2006); Culicover (1999); Sag (2007); Jackendoff (2002); Butler and Arista (2008). Construction Grammar has several natural allies in the landscape of grammatical theories, distinguished mainly because they have been developed by separate theorists, working from similar premises and with similar goals. These allied frameworks include Head-Driven Phrase Structure Grammar (HPSG) (Pollard and Sag 1994; Levine and Meurers 2006) and Word Grammar (Hudson 1984, 2007). A computational neurolinguistic implementation of construction grammar has been sketched (no more) by Dominey and Hoen (2006).

[69] Following the earlier discussion of idioms, the formulae here should represent the full hierarchical or dependency relations between the parts; to avoid visual overload, the strings shown are very schematic.

In the formula, 'NOUN' indicates that the element chosen must be of the same grammatical category, NOUN, but not necessarily the same particular word. Syntax dictates a wide range of grammatical possibilities, which are subject to non-syntactic (e.g. semantic) considerations of acceptability. *A book in the loo is worth two in the study* is fine, but ?*A book in the mistake is worth two in the error* doesn't make any obvious sense.

This example is idiosyncratic and not central to English syntax. There is a gradation of constructions from marginal ones like this to constructions that are at the heart of almost every sentence. Below are some examples of intermediate centrality, constructions known by all competent speakers of most varieties of English, but not necessarily used every day. These examples come from a subtle and perceptive article by Anna Wierzbicka (1982), entitled 'Why can you *have a drink* when you can't **have an eat*?' It's a great question, and Wierzbicka gives a good answer. Her paper predated the growth of Construction Grammar, and semantics rather than syntax was her main concern. But the solution to her intriguing question involved saying that there are items larger than a single word which have idiosyncratic meaning, and individual words can get inserted into these items. We would call these 'constructions'. First notice that *have a drink* differs in meaning from just *drink*. The multi-word construction has connotations of pleasure and some degree of aimlessness. *Have a nice drink* is OK, but ?*have a nasty drink* is not. *Have a drink in the garden* is OK, but ?*have a drink to cure my cough* is subtly weirder. There are several overlapping *have a* V constructions. One is

CONSUMPTION OF SMALL PARTS OF OBJECTS WHICH COULD CAUSE ONE TO FEEL PLEASURE. The syntactic formula is:

NP	*have* + AUX *a*	V-Inf	*of* + NP
human		two arguments	concrete
		intentional	definite
		consumption	(preferably possessed)
			no total change in the object

Examples are *have a bite, a lick, a suck, a chew, a nibble*
... if someone eats an apple or a sandwich, the object in question is TOTALLY affected.
... This is why one can *have a bite* or *a lick*, but one cannot **have an eat, a swallow* or *a devour*.   (Wierzbicka 1982, p. 771)

Other contrasts that Wierzbicka mentions without going into detail are:

give the rope a pull	**give the window an open*
give someone a kiss	**give someone a kill*
have a walk	**have a speak*
John had a lick of Mary's ice cream	?*Fido had a lick of his master's hand*

For all of these, a competent speaker of English has learned a semi-idiomatic construction, with specific semantics and pragmatics. Examples such as Wierzbicka's relate to the issue of fine-grained syntactic categories, as discussed in section 4.4.1 above. There is an open question, to my mind, of whether the **meanings** of the words which can be inserted into a such constructions are 'primitive' or whether fine-grained **lexical subcategories** are primitive, and we extrapolate some details of the meanings of the words from the meanings of the constructions they occur in.

We will come presently to more central examples of constructions, of great productivity. In general, any structure which is not itself explicitly listed in the construction store of the language is well-formed if it can be formed by combining of two or more structures that are explicitly listed. Combination depends crucially on variables. We have seen two simple examples earlier, in Figures 4.12 for the German *den Mann* and 4.13 for *has gone*. In the case of *den Mann*, the lexical entry for *Mann* mentions a context including a variable DET, and this term is present in the lexical entry for *den*, thus specifically licensing the combination *den Mann*.

Now here, pretty informally, are some more general and more widely productive examples. A basic rule of English is that finite verbs[70] obligatorily have Noun subjects which precede them. This can be conveniently diagrammed with a dependency diagram as in Figure 4.16.

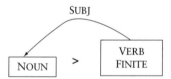

Fig. 4.16 The English Subject–verb construction, in dependency notation. The obligatory dependency relation between a finite verb and its Subject is shown by the labelled arrow. The > sign indicates obligatory linear ordering—the Subject noun must precede its verb, not necessarily immediately.

Another construction that combines with this is the English ditransitive verb construction, as in *gave Mary a book*. This is also conveniently given as a dependency diagram as in Figure 4.17.

In prose, this states that certain verbs, labelled DITRANS in the lexicon, plug into a structure with two dependent Noun elements, with the dependency relations labelled OBJ1 and OBJ2. In this case, linear order, marked here by

---

[70] A finite verb is, roughly, one that is marked for Tense and agrees with its Subject noun, as in *Mary walks*. So the verbs in English imperative sentences, for example, are not finite.

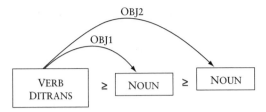

Fig. 4.17 The English ditransitive verb construction, in dependency notation. This states the essence of the argument structure of a ditransitive verb, such as *give*, with two obligatory objects dependent on the verb. These argument nouns go in the linear order shown unless overruled by the requirements of other constructions. The ≥ notation is my ad hoc way of showing 'overrulable' order of elements.

Fig. 4.18 The English Determiner-Noun construction. A Singular Common Noun requires a preceding determiner. The > symbol indicates that this local ordering cannot be overruled—the Determiner always precedes the Noun (not necessarily immediately).

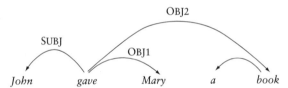

Fig. 4.19 The structure of *John gave Mary a book* in dependency notation. This structure conforms to the requirements, or constraints, specified in the three constructions given. The finite verb *gave* is preceded by a Noun subject. The verb also has its obligatory two object Noun arguments. And the Common Singular Noun *book* is preceded by its obligatory determiner.

'≥' is stipulated as preferred, but not obligatory, leaving open the possibility of this ordering being overruled by some other construction.

Presenting a third construction will allow us to show a simple case in which all three constructions combine to form a sentence. This is the English Determiner-Noun construction. English Singular Common Nouns obligatorily take a preceding determiner, such as *a, the, this* or *that*. This construction is shown, again in dependency notation, in Figure 4.18.

Now, assuming obvious information about the syntactic categories of the words involved, we can see how these three constructions go together to give the structure of *John gave Mary a book*. It is shown in Figure 4.19.

The essence of the English ditransitive verb construction, its 'argument structure', can be recognized not only in the most straightforward examples, such as *John gave Mary a book*, but also in examples such as the following:

What did John give Mary?	[*Wh-* question of 2nd Object NP]
Who gave Mary a book?	[*Wh-* question of Subject]
What John gave Mary was a book	[*Wh*-cleft on 2nd Object NP]
It was John that gave Mary a book	[*It*-cleft on Subject NP]
Who was it that gave Mary a book?	[*Wh-* question of focused item of previous example]
It was a book that John gave Mary	[*It*-cleft on 2nd Object NP]
What was it that John gave Mary?	[*Wh-* question on focused item of previous example]
A book, John gave Mary!	[Topicalization of 2nd Object NP]

As a historical note, these examples all involve what used to be called **transformations** of the basic ditransitive verb structure. Transformational Grammar[71] envisaged a sequential process in the formation of complex sentences, starting with basic forms (sometimes called 'deep structures') and a serial cascade of 'transformational' rules was postulated progressively performing such operations as re-ordering of parts, replacement of parts, insertion of new parts, and deletion of parts. Obviously, you can get to all the examples above by carrying out some of these transformational operations on the basic (or 'deep') form *John gave Mary a book*. The arsenal of available transformational operations in classical TG was very powerful. This possibly excessive power of transformations was a problem for the early theory. Construction Grammar still does not address the 'excessive power' problem to the satisfaction of some (e.g. Bod 2009).

Now in Construction Grammar, all the examples above exemplify **the same** construction, a ditransitive verb construction. Each one is also simultaneously an example of several **other** constructions, as reflected in the glosses given. For example, *What did John give Mary?* exemplifies a ditransitive verb construction, a *Wh*-initial construction, and a '*Do*-support' construction. Thus in this view particular sentences are seen as resulting from the co-occurrence of several different constructions in the same sentence. Here is an example given by Goldberg:

---

[71] Both Zellig Harris and his student Chomsky worked with ideas of transformations in linguistic structure in the 1950s (Harris 1957; Chomsky 1957). Chomsky took the ideas further and became more influential.

The expression in (1) involves the eleven constructions given in (2):

(1) A dozen roses, Nina sent her mother!
(2) a. Ditransitive construction
  b. Topicalization construction
  c. VP construction
  d. NP construction
  e. Indefinite determiner construction
  f. Plural construction
  g. *dozen, rose, Nina, send, mother* constructions   (Goldberg 2006, p. 21)

This is clearly a more complex view of syntactic combination than that of our earlier examples. (Note that individual words are counted as (simple) constructions—hence the count of eleven above.) Details of Goldberg's particular analysis of what constructions are involved in this example are not an issue here. In Construction Grammar, each construction specifies only a part of the structure of a sentence. The information given can include information about the linear order of elements, the part–whole relationships among elements, and the dependencies of elements on other elements. Any given individual construction may only be specified in terms of a subset of these types of information.[72]

I will now pick an example showing how, in principle, Construction Grammar can handle long-distance dependencies of the kind discussed in the previous section. Note that many of the examples of the ditransitive construction given above start with an initial *Wh*-word, either *what* or *who*. Four of these examples were questions, and one was a *Wh*-cleft sentence, *What John gave Mary was a book*. In the questions and the *Wh*-cleft sentence, the *Wh*-word comes at the beginning, and is understood as playing a semantic role later in the sentence, thus being a case of a long-distance dependency. Both types of sentence can be envisaged as involving a common construction, called the 'Wh-initial' construction. Informally, what needs to be specified about this construction is that the *Wh*-word (1) occurs initially, (2) precedes a structure identical to a 'normal' construction except that one of the NP arguments is missing, and (3) the *Wh*-word itself is semantically interpreted as playing the role of the missing NP. The *Wh*-initial construction is sketched in Figure 4.20.

Sketches of the structure of *Who gave Mary a book* and *What John gave Mary* are shown in Figure 4.21 (Figures overleaf).

---

[72] Crucially, semantic information on the interpretation of the parts of the construction is also included in a full account, although I do not go into the semantics here.

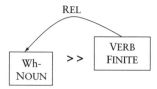

Where REL is a variable over grammatical relations such as SUBJ, OBJ1, OBJ2.

Fig. 4.20 The English *Wh*-initial construction. Here, REL is a variable over grammatical roles, indicating that the *Wh*- element takes one of the argument roles of the verb, which could be any one of SUBJ, OBJ1, or OBJ2. Whichever of these roles it takes, it obligatorily goes as far to the front of the sentence as possible, as indicated by the double >> symbol (my ad hoc notation). This treatment involves no 'movement'. The *Wh*- element is always in a front position in the construction defined here.

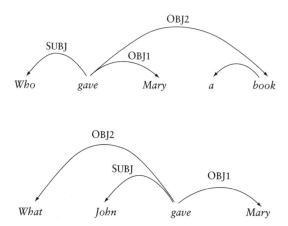

Fig. 4.21 Structures formed by combining the *Wh*-initial construction in two different ways with the Subject–verb construction and the ditransitive verb construction. Again, it is convenient to show these in dependency notation.

All the constraints stipulated by the various constructions are met by these structures. Thus

- *gave* has its regulation three arguments ;
- the *Wh*- element comes foremost;
- the Subject precedes the verb;
- the other arguments are in their default order, where not overruled by *Wh*-initial.

The strings shown could be combined with other constructions to give a variety of grammatical expressions. For instance *Who gave Mary a book* could be given appropriate questioning intonation, to give the question *Who gave Mary a book?* Or it could be used in the formation of a relative clause, as in *the person who gave Mary a book*. Similarly, *what John gave Mary* could function as an NP in a *Wh*-cleft sentence, such as *What John gave Mary was a book*. Or it could possibly, further combined with a Question construction, be part of the question *What did John give Mary?* In cases where questions are formed, the pragmatics of the *Wh*- word, not spelled out here, identify it as requesting information.

On hearing the function word *what* at the beginning of an utterance, the hearer is primed to anticipate a 'gappy' structure, and in some sense holds the *what* in mind to plug into a suitable role in the gappy structure that follows. This treatment avoids postulating two levels of structure, with a mediating 'movement' rule that moves the *Wh*-word from its canonical position to the front of the sentence.

Here is a non-linguistic analogy (with the usual reservations) of the Construction Grammar approach to sentences. Modern machinery, of all kinds, from dishwashers to cars, is assembled in complex ways from parts specified in design drawings. At the level of small components, such as screws and washers, the same items can be found in many different machines. Design drawings for larger components make shorthand reference to these widely used parts. This is analogous to words in grammatical constructions. At an intermediate level of size, some machines have similar subsystems, for instance electrical systems with batteries, alternators, solenoids, and so on. Again, the design drawings can just identify the types of components needed with incomplete, yet sufficiently distinctive information. At the largest level, each type of machine is different. A Construction Grammar is like a superbly equipped library of blueprints for interchangeable machine parts, describing components of all sizes for assembling any of an enormous set of machines, including some never assembled before, usable for novel functions. Some blueprints can afford to be very schematic, allowing a lot of freedom in how the components they describe combine with others. Crucially, any particular Construction Grammar will not allow you to assemble all possible machines, but only those of some given (vast) set. A particular store of blueprints of parts is analogous to the grammar of a particular language. The set of things assemblable from one parts-store is the language. Pushing the analogy, the low-level parts from different stores may not be interchangeable with each other, as metric and Imperial nuts and bolts are not interchangeable. This is analogous to different languages having largely non-overlapping vocabularies. No analogy is perfect, but maybe this helps.

Syntactic categories and constructions mutually interdefine each other. Thus, just as syntactic categories participate in multiple default inheritance hierarchies, so do constructions. Figure 4.10 in section 4.4.3 (p. 311) can be read as a partial multiple default hierarchy of constructions. The bulleted conditions on the syntactic categories in that diagram, for example 'can be dependent argument of verb or preposition' or 'can be modified by an adjective' are in fact references to the constructions in which the category in question participates.

Construction Grammar belongs to a large family of theories that are **monostratal**. In these theories, what you see is what you get. There are no elements in a described sentence which start life in a different 'underlying' position; that is there are no movement rules. There are no invisible word-like elements in the underlying structure which do not appear in the sentence itself. In contrast, classical Transformational Grammar described the English passive construction, as in *John was run over by a bus*, as an underlying, or 'deep', active sentence, as in *A bus ran over John*, which gets very substantially twisted around, altered and added to. The NPs are moved to opposite ends from where they started, the finite verb is replaced by its passive participial form, and the word *by* and a form of BE are inserted. In Construction Grammar, there are two separate constructions, an active and a passive one. In classical TG, English interrogatives (question sentences) were said to be formed **from** structures close to the corresponding declaratives by switching the Subject and the Auxiliary, as in *Mary can go* → *Can Mary go?* In Construction Grammar, there is a separate Auxilary–Subject construction. The relationship between corresponding declaratives and interrogatives is not lost, because they each share other properties, such as the structural relations between the particular nouns and verbs they contain. These common properties are captured by other constructions. What distinguishes interrogatives from declaratives is the involvement of the Auxilary–Subject construction in one but not the other.

A well known example of an underlying invisible element postulated by classical TG is the understood *you* in imperatives. *Get lost!* is understood as *YOU get lost!* TG postulated a deletion transformation whereby an underlying *you* in imperatives was deleted. Construction Grammar postulates a *you*-less imperative construction, whose accompanying semantics and pragmatics specifies that it is understood as a command to a hearer.[73] Most interestingly, this analysis entails that the oddness of *Shoot herself!* as an imperative is not a purely syntactic fact, but an issue of pragmatic acceptability. Classical TG accounted for this oddness as a clear case of ungrammaticality, by having the agreement rule between reflexive pronouns and their Subject antecedents apply

---

[73] Nikolaeva (2007, p. 172) gives a Construction Grammar formulation of the imperative construction.

before the *You*-deletion rule. An ordered sequence of operations from underlying structure to surface structure is not available in Construction Grammar. What you see is what you get, and some facts hitherto taken to be purely syntactic facts are seen to be reflections of semantics and pragmatics.

Monostratal theories of grammar, such as Construction Grammar, are **non-derivational**. The description of any given sentence does not entail a sequence of operations, but rather a specification of the various parts which fit together to form that sentence. See how difficult it is to avoid the terminology of processes! For a vivid description of sentence structure, locutions like 'fit together to form that sentence' are effective. But care must be taken not to equate a description of sentence structure with either of the psycholinguistic processes of sentence production and sentence interpretation. A description of sentence structure should provide a natural basis for both these processes, and should be neutral between them. Neutral descriptions of different sentences should reflect their different degrees of complexity which should correlate well with psycholinguistic difficulty, as measured, for example, by processing time. Enter, and quickly exit, the 'derivational theory of complexity'.

The derivational theory of complexity (DTC) flourished briefly in parallel with early Transformational Grammar in the 1960s (Miller 1962; Miller and McKean 1964; Savin and Perchonock 1965). The idea was that the number of transformations undergone by a sentence in its derivation from its underlying structure correlated with its complexity, as measured by psychometric methods. For example, *Wasn't John run over by a bus?* involves, in sequence, the passive transformation, the negation rule inserting *not/n't*, and the Subject–Auxiliary inversion rule to form the question. This negative passive interrogative sentence is predicted to be more complex than positive active declarative *A bus ran over John*. Early analyses showed that there was some truth to the idea. It even seemed for a while that it was possible to measure the time that each individual transformation took, with the total processing time being the arithmetical sum of the times taken by each transformational rule. You can see how this was very exciting. But the hypothesis soon ran into trouble. Fodor and Garrett (1966, 1967) argued forcefully against it on several grounds. One counterargument is that the hypothesis entails that a hearer takes in a whole sentence before starting to decode it, whereas in fact hearers start processing when they hear the first word. Another problem is that it was possible to find plenty of transformations postulated in those days that apparently turned complex structures into simple ones. For example, by the DTC hypothesis, based on transformational analyses current at the time, *For someone to please John is easy* should be less complex than *John is easy to please*. But it isn't.

A non-derivational theory of grammar, such as Construction Grammar, makes no predictions about complexity based on how many operations are serially involved in assembling the sentence. This is for the simple reason that Construction Grammar does not postulate any series of operations. The model of grammar is not **algorithmic**, in the sense of specifying finite sequences of steps. In fact, though it is very natural to talk in such terms as 'assembling a sentence', this does not represent the Construction Grammar point of view. This theory, like many other monostratal theories, is **constraint-based**. The idea is that constructions state well–formedness conditions on sentences. For example, the English ditransitive construction states that a ditransitive verb, such as *give*, must have OBJ1 and OBJ2 arguments. If a string of English words contains a form of *give*, but no nouns that can be interpreted as its OBJ1 and its OBJ2, that string is not a well-formed English sentence. Grammatical English sentences are those that conform to the constructions listed in a Construction Grammar of English.

Much earlier in this book I glossed 'syntax' crudely as 'putting things together'. But what kind of 'things'? Just words? Syntax as putting things together is still true under a Construction Grammar view, but the way things are put together is more complex than mere concatenation of words. True, some of syntax is concatenating words, but what humans can do with great ease is put **whole constructions** together in ways that involve much more than concatenation.[74] Indeed, some constructions say nothing about linear order, but only specify their necessary parts. It is left to other constructions, when combined with these, to order the constituents. In languages with freer word order than English, often this ordering may not be specified, and as long as the dependency relations between the parts are correctly represented, sentences are well-formed.

Many recent syntactic theories converge on a broad idea that a single type of combination operation lies at the heart of the grammar of any language. In Minimalism, the operation is called 'Merge'; other more computationally based theories deal in a precisely defined operation called **unification**. In Jackendoff's approach, 'the only "rule of grammar" is UNIFY PIECES, and all the pieces are stored in a common format that permits unification' (Jackendoff 2002, p. 180). The account I have presented above, being quite informal, is not a strictly unificational account, nor does it comply exactly with the Minimalist

---

[74] A major difference between Construction Grammar and Minimalism is that Minimalism only postulates single words in the lexicon, rather than larger constructions. Minimalism's Merge operation is also formally simpler than the combining operations that put some constructions together.

concept of Merge. I will leave it at that. Future work (not by me) will settle on a more precise specification of the kind of combination operation used in human grammars. I have only mentioned a handful of constructions. The grammar of a complex language has hundreds, and possibly thousands of complex constructions, that is constructions more complex than single words (which are the simplest kind).

Each construction that a person knows can have its own syntactic, semantic, and pragmatic properties peculiar to it. Smaller constructions, such as individual words, especially nouns, have little or no associated pragmatic force. Larger constructions, such as questioning or topicalizing constructions, do have specific pragmatic effects associated with them. The integration of pragmatic effect with syntactic form was identified as a problem for syntactic theory very early by John Ross. It is worth quoting him at length.

If derived force rules are taken to be rules of pragmatics, and I believe this conception to be quite a traditional one, then it is not possible to relegate syntactic and pragmatic processes to different components of a grammar. Rather than it being possible for the 'work' of linking surface structures to the sets of contexts in which these structures can be appropriately used to be dichotomized into a set of pragmatic rules and a set of semantactic rules, it seems to be necessary to postulate that this work is to be accomplished by one unified component, in which rules concerned with such pragmatic matters as illocutionary force, speaker location, and so on, and rules concerned with such semantic matters as synonymy, metaphoric extension of senses, and so on, and rules concerned with such syntactic matters as the distribution of meaningless morphemes, the choice of prepositional versus postpositional languages, and so on, are interspersed in various ways. Following a recent practice of Fillmore, we might term the study of such mixed components PRAGMANTAX.

Note that accepting the conclusion that there is a pragmantactic component does not necessarily entail abandoning the distinction between pragmatic, semantic, and syntactic aspects of linguistic structure.   (Ross 1975, p.252).

Ross's insight could not be readily incorporated into the Transformational view of syntax dominant in the 1970s. Indeed few syntacticians had yet begun to grasp much about semantics and pragmatics. Now, Construction Grammar allows the fulfilment of Ross's vision. There is not a whole large department of a grammar that deals with all the pragmatics of a language, and a separate one that deals with all the semantics, and another that handles the syntax. Instead, there is a store of constructions of varying size, each of which has its own pragmatic, semantic, and syntactic properties. Constructions combine according to a small set of combinatory rules, and their pragmatic and semantic properties may not clash, on pain of producing unacceptable sentences.

The human ability to store and combine many constructions of different shapes and sizes may be a language-specific capacity. But it may be a special case of a much broader capacity, which Fauconnier and Turner call 'conceptual integration'. 'The gist of the operation is that two or more mental spaces can be partially matched and their structure can be partially projected to a new, blended space that develops emergent structure' (Fauconnier and Turner 2008, p. 133). These authors have associated their work with Construction Grammar. (See Chapter 6 for further discussion of possible non-linguistic precursors of our ability to combine many constructions.)

Finally, a philosophical note on Construction Grammar, linking the central idea to Wittgenstein's Language Games. Wittgenstein (1953) emphasized 'the multiplicity of language-games', meaning the great range of uses, some general and some more specific, to which language is put. Some of his examples of different language-games are 'presenting the results of an experiment in tables and diagrams', 'singing catches', 'guessing riddles', 'making a joke; telling it' (¶ 23). I will add some more in the same vein, exemplifying a form of language peculiar to each activity.

Giving football results on radio: *Arsenal three, Chelsea nil* (with falling intonation characteristic of reporting a home win)

Reporting a cricket match: *At tea, India were eighty-five for one*

Describing chess moves: *Pawn to King four; rook to Queen's bishop eight*

The BBC radio shipping forecast: *Forties, Cromarty, Forth, Tyne: south or southeast 5 or 6 decreasing 4 at times, showers, good.*

Telling the time: *It's half past two*

Giving military drill orders: *Atten–SHUN; order–ARMS* (with characteristic rhythm, pausing, and intonation)

Naming musical keys: *E flat minor; C sharp major*

Counting, using numeral systems: *Two hundred thousand million; three thousand, two hundred and fifty four.* (Numeral systems have a syntax and semantics related to, but differing in detail from, the rest of their language (Hurford 1975))

Giving street directions: *First left; second right*

Officiating at Communion in the Church of England: *Hear what comfortable words our Saviour Christ saith unto all who truly turn to him.*

Air traffic control speak: *Cactus fifteen forty nine seven hundred climbing five thousand*

Ending a formal letter: *Yours sincerely,*

Each of these has at least one syntactic quirk peculiar to language about its particular activity. These are language games, and each uses some characteristic construction(s). Where linguists have found Wittgenstein's discussion of language games wanting is in its apparent lack of interest in any kind of syntactic generalization across different language games. (The same criticism would apply to Kristeva's theorizing about intertextuality, mentioned earlier.) Many of the examples above combined peculiar features with completely standard phrases, phrases which could occur in a wide range of other uses. Such very general patterns can be seen as features of the very general language game permeating a good proportion of the specialized games, namely a game we can fairly call *English*. 'I shall also call the whole [language], consisting of language and the actions into which it is woven, the "language game"' (Wittgenstein 1953, ¶7). The connection between Wittgenstein's language games and Construction Grammar has been made by Sowa (2006). He writes 'The semantics of a natural language consists of the totality of all possible language games that can be played with a given syntax and vocabulary' (p. 688). Both Wittgenstein and Construction Grammar see a language as (in part) a massive inventory of form-types, although Wittgenstein's focus was almost entirely on their semantic and pragmatic contexts. Construction Grammar follows in the syntactic tradition of seeking generalizations across all form-types, something to which Wittgenstein was not drawn. Instead of articulating cross-game generalizations, Wittgenstein stated that different language games bear **family resemblances** to each other, and he resisted the urge to generalize further. He also never went into grammatical detail. 'In this disdain for the systematic, Wittgenstein's grammar stands in contrast not only to linguistics but also to the speech-act theories of Austin and Searle' (Garver 1996, p. 151). Construction Grammar can be claimed to (try to) spell out what Wittgenstein's family resemblances consist of. Similar sentences are composed of some of the same constructions. It is possible to play several language games at once, as with Wittgenstein's own examples of 'describing the appearance of an object' and 'reporting an event'. Thus we might speak of a referring game, connected with the use of proper names or definite descriptions, and a questioning game, connected, in English, with the inversion of a subject noun and an auxiliary verb. The sentence *Has the bus gone?* can be used to play at least two language games simultaneously, referring and questioning, and correspondingly involves at least two different constructions.

Of course, there are many differences between Wittgenstein and the cognitivist, mentalist assumptions of a normal syntactician, as well as the parallels in their views of what a language consists of. Wittgenstein's insistence on family resemblances between language games denied the possibility of defining them in terms of necessary and sufficient conditions. What is less clear (to me) is whether he also denied the possibility of precisely definable discrete relationships between the constructions involved in particular games. His idea may have been that language games (and, I would add, their associated grammatical constructions) blend continuously into each other, with no possibility of clear boundaries. But there is no doubting the discrete differences between one word and another, or one grammatical pattern and another. At a fine enough level of granularity, it is possible to give precise discrete descriptions of grammatical constructions, and of how related constructions differ from each other. Grammatical change happens in discrete steps. For example, the English negative *not* switched from post-main-verb position (as in *it matters not*) to post-auxiliary position (as in *it doesn't matter*): there was no 'blended' or 'middle' position. Obviously, the statistics of usage by individuals changed continuously, but the categories between which people veered (post-main versus post-aux.) had clear discrete boundaries.

4.8 Island constraints

Finally, after considering the list of impressive linguistic feats that normal humans can learn to do with ease, I'll mention an influential claim about something that humans **can't** learn to do. I say 'claim' advisedly, because the facts concerned were long thought to be constraints on syntactic form, that is to describe patterns that no child could possibly acquire as part of her native grammar. The pioneering work was done very early on by John Ross (Ross 1967, 1986). The theoretical context was early Transformational Grammar, which postulated movement rules[75] transforming 'deep structures' into 'surface structures'. The movement rule best used as an example is the '*Wh*-fronting rule. Informally, this says 'When a *Wh*-element occurs in a sentence, move it to the front'. Thus in this theory transformations such as the following were said to occur.

DEEP STRUCTURE		SURFACE STRUCTURE
John saw WHO?	$\Longrightarrow$	*Who did John see?*
John thought WHO saw Mary?	$\Longrightarrow$	*Who did John think saw Mary?*
John thought Mary saw WHO?	$\Longrightarrow$	*Who did John think Mary saw?*

---

[75] In this section, I will use the metaphor familiar to linguists, of 'movement' describing long-range dependencies such as that between a *Wh*-word at the front of a sentence and a later 'gap'. In fact the island constraints discussed here are not constraints on 'movement', but constraints on certain kinds of long-range dependencies. Chung and McCloskey (1983) give an analysis of some of these constraints in terms of a syntactic theory which does not posit 'movement' rules (GPSG), but still treat the phenomena as essentially syntactic.

John thought Bill said WHO saw ⟹ *Who did John think Bill said saw*
    Mary?   *Mary?*
John thought Bill said Mary saw ⟹ *Who did John think Bill said Mary*
    WHO?   *saw?*

(Give the left-hand sentences here the intonation of 'echo questions', with stress and rising tone on *WHO*, as if incredulously querying a statement just made by someone else.) The important point is that a *Wh*-element can apparently move an indefinite distance, flying over many words on its journey to the front of the sentence. Given a transformational view of these structures, using a theory that permits movement rules, the facts are clear. Ross noticed that, while indeed a *Wh*-element can in some cases be 'moved' over a very great distance, there are some cases where such movement is blocked. Given below are cases where moving a *Wh*-element to the front actually results in ungrammaticality.

John saw Mary and WHO?   ⟹ **Who did John see Mary and?*
John saw WHO and Mary?   ⟹ **Who did John see and Mary?*
John believed the claim that WHO ⟹ **Who did John believe the claim*
    saw Mary?   *that saw Mary*
John believed the claim that Mary ⟹ **Who did John believe the claim*
    saw WHO?   *that Mary saw?*
John ate the sandwich that WHO ⟹ **Who did John eat the sandwich*
    gave him?   *that gave him?*
John took the sandwich that Max ⟹ **Who did John take the sandwich*
    gave WHO?   *that Max gave?*

Again, the left-hand incredulously intoned echo questions can occur. But the right-hand strings, formed by moving the *Wh*-element to the front are not well-formed. A non-linguist's response to such examples is often extreme puzzlement. 'But those sentences [the ones starting with *Who*] are gobbledygook! They don't make any sense'. Yes, indeed, the linguist replies, that is just the point; our problem as theorists is to try to explain why these particular examples 'don't make sense' when other examples moving a *Wh*-element to the front over even greater distances seem quite OK. Ross's solution, and one still widely accepted to this day, was that the starred examples are ungrammatical, that is they violate some abstract principles of pure autonomous syntax, generally labelled 'island constraints'. A few years earlier, Chomsky, Ross's supervisor, had proposed the first such constraint, labelled the 'A-over-A constraint' (Chomsky 1964). The discovery of similar facts in other languages made this seem like a discovery about **universal** constraints on the form of grammar. The conclusion, accepted for decades, and probably still held by many syntacticians, was that the innate universal language acquisition device specifically prevented children learning structures in which elements were moved across certain structural patterns. Expressed another way, children were attributed with 'knowing' these abstract constraints on movement. In favour of this idea is the fact that no child, apparently, even tries spontaneously to create sentences with movement across the proscribed patterns. Thus, the innateness theory of universal grammar not only specified the structural patterns that children are disposed to acquire easily, but also specified certain patterns that children definitely could not acquire. For the most part, the discovery of island constraints was regarded as a triumph for syntactic theory, and the purported 'explanation' was to postulate a theory-internal principle, purely syntactic in nature. Many different formulations of the required principle(s) were put forward, but most were abstract 'principles of syntax'.

From an evolutionary point of view, purely syntactic innate island constraints present a serious problem. Formulated as purely syntactic, that is essentially arbitrary, facts, the puzzle is to explain how humans would have evolved these very specific abstract aversions. One abstract grammatical principle proposed to account for some island constraints was the 'Subjacency Condition'. The details don't concern us here, but David Lightfoot (1991b, p. 69), arguing that the condition could not be functional, memorably remarked 'The Subjacency Condition has many virtues, but I am not sure that it could have increased the chances of having fruitful sex'. For a long time, no possible functional motivation was discussed, because the pervading assumption was that these are just arbitrary weirdnesses of the human syntactic faculty.

Functional explanations for island phenomena have been proposed, some within a Construction Grammar framework. Such explanations involve the pragmatic **information structure** of sentences. Information structure is about such functions as Topic and Focus. For example, the sentence *John cooked the chicken* and its passive counterpart *The chicken was cooked by John* have different information structure but identical propositional meaning. Likewise, *As for the chicken, it was John that cooked it* has another, somewhat more complex information structure. Different information structures can be incompatible with each other. For example, an indefinite noun phrase denotes some entity not assumed to be known to the hearer, as in *A tank came trundling down the street*. But the topicalized element in a sentence denotes an entity assumed to be known to the hearer. So *?As for a tank, it came trundling down the street* is not pragmatically acceptable, because it makes different assumptions about whether the hearer knows about the tank.

The idea of explaining island constraints in terms of pragmatic information structure was first proposed in a 1973 PhD dissertation by Erteschik-Shir.[76] It is a sign of the scant attention that linguists had paid to semantics and pragmatics at that time that she called her key notion 'semantic dominance'. This notion is now clearly recognized as being also pragmatic, often involving 'Focus'. Her central claim is 'Extraction can only occur out of clauses or phrases which can be considered dominant in some context' (p. 27). Note the reference to context, making extractability not a grammatical feature of sentences considered in isolation. It is fair to say that this idea, despite its respectable origins, did not feature centrally in syntactic theorizing for the next twenty years, probably due to the general slowness of the field in getting to grips with pragmatics. The idea is now being explored more widely. 'Most if not all of the traditional constraints on "movement"—i.e. the impossibility of combining a construction involving a long-distance dependency with another construction—derive from clashes of information-structure properties of the constructions involved' (Goldberg 2006, p. 132). '[T]he processing of information structure plays an important role with respect to constraints which have traditionally been viewed as syntactic constraints' (Erteschik-Shir 2007, p. 154). Here is a nice example of Erteschik-Shir's semantic dominance affecting the acceptability of a *Wh-* question. Compare the following sentences.

1. *I like the gears in that car*
2. *Which car do you like the gears in?*
3. *I like the girl in that car*
4. **Which car do you like the girl in?*   (Erteschik-Shir 1981, p. 665)

Example 2 is a reasonable question relating to example 1. But example 4 is not a reasonable question relating to example 3. The syntactic structures of examples 1 and 3 are the same. So the difference cannot be a matter of syntax. Pretty obviously, the difference is a matter is semantics. Gears are an intrinsic part of a car, but girls are not, a matter that Erteschik-Shir argues in more detail with examples based on discourse such as these:

1. *Sam said: John likes the gears in that car*
2. *Which is a lie—he never saw the car*

---

[76] A year earlier, Dwight Bolinger (1972) had shown the difficulty of explaining certain of the island constraints purely in grammatical terms, suggesting instead that a kind of semantic closeness could account for the facts.

3. *Sam said: John likes the girl in that car*
4. **Which is a lie—he never saw the car*   (Erteschik-Shir 1981, p. 668)

Example 2 is a reasonable discourse response to example 1. But example 4 is not a reasonable discourse response to example 3. Such examples show the involvement of pragmatic and semantic facts in these supposedly grammatical phenomena. See also Erteschik-Shir and Lappin (1979).

This kind of attack on the purely grammatical status of island constraints involves the interaction of Information Structure and sentence-processing. It is noted that not all word-strings apparently violating *Wh*-movement constraints are equally bad. The differences between them can be related to the amount of specific information encoded in the other parts of the sentence. Kluender (1992, p. 238) gives the following examples (originally from Chomsky, 1973):

Who did you see pictures of?

Who did you see a picture of?

Who did you see the picture of?

Who did you see his picture of?

Who did you see John's picture of?

These sentences are of decreasing acceptability going down the page. Of such examples, Kluender notes 'the increase in referential specificity' in the modifier of *picture(s)*. The differences between these examples are semantic/pragmatic, not syntactic.

Next, I give here an example from Goldberg's discussion. The arguments require a syntactician's grip of structure, and the judgements involved are subtle. Assume a conversational context in which someone asks the question *Why was Laura so happy?* and the reason is that she is dating someone new. Now a (somewhat oblique) reply might be *The woman who lives next door thought she was dating someone new*. Here the relevant information, that she was dating someone new, is in a subordinate clause, a 'complement' clause to the verb *thought*, and this is no block to the whole sentence being an acceptable, if oblique, answer to the question. But if that same information is expressed in a different kind of subordinate clause, a relative clause, as in *The woman who thought she was dating someone new lives next door*, this cannot be an acceptable answer to the original question, because it seems to be an answer to a different question, like *Who lives next door?* The information relevant to the original question is embedded in the wrong place in the attempted, but failing, answer. Now the link to 'constraints on movement' is this. Relative clauses, in particular, block 'movement' of a *Wh*-element out of them. So while you can say both the two sentences below:

The woman who lives next door thought she was dating WHO? [an 'echo question']

Who did the woman who lives next door think she was dating? [*Who* 'fronted']

only the first of the next two is acceptable.

The woman who thought she was dating WHO *lives next door?* [an 'echo question']

**That she's dating WHO is likely?*

**Who the woman who thought she was dating lives next door?* [failed *Wh-* movement]

Thus there is a correspondence between what, for pragmatic reasons, is an acceptable answer to a question and what had been taken to be an arbitrary constraint on a syntactic 'movement rule'.

Here's another of Goldberg's examples, involving the same question *Why was Laura so happy?* and acceptable answers to it. The first answer below is OK, but the second isn't an appropriate answer to that question.

It's likely that she's dating someone new

?That she's dating someone new is likely

And this corresponds with another restriction on possible '*Wh-* movement', as shown below.

It's likely that she's dating WHO? [echo question]

Who is it likely that she's dating? ['Fronting' of *Who* is OK]

That she's dating WHO *is likely?* [echo question]

**Who that she's dating is likely?* [failed *Wh-* movement]

Another early insight of a parallel between 'syntactic' island constraints and pragmatic facts is due to Morgan (1975). I'll give one last example from his discussion. Start with the sentence *John and somebody were dancing a moment ago*. Now, an allegedly syntactic fact about such a sentence, with its coordinate noun phrase *John and somebody*, is that you can't use a 'fronted' *Wh-* word to query one of the elements in this coordinate phrase. So **Who was John and dancing a moment ago?* is judged ungrammatical. In exactly parallel fashion, it is pragmatically inappropriate to query the original statement with the one-word question *Who?*, when intending to ask who John was dancing with. Arguing in the same vein against purely syntactic constraints on 'movement' ('extraction') rules, Kuno (1987) proposes a constraint rooted in pragmatics.

Topichood Condition for Extraction: Only those constituents in a sentence that qualify as the topic of a sentence can undergo extraction processes (i.e., *WH*-Q Movement, *Wh*-Relative Movement, Topicalization, and *It*-Clefting.   (Kuno 1987, p. 23)

Kuno's arguments engage in great detail with the postulates of generative syntactic theory. These are no vague claims unsupported by many examples. (See also Kuno and Takami 1993.) It takes a syntactician's facility for manipulating examples to grasp all such argumentation, and I am aware that non-linguists find it arcane. But it would be an ignorant response to dismiss it all as empty wrangling. Even our own language, so close to us, provides subtleties that it takes a trained mind to begin to penetrate analytically. These are genuine facts about the way sentences can be used, and which sentences are more acceptable in which circumstances. The linguistic argumentation that I have just gone through is aimed at showing generalizations across discourse pragmatic facts and facts hitherto regarded as mysteriously 'pure syntactic facts'. Those who focus on the communicative functions of syntax should take a special interest in them.

In an extensive literature on this topic which I have sampled, another concerted attack on the purely syntactic nature of island constraints, from the viewpoint of 'Cognitive Grammar' is found in Deane (1992). Well steeped in the relevant syntactic theory, in his first chapter Deane gives a detailed set of examples of how purely syntactic accounts of island constraints are either too strong or too weak to account for all the facts. Here and in a previous work (Deane 1991) he 'argues for an analysis which attempts to integrate Erteschik-Schir and Lappin's, Kuno's, and Takami's theories, arguing that the extracted phrase and the extraction site command attention simultaneously when extraction can proceed—and that potential topic and focus status are the natural means by which this can occur' (p. 23). From another pair of authors, note also 'Island constraints like the Complex Noun Phrase Constraint of Ross (1967) provide an example of a group of constraints that should probably be explained in terms of probabilistically or semantically guided parsing rather than in terms of grammar as such' (Steedman and Baldridge, in press).

Finally in this section, I address what might have been spotted as a possible equivocation on my part about whether violations of island constraints are ungrammatical or just unacceptable. Recall the four possible answers, proposed in Chapter 3, to the question of whether a given string of words is grammatical. Two of the possible answers are 'Definitely not grammatical' and 'Grammatical, but it's weird'. Weirdness can come from pragmatic clashes within an otherwise grammatical sentence. Now strings violating island constraints, like *Who did you see and Bill* and *What did John see the cat that caught?* have been judged as plain ungrammatical in linguistics, starting with Ross. And my intuition is also that they violate grammatical conventions. But if we can trace the problem with such examples to violations of pragmatic principles, don't we have to say that they are (apparently) grammatical but pragmatically deviant? Well, no, I can have my cake and eat it, thanks to the diachronic process of grammaticalization. What is deviant for pragmatic reasons in one generation can become fixed as ungrammatical in a later generation, and vice-versa. Recall another part of the discussion in Chapter 3, and a relevant quote from Givón: 'a language may change the restriction on referential-indefinites under negation over a period of time, from a restriction at the competence level (as in Hungarian, Bemba, and Rwanda) to a restriction at the performance or text-count level (as in English and Israeli Hebrew)' (Givón 1979a, p. 100). I would claim that canonical violations of island constraints in English have become conventionally ungrammatical. The grammaticality facts can be different in other languages, with different histories of the conventionalization of pragmatic acceptability. Hawkins (1994) gives examples of different grammaticality facts concerning constraints on 'extraction'/'movement' in three well-studied languages, English, Russian, and German. Hawkins identifies four grammatical patterns across these languages, which I will label A, B, C, and D for convenience. It does not matter here what these specific patterns are; what matters is that they are found in all three languages and that 'movement' out of them is differentially (un)grammatical across the languages. Hawkins' summary is:

WH-movement on A: always OK in English, German, Russian
    B: OK in English and Russian, not always in German
    C: OK in English, not in German (standard) or Russian
    D: not OK in English, German, Russian.
        (Hawkins 1994, p. 48) [with modified example labels]

Child learners of these three languages learn (and store) somewhat different sets of *Wh-* constructions.

4.9 Wrapping up

In this brief survey chapter, I have tried to stay reasonably theory-neutral, finding the most common ground between theories often presented as alternatives. Behind diverse terminology, I believe there lurks much significant convergence between recent syntactic theories. Linguists in particular will be painfully aware that I have barely scratched the surface of syntactic structure in this chapter. The chapter has been mostly aimed at non-linguists, with the goal of convincing them how much complex texture and substance there can be to syntactic structure. Complexity in syntax, and the ease with which humans master it, has been seen as the most crucial problem for the evolution of language. Accounts of the evolution of language that take no heed of the theoretical issues that syntacticians have struggled with are seriously missing a point. The syntacticians' struggles are not with mythical monsters summoned from the vasty deeps of their imaginations, but facts about what is (un)grammatical, or (un)acceptable, or (un)ambiguous, in languages. Many of such basic facts have been cited in this chapter. We could be resolutely uncurious about these facts. Why do apples fall? Well, they just fall, that's all there is to it. If you want to explain the evolution of the unique human capacity for grammar, you have to have a good look at it, and try to encompass all the facts in as economical and insightful framework as is possible.

CHAPTER 5

What Evolved: Languages

The last chapter was about what features of language are accessible to all human learners, give or take some individual variation and rare cases of pathology. That was all about human **potential**. Put a group of healthy children in a rich linguistic environment, and they will learn the richly structured complex language of the community. We said nothing about how complex typical languages are (or how typical complex languages are!). Languages are not all equally complex. Does this mean that humans in groups who speak less complex languages are innately lacking in the potential to learn complex languages? Obviously not. This basic point marks the difference between the topics of this chapter and the last. Languages are subject both to forces of creation and to forces of destruction, to use Guy Deutscher's (2005) evocative terms. Languages get to be complex over historical time, by cultural evolution. That is, they evolve through a cycle of learning from examples in one generation, leading to the production of examples by the learners, from which a subsequent generation can learn. In a long-term evolutionary account, the broad story must be one of complexification. Today's complex languages have evolved from simpler ones. When languages occasionally get simpler, they may revert to, or near to, some prior evolutionary state. We will look at features common to simple modern languages which seem likely to be those of the earliest languages. We will also get a glimpse, in some modern phenomena, of the early stages by which languages start to get more complex.

Languages evolve culturally, and in very diverse circumstances. Some are spoken by hundreds of millions of speakers spread around the globe, some are spoken by only a few hundred, known to each other personally. Speakers of some languages are monolingual, speakers of many other languages are practically bilingual or trilingual in their everyday dealings. Some languages have long written traditions, others have no written form used by their speakers.

Some language communities have existed with relatively limited contact with outsiders, others are used to dealing with the world as it passes through their streets. All these factors make a difference to what languages are like.

5.1 Widespread features of languages

There are in fact rather few features that all languages have in common. One strong candidate for an implicational universal is suggested by Dryer (1992): 'complementizers in VO languages seem invariably to be initial; in fact, it may be an exceptionless universal that final complementizers are found only in OV languages' (p. 101).[1] But typically, some language somewhere can be relied upon to provide a counterexample to almost any feature claimed to occur in all languages. Bill Croft puts it only a little too strongly in claiming 'anyone who does typology soon learns that there is no synchronic typological universal without exceptions' (Croft, 2001, p. 8).[2] In the same vein, Evans and Levinson (2009) argue emphatically against the idea of a closed set of 'universals' dictating the common pattern to which all languages are built. The issue is domain-specificity. 'Although there are significant recurrent patterns in organization, these are better explained as stable engineering solutions satisfying multiple design constraints, reflecting both cultural-historical factors and the constraints of human cognition' (Evans and Levinson, 2009, p. 429). Humans are ingenious and clever. Given enough motivation, they can bend themselves to conform to some very bizarre conventions, but always within limits. Humans can push up to the limits. Things get more difficult, either to learn or to use, as one approaches the limits. Mostly, such mental gymnastics are not required, and broad statistical generalizations hold about the shared systems upon which communities settle, that is their languages. This is the subject matter of linguistic typology.

Of the universally learnable features of language surveyed in the previous chapter, languages 'pick and choose' how extensively, if at all, to use them. What features, out of the total possible set, any given language possesses is a result of that language's particular evolution, in which historical accident can play a large part. Languages adapt, over the generations, to what their human

---

[1] A complementizer is a little word introducing a subordinate clause, like English *that*, French *que*, or German *dass*. A VO language is one where a verb precedes its object, as in English; an OV language is one where a verb follows its object, often coming at the end of the sentence, as in Japanese or Turkish.

[2] Croft relents on this extreme statement later on, admitting 'Proforms such as pronouns are probably universal for phrasal arguments and adjuncts' (p. 188).

users find easiest and most useful. There are many compromises between competing pressures. What is easiest for a speaker to produce (e.g. slurred indistinct speech or unclear reference) causes difficulties for a hearer. Easy production can't be pushed too far, because speakers need to be understood. What is easy for a child to learn is not the same as what is easy for an adult to learn. Children can rote-memorize from one-off experiences more easily than adults; adults tend to look for systematic regularities, rules. The synchronic state of any language is the outcome of being filtered through all these competing pressures, which are not completely uniform across societies. For example, in some small groups speakers can afford to make their meanings less explicit than in large groups where contact between strangers is more common. Likewise in some groups, at some stages in history, the burden of language transmission is carried more by younger people than in other groups at other stages.

What is uniform across societies is the distribution of innate learning abilities as discussed in Chapter 3, with respect to the saliently learnable features of languages as discussed in Chapter 4. We can expect languages richly to exemplify those features that humans have evolved to be good at. These will be in the centre of the distribution of features that languages have. We can also consider the tail(s) in the distribution of learnable features across languages in two different ways, as a tail of languages, and as a tail of features. The tail of languages will be a small bunch of structurally unusual languages, which for some reason have evolved in historically atypical ways. There are outlier languages with respect to each of the various learnable features. Indeed the most eccentric languages are outliers with respect to a number of features. We will see some such 'eccentric' languages later in this chapter. On a subjective impression, probably no language is overall very eccentric (how long is a piece of string?); all are clearly recognizable as human languages. The other kind of tail in the distribution of features of languages is a tail of features. This will include unusual properties found in very few languages. The learnable features of language surveyed in the previous chapter (massive storage, hierarchical structure, word-internal structure, syntactic categories, long-range dependencies, and constructions) are in the centre of the distribution of features that languages have. Many languages exploit these features, although to differing degrees. Examples of unusual properties found in rather few languages, statistically speaking, 'tail properties', include the high number of noun classes in Bantu languages, and the high number of case inflections in Finnish and Hungarian. These are not, in their overall structure, outlier languages, but they have (at least) one outlier property. Such outlier properties, it can be presumed, are ones which are not so readily transmitted from one generation to the next, for example because they are not easy to learn, or not easy to control in production.

5.2 Growth rings—layering

Despite the extreme rarity of exceptionless universals, there are features that languages tend strongly to have 'with far greater than chance frequency' as Greenberg (1963) put it in his ground-breaking paper. Many of these are implicational generalizations, of the form 'If a language has feature X, it has feature Y'. Some of the strong implicational tendencies have obvious evolutionary interpretations. A simple case is Greenberg's 'No language has a trial number unless it has a dual. No language has a dual unless it has a plural' (Greenberg, 1963, Universal 34). It is easy, and not wrong, to relate this with a natural path of evolution in a language. A language with a dual can only evolve out of a language with a plural; and a language with a trial can only evolve out of a language which already has a dual. Not all implicational universals can be so readily interpreted in evolutionary terms; see Hurford (2009) for some further discussion.

The plural/dual/trial example tells a diachronic story. If dual number can only evolve in a language which already has plural number, it follows that in a language with both, plural number is an older feature than dual number. This introduces the general idea that languages have **layers** of features which are a clue to their history, like the growth rings in a tree. I will illustrate with my favourite example, from numeral systems, where the facts are nice and clear.[3]

With very few exceptions, if a language has a precise expression for any number, it has a precise expression for all lower numbers.[4] We'll concentrate on the lower end of the scale. Many languages have precise words for only 1, 2, and 3. After that there may be a word translatable as 'many'. There are no languages (of course) with exact words for 4, 5, and 6, but without words for 1, 2, and 3. The lowest-valued numeral words form the foundation of a system to which later expressions are added. Now in many languages, the first few numerals, sometimes up to 2, sometimes to 3, sometimes to 4, have peculiarities that distinguish them from slightly higher-valued numeral words. In English, the ordinals of 1 and 2, namely *first* and *second* are suppletive, totally irregular in their relation to the cardinals *one* and *two*. The next ordinal *third* is also somewhat, but less, irregular. The next one, *fourth*, is perfectly regular, formed by suffixing *-th* to the cardinal. The historic roots of *first*

---

[3] There is extensive discussion of these ideas of evolutionary growth of numeral systems in Hurford (1987).

[4] An exception is noted by Derbyshire (1979a), who claims that Hixkaryana, an Amazonian language, has numerals for 1–5 and 10, but not for 6–9. (We are dealing with positive integers only here.)

and *second* are old forms, whose origin predates the introduction into the ancestor language of forms for the regular ordinals from which *fourth, fifth, sixth,* . . . are descended. See Hurford (2001a) for many more examples of how languages treat 1–4 specially. The reasoning here is a special case of internal reconstruction of earlier stages of a language.

We can see more layering a bit further up in the numeral sequence. Again, English examples will do. From 13 to 19, single numeral words are formed by prefixing a lower-valued morpheme to *-teen,* as in *thirteen, four-teen,* . . . *nineteen.* The order of elements is LOW + HIGH. After 20, numerals are also formed by addition, but now with the elements in the opposite arithmetic order HIGH + LOW, as in *twenty-one, forty-three, sixty-seven, ninety-nine.* The *-teen* expressions are older than the additive expressions over 20. These differences in age are in fact very ancient, as Proto-Indo-European had numerals at least up to 100. We can envisage an even earlier stage when the highest-valued numeral expressed 20. When numerals for numbers above 20 were first formed, they did not follow the earlier established pattern. The discontinuity in additive constructions at 20 can be seen in all Indo-European languages, from Gaelic to Bengali. Over 20, the pattern is not always HIGH + LOW, cf. German *einundzwanzig* 'one and twenty', but the pattern is not the same as for the numbers below 20.

Paul Hopper gives another example of synchronic layering reflecting diachronic growth.

Within a broad functional domain, new layers are continually emerging. As this happens, the older layers are not necessarily discarded, but may remain to coexist with and interact with the newer layer.

a. *Periphrasis: We have used it* (newest layer)
b. *Affixation: I admired it* (older layer)
c. *Ablaut: They sang* (oldest layer)   (Hopper 1991, pp. 22–4)

Hopper's example of the oldest layer, so-called 'Ablaut' or 'vowel gradation' preserves an ancient feature from Proto-Indo-European, dating from at least 5,000 years ago. In this language, the past tense and past participles of verbs were indicated by changing the vowel in the stem of the verb. In English, this survives only in a small number of verbs, for example *sing/sang/sung, drive/drove/driven, break/broke/broken.* Hopper's 'older layer' illustrates the past tense formed by adding a suffix with a dental (or alveolar) stop consonant, spelled *-ed* in English. This way of indicating past tense developed in the Germanic languages after they had split off from Proto-Indo-European about 2,500 years ago in Northern Europe, and is thus a younger feature. Finally,

Hopper's 'newest layer' reflects a development in Middle English (ME).[5] Fennell (2001) writes

There are not as many compound verbs [in ME] as in present-day English, but they do start appearing in ME. The perfect tense became common in ME with *be* and *have* as auxiliaries...

ðou havest don our kunne wo
you have done our family woe   (Fennell 2001, p. 105)

Thus modern English has preserved ways of expressing pastness which variously date back to different earlier stages in its history.

   Another example of language change leaving a modern trace is given by Nichols (1992).

We have seen several examples here where grammatical morphemes are formally renewed and the old forms remain in predictable semantic and functional ranges. Section 4.1 noted that independent pronouns frequently renew possessive affixes, and when this happens a common outcome is that the old possessive affixes remain as markers of inalienable possession while the new ones mark alienable possession.

                                                       (Nichols 1992, p. 270)

The key point here is that at some stage in the languages Nichols discusses a new possessive marker arose. It did not entirely displace the old possessive marker, but exists alongside it in the modern language, with the two possessive markers now having more specialized senses. One marker is for 'inalienable possession', the kind of possession that one cannot be deprived of, for example by theft or sale. Inalienable possession, in languages that make it explicit, involves words for bodyparts and some kinship relations. Your head is always your head; even if it should become separated from your body and taken by another person, it is still 'your' head. And your mother is always your mother (unlike your wife, who may become someone else's wife). Some languages have a special marker for this kind of inalienable possession. In the languages that Nichols discusses, the old possessive markers became specialized to this inalienable sense, while the new markers denote all other kinds of possession.

   The examples given so far reflect stages in the history of individual languages. Languages also present many examples of a more ancient kind of layering, where different types of expression reflect different evolutionary stages of the language faculty itself. In each language, we find vestigial one-word expressions and proto-syntactic (2-, 3-word) constructions keeping company with more fully elaborate syntax. Most languages have the possibility of conveying

---

[5] There were parallel developments in related languages.

propositional information without the benefit of syntax. English speakers use a single word, *Yes* or *No* and pragmatic inference identifies the particular proposition which is being confirmed or denied. Few languages lack such devices. They are a part of their language—just not of interest to syntacticians. And of course all languages have other one-word expressions used for specific pragmatic purposes, for example *Ahoy!* and *Ouch!*. Interjections, as they are called, resist integration into longer sentences. You can put *Yes* at the beginning of a sentence, as in *Yes, I will*, or, less commonly, at the end, as in *He's coming, yes*, but it won't go anywhere in the middle.[6] Despite their name, they can't be interjected into sentences.

Putting words together without any explicit marker of their semantic relation to each other (as in word soup) is, we can reasonably suppose, a primitive type of syntax. Grammatical constructions with dedicated function words indicating how they are to be interpreted came later. Mere juxtaposition is found in compound nouns, like *boy wonder*, *village chief*, and *lion cub*. Jackendoff (2002) sees compounding by juxtaposition as 'symptomatic of protolinguistic "fossils"'. Compounds are 'a plausible step between unregulated concatenation and full syntax' (p. 250). If someone comments that something is 'funny', it has become conventional to resolve the ambiguity of this word by asking whether she means *funny ha-ha* or *funny peculiar*, exploiting the ancient device of mere juxtaposition. In this case the word order has become fixed with the head word first. But similar ad hoc disambiguating compounds put the head last. I know two Toms, and we refer to one as *squash Tom* and the other as *work Tom*. Besides such noun–noun compounds, Progovac (2009, p. 204) mentions verb–noun compounds such as *pickpocket*, *scarecrow*, and *killjoy* as similar vestigial constructions.[7] Other Indo-European languages have them too, as in French *porte-avions* 'aircraft carrier' and *tire-bouchon* 'corkscrew'. However, verb–noun compounds may not be quite so vestigial. They seem to be parasitic upon more developed syntax, since they exhibit the same verb–object order as verb phrases in their respective languages. In languages where the verb follows its object (SOV languages), the order in such compounds is noun–verb, as in Burmese *hkapai-hnai*, POCKET + DIP, 'pickpocket', or Persian *jibbor* POCKET + TAKE-AWAY, 'pickpocket' (Chung 1994). In these cases, the compounding seems to have taken notice of the order of verb and object in more fully syntactic constructions.

---

[6] Of course, *yes* may be **quoted** in the middle of a sentence, as in *If the answer is yes, we'll leave at once*, but that is a different matter.

[7] I am only dealing here with verb–noun compounds with a 'nouny' meaning, not compounds with a 'verby' meaning, like *babysit*.

Those examples are referring expressions, proto-NPs. Simple juxtaposed pairs of words also convey whole propositions, predicating some property of a referent. Progovac (2009) uses a telling title, 'Layering of grammar: vestiges of protosyntax in present-day languages'. She gives the following nice examples: *Him retire?*, *John a doctor?*, and *Her happy?*, with interrogative force; *Me first!*, *Family first!*, and *Everybody out!*, with something like imperative force; and *Class in session*, *Problem solved*, *Case closed*, and *Me in Rome*, with declarative force (p. 204). These are called 'Root Small Clauses' in the literature. As Progovac notes, they lack the usual paraphernalia of 'whole' clauses, such as tense markers and subject–verb agreement. Furthermore, it is not possible to embed such small clauses into others; mostly they can only stand alone as main clauses. A few can be embedded into similarly primitive compounds, as in *a me-first attitude*. Thus these are similar to interjections. Indeed one can see them as slightly complex interjections. But they survive in languages, alongside the more elaborate machinery of complex sentence formation.

As Progovac notes, layering is common in all evolved systems and organisms. We find it in the brain, with the recently evolved neocortex co-existing with more ancient diencephalon and basal ganglia. We see layering in cities:

> Our language can be seen as an ancient city: a maze of little streets and squares, of old and new houses, and of houses with additions from various periods; and this surrounded by a multitude of new boroughs with straight regular streets and uniform houses.[8]   (Wittgenstein, 1953, ¶18)

So it's no surprise that both individual languages and the language faculty exhibit layering.

5.3 Linguists on complexity

Linguists have traditionally, and confidently, asserted that all languages are (roughly) of equal complexity. A surprisingly unguarded statement of what many linguists still teach their first-year students is: '[M]odern languages, attested extinct ones, and even reconstructed ones are all at much the same level of structural complexity or communicative efficiency' (McMahon 1994, p. 324). Evidently linguists have believed they were making a factual statement. There was public educational value in making the statement, because non-linguists might otherwise have been tempted to assume some correlation between material culture and linguistic complexity. For instance, a layperson,

---

[8] This, as it happens, was the epigraph to my first book (Hurford 1975). Déjà vu!.

unfamiliar with linguistics, might assume a tight correlation between hunter-gatherer communities, using the simplest of material technologies, and the simplest of languages. We know, of course, that this is not the case. The classic statement is Sapir's:

Both simple and complex types of language of an indefinite number of varieties may be found at any desired level of cultural advance. When it comes to linguistic form, Plato walks with the Macedonian swineherd, Confucius with the head-hunting savage of Assam. (Sapir 1921, p. 234)

The second half of Sapir's statement, featuring the Macedonian swineherd, is the more memorable and most often cited, but note the first half, which admits that 'both simple and complex types of language...may be found'. So Sapir apparently held that some types of language are simple and some complex. Difficulty of learning is naturally equated with complexity. When linguists are asked by non-linguists which is the hardest, or the easiest, language to learn, the answer they usually give is that no language is intrinsically harder to learn as a first-language learner than any other. It's only second languages that can appear hard, depending on what your first language is. Spanish comes easily to Italians; Dutch comes easily to someone who knows German. But Hungarian is a headache for a native English speaker. Maggie Tallerman (2005, p. 2) expresses this typical position: 'Greek isn't intrinsically hard, and neither is Swahili or Mohawk or any other language, although languages certainly differ with respect to which of their grammatical features are the hardest for children to learn as native speakers'.[9]

Linguists agree with Tallerman that certain parts of some languages are less complex than the corresponding parts of other languages. It is uncontroversial, for instance, that the morphology of the Chinese languages, to the extent that they have any morphology at all, is less complex than that of agglutinating languages, such as Turkish or Bantu languages. The case systems[10] of Latin, Russian, or German are more complex than anything similar in English, and take longer to acquire by children in those communities. Here the idea of compensating complexity elsewhere in the overall system is usually mentioned.

---

[9] Tallerman does not believe that all whole languages are equally complex, in sympathy with the discussion below.

[10] A case system is a system for marking nouns and noun phrases according to their grammatical role in sentences; typically, Subjects of sentences are marked with affixes of a class known as 'Nominative', Direct Objects are marked with 'Accusative' case affixes, and so on. In some languages, such as Hungarian and Finnish, these grammatical case-marking systems merge with systems for expressing meanings that would be expressed in English with prepositions such as *on*, *for*, *by*, and *to*. Such languages may have as many as sixteen different cases, which of course children must learn.

A language which marks Subject and Object with specific markers can afford to be freer in its word order than a language without such markers. Latin and German, for example, are typically freer than English to put non-Subjects first in a sentence, and postpone expression of the Subject until late in the sentence. So, it appears, the more fixed word-order system of English takes up the slack left by the absence of case-marking. And, related to issues of complexity, it is typically assumed that the claimed complexity of a more fixed word-order system balances the complexity of a case system; in short, a language can buy some way of making grammatical roles clear, and whatever system it buys, it pays roughly the same price in complexity. But no one ever quantifies the price.

Likewise, some languages have more complex systems for marking tenses on verbs than others. And tense-marking is sometimes combined with marking for other aspects of verbal meaning, such as whether the event expressed really happened, or is in some doubt, or may possibly happen, or took a long time to happen, or is just about to happen.[11] French is a familiar example, with its present indicative, present subjunctive, future, conditional, past indicative, and past historic 'tenses'. Other languages make such meanings clear using particular separate words or phrases, such as English *maybe, a long time ago, began to* and *supposedly*. Here again, it could be claimed that complexity in one part of a language balances simplicity in another part: either you have to learn complex verbal morphology, or you have to learn a bunch of separate words. Either way, what you learn takes about as much effort. But again, nobody has measured the actual effort involved in learning a whole language.

Complexity and expressive power are often mentioned in the same egalitarian, and somewhat dismissive, breath. But the two concepts should be separated. All languages, it is sometimes said, have equal expressive power. To the obvious objection that the languages of non-technological societies have no words for MICROCHIP or PLUTONIUM, an answer often given is that the statement refers to languages' **potential**, rather than to their actual capabilities. The required words, either borrowed or newly coined, could easily be added to the existing lexicon, without disturbing the structural pattern of the language. Admittedly, even English speakers have only a rough idea what *plutonium* means, as we need an expert to tell us whether something is plutonium or not.[12] But we do have a better idea of plutonium than the Macedonian swineherd, who also has no concept of nuclear fission, atomic weights, or radioactivity.

---

[11] Linguists call such features of meaning 'aspect' and 'mood', with some terminological flexibility.

[12] As pointed out by Putnam (1975), with his argument for the social 'division of linguistic labor'.

The alternative idea, that a language could, without new words, provide long circumlocutions for these meanings, is not satisfactory, because it is doubtful whether the circumlocutions would capture the same meanings accurately. So it is reasonable to conclude that some languages, due to their limited lexicons, provide less expressive power than others. A thoughtful article, with plenty of examples comparing the expressive power of languages in various domains can be found in Gil (1994a); a witty exposé of the fallacy that Eskimo languages have scores of different words for snow is found in Geoff Pullum's article 'The Great Eskimo Vocabulary Hoax' (Pullum 1989).

Beside lexical deficiencies, languages can also lack structural means of expressing concepts which can be expressed in other languages. Uncontroversially, many Australian languages don't have a numeral system at all (Dixon 1980); they may have words for TWO or THREE, but no way of combining them syntactically to express higher values, such as 273 or 5,009. Clearly, the numeral 'systems' of these languages are less complex than those of, say, European languages. The lack of expressions for higher numbers in some languages is surely correlated, at least statistically, with cultures in which trade and the accumulation of material goods are not important. Note, however, that ancient Hawaiian, dating to before the advent of Europeans, had a complex numeral system, allowing the expression of precise numbers up to multiples of 400,000, and above by addition to these.[13]

Descriptive field linguists cannot afford to assume that languages are simple, or lack expressive power. It is imperative to search for all the complexity that can be found. If, after extensive study, field linguists cannot find complexities in their chosen languages, they must report that the system is simple. This only happens extremely rarely. There have been two cases recently where a well qualified linguist, after much field study, has concluded that a language is in fact surprisingly simple, lacking many of the complex syntactic structures that linguists are used to finding. One case is that of Pirahã, an Amazonian language studied by Dan Everett (2005; 1986; 1987), and the other is Riau Indonesian, studied by David Gil (1994b; 2001; 2005; 2009). I will discuss these two cases shortly below, but suffice it to say here that these reports are controversial.[14] and that these languages have been studied on the spot by few other researchers who have published their findings. Thus, a basic scientific

---

[13] Data on the ancient Hawaiian numeral system can be found in Humboldt (1832–39); Andrews (1854); anonymous French Catholic missionary (1834); von Chamisso (1837); Beckwith (1918); Fornander (1878); Conant (1923); Judd et al. (1945). An analysis of this ancient system is in Hurford (1975).

[14] The meat of the Pirahã debate appears in Everett (2009) and Nevins et al. (2009b).

requirement, replication of results, is not yet at a satisfactory level. The matter is not helped by what Everett's opponents say are contradictions of both fact and analysis between his early work on the language and the later work in which he claimed radical simplicity for Pirahã. It seems fair to say that Gil's work and Everett's later work have drawn attention to two languages, Pirahã and Riau Indonesian, which they show to be simpler than many linguists have thought languages could be.

As a heuristic, it is always reasonable to assume that any language will turn out to have interesting complexities if we study it intensively for long enough. But given that the intuitive notion of complexity really is meaningful, despite its extreme operational elusiveness, there is no reason to expect that all languages are equally complex. Consider any naturally collected set of objects, such as oak trees, or sparrows, or blood samples, where some property of the objects, such as their height, or number of feathers, or cholesterol content, is measurable. In all cases the expectation is that the objects will vary around an average, often with a normal distribution. Why should languages be any different? A theoretical possibility is that there is some universal ceiling of complexity that all languages are pushed to by the need of speakers to communicate in some kind of standard-model human group. But there is no glimpse of such a theory being substantiated. The reasonable null hypothesis, then, is that languages vary in complexity.

A simple impressionistic way to quantify complexity in some domain is to count the elements. For instance, phonological complexity may be quantified by the number of phonemes; complexity of inflectional morphology can be quantified by the number of inflectional morphemes; and so on. Nichols (2009) has done this for some fairly large samples of languages, and arrived, in all cases except one, at bell-shaped curves for the complexity of languages in various domains. For example, in a sample of 176 languages, the most common number of inflectional morphemes was four—twenty-nine languages had this many inflectional morphemes; from zero up to four, there is a graded rise in number of languages showing the respective degree of inflectional complexity; after four, there is a graded decline in number of languages, to the extreme case where three languages have as many as thirteen inflectional morphemes. This upper end of the scale, shown as a bar chart, has a few hiccups, to be expected in a relatively small sample. But the gross shape is a bell curve, slightly skewed toward the lower end, so that the modal number of inflections is slightly lower than the average number. Nichols got similar bell curve results for phonological complexity, complexity of noun-class system, and complexity of a small subsection of the lexicon. She pooled all her data, and again arrived at a bell curve for 'total' complexity of the languages in her survey. Obviously this is crude, since only a few among many possible measures have been selected. But the study successfully establishes the point that languages, like most other natural objects, vary in their measurable properties, along roughly normal distributions. Given these assumed definitions of complexity, languages vary in complexity, with a modal value occupied by more languages than any other value, and some languages simpler than this, and others more complex.

If languages were equally complex overall, we would expect a negative correlation between the complexity of one part of the grammar and that of some other part. Complexity in one subsystem should compensate for simplicity in the other. Here again, Nichols has collected relevant data. She 'tested correlations between the different grammar domains and some of their sub-components, doing two-way correlations using all possible pairings. ... There were no significant negative correlations between different components of grammar. ... it is more telling that no negative correlations emerged on either set of comparisons, as it is negative correlations that support the hypothesis of equal complexity' (pp. 115, 119). Sinnemäki (2008) also tested the 'trade-off' hypothesis on a balanced sample of fifty languages, in the domain of strategies for marking the core arguments of a verb. He did find a significant correlation between 'free' word order and case-marking on nouns. Word order and case-marking are alternative ways of doing the same job, making clear who does what to whom. But overall, 'the results justify rejecting trade-offs as an all-encompassing principle in languages: most of the correlations were small or even approaching zero, indicating no relationship between the variables' (p. 84). Gil (2008) also tested the '*Compensation Hypothesis* that isolating languages make up for simpler morphology with greater complexity in other domains, such as syntax and semantics' (p. 109). A cross-linguistic experiment (see below in section 5.5) provided results against this hypothesis. So far then, the most systematic studies, still quite crude, point to variable overall complexity among languages. We should not be surprised. (See Gil 2001, p. 359 for a crisp summary of the expected variation in complexity of subsystems and 'overall' complexity of languages.)

In some cases, complexity in one part of a grammar necessarily implies concomitant complexity in another part.

Thus, there could hardly be a [morphological] distinction between Nominative, Dative, and Accusative case without there being syntactic rules that determine their distribution, and the [morphological] person and number distinctions in verbs entail rules that regulate the agreement between Subjects and verbs. Strangely enough, this positive correlation between certain types of morphological and syntactic complexity, which must be more or less universally valid, is rarely noted in discussions of the complexity invariance assumption.   (Dahl 2009, p. 57)

Such positive correlations, and Nichols' findings of no 'balancing' in complexity between the subsystems of languages, with the inference that some languages are overall more complex than others, also lead to the conclusion than some languages are, overall, harder than others to acquire as a first language. Slobin (1985–97), in a long-term project, has explored the 'hypothesis of specific language effects' in language acquisition. The project, with contributions from researchers on a wide range of typologically different languages, has found many instances of differential speed of learning related to the differing complexity of subsystems of languages.

One countable property of languages in Nichols' survey stands out as not conforming to the normal, bell-shaped distribution. This is 'syntax'. To be sure, the property measured was only a small fragment of the syntactic repertoire offered by any language, but it is nevertheless a central property of any language's syntax. Nichols counted the

- number of different alignments between noun arguments, pronoun arguments, and verb. Stative–active or split-S alignment was counted as two alignments. Neutral alignment was not counted.
- number of different basic word orders. A split like that between main and non-main clauses in most Germanic languages counts as two orders.

(Nichols 2009, pp. 113–14)

Glossary:

Alignment is the system of case-markings signalling the subjects of intransitive verbs and the subjects and objects of transitive verbs. Familiar European systems like Latin, Greek, German, and Russian, where subjects of both transitive and intransitive sentences both take the same, 'nominative' case, are not the only possibility. In so-called **ergative** languages, both the subject of an intransitive (e.g. *John* in *John slept*) and the object of a transitive (e.g. *John* in *I killed John*) are marked with the same case, often called 'absolutive', while the subject of a transitive is marked with another, usually called 'ergative'. There is no standard by which the ergative way of expressing relationships can be judged to be more or less faithfully reflective of the situations described than the more familiar European nominative–accusative way. Some languages have mixed systems, doing it the 'European' nominative–accusative way for pronouns and the ergative–absolutive way for nouns, or in different ways depending on the tense of the verb. Nichols would count such a mixed system as showing two syntactic alignments.

In a **split-S** system subjects of verbs are marked differently according to some property of the verb, typically the degree of volition expressed.

From a sample of 215 languages, the curve for a count of these alignment and word-order possibilities showed a clear preference for simpler systems. The greatest number of languages in the sample used only two possibilities. More complex systems, using more possible alignments or basic word-orders, were decreasingly common. The decrease in numbers from simplest to most complex was steep and smooth. There was no bell-shaped curve. So this central factor in syntax is one area where languages tend not to go for some intermediate level of complexity, as in phonology or inflectional morphology, but gravitate toward the simpler end of the scale of possibilities.

So far, all this discussion has been about complexity in the conventional code of form–meaning mappings constituting a language. I have mentioned examples where some part of the conventional code of a language might be complex, but this may be compensated by simplicity elsewhere in the conventional code, which a child must learn. But language use does not rely wholly on encoding messages and decoding signals by a conventional code. Pragmatic inference plays a large role in all language use. Mandarin Chinese, for example, does not mark tenses on verbs, but relies on occasional use of adverbs like those corresponding to English *tomorrow*, *yesterday*, and *back then*, to make it clear when the event in question happened. But it is often left to the hearer to infer from the surrounding context when an event happened. So, where an English speaker is forced to say either *Mao came* or *Mao comes*, or *Mao will come*, a Mandarin speaker can just say the equivalent of *Mao come*, unmarked for tense, and the hearer can figure out the timeframe intended, on the basis of general principles of relevance, and not by appealing to conventionalized form–meaning mappings which are part of the learned language system. When linguists mention the complexity of languages, they are thinking of the conventional codes, described in grammars, rather than any complexity in the pragmatic inferencing processes used for interpreting expressions in rich communicative contexts.

Linguists have recently returned to the idea that languages differ in complexity, after a long break in the twentieth century when a dogma of equal complexity prevailed. Quantifying the impression that one language is simpler than another has proved difficult, but not enough to abandon the inequality hypothesis. The dominant method in arguing for the relative complexity of a system involves counting its elements, as does Nichols, cited above. 'The guiding intuition is that an area of grammar is more complex than the same area in another grammar to the extent that it encompasses more overt distinctions and/or rules than another grammar' (McWhorter 2001b, p. 135). Linguists typically don't mention Information Theory in the vein of Shannon and Weaver (1963) when counting elements in some subsystem of grammar, but the intuition is fundamentally information-theoretic, as noted by DeGraff (2001b, pp. 265–74), who mounts an intensive argument against the whole idea of applying this 'bit-complexity' concept to the comparison of languages. The problems DeGraff identifies are very real. How do you weight the number of words in a lexicon against the number of phonemes or the number of inflectional morphemes? In comparing subsystems from different languages, which syntactic theory do you assume? Facts which appear complex to one theory may appear less so in another. Bit-complexity counts storage units, but does not consider ease or difficulty of processing. In Chapter 3, I touched on the topic of the relative difficulty of processing various structural configurations, with centre-embedding being notoriously difficult to parse. A bit-counting metric comparing a grammar with centre-embedding and a grammar without it would not reveal the intuitively different complexities of these grammars. These are genuine problems: 'bit-complexity may well have no basis in (what we know about) Language in the mind/brain—our *faculté de langage*. Bit-complexity, as defined [by McWhorter (2001b)] is strictly a-theoretical: this is literally bit-counting with no concern for psychological-plausibility or theoretical insights' (DeGraff 2001b, p. 268). (But see below for a counterargument.) Probably most linguists concerned with the complexity of grammars have given up on the idea of ever defining an overall simplicity metric for whole languages. But DeGraff is in a minority[15] among those concerned with complexity in his total dismissal of the idea that there can be coherent theorizing about the relative complexity of languages, even at the level of subsystems. For myself, I believe we can make factual, if limited, statements about the relative complexity of languages. In short: 'Complexity: Difficult but not epistemologically vacuous' (McWhorter 2001b, p. 133).[16]

A connection can be drawn between a bit-counting approach to simplicity and the idea of an 'evaluation metric for language' that was a prominent part of generative theorizing in the 1960s. Chomsky's (1965) goal for syntactic theory was to model the processes by which a child, confronted with a mass of data, homes in on a single grammar,[17] out of many possible grammars

---

[15] DeGraff states that he starts from assumptions of Universal Grammar, citing several works by Chomsky, 'and its Cartesian-Uniformitarian foundations' (p. 214).

[16] For statements sceptical of the possibility of developing a workable concept of simplicity in languages, see Hymes (1971, p. 69) and Ferguson (1971, pp. 144–5). Hymes and Ferguson were linguists with an anthropological orientation. Works more prepared to grapple constructively with the notion of simplicity are Dahl (2004), and Mühlhäusler (1997).

[17] It was assumed, without significant argument, that the idealized generic child would home in on a single internalized representation. Of course, different real children may arrive at different but equivalent internal hypotheses.

consistent with the data. What the child must have, the reasoning went, is an evaluation metric which attaches the best score to the best hypothesis about the language and discards other hypotheses. 'Given two alternative descriptions of a particular body of data, the description containing fewer such symbols will be regarded as simpler and will, therefore, be preferred over the other' (Halle 1962, p. 55). The linguist's task is to discover this evaluation metric. How is this to be achieved? Part of the solution was to look at typical features of languages, and arrive at a notation in which symbol-counting gave good (low) scores for typical languages, and poor scores for less typical languages. The underlying idea, not a bad one, is that what is typical of languages reflects a child's innate preferences when 'deciding' what generalizations to internalize about the language she is exposed to. It was emphasized that the task was not to apply a priori conceptions of simplicity to language data. The right kind of simplicity metric, a notation and a scheme for counting symbols, specific to language, was to be discovered empirically by looking at languages. In the spirit of the times, it was also implicit that all languages are equally complex. Thus the direction of reasoning was the exact opposite of that in the linguists' ideas about complexity discussed above. The Chomskyan idea of the 1960s was not to measure the complexity of languages by some independent objective metric, but to use data from languages to define the metric itself. And the induced metric would be part of a universal theory of grammar. In working toward the goal of this language-specific evaluation metric, it would have been unthinkable to count some languages as contributing less heavily to the theoretical work than others. Any data from any language was admissible evidence, although data atypical of languages in general would, *ex hypothesi*, attract a poorer score. All this was couched in quite abstract terms, and no one ever got near to quantifying the likelihood of different grammars being induced by the child. At most, there was informal discussion of the relative ranking of pairs of alternative grammars. The project was much more literally interpreted and pursued in phonology than in syntax. The idea of an evaluation metric for language never fully blossomed and by the 1980s it was dropped by generative linguists.

The idea of an evaluation metric lives on in computational linguistic circles. Here the closely related ideas of **Bayesian inference, Kolmogorov complexity,** and **Minimal Description Length** (MDL) (Rissanen 1978, 1989) are invoked. A grammar is an economical statement of the principles giving rise to some body of data. If the data are essentially chaotic, then nothing short of an entire listing of the data is adequate. If the data are ruly, then some shortening or compression is possible in the description, stating generalizations over the data rather than listing all the particular facts. The complexity of a grammar is its shortest description in some agreed metalanguage. Putting it crudely, write out all the rules of the grammar and count the symbols. There's the rub—the Chomskyan idea was that we have first to discover the right metalanguage, the right notation to formulate the rules in. Goldsmith (2001) describes an algorithm that takes in a corpus as a string of letters and spaces and delivers a morphological analysis of the strings between spaces as combinations of stems and affixes. The algorithm uses 'bootstrapping heuristics', which encode human ideas about how morphology actually works, and then applies symbol-counting (MDL) methods to come up with the 'right' analysis. It's not easy, either in the construction of the algorithm or in the evaluation of results. Attempting to evaluate the results shows that, at least at the margins, there is no absolutely correct analysis. 'Consider the pair of words *alumnus* and *alumni*. Should these be morphologically analysed in a corpus of English, or rather, should failure to analyse them be penalized for this morphology algorithm? (Compare in like manner *alibi* or *allegretti*; do these English words contain suffixes?)' (p. 184).

Statistical inference methods applying Bayesian or MDL criteria to grammar learning have had some success in limited areas, such as morphological segmentation. But there is little prospect of modelling what goes on in a child's head when she learns her language because we are a long way from knowing how to represent **meanings**.[18] What a child actually learns is a mapping between a space of meanings and a space of forms. Approaches like MDL, which can be implemented well on computers, are inevitably stuck in a mode which cannot take real meaning into account. Until such time as computers get a life, with human-like attention to the world, human-like drives for social approval, and human-like understanding of the attention and drives of others, no purely formal bit-counting approach can completely model what happens when a child learns her language. But after this negative note, there is also a positive message to draw from the MDL exercise.

Not surprisingly, Goldsmith's algorithm comes up with intuitively better analyses when working on bigger corpora. Consistent with this, his general conclusions on the relationship between bit-counting statistical heuristic techniques and the nature of language are interesting and valuable.

[S]trong Chomskian rationalism is indistinguishable from pure empiricism as the information content of the (empiricist) MDL-induced grammar increases in size relative to the information content of UG. Rephrasing that slightly, the significance of Chomskian-style rationalism is greater, the simpler language-particular grammars are, and it is less

---

[18] Here I disagree with Goldsmith on the heuristic value of semantics.

significant as the language-particular grammars grow larger, and in the limit, as the size of grammars grows asymptotically, traditional generative grammar is indistinguishable from MDL-style rationalism. (Goldsmith 2001, p. 190)

Of course 'in the limit' never comes, and asymptotic relationships need to be understood in the light of numbers encountered in real life. But Goldsmith's point is that complexity makes statistical approaches to grammar induction more, rather than less, likely to be successful. Maybe the grammars of human languages, and the data they generate, are so complex that statistical techniques can get a significant grip on them, without much help from very specific a priori stipulations about the form of grammars. To bring this back to DeGraff's adverse view of the value of bit-counting approaches to the relative simplicity of languages, Goldsmith's conclusions suggest otherwise. There probably is a positive correlation between the statistically defined complexity of languages and the psychological dispositions of their learners and users. Bit-counting ways of comparing the complexity of parts of languages are not wrong, but they are fraught with dilemmas about what to count and how to count it.

5.4 Pirahã

Pirahã[19] is a language spoken by less than 500 speakers in a remote group of villages in the Amazon basin. The speakers are all first-language native speakers of the language, with little knowledge or use of Portuguese. The most intensive research on this language has been done, over more than twenty years, by Dan Everett. The biggest data-oriented publications are Everett's early ones (1986, 1987), while Everett (2005) is a later, and in the event highly controversial, paper in which he reanalysed some of his earlier data, considered new data, and drew more far-reaching theoretical conclusions. The core claims for simplicity are summarized as 'the absence of numbers of any kind or a concept of counting and of any terms for quantification, the absence of color terms, the absence of embedding, the simplest pronoun inventory known, the absence of "relative tenses", the simplest kinship system yet documented' (Everett 2005, p. 621). It should immediately be said, especially for the benefit of non-linguists, that Pirahã is not simple in the sense that it could be learned by anyone without significant ability or effort. Everett stresses that only a handful of outsiders, of whom he is one, can speak the language well, and that this ability comes from

---

[19] The tilde over the final vowel indicates nasality of the vowel, as in French *sang* or *blanc*.

many years of intensive study. Pirahã is not a pidgin. It has rich morphological (word-internal) structure and a tonal system, properties which distinguish it, as we will see later, from typical creoles.

Some of the claims for simplicity attract less theoretical attention than others. Although many native Australian languages have no numeral system, Everett's claim for Pirahã is that it does not even have a form for the exact concept ONE. This is indeed surprising, but it is a **linguistic** fact and does not reflect on the non-linguistic cognitive abilities of Pirahã speakers.

We show that the Pirahã have no linguistic method whatsoever for expressing exact quantity, not even 'one.' Despite this lack, when retested on the matching tasks used by Gordon, Pirahã speakers were able to perform exact matches with large numbers of objects perfectly but, as previously reported, they were inaccurate on matching tasks involving memory. These results suggest that language for exact number is a cultural invention rather than a linguistic universal, and that number words do not change our underlying representations of number but instead are a cognitive technology for keeping track of the cardinality of large sets across time, space, and changes in modality.   (Frank et al. 2008, p. 819)

As for 'the simplest pronoun inventory known' and 'the simplest kinship system yet documented', well, some language somewhere must have the simplest system of each type, so maybe all that is surprising is that the same language should hold so many world records. Everett also claims that Pirahã is very unusual, if not unique, in lacking syntactic embedding. Outside linguistics, say in domains like swimming or long-distance running, cases of multiple world-record-holding are attributable to some generalization over the domains. Pirahã seems to make a specialty of extreme across-the-board linguistic parsimony. The language itself as an abstraction cannot be credited with any will to 'keep it simple'. The impetus must come, Everett argues, from some force acting on the individual speakers, and he identifies a population-wide social taboo on talk about anything which is outside the domain of immediate experience. I will come later to this hypothesis about the influence of a social taboo on syntactic structure.

The issue that has generated most heat in the literature concerns the alleged lack of embedding, sometimes also referred to as recursion, in Pirahã. Recursion, often undefined except in the loosest of senses, has been seen by some as a symbolic last-ditch stand for a domain-specific innatist view of human uniqueness. This is how Hauser et al. (2002) have been interpreted, and indeed possibly how their paper was intended. It is regrettable that any intellectual battle should be fought over loosely defined terms. Everett (2009, p. 407) notes correctly that Hauser et al. never define recursion, and offers a definition: 'RECURSION consists in RULE (OR OPERATION) SETS THAT CAN APPLY

TO THEIR OWN OUTPUT AN UNBOUNDED NUMBER OF TIMES [caps in original]'. This definition, from Shalom Lappin, is commonly given, especially in computational contexts, except perhaps for the factor 'an unbounded number of times'. Computer programs run on bounded hardware, so the programs themselves are absolved from specifying finite bounds on recursive processes. Biological evolution has not had the luxury of a contemplative distinction between hardware and software. What evolves is hardware (or 'meatware'), capable of complex computations which must eventually run out of scratch-pad space. I argued in Chapter 3 that no language embeds a structure within a structure of its own type an unbounded number of times. The usual appeal to a competence/performance distinction, as a way of preserving the theoretical unboundedness of language, is not evolutionarily plausible. Competence in a language and performance limitations work together, in a single package that I labelled 'competence-plus'. The human capacity to acquire competence in a language, and to make the necessary computations, evolved biologically as UG+. UG+ starts in a modern human infant with certain built-in limitations on memory and processing, which can be stretched to a certain extent by experience during language acquisition. But they can't be stretched forever. Even we humans run out of mental road.

From this viewpoint, then, there is no issue of whether any language, for example Pirahã, exhibits unbounded recursion. No language does. The question is whether there is anything particularly surprising in the very low finite limit that Pirahã apparently respects. Most of the debate in the literature has centred around two kinds of embedding, of NPs and of clauses, and it will be useful to consider these separately here. But note before we start that most of the debate thus assumes a definition of recursion in terms of specific syntactic categories, for example NP or S. A near-final word in the debate[20] takes a less restrictive view of recursion, which I will also consider soon.

Take first NP-embedding, as in English possessives. English is very permissive here, allowing such expressions as *John's brother's neighbour's wife's mother's cat*. In contrast, Pirahã is very limited:

[E]xperiments conducted by Frank, Everett, and Gibson in January 2007 attempted to elicit multiple levels of possession and found that while a single level of possession was universally produced, no speaker produced all three roles in any nonsentential construction; all complete responses were of the form in 49. So there is no way to say 48 in a single sentence.

(48)   John's brother's house. Or John's brother's dog's house. Etc.

---

[20] Hardly anyone ever gets the last word in debates among syntacticians.

To get this idea across, one would need to say something like 49 (see Gibson et al. 2009).

(49)   Xahaigí kaifi xáagahá. Xaikáibaí xahaigí xaoxaagá. Xahaigi xaisigíai.
        'Brother's house. John has a brother. It is the same one.'

        (Everett 2009, p. 420)

Nevins et al. (2009b, p. 367) note that German has a similar restriction. They point out that you can say *Hansens Auto* 'Hans's car', but you can't embed further, with **Hansens Autos Motor* 'Hans's car's motor'. Thus according to Nevins et al., this particular constraint is not so exotic. Their example is not so clear-cut, however, since even the non-recursive *??des Autos Motor* for 'the car's motor' is at best highly marginal (one says *der Motor des Autos* 'the motor of the car'). There is a further dispute about whether this limit in Pirahã might be an arbitrary syntactic fact, or whether it can be attributed to the general social taboo that Everett invokes. Everett argues that parsimony favours the more general social explanation. More on this later.

Now let's come to the eye of this hurricane in the literature—sentential embedding. The prototypical case of sentential embedding involves mental (or intensional) verbs like English *believe, want, hope, report*, and so forth. Embedded clauses occur after these as in *John believes that Mary came*. And in English, there can be quite deep embedding, as in *Mary reported that John believed that Fred wanted her to come*. Compare Pirahã:

> The work of compiling a dictionary for Pirahã (Sakel, in preparation) has produced no grounds for creating entries corresponding to the English lexemes *think, guess, believe, bet, mean*, etc. One entry is translated as 'know', but it equally translates 'see' and refers to ability rather than to abstract knowledge.
>
> Similarly there is no entry for the deontic modality markers 'wish' and 'hope', although there is a word for 'want', which lacks a counterfactual implication.
>
> Furthermore there is no entry for 'tell' or 'pretend'. We do find an entry for 'see/watch', but this verb is only used literally as a perception verb.

> (Stapert 2009, p. 235)

The Pirahã express some thoughts that we might express with embedded clauses by using affixes of uncertainty or desiredness on a main verb. Thus English *I want to study* is expressed as a single clause glossable as I STUDY-WANT, where the morpheme for WANT is an affix on the verb for STUDY. Similarly, English *I deduce that Kaogiai is going fishing* is expressed as a single clause with a suffix *sibiga* on the verb for 'fish', indicating that the speaker's knowledge of this fact is a deduction, not from direct observation (Stapert 2009). English *The woman wants to see you* is expressed with a verb–suffix combination glossable as SEE-WANT. These examples are not unlike the Hungarian use of affixes on main verbs to express meanings that in English are expressed by modal verbs; *lát* 'see', *láthat* 'may see'. Many languages, including Hungarian, Turkish, Shona, and Japanese, use a verbal affix to express a causative meaning that in English would be expressed by an embedded clause, as in *I made him write*. As another example:

The normal equivalent of a complement [embedded] clause in Inuktitut can be expressed as a morpheme within the boundaries of the verb: There are the suffixes -*guuq* (it is said that, he/she/they say that), -*tuqaq* (it seems that), *palatsi* (it sounds like), and perhaps some others. In such cases the resulting word is like a complex sentence with a complement clause [in other languages]. (Kalmár 1985, p. 159)

So the use of verbal affixes to express meanings that in English would be expressed with an embedded clause is not so unusual. Many of these affixes in Pirahã can be translated with adverbs in English. So *I hope he'll come* and *Hopefully, he'll come* are pragmatically equivalent in context, the latter avoiding sentential embedding. Similarly, *I know for sure that he'll come* is pragmatically equivalent in context to *Definitely, he'll come*, with the latter again avoiding sentential embedding. To the small extent to which there are pragmatic differences in these pairs of English sentences, that is a distinction that Pirahã cannot make.

Nevins et al. (2009b) argue at length against Everett's no-embedding analysis of Pirahã. One central issue is whether the suffix -*sai* is a marker of an embedded clause, like English *that*, which Nevins et al. say it is, or whether -*sai* is a marker of old information, as Everett claims. The debate rests upon subtle judgements about what the real meanings of sentences are for the Pirahã. For instance, Nevins et al. claim of a certain sentence that it means *I am not ordering you to make an arrow*, whereas Everett contends that 'the proper translation is "I am not ordering you. You make the/an arrow(s)", with the looseness of interpretation in Pirahã all that is implied by the English translation' (Everett 2009, p. 409).[21] Clearly, an outsider to this debate not very familiar with Pirahã cannot hope to arbitrate in such cases. It is notable, however, that even Nevins et al, in arguing for embedding in Pirahã, never give an instance of embedding at a depth greater than 1, that is there is never a subordinate clause embedded within another subordinate clause. Thus it seems likely that, even if there is some sentential embedding in the language (contrary to the analysis of

---

[21] The reliance on translation into another language presumed to be an adequate semantic metalanguage is a general problem for all such disputes. Not much can be done about it at present, if ever.

its best-informed researcher), it never gets beyond a single subordinate clause. As argued earlier, no language has unbounded embedding, and some languages (e.g. German) tolerate a greater depth of embedding than others (e.g. English) in some structural positions. This enables us to see Pirahã not as categorically different from (most) other languages, but rather at one end of a continuum of languages ranked according to the depth of embedding that they allow. Even if Everett were not right on all details, Pirahã is both simpler and has less expressive power than many other languages. (Allegedly) lacking recursion, it provides no compact means of expressing the thoughts expressed in English by *Iago convinced Othello that Desdemona was deceiving him*[22] or *John's brother's wife's house*.

Everett's claims about lack of recursion in Pirahã belong to a genre that has sprouted sporadically over the years. These claims, that certain languages have no subordination, are sometimes refuted more or less promptly. Thompson (1977) claimed that American Sign Language (ASL) has no subordination; this was refuted by Liddell (1980). An old chestnut that resurfaces occasionally is that Proto-Indo-European had no subordinate clauses—for example Benveniste (1957); Hermann (1895)—a claim routinely doubted by other Indo-Europeanists, for example Paul (1920, p. 145). For a reconstructed language, the issue depends on the assumptions made in the reconstruction. If you are determined that the underlying plan of all languages has never changed, you are more likely to reconstruct subordinate clauses in an ancient mother tongue.

In a commonly cited article, Kalmár (1985, p. 158) mentions claims for a number of modern languages lacking clausal subordination. Most of these are problematic in some way or other. Kalmár mentions 'Chafe's comment on the total lack of formal devices of integration[23] in Seneca [A North American Indian language]' (Kalmár 1985, p. 158). But according to Chafe (1993), the use of sentence integration is a matter of degree in Seneca, and is more frequent in some spoken styles, such as ritual chanting. For Kalmár's own research specialty, Inuktitut, it is certainly clear that this language uses non-subordinating devices to express many meanings that would normally be expressed with subordinate clauses in European languages. In Kalmár's view, Meillet and Cohen (1952) claim that Australian languages have no subordination; but Dixon (1980) writes at many places in his survey of Australian languages of their methods of subordination. And as for Australian languages, the waters are considerably muddied by equivocation in the literature between the terms

---

[22] Robin Dunbar's nice example of metarepresentation.
[23] 'Sentence integration' is Chafe's term roughly corresponding to clausal subordination.

'subordinate' and 'embedding'. Hale (1976) writes of a certain type of clause in Australian languages, using the term 'subordinate'; but 'other researchers have frequently interpreted Hale's discussion as suggesting that Warlpiri doesn't have syntactic embedding—that is that it does not have 'true' subordinate clauses of the type that are familiar from many other languages' (Nordlinger 2006, p. 6). Help!

Other claims for lack of clause embedding are rare and also problematic, not least because they involve languages of small communities, usually studied by few researchers and sometimes by only one. Raible (2001, p. 4) mentions spoken Louisiana French as losing 'the difference between coordination and subordination', citing Stäbler (1975b; 1975a); Louisiana French was a language in decline when it was studied. Givón (1979a, p. 306), rather famously, writes of 'a certain type of languages—those which have only coordination ("clause chaining") but no subordination', citing Longacre (1979) and Thurman (1978). In fact, Longacre's article is about 'the paragraph as a grammatical unit', and contains no statement whatsoever about lack of clausal subordination in any language. Givón's Thurman citation is to an unpublished Masters thesis, but another publication by Thurman (1975) on the same language, Chuave, a Papuan language of the East New Guinea Highlands, mentions 'dependent clauses' which on further analysis might be claimed to be in some sense subordinate. Certainly, languages of this area, among others, use clause chaining extensively, which is not the same thing as having no subordination at all. A so-far unrefuted claim for a lack of subordination is by Foley (1986, p. 177) for Iatmul, another New Guinea Papuan language. Pullum and Scholz (2010b) discuss in some detail whether Hixkaryana, an Amazonian language unrelated to Pirahã, has genuine clause embedding, based on extensive but still inconclusive data from publications by Desmond Derbyshire, who studied the language for many years (Derbyshire 1979a, 1979b, 1976). (Hixkaryana is also an extreme outlier language in its basic word order, belonging to a handful, at most, of OVS languages (Derbyshire 1977).)

Even supposing no modern language completely lacks it, it is uncontroversial that clausal embedding is rarer in the actual productions observed in some languages. Speakers of languages with written traditions import complex sentences with subordinate clauses into their speech. Generally, subordinate clauses are rarer in speech than in writing, and rarer in the speech of non-literate societies than in the speech of literate societies. In non-literate societies, subordination can be more common in ceremonial ritual speech than in normal conversation (Schlichter 1981, p. 123). Speech to certain strangers may contain more clausal embedding than speech to familiars, as this nice anecdote of Bickerton's about Guyanese Creole illustrates:

In one hour, five guys talking together produced not a single relative clause. In the first five minutes after I returned, three came out. But the mechanism there was pretty obvious. You use relative clauses to describe things you don't think the hearer will readily identify. These five guys worked together, hunted together, and had been buddies since high school; they didn't need signposts when they talked with one another. I, the outsider, did.   (Bickerton 2008a, p. 92)

Everett evidently never had a similar experience with the Pirahã.

It is clear that in the history of languages, subordinating constructions develop out of non-subordinating constructions. The general process is one of **grammaticalization**, which will be the whole topic of Chapter 9. A couple of examples will suffice here. Across languages, it is common for a complementizer, a function word specifically introducing a subordinate clause, to have developed out of a demonstrative pronoun. As an example, take the English complementizer *that*, in both its subordinating functions, introducing a relative clause, as in *This is the man that I saw*, and introducing a 'complement' clause, as in *I know that he came*. It is generally accepted that the word in these functions derived from usage as a demonstrative pronoun in an originally separate, but contiguous, sentence. Thus, for instance, and simplifying somewhat, the sources of the above sentences would have corresponded to *This is the man. THAT I saw.* and *I know THAT. He came.* Historically, over time, these once separate sentences came to be pronounceable as a single sentence-like package, analysed as a main clause with a subordinate clause (Hopper and Traugott 1993, pp. 190–4). Similarly, Guy Deutscher (2000) shows in great detail how a particular subordinating construction arose out of adverbial constructions in Akkadian, an ancient Semitic language of Mesopotamia with a continuous history of about 2,000 years, evidence of which is (miraculously) preserved. The point is that since subordinating constructions typically develop out of non-subordinating constructions (and there is no development in the other direction), earlier languages had fewer types of subordinating construction. And extremely early languages would presumably have had no such constructions. It is interesting how few, if any, modern languages reflect this ancient totally subordinationless state. But undoubtedly some languages make less use of subordination than others.

It is significant that reports of lack of subordination come from small isolated communities (or ancient proto-languages remote in time). There could well be a linguistic analogue of quantum uncertainty happening here. You can't investigate a phenomenon without simultaneously disturbing it. An academic linguist visits a small isolated jungle community with no modern conveniences, bringing his gadgets and his attitudes (and sometimes his measles). When the linguist asks questions about what a native can or cannot say, the native is faced with an artificial dilemma of a kind he doesn't normally meet in village life. And if a few more academics come to the village with their gadgets, attitudes, and questions, and possibly attempt to make small well-intentioned changes for the imagined welfare of the natives, the local culture can begin to change. Anthropologists ideally are trained to avoid such problems, but you can never be sure what happens (or doesn't happen) when you aren't looking or asking. Linguistically trained missionaries (such as Everett who was at the beginning of his career) set out with a goal of devising a writing system for a previously unwritten language and translating the Bible into the language. It is well known that writing tends to foster the growth, in usage at least, of subordination. The possible recent emergence of subordinate clauses in written Inuktitut is discussed by Kalmár (1985, p. 163): 'there is a possibility that the relative clause is developing in written Inuktitut... To my knowledge this type of construction has not previously been noticed in the linguistic literature. It seems to be a genuine innovation, hardly a borrowing from English'. The small isolated languages for which lack of subordination has been claimed have so far resisted innovation due to contact. The Pirahã seem especially resistant to outside influence. It would be interesting to see what happens to Pirahã grammar if and when writing in Pirahã were ever to become widespread. Admittedly this seems unlikely, given Everett's reports of their total lack of interest in learning to write.

Everett attributes the cause of Pirahã's simplicity to an over-arching social 'Immediate Experience Principle' (IEP) which 'constrains communication to nonabstract subjects which fall within the immediate experience of interlocutors' (Everett 2005, p. 621). 'Immediate experience' is interpreted, against the usual meanings of the words, to include things that other people have told you. Everett also stresses that the immediate experiences of Pirahã speakers differ from those of urban Westerners, in that they (claim to) see 'spirits', which are invisible to others. 'Immediate experience', then, is a factor open to interpretation, and not satisfactorily clear enough as a basis for a testable hypothesis. Everett's constant argument for his proposal is the need for parsimony in explanations. The simplicity in all the subsystems he discusses cannot be a coincidence, he argues, and looks for a common causal factor. The absence of a creation myth in Pirahã culture is a non-linguistic fact that can also be explained by this general constraint.

Interpreting 'immediate experience' in the most natural way, the IEP proposal does a poor job of circumscribing just what Pirahã grammar can and cannot do. Embedded sentences don't necessarily describe situations outside the realm of immediate experience. For example, as Nevins et al. (2009b,

p. 364) point out, the sentence *The apple that I am now looking at is rotten* describes a single situation, using the device of sentence embedding (a relative clause), and the IEP should not block the construction. It is also not clear why the IEP should block embedding in possessives as in *John's mother's hat*. The one-ness of individual objects is surely a matter of immediate experience. The large psychological literature on subitizing indicates that the concepts TWO and THREE are also accessible to immediate experience, so why shouldn't the Pirahã have words for these concepts? Kay (2005) in his commentary on Everett's article makes a similar point about the immediacy of experience of basic colour properties, so why shouldn't Pirahã have some basic colour terms? [24]

Documented cases exist of social taboos affecting language. Here is a well known case. 'In every part of Australia a person's name cannot be spoken for some time after his death. What is more, any normal vocabulary item— noun, adjective, verb, etc.—that is similar in form to the banned name must also be tabooed' (Dixon 1980, p. 28). The Pirahã case is different, because the influence is claimed to affect syntax, over which people have rather little conscious control, especially when communicating spontaneously. I, like others, am sceptical of the IEP hypothesis. One wonders how the social prohibition is maintained and transmitted. Are there language-police who discourage any embyronic move in the direction of using a word with the exact meaning of ONE, or disparage embryonic moves to use the term for BLOOD as a colour adjective? (Think of how English *orange* as a colour adjective crept into the language.)

A bad explanation is not preferable to no explanation. I have no very specific explanation for the undoubted simplicity of Pirahã in much of its grammar and lexicon. All agree that there is no biological explanation—the Pirahã are not inbred or genetically different from many other peoples of Amazonia. The explanation, then, must in some general sense be cultural, but it is not likely to be a kind of explanation that applies only to this small group. Everett elevates Pirahã to the status of an outright exception to previously held views about language, seeing it as a real intellectual wake-up call. Indeed, any linguists who still dogmatically assert the equal complexity of all languages do need waking up. Pirahã grammar and lexicon are in many ways pretty simple. The particular subsystems discussed fall within, though at the edge of, the distribution of complexity across languages. Other subsystems of the language, notably its verbal morphology and tonal system, are more complex than can be found in many other languages. Berlin (2005, p. 635) notes that these

---

[24] I don't find Everett's reply to Kay persuasive.

features 'are also typical of the languages of small, local societies with simple cultures'. Trudgill (1992) (not in connection with Pirahã) proposes a social explanation for maintenance of morphological complexity that is similar to Everett's invocation of a strict social norm. Trudgill's proposal is more general and, unlike Everett's, not tied to a single population.

In smaller, tighter communities, I would want to argue, it is easier for the community to enforce and reinforce the learning and use of irregularities by children and adolescents (see Andersen 1988). Sociolinguistic research into the influence of social network structure (Milroy 1980; Bortoni 1985) has revealed that the dense multiplex networks typical of relatively closed, stable, non-fluid communities are more likely to lead to conformity in linguistic behaviour and to the maintenance of group norms as well as the carrying through of ongoing linguistic changes. We can suppose that similar processes will be at work in the maintenance of linguistic complexity.   (Trudgill 1992, p. 204)

The Pirahã villages are certainly a small, tight community. Trudgill's appeal to close reinforcement of group norms in such a community is a more general case of Everett's specific proposal, his Immediate Experience Principle. A difference between the two proposals is that Trudgill's (1992) hypothesis aims to explain morphological complexity, whereas Everett's Immediate Experience Principle aims to explain simplicity in non-morphology. But, as seen above, these effects can be complementary—complex morphology takes over expression of meanings that would otherwise require somewhat complex syntax. Further, Trudgill's proposal is only about the **maintenance** of complexity, and does not say how complexity, morphological or otherwise, arises in the first place. And, as Everett (2005, p. 644) notes, a proposal such as Trudgill's does not explain the (non-morphological) simplicity on which Everett focuses. (More on the causes of complexity in languages later.)

Finally on Pirahã, here is what set the cat among the pigeons. 'These constraints lead to the startling conclusion that Hockett's (1960) design features of human language, even more widely accepted among linguists than Chomsky's proposed universal grammar, must be revised. With respect to Chomsky's proposal, the conclusion is severe—some of the components of so-called core grammar are subject to cultural constraints, something that is predicted not to occur by the universal-grammar model' (Everett 2005, p. 622). Yes, the Pirahã facts are interesting and perhaps even startling to some. But they in no way falsify the hypothesis that humans are biologically equipped with the capacity to acquire grammars with embedding. The key phrase is 'capacity to acquire'. An ability to acquire a case system, or a gender system, or an auxiliary verb system—all these are part of the child's innate endowment, because any normal child can learn such systems. But not all languages have case systems, or gender systems, or auxiliary verb systems. So why should recursion be any different? A newborn baby has the capacity, but has not yet acquired a grammar, let alone one with embedding; it is like tinder needing a spark and constant oxygen to get burning. Cut off the oxygen and the fire won't start. Metaphorically, Everett's claim is that a force in Pirahã culture cuts off the oxygen from the language acquisition device. The extreme case of a culturally imposed constraint on language is that of Trappist monks, who make a vow not to use spoken language at all. Nobody suggests that Trappist monks provide a counterexample to a universal disposition to acquire complex language. Even if Everett's Immediate Experience Principle were a force impinging on the practice of Pirahã speakers, it would similarly not be a counterexample to claims for the universality of a biologically given capacity to acquire certain complex features.

The generative enterprise has held itself aloof from discussion of cultural forces shaping language. But it has always sensibly assumed that experience in a cultural setting is necessary to set the acquisition device going. The Hauser et al. recursion hypothesis says nothing about the possible influence of culture. The strong form of the Hauser et al. hypothesis is that humans have a unique capacity to acquire recursive structure in their communicative behaviour. Perhaps the rhetoric of the 'language organ' which 'just grows' is misleading, because it doesn't mention the nutrients needed for growth. No organ grows without nutrients. The language organ research programme makes predictions (different predictions depending on the specific model) about what children will learn, given appropriate input in a cultural setting con- ducive to language acquisition. But the programme typically disdains interest in the possible effects of different environmental conditions on the develop- ment of language. The assumption, unresearched within the language organ paradigm, is that all societies provide input up to the level where the full innate capacities are enabled to emerge. But they don't, as languages are not all equally complex. Some languages, probably such as the Pirahã spoken by adults, provide no trigger for children to acquire embedded sentences. '[O]ur language faculty provides us with a toolkit for building languages, but not all languages use all the tools' (Fitch et al. 2005, p. 242). Not finding a property in a language doesn't mean that humans are not equipped to acquire that property, so the fuss about the lack of recursion in Pirahã is misplaced.

I will put forward a more radical interpretation of recursion, to the effect that Pirahã has recursion merely by dint of putting words together more than once. In Chapter 1, I quoted one of Nevins et al.'s arguments against Everett. Here is a longer version of what they wrote.

Hauser, Chomsky, and Fitch (2002) presupposed, rightly or wrongly, an approach to syntactic structure in which all phrase structure—not just clausal embedding or possessor recursion—serves as a demonstration of recursion. We had this in mind when we noted in [Nevins et al. 2009b] that if Pirahã really were a language whose fundamental rule is a nonrecursive variant of Merge, no sentence in Pirahã could contain more than two words. (Nevins et al. 2009a, p. 679)

Let's not rewrite history. It was certainly not clear what Hauser et al. 'presupposed' as a defining feature of recursion; their lack of a definition has attracted much criticism. But Nevins et al.'s radical and apparently novel take on recursion, that any combination of a word with something already built by combining words counts as recursion, is useful.[25] It simultaneously defuses the claim that Pirahã lacks recursion, because Pirahã obviously combines words productively more than once, while not undermining Hauser et al.'s claim that recursion is unique to human communication. No animal communication system has this property. Nor can animals be trained to take advantage of it. (This radical interpretation of recursion does not, as I noted in Chapter 1, reduce the idea of recursion to vacuity, as recursion is still distinct from iteration. And it does make the emergence of human syntax seem less of an evolutionary miracle, as I argue briefly at the end of Chapter 7, section 4.)

5.5 Riau Indonesian

This is another language claimed to be very simple. It is spoken in an utterly different social setting from Pirahã. It has about five million speakers, many living in cities. The Riau province of Indonesia comprises a strip of the east coast of Sumatra, across the Malacca Straits from Singapore, and thousands of islands. 'Riau Indonesian' is a label conveniently given to a group of closely related Malay-derived dialects spoken in the province. 'Riau Indonesian is acquired as a native language by most or all children growing up in Riau province, whatever their ethnicity' (Gil 2004, p. 374). Many of its speakers also speak other languages. 'Riau province was the target of substantial immigration for the last two generations at least, and...some contact language,

---

[25] Bickerton (2009a, p. 243) writes provocatively that 'By proposing Merge, Chomsky assassinated recursion', seeming to claim that repeated applications of the combinatorial operation Merge with products of Merge is not recursion. In a review, Arbib (2010), correctly in my view, argues that this is a mistake. Recursion is alive and well in Minimalist theory, and in fact even more basic to language than in previous theories, according to which semantically interpreted Phrase Structure grammars were not necessarily recursive.

presumably the immediate ancestor of Riau Indonesian, would have had to
have gained wide currency' (Gil 2001, p. 330). David Gil, the main researcher
on Riau Indonesian, argues plausibly 'This, then, is the best guess that can
be hazarded for where Riau Indonesian comes from: on the basis of the
arguments presented above, it is probably most appropriately viewed as the
descendant of a long and uninterrupted line of contact languages, spoken in
the region throughout the last thousand years and maybe even longer' (Gil
2001, p. 334). Thus, by the usual criteria, it is not a creole, a historically new
language created by obvious extensive borrowing from the lexicon of another,
typically socially dominant, language. (See the next section of this chapter for
more on creoles.) The discussion here will focus on Riau Indonesian, but it 'is
but one of a range of colloquial varieties of Malay/Indonesian, spoken . . . by
a total population of over 200 million people. . . . a majority of these colloquial varieties resemble Riau Indonesian in their basic grammatical structures'
(Gil 2009, p. 24).

By Gil's account, Riau Indonesian is strikingly simple. He claims that it
comes close to the extreme simple end of three separate dimensions: isolating,
monocategorial, and associational. Gil coins the term 'IMA' to refer to a
hypothetical type of language which is purely isolating, purely monocategorial, and purely associative. I will explain these terms with examples from
Riau Indonesian. That languages can be **isolating** is not controversial. Many
languages have hardly any word-internal structure (morphology). Meanings
that in other languages might be expressed by affixes are expressed in an
isolating language by separate words. 'That Riau Indonesian is not purely
isolating is evidenced by the presence of a handful of bona fide affixes,
plus various other morphological processes, such as compounding, reduplication, and truncation. None of these processes, however, are inflectional, and
none of them are obligatory in any particular grammatical environment' (Gil
2009, p. 23). In being a language near the isolating end of the spectrum of
morphological complexity, Riau Indonesian is not particularly unusual. Let's
move on.

The idea behind **monocategorial** is more striking. A completely monocategorial language is one with no distinctions at all between word categories. A
monocategorial language makes no distinction between verbs and nouns, to
mention the categorical distinction often presumed to exist in all languages.
Of course, with no separate nouns and verbs, there are no adjectives, adverbs,
or prepositions either, as these are recognized as less entrenched categories in
languages. 'Monocategorial' could in fact be paraphrased by 'acategorial'—
lacking in category distinctions. How does a language manage without a

distinction between nouns and verbs? It's actually not so difficult, to the extent that we might well ask why languages do distinguish between nouns and verbs.

Even English allows a great many words to function either as a noun or a verb. Examples are *ace, box, cut, divide, exit, function,* and so on. In a given sentence, you tell whether a word is used as a noun or a verb by the grammatical markers attached to it. Compare *Federer served sixteen aces* with *Federer aced Roddick sixteen times,* or *gifts in boxes* with *boxed gifts,* and so on. A monocategorial language takes this all the way, and allows every word to serve as either a noun or a verb. Hey, haven't I contradicted myself, with 'serve as a noun or verb' when what we are talking about is a language having no distinction between nouns and verbs? No, a monocategorial language makes no distinction **in the lexicon** between nouns and verbs. That is, a word listed in the lexicon is not given any specification to the effect that it can only be used with tense or aspect morphemes (consigning it to use only like a verb), or can only be used with determiners (restricting it to function exclusively like a noun). See the Nootka and Tongan examples soon below. Having no noun/verb distinction doesn't mean the absence of grammar, but it does make a grammar simpler in that respect.

The English example just given shows how morphological endings such as past tense *-ed* indicate the function of a word as either noun or verb in a particular sentence. An early well known claim for a language having no noun/verb distinction was made by Swadesh (1938) about Nootka, a native American language of Vancouver Island.

Normal words do not fall into classes like noun, verb, adjective, preposition, but all sorts of ideas find their expression in the same general type of word, which is predicative or non-predicative according to its paradigmatic ending. The same word can be used now as the nucleus of the predication, now as a subsidiary element in the predication by the mere adding or dropping (or changing) of the modal ending.

(Swadesh 1938, p. 78)

By a 'modal ending', Swadesh means a morphological suffix. One of his examples is as follows:[26] *qo'as* means 'man' or 'be a man' or '(be) manlike'; *mamok* means 'work' or 'working' or 'one who is working (i.e. worker)'; the suffix *-'i* is an 'indicative' marker conveying that the word to which it is attached is used predicatively, to make an assertion about a subject; the suffix *-ma* is like a definite article, but attached to the end of a word. Thus we have (Swadesh 1938, p. 78):

---

[26] I have slightly modified Swadesh's transcription here.

mamok-ma   qo'as-'i
work-INDIC   man-DEF
'The man is working'

qo'as-ma   mamok-'i
man-INDIC   work-DEF
'The worker is a man'

Schachter (1985, p. 11) gives an exactly parallel example from Tagalog, not at all related to Nootka, where 'The man is working' and 'The one who is working is a man' are rendered with the same three words, but in a different order. Jacobsen (1976) and Schachter (1985) have argued that the full Nootka facts do not stand up to a claim that a noun/verb distinction is entirely lacking. However it is clear that, by comparison with European languages, for example, much less depends on knowing the lexical class of a word; Nootka and Tagalog words are in general much more versatile. It is not widely accepted in the literature that genuine examples exist of languages with absolutely no noun/verb distinction. This could be a matter of Eurocentric bias, or due to some unwillingness to concede radical simplicity to some languages. Along with Gil's claim that Riau Indonesian is such a genuine example, there have been a number of such claims for languages from a range of different language families. Both Tchekhoff (1984) and Broschart (1997) make this claim for Tongan. Rijkhoff (2003) mentions studies of seven languages and language families[27] for which serious claims have been made that they lack a distinction between nouns and verbs in the lexicon. Foley (2005, p. 60) uses the term 'precategorial' for languages with no noun/verb distinction, with obvious evolutionary implications; Labelle (2005, p. 438), much less appropriately, uses the term 'multicategorial' for such languages. Among generativist syntacticians, there is less willingness to admit to languages without a noun/verb distinction. Baker (2003, p. 89) starts by conceding that 'It is not at all inconceivable

---

[27] Rijkhoff cites the following studies: on Salishan languages—Czaykowska-Higgins and Kinkade (1998); Kinkade (1983, 1976); Kuipers (1968); Thompson and Thompson (1980); Nater (1984); Demers and Jelinek (1982, 1984); Jelinek (1993, 1998); Jelinek and Demers (1994); on Nootka—Sapir (1921); Hockett (1958); Mithun (1999); Swadesh (1938); on Mundari Hoffmann (1903); Sinha (1975); on Santali—MacPhail (1953); on Tongan—Broschart (1991, 1997); Churchward (1953); on Tagalog—Himmelmann (1991); Sasse (1993); on Samoan—Churchward (1951); Mosel and Hovdhaugen (1992). For the Mande languages of West Africa, Delafosse (1929) identifies only three categories of word, nouns, pronouns, and particles, but no verbs; several other authors share this view of the absence of proper verbs in this language group (Kastenholz 1979; Manessy 1962); Lúpke (2005) takes a more nuanced view of the noun/verb distinction in the Mande langages. See also Foley (2005), with a section entitled 'The contrast between nouns and verbs is not universal' (p. 55).

that a human language could exist without a lexical category of verb'. But a major theme of his book is that in fact no language lacks a category of Verb. Baker's criteria for distinguishing nouns from verbs are essentially semantic, and not distributional. A noun, in his theory, 'bears a referential index' (p. 95), a criterion which he, oddly, calls 'syntactic'. His criteria for being a verb are partly theory-internal; Verb is 'a lexical category that takes a specifier' (p. 94). And the other part of his definition of Verb is that it is the only category 'that can assign agent and theme roles' (p. 94), again an essentially semantic criterion.

Nootka may have no noun/verb distinction, but it is not an isolating language. Far from it—it has complex morphology. This morphology gives signals as to whether a word is used 'nounily' or 'verbily' in a given sentence. But this way of putting it describes Nootka in terms more appropriate to languages which do have a noun/verb distinction. It is better to say that the morphology signals whether a word is used as a Subject (or Topic) or as a Predicate (or Focus). For Nootka in particular, the morphology seems likely to be signalling Topic–Focus partition of the sentence, as the morpheme -'i is glossed as 'Def'; Topics are usually definite. (See Chapter 4, section 5 for discussion of the distinctions between Topic and Subject and between Predicate and Focus.) The morphology does the Topic–Focus work (or the Subject–Predicate work) in sentences. Tongan, also claimed to lack a lexical noun/verb distinction, has function words that do the Subject–Predicate work, as in these examples, which are very similar to Swadesh's Nootka examples above. (Perhaps significantly, both Nootka and Tongan put the predicative 'verby' element first in a sentence, with the arguments or 'nouny' referring expressions later.)

na'e	lele	e	kau	fefiné
PAST	run	ART	PL.HUM	woman.DEF

'The women were running'

na'e	fefine	kotoa	e	kau	lelé
PAST	woman	all	ART	PL.HUM	run.DEF

'The ones running were all female'   (Broschart 1997, p. 134)

But Riau Indonesian has neither morphology nor (more than a few) function words to do the noun–verb or Subject–Predicate work. Thus this language appears to be even simpler than Nootka or Tongan. In a purely monocategorial language, since all words belong to a single category, they all have the same syntactic distribution. There are no syntactic subclasses with special distributional privileges. Therefore, in such a language, any word can be combined with any other word, or any other sequence of words, to form a grammatical sentence (not necessarily meaningful). Riau Indonesian is not quite as free as that, but, Gil claims, it does approach this extreme.

The Riau Indonesian words *makan* and *ayam* can be translated as *eat* and *chicken* respectively. One word prototypically denotes a kind of activity, the other a kind of object. But there is no syntactic difference between them. 'Words such as *makan* "eat" and *ayam* "chicken" have the same distributional privileges and, more generally, identical syntactic behaviour' (Gil 2005, p. 247). These two words are typical of the whole vocabulary. Words denoting actions, objects, qualities, and relations all behave identically syntactically. Gil chooses to say that all these words belong to the single category **sentence**. This is appropriate because any one of these words can stand on its own and express a sentential meaning. There are a few exceptions.

That Riau Indonesian is not purely monocategorial is due to the fact that in addition to the single open syntactic category sentence, it also contains a single closed category containing a few dozen semantically heterogeneous words whose grammatical behaviour sets them apart from words belonging to the category of sentence. However, although most members of this second, closed syntactic category are what are generally considered to be grammatical function words, none of these items are obligatory in any specific grammatical construction.   (Gil 2009, p. 24)

Consider a colloquial form of this language, in which no items from Gil's second, closed class of words occur. That is, in utterances in this form of the language, there are no words giving specific clues to grammatical structure. Interpretation is all done by inference from the meanings of the words. According to Gil (2005, p. 246), both *makan ayam* and *ayam makan* can be translated into English as any, and more, of the following:[28]

> The chicken is eating
> The chickens are eating
> A chicken is eating
> The chicken was eating
> The chicken will be eating
> The chicken eats
> The chicken has eaten
> Someone is eating the chicken
> Someone is eating for the chicken

---

[28] Too late for a major change, I found a native Riau Indonesian informant of my own, who told me that *ayam makan* could only mean 'the chicken is eating'. This person was an educated bilingual English/Indonesian, which may have affected her judgement. David Gil's data is more likely about a less educated vernacular.

Someone is eating with the chicken
The chicken that is eating
Where the chicken is eating
When the chicken is eating

As these examples show, the language does not obligatorily signal number (singular/plural), (in)definiteness, tense (past/non-past), aspect (whether the action is ongoing or has finished), or thematic roles (who did what to whom), and much else. *Ayam makan* means vaguely 'anything to do with a chicken and eating'. This illustrates the third concept in Gil's trio isolating/monocategorial/associational (IMA). A language is **associational** (Gil's term) if semantic interpretation works by this simple principle: 'For any expression X and Y belonging to S, the construction XY may be associated with any interpretation derived by straightforward compositional means from the interpretations of X and Y' (Gil 1994b, pp. 188–9). This is how *ayam makan* can mean anything in the list above. Riau Indonesian is not purely associational. This 'is clear from the presence of additional rules of compositional semantics that make reference to specific lexical items or to particular syntactic configurations, for example, word order. Still, the effect of such rules is much more restricted than is the case in many other languages' (Gil 2009, p. 24).

To a student of European languages, this extreme flexibility is surprising. Gil is describing a genuine form of a language widely used for practical everyday spoken communication. Further, *ayam makan* 'is a typical sentence in Riau Indonesian; it is not "telegraphic" or otherwise stylistically marked in any way' (Gil 2009, p. 23). There exist grammatical means of making meanings more precise, but these are not obligatory.

Although colloquial varieties of Indonesian do not have bona fide relative clauses, the grammatical behaviour of *yang*—it can only occur in front of another expression which functions as its host—places it outside the single open syntactic category and therefore beyond the limits of monocategoriality. However, its use is always optional; for example, 'the chickens that were eaten' can be rendered as either *ayam yang makan* or simply ... *ayam makan*. (Gil 2009, p. 29)

Ayam yang makan can also mean 'the chickens that will eat' or 'the chicken that has eaten'. But at least the inclusion of *yang* narrows down the range of meanings somewhat.

In a language with no noun/verb distinction and no inflectional morphology or function words, it is particularly important that the words in a sentence cannot be freely scrambled. Remember the Latin poetic line quoted in the previous chapter:

*Quis multā gracilis te puer in rosā perfusus liquidis urget odoribus grato,
Pyrrha, sub antro?*
*What many slender you boy in roses sprinkled liquid courts scents pleasant,
Pyrrha, in grotto?*

The poet Horace could get away with this flagrant scrambling by relying on
inflectional morphology as a clue to which words depend on which others. In
Riau Indonesian (RI), that device is not available. Semantically closely dependent words are juxtaposed. For example, there are various negative particles,
and they are positioned immediately before the expression over which they
have scope. Possession is expressed by putting the word for the possessor after
the word for the possessed. 'Moreover, adpositions invariably occur before
their NPs' (Gil 2000, p. 6). RI has some strict rules of word order.

The expressive power of simple juxtaposition can be illustrated with the
word *baru*, whose basic meaning is 'new'. Most commonly *baru* occurs
together with an object-denoting expression, for example:[29]

Aku   dapat   gitar   baru
1SG   get   guitar   new
'I got a new guitar'

However, *baru* may also occur in construction with an event-denoting expression, in which case it is most appropriately understood as meaning 'newly',
'(only) just', 'recently' or 'finally', for example:

Aku   baru   dapat   gitar
1SG   new   get   guitar
'I just got a guitar'

Further examples show the versatility of this word, typical of many in the
language, and how the meaning depends on the adjacent words and the pragmatic context. The word can be used twice in the same sentence with different
functions, qualifying an object and a whole event.

Aku baru   dapat   gitar   baru
1SG   recent   get   guitar   new
'I just got a new guitar'

In the above example, *baru baru* is not a constituent, but in other cases it could
be. First consider:

[29] The next five examples and the comments on them are a personal communication
from David Gil.

Ini   baru   gitar   baru
this   final   guitar   new
'This finally is a new guitar'

[Context: you asked for a new guitar, but were presented, repeatedly, with a series of old ones. Finally, you are are presented with a new one.]

Now take the above sentence, and, in a context where 'guitar' is understood, delete *gitar*:

Ini   baru   baru
this   final   new
'This finally is a new one'

[It's not clear to me why David Gil should consider *baru baru* a constituent phrase in this last example.]

Evidently, RI speakers enjoy a freedom from European-style grammatical fussiness, and as these examples show, subtleties of meaning can be expressed, given suitable inference from the context of an utterance. Words like *baru* can be put to multiple uses. 'Multiple uses' may reflect a Eurocentric perception of the data. Gil (2004) argues, in connection with another word, *sama*, for the **macrofunctionality** of words in RI. That is, rather than a word having many different uses which can be separated out and classified, Gil explores the possibility that a word has one 'large' function. Which aspect of this big meaning is intended by a speaker and understood by a hearer depends on the context of use. In a previous chapter, I have mentioned the difference between 'lumpers' and 'splitters', reflecting a difference in preferred analytical style. Among European lexicographers, splitters carry the field. Any sense of a word that can possibly be individuated is listed and defined separately. Very often, however, allegedly different senses of a word are closely related, and one wonders whether a macrofunctional treatment might be psychologically more plausible. Take the example of English *must* as in *You must wash your hands* or *You must be tired*. It is customary to separate the meanings of *must* into 'deontic', for a kind of social obligation, and 'epistemic', for probable inference. A macrofunctional analysis would attempt to lump these meanings into one large pie, with speakers choosing which slice of the pie to understand on the basis of context. I will not debate here how to analyse English *must*. Gil is clearly of the lumping persuasion, and emphasizes the macrofunctionality of words in RI, as we have seen with *baru*. Gil's (2004) paper on *sama* is a masterpiece of close attention to what might be called variation of meaning according to discourse context, except that of course Gil proposes not many meanings but a single big meaning. Very briefly, *sama* is used to convey meanings that in English are expressed by *and*, *with* (both comitative and instrumental), *by* (as in English passives), various locative prepositions such as *on*, *from* as an animate source, *to* marking an English indirect object, *about* (as object of intention or source of emotion), *each other*, *together*, *all*, *same as*, and *than* (as in English comparatives), among others. English prepositions have some versatility (count the 'meanings' of *of* or *to*) but not as much as Gil finds in RI *sama*.

Word order is to a limited degree fixed, and related to meaning, in RI. 'In a nutshell, the range of possible interpretations of *David sama* is a subset of those of *sama David*' (Gil p.c.). Syntactically, when *sama* stands on its own, in no immediate dependency with another word, it can mean *together*, *same*, etc. When closely combined with a following word, as in *sama David*, it can be translated as *and*, *with*, etc. I asked David Gil about details of RI, and I give our exchange on word order and meaning, in an edited form, below.

Question, JRH: Is *baru gitar* lit. 'new guitar' also possible?

Answer, DG: Like *ayam makan*, *baru gitar* is vague between predicative and attributive semantics. But when understood attributively, e.g., in a context such as 'I bought a...', there is a very strong preference for the order *gitar baru*. But, very rarely, the opposite order does surface, and you may get *baru gitar*.

Question, JRH: Are *sekali susa* lit. 'very difficult', and *sekali marah* lit. 'very angry' OK in the same sense as *susa sekali* and *marah sekali*?

Answer, DG: Again, reference needs to be made to the polysemous nature of *sekali*. As an intensifier meaning 'very', it can only occur after the word that it modifies. But as a word meaning 'once', it can occur either before or after the expression that it modifies.

Although in general semantically related words are juxtaposed in Riau Indonesian (as indeed in many other languages), some long distance dependencies are possible. Topicalization[30] works by putting the topicalized element at the front of a clause (again, as in many other languages), with a 'resumptive' pronoun later on indicating the role of the topic referent in the event being described. Here are two examples from (Gil 1994b, p. 186):[31]

---

[30] I use the term 'topicalization' in a broad sense to include what is sometimes called 'left-dislocation'. For some syntacticians, the difference rests on whether there is a later constituent in the sentence overtly marking the place of the 'dislocated' element.

[31] Almost all of Gil's examples were observed in conversation by speakers of RI. The situational context, which Gil usually gives, is often crucial to the interpretation of the examples.

saya ada beli kaca mata dulu, mana dia?
1:SG exist buy glass eye DIST.PAST where 3
'The eyeglasses that I bought before, where are they?'

Here the 3rd-person pronoun *dia* is understood as the object of *beli* 'buy', coreferential with *kaca mata* 'eyeglasses'.

ada perempuan tadi, ininya nampak
exist woman PROX.PAST this-3 see
[talking about a woman who had just passed]
'The woman before, her *this* [speaker points to his own chest] was showing'

Here the demonstrative pronoun *ininya* is understood as associated with the woman mentioned earlier.

Overall, a student of European languages is likely to be taken aback by the grammatical simplicity of RI. Being keen to locate this language among others in the space of existing languages, I asked Gil some further questions of a more general nature. Here, again in an edited form, is our exchange.

Question, JRH: Are there fixed phrases, like English *sooner or later*?

Answer, DG: Sure. (And the existence of such expressions provides evidence that, in accordance with John McWhorter's criteria, Riau Indonesian is an 'old' language as opposed to a newly created creole.)

Question, JRH: More generally, are there multi-word constructions (in the sense of Construction Grammar), with variable slots for a range of insertable items, such as *the COMPARATIVE the COMPARATIVE*, e.g. *the more the merrier, the more it rains, the wetter I get*, etc.?

Answer, DG: Yup, there are such things; even one that corresponds to your example:

makin hujan makin basah
increase rain increase wet

Though come to think of it, the Riau Indonesian example differs from the English in that it is formally completely regular—no morphosyntactic peculiarities like its English counterpart. Since there's so little morphosyntax in Riau Indonesian, it's hard to imagine what a 'morphosyntactic idiom' might look like.

Question, JRH: Do RI speakers seem aware (or can they be made aware) of examples like the classic *Colorless green ideas sleep furiously*, i.e. cases where they may say you could say that but it would be a bizarre thing to say. That is, can one make a distinction, for RI, between conventionalized grammaticality and semantic meaningfulness?

Answer, DG: Sure one can make the same distinction in Riau Indonesian; the main difference between Indonesian and English is a quantitative one, namely that in Indonesian there are so few ungrammatical sentences.

Also, one can get such effects through the application of preference rules. In the psycholinguistic experiment described in Gil (2008), speakers of Riau Indonesian (and, so far, 30 other languages) are presented with stimuli consisting of a sentence in their language, plus two pictures, and are asked which of the two pictures is appropriately described by the sentence. An example of a test stimulus in Riau Indonesian is:

orang   makan   kayu
person   eat   tree

Picture 1: Person eating under a tree
Picture 2: Person eating a tree

If Riau Indonesian were a pure IMA (isolating-monocategorial-associational) language, i.e. lacking in any more specific preference rules, one might expect subjects to opt for Picture 1, as it conforms with associational semantics ('eating associated with a tree') and is the most natural. In fact, some subjects do opt for this interpetation. However, many subjects point to the bizarre Picture 2, showing that speakers are sensitive to the semantic case frame of *eat* and prefer to see it followed by an element within its case frame, in this case the patient, rather than an extraneous element such as a locative.

This shows, then, that you can express bizarre notions in Riau Indonesian. And here's my bash at the mother of them all:

Ide   hijau   yang   tak   ada   warna   tidurnya   marah
idea   green   REL   NEG   exist colour sleep-ASSOC   angry

My guess is that the most readily available reading of the above sentence is the famous one. But it could probably also have non-bizarre readings as well, such as 'The colourless guy's sleeping infuriated the guy with the idea about the green thing'.

Question, JRH: Finally, if RI can be adequately described by the 3 principles in your 1994 article, what is there to learn, beside vocabulary? How come you need a full-time teacher?

Answer, DG: The grammar, in the narrow Chomskyan sense of 'set of well-formed strings', can be learned in less than an hour. But still, in order to be able to be mistaken for a native speaker down a dark alley, you'd need to spend years learning: lexicon, phonetics, and, most interestingly, that nebulous domain that is sometimes referred to as idiomaticity—being able to say something that is not just grammatical but also stylistically felicitous in the appropriate context.

Question, JRH: I'm pondering what you mean by 'idiomaticity'. It would seem to mean either that you have to learn many subtle details of the meanings of words, or that you have to learn a large number of idiomatic constructions with subtly special semantics and pragmatics. It is probably the latter.

Answer, DG: No, it's definitely not the latter, and only to a certain extent the former. It's more something else, to do with the myriad choices that speakers make whenever they take a 'thought', or a conceptual representation, and cast it in words. How they do this, in different languages, depends not just on the grammatical devices that each language makes available, but also on various constraints, which, for want of a better term, I called 'stylistic', which govern the choice between alternative linguistic renditions of the same or similar thought.

For example, I am a native speaker of both English and Hebrew. Both languages permit stacked attributive adjectives. However, whereas in English stacked adjectives occur relatively frequently, in Hebrew they're kind of odd. No question about their grammaticality, they're perfectly well-formed. But you just don't say things that way. You could if you wanted to, and your grammar teacher wouldn't be able to correct you for doing so, but using stacked adjectives all over the place in Hebrew would still mark your language as being strange, stilted, and non-idiomatical. It's things like this, and they're really ubiquitous, in every nook and cranny of language, that I meant with the term 'idiomaticity'. And not surprisingly, my impression is that with respect to idiomaticity, Riau Indonesian is more different from both English and Hebrew than either of these two languages are from each other. You can speak perfectly grammatical Riau Indonesian but still be easily recognizable as a foreigner if you haven't yet acquired idiomaticity.

There you have it. My take on it is that the grammar of Riau Indonesian is a large collection of special constructions that are known to its speakers as good style (part of the pragmatic specification of constructions). Unlike (say) English, the RI grammar has few if any more general constraints/constructions governing what strings are grammatical—constructions at the level of generality of the English subject–verb construction (Figure 4.16 on p. 350). Riau Indonesian syntax is relatively simple by European standards, but far from being just word salad or semantic soup. The grammatical simplicity is a matter of degree. Many linguists are sceptical of the simplicity that Gil attributes to RI. Mark Baker is typical in his scepticism, but atypical in expressing it in print. '[O]ne can legitimately wonder how hard [Gil] has looked. Has he looked hard enough to discover a difference like Agent Raising, if something comparable were to exist in RI?...I do not want to convey disrespect for Gil' (Baker 2005, p. 426). But Baker himself concedes what I take to be the crucial fact. '[I]t remains true that these distinctions are much more subtle in some languages than in others. We can still ask what is the difference between a language like English or Latin, where no one could miss the distinction between a noun and a verb, and Austronesian languages and sign languages, where it is very easy to miss. This difference seems real' (p. 427).

Gil emphasizes how effective this simply structured language is for practical everyday communication.

[T]he restriction to IMA Language does not impose any constraints on the range of things that can be talked about, or on what can actually be said about those things. ...IMA Language is enough to talk about school, sports, love, and life. And it is sufficient to support most daily activities throughout one of the world's largest countries, from the giant metropolis that is Jakarta to the most far-flung of island provinces.

...there may exist some domains for which the Relative IMA character of colloquial Malay/Indonesian is functionally inadequate. However, in many cases at least, the use of the standard language is motivated not by any functional gain in expressive power but by social conventions. For example, the president addressing the nation on television could easily get his message across in colloquial Jakarta Indonesian, but to do so would result in loss of face, thereby endangering his elevated standing.

(Gil 2009, p. 30)

As Gil notes, these facts cast doubt on a functionalist argument that complexity in language arises because it is needed to convey complex meanings. The usefulness of such a simple code in a society making and using complex artefacts also means that we cannot infer modern-type complexity in earlier stages of human language from remains of the artefacts of very early *Homo sapiens*. Linguists have always been sceptical of archeologists' attempts to infer complex language from excavated relics, in the face of the truism that complex language leaves behind no fossils. A recent discussion of such theorizing, citing many precursors, is Henshilwood and Dubreuil (2009). It is noteworthy that these authors mostly enclose 'syntax' in double scare-quotes, thus carefully distancing their concept from modern exemplars of syntactic language. Their broad characterization of 'syntax' is 'the ideas or emotions that were communicated by means of symbolic elements... these elements can be recombined according to systematic, conventionalized criteria to create meaning' (Henshilwood and Dubreuil 2009, p. 41). At this broad level, with 'syntax' not going beyond

Bickertonian protolanguage[32] or Gil's IMA properties, archeologists and linguists interested in language evolution can agree.

Riau Indonesian as Gil describes it is interesting for speculation about
the nature of very early prehistoric languages. Gil (2006) notes that a language with his IMA trio of isolating, monocatecategorial, and associational
properties is almost exactly the same concept as Bickerton's construct 'protolanguage' (Bickerton 1990, 1995). On grounds of pure simplicity and the
productions of human two-year-olds, language-trained apes, a few language-
deprived people such as Genie, and pidgin users, both Gil and Bickerton
argue the likelihood that the very earliest human languages had the properties
of protolanguage, or the IMA properties that we see approximated in Riau
Indonesian.

5.6 Creoles and pidgins

5.6.1 Identifying creoles and pidgins

The classic exemplars uncontroversially recognized as creoles share characteristic historical origins. They are new languages, often emerging over a relatively
short period as a result of drastic population movements, such as slavery. The
emergence of creoles, though often fast, is not absolutely abrupt, of course. It
is a matter of individual speakers gradually adjusting their own behaviour, and
of the behaviour of individuals gradually getting coordinated across a whole
community. 'Gradual' can be relatively fast or slow. The most extreme claim
in the literature (Bickerton 1981) is that creolization can happen in a single
generation, a claim which has attracted widespread criticism.[33] Examples of
creoles are: Haitian creole, with obvious French input; Saramaccan, spoken
by descendants of escaped slaves in Surinam, influenced by English and Portuguese; and Nubi, an Arabic-based creole spoken in parts of Uganda and
Kenya by descendants of empressed Sudanese soldiers.

In a nutshell, the simplicity found in creoles is due to language contact and
simplification of the more complex languages in contact. It is this history of
contact that identifies creoles as a (fuzzy) class. Creoles are languages, and
their formation is subject to the same social and cognitive influences as apply
to all languages. The cognitive influences that apply are the same as those

---

[32] There is further discussion of Bickertonian protolanguage in the next chapter,
Chapter 6.

[33] See, for example Goodman (1985b); Singler (1992); Arends (1995); McWhorter
(1997); Roberts (2000).

that apply across all languages—humans are humans. But the **social** situations historically giving rise to creoles are atypical of those that apply, at least now, to most of the world's 6,000-odd languages. DeGraff (2001b) criticizes talk of creoles as 'new' languages, insisting correctly that their roots are as old as those of the languages from which they are formed. In fact Hurford and Dediu (2009) argue that any talk of the relative age of languages is problematic, in that their features come from different sources and date from different times, some recent and some remote. But creoles are new in the sense of clearly being distinct languages from any that existed just a few generations before. If transported back 300 years in time, I could find people whom I could immediately and easily understand and be understood by in my native language, despite intervening changes. Given the same chance of time travel, no speaker of a classic creole could do that. Once they exist, creoles are subject to the same diachronic tendencies as other languages. The greater the time that has elapsed since the social situation giving rise to a creole, the less it is likely to show any particular signs of its origin. Thus in making statements about creoles, it is important to catch them early, before they become the generations-old traditions of stable communities. Where new creoles have features not attributable to either superstrate or substrate languages (not a common situation) these features plausibly represent natural, most biologically entrenched, preferences for language in general. Such features are clues to what early prehistoric languages were like. Bickerton (1990) links the pidgins, from which creoles can evolve when they get a grammar of their own, with his 'protolanguage' stage of language evolution. Creole languages have been said to have 'the world's simplest grammars' (McWhorter 2001b). It is worth considering the relationship between creolization and prehistoric language evolution.

Terminology in this area is applied rather haphazardly. One reliable constant is that the three terms 'jargon', 'pidgin', and 'creole' identify forms of language ranked in that order on a continuum, jargons being the crudest form, with no conventional grammar, and creoles said to be 'full' languages.[34] Pidgins are more systematic and conventionalized varieties than jargons, but less so than creoles. In the literature, especially where the term 'jargon' is not used, the term 'pidgin' can also imply a lack of any conventional grammatical organization. Conversely, some languages which clearly have grammatical organization, and are spoken as native languages, are sometimes referred to as pidgins. Linguists

---

[34] See Winford (2003); Wardhaugh (2005); Holm (2000) for introductions to the various types of pidgins and their historical origins.

have devoted much more attention to creoles than to pidgins, and more to pidgins than to jargons, because of their relative stability and interesting complexity. The earliest stages of prehistoric languages are more likely to resemble pidgins and jargons than creoles. The rich literature on creoles nevertheless provides relevant material for speculation about what the earliest languages may have been like.

On going afresh into a new linguistic community, without knowing its history, there is no way that one can diagnose from the structure of the language that it belongs in a 'creole' category, as opposed to a non-creole category (Gil 2001; Ansaldo and Matthews 2001). Bickerton (1981, p. 2) writes that 'languages known as creoles . . . do not constitute a proper set', but people still continue to generalize about creoles. Winford puts it more colourfully:

creoles constitute a motley assortment of contact vernaculars with different histories and lines of development, though of course they still have much in common . . . there are no structural characteristics that all creoles share . . . no structural criteria that distinguish creoles from other types of language. (Winford 2003, p. 307)

This confusion is a pity, especially for public understanding of language. The research literature suffers from this lack of an independent definition of 'creole'. For example, in one debate, McWhorter's claim, quoted above, that the world's simplest grammars are creole grammars, is countered by David Gil with a description of Riau Indonesian showing it to have a grammar of comparable simplicity to McWhorter's creole examples. Gil describes at length the historical and social background of Riau Indonesian, with a view to making it very clear that it is not a creole. But this counterexample is easily waved away by McWhorter in his reply:

David Gil finally comes through with Riau Indonesian. I fully acknowledge that this language displays no more complexity (according to my metric) than Saramaccan or many other creoles . . .

In this light, my honest response to the fascinating data Gil presents is that, in paralleling Saramaccan and other creoles so closely in relative lack of over-specification, Riau Indonesian is a creole. (McWhorter 2001a, pp. 405–6)

Without a definition of 'creole' independent of the properties creoles are hypothesized to have, any hypothesis runs the risk of circularity. A satisfactory definition of creoles should be in terms of either the socio-historical context in which they arise, or their structural linguistic properties, **but not both**. Any interesting hypothesis could then use such a definition to try to establish correlations between the socio-historical context and the linguistic properties, independently defined. Research on creoles does indeed circle around trying to see such correlations. But it is often tempting not to question the assumption that a specific language deserves the label 'creole' before plunging in with data aimed at supporting or falsifying some claim about 'creoles' in general. Bickerton (1981) gets over the problem by severely restricting his theorizing about creoles to

languages which

1) Arose out of a prior pidgin which had not existed for more than a generation.
2) Arose in a population where not more than 20 percent were native speakers of the dominant language and where the remaining 80 percent was composed of diverse language groups.   (Bickerton, 1981, p. 4)

This restriction allows Bickerton to make some very specific claims. But in the secondary literature following Bickerton's work it is often not recognized that his claims do not apply to all languages that have been (unsystematically) labelled as 'creoles'. His claims have been given a more general and less sustainable interpretation.

Most definitions of creoles mention that they are 'full' languages, as opposed to pidgins. Lightfoot (2006, p. 140) is typical: 'All the evidence suggests that creoles have the structural properties of well-established languages'. Such statements lack detail; as we shall see, there is some question of **which** structural properties of well-established languages can be found in languages known as creoles. Most students of creoles agree that they are in certain senses simpler than languages with longer histories. Wardhaugh (2005) several times contrasts creoles with 'fully-fledged' languages, albeit always with scare-quotes around this term. And there is consistency about the importance of contact between different language communities in the formation of creoles. No one would apply the term 'creole' to a language that has been isolated, or resisted borrowing, for hundreds of years.

Despite the terminological problems, relatively coherent discourse about creoles survives. There is some phenomenon, some facts of the matter, some real tendencies to chart. Of particular interest here are the ways in which creoles are simpler than other languages; these can shed some light on possible early human language, as Mufwene insightfully, yet somewhat grudgingly, states:

More interesting about incipient pidgins is the fact that they represent simplifications, reductive developments of some sort, from full-fledged languages. Evolutionarily, they [and creoles] have evolved in the opposite direction of proto-Language, which started from non-linguistic means of communication. At best, what they teach us about the evolution of language is that not all structural components of modern linguistic systems are as deeply entrenched. Those morphosyntactic components that survive the 'break down', so to speak, that produces incipient pidgins may be the most deeply entrenched in the architecture of language.   (Mufwene 2008, p. 79)

Jargons (or pidgins) arise when people who need to communicate have no language in common. They manage to pick up a few of the words of the other's language and string them together with little or no grammatical organization. Holm's (2000, p. 5) example is 'New Yorkers buying sunglasses in Lisbon'. If the contact situation persists, the mode of communication gets more conventionalized. An example is Russenorsk, a simple form of communication used in the nineteenth century between Russian traders and Norwegian fishermen (Broch and Jahr 1984b, 1984a; Jahr 1996). Russenorsk is referred to as a pidgin. A common criterial property of pidgins is that they are not spoken as native languages by anyone.

If a pidgin situation persists even longer, such that children grow up with a pidgin spoken around them, a creole may be formed by the new generation. Bickerton claims that this can happen in a single generation, and that the children are by far the principal innovators. For the transition from Hawaiian Pidgin English to Hawaiian Creole English, he writes 'we can place the time of creolization somewhere around 1910, and certainly no later than 1920' (Bickerton 1981, p. 8). Wow! It can't have been a uniform transition, though overall it may have been relatively fast. Other creolists disagree with Bickerton's dates. Goodman (1985b) in a highly critical review of Bickerton's book, puts the emergence of Hawaiian Creole English in the last quarter of the nineteenth century; and Tryon and Charpentier (2004, p. 14) have the creolization 'peaking in the 1930s'. McWhorter (1997) also argues in detail, against an abrupt transition into Hawaiian Creole English, on grounds of relevant aspects of the social history of the islands. Bickerton's has been the dominant story about creoles propagated in introductory linguistics books— that they are historically derived from pidgins. Hall (1962) wrote of the 'life cycle of pidgins', whereby pidgins sometimes become nativized into creoles. But he did not actually say that this was the only source of creole languages. Not all languages known as creoles originate from pidgins, and certainly not all emerge in the rapid one-generation manner that Bickerton claims for the emergence of Hawaiian Creole English. Mufwene expresses a counterposition:

Both creoles and pidgins developed gradually, from closer approximations of the initial targets to varieties more and more different from them. ... They are creations no more of children exclusively than they are of adult L2-learners exclusively. Actually, substrate influence in creoles would be difficult to account for if the role of adult nonnative speakers as carriers of xenolectal features were not factored in our hypotheses. The role of children in the development of creoles involved selecting some of those substrate features into their idiolects and making them available to future learners.

(Mufwene 2008, p. 78)

5.6.2 Substrates and superstrates

A classic creole has both 'substrate' and 'superstrate' elements. The most prominent superstrate element is the vocabulary, taken from the 'lexifier' language, often the language of the colonial power, such as Portuguese, English, or French. Opinions are divided over where features of grammatical organization in a creole come from. Some researchers stress the contribution of innate dispositions in the children creating the creole out of the pre-existing adult pidgin. A prominent advocate of this line of thought is Derek Bickerton, who has invoked a Chomsky-style 'Language Bioprogram' as explaining the common features of many creoles (Bickerton 1981, 1984, 1999a). An alternative theory of the origin of creole grammars is that the syntactic and semantic properties of lexical items are inherited from the substrate languages of the adults speaking the pidgins. Any claim for substrate influence needs evidence of real population contact during the relevant period. It is not enough merely to show that a creole shares some feature with a language from an area where the ancestors of the creole speakers came from. Unfortunately, the necessary historical records are usually very sketchy.

An example of a substrate theory is the Relexification Hypothesis, of which Claire Lefebvre is a prominent advocate (Lefebvre 1998, 2001a, 2009). For example, 'the relexification account of creole genesis predicts that Atlantic creoles will reproduce the properties of their West African substratum languages, while Pacific ones will reproduce those of their Austronesian substratum languages. Atlantic and Pacific creoles are thus expected to differ in the same areas of lexicon and grammar as West African and Austronesian languages do among themselves' (Lefebvre 2001b, p. 197). At this least enlightening, the exchanges are an all-or-nothing tussle between 'universalists' and 'substratists'—Bickerton (1981) calls them 'substratomaniacs'. The debate over the origins of grammatical features in creoles mirrors a fundamental divide in linguistic theory more generally, with the Language Bioprogram hypothesis emphasizing the contribution of innate dispositions, and the Relexification hypothesis emphasizing the influence of input from the prior linguistic environment. It is not necessary to see these theories as in stark competition. Clearly, in creoles as in the case of all languages, both innate dispositions and the pre-existing language of the community play a part. 'The universalist and substrate hypotheses complement one another' (Mufwene 1986, p. 129).

In the classic cases of creoles, the prior linguistic environment is mixed and inconsistent, and the creators of the creole are thrown more upon their instinctive resources. In remote human prehistory, the first languages with any grammatical structure were presumably formed on the platform of pidgin-like systems with a stock of words but no complex constructions. We get a clearer insight into the untrained language-forming dispositions of humans by looking at the properties of languages emerging from situations in which no grammar was exemplified enough to provide the same consistent basis as is given to children in non-creole situations. This approach gives some credence to the Language Bioprogram hypothesis. Only if **all** grammatical properties of creoles are inherited by cultural transmission from grammars of pre-existing languages, that is if the Language Bioprogram hypothesis is completely wrong, would creolization shed no light on the prehistoric evolution of languages with complex syntax. Creole languages do have certain striking similarities. Let's have a look at a selected sample of their prototypical properties. What we are looking for are properties which cannot have come from either substrate or superstrate languages.

5.6.3 Properties of pidgins and creoles

First, basic **word order**. Creole languages are indeed typically SVO.[35] That is, they have dominant Subject–Verb–Object word order, like English. In many cases, SVO word order in creoles can be seen simply as inherited from the superstrate languages. 'SVO is the usual word order in the superstrate languages (except for SOV with object pronouns in the Romance languages, and in Dutch subordinate clauses)' (Holm 2000, p. 173). A possible case of creolization turning a non-SVO word order into SVO is that of Colloquial Arabic dialects. All Colloquial Arabic dialects have SVO word order. Versteegh (1984) argues that all modern Colloquial Arabic dialects arose through a process of creolization from Classical Arabic, which was and remains VSO in its word order. The modern dialects are certainly not creoles any longer, so this claim is controversial. Hence, the idea that creole SVO word order comes from an innate preference, rather than the superstrate language, is not particularly persuasive. A convincing case would be one where an SVO creole was formed from substrates and superstrates all of which were non-SVO. To my knowledge, no such case exists.

---

[35] As we shall see, it is not the case that 'all Creoles are SVO languages' (Nicolis 2008, p. 277), a statement that perhaps betrays an author's commitment to an innate (or 'universal') determinant of the properties of languages.

Further, apparently not all creoles are SVO. Barrios (2006) describes the case of Philippine Creole Spanish, otherwise known as Chabacano, whose dominant word order is VSO, like its substrate Philippine languages, Tagalog and Cebuano. The basic vocabulary of Chabacano is obviously derived from Spanish, making it prima facie a creole.[36] Another likely counterexample is Nagamese, spoken in Nagaland in Northeast India. Although I have not been able to see primary sources for this language, it is typically referred to as a creole. It evolved, around the 1930s, as a lingua franca in a situation where over 20 mutually unintelligible languages were spoken. Its vocabulary is based on words from Assamese, English, Hindi, and Naga. The official language of Nagaland is English, but Nagamese is used widely in trade, education, religion, and law-making. Nagamese has SOV word order, like its main superstrate languages, Assamese and Hindi.[37] Defenders of an innate disposition leading to creole SVO word order may object that Chabacano and Nagamese are not 'proper' creoles; at this point the argument risks becoming circular.

The susceptibility of word order to substrate influences is nicely illustrated by Pidgin Fijian. Standard Fijian is VSO, but Pidgin Fijian has the SVO word order of the early European settlers and traders, who adopted a pidginized form of Fijian. But as Siegel (2008, p. 16) notes 'SOV ordering, as in Fiji Hindi, can also be found in the speech of some Indian speakers'. Comrie (1997) also briefly surveys evidence that creole basic word order comes from the superstrate languages. On the whole, I conclude that the frequency of SVO word order in creoles is due mostly to superstrate and perhaps occasionally to substrate effects, and is not due to some natural preference for SVO.

Looking at languages for signs of what earlier languages may have been like, Givón (1979a), Newmeyer (2000) and Gell-Mann (2005) have independently argued that all prehistoric languages had SOV word order. In brief, this is based on the facts that (1) SOV is the most common word order across languages today (Dryer, 1996), and (2) diachronic switches from SOV to other word orders are well attested, but changes in the other direction are rare and perhaps do not occur at all, except in obvious cases of language contact. See also pp. 451–3 and pp. 456–9 on SOV order in new sign languages.

Next, consider **morphological complexity**. Creoles tend strongly to be isolating languages, with little word-internal structure (morphology). That is, words are simple, with few added affixes, if any. Creolists, despite their many differences, are almost unanimous on the tendency of creoles to be isolating

---

[36] Bickerton (1988, p. 282) admits the exceptionality of Spanish-based Philippine creoles in a footnote.

[37] Sreedhar (1974, 1976, 1977); Borua (1993); Bhattacharjya (1994).

languages. Non-creoles can also be isolating, for example the Chinese languages, so this is not a distinguishing feature of creoles. English is toward the isolating end of the spectrum of morphological complexity. Creoles are never morphologically more complex than their superstrate or substrate languages, and are usually simpler. Creoles based on French, Portuguese, or Spanish lack the complex tense markings on verbs found in those languages. In some creoles, the time of the action is not expressed at all. Here is an example from Holm:

A speaker of Nicaragua's Miskito Coast C[reole]E[nglish] is discussing how each jungle spirit guides the animals under his protection to hide them from hunters: 'Him a di uona. Him *tek* dem and *put* dem an dis wie... die *kom* and him *liiv* dem all hiia and *guo* de', i.e. 'He is their owner. He *takes* them and *puts* them on the right path ... They *come* and he *leaves* them all in that place and *goes* off. ...

On the other hand, unmarked verbs can also refer to past actions which in English would be expressed in the simple past tense. In the following passages another speaker of the same creole is relating how he and his family moved to town so he could go to school: 'Wi *liiv* from der an *kom* doun hiir fo stodi. Ai *staat* to pas my gried-dem' i.e. 'We *left* that place and *came* down here so I could study. I *started* to pass from one grade to the next'. (Holm 2000, p. 175)

There are plenty of examples of such plain omission of tense-marking affixes in other creoles, though in some cases a plain verb form with no affixes cannot have the whole range of possible time meanings. For example, Holm (2000, p. 177) mentions that unmarked verbs in Papiamentu Creole Spanish and Haitian Creole French cannot be used to indicate past states (e.g. 'He slept/was sleeping' in English).

When creoles explicitly express the time or duration ('aspect') of an action or state, it is often done, not with an affix, but with a separate word. To simplify somewhat, in Tok Pisin, a creole of Papua New Guinea, past tense is marked by *bin* before the verb, future is marked by *bai* before the verb, continuous aspect (as in English *is working*) is marked by *stap* after the verb, and completed action (as in English *has worked*) is marked by *pinis* after the verb (Romaine 1992).

It is not only with verbs that creoles tend to lack morphology. In Tok Pisin, possession (and many other relations) is signalled by *bilong*. *My friend* is *pren bilong mi*. Here English has a fused morpheme *my* expressing both 1ST PERSON SINGULAR and POSSESSIVE; Tok Pisin separates these meanings out into two separate words *mi* and *bilong*. English has both morphological and periphrastic ways of forming comparatives, as in *bigger* and *more important*. Tok Pisin has several ways of expressing comparison, none of them involving morphological modification of the adjective. One way to say *He is bigger than me* is *Em i moa bik olsem mi.* Where English adds a plural suffix *-s* to a noun, Tok Pisin has a separate word before the noun. Thus *men* is *ol man*. The *ol* is omitted if the plural information is redundant, as in *tripela man—three men*.[38]

In some features, creoles can have more complex morphology than one or other, but not both, of their substrates or superstrate. For example, Tok Pisin has a more complex system of personal pronouns than English. Where English *we* is ambiguous between *you and I* and *I and others, not including you*, Tok Pisin has two clear forms *yumi* and *mipela*. Further, beside plural number, Tok Pisin can signal dual and trial number with complex pronouns, giving for example:

mitupela	*I and one other, not you*
yumitripela	*we three, including you*

Krifka (2006, p. 80), drawing on primary sources, traces complex Tok Pisin pronouns to a substrate influence. 'The structure of the pronoun system of Tok Pisin is very similar to the system of Austronesian substrate languages, in particular Tolai, presumably the most influential one of these languages (cf. Mosel 1980; Keesing 1988)'. The original Austronesian forms did not, of course, use morphemes borrowed from English, but the internal structure of their pronouns was like what emerged in Tok Pisin. In similar vein, Lefebvre (2001b) shows that Haitian Creole French preserves semantic distinctions from a West African substrate language, Fongbe, while expressing these with phonological forms taken from French.[39] Further, the substrate Tolai complex pronouns are less transparent than the newly forged Tok Pisin pronouns, in which clear agglutinating structure can be seen—for example in *yumitripela* the separate morphemes are easily dissected out.[40] 'Creoles tend to be very low on INFLECTIONAL morphology (and . . . what inflection there is is almost always agglutinative rather than fusional)' (McWhorter, 2001a, p. 394).

Both Tok Pisin and Bislama (a creole of Vanuatu) have a verbal suffix *-im* (or *-em*) marking transitive verbs, for example Bislama *mi ridim buk* 'I read the book'. Intransitive verbs don't have this marker. This is clearly more

---

[38] Tok Pisin is a well known creole, now getting standardized, but (so far) not losing much of its creole character. There is a wealth of information and examples collected at first hand, to be found in books and on the internet.

[39] My argument is that a new creole never has more complex morphology than can be found in any of its parent languages. So it is immaterial whether some Haitian complex morphology comes from an African substrate, or from French, as claimed by DeGraff (2001a, 2001b); Becker and Veenstra (2003). If complex morphology comes, it comes from somewhere. But sometimes it is not picked up from anywhere, so the creole ends up without it. New creoles do not **create** complex morphology.

[40] *-pela* is a suffix that Tok Pisin also puts on all modifiers of nouns, such as adjectives and demonstratives.

complex than English, the superstrate, which does not take the trouble to mark transitive verbs specifically as such. It seems that the historical seeds of this marking pattern can be found in substrate Oceanic languages and Australian pidgin, though its diachronic trajectory is very complex (Crowley 2003). Another morphological complexity in Tok Pisin is the suffix *-pela* which marks adjectives, and noun modifiers generally, as in *bik-pela haus* '(a) big house', or *faiv-pela haus* 'five houses'. The phonological form of this suffix comes from English *fellow*, but where does this grammatical feature of marking noun modifiers come from? At least some substrate influence seems possible, as Tolai, a relevant Austronesian language, marks noun modifiers with a special form (Faraclas 1989, pp. 129–31). Jeff Siegel (1998) notes that the substrate influence for *-pela* is not straightforward and suggests that this suffix may have originated in English speakers using 'foreigner talk' in talking down to non-native speakers, and the pattern being reinforced by the substrate construction. Whatever is the case, there is no suggestion that transitive-verb-marking *-im* and adjective-marking *-pela* arose due to any innate dispositions in favour of such constructions.

It is clear that the direction of simplification taken by creoles is toward more isolating language, that is in the extreme, total absence of complex word-internal structure. Where such structure persists, it comes from the substrate or superstrate language (or the L1 or L2 of the language learner). This direction of simplification is a clue to the form of language to which humans naturally gravitate in the absence of sufficiently consistent environmental influence from another language, or when the humans are too old to master the full complexities of the ambient language. This is entirely natural. In the absence (or weak presence) of existing cultural norms, there is a preference for more transparent forms of language. Isolating language, in which each separate meaningful unit is a free-standing form, is more transparent than language with inflectional morphology. Given some word-internal structure, agglutinating structure is more transparent than morphology with fused, or portmanteau, forms. Typically, the phonetically salient parts of complex words are the stems, and the stems of words are what remain constant across variation by addition of different affixes.

We also have a good account of where complex inflectional morphology comes from. It arises through historical processes of grammaticalization, by which languages develop function words and grammatical affixes from previously existing content words—see Chapter 9. Grammaticalization is almost entirely a unidirectional historical process. Content words metamorphose into function words and grammatical affixes, but the reverse hardly ever happens. In creoles that evolve out of pidgins, the earlier pidgins have little or no word-internal structure, and part of the creolization process is the metamorphosis of selected content words into function words or affixes with grammatical function. Given these facts, and the fair assumption that the very first human grammars were simpler, it is reasonable to hypothesize that the earliest human languages were isolating languages, with no complex word-internal structure.

The 'transparency' idea appealed to above is different from the Semantic Transparency of Seuren and Wekker (1986). Their idea is a version of a 'one form—one meaning' principle claimed for creoles (Kay and Sankoff 1974). A problem with semantic transparency is identifying what we mean by 'one meaning', leading into the whole minefield of 'semantic primitives'. Rather, what I have in mind is **phonetic** transparency. Bickerton (1988 pp. 276–7) expresses the same idea with the term 'phonological salience'. The forms that are easiest to pick out from the flow of speech in the superstrate language are those taken up by a creole or pidgin. Sometimes picking out a salient stretch of speech from the superstrate language involves a re-analysis, as when Haitian creole made *zwazo* 'bird', taking it from French *les oiseaux*; another example is Haitian creole *zetwal* 'star', from French *les étoiles*. In both cases the creole *z-* is from the last consonant of the original French definite article. Where a creole reinvents some structure, perhaps mirroring substrate structure (as with Tok Pisin pronouns) the meaningful elements are expressed as easily dissectable segments of form. Extrapolating phonetic transparency back to the shape of prehistoric languages, I would not claim that they adhered to a 'one form—one meaning' principle, because of the difficulty in defining the 'meaning' side of such a principle. I would claim that the earliest prehistoric languages were probably phonetically transparent, with no fusion of morphemes, and few, if any, unstressed meaningful elements such as function words and affixes.

Use of **Compound nouns** and other compound forms is typical of pidgins (Mühlhäusler 1986). Sebba (1997, p. 50) gives these examples from Sranan Tongo.

wrokoman	'work+man' = 'worker'	
wakaman	'walk+man' = 'drifter'	
wrokosani	'work+thing' ='tool'	

We can put the use of compounds down to a paucity of vocabulary. If you don't have a word for something, make one up, in a transparent way. Compounding, by definition, involves simple juxtaposition of content words, with no grammatical markers binding the juxtaposed items. Developed creoles may keep the members of a compound noun expression but insert a grammatical marker, as in the Tok Pisin expression for 'hair', *gras bilong hed* and for 'beard' *gras bilong fes*. Pidgins and creoles also have more than the usual share of bi-morphemic question words, for example Guyanese Creole *wisaid* (from *which side* = 'where'), Haitian *ki kote* (from *qui coté* = 'where') (Bickerton 1981, p. 70). Bi-morphemic question words are a kind of compounding, also quite transparent in their meaning.

Next, **serial verbs**[41] are a feature characteristic of some, but not all, creoles. Serial verbs share with compound nouns the basic trait of expressing a meaning with two (sometimes more) content words in a conventional linear order. In a serial verb construction, several verbs are strung together in the same clause, typically all having the same understood subject, and sometimes all having the same agreement or tense and aspect markers. Payne (1997, p. 307) mentions that English has examples, albeit marginal, as in *Run go get me a newspaper*. Defining exact criteria for what counts as a serial verb construction is problematic, and some scholars include more examples in the category than others—see, for example Crowley (2002); Aikhenvald and Dixon (2006); Durie (1997); Newmeyer (2004). Nevertheless there is definitely a 'serial verb phenomenon', with a core of agreed examples.[42] Serial verb constructions are similar across languages. But each language with serial verbs has its own particular version. In each language with serial verbs, there are restrictions on which verbs can appear in these constructions. Verbs corresponding to English *take*, *give*, *go* and *come* are especially common in serial verb constructions. And in each language there are constraints on the ordering of verbs in serial constructions in relation to other parts of the sentence. Having a serial verb construction is not just having the possibility to string any sequence of verbs together. Part of the problem with a watertight definition of serial verb constructions is that they (like so much else in language) are a moving target. They represent a transitional stage between a kind of 'pre-structural' organization and a stage to which traditional linguistic structural analyses can apply. I hope to substantiate that view briefly in what follows.

Below are some creole examples, taken from Bickerton (1981, pp. 118–28). Here, the italicized words are the verbs:

Sranan[43]   a *waka go* a wosu Lit: He walk go to house.
                                    'He walked to the house'

---

[41] For an excellent concise summary of the facts and issues concerning serial verbs, I recommend the concluding chapter of Sebba (1987).

[42] The view that serial verb constructions are just a myth (Delplanque 1998) is an extreme outlier in the literature.

[43] Sranan is a creole of coastal Surinam, with largely English-based vocabulary; São Tomense is a creole of São Tomé, an island off the coast of West Africa, with a largely Portuguese-based vocabulary; Guyanais is a creole of French Guiana, with a largely French-based vocabulary; Djuka is an English-based creole of inland Surinam.

São Tomense   e *fa da* ine   Lit: He talk give them.
                                      'He talked to them'

In some cases, the object of the first verb intervenes between the verbs.

Guyanais   li *pote* sa *bay* mo   Lit: He bring that give me.
                                            'He brought that for me'
Djuka   a *teke* nefi *koti* a meti   Lit: He take knife cut the meat.
                                            'He cut the meat with a knife'

Serial verbs do not occur in all creoles but they are proportionately somewhat more common in creoles than in non-creole languages. Many Atlantic creoles, with African substrates, have serial verbs, as do many of the African substrate languages. Outside the Atlantic domain, Sankoff (1994) showed a similarity between serial verbs as used by Tok Pisin children and patterns in Austronesian languages. In such cases, appeal to substrate influence seems obvious. But there is a dilemma. Mostly the features characteristic of creoles are very common, even the most common across all languages. For instance, most creoles have only the simplest consonant–vowel (CV) syllable structure found in an overwhelming majority of languages. But verb serialization, though it exists outside creoles, is nevertheless a rather rare, or 'marked' feature of languages. And yet creoles tend to have it more often than other languages. A debate has raged over whether verb serialization in creoles is entirely due to substrate influence, or whether some factor from creole circumstances also plays a part. The relationship between Caribbean creoles and African substrate languages is usually cited in favour of substrate influences. Outside the Atlantic domain, it has been argued that Bislama, a creole spoken in Vanuatu, has properties of serial verbs that derive from substrate Oceanic languages (Meyerhoff 2001). Also outside the Atlantic domain, Bickerton (1989) argues that Seychelles Creole French, Seselwa, has serial verbs that could not have come from a substrate, and therefore are 'pro-universalist' evidence for the natural spontaneous emergence of such structures. Seuren (1990) argues that the phenomena in question are not genuine serial verb constructions. We should remember Mufwene's wise words: 'The universalist and substrate hypotheses complement one another'. Both substrate influence and the natural tendencies of people in creolizing situations may play a part.

There is a correlation between the absence of complex morphology in a language and the presence of serial verb constructions, both in creoles and non-creoles. This correlation is widely noted (Lefebvre 2004; Baker 1991; Muysken 1988b; Payne 1997; Aikhenvald and Dixon 2006). Payne (1997,

p. 307) cautiously notes 'Serial verbs occur in all types of languages, but may be more common in languages that have little or no verbal morphology (isolating languages)'. Aikhenvald and Dixon (2006, jacket) state 'Serial verb constructions are a pervasive feature of isolating languages of Asia and West Africa'.

What could be the reason for this correlation? Some accounts (e.g. Lefebvre 2004; Baker 1991; Muysken 1988b) are couched in the terminology of Principles and Parameters grammar, invoking the setting of parameters, an operation called 'raising to INFL', 'Theta Theory', and the 'Projection Principle'. In fact, the naturalness of the correlation can be expressed in less theory-laden terms. Assume you speak an isolating language with no complex morphology. For example you have no way of forming causative verbs; and no way of marking semantic roles, such as the beneficiary of an action, or the source or goal of an action, on nouns. But you do have words. You use words to express the meanings that are expressed in other languages by affixes on verbs and nouns. We have already seen instances in the examples above. For instance, São Tomense *E fa da ine*, literally 'He talk give them', meaning 'He talked to them', uses the word *da* 'give' to convey the meaning that in languages such as Latin or German would be expressed by a Dative case inflection on the pronoun for 'them'. One of Baker's (1991, p. 79) many examples compares Yoruba, an isolating language of Nigeria, with Kinyarwanda, a Bantu language of Rwanda with complex verbal morphology:

a. *Olè   fi   ọbẹ   gún   ọba.*
   Thief use knife stab chief
   'The thief stabbed the chief with a knife.' (Yoruba (George 1985))

b. *Umugabo   a-ra-andik-iish-a*   *íbárúwa   íkárámu.*
   Man   SP-PRES-write-INSTR-IND   letter   pen
   'The man is writing the letter with a pen' (Kinyarwanda (Kimenyí 1980))

Here, Kinyarwanda has a way of building the notion of instrumentality into the verb, rather as if some version of English had a verb glossed as 'write-with', which could be used in a sentence such as *Man write-with letter pen*. Expression of instrumentality need not be in the morphology of the verb. It can be in the morphology of the relevant noun, as in Russian, where (in this example), the noun for 'pen' would be marked with an instrumental case ending—*per-om* 'pen-with'. Yoruba lacks these morphological resources and uses a whole word, a verb glossable as 'use'. Here, the result is a version of a serial verb construction. Mufwene (1999, p. 118) puts the simple idea well: 'the general loss of inflections during the development of creoles is an important factor in accounting for the prominence of serial verb constructions in their systems—without inflections, *went/came fishing* becomes *go/come fish* as typically attested in creoles'. Bickerton expresses a similar thought, rather too strongly: 'Without prepositions and without inflectional morphology, how else could oblique cases be distinguished if not by serial verbs?' (Bickerton 1981, p. 121). Indeed; but Muysken (1988a, p. 296) weakens that argument with a killer fact: 'all creole languages, including those with extensive serialization, have the category preposition'. That is, creoles are not 'without prepositions', a premiss of Bickerton's argument. Bickerton's idea can, however, be half-rescued by a weaker inference. Without inflectional morphology, the task of distinguishing oblique cases, if it must be done at all, must be done by a word, and the word chosen can be either a preposition or a verb. As Bickerton points out in his reply to Muysken (Bickerton and Muysken 1988), the simple existence of prepositions in a creole does not necessitate that they be used in all the functions (such as case-marking) observed in the superstrate language. This weaker argument has the merit that it accounts for the fact that serial verbs are not found in all creoles. It must also be pointed out that not all languages without inflectional morphology use either prepositions or serialized verbs to express oblique cases. Riau Indonesian, as we have seen, leaves interpretation of oblique cases (e.g. location, instrument) to pragmatic inference from context, and does not have anything that would be called serial verbs.

There is a connection between serial verb constructions and **single-valence verbs**. The valency of a verb is the number of arguments that it licenses. For example, English *sleep* is a single-valency verb; sleeping conceptually only involves one participant, and the semantics of a verb often mirrors its grammatical valency. English *hit* is a di-valent verb, requiring an Agent (the hitter) and a Patient (the 'hittee'). In serial verb constructions, the ratio of verbs to arguments is increased closer to 1:1, so that each verb is paired with a single argument. Serial verb constructions involve 'multi-verb propositions whose arguments are distributed singly over the verbs' (Hopper 1985, p. 74). In the early stages of language acquisition, when a child's sentences are very short, verbs that in adult language are di-valent are often produced with one argument missing. Often a Subject is missing and the verb is accompanied by its Object. Attested examples of child two-word utterances are *Want baby*, *Want Car*, *Get ball*, *Get doll*, *See doll*, *See ball* (Braine 1963, p. 7). In the child's actual practice, these verbs are used as single-valence verbs. If two sentences with such single-verb valences are combined to express a somewhat more complex meaning, we can get strings like *use knife stab chief*. Interestingly, Genie, the girl deprived of language input until the age of thirteen, also occasionally juxtaposed single-valence verbs in a similar way, as in *father hit Genie cry long time ago* (MacSwan and Rolstad 2005, p. 232). We will see the connection between serial verbs and single-valence verbs again in connection with Nicaraguan Sign Language.

Serial verbs often undergo a historical process of grammaticalization to prepositions (or postpositions), and later to case inflections on nouns. By this route, serial verb constructions can disappear from a language. Givón gives an example: 'Ute derives all locative case-markers from historically-still-traceable precursor verbs. But these erstwhile verbs cliticize as noun suffixes, are in most cases phonologically reduced, and carry no discernible residue of verbal properties' (2009, p. 84). Somewhat more generally, 'Lexical categories intermediate between verb and preposition are a common feature of Oceanic languages, well known to Oceanicists for over one hundred years (see Codrington 1885). The complex typology of these categories can be given a coherent account if they are assumed to arise in the context of a diachronic drift from serial verb to preposition' (Durie 1988, p. 1). Lord (1993) gives a book-length survey and discussion of the directional diachronic processes leading from serial verbs to prepositions and case markers. Serial verbs can also get grammaticalized as auxiliaries; Meyerhoff (2001, p. 261) mentions a possible instance in Bislama. Grammaticalization of verbs into auxiliary verbs is a well known phenomenon: think of English *have* in *They have gone*. The connection between serial verbs and single-valence verbs, with the subsequent diachronic shift away from these constructions, is succinctly summarized by Givón:

What is involved, diachronically, is a slow process of reanalysis, by which the description of an event—that is, a proposition—is first assembled as a concatenation of small propositions in which, roughly, a one-to-one correlation is maintained between verbs and nominal arguments, so that in essence the function of each nominal argument is marked by the verb which precedes or follows it. In the course of time, however, a slow and gradual reanalysis by which the verbs *except for one* become grammaticalized as case-markers. The loosely concatenated paratactic expression then becomes a single sentence, falling under a single intonation contour, with *one* complex verb.

(Givón 1979a, p. 220)

Such diachronic shifts and reanalyses present problems for purely synchronic descriptions of languages, giving rise, for example, to such apparently paradoxical entities as 'tensed prepositions' (e.g. Bowern 2002). Synchronic complexity arises through diachronic processes. In another example giving rise to the same kind of synchronic descriptive dilemma, serial verbs can get grammaticalized into complementizers, little words introducing certain subordinate clauses. Bickerton (1981, p. 105) gives these examples from Guyanese Creole.

i   taak se i na si am
'He said that he didn't see it'

mi no   se i na si am
'I know that he didn't see it'

Se derives from English *say*. Thus we have the creole counterparts of *talk say* and *know say*. We are not licensed to say that these are serial verbs in the creole simply on the basis of the English forms. But these creole examples do string together words denoting actions and mental states. At the same time, *se* is beginning to look like a complementizer, as it introduces a subordinate clause. Bickerton goes into the descriptive problem of whether *se* is, or is not, a complementizer and concludes, after twelve pages of struggling with the generative formalism of the day, 'We can therefore only conclude that *se* is something other than a complementizer' (p. 116). At the beginning of his discussion, Bickerton had already pinpointed the source of his problem, with characteristic vigour and eloquence.

[W]e are not going to get very far with the study of creoles—or of child language acquisition, or of language origins—if we allow ourselves to remain trapped within the static, antiprocessual framework which has dominated linguistics since de Saussure. The emergence of creole languages is a process; the original growth and development of human language was assuredly a process. To apply to processes those methods expressly designed to handle static-synchronic systems is simply absurd.

(Bickerton 1981, p. 104)

There is a growing awareness that little in language makes sense except in the light of diachrony. Givón (2009, p. 61) states the same axiom: 'A synchronic typology, of whatever syntactic domain, can only make sense from a diachronic perspective; that is, as a typology of the diachronic pathways that gave rise to the extant synchronic types'. The key phrase here is 'make sense', referring to **explanation** rather than description. In some ways, even description involves making sense of data, because there are more or less insightful ways of describing data. But synchronic descriptions of languages can never be fully explanatory, I claim, with Givón and others, because they do not explain how the languages got to be the way they are. Languages get to be the way they are through diachronic processes. To the extent that we can also explain why the diachronic processes are the way they are, based for example on functional (communicative) or psychological principles, we can make sense of the language data in a way that would escape us if we are restricted to synchronic description. None of this is to minimize the value of good synchronic description or typology, without which diachronic explanations could not be approached.

The diachronic tendency in languages to shift away from serial verb constructions accounts for the relative rarity of these constructions across the world's languages. Diachronic grammaticalization is a common, but not a necessary process. Some languages for some reason resist grammaticalization trends and hold onto archaic features. The move from serial verbs to other types of grammatical organization is one-directional. We do not have examples of languages developing serial verbs out of pre-existing prepositions, case inflections, auxiliary verbs, or complementizers. Where a historic source for serial verbs can be seen, as with creoles, the verbs typically come from verbs in the superstrate language. Together, the correlation of serial verbs with isolating languages, and the uni-directional diachronic shift away from serial verbs into more complex constructions with prepositions and inflectional morphology, suggest that some very early prehistoric languages probably had some constructions concatenating words denoting actions or mental states (proto-serial-verb constructions).

Function words can be distinguished from content words in creoles, as in non-creoles. But typically, creoles have fewer function words than non-creoles. Function words in creoles come from a variety of sources. Some are borrowed directly from the superstrate or substrate languages. They may also originate by a process of grammaticalization of content words, as with the Tok Pisin preposition *bilong*, with many of the functions of English *of*, derived from the English content word *belong*. Another example is the Tok Pisin subordinating conjunction used with conditional clauses, *sapos*. This has roughly the same function as English *if*, but is derived from the English verb *suppose*. Siegel (2008, p. 32) notes that restricted pidgins lack function words altogether. Bickerton (1999b, p. 53) reports for the pidgin preceding Hawaiian Creole English 'an almost complete absence of grammatical items (including a complete absence of tense, modality, and aspect (TMA) markers)'. As for creoles which evolve from pidgins, in their early stages these have fewer function words than non-creole languages. Myers-Scotton (2001, p. 221) assumes that 'in contexts where a known pidgin preexisted a present-day creole there is a structural continuum with far fewer slots filled in an abstract grammatical frame in pidgins than in creoles'. This implies that at least some creoles have fewer function words (closed class items) than non-creoles. In the process of language growth, development of a set of function words proceeds quite rapidly. This growth is attested, and is generally unidirectional, so it is reasonable to surmise that the earliest human languages had few or no function words.

Among the function words found in many creoles are 'TMA' particles, little words expressing tense, modality, and aspect. Tense distinctions usually involve past time versus non-past[44] time. Modality distinctions usually involve 'realis' versus 'irrealis', that is whether the proposition expressed describes an event that actually happened or one that is merely spoken about, as with wished-for events or perhaps future events. Aspect distinctions usually involve the difference between an ongoing action or one that has been completed; the English progressive as in *She is going* and the English perfective as in *She has gone* express different aspects.

'A majority of creoles...express, tense, modality, and aspect by means of three preverbal free morphemes, placed (if they co-occur) in that order' (Bickerton 1981, p. 58). Bickerton argues that this ordering of these particles, together with details of their semantics, belongs to a set of innate dispositions in language acquirers and language creators. Holm, who is generally averse to the Bioprogram hypothesis, concurs mostly on the facts, but is somewhat more cautious in his generalization.

First, the creoles indicate tense, mode and aspect with verbal markers rather than inflections, and most of these markers occur before the verb. Secondly, there are striking semantic and syntactic similarities among the corresponding markers of each category that cannot be explained adequately by referring only to the creole's lexical source languages. Although these have usually provided the lexical forms of the markers (derived from European auxiliary verbs with partially similar semantic and syntactic features), the creole markers are part of a verbal system that is quite different from that of the European lexical source language in many respects.   (Holm 2000, p. 190)

Lexical source languages are the superstrate languages. Several authors have pointed out similarities between creole TMA systems and the relevant substrate languages. For Haitian creole TMA markers taken from African substrate (see Lefebvre 2001b, p. 192). Winford (2006, p. 104) writes 'Finally, the ordering of preverbal auxiliaries in SN [Sranan] also matches that of its Gbe substrate to a significant degree. For instance, it is well known that SN, like other radical creoles, displays a Tense–Mood–Aspect order of auxiliaries (among others)'. Faraclas et al. (2007, p. 257) argue that 'Papiamentu TMA operates essentially on the basis of the same system found in most Atlantic Creoles as well as in most of their West African substrate languages'. TMA markers like those in the Atlantic creoles are found in Nubi, an Arabic-based creole far from the Atlantic (in Kenya). Here, however, a superstrate influence from Arabic is definitely arguable (Thomason and Elgibali 1986.)

---

[44] I will not delve into Bickerton's arguments for distinguishing between 'past' and 'anterior' tenses.

Muysken (1981) is a detailed attack on the TMA aspect of the Bioprogram hypothesis, an attack which Bickerton (1981, pp. 73ff) rebuts. Bickerton's counterarguments in many cases dismiss the relevance of Muysken's examples, because they are not taken from 'classic' creoles which developed in circumstances of drastic social and linguistic upheaval. The problem with this argumentative strategy is that it narrows down the relevant empirical sample of languages to the point where any recurring patterns may not be statistically significant. Certainly some languages known as creoles deviate from Bickerton's generalization that TMA particles are preverbal. In Cape Verdean Creole, the 'anterior' (past) marker is suffixed after the verb (Baptista 2003, p. 95, citing Silva 1985, 1990). Also 'the Papiamentu irrealis marker *lo* is postverbal, against the LBH [bioprogram] prediction that it would appear preverbally' (McWhorter 1997, p. 57). Muysken (1988a, p. 291) seems to concede that something beyond substrate influences may play a part—'Still, there is no doubt that the very existence and overall similarity of the preverbal particle systems needs to be explained by a theory of creole genesis'. The most recent overview (Siegel 2008) is generally negative about the Bioprogram hypothesis, even for the limited set of creole situations (e.g. Hawaiian Creole English) at the heart of Bickerton's arguments. Research subsequent to Bickerton's has shown both the population movements and the linguistic facts to be more complex than his original account.

As far as TMA markers may be relevant to speculation about the earliest human languages, note that pidgins generally lack such markers, using instead various adverbial forms to convey these meanings. TMA markers are not likely to have figured in distant prehistoric languages.

Tone languages are recognized as a relatively clear language type. These are languages in which the musical pitch of a word is crucial to distinguish it from other words with the same sequence of consonants and vowels. Mandarin Chinese is the best known example, where a single syllable with the same consonants and vowel can mean four different things, depending on its tone (high level, rising, fall-rise, falling). Perhaps as many as half of the world's languages make some use of tone to distinguish words (Maddieson 2008). The distribution of tone languages is strongly skewed geographically. All Atlantic creole superstrate languages (European languages) are non-tone, and most of their substrate languages (African languages) are tone languages. It has occasionally been suggested that some creoles are tone languages. Holm (2000 pp. 166–9) cites a number of cases, without making any statement about the commonness or rarity of lexical tone systems in creoles. Prima facie, there are clear cases where minimal pairs of words exist distinguished by tone. For example, Günther (1973, pp. 48–51) writes that Principe Creole

Portuguese distinguishes *kwê* (rising tone) 'run' from *kwé* (high tone) 'rabbit'. Ferraz and Traill (1981) argue against Günther's analysis of this creole as a tone language, although it is not clear to me how the above monosyllabic pair can be interpreted synchronically as anything but a tonal minimal pair. I will come to the diachronic origin of such examples below. De Groot (1984, p. 1) writes simply that Ndyuka, a creole of Surinam, is a tone language, and indeed it does have some tonally distinguished minimal pairs. But Huttar and Huttar (1997, p. 396) note that tone 'is a marginal feature in Ndyuka'.

In fact, the use of tone in creoles is sparser than across languages generally. '[A]mong languages known as creoles, tone generally carries a relatively low functional load. More specifically, languages known as creoles make very little or no use of tone to (a) lexically contrast phonetically identical monosyllables, ... or (b) encode syntactic distinctions' (McWhorter 1998, p. 793). The suggested explanation for this rarity is 'Like inflections, [uses of tone] require a subtlety of perception unlikely to develop amidst the rapid, utilitarian acquisition typical of settings which give birth to a contact language' (p. 794). The 'subtlety of perception' idea is a testable hypothesis. It implies, for example, that distinguishing among tones is more difficult than distinguishing among vowels. Certainly languages typically make more vowel contrasts than they do tone contrasts, so this suggestion might be on the right track. If you want to distinguish words, it is preferable to do it primarily with non-tone contrasts, only using tone as a backup.

The actual words which the first pidgin or creole speakers used, if taken from a European superstrate lexifier language, would not have been distinguished by tone. In picking up the words, there were no accompanying tones to pick up. Any use of lexical tone in a creole cannot come from the superstrate language. How did the limited use of tone in creoles arise? The use of tone would have been familiar to speakers of the substrate languages of many creoles. A plausible suggestion, which works for some cases, is that distinctions of **stress** in the lexifier language(s) got interpreted as tonal distinctions. Stress on a syllable is distinct from tone, and is realized mostly as some combination of loudness and length. Stress and tone can be varied independently, though they are perceptually related. Now, the Portuguese words for 'rabbit' *coelho* and 'run' *correr* are disyllabic words with stress on their first and second syllable, respectively. A speaker of a tone language might have perceived this as a difference of tone, simplifying both to a monosyllable, but with different tones, *kwé* and *kwê* (Günther 1973, cited by Holm 2000, p. 166). Such an explanation won't work for words which were monosyllabic in the original superstrate language. Alleyne (1980, p. 73) suggests another explanation for the emergence of distinctive tone in creoles. His idea is that creoles adopt tone to distinguish otherwise homophonous words from different sources. A minimal pair in Saramaccan is *kai*, from English *call*, contrasted with *kaí*, from Portuguese *cair* 'fall, drop'. This functional suggestion is not persuasive, as languages, and especially isolating languages, are usually extremely tolerant of homophony—think of English.

Languages develop and lose lexical tone during their histories. Rise and loss of lexical tone are attested historical changes. Once a creole gets established, it may develop tonal distinctions, although very few have done so. The limited use of lexical tone in early creoles is most plausibly attributed to indirect substrate influence, as suggested above. The relative rarity of lexical tone distinctions in creoles suggests that tone is not the first natural resource exploited by humans for making semantic distinctions. It seems likely that the earliest human languages would not have exploited this resource, and were not tone languages.

'Tone', as linguists use the term, is different from **intonation**. Intonation patterns stretch over whole short sentences. English is not a tone language, but makes extensive use of intonation, for example to distinguish questions from statements, among many other uses connected with the pragmatic functions of utterances. The difference between asking a question and making a statement is very important in discourse, and creoles tend to use intonational means, rather than specific grammatical markers, to encode this difference. This is particularly true for *Yes/No* questions. Bickerton (1981, p. 70) cites *i bai di eg-dem* as meaning both 'He bought the eggs' and 'Did he buy the eggs?' in Guyanese Creole. We can do this in English, too, of course, with suitable intonation. Where a specific grammatical marker of a *Yes/No* question is used, it does not need to match up with any of the internal structure of the sentence. Holm (2000, p. 234) cites Miskito Coast Creole English *Das waz a swiit stuori, duonit?* meaning 'That was a nice story, wasn't it?' Note that in English, but not in the creole, the tag question *wasn't it?* has to agree with the subject of the sentence (hence *it*), with the tense of the verb (hence *was*), and be opposite in positive/negative polarity (hence *-n't*). All this complication is lacking in creole tag question markers.

We can presume that the difference between questions and statements was as important for early humans as it is for us, and that their languages had ways of expressing this difference. But it seems likely that little grammatical machinery was involved, and that intonation mainly carried the load. It would be going too far to infer whether such early languages had specific *Wh-* question words, as the creole versions all derive from one or other of the source languages, including in their positioning. It seems that it would have been useful to have such words, but such intuitions are notoriously unreliable. We often find modern languages lacking features that we think would be useful, as we have seen in the last few sections.

It can also be very useful to a hearer to distinguish with emphasis what you are talking about from what you have to say about it, that is to indicate the **Topic** and/or **Focus** of your utterance. Many creoles are reported as having topicalization and focusing devices, and I have not found a claim that any specific creole lacks the means of highlighting the Focus of a sentence. But 'Among creole languages, there are on the whole fewer formal devices to syntactically emphasize constituents than in older, longstanding languages with more diachronic depth' (Byrne et al. 1993, p. x). And it seems that having a focusing device is a higher priority for developing creoles than having a topicalization device. 'Indeed, it is not clear whether...the creoles we shall be discussing in this paper have or ever have had a clearly-defined formal topicalization device. . . . What all creoles do have is some focussing device (or devices)' (Bickerton 1993, pp. 191–2). Unfortunately, the literature does not always consistently distinguish topicalization from focusing. Both are high-lighting devices, but they have complementary functions. A favoured method is to place the highlighted element at the front of the sentence. Holm (2000, p. 234) gives the example of *An kwéschon dem di yúustu gí wí*, 'QUESTIONS, they used to give us', from Miskito Coast Creole English. Holm mentions this as topicalization, but it seems possible that it is a case of focusing, with 'QUESTIONS' the new, rather than the given information. Given Holm's gloss on this example, I find it hard to imagine a situation in which the idea of questions is already familiar to the hearer. But it's one example with limited context given, and I don't know the Miskito language. Kouwenberg (1994, pp. 423ff) has extensive discussion of 'contrastive focus' in Berbice Dutch Creole, which uses the front position in a sentence to signal this kind of highlighting. In a different section, the same author (pp. 47ff) also gives many examples of 'left dislocation' which clearly signal the Topic status of the element put at the front of the sentence. The difference between the two fronting constructions is that the topicalization construction has a resump-tive pronoun later in the sentence, marking the role the topicalized element plays in the whole sentence; Focus constructions lack this resumptive pronoun and are often marked by a special particle, *da* or *sa*. Thus Berbice Creole Dutch, with origins in the seventeenth century, progressed to a quite sophis-ticated stage before its probable extinction around the end of the twentieth century.

It also seems that creoles are somewhat freer than non-creoles in what kind of element can be topicalized or focused. Here are some examples from Cape

Verdean Creole (Baptista 2003, p. 148), showing that not only noun phrases, but also verbs and adjectives can be topicalized.

Fidju, N ten txeu, es e oitu
child I have a lot they COP eight
'Children, I have a lot of them, there are eight of them'

Ma sabi, N ka sta
But happy I NEG be
'But happy, I am not'

Kume, dja' N ka meste fla
Eat, PERF I NEG need say
'Eat, I don't need to tell you about'

All of these examples were recorded in natural conversation. One would need to know their discourse context to judge whether they are genuine instances of topicalization, and not focusing. Baptista calls them all 'topicalization'. A clear case of the flexibility of focusing in creoles is the Haitian Creole 'Predicate cleft' construction, by which a verb is located at the front of the sentence. Harbour (2008, p. 853) gives this example:

Se kouri Bouki ap kouri
SE run Bouki PROG run
'Bouki is RUNNING'

The meaning conveyed is 'that Bouki is running flat out or that Bouki is running, as opposed, say, to walking' (p. 854). This would be the approximate equivalent of English being able to have **It's RUNNING that Bouki is*. English can't focus on verbs with the *It*-cleft construction, but it can with the *What*-cleft construction, as in *What Bouki is doing is RUNNING*. The copying of the verb in Haitian is similar to the English use of a generic verb *do* in verb-focusing *What*-cleft constructions. Here is a similar example from a different language, Carribean English Creole, also involving Focus on the verb by putting it at the front after a Focus marker, and having a copy later in the sentence (Winford 1993, p. 275).

a gi Jan bring fuud gi dem
FOCUS give John bring food give them
'John brought food and GAVE (it to) them'

The more equal treatment of different parts of speech in creole topicalization and focusing constructions is reminiscent of Gil's **monocategorial** property, discussed in the previous section. It is clear from Bickerton (1981) and several other sources that topicalization in creoles is somewhat limited in the elements that can be put in front position. The limitation involves how the topicalized element is understood in relation to the rest of the sentence. It cannot be understood as too deeply embedded or too large a constituent. One of Bickerton's examples (p. 107) is from Guyanese Creole. *Mi no aredi se dem gaan* 'I know already that they've gone' cannot be more emphatically expressed as **se dem gaan mi no aredi* 'That they've gone, I know already'. We see the beginnings of Island Constraints in creoles.

McWhorter (1997, p. 116) describes how 'in the Atlantic creoles and many other languages, copulas tend to emerge diachronically from demonstratives used as NP resumptives in topic–comment constructions'. To illustrate, here is a version of the reanalysis which McWhorter suggests took place in Saramaccan (McWhorter, 1997, p. 98):

hen	*da*	*dí*	*Gaamá*	
he	that	the	chief	—EARLY CREOLE ANALYSIS—EMPHATIC, TOPICALIZED
he	is	the	chief	—LATER CREOLE ANALYSIS—NEUTRAL, NOW WITH COPULA

The evolution of copulas from the resumptive pronouns in topicalized sentences is also seen by researchers in other creoles, for instance by Arends (1989) in Sranan. What this shows for my purpose here is that topicalization was a feature of these creoles in their early form. It seems likely that some means of topicalization existed in systematic languages from a very early stage, and that placing the topicalized element at the front of the sentence was a naturally favoured method. It also seems likely that the earliest languages were less selective than some modern languages in the kind of element that could be topicalized. It could be an object-word (proto-noun), action-word (proto-verb), or a property-word (proto-adjective).

Beside Berbice Creole Dutch, other creoles have introduced a specific Focus marker. For example Jamaican CE has *A Jan wi a taak bout* 'It's JOHN we're talking about' (Bailey 1966, pp. 88–9) has the Focus marker *a* placed immediately before the focused element. This particular example makes it very clear that it involves Focus. In any conversational context, it must be common knowledge between speaker and hearer that they are talking. So the information that 'we are talking' must be given information. What they are talking about, namely John, is the Focus here. 'This *a*-element obligatorily precedes focalized XPs' (Bailey 1966, p. 84).

The front position in a sentence is salient, and languages exploit it for several 'highlighting' purposes, the main ones being topicalization and focusing. Pragmatically these are complementary functions. A Topic cannot be in Focus, and vice-versa. So there is competition between these functions for front position in a sentence. Creoles and other languages resolve this competition by marking the different functions with specific grammatical markers. Often topicalized elements at the front of a sentence have an 'echoing' resumptive pronoun later in the sentence. Jamaican CE marks focused elements with the particle *a*, Berbice Dutch Creole uses a focusing particle *da* or *sa*, and Haitian Creole uses a focusing particle *se* in a construction in which the front-focused element is echoed by a copy later in the sentence. Without such grammatical devices, the front position in the sentence is pragmatically ambiguous. It seems reasonable to surmise that the earliest languages, before the rise of such specific grammatical devices, used front position for an underspecified pragmatic highlighting purpose.

Several of the focusing or topicalization examples that we have seen involve constructions in which a somewhat long-range dependency exists. In the Haitian Predicate-clefting construction, there is a dependency between the emphasized verb near the beginning of the sentence and a copy of it later in the sentence.

Finally, although creoles are said usually to lack 'encrustation' with irregularities and idiosyncrasies, it doesn't take long for speakers of a new language to invent **idioms**. Here are some from Bislama, an English-based Creole of Vanuatu:[45]

rat i   sting long bed?
rat AGR   stink PREP bed
lit. does a rat stink in your bed?
means: 'What are you doing here now?/Why aren't you at home?'

solwora   i   drae/kamsoa
salt-water AGR   dry/comeashore
lit. The tide is out/in
means: 'I'm broke/flush'

Most, and possibly all, creoles have longer histories than the popular 'single generation' account admits. Language change happens quite fast. Many creoles have had time to evolve toward the kind of complexity found in non-creoles. If a creole can be observed very early in its development, it can give some clues to the shape of earliest human languages. Otherwise, pidgins are likely to be closer in shape to languages of that prehistoric stage. On this basis, we cannot reasonably speculate very much, but given that we are looking for a simple form of language anyway, this is not too frustrating. It seems very

---

45 Thanks to Miriam Meyerhoff for these examples.

plausible that the earliest languages with any hints of grammatical organization (1) were isolating, with no word-internal structure, (2) had very few
function words, (3) made productive use of juxtaposition of content words,
as in noun–noun compounding, (4) may have strung words denoting actions
and mental states (proto-verbs) together in a somewhat systematic way, (5)
did not use tone to distinguish words, (6) used intonation to distinguish the
pragmatic functions of sentences, such as questions or statements, (7) put
pragmatically highlighted elements of a range of sorts, Topic or Focus, action-
words as well as object-words, at the front of sentences, and (8) already
had some stock of conventional multi-word idioms. Individually, none of
these conclusions is very new, but collectively they start to build up a bigger
picture.

5.7 Basic Variety

There is a connection between pidgins/creoles and the interim forms of a
language produced by second language learners before they have fully mastered
the target language (Schumann 1978; Kouwenberg and Patrick 2003; Siegel
2003).[46] In second language acquisition (SLA), parallel to the debate in creole
studies, the question arises 'Where do L2 learners' consistent errors come
from?'. If a Vietnamese learner of English produces strings of English words
with features of Vietnamese grammatical organization (e.g. word order), this
can be seen as parallel to substrate influence in creolization (Helms-Park 2003).
But where L2 learners' errors are unlike anything in either the learner's native
language or the target language, this can be seen as due to some natural
instinctive bias coming from within the learner himself. In SLA, Pit Corder
pioneered the idea of an 'interlanguage', the language of language learners,
formed at least in part by natural biases in learners, and not necessarily
by transfer from the native language (Corder 1971; Selinker 1972). Both in
creolization and the intermediate productions of language learners, various
kinds of simplification are apparent, reinforcing the parallel. Klein and Perdue
(1997) use the term 'Basic Variety'[47] (BV) for a simple form of language
used effectively for communication by second language learners who learn the
second language outside the classroom. 'The BV is a type of language which, as

---

[46] A special issue of *Studies in Second Language Acquisition* (2003, Vol.25(2)) is
devoted to exploring the connection between creoles and second language acquisition.

[47] A special issue of *Second Language Research* 13(4) (1997), is devoted to the Basic
Variety.

far as we know, regularly develops during second language acquisition (outside the classroom)' (Klein and Perdue 1997, p. 305). 'The BV is a highly efficient system of communication, and in this sense it is surely a real language; at the same time, it lacks some of the structural characteristics which we typically find in fully fledged languages' (p. 333).

A note of caution must be expressed on putative parallels between creolization and SLA. People in pidgin and creole situations are not necessarily aiming to acquire the superstrate language. Rather they are just trying to communicate with each other. If two pidgin speakers need to communicate, this communicative goal has priority over conformity to the norms of the superstrate language. On the other hand, the emphasis that BV arises outside the classroom in discourse between non-native speakers of a 'target' language means that communication, rather than approximation to the 'target' language, may also be their highest priority. In what follows, I will mention features of BV where they appear to coincide interestingly with features of creoles, and where they appear to reflect some natural dispositions not traceable to the speakers' L1 or L2. A criticism of BV (Vainikka and Young-Scholten 2006) is that it describes a single (intermediate) stage in L2 acquisition, whereas some of its features are more prominent at early stages of learning and other features are more prominent at later stages. From the point of view of seeking natural, relatively input-free, dispositions of language creators, it will be advisable to focus on those features more associated with the earliest groping efforts of L2 acquirers.

BV uses a simple semantically based principle of word order, 'Agent First': 'The NP-referent with the highest control comes first' (Klein and Perdue 1997, p. 315). Differences in 'control'[48] range 'from clear agent–patient relations at one extreme (with verbs such as *hit, break*) to weak asymmetries (with verbs such as *kiss, meet*) and finally to complete absence at the other extreme (as in copular constructions)' (p. 315). Thus, for example, a BV speaker's clear preference for describing an attacking event is to put the expression for the assailant before the expression for the victim. This is also, of course, a clear tendency across fully-fledged languages. This makes no mention of the position of the verb, which in BV tends to come between an Agent expression and a Patient expression, and so BV is SVO. Comrie (1997, p. 368) notes that in the data from which the BV conclusions were drawn, the second 'target' languages were all SVO. So it is likely that SVO order in BV reflects the influence of the second language, rather than any instinctive preference for SVO order. SVO

---

[48] This is a different use of the term 'control' from that used in generative grammar.

order is also a feature that Vainikka and Young-Scholten (2006) identify with later stages of BV, by which time the influence of the L2 has penetrated further into the learner's behaviour.

One of Klein and Perdue's BV principles is 'Focus expression last' (p. 317). Their discussion is in terms of a Topic–Focus system, in which Topic and Focus are complementary. If a sentence is dichotomously conceived as split into two parts, then 'Focus last' equates with 'Topic first'. Klein and Perdue could have expressed the same principle in this alternative way. Perhaps they did not wish to invite the immediate appearance of conflict with their 'Agent first' principle. They do recognize that conflict between their principles arises. When it does, either '(a) learners "override" one of the constraints, or (b) they develop specific means to accommodate the "competition"' (p. 330).

Option (a) is the crude solution adopted early by L2 learners. If Topic and Agent differ, just choose one of them to put first, and hope that putting the other one later will not cause too much of a communicative problem. Klein and Perdue (p. 330) give examples of such a conflict being resolved in both possible ways by learners, influenced by preferred strategies in their native language. A Punjabi learner of English used *stealing bread girl* in a context where an English speaker would have used Agent-first order, with additional Focus-signalling stress on the Agent, as in *The GIRL stole the bread*. Or an English speaker might have used a dedicated Focus construction, as in *It was the GIRL that stole the bread*. The Punjabi speaker put the Topic expressed by *stealing bread* first, and hence the Focus expressed by *the girl* last. In another example, an Italian learner of German sacrifices the Focus principle (aka the Topic-first principle).

Klein and Perdue's option (b) is a later step, and clearly mirrors the emergence of specific Topic- and Focus-signalling constructions seen in creoles (previous section). They describe another learner coming up with an 'embryonic cleft construction', using *is the girl pinching the bread*, as a declarative, with *is* as a spontaneously made-up Focus marker. This kind of evidence nicely reinforces the idea that the earliest grammar creators would have used the salient front position in a sentence to highlight both semantic roles (e.g. Agent) and pragmatic functions (e.g Topic), and that specific grammatical markers of these roles and functions developed later.

The Basic Variety resembles pidgins in morphological simplicity. 'There is no inflection in the BV, hence no marking of case, number, gender, tense, aspect, agreement by morphology. Thus, lexical items typically occur in one invariant form' (Klein and Perdue 1997, p. 311). That is, BV is like an isolating language. BV also lacks function words. 'Strikingly absent from the BV are ... free or bound morphemes with purely grammatical function' (p. 332). Creoles do not lack function words, although they may have fewer than older languages. In this respect, the Basic Variety is more like a pidgin (or jargon) than a creole. Vainikka and Young-Scholten (2006) mention these features as belonging to earlier stages of L2 learning.

BV, according to Klein and Perdue, typically has only a few prepositions, and no complementizers, and lacks 'complex hierarchical structures, in particular subordination' (Klein and Perdue 1997, p. 332). Again, Vainikka and Young-Scholten (2006) identify these features with earlier stages of L2 learning. Thus BV in these further respects resembles a pidgin or early creole. 'In a well-documented study, [Broeder, et al.] (1993) observe that the BV favours noun–noun compound constructions over derivational word formation (as do pidgins; cf. Mühlhäusler, 1986)' (Klein and Perdue 1997, p. 312). Noun–noun compounds are formed by simple juxtaposition of words, rather than any internal structuring of words.

In brief, the intermediate language of second language learners who learn it outside the classroom in communicative situations strongly resembles pidgins and early creoles in a number of features (many of which were listed at the end of the previous section). This reinforces the picture we are building up of the likely shape of the very earliest languages with the beginnings of grammatical organization—isolating, monocategorial or nearly so, exploiting initial position for undifferentiated pragmatic functions (Topic and Focus), with few, if any, specific constructions dedicated to particular pragmatic purposes, correspondingly few, if any, function words, and compound nouns. The speed with which creoles develop specific dedicated constructions, and the readiness of BV speakers to invent ad hoc constructions to signal pragmatic functions, suggest that the simple stage does not last long in modern humans. The very earliest humans, say 300,000 years ago, may not have had exactly the same capacity for extension of the primitive variety, and linguistic expansion back then may have been slower. The co-evolution of more intricate grammatical structures within groups, and the biological capacity to acquire such structures, will be discussed in Chapter 8.

5.8 New sign languages

With creoles, as we saw, there is the perennial problem of disentangling 'universal' influences from substrate or superstrate influences. There are a few cases where a new language has recently emerged, apparently from no prior significant substrate or superstrate. These are new sign languages of the deaf. There are very few of these, and by far the best documented are Nicaraguan

Sign Language (Idioma de Señas de Nicaragua—ISN)[49] and Al-Sayyid Bedouin Sign Language (ABSL).[50]

ISN and ABSL are the most recently developed sign languages.[51] But the way in which they emerged almost certainly holds of sign languages with longer pedigrees, such as American Sign Language (ASL). The ultimate origins of these languages are undocumented, which is partial evidence for their spontaneous vernacular emergence. Hearing teachers, aristocrats, and priests have at times been instrumental in encouraging systematic use and teaching of manual/visual communication systems for the deaf, and we can often date such interventions. One instance is that of the Abbé de l'Epée who, in the eighteenth century, devised a method for signing meanings corresponding to French grammatical morphemes added to probably pre-existing signs for objects and actions. This is clearly parasitic on a spoken language, and is now called 'Old Signed French'. But it didn't catch on among the deaf community.

> In Paris, Sicard had learned from Epée's attempts that merely translating a French sentence into Signed French did not assist its understanding; therefore the meaning of each sentence was first explained in FSL [a pre-existing 'natural' sign language, JRH]. It remained only for Sicard's intellectual successor, Bébian, to propose dropping the intermediate step and using FSL as the language of the school as well as of everyday life.
>
> (Lane 1980, p. 126)

The outline of this story has been repeated many times, with well-intentioned hearing benefactors ignoring the naturalness and expressive power of sign languages which have evolved without central design in Deaf communities. There can be some lasting influence of spoken languages on sign languages, sometimes originating when hearing people attempt to translate 'word-for-word' from one medium to the other. 'One cannot fail to notice that the high incidence of question particles in East Asia corresponds to a prevalence of question particles in the spoken languages in the region' (Zeshan 2008).

It ought to be obvious, but often is not, that a language whose output modality is movements of the hands, arms, head, and face-parts can in principle be just as expressive of ideas of all sorts as a language whose output modality is movements of the vocal cords, tongue, velum, jaw, and lips. Nevertheless, either due to the relative historical newness of sign languages or to the difficulty

---

[49] References for ISN include Kegl and Iwata (1989); Kegl et al. (1999); Kegl (2002); Senghas (1995a, 1995b, 2001, 2003).

[50] References for ABSL include Aronoff et al. (2004, 2008); Sandler et al. (2005); Meir et al. (2007, 2010); Al-Fityani and Padden (2010); Padden et al. (2010).

[51] Meir et al. (2010) discuss the origins and social circumstances of many other relatively new sign languages.

of researching language in a new medium, there remains some question as to how much of meaning is made grammatically explicit in sign languages, rather than being left to pragmatic inference. For instance, according to Zeshan (2008), twenty-five out of thirty-eight sign languages surveyed had no known sign 'whose main function is to indicate that an utterance is a question'. The figure of twenty-five 'also includes sign languages for which no clear evidence for question particles has been found so far. In particular, in some sign languages there may be a process of incipient grammaticalization of question particles, but the evidence is not conclusive to speak of bona fide question particles'.

The crucial, and very obvious, point about deaf people is that they cannot hear. So the sounds of spoken languages used around a deaf child or adult are a completely closed book to them. Lip movements can be observed, but they are not an adequate clue to what is being said. A single deaf child raised in a speaking community without concessions to signing acquires no language at all.[52] If a deaf child learns to read a written language, its written form is all she knows. The fact that the written symbols correspond to oral sounds does nothing for her. Where preliterate deaf children acquire a sign language, there is no way that the sounds of any spoken language can influence them. Most crucially for our purposes, where illiterate deaf people spontaneously develop a language among themselves, as with ISN and ABSL, there is no way that it can be parasitic upon the flow of sounds of any spoken language in their environment, although there can be very limited influence due to lip-reading. American Sign Language is closer to French Sign Language, from which it developed, than it is to British Sign Language. Various mutually unintelligible sign languages exist in the Arabic-speaking world, and there is resistance to the idea of developing a single 'pan-Arabic' sign language (Al-Fityani and Padden 2010). If such a language were to come into existence, it would be no more 'Arabic' than ASL is 'French' or 'English', where these terms refer to spoken languages. In this way, the origin and evolution of sign languages

---

[52] Schaller (1995) describes the case of deaf man who lived for 27 years, she claims, without acquiring any language at all, due to his deafness. She describes a Eureka moment when he apparently realized for the first time, at the age of 27, that some action could actually refer to some entity in the world. This 'naming insight' comes to normal children some time around the beginning of their second year. Helen Keller describes suddenly gaining this insight at the age of six (Keller et al. 1903). The term 'insight' has connotations of awareness; it is hard to know how much awareness is involved in the earliest exploitation of a regular form–meaning correspondence. I take Schaller's account with some scepticism, as her subject 'Ildefonso' had deaf relatives who supported him and she describes fairly elaborate story-telling sessions in a group of these people, including Ildefonso.

are the closest case we can find to the circumstances in which the first human languages originated and evolved.

> Where sign language is concerned it is important to realize that the deaf individuals who have created communication systems within hearing-speaking populations did not have access to the existing spoken languages (Kegl et al. 1999); thus, an examination of the formation of sign in their different communities offers a unique glimpse into language genesis in real populations.   (Ragir 2002, p. 272)

> [T]he language-emergence process in Nicaragua constitutes one of the few cases in which ... innate human language capacities, by virtue of no co-existing language input, have been forced to take a singular role in shaping the emergent language. ... We have been able in Nicaragua to witness first hand the source point of language genesis. We have discovered that the source of language is within us but that the conditions for its emergence crucially depend upon community.   (Kegl et al. 1999)

New sign languages are our best clue to how the earliest languages got started. Nevertheless, certain reservations must be expressed about their direct applicability. First, the medium makes a difference. I focus in this book on the origin and evolution of language in its prevalent modern form, speech. Where there are significant differences between signed and spoken syntax, I will mention them. Secondly, modern deaf people are surrounded by hearing people who obviously communicate, so they are more aware than our earliest ancestors of some of the richness of social life made possible by some form of communication.[53] Thirdly, if there has been any gene-culture co-evolution of humans in the last 300,000 years (see Chapter 8), then modern deaf people are genetically more capable of acquiring a complex modern language than our earliest human ancestors. Despite all these reservations, the case of new sign languages of the deaf is obviously relevant in our search for clues to how early human languages came into being.

5.8.1 Nicaraguan Sign Language

Idioma de Señas de Nicaragua (ISN) sprang into existence in a period of about fifteen years starting in the 1980s. The process is summarized by Kegl et al. (1999) and in many other publications. Under the Somoza dictatorship from 1934 to 1979, deaf people were isolated, often hidden away, and there was no Deaf community. A substrate of sorts existed in the form of limited 'homesigns' used within families before deaf children were brought together in

---

[53] This is what I find rather incredible about Susan Schaller's account of Ildefonso living to the age of 27 with no inkling of what the people around him were doing when communicating.

one school after the 1979 Sandinista revolution. The school situation makes ISN a 'community sign language', as opposed to a 'village sign language', in the terms of Meir et al. (2010). This difference affects the speed at which a new sign language can develop. Bringing deaf Nicaraguan children together lit a fuse, and it was the natural spontaneous interaction of the kids that fuelled the explosion, not any deliberate intervention from their teachers. The school's policy was to encourage oral communication; signing was forbidden in the classrooms. Signing flourished and grew among the deaf children outside the classroom. Kegl et al. (1999) trace an extremely rapid evolution through stages from 'mimicas', the result of immediate pooling of the diverse homesigns that children brought with them, through Lenguaje de Señas de Nicaragua (LSN), equivalent to a pidgin or jargon, to fully-fledged ISN. The whole process to get to a recognizably 'full' sign language took about fifteen years. The language continues to evolve, of course. On the side of this process, and in parallel, a 'Pidgin de Señas de Nicaragua' (PSN) also emerged, by which hearing Spanish speakers and deaf signers interacted. Kegl et al. (1999) state that this had minimal effect on the evolution of ISN. Spanish, the only candidate superstrate language, played a negligible, but not quite zero, part in this story. After the emergence of ISN and increased general interaction between signers and the hearing population, Spanish had some influence, for example with signers finger-spelling Spanish words. A crucial difference between the Nicaraguan situation and other creolization processes is that any 'substrate' known to the Nicaraguan children was not a fully formed language, unlike the West African languages which were substrates for Atlantic creoles. The assorted homesign conventions that the children brought from their homes were limited in scope, variable, unstandardized, even informally, and not fluent. The Nicaraguan children were thus thrown much more on their own innate resources in developing an effective communication system.

The Nicaraguan Sign Language phenomenon gave us a marvellous window on language creation as it was happening. Fortunately, expert researchers were on hand from the beginning to record and test the young creators. The main research leaders were Judy Kegl and Ann Senghas. Successive cohorts of deaf children came into the central deaf school in Managua. The most developed forms of the language were observed in children who had come to the school (a) early in their own lives, well before the age of seven, and (b) late in the period over which the language developed, that is in the 1990s. The children who had arrived in the early 1980s made a start at inventing the language. The children who arrived later in the 1980s, if they were still young enough, picked up the baton and pushed development of the language further. It seems that the population turnover and age structure were just right for this to happen.

I will first dispatch a couple of features in which the manual/visual medium does make difference, so that we can make no inference from sign languages to the probable shape of early spoken languages. One such feature is morphology, where we have seen a preference for isolating, morphologically simple forms in spoken language. Sign languages are different, partly because of the possibility of simultaneous movements of the various signing organs, and partly due to the relative slowness of visual processing compared to auditory processing.

[I]t is reasonable to ascribe the dearth of sequential affixation in both creoles and sign languages to their youth. Despite these similarities, however, unlike creoles, all sign languages that have been investigated in any detail so far have complex morphology. The morphology of sign languages tends to be nonconcatenative or 'simultaneous' rather than sequential   (Aronoff et al. 2003, p. 54)

The visual system, which is the typical modality for reception [of signed languages], is not suited to the same rapid linear processing that the auditory system can handle (Poizner and Tallal 1987). As a consequence, signed languages favor packing more information into a single sign (more agglutinative morphology, with the potential for this morphology to be simultaneously realized, or nested). The demands of the modality override many of the spoken-creole generalizations, particularly those favoring isolating morphology.   (Kegl et al. 1999, p. 214)

If it should turn out that the earliest human languages with a grammatical system were in the manual/visual modality, then my claim that early languages were isolating, without word-internal structure, would have to be limited to the earliest spoken languages, that is after the putative transition into the vocal/auditory modality.

There is a tendency in sign languages for simultaneous, rather than sequential coding of information. But the tendency is not taken to the extremes that one could imagine. One could imagine a highly agglutinating form of sign language, with 'one-word sentences' consisting of up to a dozen morphemes signed simultaneously. But this doesn't happen. In all sign languages, it is possible to discern a sequential order of the main parts of a sentence, for example Subject, verb, and Object. A disposition to concatenate some signs seems to come naturally, even when a more iconic representation would involve simultaneous actions.

A development from simultaneous gestures to sequential gestures is seen in the early history of ISN. Senghas and Littman (2004) showed videos of simple dynamic events to first-cohort ISN signers and to second- and third-cohort ISN signers. These videos involved, for example, an animated cartoon of something rolling downward. Downward motion can be signalled iconically and holistically by a hand-over-hand rolling motion while simultaneously leaning forward and down to shift the place where this hand action is happening. Alternatively, the event can be segmented into its manner (e.g. rolling) and its path (e.g. downward), and the hand-over-hand rolling gesture is now separated in time from a gesture indicating downward motion, typically a one-hand pushing motion down and away from the body. In this case, the ROLLING gesture and the DOWN[54] gesture are produced in sequence. Senghas found that

> The groups differed dramatically in the means used to express both manner and path. In . . . the signs of first cohort NSL [=ISN, JRH] signers, manner and path were expressed primarily simultaneously; in the descriptions produced by the second and third cohorts of NSL signers, they were expressed primarily as sequences of simple manner and path units. (Senghas and Littman 2004, p. 161)

This shows a progression in the very early development of ISN from simultaneous expression of semantic elements to sequential expression. Even though the medium permits simultaneous expression, second- and third-cohort ISN signers preferred a sequential form. The authors also note that in Spanish Sign Language, a 'mature' sign language, the same event is again signalled simultaneously, but now using grammatical devices which had not yet developed in ISN. We see a microcosm reflecting initial pidgin-like serial juxtaposition of words, followed by creole-like grammaticalization of one of the meaningful elements, which in the manual/visual medium can be expressed simultaneously with the other element.

I noted above a preference for compounding of nouns in pidgins. Here are some LSN/ISN examples of juxtposition use to form compound nouns, or noun-classifier sequences (from Kegl et al. 1999, p. 193). (The ˆ mark indicates concatenation, a hyphen indicates simultaneity.)

OVOID-large-longˆCUT-LENGTHWISE	'papaya'
OVOID-largeˆHANDLE-OVOID-largeˆWHACK-OFF-	
TOPˆDRINK	'coconut'
REDˆOVOIDˆCUT-WIDTHWISE	'pitaya, cactus fruit'

Word order, especially in early cohorts of ISN signers is significantly verb-final. Senghas et al. (1997) give a list of fifteen common word orders in the first generation. They are all verb-final. In the second generation the most common word orders are also all verb-final. At these stages, however, the language had not developed to a stage where a single verb could be used with two nouns, a

---

[54] Following the sign language notational conventions, I use capitals to represent signs in sign languages.

Subject and an Object, so we cannot conclude that ISN at this stage was SOV. But the preferred verb-final order is interestingly similar to SOV.

Serial verbs also arise in the Nicaraguan data. In LSN, 'only one full noun tends to be signed per verb. Multiple-argument propositions are often expressed using separate verbs to support each NP argument. We will argue that these sequences of *single-valence verbs* are precursors of a grammaticized serial verb construction' (Kegl et al. 1999, pp. 183–4). Senghas et al. (1997) showed videos of four kinds of simple event to first-generation[55] LSN/ISN signers. The event types were (1) one-argument, e.g. *a man cries*, (2) two-argument, one animate, one inanimate, e.g. *a man taps a cup*, (3) two-argument, both animate, e.g. *a man pushes a woman*, and (4) three-argument, e.g. *a man gives a cup to a woman*. Subjects were asked to describe the actions in signs. There was an interesting difference between the first two types (1, 2) and the last two types (3,4). The results are worth quoting at length.

Signers from the first generation produce predominantly NV sentences for verbs with one animate argument (e.g., MAN CRY), and NV or NNV sentences (e.g., CUP MAN TAP) for verbs with one animate and one inanimate argument. While the nouns in these sentences always precede their verbs, there is no contrastive word order used to distinguish the subject (or agent) noun versus the object (or theme) noun, as long as the nouns differ in animacy. In contrast, when there are two animate arguments, a quite different construction appears. Events with two animate arguments require two verbs, one of which carries the agent and the other of which carries the experiencer, and observe a NVNV word order in which the first noun is always the agent (e.g., MAN PUSH WOMAN FALL). While the nouns are not obligatory in these sentences, if two animate nouns are expressed, both verbs must be present. No sentences occur in which a single transitive verb has both an animate subject and an animate object. Class 4 events, with two animate arguments plus an inanimate theme, appropriately show the combined syntactic patterns of classes 2 and 3. These events also require two verbs, one of which may take both a subject/agent and theme, and the other taking the recipient. Such sentences are signed NOVNV (e.g., MAN CUP GIVE WOMAN RECEIVE).   (Senghas et al. 1997, p.555)

This passage is rich in echoes of findings that I have surveyed from other domains. Recall first Klein and Perdue's 'Agent-first' principle for the Basic Variety. Where two participants are animate, and therefore both potential Agents, these signers used an Agent-first principle to make it clear who did what to whom. Where only one participant is animate, and thus almost certainly the Agent, the order of nouns is not fixed as a receiver of a signal

---

[55] The literature alternates between the terms 'cohort' and 'generation', apparently with no difference in meaning.

can apply normal pragmatic inference to work out which participant initiated the action. Note also the verb-final word order in all sentence types here; SOV order is the commonest across modern languages, and has been argued by Givón (1979a) and Newmeyer (2000) to be the most likely prehistoric order. Finally, sentences like MAN PUSH WOMAN FALL and MAN CUP GIVE WOMAN RECEIVE are clearly examples of serial verbs, at least under some definitions of serial verb. My speculation about these latter examples is that they may derive mentally from sequences of two sentences, describing two events, albeit events inextricably linked in the videos. If a pause were inserted after the first verb, they would be indistinguishable from two-sentence sequences. Possibly, in marshalling their thoughts to describe these events (what Slobin calls 'thinking for speaking' (1996)) these first-cohort signers have available a rudimentary code that is only capable of encoding the complex event of a man pushing a woman down by its two separate parts. However, it seems clear that utterances like MAN PUSH WOMAN FALL are single-sentence serial verb constructions, because one of the noun arguments can be topicalized and placed at the front of the sentence, optionally with a copy later in the sentence (Kegl et al. 1999, p. 218). A consideration of ambiguity-avoidance also seems relevant to this two-verb construction. Where only one participant is animate, a two-participant event is encoded with only one verb/sentence, and who-does-what-to-whom is clear from pragmatics. This method of interpretation won't work in a single sentence describing an event with two animate participants. Having two verbs, each with its own referring expression, solves this problem.

The development of serial verbs in the second generation is interesting and suggestive. In this study, 'The subjects...were eight Nicaraguan signers (four first-generation and four second-generation), all of whom entered the signing community before the age of six. The four first-generation signers entered the community in 1980 or earlier, and had a mean age of 24 years at the time of testing. The four second-generation signers entered in 1985 or later and had a mean age of 12 years at the time of testing' (p. 552). A comparison of results from the two generations is striking, enabling us to see, in a way unique to this large research project, possible phases in the growth of a language from its very earliest grammatical stages to a subsequent, but still not 'fully fledged' stage. The results above were from the first-generation signers. Second-generation signers described events of the first two types similarly to the first-generation signers. But there were interesting developments in how they described events of the last two types. '[T]he most common, basic word orders from the first generation are much less frequent.... [T]he new orders that replace them often have the two verbs adjacent to one another. This new pattern is not merely the consequence of the production of fewer nouns. ... Thus we now observe sentences such as MAN WOMAN PUSH FALL, and MAN PUSH FALL WOMAN' (p. 558). Here are serial verbs, by anyone's definition. The two verbs have been brought together, and this two-verb package can occur after or between the two noun arguments. A little later in the development of ISN, signers start to produce genuine two-valence verbs, like English transitive verbs, with sentences such as MAN PUSH WOMAN. Here is my illustrative summary of the whole course of (very rapid) development.

1st cohort		2nd cohort		later ISN
MAN PUSH WOMAN FALL	>	MAN WOMAN PUSH FALL/ MAN PUSH FALL WOMAN	>	MAN PUSH WOMAN
(Sequence of two Noun–Verb clauses with single-valence verbs)		(Verbs brought adjacent, serial verbs)		(Adjacent verbs collapsed to one— transitive verbs)

Kegl et al. conclude with:

> The use of single-valence verbs seems to be a natural stage in the emergence of serial verbs and the emergence of transitivity in language. Single-valence verbs circumvent the need to use syntactic means of identifying grammatical relations. They are an expected grammatical characteristic of early stages in the emergence of a language and may be expected in spoken-language pidgins as well. (Kegl et al. 1999, p. 221)

Next, there are long-range dependencies in ISN. In spoken language these are defined in temporal terms. The dependent words are separated in time by the occurrence of other intervening words. Sign languages exploit space, rather than time, to capture some dependencies between elements. In beginning to describe an event with several participants, signers allocate regions of the signing space (e.g. top left, lower right) to individual entities, and when referring to these entities later, they pick out the appropriate regions. Thus in a sense the entities mentioned in a discourse are ever-present. In LSN, 'a brow raise over a single sign can mark it as a topic' (Kegl et al. 1999, p. 183). This also illustrates the exploitation of simultaneity in sign languages; it is parallel to the use in a spoken language of intonation to indicate a topic, rather than any device involving a linearly separated marker or construction involving a nonstandard order of elements. The brow raise does show that the need for some topicalization device is felt early in the development of a new language. Linear devices have also emerged in ISN for discourse highlighting of selected elements. These, unsurprisingly, involve exploiting front position, which thereby enters into a long-range dependency with later elements in the sentence. I give below Kegl et al.'s examples (p. 218), simplified and with my own glosses to indicate the Topic meanings.[56]

MAN, WOMAN PUSH MAN GET-PUSHED
'As for the MAN, the woman pushed him'

MAN GET-PUSHED, WOMAN PUSH MAN GET-PUSHED
'As for PUSHING THE MAN, it was the woman that did it.'

Another long-range discourse phenomenon in ISN, involving anaphoric reference, can also be interpreted as showing a kind of **monocategoriality**, as described earlier in connection with Riau Indonesian. In the ISN case, a form of the same lexical item is used, according to discourse circumstances, as either a noun or a verb.

> One striking characteristic of both LSN and ISN is the fact that anaphora is frequently realized via a reduced verb form, a construction that appears to be unique to Nicaraguan Sign Language. To produce this form, a verb is truncated to its uninflected form and reduced significantly in amplitude. This reduced form is then used to refer back to the referent in the narrative that last served as subject of that verb. Thus, the reduced form used to pick out a specific referent changes as the narrative unfolds.
>
> (Kegl et al. 1999, p. 190)

I give their example below, simplified and modified to pick out the relevant point. This is a narrative about a person, X. The two verb forms in boldface actually refer back to this same person, X; the underlined verbs are those which link this person to the 'verby' referring expressions used later in the discourse.

X <u>collected</u> feathers from the chickens. The chickens looked up, naked. **Collect** jumped off the mountain. Tried to <u>fly</u>. Crashed into the mountain. The mountain crumbled. **Fly** raised his arm, still covered with feathers, from the rubble and had an idea.

It is perhaps significant that this monocategorial use of a word involves its bare uninflected form; monocategoriality and lack of inflection are both features that we are coming to expect in simpler varieties of language.

---

[56] I assume that Kegl et al. have not conflated topicalization with focusing. Even if they have, the examples still show the use of front position for discourse highlighting, with concomitant long-range dependencies.

5.8.2 *Al-Sayyid Bedouin Sign Language*

Another newly emerged sign language, arguably a creole, Al-Sayyid Bedouin Sign Language (ABSL), also reveals properties echoing those we have already seen. The literature on this language is less extensive than that on ISN. It is older than ISN, having emerged in the 1930s in a Bedouin community as a response to the rise of congenital deafness in a subpopulation. There are about 140 deaf people in the community. ABSL is a village deaf sign language. Many hearing villagers are more or less fluent in the sign language. ABSL is used among the deaf people and between deaf and hearing people. The first generation that used ABSL are now dead. The second generation[57] were in their thirties or forties when observed, and the third generation 'range from teenagers to young children' (Sandler et al. 2005, p. 2662).

The predominant word order in ABSL is SOV, unlike any of the nearby languages, spoken Israeli Hebrew and Arabic and Israeli Sign Language, all SVO. The creators of ABSL would appear to have had a natural preference for SOV word order.

Overall, we find statistically significant structural regularities in the order of signs in the language: S-O-V order within sentences. . . . These word orders cannot be attributed to the ambient spoken language. SOV word order is not characteristic of any language that ABSL signers may have had contact with. The basic word order in the spoken Arabic dialect of the hearing members of the community, as well as in Hebrew, is S-V-O. This generation of signers had little or no contact with [Israeli Sign Language], whose word order appears to vary more widely in any case.

(Sandler et al. 2005, p. 2664)

The predominance of verb-final orders was confirmed by further data collected later (Padden et al. 2010). This preferred word order may be due to special properties of signed languages. It could be seen as supporting the general idea of a natural tendency to create SOV word order, notably different from the SVO order claimed by Bickerton, on the basis of creoles, to be innately preferred. Fischer (1975) studied old films of ASL, and proposed that ASL changed over time from SOV to SVO. On the scant evidence available, from new sign languages, typological universals and uniform direction of change, SOV may have been the proto-word order.

Beside SOV order, there are hints in the ABSL data of serial verbs, or single-valence verbs. 'Most clauses contain one argument per verb, with the argument preceding the verb' (Sandler et al. 2005, p. 2663). This is true of

---

[57] It is important to note that 'generation' here has a different sense from the same term in the studies by Senghas, Kegl and others on ISN.

many two-place (transitive) events, where either the subject term or the object term was omitted. On describing a scene from a video clip, one signer produced WOMAN APPLE GIVE; MAN GIVE, and another produced WOMAN GIVE MAN TAKE (Sandler et al. 2005, p. 2664). The strong preference for single-valence verbs (or single-argument clauses) was also confirmed by more data collected later. For example, 'an event in which a girl feeds a woman may be described as: WOMAN SIT; GIRL FEED' (Padden et al. 2010, p. 395). The semi-colon here indicates a 'prosodic' break between separate sentences, realized as a slight pause in signing or brief resting of the hands. These observations echo those of Goldin-Meadow and Mylander (1998), who studied Chinese and American homesigns used by deaf children. They used predominantly two-gesture 'sentences' in which the gesture denoting the action followed the gesture denoting one of the participants in the action, whether an intransitive actor (as in MOUSE EAT) or a transitive patient (as in CHEESE EAT). As in the ISN and ABSL cases, there was little likelihood that these children had been influenced by any other language, spoken or signed. And moreover, the homesigns used by these children tended to be more complex than those used by their mothers. The children were leading the development of these simple systems. Of course, both in ABSL and the homesign systems, despite the significant statistical tendencies, there was some variability among individuals.

The facts above are sometimes expressed in grammatical terms, for example 'noun', 'verb', and 'SOV'. But there is no need, as far as we have seen yet, to assume that the deaf signers and gesturers are guided by some specifically **syntactic** template. It could well be that discourse-related factors like Topic and Focus are influencing the behaviour. Padden et al. (2010) give convincing arguments that ABSL discourse is chunked into very short sentences. The choice and sequencing of such sentences is determined by discourse-motivated considerations such as 'background precedes foreground' (Talmy 1983). But within the short sentences the order of elements is more fixed. '[I]f an event is described in a sequence of clauses, signers often describe the patient (stationary argument) first; but if the same event is described by a single clause, then the active argument, the agent, is introduced first, typically yielding SOV order' (Padden et al. 2010, p. 397). An example showing this is a two-sentence sequence describing a video clip in which a man is showing a picture to a woman: WOMAN LOOK. MAN PICTURE SHOW. (p. 395). Another example describes a woman giving a shirt to a man: MAN STAND. WOMAN SHIRT GIVE. MAN TAKE. (p. 395).[58] This simple language has already

---

[58] This argument and these data are also found, almost verbatim, in Aronoff et al. (2008).

settled on simple clauses with consistent internal structure. The clauses are juxtaposed, with prosodic breaks in between them.

So far, no overt grammatical mechanisms for embedding one clause inside another have developed. Aronoff et al. (2008) describe instances where a signing episode can be translated into another language using recursive devices such as marked subordinate clauses. '[W]e do not find overt syntactic markers such as complementizers introducing embedded clauses, but we do find that signers convey messages which are multi-clausal in nature, such as conditionals, . . . adverbial clauses with similar dependency . . . and reported speech' (Aronoff et al. 2008, p. 145). We must not confuse sentences with messages. Of course, it is possible to 'translate' an utterance from a pidgin, or even a jargon, into grammatical English with a full panoply of grammatical markers. It is not clear to me that the ABSL signers themselves are deploying consistently conventionalized explicit means of conveying their meaning, rather than relying on the pragmatics of the situation. At most, the indications of subordination are 'prosodic' using facial expressions, rather than manual signs.

Although we have found very few syntactic markers in ABSL—no subordinators, relative pronouns, or other complementizers, no lexical forms to mark conditionals, no syntactic structures to mark questions, all of these functions are expressed in the language. Through painstaking slow-motion viewing of a conversation between two women and analysis by means of a minutely detailed coding system, we have been able to identify some consistent prosodic markers of syntactic structure. . . . Not only do prosodic signals serve to separate clauses into intonational phrases, they can also link them to one another to form complex propositions. This linkage is typically signaled by raised eyebrows and head/body forward or down at the end of the first constituent, followed by a change in head/body position and facial expression for the next.

(Aronoff et al. 2008, p. 140)

We cannot tell from this subtle analysis how widely conventionalized this signalling behaviour has become in ABSL. Although regular, and reflecting these individuals' competences, it could be idiosyncratic to the particular women. And we don't know whether the same signals were given by both women in the conversation. The same authors write in a later paper that 'there are no reports of a village sign language with syntactic embedding, that is, the embedding of a clause inside another, as in '*He told me that he is coming*', or '*The boy that you met yesterday is my son*'. (Meir et al. 2010, p. 15). What seems likely is that individuals are just beginning uncon-sciously to explore ways of expressing meanings with subordinate clauses, not using the most saliently dynamic instruments, the hands. We don't know to what extent these tentative individual efforts have yet caught on and become more widely conventionalized. Meir et al. (2010) note that lexical variability is a feature of village sign languages generally. 'For example, in ABSL three lexical variants exist for commonly used words such as *cat*, *lemon*, *train*, and *morning*, and many signs have two variants, such as *fish*, *white*, *red*, *tree*, and many others' (p. 16). The simplicity and variability of this language does not reflect on the grammatical capacities its speakers were born with, but rather on the abnormal date and place of their birth. It takes more than innate grammatical capacity in individuals to make a language. It takes a certain kind of community, and it takes time, usually at least several generations.

Condensing a message from the sections of this chapter so far, creoles and pidgins, the Basic Variety, and new sign languages give us a window on how humans with normal innate capacity for language go about constructing new languages when the ambient languages are mixed and inconsistent, or insufficiently exemplified, or just plain absent. The most basic characteristics of historically new languages are a relative lack of inflectional morphology and function words. These traits bring with them some concomitant features, particularly the use of single-valence verbs and serial verb constructions, motivated by the lack of morphology and grammatical marking devices. Subordination is rarer than in older languages. These new languages find ways, early in their development, of highlighting some sentence elements for discourse purposes, typically by exploiting the front position. The more recent research surveyed here reinforces the vision articulated over thirty years ago by Talmy Givón (1979a, p. 296), when he listed the 'major salient properties of the presyntactic, pragmatic mode of discourse' as (1) Topic-comment word order, (2) Concatenation, (3) Low noun per verb ratio, (4) Lack of grammatical morphology, (5) Intonation, and (6) Zero anaphora.[59] Givón was ahead of his time, and these are now ideas whose time has gradually come, to some sooner than to others.

These features of new languages can also be found in some, but not all, older languages. The contrast between Pirahã and Riau Indonesian, both old languages, is striking. Both are simple in many ways. But Pirahã has complex verbal morphology, quite lacking in Riau Indonesian. Riau Indonesian is more like a new language. The social environments of these two languages could hardly be more different. The linguistic and social differences suggest that idiosyncratic and complex morphology, in particular, can develop and be maintained in close-knit and isolated communities. Conversely, in large populations with great geographical mobility and contact with other languages there

---

[59] I have said nothing much about this last, but it is implicit in mentions of pragmatic inference, and in later discussion of holophrastic utterances in Chapter 8.

are simplifying tendencies resulting in much less morphological complexity. The richness of syntactic (as opposed to morphological) marking devices in languages with a history of contact varies, with Riau Indonesian having very little, like a new language. The next section will explore correlations between grammar and population structure.

5.9 Social correlates of complexity

So languages vary in complexity, and in expressive power. It has not been shown that any population has a distinctive potential for acquiring any particular type of language.[60] The variability is a **cultural** property of conventional systems (languages), and not a biological property of their speakers, and so has to be explained by their cultural histories as languages. All kinds of sociocultural factors may be relevant, but biology will not play a part in explaining differences in complexity among languages. Any connection between social structure and language structure arises through historical processes. Explanations for synchronic facts lie in diachrony. For expository reasons, the present chapter has been as doggedly synchronic as is reasonable, describing what languages can be like, and incidentally mentioning relevant diachronic processes such as grammaticalization, pidginization, and creolization. I will stick with this artificial division at the end of this chapter and briefly summarize some synchronically observable correspondences between type of society and type of language. Diachronic implications of these correspondences will be seen in Chapter 9, section 1.

A disclaimer first. What can be called the 'content' of a culture can be weakly correlated, for purely contingent historical reasons, with structural features characteristic of some language families. For example, there is a probabilistic correlation between the Islamic religion and template-based morphology as found in Semitic languages. A person who speaks such a language is more likely to be a Muslim than someone who doesn't speak such a language. As an implication in the other direction, a Protestant Christian is likely to speak an SVO language, with greater than chance probability. The causes of such correlations are easy to see; they are historical accidents and are of no concern here. I include in the idea of 'content' the social hierarchy of a society and the ways in which this may be reflected in lexicon and grammar. In Japanese and Korean society, for example, considerations of the relative status of interlocu-

---

[60] With the possible minuscule exception argued in Dediu and Ladd (2007), mentioned in the footnote to p. 260.

tors correlate with choice of words and to some extent with choice of sentence form. In Japanese, there are 'respect words ("sonkeigo"), condescending words ("kenjougo"), and polite words ("teineigo")' (Maeda et al. 1988, p. 140). In Japanese grammar, respect or politeness may be shown to the addressee, to whatever is denoted by the Subject of a sentence, or to whatever is denoted by the Object of the sentence. These pragmatic nuances are signalled by affixes on the verb or either of the nouns concerned (Harada 1976). Whether to use these honorific forms is at the discretion of a speaker (subject to some social sanction). The range of grammatical devices that happens to be used for expressing respect, politeness, or condescension is not part of a correlation between type of society and type of language, except in the obvious sense that a language must have some way of expressing these pragmatic nuances if the society requires it. Also at the level of content are lexical differences between languages. The languages of technologically developed societies differ from those of hunter-gatherer groups.

What will interest us, however, is the possibility of gross correlations between types of populations and some very basic features of language, such as how complex their morphology is. In line with discussion at the beginning of this chapter, there will be no attempt to quantify the overall complexity of languages. And clearly, any attempt at quantifying the overall 'complexity' of a society is well beyond my remit. But we can isolate a few raw properties of both languages and societies and ask whether any correlations exist.

A recurring broad idea, variously worded, links a certain kind of language evolution or change to a certain feature of a community, as summarized in the dichotomies below:

'tightly knit communities'	'loosely knit communities'	(Trudgill 1992)
'esoteric communication'	'exoteric communication'	(Wray and Grace 2007)
'esoteric niche'	'exoteric niche'	(Lupyan and Dale 2010)
a 'society of intimates'	a 'society of strangers'	(Givón, 1979a, 2005)
'contextualized language'	'decontextualized language'	(Denny 1991; Snow et al. 1991)
'non-autonomous communication'	'autonomous communication'	(Kay 1977)
'local languages'	'world languages'	(Swadesh 1971))
'residual zones'	'spread zones'	(Nichols 1992)
'Type 1 communities'	'Type 2 communities'	(Kusters 2003).

Three different factors are variously emphasized by those claiming a connection between tightly/loosely knit societies and language evolution. These are:

(1) degree of shared background knowledge among speakers, (2) whether the language is learned mainly by children or by adults, and (3) the inherent conservatism of the group's identity, allowing perpetuation of complexity across generations. Factors (2) and (3), in particular, are interwoven; and I would add a further interwoven factor, namely (4) the age-structure of the group. These factors sometimes work in the same direction, and are sometimes in tension. I will discuss them in turn.

5.9.1 *Shared knowledge and a less autonomous code*

Snow et al. (1991, pp. 90–1) offer a definition: '*decontextualized language use*—language used in ways that eschew reliance on shared social and physical context in favour of reliance on a context created through the language itself'. Written language is clearly more decontextualized than spoken language. When you write, your audience is in a different place, and will be in a different time when they read your message. It is widely accepted that a factor influencing a difference between writing and speech is the need to spell out assumptions that could be taken for granted in a spoken conversational situation. Given this acceptance, the same reasoning applies between different types of speech situation. A context is 'created through language itself' every time we speak, but to differing degrees. 'I was in the bar of the Red Lion at 9.30 on the night of the murder' spells out a lot of the context of a conversation. A simple 'Yes' hardly creates any context, but could express exactly the same message.

When people know each other well, a lot of what they communicate can be left to pragmatic inference. People only communicate at all, of course, because they don't know each other's minds perfectly at the time of speaking. What sort of things typically need to be made explicit, and what can usually be left implicit? We can take some clues from Riau Indonesian, which lacks most of the main grammatical markers that linguists look for in a language, for instance case-markers indicating who did what to whom, number (singular/plural), definiteness of reference, tense, aspect, and modality. In addition, RI words are versatile as to whether they are used referentially (as 'nouns'), predicatively (like verbs) or attributively (like attributive adjectives). RI gets close to semantic soup in everyday conversation. The **lexical** information contained in a word (e.g. *ayam*, something to do with a chicken, or *makan*, something to do with eating) is crucial, but the rest of the burden of interpretation is taken by pragmatic inference, with no or very few grammatical signals.

The lesser syntactic complexity of Riau Indonesian is undoubtedly due to its role as a basilectal language variety. The prototypical use of Riau Indonesian is to talk about the here and now; it thus contrasts with Standard Indonesian, which must also be able to convey, in speech or writing, information about matters that are remote in space and time—as in a politician's speech or a newspaper article. Accordingly, Riau Indonesian can permit itself to leave more aspects of meaning without formal encoding. Context will usually disambiguate, and in those rare cases when it does not, a simple 'What do you mean?' will elicit the necessary clarification.   (Gil 2001, p. 364)

The prototypical usage that Gil describes is what Wray and Grace (2007) label 'esoteric' communication. They contrast this with 'exoteric' communication.

Exoteric communication is outward-facing, and conducted with strangers—that is, members of other groups, or members of one's own group with whom one is unfamiliar in the sense of not sharing their knowledge of people, places, cultural practices, professional specialism, and so on. Insofar as information is not shared, there is a necessary assumption on the part of the speaker that the hearer may not understand the content of a message that is too implicitly expressed. More crucially, the speaker must encode the message in a form that makes it possible for the hearer to work out what is meant in some systematic way. . . .

   Thus, languages that are customarily used exoterically will tend to develop and maintain features that are logical, transparent, phonologically simple and, significantly, learnable by adults. The meanings of expressions can be determined from their composition, because the system approximates a one-to-one relationship between forms and meanings, and because it eschews allomorphy, particularly morphologically-conditioned allomorphy.   (Wray and Grace 2007, p. 551)

Kay (1977) expresses very similar ideas, using the terms 'autonomous language' and 'nonautonomous language'. George Grace explains the idea of autonomy very clearly and forcefully:

The term 'autonomous text' refers to linguistic expressions whose content is encoded so completely and unambiguously into the expression that it will be forever available without distortion to anyone who approaches that expression with the necessary knowledge of language, i.e. with the only requisite knowledge being narrowly linguistic in nature.   (Grace 1987, p. 42)

No language is completely autonomous in this sense, or decontextualized, of course; context always helps in figuring out exactly what someone means. But there can be degrees of autonomy. Using a proper name instead of a pronoun, or marking tense on a verb (as opposed to not marking it at all) gives a more autonomous expression. Grammatical structure generally increases the autonomy of expressions available in a language.

   Beside 'autonomous' and 'nonautonomous', Kay also uses Swadesh's terms 'local language' and 'world language'. The implication is that local languages, spoken by small communities, are less autonomous, because everyone in a small community shares the same background knowledge. World languages, on the other hand, tend to be more autonomous, because their speakers cannot always be sure what to take for granted. Kay sets out a number of admittedly speculative suggestions about formal differences between local/nonautonomous and world/autonomous languages. Many of his suggestions concern the rise of abstract vocabulary. He has little to say about syntax or morphology.

Kay's firmest morphosyntactic example is this: 'In goal attainment verbs, semantic incorporation of the object into the verb is a common, though not universal, feature of local languages' (p. 25). This refers to a kind of construction known as 'noun incorporation' whereby the object of a verb is phonetically reduced in some way and affixed as a bound morpheme to the verb. English has no clear cases. Imagine a verbal phrase like *to cow-milk* (i.e. to milk a cow) or *to tree-climb*, but in which, unlike these English examples, the nouns have reduced stress and are merely affixes on the verb. Mithun (1984) gives a very extensive survey of types of noun-incorporation across languages in all regions of the world. She shows ample evidence of an evolutionary process by which the most extreme types of noun incorporation evolve through a succession of three prior stages from more obviously syntactic Verb+Object combinations. The diachronic progression is from a syntactic construction to a complex lexical item preserving a phonetically reduced and semantically specialized historical trace of the original noun.[61] Of the aspects of Mithun's analysis that interest us most here, the foremost is that full noun incorporation results in complex and often irregular verbal morphology. Mithun is not concerned with any correlation between social circumstances and morphosyntactic structure. However, impressionistically, at least, the great majority of languages that she mentions fall into the type that Swadesh called 'local' and alternatively 'folk' and 'tribal' languages. Kay's remark that noun incorporation is a feature of local languages seems to be confirmed, at least as a tendency. This is consistent with the view explored here, that the languages of small relatively isolated communities tend to develop complex and irregular verbal morphology over time.

A second idea of interest here can also be gleaned from Mithun's discussion of noun incorporation. One type of incorporation construction (the 'compounding' type) typically denotes an institutionalized activity or event. Mithun's illustration is: 'If you ask where my brother is, I might reply, *He is out berry-picking* or *He is off mountain-climbing*, but probably not *He is out ladder-climbing*, even if he is in fact climbing a ladder. . . . Ladder-climbing

---

[61] This is also the gist of a later analysis of noun incorporation constructions by Rosen (1989).

is not an institutionalized activity' (Mithun 1984, p. 848). In a closely-knit traditional society, there is arguably more consensus about which types of action-object event are part of the everyday habitual fabric of life, and so candidates for description by these very compressed, and not very transparent, constructions. In a more flexible, socially mixed society, standardized collocations of verb and object noun are not so predictable, and so, my argument goes, the languages of these societies tend to keep to the more transparent syntactic Verb+Noun structures.

Another area where a correlation between culture and linguistic structure has been found is the area of **deixis**. 'Deixis' literally means 'pointing'. We can point linguistically most obviously by using demonstrative pronouns such as *this* and *that*. It is important to note that such words actually do the work of manual pointing, so they do not need to be accompanied by manual pointing. The words themselves are 'pointing words'. Deictic words work because they are interpreted according to their context of use. Personal pronouns such as *I* and *you* refer to different people depending on who is using them. In a speech by Barack Obama, the personal pronoun *I* means the president himself. In Darwin's writings, the same pronoun meant Darwin himself. Tense markers (past/present/future) are also deictic because they indicate the time of the event described in relation to the time of utterance. *John is singing* is true just if John is singing at the time when the sentence is used. Deictic elements, then, depend on shared background assumptions between speaker and hearer, for example about the time and place of the utterance, who is speaking, who is being addressed, and who is being spoken about. The more speakers routinely share such assumptions, the more use can be made of deictic elements. By contrast, if two people only communicate in writing, and have never met each other, elements that depend for their interpretation on common knowledge are less likely to be useful. For instance, in spoken conversation we can make an appointment by using the deictic word *tomorrow*, but in an email confirming the day of an appointment it is more sensible to use an exact non-deictic phrase, like *October 9th*. Further, in a community where deictic elements are in common use, we can expect them to be expressed in a compressed way, in morphological affixes, rather than as separate words. And this expectation is confirmed. Perkins (1992) looked for a relation between deixis as morphologically expressed by affixes on nouns and verbs and social complexity, and he found it. Cultural complexity was scored according to a combination of twelve criteria relating to such features as subsistence methods, permanence of settlements and social stratification. Summarizing a mass of careful statistical analysis on a sample of fifty cultures and their languages, he writes,

The variable DTSP is the sum of values for the variables Tense on Verbs, Person Affixes on Nouns, Person Affixes on Verbs, Non-person Deictic Affixes on Verbs, and Non-person Deictic Affixes on Nouns. The association between the composite measure and cultural complexity is even more sizeable than the individual associations except for Person Affixes on Nouns. . . .

There are very few languages that are spoken at the lowest levels of cultural complexity that do not rank at least on the second level of the DTSP variable. On the other hand, at the highest levels of cultural complexity there are very few languages that are even at the third or fourth rank for this variable.   (Perkins 1992, p. 161)

Thus, as a statistical tendency, in languages of less complex cultures, in which one would expect more talk to be between intimates than between strangers, more deictic distinctions are expressed in the morphology, and the morphology is more complex. As an example of how deictic morphology can be complex, recall such examples as *yumitripela* 'we three, including you' from Tok Pisin, a distinction most probably brought in from a substrate Austronesian language (section 5.6).

In connection with deictic expressions, it is interesting to note that some languages of relatively small populations use terms relating to the local landscape instead of terms for *left* and *right* for expressing directions and spatial relationships. Pirahã has no words for 'left' and 'right' (Everett 2008). Out in the woods, Pirahã hunters give directions like 'toward the river'. Another example: 'Tenejapan speakers of Tzeltal speak as if the whole world tilted down northwards: thus one can speak of the "uphill" end of a table, for example, using the general North/South slope of the land as a frame of reference for describing spatial relations on the horizontal' (Brown 2001, p. 512). 'Tenejapans themselves do not think in terms of North/South/East/West' (p. 537).

[D]eictics often contain information in an absolute frame of reference, that is an allo-centric frame of reference hooked to geographical features or abstract cardinal directions. Thus the large Yup'ik series of demonstratives has 'upstream/downstream/across river' oppositions, West Greenlandic has north/south (Fortescue 1984), and languages used by peoples in mountainous areas of Australia, New Guinea or the Himalayas often contain 'uphill'/'downhill' oppositions (see Diessel 1999: 44–5 for references).

      (Levinson 2003, p. 117)

Use of 'absolute' directional terms related to the local landscape is no less anchored in speakers' shared experience than terms corresponding to 'left' and 'right'. Indeed it avoids the confusion caused by your left hand being on the same side of us as my right hand when we are face to face, as partners in a conversation usually are. Terms rooted in a local landscape would obviously be less functional in a global language, whose speakers inhabit different landscapes.

We'll move on now from morphological phenomena to syntactic ones, in particular to relative clauses. If you want to talk about a particular man (say), and your hearer is likely to know which man you have in mind, you don't need to modify *the man* with a relative clause. But with less shared information between speaker and hearer, relative clauses as in *the man that's near the window* or *the man that Mary lives with*, become increasingly useful. A relative clause helps identification of a referent if it is not obvious from context. I quoted above, in connection with Pirahã, an observation of Bickerton's that the use of relative clauses increased when a stranger entered the room. That was a matter of frequency of use of an existing resource. However, languages differ in the resources they offer. Relevant here is that languages differ according to the extent to which they allow relative clauses with the understood noun in different grammatical positions. Keenan and Comrie (1977) discovered a 'noun phrase accessibility hierarchy' which ranks relativizable positions. I give examples below:

	Noun understood as ...
the man that came yesterday	Subject of relative clause
the man that Jack saw	Direct Object of relative clause
the man that I gave a book to	Indirect Object of relative clause
the man that I play squash with	Object of a preposition (*with*) in the relative clause
the man whose bike I stole	a possessor in the relative clause
the man that I am taller than	Object of a comparative (*taller than*) in the relative clause

It is noteworthy that the last example here is a little awkward in English, but all the others are acceptable. French actually won't allow the equivalent of the last example—**Voici l'homme que qui je suis plus grand*. But French equivalents of all the others, for example *Voici l'homme dont j'ai piqué le vélo* are acceptable. As a general rule, Keenan and Comrie discovered, languages have a cut-off point somewhere on this hierarchy. The cut-off point for English is at the very bottom of the list above, as all possibilities are allowable in English. For French, the cut-off point is just before the bottom line, as it allows relativization on a possessive but not on a comparative. Other languages are more restricted. For Toba Batak, spoken in Sumatra, the cut-off point is immediately after the first, Subject, position on the hierarchy. In this language, there is a direct equivalent of *the woman who washed the clothes*, but there is no direct equivalent of *the clothes that the woman washed*. Toba Batak cannot relativize on Direct Objects or on any other structural position lower down the hierarchy. There is a general rule holding strongly across languages, that if they can relativize on a given position in the hierarchy, then they can also relativize on positions further up in the hierarchy, but not necessarily on positions further down. Conversely, if a language cannot relativize on a given position in the hierarchy, then it cannot relativize on any position further down in the hierarchy. Thus languages can be characterized by how far down the hierarchy they can do relativization. Some languages allow more types of relative clause than others.

What is of interest here is that this structural characterization of languages correlates with a social characterization of the communities that speak them. Some years earlier, Marsh (1967) had devised a measure of cultural complexity for thirty-six of the forty-nine communities whose languages Keenan and Comrie studied. Marsh's scores were based on (1) degree of political organization; (2) degree of social stratification; (3) percentage of adult males involved in non-agricultural occupation; and (4) gross energy consumption per capita (Perkins 1992, p. 190). These criteria are clearly far from considerations of language structure. Yet Perkins (1992) found a correlation between Marsh's scores and the range of clausal positions that languages allowed relativization on. He cross-tabulated relativizable positions according to Keenan and Comrie with Marsh's scores for cultural complexity. The results were statistically significant ($p < 0.0495$ on one test, and $p = 0.0071$ after a correction for possible bias in the sample of languages). 'As cultural complexity increases, so does the number of noun phrase positions that are relativizable by a major strategy' (Perkins 1992, p. 191).[62] Perkins' explanation for this correlation is the same as I have suggested here: 'As such forms [e.g. relative clauses] become more and more relevant to the conversational neeeds of speakers in increasingly complex cultures, their use is extended even further to cover more grammatical functions' (Perkins 1992, p. 188). It seems fairly straightforward to associate lack of social complexity on Marsh's scale with small isolated communities, or 'local' languages.

In this subsection I have suggested two kinds of correlation between a language feature and a community of intimates. Noun-incorporation, more common in small 'local' languages, is a way of compressing a message into a single word, resulting in a less transparent way of expressing the meaning. The decreased transparency can be tolerated in a group where certain action-object combinations are more predictable from the community's habitual way of life. (So my argument goes, but it needs more empirical work to bolster the idea.) A correlation was also noted between less complex cultures and increased

---

[62] Much of the work in Perkins' 1992 book was completed much earlier in Perkins (1980).

morphological expression of deictic distinctions, which are rooted in shared assumptions about the speech situation. These were correlations between small 'local' languages and **increased morphological complexity**. The other kind of correlation involved syntax, the range of clausal positions over which relative clauses can be formed. The correlation that Perkins found was between small 'local' languages and what can be seen as **decreased syntactic complexity**, if each way of doing relativization is taken as a separate construction. Viewed this way, some languages, which tend to be the languages of small communities, have fewer syntactic constructions, at least of the relative clause type. Commenting on these and similar results, Denny (1991, p. 74) writes, 'As the community increases in size with the development of agriculture, speakers cannot rely on hearers having such contexts available, so the context is specified in the utterance by relative clauses. . . . Relative clause formation amounts to decontextualization because it allows contextual information to be included in the message instead of being added from context by the recipient. We see from these studies that relative clauses as a decontextualizing device increase as community size increases among preliterates'.

In short, the facts reviewed suggest the following broad tendencies:

• Small community languages tend to have more complex morphology and simpler syntax, especially after a long history of relative isolation.

• Languages of large communities where people often talk to strangers tend to have simpler morphology and more complex syntax.

It is suggested only that these are statistical tendencies. The validity of the statistical correlation between morphological complexity and small groups has been convincingly shown by Lupyan and Dale (2010):

We conducted a statistical analysis of >2,000 languages using a combination of demographic sources and the World Atlas of Language Structures [WALS]—a database of structural language properties. We found strong relationships between linguistic factors related to morphological complexity, and demographic/socio-historical factors such as the number of language users, geographic spread, and degree of language contact. The analyses suggest that languages spoken by large groups have simpler inflectional morphology than languages spoken by smaller groups as measured on a variety of factors such as case systems and complexity of conjugations.

(Lupyan and Dale 2010, p. 1)

Population, and to a lesser extent area and number of neighboring neighbors, was a significant predictor for 26/28 of the WALS features that were most relevant to inflectional morphology. Of these, 23 remained significant when language family was partialed out. For 22/28 the demographic variables (population, area over which a language is spoken, and degree of linguistic contact) combined with geographic covariates (latitude/longitude) proved to be better predictors of the linguistic features than geographic location alone. Across a wide range of linguistic features, a systematic relationship...between demographic and typological variables was found, providing overwhelming evidence against the null hypothesis that language structure is unrelated to socio-demographic factors.   (Lupyan and Dale 2010, p. 3)

Counterexamples to the statistical tendencies certainly exist, and further empirical systematic comparisons, involving more languages and more morphosyntactic phenomena, need to be carried out. Riau Indonesian fits neither generalization neatly, as it is a language of a large community in which discourse is nevertheless, according to Gil, mostly between non-strangers. We can expect non-conforming cases, as many other factors doubtless complicate the picture. Lupyan and Dale borrow Wray and Grace's terms 'esoteric' and 'exoteric' and use them of the 'niches' provided by small and large populations, respectively. They also associate small populations with language-learning preponderantly by children, and large populations with language-learning more by adults. In the next subsection we will meet the same general ideas from a different perspective.

5.9.2 Child and adult learning and morphological complexity

In light of the subtlety of the issues here, it is worth spelling out some relevant premisses. The statements below reflect an uncontroversial consensus—indeed, they are almost tautologous.

Premiss 1: In small isolated communities, learning the language of the community is almost entirely by children, who normally learn no other language as children, and perhaps not even as adults. Children learn from the model of older members of the community. The motivation to become an acknowledged member of the community plays a larger role in learning the language than in a language contact situation.

Premiss 2: In small isolated communities, the language input to the child learner is not inconsistent. There may be much irregularity, but it is consistent irregularity. Each adult model produces the same regular and irregular forms, from one occasion of use to the next. There is little or no inconsistency between speakers or within speakers.

Premiss 3: In language contact situations with many ambient languages, there is much second language learning by adults, who consequently arrive at non-native competence in one or more languages. The models for learning may also be non-native speakers, of a similar age to the learners. The motivation to communicate in practical situations plays a larger role in learning the language than in a small isolated community.

Premiss 4: In language contact situations with many ambient languages, the experience of all people is inconsistent and variable, due to the presence of several ways of expressing every message, i.e. several languages. Each language in the community may or may not have irregularities. Within a single language, any irregularities are consistently and invariantly produced. Across the languages of the community, the same meaning is expressed in varying and mutually inconsistent ways.

The two types of situation mentioned here are extremes. Many languages exist in intermediate situations.

I noted above relative commonness of noun incorporation (NI) in local languages, or the languages of tight-knit communities. Mithun also mentions a pertinent fact relating to the acquisition of these constructions. NI 'is one of the last operations to be learned by children acquiring their native tongue' (Mithun 1984, p. 879). She also gives many examples of the loss of NI constructions in circumstances of language contact and language decay. Where a small language community is invaded by another dominant language, younger members of the community may not persist with learning the original local language to the point where such morphological complexities as NI are mastered. The inherent difficulty of NI constructions also prevents them from being competently acquired by any adults who may try to learn a language with them. If a local language community remains relatively uninvaded by other languages, the community can preserve its linguistic traditions, including those which take rather more time for children to acquire. This section pursues this theme of child versus adult language learning and its effect on morphological complexity.

Trudgill (1992) argues that morphological complexity and irregularity are features of 'tightly knit communities', based on a comparison of Norwegian and Faroese. These languages had a common ancestor over a millennium ago, but have diverged to the point where they are mutually unintelligible. Faroese is spoken by a small, isolated community, whereas Norwegian speakers have been much more in contact with the outside world. Faroese has much more complex morphology, and more morphological irregularity, than Norwegian. The ancestor language of both Faroese and Norwegian, it is universally assumed, had complex morphology which the continental descendants (Danish, Swedish, and Norwegian) have largely lost. This one case strongly supports the idea that contact tends to bring about simplification of morphology, due to the language being more often acquired by adult, rather than child, learners. This is completely consistent with the evidence from pidginization, which involves learning by adults. (See also Trudgill 2002, 2003).

Trudgill traces the source of the Norwegian/Faroese difference to a difference between child (L1) learners and adult (L2) learners.

If we ask of the imperfect learning that occurs in language contact situations: imperfect learning by who?, the answer is fairly apparently [*sic*]: imperfect learning by non-native adults and post-adolescents. Everything we know about young children indicates that in general they are such good language learners that they normally learn perfectly any language variety that they have sufficient exposure to. Imperfect learning, and thus simplification, does not result from non-native language learning as such but from adult non-native language learning.   (Trudgill 1992, p. 130)

In another paper, relevant differences between other Germanic languages are cited to invoke reduction in morphological complexity due to adult learning.

The correct generalization in fact seems to be that gender marking reduces or disappears only in high-contact adult-learning situations. The standard koineized forms of Swedish and Danish, for instance, have only two genders, while many non-standard dialects of these languages still have three. English and Afrikaans, the Germanic languages with the greatest history of contact, have lost grammatical gender altogether. It is also typical of creoles that they do not have it.   (Trudgill 2002, p. 725)

Also in the Germanic sphere, Dahl (2009) carefully compares the grammars of Standard Swedish and Elfdalian, 'an endangered vernacular spoken by about 3,000 persons in Älvdalen in the Swedish province of Dalarna. It is sufficiently far from Swedish not to be mutually comprehensible with it' (p. 52). Dahl concludes that Elfdalian is more complex in both morphology and syntax, confirming the hypothesis of a tendency to more complex morphology in small communities (but admittedly disconfirms the hypothesis of a tendency to simpler syntax in small communities).

The contrast between languages transmitted more by adult learning and those transmitted more by child learning is also emphasized by Wray and Grace. The contrast between the two learning styles, as they see it, is encapsulated in the following:

Consistent engagement by adult learners with the language will lead to unconscious and/or conscious strategies on the parts of both learner and native speaker to effect the regularisation of irregularities, the rationalisation of partial patterns, the re-expression of impenetrable conventionalised expressions.   (Wray and Grace 2007, p. 557)

Wray and Grace's view is consistent with Trudgill's, quoted just above. A language with fewer genders is more regular than one with more genders. In a language with no gender, one pattern fits all nouns, rather than several different patterns, which need to be learned. Wray and Grace see adult learners as tending to seek out, or even impose, regularities and systematic correspondences, while children are content to memorize useful expressions, such that their knowledge ends up being only partly representative of the full paradigmatic potential of the language, and hence tends to be irregular. Children are faithful transmitters of an already morphologically complex language. Any innovation from adult learners, in Wray and Grace's view, is in the direction of simplification, a view that is consistent with a mass of data on pidginization. Of course, this leaves the question of how languages get to be morphologically complex in the first place, a topic to be addressed in Chapter 9, under the broad heading of grammaticalization.

Such a contrast between adult and child learners is also argued at length by Kusters (2003). His 'hypothesis indicates that a language which is more "adapted" to an outsider, or in my terminology, less complex, is one where the speech community has had many L2 learners' (p. 7). In an impressive dissertation, now a book, Kusters compares varieties within four different language families: Arabic (Classical Arabic, Najdi Arabic, Moroccan Arabic, Nubi Arabic); Scandinavian (Old Norse, Icelandic, Faroese, Norwegian); Quechua (Quechua II,[63] Cuzco Quechua, Bolivian Quechua, Argentinian Quechua, Ecuadorian Quechua); and Swahili (Standard Swahili, Katanga Swahili, Kenyan Pidgin Swahili). The idea is to compare, within each language group, languages of 'Type 1', whose speakers are mostly native (L1) speakers, with 'Type 2' languages, many of whose speakers learn the language in adulthood, as an L2. Kusters finds a general tendency for Type 1 languages to be morphologically complex, and for Type 2 languages to be morphologically simpler. Kusters summarizes the social conditions for morphological simplification as follows:

The kind of simplification process studied here is related to several necessary social conditions: 1) a language must spread rapidly outside its initial sphere of use to a domain where it is predominantly used in its communicative function by second language learners, 2) to be simplified it must remain in use for a longer period, and be learned by a next generation, 3) contact between the source language and the variety spoken in the new domain must be not too extensive, otherwise simplifications may be levelled out, especially when the source language is dominant. (Kusters 2003, p. 367)

---

[63] Quechua II is one of two early Quechua varieties, from which a number of modern dialects are descended.

As a stimulus to deeper and clearer thinking about these matters, this common view of the contrast between adult and child learners can seem to be the exact opposite of conclusions derived from experiments by Hudson Kam and Newport (2005). They taught children and adults an artificial language, and summarize their results as follows:

> [T]he adults did not regularize the language. However, many children did regularize the language, imposing patterns that were not the same as their input. These results suggest that children and adults do not learn from variable input in the same way. Moreover, they suggest that children may play a unique and important role in creole formation by regularizing grammatical patterns.   (Hudson Kam and Newport, 2005, p. 151)

The apparent clash is this. Trudgill and Wray and Grace attribute 'regularization' to adult learners, and not to child learners; Hudson Kam and Newport attribute 'regularization' to child learners and not to adult learners. The key, as implied by my scare quotes, is in that word 'regularization': it means different things to the two sets of authors. Another clue is in the second sentence of that last quotation, where Hudson Kam and Newport write of 'variable input'.

Hudson Kam and Newport taught their subjects a language that was inconsistent. Sometimes a determiner was present with a noun, and sometimes it wasn't, for no apparent reason. This was a case, as far as the subjects could see, of genuinely free variation. No difference in meaning was attached to the inclusion or omission of the determiner, and its presence or absence was not correlated with any other grammatical feature of the language. Most adult learners, who learned this little 'language' in a week, roughly preserved the statistical distribution of this unmotivated variability. The adult learners did **probability matching**. Most children tended not to, going for an 'all or nothing' solution, either always using a determiner or never using one. The child learners didn't do probability matching.

The kind of 'regularization' studied Hudson Kam and Newport involved reducing two different yet apparently absolutely synonymous patterns, involving the same words, to a single pattern, either with or without the determiner. Before such regularization, there are two ways to say something; after the regularization, there is only one way. The kind of 'regularization' that Trudgill and Wray and Grace have in mind is the smoothing into conformity of ways of expressing meanings so that they more closely resemble ways of expressing other similar meanings. Before such regularization there is one idiosyncratic way of expressing some particular meaning (e.g. English *came*); and after the regularization there is still one way of expressing this meaning, but it is less idiosyncratic (e.g. *comed*).

An experiment subsequent to Hudson Kam and Newport's, by Reali and Griffiths (2009), placed the learning in the context of **iterated learning**.[64] This experimental paradigm seeks to emulate the cultural transmission of a language across several generations. In Generation 1, learners are trained on whatever data the experimenters decide to start with. It can be random or structured, according to the goals of the experiment. In the next generation, Generation 2, learners are trained on a sample of data produced by the prior generation of learners. And so on, with each Generation $N + 1$ being trained on (a sample of) the output of Generation N. Often, over time, learners converge on a 'language' with some specific characteristic. The point is that simulated cumulative cultural evolution can yield results that are not observable from the learning of a single generation. Reali and Griffiths did experiments like Hudson Kam and Newport's with this kind of iterated learning across several generations of adult learners (university undergraduates, of course!). Their experiments 'demonstrate that a bias toward regularization exists that is not obvious in a single generation. More generally, these results show that iterated learning provides a way to test whether weak biases operate during individual learning, as well as the consequences of these biases in shaping the form of languages over time' (pp. 323–4). So adults, even though they may do some probability matching, nevertheless slightly skew the statistical distribution from their experienced training data. Over generations, the accumulation of such skewings results in complete 'regularization', in Hudson Kam and Newport's sense.

It should also be noted that Hudson Kam and Newport's subjects were told that their task was to learn a language, over a week, and they were not embedded in any situation where they had to use the language communicatively. Recall the key social property of Klein and Perdue's Basic Variety, that it is acquired and used outside the classroom, in communicative situations.

So, after an initial scare from apparent experimental counterevidence, the hypothesis of adult regularization (in the appropriate sense) and children's faithful replication of complexifying irregularities is not challenged. It is well known that children do, for a while, overgeneralize, and smoothe out irregularities, saying at one point *comed*. But they get over it, and end up saying *came* like the adults around them. All learners, adults and children, have a

---

[64] An early computational model of iterated learning (although it wasn't called that) in the evolution of a feature of language is found in Hurford (1987). The baton was picked up by Simon Kirby, in many publications on iterated learning (e.g. Kirby 1999b, 2000, 2001, Kirby and Hurford 2002). These studies were all computational simulations. More recently, the iterated learning paradigm has been implemented with experimental learning of artificial mini-languages by successive 'generations' of real human learners, as in Reali and Griffiths' study reported here.

tendency to smoothe out irregularity. In children L1 learners this tendency is more easily overridden by counterevidence from persistent ambient irregularity. Comrie (1992) briefly surveys first language acquisition looking for features of the child's production that deviate from the surrounding language. He finds a sequence 'of increasing morphological complexity: first, no bound morphology; second, only readily segmentable, regular, and productive morphology; and third, the full complexity of adult morphology, with its historically accreted idiosyncrasies' (p. 194). Child L1 learners mostly go all the way. Adult L2 learners have a tendency to stop around the middle stage that Comrie mentions. Given enough time, children are better than adults at learning complex and irregular morphology. In a tightly knit society persisting through time with little outside influence, grammaticalization produces increasingly complex morphology.

5.9.3 Historico-geographic influences on languages

Johanna Nichols' work is more geographically oriented than other work discussed here. Nichols (1992) introduced a distinction between 'spread zones' and 'residual zones'. This is not a direct binary classification of types of language community, but rather makes a distinction between different geographical areas of the world. She characterizes **spread zones** in terms of seven criteria, not repeated here in full. More succinctly, she defines a spread zone 'as the combination of language spread, language succession, and low genetic[65] density over some sizeable area (at least a quarter of a million square miles)' (p. 17). Her examples of spread zones are western Europe, central Australia, interior North America, Mesoamerica, the Ancient Near East, and central insular Oceania. It will be noticed immediately that languages in spread zones may be spoken by small communities, as in central Australia, or by large communities, as in western Europe. Thus Nichols' historico-geographical dichotomy cuts across the social features considered in the subsections above. Nichols' characterizes **residual zones** in terms of seven criteria again, and defines a residual zone succinctly as 'a dense grouping of genetically diverse languages with ongoing accretion, increasing diversity, and no center of innovation. Again, the area should be sizeable (perhaps a hundred thousand square miles or more)' (p. 21). The residual zones she selected for study are 'Ethiopia and Kenya; the Caucasus; the Pacific coast of northern Asia (from Japan to the Bering Strait); northern Australia; and the Pacific coast of North America, here

---

[65] 'Genetic' here relates to membership of language families, not any biological property.

represented by California' (p. 21).[66] The languages in residual zones do tend to be spoken in small, but not necessarily isolated, communities.

Nichols found a connection between residual zones and greater morphological complexity. As she notes, the definition of morphological complexity is itself complex. A language may use affixes only or mainly on the head of a phrase or sentence, a case of 'head-marking', or on the dependent elements in a phrase or sentence, a case of 'dependent-marking'.[67] For example, taking the verb to be the head of a sentence, and argument noun phrases to be dependents, languages can express the same semantic distinction either by marking the verb (head marking) or marking one or more of the noun phrases (dependent marking). Compare English with Finnish in this respect:

Kalle   *lämmittää*   *saunaa*
Kalle+Nominative   warm+3SG.PRES   sauna+Partitive
'Kalle is warming up the sauna'   (Karlsson 1983, p. 80)

What English achieves by marking the verb for progressive aspect, with BE+ -*ing*, Finnish achieves by marking the Object of the verb (in this instance) with the 'Partitive' case. In this example, English is head-marking and Finnish is dependent-marking. Now here is another example, in which English is dependent-marking and another language, Hungarian, is head-marking.

Péter   *édesapja*
Peter   father+Possessive
'Peter's father'

English marks the possessor, here *Peter*, with an -'*s* suffix, whereas Hungarian marks the possessed, here the word for 'father', with a possessive suffix. Languages can be both head-marking and dependent-marking in some constructions—a 'belt-and-braces' approach. And languages may not mark either head or dependent. Hence languages differ in the extent to which they mark heads and dependents. Nichols' measure of morphological complexity reflects the total amount of head- and dependent-marking in a language. She found a statistical connection between morphological complexity and residual zones. 'Residual zones show relatively high complexity, equal to or greater than that of their respective continents. Spread zones show somewhat lower average complexity, equal to or lower than that of their respective continents' (p. 192).

---

[66] Of course this relates to the indigenous languages of California, now swamped by European languages, and now dead or dying. Records exist of these Native American languages.

[67] This distinction between head-marking and dependent-marking was introduced in Nichols (1986).

To illustrate the multi-factorial intricacy of this topic, note that Nichols makes a connection between language contact and the fostering of complexity, going against the tendencies that have been accumulating in this chapter. 'Independently of whether they are in residual or spread zones, however, almost all of these high-complexity languages are in areas of considerable linguistic diversity and contact. It can be concluded that contact among languages fosters complexity, or, put differently, diversity among neighbouring languages fosters complexity in each of the languages' (Nichols 1992, p. 193). It should be noted that the generalization here is over rather few languages, twenty-six, of which two are long-dead languages of the Near East, Sumerian and Akkadian.

Noonan (2008) studied the effects of contact in the Tamangic languages, a small group of Tibeto-Burman languages spoken in Nepal. These languages have a long history of contact. He lists a large number of borrowings at all linguistic levels, including morphosyntax. The most contact and borrowing has been between Nepali, the Indo-European (Indic) language encouraged by the government, and Chantyal, a Tamangic language once the language of a prestigious mining community. Of eleven contact-induced changes in Chantyal, seven are judged to have increased the complexity of the language by adding new constructions, while two changes have decreased the amount of choice among constructions, and two changes are neutral. One of the lost constructions involves honorific verb stems, a change which may well be influenced by general changes in the society. The other loss is in variety of Adjective–Noun (versus Noun–Adjective) order. Writing of Nichols' hypothesis that contact fosters complexity, Noonan (2008, p. 99) writes 'The Chantyal data would seem to confirm this, at least in the areas of morphosyntax and rhetorical strategies, which became more complex overall'.

We need to distinguish different kinds of language contact, involving acquisition at different ages and in different social circumstances (Tollefson 1980; Bentahila and Davies 1995; Thomason 2001). In one type of contact, languages remain for long periods the cultural property of their original communities, with strong internal cohesion, sense of identity, and normal learning by children. In this case, neighbouring languages stably cohabit the same region. In a very different kind of contact, at least some of the languages are learned by adults divorced from their original communities, as in the extreme case of creole or pidgin situations. The connection between contact and greater complexity noted by Nichols most probably involves the former stable kind of contact.

Stable contact over generations can give rise to grammatical variety. In the first instance, this would be a case of a language borrowing a construction with roughly the same meaning as a construction it already has. A well known example is the co-existence in English of the 'Saxon genitive' (e.g. *my brother's wife*) with the 'Norman genitive' (e.g. *the wife of my brother*). By now, these two constructions have to some extent diverged in purpose. But some overlap persists, as the examples just given show. Languages with a history of stable contact can have more grammatical constructions, often deployed to express finer pragmatic distinctions.

A well known example of contact modifying the grammatical structures of neighbouring languages is found in the 'Balkan Sprachbund'. In this geographical area, languages from different subfamilies of Indo-European, that is Greek (Hellenic), Romanian (Romance), Bulgarian (Slavic), and Albanian, have grown alike in certain grammatical features. The borrowings have been piecemeal and result from pairwise contacts between the languages, sometimes transmitted further by subsequent pairwise contact. Not all generalizations apply equally widely across all Balkan languages. Some of the areal features, attributed to contact, are: loss of a distinction between Dative and Genitive case; expression of future and perfect tenses by separate words, rather than by morphological inflections; loss of a specifically marked infinitive form; definiteness on nouns marked by a suffix; and marking of comparison for adjectives by separate words rather than by morphological inflections. Note that some of these contact-induced changes are simplifications of the morphology, with the burden of carrying the meaning shifted to free-standing words. But at least one change, the definiteness affix on nouns, involves complexification of the morphology.

Another classic case is that of Kupwar, an Indian village at the border between the areas of two language families: Indo-European, represented by Urdu and Marathi, and Dravidian, represented by Kannada. Here, 'the local varieties of (Indo European) Urdu and (Dravidian) Kannada have undergone radical restructuring on the model of (Indo-European) Marathi to the extent that there is morpheme-for-morpheme intertranslatability among the three varieties (Gumperz 1969; Gumperz and Wilson 1971)' (Ross 2007, p. 116). Thomason and Kaufman (1988, pp. 86–8) consider the sixteen contact-induced morphosyntactic changes among the Kupwar languages, concluding that only one is clearly an increase in complexity. This is the development of an inclusive/exclusive 'we' distinction in Kupwar Urdu. Three other changes are losses of morphological distinctions, and so are simplifying. Other changes are neutral as far as complexity is concerned.

A good generalization about whether contact induces simplification or complexification is elusive. Just mentioning instances, one way or the other, won't settle the general case (if there even is one). An authority on language contact, Thomason (2001), writes, 'The general idea is that contact-induced change leads to simplification, not complication. There are many examples that support this view, but here too there are many examples that go against it' (p. 64). Further, 'T. Givón, in a section entitled "Why languages do not borrow grammar" in a 1979 article, is one prominent author who argues that contact-induced change simplifies the grammar, and C.-J. N. Bailey (e.g. in a 1977 article) is probably the most prominent author who argues that interference always complicates the grammar' (p. 96). The jury is still out.

In this chapter we have seen how languages vary in complexity, often making much less use of the human potential for language learning than is theoretically possible. The social environment in which a language is embedded affects the complexity that develops. 'Only through the course of time can a language accumulate all of the features, phonological, syntactic, grammaticalized, and inflectional, which together contribute to its characterization as more highly complex' (Gil 2001, p. 358).

In this part of the book, we have finished the stage-setting for what most probably happened since our species diverged from our closest biological relatives. The human capacity for grammar, as set out in Chapter 4, evolved biologically. Individual languages, within this biological envelope, have evolved to exploit it in different ways and to different extents, as has been explained in Chapter 5. Now, finally, we are ready to take a shot at a story of the changes in our species and in our cultures that have landed us in our present situation, so spectacularly different from anything recognizable in other animals.

Introduction to Part III: What Happened—The Evolution of Syntax

The theme in this part of the book is the gradualness and continuity of the evolution of language and languages, once two necessary capacities were in place in rudimentary form in new-born humans and began to be exploited in their communities. These capacities, to learn arbitrary connections between forms and meanings, and to concatenate the forms into longer expressions, almost certainly did not appear in the earliest humans in their modern advanced form. Being able to store about a hundred items, and to put just three of them together in a systematic way, would give an advantage not previously experienced. After the qualitative introduction of these capacities in a primitive form, the rest of language evolution is a quantitative story—greater storage capacity, and greater facility for combining longer and longer strings expressing compositionally interpreted complex meanings.

CHAPTER 6

The Pre-existing Platform

6.1 Setting: in Africa

First, a little geo-historical scene-setting is in order.

'Why only humans?' is a challenge often put up to language evolution researchers. It is not the kind of fact that can receive a general scientific explanation, because it is a particular unique fact. A historical explanation could be given, along the same lines as answers to such questions as 'Why are the only humans to walk on the Moon American?' or 'Why is Earth the only planet in the solar system that supports complex life?' There must be a story here, starting in Africa. It possibly continues in Asia and Europe if part of the answer is that we somehow eliminated all our nearest competitors. But it is not my task here to tell that very particular story.

Here are some background facts about human evolution and migration. Very rough dates, and mostly no dates at all, are sufficient for my purposes. My concern is with the 'Why?' and 'How?' of the origins of syntax, not the 'Where?' or 'When?' It is quite possible that *Homo erectus*, perhaps for over a million years, had symbolic pre-syntactic communicative behaviour. They may have had inventories of learned conventional 'words' referring to things and events. *Erectus* brain size was on average about two-thirds of modern human brain size, with the largest *erectus* brains verging on the modern human range. A recent study of a well-preserved juvenile *erectus* skull concludes, on the basis of pelvic inlet size and skull size, 'These data also suggest that in *H. erectus* only a short period of brain maturation took place in the extra-maternal environment. This makes it unlikely that early *Homo* had cognitive skills comparable to those of modern humans, and it also implies that complex human language emerged relatively late in the course of human evolution' (Coqueugniot et al. 2004, p. 301). The link between language and the archaeological remains of these and later hominins[1] is tenuous. The evidence of fire, campsites, personal decoration, and trade over several hundred kilometres is not convincing that their users had anything more than a shared vocabulary. 'How much grammar does it take to sail a boat?' asks David Gil (2009): 'Virtually none' is the answer. Practical tasks may be made easier with grammatical communication, but humans can manage with much less.

Genetic evidence shows that more people stayed behind in Africa than left it. There is more genetic variability in Africa than in the rest of the world, and some genetic variants found in Africa are not found elsewhere. As far as can be seen after extensive study of the world's languages, modern populations of African stock do not differ from others in their capacity for complex syntax. It follows that our species became ready to develop fully syntactic languages before some ancestors of modern humans moved out of Africa less than 200,000 years ago. In possible conflict with this view, Coolidge and Wynn (2009) have recently claimed to identify a 'second major leap in [human] cognition', dating to between 14,000 and 60,000 years ago, based on a mutant form of the *Microcephalin* (MCPH1) gene that spread extremely rapidly through most parts of the world, evidently under positive selection.[2] Extrapolating from a sample of 1,184 individuals, the new C allele in this gene is rare in Africa, much more common than non-C alleles in Europe and Asia, and almost the exclusive variant in the indigenous populations of the Americas (Evans et al. 2005, p. 1719). Coolidge and Wynn associate this genetic shift, which has swept the world, except for most Africans and some Eurasians, with 'enhanced working memory and the evolution of modern thinking'. Oddly, given the distribution of the positively selected variant of MCPH1, they suggest that 'the alleles that enhanced working memory capacity' were present in the gene pool of recent African origin (p. 205). The essence of their idea, as it relates to syntax, is expressed in the following passages.

However it is done, working memory plays an important role in deploying and receiving the words and syntax of language. Any enhancement of working memory capacity would have increased the potential complexity of utterances. . . .

---

[1] Throughout this book, I use 'hominin' for humans and all their ancestors and close relatives, going back only as far as *Australopithecus*, thus including Neanderthals, *Homo erectus*, and *Homo habilis*. 'Hominid' is now a broader term, including extant great apes. 'Hominid' has recently changed its usage, with 'hominin' taking over some of its previous range. Many of the authors I quote use 'hominid' in the earlier narrower sense. See http://www.madsci.org/posts/archives/2003-04/1050350684.Ev.r.html for a note reflecting the terminological confusion in this area.

[2] An early sketch of these ideas appeared in Coolidge and Wynn (2005).

There is empirical evidence that recursion not only requires greater working memory capacity but also greater phonological storage capacity. One possibility, then, is that an additive genetic neural mutation or epigenetic event enhanced phonological storage capacity.   (Coolidge and Wynn 2009, pp. 217–18)

Coolidge and Wynn's hypothesis predicts that individuals lacking the now predominant MCPH1 allele (most of whom are Africans) tend to have shorter working memories than others (in comparable environmental conditions). There is little, if any, reliable evidence that this is true. Reliable evidence would control for differences in cultural context. Dobel et al. (2003) found that African-American schizophrenic patients performed worse on some measures of working memory than European-American schizophrenic patients, but concluded on other evidence that this may have been due to '[m]ediating variables of culture and socio-economic status in ethnic minority populations' (p. 132). The likely significance of environmental factors is borne out in a study by Manly et al. (1998). They reported 'After controlling for the effects of age, education, and sex, medically healthy African Americans who reported less acculturation obtained lower scores on the WAIS-R Information subtest and the Boston Naming Test than did more acculturated individuals. . . . there are cultural differences within ethnic groups that relate to neuropsychological test performance' (p. 291). To test the Coolidge/Wynn hypothesis more thoroughly, tests should be done in Africa, as people classified as African American often have partly non-African ancestry. Any such tests would need to control somehow for differences between African cultures and the cultures of the comparator individuals. African languages are not notably lacking in recursion, compared to languages of other regions. Coolidge and Wynn have proposed a bold hypothesis, not centrally targeted at language, but nevertheless with significant implications for the evolution of syntax. The hypothesis deserves further consideration. For the reasons given, I can see no grounds as yet for doubting that a universal human capacity for syntax was in place in all of our species at the time when the first migrants wandered out of Africa.[3]

Coolidge and Wynn are on one side of a continuing debate about the recency of modern human cognition. Others supporting a relatively recent date for its origin (roughly 50,000 years ago) include Fauconnier and Turner (2008), Noble and Davidson (1996), and Klein (1995, 1999). On the other side, debaters include McBrearty and Brooks (2000). My concern is with the process by which complex human syntax could have arisen, and not with dates. The

---

[3] Just possibly, phonology may be another matter. Dediu and Ladd (2007) argue for a correlation between variants of the MCPH1 gene and tone languages. Coolidge and Wynn do not mention this study.

universality of syntax-learning among Africans and non-Africans alike, and the dating of the alleged 'second major leap in human cognition' **after** the dates commonly cited for the migration out of Africa (in the range 90,000–45,000) are not easily reconcilable.

So, by far the greatest part of our biological evolution relevant to language happened in Africa.[4] The extent to which the biological capacity was exploited by the human groups in Africa before the time of the exodus is unknown. Parallel evolution of the most basic aspects of the language capacity in separate regions after the exodus from Africa is unlikely. After the exodus, both within and outside Africa, there could have been some tiny quantitative adjustments in the biological capacity, but not enough (or not different enough) to create any regional differences in language capacity observable in the modern world. Whether or not there was any trickle of gene flow between the modern humans fanning out from Africa and the pre-existing populations in Europe and Asia, or between human and pre-human populations in Africa, is immaterial to my purpose here. All modern humans share roughly the same capacity for language, by whatever biological means we got it. On genetic evidence for dates and routes of human migration, including some gene-flow from earlier settlers, see Zegura (2008), Green et al. (2010), and references in Hurford and Dediu (2009).

6.2 General issues about evolutionary 'platforms'

Chapter 1, on animal syntax, explored a possible platform on which human syntactic ability evolved, an ability to control fairly complex, learned, and phrasally organized stretches of sounds, like birdsong or whalesong. Those 'songs' had no compositional semantics, because the basic individual elements carried no meaning from which any meaning of the whole song could be composed. This was a chapter about meaningless syntax. Chapter 2, conversely, was a chapter on syntaxless meaning. It explored an undoubted evolutionary platform for the emergence of language, a first shared lexicon. Beside those generic platforms, we will look in this chapter for evidence that pre-humans might have had any capacity to manage the more specific features that I singled out in Chapter 4 as most distinctive of modern language, features such as massive storage, hierarchical structure, syntactic categories, long-range

---

[4] And some of the deepest features of the language capacity, in the broad sense, are ancient enough to have originated even before there was a separate continent of Africa—see Hurford and Dediu (2009).

dependencies and constructions. In these explorations, it must be borne in mind that as soon as we start to consider language in the light of evolution, the terms 'extralinguistic' or 'non-linguistic' can act as a barrier to pursuing explanations for linguistic facts. Facts about language fit into a broader picture of facts not strictly linguistic. It is necessary to disentangle two layers of non-linguistic phenomena. An earlier layer is found in non-human (e.g. chimpanzee or bird) behaviour. Here we can look for ape abilities that could have been exapted for language. The fact that human brain evolution continues a trajectory already started by other primates (see Chapter 7) suggests that we should be able to find some. If apes can do tasks that are somehow similar to those involved in language-processing, it may be reasonable to treat these ape abilities as evolutionary precursors to human syntax. A later layer of non-linguistic phenomena is found in specifically human activities that apparently don't involve language. An old-fashioned idea was that humans have language because they are generally smarter—just being a super-intelligent ape gives you language for free. The intelligence–language connection is at least somewhat separate from matters of brain size. A bigger brain helps with language only if it is structured in the right way. One needs to consider the possibility that the intelligence–language connection was the other way around, that having language enhanced thinking power, an idea for which we have seen some support in Chapter 2, section 6.

This raises the issue of **domain-specificity**. It has been part of generative theorizing over the past decades to assume that humans have a modular, compartmentalized knowledge of language, and correspondingly modular, compartmentalized language processing skills, separate from other perceptual processing skills. Opponents of this kind of modularity have stressed the overlap between linguistic abilities and non-linguistic abilities. An extreme antimodular view would hold that there are no abilities specifically applied during language behaviour alone, and never in non-linguistic behaviour. On this view the spectacular human ability with language is just a case of humans' spectacular cognitive abilities generally. At the other extreme is a view that there is a significant set of specifically linguistic abilities which are not deployed in any non-linguistic activity. It will be no surprise that I steer a middle course between these extremes, not because I want to keep both sides happy (some hope!), but because a middle position best reflects the facts, mostly from comparative psychology.

Regarding domain-specificity, a special issue of *Cortex* (42(4), 2006), was devoted to position papers on the functions of Broca's area and the closely adjacent ventral premotor cortex (vPMC). This shows the continuing disparity in the field between those arguing for a specifically linguistic module functionally distinct from more general action schemas (e.g. Grodzinsky 2006; Caplan 2006), and others suggesting that 'an important computational role of Broca's area may be to process hierarchic structures in a wide range of functional domains' (Tettamanti and Weniger 2006, p. 491), including object manipulation, visuospatial processing, and music. We can broaden the issue of domain-specificity by considering any brain areas involved in language processing, of which Broca's area, clearly, is an important instance. It is clear that some aspects of language processing deal in content of a specifically linguistic type. This is nothing more controversial than saying that language itself is a nonarbitrary domain. Syntactic categories (Noun, Verb, Determiner, etc.) and grammatical dependency relations (Subject, Modifier, Agreement, etc.) are not found outside language. This is parallel to saying that the content of visual processing (e.g. colour, brightness) is of a specifically visual type. We know that there are some parts of the brain that deal only in visual information. Our question is whether some parts of the brain deal only in grammatical information. The alternative is that all parts of the brain involved in syntactic processing also, perhaps at other times, are involved in non-linguistic tasks. Grodzinsky (2006, p. 467), advocating a domain-specific position, notes 'relatively clear signs that specific linguistic rules have an identifiable brain locus', but continues 'there seem to be some findings to suggest that non-linguistic, potentially motor, functions are represented in the same region as well'. This kind of conclusion is common. 'These results suggest that semantic and syntactic language functions are mediated by partly specialized brain systems but that there nevertheless exists a substantial functional overlap of the involved brain structures' (Röder et al. 2002, p. 1003). From an evolutionary point of view such overlap could be helpful, as it suggests that the non-linguistic functions (not necessarily restricted to motor functions) could be precursors which were recruited for linguistic purposes. And, given the impressive speed of language processing, these brain regions, while not losing their earlier non-linguistic functions, adapted to be particularly efficient at the new linguistic work.

For the evolution of language, the difference between earlier (i.e. non-human) layers of non-linguistic behaviour and later (specifically human) layers is important because it has implications for timing. With the earlier layers, if for some plausible chimp (say) language-like behaviour can be established, there is little question that this can be taken seriously as a chronological precursor to language. But in the case of human non-linguistic, but plausibly language-like, behaviour, we face the 'which came first?' question. The 'which came first' issue has been raised by several scholars. Bickerton asks whether language or shared intentionality came first; Sperber asks whether language or metarepresentational capacity came first. These are the sorts of issue that will be raised several times in the following sections.

6.3 Pre-human semantics and pragmatics

General primate evolutionary trends, especially in brain structure and development, have been pushed much further in the human lineage. In this and the following sections, we will try to see how far toward fully modern syntactic capacities our near pre-*sapiens*[5] ancestors seem likely to have got. And correspondingly we will see the gap across which our own modern species had to evolve. I will discuss the various properties of syntactic language in sections under the same headings as were used in Chapter 4, describing 'What evolved: Language Learning Capacity'. But before that, I will briefly remind the reader of the semantic and pragmatic abilities that I claimed for apes in the earlier book *The Origins of Meaning*. The motivation should be obvious. Modern human syntax is meaningful. Sentences have propositional content about states of the world; this is **sentence meaning** which I gloss as 'semantics'. And our sentences are uttered with a view to affecting the responses of our hearers; this is **speaker meaning**, glossed as 'pragmatics'. In the earlier book, I claimed to be able to see, in languageless animal behaviour, precursors and evolutionary seeds of linguistic semantics and pragmatics.

On the semantic side, non-human animals have rich representations of the world. There is no doubt that in the wild, animals form conceptual categories (or categorical concepts, if you will) of the types of object, event, and situation that are relevant to them. As they are ready at any time to respond in the appropriate way, these representations must be in waiting in their minds even when not activated or attended to. It has been argued that some animals show evidence of meta-cognition—that is, being able to become aware of their own states of attention.[6] This evidence is patchy at best, only applies to a few animals, and can only be induced in lab conditions. But some little seed that can evolve into full-blown awareness of our own concepts can be dimly glimpsed in non-humans. The concepts that animals have are mostly concrete, but it has been reliably shown, for a wide range of animals, that they can form more abstract relational concepts, in particular concepts SAME and DIFFERENT, and

---

[5] I will not distinguish between modern humans and Neanderthals. We know nothing about differences between these (sub)species relevant to syntax.

[6] See Ch. 2, sec. 2 of *The Origins of Meaning*.

that they can generalize these conceptual relations over a wide range of novel stimuli.[7] Troop animals such as baboons and chimpanzees know hierarchical social relations that we would express as propositions, for example X is dominant over Y. Animals are often said to live only in the here-and-now, whereas a salient property of language is our ability to talk about things distant in time and space. But this again is not an absolute difference. Object-permanence experiments show that many different species can keep a representation of an object in mind even when it is not present to the senses. The dog remembering for five minutes where a bone has been stashed, a bone that it can no longer see or smell, knows about an object that is not here now. A chimpanzee has been shown to recall the presence of hidden food overnight, so again knowing about an object that is not in the here and now. The difference between humans and others is again a matter of degree. We are vastly better at mentally representing things that are not here and now, as I am currently trying to imagine you, the reader, a long distance away, and at least a year away in time.[8] (Hi there!) Closely related to representation of objects away from the here and now is the issue of episodic memory, a memory for specific experienced events. Certain animals have shown an ability in this respect, limited to domains, in particular food, that are of great interest to them. Humans have much better abilities in this sphere of mental time travel, but again it is a matter of degree. Finally, chimpanzees and orang-utans clearly show some ability to plan for the future (Osvath and Osvath 2008; Osvath 2009), so this mental time travel can be, like ours, both retrospective and prospective.[9]

On the pragmatic side, all animals communicate at a basic level by doing things to each other, and much of this communication is ritualized.[10] I compared this pragmatic aspect of communication to Austin's *How to Do Things with Words*. Some simple human sentences are still limited to this doing-things-to-each-other kind of meaning, like the greeting *Hello!*, which has no propositional content (although what the speaker means by it can be described in propositional terms by an analyst). All human utterances are intended to do something to a hearer, otherwise what would be the point of making an utterance? So syntactically complex sentences retain this ancient illocutionary or performative aspect of meaning. We humans have found ways to incorporate detailed propositional content into the utterances we use to do things to each

---

[7] See Ch. 2, sec. 1 of *The Origins of Meaning*.
[8] See Ch. 2, sec. 3 of *The Origins of Meaning*.
[9] See Ch. 3 of *The Origins of Meaning*.
[10] See Ch. 6, sec. 3 of *The Origins of Meaning*.

other. In other words, we can manipulate each other's minds in far richer ways by drawing our hearers' attention to present, distant, or even non-existent imaginary or fictional objects and events. The manipulation and mind-reading aspects of language have ancient pre-human roots. Some animals are capable of tactical deception, which requires knowing how another animal will respond to a certain action. There is experimental evidence that a chimpanzee can know what objects another chimpanzee knows about, in limited domains such as food.[11] And a chimpanzee can discern the intentions, at least insofar as distinguishing between deliberate teasing and fumblingly cooperative, of other agents, human or chimp. What apes are far less, if at all, disposed to is what Tomasello et al. (2005) call 'shared intentionality', a natural capacity to discern the interests of others and a willingness to participate cooperatively in their intended actions. The elaborate structured utterances of humans clearly reflect this cooperative disposition, and I hypothesize that it was this[12] that opened the door a first crack for the evolution of syntax. But it was not a simple 'first shared intentionality, then syntax' story. Presumably both the capacity and willingness to share intentions and the capacity to construct and understand complex sentences grew in parallel, in what Bickerton (2005) has aptly called 'a beneficent spiral'. Trying to say which came first gets us into the logical chicken-and-egg bind. Whichever it was, it was tiny and different from the modern evolved capacity, so the question becomes essentially terminological.

Also in the realm of pragmatics is the question of whether the recipient of a signal interprets it as conveying an intention to communicate on the part of the sender. This is central to language. A speaker communicates not only some proposition about the world (say) but also implicitly communicates, by virtue of deliberately speaking the same language, or playing the same language-game as her hearer, that she intends to communicate that proposition. And a human recipient of such a message understands that the speaker intends him to understand that she intended to communicate something to him. This is a central theme of Relevance Theory (Sperber and Wilson 1986). In this connection, Thom Scott-Phillips has coined the useful phrase 'signalling signalhood' (Scott-Phillips et al. 2009). There is evidence in non-human primates of the seeds of a system for recognizing signalhood, or at least treating meaningful actions

---

[11] See passages indexed under 'mind-reading' and 'manipulation of attention' in *The Origins of Meaning*.

[12] Amongst other factors, including a capacity for metarepresentation, to be discussed below.

by others differently. For an evolutionary start, recall the left-lateralization of processing of conspecific calls in monkeys, noted in Chapter 2, section 1.1. Closer to humans, that section also noted studies showing a left-hemisphere preference in chimpanzees for processing learned meaningful symbols—the chimpanzee brain distinguishes meaningful symbolic actions from other input. In humans, I have also noted (Chapter 2, section 1.2) activation of Brodmann areas 44 and 45 (constitutive of Broca's area) on viewing meaningful manual gestures. The neural specialization for meaningful signals in non-human primates falls short of full-blown modern human recognition of an intention to communicate, or **metarepresentational** ability, but it is an evolutionary seed from which this ability is likely to have grown. Non-human animals show only little signs of such ability. 'Other primates may have some rather rudimentary metarepresentational capacities. We humans are massive users of metarepresentations, and of quite complex ones at that' (Sperber 2000, p. 117). Sperber also links the evolution of metarepresentational capacity with the evolution of language, and his approach poses a similar chicken-and-egg dilemma to that posed by Bickerton's approach to the relationship between shared intentionality and language.

If one accepts, as I do, the existence of two dedicated mental mechanisms, one for language, the other for metarepresentations, it seems reasonable to assume that, in humans, they have coevolved. While the fully developed version of each of these two mechanisms may presuppose the development of the other, it still makes sense to ask which of these two, the linguistic or the metarepresentational, might have developed first to a degree sufficient to bootstrap the coevolutionary process.

(Sperber 2000, p. 121)

Here again, while agreeing with the coevolution point, I would argue that the 'which came first' question is deceptive. I will discuss the role of metarepresentations further in the next chapter. For the present, it is enough to note that metarepresentational abilities of apes are at best very slim compared to what humans can do.

All this semantic and pragmatic ability was in place before humans started using syntax. Syntactic structuring of messages made it possible to expand massively the range of what is communicated. In the following sections I will look at other possible abilities of pre-humans, non-semantic and non-pragmatic, that could have helped to lay the foundations of human syntactic capacity. As pre-syntactic creatures, by definition, had no syntax, the capacities that I will be discussing below are not specifically linguistic capacities.

6.4 Massive storage

In Chapter 2, we have already seen how limited is the capacity of apes, even symbol-trained apes, for vocabulary acquisition. The difference between humans and apes is on (at least) two dimensions. There is the dimension of sheer numbers. The vocabularies of trained apes only get into the hundreds, never above a thousand items. This can be ascertained simply by counting the stimuli (object or symbol) that an ape successfully responds to. Humans, compared to chimps, have massively expanded their storage capacity for object–symbol associations. A typical speaker knows many tens of thousands of words and their meanings.

In the wild apes learn no extensive vocabulary. Given a human lab environment, they show themselves to be surprisingly good at acquiring vocabulary, well beyond anything observable in the wild. The apes have latent ability not tapped for this purpose in the wild. But why should any animal in its natural environment have such spare capacity? We would expect natural selection to trim down an animal's toolkit to just what it is likely to meet. Apes did not evolve to survive, or reproduce more, in circumstances of human training. The most plausible answer is that the abilities we have found in apes are not unused or unusable spare capacity. Apes' abilities are not specifically vocabulary-learning abilities, but more general learning abilities that can be applied to picking up vocabulary if the occasion demands. In other words, these abilities in apes are not domain-specific to language. 'Despite its obvious homology with memory systems in non-humans, the huge number of words that every child learns dwarfs the capabilities of the most sophisticated of non-humans. This suggests that, despite a broadly shared neural basis, even the lexicon has undergone some special modifications in humans' (Hauser and Fitch 2003, p. 159).

Vocabulary is just one domain in which human information storage has dramatically increased. This ape/human difference is a matter of degree. Of course nobody knows how to measure all the other knowledge stored in an ape brain, but it is surely safe to say that, whatever plausible metric might be devised, apes cannot store as much knowledge as humans. Chimpanzees' episodic memory is known to be very limited, by comparison with humans'. A chimpanzee knows all the members of its troupe, and many features of its geographical range. But this knowledge is small compared to how many people humans typically know (Dunbar 1996a, 1996b). It is also possible that human knowledge of different places exceeds chimpanzees' knowledge of their range, although this is difficult to quantify. Beside vocabulary, bonobos and chimpanzees can learn arbitrary conventional non-linguistic facts. Kanzi, for example, knows to turn a water tap anti-clockwise to turn it on, and to turn a doorhandle the other way to open a door.

It is not difficult to imagine that some of the increased brain size of humans is devoted to storage, conceived in this straightforward quantitative way. Recall from Chapter 1 the correlation between the size of the higher vocal centre (HVC) in a songbird's brain and the number of songs in its repertoire. The first computer I ever worked with, a Q32, had a core memory of 256k 48-bit words. This capacity is tiny compared to the terabytes of storage now cheaply available. Computers with less memory cannot do such complex computations as machines with more memory. By modern standards, we were extremely limited in trying to work within the capacity of the old Q32. The computer analogy is salutary, however, in that it reminds us that physical size does not simply correlate with amount of storage. The ancient Q32 occupied a whole basement; now a chip the size of a thumbnail houses much more data. This miniaturization is due to successive inventions of radically different technologies, from big drums to tiny semiconductor chips. But the evolution of ape brains into human brains did not involve any such technological shift. Ape and human brains work on the same basic principles. So pure expansion in physical size probably has something to do with how much information we can store, compared to apes.

A more interesting dimension is the richness of the internal representation formed by a trained ape in learning the naming task. As mentioned in Chapter 2, the chimpanzees Sherman and Austin were very laboriously trained to be able to make generalizations across lexigrams, building, as Deacon and others argue, not just a set of object–lexigram associations, but a network of concepts behind these object–lexigram pairings. In this way these chimpanzees showed that with great effort they could be induced to form something like human concepts. The difference between simple object–symbol pairings and a network of inferential relations between object–symbol pairings is indeed a qualitative difference. But the difference between chimpanzees and humans in this area is not a qualitative difference, but a matter of degree. Chimps, with great effort on their and their trainers' parts, can learn to acquire the same kind of representations, as far as we can tell, as humans. They just can't do it anything like so easily, and they can't do it for anything like so many concepts. But they can (be made to) do it. Ape brains have the potential to develop in an individual's lifetime the weak machinery, creakily implemented, to do something humanlike, in a quantitatively very restricted way. It doesn't come naturally to them in normal circumstances. Nothing in wild chimpanzee life brings out this capacity. Humans from infancy are strongly disposed to form such representations and we live in cooperative social environments which foster this growth.

6.5 Hierarchical structure

In this section, we'll first consider Kanzi's apparent inability to comprehend a basic kind of hierarchical structure, a coordination of two noun phrases. Then we'll look elsewhere at two kinds of hierarchical structure: hierarchical structure in non-linguistic routine activities of humans and non-human animals; and the possibility of some hierarchical structure in thoughts, which can get naturally externalized as expressions showing hierarchical structure in their syntax.

6.5.1 *Kanzi doesn't get NP coordinations*

This subsection concerns the earlier layer of non-linguistic phenomena, because it is about what an ape can, and cannot, do. To fairly general amazement, it turned out that Kanzi can understand some spoken English. The ape vocal apparatus can't produce human-like vowels and consonants, which is why researchers have resorted to sign language and lexigram boards. But ape hearing is well enough tuned to human speech that Kanzi can extract some meaning from spoken English. At age eight, he obeyed simple requests spoken in English somewhat better than a comparator two-year-old child. Savage-Rumbaugh et al. (1993) give a complete corpus of the 653 simple English requests spoken to Kanzi and Alia, the child, with a record of whether they successfully complied with the requests. Examples of these requests are *Can you put your collar in the backpack?*, *Can you put some toothpaste on your ball?*, and *Carry the rock to the bedroom*. Kanzi was judged to have carried out the request 72 percent of the time. This is highly significant. 'Even in object-location sentences, if a mean of seven objects and six locations is assumed, the probability of getting any such sentence correct by chance is 2.4 percent. The probability of being correct on other sentence types would be less as the potential for error is higher. The possibility that, with each trial represented by different tokens, either subject would be correct on a majority of sentence types by chance approaches zero' (Savage-Rumbaugh et al. 1993, p. 76).

If one is so inclined (a crucial precondition in this sensitive area), one may even find a sense of humour in some of Kanzi's responses. When asked *Put some water on the carrot*, he tossed the carrot outdoors, where it was raining heavily. Well, the result was getting water on the carrot! When asked

Put the carrot in the water, he did the expected thing. The experimenters used twenty-one pairs like this, to test Kanzi's comprehension of word order. Another pair was *Put the tomato in the oil* versus *Put some oil in the tomato*. For twelve of the twenty-one pairs, he successfully complied with both requests. Not too impressive, but a lot better than Alia, the two-year old child.[13] Both Kanzi and Alia, when they got it right, were possibly doing no more than applying a 'word soup' strategy boosted by pragmatic inference from context and an iconic factor. When asked to put the tomato in the oil, you naturally pick up the first thing mentioned, the tomato. Note that this doesn't account for Kanzi's (humorous?) tossing the carrot outside into the rain when asked to put some water on the carrot. As discussed in Chapter 3, Section 3.4, even adult humans often resort to a 'Good Enough' parsing strategy, ignoring grammatical markers. It is possible to get away with such a minimal strategy much of the time.

Rob Truswell (2009) has argued for signs that Kanzi has more than a simple 'semantic soup' understanding. Kanzi acts appropriately when asked to put something 'on' something else, as in *Put some oil on your ball*. So, the argument goes, he understands this meaning of *on*. He doesn't put the oil by the ball, or near the ball, or under the ball, but on it. OK, you may say, but after *put* and especially with oil, this interpretation is the most natural, because that's what you do with oil. But it gets more interesting. When asked *Put your collar on*, Kanzi does so. He doesn't look around for some other object to put his collar on—he puts it on himself. By contrast, when asked *Put your collar in the refrigerator*, he does so. Truswell writes 'Although relevant data are quite sparse, Kanzi responded correctly in 10 of the 12 items (83%) involving particles or intransitive prepositions, again suggesting that these pose no particular problem for him'. A semantic soup strategy could still be uppermost here. Given what you normally do with a collar, and if no other object, like a refrigerator, is mentioned, what else are you going to do if asked to put your collar on? Truswell attributes to Kanzi a nuanced knowledge of the meanings of the preposition *on*, because Kanzi does (more or less) the right thing in response to all of *Turn the flashlight on*, *Put your collar on*, and *Put the ball on the telephone*, in which the meanings of *on* are clearly different. However, again a semantic soup strategy will do. If you only know two words of German *mach* 'make' and *Licht* 'light', and the light is off, and someone

---

[13] Sue Savage-Rumbaugh is widely suspected of over-generous interpretation of Kanzi's performances, and there may be a degree of truth in this. I believe that the Kanzi/Alia comparison experiment did show some ability in Kanzi at least comparable to that of the child. See Chapter 8, section 4 for a bit more discussion of this.

says *Mach das Licht auf*, you can make a pretty good guess at what they want you to do. So I think Rob Truswell here is giving Kanzi too much credit.

With other examples, Truswell makes a convincing case that Kanzi does not understand some basic features of English grammar, such as the singular meaning of the article *a* and coordinated noun phrases (NP+NP). When asked *Kanzi, go get a carrot for Rose*, Kanzi (in the end) gives Rose several carrots. (The experimenters generously classed this as a kind of correct response.) In another case, *get a tomato*, Kanzi responds by handing over a whole bag of tomatoes. Examples of coordinated NPs are *the water and the doggie* and *the lighter and the shoe*. Thus English grammar provides a way of referring to a collection consisting of two or more things. Just as the collection has a hierarchical part/whole structure, so does the whole coordinate NP, consisting of two embedded NPs joined by the conjunction *and*. Truswell eliminated some of the experimenters' trials on methodological grounds. Then:

This leaves 18 unproblematic NP-coordination trials. Of these, Kanzi ignored the first NP on 9 trials, as in (25a), ignored the second NP on 5 trials, (25b), and responded correctly to 4 trials (25c).

(25) a. 428. (PC) *Give the water and the doggie to Rose.* (Kanzi picks up the dog and hands it to Rose.) [PC = partially correct]

b. 526. (PC) *Give the lighter and the shoe to Rose.* (Kanzi hands Rose the lighter, then points to some food in a bowl in the array that he would like to have to eat.)

c. 281. (C) *Give me the milk and the lighter.* (Kanzi does so.) [C = correct]

Kanzi's overall accuracy on this construction is therefore 22.2%. In comparison, Savage-Rumbaugh et al. (1993, p. 77) give his overall accuracy across the corpus as 72%. The same trials were presented to a human infant, Alia. Alia's accuracy across the corpus was slightly lower, at 66%, but her accuracy on the NP-coordination trials is around $\frac{13}{19}$, or 68.4%. We have, then, a clear case of a species-specific, construction-specific deficit. Kanzi does not perform worse than a human infant across the whole corpus, but he performs much worse than both his usual standard (2-tailed Fisher exact test, p = 0.00002), and the human control (p = 0.008), on this one construction.

(Truswell 2009, unpublished, p. 24)

So Kanzi doesn't reliably interpret hierarchically structured examples, even of a simple NP+NP kind. Savage-Rumbaugh et al. (1993), interestingly, resort to a Chomsky-like strategem for interpreting this: 'Kanzi's difficulty was perhaps due more to short-term memory limitations on the overall amount of information than to processing limitations on the information that was available to him' (p. 85). What I think this means is that Kanzi may have understood the coordinate NP+NP construction, but was then unable to keep in mind all the things (all two of them) that he had been asked to deal with. (That's why we make shopping lists.) Peter Gärdenfors (2003, p. 154), against this, notes 'but there are so many other things that indicate that his memory is excellent'. But maybe that is not what the authors meant. With my concept of **UG+**, processing limitations are an integral part of the evolving linguistic capacity. Kanzi's UG+ doesn't stretch to this much hierarchical structure.

Much earlier, Premack and Premack (1972) had also sketchily investigated the possibility of a chimpanzee understanding hierarchical syntax. Their chimpanzee, Sarah, had been taught to associate plastic chips with objects and actions. She was given the string corresponding to *Sarah insert apple pail banana dish*. She duly put the apple in the pail and the banana in the dish. While linguists would draw a hierarchical tree structure over such an example, the string can be interpreted without appeal to such structure. The only somewhat impressive thing here is that when Sarah came to *banana*, she remembered the instruction *insert* from three words 'earlier'. But then again, the whole string of chips was still in front of her, and she had only just finished another inserting act. Concluding an earlier survey of chimp 'language' experiments, Dwyer (1986, p. 41) writes 'we are led to the conclusion that to date, chimpanzees only clearly show an ability for paratactic signing'. 'Paratactic signing' is stringing signs together with no hierarchical structure, that is semantic soup. Dwyer's conclusion echoes Givón's:

> More related to phylogenetic evolution is the observation that chimpanzees, when taught human language via ASL (Gardner and Gardner 1969, 1974), colored magnetic chips (Premack 1976) or computer console (Rumbaugh and Gill 1977) find it quite easy to handle coordination, but almost impossible to handle subordination.
>
> (Givón 1979a, p. 298)

The 'coordination' that Givón mentions here is not the hierarchical organization of two or more phrases into a larger phrase, as with *the water and the doggie*, where the overall phrase denotes a collection. It is 'coordination' in a looser sense that can be handled by a semantic soup strategy.

6.5.2 *Hierarchical structure in non-linguistic activities*

A linguist who has discussed a parallel between hierarchical syntactic structure and the hierarchical structure of human non-linguistic activities is Ray Jackendoff (2007). He delves at length into the structure of the task of making coffee.[14]

---

[14] Jackendoff's Chapter 4 'The Structure of Complex Actions' is well worth reading in this context, but can't be quoted in full here.

He makes a convincing case that many of the modules of action involved are not specific to the coffee-making task, and furthermore can be rather freely re-arranged in various orders. Coffee-making and many other human activities are hierarchically ('phrasally') structured. When problems occur in the coffee-making ritual, like the coffee-jar being unexpectedly empty, he inserts another whole routine, namely going to the store to buy coffee, a task that involves many other subroutines, like finding car keys, going to the car, and so on and so on. On getting back home with the coffee he can pick up coffee-making where he left off. All this activity is hierarchical in a clear sense, with routines embedded in other routines to some considerable depth. A crucial question is: does language itself makes such deeply nested activities possible?—the 'which came first?' question. Do we always talk to ourselves, even if only subvocally, at key transition points when carrying out such complex activities? We know that languageless creatures, infants and apes, are not much good at such activities (except innately built-in activities like birds' nest-building). Based on my own introspection, I can't help thinking that language at least plays a significant part in the social transmission of complex activities by learning. Someone once explained to me verbally, along with a practical demo, how to make coffee. The practical demo is also important, as it invokes imitative capacities, which interestingly involve circuits including Brodmann's area 44 within Broca's area (Iacoboni et al. 1999). The conceptual (= verbal) and practical components of complex tool use are dissociable but work together (see Johnson-Frey 2004 and references therein). '[T]he very same brain areas involved in representing familiar tool-use skills also show increased activity when retrieving and planning communicative gestures' (Frey 2008, p. 1955). Once learned and practised routinely, complex practical activities, typically involving tools, don't require verbal rehearsal, not even subvocally; think of driving a car. This points in the direction of 'language came first' as the answer to our recurring question in this case. Many complex human hierarchically structured non-linguistic activities are mediated in the first instance by language, either in the private thought of an inventor or in public teaching. When, later, they get routinized so that one can do them without thinking, they possibly use some of the same brain circuits as language processing.

In research on how humans carry out everyday routine actions, the passage below expresses a solid consensus.

There are two main modes of control: an unconscious, automatic mode best modeled as a network of distributed processors acting locally and in parallel; and a conscious control mode acting globally to oversee and override automatic control. Automatic and conscious control are complementary: the unconscious mode is fast, parallel, and context-dependent, responding to regularities in the environment in routine ways, whereas the conscious mode is effortful, limited, and flexible, stepping in to handle novel situations. (Sellen and Norman 1992, p. 318)

This is strikingly reminiscent of the situation with language. Much of the time we speak fast and automatically—the words just flow out. When faced with a need to express thoughts very carefully, or during our early steps with a new language, we proceed much more deliberately. In this respect language behaviour is very similar to non-linguistic behaviour.

In a pathological condition known as 'Action Disorganization Syndrome' (ADS), sufferers get mixed up in routine actions like making coffee, for instance putting the water where the beans should go. It is clear that this condition is associated with much more general brain damage than just to those areas that cause language deficits. ADS 'tends to occur in etiologies associated with diffuse and widespread cerebral damage: closed head injury, anoxia, Alzheimers disease' (Schwartz 1995, p. 332.) This suggests that an ability to carry out complex everyday, but non-linguistic tasks is a less compartmentalized ability than language. This was a discussion of the later layer of non-linguistic phenomena, because it deals with specifically human behaviour that seems in some way language-like. It raised the 'which came first?' question, to which I gave a tentative answer, 'language'.

I turn now to the earlier layer of non-linguistic behaviour in connection with the (non-)abilities of apes at what we regard as everyday activities. Such human activities as coffee-making require a degree of planning and imagination that seems to be lacking in apes. Köhler (1925, pp. 53–5) describes chimpanzees desperate to reach fruit suspended from the ceiling but unable to figure out that a box or ladder in a nearby corridor could easily be used for access. The animals had seen the ladder and the box, but as it was out of sight, it also seemed to be out of mind. The immediacy of the fruit above them dominated their thinking. Thus there is an emotional component to our ability to carry out complex hierarchical activities. Humans can keep an ultimate goal in mind while patiently carrying out other actions not immediately resulting in gratification. Heightened emotions like fear or anger can have a paralysing effect on careful thinking. It is an intriguing thought that levels of neurotransmitters, as well as brain architecture, may play a large part in our capacity for complex planning. Indeed, based on the role of dopamine in language dysfunctions associated with Parkinson's Disease, McNamara and Durso (2000) propose a 'neurochemistry of language'.[15]

---

[15] See The Origins of Meaning, pp. 327–9 for a discussion of the role of oxytocin in fostering trustful attitudes, necessary for linguistic interaction.

It is in fact very widely recognized, especially within neuroscience and by computational modellers, that any complex behaviour is hierarchically organized.

> Research on human and animal behavior has long emphasized its hierarchical structure—the divisibility of ongoing behavior into discrete tasks, which are comprised of subtask sequences, which in turn are built of simple actions. The hierarchical structure of behavior has also been of enduring interest within neuroscience, where it has been widely considered to reflect prefrontal cortical functions.
>
> (Botvinick et al. 2009, p. 262)

(The allusion to prefrontal cortex, comparatively over-developed in humans, is notable. The role of the prefrontal cortex will be discussed further in Chapter 6, section 8 and Chapter 7, section 2.) Our question is not whether hierarchically organized behaviour exists in non-humans—it is clearly widespread. Rather, we should ask to what extent the actions of non-humans are hierarchically structured in specific ways which could provide a possible evolutionary foundation for human syntax. I will note some differences between apparently hierarchical behaviour by animals and the hierarchical production and comprehension of human sentences.

A parallel is often drawn between the hierarchical structure of sentences and the hierarchical organization of sequences of actions on physical objects. Routine activities by many animals, including humans of course, seem intuitively to a human observer to be hierarchically organized. A well known example is the way mountain gorillas prepare nettles for eating. Byrne and Russon (1998, p. 673) give the diagram in Figure 6.1 (overleaf) for this activity, based on their field observations. These authors are not concerned to draw a parallel between animal activities and human syntax. Several other researchers have drawn such a parallel. A prominent example is in an important article by Patricia Greenfield (1991), who surveys a number of studies, including her own, comparing the ways in which babies and children manipulate physical objects, such as spoons, sticks, toys, and little plastic pots. The interest is in seeing whether the subjects make 'subassemblies' while building play structures, or while carrying out some goal-driven activity, such as eating. To take a simple example, a baby merely grasping a spoon is not taken to be a hierarchically organized action.[16] A baby putting a spoon in its mouth is still not counted as a hierarchically

---

[16] All the actions discussed in this literature are analysed with the discrete physical objects taken as dictating the basic building blocks of the activities. The motor programme for grasping a spoon is itself hierarchically organized, of course, involving moving the arm and hand toward the spoon, opening the hand, and then closing the fingers around the object. This motor level of hierarchy is apparently not considered relevant.

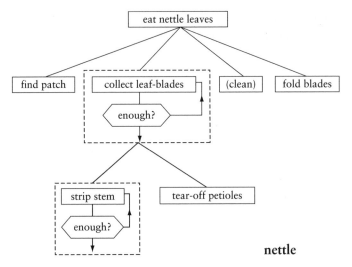

Fig. 6.1 Claimed hierarchically organized food preparation by mountain gorillas.

Source: From Byrne and Russon (1998), who analyse this activity into four main subroutines, with the second subroutine analysed into two sub-subroutines. Note the close formal similarity of this diagram with those used for many birdsongs in Chapter 1. This sequence of actions can be generated by a grammar of lesser power than a Phrase Structure (i.e. hierarchical) grammar. In fact this sequence of actions can be generated by a Strictly 2-Local set of transitions from one basic element to the next, with no implicit appeal to hierarchical organization.

structured action. But loading the spoon with food, then putting the sub-assembly consisting of spoon-with-food into the mouth, is considered a case of hierarchically organized action. One sees the point. Greenfield diagrams this last activity as in Figure 6.2, deliberately evocative of linguists' tree diagrams.

The methods of linguists, especially those attentive to Formal Language Theory (FLT), entail more disciplined reasoning than just eyeballing some complex activity, such as a gorilla preparing nettles, and declaring the activity hierarchical. The possibility of a description in hierarchical terms does not necessarily entail that representation of the activity is hierarchically structured

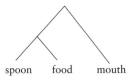

Fig. 6.2 Simple hierarchical organization in the act of feeding oneself with a spoon. Loading the spoon with food creates a subassembly, which is then carried to the mouth.

Source: Diagram from Greenfield (1991 p. 540), based on data from Connolly and Dalgliesh (1989).

in the brain of the animal. Recall the discussion of various birdsong repertoires in Chapter 1. It was shown that many repertoires could be described with a strictly linear grammar, entailing no phrasal (i.e. hierarchical) organization. Nevertheless, many of the intuitive descriptions by birdsong researchers ascribed phrasal organization to the songs. In one case, zebra finch song, I mentioned neuroscientific evidence for phrasal organization, even though the observable repertoire could be described with a less powerful linear grammar. Evidence other than the form of an individual song itself was needed to decide the issue. Applying the FLT kind of reasoning to cases like gorilla nettle-eating, one has to ask whether the activities could possibly be described without invoking hierarchical organization. That is, could it be that the gorilla, for example, has no overall hierarchical plan in mind, but simply goes to each next stage in the routine, triggered probabilistically by the immediately previous sub-action? From Figure 6.1, it is clear that an alternative description using a less powerful kind of descriptive device, implying no hierarchical organization, would be sufficient to describe what the gorilla does.

The case for hierarchical organization of gorilla nettle-eating would be strengthened if it could be shown that each alleged subroutine is an action module embedded in various other activities with different surrounding actions. For example, does the gorilla sometimes strip the stems of some non-food plant, for a purpose other than eating, and without automatically going to the next 'tear off petioles' step? If so, this would suggest a separately stored action schema with some versatile potential for being plugged into a variety of different overall actions. In a scientifically ideal world, we would also be able to scan the brain of the gorilla, as can be done with zebra finches, and see whether sparsely coded instructions are sent from 'higher' regions, triggering premotor activity and ultimately the detailed movements. It is likely that nettle-eating by gorillas is strongly automatized and that the animal's brain has developed a linear routine. But birds' songs are also strongly automatized, and yet we found reason to argue from the neuroscientific evidence for organization resembling phrase structure.

It is certainly safe to grant that some, but not all, physical activities with objects by gorillas, children and many other animals are hierarchically structured in the minds of the actors. But there is a key difference between such physical activity and the act of producing a hierarchically structured string of words. For the physical manipulations of objects, the current state and position of the objects themselves provide immediate sensory information about the stage reached so far in the overall process. Note the test labelled 'enough?' which occurs twice in Figure 6.1. The gorilla sees the stripped nettle stem; could a gorilla do its nettle-processing routine in the dark? The baby sees or feels the loaded spoon; what it sees prompts it to do the next thing. When Ray Jackendoff makes coffee, he is reminded of where he has got to in the process by sensing some current state of the world, such as the unground beans or the empty water holder. This is in marked contrast to the utterance of a spoken sentence. The words already spoken are no longer physically present to the senses, though they may be held briefly in a memory buffer. The difference is like the difference between navigating by familiar landmarks at every turn and navigating by dead reckoning in an open and featureless sea. Dead reckoning involves keeping a record of all time travelled, and in which directions, with no feedback other than from celestial bodies. Producing a grammatically structured utterance happens very much faster than navigation at sea, of course. But producing grammatical output does not even have the benefit of stars to sail by, or any kind of sensory feedback which might give a clue what to say next. Short-term auditory feedback is important in speech production insofar as it helps the speaker to monitor the words as they are uttered. But the acoustic/sensory properties of the words just said do not generally act as a stimulus triggering the next step in the serial action. What to say next when midway through a complex novel sentence is all determined by an internally kept memory of what has been said so far and the intended meaning; no external stimulus gives a prompt. In fact, external stimuli can be positively distracting: a person who happens to see a salient printed word at some crucial point while speaking can be induced to make a slip of the tongue and say the word printed rather than what she really intended to say.

A related crucial difference between routine physical activities, such as making coffee, eating with a spoon or stripping nettles, and producing a sentence, is that the components of a sentence (words and phrases) are **arbitrary symbols** for other things. Physical spoons or jars of coffee beans or handfuls of nettles have certain affordances, prompting further action. But the **words** *jar*, *coffee*, and *beans* do not have the same affordances. The word *jar* is not something you can put beans into; the word *beans* cannot be put into a jar. If you put a slip of paper with the word *beans* written on it into a jar, the actual word, a reusable item in the language, does not need to be taken out of the jar if you want to use it again. What went into the jar was a slip of paper, not the word. When producing a sentence, say about coffee-making, you most directly organize these abstract symbols, not the objects they refer to. Certainly, the relations between the real-world objects have some influence on the structure of sentences describing them. We expect a sentence about someone handling a jar of coffee beans to have the words for COFFEE and BEANS adjacent or linked by some grammatical marker; and likewise we expect this pair of words to be close, or somehow grammatically linked, to the word for JAR. But the relations between the objects referred to do not fully determine how a sentence describing the scene is to be organized. Languages do it different ways. To talk about beans in English you have to know that it/they is/are referred to using a plural count noun; to talk about beans in Arabic, you have to know that it/they is/are referred to using a singular mass noun; and in each language, you have to make other words, such as verbs and adjectives, agree in number accordingly. The kind of mental manipulation involved in sentence production is, obviously, more abstract and symbolic than manipulation of physical things.[17]

Arguments against domain-specificity of hierarchical organization in grammar typically invoke non-linguistic tasks (such as coffee-making) which have hierarchical structure, and point to the ease with which humans can manage such tasks. Therefore, the argument goes, it should be no surprise that we can manage hierarchical structure in grammar. Conversely, an argument in favour of domain-specificity shows a non-linguistic hierarchical task that humans actually find difficult. Cummins (1998) gives such an example.

Can humans form hierarchically embedded mental representations? The depth of recursive embedding in the five-disc Tower of Hanoi problem described above is trivial compared with the embedding depth one typically finds in the grammatical structure of human language. Yet the Tower of Hanoi problem is notoriously difficult for adult humans to solve, whereas parsing sentences with equal or greater grammatical structures is trivial for most native speakers. Focusing solely on performance in either of these domains would lead one to draw very different conclusions about the human capacity to traffic in hierarchically complex mental representation.

(Cummins 1998, p. 687)

This argument is flawed. The Tower of Hanoi problem[18] involves a kind of self-embedding, keeping track of (or anticipating) a certain physical move operation within the same move operation at a higher level, itself embedded in the same move operation at an even higher level, and so on.[19] As argued in Chapter 3, section 6, humans do have great difficulty in parsing sentences with more than one degree of centre-self-embedding.

---

[17] We could perhaps usefully stretch the use of the Gibsonian term *affordances* to the conventional grammatical relations between words in a language. The phrase *grammatical affordances*, describing how words and constructions fit with each other in a language, has been used by Cameron and Deignan (2006), by K. Y. Ohara, and by M. Fortescue in several unpublished essays relating to Construction Grammar.

[18] You can play the Tower of Hanoi game online at http://www.dynamicdrive. com/dynamicindex12/towerhanoi.htm.

[19] See Anderson and Douglass (2001) for an analysis of the costs of storage and retrieval in a version of the Tower of Hanoi problem.

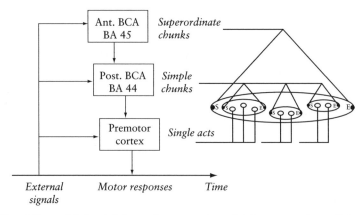

Fig. 6.3 Koechlin and Jubault's (2006) proposed model for processing of hierarchically structured tasks.

Note: BCA = Broca's area and its right hemisphere counterpart. BA = Brodmann's area.

A degree of domain-specificity is compatible with exaptation of a capacity in a pre-existing domain for use in a new domain. Many studies testify to the activation of Broca's area in humans during processing of hierarchically complex sentences.[20] How and to what extent is Broca's area involved in non-linguistic hierarchical tasks? I will mention one prominent recent study that purports to give an answer, noting some problems with its interpretation in the context of syntax evolution. Koechlin and Jubault (2006) gave human subjects tasks involving three hierarchical levels, which they gloss as 'single motor acts', 'simple action chunks', and 'superordinate action chunks', items on each level being composed of sequences of items on the next lower level. The input stimuli in their experiment at the bottom level were letters, to which subjects had to respond with left or right button-presses. The 'correct' button press varied depending on which middle-level task subjects were completing at the time. There were three different middle-level tasks, involving different mappings from letters to button-presses. The top-level task was to carry out the three middle-level tasks in sequence, with some repetitions. The overall structure of the superordinate task was thus interestingly similar to the formal structure of some complex birdsongs, with their sequences of sometimes repeated phrases, each phrase consisting of a sequence of basic notes (a comparison the authors do not make). Furthermore, the tasks, subtasks and sub-subtasks were arbitrary and meaningless; they were just things that the subjects had been

[20] Some example studies are Friederici et al. (2006a, 2006b); Röder et al. (2002); Ben-Shachar et al. (2003); Musso et al. (2003); Bahlmann et al. (2008).

trained to do, with no associated use or meaning. Thus the task was neither completely like making coffee, with a desired end reward, nor completely like a hierarchically structured sentence, being devoid of meaning. The experimental task, though it involves letters, is not overtly linguistic, and so is arguably not in the domain of language. Based on fMRI data, Koechlin and Jubault propose a division of labour in Broca's area as shown in Figure 6.3. This model is very reminiscent of neural models of birdsong control as described in Chapter 1, with HVC (in birds) controlling top-level structure of the song, and sending messages to the bird's RA, which sends signals to the motor areas that produce the notes. Unfortunately, this model and the tasks on which it is based don't get us very far in understanding the basis for human processing of either non-linguistic tasks such as coffee-making or processing of meaningful sentences: both these latter tasks involve more levels than there is room for in Koechlin and Jubault's model. The question arises: what brain areas would be activated in carrying out a four-level task, or a five-level task? It seems unlikely that there is a further 'stack' of brain areas waiting to be activated just for even more complex tasks. The question of recursion obviously arises. Is there some processing circuit in the human brain that can process its own output? Nevertheless it is possible that Koechlin and Jubault's model, or something like it, is involved in 'first-pass' parsing of complex sentences, of the kind proposed by Ferreira and colleagues ('Good Enough parsing') and by Townsend and Bever (Late Assignment of Syntax Theory—LAST)—see Chapter 3, section 4.2.

6.5.3 Hierarchical structure in the thoughts expressed

In *The Origins of Meaning*, I argued that non-human animals are capable of mentally representing scenes in a hierarchical way. They pay global attention to a whole scene or event, which may have one, two, or three salient participants, and they pay local attention to each of these participants. Information about each participant is embedded as a separate bundle of properties within the representation of the whole event, which has its own event-level properties. Here, for example, is the representation of the type that I proposed for a scene in which a quick brown fox is jumping over a lazy dog.

	QUICK BROWN FOX	LAZY DOG
JUMP-OVER	AGENT	PATIENT

Within each box the elements are unordered—they could have been printed in any order.[21] The only structure of any kind is the nesting of boxes representing individual participants inside a box representing the whole event. See Chapter 5 of *The Origins of Meaning* for arguments for this notation. In any natural notation, the individual participants in an event are represented separately, and representation of the event as a whole embraces the representations of the individual participants. In the earlier book, I argued that this representation was faithful to certain neural facts, in particular a separation between mechanisms of global and local attention. And it was also argued there that this degree of pre-existing hierarchical conceptual 'semantic' mental structure can be ascribed to some animals, including apes.

We have seen how in Nicaraguan Sign Language descriptions of events are at first packaged into small sentences, as in MAN PUSH; WOMAN FALL. Then later, longer sentences are used, with the core elements of the previously separate sentences now brought into a single description. The resources of the current language to some extent dictate the packaging of how an event is described. But if any attempt is made to package information from a whole event with several participants into a single sentence, it is natural to bundle the expressions for the properties of the individual participants together. Sentence structure with clearly bounded noun phrases inside a whole sentence, thus with a degree of hierarchical organization, is a natural expression of pre-existing mental representations of events with several participants. This generalization states a tendency, to which languages conform to some degree or other. Non-configurational (roughly 'free word order') languages, with discontinuous noun phrases linked by extensive case-marking, are the exception.[22] In more complex constructions, constituents such as NPs can get broken up, as in *That man came that I was telling you about*, but this is usually a stylistic option and seldom, if ever obligatory. So *That man that I was telling you about came* is also grammatical.

It might be thought that to the extent that animals can know the contents of minds of other animals, their hierarchical representations are more deeply nested. This is not necessarily true in all cases. (Hare et al. 2001, p. 139) conclude from experiments that 'at least in some situations (i.e. competition with conspecifics) chimpanzees know what conspecifics have and have not seen

---

[21] And, of course, the labels I have used in the boxes stand for concepts in an animal's mind, not for words in any language.

[22] Givón (2001, p. 283) notes, however, that 'none of the studies purporting to describe (non-)configurationality have ever supported their claims with comparative frequencies of adjacent vs. non-adjacent VPs and NPs in "configurational" vs. "non-configurational" languages—in texts from any genre'.

(do and do not know)'. What a subordinate chimpanzee evidently knew in these experiments was that another chimpanzee, dominant to him, could see a certain food item (say a banana), but could not see another food item (say an apple). In my notation, we could diagram the subordinate's representation of the positive aspect of the scene as

This puts the predicate SEE on a par with the predicate EAT, for example. Seeing you see a banana is no more mind-reading than seeing you eat a banana. The subordinate chimpanzee witnesses a scene in which a two-place relation, seeing, holds between the dominant chimp and the banana. This is apparently no more complex than witnessing a scene in which a different, more concrete, two-place relation, eating, holds between the dominant and the banana. One may not be entirely happy with this analysis, because presumably more mental work must be done by the witness to discern a seeing event than would be needed to recognize an eating event. We all know that we can be looking at something right before our open eyes without seeing it. One may be daydreaming, or just not attending to the right properties of the input visual stream. For the witnessing chimpanzee to judge that the other animal is really seeing, it must do some inference based on observations of the spatial layout of the compound and the dominant's gaze. This may be crediting the animal with too much. It could have a well-adapted response to more superficial information, namely that the dominant only gazed in the direction of the banana (but not the apple). Even if we grant that the witnessing chimpanzee does infer that the dominant animal sees the banana, the conclusion reached by chain of inference, namely that the dominant sees the banana, is not itself a proposition within a proposition.

Evidence that an ape can mentally entertain a proposition within a proposition would indicate a pre-linguistic capacity for some degree of hierarchical structuring of representations that could, at a later stage in evolution, get expressed in language. For example, we can look for evidence that a chimpanzee knows that another individual knows that X, where X is a whole situation or state of affairs. In a human langue, this might come out as, for example, *Bill knows that the key is behind that bolt* (rather than the simple first-order *The key is behind that bolt*). Whiten (2000a) describes experiments in which Panzee, a symbol-trained chimpanzee well accustomed to interacting with humans, was allowed to observe food being placed in one of two boxes, which she saw being locked with a key by one human. The experiment was designed so that another human, the 'Helper', would sometimes know, and sometimes not know, where the key to the baited box was. Whiten reports

In sum, Panzee entered the experiment with a capacity already in place [i.e. she needed no training, JRH] to discriminate those occasions on which the Helper was ignorant from those in which he was knowledgeable about the key location. She appeared to appreciate that in the ignorant condition, he needed information and she supplied it to him.   (Whiten 2000a, p. 152)

Thus, some non-human animals can, at least in lab conditions, but without being trained on the task, entertain thoughts that we can naturally describe as hierarchically structured. Evidence that an ape can entertain knowledge of a **false** belief on the part of some other individual has not yet been found. This would be a case, for example, of knowing that Bill thinks the key is in the box, when in fact the key is not in the box. This is harder to do. Some humans, severe autists, can't do it. Keep in mind a theme of this whole book, that differences between humans and closely related non-humans are often matters of degree. Evidence that Panzee can entertain a second-order thought about someone else's knowledge does not open the floodgates to indefinite possibilities of embedding. This is biology, not philosophy. One level of embedding is probaby about as far as an ape can get.

I give the penultimate word on hierarchical structure to Ray Jackendoff: 'So the conclusion is mixed: The wondrous recursive creativity in language is not as special as it is often claimed to be. Nevertheless, language *is* a special system because of what it does and the particular structural materials it uses to do it' (Jackendoff 2007, p. 143). On the whole, I am perhaps slightly more on the domain-specific side of the debate than Jackendoff. For sure, there are precursors of hierarchical grammatical structure, but modern humans emerged with a far more elaborate and abstract capacity than can be seen in any non-linguistic activity, human or non-human. Very complex hierarchical non-linguistic activities are at least in part scaffolded by language.

6.6 Fast processing of auditory input

Impressionistically, we process language amazingly fast. The speed of our speech production is limited by having to move the articulators around. We can actually take in and comprehend even faster speech. A blind student of mine, John Burling, tells me that he routinely speeds up audiotapes by a factor of about 30 percent. The literature on perception of time-compressed speech bears this out.[23] Kanzi, as noted above, can comprehend some spoken English, so a degree of sentence-processing is within the grasp of some apes. But, as also noted, he can't manage any hierarchically nested syntactic structure. Speech perception involves keeping strings up to a certain length in a short-term memory buffer, while higher-level decoding processes get to work on them. How much of the spoken signal gets through Kanzi's peripheral auditory apparatus? Can he take in and hold a fairly full phonological representation of a stretch of, say, seven words? If he does, then his limited comprehension of such stretches is clearly a morphosyntactic deficit. An alternative is that he picks out a few content words as islands in the speech stream identified by their phonetic stress, missing the function words, and uses a 'semantic soup' strategy to interpret them. We'll have a look at this issue.

Two authors who have committed themselves elsewhere to the view that syntactic recursion is the only uniquely human trait of language[24] assert, as would be expected, that perception of speech is not a special human ability. 'If we had to place a wager, we would bet that humans share with other animals the core mechanisms for speech perception. More precisely, we inherited from animals a suite of perceptual mechanisms for listening to speech—ones that are quite general and did not evolve for speech' (Hauser and Fitch 2003, p. 179). This view is based on lab studies which isolate particular features of speech and show that animals perform like humans, though often after extensive training. For example, Kojima et al. (1989) compared the perception of syllables like [ga], [ka], [ba], and [da] by humans and chimpanzees, and found 'that the basic mechanism for the identification of consonants in chimpanzees is similar to that in humans, although chimpanzees are less accurate than humans in discrimination of consonants' (p. 403). In a related study, Kojima and Kiritani (1989) found that although humans and chimpanzees made different perceptual groupings of vowels, chimpanzees could do vocal tract normalization, that is recognizing the same vowel from different (male and female) speakers, about as well as humans. Similarly, Tincoff et al. (2005) compared the perception of rhythm in tamarins and human new-borns, concluding 'language discrimination in tamarins is facilitated by rhythmic differences between languages, and... in humans, this mechanism is unlikely to have evolved specifically for language' (p. 26). The experimental tasks involved making same/different judgements when exposed to samples from different languages, such as English and Dutch (same rhythm-type) or Polish

---

[23] For example, Wingfield (1975); Pallier et al. (1998); Arons (1992).
[24] See Hauser and Fitch (2003).

and Japanese (dfferent rhythm-types). Most famously, Kuhl and Miller (1978) compared the sensitivity of chinchillas and humans to syllables with different voice onset times, like [ba]/[pa] or [ga]/[ka]. 'No significant differences between species on the absolute values of the phonetic boundaries were obtained, but chinchillas produced identification functions that were slightly, but significantly, less steep' (p. 905). In training, which lasted many days, the water-deprived chinchillas were rewarded with water and punished with mild electric shocks. Such results do not establish that the **whole** of human speech perception is similar to that by non-humans, a point made forcefully by Pinker and Jackendoff:

[Humans] can process a continuous, information-rich stream of speech. In doing so, they rapidly distinguish individual words from tens of thousands of distracters despite the absence of acoustic cues for phoneme and word boundaries, while compensating in real time for the distortions introduced by coarticulation and by variations in the age, sex, accent, identity, and emotional state of the speaker. And all of this is accomplished by children as a product of unsupervised learning. A monkey's ability to be trained to discriminate pairs of phonemes provides little evidence that its auditory system would be up to the task accomplished by humans.   (Pinker and Jackendoff 2005, p. 207)

Backing up the idea that ape speech perception does not match up to human performance in real fluent speech situations, Hashiya and Kojima (2001) found that chimpanzees' working memory for auditory stimuli is very poor, significantly worse than their working memory for visual stimuli. While a visual stimulus could be recalled with above 90 percent accuracy after a delay of up to sixteen seconds, auditory recall decayed to below 80 percent after two seconds, below 70 percent after eight seconds and below 60 percent after sixteen seconds (p. 176). The authors write of chimpanzees' 'limited ability to store auditory information' (p. 175). In relation to processing of speech, they comment 'Speech signal processing requires rapid computation of changing auditory input and sufficient memory capacity to store verbal information. . . . Chimpanzees are not endowed with a capacity in such aspects, in contrast to their ability for consonant perception and for vocal tract normalization' (Hashiya and Kojima 2001, p. 186).[25]

Thus it seems that chimpanzees (and almost certainly bonobos) don't have the short-term memory store appropriate for speech. But we cannot rush from this fact to the conclusion that Kanzi's (for example) only problem with

---

[25] Chimpanzee visual working memory, on the other hand, compares extremely favourably with humans, at least in one experimental paradigm (Inoue and Matsuzawa 2007).

comprehending speech is an auditory problem, and not a syntactic problem. Imagine that Kanzi, somehow miraculously, could be furnished with full phonological representations of input stretches of about seven words. It is extremely unlikely that any grammatical machinery is ready in his head to do a better analysis of them than he can of the partly ordered bags of content word islands that he probably hears now. The point is that grammatical ability and speech perception ability almost certainly coevolved to be compatible with each other in normal individuals. If the syntactic machinery can only do 'semantic soup' analysis, the speech perception machinery is likely only to adapt to pick out the salient content word lumps from the soup. Conversely, if the speech perception apparatus only delivers a partly ordered bag of a few stressed words, we don't expect higher-order grammatical processing. This is in tune with my arguments in Chapter 3 for a coevolved unified package, UG+, incorporating features from domains traditionally separated into competence and performance. It puts the matter slightly more strongly than Hauser and Fitch (2003, p. 160): 'During human evolution, it was minimally necessary for the faculty of language to coexist with the extant vocal communication system'.

I have stressed the coevolution of a specifically language-oriented working memory with representation of complex grammatical structures. This applies to normal individuals, clear exemplars of the evolved phenotype. Stressing the coevolution of the components of UG+ does not imply that the components are the same thing, implemented, for example, in indistinguishable brain mechanisms. One of many analogies would be the coevolution of speech production and speech perception. To a first approximation, we can produce the same range of sounds that we can distinguish; yet production and perception are separate macro-mechanisms, that can be subject to pathology independent of each other.

A link between grammatical ability and auditory processing comes out in many individuals with 'specific language impairment' (SLI). This broad clinical category is associated with difficulties across much of the spectrum of language, including smaller vocabularies, word-finding difficulties, poor comprehension especially of more complex sentences, and shorter produced sentences. Somewhat surprisingly, and despite early cautionary advice (e.g. by Leonard 1982), SLI has kept its place in the literature as a single condition, rather than as a collection of related conditions. This may be changing. Researchers focus on different aspects of the condition. Advocates of both domain-specificity and domain-generality haunt the field. On the side tending toward domain-specificity, researchers emphasize poor control of features which I have identified as central to grammar, such as function words, inflectional morphology, and long-distance dependencies.[26] Some of these authors propose grammatical problems with agreement and auxilaries as clinical markers of the SLI condition. Others focus on problems with long-distance dependencies, such as those involved with English *Wh*-questions. For all these authors, SLI is seen as a deficit specifically affecting the capacity for acquisition of complex syntax. On the other hand, other researchers have accumulated substantial evidence that many SLI children have particular auditory processing difficulties. I will illustrate these processing problems in the present section, leaving the more clearly domain-specific cases until section 8, on long-range dependencies.

Many SLI children have problems in discriminating sounds that occur too close together. Tallal et al. (1993) presented children with pairs of tones separated by intervals of between 8 and 4000 milliseconds. The children had to say whether the tones were the same or different. Not surprisingly, all children performed well when the tones were separated by one second or more. With inter-stimulus intervals of less than half a second, children with SLI performed very significantly worse than controls. With intervals of 30 or 60 milliseconds, SLI children performed slightly better than chance (about 65 percent correct), whereas the control children performed at over 95 percent correct. Sounds in normal speech come in very rapid succession. Consonants in a consonant cluster can last for as little as 50 milliseconds. A later study finds similar evidence of an auditory deficit in SLI childen.

Here we report the results of psychophysical tests employing simple tones and noises showing that children with specific language impairment have severe auditory perceptual deficits for brief but not long tones in particular sound contexts. Our data support the view that language difficulties result from problems in auditory perception.

(Wright et al. 1997, p. 176)

The experiments involved 'backward masking' of sounds. A sound that occurs a very short interval before another may not be detected because the following sound 'masks' it. Dorothy Bishop (1997) summarizes Wright et al.'s experiments and results in non-technical terms:

Wright *et al.* show that there is massively enhanced backward masking in children with SLI. Whereas control children could reliably detect a 45-decibel, 1,000-Hz tone that was immediately followed by a broad-band masking noise (a hissing sound), children with SLI could not: the volume of the stimulus tone had to be increased to nearly 90 decibels for them to achieve control performance levels. . . .

---

[26] e.g. Rice et al. (1995, 2004, 2009b); van der Lely and Battell (2003); van der Lely (2005).

Excessive backward masking could play an important role in causing SLI, by inter-
fering with the development of the ability to discriminate between speech sounds such
as 'pa', 'ta' and 'ka' where a brief consonant portion is immediately followed by a
vowel.   (Bishop 1997, p. 130)

Chimpanzees have limited auditory memory. Many children with SLI have
auditory problems that could prevent them taking in a fast stream of speech
in all its detail. The implication for the evolution of morphosyntax is that
humans needed to evolve suitable peripheral processing abilities in tandem with higher-level capacities for processing linear input into hierarchical
structure.[27]

6.7 Syntactic categories and knowledge representation

Apes know no syntactic categories. No seed of a specifically linguistic platform
here. But apes know a lot, and we can ask whether the structure of their
knowledge resembles the structure of human knowledge of language. If the
answer to that question is negative, we can, closer to home, ask how closely
the structure of human linguistic knowledge resembles the structure of our non-
linguistic knowledge. The structural aspect of knowledge systems that I will
focus on is their organization in terms of multiple default inheritance hierarchies, as explained in Chapter 4, section 4.3. We saw that a human's knowledge
of the syntactic categories of her language could naturally be organized in
terms of (multiple) default inheritance hierarchies. As syntactic categories and
constructions mutually interdefine each other, it follows that knowledge of
constructions also takes the form of default inheritance hierarchies. We will
see at the end of this section that there is a neat evolutionary explanation for
default inheritance hierarchies.

A classic human example of default inheritance is our knowledge of birds.
Take a folk-taxonomic tree of birds, with several layers in it specifying (folk)
subcategories of birds, and sub-subcategories, and so on. At the top of the tree,
some general properties assigned to the top-level concept BIRD are CAN-FLY and
HAS-FEATHERS. These features are inherited by concepts further down the tree,
so it does not need to be explicitly stated that, for example, crows and swallows
can fly. It is economical to let the top-level statements about birds in general

---

[27] This section has been on processing speed in language perception. Clearly humans
produce language very fast, too. Bickerton (1998, p. 352) writes in passing of the rise
of a 'neo-cerebellar speeder-upper' that would be necessary to give us our modern
production speeds.

do the work. But not all birds can fly, and here is where the option to overrule the default value kicks in. At a particular point in the tree is a node PENGUIN, with different species of penguin (KING, EMPEROR, FAIRY,...) below it. The PENGUIN node is assigned a property CAN'T-FLY, which explicitly overrides the default property CAN-FLY inherited from above. This is the new default value for all lower nodes and so is assigned to all types of penguin. Conceivably, this default could itself be overruled by another specific statement even lower down the tree, though this doesn't actually happen often.

Two questions arise now. First, are such examples only and specifically linguistic? That is, in the example above, for instance, are we only dealing with the senses of verbal expressions, such as *bird, crow, swallow, penguin, can-fly*, and *can't fly*? Could we have such hierarchies of knowledge without any words denoting the concepts involved? Then, second, if indeed non-verbal knowledge is organized by default hierarchies, do apes know the world in this way, too? If a case can be made that chimpanzee knowledge of the world is organized as default inheritance hierarchies, we have a formal precursor of the kind of organization seen in our tacit knowledge of syntactic categories. If such a case cannot be made, then it would seem that this kind of structure evolved first with humans, and, given that much human non-linguistic knowledge is organized in this way, then we have to ask the 'which came first?' question. This outlines the ensuing discussion.

Is an ape's knowledge of the world organized in a way suggesting a default inheritance hierarchy? A bold question to ask, perhaps, but I think we can tentatively claim to see reasons for an affirmative answer. Recall Rob Truswell's discussion (section 6.5.1) of Kanzi's responses to *put your collar in the backpack, put your collar in the refrigerator*, and *put your collar on*. Kanzi mostly seemed to understand these instructions right. Now, given that he can carry out these instructions, we may consider that he knows something like the following. If a specific receptacle (e.g. a fridge, a backpack) is named, then put the collar in (or on, etc.) it; when no receptacle is named, if the object to be put is a collar, put it on yourself. The default option is to put the object in a location named. If it happens that no location is named, this default option is overridden and an alternative target for the putting is chosen. We can consider the larger question away from such possibly problematic examples. More generally, the question is: do animals, especially apes, have hierarchies of fallback behaviours? Put this way, it seems rather obvious that they do. A chimp will prefer, other things being equal, certain foods over others. If the preferred food isn't available, they will take the next-most preferred food, and if that isn't available, they move on down their hierarchy of food preferences. Animals have 'high-level' default behaviour in normal circumstances.

In somewhat abnormal circumstances, they resort to first-alternative default behaviour. In even more abnormal circumstances, they take lower-order default actions.

There is a philosophical issue of how this kind of 'knowing what to do' in animals relates to the kind of propositional knowledge usually associated with default inheritance hierarchies seen in human knowledge. Knowing what to do might seem to be qualitatively different from knowing what is the case, for example that penguins are an exception to the rule that birds fly. There has been a tendency to forget that cognition is adaptive for purposeful action. What use is it to know that most birds fly but penguins don't? We humans delight in arcane knowledge for its own sake. One possible evolutionary basis for this is some advantage in showing off one's knowledge to others. But surely, equally important is the value of detailed knowledge in guiding our negotiation in the world. The more we know about crucial aspects of the world, the more successful we are as individuals. Fallesen and Halpin (2004) develop this view in a paper titled 'Representing cognition as an intent-driven process'. They include default reasoning as an important feature of human cognition, and quote an example which nicely relates knowing what to do to knowing what is the case.

Default values refer to the fact that we readily assume certain aspects of the situation without being told them directly. ... Although we do not know that these attributes of [some unfamiliar machine] are necessarily true, we often find communication and learning facilitated by making the inference that they are true, unless we are told otherwise. (Kyllonen and Alluisi 1987, p. 127)

Struggling with any practical problem, given that our goal is to find a solution that works, knowing what to do is equivalent to knowing what works, that is to say, what is the case. In a complex problem, what works may well be structured as a default hierarchy. In general, try this; if this doesn't work, try that; if that doesn't work, try the next thing.

The similarities between an animal's hierarchy of default solutions to practical challenges and the default inheritance hierarchies used to describe human knowledge can be illustrated by a more vivid example, hopefully not too fanciful. Imagine you are a hunter-gatherer starting out after game of some kind. GAME is at the top of your mind, your general-level goal, so you make certain preparations appropriate for game of any kind. Later, you come across tracks of a certain kind of prey, which causes you to make some small changes to the general plan, appropriate to this specific kind of prey. Further along the trail, you spot the animal and realize that it's an unusually big one, so you make further changes to your plan for this type of animal. It seems likely that some apes have knowledge of what works for their everyday challenges in terms of a hierarchy of default solutions. Any such hierarchy is probably not at all deep, given animals' generally limited ability in problem solving. What animals can do is a long way short of human abilities. I have tried to make a case that default inheritance hierarchies, however small and simple, might appropriately represent an ape's practical knowledge for negotiating their world. If this is right, we can see in apes' practical knowledge of the world the tiny seeds of our own efficient way of storing knowledge. Of course, the content domain (nouns, verbs, determiners, prepositions, and all such things) of our human knowledge of grammatical categories is far over the horizon for apes.

Perhaps I am wrong, and no non-humans store knowledge in default inheritance hierarchies. In that case, the capacity to store knowledge in this way has evolved uniquely in humans. Many have argued that the form of our grammatical knowledge is of a kind with non-grammatical knowledge. Hudson (2000) argues in detail for the equivalence of grammatical and non-linguistic knowledge in terms of default inheritance hierarchies. The idea is central to the school of thought known as 'Cognitive Grammar'. In sympathy with this idea, Goldberg (1995, p. 5) writes 'knowledge of language is knowledge'. It must be said, however, that the use of this knowledge in the grammatical domain is unlike any practical use of default inheritance knowledge outside language. A child who learns a complex human language has routinized the productive use of a highly complex array of constructions, which it seems correct to describe in terms of default inheritance hierarchies. The online use of this knowledge in speaking and listening is extremely rapid. Nothing else we do compares in its complexity and speed. Given this disparity between language and non-language, neither answer to the 'which came first?' question is very plausible. It is not easy to make the case that our language ability simply reflects our general capacity for complex knowledge, because the use of our linguistic knowledge is orders of magnitude faster and more complex than applications of our non-linguistic knowledge. Nor does it seem plausible to argue the other way around, that is, that a capacity to acquire complex knowledge of grammatical categories and constructions, involving default inheritance hierarchies, gives us a more general ability to represent our knowledge of the world, again because of the great difference in complexity and fast automatic use. It might be that, for reasons having to do with the mathematical complexity of computational systems, a default inheritance framework is a natural attractor for complex systems of various kinds, both for rather abstract representation of knowledge and for organization of skilled productive routines applicable in diverse situations, like language. But here below is a better idea.

It seems rather obvious that default inheritance is a natural property of systems that evolve by descent with modification. Each modification introduces a change from the parent entity. The modified offspring inherits most of its properties from its parent, but its modified (mutated) trait is new, not inherited, and hence needs to be described by an overruling statement. In the evolution of animals, penguins have inherited many features from the ancestral protobird (feathers, wings, beaks, egg-laying), but the modification that made them flightless overrules the 'can-fly' feature. Our human folk knowledge of birds and other evolved domains is accurate enough to reflect this biological descent with modification, in a default inheritance structure. This is a case where the structure of human knowledge mirrors biological evolution somewhat faithfully.[28] Descent with modification can apply to cultural entities such as games, religions, and languages. Much of the history of such institutions involves schism, with several descendants of a common ancestor sharing many properties which they inherit from the ancestor, and differing in some novel detail. An evolutionary perspective on grammatical categories tells a similar story. As we will see in Chapter 9, on grammaticalization, the great ramification of grammatical categories is a product of linguistic evolution. Original verbs spawned a subset of auxiliary verbs with special characteristics, overriding some of the distributional traits of the original verbs, but also maintaining enough traits to be still recognizable as a sort of verb. Default inheritance is characteristic of systems evolved by descent with modification, whether the replication is biological or cultural.

6.8 Constructions and long-range dependencies

The features considered in this section are the most central to the human capacity for syntax; there is some overlap with the earlier section on hierarchical organization. To anticipate the conclusion, no phenomena, either in apes or in human non-linguistic behaviour, resemble our extremely fluent and flexible combination of constructions closely enough to suggest any obviously plausible pre-existing evolutionary platform. Logically, there had to be a pre-existing platform, somewhere between australopithecines and modern humans, but it has left no traces. Nevertheless, we are obliged to consider the possibilities that have been suggested. In the area discussed in this section, I will come to a domain-specific conclusion about twin ingredients of human syntax. First to be

---

[28] Folk taxonomies sometimes get it wrong, as when whales are classified as fish.

discussed is our capacity to acquire and quickly routinize a massive number of constructions. The constructions of interest will be those exhibiting some kind of long-range 'planning', rather than simple lexical items. Then I will turn to our ability to combine constructions productively and rapidly in spontaneous speech. After considering some suggestions, I will conclude that neither ability has any obvious parallels outside language.

6.8.1 Constructions and plans for action

A construction is some part of a sentence that can be 'filleted out' of the whole as making a systematic contribution to its well-formedness. Every sentence is a combination of constructions. For example in English, one construction in a sentence specifies that a verb agrees with its subject, leaving the rest of the work of sentence-specification to other constructions. There may be (usually is) some distance between the Subject noun and the verb, filled by other material licensed by other constructions. This, in general, is how Construction Grammar accounts for long-distance dependencies. The distance between an item and its dependent item may be indefinitely long, subject to working memory limits. Working memory imposes a general constraint on the grammar, and need not be specified in connection with any particular individual construction.

Can we find anything like this in behaviour outside language? The criterial features to look for are (1) some dependency between an early part of an activity and a later part, and (2) ideally with some other sub-actions in between. This last ideal criterion, which in language gives us dependencies between distant parts of a sentence, is hard, if not impossible, to find in animal behaviour. But we can find examples fitting the first criterion. There are well documented cases of animal action where some property of the latter part depends on a property of the former part. These are simple cases where the property in question is simply length. The lengths of early and late parts of an action are interdependent. In Chapter 1, I gave an instance, in chaffinch song, requoted here: '...the two song parts must be traded off against each other as either long trills or long flourishes can only be achieved by shortening the other part of the song' (Riebel and Slater 2003, p. 283). In the case of chaffinch song, there is no need to invoke planning of the whole song at its outset. The precise length of the initial trill segment can be unplanned, only aiming roughly at the canonical median target of seven iterations; then the inversely proportioned length of the flourish is determined when the initial trills are finished. A better case for planning of a whole action is given by Schleidt and Kien (1997):

Further evidence that segmentation in behavior is related to planning is that, in natural behavior, action units containing one repetition of a movement are not longer than those without repetitions (Feldhütter et al. 1990; Kien et al. 1991). The distributions of durations of these two types of action unit are almost identical over their whole range. This renders it unlikely that a second movement is simply added to the first movement. Instead, the obvious interpretation is that the addition of a second movement requires a speeding up of the first movement. This can only be achieved at the planning stage. It indicates that the whole segment is held in the motor planning circuits before execution and that these circuits are capable of altering and manipulating individual elements of the segment. Altering an early element because of addition of a later element can be described as 'later modifies earlier,' which resembles a syntactical rule in language grammars. This process has therefore been named presyntactical motor planning (Kien et al. 1991). This effect is seen only when the movements are repeated once.

(Schleidt and Kien 1997, p. 90)

This effect is observed in humans and chimpanzees, but not in baboons.

Chimpanzees, like humans, show the ability to reorganize motor elements within a temporal unit; they show presyntactical motor planning. Baboons, in contrast, do not. If movements are to be repeated once, then chimpanzees, like humans, compress both movement repetitions to fit into one action unit (Kien et al. 1991), and so action units with one repetition are not longer than those without repetition. However, in baboons (Ott et al. 1994), all repetitions, particularly of goal-directed movements, result in a lengthening of the action units; i.e., action units with one repetition are longer than nonrepetitive ones. This suggests that baboons, unlike chimpanzees and humans, need to replan a repetition of a set of movements. (Schleidt and Kien 1997, p. 91)

The term 'presyntactical motor planning' used by these authors is suggestive of a connection between non-linguistic actions and sentence production. The connection in fact only serves to emphasize the great gap between ape action planning and human syntax. These data are more relevant to the evolution of phonological phrasing than anything in syntax. In particular, the focus on length phenomena has little to do with human syntax. In the hunt for homologues of long distance dependencies in animals, we are looking for cases where the **form** of some early part of an action is predictive of the form of some later part, with a gap in between. We saw a striking example of this in humpback whalesong (Chapter 1). The whale's song, which lasts up to about twenty minutes, is repeated over and over without a break, so that passages in the whole song bout are predictable from earlier passages. But I gave in Chapter 1 some reasons why this predictability of patterns in whalesong is very different in kind from the long distance dependencies found in language—see pp. 63–71.

Nothing in animal communication or action is quite like the long-distance dependencies in human syntax. The complexities, such as they are, of bird- and whalesong are strongly routinized and stereotypic. Further, the songs have no propositional content (as far as we know), so there is no scope for any kind of semantic dependency between distant elements. Can we find in these routinized stereotypic systems any of the capacities out of which human syntax evolved? The main link is in routinization itself, a topic which raises a paradoxical aspect of human sentences.

Human spoken sentences are paradoxically both deliberate and automatic. Take a sentence like *Who was Mary talking to on the phone when I came in?* It is specific enough in its content to indicate careful choice of words and structure to suit the situation and the intention. Composing a sentence as specific as this is not just a knee-jerk reflex. The sentence is crafted to convey and to elicit very detailed information. This example sentence (in case you hadn't noticed) has a long-distance dependency in it, with the initial *Who* understood as the indirect object of the later verb *talking to*. And yet such a sentence would be uttered fluently without apparent effort, perhaps while doing something else, like taking off one's coat or shifting a chair. Sentence production can be separated into two phases, a 'deliberate' phase and an 'automatic' phase. These phases are largely sequential, but can be somewhat interleaved and overlapping in the production of a sentence—no need for detail here. The deliberateness comes in making semantic and pragmatic choices. These include all the considerations discussed in connection with the packaging of messages into sentence-like units, back in Chapter 3. In the case of *Who was Mary talking to on the phone when I came in?*, the speaker decides to mention the time when he came in; he decides to specify 'on the phone'; he chooses to refer to Mary by name rather than with a pronoun (*she*) or definite description (*that woman*); he chooses to ask about Mary 'talking' rather than 'blethering';[29] he chooses a direct speech act, rather than an indirect hint at what he wants to know, for example *I heard Mary talking to someone when I came in*; first of all, he chooses speech rather than silence. This is the 'Conceptualizer' stage in sentence production (Levelt 1989). Certainly all these decisions are made very fast, and there may be elements of automaticity in some of these choices. But once these decisions are made, the die is cast: out comes the sentence, automatically, strictly following the grammar of the language. Before phonological and phonetic encoding, Levelt's model of speech production, widely accepted in essence, has these two components:

---

[29] Scots for *gossiping* or *yakking*, roughly.

(i) *A Conceptualizer, which generates preverbal messages.* These messages consist of conceptual information whose expression is the means for realizing the speaker's intention. (ii) *A Formulator consisting of...* The Grammatical Encoder retrieves lemmas from the lexicon and generates grammatical relations reflecting the conceptual relations in the message. Its output is called 'surface structure'. ...

Message generation and monitoring [are] described as controlled activities requiring the speaker's continuing attention. Grammatical encoding, form encoding, and articulating, however, are assumed to be automatic to a large degree. They are speedy and reflexlike, requiring very little attention, and can proceed in parallel.

(Levelt 1989, pp. 27–8)

'Lemmas' that the Grammatical Encoder retrieves from the lexicon include entries for single words and 'superlemmas' for idioms and other formulaic expressions. I suggest that they also include grammatical constructions.

Each grammatical construction can be regarded as a stereotypical pattern, executed automatically, in some ways like a bird's song. The big differences between human grammar and birdsong are (1) a bird, even one with a large repertoire of songs, cannot combine one song with another or embed one song in another, and (2) obviously, for the bird, having no Conceptualizer stage, combining different songs as human constructions combine to form sentences would have no function—impressing the females can be achieved with a big repertoire of different uncombinable songs; indeed their uncombinability emphasizes the individuality of each song.

We can see neural correlates of the distinction between deliberate message planning and relatively automatic conversion into grammatical utterances. Terry Deacon notes that production of everyday speech and the comprehension of others' speech

are only minimally affected by damage to prefrontal cortex;[30] such damage seldom produces permanent difficulty producing speech, comprehending speech, or analyzing grammar. Disruption of these basic language abilities—aphasias—typically results from damage to areas more closely associated with motor and auditory analysis: Broca's and Wernicke's areas, respectively. ... Prefrontal areas seem instead to be recruited during such tasks as planning complex behaviors. (Deacon 1997, pp. 255–6)

The functions of prefrontal cortex are more general-purpose than those of the classical areas more specifically associated with language processing. Computations in prefrontal cortex are abstract, being only indirectly connected to primary sensory and motor cortex. Novoa and Ardila (1987, p. 207) mention that

---

[30] In passages such as this 'prefrontal' is understood to exclude language-related parts of the left inferior frontal gyrus [JRH].

prefrontal lesions produce a disorder 'characterized by a change in narrative abilities, an inability to use language in conceptual or categorization activities, and an inability to express one's own thoughts'. Prefrontal cortex is where a lot of the work of the deliberate Conceptualizer for framing and packaging a sentence is done. (See Miller and Cohen 2001 for a recent account of prefrontal function.) Some descriptions of transcortical motor aphasia suggest that the deficit may be in the connection between the Conceptualizer and the Grammatical encoder.

According to Luria, the underlying deficit is a difficulty in translating thought into words, that is, a disconnection between language and nonverbal thinking. The patient with transcortical motor aphasia can correctly perform all linguistic tasks: speech is well articulated, oral and written comprehension is normal or only mildly impaired, and all transcoding tasks are correctly performed. The patient, however, does not use language spontaneously and when he/she does so, uses only isolated words or short sentences; there is a remarkable dissociation between the patient's capacity to describe an event (severely impaired) and his/her capacity to repeat long and complex sentences.

(Basso and Cubelli 1999, p. 187)

Incidentally, relating language to non-language, the same division between deliberate and automatic processes is seen in simple actions, such as grasping a cup. In that field, the commonly used terms are 'planning' and 'control'.

Woodworth (1899) was the first to propose a distinction between the planning and control stages of action, based on his seminal study examining the use of visual feedback in on-line control. Since Woodworth's time, the distinction between planning and control has been the subject of much investigation (...see Elliott et al. 2001, for a review), and the existence of these two stages has generally become accepted as an underlying principle of human motor behavior. (Glover 2004, p. 3)

Glover claims to have located separate brain centres serving these distinct functions, a claim that received a mixed response among commentators. But the distinction itself was not seriously questioned.

The distinction between deliberate and automatic components of sentence production presents a problem for arguments that human syntax evolved out of planning for action (e.g. Steedman 2002). Planning for action is deliberate, but the grammatical encoding stage of fluent sentence production is automatic. Mark Steedman draws attention to a formal parallel between logical operations involved in semantic interpretation and in planning to solve practical problems. The logical operations are 'functional composition' and 'type raising', both, in Steedman's model, involved in the semantic interpretation of sentences. I will informally illustrate the simpler of the two, functional composition, and explain the parallel that Steedman sees with semantic interpretation.

For this example, assume that in a given context *in London* identifies the same location as the deictic pronoun *there*. Putting it in mathematical terms, we can see *in* as a **function** applied to the referent of *London*, giving the location denoted by *there*. This may sound unnecessarily mathematical, but something of the sort must go on when we understand an expression such as *in London*, precisely because we know what *London* refers to and we know the meaning of *in*. This is functional application, applying a function denoted by one expression (here *in*) to the denotation of another expression (here *London*), to give a derived meaning (here equivalent to *there*). Now consider the longer expression *lives in London*. We know what part of it means, by the route that I have just described. To understand the longer expression, we must combine the meaning of *lives* with the derived meaning of *in London*. Again, think of this as applying a function, the function corresponding to *lives* applied to the meaning of *in London*. So far, this is just a sequence of two functional **applications**. We can define a new function corresponding to *lives-in* as a kind of short cut combining the two previous operations. So *lives-in(London)* equals *lives(in(London))*. This is functional composition; we have composed a new function out of two primitive ones.

Informally, functional composition involves being able in one step to envisage the result of one operation and to apply another operation to this result. The parallel with planning should be clear. Steedman's paper takes a break from fierce logical formalisms to reproduce two engaging photos of a chimpanzee solving the problem of reaching a banana using stacked boxes or a pole. The idea is that the chimpanzee has had the foresight to put several operations together in his mind to solve the practical problem. Steedman acknowledges the very limited planning powers of non-humans, and invites us to ascribe both our language capacity and our own superior planning powers to the same mental ability. Towards the end of his paper, he indicates another difference between practical problem solving with physical objects and the calculations involved in processing language. Practical planning involves envisaging applying actions to states of the world. Sentence interpretation involves applying qualifiers to thoughts (my way of putting it, not Steedman's). On the difference between us and apes, he speculates 'Perhaps a theory of other minds and the associated propositional attitude concepts are *all* that is missing' (p. 748).

Steedman makes no distinction between deliberate and automatic aspects of action. As well as the business of stacking boxes to reach a banana, which requires some deliberate thinking even for humans, he mentions that 'the onset in the child of the ability to compose motor plans such as those needed for composite reaching around an obstacle precedes the onset of productive language use' (p. 747). Reaching around an obstacle comes much more automatically. Of course, even reaching round an obstacle has a planning stage and an execution stage, but these are very compressed in time, and subconscious, compared to the pondering required to imagine stacking boxes to get a banana. Chimpanzees can reach around an obstacle without pondering.

The issue here is the same as with Jackendoff's comparison of making coffee to the hierarchical organization of grammar. Coffee-making and a chimp's figuring out how to reach a banana are under much more conscious control than uttering *Who was Mary talking to on the phone when I came in?*, once you've decided this is what you want to say. The words just come out in the right order, with all the right function word signals—fronted *Who*, auxiliary *was* inverted round its subject, agreeing in number (*was*, not *were*), 'gap' after *to*, and so on. English speakers have learned a host of grammatical routines that they interleave effortlessly and automatically. As linguistics lecturers know, it takes some effort to make native speakers aware of the complexity of what they do without thinking.

Many human activities at first demand careful attention and deliberate rehearsal and then get routinized as 'second nature'. Careful attention and deliberate rehearsal are not conspicuous in child language learning. Children seem to go straight to automatic control of a gradually expanding repertoire of constructions. The neural processes by which this happens are basically not known. We know something about the neural correlates of the end adult state, but there are no studies of what happens in a child's brain over the brief period when she learns a new construction. (How could there be?)

Recently, a wide-ranging provocative work has made some general suggestions about routinization. 'Over the last few years, several dichotomies have become prominent in the computational and neuroimaging communities that broadly approximate the distinction between cognitive novelty and cognitive routinization' (Goldberg 2009, p. 78). Goldberg makes a case for 'right-to-left and frontal-to-posterior shift in the center of cognitive gravity with familiarization' (p. 78).[31] Goldberg cites a number of imaging studies, using various technologies that detect increased activity in the right hemisphere on learning a new task, with progressive decrease in right activation and increase in left activation as the subject becomes more familiar with the task. Typically with familiarization, the overall levels of activation also decrease, as one might expect. The brain finds a cost-efficient way of doing a job that it is likely to

---

[31] Goldberg's is a serious work, relating to solid empirical research—it is not of the oversimplifying soppy popular 'right hemisphere = emotion and left hemisphere = logic' genre.

have to do again. The brain areas mentioned in the studies that Goldberg cites are various. His hypothesis is quite broad-brush. He does not specifically cite any work on language learning, but a couple of studies involve learning little 'grammars' or a task finding verbs for given nouns. Goldberg makes some general comments that apply to our concerns.

The shift of the locus of cognitive control from the right to the left hemisphere occurs on many time scales: from minutes or hours, as in experiments using within-experimental learning, to years and decades, as in learning complex skills and codes, including language. This shift may even be discerned on the scale transcending the life of an individual. It can be argued that the whole history of human civilization has been characterized by a relative shift of the cognitive emphasis from the right hemisphere to the left hemisphere, owing to the accumulation of ready-made cognitive 'templates' of various kinds. These cognitive templates are stored externally through various cultural means, including language, and are internalized by individuals in the course of learning as cognitive 'prefabricates' of sorts. (Goldberg 2009, p. 80)

This sounds very much like the story of language and languages, although Goldberg's canvas is much wider. His 'ready-made cognitive templates, stored externally through cultural means' can be interpreted, in the case of language, as grammatical constructions in frequent use by the community. Children learning a language internalize these constructions as 'cognitive prefabricates', by a process of routinization. What distinguishes human language from other learned behaviours is that children acquire the automatic routinized use of grammatical constructions without apparently going through any stage of more deliberate or conscious rehearsal. No pre-existing platform for this ability can be seen in ape or human non-linguistic problem-solving.

6.8.2 Syntax, navigation, and space

I turn now to the capacity for combining constructions productively. Nightingales learn up to about 200 different 'constructions', that is songs, but they don't combine them. Human children learn many more, and start to combine them productively and creatively as soon as they know just a few. Constructions are involved in sentence production in the following way. Almost every construction is a form–meaning pairing. The word *Mary* is paired with the speaker's concept of the individual Mary. The *Wh-* question construction pairs a particular template of words and categories with the pragmatic intention to enquire about someone's or something's involvement in a situation or event. The 'almost' above is there because of a tiny minority of constructions that are purely grammatical, like the English Subject–Verb agreement construction. Making the verb agree with its Subject does not reflect any part of the meaning of a sentence. At the Conceptualizer stage of sentence production, a bunch of semantic and pragmatic entities are assembled. The speaker wants to know something about Mary talking to someone on the phone when he came in. That 'someone' is unknown to him and he wants to know who it is. Each aspect of meaning in this ad hoc conceptual/intentional representation is the semantic or pragmatic part of at least one construction in the speaker's grammar, a construction which pairs it with its conventional grammatical form in the language. So the collection of semantic and pragmatic entities brings along with it a corresponding collection of grammatical patterns, some big, some small. Producing the appropriate sentence consists of unifying these constructions in permitted ways. The (grammatical parts of) constructions themselves dictate the ways in which they may be fitted together. This is the apparently automatic part of sentence production, Levelt's Grammatical Encoder.

Can we find anything outside language which creatively fits together, or unifies, somewhat complex structures to produce a whole that is consistent with them all? Remember that we have excluded activities like making coffee on the grounds that they (1) are fairly deliberate, and (2) are guided by constant sensory feedback from the objects involved in the task (e.g. the empty water jug, the full coffee scoop).

Fauconnier and Turner (2008) also see the capacity to combine constructions as central to the language capacity. They link this to a domain-general unique human capacity for 'double-scope conceptual integration', the ability to mix ideas creatively, like imagining an octopus who can predict soccer results. Their answer to the 'which came first? question is unequivocally double scope conceptual integration. I see no compelling reason why it had to be this way round. Our capacity to imagine (say) a horse with a single horn in its forehead may derive from our capacity for unconstrained combination of constructions with the relevant nouns (*horse*, *forehead*, and *horn*) and other relevant words.

Above, I used the analogy of navigation by dead reckoning, and route-planning in navigation has been suggested as a possible evolutionary antecedent of syntactic ability. I will consider first an austere aspect of navigation known as 'path integration'. An animal or a person can wander in a C-shaped trajectory, say going from one corner of an imagined square along three sides, turning 90° left at two corners. After this, they can return directly to the starting point without retracing their steps. In some circumstances they can do this without using landmarks, by 'dead reckoning'. Dead reckoning involves keeping track of one's movement (e.g. by proprioception) and constantly updating a 'return vector', the shortest route between one's current position and the starting point. This is path integration. 'In rodents and other mammals, this path integration process (dead reckoning) can occur on the basis of purely internal signals, such as vestibular or proprioceptive (re)afferences' (Etienne et al. 1998, p. 161). The term 'path integration' is appropriate because the computation requires integrating the most recent movement with the previously current return vector to produce a new vector. Experiments with animals have produced mixed results, with no great surprises about the animals' ability. For instance, 'the large directional errors made by rats and hamsters even after a small turning amount (presumably because of large inaccuracies in the rotation measure systems) dramatically limit their use of path integration to short outward paths' (Benhamou 1997, p. 327). Humans are also not particularly impressive over medium-to-long distances, with many turns and in the absence of landmarks (Loomis et al. 1993). Using landmarks is cheating in a test of dead reckoning ability.

Path integration is not a close analogue of construction-combining. It does not operate on a set of many representations at a time, as construction-combining does. And humans are not as impressively good at path integration as they are at combining constructions. A more appropriate parallel between navigation and construction-combining has been suggested by Robert Worden (1992). Worden's proposal is mostly theoretical, based on computational modelling. It does a fair job of modelling animal navigation abilities, using landmarks, as animals do. Here is the essence of the model:

In the theory, mammals store memories of their geographical environment as a large number of independent fragments. A typical fragment denotes a few prominent landmarks in some region, their geometric relations, and their nongeometric properties, such as smells and visual cues. Navigation involves piecing together current sense data and relevant fragments to form a local map of the animal's surroundings; this is like solving a jigsaw puzzle. (Worden 1992, p. 165)

The parallel with combining syntactic constructions should be evident. The computational operation at the core of Worden's model is unification, an operation widely used in the computational linguistic literature for modelling sentence generation from grammars.

The multiple matching function required for navigation is one case of a capability for element-by-element matching of two structures, which has been extensively studied by computer scientists under the name of *unification*. This has become an important topic in the study of computer logics and, interestingly, natural language. Unification is at the heart of most current computational formalisms for handling both the syntax and semantics of natural language (Pollard and Sag 1987). We may conjecture that a multiple matching capability, evolved in the hippocampus for navigation, may be used in the left hippocampus of humans for other purposes. (Worden 1992, p. 175)

Peter Hagoort (2009), in an analysis of the functions of Broca's area and related parts, invokes a linguist's model of processing by unification (Vosse and Kempen 2000), and writes that 'Recent neuroimaging studies indicate that Broca's complex contributes to the unification operations required for binding single word information into larger structures' (p. 285). Formally, unification of fragmentary form–meaning pairings is useful because it can serve both in sentence production and in parsing. In another computational model, Worden (1998) has himself made extensive use of unification of stored grammar fragments to generate sentences. The formal parallel between this version of animal navigational ability and linguistic construction-combining is quite clear. At present, fragment-fitting is no more than a hypothesis about navigation, and it has not been focused on in neuroscientific work on navigation. The brain regions that Worden speculatively identifies as doing fragment-fitting are the hippocampus and nearby structures, not notably language-related areas. There is no known correlation between specifically navigational deficits and specifically grammatical deficits. It is an interesting possibility that human linguistic construction-combining evolved on the back of more general animal navigation strategies, in particular using fragment-fitting. A lot more relevant evidence needs to be accumulated. We have to leave it at that.

Another proposal for navigation as an evolutionary platform for syntax is by Bartlett and Kazakov (2005): 'The origins of syntax: from navigation to language'. Their model is a device for making a list of places visited, which is 'parsed' in the same way that strings generated by a State Chain grammar are parsed. There is no interesting connection to hierarchical structure and the recursive combination of constructions central to human syntax. And as with computer simulations generally, this is a proof of concept, showing what could have happened, given certain conditions, but not necessarily what did happen.

Van der Velde and de Kamps (2006) propose that a common neural 'blackboard' architecture can be used in both sentence processing and vision. They concede that 'there are clear structural differences between these architectures, which derive from the nature of the information processing in which they are involved (in this case, the spatial arrangement of visual features in a visual display versus the sequential arrangement of words in a sentence)' (p. 67). The similarities that they note are properties of any system designed to solve complex combinatorial problems, which undoubtedly occur in vision as well as in language. Phillips and Wagers (2006) argue that the architecture proposed does not handle the central structural properties of human syntax such as hierarchical structure and long-distance dependencies. Van der Velde and de Kamps reply that recognition of hierarchical structure is 'not a state but a process'. (This is reminiscent of the approach to syntactic structure taken by the Dynamic Syntax that I discussed in Chapter 4.) The blackboard architecture is a particularly powerful general information-processing framework, not specialized for any particular domain. The brain regions that van der Velde and de Kamps identify as instantiating the blackboard architecture in the case of vision are well-known from the neurology of vision, and do not correspond to language-processing areas. Further, though human vision is substantially similar to non-human primate vision, in terms of the combinatorial challenges that it faces, this paper offers no explanation why non-human primates have not exapted their visual apparatus to deal with language.

Finally, another proposal relating syntax to a non-linguistic domain is Lakoff's Spatialization of Form hypothesis, stated thus: 'the Spatialization of Form hypothesis requires a metaphorical mapping from physical space into a "conceptual space". Under this mapping, spatial structure is mapped into conceptual structure' (Lakoff 1987, p. 283). This is part of Lakoff's wider theories on the metaphorical and analogical mapping of concrete spaces onto abstract spaces. Our discourse about abstractions preserves the structural relations inherited from the concrete domain which is the source of the metaphor. Since Lakoff coined it, the Spatialization of Form hypothesis has been most extensively advocated by Paul Deane (1992, 1995). There are two major strands to Deane's argumentation. One strand is based on the metaphor idea, and I will explain why I find this idea misconceived. The other strand draws on neurological evidence for brain areas devoted to spatial cognition being exapted for grammar. This neurological argument is intriguing and may have some truth in it. I will deal with the metaphor idea first.

The metaphor idea is that grammatical structure is a projection of concrete spatial properties and relations that hold of physical objects into a more abstract realm. 'The abstract nature of syntax precludes any direct perceptual grounding; thus syntactic representations are metaphorical *ex hypothesi*. That is to say, each of the structural relations of syntax functions as the metaphorical projection of a particular embodied schema' (Deane 1992, p. 96). In Chapter 4, I distanced myself from the 'bike analogy' for syntactic structure, thus implicitly rejecting the metaphor strand of the Spatialization of Form Hypothesis. The clearest example of a spatial metaphor occurs when we speak of the 'parts of a sentence'. Part–whole relations occur in their most basic form in physical objects, as with the parts of a bicycle. It is virtually impossible to speak about abstractions without importing concrete terms into the discourse. And very often, spatial properties (e.g. length) and relations (e.g. distance, relative direction) can be fruitfully applied in discourse about abstractions. Metaphor and analogical thinking are extremely useful in getting to grips (see what I mean?) with realms not perceptible by the senses. Syntactic theory is riddled with spatial metaphors—'tree' diagrams, 'higher' nodes, phrases 'inside' other phrases, 'raising', 'gaps', and so on. But space is not the only useful source of metaphor—we talk of 'heavy' NPs and 'light' verbs; of 'mother', 'daughter', and 'sister' constituents; and of 'dominance', 'command', 'control', 'government', and 'binding'. None of these latter metaphors is inherently spatial, but linguists have found them useful in theorizing about mental happenings.

My objection to this line of argument is that it is not about what happens in the minds of ordinary language users, but describes the theoretical discourse of analysts. Deane (1992, p. 98) asks 'But what if the metaphor is not just the theoretician's metaphor, but is an aspect of linguistic competence?' This invites us to believe that the metaphor-producing process of theoretical discourse happened, unconsciously of course, and presumably gradually over millennia, in the minds of our ancestors in whom a grammatical capacity evolved. (Here I must get a bit convoluted, but stay with it.) As a metaphor itself, the metaphor story may be a helpful way of communicating what you think happened. In the same way as expressions like 'evolutionary bottleneck', 'floodgates', and 'cascade of consequences' are useful metaphors, so 'metaphor' in this context might be useful. But just as there was no literal cascade, or physical bottleneck, there was no actual process of metaphorical extension in the evolution of grammar. Metaphorical extension is essentially a linguistic device. We extend the use of a word from a concrete to an abstract domain. Underlying the linguistic extension is a dim awareness of the abstract domain, and strapping it about with terms that we already understand from their concrete usage is a means of trying to make the abstract domain itself more understandable. Myself, while I can understand a 'cascade' metaphor, I don't buy the usefulness of the 'metaphor' metaphor because its recursive convolutedness is hard to get my head around. Also, the specific focus on spatial metaphors leaves out the other possible source domains that I have mentioned. Pre-humans surely had a good grasp of kinship relations like MOTHER, SISTER, and DAUGHTER, so why not claim, on the basis of their usefulness in theoretical discourse about syntax, that the syntactic relations in question are derived from these kinship concepts? There are good reasons, to be discussed immediately below, why spatial cognition in particular is privileged over other domains as a possible platform from which complex syntax sprang, but the mere usefulness of spatial terms in linguists' discourse doesn't swing the argument.

Now, escaping metaphors (as far as possible), there is a serious neural aspect to Deane's claims for grammar being an exaptation of our spatial cognition.

Deane does not use the terms 'exaptation' or 'evolution'. The closest he gets to explicit evolutionary terms is in: 'The properties of grammar derive from two sources: from the target domain (the inherent semiotic properties of language), and from the source domain (spatial schemata and their associate inferential patterns)' (1992, p. 96). I can translate this into words more familiar to theorists of language evolution as 'The properties of grammar evolve to suit the inherent requirements of communication, out of spatial cognition'. On this evolutionary interpretation of his ideas, let's look at Deane's neurological evidence.

The essence of the idea is stated in this long quotation:

It would be easy to interpret the Spatialization of Form Hypothesis as claiming that all grammatical concepts must be explicitly modeled as spatial concepts. There are obvious problems with such an account, for it is far from clear that spatial and linguistic processing operate in tandem. If anything, a negative correlation could be claimed, since linguistic processing is primarily a left-brain function, whereas ordinary spatial reasoning is if anything localized more in the right brain than the left (Le Doux, Wilson and Gazzaniga 1977).

... There is, however, another possibility. Given the biological importance of spatial cognition, it is plausible to postulate that the brain is hardwired to process spatial information, with specific brain regions specifically adapted to process spatial information. However, hardwiring creates processing structures, not representations; a particular region of the brain is a processor of spatial information only because it receives information about spatial position. The very same region, connected differently, could function as a processor of linguistic information—but it would process that information in spatial terms, using the same schematic structures, using the same inferential routines it would have applied to spatial patterns. (Deane 1995, p. 63)[32]

Deane pays particular attention to the (left) inferior parietal lobule, which plays an important role in language processing, with connecting pathways to other language-related areas, in particular the nearby Wernicke's and the more distant Broca's. The inferior parietal lobule sits at the 'POT junction', where parietal, occipital and temporal lobes meet. Neurons in this lobule can simultaneously process and associate information coming in from stimuli in different modalities, for example touch, acoustic, or visual. This lobule was differentiated late in phylogeny (Aboitiz and García V. 1997), is differentiated

---

[32] Contrast this careful statement with the rhetorical flourish with which Deane concludes his paper: 'The analysis which results suggests that grammar, far from being an independent module of mind, is simply one instantiation of the general human capacity for spatially structured thought' (p. 107). It is possible, with some ingenuity and goodwill, to reconcile these passages, but this final rhetorical statement lays traps for tender minds coming into the subject.

late in foetal growth (Chi et al. 1977) and does not mature in childhood until three or four years or even later (Geschwind 1964, p. 99, citing Paul Yakovlev). Norman Geschwind, an early proponent of the importance of the IPL for language, appealed to its known function in associating stimuli in different modalities, for example associating a sound image with a visual image. This, of course, is a necessary component of learning the form–meaning pairings of a language. But we are concerned here with the syntactic capacity to **combine** form–meaning pairs (constructions) into larger units. This work is all done in a single, linguistic, modality.

Deane's target is complex combinatory syntax. One fulcrum of his argument is this:

...the inferior parietal lobe displays different functions in the left hemisphere of the [human] brain than it does on the right. In the left hemisphere of normal right handed individuals, it is a linguistic center; in the right hemisphere, it is a purely spatial center. A variety of authors have argued that linguistic function is a secondary specialization of the left inferior parietal lobe, since in nonhuman primates the inferior parietal lobe is a spatial center on both sides of the brain. ...

These considerations lead naturally to the idea that our sense of grammatical structure is based upon our sense of spatial structure, with the implication that the inferior parietal lobe is the true seat of grammatical competence.   (Deane 1995, p. 58)

This last remark about the 'true seat of grammatical competence' should be dismissed, as the capacity for grammar is now acknowledged to be distributed in many centres of the brain; no single area is its 'true seat'. As Deane implies, the left inferior parietal lobule does multiple work. It is 'still' involved in spatial manipulation.

Left inferior parietal cortex (area 40) is activated when participants imagine grasping either a real (Grafton et al. 1996) or a virtual (Decety et al. 1994) three-dimensional object with the right hand. This same region is activated when actual reach-to-grasp actions are performed with real objects (Rizzolatti et al. 1996[a]).

(Castiello et al. 2000, p. 91)

It may be argued that involvement of the right hand is a special case, but Castiello et al. (2000), using PET scans, found bilateral activation of the inferior parietal cortex during real and imagined grasping of a sweet both with the mouth and with a hand (four separate conditions). Deane's case can survive this because there are different subparts of the inferior parietal lobule, only some of which may be specialized for language. Alternatively, the parts involved in grammar processing may also be involved in spatial processing (which would even strengthen his case). We just don't know enough yet.

Deane makes a convincing case that lesions to IPL in many cases bring about specifically grammatical deficits, including typical problems with function words and long-distance dependencies. Complicating the picture is the fact that many aphasics with function word problems, classic Broca's cases, have no damage to IPL. The confluence of linguistic and spatial processing in the same part of the brain (or in some very close subparts), and the correlation of lesions in this area with core aspects of syntax in some patients, certainly start to build a case for a link between spatial reasoning and grammatical processing. But I stick at the formal differences between spatial and grammatical processing. Deane gives considerable weight to what I have called the 'metaphor strand' of his argument, and it is in the end crucial.

> . . . if grammatical structure is a metaphorical projection of this [spatial] system, then linguistic expressions are being processed as if they were physical objects, that constituency and head-adjunct organization is being perceived as if it were an object's internal configuration, and that the entire grammatical system is based on the processing of grammatical relationships as if they were linkages between physical objects.
>
> (Deane 1995, p. 62)

An important difference between the grammar in a person's head and spatial cognition is that the grammar is used in both production and perception. Spatial analysis is in a crucial sense limited to perception. We perceive objects and their spatial properties and relationships, but we don't use our visuospatial system in any way to produce objects and scenes. Sentence production, on the other hand, actually creates physical events outside the body. Thus there is a motor component to grammar that is not present in vision. Imagining visual scenes may be considered a kind of production, but it activates broadly the same brain areas as real perception.

Among the first steps in visual analysis of a scene are individuation and recognition of objects. This is parallel to the step in language processing of individuating and recognizing words. Both linguistic and spatial resolution of individual entities are partly top-down and partly bottom-up, and context-driven. Some grammatical analysis helps us to 'hear' a word that was not clearly articulated. Likewise, some analysis of parts of a scene help us to know what we are seeing—that dark shape is probably a hat because it is above a face. So far, so similar.

But spatial and linguistic analysis diverge in many ways. Analysing a sentence involves grappling with symbols. Each content word and larger contentful expression is 'looked up' in the hearer's lexicon and paired with a meaning (more usually several meanings). The form–meaning linkages are arbitrary and conventional. While it is true that what we see is influenced by conventional expectations, the pervading Saussurean arbitrariness of language is far from anything involved in visual analysis of a scene. The overriding imperative of sentence analysis is to arrive at a meaning. We penetrate through the words and the grammatical structure of sentences to their meanings extremely rapidly and automatically. We do not 'read' a visual scene in this symbolic meaning-seeking way. In focusing on the form of sentences, analogous to the shapes of physical objects, Deane is, paradoxically for a person of his general school of thought, taking a quite syntacto-centric view.

Linear order is crucial to much sentence analysis. The uttered sentence unfolds in real time. Short stretches can be held in working memory, and are perhaps reviewed in something like the way a visual scene is briefly perused. The uttered sentence is ephemeral. Some visual scenes are necessarily taken in at a glance. Any parallel between vision and sentence processing would have to involve such rapidly analysed scenes. There is no clear analogue of long-distance dependencies in visual analysis. On hearing a *Wh*-word, an English speaker is set up to expect a structure which is in some sense incomplete and waiting for the 'gap' to be filled by the *Wh*-word. The *Wh*-word and the 'gap' may be as much as twenty words apart.

Visual analysis of a scene involves coordinated work by two separate information streams, the dorsal and the ventral (Ungerleider and Mishkin 1982). The dorsal stream, nicknamed the 'where' stream orchestrates focal attention to the prominent objects in a scene, without delivering any information about what those objects are. The ventral stream, nicknamed the 'what' stream, is responsible for object recognition—'Aha, it's a bird'. There is nothing like this in grammatical processing.[33]

The issue here must be separated from the activation of visuo-spatial images on hearing a sentence about physical objects. On hearing, for example, *The cat sat on the mat*, a visual image is conjured up. Bergen et al. (2007) investigated this effect, concluding 'either subject nouns or main verbs can trigger visual imagery, but only when used in sentences about real space—metaphorical language does not yield significant effects' (p. 733). This implies that (1) grammatical processing of a sentence must be complete before a visual image is evoked, and (2) nothing in the ongoing specifically grammatical processing calls up a visual image.

In sum, Deane's advocacy of the Spatialization of Form Hypothesis makes the best case that I have found for an evolutionary relationship between

---

[33] My own claims (Hurford 2003) that the ventral and dorsal streams correlate with semantic PREDICATE(*argument*) structure are not related to this point.

grammar and visuo-spatial cognition. I believe that there may indeed have been some neurological exaptation of spatial capacities to give, ultimately, a capacity for grammar. But the big differences between grammar and visuo-spatial cognition show what great evolutionary changes have taken place since the inception of this exaptation. Grammar has taken on a life of its own, and evolved into a clearly independent domain.

Now to wrap up this chapter. As far as we can tell from studies of apes, several diverse minimal seeds of the language faculty had accumulated in our pre-human ancestors, especially in conceptual (semantic) and interpersonal (pragmatic) realms. In these realms, on the one hand, the difference in degree between humans and apes is enormous. On the other hand, the difference is clearly not so great that only some incomprehensible process could bridge the gap. Somehow in the space of no more than four million years, our species bridged that gap. We will ask how in the next chapters.

Where we have not found plausible precursors to human language, either in ape behaviour or in human non-linguistic behaviour (such as navigation and spatial reasoning), is in our unique capacity for productive combination of constructions, some quite abstract, drawn from a massive store. This agrees with one facet of the famous claim by Hauser et al. (2002) that recursion is only found in human language—that is, not in animals and not in human non-linguistic behaviour (unless this is derivative of language). Where I part company with Hauser et al. is in their claim that recursion is all there is to human language (in the narrow sense). Our combinatorial ability is as impressive as it is because we have massive stores of constructions to combine. There could be a system of just two constructions (or even just one) with a principle of combination limited only by working memory. But this would not be a human language (except in a sense so 'narrow' as to make it a virtually terminological claim). How could such an apparently great leap to massively productive combining of constructions have happened? I suggest, perhaps disappointingly, that the move to combinatoriality itself was no big deal. In a framework which posits a lexicon–syntax continuum, as does Construction Grammar, inserting a word (the simplest kind of construction) into a simple syntactic template (a slightly more complex kind of construction) is the beginning of syntactic combinatoriality. It is a desire to communicate a variety of meanings that drives the combining of constructions. **Semantically driven** combinatoriality is what distinguishes human language from birdsong. The only difference between *Daddy says yes* and *Daddy says we can* is a slight difference in the complexity of the embedded object of the verb *says*. There is no qualitative rubicon here. Actually, the real rubicon was crossed much earlier, with the first use of 'one-word' noises (or gestures) systematically paired with commonly understood meanings.

In the following chapters, I will try to sketch a plausible path by which complex combinatorial systems (languages) could have coevolved with the capacity to manage them. The required capacity, given the size of the set of constructions that modern humans have found it profitable (in some sense) to use, and an understandable pressure for fast processing, necessitated radical adaptations to brain structure.

CHAPTER 7

Gene–Language
Coevolution

7.1 Fast biological adaptation to culture

Cultural and biological evolution proceed on different timescales.[1] Modern
humans took over 4 million years to evolve from their first bipedal ancestors,
the australopithecines. Modern internet use, a global market economy, space
exploration, and mass literacy took less than 10,000 years to evolve out of
tribal Stone Age cultures. That's a ratio of about 400 to 1. This is the usual
picture described. Both the biological and cultural sides of this story need some
qualification. In fast-breeding species, biological evolution can be observed
over quite short timescales, especially where humans have intervened with
artificial selection. Evolution can be observed in the lab with such species as
fruit flies and guppies. Evolution is still evolution, whether the selection is
natural or artificial. Modern domestic dogs are so varied in shape and size that
they would surely be judged by an uninformed observer to be many different
species. A great dane and a chihuahua are as different to the eye as a cheetah
and a rat. Yet both have evolved, under artificial selection, from wolves in less
than 15,000 years, about the same period as it took modern human cultures
to evolve from the later Stone Age. The coincidence in timescale is no accident.
The breeding of dogs was a part of human culture, and in man-made conditions
the biological evolution of dogs and the cultural evolution of humans kept
pace with each other. A commonly-cited example of fast biological evolution
in humans driven by cultural changes is the evolution of lactose tolerance:

[1] Pioneering works in the now extensive literature on gene–culture evolution include
Cavalli-Sforza and Feldman (1981); Boyd and Richerson (1985).

Genetic analyses by Sarah Tishkoff and others have shown that African and European groups converged on the same adaptation independently. Each group uses a variant of a regulatory gene...to control the genes for lactase production, which is called *LCT*. So far there are four different mutations that keep the lactase gene switched on. Each allele occurs in much higher frequency in populations that have long histories of dependency on domestic dairy animals. (1) Dutch and Swedes who are related to the ancient 'Funnel Beaker' cattle-raising people of north-central Europe, (2) Nilo-Saharan-speaking groups in Kenya and Tanzania, (3) the Beja people of northeastern Sudan, and (4) Afro-asiatic-speaking groups living in northern Kenya. The evolutionary tale of lactose tolerance is a powerful one because it highlights the influence of culture on biological evolution. Even more importantly, lactose digestion is a shining example of how quickly the biology of humans can adapt in order to survive better

(Dunsworth 2007, p. 107)

(Lactose is a sugar found in cow's milk, among other things; lactase is an enzyme that breaks down lactose.) Selection of lactose tolerant alleles is reckoned to have happened within the last 5,000 years (Aoki 1991) or at most the last 7,000 years (Tishkoff et al. 2007).

Another commonly cited case of gene–culture coevolution involves sickle-cell anaemia, a genetic condition that gives some immunity from malaria. Durham (1991) gives a very thorough discussion of this topic, based on his own and earlier research. One of his conclusions is that 'culture, specifically the know-how of slash-and-burn agriculture, has played an instrumental role in the genetic evolution of West African populations. Our analysis indicates large and statistically significant differences between the S [allele] frequencies of populations with a long cultural tradition of cultivation and those who have adopted this technology much more recently' (p. 146).

Another suggested biological response to the rise of agriculture is the development of light skin in people living further from the equator. More cereal and less meat in the diet lowered the amount of vitamin D in the body, and light skins evolved as a way of synthesizing vitamin D on exposure to sunlight (Heaney 1997). Cochran and Harpending (2009) devote a very readable book to *The 10,000 Year Explosion: How Civilization Accelerated Human Evolution*, mentioning the role of agriculture in the evolution of different skin colours. Some of their other arguments are controversial, but the general case for an influence of cultural practices on biological evolution is well surveyed and by now uncontroversial. The evolutionary link between skin colour, sunlight and vitamin D is made by Jablonski and Chaplin (2000), who do not mention agriculture, but do cite recent migration as a factor and accept the role of culture in biological evolution. Living in a less hospitable climate as a result of migration can be counted as a cultural factor. Human migrations are relatively recent in evolutionary terms, and there is other evidence of adaptive biological response to new climates. Mishmar et al. (2003) and Ruiz-Pesini et al. (2004) found significant changes in mitochondrial DNA, not attributable to neutral drift, in populations in colder climates.

One more case is the evolution of human digestion with the cultural practice of cooking food. A diet of only raw food in humans is correlated with weight loss and, more importantly for evolution, significant diminution of female fertility. 'About 30% of the women under 45 years of age had partial to complete amenorrhea; subjects eating high amounts of raw food (> 90%) were affected more frequently than moderate raw food dieters' (Koebnick et al. 1999, p. 69). Wrangham and Conklin-Brittain (2003) argue that a pure raw food diet cannot supply the energy needs of human hunter-gatherers, and that this constitutes a case of gene–culture coevolution: 'If cooking is indeed obligatory for humans but not for other apes, this means that human biology must have adapted to the ingestion of cooked food (i.e. food that is tender and low in fiber) in ways that no longer allow efficient processing of raw foods. Cooking has been practiced for ample time to allow the evolution of such adaptations' (p. 35). Control of fire, probably for cooking, since many burnt animal bones were involved, has been dated to at least 1 million years ago, in the Swartkrans cave in South Africa (Brain and Sillen 1988). Gowlett et al. (1981) claim evidence of human-made fire dated to at least 1.35 million years ago for a Lower Pleistocene Oldowan site in Kenya; this evidence is disputed (Isaac 1982; Gowlett et al. 1982). A survey by James (1989), written before publication of the Swartkrans data, is more cautious, as are commentators on that survey. The most that can be asserted with complete confidence is that *Homo* controlled fire toward the end of the Middle Pleistocene stage, about 300,000 years ago. Even this late date would give time for biological coevolution of the human digestive system to adapt to the cultural practice of cooking. The human gut is significantly smaller than the ape gut (Aiello and Wheeler 1995). The chimpanzee gut is adapted to processing meat. The human gut has evolved a step further and is adapted for processing cooked food, both meat and tubers. Correlated with their cultural practices, some populations are genetically better at digesting starchy tuber food than others (Perry et al. 2007). These biological changes could have been very fast, or somewhat slower, but at the slowest, over roughly the same period as any biological adaptation for language.

Aiello and Wheeler (1995) propose an 'Expensive-Tissue Hypothesis', by which 'there has been a coevolution between brain size and gut size in human and other primates. ... no matter what is selecting for brain-size increase, one would expect a corresponding selection for reduction in the relative size of the gut. This would be essential in order to keep the total body BMR [basic metabolic rate] at the typical level' (p. 205). Fish and Lockwood (2003) found supporting evidence for this hypothesis in positive correlations between brain mass and quality of diet, across all primates. In humans alone, cooking (of the right kind) further enhances dietary quality, and humans maintain a BMR typical of other primates, through having compensated for a larger energy-consuming brain by a reduced energy-consuming gut. So this last example of biological adaptation to a cultural practice (cooking) brings us close to facts relevant to language, namely brain size, discussed in the next section.

Finally, note that convergent phenotypic responses to similar environmental pressures by different populations may have different underlying genetic mechanisms. The various lactose-tolerant populations mentioned above have become lactose-tolerant by different genetic routes. And Norton et al. (2007) show different genetic correlates of light skin colour in European and East Asian populations.

Such cases leave little doubt of the possibility of cultural practices influencing and accelerating the course of biological evolution. I have mentioned the domestication of dogs by humans. A hypothesis gaining increased currency, couched in diverse terminology, is that modern humans have also **domesticated themselves**. I briefly raised the possibility of self-domestication by humans in *The Origins of Meaning* (p. 219). This was in connection with the emergence of cooperative attention-guiding and attention-following. The idea of human self-domestication has a quite long, and chequered, history. Brüne (2007) recounts how Darwin, in *The Descent of Man*, toyed with the idea that humans are domesticated. He rejected it on the strict grounds that no other species had domesticated us, and no deliberate or conscious policy can be seen. But Darwin did concede that humans have some characteristics of domesticated species, including variability between individuals and behavioural plasticity. Brüne describes how the self-domestication idea was adopted by eugenicists, including the Nazi regime. In this light, self-domestication has got a bad name. Brüne suggests a neutral term 'adaptation to sedentism'. For myself, I prefer to consider the possibility of human **adaptation to complex culture**.

Humans have constructed complex cultures, and obviously had the biological dispositions to do so. We are animals, but we do not live like animals. Humans have developed thick mantles of culture to overlay their animal instincts. The animal instincts occasionally erupt like volcanoes from under the mantle. But mostly humans are adapted to living engaged with the conditions defined by their highly developed cultures. The cultures bring them significant material benefits, like being able to survive in the most inhospitable regions of the earth, and to live in previously unimaginable comfort and safety. We have become adapted to high levels of long-term planning, conformity to elaborate social convention, and trust in strangers from our own cultural groups. We humans are engaged in a great natural experiment, testing whether an evolutionary strategy so conceived can long endure. Culture has taken us on an extraordinary journey so far, but will our species outlive the cockroaches and bacteria? That question is not my department.

It is unlikely that culture-forming dispositions arose abruptly out of the blue. As cultures began to emerge (beyond any stage like that found in chimpanzee groups), humans, by this hypothesis, began biologically to adapt to living with more complex cultures, and to push the boundaries of their cultures toward greater complexity, in a coevolutionary gene–culture cycle.[2]

Accepting in general the likelihood of recent fast gene–culture coevolution in humans, I will focus on the more specific possibility of gene–culture–**language** coevolution. The idea is already often found, couched in broad terms. 'A genetic predisposition for language may well have co-evolved with language itself' (Dahl 2001, p. 376); '[L]anguage is a bio-cultural hybrid, a product of the intensive gene–culture coevolution over perhaps the last 200,000 to 400,000 years' (Evans and Levinson 2009, p. 431). Terry Deacon has been a consistent advocate of brain–language coevolution (Deacon 1992, 1997). Dor and Jablonka (2000) argue for a model of culturally-driven genetic assimilation. Interestingly, the most prolific writer on language evolution, Derek Bickerton, has vacillated from pro to con and back to pro on brain–language coevolution. In Bickerton (1995, from p. 46 onwards) he argues very strongly against brain–language coevolution, arguing instead for a qualitative structural change in the brain. This is at odds with his earlier position (in Bickerton 1981, p. 295), although this is expressed in quite general terms. More recently Bickerton (2009a), he has become a convert to niche-construction (see section 7.4.2 below), more compatible with a gene–culture coevolutionary view. Even in non-human species with very limited 'culture' (birdsong transmitted across generations by learning), some authors have argued for 'the coevolution of cultural signals and genes encoding learning preferences' (Lachlan and Feldman 2003).

---

[2] Among many other authors who have written on gene–culture coevolution, see especially Boyd and Richerson (1985); Enfield and Levinson (2006); Laland et al. (2000); Lumsden and Wilson (1981).

7.2 Phenotype changes—big brains

First, the basic facts about human brain size.[3] Our cranial capacity has roughly tripled in the last 3 million years. Some expansion of brain capacity is not uniquely human, but humans have gone further than other primates in evolving a larger brain. '[T]he average human has a brain that is 4.6 times the size expected for the average mammal and the average non-human primate anthropoid has a brain almost twice as large as that of the average mammal' (Aiello and Wheeler 1995, p. 200). 'Even though absolute brain size is significantly larger in pongids (chimpanzee, bonobo, gorilla, orangutan) than in all other anthropoids except humans, they do not have substantially larger EQs,[4] indicating their brains are scaling approximately similar to other anthropoids. Human brain sizes, by contrast, are not explained by brain/body scaling in either mammals or primates' (Schoenemann 2006, p. 381).

Paleontological evidence indicates that the rapid brain evolution observed with the emergence of *Homo erectus* at approximately 1.8 million years ago was likely associated with important changes in diet and body composition.
   ... humans allocate a much larger share of their daily energy budget to 'feed their brains'. Brain metabolism accounts for ~20–25% of resting energy demands in an adult human body. This is far more than the 8–10% observed in other primate species, and still more than the 3–5% allocated to the brain by other (non-primate) mammals (Leonard and Robertson 1994).   (Leonard et al., 2003, p. 5)

A difference in detail about timing, not enough to affect my argument here, appears in 'the major increase in encephalization within *Homo* [which] occurred earlier during the Middle Pleistocene (600–150 thousand years before present (kyr BP)), preceded by a long period of stasis extending through the Early Pleistocene (1,800 kyr BP)' (Ruff et al. 1997, p. 173). Further on timing, Schoenemann (2006) writes that 'there is no compelling reason to assume anything other than a reasonably constant trend toward increasing brain size over time' (p. 390). And, somewhat surprisingly 'results also indicate that a decrease in average absolute brain size over the past 35,000 years within *H. sapiens* was paralleled by a corresponding decrease in average body size' (Ruff et al. 1997, p. 175). This recent decrease in brain size is not a decrease in the ratio of brain mass to body mass, and appears to be due, again, to a recent change in diet. All the brain evolution relevant to syntax took place before the dispersal of *Homo sapiens* out of Africa. Both the humans who moved out

---

   [3] I recommend Schoenemann (2006) as a most useful survey article on the evolution of human brain size and function.
   [4] EQ = encephalization quotient, the ratio of an animal's brain size to its brain size as expected from its body size by some accepted reference species.

of Africa and the humans who stayed behind had developed languages in the modern range, and (of course) the natural capacity to acquire them.[5] We don't see any significant regional biological differences among humans relevant to the acquisition of complex modern syntax.

The human brain has expanded more in certain features than in others. Norman Geschwind makes a useful overall generalization.

> If we contemplate the brain of a subprimate mammal, such as a rabbit or a cat, we find that these primordial [i.e. early maturing, JRH] zones become increasingly separated by new areas of cortex. The cortex separating the primordial zones occupies a greater percentage of the surface in the primates and achieves its greatest extent in man where it clearly occupies most of the surface of the hemispheres. It is indeed the development of this **association cortex** which is responsible for the higher functions of the nervous system.
>
> (Geschwind 1964, pp. 92–3)

The most notable disproportionate increase is in the prefrontal cortex. 'According to extrapolations derived from two different data sources (Deacon 1984, 1988), prefrontal cortex is at least twice the size that would be predicted in an ape brain of this size' (Deacon 1996, p. 112). Although 'prefrontal lesions do not cause aphasia' (Novoa and Ardila 1987, p. 206), prefrontal cortex is involved in more conceptual aspects of language use, with some knock-on effect on related abilities.

> The language abilities of 21 patients with prefrontal lesions (11 right and 10 left) and 15 matched normal subjects were analyzed, using a linguistic ability test designed to evaluate performance in six areas: automatic language, language production, verbal memory, syntax, derivative words, and comprehension of logical grammatical structures. Significant differences in the obtained scores of all groups were found. In spite of formal conservation of language in patients with frontal damage, their complex and conceptual verbal abilities were severely compromised.
>
> (Novoa and Ardila 1987, p. 206)

Among many papers testifying to the role of prefrontal cortex in language is Goldberg et al. (2007); these authors found increased left prefrontal activation for processing of abstract, verbally mediated knowledge about objects. White matter is the longer-distance cabling connecting non-adjacent brain regions. Schoenemann et al. (2005, p. 242) found that 'Prefrontal white matter volume is disproportionately larger in humans than in other primates'.

The prefrontal cortex is not the only part of the human brain disproportionately expanded. The inferior parietal lobule, an important junction area with thick fibre tract connections to several other language areas, is recently

---

[5] See my discussion of Coolidge and Wynn's (2009) hypothesis near the beginning of the pevious chapter.

differentiated in phylogeny. Aboitiz and García (1997, p. 386) 'suggest that the inferoparietal region has suffered a progressive differentiation in primate phylogeny and that areas 40 and 39 of the human inferior parietal lobe arose as a consequence of the further subdivision of inferior moiety of area 7 in the monkey'. Comparing postnatal growth, rather than size, Norman Geschwind (1964, p. 99), a leading figure on the importance of the inferior parietal lobule, writes 'the greatest relative growth of the human brain compared to that of the subhuman primates is in the inferior parietal region'.

Rilling and Seligman (2002) associate the temporal lobes with language comprehension and note that 'Within the temporal lobe, overall volume, surface area, and white matter volume were significantly larger in humans than predicted by the ape regression lines. The largest departure from allometry in humans was for the temporal lobe white matter volume' (p. 505). Schenker et al. (2005) looked for human brain features differentially enlarged, comparing humans with apes of several species. They found that gyral white matter volume, immediately underlying the cortex, is larger than expected in humans. I have already noted the strong modification in human evolution of the arcuate fasciculus, a white matter pathway linking Broca's and Wernicke's areas, in Chapter 2, section 1.

'The human cerebellum is ~2.9 times as large as expected for a primate of our body size... and as such has increased only slightly more slowly than the brain as a whole. ... The cerebellum's participation in language presumably explains why it has not lagged behind as has the olfactory bulb, for example' (Schoenemann 2006, p. 384). The cerebellum clearly is involved in language processing. De Smet et al. (2007) surveyed a number of studies of damage to the cerebellum, concluding

A variety of linguistic disorders were found to occur following acquired cerebellar lesions: (1) impaired phonological and semantic fluency; (2) agrammatism (at morphological and sentence level); (3) naming and word finding difficulties; (4) cerebellar-induced aphasia; (5) reading difficulties; (6) writing problems; and (7) higher-level language deficits, including disturbed listening comprehension, impaired language proficiency and metalinguistic ability.   (De Smet et al. 2007, p. 165)

Belton et al. (2003) also found that affected members of the KE family[6] had significantly reduced grey matter density in their cerebella. The wide dispersion around the brain of disproportionately expanded features emphasizes the dis-

---

[6] The KE family is a London family, about half of whom have an inherited language disorder, now traced to a mutation in a single nucleotide base (Hurst et al. 1990; Enard et al. 2002; Lai et al. 2001, 2003).

tributed nature of language representation and processing. There is no single 'language area' in the brain.

Overall size matters, as a cross-species analysis reveals.

A comparative analysis of 533 instances of innovation, 445 observations of social learning, and 607 episodes of tool use established that social learning, innovation, and tool use frequencies are positively correlated with species' relative and absolute 'executive' brain volumes, after controlling for phylogeny and research effort. Moreover, innovation and social learning frequencies covary across species, in conflict with the view that there is an evolutionary tradeoff between reliance on individual experience and social cues. These findings provide an empirical link between behavioral innovation, social learning capacities, and brain size in mammals. The ability to learn from others, invent new behaviors, and use tools may have played pivotal roles in primate brain evolution.
(Reader and Laland 2002, p. 4436)

Thus, even before language, increased encephalization in related species brought some of the advantages that we tend to think of as particularly characterizing our own species. The emergence of language enabled our species to capitalize, spectacularly further, on reasoning and learning abilities that were already present to some degree before language.

Within non-human species, the correlation between brain size and ability in mental tasks is well known. Early and recent experiments on rats established a significant correlation between brain size and performance on tasks such as learning the layout of a maze (Hamilton 1935; Anderson 1993).[7] In humans, it is also clear that brain size in individuals, as can be accurately measured with MRI scans, covaries significantly with performance on a range of psychometric tests, such as standard tests for IQ.[8]

Specifically linguistic performance is correlated with brain size, with an interesting quirk: a study of 100 brains concluded 'General verbal ability was positively correlated with cerebral volume and each hemisphere's volume in women and in right-handed men accounting for 36% of the variation in verbal intelligence. There was no evidence of such a relationship in non-right-handed men' (Witelson et al. 2006, p. 386). A study of forty healthy right-handed women found that '[B]rain size correlated more highly with verbal ability as opposed to performance/spatial ability' (Wickett et al. 1994, p. 831).

Chomsky mentions brain size and language together, in a notorious passage:

---

[7] Thanks to Tom Schoenemann for alerting me to these sources and several others cited below.

[8] Andreason et al. (1993); Raz et al. (1993); Wickett et al. (1994); Willerman et al. (1991); McDaniel (2005).

We know very little about what happens when 10^{10} neurons are crammed into something the size of a basketball, with further conditions imposed by the specific manner in
which this system developed over time. It would be a serious error to suppose that all
properties, or the interesting properties of the structures that evolved, can be 'explained'
in terms of natural selection.   (Chomsky 1975b, p. 59)

True, we know very little about the representation of language in the brain
(but we are getting to know more). Also true is that conditions imposed by
the specific manner in which systems develop over time, both ontogenetic and
phylogenetic time, are crucial to the final shape of the system. This clause is
a clear recognition that considering evolution or development by stages from
small and simple beginnings must play a central role in any theory of language.
Sadly, until very recently, such developmental/evolutionary considerations have
played no part in syntactic theorizing. Chomsky offers no justification for the
opinion that interesting properties may not be explainable in terms of natural
selection. In debate among social scientists discussing evolution, a couple of
rhetorical labels get tossed around. Any adaptationist proposal runs the risk
of being labelled a 'Just So story', and the counterproposal is that the trait in
question is a 'spandrel'. Evolutionary psychology, in particular, often comes in
for this accusation and counterclaim, which may be right or wrong. But how
would we know? Genetics has moved beyond impressionistic arguments that
apparently adaptive traits have been selected. As we will see below, regions of
the genome can now be tested by various techniques for signatures of positive
natural selection.[9] Of course, a genetic 'signature' is not an absolute proof, but
it adds a powerful new type of evidence for positive selection or lack thereof. As
always, Chomsky has his own views as to what the interesting properties are,
and they don't necessarily coincide with what other linguists, psycholinguists,
and philosophers find interesting. And the scare quotes around 'explained' are
just a dismissive rhetorical move. As brain tissue is so expensive of energy, it
would be surprising if its growth and maintenance were not selected for by
some advantageous function. A useless but energetically inexpensive bodypart
can be cheaply carried along during evolution,[10] but carrying a costly and
useless 'organ' would be selected against. So the massive expansion in brain
size is relevant to the evolution of our language faculty. But we have to ask
'How exactly?' (or as exactly as can be expected at present).

---

[9] Two papers (Hancock and Di Rienzo 2008; Kelley and Swanson 2008), give very
thorough surveys of methods of detecting the genetic signature of natural selection.
Their examples are all from human genetics, but the methods are quite general.

[10] Until recently, many, including Darwin, thought the appendix to be one such
useless but cheap vestige, but see Smith et al. (2009).

Evolution did not just produce more of the same homogeneous stuff as brain size increased. The architecture increased in complexity in certain areas, including polysensory and high-order association areas of cortex, as testified, for example, by Shaw et al. (2008). They studied longitudinal changes in cortical thickness in 375 typically developing children and young adults.

> We find differing levels of complexity of cortical growth across the cerebrum, which align closely with established architectonic maps. Cortical regions with simple laminar architecture, including most limbic areas, predominantly show simpler growth trajectories. These areas have clearly identified homologues in all mammalian brains and thus likely evolved in early mammals. In contrast, polysensory and high-order association areas of cortex, the most complex areas in terms of their laminar architecture, also have the most complex developmental trajectories. Some of these areas are unique to, or dramatically expanded in primates, lending an evolutionary significance to the findings.
>
> (Shaw et al. 2008, p. 3586)

7.3 Genotype changes—selection or drift?

First, a brief and simple genetics tutorial update. Until about fifteen years ago, what was understood about the working of DNA was that long sequences of contiguous nucleotide bases get translated into particular proteins or enzymes via triplets of bases (codons) coding for amino acids which then string together into long protein molecules. The protein formed from the FOXP2 gene, for example, is a 715-long sequence of amino acids. The earliest idea about DNA translation into proteins was that the proteins produced are the actual protein building blocks of the body. Any DNA that didn't code for a protein was thought to be 'junk DNA', and there appeared to be a lot of it. Within the last fifteen years this relatively simple story or 'central dogma', with 'genes' and proteins at its centre, has become much more complicated.

> The central dogma has therefore not only been taken to mean that most genes encode proteins, but also that proteins are sufficient in themselves to specify and organize the autopoietic[11] programming of complex biological entities, an assumption that has pervaded molecular biology for decades. This assumption must now be reassessed.
>
> (Mattick 2003, p. 937)

---

[11] Maturana and Varela (1980), who coined this term, gloss 'autopoiesis' as 'self-reproduction'. 'Ontogeny is the history of the structural transformation of a unity. Accordingly, the ontogeny of a living system is the history of maintenance of its identity through continuous autopoiesis in the physical space' (p. 98).

All mammals are built from essentially the same set of protein types; the proteins are just arranged very differently in mice and men. As early as 1975, King and Wilson, comparing human and chimpanzee 'structural genes', noted that 'their macromolecules are so alike that regulatory mutations may account for their biological differences' (p. 107). What the genes do is not just produce proteins but mostly act as traffic controllers during the complex body-building process, organizing which proteins are produced in which order and in what quantities in various bodily contexts. The detailed mechanisms are extremely complex and as yet only partially understood. Some bits of double-stranded DNA get copied into single-stranded scraps of RNA, which interfere, in either a facilitatory ('upregulating') or an inhibitory ('downregulating') fashion, with the productions of other parts of the genome. Some proteins also have the same role. The human FOXP2 gene, for example, is a 'transcription factor' giving rise to a protein which affects the workings of many other genes. Konopka et al. (2009) investigated the differences made by the two amino-acid changing mutations in FOXP2 distinguishing humans from chimpanzees. They 'identified 61 genes significantly upregulated and 55 genes downregulated by FOXP2$^{[human]}$ compared to FOXP2^{chimp}' (p. 213). Thus, it turns out, much DNA is not junk after all, but acts indirectly in the body-building process. And some acts very indirectly, turning on (or off) genes which themselves turn on (or off) still other genes, and so on. It's all fantastically complicated, and more or less completely destroys any old-fashioned ideas about 'a gene for X', where X is your favourite trait. In fact this means that the very concept of a gene is evolving. '[T]he sharper resolving power of modern investigative tools makes less clear what, exactly, is meant by a molecular gene' (Fogle 2000, p. 4).[12] The term 'gene' is still used and useful, but must be treated with great caution, especially by non-biologists. Most DNA is 'non-coding' DNA, not directly translating into a protein. End of tutorial update.

The marked differences in behavioural phenotype between humans and apes are paralleled, not surprisingly, by marked differences in the genomes. But because of the complex way in which DNA relates to body-building, one way to study genomes is to start with the whole DNA sequence, rather than being selectively guided to regions known to link to phenotypic traits. Put informally, a researcher in this strong bioinformatic style starts with the 3 billion base pairs of the human genome, or the slightly larger chimp genome, and looks for

---

[12] The whole collection (Beurton et al. 2000) in which this chapter appears is a useful discussion of the concept of a gene.

patterns, either within or across genomes, and subsequently asks about possible function.[13] Modern gene sequencing and massive computational power for searching and comparing billions of bits of information make it possible to identify 'human accelerated regions' (HARs)[14] in the human genome. These are sequences of nucleotide bases which are highly conserved in other mammals, but markedly different in humans. A HAR can be nearly identical in chimpanzees and mice, for example, but the corresponding region in humans is strikingly different from the chimp region. Naturally, such judgements as 'nearly identical' and 'strikingly different' need to be quantified and evaluated for statistical significance. All this has been done for 202 HARs identified by Pollard et al. (2006a). 'We have scanned the whole human genome and identified the most extreme examples of recent, rapid molecular evolution. After careful screening to remove alignment and assembly errors, we found 202 significantly accelerated elements'. These genomic elements are mostly in non-coding DNA, so there is no prospect of any simple story of accelerated evolution of the human DNA giving rise directly to particular brain structure. Nevertheless, there is evidence that some of the most highly accelerated regions make a contribution to the building of the cortex.

Pollard and her colleagues labelled the DNA region showing most accelerated evolution in humans 'HAR1'. It does not code directly for a protein. What HAR1 does is dauntingly complex. 'HAR1, is part of a novel RNA gene (HAR1F) that is expressed specifically in Cajal-Retzius neurons in the developing human neocortex from 7 to 19 gestational weeks, a crucial period for cortical neuron specification and migration. HAR1F is co-expressed with reelin, a product of Cajal-Retzius neurons that is of fundamental importance in specifying the six-layer structure of the human cortex' (Pollard et al. 2006b, p. 167). Trying to unpack this technical description doesn't yet, unfortunately, shed much clear light on the function of this accelerated area. From what I have been able to discover, there may in fact be two types of cell, Cajal cells and Retzius cells,[15] both of which play a role in the building of the cortex during gestation (Meyer et al. 1999). According to these authors, Retzius cells, presumably having done their work, die off during gestation; Cajal cells may

[13] Beside the work discussed below, other work in this bioinformatic style, reflecting a broad consensus on recent positive selection in humans, includes Sabeti et al. (2006, 2007); Voight et al. (2006); Nielsen et al. (2007); Wang et al. (2006).

[14] Naming at the frontier of biological research is still like a Wild West land grab. HAR has also been used for human androgen receptor, hyperacute rejection, and human aldose reductase, among others, nothing to do with the DNA regions that Pollard and colleagues explored.

[15] Named after their late nineteenth-century discoverers.

succeed Retzius cells and can sometimes persist into adulthood. Some form of Cajal-Retzius cells are found in the developing neocortex (such as it is) of non-primates, such as rats (Radnikow et al. 2002). Finally, all mammals have a six-layer cortex, although the human cortex is most finely differentiated into sublayers. So, alas, we are in the frustrating position of knowing about dramatically accelerated evolution in humans of a region of the genome, HAR1, but nobody yet has much of a clue what exactly it does. The most we can say, at least in non-technical terms, is that it has something to do with brain development. Why this region has evolved so fast in humans is still a mystery, as Pollard (2009) readily admits. She describes its role less technically as follows:

HAR1 is active in a type of neuron that plays a key role in the pattern and layout of the developing cerebral cortex, the wrinkled outermost brain layer. When things go wrong in these neurons, the result may be a severe, often deadly, congenital disorder known as lissencephaly ('smooth brain'), in which the cortex lacks its characteristic folds and exhibits a markedly reduced surface area. Malfunctions in these same neurons are also linked to the onset of schizophrenia in adulthood.

HAR1 is thus active at the right time and place to be instrumental in the formation of a healthy cortex. (Other evidence suggests that it may additionally play a role in sperm production.)   (Pollard 2009, p. 45)

(That last bit about HAR1 being involved in sperm production, too, is typical of the tangled web of relations between DNA and phenotype.) '[T]he changes in HAR1 clearly occurred on the human lineage, but probably took place more than 1 Myr ago' (Pollard et al. 2006b, p. 168b).

The second most accelerated region on Pollard's list, HAR2, also known as HACNS1, does not affect the brain or its development, but the thumb, wrist, ankle, and big toe! (Prabhakar et al. 2008). It probably plays a role in the unique degree of opposability of the human thumb and our bipedality. HAR1 and HAR2, considering their role in adaptive human traits, have probably undergone positive natural selection (but see below for the elusiveness of evidence for positive selection in general).

No specific functions have yet been identified for Pollard's next three most accelerated regions, HAR3, HAR4, and HAR5. They yield mixed evidence for and against positive selection, depending on the time period targeted by the test concerned. Non-deleterious variation at a locus across individuals (polymorphism) is evidence of neutral mutation, that is, not affecting fitness. Pollard and colleagues looked at variation among humans living today. Applying a test that measures polymorphism (Hudson et al. 1987), they 'found no evidence of departures from neutrality for HAR3, HAR4, and HAR5'. 'If there has been a strong selective sweep[16] in the last ~200,000 years then we should be able to see a signature in the variable sites nearby the region that was affected by adaptive evolution. We do see signatures like this for HAR1 and HAR2, but not for HAR3–5' (K. Pollard, p.c.). But another test, across all HARs, considered a much longer time period (since the chimp–human ancestor) and compared the rate of DNA changes in humans to what is expected for neutrally evolving sequences over the same period of time. On this test, 'the human substitution rate exceeds the human–chimp neutral rate in 201 of the 202 HARs, whereas the chimp rate does so in only 33 HARs (16%). This evidence suggests that the HAR elements were not created by relaxation of functional constraint' (Pollard et al. 2006a). Neutral drift through relaxation of functional constraint is the opposite of positive selection. So on the evidence of these tests, HAR1 and HAR2 have been positively selected in the last 200,000 years, while positive selection for HAR3, HAR4, and HAR5 occurred earlier, during some period after the chimp–human split.

Positive selection typically triggers accelerated evolution, but highly accelerated evolution is not in itself evidence of positive selection. Neutral drift can conceivably sometimes be accelerated, although with lower probability than positive selection. It appears that regions near the ends of chromosomes ('subtelomeres', where HAR1, HAR3, and HAR5 lie) are hotspots for evolutionary change through recombination and duplications, not necessarily driven by selection (Linardopoulou et al. 2005). Further, a significant factor in human–chimp differences in regions HAR1–HAR5 is a very pronounced bias away from A and T alleles towards G and C alleles. This process is known as 'biased gene conversion' (BGC), a mechanical effect of the recombination of mismatched alleles during meiosis, the production of sperm and ovum cells. An individual with A or T in one chromosome and G or C at the corresponding locus in its partner chromosome is more likely to produce a G or C gamete than an A or T one. Galtier and Duret (2007) have argued that BGC, rather than positive selection, may be the dominant factor at work in the HARs identified by Pollard et al. They suggest several ways of testing whether accelerated regions are subject to neutral BGC or adaptive selection. No such tests have yet been carried out. It is also not clear why BGC should have occurred significantly more in humans than in chimpanzees. The HAR discoveries are

---

[16] If a particular region of the genome produces a phenotype that is advantageous and therefore selected, not only that region, but also its close neighbours on the chromosome will be more frequent in subsequent generations. If these neighbours do not themselves appear to convey any particular advantage, the conclusion is that they have 'hitch-hiked' in the 'wake' of the selected region, or been involved in a 'selective sweep'.

definitely exciting, but as yet we cannot be certain beyond reasonable doubt that these regions point us to particular adaptive changes in humans.

Accelerated evolution in some regions of the human genome does not, of course, imply, that the whole human genome has accelerated faster than expected. Indeed, measured in years, human evolution has **slowed down**, a phenomenon known as the 'hominoid slowdown'. Li and Tanimura (1987) use as their title 'The molecular clock runs more slowly in man than in apes and monkeys'. Human generations are longer than ape generations. But calibrating the clock in terms of generations rather than years is not enough to account for the slowdown.

There is reason to expect that the rate of molecular evolution decelerated in the primate lineage to humans. First of all, an increasing complexity of the molecular machinery of life left fewer sites in coding DNA where neutral mutations could accumulate, i.e. the probability increased that any mutation in a protein would be harmful and therefore selected against. Secondly, rates of occurrence of *de novo* mutations decreased as enhanced DNA repair mechanisms and longer generation times evolved.

(Goodman 1985a, p. 10)

This suggests that hominoids were reaching an evolutionary near-plateau of complexity where only very fine tuning could yield any small advantages. There is no reason to believe that evolution has altogether stopped affecting humans. And any such slowdown could be drastically reversed by entry in a new niche. I will argue in the next section that humans did indeed enter a new niche. The apparently paradoxical situation is expressed by Cooper (1999, p. 71): 'The *hominoid slowdown* is at its greatest in humans although anatomically, humans are quite divergent. Clearly, changes in certain key genes must have assumed a critical importance'. This brings us to a study looking for such critically important key genes.

An approach complementary to that of Pollard and her colleagues was taken by Dorus et al. (2004). Rather than beginning with the whole genome, they started with a list of genes known to be involved in building and maintaining the nervous system.

We found that these genes display significantly higher rates of protein evolution in primates than in rodents. Importantly, this trend is most pronounced for the subset of genes implicated in nervous system development. Moreover, within primates, the acceleration of protein evolution is most prominent in the lineage leading from ancestral primates to humans. Thus, the remarkable phenotypic evolution of the human nervous system has a salient molecular correlate, i.e., accelerated evolution of the underlying genes, particularly those linked to nervous system development. In addition to uncovering broad evolutionary trends, our study also identified many candidate genes—most of which are implicated in regulating brain size and behavior—that might have played important roles in the evolution of the human brain.   (Dorus et al. 2004, p. 1027)

These researchers compared primates with rodents, and humans with non-human primates. It is clear that human brain evolution continues a trend that was already under way in our primate ancestors. Whereas Pollard et al. focused on human genome **regions** identified by accelerated evolution, irrespective of function, hence almost entirely non-coding DNA, Dorus and colleagues surveyed **genes**, chosen for their known involvement in brain development or maintenance in rats, mice, macaques, chimpanzees, or humans.

Dorus and his co-authors lean heavily on a particular test for positive selection. This is the K_a/K_s test. I will explain. Triples of nucleotide bases (codons) code for specific amino acids. In RNA, transcribed from DNA, there are four types of base, A, U, G, and C, so there are $4^3 = 64$ possible codons. But there are only twenty-two amino acids. This means that some amino acids are encoded by several different codons. For example, the amino acid Arginine is encoded by any of CGU, CGC, CGA, CGG, AGA, or AGG; Histidine, on the other hand, is encoded by just two RNA codons, CAU and CAC. Different strings of amino acids make different proteins. The mutation in the FOXP2 of the KE family was a point mutation substituting an A (adenine) for a G (guanine); thus CAC encoding for Arginine became CGC encoding for Histidine, ending up making a different protein, with the deleterious results seen in affected members of the KE family. Because this mutation changed the resultant amino acid, this was a 'nonsynonymous' substitution. If CAC had mutated to CAT (CAU in RNA) instead, this would have been a 'synonymous' substitution, as it would not have altered the resultant amino acid, and presumably not produced a disadvantaged phenotype.

Over time, substitution mutations accumulate, and some are synonymous neutral substitutions, presumed to have no phenotypic effect, while others are nonsynonymous, amino-acid changing substitutions, almost certainly affecting the phenotypic outcome. Comparing corresponding regions in the genomes of related species, one can count the two types of substitutions that have happened since descent from a common ancestor genome. The ratio of non-synonymous substitutions, K_a, to synonymous substitutions, K_s, is the K_a/K_s ratio. A high K_a/K_s ratio is a sign that more amino-acid-changing substitutions have occurred, and survived, presumably not detracting from fitness. In much of the genetics literature, on the rationale that mutations are like random coin tosses, and synonymous and nonsynonymous mutations are equally likely, a K_a/K_s ratio higher than 1 is taken to be evidence of positive selection.[17]

[17] Surely, as Geoff Sampson has pointed out to me, the expected ratio of synonymous to nonsynonymous mutations depends in the actual precise distribution of various numbers of codons against different acids. The coin toss is not a simple heads/tails one. This does not affect the gist of my argument here.

This sets the bar very high, perhaps too high, because if any nonsynonymous mutation has survived at all, it must at least be non-deleterious. Most K_a/K_s ratios are well below 1. A K_a/K_s ratio above 1 is strong evidence of positive selection. (For ease of reading in what follows, I will abbreviate 'K_a/K_s ratio' to 'K-ratio'.) A disadvantage of the K_a/K_s test is that it can only be applied within protein-coding genes, which constitute only about 2 percent of the genome. Nevertheless some interesting results have been obtained using this test.

Dorus et al. compared housekeeping genes with nervous system genes. Housekeeping genes are those involved in 'the most basic cellular functions such as metabolism and protein synthesis' (p. 1030). For housekeeping genes, primates and rodents show the same K-ratios, whereas for nervous system genes, primates show higher K-ratios than rodents. The number of high-K-ratio nervous system genes in primates differs significantly from that in rodents ($p = 0.004$), but there is no significant primate/rodent difference in the number of high-K-ratio housekeeping genes. Across the whole distribution of K-ratios for nervous system genes, primate ratios were significantly higher than rodent ratios ($p < 0.0001$). For housekeeping genes there was no significant primate/rodent difference in the overall distribution of K-ratios.

Next, Dorus et al. partitioned nervous system genes into two categories. 'One comprises genes whose functions are strongly biased toward nervous system development. The other consists of genes biased toward the routine physiological operations and maintenance of the nervous system' (p. 1030). The 'physiological' nervous system genes affect such things as the production of neurotransmitters and the details of how synapses keep working. Here a similar primate–rodent difference appeared. The number of high-K-ratio nervous system development genes in primates differs significantly from that in rodents ($p = 0.0002$), but there is no significant primate–rodent difference in the number of high-K-ratio nervous system 'physiological' genes. Across the whole distribution of K-ratios for nervous system development genes, primate ratios were significantly higher than rodent ratios ($p < 0.0001$). For nervous system physiological genes there was no significant primate–rodent difference in the overall distribution of K-ratios.

If high K-ratio is a sign of positive selection, primate nervous system genes have undergone more positive selection than rodent nervous system genes, whereas their bodily housekeeping mechanisms have adapted to about the same degree. And, with the same conditional caveat, within nervous system genes, those involved in development of the system, rather than those involved in routine maintenance of the system, have been most positively selected.

Dorus et al. next homed in on those genes showing the greatest difference between primates and rodents, calling these the 'primate-fast' genes.

It is remarkable that 17 out of the 24 primate-fast outliers are linked to the regulation of either brain size or behavior. This trend suggests that genes controlling brain size or behavior are preferential targets of positive selection during primate evolution. The functional specificity of these outliers adds additional credence to the notion that the higher K_a/K_s of nervous system genes in primates is likely the consequence of adaptive evolution.   (Dorus et al. 2004, p. 1032)

Finally, humans were compared with macaques and chimpanzees, with specific reference to the primate-fast nervous system genes. In short, significant K-ratio differences were found in the genes relating to nervous system development, with humans having higher values. The overall conclusion of these researchers is summarized as follows:

[A]ccelerated protein evolution in a large cohort of nervous system genes, which is particularly pronounced for genes involved in nervous system development, represents a salient genetic correlate to the profound changes in brain size and complexity during primate evolution, especially along the lineage leading to *Homo sapiens*.
                                                                    (Dorus et al. 2004, p. 1037)

Dorus and colleagues did not include in their study a number of genes that are known to affect brain development or language. For these other genes there is also evidence of recent positive selection in primates, and particularly in humans. Kouprina et al. (2004) investigated ASPM, a gene affecting brain development. Mutations to ASPM result in microcephaly, a 70 percent reduction in brain size.

[W]hereas much of the sequence of ASPM is substantially conserved among primates, specific segments are subject to high Ka/Ks ratios (nonsynonymous/synonymous DNA changes) consistent with strong positive selection for evolutionary change. The ASPM gene sequence shows accelerated evolution in the African hominoid clade, and this precedes hominid brain expansion by several million years. Gorilla and human lineages show particularly accelerated evolution in the IQ domain of ASPM.
                                                                    (Kouprina et al. 2004)

Among the accumulated mass of literature on ASPM, see for example Zhang (2003) for evidence that 'human ASPM went through an episode of accelerated sequence evolution by positive Darwinian selection after the split of humans and chimpanzees but before the separation of modern non-Africans from Africans' (p. 2063). This is corroborated by Evans et al. (2004), who conclude 'that, on average, *ASPM* fixed one advantageous amino acid change in every 300,000–400,000 years since the human lineage diverged from chimpanzees.

We therefore conclude that *ASPM* underwent strong adaptive evolution in the descent of *Homo sapiens*' (p. 489). Ali and Meier (2008), also arguing for positive selection on ASPM, show that some of the amino acid changes in ASPM affect cerebral cortex specifically, not merely gross brain size. ASPM and another gene affecting brain size, Microcephalin (MCPH), continue to evolve in modern humans (Evans et al. 2005; Mekel-Bobrov et al. 2005). Dediu and Ladd (2007) have suggested a link between variation in these genes and tone languages. At present there is no sign that this variation affects syntactic ability. GLUD2 is another brain-related gene, which evolved roughly in tandem with ASPM and MCPH1. Based on K_a/K_s ratios, Burki and Kaessmann (2004) argue that this gene, too, has undergone positive selection in the hominoid lineage. They conclude 'GLUD2 probably contributed to enhanced brain function in humans and apes by permitting higher neurotransmitter flux' (p. 1062).

AHI1 is another gene affecting brain development, including development of motor control. Mutations to this gene are associated with schizophrenia. 'Comparative genetic analysis of *AHI1* indicates that it has undergone positive evolutionary selection along the human lineage. Therefore, changes in *AHI1* may have been important in the evolution of human-specific motor behaviors' (Ferland et al. 2004, p. 1008). Linguistic behaviour is included among human-specific motor behaviours.

The best known language-related gene is of course FOXP2, and I will not go into much detail about it. Its precise working is not known, but mutations breaking the fixed human version of FOXP2 result in severe speech problems, attributed to orofacial apraxia, an inability to work the lower face muscles wth precision (Hurst et al. 1990; Vargha-Khadem and Passingham 1990; Vargha-Khadem et al. 1995). Affected people have detectable problems with syntactic and morphological tasks such as judging grammaticality, forming past tenses, and transforming sentences (Gopnik 1990; Gopnik and Crago 1991). Affected people also have a smaller Broca's area and smaller caudate nuclei, deep within the brain's basal ganglia on both sides (Watkins et al. 2002). The basal ganglia as a whole are involved in the control of movement, acting in an inhibitory 'braking' way. Remarkably, the caudate nucleus is selectively activated when subjects are reminded of an intensely loved relative or partner (Aron et al. 2005; Bartels and Zeki 2004), and is more active in smokers temporarily deprived of a chance to smoke (Wilson et al. 2008). More closely related to language behaviour, the caudate nucleus is activated selectively when a player in a lab game exhibits trust in another player or has the opportunity to apply altruistic punishment (King-Casas et al. 2005; de Quervain et al. 2004). Beside clearly affecting language, FOXP2 is expressed in several other body parts outside the brain during development, particularly in the lungs, intestines, and heart (Shu et al. 2001).

Human FOXP2 has undergone two amino-acid-changing mutations since the chimp/human split, whereas the chimpanzee version has remained conserved with no amino-acid-changing mutations since the last mouse–primate common ancestor. Neanderthals, who split off from *Homo sapiens* between 400,000 and 300,000 years ago, had the same two amino-acid-changing mutations as modern humans (Krause et al. 2007). Thus we can date these changes to between the chimp–human split and the Neanderthal–*sapiens* split. Evolution of this gene in humans has been highly accelerated. Zhang et al. (2002) found that 'human FOXP2 experienced a >60-fold increase in substitution rate' and wrote of 'possible adaptive selection' (p. 1825). Enard et al. (2002) consider the possibility that the human variant of FOXP2 may result from a relaxation of constraints rather than positive selection. They conclude in favour of positive selection, on the grounds of a selective sweep around the locus of FOXP2, and the disadvantages observed in humans with a mutated version: affected members of the KE family. The discovery of the specific FOXP2 mutations in humans is not a final key to understanding language evolution. That discovery is just one step in what will turn out to be an extremely complicated story.

In short, you only have to scratch the surface of twenty-first century genetics to find a huge number of papers citing diverse detailed molecular evidence for positive selection of genes relating to brain size, brain workings, and brain development, including some with likely links to language. Delving deeper than the surface, you won't find serious contradicting arguments against the existence of positively selected brain- and language-related genes. In the literature, one finds cautious 'glass-half-empty' comments, such as 'At present, strong evidence of positive selection unique to the human lineage is thus limited to a handful of genes' (Chimpanzee Sequencing and Analysis Consortium 2005, p. 80). But against this, Vallender and Lahn (2004) give a list of 'genes showing evidence of positive selection in humans and/or primates' (p. R246). Of these, they classify thirty-three as 'hominid', 'human', or 'recent human'. For these authors the glass seems more like half-full. Many of these adaptive changes apply to all primates, but human evolution has continued further along the trajectory initiated by primates. Fisher and Marcus (2005), in a review of the state of knowledge about genes, brains, and the evolution of language, argue that 'language should be viewed not as a wholesale innovation, but as a complex reconfiguration of ancestral systems that have been adapted in evolutionarily novel ways' (p. 9). That, in broad terms, is as much as we know. The detailed workings of the clearly relevant genes, especially any role they play in language, are typically not well understood. These modern studies have started at the opposite end of matters from Darwin. He noted phenotypes and saw their obvious adaptation to environmental conditions. The studies cited here start with genotypes and look for signatures of selection, often without a clear idea of what the full phenotypic correlates are. In coming years this gap in our knowledge will close to some extent.

7.4 The unique symbolic niche

There has been positive selection for brain development in areas relevant to language. Humans have adapted to language. But how can this be, because in the beginning there was no language to adapt to? As generally in evolution, some small change turned out to be very useful, and was widely adopted by pre-humans, thus changing their social behaviour. From that point there was a coevolutionary spiral of change and adaptation to change, enabling further change. In this section I will describe a possible route to the construction of a uniquely human niche, to which humans have adapted by evolving their unique capacities. I will focus, of course, on our syntactic capacities, specifically the ability to store massive repertoires of constructions and to combine them productively. Construction of the niche itself was not a sharp discrete process, and the topics of the subsections below (relaxation of constraints, positive selection) should be thought of as happening in a spiral, from small beginnings all round.

7.4.1 Relaxation of constraints

An alternative to positive selection is relaxation of functional constraints.[18] The struggle to survive and reproduce brings adaptation to adverse conditions. Selection can 'purify' the genome. But if for some reason conditions become less adverse, mutations that would have otherwise been deleterious can survive, as harmless variants. Populations in these cases become polymorphic in the relevant parts of the genome, and in the phenotype. Purifying selection is relaxed. Animals in captivity are typically under weaker purifying selection than animals in the wild, in aspects of the phenotype that are not subject

---

[18] At various places in this book, but particularly here, it will be evident that I have learned a lot from reading and listening to Terry Deacon. His 2010 paper is especially clear and convincing. Mike Oliphant was also an early and insightful prophet of the importance of symbolic reference in the evolution of language; he left academic life.

to artificial selection. The 'wild type' of a species is less varied than varieties protected from the rigours of the wild by human intervention. And the captive type can be free to develop complexities of behaviour that would have been selected against in the wild. Complex behaviour is usually costly in metabolic terms, like the complex behaviour sustained by bigger brains.

Kazuo Okanoya (2004) has suggested that relaxation of functional constraints is responsible for the song of Bengalese finches being more complex than that of the wild birds from which they were bred, starting about two and a half centuries ago (about 500 generations). The original wild type strain was the white-rumped munia. These birds were bred in captivity and artificially selected for colourful plumage. They were not selected for their song, according to Okanoya. This is plausible, as even the complex song of Bengalese finches is not attractive to the human ear. Detailed analysis of the song shows that it cannot be fully described by simple transitions between adjacent notes (see Chapter 1). In captivity, the parts of the genome determining the innate song template have been free to evolve in a direction yielding a somewhat more complex song. There has been some indirect sexual selection, as the captive females respond sexually more to the complex song than to a simpler song (artificially generated from real song parts), and display more nesting care. The human breeders also selected birds for better parenting behaviour. The female preference for complex song would have been present in the wild, Okanoya speculates, but complex song in males did not evolve because the cognitive cost was outweighed by the risk of predation. Captive male Bengalese finches also sing louder than the wild type.

Pre-humans were freer in mate choice than the captive Bengalese finches, for whom their captors dictate who mates with whom. The logic of the Bengalese finch example suggests a further experiment. Instead of human captors determining who mates with whom, we simply let the birds get on with it in an environment with no predators and free food, nest sites, and nesting material. This would be almost pure relaxation of constraint. Sexual selection would presumably still operate, and this, combined with the logic of Okanoya's argument, predicts even more complexification in the song than we see now.[19] It might not take as long as 240 years to notice any significant change. However, one thing would be missing in this experiment, a feature that almost certainly applied in human evolution, namely intergroup competition. On intergroup competition among primates, see, for example, Cheney and Seyfarth (1987) and Isbell (1991). Intergroup competition, usually motivated

---

[19] And they might evolve to watch TV all day and grow obese.

by food resources, is positively correlated with group size. The factor of inter-group competition is important for the human case, as I will argue below. Mere syntactic complexity of song can be a factor in sexual selection of individuals, as with many birds. Combining compositional meaning with syntactic complexity, whereby detailed messages about the world can be exchanged, permits more complex kinds of cooperation between members of a group, involving things away from the immediate here and now, to the general benefit of the group.

The finch example is suggestive that some complexification of human behaviour was made possible, though not necessary, by a relaxation of functional constraints. I have mentioned earlier (in this and in *The Origins of Meaning*) the likely effect that dispositions to greater altruism, cooperation, and shared intentionality had on pre-human social life. As social groups got larger, social relationships became more flexible and negotiable. The overall success of the group deriving from cooperation gave benefits to individual group members, relieving them to some degree from the constant need to attend to their purely material welfare. There was more time to socialize. A Darwinian imperative still urged individuals to pass on their genes. But now, with material needs somewhat less pressing, the means to enduring reproductive success could be less direct.

We can imagine a relaxation of constraints applying in the evolution of the reciprocal trust that paved the way for cooperative communication. In a social situation where reciprocation of cooperation cannot be relied on, animals must continually be on their guard. Better to be safe by not cooperating than sorry through being exploited. Genes determining watchful, suspicious behaviour leading to not spontaneously cooperating with others could take a break if the emergence of greater degrees of trust tended to guarantee reciprocation.

In the Bengalese finch case, a relaxation of constraints on biological selection was artificially imposed, by humans removing food insecurity and predation. Another important route for the relaxation of constraints is by learning replacing instinctive behaviour. If young animals can learn useful behaviour without too much cost, then strains which substitute learning for instinctive behaviour will not be selected against, and the genes can drift. This is a general trend in evolution.

On the whole, and certainly among the higher vertebrates, there has been a tendency to replace rigidly closed programs by open ones, or as the student of animal behavior would say, to replace rigidly instinctive behavior by learned behavior. This change is not a change in an isolated character. It is part of a whole chain reaction of biological changes. Since man is the culmination of this particular evolutionary trend, we naturally have a special interest in it. (Mayr 1976, p. 24)

It is conceivable that the combined effects of increased group size, increased cooperation within groups, increased trust, and shared intentionality permitted some relaxation of genetic control of instinctive alarm and other functionally referential calls, so that they began to be learned and more variable. Thus the first learned arbitrary symbols could have emerged. Learned symbols are more subject to variability across groups and so could assume a secondary function of marking group identity. And a general symbol-learning capacity, however initially restricted by memory, could have begun to enlarge the set of referent situations that calls were used for.

Keightley et al. (2005) report 'widespread degradation of the genome during the evolution of humans and chimpanzees' in regulatory regions. They attribute this surprising degradation to low effective population sizes. They do not mention learning, but their work is interpreted by Varki et al. (2008, p. 761) as fitting with ideas about 'relaxation of constraints on genomic diversity owing to buffering by culture and learning'. Varki et al. give the following generalizations about replacement of genetic constraint by learning and culture:

The phenotype of a fly or worm can be affected by its external and internal environment, but behavioural responses tend to be relatively hard-wired and stereotyped. With warm-blooded animals one sees a greater impact of postnatal care and of influence of learning from the prior generation—with humans being at one extreme end of this trend. . . .

In this regard, it is notable that even stereotyped mammalian behaviours that are considered crucial for species survival, such as effective mothering, seem to require observational learning in primates. (Varki et al. 2008, p. 758)

The buffering (shielding, masking) of the genes by culture and learning that Varki et al. mention depends on properties of the learned culture. 'Under neutral cultural evolution, where no cultural trait has any inherent advantage over another, there is selection in favour of less restrictive genes (genes that allow a wider range of signals to be recognized)' (Lachlan and Feldman 2003, p. 1084). Kirby et al. (2007) also describe shielding of genes by cultural evolution, allowing the genes to drift.

7.4.2 Niche construction and positive selection

Relaxation of functional constraints cannot be the whole story for the spectacular emergence of human language. In the genetics literature, as we have seen, relaxation of constraints is contrasted with positive selection. And as we also saw in the previous section, there is ample evidence of recent positive selection in humans. A general genetic model for the relationship between relaxation of constraints and subsequent positive selection is sketched by Sidow (1996):

> Phylogenetic analyses and sequence surveys of developmental regulator gene families indicate that two large-scale gene duplications, most likely genome duplications, occurred in ancestors of vertebrates. Relaxed constraints allowed duplicated and thus redundant genes to diverge in a two stage mechanism. Neutral changes dominated at first but then positively selected regulatory changes evolved the novel and increasingly complex vertebrate developmental program.   (Sidow 1996, p. 715)

Relaxation of constraints gives brief respite from evolutionary struggle, allowing genomes and phenotypes to drift in ways not permitted by a previous tightly constraining niche. The new variability is subject to selection by new pressures. Think, by analogy, of a poor family winning £50m in a lottery. Suddenly all the old pressures of daily life are gone, soon to be replaced by the equally fraught problems of adapting to the new moneyed niche. Putting it figuratively, the first beaver to build a dam might have thought he had freed himself from a host of worries that plagued his pre-dam-building life. But he could not rest in his lodge for long, as the rest of nature began to react to beaver dams. Solving one problem creates previously undreamed-of problems. And there is no going back. Less figuratively, the first hominins to reap substantial group benefits from enhanced cooperation, including the exchange of 'one-word' symbolic messages, were to some extent freed from constant concerns about food and safety. But being a member of a group means you have to find a modus vivendi with your constant companions. There always was, and still is, competition with your fellows to promote your genes, but now, due to the cooperative social setup, the competition has to take a more subtle form. This is the social niche.

Chimpanzees, of course, also live in a social niche, but the scenario that I have sketched for pre-humans includes a factor unique to humans. Only humans in their natural habitat learn arbitrary form–meaning mappings and use them communicatively. This means that the arsenal of tools for negotiating with neighbours in your group includes a powerful device previously unseen in evolution. Pre-humans were now in the **symbolic niche**.[20] The evolution of language

> …ushered in a new, unique way of life consisting of what is termed a 'symbolic niche'. … In other words, it established a totally different conceptual way of life (from earlier hominids) that featured individuals living in communities of rules and contracts,

---

[20] This term was usefully adopted by Deacon (2010).

notions of personal identity clearly profiled, patterned obligations to one another constituting a social order, and myths, systems of beliefs, and rituals that rationalized the position of the group in the world. (Fabrega 2004, p. 25)

The effects that Fabrega describes are all certainly true of modern humanity, but they evolved slowly from smaller beginnings. What is important here is that once the symbolic niche had been entered, there was an inescapable progression toward this complex modern state of affairs. In the view advanced here, the route to complexity followed by symbolic communication was a balanced path between use in cooperation promoting the interests of the group and use by individuals in promoting their own interests. As soon as creatures started to exchange one-word conventionally-learned messages for cooperative purposes, a new niche had been established. Now it became important to be able to profit by the exchange of information in the group, and (as a cheater-policing mechanism) to be seen to be willing and able to contribute to the exchange of information. The group benefits, and within the group individuals are selected according to their ability to keep up with the ambient level of public communication. People who don't understand much of the ongoing discourse don't do well, as they can't profit by the information offered. And people who positively contribute useful and surprising information gain status. Any particular instance of the use of language is partly in conformity with group norms and meant to be helpful, and partly an idiosyncratic ploy in negotiating an individual's place in the group.[21] Increases in complexity could be used to the benefit both of the collectivity and of individuals. It is in this sense that the progression to complexity was inescapable. The benefits to individuals could be reaped not only in speech acts negotiating social position, but also in aiding thought, of which more below.

The term 'niche' is subject to theoretical discussion, which I will not address in detail here. Obviously ecological, or evolutionary, niches, are multidimensional. Humans share much of their niche with other animals, as we eat carbohydrates and proteins, drink water, and breathe air. By modern times, most humans also live in towns or cities and deal with complex machines. But, I hypothesize, before any such modern developments happened, the most important feature distinguishing pre-human hunter-gatherers from their close ape cousins was their occupation of the symbolic niche. The term 'symbolic niche' extends the niche concept beyond what it has been conventionally used for in biology. Non-human biology has scarcely been interested in symbols.

---

[21] This is related to the distinction that I made in *The Origins of Meaning* between 'communicative cooperation' and 'material cooperation' (pp. 270–1).

Niches have been conceived of in terms of physical habitat. 'Symbolic niche' is an appropriate concept to describe the uniquely human predicament, because the use of symbols by others around us affects our lives profoundly. A human living isolated in the wild, fending for himself with no contact with other humans, could only be said to occupy a symbolic niche to the extent that his thinking and problem-solving is enhanced by having inherited a capacity for language and having once learned a language. Symbol use by others would not impinge on such a character (assuming he had no reading material). And he wouldn't propagate his genes.

I am using 'symbolic' here in the narrow sense in which linguistic elements, such as words, are symbols. The term 'symbol' is often used, especially by archeologists, in a wider sense, embracing both language and such artefacts as personal ornamentation, cave paintings, carved figurines, and even obviously functional items such as well-crafted spearheads. Archeologists (e.g. Henshilwood and Dubreuil 2009) often like to infer a date for the emergence of language from dates of the earliest such artefacts. This is despite the accepted wisdom that language leaves no material fossils of itself that can be dug up. I am sceptical about the possibility of dating the onset of language from artefacts. See Case and Dibble (1987) and Dibble (1989) for some sensible discussion of this issue.

The idea of **niche construction** has rightly gained credence lately.[22] Previous evolutionary discussion focused on organisms' adaptation to constant environments. The different Galapagos islands in Darwin's account had longlasting ecological conditions to which the finches and tortoises had adapted over many thousands of years. The conditions on each island provided different ecological niches. The behaviour of the birds and reptiles didn't do anything to upset the basic conditions. For many animals, a constant relationship with their environment keeps both animals and environment in the same state, to a first approximation. It is clear, however, that animals change their environments. When they do this in such a way as to improve their own chance of success, this is called 'niche construction'. In the most interesting cases, this sets off a feedback loop, with exaggerated changes to the environment producing further biological adaptations in the animal species. As Bickerton (2009a, p. 103) puts it 'it's not just the species that makes the niche: it's the niche that also makes the species'. The classic case is of beavers building dams, which radically change the flow of water, making lakes. Humans have radically

---

[22] Key works on niche construction include Odling-Smee et al. (1996, 2003); Laland et al. (2000). There's a very lively introduction to the idea in Bickerton (2009a).

changed their environment, and can now thrive in places where our primate ancestors could not have survived. Niche construction is not, of course, the outcome of any deliberate plan by an enterprising individual or group. It just happens, and when it does, it is game-changing. The relaxation of constraints, I have suggested, allowed a drift to happen whereby meaningful calls became learned, by degrees. At this point, the most rudimentary seeds of the symbolic niche had been planted, changing a species' evolutionary trajectory as never before.

Now, the big question. What was the selective advantage of staying in this rudimentary symbolic niche, once we had strayed into it, and in time pushing its boundaries to the fantastic level that we have? A number of essentially practical suggestions have been made, and I do not think that any of them really explain why a system as rich as one with learned symbols was necessary for the task. Terry Deacon sums up the general problem well:

From the perspective of hindsight, almost everything looks as though it might be relevant for explaining the language adaptation. Looking for the adaptive benefits of language is like picking only one dessert in your favorite bakery; there are too many compelling options to choose from. What aspects of human social organizatiion and adaptation wouldn't benefit from the evolution of language? ...A plausible story could be woven from almost any of the myriad advantages that better communication could offer: organizing hunts, sharing food, communicating about distributed food sources, planning warfare and defense, passing on toolmaking skills, sharing important past experiences, establishing social bonds between individuals, manipulating potential sexual competitors or mates, caring for and training young, and on and on.

(Deacon 1997, p. 377)

By analogy, consider electric current. One might surmise that electric current became widespread in human artefacts because of its use for lighting, or for cooking, or for protective fencing, or for turning rotary machines, and so on. But these specific uses all depend on the primary, more 'abstract', property of an electric current, namely the efficient conduction of energy to specific targets. Communication using symbols, like electricity, is useful for a great range of practical purposes. I will briefly discuss a couple of the suggested specific selection pressures for the evolution of language, group bonding, and foraging.

Aiello and Dunbar (1993) argue that group size was the key factor.

The close relationship between encephalization and group size allows us to predict the point in hominid evolution at which groups became so large that language would have been necessary to maintain social cohesion. When this model is applied to the hominid fossil record, it suggests that the necessity for both large groups and (at least

rudimentary) language appeared early in the evolution of the genus *Homo* and began
to increase rapidly in the second half of the middle Pleistocene.

(Aiello and Dunbar 1993, p. 184)

One must of course beware of teleologic thinking. A need to maintain social
cohesion does not necessarily trigger an evolutionary change meeting that need.
In another possible evolutionary course of events, group sizes would have
settled at lower levels without language to maintain social cohesion. In fact
this is what happened in the evolution of all our primate cousins, who maintain adequate social cohesion with smaller groups than humans and without
language. Larger group size does not automatically produce language. The first
evolutionary rudiments of language permitted somewhat larger group size, and
there could have been a coevolutionary spiral after that. Such a coevolutionary
spiral would of course have also involved increases in other traits, including
shared intentionality (Tomasello et al. 2005) and a capacity for more abstract
thought and reasoning. Aiello and Dunbar don't consider these other traits;[23]
their conclusion is that 'language evolved as a form of bonding mechanism
in order to use social time more efficiently' (p. 184). The obvious and central
function of language to interact with others using utterances that describe the
world is something over and above what would be needed for social bonding
alone—unless we have a very extended notion of social bonding. One can
imagine instinctive mechanisms that do the task of identifying rivals or allies
over larger numbers than 150 (which is Dunbar's favourite size for human
groups, and bigger than any other primate group).

Bickerton (2009a) argues that pre-humans, uniquely, occupied a 'territorial
scavenging' niche. Actually, he writes in places that they constructed this
niche, and at other places they they merely moved into this niche. Territorial
scavenging is roaming a large territory in search of very large dead animals,
so big that you have to feast on them on the spot rather than trying to carry
them back to a home base. His argument that this was game-changing is that
it necessarily involved cooperation with non-kin for the first time. You need
more than just your family to defend a large carcass from hyenas. And for this
reason Bickerton identifies territorial scavenging as the crucial function that
stimulated adoption and extended use of protolanguage. I'm not convinced.[24]
Territorial scavenging may well have been done more efficiently with better
communication, but it was just one of the activities that pre-humans engaged
in. If this one activity was the sole trigger for better communication, evolution

---

[23] One searches their article in vain for any instances of the terms 'cooperation',
'thought', 'thinking', 'abstract(ion)', 'meaning', 'semantic', and even 'cognition'.

[24] And nor is Michael Arbib—see his reviews of *Adam's Tongue* (Arbib 2010, 2011).

could have, and would have, honed an instrument more finely tuned to this specific purpose, and the mechanism might have been more instinctual, like bee communication, only possibly a bit more detailed. Given that everyone has a shared interest in finding and eating the fallen beasts, it's not clear how much detailed communication would have been necessary. On the face of it, hunting a moving target, such as a colobus monkey, as chimpanzees do, would seem to be at least as difficult to coordinate as finding dead animals. Dead animals don't hide or run away. The argument that territorial scavenging involved non-kin is also speculative.

Why does Bickerton, or anyone else, need to identify a particular dedicated function for the first language, be it social bonding, or cooperative scavenging, or whatever? The great thing about learned symbolic communication is that it can be used for **anything**. Once we had entered the symbolic niche, words could be invented for anything the ancestors wanted to talk about—fire, sunrise, night, sex, food. Bickerton himself seems to acknowledge as much: 'the creation of protowords may have been enough, alone, in and of itself, to trigger the large variations in the long-term behavior of that system that would eventually give us full language, human cognition, and (almost) unlimited power over earth and all its other species' (Bickerton 2009a, p. 168). Bickerton is a late convert to the idea that symbolic behaviour, rather than syntax, was the key initial step in the evolution of language.

7.4.3 Metarepresentation and semantic ascent

No particular practical topic of communication is sufficient to explain the power of language. Indeed, we can use language to talk about shoes, ships, sealing wax, cabbages, and kings. Try, if you can, to imagine a communication system between intentional agents enabling discourse on any concrete topic (objects, events, situations), but on nothing other than these. Here is a letter from an autistic adult who was regularly helped and encouraged to write letters. Without such help and encouragement, he would not have written anything.

Dear Marion,
I fed the chickens this week. I collected the eggs. I helped to make a bonfire with branches. I have been to Sandpoint. I collected rubbish in the black bag. I went horse-riding on Tuesday. I went to tea with Bryan and Wayne and shopping and the aromatherapy. I ate chocolate cake.
Lots of love,
Joe   (Glastonbury 1996, p. 119)

Even this letter, no doubt due to the encouragement of Joe's carers, volunteers a lot of information, as if Joe knew the hearer was interested. But that probably credits autistic Joe with too much understanding of normal human communication. We can imagine that the first uses of public symbols were extremely matter-of-fact, no-nonsense, and only about the concrete practicalities of life. And at the earliest stages, it seems reasonable to assume that the users lacked our present depth of understanding of communication. Apes are capable of a very limited degree of mind-reading. In the wild they engage in tactical deception (Byrne 1995; Byrne and Corp 2004a), which implies some degree of understanding of the thoughts of the deceived animal. In the lab, chimps have been shown to discriminate between different intentions (fumbling versus teasing) of a human experimenter, again implying some mind-reading (Call et al. 2004).

The full power of language comes with an understanding (which can be tacit) of its symbolic nature. Communicative utterances themselves are real-world public observable events. Uttering *Lion!* causes sound waves to pass through the air, forming an auditory event-image in the mind of a hearer for a brief time. The hearer can hold this event in memory, can know who said it, and given enough Theory of Mind, can understand why it was said. Fulfilment of this last condition opens up a whole new universe. A capacity for metarepresentation, mentally representing the content of others' (or ones own) mental states **as** their mental states, is one facet of a Theory of Mind. If the chimpanzee who realizes that he is being teased goes through the same process as a human realizing that 'he's teasing me', then the chimp has a capacity for metarepresentation at first-order level.

Sperber (2000, p. 121), while acknowledging that modern well-developed capacities for language and metarepresentation have coevolved, asks 'Which came first: language, or metarepresentations?'. Such chicken-and-egg questions are a nice game, relying on the current conventional meanings of terms for the 'chicken' and the 'egg'. What is really being asked is 'Did everything that we would now recognize as a chicken hatch out of something that we would now recognize as an egg?'[25] So for Sperber's 'which came first?' question, we have to ask 'Did anything that we would now call metarepresentation precede everything that we would now call language, or vice-versa?' But everything evolves. Metarepresentation evolved out of something that was not metarepresentation, and language evolved out of something that we would not call

---

[25] In fact, put this way, the traditional dilemma has a clear answer. Eggs came first, because birds evolved from non-birds (reptiles) which laid what we are happy to call eggs, as I pointed out in my semantics textbook (Hurford and Heasley 1983).

language. On the metarepresentation side, Sperber distinguishes several degrees of metarepresentation. *Peter believes that Mary believes that these berries are edible* attributes first-order metarepresentation to Peter. *Peter believes that Mary intends that he should believe that these berries are edible* attributes second-order metarepresentation to Peter. And so on. The degrees can be nicely quantified because of the discrete linguistic structure of the examples —we can count subordinate clauses. It is an open question whether the mind works in this neat clockwork discrete language-like way. Peter may have a faint suspicion about what Mary intends, or he may half-believe something about her intentions. Does he have these propositional attitudes, suspecting and believing, or not? Well, yes and no. He 'sort of' suspects that she does, or as we might say, he 'is inclined to' suspect, or 'inclined to believe'. If he is inclined to suspect or to believe, does he suspect or believe, or not? A lawyer could make hay with questions like this. Just as modern humans have partial fuzzy higher degrees of metarepresentation, so our ancestors would also have had fuzzy partial lower degrees of metarepresentation. There was not a 'click' when the first clear case of metarepresentation happened. The first glimmerings of metarepresentation would have been vague, sporadic, and narrowly focused on particular content domains, such as sex and food. But I don't doubt that we have greater capacity than apes and early hominins.

The same kind of argument can be applied to the language end of the 'which came first?' question. Here a particular feature of modern language is crucial to Sperber's argument that metarepresentation came first. In modern language use, a speaker's meaning is underdetermined by the meaning of the sentence he uses. In almost every case, a hearer uses inference from context to figure out what the speaker means. Certainly, the words and grammatical structure do provide a clue, often a substantial clue, but in almost all cases pragmatic inference is necessary. Sperber contrasts this with a simple 'coding–decoding' system. If a spy's signal is encrypted in a code, we only need to know the code to get at the original signal. There is a mechanical procedure of translating symbols into other symbols, with no inference from context. A large part of Sperber's research programme emphasizes that language is not like this, and he is right. We use context and our assumptions about speakers' intentions all the time in interpreting what they say. This is the difference between interpreting and decoding. A paleontologist interprets fossils in the light of their context and his theories. By contrast, and in theory at least, a geneticist working with a DNA sequencing machine, decodes a DNA molecule into its sequence of nucleotide bases. Sperber argues:

If the ability to communicate linguistically had preceded the ability to use metarepresentations, then this pre-metarepresentational, ancestral verbal ability would have been radically different from the kind of verbal ability we modern humans use, which is metarepresentational through and through. The ancestral language would have been a coding–decoding affair, as are the many forms of non-human animal communication of which we know. This, in itself, is an unattractive speculation, since it implies a radical change in the mechanism of human linguistic communication at some point in its evolution. . . .

If our ancestors were such coders–decoders, and had no evolved disposition to metarepresent, then there is no sensible story of how the presence of utterances in their environment would have led them to discover their representational character, to metarepresent their content, and to use for this their own mental representations in a novel, opaque, manner. Out goes the language-first hypothesis.

(Sperber 2000, pp. 122–3)

Language as we know it evolved from non-language. It seems quite plausible that the early precursors of language were much more, perhaps almost entirely, coding–decoding in nature. The contexts in which signals were given would have been so limited and so stereotyped that little or no contextual inference would have been necessary. There are degrees of 'coding–decodingness'. Indeed there has been a radical change in evolution, but this change has taken place slowly over millions of years. We do not need to locate a point, as Sperber seems to think we must, in relatively recent, specifically human history.

I agree with Sperber that capacities for metarepresentation and language coevolved (even if I think we can't answer the 'which came first?' question as straightforwardly as he does). I interpret this coevolution as meaning that (1) there was advantage in greater metarepresentational capacity, and (2) more complex language enabled greater metarepresentational capacity. In other words, the driver was not linguistic complexity per se, but the advantage for expression and thought that such complexity could bring. Put like that, the matter is rather obvious. Being able to calculate your social moves by anticipating the attitudes of others to the further attitudes of yet others is advantageous. Machiavellian intelligence is adaptive (Byrne and Whiten 1988). The implication of the above is that we could not have reached higher degrees of metarepresentation without more complex language.

Along with this is the more general proposition that we use linguistic objects in our more complex thought. In other words, in complex cases, we are helped in thinking about things by thinking about the words or sentences that describe these things. Thinking about bits of language, or using language about bits of language is what Quine (1960, pp. 270–6) calls **semantic ascent**. Quine saw semantic ascent as a tool in philosophical discourse. He contrasts discussions of the existence of unicorns and wombats with discussions of the existence of points, miles, numbers, attributes, propositions, facts, or classes. These latter are abstractions, and Quine's point is that when we talk about these, we are essentially talking about words. Away from philosophical discourse, abstract terms like *mile* are undoubtedly useful, and language allows us to treat miles as if they were as real as wombats (just as it allows us to treat unicorns as if they were as real as wombats). In fact, we could not even entertain the (exact) concept of a mile unless it had been made available to us through language. True, talk of miles is cashed out in concrete terms, but the concept MILE is an abstraction that allows us to get a better handle on concrete experiences. In a book mostly devoted to arguing the case for the possibility of some thinking without words (and thus very much in line with my own claims about the origins of meaning), Bermúdez (2003, pp. 150–1) writes 'there is an important class of thoughts that is in principle unavailable to nonlinguistic creatures. . . . all thinking that involves intentional ascent (roughly, all thinking that involves thinking about thoughts) requires the capacity for semantic ascent (roughly, the capacity to think about words)'.[26]

Joyce (2006, p. 83) illustrates semantic ascent with a comparison between the English words *German* and *kraut*. The former is only denotative. People can be described as German if they satisfy certain criteria. It's a matter of fact whether someone is German or not. But it's not entirely a matter of fact whether someone should be described as a kraut, as this is derogatory. Knowing that a word is derogatory is knowledge about a word, a step up from knowledge about non-linguistic facts. Joyce argues that ethical concepts and the corresponding words are only achieved through the medium of language, involving semantic ascent. (He does not disagree with Frans de Waal who has argued that chimpanzees may have some of the basic building blocks of morality (de Waal 1996); but full human moral sense comes with language and semantic ascent.)

The externalization of linguistic expressions in physical (sensorimotor) form creates an object (a temporal event) which can be usefully recalled later. Tecumseh Fitch expresses well how this can work in day-to-day experience, stressing the hearer's sensorimotor representation of an utterance that has been put 'out there' in the world by a speaker.

The ability to retrieve the utterance (silently or out loud) along with its context, long after the communicative act is over, perhaps in concert with new information, provides a very important advantage in trying to make sense of others' minds. At the very

[26] Different cultures have different ways of expressing thought about thought or thought about words. The Pirahã don't use subordinate clauses to do it, for example. But Pirahã speakers can clearly think about words and sentences, as when they tell Everett that a particular expression is not the Pirahã way of saying things. And there is no indication that speakers of Riau Indonesian can't think about thoughts or talk about words.

least, the ability to encode part of a communicative event in the concrete realm of
sensorimotor memory aids the encoding and retrieval of the event. More generally, the
phonological and syntactic structure of the remembered utterance can act as a scaffold
for a slow but steady increase in the understanding of the intended meaning. Anchored
by the sensorimotor representation, the semantic and pragmatic interpretation process
can continue days or even years after the utterance itself has faded. ...

   Thus the coevolutionary relationship between quoting and theory of mind might
have long predated language in its fully modern form, and provides a plausible,
persistent selective force in the evolutionary path to language.   (Fitch 2004)

The availability of **public** tokens for private thoughts made it possible for
further private thoughts to achieve greater complexity. Andy Clark (1998, pp.
170–3) lists the ways. In the list below, I give Clark's headings, but abbreviate
and interpret his more substantial explanations of them. The six ways seem to
me to overlap somewhat at the edges, but nevertheless are centred around six
different foci.[27]

   (i) *Memory Augmentation* We leave notes for ourselves. Written notes substi-
        tute for long-term memory. I can't think of spoken examples that are not
        covered by Clark's item *(v)* below.

  (ii) *Environmental Simplification* We assign labels to expected bits of structure
        in the environment. For example, we expect a city to have a certain kind
        of centre, so we confidently use *city centre* in advance of any actual
        acquaintance of the centre of a new city. See also my earlier discussion
        in Chapter 2, sections 5 and 6.

 (iii) *Coordination and the Reduction of On-Line Deliberation* We use verbally
        expressed plans to coordinate action with others. And we use language in
        complex collaborative problem-solving.

  (iv) *Taming Path-Dependent Learning* Complex and abstract ideas, as in the-
        oretical physics, can only be approached in small steps, from far-away
        beginnings. The history of the culture's discovery of such abstract ideas
        is preserved in verbal traditions, used in pedagogy. Without language, no
        such intellectual odyssey would be transmissible, and the abstract ideas
        would not be attained.

   (v) *Attention and Resource Allocation* We verbally rehearse spoken directions
        ('left at the traffic lights') to help us remember what we have to do. An
        externalized phrase substitutes for medium-term memory, and allows us
        briefly to attend to other things, creating an external 'control loop'.

----

[27] Bermúdez (2003, p. 151) also lists these six ways of Clark's with his own abbreviations and interpretations and occasional rewording.

(vi) Data Manipulation and Representation 'Extended intellectual arguments and theses are almost always the product of brains acting in concert with multiple external resources. These resources enable us to pursue manipulations and juxtapositions of ideas and data which would quickly baffle the un-augmented brain'. Many people composing extended intellectual arguments do not know what they think until they have written something down, and then what they think develops as the text grows through a series of additions, deletions, cuttings, and pastings.

Bermúdez (2003) discusses these six ways of Clark's at some philosophical length. He points out that for the first four, the same function could also be achieved by non-linguistic means. For example, instead of leaving a note for oneself, one can leave an empty olive oil bottle near the door to remind oneself of the need for olive oil as one departs for the shops (Clark's own example). Nevertheless, it is clear that linguistic objects, words, and sentences, can be used for these purposes, and for humans, language may be the most frequently used tool. Bermúdez' point is that while public language is a powerful thought-enhancing technology, it is not the only conceivable tool for the purposes identified by Clark: 'all [Clark] really offers is an account of how, given that we have language, we are able to engage in second-order cognitive dynamics[28]— whereas what we need is an argument that second-order cognitive dynamics can only be undertaken by language-using creatures' (p. 158). Bermúdez focuses on thoughts with complex structure and argues, by a careful process of elimination, that specifically linguistic representations are the only possible means of achieving thoughts about such complex thoughts. The other vehicles of thought he eliminates as possible tools in thinking about thinking are the 'language of thought' in the classic Fodorian sense (Fodor 1975) and 'mental models' as theorized by Johnson-Laird (1983). In brief, the Fodorian language of thought is not accessible to consciousness, so not public. And mental models lack the articulated structure to make them good candidates for thoughtful inferences, which depend on the structure of the entities manipulated in the inferring process. 'By a process of elimination, therefore, we have reached the conclusion that...there can be no intentional ascent without semantic ascent. We think about thoughts through thinking about the sentences through which those thoughts might be expressed' (p. 164).

To relate this discussion to the topic of recursion, language about language, or thoughts about thoughts, are both kinds of **recycling**. They are not what

---

[28] Second-order cognitive dynamics seems to be what others call 'metacognition', a term that Bermúdez does not use.

syntacticians consider when discussing recursion, but they share an essential ingredient with recursion as linguists use the term. Recursion is forming a constituent of type X out of other (smaller) constituents of type X. Or in terms of parsing, recursion involves processing a constituent of type X while already engaged in processing a constituent of type X. To use language about language in a way involving full analysis of the object language is to be engaged in (imagined) language use while engaged in language use. So this kind of thinking is recursive in nature. If I (truthfully) say *John told me he was coming*, I have analysed John's words and made their content the object of a sentence of my own. On the contrary, if I (again truthfully) say *John said 'amäsägnalähu'*, without having a clue what *amäsägnalähu* means, I am not using language about language in the full sense of language as a pairing of meanings and forms. This latter example is no more second-order, or recursive, than *John coughed*. I claim that only humans think about thinking, beyond the vaguest inklings that apes may have about other minds. And only humans can converse about each other's thoughts. And I claim that this uniquely developed human trait derives from our (also unique) ability to embed constructions inside constructions, used in public discourse. In the Construction Grammar view of language, embedding constructions inside constructions occurs as soon as two words are put together in a sentence package. As I noted in Chapter 1, this is consistent with a view adopted by workers in the Minimalist school: 'if Pirahã really were a language whose fundamental rule is a nonrecursive variant of Merge, no sentence in Pirahã could contain more than two words' (Nevins et al. 2009a, p. 679).

7.5 Learning and innateness

Evolutionary talk of niches, as in the last section, generally supposes that species adapt to them biologically, through changes in their DNA. Yet the seeds of the symbolic niche, I argued, germinated in the fertile ground created by relaxation of functional constraints on the genome, permitting learned behaviour to replace strongly genetically channelled behaviour. This transition, from 'innate' to learned behaviour, is a general trend among the higher vertebrates. We might say that the symbolic niche is a special case of a more general class of niches, all of which could be labelled 'learning niches'. For fear of needlessly distorting the usefulness of the niche concept, I will not pursue this idea further. But the issue arises of the extent to which the use of symbols in the symbolic niche must be learned, rather than innately determined. Put another way, how does a balance between learned and genetically channelled behaviour come about, and what does that balance look like?

Could a system as complex as a modern language be entirely innate? In principle, yes. This would be a truly universal grammar. All vocabulary would be the same across the species, as would all constructions and rules for combining them. There would be no learning, but there might be maturation, with the system growing along identical lines across the species as individuals grow. In principle, such a system could be rich enough to express thought about thought, and have the properties of metarepresentation and semantic ascent identified in the previous section. In this case the users would also have an innate Theory of Mind capacity, also possibly maturing as the infant grows. As we know, language is not like that. Why not? I will sketch a tentative answer before moving on to the question of how a balance between innateness and learning can evolve.

Basically, the genome might not be big enough to represent a system as complex as a modern language in its entirety. The genome has a lot of other work to do, catering for the development of the whole body and its intricate mechanisms of control. Evolution strikes many balances. Why do living organisms age and eventually die of decrepitude, barring prior accidents? The genes do a brilliant job of body-building, from a single cell to a complex adult animal. If genes can do morphogenesis so well, why can't they perfect the repair mechanisms to keep us alive for ever, or at least for much longer? There are several answers. One is that if we lived for ever, we would compete with our descendants, some of whom would have mutant, better adapted genes. Sooner or later there would not be enough resources for us all, and the less well adapted would succomb to shortages before the better adapted. Evolution has found a balance in the typical life-span, between preserving a viable organism long enough for it to reproduce and letting it die to make room for possibly better adapted descendants. Why not let organisms live for ever and not reproduce, so there is no possible competition from better adapted descendants? Here the inevitability of accidents, predators, and diseases gives the answer. Even the best designed organism cannot be guaranteed against these, so death is inescapable. Reproduction is nature's way of providing life after death.

That may all seem a fanciful digression, but I think there is a rough analogy with the balance that nature strikes between innate instincts and learning. Environments are never 100 percent predictable. Given an organism of a certain complexity, and an environment of a certain predictability (less than 100 percent), it is adaptive to have a balance between strongly genetically fixed traits and more plastic traits, malleable by learning. Further, the size of the genome may be a relevant factor (as Robert Worden suggests—see below). It may be easier for evolution to reach a genome that builds a learning mechanism than one that specifies all the details of a complex language. In social species that construct social parts of their environments, many of those social aspects of the environment are not predictable on a time scale that biological evolution can readily respond to. So learning is the best solution. This tallies with the correlation between larger group sizes, more complex social arrangements and greater capacity for learning.

A strand of work in theoretical biology considers the amount of information that can be coded in a genome. This relates to the issue of how much of the genome really is 'junk', an issue still empirically unresolved. Early contributions to this strand include Kimura (1961) and Williams (1966). Maynard Smith (2000) is a methodological and somewhat philosophical overview. Information is measured in bits, as in Information Theory (Shannon and Weaver 1963). Kimura, for instance, argues that the amount of information in genomes increases cumulatively through natural selection. Williams disputes this—'no genetic information is accumulating in modern organisms' (Williams 1966, p. 37). Clash of the Titans! This work is highly theoretical and mathematical, and the premises from which arguments start tend to be up for grabs. Nevertheless it is clear that the information coded into a genome is finite, and in theory, if not in practice, measurable. The information coded into a genome cannot be less, and in fact surely is much more, than the amount of information it takes to specify the corresponding phenotype, putting aside the contribution of the environment.

Relevant to the evolution of language, Robert Worden (1995) theorizes about 'a speed limit for evolution' in terms of how many bits of information can have changed in the human genome compared to the chimpanzee genome. Worden estimates, not the size of the genome, but the amount of distinctive information in the phenotypes of humans and chimpanzees, based on the number of generations since divergence of the species. As you will see, the argument is highly theoretical:

Our antecedents and the antecedents of chimpanzees diverged some 5–7 Myr ago, so there have been of the order of 350 000 generations since the split. Suppose that the average number of children per couple is three, giving $\gamma = 1.5$. The practical limit on total GIP growth implies that our phenotype differs from that of chimps by at most $175\,000 \log_2 \gamma \cong 100\,000$ bits of GIP.   (Worden 1995, p. 147)

GIP is Worden's term for 'genetic information in the phenotype'. The term γ is the average offspring of each individual. I will not go into his justification for the use of $\log_2$. The overall argument is highly mathematical, invoking terms for such assumed factors as the number of independent 'subphenotypes', the proportion of animals that survive to adulthood, and so on. Brain design is a 'subphenotype', so only part of the genomic difference between chimpanzees and humans is reflected in brain design. From his calculation, Worden concludes 'The amount of extra design information in the human brain, compared to the chimpanzee brain, is less than 5 Kbytes. This is not enough to define a language faculty *ab initio*; so language must be built largely on cognitive faculties we share with chimps' (p. 138). In a personal communication, Worden says that 5 Kbytes is about as much information as is given on one normally printed sheet of A4 paper—not much is the implication. Of course, we don't know how many bits it would take to specify a complex UG of the type envisaged in the 1960s and 1970s. Worden's point is that there have not been enough generations since we diverged from the chimpanzees for a richly structured innate specification of the language faculty to evolve. Frankly, I can't tell how much credence to give to such calculations. Despite their mathematical sophistication, they have a back-of-the-envelope flavour, as they make so many simplifying assumptions and idealizations. But Worden takes the innateness argument seriously enough to try to figure out if the genes could have delivered a complex UG in the time available, which is surely a legitimate question to ask. His answer may be right. This work has not been followed up in the literature.

The question of how much the genome could possibly have adapted for human language is also taken up by Chater et al. (2009).[29] Their simulations do not involve niche construction, but model a situation where a language already exists in a community (how did it get there?), and initially this language is wholly or mostly learned. They simulate (in the idealized way of all such modelling) individuals who either learn a particular property of a language or else are innately disposed to 'know' the property without the need for learning. This information is coded into the genes of the simulated individuals. Individuals mate and reproduce according to their success in acquiring the language. And their genes can mutate, either in the direction of learning more properties of the language or in the direction of having more properties innately specified. When the language stays fixed, that is when there is no (simulated) historical language change, the genes in the population gradually evolve in the direction of having more properties of the language innately specified. This

[29] The design of this work is substantially based on earlier simulations, in particular by Hinton and Nowlan (1987) and to a lesser extent Briscoe (2000), whom they acknowledge. It also closely echoes other earlier work Turkel (2002); Yamauchi (2001, 2004) on the Baldwin Effect in the evolution of language.

result is entirely as expected, since there is a natural cost to learning; learners tend not to be so successful as individuals who don't need to learn because of already innately 'knowing' the relevant aspect of the environment, in this case a property of the language. This is simply a case of organisms tending to adapt to a fixed environment. Next, these authors ran simulations like the above, but in which the language of the community changed, as real languages do, and quite fast, certainly faster than genes can evolve. In this situation, again quite unsurprisingly, there was no shift toward innate specification of properties of the language, because the language changed too fast to be adapted to biologically. If the language, or any aspect of the environment, is a fast-moving target, biological evolution can't react fast enough.

What conclusions do Chater et al. draw? The paper summarized above is in line with a further paper by two of the same authors (Christiansen and Chater 2008). This 2008 paper makes many of the same arguments, 'Specifically, as the processes of language change are much more rapid than processes of genetic change, language constitutes a "moving target" both over time and across different human populations, and, hence, cannot provide a stable environment to which language genes could have adapted. We conclude that a biologically determined UG is not evolutionarily viable' (p. 489). This latter paper is titled 'Language as shaped by the brain'. Note the description of a one-way process, contrasted with Bickerton's aphorism quoted earlier: 'it's not just the species that makes the niche: it's the niche that also makes the species' (Bickerton 2009a, p. 103). In other words, there is coevolution from the beginning. Barrett et al. (2008, p. 511), in a commentary on Christiansen and Chater, pinpoint this flaw succinctly: 'It is a mistake to think either that language leaps fully formed upon the stage, and genes evolve to it, or that a genetic apparatus for language evolves, and then language sprouts from it. The process is likely to have been coevolutionary, all the way up'. Fitch (2008), in a more fiercely worded commentary, makes the same coevolutionary point.

Chater and Christiansen, if classified, would clearly belong in the function-alist camp that has argued against generative grammar since its inception. In many publications, together and individually, they attack the classic view of UG, as promoted by generative linguists, especially from the 1960s to the 1980s. Here they single out the specifically arbitrary features that languages may have, as opposed to their functional features. Arbitrary features include facts about the binding of reflexive pronouns and island constraints such as I have discussed in Chapter 4, section 8. Their argument about what innate features of language can evolve is directed at these arbitrary features. '[O]ver time, functional aspects of language might be expected to become genetically encoded across the entire population. But UG, according to Chomsky (e.g.

1980b, 1988), consists precisely of linguistic principles that appear highly abstract and arbitrary—that is, they have no functional significance' (p. 492). Chater and Christiansen's critique would have been well-aimed in a former era, but generative grammar, following Chomsky, has moved on, and its Minimalist version now claims that the innate language faculty consists only of the recursive Merge operation. This single principle captures what Chater and Christiansen call 'the compositional character of language', which they correctly say has 'great functional advantages' (p. 492).

So we can expect humans to be biologically adapted to constant functional properties of language. For me, the most salient evolved traits in the syntactic domain are a capacity for massive storage of both simple and more complex constructions, a capacity to combine these very freely and productively, and a capacity to process these combinations at great speed, in both production and perception. The symbolic niche gradually created by humans contained increasing numbers of constructions. Humans adapted by a gradual growth in the natural limits of their storage space for learned meaning–form pairings. They also gradually increased the level of abstractness of the constructions they could store, with increasing use of variables over syntactic categories and other constructions. The capacity to combine constructions probably started with small combinations of only two or three words (see the next chapter). These combinations and longer productions which were occasionally spontaneously produced became part of the niche, to which humans duly adapted by stretching their combinatorial capacities and the speed at which combinations could be processed.

The relationship that I envisage between learning and innateness is that innovations, such as new words, and larger and more abstract constructions, would have been first produced with some effort, not the facility with which they came to be used later. This facility arose in two related ways. In the lifetime of an individual, constant re-use of a new form leads to habituation, and an ability to process it faster and with less effort. In phylogeny, the common use of forms of slightly greater complexity than before would have led to selection pressure for forms of this greater complexity to be acquired more easily, and processed more easily. What is now innate is a capacity to acquire and use complex forms, up to a certain level constrained by our memory and processing limitations (the 'plus' of competence-plus). When forms of a certain complexity were first used way back in time, these forms at the frontier of advancing language evolution did not come so easily to their users and were learned and used with greater effort. Indeed this is still the case with very complex sentences. We get tangled up, trying to compose overlong complex sentences. Dor and Jablonka (2000) propose a theory of language evolution identical in

all significant respects to that outlined here. Rather than using the term 'coevolution', they write of 'culturally-driven genetic assimilation', an equally apt
expression.[30]

It is helpful here to compare modern first language acquisition with adult
second language acquisition. Children, up to just before puberty, are ace
language learners. And they do it without apparent conscious effort. It comes
naturally. Adults, by comparison, have to spend greater conscious effort. They
hardly ever get to be as proficient as children at the phonetic end of language—
they speak with a non-native accent. In syntax, adults typically still seldom
achieve native-like competence, except for a few outliers like Joseph Conrad
and Vladimir Nabokov. In struggling to master a new language, adolescents
and adults put a lot of thought into encoding and decoding. I remember at
the age of thirteen spending a couple of minutes figuring out where to put
the pronouns in the French sentence *Est-ce que vous voulez vous asseoir?*,
to offer a seat to a lady in a French bus. (After all my effort, she merely
replied politely *Merci, non.*) Adult learners of a new language speak haltingly,
with pauses, and conscious effort. A few shorter formulaic phrases come more
easily because of their frequency and usefulness. It would have been like this
at the frontiers of language evolution. Children observing the halting efforts
of adults manage to put similar sentences together faster and with much less
obvious effort. This is evident today in the transition from pidgins to creoles,
and in the growth of a totally new language like Nicaraguan Sign Language.
Anne Senghas shows a video of a deaf Nicaraguan boy, fluent in ISN, good-
naturedly mocking the efforts of an elder deaf relative to express herself in the
same idiom.

Both children and adults learn a language. The difference is that children
do it with far greater ease. The human genome has programmed the pre-
pubertal developmental trajectory with a great facility for learning masses
of form–meaning pairings and learning to combine them productively. After
that age, the facility declines. The evolution of the critical period for language
acquisition is a result of genes affecting development being tailored to cope
well with language at the crucial period in an individual's life. The social
environment in which humans evolved made it beneficial for children to learn

---

[30] The term 'genetic assimilation' was used by Waddington (1953) to describe a
process by which traits acquired during an individual's lifetime in response to various
shocks (heat, ether) could be made innate by a programme of selective breeding.
Waddington's work does not relate to a transition from learned behaviour to innate
behaviour, but there are interesting similarities between the effect he achieved and the
Baldwin Effect—see below.

the language of the group at the beginning of life, and certainly by puberty. In a self-contained group of hominins there was only the language of the group. There was no 'foreign' language around. Occasional contacts with other groups would have invoked wariness and suspicion. The codes of other groups may well have been held to ridicule, as a solidarity-promoting device. Even the Greeks derided speakers of other languages as barbarians, those who merely uttered *ba, ba.*

Hurford (1991a) gives a simulation of the biological evolution of a critical period for language acquisition. At the beginning of the simulation no individual has any language-learning capacity at all, at any period of life. Consistent with this, the group has no language at all, at the beginning of the simulation. Ability to learn a bit of language at a certain time in life is determined by genes, with one locus for each tenth of the lifespan. There is sporadic invention of little bits of language, and individuals, if they are genetically so endowed and at the right age for learning, according to their genes, can learn these scraps of language. There is random mutation in the genes determining how much language an individual can acquire at its particular stage in life—always provided that by then there is also enough ambient language around in the group to learn from. Individuals who acquire most language have proportionately more offspring. But of course, pre-pubertal individuals, those in the first two-tenths of the lifespan, are not in the mating competition. But when they pass puberty, they had better be ready if they want to beget children. Accordingly, what evolves in the simulation is a developmental profile in which language-learning capacity is switched on for the first two-tenths of the lifespan, and never gets significantly switched on for later ages. See Hurford (1991a) for details. The sporadic inventions of bits of language in this model are cultural innovations to which the genome adapts over time. This was an early model of gene-language coevolution. It was followed up by a somewhat more elaborate model, more explicitly focusing on gene—language coevolution, in Hurford and Kirby (1999). As with all simulations, these were proofs of concept, demonstrations that the logic of the ideas are consistent, making the necessary assumptions quite precise, and showing what follows from what, given the assumptions. Since the underlying assumptions may be false, such simulations do not necessarily prove what actually happened. See what you think—I believe the assumptions are a close enough approximation to reality to give credence to the general framework of gene-language coevolution that I have outlined.

The evolutionary transition from learned behaviours to corresponding genetically 'hardwired' behaviours goes under the general rubric of the

'Baldwin Effect'.[31] The idea of niche construction is orthogonal to the Baldwin Effect. Niche construction can happen without any involvement of learning. For example, some termite species have evolved to build huge termite towers, and they have adapted to living in the towers. No learning is involved; each termite reacts instinctively to its surroundings, resulting in the complex social structure of the community. But equally, niche construction can, as we have seen, involve learned behaviours. Complex cultural practices, handed on from one generation to the next by learning, are the best case of niche construction involving learning, with humans by far the most salient example. There can also be a Baldwin Effect, that is genetic assimilation of previously learned behaviours, without niche construction. This is the effect simulated by Chater et al., as discussed above. For the Baldwin Effect without niche construction, that is 'pure' genetic assimilation, to work the environment that it is adapted to must be stable for a long time. Thus this version of the Baldwin Effect is not applicable to the evolution of syntax, which was a case of a socially created niche continuously evolving in parallel with the evolving biological adaptation to it.

---

[31] The original idea was suggested by Baldwin (1896). The effect was only named much later by Simpson (1953), who was sceptical about it. Griffiths (2003) and Pigliucci and Murren (2003) give some history of the effect. For good explanations of various manifestations of the effect, see Mayley (1996) and Papineau (2005). Hinton and Nowlan (1987) give an ingenious and influential simulation of the effect.

CHAPTER 8

One Word, Two Words, . . .

8.1 Syntax evolved gradually

The title of this chapter gives the message. Syntax started by putting words together in the smallest ways, and then moved on to slightly bigger ways. It is reasonable to think of a 'one-word stage' followed by a 'two-word stage', the first manifestation of productive combination. After that the pace accelerated. Once the possibility of combination had been realized, it did not proceed in a neat arithmetical succession. So there is less sense in talking about a 'three-word stage', and little reason at all to talk of a 'four-word stage', as if these exact numbers played some formal role in the developing language capacities. As is evident from my concept of competence-plus (Chapters 1 and 3), the language capacity has been constrained throughout its evolution by quantitative limits on processing. Social norms also affect the typical lengths of sentences. In a community where people habitually speak in short sentences, children will grow up speaking in short sentences. The earliest members of our species (or later pre-*sapiens* members of our genus) would have had limited processing capacity, more limited than modern capacity. This would have constrained their sentences to a few words each, and their children would have tended to observe the same rough quantitative limits. Over hundreds of generations the capacity increased, by mechanisms discussed in the previous chapter.

The gradual continuity[1] view taken here contrasts with that typical of linguists close to Chomsky. For example, I do not agree with Berwick (1997,

---

[1] Saltationist views of evolution have been called 'evolution by jerks'; in reply the position of gradualists is called 'evolution by creeps'. I am a creep, not a jerk.

p. 248) that 'There is no possibility of an "intermediate" syntax between a non-combinatorial syntax and full natural language syntax—one either has Merge in all its generative glory, or one has effectively no combinatorial syntax at all, but rather whatever one sees in the case of agrammatic aphasics: alternative cognitive strategies for assigning thematic roles to word strings'. Note several conceptual problems here. Berwick uses the phrase 'non-combinatorial syntax', which is a contradiction; syntax is by definition combinatorial. Also, on one definition of 'combinatorial', it would be a tautology to say that there is no possibility of an intermediate kind of system between combinatorial systems and non-combinatorial 'systems'. In linguists' implicit use of the term, either something is combinatorial or it is not. But outside linguistics, mathematical approaches in quite diverse fields find the term 'semi-combinatorial' useful, for example in musical theory (Lewin 2007), metalogic (Hughes 2006), chemical physics (Temme 1993), and molecular biology (Mayrose et al. 2007). I make no claim to understand any of those references, but unless the term is opaque, 'semi-combinatorial' suggests that these fields have found some value in conceiving of degrees of combinatoriality. Back in linguistics, and doubtless using the term in a different way from these, it would be reasonable to see the various levels of the Formal Language Hierarchy as defining successive degrees of combinatoriality. First-order Markov languages require less combinatorial power than State Chain languages, which in turn require less combinatorial power than Phrase Structure languages. Indeed such a scale of combinatorial power motivated the experiments comparing tamarins with humans, discussed in Chapter 1, section 3.5 (Fitch and Hauser 2004). But there is another way of interpreting degrees of combinatoriality within a single rank of the Formal Language Hierarchy. For example, one may think of different Phrase Structure grammars, where some of them contain few rules and allow only fairly short sentences while others have lots of rules and permit very long, perhaps unboundedly long sentences.[2] These grammars could reasonably be said to exhibit different degrees of combinatoriality. And this idea is consistent with my idea of evolving UG+ and competence-plus, which have quantitative as well as qualitative information.

Again outside linguistics, there is a large literature on combinatorial complexity, based on the possibility of different degrees of combinatorial complexity. I am concerned with quantitatively expressed degrees of combinatoriality. A combinatorial system with an upper bound of N on the size of its productions or the length of its derivations has less combinatorial power than one of the

---

[2] I thank Geoff Sampson for this wording.

same type with an upper bound greater than N. In computer science, **bounded combinatorial** systems or procedures work within finite limits (e.g. Della Croce and Paschos 2008; Smania 2001). Dinneen (1995) explores a bounded combinatoriality of just this sort in a practical thesis on ways of computing families of graphs in graph theory. It is noteworthy that his concern is practical, to be implemented in a physical working system (a computer). Humans are physically real computing systems too. From an evolutionary point of view, it is sensible to hypothesize that humans have progressively evolved greater combinatorial powers. This is more plausible than a tale of an evolutionary jump, such as Berwick envisages, to the infinite products of 'Merge in all its generative glory'. Hence I envisage that the sentence-forming word-combining powers of humans started small, and evolved to be more extensive.

Among many others, Fauconnier and Turner (2008) also argue, at the beginning of their paper, against a gradualist view of the evolution of language, on the grounds that 'we can point to no simple languages, or even ones that are simpler than others'. But we can, as I have shown in some detail in Chapter 5. And later in the same paper, Fauconnier and Turner identify 'a continuous path of evolutionary change over a very long period as the cause of language, since that is how evolution almost always works'.

Bickerton's idea of protolanguage presupposes a clear distinction between the lexicon of a language and its syntactic system. Protolanguage reflects a hypothetical stage in language before 'syntax evolved'. In some publications (e.g. Bickerton 1998) it was proposed that syntax arrived by 'catastrophic evolution' in 'a single step from protolanguage'. In Chapter 4, section 7, I adopted more recent proposals in syntactic theory, generic Construction Grammar, according to which there is not a firm distinction between lexical items and grammatical constructions. What a modern language learner acquires is a set of constructions. Some of the acquired constructions have no internal morphosyntactic structure or variables in them—these are words. And some of the learned constructions are very general with many slots filled by variables– these are grammatical constructions in the traditional sense. There is a **syntax–lexicon continuum**. Given this continuum, the Bickertonian idea of protolanguage as a discrete stage with lexicon but no syntax loses its bite, and the possibility opens up of a more continuous, less catastrophic, account of language evolution. There was no phase-shift, like the boiling or freezing points of water, between stringing a few words together and more complex syntax. The protolanguage idea can still be useful as describing a stage in which all linguistic knowledge was in terms of specific lexical items, containing no variables at all, that is, there was no knowledge of constructions other than words. So in this hypothetical, yet plausible, stage of language evolution, there were no big constructions, only (proto-)words, with a specific phonological shape and a specific meaning (which could be simple or complex).

Generative approaches have tended to assume categorical boundaries between different types of system. This leads to an evolutionary problem. A categorically new type of system has to appear by an evolutionary leap, rather than evolving out of pre-existing systems by gradual steps. We see the mindset and the problem in some language acquisition studies, paralleling Bickerton's envisaged gap in language evolution between protolanguage and syntax. In the specific context of one-word utterances, Atkinson (1985) asked 'How linguistic is the one-word stage?' To me, this is a silly question. Words **are** linguistic objects. A language is a system of meaning–form mappings, with the simplest mappings involving just words. Atkinson paraphrases what he takes to be Chomsky's position:

... unless we have evidence pointing to the child having internalized the principles of X̄-theory, levels of D-structure, S-structure and logical form, Principles of Government, Binding, Bounding, etc., we withhold the label 'linguistic' from the child's representational system.   (Atkinson 1985, p. 297)

Atkinson quotes Chomsky in similar vein: 'It might be, for example, that the bulk of the work on child language acquisition, which is limited to very early stages, is not really studying language at all, in a serious sense of the term' (Chomsky 1980b, p. 264). 'Serious'?! It would be equally preposterous to say that biologists who study bacteria are not really studying life at all, 'in a serious sense of the term', or that study of the month-old human foetus is not really about human life at all,[3] 'in a serious sense of the term'. In this chapter, I will have no qualms about discussing the one-word stage in children as the ontogenetic beginnings of language, and speculating that there was a similar stage early in the phylogenetic beginnings of language. The one-word stage is not yet syntactic, of course, but that is another matter.

'Large-scale theories and approaches to child language acquisition are mainly characterized by the theory of linguistics that they assume as their foundation' (Tomasello 2006, p. 256). Many works on grammar acquisition have started with syntax as defined by linguists as their target. This is evident in the quotation from Atkinson above. It was more true in the 1970s and 1980s than it is now, and authors showed some discomfort in adapting

---

[3] How you stand on this issue should be a component of your position on abortion. Relatedly, if you believe in souls, this is like the issue of when 'the soul enters the body'. Any debate about whether 'language appears in the child' with the onset of specific landmarks in development would be more terminological than empirical.

to the linguist's frameworks. De Villiers and de Villiers (1978, pp. 115–16) devote a section to 'The Acquisition of Transformations' and go along with the view that 'prior to the age of 6 years, a transformational grammar is unnecessary to describe children's speech, but thereafter the child acquires productive transformational rules'. More recent examples of studies taking the linguist's theoretical constructs as defining the questions to be asked in language acquisition are 'Parameters in Acquisition' (Meisel 1995), 'Phrase Structure and Functional Categories' (Radford 1995) and 'Empty Categories and Complex Sentences' (de Villiers 1995). I think it is fair to say that all such studies, in grappling with the difficulties of reconciling actual child behaviour with the chosen theoretical abstraction, adopt one or more of the following strategies: (1) decide that the theoretical construct needs refinement or modification; (2) postulate discontinuities in development when control of various constructs 'come online' or 'mature'; or (3) postulate that despite appearances to the contrary, young children really do show evidence of the constructs from an early age. All these strategies are perfectly respectable, as long as they give rise in the longer term to convincing analyses. Over the years, there have also been many studies of acquisition which do not take linguists' constructs as defining the problem. But until recently any flow of information between theoretical syntax and language acquisition has been from the former to the latter. Theoretical syntacticians have not been influenced in their theorizing by detailed data from language acquisition. Of course, at a gross level, the theorists have stated that their goal is to explain language acquisition, but only conceived in the bare terms of systems acquiring competence on the basis of limited, and positive only, input. Almost all the theorists' attention has been focused on details of the adult's acquired state, and not on the day-by-day process whereby that state is achieved. Academic subjects don't change overnight, but Construction Grammar is a syntactic framework that is more guided by the detailed processes of acquisition than others have been (e.g. Clark and Kelly 2006). The flow of information and ideas has slowly begun to go in both directions, as it should. Tomasello (2006) gives an overview of the course of a child's grammar acquisition, couched in terms of acquiring constructions. It works. Watching children acquire syntax, it appears to happen one construction at a time, and each construction itself goes through increasing stages of productivity. I will re-quote Anderson's conclusion about syntactic theory conducted in isolation: 'We cannot assume that the tools we have are sufficient to support a science of the object we wish to study in linguistics' (Anderson 2008b, p. 75). Syntactic theory needs input from language acquisition, and, I suggest, from considerations of how languages and the capacity for language could possibly have evolved.

I would agree that the very first communicative noises made by babies are not words. At some later point it becomes reasonable to speak of the infant's utterances as words. This is the perennial dilemma of any study, including phylogenetic and ontogenetic studies, that traces a passage through time from non-X to X. At what date did the French language appear? Don't ask. Once there was no French, now there is French; in between, something evolved. Drawing an exact boundary is artificial, although demanded by the need to use discrete terms. The earliest infant behaviour is pre-verbal, later it is verbal, with recognizable words; in between, something develops. Here is where my basic assumptions differ from Atkinson's, who was writing over twenty years ago, and against a different theoretical linguistic background. The lexicon was peripheral to most linguistic theorizing. The real action was in syntax, as it was then conceived. The store of meaning–form mappings is now conceived by Construction Grammar as encompassing all of what was previously separated into lexicon and syntax. Some lexical entries are simple, some are more complex, with hierarchical structure and variables. So in my view, when you have words, you're already over the threshold and into language. The journey doesn't stop there of course.

I take language acquisition as the most promising guide to what happened in language evolution. This is a special case of following the old adage that ontogeny recapitulates phylogeny (Haeckel 1866). In the case of physical morphology of animals, there is a rough parallelism in many cases between phylogeny and ontogeny. The earliest organisms were single-celled, and modern complex animals start life as a single cell. Mammals evolved from fish, and a human foetus has gill-like arches. Examples like this don't prove the general principle, and there are counterexamples. There is no absolute necessity for the course of embryonic development to echo the evolution of a species, but it often does. In the case of learned behaviour, we have no precedents, no fossils of the sequences in which earlier animals learned. Some conclusions can be drawn from parallels between brain growth in the species and in infants. 'Limited recapitulation, however, does characterize human neural maturation. Specifically, the neocortical association areas are late to mature and have demonstrated the greatest phylogenetic expansion. This parallel provides a basis for attempts to unravel the evolution of language phylogeny by examining its ontogeny' (Gibson 1996, p. 407). Gibson's article is a thorough and balanced argument for limited inferences from ontogeny to phylogeny.

In the case of bodies of acquired knowledge, it can be argued that they have an inherent structure dictating the sequence in which they are acquired.[4] At a gross level, this kind of 'structural' recapitulationism is true. The simpler theorems of Euclidean geometry are a basis for proofs of more complex theorems. Words must be acquired before sentences can be assembled by putting words together. It is not clear, however, that there is a logical necessity for a learning system to master three-word sentences only after it has mastered some two-word sentences. There are a number of studies of artificial learning systems which conclude that gradually relaxing a limit on the complexity of input data facilitates, or even enables, learning of a whole complex system. Elman (1993) describes experiments which show that acquisition of a small but naturalistic context-free language is significantly facilitated by arranging the acquisition device (a recurrent neural net) in such a way that its 'working memory' is small at the outset of learning, and grows incrementally during the learning process.

The networks are trained to process complex sentences involving relative clauses, number agreement and several types of verb argument structure. Training fails in the case of networks which are fully formed and adultlike in their capacity. Training succeeds only when networks begin with limited working memory and gradually mature to the adult state. This result suggests that rather than being a limitation, developmental restrictions on resources may constitute a necessary prerequisite for mastering certain complex domains. Specifically, successful learning may depend on starting small.

(Elman 1993, p. 71)

In a similar vein, working with a different language-learning task and a different computational system, Goldowsky and Newport (1993) devised a programme that learned meaning–form mappings from input sequences of forms paired with unordered sets of meanings. This learning programme takes in meaning–form pairs, as extracted in all logically possible ways from the simulated utterances, and builds a table of their correspondences. Their general conclusion is

We have shown that a limitation on the ability to perceive or remember the full complexity of linguistic input, as seems to occur in young children, may have unexpected benefits for the learning of morphology. If the child begins acquisition with a very restricted input filter, it will obtain the optimally clean data for the smallest meaningful units in the language. Learning larger units will require a less restrictive filter, but as we mentioned earlier, for *any* structure in the language there is a filter that produces

---

[4] Herbert Spencer may have had this in mind, although the direction and force of his inference is not completely clear: 'If there be an order in which the human race has mastered its various kinds of knowledge, there will arise in every child an aptitude to acquire these kinds of knowledge in the same order' (Spencer 1861, p. 76).

optimal learning of that structure. If you start with very limited capabilities and then mature, you will have each size of filter in turn, and therefore have the chance to learn each structure in the language at the time appropriate for that structure—and you end up learning the entire language optimally.   (Goldowsky and Newport 1993, p. 134)

Because the evolution of language involved successive episodes of learning by each generation, the same logic applies to phylogeny as is shown by these studies applying to ontogeny. The same property in the structure of a complex system such as a language that makes it necessary to learn it incrementally from small beginnings also entails that it can only grow by successive acts of learning incrementally from small beginnings. Of course, no whole language system was in place for our ancestors to learn from, but the logic applicable to learning from given exemplars also applies to the evolutionary growth of a system by innovations that are to be learned by each generation. The innovations must make small increments to the complexity of the system.

We generally assume that modern apes are still fairly close in cognitive ability to our most recent common ancestor. Symbol-trained apes reach about the same level of performance in symbol-use as children just over two years of age. There is of course one absolutely crucial difference between language evolution and language development. Modern children and the trained apes have care-givers and/or peers to learn from. In evolution, our ancestors had to make it up for themselves—they had no models. This difference could account for the slowness of the evolutionary process. But it also introduces the possibility of exceptions to phylogeny/ontogeny parallelism. Here is an analogy. In the Indus-trial Revolution and its aftermath, trains were invented before aeroplanes. In Britain and the other early industrialized countries, trains historically preceded aeroplanes. Let's say this order of invention was necessary. But jump forward to the settlement of Alaska in the twentieth century, after planes had been invented. Now there are towns in Alaska accessible only by air, and not by train. Planes came first to these towns, and trains will never come. Because of learning (about flight), it was possible for the later development to leapfrog over a stage which had been necessary when the evolution was moved on by innovative invention, not by learning from examples. More tragically, modern hunter-gatherers who migrate into cities skip the intermediate agricultural stage in human evolution. One last example: arithmetic on paper or in the head preceded electronic calculators, but children nowadays resort to calculators, ignoring the paper or mental arithmetic stage. Culture and technology, passed on quickly by learning, allow people to skip straight to levels that historically took many generations to achieve by cumulative invention.

Here is a linguistic parallel. The child inventors of Nicaraguan Sign Language (Idioma de Señas de Nicaragua—ISN; see Chapter 5) are the closest we have to people who have created a new language from scratch, without learning it from any external source. We can compare their three- and four-word utterances with those of children acquiring language normally. One difference stands out. In normal language acquisition, children begin earlier to use grammatical morphemes and inflections. 'The process [of acquiring grammatical morphemes] begins early, as soon as the MLU[5] approaches 2.0' (Tager-Flusberg 2005, p. 165).

In this period ['Stage II', when the MLU is between 2 and 2.5], in Adam, Eve, and Sarah, a set of little words and inflections begins to appear: a few prepositions, especially *in* and *on*, an occasional article, an occasional copular *am*, *is* or *are*, the plural and possessive inflections on the noun, the progressive, past, and third person present indicative inflections on the verb. All these... begin to grow up between and upon the major construction blocks, the nouns and verbs, to which Stage I is largely limited. (Brown 1973, p. 249)

By contrast, three- and four-word utterances in the first cohort of ISN signers consisted only of content words. Examples are MAN PUSH WOMAN FALL (Senghas 2000, p. 698) and MAN CUP GIVE WOMAN RECEIVE (Senghas et al. 1997, p. 555). This is a difference in degree. Normal children do use 'telegraphic' all-content-word utterances, such as *man clean car* and *goat try eat lid* without grammatical markers. But ISN signers in the first stages did not invent any grammatical morphemes at all. Admittedly, this difference may be due to the difference in modality. Much of the work done in spoken languages by function words is done in sign languages by concurrent facial expression and whole body orientation.

So child language development in languages with grammatical morphemes and inflections cannot be taken as a completely reliable model for the original creation of languages. Children who use grammatical morphemes, even in short utterances, have learned them from older speakers. Children acquiring Riau Indonesian, as described in Chapter 5, section 5, would not use grammatical morphemes and inflections because the adult language has none, or very few. The original appearance of grammatical morphemes in the earliest languages seems likely to have come somewhat later than the first use of three- and four-word utterances by children acquiring European languages.

---

[5] MLU = mean length of utterance, typically counted in words, not morphemes.

Another likely difference between original language creation and modern language acquisition is in the emergence of idioms and stock phrases. Some modern young children pick up some complex expressions holistically. Learning strategies differ. Children labelled as adopting a 'Gestalt' or 'expressive' style use whole formulaic phrases at an early age.[6] Nelson (1981, p. 174) gives the following examples, collected from several other observers.

I don't know where it is
I'll get it
Is it go back? (Jonathan, 17–20 months, from Brannigan 1977, note 1)

Open the door
I like read Good Night Moon
Silly isn't it? (Minh, 14–19 months, from Peters 1977)

These examples were articulated fluently in one intonation contour, but not very distinctly, though it was apparently clear what adult expressions they had been modelled on. Clearly there is a difference between children learning by such a strategy and the earliest creators of languages, since the earliest creators had no such models to imitate.

The existence of different learning styles and strategies is a kind of polymorphism. As in biology, stable polymorphism can foster the maintenance of group-wide social structure, which would not survive without this polymorphism.[7] In our case, the socially maintained, and evolving, structure is a language itself. If a few elementary words are put together in one generation, and if this combination of words is frequent enough, learners with a holistic strategy in the next generation can learn the whole combination **as an elementary unit**. They presumably will have the same kind of redundant representation of this unit as was seen in Chapter 4 in the case of idioms. Idioms are indexed in mental storage both by their overall idiomatic meanings, and by the literal meanings of their individual parts. I will take up the idea of language growth by iterated learning across generations again in Chapter 9.

To recap this section, I have argued for a gradualist view of the evolution of syntax. A study of the ongoing creation of a new language, Al-Sayyid Bedouin Sign Language (see Chapter 5, section 8.2), backs this up. 'What can these findings tell us about the evolution of language? First, the existence of certain syntactic mechanisms and the lack of others suggest that language does not

---

[6] For more on individual differences in learning styles, see Stoke and Holden (1980); Bates et al. (1988); Lieven et al. (1992).
[7] Wilson (1975); Skyrms (2004).

appear all at once, but rather develops incrementally. Even syntax is not an "indecomposable bloc"; instead, it builds up over time' (Aronoff et al. 2008, p. 149). I have also pinned my colours to a recapitulationist view, assuming that, with the exceptions noted above, the evolution of language in our species took a similar course to what we see in the development of language in children today. The language acquisition literature is vast, and our focus here is, rather, on language evolution. I will not rehearse the consensus that has emerged in language acquisition studies about the general trajectory a child follows from around one year until a good grip of syntax has been acquired. Looked at in sufficient detail, the child's day-to-day development is gradual and continuous. It seems safe to assume that the trajectory of language evolving among early humans was very similar, but very much slower. The main issue in language evolution, as opposed to language development in modern children, is where the innovations came from. I will devote several later sections to the features in which language evolution probably did not follow the same course as modern child language acquisition.

We have good general descriptions of the stages that modern children go through in acquiring syntax. It takes a child about ten years. Let's say it would have taken our ancestors somewhere between 50,000 and 2 million years[8] to evolve from no capacity for learned symbols or syntax to the modern capacity. Therefore, applying recapitulation, one aspect of building an evolutionary story is to stretch the timescale of the modern developmental stages by a factor of between 200,000 and 5,000. We can imagine reconstructing periods of apparently slow language growth, like the child's first year, and some explosions, like the syntax explosion seen after about age two in modern children. If you film a bomb exploding in ultra-slow motion, it is seen to be a gradual process. In that light, stretched over perhaps two million years, or even as little as 50,000 years, and with exponential growth later in the period, the evolution of the modern syntactic capacity seems less amazing than many linguists over the past fifty years have taken it to be. (A minority of scholars who have argued that the development of syntax is a matter of cultural rather than biological evolution have naturally not been so amazed.) An apparently explosive efflorescence of languages is what one might expect, given the parallel evolution of complex cultures among humans. It is not hard to imagine a succession of small culturally produced innovations in a language accumulating over such a period, accompanied by some gradual growth in memory and processing speed, paralleling what we see in children (see Chapter 9).

---

[8] A big difference in numbers, but it doesn't matter. Both numbers are big enough for the argument here. These are lower and upper limits implied by external considerations.

8.2 One-word utterances express propositions

Scene-setting reminder: Recall from earlier chapters the discussion of the pack-aging of language into sentence-like units[9] (Chapter 3, section 4) and the idea of autonomous language (Chapter 5, section 9.1). The key points to bring forward here are that

1. the sentence-like packages express propositions—their meanings are partly about the world;
2. they also have illocutionary force, or interpersonal meaning. Propositional and illocutionary meaning are both carried by any typical utterance;
3. the interpretation of every utterance is partly a function of its context of use—much is left to pragmatic inference by a receiver.

Single words used by children and apes are not syntactically structured sen-tences. In this section I will argue that their semantics, their relation to a world that is commented on, is essentially the same as the semantics of sentences. Full sentences are more explicit, leaving less to pragmatic interpretation by a hearer, and they have grammatical structure in addition to the semantics that they convey. Single-word utterances, as all agree, have illocutionary force, just as whole-sentence utterances do. A child or an ape uses a one-word utterance to **do** something: for example, a single word may function as an imperative, demanding action. This is entirely compatible with the utterance also having propositional content, predicating **about** something. What is the point of an order if it is not about something, not necessarily only the addressee? Harms (2004) suggests that the best rough-and-ready translation for the vervet leopard alarm call is a conjunction of declarative *There's a leopard around* and imper-ative *Do something about it!* The problem in arguments about the meaning of vervet calls is that we are trying to translate from a simple system with three calls into a human language with a vast array of calls. In English, the single word *leopard*, considered as a noun in the lexicon, clearly does not mean the same thing as the whole compound sentence *There's a leopard around and do something about it!* Considered as a noun in the lexicon, the form *leopard* is an abstraction, stripped out of its possible contexts of use. But say the single word *Leopard!* in a real-life situation like that of a vervet, and what it conveys is 'There's a leopard around and do something about it'. If you didn't know this, you wouldn't last long. Vervets don't have the luxury that English speakers have of comparing sentence-like meanings with the theoretical denotations

---

[9] Or, more technically, clause-like units.

of words considered purely as lexical items. A child at the one-word stage who is frightened of dogs may say *Dog!*, intending 'There's a dog here, and do something about it!'. Indeed that's the kind of thing we intend when we (seriously) shout *Fire!* Utterance of a single word which happens to be a noun in adult language has both illocutionary force (e.g. imperative) and propositional content, predicating something of the current situation. Perhaps the first one-word utterances of our ancestors had mainly imperative force, like the majority of utterances of modern trained apes. But if they were like the one-word imperatives of modern children (which I assume), they also conveyed predicative meaning. Predicative meaning is involved whether or not the hearer is assumed already to know the applicability of the predicate to the object concerned. Thus the predicate CAT is involved both in the assertive *That is a cat*, giving new information about the thing pointed to, and in *That cat is hungry*, where the hearer is assumed to know that the thing being spoken about is a cat.[10]

Emphasizing the semantic and pragmatic similarities between single-word utterances and fully syntactic sentences/clauses shows a continuity of function. The passage from one-word utterances to syntactically structured sentences does not involve any significant functional break. One-word utterances convey the same kinds of meaning, referential/predicative and interpersonal/illocutionary as full sentences. But a one-word utterance, like a simple digging stick, is not a structured tool; by the same analogy, a full grammatical sentence is structured with parts joined together, like a hoe or a spade.[11] The functional continuity between one-word utterances and structured sentences, the fact that they convey the same kind of semantic and pragmatic meanings, does not entail that the structural relations within sentences are 'derived from' any structure that may be found in the meanings. The structural relations within sentences, for example the Subject–Predicate relation found in many languages, are used to convey meaning, but are not the meanings themselves. Following the digging-stick/hoe analogy, the two-part handle-plus-blade structure of the hoe is adaptive for digging, but is not the same structure as anything in the digging person or the soil that is being dug. Likewise, any grammatical Subject–Predicate relation between the words in a sentence is not the same thing as the private psychological semantic PREDICATE(*argument*) structure that it may publicly express. The medium is not the message; nor is

---

[10] It must be clear that since this section is about one-word utterances, the term 'predicate' is used in its semantic (Fregean) sense, and not in any grammatical sense. Some animals, I argued in *The Origins of Meaning*, think in PREDICATE(*argument*) terms, though they have no language.

[11] This only an analogy, not implying that grammar 'derives from' tool construction, a case that needs more careful consideration and is certainly not wholly right.

the signal the message. If the signal were the message, there wouldn't actually be any distinction between signal and message. But there is a distinction, and this is a *reductio ad absurdum* of the proposition that the signal is the message. Of course, since the signal expresses the message, there is some systematic relationship between elements of a public signal and elements of a privately conceived and interpreted message. As languages get more complex, this relationship becomes less direct. For example, as discussed earlier, in English there is not a perfect correspondence between the syntactic category of Noun and the class of physical objects. At one-word and two-word stages there is little, if any, divergence between semantic categories and grammatical categories. In a useful and insightful approach Greenfield and Smith (1976, pp. 16–17) write 'a semantic approach to language which derives grammar from relations among perceived aspects of the real world opens the way to a theoretical treatment of one-word speech as structurally continuous with later grammatical development'. But I must sound a note of caution. For more complex language this straightforward view that grammar derived from semantics will not hold. Yes, there is functional (semantic and pragmatic) continuity, but the very fact of going from one word to two, packaged into a communicative unit, introduces the possibility of a new kind of structure, syntactic structure. At first, for example at a two-word stage, any divergence between syntax and semantics may be absent, but for longer sentences the existence of a conventional structure brings with it categories for the planning of behaviour that are not solely rooted in semantics or pragmatics, for example grammatical markers of various kinds. You may find objects and actions out there in the world, but you won't find conjugations of verbs or declensions of nouns, for example.

Language beginners of all sorts, babies and trained apes, start with one-unit signals, and it seems most likely that there was a stage in which remote human ancestors also used one-unit signals, before a stage in which they began to concatenate them. This is not quite a conceptual necessity; one can logically conceive of the first utterances being already multi-parted. But beginning with one-unit signals is surely conceptually by far the most plausible course of events. 'This principle is simple to the point of being trivial; one cannot erect the superstructure without having provided the foundation' (Jakobson 1941, p. 93).

Some single-unit utterances would have had the same function as primate calls, used for dyadic interaction between animals, for example as threats, submission signals, and courtship signals. In early child language too, some one-word utterances have 'performative' significance only, like *Bye!*, a conventional leave-taking. Such utterances had no content referring in any way to objects or situations beyond the sender and receiver. But this is not an intrinsic limitation of one-unit signals. Such simple signals can also be used to pass comment about things in the world other than the speaker or hearer, as I will now show.

In *The Origins of Meaning*, the discussion of propositions was mainly in the context of immediate perceptual experiences, like what happens in the brain of a baboon at the moment it attends to a crouching lion. I hypothesized a convenient representation of such an experience as $\boxed{\begin{array}{c}\text{LION}\\\text{CROUCH}\end{array}}$. I will briefly recap the essential idea from that book. The proposal there was about mental representations that are **pre**-linguistic, that is the labels used in such diagrams do not correspond (yet) to public signals shared by an animal's social group. These are private representations, individually acquired, but because animals in a social group share most of their genes and most of their basic experiences, the representations are likely to be of categories of experience that are very similar from one animal to the next. The use of suspiciously English-like labels in my notation does not imply, of course, that English speakers' ways of carving up experience are in any way privileged. I just need to convey some representation of the bundles of categories in an animal's mind when it experiences an object or event. For the moment, we'll stay with the simple case of an animal contemplating a single object. The processes involved are all no doubt unconscious, but something happens in an animal brain when it encounters an object and has to decide how to respond to it. It may sniff the object, or turn it over with its paw, or suddenly draw back from it only to re-approach it cautiously. All the time, impressions about the properties of the object are being formed in the animal's mind, some more saliently than others, mostly depending on their relevance to the animal's well-being. Each fleeting impression is the result of long-term potentials established in the animal's brain. Several impressions can be formed at once. So I envisage bundles of categories, or predicates, as I have identified them, like these three objects illustrated below.

$$\boxed{\begin{array}{l}\text{CONSPECIFIC}\\\text{MALE}\\\text{DOMINANT-TO-ME}\end{array}} \qquad \boxed{\begin{array}{l}\text{APPLE}\\\text{RED}\\\text{TASTY}\end{array}} \qquad \boxed{\begin{array}{l}\text{FINGER}\\\text{BLEEDING}\\\text{PAINFUL}\end{array}}$$

I emphasize that this is not thought-in-language. In a child near the end of the first year of life, the mental categories may already have begun to be shaped socially, but this is so far just a matter of re-adjusting the boundaries of categories already developed largely free of social input. The bundles of predicates above could also figure in the experience of a pre-linguistic child. In particular, note that there is absolutely no grammatical Subject–Predicate structure in these bundles. The predicates present to an animal's or a child's mind when pondering an object may differ in salience or urgency, but that is the only difference among them. We'll consider now what may happen when children want to communicate their experience of some object, and will assume that some very similar process took place when the first proto-humans likewise felt the urge to communicate some experience of an object.

Some human utterances are reports of present experience. Young children sometimes can't suppress a running commentary on events they are watching. I find myself doing it when talking to myself—say I unexpectedly find a door locked, I might mutter 'Hmm, locked'. Or I might notice that some women a block away have unexpectedly started running, and mutter 'Huh, running (I wonder why)'. We do it too when describing immediate experiences not available to our interlocutors, because the experience is not in a public sensory modality; thus, on my first taste of a curry one evening, I might say to my friend 'Hot!'. And in moments of communal phatic experience-sharing, we also do it, as when exclaiming about the beauty of a view or the dampness of the weather, or noting that the cat we are stroking is purring. These examples all involve some degree of intimacy between speaker and hearer (the ultimate intimacy in the case of talking to oneself!). Less intimately, and more artificially, radio sports commentators (a dying breed) and subjects in some psychological experiments ('Tell me what you see') also describe their immediate experiences.

So in modern human language, there is a place for reports of immediate experience, especially in social contexts where some kind of sharing of the experience is appropriate. 'Hmm, locked', 'Hot!', 'Beautiful!', 'Driech!',[12] 'He's purring'. Note that a typical form for such utterances omits any grammatical Subject term identifying what the utterance is about, such as the door I just found locked, the curry we are having, the view we have just come across, the weather we are both enduring, or the cat. When a Subject term is used, for grammatical form's sake, it is a pronoun, with little or no descriptive content. In cases such as these, it is possible to envisage a direct translation from the proposed non-linguistic mental representation. The procedure is: just say the 'word' associated with one of the prelinguistic predicates applying to the object in question, choosing this predicate from among the several available as being the one most likely to interest the hearer; don't bother saying anything identifying the object in question, as the context of the utterance makes it likely that the hearer is also attending to just this object. So internal mental representations get externalized publicly like this:

---

[12] *Driech* is a great Scottish word describing an all-too-common kind of Scottish weather. Pronounce it to rhyme roughly with *reek* but with a good long hissing voiceless fricative at the end. You can guess what it means. The spelling is variable with *dreich*.

WOMEN RUN	→	'Run'	or	→	'Women'
HOT CURRY SPICY	→	'Hot!'	or	→	'Spicy'
CAT TABBY PURR	→	'He's purring'	or	→	'a tabby'
DRIECH COLD DARK	→	'Driech!'	or	→	'Cold!'

(In the last example, there is no particular object that the judgements are about; rather, the judgements are just about the whole immediate ambient environment. Weather terms, like *snowing*, *raining*, *windy*, and *sunny*, have no logical subject; they express logically zero-place predicates.) In a study of children's one-word utterances, Greenfield (1979) finds support for the hypothesis that 'What, from the child's point of view, can be assumed is not stated, what cannot be assumed or taken for granted is given verbal expression by the single word' (p. 160). It seems entirely natural that this was also the case for the first of our ancestors who used single word expressions to convey information about the states of affairs or events around them.

A lot is taken for granted here, most prominently answers to the following questions. (1) Why should a creature feel motivated to share its experiences anyway? (2) How did 'words' get associated with the prelinguistic concepts? I have addressed the first question in Chapters 8 and 9 of *The Origins of Meaning*, under the headings 'Why communicate?' and 'Cooperation, Fair Play, and Trust'. The second question was addressed in Chapter 2 of this book, 'First Shared Lexicon'. We move on, regardless. Note that the proposed format for pre-linguistic propositions, in the PREDICATE form, is very easy to translate into simple public utterances. All you do is say the word associated with the salient feature or category of the thing you are attending to. You don't say anything corresponding to the box, or what Pylyshyn (2000, p. 206) calls the 'visual objects or proto-objects' identified (in the case of seen objects) by your dorsal stream.

Such examples are very familiar, of course, from classic observations by Vygotsky:

Now let us imagine that several people are waiting for a bus. No one will say, on seeing the bus approach, 'The bus for which we are waiting is coming.' The sentence is likely to be an abbreviated 'Coming,' or some such expression, because the subject is plain from the situation.   (Vygotsky 1986, p. 236)

[We] found that as egocentric speech develops it shows a tendency toward an altogether specific form of abbreviation, namely: omitting the subject of a sentence and all words connected with it, while preserving the predicate. This tendency toward predication appears in all our experiments with such regularity that we must assume it to be the basic syntactic form of inner speech.   (Vygotsky 1986, p. 236)

Predication is the natural form of inner speech; psychologically, it consists of predicates only. It is as much a law of inner speech to omit subjects as it is a law of written speech to contain both subjects and predicates.[13]   (Vygotsky 1986, p. 343)

Inner speech is almost entirely predicative because the situation, the subject of thought, is always known to the thinker.   (Vygotsky 1986, p. 182)

It is good that Vygotsky gives prominence to these examples of bare-predicate utterances, and I share his analysis of the motivation for them ('the subject of thought is always known to the speaker'). But I disagree with his account of the origin of this bare-predicate form, and favour a different explanation (as may already be plain to those who have read *The Origins of Meaning*). For Vygotsky, keen to emphasize the essentially social origins of language, inner speech is public speech gone underground. First in his view, apparently, come public whole Subject–Predicate sentences; in the process of these becoming the vehicles of inner thought, they lose their Subjects, while still being publicly (sometimes) uttered; the last stage, silent inner speech (i.e. thought) is taken to be of pure Predicate-only form. 'In the beginning, egocentric speech is identical in structure with social speech, but in the process of its transformation into inner speech, it gradually becomes less complete and coherent as it becomes governed by an almost entirely predicative syntax' (Vygotsky 1986, pp. 243–4). Metaphorically, imagine a sea-creature with a tail in full view basking on the surface; then it dives below the surface, away from view, and as it dives, sheds its tail, so that for a moment we see it without its tail before it disappears below the waves forever. It is a fair inference that, down below, it lives on without its tail. Vygotsky's idea is that things start in the social, public realm with whole Subject–Predicate statements, and that these live on in the private world without their Subjects.

    Vygotsky, despite his dates, belonged to the pre-Fregean Aristotelean tradition which held that the complete form of meaning conforms to the gram-

----

[13] Here Vygotsky is quite Eurocentric. It is not a 'law of written speech' in all languages to contain both subjects and predicates. In some cultures (e.g. Classical Chinese) writing style can be more elliptical.

matical Subject–Predicate partition, a tradition with which, following Frege, I have disagreed. The artificiality of the Subject–Predicate partition has been commented on by many. Here, for example, is Nietzsche:

[T]he seduction of language (and the fundamental errors of reason petrified in it), which understands and misunderstands all action as conditioned by something which causes actions, by a 'Subject.'
...people separate lightning from its flash and take the latter as an action, as the effect of a subject, which is called lightning,...People basically duplicate the event: when they see lightning, well, that is an action of an action: they set up the same event first as the cause and then again as its effect.   (Nietzsche 1887, XIII)

Descartes has been extensively criticized for the same kind of error in his 'Je pense donc je suis', inferring a thinking subject from the activity of thinking (Descartes 1637; Kierkegaard 1985; Williams 1978). Language evolution's own Derek Bickerton expresses the same idea: 'The subject–predicate distinction in language is so fundamental, and so much taken for granted, that it is perhaps worth emphasizing that it corresponds to nothing in nature' (Bickerton 1990, p. 39). It is essential here to distinguish between the PRED-ICATE(*argument*) structure of private thought and the Subject–Predicate structure of public grammatical utterances. They are not the same thing, although they are related. The linguistic Subject–Predicate partition, I will argue later, comes not from thought, but from communication. But in this section, we are only dealing with single-unit utterances, like 'Hot!' or 'Purring', so that the issue of any Subject–Predicate partition does not arise.

Many aspects of Vygotsky's social approach to language are valuable, but his account of the origins of bare-predicate form of egocentric speech has several flaws. In the first place, not only is the subject of thought always known to the thinker, but so, obviously, is the predicate. So why not drop the predicate? In my PREDICATE account, the predicate part of the semantic representation is the only part which has any permanent semantic content, relating systematically to some class of things in the world, whereas the 'Subject' part of the representation, the box itself (corresponding to a variable such as x in a traditional logical form) only has temporary, deictic reference, and no permanent semantic content. So it is not surprising to find predicate-only utterances. Vygotsky also implies an observed change in child speech, from public full Subject–Predicate utterances to predicate-only utterances. That is, a 'progression' is implied from two-part utterances to simpler holophrastic or 'one-word' utterances. But of course the normal course of development is in the other direction, starting with holophrastic utterances and progressing to two-part utterances. It would be easier to assume that the very first holophrastic utterances are purely predicative, reflecting Vygotsky's own view that 'inner

speech is almost entirely predicative'. We agree on the Subject-less nature
of 'inner speech', which I equate with thought; but we differ on its origins.
Vygotsky, with his Soviet background, wished to argue for the social formation
of human thought.[14] I agree that **some** human thought is socially formed, but
not its basic PREDICATE(x) form (here re-notated as $\boxed{\text{PREDICATE}}$), which has
far more ancient roots in preattentional and attentional mechanisms common
to many mammals, as argued in detail in Hurford (2003). Vygotsky also did
not have the benefit of modern research into animal mental categorization
capabilities.[15]

One-word utterances can express predicates, that is properties of objects,
situations, or events. On any given occasion, a suitably minded hearer can
extrapolate a whole proposition from what is expressed in a one-word utterance, using shared background information and clues from context. When a
toddler says 'Daddy', this may be taken (as intended) to convey that Daddy
has just driven up outside the house, or that the object the child is attending to
is Daddy's, or that the child wants help from Daddy, and so on. What all these
meanings have in common is **something to do with Daddy**. When the child
wants his Mummy, he does not call 'Daddy'.[16] Human hearers are disposed to
take one-word utterances and construct pragmatically motivated propositions
based on the predicate expressed by the utterance. And human speakers are
disposed to take advantage of a hearer's powers of interpretation. Children
start with one-word utterances as their first simple attempts at joining in the
language game. In emergencies and time-constrained situations, adults resort
to one-word utterances with the same kind of effect. Obvious examples are
'scalpel', 'forceps', used by a surgeon, 'Gas!' on smelling gas in the house,
'lights' used by a film director, or 'Ready?' just before some planned joint
action. Part of the speaker's intention, and the hearer's interpretation, is the
pragmatic force of the utterance, that is whether it is to be taken as a request
(as with 'scalpel' and 'lights') or as a statement (as with 'Gas!') or as a query
(as with 'Ready?'). One-word utterances are also naturally used as vocatives,
just specifying the person addressed and commanding her attention, for example 'Mummy!' Thus, one-word utterances are semantically and pragmatically
versatile. A one-word utterance partitions the world into a set of possible
situations which can plausibly be connected with the conventional meaning
of the word uttered, distinguished from the much larger set of other possible

[14] Even so, the Soviet authorities pronounced Vygotsky's work 'eclectic' and 'erroneous' (Kozulin 1986, p. xliii).

[15] Disagreeing with Vygotsky does not, of course, make me a Piagetian. I certainly
don't hold with Piaget's (1973, p. 51) contention: 'The First Stage: Thought is with the
Mouth'.

[16] Unless, like some kids, he has a single word for both parents at this stage.

situations. There is no reason to suppose that the first one-word utterances used by early humans were any less versatile than this. It is plausible that they were multi-purpose. The hearers could be relied on to interpret them appropriately in the situation.

Symbol-trained apes use one-sign utterances in a variety of meanings, depending on the situational context. 'One-word sentences are the same way—their meanings vary considerably from one instance to the next. Kanzi and Pan-banisha often come up with a completely new meaning for a well-worn word, simply as a function of how they use it' (Savage-Rumbaugh 1999, pp. 139–40). Of course the 'new meanings' are not random, but novel applications of a lexigram to a referent or situation related in some way to the meanings for which it had been used before. This is just like human versatile use of one-word utterances (and I do not believe that Savage-Rumbaugh is over-interpreting the apes' behaviour in this instance).

I have argued that single-unit utterances could (and still can) express the predicating component of propositions, given suitable pragmatic inference. The meanings expressed were (and are) not necessarily the simplest concepts we can imagine. Some meanings expressed by single words are complex, in that they bring with them impressions that can also be expressed by other single-unit utterances. For example, the idea expressed by the English word *dinner* entails the idea of FOOD and (for many people) a certain rough time of day, a degree of communality, and perhaps formality. Assuming original single-unit utterances does not commit one to their meanings being in any way primitive or atomic in the minds of their individual users. But the use of single units in communication establishes their meanings as the basic units in the currency of communication within the social group.

Givón (1979a) postulates three evolutionary stages of language:

> 'monopropositional' > 'pragmatic mode' > 'syntactic mode'.

The earliest hominin descendants of apes, he speculates, would have used 'monopropositional' single-unit utterances, not strung together. Independently, I concur with Givón that single-unit utterances can express propositions, even though they don't have overt Subject–Predicate form. The stage I have argued for here is Givón's 'monopropositional' stage. In the next section I will describe something close to Givón's 'pragmatic' stage, also a natural progression.

8.3 Shades of protolanguage

The term 'protolanguage' was used by Hewes (1973) and perhaps by others before him to describe a primitive pre-modern stage in the evolution of language. The idea behind the term has been considerably fleshed out by Derek Bickerton (1990, 1995) describing a hypothetical stage in the evolution of human language, with lexical items ('words') that could be strung together but without syntactic organization. Protolanguage is envisaged as a discrete intermediate stage between no language at all and full human language. Especially in his earlier work on language evolution (e.g. Bickerton 1998), Bickerton envisaged a catastrophic change from protolanguage to full language with syntax. I will argue for a more gradualist view. Conceived as a syntaxless stage in language evolution, protolanguage has been a fruitful focus for discussion. It has mostly been accepted as a reasonable, even necessary, stage. It is simply characterized as a stage when there was a lexicon but no syntax. In a protolanguage, the 'words' could be uttered in sequence, but not in any regular order, and with no markers of grammatical structure. Bickerton's conception is of protolanguage as a general class of simple communication systems, separate from 'protolanguages', particular systems used by particular populations. Protolanguage is not hypothesized as a single communication system used by any particular group. Protolanguage is a **type**, defined as having single meaningful units but no systematic way of organizing them into longer signals expressing complex messages. If indeed *Homo erectus* had protolanguage, different geographically separated tribes would have had different protolanguages, probably mutually unintelligible. Protolanguage is beyond the capacities of wild animals, and producing it is just within the reach of captive, home-reared apes. We have no way of knowing for how long protolanguage existed as a long stable equilibrium stage. The creatures that (may have) used protolanguages would have been able to string lexical items together in pragmatically guided short sequences.

As Bickerton points out, even nowadays we can see parallels with this hypothetical protolanguage type in the language of human toddlers (e.g. *Mommy sock, red me eat*), the attempts at English of Genie, a girl deprived of language until she was thirteen years old (e.g. *applesauce buy store*[17]), and the utterances of a language-trained chimpanzee, Nim (e.g. *hug Nim hug*[18]). The utterances of severely affected agrammatic aphasics can also look like protolanguage, for example ... *Hahnemann Hospital ... uh, uh, I ... uh uh wife, Rosa ... uh ... take ... uh ... love ... ladies ... uh Ocean uh Hospital and transfer Hahnemann Hospital ambulance.*[19]

---

[17] Curtiss (1977).
[18] Terrace (1979).
[19] Menn (1990, p. 165).

So that's the simple protolanguage idea. Now I'm going to modify it, to depict it not as a discrete uniform stage, but as having the possibility within it of gradual continuous growth towards syntactic organization. I argued in section 8.1 that, assuming a framework of Construction Grammar, the distinction between lexicon and syntax dissolves, and with it the idea of a discrete stage 'between' lexicon and syntax. At a broad level the protolanguage concept is still useful. But within the set of examples typically lumped together as protolanguage, there are differences in degree of organization, so that even within a 'protolanguage stage' some gradual growth along a continuum can be hypothesized. One should actually make a distinction between human productions like *red me eat* and *applesauce buy store* and Nim's productions such as *hug Nim hug*. The former may be protosentences, while the latter is just a string of words. Further, one should not classify all productions by trained apes homogeneously as 'protolanguage'. Some ape utterances, for example Kanzi's, are closer to sentencehood than some others, for example Nim's, as I will argue in a later section.[20] Pushing a view of gradual and continuous evolution, in line with the adoption of Construction Grammar as most appropriate for modern language, I do not envisage a discrete evolutionary jump between no-syntax and syntax.[21]

The crudest form of sequential stringing together of words is dictated by a principle such as 'Say first what is most urgent to convey, then what is next uppermost in your mind, and so on'. Such an ordering of symbols is seen in a sequence of lexigrams used by Panzee, a chimpanzee, to direct a human to the location of some hidden kiwi fruit. While pointing, she signalled *hide, stick, hide, stick, stick, stick, hide, kiwi, kiwi* (Menzel 2005, p. 203). The first objective was to tell the human that something was hidden, hence *hide*; the second objective was to get the human to use a stick to poke about for the hidden object; then as the human homed in on the target, she told him what it was—kiwi fruit. There is no reason to think of Panzee's utterance as anything more than a disjointed monologue, perhaps guided along by the sequence of events she was responding to. The many repetitions are not like anything systematically seen in human sentences. Such repetitions are also characteristic of many of Nim's productions. If we delete the repetitions, getting just *hide stick kiwi*, it is not easy to relate this to a single coherent event. True, a kiwi had been hidden, but the stick was not part of the hiding

---

[20] Kanzi is a bonobo or pygmy chimpanzee (*Pan paniscus*); Nim, now dead, was a common chimpanzee (*Pan troglodytes*). We will see more of them.

[21] Michael Arbib (2008) also invokes Construction Grammar in arguing for a continuous 'protolanguage spectrum'.

event. Just possibly what Panzee meant was something like 'Find the hidden kiwi with a stick'. We can't tell. We also don't know whether Panzee paused between any of her 'words'. In analysing newly emerging sign languages, as seen in Chapter 5, pauses are plausibly taken as indicating boundaries between sentences.

Contrast Panzee's utterance with Tervoort's (1968) example *You me downtown movie fun*. This was an utterance signed by a deaf student asking a girl out for a date. The deaf students and their teachers that Tervoort studied had not developed a full sign language, such as ASL or BSL, as far as can be seen. 'During some fifteen years of studying some twenty thousand sentences of deaf children, I have noticed a very great freedom of sequence in the signs. The counterpart of this freedom, of course, is the great dependence on the situation with the visible partner as centre' (p. 309). These children's signing, in other words, was very much guided by pragmatic principles. Taking the string *You me downtown movie fun*, which has five elements, Tervoort tested all 120 possible permutations of these five words with teachers of the deaf, to see how acceptable they were. All the first forty-eight permutations, in which *you* and *me* were kept together, in either order, were judged equally acceptable and clear in meaning, given the situation of a boy talking to a girl. The six permutations of *downtown*, *movie*, and *fun* were all judged 'identical in meaning' (p. 313). 'Of all one hundred and twenty permutations some were more ambiguous than others but none was considered to be esoterically ungrammatical by the majority'. *You me downtown movie fun* was apparently signed as a sequence without pauses. It has no repetitions, and can be easily interpreted. Anyone who hears it knows immediately what is being proposed.

There is an important difference between the chimpanzee's *hide, stick, hide, stick, stick, stick, hide, kiwi, kiwi* and the human *You me downtown movie fun*. At some point in the evolution of language, discourse began to be chopped up into **sentence-sized units**, in the sense of Chapter 3. These units have an internal coherence distinguishing them from any kind of looser discourse-level organization. At its simplest this coherence is marked by pauses at the boundaries of the units. (Recall that birdsong is organized into repertoires of discrete songs, intriguingly roughly human sentence-sized in physical duration, but without the propositional content, of course.) If there was any discrete step around the hypothetical protolanguage era, it was the introduction of this kind of hierarchical packaging of discourse into units longer than the elementary notes or words, and shorter than a whole discourse. Also, in *You me downtown movie fun* the apparently obligatory grouping of *you me* together shows the beginning of phrase-sized subunits within sentence-sized units. This point is implicit in discussions of examples such as *Mommy sock*, *red me eat*, and *applesauce buy store*, all produced by humans. The elements in these utterances are not ordered conventionally, but they are cited by their sources as if seen as packages, perhaps pronounced in a single intonation tune and bounded by pauses. But Nim's *hug Nim hug*, often mentioned on the same page as an example of protolanguage, is not necessarily of the same kind. It is repetitive and though we can't know for sure, observers have given the impression that his utterances were not packaged into chunks with clear boundaries.

Genie's *applesauce buy store* is in no way good English. But some of her other utterances show signs that she has acquired English word order: examples such as *Want milk*, *Mike paint*, and *Big elephant*. These examples show a little more acquired syntactic organization. The example that Bickerton (1990) gives from Hawaiian Pidgin *Ifu laik meiki, mo beta make time, mani no can hapai*[22] clearly has some syntactic structure, with a conditional clause introduced by *If*, and the last four words constituting a clause with a subject *mani* first, and an auxiliary verb *can* preceding a main verb *hapai*; this utterance is clearly more grammatically structured than the other examples. I therefore prefer not to count it as an example from a protolanguage; this speaker of Hawaiian Pidgin was already a long way towards a full Creole.

The insistence on no syntactic, but only pragmatic, organization in protolanguages means that one cannot speak of protolanguage utterances containing nouns and verbs, let alone adjectives, adverbs, prepositions, or proper nouns. In the modern 'fossils of language', with words borrowed from existing full languages, one can of course identify the source of the word and its grammatical category in the lexifier language. Thus in Genie's *applesauce buy store* we can recognize two words which in standard English function as nouns and one that functions as a verb.[23] But there is no hint that in Genie's mind at the time these words were associated with any syntactic categories and rules determining how they should be inserted into longer sequences. That is what makes it a good candidate for evidence of an early primitive stage when there was no syntactic organization.

Here, apparently, I part company with Bickerton. Taking issue with Carstairs-McCarthy (1999), he writes 'a verbless protolanguage seems intrinsically implausible. While most of the first words children learn are nouns, there

---

[22] The underlined words here are from the Hawaiian language, embedded in a string of otherwise English-based words. *make* means roughly 'die' and *hapai* means 'carry'. The whole thing means roughly 'If you want to make something, better do it before you die, you can't take money with you!'

[23] Assuming, naturally, that Genie was referring to a foodstore, and not to the activity of storing.

are always a few verbs among them, and apes seem to learn verbs (with actions as referents) as easily as nouns (with entities as referents)' (Bickerton 2007, p. 516). This is to confuse syntax with semantics. We spend time in first year linguistics classes dispelling the traditional erroneous ideas that 'A Noun is the name of a person, place or thing' (counterexamples: *action, ambition, virtue, redness, million*, etc.) and 'A Verb describes an action' (counterexamples: *sleep, own, have, be, consist*, etc.). Syntactic categories such as Noun and Verb are defined in each separate language according to the way they fit into the grammatical patterns of the language. Very often, a noun in one language will be translated by a noun in another language, and a verb by a verb, but not always. English *have* in the sense of *own* is translated into Arabic and Russian with a preposition and no verb, for example 'to me a book'. Cross-linguistically, it is possible to make generalizations about nouns and verbs because of the strong statistical correspondences. But looking at the productions of trained apes, language-deprived children or under-twos, like *Hug Nim hug, applesauce buy store*, or *Mommy sock*, there is no evidence that the producers of these strings have categorized the words in any way that bears upon their conventional insertion into standardized sentences. *Mommy* and *sock* are nouns in the adult language that the child is attempting to learn, but so far the child, although having acquired the meanings of the words, has not acquired this grammatical information about them. At this stage, under-twos and trained apes have no syntax, and appear simply to string words together according to pragmatic principles.

Bickerton (2007, p. 516) claims that 'protolanguage had proper as well as common nouns'.[24] In English, proper nouns like *Peter* have a different grammatical distribution from common nouns like *scholar*, and this fact entitles us to say that English has two syntactically distinct subcategories of noun. Undoubtedly most modern languages distinguish a syntactic category of proper nouns, distinct from common nouns. But not all languages make this distinction. Machiguenga (or Matsigenka), an Arawakan language, lacks proper names. (See Hurford 2003, sec. 1.3 for excerpts from primary sources; Johnson 2003 and Snell 1964 describing this fact.) Dixon (1980, pp. 27–8) also notes that Australian languages typically lack proper names. If some languages spoken in the twentieth century[25] make no syntactic distinction between proper

---

[24] This claim was discussed in Hurford (2007, pp. 133–6). I have argued for the absence of proper names in some languages and the absence of individual constants in protothought in several places (Hurford 2003, 2001b). I will not rehearse these arguments here.

[25] I hope they have survived into the twenty-first century.

and common nouns, it would be odd (not to say contradictory) to claim that this distinction was made in pre-syntactic systems. This does not mean, of course, that users of such systems did not have words which characteristically referred to individuals (mentally represented as very specific bundles of features); they just did not distribute these words in their utterances in any way different from other words, except insofar as reference to people may be statistically correlated with certain pragmatic preferences. A similar argument applies to the question of whether protolanguages distinguished nouns from verbs. Defined as having no syntax, and therefore no syntactic categories, protolanguages could have had no distinction between nouns and verbs, which is not to say that many two-word utterances didn't contain an action-denoting word and an object-denoting word, for purely pragmatic reasons.

I have stressed the purely asyntactic conception of protolanguage. Undoubtedly some further ramifications of human meaning coevolved with the rise of syntax. But at least one fundamental feature of the relation between syntax and semantics, namely **compositionality**, is already rudimentarily present in purely asyntactic protolanguage. The principle of compositionality is that **The meaning of an expression is a function of the meanings of its constituent parts and the way they are put together**. In the purely pragmatic mode, with no grammatical rules or conventions for putting words together (beyond mere concatenation), there is already a simple systematic relationship between the meaning of a whole string and the meanings of its constituent words. For example, the meaning of *Mommy sock* is something to do with Mommy **and** something to do with a sock. The meaning of the whole is any proposition that a hearer can extrapolate from shared background knowledge and contextual clues, provided that this proposition is somehow about Mommy and a sock. The meaning of *Daddy car* is not the same as the meaning of *Mommy sock*, exactly because of differences among the meanings of *Mommy*, *Daddy*, *sock*, and *car*. Expressions in this mode are compositional in the same rudimentary sense as, apparently, most expressions in Riau Indonesian as described in Chapter 5. Gil described the relationship between form and meaning in that language as 'associational'. If a present-day language can work largely by means of such a simple principle, there is no reason to doubt that earlier forms of human language generally worked that way too, like the productions of modern two-year-olds and trained apes.

In pragmatic mode, though any order of words is possible, it is likely that some word-orders will be more frequent than others. Utterances with Topic-first and/or Focus-last, as in the Basic Variety (Chapter 5, section 7) were probably common. Also words for concepts belonging together, for example describing the same referent, as in *big cow brown*, were probably continuous.

By definition of this stage, there were no function words and no morphological inflections.

8.4 Packaging in sentence-like units

Preamble. Recall Chapter 1 and its discussion of birds' capacity to learn to produce complex sequences of notes, without any compositional semantic interpretation. The abilities explored in the present chapter also involve an ability to learn to produce complex sequences, in this case of meaningful words. For sure, the addition of meaning would have made a significant difference, facilitating the learning task. But a pre-existing ability to mimic initially meaning-free sequences would also, reciprocally, have facilitated the task of learning to produce somewhat complex meaningful sequences. We saw in Chapter 1 that there is good reason to attribute hierarchical 'phrase' structure to birdsong, as well as to think of birdsong in terms of **competence** and **performance**, concepts usually reserved for discussion of human language only. In this book, we have travelled a long way from where we started, with animal meaningless syntax. Darwin's and Jespersen's quaint picture of humans singing to each other like birds may have an element of truth in it. I doubt that we will ever know. But put aside the quaintness and the jolly connotations of 'song'. Just keep in mind that the semantically motivated 'putting words together' that I will describe in this chapter was done by creatures with at least an ability to organize element-strings into units with a canonical size and structure, as birds do. Further, as with birds, this ability was based on learned templates stored in declarative memory, rather than being only procedural reflexes. Some very elementary aspects of syntax, for example hierarchical 'phrasal' structure and behaviour based on stored declarative knowledge, have very ancient origins in birds, with lineages separate from our own. We do not know whether our own lineage has, much more recently, independently converged on a similar solution to complex learned vocal signalling. It certainly would have helped. The birds are a long way from us, and will hardly be mentioned further.

In the last section I ran ahead to contrasting *You me downtown movie fun* with the chimpanzee Panzee's *hide, stick, hide, stick, stick, stick, hide, kiwi, kiwi*. The former, produced by a modern teenage human, is arguably a sentence-like unit. The latter is more probably just a stretch of discourse produced by iterated following of the instruction 'utter a word'. The longest utterance by another trained chimp, Nim, was *Give orange me give eat orange me eat orange give me eat orange give me you* (Terrace 1979). Koko, a gorilla, came up with *please milk please me like drink apple bottle* (Patterson 1979,

p. 345). These animals have learned to produce words, and they can string them together. But there is no evidence from them that they package their long utterances in any units smaller than a discourse turn. There is no doubt that these long utterances can be interpreted by a human as having propositional content—'Please give Nim an orange' or 'Please, I [Koko] would like a drink of milk'.[26] But as far as we can see, they are unconstrained in structure; any list of signs naming the same ideas could be expected. There is no evidence that these particular apes produce anything that could reasonably be counted as a sentence.

But some apes may do better. On some interpretations, Kanzi compares reasonably well with two-year-old children and other humans just starting out on syntax. Children start syntax-like behaviour with two-word utterances, and so do trained apes—that's an obvious similarity. An equally obvious difference is that children rapidly go on to far greater complexity and productivity, while apes remain stuck at best around the two-word stage. In accordance with my concept of UG+, the language capacity incorporates a quantitative constraint on what is processable. Children at first can only produce two-word sentence-like utterances, but they progress past the two-word stage. Child brains are plastic, up to limits well beyond what apes can ever manage. I suggest that a quantitatively limited forerunner of human UG+ existed in early hominins, as it may now exist in apes with no plasticity allowing the ape to progress to structured sentences longer than two words. This presupposes that we can find good reasons to classify ape two-word productions as sentence-like. Some systematic rules of word-order, and some sign of productivity in using common patterns are the features to look for. In the cases of humans limited temporarily to a two-word stage, most researchers[27] have no hesitation in seeing two-word utterances as the first step on a ladder to more complex sentences. This applies, for example, to early Nicaraguan Sign Language MAN PUSH and to hosts of examples from normal acquisition. Anisfeld (1985, pp. 133–49) classifies the uses of early child sentences six ways, with examples. I will give just one example of each of his six semantic types.

here flower	'demonstrative naming'	(Braine 1976, p. 43)
funny man	'attributive'	(Bloom et al. 1975, p. 60)
Lois scarf	'possessive'	(Bloom et al. 1975, p. 56)
Gia push	'action'	(Bloom et al. 1975, p. 50)
more clown	'recurrence'	(Bloom et al. 1975, p. 57)
no bib	'negation'	(Bloom et al. 1975, p. 46)

[26] Ignoring the 'apple' sign'.
[27] Except those stuck with theory-dependent definitions.

These are **early child sentences**. We saw in Chapter 5 some examples like *makan ayam* 'eat chicken', *ayam makan* 'chicken eat', and *baru gitar* 'new guitar'; these are **adult Riau Indonesian sentences**. Now here is what Kanzi does with the limited number of symbols (256) on his keyboard:

when Kanzi says 'peanut hide' and looks at your pocket, he is asking you if you have peanuts. If he says 'peanut hide' and drops some peanuts on the ground into a clump of grass, he is talking about what he is doing—hiding peanuts. And if he says 'peanut hide' and takes you to the staff office and points to the cabinets, he is trying to tell you that he wants some of the peanuts that are kept there.

(Savage-Rumbaugh 1999, p. 139)

If Kanzi had been a human child, many researchers would not have hesitated to call his *peanut hide* an early child sentence. If the term 'sentence' can be modified by 'early child' or 'adult Riau Indonesian', there is no reason not to label novel two-word sequences produced fluently by an ape, bounded by pauses, as **ape sentences**. The clear fact is that Kanzi mostly does not get beyond two-word sentences, due to his limited plasticity as compared with human children. He occasionally manages three-word sentences. Kanzi's sentences are very short, but, unlike the utterances of Panzee and Nim, they may qualify as sentence-like and not just structureless listings of words.

The two-word child utterances given above have word order following an adult English model. Kanzi's word order in two-word utterances is more variable, but with statistically significant preferences for one order over another. Here are some examples—compare the numbers in each line.

Relation	No.	Relation	No.
Action-agent	119	Agent-action	13
Action-object	39	Object-action	15
Object-agent	7	Agent-object	1
Entity-demonstrative	182	Demonstrative-entity	67
Goal-action	46	Action-goal	10

(Greenfield and Savage-Rumbaugh 1990, p. 557)

It is possible that the biased frequencies here reflect the pragmatics of the different situations in which they were uttered. Or possibly Kanzi was beginning to follow some word-order rules not immediately dictated by the pragmatics of the situations. We can't tell for sure. But it is noticeable that Kanzi did not go in for the repetitions we have seen in Nim's and Panzee's utterances. 'There were no purely repetitious two-symbol utterances in the two-symbol corpus' (Greenfield and Savage-Rumbaugh 1990, p. 557). In his occasional three-term utterances Kanzi also does not repeat elements as Nim did. There are several possible explanations for this. One is that the affordances of the lexigram board do not lend themselves naturally to repetitions.[28] Another possibility is that the lack of repetition indicates that Kanzi is somehow aware of a canonical principle of two- and three-word utterances, that the information in each part is combined to convey a more specific meaning, something that repetition does not achieve. From the corpus of Kanzi's two-element combinations (Savage-Rumbaugh 1990), it is also noticeable that in four of the relations in which a lexigram was sometimes combined with a pointing gesture (Action-agent, Goal-action, Action-object, and Object-agent) the second element was always the gesture. This reflects a rule sensitive to the modality, lexigram, or gesture, of the symbols used. Kanzi seems to have invented this rule for himself. The authors insist that he was not trained to present information in this order, but he did so extremely consistently. Greenfield and Savage-Rumbaugh discuss this 'gesture follows lexigram' rule in detail and give many examples. They mention the occasional inconvenience of this ordering:

The rule that 'gesture follows lexigram' does not seem to have any basis in functional convenience. At one point Kanzi was observed to move away from a person he would later indicate as agent, go to the board (where he indicated an action lexigram), and then return to the person (using a gesture to designate her as agent). In that situation, the rule Kanzi had invented demanded extra motor steps and therefore seemed purely arbitrary.   (Greenfield and Savage-Rumbaugh 1990, p. 564)

A reservation must be expressed: in Kanzi's 'Demonstrative-entity' combinations, this rule was not applied, and the gesture corresponding to 'Demonstrative' always came first, naturally by definition of 'Demonstrative' here. However, almost three times as frequently he used the reverse order of these elements, in which the gesture followed the lexigram, conforming to the rule he applied in other combinations.[29] Combining gestures with lexigrams in two-element utterances was also observed in Panbanisha, a bonobo, and Panpanzee, a chimpanzee, as reported by Greenfield et al. (2008, p. 40). All these apes produced many such combinations. In most cases the gesture involved was deictic (pointing), but in some cases it was 'representational' (iconic). Panbanisha and Panpanzee resorted to the gesture+lexigram (in either order) tactic proportionately less than Kanzi. Something over half of their two-element utterances were lexigram+lexigram. Over a year and a half, observed only part of each day, all these apes produced numbers of such combinations

---

[28] This point was made to me by Adele Abrahamsen.
[29] This particular combination is reminiscent of English equative sentences such as *My mother is her sister* and *Her sister is my mother*, which express the same proposition but differ pragmatically according to the order of phrases.

in the high hundreds. The only ones counted here were created by the apes themselves, not repeats or imitations of caregiver utterances. Greenfield et al. (2008) note that children also go through a stage where they make two-element utterances combining a gesture with a spoken word, citing Capirci et al. (1996) and Pizzuto and Capobianco (2005). In children the gesture is usually a pointing gesture, but can be an iconic representational gesture. A slightly more complex two-element utterance occurs when a child uses a deictic pronoun accompanied by a pointing gesture, in combination with some other word, as in *That bad*, that is, 'that is bad'. After a while, pointing accompanying deictic pronouns decreases, leaving the deictic word itself to do the attention-drawing work.

The combination of gestures with other kinds of symbols shows how any transition from a gestural modality to a vocal modality could have been gradual in human evolution, with such mixed utterances characteristic of the transition. Indeed we modern humans occasionally substitute a gesture for a word in a sentence, and gesture meaningfully interpenetrates speech in many ways (Goldin-Meadow 2003).

It seems likely that human ancestors went through a Kanzi-like stage where they could not have managed to produce sentences more than two words long. Even at that stage, however, our ancestors differed from modern wild bonobos, in that they lived in a culture where exchanges of such two-word utterances were part of the social fabric. The reasons for the evolution of that cooperative social fabric have been discussed earlier. The existence of the cooperative culture could be the main reason why we and our languages evolved beyond the two-word stage.

Opinion is very polarized on the implications of 'ape-language' research. For myself, I am prepared to grant primitive sentencehood to many of Kanzi's two-lexigram productions, meaning that I think it likely that he pre-plans a short message, finds two or three appropriate lexigrams or gestures, and uses them in a somewhat conventionalized order. Of course, there is no evidence of hierarchical structuring, or an identifiable grammatical category of Subject, let alone long-range dependencies, in Kanzi's productions, just as these features cannot be found in a child at the two-word stage. Kanzi's performance is markedly different from Nim's. Here is a summary of Nim's performance, in an article entitled 'Can an ape create a sentence?':

More than 19,000 multisign utterances of an infant chimpanzee (Nim) were analyzed for syntactic and semantic regularities. Lexical regularities were observed in the case of two-sign combinations: particular signs (for example, more) tended to occur in a particular position. These regularities could not be attributed to memorization or to position habits, suggesting that they were structurally constrained. That conclusion, however, was invalidated by videotape analyses, which showed that most of Nim's utterances were prompted by his teacher's prior utterance, and that Nim interrupted his teachers to a much larger extent than a child interrupts an adult's speech. Signed utterances of other apes (as shown on films) revealed similar non-human patterns of discourse. (Terrace et al. 1979, p. 891)

The difference between Kanzi and Nim may be partly attributable to a bonobo/chimpanzee difference. But it is more likely that the difference results from the very different experiences each ape had. Kanzi and his trainer, Sue Savage-Rumbaugh, have built up a rapport similar to a human child–parent relationship. Kanzi's humane and supportive environment is more conducive to human-like behaviour than Nim's was. Kanzi had a fifty-acre wood to roam in, often accompanied by a human who 'chatted' with him to the low limits of his ability. By contrast, 'Nim was exposed to 60 different teachers, most of whom were not fluent in sign language. . . . Nim's learning environment may have had deleterious effects on his signing' (Patterson in Bindra et al. 1981, p. 87).

The room used as Nim's classroom was bare and small, a mere eight feet square. This was by design. I felt that Nim would not romp around too much in a small area and would be more likely to concentrate on the activities introduced by his teachers. I also felt that a bare room would minimize distractions. . . . Nim's nursery school contained nothing familiar. (Terrace 1979, pp. 49–50)

Five days a week, for five to six hours a day, volunteer teachers worked with him in the classroom on what proved to be a rather grueling schedule. (Terrace 1979, p. 56)

A 'realization' that discourse is packaged into units longer than the most basic element, a word, and shorter than a whole discourse, was a key step in language evolution, I suggest. And we can perhaps see the dim beginnings of it in the patternings of Kanzi's two-element utterances, but not in Nim's.

As I have said, the 'ape language' literature is extraordinarily polarized. Given that strict experimental lab conditions are not conditions under which language normally develops in children, we have to try our best to interpret data collected in less formal circumstances. (Linguists should be especially sympathetic to this point.) I am aware that I fall on the side of the fence that attributes **some human-like**[30] capacity to Kanzi. It is true that Savage-Rumbaugh's criteria for successful carrying out of a request are generous, as Wynne (2004, p. 125), among others, has pointed out. The 'PC' in the examples

---

[30] Please note the deliberately moderate wording.

cited in Chapter 6 by Truswell means 'partly correct', which seems fair when Kanzi only brought one of the items requested. The same criteria were applied to the responses of Alia, the child, and Kanzi outperformed her. And as Wynne also writes, about Kanzi's two- and three-element productions 'Note too how the transcriber has added periods after almost every word that Kanzi utters. These words just refuse to string together into sentences' (Wynne 2004, p. 124). This makes Kanzi seem more like Nim.

If it should be established somehow that Kanzi has absolutely no sentence-like behaviour, we could not appeal to him as a living example of what our remote ancestors' language capacities may have been like. Researchers critical of the experimenters' interpretations of Kanzi's behaviour hold the view that it is further from human behaviour than the experimenters like to think. If the critics are right, that takes away a modern living 'fossil' of early human language-like behaviour. If the common ancestor of chimpanzees, bonobos, and humans did not even have this much language capacity, the implication is that more of our own language capacity evolved more recently. What follows? To find a massive gap between Kanzi's behaviour and ours (and it really is big, if not massive) does not entail any catastrophic evolutionary leap or discontinuity after the split from our common ancestor with chimps. It just means that all of our impressive syntactic capacities evolved in a shorter time, after the chimp–human split. But they did evolve, and it is consistent with all we know about evolution, and about the genetics of the language faculty, that it happened in a gradual quantitative manner. If he really can't do all the things claimed for him (and I believe he can do at least some of them, especially in his simple two-element productions), a fictional hominid Kanzi-like character who could do these things would be a reasonable construct for speculation about the evolution of syntax.

Beside trained apes, a further source of clues to the form of the earliest syntax can be found in the rudimentary systems that develop in households with deaf children of hearing parents who don't use an established sign language. A possible advantage of such data is that it is produced by members of our own species, as opposed to apes who might have evolved in different ways after the chimp/human split. Susan Goldin-Meadow has studied these 'homesign' systems. In her work, we can see clearly the boundaries of the packages into which the children segment their discourse. 'Relaxation of the hand signals the end of a sentence' (Goldin-Meadow 2005, p. 97). She gives many examples which are reminiscent both of Kanzi's two-element combinations and of the early productions in Nicaraguan Sign Language and Al-Sayyid Bedouin Sign Language, discussed in Chapter 5. These deaf children often combine an iconic (imitative) gesture with a deictic (pointing) gesture. Here are some examples

(Goldin-Meadow conventionally represents pointing gestures in lowercase and iconic gestures in capitals).

train CIRCLE	[describing motion of a toy train]
TRANSFER *puzzleboard*	[before moving a puzzle piece to the board]
COME *mother*	[asking mother to come to his side]
ketchup-bottle LITTLE	[commenting on unusual size of a ketchup bottle]

(from Goldin-Meadow 2005, pp. 98–9)

Notice that these utterances, by several children, often share information for no immediately selfish purpose, unlike many of the communications of trained apes. Goldin-Meadow argues that these utterances have the simple sentence-like property of expressing propositions, but are, for some children, restricted in length to two elements.

All of the deaf children produce sentences about transferring objects and, at one time or another, they produce gestures for each of the three arguments that we would expect to underlie such a predicate. They never produce all three arguments in a single sentence but, across all their sentences, they produce a selection of two-gesture combinations that, taken together, displays all three of the arguments. For example, David produces the following two-gesture sentences to describe different events, all of which are about a person transferring an object to another person. In the first three, he is asking his sister to give him a cookie. In the fourth, he is asking his sister to give a toy duck to me so that I will wind it up to make it go.

cookie GIVE [patient—act]
sister David [actor—recipient]
GIVE *David* [act—recipient]
duck Susan [patient—recipient]

By overtly expressing the actor, patient, and recipient in this predicate context, David and the other children exhibit knowledge that these three arguments are associated with the transfer-object predicate. (Goldin-Meadow 2005, pp. 99–100)

Note that several of these utterances combine two pointing gestures (lowercase). Even in this simple system, there are ways of telling who did what to whom, the Agent and Patient roles: '...likelihood of production distinguishes thematic roles. All ten of the children are more likely to produce a gesture for the patient (e.g. the eaten cheese) in a sentence about eating than to produce a gesture for the actor (e.g. the eating mouse)' (p. 104). Goldin-Meadow argues convincingly that the frequency effects here relate to the thematic relations of Agent and Patient, rather than being determined by Information-structure considerations like Topic and Focus. Further, one child, David, signals thematic roles by word order. 'David thus treats patients and intransitive actors alike (both precede the act) and distinct from transitive actors (which follow the act)' (p. 111).[31] These deaf child homesigners are able, like users of deaf sign languages, to use a spatial device for marking the roles played by participants in an event. If, say, a jar is intended as the patient of a twisting motion, the TWIST gesture is performed in a space nearer the jar, not in 'neutral' space nearer the signer's chest. Goldin-Meadow, following the sign language literature, calls this 'inflection'. Such a method is not available in spoken language, and use of the term 'inflection' here is related to inflections in spoken language by function, but not, obviously, by form.

Goldin-Meadow has also studied gesture+word combinations in hearing children. 'There is, however, evidence, that children in the one-word period can produce two elements of a proposition in one communicative act—but only if one looks across modalities. One-word children can utter a word—*drink*—and indicate the object of that action through their gestures—a point at a bottle' (Goldin-Meadow and Butcher 2003, p. 86). These authors also note a transition from pointing+speech where the point and the speech are consistent, for example *bottle*+point-to-bottle, to pointing speech where the information in the point is different, for example *go*+point-to-turtle. This transition is a step toward syntax.

One of the key messages that Goldin-Meadow draws from her data fits nicely with my own emphasis in this section on the natural packaging of discourse into sentence-like units. 'Children come to the language-learning situation with actions organized into frameworks—predicate frames. Those frameworks serve as the organizing structure for children's earliest sentences, whether those sentences are learned from conventional language models or invented *de novo*' (Goldin-Meadow 2005, p. 113).

Wrapping this section up, and with a nod back to Chapter 5, section 8, language-beginners of many kinds, trained apes, normal children, child deaf homesigners, and creators of sign languages (e.g. ISN, ABSL), start syntax with two-element combinations, which have a kind of unity both in form and function. In form, they are bounded by pauses, or relaxation of the hands. In function, they convey simple propositional meanings, with some statistical tendency to associate element-order with the roles of the participants in the event described. Two-element utterances may be followed, depending on the user's capacity, by three-element utterances. The three-element utterances package the same propositional information, but add more detail, and start to

---

[31] Goldin-Meadow notes that this pattern is like that found in languages with an ergative case-marking system.

look more like sentences in familiar modern languages. This progression has been suggestively compared to the use of serial verbs, as discussed in Chapter 5.

> Early in training, Sarah [a chimpanzee] was given only one action name at a time, one appropriate to the point in the sequence to which the action had progressed. Later, several verbs were made available to her at the same time, enabling her to write, 'Wash apple, cut apple,' or 'Cut apple, give apple,' etc. But Sarah did not write pairs of sentences of this kind; rather, she wrote instead 'Cut give apple,' and 'Wash give apple,' even if not always observing the correct order (Premack 1976: 244, 321). Such complex forms involving sequences of two verbs might be suggestive of verb serialization, which did not occur until after she had first produced equivalent outcomes by using multiple simpler sentences; for example, she did not write 'Wash give apple' until she had written 'Wash apple' and 'Give apple' many times before (Premack 1976: 324). Much the same behavior was shown by the other two chimpanzees Peony and Elizabeth, who wrote, for example, 'Elizabeth apple wash cut' in describing their own action or 'Amy apple cut insert' in referring to the trainer Amy as an agent.
>
> (Heine and Kuteva 2007, p. 149)

Of course, we absolutely do not want to suggest that the language capabilities of speakers of creoles with serial verbs are no greater than those of trained apes. But the similarity noted by Heine and Kuteva is more than a coincidence. In human languages, serial verbs are a creative solution to a problem in basic communication when a sender only has limited conventional grammar at her disposal. If a sender aims to convey a message about two separate events involving the same participant (such as the apple Sarah was signalling about), and if she has words for the participant and predicates involved, it is natural to utter those words together. In the case of trained apes, we would not want to attribute syntactic categories such as Noun and Verb to them. It is better to say that the apes serialize words, and that naturally some of the juxtaposed words denote actions. The progression from two-word productions to three-word productions noted by Premack need not be seen as involving a hierarchical 'subassembly', embedding the two-word sequence as a constituent in the longer sequence, although this is a possibility.

8.5 Synthetic and analytic routes to syntax

This section deals with one of two aspects of language evolution which may not closely follow the path of language acquisition in modern children. These are cases where the modern child can take advantage of being surrounded by a language already fully formed, and can 'leapfrog' past stages which our ancestors had to go through because they were inventing language *de novo*.

(The other aspect, involving grammaticalization, will be given a chapter of its own after this one.)

The origins of syntax, as I have presented it, lie in putting words together (and I expanded the idea to putting larger constructions together). There is another way of seeing the origins of syntax, not as putting things together, but as taking things apart. We see the difference between a putting-together strategy and a taking-apart strategy in modern language acquisition. Greenfield et al. (1985) write:

> successive single-word utterances are used as a transitional mechanism to two-word utterances. This can be classified as a constructive or building-up process. The contrasting side of this process is where children produce unanalysed sequences and later break them into their component parts which are then used independently in combination with other lexical items. ... These two complementary processes (build-up constructions and amalgam analysis) have been summarized by Garman (1979) as *synthetic* or *analytic* approaches on the part of the child.
>
> (Greenfield et al. 1985, p. 240)

Terminological note: Very unfortunately, the term 'analytic' is used in diametrically opposing ways in the child language literature. Peters (1977) uses 'analytic' for a strategy 'which proceeds from the parts to the whole' contrasted with a 'Gestalt' strategy which proceeds 'from the whole to the parts'. Consistent with this, Wells (1986) contrasts 'analytic' with 'holistic' or 'Gestalt' styles of learning. But for Garman (1979) and for Greenfield et al. (1985), as we see, the 'analytic' strategy is the strategy by which a form previously learnt as a unit is broken down into parts, while a 'synthetic' strategy is one of putting words together. Independently, and in connection with language evolution, I used 'analytic' in the 'breaking-apart' sense and 'synthetic' in the 'putting together' sense in (Hurford 2000a, 2000b). Andrew Smith (2008a) uses 'analytic' and 'synthetic' in my sense. I will keep to this usage here. It is also important to distinguish between 'analytic' as applied to the diachronic processes giving rise to a language system and 'analytic' as applied to the synchronic systems themselves. When comparing the hypothetical analytic and synthetic routes to modern syntax, one is obviously dealing with diachronic processes. The term 'analytic' has also been applied, not to the process, but to the resulting system, as in a contrast between 'analytic protolanguage' and 'holistic protolanguage' (Wray 2002a). Whether for some period in the past pre-humans spoke languages that were holistic is a matter of the synchronic nature of those communication systems. Not helping to escape the terminological mix-up, both Kenny Smith (2008b) and Maggie Tallerman (2007) ask a question about the existence of 'a holistic protolanguage' in the titles of their articles, but the articles themselves address the diachronic process whereby modern syntactically combinable words emerged. In fact, if 'protolanguage' is defined as a stage when words were uttered in sequences, even if only short ones, the very phrase 'holistic protolanguage' is a contradiction. Only a one-word stage of evolution or development can be called 'holistic'. To avoid confusion, I will contrast 'holistic' with 'atomistic' when talking about synchronic systems. Any stage beyond the one-word stage is atomistic, with the words being the 'atoms'. The diachronic processes leading from a holistic state to an atomistic state have been a matter of contention. I will set out this debate, and give reasons why I end up on one side of it.

You might think that the analytic break-down route to multi-word sequences is one where ontogeny is not a sure guide to phylogeny. As I mentioned above, in the case of language acquisition, it is safe to assume pre-existing two-word sequences (by adults), which are first adopted holistically by a child, who then 'realizes' their two-word structure. But in the case of language creation these two-word sequences are produced for the first time ever, from sequences which were not two words before. Nevertheless, several thoughtful and distinguished authors have advocated the analytic, or break-down, route to the first syntactic combinations. In grammar evolution, the debate between putting-together or taking-apart goes back a long way.

Thinkers prior to Jespersen assumed an evolution of language from the simple to the complex. They held that man must have begun to communicate with monosyllables and afterward learned to combine them into longer words and sentences. Jespersen thought it might have happened the other way around. He suggested that man first expressed himself in snatches of song, which gave vent to his feelings of success or failure, joy or despair. Some of the spontaneous outbursts were repeated to recall the occasion when they were formed or to express similar events. When two songs were partly alike and partly different, the like portions became associated with the common features of two situations. In this way, words were extracted from primeval unbroken songs. Unquestionably this is a clever theory, and it fits the observed fact that some animals sing in phrases and melodies. It fails, however, to account for the fact that animals also grunt, squeal, and chirp. Perhaps some signals were crystallized out of primordial phrases, but others must have come from short bursts of voice, including one- and two-consonant monosyllables. (Swadesh 1971, p. 132)

Swadesh's summary applies exactly to a debate still current in the twenty-first century. For the earliest origins of syntax, I am on the 'putting-together' side, for reasons which I will give. It is notable that recent advocates of the 'breaking-apart' view also tend to be the ones who, like Jespersen, regard bird-like song as a possible antecedent facilitator of human syntax. The language-evolution version of the break-down story posits original one-word utterances which are long enough to break down, that is consist of more than one syllable. Further, these words (or songs) express somewhat complex meanings that can be later decomposed into several different semantic components, typically the predicate and argument(s) of a proposition.

Simon Kirby's computer simulations of the emergence of semantically compositional syntax (Kirby 2000, 2001; Kirby and Hurford 2002) model the analytic, breaking-down, route to syntax. The models show that this scenario is logically possible; there is nothing contradictory or inconsistent in this story of how syntax arose. But these models, like any models, don't necessarily show what did happen. In these models it is assumed that the simulated agents have mental access to sets of fairly complex propositional meanings, conceived in a predicate logic framework. One such 'thought' that a simulated agent could entertain, and be prompted to express, is '< Agent = Zoltan, Patient = Mary, Predicate = Knows >' (translatable as Zoltan knows Mary) (Kirby 2000, p. 306). The simulated agents have at their disposal 'a semantic space of 100 possible meanings'. This semantic space is by design already ripe for decomposing; each proposition is in fact synthesized from basic semantic terms, individual constants (e.g. Zoltan, Mary) and predicates (e.g. Knows). Kirby's modelling of the phonetic space available to simulated speakers is equally amenable to segmentation. The utterances are just strings of letters, like **aceabbceeeabeea**. At the beginning of each simulation, the agents produce random strings of letters for whole propositional meanings, like 'Zoltan knows Mary'. The agents in Kirby's model are given an ability to notice chance coincidences in randomly generated holistic meaning–form pairs, and to induce that some part of a phonetic string corresponds to some atomic semantic term, and also given an ability to assemble this information into simple semantically interpreted Phrase Structure grammars. Then these agents, over many simulated generations, arrive at a neat economic system in which each atomic concept (e.g. MARY, KNOWS) is expressed by a single string of letters, and there are a couple of general Phrase Structure rules generating sentence-like expressions for all the one hundred meanings that the agents can conceive of. This is a proof of concept,[32] showing that the idea of a simple grammatical language emerging by an analytic process of breaking holistic utterances into their parts can work in principle. This shows that it could have happened; it does not of course show that it must have happened this way. And it works given the prior

---

[32] There is a fine line between proofs of concept and Just So Stories. All proofs, of any kind, assume premises and deduce conclusions. If purported proofs of concept assume unrealistic premises, they verge on Just So Stories, because the concept they 'prove' is unlikely to bear much relation to reality. Proofs of concept do, however, require logical consistency, which literary Just So Stories are not obliged to respect.

assumptions about the form of the semantic and phonetic representations, which are already, in the simulation, highly amenable to decomposition.

In non-computational theorizing, there are some more examples of the analytic, breaking-down scenarios. I'll mention the most prominent, in decreasing order of plausibility.

Homo heidelbergensis and other early humans could have had a great many holistic messages, ranging from the general 'come here' to the more specific 'go and hunt the hare I saw five minutes ago behind the stone at the top of the hill'. The key feature of such phrases is that they would not have been constructed out of individual elements that could be recombined in a different order and with different elements so as to make new messages. Each phrase would have been an indivisible unit that had to be learned, uttered and understood as a single acoustic sequence. (Mithen 2005, p. 172)

Unitary utterances such as 'grooflook' or 'koomzash' might have encoded quite complex descriptions such as 'The alpha male has killed a meat animal and now the tribe has a chance to feast together. Yum, yum!' or commands such as 'Take your spear and go around the other side of that animal and we will have a better chance together of being able to kill it.' (Arbib 2005, pp. 118–19)

Flintstone-type examples like these give language evolution a bad name.[33] I can imagine a word for 'dinner' being used on a specific occasion such that the context brings to mind all the other ideas that Arbib envisages, the alpha male, the killed animal, and the communal feasting. But it seems unlikely that this very specific combination of circumstances was common enough to have been given its own unitary label. '[I]t is implausible... that any meaning could be reconstructed [by a hearer] to such a degree of specificity, complexity and intricacy. On the contrary, it seems reasonable that, without linguistic clues, the more complex and elaborate the semantic representation, the *less* likely the meaning can be faithfully reconstructed' (Smith 2008a, p. 108). Alison Wray (2002a, pp. 120–1) makes the same point, adding the factor of frequency: 'To stay on the inventory, a message must establish a balance between specificity and resultant frequency. Suppose a message needs to be said ten times a month for it to remain active in the protolanguage. Many specific messages will not reach the threshold, because the circumstances for their appropriacy will not arise that often'. The colourful specificity of Mithen's and Arbib's examples lets down an idea worth considering.

Alison Wray (1998, 2000) advocates the same idea with less flamboyant, and therefore more plausible, examples.

---

[33] Arbib (2006, p. 35) admits that this is a Just So Story.

Going back to our examples, in a protolanguage where *tebima* meant *give that to her*, the individual might ask which part of it meant *to her*. The answer, of course, is none of it, because the sequence is arbitrary. But if in two or more sequences there were chance matches between phonetic segments and aspects of meaning, then it would seem as if there was a constituent with that meaning. So if, besides *tebima* meaning *give that to her*, *kumapi* meant *share this with her*, then it might be concluded that *ma* had the meaning *female person + beneficiary*.   (Wray 2000, p. 297)

Arbib calls this process 'fractionation' (Arbib 2005, 2006), but doesn't envisage that this was the only diachronic mechanism by which separate, combinable words could have emerged. I call it the 'analytic' route toward syntax. Wray's examples are more plausible than Arbib's because they lay less stress on the descriptive content of the utterances than on their function to manipulate the hearer into action. In a small social group, at the protolanguage stage, maybe halfway between the present and the chimp–human split, the most useful messages for social cohesion would have had clear pragmatic, illocutionary import, and their propositional content would have been a less prominent component of their meaning. In Wray's *tebima* example the meaning conveyed is of a three-place predicate GIVE, whose arguments are provided by the context, the addressee as Agent, some contextually or deictically indicated object as Patient, and some contextually or deictically indicated female person as the Beneficiary. Thus the propositional content of *tebima* describes a generic event-type. The understood illocutionary force of *tebima* is a command.

There are thus two distinctive aspects of the analytic/fractionation account. One is the postulated complexity of the meanings conveyed by the holistic forms—whole generic event-types or situation-types, with some specific information encoded about both the predicate and its arguments. The other aspect is the fractionation process whereby the holistic form gets analysed into separate parts which are then associated with parts of the complex meaning. How likely is the analytic/fractionation story? One question is whether our remote ancestors were likely to have used holistic forms for these relatively complex meanings. The other question is whether they were exposed to enough data to be able to do the appropriate induction. We have only modern humans to judge by. If we assume that the fractionation of holistic forms into smaller elements happened quite late, after the speciation of *Homo sapiens*, it is fair to judge by modern standards. Modern children, given exposure to already well organized data from adult speech, can spot relevant correspondences and learn to pick out the words from continuous streams of adult speech and to pair these words with appropriate meanings, gleaned from the situations in which the adult utterances are used. It is worth looking in some more detail at how they do this. I will pass over the non-trivial phonetic problem of detecting word boundaries in the speech stream. I will focus on how a child, once words have somehow been dissected out of the speech stream, associates these words with appropriate meanings.[34] Note that this process, which undeniably happens in modern language learning, is similar to what is postulated to have happened under the analytic fractionation account of language evolution. But there are differences, too, which I will come to after coming to some relevant conclusions about the modern process. I will address the 'complexity of meanings' issue first, and come later to the 'sufficiency of data' issue.

The foundational puzzle for learning the meaning of a word from experience was defined by the philosopher Quine (1960), and is known as the 'Gavagai' problem, or more formally the problem of 'indeterminacy of translation'.[35] Imagine an anthropologist in a remote village interviewing a native. A rabbit runs by and the native says 'Gavagai!'. We cannot jump to the conclusion that *gavagai* means RABBIT. Quine mentions some rather arcane possibilities, such as 'undetached rabbit part'. But for all we know, the native might have meant 'the spirit of my ancestor' or 'lunch' or even 'the rabbit I saw five minutes ago behind the stone at the top of the hill', to pick up Mithen's very complex example. And the native might not have been talking about the rabbit at all, although we could guess from his gaze that he probably was. In the limit, there is no absolute guarantee that you and I attach the same private concept to the word *rabbit*, or any other word. But we get by in the vast majority of practical situations, interacting about things in the world to all parties' mutual satisfaction. (I have trouble with the words *blue* and *green*.) Language learners must induce from their everyday experience of language around them enough knowledge of the uses of words to be able to interact satisfactorily using the words. Quine's philosophical problem is about the absence of an absolute guarantee, a not uncommon philosophical will-o'-the-wisp. He agrees that it is not a **practical** problem. The Gavagai problem is a subcase of the more general problem of induction—how do we jump to apparently justified conclusions on the basis of logically inconclusive evidence? We do it all the time, and often we are right. We'll concentrate here on the more specific question of how the meanings of words can be adequately learned from observations of their use. A number of psychological studies have established dispositions in children which help them to home in on the same meaning of a word as the adult

---

[34] This is not to suggest that there is a neat sequential process, with all phonetic dissection preceding assignment of meaning to the bits dissected out. No doubt the phonetic and semantic processes are interwoven.

[35] In several places in this book, we have already encountered the indeterminacy of translation problem, for example, in the dispute over the 'true meaning' of an expression in Pirahã (Chapter 5).

speakers around them. These studies give us some idea of how relatively simple or complex the kinds of meanings are that children naturally associate with words. Three relevant dispositions are (1) the effect of shared attention, (2) the 'whole object bias', and (3) the 'taxonomic bias'. Together, these aspects of a child's word-learning point in the direction of first learning the names of types of objects, rather than names of whole generic event-types or situation-types. I will explain.

Saint Augustine in the fourth century came pretty close in his introspections:

When they [my elders] called some thing by name and pointed it out while they spoke, I saw it and realized that the thing they wished to indicate was called by the name they then uttered. And what they meant was made plain by the gestures of their bodies, by a kind of natural language, common to all nations, which expresses itself through changes of countenance, glances of the eye, gestures and intonations which indicate a disposition and attitude—either to seek or to possess, to reject or to avoid. So it was that by frequently hearing words, in different phrases, I gradually identified the objects which the words stood for.[36]   (Augustine 397, Book 1, ch. VIII)

Children learn the names of types of objects by observing how caregivers attend to those objects while using their names. 'Parents readily provide attentional cues such as line-of-regard and gestures while speaking (e.g. Messer 1983), and infants are able to make use of such cues from a relatively early age: They follow line-of-regard and pointing gestures to nearby objects by roughly 9–12 months'[37] (Baldwin 1995, p. 131). Tomasello and Farrar (1986) found a positive correlation between a mother and child's joint attention to an object and the child's word-learning. Both this study and another (Tomasello and Todd 1983) found that word-learning was enhanced when the mother followed the child's attention, rather than trying to redirect it. The relevant point here is that in word-learning attention is given to individual objects, rather than to whole events or situations. Given this kind of attention, it comes naturally to modern children to learn word-meanings that denote object types, and not generic event- or situation-types. This leads to another observed bias in modern children's word-learning. 'One way children initially constrain the meanings of terms is to honor the *whole object assumption* and thereby assume that a novel label is likely to refer to the whole object and not to its parts, substance or other properties' (Markman 1990, pp. 58–9). So children, on attending to

---

[36] We can accept what is right about Augustine's idea, while acknowledging some of Wittgenstein's critique at the beginning of the *Philosophical Investigations*.

[37] Baldwin cites the following sources: Butterworth 1991; Butterworth and Jarrett 1991; Corkum and Moore 1992, [1995]; Murphy and Messer 1977; Scaife and Bruner 1975.

a rabbit running, and hearing adults say *rabbit* (or *gavagai*) assume that the word denotes not the running but the rabbit.

A further bias in modern children's word-learning is the 'Taxonomic Assumption'. Taxonomic relations between concepts are relations of category inclusion. A partial taxonomy of animal concepts includes the hierarchy VERTEBRATE > MAMMAL > DOG > POODLE. It may be useful to think of these as 'vertical' conceptual relationships. The relations between the words concerned are relations of **hyponymy**. On the other hand, there are 'horizontal' relationships between concepts, established by common co-occurrence in events or situations. Markman and Hutchinson (1984) call these 'thematic' relations. Examples of thematically related concepts are MOTHER and BABY, or PREDATOR and PREY, or BUILDER and HOUSE. There is evidence that when children learn the meanings of words, they do not assume that a word means a cluster of thematically related concepts. 'To take a concrete example, imagine a mother pointing to a baby and saying "baby." Based on the sorting studies, we should assume that the child will be attending to the baby shaking a rattle or to the baby being diapered. Why, then, doesn't the child infer that "baby" also refers to the rattle or to the diaper, in addition to the particular baby?' (Markman and Hutchinson 1984, p. 4). And, one can add, why doesn't the child assume that *baby* refers to the whole event of the baby shaking a rattle or being diapered? As Markman (1990, p. 59) writes 'Moreover, *dog* could also refer to "the dog and his bone" or "Mommy petting the dog" or "the dog under a tree"'. Children don't assume such word meanings. Markman and Hutchinson's solution is that children are disposed to make a 'Taxonomic Assumption', that is 'children expect labels to refer to objects of the same kind or same taxonomic category. This assumption would allow them to rule out many potential meanings of a novel term, in particular, many thematic meanings. Even though children consider thematic relations good ways of organizing objects themselves, they do not consider thematic relations as possible meanings for words' (Markman 1990, p. 60).

In sum, modern children are strongly disposed to assume that words denote individual object-types and not generic event-types or situation-types. If the first creators of atomic words had similar dispositions, the very first descriptive words would have been names for object-types. I emphasize 'descriptive' here because I agree with Wray that there almost certainly were also, in parallel, single-unit utterances with mostly illocutionary force, meaning things like 'get away', 'sex?', 'help!', and 'run!'.

Children don't all learn in the same way. Peters (1977) describes a child with parallel speech styles, which she calls 'Gestalt' and 'analytic'. This child was aged between seven months and two years, three months while Peters

studied him. Sometimes (and it depended heavily on who he was talking to)
he spoke in stretches as long as short adult sentences in a slurred way, which
Peters frequently found unintelligible, although his mother could understand
these utterances. These longer utterances were hard for Peters to segment in
any standard way. Many of them, to judge by Peters' examples, had a more
manipulative than descriptive purpose. This child might be a microcosm of an
early form of language, with unsegmented utterances with mainly illocutionary
force, in parallel with other short sentence-like utterances formed by putting
one or two atomic words together. Peters' child subject did not go through
a 'fractionation' process whereby he took apart the longer apparently unsegmented holistic utterances to discover the words that had lain unrecognized
within them. There is certainly evidence of both a Gestalt or holistic synchronic
state in the early language of some children, sometimes co-existing for a while
alongside an 'analytic' or atomistic synchronic state. And indeed, we adults
all maintain such a parallelism, using formulaic utterances, sometimes a bit
slurred, especially for more socially interactive purposes, like *Howdyado?*,
and *Knowa'Imean?*, and *Innit?*. Other authors have distinguished between
'referential' and 'expressive' learning styles in young children (Goldfield 1986;
Goldfield and Snow 1985). 'Referential' children concentrate more on learning
the names of objects, while 'expressive' children concentrate more on socially
interactive expressions like *Bye* and *Hi*. All normal children eventually learn
names for actions and qualities, too, plus the function words of their language.
What we don't find in any child learning strategy is evidence that young
children assume that holistic forms can mean anything like Wray's hypothetical
tebima 'give it to her', and *kumapi* 'share this with her' denoting whole quite
specific event-types with some detail of the fillers of their argument slots
understood as encoded. I am in the same ball-park as Andrew Smith (2008a)
commenting on this debate and noting 'the implausibly elaborate semantic
structures proposed for unstructured utterances' (p. 113).

Now we'll come to the other problematic aspect of the analytic/fractionation
story, the process of fractionation itself. It is common for children to acquire
first some formulaic expressions, like *Allgone milk* or *Where Teddy?* They later
generalize these so that one part can be somewhat productively replaced by
a variety of other words, giving, for example *Allgone soup*, *Allgone apple*,
Allgone banana, and so on or *Where Daddy?*, *Where doggie?*, *Where Mama?*,
and on on. The once holistic expression has been fractionated into a fixed part
and a variable part. Children typically get some encouraging feedback in the
shape of adult repetitions of these same phrases. Sometimes, though not often,
children misfractionate holistically learned expressions into the wrong words.
Bob Ladd's son Andrew knew the phrase *a long time ago* and analysed it later

as *a long time of go*. But the misfractionated element *of* was already an existing word that he had no doubt heard many times. There are historical cases of **back formation** where a word comes into existence by the fractionation of an existing larger word. One example is *pea*, the pulse vegetable. This is now a singular count noun, with a plural *peas*. Originally, the form *pease* was a mass noun, like *rice* or *water*. It just happened to end in the /z/ phoneme, and this was enough for it to be (mis)taken as a plural count noun, whose singular was taken to be *pea*, in fact a new word. The verb *edit* is another example, back-formed from the pre-existing noun *editor*. Humans can do taking words apart, but what they do overwhelmingly more is putting words together. That's syntax. Heine and Kuteva (2007) address the same problematic aspect of the fractionation hypothesis, and write:

[W]e are not aware of any diachronic evidence to the effect that such a segmentation process can commonly be found in language change. . . . Accordingly, we consider this hypothesis to be less convincing for reconstructing language evolution. . . .

To be sure, it may happen that unanalyzable lexemes, such as *Watergate, Hamburger* or *lemonade* in English are segmented and give rise to new productive morphemes (*-gate, -burger, -ade*), and folk etymology also provides examples to show that segmentation is a valid process of linguistic behavior. But such a process is . . . fairly rare (i.e. statistically negligible). (Heine and Kuteva 2007, p. 26)

There is also no doubt that modern children do dissect words out of the continuous adult speech stream and manage to associate meanings with them, induced from the contexts in which they have been used. Cross-situational learning is a research area studying how learning is possible from a range of partially overlapping experiences. A number of mathematical and computational studies show that it is a viable process. Siskind (1996) is a seminal paper; Hurford (1999) also implements cross-situational learning in a simulated child learning a grammar by fragmented observation of his mother. Two impressive models are presented in Yu et al. (2005) and Frank et al. (2009). These models only deal with relatively small numbers of words and their induced meanings. Just recently, Blythe et al. (2010) 'demonstrate mathematically that cross-situational learning facilitates the acquisition of large vocabularies despite significant levels of referential uncertainty at each exposure'. Indeed, if cross-situational learning in some form did not work, even if augmented with some hefty innate mechanisms, we would be left with the absurd conclusion that children don't learn language. Some kind of cross-situational learning must be part of the modern language acquisition story. But was it a part of the story of the evolutionary transition from holistic one-element signals to a system in which words are concatenated? Did some early hominins manage to dissect parts out of holistic signals and associate them with parts of the original meanings?

The crucial difference between modern child word–learning and our ancestors' very first use of multi-word (probably only two-word) meaning–form mappings is that modern children are exposed to very regular and systematic data. Maggie Tallerman (2007) mounts a fierce attack on the fractionation story. One of her central points is the 'fractionability' of the set of holistic utterances that early hominins had at their disposal. This raises a number of phonetic and phonological questions. For the fractionation story to work, there have to be obvious break points in the individual holistic utterances. The studies by Kirby, Wray, and Arbib all assume a fairly modern language-like situation, typically with 'phonemes' or 'syllables' strung together. The pre-existing raw material that fractionation works on in these models is usually sets of polysyllabic utterances, with the syllables already composed of 'phonemes', just like a modern language. We don't know at what stage phonological organization into discrete phonemic consonants and vowels took place. And we certainly don't know how this phonological development was timed with respect to developments in syntax. It doesn't seem unreasonable to me that there could be a set of about a hundred holistic signals in which some phonetic (or manual) gestures were re-used, so that one might be able to notice repeated elements. If there were more than a hundred signals, even if their assignment to meanings was still totally unsystematic, it seems more likely that principles of economy would tend to push in the direction of re-usable phonetic segments. On the other hand, this is by no means a necessity, as the example of nightingale song shows. Recall from Chapter 1 that the nightingale has about two hundred different songs, but uses about a thousand different notes to form them. If (counterfactually for the sake of this argument) each of the nightingale's two hundred songs carried a different meaning, there would be hardly any raw material for the fractionation process to work on. Hominins are not birds, but *Homo erectus* could have had a memory good enough to store hundreds of holistic meaning–form pairs, and perhaps fine enough hearing (or vision) and vocal (or manual) nimbleness to store hundreds of phonetically (or visually) dissimilar utterance-types. We don't know what they had.

Tallerman makes the point that even if there were some chance correspondences between a bit of meaning and a bit of an utterance, there would also be many cases where such correspondences failed to hold. For instance, in Wray's example *tebima* and *kumapi* both happen to have the syllable *ma* and both happen to mean something to do with 'to her', so the protolanguage creator induces that *ma* means 'to her'. But as Tallerman points out, there could be many counterexamples, where some utterance meaning something to do with 'to her' (e.g. 'don't give it to her') does not contain the syllable *ma*, or where some utterance containing *ma* does not mean anything to do with 'to her'.

The likelihood of the kind of chance correspondences required by the fractionation story all depends, of course, on the size of the 'alphabet' of possible atomic components in a signal, and the length of signals. With a smaller alphabet, the probability of happenstance overlaps between utterances is higher, and this increases as utterances are allowed to be longer. Kenny Smith (2008b) has done some relevant calculations. He ran Monte Carlo simulations generating pairs of utterances at random 10,000 times. He did this for various alphabets and with various permitted utterance lengths. He counted the ratio of overlaps (pairs containing an identical substring) to non-overlaps (pairs not containing any identical substring). Looking for a substring of length 1, the ratio of overlaps to non-overlaps, that is the ratio of confirming cases to counterexamples to the fractionation story, hits 1:1 with utterances three elements long made from an alphabet of five. With a larger alphabet, of 20 elements, utterances have to be thirteen elements long before the ratio of confirming cases to counterexamples hits 1:1. To work well, fractionation needs small sets of recognizable discrete phonetic elements and longish utterances. Smith points out that even a high ratio of counterexamples to confirming cases is not necessarily a barrier to induction of atomic meaning–form pairs by a learner. He gives the example of English past tenses. Children learning English are able to figure out that the *-ed* suffix, in its various phonetic forms, means PAST, despite the fact that, by his calculations, the number of counterexamples, i.e. irregular verbs like *came*, *went*, and *did*, outnumbers the confirming cases, when counting tokens in discourse.

The moral that Kenny Smith draws is that, as far as the numbers are concerned, it could happen, but it is unlikely. '[U]nder the (reasonably plausible) assumptions that utterances are relatively short and do not consist of a very small number of segments, counter-examples should, on average, outnumber confirming cases. The counter-example problem is particularly marked if we assume that analysis requires matching of longer substrings ($l > 1$), at which point counter-examples tend to outnumber confirming cases for all but the most contrived of cases' (Smith 2008b, p. 9). The utterances in Kirby's simulations described above were not short. The ten examples that he gives (p. 313) have an average length of 9.9, with some as long as seventeen elements. They are composed from a very small alphabet of five elements, **a, b, c, d, e**. By Smith's calculations, in this simulation, confirming cases are likely to outnumber counterexamples by about six to one. The dice were loaded in favour of chance coincidences in the phonetic forms of utterances.

It seemed to me that Smith's numbers are too generous to the fractionation story, because one also needs to calculate the likelihood of any phonetically overlapping pair also being a semantically overlapping pair. I put this point to Kenny Smith, who replied 'Indeed, so those calculations are just for one side of the question' (personal communication). To evaluate the viability of the fractionation account, one must calculate the likelihood of the required phonetic-semantic coincidences for a given random phonetic space (alphabet + length of utterances), and a given random semantic space (inventory of basic terms, and permitted complexity of semantic formulae). A standard technique for doing this exists, the Mantel test (Mantel 1967; Sokal and Rohlf 1995), which measures the correlation between similarities in one space and similarities in another space. I have not done the sums, but it is clear that the probability of such coincidences, 'confirming cases' would be lower than Smith's calculations suggest.

The numbers are crucial. Presented with a relatively orderly corpus of utterances, such as a modern child receives, the child is able to detect the orderly correspondences, despite noise from irregularities which are counterexamples. Any system which is transmitted relatively faithfully from one generation to the next by learning, as languages are, must have a certain level of regular form–meaning correspondence. Irregularity can be tolerated, that is passed on to the next generation, only if the examples are frequent enough. That is why there is a correlation between irregularity and word-frequency. The irregular verbs are the most frequent ones. We have to suppose that any accidental level of form–meaning correspondence in a holistic system would have been orders of magnitude lower than in modern languages. For this reason, it seems to me that the statistical odds are highly stacked against the holistic system being so conveniently amenable to fractionation.

There might be one last desperate throw against this numbers argument. Over time, any holistic system would drift around in the space of possible holistic meaning–form pairings. At any given moment in time the chances of a holistic system being statistically likely to offer the right number of correspondences are small. But given a few hundred thousand years in which to mutate randomly, the chances are higher that, at some point, the correspondences would reach the critical level, making fractionation a possibility. At this point, our ancestors might have grabbed the lucky opportunity, and the rest is history. For this case, even Kenny Smith could not do the required sums, because we can't make realistic assumptions about the rate of change in a holistic system.

Wray published another article (2002a) two years later than the main one I have been citing. Here again she stresses the parallel existence in modern adult language of formulaic expressions and atomistic (my term) or 'analytic' (her term) expressions, that is novel phrases and sentences. This is surely a correct picture, consistent with my own emphasis on massive storage in Chapter 5, section 1. Wray suggests that there was a very long period when hominins had only formulaic expressions, perhaps almost a million years, and this was a force for mental conservatism, possibly accounting for the suprisingly static nature of *Homo erectus* culture, as far as we can glimpse it through the uniformity of the stone tools they have left us. This seems very plausible. Only with the advent of atomistic/'analytic' language could our ancestors begin to talk more productively about novel events, albeit events with familiar participants. After this advent, both kinds of system co-existed, each with its own peculiar advantages. The holistic system was useful as an economical and direct shorthand for common interpersonal interactions. The new productive system began to grow the advantages that we recognize in productive syntax today. And, as said before, both kinds of language continue to coexist. Only the balance has shifted in favour of productive grammatical language. Wray emphasizes that the modern balance is much less weighted in favour of atomistic/'analytic' language than work in syntactic theory would have us believe.

Wray's 2002 article only mentions the segmentation (aka fractionation) route from a holistic system to an atomistic system in a footnote (p. 118). Elsewhere in the paper she envisages a different kind of transition, actually involving putting elements from the holistic language together. Here is the scenario she envisages:

The message inventory will include a separate message form for each of 'W I S W I W Y T[38] fetch N', where N is every member of the group (or at least every member that might be fetched). In other words there is a distinct phonetic form associated with each individual in the group, for the context of 'fetch that person'. Once you have *any* message for which each individual has his or her own personal referential form, you have attained proper names by the back door, even if, in the first instance, there is additional message material tagged on. (Wray 2002a, pp. 123–4)

Let's pause there to take stock. The members of this tribe have N specific expressions for 'fetch someone', varying systematically with the identity of the person to be fetched. And if they have these, nothing in this approach would suggest that they don't also have another N specific holistic expressions for 'share this with someone', again mapping systematically onto the people

---

[38] This is Wray's abbreviation for 'what I say when I want you to', a device adopted to emphasize the imperative force of the following expression, and to discourage any temptation to parse it into bits.

to be shared with. And so on, for 'Don't tell someone', 'Avoid someone', for all the other gossipy, Machiavellian alliance-forming formulae that would be useful in a group of hominins somewhere between chimpanzees and modern hunter-gatherers. And, by Wray's hypothesis, none of these holistic expressions about a particular individual would necessarily have anything in common. 'Fetch Mary' need not be at all similar to 'share this with Mary'. Wray says these people have 'attained proper names by the back door'. But they would probably have attained a whole lot of different proper names for each person by this back door, one for every formula-type. This seems to me a circuitous and inefficient route to attaining proper names. I prefer the front door—call Mary *Mary*. (And anyway, as I have argued elsewhere,[39] proper names are actually originally derived from descriptions, like 'fat woman' or 'walks funny' or 'loud talker'.) The 'additional message material tagged on' to each back-door proper name seems now like an embarrassing side-effect of a creaky theory. Wray continues,

Let us next imagine that a speaker wishes to get a hearer to give an apple to Mary, but, though the apple is in plain view, Mary is not present and so cannot be indicated by gesture. The speaker resolves the problem by saying first *baku*, 'w I s w I w y T fetch Mary', and then *tebima* 'w I s w I w y T give specified object (distant) to specified female person.' Since only one of the two variable referents (the apple) has been indicated by gesture, the hearer is seeking local information that will indicate who the recipient of the apple is. Provided *baku* is viewed as somehow relevant to this quest, the effect (whether on this first occasion or only after repeated usage) will be to interpret 'w I s w I w y T fetch Mary' as a perceptual rather than physical manipulator ('conjure up an image of Mary').   (Wray 2002a, p. 124)

Right, so the effect is achieved by juxtaposing two elements from the holistic system—you say *baku tebima*. No fractionation here, but some rather convoluted semantics to get from the dogmatic position that the holistic signals originally encoded generic whole event-types. How much simpler is an account where *baku* means MARY and *tebima* means GIVE, and the speaker utters *baku tebima* gesturing toward the apple, as in Wray's account.

Wray's account here envisages the combination of gestures with words. That is already a kind of putting together. As the work of Goldin-Meadow and her colleagues shows (Iverson and Goldin-Meadow 2005), such gesture+word combinations in young children pave the way to word+word combinations a few months later. (See also Mayberry and Nicoladis 2000; Nicoladis et al.

---

[39] Hurford (2003, 2001b).

1999.) Kanzi's researchers also count his gesture+lexigram combinations as sentence-like.

The synthetic route from a holistic stage to atomistic word-strings has its computational proof of concept, too, in a simulation in Hurford (2000b). This simulation was very like Kirby's, cited above, in assuming that the simulated agents could mentally represent whole propositions in PREDICATE(*argument(s)*) form. And as in Kirby's simulation, a population that started with no systematic meaning–form mappings ended up after some generations with a shared little grammar and lexicon adequate for describing the semantic space involved. The overall message of the work was essentially similar to Kirby's— a model of how a systematic language can emerge from initially random behaviour over generations of iterated learning in a population. But crucially, the route by which these simulated agents got to that result was the synthetic route. They could learn the names of predicates and arguments in isolation, and were able to put them together to form sentences. As is typical of computational models in the area, this showed what could happen, not what must have happened. Thus simulations have shown that both the analytic and synthetic routes to syntax could have worked, if the premises on which they are based really were true of our ancestors' abilities and dispositions.

The discussion so far has been between two extremes. Either all one-word utterances denoted whole complex propositions or they all denoted more atomic concepts, the predicates and arguments of propositions. There could have been an intermediate situation, in which some words denoted whole complex propositions and some other words denoted the more atomic concepts. Mike Dowman (2008) has carried out iterated learning simulations which can be tweaked to give any outcome you want, from extreme holophrastic, through intermediate possibilities, to extreme atomistic. His simulations are not of the emergence of syntax, like Kirby's and Hurford's mentioned above. Dowman simulated the rise of 'single-word' codes in populations that had various capacities for conceptual representation and articulation of signals. In conditions where the agents had limited ability to produce signals (e.g. only ten different 'words'), but a rich set of conceptual representations (e.g. 120 complex meanings composed from ten atomic concepts), an atomistic code emerged, with one word per atomic concept. On the other hand, when the semantic and phonetic abilities were in a different relationship, the opposite result was obtained. That is, in conditions where the agents had versatile abilities to produce signals (e.g. 150 different 'words'), with the same conceptual representations (e.g. 120 complex meanings), a holophrastic code emerged in which each complex situation was signalled by its own word. Naturally, with intermediate-sized vocabularies of signals, intermediate situations emerged, with some words expressing holophrastic meanings and other words expressing atomic meanings. This is very elegant work.

Dowman considered two further extensions to his basic model. In one, certain of the complex meanings were called into use much more frequently than the others. He found that '[m]aking some meanings especially frequent ... seems to have had little effect on the nature of the emergent languages' (p. 455). The other extension of the work was to model evolutionary increases in either the set of conceptual representations or the set of possible signals, or a coevolutionary scenario where both semantic and phonetic abilities expand. These dynamic results were consistent with the earlier static results. The emergent codes depended on the final ratio of possible meanings to possible signals. Dowman summarizes:[40]

> If communicative ability evolves more rapidly than conceptual capacity, we would expect a move towards more holophrastic protolanguages, while if conceptual capacity evolves more rapidly than communicative ability, we should expect a move towards less holophrastic protolanguages. As these two abilities likely evolved at different rates at different points in the course of human evolution, there may well have been multiple transitions between holophrastic protolanguages and protolanguages where the words had atomic meanings.   (Dowman 2008, p. 459)

Given what we know about apes' conceptual abilities and their vocalization abilities, it seems likely that our post-ape ancestors had relatively meagre signal production capacity compared to the events and situations that they could mentally represent. This makes an atomistic pre-protolanguage more likely, by Dowman's results. Even if this were not the case, and there was a more holophrastic pre-protolanguage, the numerical problem remains of the low likelihood of chance coincidences between segments of the signals and components of the meanings (as estimated, for example, using the Mantel test).

In sum, for the reasons given, I find the synthetic putting-things-together route from a one-element stage to a multi-element stage more plausible than the alternative analytic fractionating route. Indeed, modern children do dissect the prefabricated expressions of their elders; but the first humans to produce systematically meaningful two-word strings had no prior generation of elders to feed them prefabricated expressions. They did it by stringing their existing

---

[40] In this quotation, 'protolanguage' should be read as 'one-word language'. In my usage, 'protolanguage' describes a stage where words are already concatenated, albeit with no syntactic organization. Dowman's simulations are thus about a pre-protolanguage, one-word, stage. And 'communicative ability' might be better glossed as 'signal production ability'.

words together, as we see in the beginning stages of Nicaraguan Sign Language, pidgins, the early language of many modern children, and Kanzi's productions. As soon as a multi-word stage is up and running, it is to be expected that some frequent utterance-types will be taken as holistic by at least some users in the next generation. At that point, an interesting cycle of language growth can begin.

CHAPTER 9

Grammaticalization

We know a lot about how languages have changed in the last several millennia. Historical linguistics has built up histories of many different language families, sometimes appealing to documentary evidence, but more often proceeding on the basis of certain assumptions about the nature of language change. It is generally agreed that it is not possible to reconstruct the grammar of any 'Mother language' beyond a time depth of about 5,000 years at the most. The evidential trail for traditional historical linguistic reconstruction peters out, because languages change so much that the premises on which hypotheses are based get weaker and weaker. In parallel with traditional reconstructive methods, a body of theory labelled 'grammaticalization' has grown up which gives reasonable grounds for speculating about what the grammars of the very earliest languages were like. This chapter will introduce the basic ideas of grammaticalization theory and apply them to devising an account of the very beginnings of syntactical organization in languages. But first, it is appropriate to set the scene by sketching the relevant history of humans, along with some previous ideas about how languages have changed in relation to this history.

9.1 Setting: in and out of Africa

I assume that humans moved out of Africa in small hunter-gatherer bands, and that small hunter-gatherer bands also dispersed through Africa. For a very long time, before the world started to fill up with humans, these small groups would have occupied their own proper small territories. No doubt there was some trade, exogamy and warfare between groups, but not enough to weaken their identity as groups. The group territories may have shifted and subgroups would have split off to occupy new territories. The history of the diversification of languages is one of successive relative geographical isolation of groups. That's how we got so many different language families and so many different languages within the families.

Givón locates his society of intimates far back in evolution, starting even with dog packs (Givón 1979a, p. 287). He argues that the social structure of early human groups was similar, being small, kin-related, living in a familiar, stable natural environment (however tough), with largely undifferentiated needs and roles. Societies of intimates have persisted throughout human evolution, as even some modern groups, such as the Pirahã among many others, fit this description rather well. Since the beginning of human evolution, there have always been tightly knit groups of intimates, and some modern ones (e.g. Andaman Islanders) may possibly have a continuous history going back 100,000 years, although not necessarily always in the same location. The earliest humans lived and wandered in such groups for tens of thousands of years. Occasionally groups divided, never again to re-unite until modern times. As they penetrated new lands and established new homes across the globe, staying relatively self-sufficient and jealous of their group identities, their languages changed, giving us the diversity we can still see today.

The languages that exist now are a small subset of all that have existed in the past. Pagel (2000a) worked with mathematical models to get rough estimates of the number of languages ever spoken.

The total number of languages ever spoken dramatically exceeds the number of extant languages, ... Choosing the middle figure of 100,000 years ago for the origin and one language per 1,000 years still yields a figure of about 130,000 languages ever spoken. Throughout history, the overwhelming majority (80–99%) of the languages humans have invented have gone extinct. ... These figures are intriguingly similar to estimates of the fraction of biological species that have gone extinct. Raup (1991) estimates that up to 99% of all species that have ever lived are extinct.   (Pagel 2000a, p. 395)

Human dispersion and concomitant language creation went on for possibly as long as 150,000 years. During this time, probably no separate language community numbered more than a few thousand people. Givón's idea is that human language originated in such small human groups; Trudgill's and Wray and Grace's idea (Trudgill 1992, 2003; Wray and Grace 2007) is that morphosyntactic complexity grew and flourished in such groups, in the absence of large-scale contact with, and influence from, other groups.

Then, quite recently in human history, conditions changed. The habitable world began to fill up with humans, and first agriculture, and then cities and empires began to appear. Where previously there had been little contact between different language communities, now there began, in different parts of the world at somewhat different times, to be substantial contact between language communities. This contact ranged from extreme suppression, even extermination, of language communities, to stable coexistence, with trade and bilingualism or multilingualism. Some language communities grew very large, some even getting into the millions of speakers.

The implication for language evolution is that it has in some aspects followed a curvilinear trajectory. The early languages of small bands gradually developed complex morphology (by means to be described) and somewhat complex syntax, perhaps over as long as 100,000 years. Some of these small languages developed 'exotic' features not typical of languages in general. The social cohesiveness of the small groups helped to preserve any such idiosyncratic features. With the advent of increased contact and larger language communities, there was simplification of morphology and exchange of syntactic constructions tending to weed out the more exotic and less functionally efficient ones. Here 'functionally efficient' refers to such factors as learnability, parsability, and producibility. In modern times, with the rise of empires, communication, and increased trade, groups have integrated into larger communities, losing their small-group identities. With these modern developments individuals had to face for the first time the prospect of dealing every day with strangers, whose native languages or dialects they do not share. In these circumstances, morphosyntax is simplified, in the way we have seen for pidgins, creoles, and the Basic Variety. That is the basic simple story—steady prehistoric accumulation of idiosyncratic linguistic complexities in small groups, followed by a tendency in historic times to lose at least some of this complexity in large modern communities. **Of course** it's not as simple as that when we get down to details of individual languages and communities. There are counterexamples and complicating factors.

There is a mistaken tendency to think that evolution, of any kind, proceeds in a uniform direction. But as environments change, the path of evolution may change. The natural environment of a language is its social group. To some, there has appeared to be a puzzle, in that the recent known history of Indo-European languages involves steady simplification of morphology.

All the signs, then, seemed to point to some Golden Age lying somewhere in the twilight of prehistory (just before records began), when languages were graced with perfectly formed structures, especially with elaborate arrays of endings on words. But at some subsequent stage, and for some unknown reason, the forces of destruction were unleashed on the languages and began battering the carefully crafted edifices, wearing away all those endings.   (Deutscher 2005, p. 7)

This is certainly how the widely knowledgeable August Schleicher (1850, ch. III) saw the life of languages: 'the further we trace a language back, the more perfect we find it. ...In historic times, we know from experience, it is all downhill with languages, and we don't see any new ones arising. ...The development of languages occurs in pre-history, the decay of languages by contrast in historical times' (pp. 11–13).[1] This is a Eurocentric view, as Chinese, for example, has been an isolating language without serious inflectional morphology for all of its history, dating back several thousand years. To us, it is hard to see why one should equate morphological complexity with perfection.[2] It also is hard to see how the dawn of history could have had a causal effect on languages. But if we replace 'history' by 'extensive language contact', we get a quite plausible story. With the great benefit of hindsight, we may think it odd that the nineteenth-century linguists did not see this. Seventy years later, the same facts were recognized, but now without the fatalistic historicist overtones. Jespersen, a linguist of undoubted care and knowledge, saw positive salutary progress in the same trend:

We have found certain traits common to the old stages and certain others characteristic of recent ones, and have thus been enabled to establish some definite tendencies of development and to find out the general direction of change; and we have shown reasons for the conviction that this development has on the whole and in the main been a beneficial one, thus justifying us in speaking about 'progress in language'. The points in which the superiority of the modern languages manifested itself were the following:

(1) The forms are generally shorter, thus involving less muscular exertion and requiring less time for their enunciation.

(2) There are not so many of them to burden the memory.

(3) Their formation is much more regular.

(4) Their syntactic use also presents fewer irregularities.

(5) Their more analytic and abstract character facilitates expression by rendering possible a great many combinations and constructions which were formerly impossible or unidiomatic.

(6) The clumsy repetitions known under the name of concord have become superfluous.

(7) A clear and unambiguous understanding is secured through a regular word order.

---

[1] My translation: the original German was 'Je weiter zurück wir eine Sprache verfolgen können, desto vollkommener finden wir sie...In historischen Zeiten, das wissen wir aus Erfahrung, geht es mit den Sprachen als solche abwärts...Die Bildung der Sprachen fällt also vor die Geschichte, der Verfall der Sprachen dagegen in die historische Zeit'.

[2] But then, even now, some people have weird ideas about perfection in language.

These several advantages have not been won all at once, and languages differ very much in the velocity with which they have been moving in the direction indicated; thus High German is in many respects behindhand as compared with low German.

(Jespersen 1922, p. 364)

This is the prescription of a busy modern no-nonsense man who wants his information fast and free from complications of speaker identity. But life is different if lived entirely in a low-tech village with only a few hundred other people you ever deal with cooperatively. Here, a large slice of the function of language is to **fit in**, not to stand out too much, to conform successfully to the subtle and idiosyncratic norms that have evolved in the community. The propositional informative function of language is still important, but it must be dressed in clothes that everyone else recognizes as conforming to the communal norms. Everett's Pirahã informants often said 'we don't do that because we are Pirahã'.

Jespersen further wrote 'The evolution of language shows a progressive tendency from inseparable irregular conglomerations to freely and regularly combinable short elements' (p. 429). The obvious question is 'But how did those inseparable irregular conglomerations evolve?' The outline given above suggests the answer. The social environments of languages changed around the dawn of history. Before that, with relatively isolated language communities, the conditions were conducive to the accumulation of complex morphology, with not a great deal of pressure to develop highly recursive syntax. After that, with decreasing isolation of language communities, conditions were less conducive to the maintenance of this kind of complexity, and it dwindled, to be replaced by periphrastic syntactic devices. Later still, in those societies which developed writing, more syntactically hierarchical constructions emerged, with the possibility of more deeply hierarchical structured sentences. This is of course a very broad-brush sketch of what happened, correct, I believe, in outline, but do doubt with many complicating wrinkles and local counterexamples.

It is a better story than Schleicher's. The great German nineteenth-century scholar believed that each language had a life, just like an individual animal or plant. 'Languages are organisms of nature;...they rose, and developed themselves according to definite laws; they grew old, and died out' (Schleicher 1863, pp. 20–1).[3] A language is only a living organism in a metaphorical sense. It has no physical body, has no DNA, no constant cell division and cell decay, and suffers no traumas from war, disease, or hunger, except in that metaphorical sense. One should not be misled by the metaphor.

---

[3] Schleicher also wrote, foreshadowing *Language in the Light of Evolution*, 'so long as we are ignorant of how a thing arose we cannot be said to know it' (p. 26).

The changing nature of languages over tens of millennia brings up the topic of **uniformitarianism.** The idea was applied systematically in geology before it was applied to language. James Hutton, known as the father of modern geology (and an Edinburgh man), argued that the processes that shape the earth have been constant throughout the ages (Hutton 1788). This does not mean, of course, that the nature of the earth has been constant for all time. Once, the earth did not even exist, just as languages once (much more recently) did not exist. **Static** uniformitarianism, applied to language is the doctrine that languages have always had the same essential nature. If we believe that the language capacity and languages evolved, this doctrine is untenable. **Dynamic** uniformitarianism, akin to Hutton's geological vision, applied to languages, holds that the cognitive and social pressures that shape languages have always acted according to the same fundamental principles. This is tenable in the face of evolution. The cognitive, and particularly the social contexts in which these principles apply may differ, and therefore the principles will yield different outcomes. Analogously, in geology, the laws of physics have been constant through the shaping of the earth. But the recent earth is a lot cooler than the early earth, yielding different geological phenomena. Again analogously, it is reasonable to suppose that natural selection has operated since the beginnings of life. But the nature of life on earth has changed since life started. So too with languages.

9.2 Introducing grammaticalization

We pick up now from the previous chapter in discussing an aspect of language evolution that cannot be expected to follow closely the same course as language development in a modern child. A modern child is exposed to grammatical speech with (depending on the language) many function words and morphological inflections, and rules of word order. Thus, even in short utterances, children may start to use function words, inflections, and word order following the adult model. From what we have seen of modern cases of language invention, function words do not appear in new languages until a solid base of expressions with juxtaposed content words has been built up. Function words, morphological inflections, and word order, and the complex constructions they signal, are characteristic of modern complex syntax. How, in the first wave of human languages after they started to put words together, did function words and inflections, and fixed orderings of words first appear? A large body of theory, **grammaticalization theory** has investigated the corresponding general question in relation to today's languages. 'Grammaticalization'[4] is a broad label for several different facets of the cultural evolution of languages. Grammaticalization is a process whereby the effects of frequent use, for example routinization of set expressions and phonetic erosion, become entrenched as part of the learned structure of a language. It is a case of the accumulated effects of linguistic performance over generations shaping the competence of later generations.

Under the heading of grammaticalization, several unidirectional processes have been studied. One is the process recruiting a content word as a more specialized grammatical morpheme, or functional item. This was Meillet's emphasis in one of the earliest grammaticalization studies (Meillet 1912), and dubbed the 'lexical item > morpheme model' by Traugott and Heine (1991). Another, two-stage, process adopts a frequent discourse pattern as a learned syntactic construction, which may then undergo a change to a morphological pattern; Givón (1979a, p. 209) summarizes this as 'Discourse → Syntax → Morphology'. These two processes are mutually compatible. In what follows I will draw on examples of both kinds of process. Hopper and Traugott (1993, p. 7) write of a 'cline of grammaticality' as follows:

content item > grammatical word > clitic > inflectional affix

'...Each item to the right is clearly more grammatical and less lexical than its partner to the left'. The examples I will discuss fit into this scheme (I will not go into the nicety of the difference between clitics and inflectional affixes). Under the dynamic uniformitarian assumption that early human linguistic behaviour was guided by the same principles as modern behaviour, we can use the revelations of grammaticalization studies to reverse-engineer back from modern syntactic structures through the unidirectional processes that built them up. If protolanguage is words strung together without grammar, and modern mature languages use grammar to put words together, grammaticalization, as I exploit it here, is the process bridging that gap. It is a gradual cultural alternative to any putative 'syntax mutation'. Languages, under most social conditions, grow more grammatical over time, meaning that they develop more specific constraints on how words are put together (involving a growing number of word classes) and how the resulting sentences are interpreted. I will focus on the more particularly syntactic aspects of grammaticalization, in particular the rise of function words, inflections, and word order.

---

[4] Sometimes also 'grammaticization'; the terms are pretty much equivalent.

It must be noted at the outset that different languages have followed different routes of grammaticalization. In some, like English, word order has become relatively fixed, and English has no inflections on nouns marking case (who did what to whom). In other languages, most notably the 'non-configurational' languages, word order is relatively free, and case inflections take up the communicative load of making clear who did what to whom. Different languages have become grammaticalized in different ways, and to differing degrees. In Riau Indonesian, either grammaticalization has hardly happened, or contact has brought about a process of degrammaticalization,[5] whereby complexity is lost. Grammaticalization is not an inexorable force. In the right social circumstances it proceeds in one general direction, but its effects can be demolished by upsets in the social structure, most obviously by drastic mixing of populations.

Up to here, we have only got to about a two-word stage with the 'One word, two words...' theme of the previous chapter. Getting a shared vocabulary and then stringing the words together into very short sentence-like units were probably the slowest steps in language evolution, perhaps taking as much as a million years. Given the expressive potential of two- and three-word utterances, with a decent vocabulary, there was then inevitable pressure to use longer expressions. For longer expressions to be less ambiguous, they need some internal organization to allow users to handle them and to navigate inside them. Function words and inflections provide that scaffolding. But no individual speaker foresaw the usefulness of function words and inflections, decided they would be a good thing, and invented them. Language change doesn't work like that. Rather, grammaticalization, a kind of language change, occurs by patterns of use that happen to be frequent becoming entrenched as fixed conventions that speakers follow. When such conventions become fixed, speakers tend to notice if they are violated. Breach of the conventions marks a speaker as an outsider or a beginner. The main point of speaking is still communication, but a new aspect is introduced, communication using the adopted norms of the group. Pidgins and Basic Variety may get a message across, but users of full languages typically expect more than just getting a message across—the message should be framed in a certain way, and use the constructions that have come to be followed and accepted by the group. An important step occurs between merely putting words together (as in *hug Nim*

---

[5] Degrammaticalization is not the reverse process of grammaticalization, just as the demolition of a house is not the reverse in strict order of the processes involved in building the house.

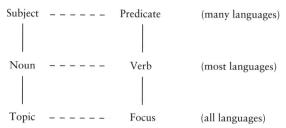

Fig. 9.1 Common binary grammatical contrasts. The horizontal dashed lines represent a relation of opposition within a binary distinction. All languages mark the Topic–Focus distinction somehow. Most, but not all, languages make a distinction between nouns and verbs. And many, but not all, languages mark Subjects as a special element. The Subject and Topic of a sentence often coincide, and the Topic element is typically a noun or noun phrase. The Predicate and Focus (or 'Comment') of a sentence often coincide, and the Predicate element is typically a verb or verb phrase. The vertical solid lines indicate these coincidences, and an evolutionary relationship, upward in the diagram, between these features of a fully developed grammatical system.

Source: Substantially adapted from Foley (2005, p. 49).

hug) and putting words together in a conventionally structured package (as Kanzi appeared to with his 'gesture follows lexigram' rule.[6]

9.3 Topics give rise to nouns

The most basic grammaticalization steps in the evolution of languages involve the network of concepts in Figure 9.1.

This section and the next will set out the view, common in the literature, that the most basic communicatively functional distinction is between Topic and Focus (or Comment), and that the Subject–Predicate distinction is derivative of it. This argument is fairly common; it is less common to argue, as I will, that the Noun/Verb distinction also derives, in the evolution of language, from the Topic–Comment distinction.[7] The connection between evolution and

---

[6] Kanzi's rule was a 'one-user convention', idiosyncratic to him. I can stretch the idea of 'convention' to one-person behaviours if the behaviour follows some rule that is not dictated by outside influences. Many people have speech idiosyncrasies that they follow as regularly as they follow rules that other people observe. Our concern here will not be with personal idiosyncrasies but with the emergence of conventions that everyone in the group follows.

[7] You may have noticed the difference in my notations for two kinds of related distinction: Noun/Verb, Topic–Comment, and Subject–Predicate. The Noun/Verb distinction is what linguists call a **paradigmatic** difference, here a difference between words as listed in a lexicon. In a language that follows a strict distinction between nouns and verbs, a given noun, for example, is always a noun, whatever sentence it is used

acquisition is nicely summed up by Bates and MacWhinney (1979): '[C]hildren can indeed discover the structure of grammar by rediscovering the same solutions mankind has always had to apply to the set of converging constraints on communication' (pp. 209–10). This 'rediscovery' is true of cases where children are not simply following the model of their elders' usage.

In the last chapter, adapting an example from Chapter 5, I imagined a situation where a speaker uses a one-word utterance, repeated here:

| RUN |
| WOMEN | → 'Run' or → 'Women'.

It was envisaged that the speaker would not feel the need to say anything identifying the object in question, as the context of the utterance makes it likely that the hearer is also attending to just this aspect of the scene. But in many cases, the context is not so helpful, and the hearer needs explicitly to identify what he is talking about. Now imagine (1) you are cognitively able to package two words together into a unified signal, and (2) you have seen this same scene of women running, and want to comment on it to a person who you are not sure has identified the same aspects of the scene as you. Depending on your assessment of what the hearer is most aware of, you might package the appropriate words together in either of the following ways:

| RUN |
| WOMEN | → 'Run women' or → 'Women run'.

This is parallel to the versatility, noted in Chapter 5, of words in some languages, for example Nootka and Tongan, to serve in either a Noun/Subject/Topic role or a Verb/Predicate/Focus role. The difference between those languages and my hypothetical example is that Nootka and Tongan have inflections or function words that explicitly mark the roles played by the words in the sentence. At the protolanguage stage, it is likely that two uninflected content words were strung together without helping function words, in a linear order that began to signal which word identifies the

---

in. For example, *rice* is a noun in English, and you know this without seeing it in an example sentence. By contrast, you can't sensibly ask of a given word, out of a sentential context, whether it is a Subject or a Topic. It depends on the structure of a sentence that the word is used in. For instance the word *rice* is the Subject in *Rice is cheap*, but not in *We boiled rice*. Likewise, you can't sensibly ask whether *rice* is a Topic, without mentioning the sentence you have in mind. *Rice* is the Topic in *Rice, it grows in China*, but not in *Wheat is cheaper than rice*. The Subject–Predicate and Topic–Comment distinctions express **syntagmatic** structural relations within a given sentence. The Noun/Verb distinction expresses a paradigmatic distinction within the overall language system, here within the lexicon.

Topic. The natural position for a Topic, attested across the great majority of constructions in the great majority of languages, is sentence-initial. We see this in new sign languages and in two-word child language.

In an early study of topicalization in child language, Gruber (1967) found a child systematically using utterance types which were not patterned on the usage of his parents or any adult around him. The child, Mackie, produced these: *him bear, him bad dog, them eyes, me no bear*. In the first three cases the intended meaning was predicating some one-place concept(s) (BEAR, BAD & DOG, EYES) of an entity picked out by the pronoun. In the fourth case, the predication of BEAR is negated. These pronouns were not used with this function by Mackie's adult models. Mackie is not an isolated case. I, like many others, have noticed English-learning children coming out with such utterances. Vainikka (1993/1994, p. 263) cites a child of just over two saying both *I get Bozo* and *Me get John* in the same recording session. I remember *me come to party* by a child wanting to come to a party.[8] These uses of the accusative pronoun are spontaneous child productions not modelled on the adult language. The child seems to select these pronouns as expressing the Topic of a message, and puts them first in a short utterance, often just two words. In starting to communicate, Mackie seems to use two different grammatical systems in parallel. One is consistent with the English he is picking up from his environment; the other is his own instinctive invention (using English words). Thus we have the contrasts below:

I wanna	*me wanna truck*
he take the wheel, fire engine	*me take the wheel*
I show you?	*me show you?*
I write	*me draw*
I see the tree	*him go right back*
he bites anyone	*no him no bite*

(From Gruber 1967, p. 53)

The utterances starting with *me* and *him* were not like anything Mackie had heard around him. Gruber notes that the third example, the questioning *me show you?* had declarative falling intonation on the pronoun, then an intonation break and rising question intonation on the rest of the utterance. Mackie here seems, in my terms, to be putting his message into two short packages. Then later the two elements get rolled into a single package, as 'later repetitions of "me show you?" have a continuous rise' (p. 53). Gruber

---

[8] Further instances are noted by Fromkin et al. (2000); Budwig (1989, 1995); Huxley (1970); Powers (1995); Rispoli (1994); Tanz (1974).

interprets the utterances beginning with *me* and *him* as Mackie's spontaneous solution to the problem of drawing some emphatic attention to the entity picked out. He calls it 'Topic', but it seems likely that there is also an element of contrastive meaning. Gruber's conclusion is 'It would seem then that the topic–comment relation is the precursor of the subject–predicate relation. ... a child learning a language for the first time first produces sentences without subjects. Then he uses the innately known topic–comment construction to compose richer sentences. Later, if he is learning English, he comes to give the construction its special characteristics, ultimately arriving at the subject–predicate construction' (pp. 64–5). Gruber was writing in the 1960s, in the conceptual mindset of the syntactic theory of that era. Hence the mention of an 'innately known construction'. There is no mention of a basic communicative function as opposed to the innate construction. And Gruber, like linguists of that time, tried to attribute various somewhat abstract tree structures and rules to the child on the basis of his behaviour. He was trying to make sense of the data in terms of the dominant theories of the decade. But the move to emphasizing the basicness of the Topic–Comment relation reflects a seminal insight. There is no justification for applying the Noun/Verb or Subject–Predicate terms to Mackie's *him bear* or *me draw*. Nouns and verbs, Subjects and Predicates are defined in relation to other parts of a more developed system than a simple two-element system. At this stage, Mackie has a system that places a Topic word such as *me*, *him*, or *them* first, and then follows it with **any other informative word or small phrase** that he has learned, like *bear*, *draw*, or *wanna truck*. The likelihood is that at this stage a string like *wanna truck* is learned as a holistic unit. For this simple system, no insight is gained by applying labels like 'Noun', 'Verb', 'Subject', or 'Predicate'. In the adult language *bear* is a noun, *draw* is a verb, and *wanna truck* is a verb phrase. But not for Mackie; they are just things that you say after your Topic expression, *me*, *him*, or *them*. Since Topic–Comment is a distinction rooted in function, we can reasonably recognize these utterances of Mackie's as having Topic–Comment (or Topic–Focus) structure, because we (think we) understand why he was speaking like this. Although his parents did not use these expressions, they understood him when he used them.

An interesting question, not directly related to language evolution, is why English-learning children pick the Accusative case for their Topic marker. In English, the Accusative (e.g. *me*, *him*, *her*) is the **default case**, as opposed to the Nominative (*I*, *he*, *she*) (Marantz 1991; Schütze 2001; Fromkin et al. 2000). These Accusative forms are those most often used in the adult language in phonetically stressed positions and where they are not tightly bound into the structure of a sentence. For example, Question: *Who's there?*; Answer: *Me*. The Accusative forms are also used as Topic in the adult language, as in *Me*,

I'm hungry and *Him, he's crazy*. The English-learning child presumably finds
these pronouns the most salient and adopts them as his own Topic versions.
In other languages, different cases are the default. Our earliest ancestors, of
course, had no model to follow, and no language around them with any
developed case system, so for them talk of 'Accusative' or 'Nominative' case
is irrelevant. To make a statement about a person, they would presumably
have used any referring word that had by then been developed. Note that these
child expressions like *him bear* and *me draw* are like the Root Small Clauses
mentioned in Chapter 5, section 2 as vestiges of ancient forms in modern
language; examples were *Me first!*, *Him retire?*, and *Her happy?*.[9]

   Mackie's simple system was perhaps a little more flexible. When *him*, *me*,
and *them* were used as Topic, the Topic always came first in his utterance. But
he also used words which are nouns in adult English as Topics, and in Gruber's
analysis these could come either before or after the Comment expression, as
these examples, sorted by Gruber's analysis, show.

Topic after the Comment	Topic before the Comment
all broken wheel	*dump truck all fixed*
break pumpkin	*other wheel broke*
in there wheels	*truck broke*
in there baby	*wheel in there*
go truck	*Mama goes*

(From Gruber 1967, pp. 49–50)

Gruber clearly tended to envisage the child's emergent grammar in terms of
the adult target language. In the examples above, he systematically classified
a word as a Topic only if it was a noun in the adult language. Hence he was
obliged to say that in Mackie's system the Topic could either precede or follow
the Comment. Gruber mentions no possible nuance of meaning carried by these
alternative orders. But there is an alternative analysis: that all the examples
above have the same Topic–Comment order, with Topic expression first in all
cases. It's just that, at this stage, Mackie used any content word as a Topic,
regardless of its syntactic category in the adult language. Recall the Nootka
and Tongan examples of Chapter 5, glossed as 'the man is working' versus
'the worker is a man' and 'the women were running' versus 'the running ones
were all women'. Mackie could have been making a similar distinction between
truck broke and what we have to gloss as 'the breaking thing is a pumpkin'
(*break pumpkin*). Likewise his *go truck* could be glossed as 'the going thing is

---

[9] *Me Tarzan* and *You Jane* are no accident.

a truck'. These English glosses are clumsy, because we are stuck with the rigid adult language, in which this is the only way to make entities identified by their movement (e.g. going, breaking) the Topic or Subject of a sentence.

I am assuming that language evolution followed a similar course to what we see in language acquisition, especially where there is evidence of spontaneous construction-building by the child. So I conclude that our earliest ancestors who strung two words together did so in Topic–Comment structures, with no rules requiring mention of nouns or verbs or Subjects or Predicates. And at an early stage words denoting motions and actions, for example *work* or *run* could be Topics, as well as words denoting things, for example *man* or *women*. We can imagine a simple system juxtaposing two words, always in Topic–Comment order, with no restriction on which words could express Topic, but probably certain demonstrative or deictic words, like Mackie's *him, me, them*, not occurring as Comments.

I have argued that Topic–Comment was the first syntactic construction, manifesting itself in two-element stand-alone clauses. These are the simplest of sentences. You might want to call them only 'protosentences'. They are the evolutionary precursors (I claim) of more elaborate sentences. At this stage, language still has a long way to go. The only conventionalized features of this rudimentary construction are its word order and possibly its singling-out of several specific deictic words that can only act as Topics, never as Comments. This primitive Topic construction is different from more grammatically developed Topic constructions in modern languages. For example, English has a specialized grammatical particle *As for* marking a Topic; Japanese marks a Topic with a special particle *wa* immediately after the topicalized phrase, and puts the whole assembly at the front of the sentence. In developed languages, there are often many different constructions that have a topicalizing effect. In English, for instance, the Passive construction is a way of making the Patient of a transitive verb the Topic of a sentence, as in *John was bowled over*. I assume that all such more complex constructions arose by historical processes of grammaticalization. There is no space to explore the sources of the myriad modern constructions which have arisen through grammaticalization. I want to concentrate on the emergence, via grammaticalization, of two of the most salient distinctions found in modern languages, the Noun/Verb and Subject–Predicate distinctions.

If I am right, this first construction already exemplifies a feature found in all modern languages, a distinction between a small closed class of words and a larger open class—a small set of function words and a larger set of content words. The ancient deictic counterparts of *him, me, that*, etc. had a restricted distribution, only occurring in the Topic slot of the construction, while all the other words that these people had could be used in both the Topic and the Comment slots. The pragmatic motivation for this division into two word-classes is obvious. Deictic words are those which draw on the immediate context of situation for their interpretation, and hence are the most likely to be used to indicate something already known to the hearer.

At the early stage hypothesized here, the class of content words was not sub-divided. 'Translating' into English, you could say *Me Tarzan*, *Me run*, *Me man*, *Me stink*, *Him Tarzan*, *Him run*, *That man*, *That stink*, *Run Tarzan*, *Tarzan run*, *Run stink*, *Stink run*, *Man stink*, *Stink man*, and so on, with the order determined by what the hearer was likely to be already aware of, the Topic. Languages without a Noun/Verb distinction, or any other syntactic distinction between content words, such as possibly Nootka or Tongan, are still like this in the freedom of any content word to occupy the Topic slot. But of course Nootka and Tongan have in addition developed syntactic and morphological markers clarifying and elaborating on the meanings of sentences.

Despite this grammatical freedom, there certainly would have been a skewed frequency distribution in the words that filled the Topic slot. You are more likely to want to tell me that Tarzan is running than that the running one is Tarzan. There are some words that denote stable objects which do not change their object type. A man is always a man, never a woman, never a tree, never a lion. Other words denote changing features of objects. What is running now will soon be sitting or standing. This is the object/action distinction loosely correlated with the syntactic Noun/Verb distinction. So statistically, certain words are more likely to be used in the Comment slot than others. This skewed frequency distribution may, over time, be taken as conventional by new generations, and become fixed so that certain content words are Comment-slot-only. The deictic forms like *him*, *me*, and *that* are, as noted above, Topic-slot-only words. Words denoting object types, like *man*, *lion*, and *tree* are likely to occur in the Topic slot, but also in the Comment slot if the Topic slot is filled by a deictic term, giving the equivalent of predicating nominals, as in *Me Tarzan* and Mackie's *Him bear*. The Comment-slot-only words are likely to include those denoting actions or transient states, like *run*, *stand*, and *hungry*. Thus all the logical possibilities for subdivision of the word-store in terms of allowed position in a two-word sentence are exploited. We have Topic-slot-only words, the deictics like *me*, *him*, *that*; Comment-slot-only words, those involving changing or temporary states, like *run*, *sleep*, *angry*; and 'anywhere' words denoting more permanent object types, like *man*, *lion*, *tree*. In a simple language becoming conventionalized in this way, we see the emergence, via grammaticalization, of two syntactic classes of content words, nouns and non-nouns. It is a case of grammaticalization because it is a process whereby a pattern of frequency in discourse gets fixed as a conventional grammatical pattern. I suggest that this happened in the very earliest history of languages. At this stage, certain word-sequences would not have conformed to the grammatical norm, sequences like *Me him, *Tarzan him, *Run Tarzan, and *Run work.

The claim here is that the bipartite organization of clauses stems from a central communicative function of language, namely (1) to identify what you are talking about, and (2) to give new information about what you are talking about.[10] I will label this a 'pragmatic' hypothesis. It contrasts with a 'semantic' hypothesis, which is that humans instinctively encode the difference between actions and objects into major syntactic categories, which become the basis of the bipartite organization. According to this semantic hypothesis, an innate template for sentence organization determines the two main parts of a sentence, and items denoting objects (i.e. nouns) occupy the Subject part, and items denoting actions (i.e. verbs) occupy the Predicate part.

The pragmatic hypothesis is that speakers identify what is **constant** in a changing world, and assume that a hearer will be aware of this constancy. The speaker then uses a term identifying the constant factor to indicate what he is talking about. The speaker also identifies what is **changeable** in the world he is communicating about, and assumes that the hearer does not know of the change that the speaker has observed. The speaker uses a term identifying the changing element in the world. Thus the bipartite organization of sentences reflects, I claim, a distinction between constant and changing, and not between objects and actions. Of course, in the world that we live in, objects are mostly constant and actions involve change. So how can the two hypotheses be teased apart? Modern technology provides an experimental possibility. What follows describes an experiment in progress, aimed at testing the pragmatic hypothesis.

Imagine a world in which objects, like trees, cows, pigs, and rocks, frequently morph into other objects. This would be a superfast and completely general version of our world in which tadpoles morph into frogs and caterpillars into butterflies. In this weird world, something is a tree one minute, then it is a cow, then it is a rock, for example. Object types exist—there are distinct categories of object which remain stable for short periods. The morphing from one type to another is fast. Nothing stays for long in a state between categories during the morphing process. So in this world, objects keep changing into other objects of other types. Symmetrically, in this odd world, motions are constant.

---

[10] It doesn't matter that many complex sentences in modern languages may not split neatly into sequential Topic and Comment parts (although they do almost always split into two parts). Subsequent linguistic evolution has elaborated and ornamented the original pragmatically motivated structures.

Some things are always bouncing, some are always swaying, some are always spinning. A thing that sways never stops swaying, even while it morphs its object type into another object type. Now imagine observing this world and commenting on it to another person. Your job is to keep this other person updated on what is happening, using two-word utterances. The pragmatic hypothesis is that in this situation, the Topic part of a two-element utterance will tend to denote constant actions, such as swaying, bouncing, and spinning, while the Comment part of an utterance will denote the changing object types, such as tree, rock, and cow. Modern morphing technology makes it possible to set up an unreal world like this on a computer screen. We can get experimental subjects to describe this world to each other. The strange world needs to be compared with a real world as a control condition. A difference is predicted between the utterances used in the two conditions something like this: in the 'real' world, the control condition, subjects will use forms like *cow spin*, to describe a cow that has just started to spin; in the 'unreal' world, subjects will use forms like *spin cow*, to describe a constantly spinning thing that has just morphed into a cow. This is an experiment in progress. Stay tuned. Very preliminary results are reported in Scott-Phillips et al. (2010).

To briefly recap this section, a category of Noun emerges in two-word utterances by a statistical pattern getting interpreted as fixed and conventional. So a word that tended to come second, in Comment position, at an earlier historical stage, now always comes second, by convention. In this way, a conventional word order emerges alongside the new subdivision of the lexicon. This subdivision is into (1) words that can only come first, in the Topic slot— call them (proto-)pronouns; (2) words that can only come second, in the Comment slot—call them (proto-)Predicates; and (3) words that can function either to identify a Topic or to pass comment on something already iden- tified deictically—call them (proto-)nouns. Routinizing a fixed conventional pattern has its advantages. As with any routinized activity, less mental effort is required in carrying it out. But convention has its disadvantages, too. What is conventional is, by definition, less informative. If a word always occupies the Topic slot by convention, a speaker cannot be interpreted as having made an informative choice to put that word first in his utterance. This brings us to a further step in the early grammaticalization of languages.

9.4 Topics give rise to Subjects

I will deal with Topic here as a broad category, and sweep over many nuances of how this notion is interpreted in different languages and different construc- tions. In its core, Topic is undeniably a functional notion, relating to how a message is tailored to a particular conversational situation and speaker's goal. Subject, on the other hand is much less clearly functional. In some grammatical traditions, Subject and Object are confusingly called 'grammatical functions', but this is a nonstandard use of the term 'function'; 'grammatical relation' or 'grammatical role' are preferable terms. As mentioned before, the Subject of an English sentence does not necessarily identify the doer of an action (the Agent), nor the thing that is overtly marked as what the sentence is about (the Topic). In grammatically boring neutral sentences such as *Rambo killed the cat*, indeed Topic, Agent, and Subject do coincide. But they don't have to. So what is a Subject? Ed Keenan (1976) surveys a wide range of phenomena across languages in an attempt to arrive at a universal definition. It is clear that a great many languages converge on similar semantic and formal patternings involving the pretheoretical notion of Subject. There is a strong connection between the semantic notion of Agent and the grammatical notion of Subject. The Agent in an event is more often expressed as the Subject of a sentence than in other structural positions. But, as explained earlier, the correlation is not necessary or absolute, and Subject and Agent are distinct categories. It is also clear that Subject is a fuzzy category. Not all languages have Subjects. Mark Durie (1985) argues in detail that Acehnese, spoken in Sumatra, has no category of Subject. Li and Thompson (1976) distinguish between 'Subject-prominent' languages and 'Topic-prominent' languages. Even in languages that do have Subjects, some constructions mark them more distinctly than other constructions. In a language with Subjects, the Subject of a sentence can be marked by special morphology, occupy a special linear position in a sentence, be typically of a certain syntactic category (almost always a noun), and enter into typical formal relationships with other parts of the sentence, for example agreement with a verb and acting as an antecedent for a reflexive pronoun.

How do Subjects arise in languages? The typical word order position of Subjects can easily be seen as derivative of former Topics. Topics favour initial position, and Subjects, where they are not upstaged by specially marked Topics, also favour initial position, except in the small proportion of languages which put the verb first (VSO). Even in VSO languages, as the label suggests, Subjects come earliest among the noun phrases.

I will now focus on another prominent aspect of Subjecthood, agreement with a verb, and ask specifically 'How do languages acquire a special part of a sentence with which the verb agrees?' At this stage in our hypothetical broad-brush prehistory of languages, we have two-element utterances, with a conventional Topic-first word order, and a syntactic class of words conventionally privileged to occur in the Topic position. With this, you can say, for example, *Boy bad*. But by the conventionalization of the Topic slot, this utterance has lost some of its spontaneous attention-directing power. A hearer can't tell whether the word *boy* has been singled out for special attention or just put in its place by convention. A further, explicit Topic-marking device is needed. As often, Givón (1976) has an insightful and persuasive account of how this process gives rise to agreement markers. My suggested story will blend his account with the terms in which I have already begun. In my story, a two-package discourse contribution by one speaker could consist of a one-word utterance *Boy*, drawing attention to some boy in the situation, followed by a two-word package *He bad*. So we get *Boy, he bad*. Givón's version, re-labelled slightly, is:

Topic-Shifted ('Marked')				Neutral (Re-analysed)	
The man	*he*	*came*		*The man*	*he-came*
TOPIC	PRONOUN	VERB	⇒	SUBJECT	AGREEMENT+VERB
				(After Givón 1976, p. 155)	

Givón's summary is

A subject topic-shift construction is over-used in a weaker context. Speakers eventually recognize the context as being much too weak to justify a marked status for the TS [Topic-Shift] construction. Thus they re-analyze it as the <u>neutral</u> syntax. The erstwhile topic-subject gets reanalyzed as 'mere' subject, while the topic-agreement anaphoric pronoun gets re-analyzed as subject-agreement. . . . The morphological binding of the pronoun to the verb is an inevitable natural phenomenon, cliticization, having to do with the unstressed status of pronouns, their decreased information load and the subsequent loss of resistance to phonological attrition.   (Givón 1976, pp. 154–5)

In the context of language evolution at a very early stage, I would prefer to re-word this slightly. A discourse Topic construction, for example *Boy, he bad*, is frequently used. The former discourse-level Topic *Boy* gets re-analysed as a 'mere' Subject, while the former sentence Topic pronoun *he* gets re-analysed as an agreement marker on the following word. By this route an element emerges which conventionally imposes agreement on a subsequent word, that is an element with one typical feature of the common linguistic category of Subject. Here again, the process of grammaticalization involves a markedly informative structure becoming conventional, and therefore less immediately informative.

Givón gives examples where one can see obvious traces of the transition from pronoun to agreement marker. In Tok Pisin a particle *i* derived from English *he* occurs between a Subject and its verb, and is fairly analysed as a marker of Subject agreement prefixed to the verb. Examples are

ol   *i*   *sindaun*
all   he   sit-down
'They sat down'

em   *i*   *paitim*
him   he   fight-him
'He beat him'

mipela   *i*   *go go go*
me-fellow   he   go go go
'I went for a long journey'   (Givón 1976, p. 155)

Meyerhoff (2000) discusses similar data in Bislama, a creole of Vanuatu, closely related to Tok Pisin. Here again it is clear that English pronouns have been grammaticalized as agreement markers. But Meyerhoff's data make it clear that the passage from discourse to grammar has not been uniform across all persons (1st, 2nd, 3rd) and numbers (singular, dual, trial, plural). This is consistent with a grammaticalization analysis, according to which frequency in discourse affects the likelihood of a pattern being 'frozen' into the grammar of a language. Meyerhoff also suggests that a factor encouraging the emergence of agreement markers was similar patterns of agreement in substrate languages; the first human grammaticalizers of pronouns into agreement markers would of course have had no substrate model. Lambrecht (1981, p. 40) gives a nice example of this same type of exaptation of a pronoun as an agreement marker from nonstandard French: *Ma femme il est venu* 'My wife has come'. In the Bantu languages, the source of agreement markers in Subject pronouns is, Givón writes, 'established beyond a shred of doubt' (p. 157). In these languages there is still often a clear phonological similarity between a marker on the Subject noun indicating its noun class, or gender, and the agreement marker affixed to the verb. This is not exactly the same as a similarity between a surviving pronoun and an agreement marker. Writing of pronouns and agreement markers in Tibeto-Burman[11] languages, LaPolla (1992, p. 303) notes 'the etymological transparency of most of the Tibeto-Burman verb agreement systems (the independent pronouns become attached to the verb) show that these agreement systems are relatively recent grammaticalizations of discourse prominence'. He further notes the 'transparent system where the markings on the verb correspond exactly to the free pronouns in phonological shape' (p. 304) in Tangut, one of the languages in this family. More generally, Jacques

---

[11] Also more often called the Sino-Tibetan language family.

(2007, fn. 3) writes 'In all these [Sino-Tibetan] languages [that have agreement systems], most verbal agreement markers are nearly identical with independent pronouns'. Bresnan and Mchombo (1987) comment that the incorporation of pronouns into verbs as agreement markers has been noted in American Indian languages since the nineteenth century. While there is widespread agreement about the sources of agreement markers as pronouns, it must be said that the current synchronic evidence is absent in many, if not most, languages. Explanations of the general form of Givón's, outlined above, work more naturally for prefixed agreement forms. When agreement affixes are postverbal, as in English *walk+s*, a grammaticalization account would need to make some link with a preverbal pronoun. Grammaticalization theory does not insist on unique pathways. There could be other sources for agreement markers in some languages. And probably most languages are so old that the origins of their agreement markers, if they have any, are lost in the depths of the past. What I have done here is outline a historical process by which a common characteristic of grammatical subjects, and hence the category of Subject itself, could have first arisen in the prehistory of languages. They arose, it seems likely, by the grammaticalization of originally Topic pronouns.

I have put forward ideas about the origin of several features of the grammatical category of Subject, in particular early position in a sentence, restriction to the emergent syntactic category Noun, and participation in rudimentary Subject–Predicate agreement relations. One other common property of Subjects across languages is marking by a designated case, usually called 'Nominative'. Not all languages use case marking, which is to a large extent an alternative to more fixed word order. But in case-marking languages, the Subject of a sentence is systematically identified by a characteristic case (e.g. Nominative), and this is one more aspect of Subjecthood that needs explanation. Case markers are commonly said to originate in **adpositions**, little function words like English *to*, *from*,and *ago*. The overall rise of case markers involves at least three steps: (1) the prior rise of a syntactic class of adpositions, itself not a simple matter, (2) the change of some members of the class of adpositions into words marking case relations, and (3) the compressing of these case-marking words into morphological affixes. These processes are all examples of grammaticalization in a broad sense. These types of grammaticalization will be illustrated in the sections that follow, and we will eventually come back to the evolution of case-marking inflections in particular, filling out the account of how the major distinguishing characteristics of Subjects, in languages that have them, arose. The implication is that the case-marking property of grammatical Subjects arose in the earliest languages later, and possibly a lot later, than the other main features, early word order, restriction to nouns and participation in Subject–Predicate agreement patterns.

9.5 Emergence of more specific word classes

Things can go faster now. Heine and Kuteva (2007) have capitalized on a generation of grammaticalization studies, and provided a long list of pathways by which modern languages have acquired more specialized syntactic categories. It is not possible or necessary here to show how all the syntactic categories of the world's languages (could) have arisen through grammaticalization. The hypothesis proposed implicitly or explicitly by many grammaticalization researchers is that all syntactic categorization arises through this mechanism, starting from pragmatically motivated discourse patterns. In the previous sections, I have been bolder than most, and proposed that the most basic categories of all, (proto-)nouns and (proto-)Predicates, can also be accounted for in this way. A basic Noun/Verb distinction is Heine and Kuteva's starting point. 'they [nouns and verbs] can be called evolutionary primitives in that they are not derived productively from any other morphological or syntactic categories while they themselves commonly develop into other categories' (Heine and Kuteva 2007, pp. 59–60). I will give below some examples beginning to show how languages can evolve out of the simple two-word stage discussed so far. This section will give examples of the rise of syntactic categories of the kind illustrated in Chapter 4, section 4, focusing most specifically on functional categories or closed word-classes.

Many languages have no adjectives, and in those languages that have them, they often form a small closed class of as few as a dozen words (Dixon 1982). Some adjectives emerge by grammaticalization of nouns. Sometimes a single word is not enough to identify the Topic of a sentence. If you have words for MALE, YOUNG, and RUN, and you want to say that the young male, but specifically not any older male in the context of situation, is running, you could combine a two-word Topic phrase with a Comment word, giving *Young male run*. But given the conventions developed so far, this is ambiguous. It could be interpreted as making two comments about a young person, that he is male and that he is running. In other words, the phrasal breakdown of this utterance is unclear. The ambiguity can be resolved by a device marking how one word belongs as a modifier to a noun, that is by the emergence of a marked class of attributive adjectives. Heine and Kuteva (2007) give an example.

Another group of nouns widely grammaticalized to adjectives concerns sex-specific human items such as 'man' and 'woman' or 'father' and 'mother', which in many languages are recruited to express distinctions in sex. Thus, in the Swahili examples [below], the nouns *mwana(m)ume* 'man' and *mwanamke* 'woman' are desemanticized and decategorialized in that their meaning is restricted to denoting the qualities 'male' and 'female', respectively, and they occur in the syntactic slot reserved for adjectives, namely after the noun they modify, and they agree in number with their head noun. ...

kijana	*mwana(m)ume*	'boy'
youth	man	

kijana	*mwanamke*	'girl'
youth	woman	

(Heine and Kuteva 2007, pp. 60–1)

When this process happened for the first time in a language, a new syntactic category, Adjective, was born in that language. And simultaneously a new type of phrasal construction arose, a noun phrase in which an adjective is placed in a conventional order with a noun and may be marked as agreeing with it. In the Swahili case above, the adopted conventional order is Noun–Adjective, and the adjective agrees in number with the noun. Grammaticalization of this sort is widely attested across many different language families, so parallel and independent evolution of adjectives by this process, after the beginning of the human diaspora, can be envisaged without problems.

The paths of grammaticalization in the history of a language are often preserved transparently by the same, or similar, words performing different functions. Deictic pronouns in many languages have the same form as definite determiners, or demonstratives. We see it in English *this* and *that*, which can be used referentially on their own (e.g. *This is a cat*, *That is a dog*), and as a modifying 'prop' in a larger referring expression (e.g. *This cat is docile*, *That dog is fierce*). We also see it in some nonstandard English expressions such as *them flowers*, *they people*, and in standard English *we men* and *you boys*. In German, the definite article can stand on its own, functioning as a pronoun, as in *Der kommt später* 'he's coming later' or *Die sind schön* 'they are beautiful'. In Hindi, the demonstrative pronouns are identical in form with the definite determiners. A well-documented case of the rise of definite determiners by grammaticalization from independent demonstrative pronouns is that of Romance definite articles (e.g. French *le*, *la*, deriving historically from the Latin demonstrative pronouns *ille*, *illa* (Harris 1978)). The synchronic traces of this history are seen in the correspondence between articles and Object pronouns (e.g. French *le*, *la*, *les*). In the case of Latin > Romance, written documents from across the centuries testify to the grammaticalization of *ille* and *illa* as definite articles. When a language for the first time co-opted an independent pronoun as

Fig. 9.2 Two constructions emerging through grammaticalization of the new categories of Determiner and Adjective (in dependency notation). The word order in other languages could be different.

a determiner modifying a noun, it introduced the novel category of Determiner into the language, and simultaneously introduced the language's own particular Determiner–Noun construction. This particular grammaticalization process, producing definite determiners could have happened many times independently in the histories of different languages.

Another common path of grammaticalization is from the numeral for ONE to an indefinite article. This is still transparent in French *un*, *une* and German *eins*, *ein*, *eine*. Indefinite articles would typically have appeared in the first languages later than definite articles, as indefinite articles usually arise from a pre-existing numeral, and it takes a while for languages to develop numerals. Among modern languages there are languages with a definite article but no indefinite article, for example Arabic, but the reverse situation is not found, as far as modern typological surveys show. Dryer (2008) surveyed 473 languages, and found eighty-one with a definite article and no indefinite article, but no languages with the converse situation.

As argued in Chapter 4, section 4, constructions and syntactic categories mutually interdefine each other. '[G]rammatical morphemes do not arise just from words, but from words in specific **syntactic constructions**. . . . What grammaticalization gives rise to, then, are morphologically marked syntactic constructions' (Givón 2009, p. 328). The appearance of adjectives means the appearance of at least one adjectival construction. The appearance of determiners means the appearance of a determiner–noun construction. Given the emergence of two categories of noun-modifiers, adjectives and determiners, we have some hierarchical structure, a noun-phrase constituent in Subject position.[12] Using Noun–Adjective word order (e.g. Spanish) for convenience to make the point, we could have two constructions as sketched in Figure 9.2.

Given these constructions, a short phrase with dependencies like that shown schematically in Figure 9.3 is possible. And given the emergence of agreement along with somewhat complex noun phrases, we have the potential for some

---

[12] Subject position is the only position so far considered. By the time noun phrases with adjectival and determiner modifiers evolved, it is possible that other argument slots (e.g. Object) had also become defined, but I have not explored this avenue here.

El	hombre	gordo	
The	man	fat	'The fat man'

Fig. 9.3 The structure of a newly available noun phrase (in dependency notation), glossed in Spanish.

slightly long-range dependencies. Meyerhoff (2000, p. 209) gives the following example from Bislama (I have adapted her glosses slightly).

woman	blong	yu	i	kam	long	wea
woman	of	you	AGREE	come	from	where

'Where does your wife come from?'

In this Bislama example the agreement particle *i* is a couple of words distant from the noun (*woman*) that it agrees with. Obviously, as noun phrases potentially get longer and longer, dependencies involving agreement can stretch accordingly.

The Bislama *woman blong yu* 'your wife' illustrates another common grammaticalization process, the rise of adpositions, in this case from a verb *belong* in the superstrate language, English. (Adpositions include prepositions, which precede their dependent noun phrase, like *after* in *after five years*, or postpositions, which follow their dependent noun phrase, like *ago* in *five years ago*.) Heine and Kuteva (2007) give many examples from different languages of adpositions deriving historically from verbs. For example, 'In English, prepositions are most commonly derived from present participle forms (*barring, concerning, concerning, during, excepting, failing, following, notwithstanding, pending, preceding, regarding*) or past participle forms (*given, granted*)' (p. 72). Examples like these derive the adposition from a morphologically complex form of the verb. The very first languages probably had no complex morphology. There are examples of the pathway Verb > Adposition in isolating languages, where the source verb is uninflected. Heine and Kuteva give an example from Ewe, a language of Ghana. '[T]he verb *tsó* "to come from" has been grammaticalized to a source preposition "from" ' (p. 73). They give further examples from Swahili, Japanese, and Haitian creole French. In English, we can see this particular grammatical transition in progress in expressions with *come* as in *Come Christmas, I'll be there*, synonymous with *By Christmas, I'll be there*. The most common historical source of adpositions is nouns, and here Heine and Kuteva also give many examples. Here is one: 'the Icelandic body-part noun *bak* "back" was grammaticalized to a locative preposition *bak(i)* "behind", but also to a temporal preposition "after" ' (p. 63). For many further instances, see Heine (1989); Bohoussou and Skopeteas (2008); Matsumoto (1999); Rubba (1994).

Another functional category widespread in languages is the copula, exemplified in English by forms of *be*, in French by forms of *être*, and in Spanish by forms of *estar*. This Spanish form suggests a relationship with Latin *stare* 'stand', and indeed there is a common grammaticalization path from such verbs to copulas. 'It appears that Australian languages show a recurrent tendency to create copular verbs (generally by grammaticalization of stance verbs "sit", "stand", and "lie", or of "stay" or "go")' (Dixon 2002, p. 1). To illustrate the non-deterministic nature (as far as we can see) of grammaticalization, such posture verbs have also alternatively been grammaticalized in many languages as markers of progressive aspect (Bybee et al. 1994, pp. 129–31). Indeed in Spanish, the progressive aspect is marked by a form of *estar*, as in *estoy bebiendo* 'I am drinking'.

One source for case markers (in this case a freestanding word) is the origin of the Chinese *bă*, which marks a Direct Object in some constructions. This derives historically from a verb meaning 'take hold of'. This verb became serialized in expressions like pseudo-English *man take stick break*, and is now simply a marker of Direct Object (Slobin 2002, pp. 381–2).

As one more illustration of the origins of functional categories, consider certain English auxiliary verbs, including modal verbs such as *will* and *can* and the perfective auxiliary *have*. English modals are now a closed functional class as they take no agreement markers, are inverted in questions (*Can I go?*) and take the negative *not* immediately after them (*I will not go*), unlike the thousands of main verbs in English. *Will* as a future marker is grammaticalized from Old English *willan* 'want to'. *Can* is derived from Old English *cunnan* 'know, be acquainted with'. The auxiliary verb *have* is transparently related to *have* as a main verb denoting possession; this relationship is mirrored in other Indo-European languages. Note also the divergent grammaticalization of this same main verb to express obligation, as in *I have to go*, pronounced [haftə].

In the earliest languages, grammaticalization would have produced new categories, emerging for the first time. But the process continues in modern langages, so that individual words can undergo historical change from one established category to another. Peter Trudgill gives some nice examples:

For example, *more* is used in traditional East Anglian rural dialects as a conjunction equivalent to Standard English *neither* as a result of contraction from an original *no more*:

The fruit and vegetables weren't as big as last year, more weren't the taters and onions

Similarly, *time* has become a conjunction equivalent to Standard English *while* as a result of the phonological deletion of lexical material such as *during the*:

Go you and have a good wash and change, time I get tea ready

(Trudgill 2002, p. 717)

This section has given examples, selected from thousands in the literature, of grammaticalization processes giving rise to new syntactic categories, with the emphasis on functional categories (closed word-classes). By implication, these same processes also give rise to new constructions in which these new syntactic categories play their characterizing part. In Figure 9.4 is a diagram from Heine and Kuteva, in which they summarize just a few of the major pathways of grammaticalization commonly found in languages across the world. Their work is conceived in the context of language evolution, and they speculate, as

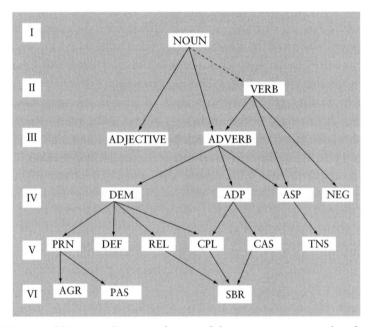

Fig. 9.4 Heine and Kuteva's diagram of some of the most common paths of grammaticalization. There are many more such pathways, not shown.

Abbreviations: I, II, etc. = layers; AGR = agreement marker; ADP = adposition; ASP = (verbal) aspect; CAS = case marker; CPL = complementizer; DEF = marker of definiteness 'definite article'; DEM = demonstrative; NEG = negation marker; PAS = passive; PRN = pronoun; REL = relative clause marker; SBR = subordinating marker of adverbial clauses; TNS = tense marker. The general message is that more abstract, specifically grammatical categories arise historically, deriving from more concrete, more semantically or pragmatically based categories.

Source: From Heine and Kuteva (2007, p. 111).

I do, that the first languages would have followed these and similar pathways from simple beginnings, with few if any distinct syntactic categories, to the complex systems that we see today.

9.6 Morphologization

A strong hypothesis of grammaticalization theory is that all morphological inflections derive from once independent lexical items, either function words or content words. This hypothesis is supported by many examples.

> [T]he universal principle would appear to be that affixation is not simply created out of the blue: it emerges from the grammaticalization, reanalysis, or reinterpretation of material which was not originally inflectional. It follows logically that THE FIRST LANGUAGE HAD NO AFFIXES (cf. Comrie 1992).   (McWhorter 2001b, p. 158)

I will give some classic examples of the growth of morphology through grammaticalization. I'll start with inflections marking tense on verbs.[13]

In modern Romance languages, the future tense is indicated by a suffix on the verb. When I was taught how to memorize the future suffixes in French, we were told that the endings were the same as those of the irregular verb *avoir* 'have'. Here are the endings on (present) *avoir* and future *dormir* 'sleep'.

j'ai	*je dormirai*	*nous avons*	*nous dormirons*
tu as	*tu dormiras*	*vous avez*	*vous dormirez*
elle a	*elle dormira*	*elles ont*	*dormiront*

This curious fact is no accident. It results from the compression of a once independent auxiliary verb into a suffix. From Latin to Spanish (more transparent than the French), the historical path was

Latin *cantare habemus* 'we have to sing' → *cantarabemus* → Spanish *cantaremos* 'we will sing'.

Note some apparent capriciousness in the choice of lexical item recruited to do tense/aspect-marking work; the verb for HAVE is also co-opted (though not morphologized) to express perfect aspect as in French *nous avons payé*, Italian *abbiamo pagato*, and Spanish *hemos pagado* 'we have paid'.

---

[13] Bybee et al. (1994) is a book-length extensive survey of grammaticalization processes leading to functional categories and inflections marking tense, aspect, and modality.

A more deeply buried lexical source of a tense-marking suffix is an ancient Indo-European form for 'do', which became a dental suffix on verbs, expressing past tense, in the Germanic languages. In English this dental suffix is the past tense ending spelled -ed (as in *spelled*). In German it is the 'weak preterite' ending -te, as in *sagte* 'said'. Lahiri (2000) expresses a fairly traditional view of what happened:

> The claim is that the fully inflected form of 'do' was added to the weak verbs along with the suffix /j/ to mark past tense. Later, due to grammaticalisation and reanalysis, the verb root became a suffix and is now present as the productive tense marker in all the Germanic languages.   (Lahiri 2000, p. 91)

This theory is somewhat controversial, but the derivation of the past tense ending from an ancient word for DO is the most widely accepted account; Tops (1974) surveys all the contending theories.

I turn now to the sources of inflections on nouns, specifically case markers. It needs to be said at the outset that in languages with many 'case' markers, such as Hungarian and Finnish, a small number serve clearly grammatical purposes such as marking the Subject or Direct Object of a verb, while others carry semantic information, typically spatial. In Hungarian, for instance, the Accusative suffix -at marks the Object of a verb, as in *tudom a házat* 'I know the house'—I will call this type 'grammatical case-marker'. By contrast, the Hungarian suffix -ben[14] which patterns in many ways like -at and so is reasonably also called a 'case' marker, expresses the spatial notion translatable by the English preposition *in*, as in *a zsebemben* 'in my pocket'—I'll call this type 'semantic case-marker'.

In analysing Hungarian there are good reasons to distinguish case markers from postpositions, even though many case markers and many postpositions express the same kind of meanings, often spatial. Case markers vary phonologically according to the vowel in the nouns they are suffixed to; postpositions do not undergo this vowel harmony. Demonstratives modifying case-marked nouns must also be case-marked, thus agreeing with their noun in case; postpositions do not affect demonstratives in this way. And in written Hungarian, case markers are written attached to their nouns, whereas postpositions are separated from their nouns by a space. Hungarian is a literary language, used by school-educated speakers, so the rigid distinction between case markers and adpositions can be maintained. In Lakota, a Siouan language of the American plains, a less literary language, usage is more varied and there are hybrid forms

---

[14] For simplicity, I only give one form for each of these suffixes; their vowels vary in predictable ways when combined with other words.

between case-marking suffixes and adpositions. '[T]he realization of individual case markers as either postpositions or suffixes in Lakota is controlled by their collocational frequency in discourse' (Pustet 2008, p. 269). Pustet's title includes 'the collapse of the adposition vs. affix distinction in Lakota', but the collapse is not total, as she mentions 'three case markers which always figure as suffixes and never as postpositions' (p. 272). Nevertheless, such data show us (1) how structurally close postpositions and case-marking affixes are, and (2) how factors of discourse frequency influence the variation between them. This is a situation ripe for grammaticalization of postpositions into case-marking affixes. If Lakota were to survive and become more codified in this part of its grammar we might expect to see more case-marking suffixes clearly emerging from postpositions.

In languages that distinguish case markers from adpositions, case markers of both sorts, grammatical and semantic, are most widely derived by grammaticalization from adpositions. And the same grammatical/semantic distinction applies among adpositions. The English preposition *of*, for example, serves a much more grammatical purpose (in fact a great range of different grammatical purposes) than the preposition *in*. In the nominalized phrase *the destruction of the city*, *of* expresses the same relation between *destruction* and *city* as is expressed by word order in the corresponding clause *Hannibal destroyed the city*; we may say that *of* here marks Direct Objects in nominalized transitive clauses. In nominalized intransitive clauses, like *the arrival of the train*, the same preposition marks a Subject,[15] corresponding to *the train arrived*. The preposition *in*, on the other hand, is not recruited to serve any such grammatical purpose, and just expresses a spatial relationship (sometimes metaphorically extended).

An early stage in the grammaticalization of adpositions as case markers involves adpositions which do not previously express grammatical relations becoming bleached of some of their semantic (e.g. spatial) content and starting to mark grammatical relations. A well known example is the passage from Latin prepositions *de* and *ad* to the French prepositions *à* and *de*. 'In many contexts in which Latin *de* occurs, it is substitutable by *ab* "from" or *ex* "out of", or even omissible; cf. *cadere (de/a/e) manibus* "to drop from the hands". French *de*, on the other hand, is typically neither substitutable nor omissible in contexts such as *le début de l'année* "the beginning of the year"' (Lehmann 1985, p. 448). These French grammatical adpositions *à* and *de*

---

[15] In this respect, English nominalized clauses reflect an **ergative** system, in which the Subjects of intransitive verbs are treated grammatically in the same way as the Direct Objects of transitive verbs.

are prepositions. Had they been postpositions, they could have been easily grammaticalized into case-marking suffixes. 'Subject (nominative) and direct-object (accusative) case-markers are central in the grammar of referential coherence...most commonly these "pragmatic" case markers are not grammaticalized directly from lexical words. Rather, they are derived indirectly from previously-grammaticalized semantic case-markers' (Givón 2009, p. 329). We can, then, see a grammaticalization pathway:

Semantic postposition → Grammatical postposition → Case-marking suffix.

An instance of the trajectory from postposition to case-marking suffix is given by Kiparsky (in press). He offers a generalization: 'In Finno-Ugric languages, new case forms arise by grammaticalization of postpositions'. This trajectory is illustrated in Hungarian by the development of the word *pälV-k* 'to the inside' (a reconstructed Finno-Ugric source) into the Hungarian illative case suffix -*be*.

    As one more example of morphology arising out of previously freestanding words, the English adverb-forming suffix -*ly* is derived historically from a freestanding Old English word *lic*, itself originally derived from a noun meaning 'body' (cf. German *Leiche* 'corpse'). And so on. The examples I have given here of emergent morphology are among the best known. The origins of many affixes are not so transparent. But we have no reason to doubt that, in general, affixes on words are historically derived from non-affixes, independent words. The examples of this section show how, in general, morphology could have arisen in the earliest languages. 'Today's morphology is yesterday's syntax' (Givón 1971, p. 413).

9.7 Cognitive and social requirements for grammaticalization

The processes lumped under the heading of 'grammaticalization' happen in all known languages. They are sometimes claimed to be absolutely irreversible (Haspelmath 1999; Lehmann 1982; Heine et al. 1991). Fritz Newmeyer (1998) has very thoroughly refuted this absolute claim, giving plausible examples of the reverse of every type of grammaticalization typically cited, for example affix > word and functional category > lexical category. Newmeyer does not question the great weight of examples going in the 'usual' direction, only the absoluteness of the unidirectionality claim. His conclusion is that 'unidirectionality is *almost* true...nobody is in a position to offer statistics on the matter, but a rough impression is that downgradings have occurred at least ten times as often as upgradings' (pp. 275–6). This highly significant tendency is enough to provide valuable insight into the ways in which the earliest languages probably evolved.

Appealing to grammaticalization is not a handwaving exercise invoking a mysterious force. Indeed grammaticalization is not a **primitive** force in the evolution of languages at all. It is the result of several interacting tendencies of the users of languages. One such factor is the routinization of frequent actions. A routinized action does not need to be assembled afresh each time it is used, but can be pulled whole from the user's memory. Being routinized, an expression tends to be compressed into a single phonologically convenient package, for example a word-length package, with a single stress, and perhaps vowel harmony. Thus morphological affixes are born from originally freestanding words. Getting incorporated into a word has the effect of subjecting the newly affixed form to the phonological influence of its stem.

Only humans do grammaticalization. Cultural conventions can be found in ape populations,[16] but they do not build upon each other, leading to accumulations of complex culturally transmitted behaviour. This relates to another factor contributing to grammaticalization, the almost slavish disposition of children to replicate the linguistic patterns they observe. Human children are impulsive imitators. Where telegraphic expressions with little grammatical organization will serve a child's needs, and indeed are used in the earliest stages of childhood, the child soon learns to dress her productions in the conventional code of the community. Thus given a reasonable context, an expression such as *goat try eat lid* (Halliday 1975) is perfectly understandable, but a child readily moves past this stage and ends up able to express the same meaning as *The goat tried to eat the lid*, with all its grammatical details. The patterns acquired by children include those that have been routinized by previous generations, so morphology, for instance, is passed on, unless subject to further routinizations.

In a conservative social group, relatively isolated from outside contact, with an age structure in which there are plenty of adults to provide exemplary behaviour, and where the environment of daily life has been stable for many generations, we can expect a high degree of routinization in language, hence quite complex morphology. No human group, however, is so stuck in its ways that a complete set of useful utterances can be rote-memorized, and so a level of generative productivity is maintained for the expression of relatively infrequent meanings. Indeed, occasionally a new construction may be innovatively introduced, and if it turns out to be useful enough, it will be acquired by subsequent generations. But innovations make novel use of old material.

---

[16] Whiten et al. (1999); Whiten (2000b); Whiten et al. (2005).

New constructions are crafted out of old pieces and are never new in their entirety. Thus the main verb of possession (e.g. *have*) was recruited to do the auxiliary work of expressing futurity (e.g. *cantare habeo*) and perfective aspect (e.g. *I have sung*). In the former case it later underwent further change to a morphological affix. Thus grammaticalization is not a story of irrevocable decline, but of recycling old material for new purposes, with the language moving toward an asypmtote of an optimal balance between least effort (in speaking, understanding, and learning) and the expressive power that serves the community's needs. The process is relatively slow, except in abnormal social situations. The circumstances of the tribe may shift before a movement in one direction is complete, for example, by some new contact, by a change in the age structure resulting from disease or famine, or by expansion of the group making encounters with strangers more frequent. Populations can be expected to respond, by cumulative individual action, some routinizing, some innovative, in ways that keep a level of useful communicative activity going. What is communicated includes both practical information about the environment, but also rich 'shibboleth' information about membership of the group by conforming to its established ways of speaking.

Fritz Newmeyer (1998) has mounted a detailed examination of grammaticalization theory, from the viewpoint of a scholar more immersed in the generative tradition than in any other. He is thus drawn to react to some extreme claims put forward by grammaticalization researchers. One such extreme, and ultimately paradoxical, claim is Paul Hopper's (1987, p. 148) 'There is...no "grammar" but only "grammaticization"—movements toward structure'. But if grammaticalization is defined, as it usually is, as a movement toward grammatical structure, we are in a circular bind. We could not recognize a process as grammaticalization unless we had a prior idea, ideally with some concrete examples, of what grammatical structure actually is. It might be possible to maintain that such a prior idea is a kind of Platonic ideal, not realized on this earth. But in fact Hopper rescues himself from the Scylla of paradox and the Charybdis of Platonism by a sensible continuation, right after the remark quoted above: 'It goes without saying that many phenomena which we would agree to call grammatical are relatively stable and uniform. That is not in dispute. The point again is that any decision to limit the domain of grammar to just those phenomena which are relatively fixed and stable seems arbitrary'. Yes, but there is no legislation preventing some scholars from investigating just the phenomena that are relatively fixed and stable, any more than others are bound only to study the transient processes. Think of geology. The earth is the way it is, and always changing. Geology makes sense by saying how stable features, igneous intrusions, sedimentary strata, and metamorphic rocks, get to be the way they are. Geologists don't deny the stability of some features nor the dynamic forces that made them.

Newmeyer did not quote Hopper's rescuing clause, and comes up with an equally provocative statement of his own: 'In this chapter I will put grammaticalization under the microscope and conclude... that *there is no such thing as grammaticalization*, at least insofar as it might be regarded as a distinct grammatical phenomenon requiring a distinct set of principles for its explanation' (Newmeyer 1998, p. 226). This is what I meant in saying that grammaticalization is not a primitive force. Newmeyer calls grammaticalization an 'epiphenomenon', a result of the interaction of 'Downgrading analysis', 'Appropriate semantic change', and 'Phonetic reduction' (p. 260). Use of the term 'epiphenomenon' in linguistics is a rhetorical move, implying that the effect in question is somehow not real. Chomsky even states that languages in the traditional sense are epiphenomena: 'The E-language that was the object of study in most traditional or structuralist grammar or behavioral psychology is now regarded as an epiphenomenon at best' (Chomsky 1987, p. 25). (What might it be 'at worst'?) Outside linguistics, and more generally, it is not denied that epiphenomena are phenomena, that is observable. The judgement is theory-specific. A phenomenon that can be shown to be completely a result of principles accounting for other phenomena is labelled an epiphenomenon. By this criterion, anything observable might be an epiphenomenon, the tides, the seasons, eclipses, global warming, and so on. Let's not ignore global warming because it is an epiphenomenon! You may label grammaticalization an epiphenomenon, but it is as real as the heat of summer and the cold of winter. Hopper's point, and the main point of all grammaticalization theorists, is that performance can have long-term effects on competence. Today's frequency in discourse can become tomorrow's entrenched grammatical pattern; today's erratic phonetic erosion can become tomorrow's canonical form.

Grammaticalization is the only theory in town purporting to explain how languages, in their syntax and morphology, get to be the way they are. A theory of an innate universal grammar does not explain how or why languages get to be as complex as they do. Such a theory may account for children's amazing ability to pick up complex syntactic constructions, given that those constructions are already present in the adult language. Innovation occurs, but is rare. Mostly children grow up speaking a form of language very close to that of their parents.

Synchronic analysts have noticed the pronoun–determiner correspondences discussed in section 9.5, and resorted to various formal devices to capture the partial similarity between modern pronouns and determiners (Postal 1966; Hudson 1984; Abney 1987; Radford 1997). These synchronic analyses are ingenious and continue to be wrangled over. They neglect the diachronic dimension. Grammaticalization is a diachronic process in which a form used for one purpose is recruited for another, more grammatical, purpose. Thus forms related by grammaticalization are partly similar (reflecting common origin) and partly different (reflecting innovation). Synchronic analyses partial out the common features, but inherently miss the clear diachronic explanation of the similarities, which is that determiners in many languages are historically derived from independent (typically demonstrative) pronouns. We **know** why there are synchronic similarities between determiners and pronouns, just as we know why there are synchronic similarities between adpositions and case markers, between auxiliaries and some main verbs, and between subjects and topics. Purely synchronic descriptions, or whatever formal stripe, don't mention in any way what we know to be the historical source of the facts.

All explanatory theories rely on a diachronic dimension. The laws of physics predict what happens as time unfolds. If there were no time unfolding, the laws of physics wouldn't operate. In the Chomskyan theory of Universal Grammar, the relevant timeframe is compressed into the short period of an individual's life during which the bulk of language learning happens. This limits the theory to explaining regularities, as the child is seen as a little generalizing machine making sense out of messy input data, according to innate biases of Universal Grammar. But such a theory can't explain how languages get to be so messy in the first place.[17] A paper by Comrie (1985) is typical of authors using diachrony to explain recalcitrant idiosyncratic facts.

> At first sight, and from a purely synchronic perspective, the inflectional morphology of the Chukchi verb presents a bewildering array of idiosyncrasies, in addition to a relatively simple general pattern that can be discerned once one abstracts away from these idiosyncrasies. The present paper is part of an ongoing attempt to explain these idiosyncrasies from a diachronic perspective by showing that features of the system which are arbitrary from a synchronic point of view can readily be accounted for in terms of the reanalysis of patterns that were quite regular at an earlier period in the history of the language.
>   (Comrie 1985, p. 85)

Within grammaticalization theory, there are debates and differences of detail about the precise mechanisms. One such debate concerns who, adults or children, are the principal agents of change through grammaticalization. Here, perhaps not surprisingly, the debaters tend to be aligned along theory-driven lines. Scholars more closely associated with generativist linguistics[18] argue that

---

[17] See Hurford (2009) for elaboration of this point.
[18] For example, Kiparsky (1968); Lightfoot (1979, 1991a, 1999).

language change is mainly driven by young language acquirers reanalysing the data they observe. This is consistent with the generativist emphasis on the child's instinctive contribution to the shape of language, and the poverty of the input data. On the other hand, another view holds that language change stems from innovation by adolescents and adults. Heine and Kuteva (2007, pp. 331–8) review the debate and conclude 'there is a fairly clear answer to the question of who were the creators of early language: On account of all the observations made above they must have been adolescents and adults, and it seems unlikely that young children were the driving force in creating early language' (p. 337). Bybee and Slobin (1982) collected data on misrenderings of the past tenses of English verbs, examples such as *lended for lent, *slank for slunk, and *thunk for thought. They collected such examples, or elicited them under stressful conditions, from pre-schoolers, third-graders, and university students. They compared the misrendered examples to known kinds of change in English past tense forms, and concluded that members of all three groups produced forms that were of a kind that could possibly get entrenched in future usage. In some cases, it was the adults who produced versions more likely to 'stick' as innovative forms. For my account, it is not crucial to resolve this debate. Grammaticalization happens, and we can see clear pathways along which grammar emerges and develops.

Grammaticalization rests on uniquely human cognitive abilities. Only humans can compose complex messages by putting words together, and only humans can interpret the more complex of such messages. Only humans occasionally innovate new ways of stringing words together for some new effect. Only human children rapidly acquire productive competence, mastering the regularities in the ambient language. This chapter has presupposed that the agents of grammaticalizaton, whether child or adult, had modern linguistic capabilities. The story outlined in this chapter is one of the cultural evolution of languages in biologically modern humans. This was a convenient division of labour. It seems likely that there was coevolution of the language faculty and actual languages—gene-language coevolution as discussed in Chapter 7.

Sendoff

In this final part of the book, we have built on the foundations laid in the first two parts to tell a story of what happened over the last few million years, but most rapidly in the past few hundred thousand years, to make us the most astonishingly creative (and hence destructive) organisms that have ever appeared on the planet. The evolution of grammar was not a Big Bang, but once the necessary conditions were in place, the efflorescence of language and languages went at an unprecedented pace, reaching unprecedented heights of subtlety and complexity. We are what we are, animals subject to constraints of the flesh, but with unique foresight, curiosity, and critical powers. You even have enough capacity for deferment of reward to read bloody great books like this one to the finish, and to imagine alternatives.

Bibliography

Aarts, B. (2007). *Syntactic Gradience: The Nature of Grammatical Indeterminacy.* Oxford: Oxford University Press.

—— (2008). Approaches to the English gerund. In G. Trousdale and N. Gisborne (eds.), *Constructional Approaches to English Grammar*, pp. 11–31. Berlin: Mouton de Gruyter.

Abeillé, A. and O. Rambow (eds.) (2000). *Tree Adjoining Grammars: Formalisms, Linguistic Analysis and Processing.* Stanford, CA: CSLI Publications. (Distributed by the University of Chicago Press.)

Abeles, M. (1991). *Corticonics—Neural Circuits of the Cerebral Cortex.* Cambridge: Cambridge University Press.

Abney, S. (1987). *The English Noun Phrase in its Sentential Aspects.* Ph.D. thesis, MIT.

Aboitiz, F. and V. R. García (1997). The evolutionary origin of the language areas in the human brain. A neuroanatomical perspective. *Brain Research Reviews* 25(3), 381–96.

Adret, P. (2004). In search of the song template. *Annals of the New York Academy of Sciences* 1016, 303–24.

Aiello, L. C. and R. I. M. Dunbar (1993). Neocortex size, group size, and the evolution of language. *Current Anthropology* 34(2), 184–93.

—— and P. Wheeler (1995). The expensive-tissue hypothesis: The brain and the digestive system in human and primate evolution. *Current Anthropology* 36(2), 199–221.

Aikhenvald, A. Y. and R. M. W. Dixon (eds.) (2006). *Serial Verb Constructions: A Cross-Linguistic Typology.* Oxford: Oxford University Press.

Airey, D. C. and T. J. DeVoogd (2000). Greater song complexity is associated with augmented song system anatomy in zebra finches. *Neuroreport* 11, 2339–44.

Aitken, P. G. (1981). Cortical control of conditioned and spontaneous vocal behavior in rhesus monkeys. *Brain and Language* 13, 171–84.

Ajdukiewicz, K. (1935). Die syntaktische Konnexität. *Studia Philosophica* 1, 1–27. (Translated and reprinted in Storrs McCall (ed.), *Polish Logic 1920–1939*, pp. 207–31. Oxford: Oxford University Press, 1967.)

Akhtar, N. and L. Montague (1999). Early lexical acquisition: The role of cross-situational learning. *First Language* 19, 347–58.

Al-Fityani, K. and C. A. Padden (2010). Sign languages in the Arab world. In D. Brentari (ed.), *Sign Languages*, pp. 433–50. Cambridge: Cambridge University Press.

Ali, F. and R. Meier (2008). Positive selection in *ASPM* is correlated with cerebral cortex evolution across primates but not with whole-brain size. *Molecular Biology and Evolution* 25(11), 2247–50.

Alleyne, M. C. (1980). *Comparative Afro-American*. Ann Arbor, MI: Karoma.

Andersen, H. (1988). Center and periphery: adoption, diffusion and spread. In J. Fisiak (ed.), *Historical Dialectology, Regional and Social*, pp. 39–83. Berlin: Mouton de Gruyter.

Anderson, B. (1993). Evidence from the rat for a general factor that underlies cognitive performance and that relates to brain size: Intelligence? *Neuroscience Letters* 153, 98–102.

Anderson, J. M. (2005). The non-autonomy of syntax. *Folia Linguistica* 34(3-4), 223–50.

Anderson, J. R. and S. Douglass (2001). Tower of Hanoi: Evidence for the cost of goal retrieval. *Journal of Experimental Psychology: Learning, Memory, and Cognition* 27(6), 1331–46.

Anderson, S. R. (2004). *Doctor Dolittle's Delusion*. New Haven, CT: Yale University Press.

—— (2008a). The logical structure of linguistic theory. *Language* 84(4), 795–814. (This is a fully written-up version of Anderson's Presidential address to the Linguistic Society of America, January 2008.)

—— (2008b). The logical structure of linguistic theory. In *Meeting Handbook*. Linguistic Society of America.

Andreason, N. C., M. Flaum, V. Swayze, D. S. O'Leary, R. Alliger, G. Cohen, J. Ehrhardt, and W. T. C. Yuh (1993). Intelligence and brain structure in normal individuals. *American Journal of Psychiatry* 150, 130–34.

Andrews, L. (1854). *Grammar of the Hawaiian Language*. Honolulu: Mission Press.

Anisfeld, M. (1985). *Language Development from Birth to Three*. Hillsdale, NJ: Lawrence Erlbaum Associates.

Anonymous French Catholic missionary (1834). *Notes Grammaticales sur la Langue Sandwichoise*. Paris. (British Library catalogue no. 12910.bb.47.(1.)).

Ansaldo, U. and S. J. Matthews (2001). Typical creoles and simple languages: The case of Sinitic. *Linguistic Typology* 5, 311–25.

Aoki, K. (1991). Time required for gene frequency change in a determinist model of gene culture coevolution, with special reference to the lactose absorption problem. *Theoretical Population Biology* 40(3), 354–68.

Arbib, M. (2004). How far is language beyond our grasp? A response to Hurford. In D. K. Oller and U. Griebel (eds.), *Evolution of Communication Systems*, pp. 315–21. Cambridge, MA: MIT Press.

—— (2005). From monkey-like action recognition to human language: An evolutionary framework for neurolinguistics. *Behavioral and Brain Sciences* 28(2), 105–25.

—— (2006). The Mirror System Hypothesis on the linkage of action and languages. In M. A. Arbib (ed.), *Action to Language via the Mirror Neuron System*, pp. 3–47. Cambridge: Cambridge University Press.

——(2008). Holophrasis and the protolanguage spectrum. *Interaction Studies* 9(1), 154–68. (Special issue, edited by Derek Bickerton and Michael Arbib, entitled *Holophrasis, Compositionality and Protolanguage*).

——(2010). Review of Derek Bickerton's *Adam's Tongue*. *Language* 86(2), 431–5.

——(2011). Niche construction and the evolution of language: Was territory scavenging the one key factor? *Interaction Studies* 12(1).

Arends, J. (1989). *Syntactic Developments in Sranan*. Ph.D. thesis, University of Nijmegen.

——(ed.) (1995). *The Early Stages of Creolization*. Amsterdam: John Benjamins.

Armstrong, D. F., W. C. Stokoe, and S. E. Wilcox (1995). *Gesture and the Nature of Language*. Cambridge: Cambridge University Press.

Arnold, K. and K. Zuberbühler (2006). Language evolution: Semantic combinations in primate calls. *Nature* 441, 303.

——and——(2008). Meaningful call combinations in a non-human primate. *Current Biology* 18(5), R202–R203.

Aron, A., H. Fisher, D. J. Mashek, G. Strong, H. Li, and L. L. Brown (2005). Reward, motivation, and emotion systems associated with early-stage intense romantic love. *Journal of Neurophysiology* 94, 327–37.

Aronoff, M., I. Meir, C. A. Padden, and W. Sandler (2003). Classifier constructions and morphology in two sign languages. In K. Emmorey (ed.), *Perspectives on Classifier Constructions in Sign Languages*, pp. 53–84. Mahwah, NJ: Lawrence Erlbaum Associates.

——,——,——, and——(2008). The roots of linguistic organization in a new language. *Interaction Studies* 9(1), 133–53. (Special issue, edited by Derek Bickerton and Michael Arbib, entitled *Holophrasis, Compositionality and Protolanguage*).

——, C. A. Padden, I. Meir, and W. Sandler (2004). Morphological universals and the sign language type. In G. Booij and J. van Marle (eds.), *Yearbook of Morphology 2004*, pp. 19–40. Dordrecht, Holland: Kluwer.

Arons, B. (1992). Techniques, perception, and applications of time-compressed speech. In *Proceedings of the Conference of the American Voice I/O Society*, pp. 169–77. American Voice I/O Society.

Atkinson, M. (1985). How linguistic is the one-word stage? In M. D. Barrett (ed.), *Children's Single-Word Speech*, pp. 289–312. Chichester, UK: John Wiley and Sons.

Augustine, S. (397). *Confessions*. (English translation by Albert C. Outler, online at http://www.ccel.org/a/augustine/confessions/confessions.html).

Austin, J. L. (1962). *How to Do Things with Words*. Cambridge, MA: Harvard University Press.

Bahlmann, J., R. I. Schubotz, and A. D. Friederici (2008). Hierarchical artificial grammar processing engages Broca's area. *NeuroImage* 42(2), 525–34.

Bailey, B. L. (1966). *Jamaican Creole Syntax: A Transformational Approach*. Cambridge: Cambridge University Press.

Bailey, C. N. (1977). Linguistic change, naturalness, mixture, and structural principles. *Papiere zur Linguistik* 16, 6–73.

Bak, T. H., D. G. O'Donovan, J. H. Xuereb, S. Boniface, and J. R. Hodges (2001). Selective impairment of verb processing associated with pathological changes in Brodmann areas 44 and 45 in the motor neurone disease-dementia-aphasia syndrome. *Brain* 124, 103–20.

——, D. Yancopoulou, P. J. Nestor, J. H. Xuereb, M. G. Spillantini, F. Pulvermüller, and J. R. Hodges (2006). Clinical, imaging and pathological correlates of a hereditary deficit in verb and action processing. *Brain* 129, 321–32.

Baker, M. C. (1991). On the relation of serialization to verb extensions. In C. Lefebvre (ed.), *Serial Verbs: Grammatical, Comparative and Cognitive Approaches*, pp. 79–102. Amsterdam: John Benjamins.

——(2003). *Lexical Categories: Verbs, Nouns, and Adjectives*. Cambridge: Cambridge University Press.

Baker, M. C. (2005). On syntactic categories. In H. Cohen and C. Lefebvre (eds.), *Handbook of Categorization in Cognitive Science*, pp. 423–30. Oxford: Elsevier.

Balaban, M. and S. Waxman (1992). Words may facilitate categorization in 9-month-old infants. *Journal of Experimental Child Psychology* 64, 3–26.

Baldwin, D. A. (1995). Understanding the link between joint attention and language. In C. Moore and P. J. Dunham (eds.), *Joint Attention: Its Origins and Role in Development*, pp. 131–58. Hillsdale, NJ: Lawrence Erlbaum Associates.

Baldwin, J. M. (1896). A new factor in evolution. *American Naturalist* 30, 441–51, 536–53.

Bancel, P. J. and A. Matthey de l'Etang (2002). Tracing the ancestral kinship system: The global etymon KAKA. Part I: A linguistic study. *Mother Tongue* VII, 209–43.

——and ——(2005). Kin tongue. a study of kin nursery terms in relation to language acquisition, with a historical and evolutionary perspective. *Mother Tongue* IX, 171–90.

——and ——(2008). The millennial persistence of Indo-European and Eurasiatic pronouns and the origin of nominals. In J. D. Bengtson (ed.), *In Hot Pursuit of Language in Prehistory: Essays in the Four Fields of Anthropology—in Honor of Harold Crane Fleming*, pp. 439–64. Amsterdam: John Benjamins.

Baptista, M. (2003). *The Syntax of Cape Verdean Creole: The Sotavento Varieties*. Amsterdam: John Benjamins.

Bard, E. G., D. Robertson, and A. Sorace (1996). Magnitude estimation of linguistic acceptability. *Language* 72(1), 32–68.

Baron-Cohen, S. (1996). Is there a normal phase of synaesthesia in development? *PSYCHE* 2(27). (Online journal: http://psyche.cs.monash.edu.au/v2/psyche-2-27-baron_cohen.html).

Barrett, H. C., W. E. Frankenhuis, and A. Wilke (2008). Adaptation to moving targets: Culture/gene coevolution, not either/or. *Behavioral and Brain Sciences* 31(5), 511–12.

Barrios, A. L. (2006). Austronesian elements in Philippine Creole Spanish. Paper presented at the Tenth International Conference on Austronesian Linguistics, January 2006. Puerto Princesa City, Palawan, Philippines. Online at http://www.sil.org/asia/Philippines/ical/papers/barrios-austronesian%20elements.pdf.

Bartels, A. and S. Zeki (2004). The neural correlates of maternal and romantic love. *Neuroimage* 21, 1155–66.

Bartlett, M. and D. Kazakov (2005). The origins of syntax: From navigation to language. *Connection Science* 17(3-4), 271–88.

Barton, S. B. and A. J. Sanford (1993). A case study of anomaly detection: Shallow semantic processing and cohesion establishment. *Memory and Cognition* 21, 477–87.

Basso, A. and R. Cubelli (1999). Clinical aspects of aphasia. In G. Denes and L. Pizzamiglio (eds.), *Handbook of Clinical and Experimental Neuropsychology*, pp. 181–94. London: Psychology Press.

Bates, E. and J. C. Goodman (1997). On the inseparability of grammar from the lexicon: Evidence from acquisition, aphasia and real-time processing. *Language and Cognitive Processes* 12(5/6), 507–84.

—— and B. MacWhinney (1979). A functionalist approach to the acquisition of grammar. In E. Ochs and B. Schieffelin (eds.), *Developmental Pragmatics*, pp. 167–211. New York: Academic Press.

——, L. Benigni, L. Bretherton, L. Camaioni, and V. Volterra (1977). From gesture to the first word. In M. Lewis and L. Rosenblum (eds.), *Interaction, Conversation, and the Development of Language*, pp. 247–307. New York: Wiley.

——, I. Bretherton, and L. Snider (1988). *From First Words to Grammar: Individual Differences and Dissociable Mechanisms*. Cambridge: Cambridge University Press.

——, P. Marangolo, L. Pizzamiglio, and F. Dick (2001). Linguistic and nonlinguistic priming in aphasia. *Brain and Language* 76(1), 62–9.

Bauer, R. H. (1993). Lateralization of neural control for vocalization by the frog (*Rana pipiens*). *Psychobiology* 21, 243–48.

Baum, S. R. and M. D. Pell (1999). The neural bases of prosody: Insights from lesion studies and neuroimaging. *Aphasiology* 13(8), 581–608.

Beaken, M. (1996). *The Making of Language*. Edinburgh: Edinburgh University Press.

Becker, A. and T. Veenstra (2003). The survival of inflectional morphology in French-related creoles. *Studies in Second Language Acquisition* 25(2), 283–306.

Beckwith, M. W. (1918). *The Hawaiian Romance of Laieikawai*. Washington, DC: Bureau of American Ethnology.

Belin, P., S. Fecteau, I. Charest, N. Nicastro, M. D. Hauser, and J. L. Armony (2007). Human cerebral response to animal affective vocalizations. *Proceedings of the Royal Society Series B* 275, 473–81.

Belletti, A. and L. Rizzi (1988). Psych-verbs and θ-theory. *Natural Language and Linguistic Theory* 6(3), 291–352.

Belton, E., C. H. Salmond, K. E. Watkins, F. Vargha-Khadem, and D. G. Gadian (2003). Bilateral brain abnormalities associated with dominantly inherited verbal and orofacial dyspraxia. *Human Brain Mapping* 18(3), 194–200.

Ben-Shachar, M., T. Hendler, I. Kahn, D. Ben-Bashat, and Y. Grodzinsky (2003). The neural reality of syntactic transformations: Evidence from functional magnetic resonance imaging. *Psychological Science* 14(5), 433–40.

Benhamou, S. (1997). Path integration by swimming rats. *Animal Behaviour* 54(2), 321–27.

Bentahila, A. and E. E. Davies (1995). Patterns of code-switching and patterns of language contact. *Lingua* 96(2-3), 75–93.

Bentley, M. and E. Varon (1933). An accessory study of 'phonetic symbolism'. *American Journal of Psychology* 45, 76–86.

Benveniste, E. (1957). La phrase rélative, problème de syntaxe générale. *Bulletin de la Société Linguistique de Paris* 53, 39–54.

Bergen, B. K., S. Lindsay, T. Matlock, and S. Narayanan (2007). Spatial and linguistic aspects of visual imagery in sentence comprehension. *Cognitive Science* 31, 733–64.

Berlin, B. (1994). Evidence for pervasive synesthetic sound symbolism in ethnozoological nomenclature. In L. Hinton, J. Nichols, and J. Ohala (eds.), *Sound Symbolism*, pp. 76–93. Cambridge: Cambridge University Press.

——(2005). Commentary on Everett (2005). *Current Anthropology* 46(4), 635.

Bermúdez, J. L. (2003). *Thinking without Words*. Oxford: Oxford University Press.

Bernardis, P. and M. Gentilucci (2006). Speech and gesture share the same communication system. *Neuropsychologia* 4(2), 178–90.

Berndt, R. S., A. N. Haendiges, M. W. Burton, and C. C. Mitchum (2002). Grammatical class and imageability in aphasic word production: Their effects are independent. *Journal of Neurolinguistics* 15, 353–71.

Berwick, R. C. (1997). Syntax facit saltum: Computation and the genotype and phenotype of language. *Journal of Neurolinguistics* 10(2-3), 231–49.

Beurton, P. J., R. Falk, and H. Rheinberger (eds.) (2000). *The Concept of the Gene in Development and Evolution: Historical and Epistemological Perspectives*. Cambridge: Cambridge University Press.

Bhattacharjya, D. (1994). Nagamese: Pidgin, creole, or creoloid? *California Linguistic Notes* 24(2).

Bhattacharya, H., J. Cirillo, B. R. Subba, and D. Todt (2007). Song performance rules in the oriental magpie robin (*Copsychus salauris*). *Our Nature* 5, 1–13.

Bickerton, D. (1981). *Roots of Language*. Ann Arbor, MI: Karoma.

——(1984). The language bioprogram hypothesis. *Behavioral and Brain Sciences* 7, 173–88.

——(1988). Creole languages and the bioprogram. In F. J. Newmeyer (ed.), *Linguistics: The Cambridge Survey, Vol. 2, Linguistic Theory: Extensions and Implications*, pp. 268–84. Cambridge: Cambridge University Press.

——(1989). Seselwa serialization and its significance. *Journal of Pidgin and Creole Languages* 4(2), 155–83.

——(1990). *Language and Species*. Chicago: University of Chicago Press.

——(1993). Subject focus and pronouns. In F. Byrne and D. Winford (eds.), *Focus and Grammatical Relations in Creole Languages*, pp. 189–212. Amsterdam: John Benjamins.

——(1995). *Language and Human Behaviour*. London: UCL Press.

Bickerton, D. (1998). Catastrophic evolution: The case for a single step from pro-tolanguage to full human language. In J. R. Hurford, M. Studdert-Kennedy, and C. Knight (eds.), *Approaches to the Evolution of Language: Social and Cognitive Bases*, pp. 341–58. Cambridge: Cambridge University Press.

——(1999a). Creole languages, the Language Bioprogram hypothesis, and language acquisition. In W. C. Ritchie and T. K. Bhatia (eds.), *Handbook of Child Language Acquisition*, pp. 195–220. San Diego, CA: Academic Press.

——(1999b). How to acquire language without positive evidence: What acquisitionists can learn from creoles. In M. DeGraff (ed.), *Language Creation and Language Change: Creolization, Diachrony, and Development*, pp. 49–74. Cambridge, MA: MIT Press.

——(2005). Language first, then shared intentionality, then a beneficent spiral. *Behavioral and Brain Sciences* 28, 691–2.

——(2007). Language evolution: A brief guide for linguists. *Lingua* 117(3), 510–26.

——(2008a). *Bastard Tongues: A Trail-Blazing Linguist Finds Clues to Our Common Humanity in the World's Lowliest Languages*. New York: Hill and Wang.

——(2008b). But how did protolanguage actually *start*? *Interaction Studies* 9(1), 169–76. (Special issue, edited by Derek Bickerton and Michael Arbib, entitled *Holophrasis, Compositionality and Protolanguage*).

——(2009a). *Adam's Tongue: How Humans Made Language, How Language Made Humans*. New York: Hill and Wang.

——(2009b). Syntax for non-syntacticians: A brief primer. In D. Bickerton and E. Szathmáry (eds.), *Biological Foundations and Origin of Syntax*, pp. 3–13. Cambridge, MA: MIT Press.

——and P. Muysken (1988). A dialog concerning the linguistic status of creole languages. In F. J. Newmeyer (ed.), *Linguistics: The Cambridge Survey, Vol. 2, Linguistic Theory: Extensions and Implications*, pp. 302–6. Cambridge: Cambridge University Press.

Biehler, E. (1913). *English–Chiswina Dictionary with an Outline Chiswina Grammar*. Chishawasha, Zimbabwe: Jesuit Mission.

Bindra, D., F. G. Patterson, H. S. Terrace, L. A. Petitto, R. J. Sanders, and T. G. Bever (1981). Ape language. *Science* 211, 86–7. (Not co-authored—a contentious exchange of three short notes by the first, second, and last four authors named.).

Bird, H., S. Franklin, and D. Howard (2002). 'Little words'—not really: Function and content words in normal and aphasic speech. *Journal of Neurolinguistics* 15(1-3), 209–37.

——, D. Howard, and S. Franklin (2003). Verbs and nouns: The importance of being imageable. *Journal of Neurolinguistics* 16, 113–49.

Bird, S. and M. Y. Liberman (2001). A formal framework for linguistic annotation. *Speech Communication* 33(1-2), 23–60.

Bishop, D. V. M. (1982). Comprehension of spoken, written and signed sentences in child language disorders. *Journal of Child Psychology and Psychiatry* 23(1), 1–20.

——(1997). Listening out for subtle deficits. *Nature* 387, 129–30.

Bishop, D. V. M. (2003). Genetic and environmental risks for specific language impairment in children. *International Journal of Pediatric Otorhinolaryngology* 67, Supplement 1, S142–S157.

——, C. V. Adams, and C. F. Norbury (2006). Distinct genetic influences on grammar and phonological short-term memory deficits: Evidence from 6-year-old twins. *Genes, Brain and Behavior* 5(2), 158–69.

Blaubergs, M. S. and M. D. S. Braine (1974). Short-term memory limitations on decoding self-embedded sentences. *Journal of Experimental Psychology* 102(4), 745–8.

Bloom, L., P. Lightbown, and L. Hood (1975). *Structure and Variation in Child Language*. (Monographs of the Society for Research in Child Development, 40(2), Serial No. 160.).

Bloomfield, L. (1933). *Language*. New York: Holt.

Blythe, R. A., K. Smith, and A. D. M. Smith (2010). Learning times for large lexicons through cross-situational learning. *Cognitive Science* 34(4), 620–42.

Bod, R. (1998). *Beyond Grammar: An Experience-Based Theory of Language*. Stanford, CA: CSLI Publications.

—— (2009). Constructions at work or at rest? *Cognitive Linguistics* 20(1), 129–34.

——, J. Hay, and S. Jannedy (2003a). Introduction. In R. Bod, J. Hay, and S. Jannedy (eds.), *Probabilistic Linguistics*, pp. 1–10. Cambridge, MA: MIT Press.

——, J. Hay, and S. Jannedy (eds.) (2003b). *Probabilistic Linguistics*. Cambridge, MA: MIT Press.

Boersma, P. and B. Hayes (2001). Empirical tests of the gradual learning algorithm. *Linguistic Inquiry* 32(1), 45–86.

Bohoussou, A. and S. Skopeteas (2008). Grammaticalization of spatial adpositions in Nànáfwê. In E. Verhoeven, S. Skopeteas, Y.-M. Shin, Y. Nishina, and J. Helmbrecht (eds.), *Studies on Grammaticalization*, pp. 77–104. Berlin: Mouton de Gruyter.

Bolinger, D. (1972). What did John keep the car that was in? *Linguistic Inquiry* 3(1), 109–14.

Bonvillian, J. D., A. M. Garber, and S. B. Dell (1997). Language origin accounts: Was the gesture in the beginning? *First Language* 17(51), 219–39.

Booth, A. E. and S. R. Waxman (2002). Object names and object functions serve as cues to categories in infancy. *Developmental Psychology* 38(6), 948–57.

Boroditsky, L. (2001). Does language shape thought? Mandarin and English speakers' conceptions of time. *Cognitive Psychology* 43, 1–2.

—— (2003). Linguistic relativity. In L. Nadel (ed.), *Encyclopedia of Cognitive Science*, pp. 917–21. London: Macmillan Press.

Borsellino, A., A. De Marco, A. Allazetta, S. Rinesi, and B. Bartolini (1972). Reversal time distribution in the perception of visual ambiguous stimuli. *Biological Cybernetics* 10(3), 139–44.

Bortoni-Ricardo, S. (1985). *The Urbanisation of Rural Dialect Speakers: A Sociolinguistic Study in Brazil*. Cambridge: Cambridge University Press.

Borua, B. K. (1993). *Nagamese, the Language of Nagaland*. New Delhi: Mittal.

Botvinick, M. M., Y. Niv, and A. C. Barto (2009). Hierarchically organized behavior and its neural foundations: A reinforcement learning perspective. *Cognition* 113(3), 262–80.

Bowerman, M. and S. Choi (2001). Shaping meanings for language: Universal and language-specific in the acquisition of spatial semantic categories. In M. Bowerman and S. C. Levinson (eds.), *Language Acquisition and Conceptual Development*, pp. 475–511. Cambridge: Cambridge University Press.

Bowern, C. (2002). Grammatical reanalysis and verb serialization: The unusual case of Sivisa Titan. (MIT Working Papers in Linguistics, vol. 44.)

Boyd, R. and P. J. Richerson (1985). *Culture and the Evolutionary Process*. University of Chicago Press.

Böye, M., O. Güntürkün, and J. Vauclair (2005). Right ear advantage for conspecific calls in adults and subadults, but not infants, California sea lions (*Zalophus californianus*): Hemispheric specialization for communication? *European Journal of Neuroscience* 21(6), 1727–32.

Bradley, D. C. (1978). *Computational Distinctions of Vocabulary Type*. Ph.D. thesis, MIT.

Bradshaw, J. and L. J. Rogers (1993). *The Evolution of Lateral Asymmetries, Language, Tool Use, and Intellect*. San Diego, CA: Academic Press.

Brain, C. K. and A. Sillen (1988). Evidence from the Swartkrans cave for the earliest use of fire. *Nature* 336, 464–6.

Braine, M. D. S. (1963). The ontogeny of English phrase structure: The first phase. *Language* 39(1), 1–13.

——(1976). *Children's First Word Combinations*. (Monographs of the Society for Research in Child Development, 41(1), Serial No. 164.)

Branigan, H. P., M. J. Pickering, and A. A. Cleland (2000). Syntactic co-ordination in dialogue. *Cognition* 75(2), B13–B25.

Brannigan, G. (1977). If this kid is in the one-word period, so how come he's saying whole sentences? (Paper presented at the second annual Boston University Conference on Language Development).

Bråten, S. (2009). *The Intersubjective Mirror in Infant Learning and Evolution of Speech*. Amsterdam: John Benjamins.

Brenowitz, E. A. and A. P. Arnold (1986). Interspecific comparisons of the size of neural control regions and song complexity in duetting birds: Evolutionary implications. *Journal of Neuroscience* 6, 2875–9.

——and D. E. Kroodsma (1996). The neuroethology of birdsong. In D. E. Kroodsma and E. H. Miller (eds.), *Ecology and Evolution of Acoustic Communication in Birds*, pp. 285–304. Ithaca, NY: Comstock Publishing Associates, a division of Cornell University Press.

——, A. P. Arnold, and R. N. Levin (1985). Neural correlates of female song in tropical duetting birds. *Brain Research* 343, 104–12.

——, D. Margoliash, and K. W. Nordeen (1997). An introduction to birdsong and the avian song system. *Journal of Neurobiology* 33(5), 495–500.

Bresnan, J. and S. A. Mchombo (1987). Topic, pronoun, and agreement in Chicheŵa. *Language* 63(4), 741–82.

——, S. Dingare, and C. D. Manning (2001). Soft constraints mirror hard constraints: Voice and person in English and Lummi. In M. Butt and T. H. King (eds.), *Proceedings of the LFG 01 Conference The University of Hong Kong, Hong Kong*. Stanford, CA: CSLI Publications.

Briscoe, E. J. (2000). Grammatical acquisition: Inductive bias and coevolution of language and the language acquisition device. *Language* 76(2), 245–96.

Briscoe, E. J. and J. Carroll (1997). Automatic extraction of subcategorization from corpora. In *Proceedings of the Fifth Conference on Applied Natural Language Processing*, Washington, DC, pp. 356–63.

——, V. de Paiva, and A. Copestake (eds.) (2003). *Inheritance, Defaults, and the Lexicon*. Cambridge: Cambridge University Press.

Broch, J. and E. H. Jahr (1984a). Russenorsk: A new look at the Russo-Norwegian pidgin in northern Norway. In P. S. Ureland and I. Clarkson (eds.), *Scandinavian Language Contacts*, pp. 21–65. Cambridge: Cambridge University Press.

—— and —— (1984b). *Russenorsk: et pidginspråk i Norge*. Oslo: Novus.

Broeder, P., G. Extra, R. van Hout, and K. Voionmaa (1993). Word formation processes in talking about entities. In C. Perdue (ed.), *Adult Language Acquisition: Cross-linguistic Perspectives, Vol. 1, Field Methods*, pp. 41–72. Cambridge: Cambridge University Press.

Broschart, J. (1991). Noun, verb, and participation (a typology of the noun/verb distinction). In H. Seiler and W. Premper (eds.), *Partizipation: das Sprachliche Erfassen von Sachverhalten (Language Universals Series 60)*, pp. 65–137. Tübingen: Gunter Narr.

—— (1997). Why Tongan does it differently: Categorical distinctions in a language without nouns and verbs. *Linguistic Typology* 1, 123–65.

Brown, E. K. and J. E. Miller (1991). *Syntax: A Linguistic Introduction to Sentence Structure*. London: Routledge. (2nd edition).

Brown, J. W. (1975). The problem of repetition: A study of 'Conduction' Aphasia and the 'Isolation' Syndrome. *Cortex* 11(1), 37–52.

Brown, P. (2001). Learning to talk about motion up and down in Tzeltal: Is there a language-specific bias for verb learning? In M. Bowerman and S. C. Levinson (eds.), *Language Acquisition and Conceptual Development*, pp. 512–43. Cambridge University Press.

Brown, R. W. (1958). *Words and Things*. Glencoe, IL: Free Press.

—— (1973). *A First Language*. Cambridge, MA: Harvard University Press.

——, A. H. Black, and A. E. Horowitz (1955). Phonetic symbolism in natural languages. *The Journal of Abnormal and Social Psychology* 50(3), 388–93.

Brumm, H. and P. J. B. Slater (2006a). Ambient noise, motor fatigue, and serial redundancy in chaffinch song. *Behavioral Ecology and Sociobiology* 60, 475–81.

—— and —— (2006b). Animals can vary signal amplitude with receiver distance: Evidence from zebra finch song. *Animal Behaviour* 72, 699–705.

——, S. Kipper, C. Riechelmann, and D. Todt (2005). Do Barbary macaques 'comment' on what they see? A first report on vocalizations accompanying interactions of third parties. *Primates* 46(2), 141–4.

Brüne, M. (2007). On human self-domestication, psychiatry, and eugenics. *Philosophy, Ethics, and Humanities in Medicine* 2, 21. (online publication).

Budwig, N. (1989). The linguistic marking of agentivity and control in child language. *Journal of Child Language* 16, 263–84.

——(1995). *A Developmental-Functionalist Approach to Child Language*. Mahwah, NJ: Lawrence Erlbaum Associates.

Burki, F. and H. Kaessmann (2004). Birth and adaptive evolution of a hominoid gene that supports high neurotransmitter flux. *Nature Genetics* 36(1), 1061–3.

Burling, R. (2005). *The Talking Ape: How Language Evolved*. Oxford: Oxford University Press.

Butler, C. and J. M. Arista (eds.) (2008). *Deconstructing Constructions*. John Benjamins.

Butterworth, G. E. (1991). The ontogeny and phylogeny of joint visual attention. In A. Whiten (ed.), *Natural Theories of Mind: Evolution, Development and Simulation of Everyday Mindreading*, pp. 223–32. Oxford: Blackwells.

——and N. L. M. Jarrett (1991). What minds have in common is space: Spatial mechanisms serving joint visual attention in infancy. *British Journal of Developmental Psychology* 9, 55–72.

By, T. (2004). English dependency grammar. COLING: 20th International Conference on Computational Linguistics, 28 August 2004. (Online at http://acl.ldc.upenn.edu/coling2004/W4/pdf/9.pdf).

Bybee, J. L. and J. Scheibman (1999). The effect of usage on degrees of constituency: The reduction of *don't* in English. *Linguistics* 37(4), 575–96.

——and D. I. Slobin (1982). Why small children cannot change language on their own: Suggestions from the English past tense. In A. Ahlqvist (ed.), *Papers from the 5th International Conference on Historical Linguistics*, pp. 29–37. Amsterdam: John Benjamins.

——, R. Perkins, and W. Pagliuca (1994). *The Evolution of Grammar: Tense, Aspect and Modality in the Languages of the World*. Chicago: University of Chicago Press.

Byrne, F., A. F. Caskey, and D. Winford (1993). Introduction: Focus and grammatical relations in creole languages. In F. Byrne and D. Winford (eds.), *Focus and Grammatical Relations in Creole Languages*, pp. ix–xvi. Amsterdam: John Benjamins.

Byrne, R. W. (1995). *The Thinking Ape: Evolutionary Origins of Intelligence*. Oxford: Oxford University Press.

——and J. M. E. Byrne (1991). Hand preferences in the skilled gathering tasks of mountain gorillas (*Gorilla g. beringei*). *Cortex* 27, 527–46.

——and N. Corp (2004a). Neocortex size predicts deception rate in primates. *Proceedings of the Royal Society of London, Series B* (published online).

——and ——(2004b). Sex difference in chimpanzee handedness. *American Journal of Physical Anthropology* 123, 62–8.

Byrne, R. W. and A. E. Russon (1998). Learning by imitation: A hierarchical approach. *Behavioral and Brain Sciences* 21(5), 667–84.

——and A. Whiten (1988). *Machiavellian Intelligence: Social Expertise and the Evolution of Intellect in Monkeys, Apes and Humans*. Oxford: Clarendon Press.

Cacciari, C. and P. Tabossi (1988). The comprehension of idioms. *Journal of Memory and Language* 27, 668–83.

Call, J. (2006). Descartes' two errors: Reason and reflection in the great apes. In S. Hurley and M. Nudds (eds.), *Rational Animals?*, pp. 219–34. Oxford: Oxford University Press.

——, B. Hare, M. Carpenter, and M. Tomasello (2004). 'Unwilling' versus 'unable': Chimpanzees' understanding of human intentional action. *Developmental Science* 7, 488–98.

Cameron, L. and A. Deignan (2006). The emergence of metaphor in discourse. *Applied Linguistics* 27(4), 671–90.

Cangelosi, A. and S. Harnad (2000). The adaptive advantage of symbolic theft over sensorimotor toil: Grounding language in perceptual categories. *Evolution of Communication* 4(1), 117–42.

——, A. Greco, and S. Harnad (2000). From robotic toil to symbolic theft: Grounding transfer from entry-level to higher-level categories. *Connection Science* 12(2), 143–62.

Cann, R (2001). Functional versus lexical: A cognitive dichotomy. In R. D. Borsley (ed.), *The Nature and Function of Syntactic Categories*, pp. 37–78. Academic Press.

——, R. M. Kempson, L. Marten, and D. Swinburne (2004). On the left and on the right. In D. Adger, C. de Cat, and G. Tsoulas (eds.), *Peripheries: Syntactic Edges and their Effects*, pp. 19–47. Dordrecht, Netherlands: Kluwer.

——, R. M. Kempson, and L. Marten (2005). *The Dynamics of Language*. New York: Academic Press.

Capirci, O., J. M. Iverson, E. Pizzuto, and V. Volterra (1996). Gestures and words during the transition to two-word speech. *Journal of Child Language* 23, 645–73.

Caplan, D. (2006). Why is Broca's Area involved in syntax? *Cortex* 42(4), 469–71.

——and C. Futter (1986). Assignment of thematic roles by an agrammatic aphasic patient. *Brain and Language* 27, 117–35.

——and G. S. Waters (1999). Verbal working memory and sentence comprehension. *Behavioral and Brain Sciences* 22(1), 77–94.

——, L. Stanczak, and G. Waters (2008). Syntactic and thematic constraint effects on blood oxygenation level dependent signal correlates of comprehension of relative clauses. *Journal of Cognitive Neuroscience* 20(4), 643–56.

Cappa, S. F. and D. Perani (2002). Nouns and verbs: Neurological correlates of linguistic processing. *Rivista di Linguistica* 14(1), 73–83. (Available online at http://alphalinguistica.sns.it/RdL/14.1/Cappa_Perani.pdf).

Caramazza, A. and A. Hillis (1991). Lexical organization of nouns and verbs in the brain. *Nature* 349, 788–90.

Caramazza, A. and E. Zurif (1976). Dissociation of algorithmic and heuristic processes in sentence comprehension: Evidence from aphasia. *Brain and Language* 3, 572–82.

Carey, B. (2006). Grammar revealed in the love songs of whales. *Live Science* (22 March 2006).

Carlson, K. (2002). *Parallelism and Prosody in the Processing of Ellipsis Sentences*. London: Routledge.

——, M. W. Dickey, and C. Kennedy (2005). Structural economy in the processing and representation of gapping sentences. *Syntax* 8(3), 208–28.

Carnie, A. (2002). *Syntax: A Generative Introduction*. Oxford: Blackwell Publishing.

Carstairs-McCarthy, A. (1999). *The Origins of Complex Language*. Oxford: Oxford University Press.

—— (2010). *The Evolution of Morphology*. Oxford: Oxford University Press.

Case, P. G. and H. L. Dibble (1987). Middle Paleolithic symbolism: A review of current evidence and interpretations. *Journal of Anthropological Archaeology* 6(3), 263–96.

Castiello, U., K. M. Bennett, G. F. Egan, H. J. Tochon-Danguy, A. Kritikos, and J. Dunai (2000). Human inferior parietal cortex 'programs' the action class of grasping. *Journal of Cognitive Systems Research* 1(2), 89–97.

Catani, M. and M. Mesulam (2008). The arcuate fasciculus and the disconnection theme in language and aphasia: History and current state. *Cortex* 44(8), 953–61.

Catani, M. C., D. K. Jones, and D. H. ffytche (2005). Perisylvian networks of the human brain. *Annals of Neurology* 57, 8–16.

Catchpole, C., B. Leisler, and J. Dittami (1986). Sexual differences in the responses of captive great reed warblers (*Acrocephalus arundinaceus*) to variation in song structure and repertoire size. *Ethology* 73, 69–77.

Cavalli-Sforza, L. L. and M. W. Feldman (1981). *Cultural Transmission and Evolution: A Quantitative Approach*. Princeton, NJ: Princeton University Press.

Chafe, W. (1993). Seneca speaking styles and the location of authority. In J. H. Hill and J. T. Irvine (eds.), *Responsibility and Evidence in Oral Discourse*, pp. 72–87. Cambridge: Cambridge University Press.

Chastaing, M. (1965). Dernières recherches sur le symbolisme vocalique de la petitesse. *Revue Philosophique* 155, 41–56.

Chater, N., F. Reali, and M. H. Christiansen (2009). Restrictions on biological adaptation in language evolution. *Proceedings of the National Academy of Sciences of the U.S.A.* 106(4), 1015–20.

Cheney, D. M. and R. M. Seyfarth (1987). The influence of intergroup competition on the survival and reproduction of female vervet monkeys. *Behavioral Ecology and Sociobiology* 21(6), 375–86.

Chernigovskaya, T. V., N. D. Svetozarova, T. I. Tokareva, D. A. Tret'yakov, P. V. Ozerskii, and K. N. Strel'nikov (2000). Specialization of cerebral hemispheres in the perception of Russian intonations. *Human Physiology* 26(2), 142–7.

Chi, J. G., E. C. Dooling, and F. H. Gilles (1977). Gyral development in the human brain. *Annals of Neurology* 1(1), 86–93.

Chimpanzee Sequencing and Analysis Consortium (2005). Initial sequence of the chimpanzee genome and comparison with the human genome. *Nature* 437, 69–87.

Chipere, N. (2003). *Understanding Complex Sentences: Native Speaker Variation in Syntactic Competence*. Basingstoke, UK: Palgrave Macmillan.

——(2009). Individual differences in processing complex structures. In G. Sampson, D. Gil, and P. Trudgill (eds.), *Language Complexity as an Evolving Variable*, pp. 178–91. Oxford: Oxford University Press.

Chomsky, N. (1956a). On the limits of finite state description. *MIT Research Lab in Electronics Quarterly Progress Report* 42, 64–5.

——(1956b). The range of adequacy of various types of grammars. *MIT Research Lab in Electronics Quarterly Progress Report* 41, 93–6.

——(1956c). Three models for the description of language. *IRE Transactions on Information Theory IT-2, no. 3*, 113–24. (Reprinted in *Readings in Mathematical Psychology* 2, edited by R. Luce, R. Bush, and E. Galanter, pp. 105-24. New York: Wiley and Sons, 1965.)

——(1957). *Syntactic Structures*. The Hague: Mouton.

——(1958). Some properties of phrase structure grammars. *MIT Research Lab in Electronics Quarterly Progress Report* 49, 108–11.

——(1959a). A note on phrase structure grammars. *Information and Control* 2, 393–5.

——(1959b). On certain formal properties of grammars. *Information and Control* 2, 137–67. (Reprinted in *Readings in Mathematical Psychology* 2, edited by R. Luce, R. Bush, and E. Galanter, pp. 125–55. New York: Wiley and Sons, 1965.)

——(1962a). Context-free grammars and pushdown storage. *MIT Research Lab in Electronics Quarterly Progress Report* 65, 187–94.

——(1962b). Explanatory models in linguistics. In E. Nagel, P. Suppes, and A. Tarski (eds.), *Logic, Methodology, and Philosophy of Science*, pp. 528–50. Stanford, CA: Stanford University Press.

——(1963). Formal properties of grammars. In R. Luce, R. Bush, and E. Galanter (eds.), *Handbook of Mathematical Psychology* 2, pp. 323–418. New York: Wiley and Sons.

——(1964). *Current Issues in Linguistic Theory*. The Hague: Mouton.

——(1965). *Aspects of the Theory of Syntax*. Cambridge, MA: MIT Press.

——(1973). Conditions on transformations. In S. Anderson and P. Kiparsky (eds.), *A Festschrift for Morris Halle*, pp. 232–86. New York: Holt, Rinehart and Winston.

——(1975a). *The Logical Structure of Linguistic Theory*. New York: Plenum.

——(1975b). *Reflections on Language*. Glasgow: Fontana/Collins.

——(1980a). Reply to question by Papert. In M. Piattelli-Palmarini (ed.), *Language and Learning: the Debate between Jean Piaget and Noam Chomsky*, pp. 175–6. London: Routledge and Kegan Paul.

——(1980b). *Rules and Representations*. London: Basil Blackwell.

——(1981). *Lectures on Government and Binding: the Pisa Lectures*. Dordrecht, Netherlands: Foris.

Chomsky, N. (1986). *Knowledge of Language*. New York: Praeger.

——(1987). *Knowledge of Language: Its Nature, Origin and Use*. Dordrecht, Netherlands: Foris.

——(1988). *Language and Problems of Knowledge*. Cambridge, MA: MIT Press.

——(1995a). Bare phrase structure. In G. Webelhuth (ed.), *Government and Binding Theory and the Minimalist Program: Principles and Parameters in Syntactic Theory*, pp. 383–439. Hoboken, NJ: Wiley.

——(1995b). *The Minimalist Program*. Number 28 in Current Studies in Linguistics. Cambridge, MA: MIT Press.

——and G. Miller (1958). Finite state languages. *Information and Control* 1, 91–112. (Reprinted in *Readings in Mathematical Psychology* 2, edited by R. Luce, R. Bush, and E. Galanter, pp. 156–71. New York: Wiley and Sons, 1965.)

——and —— (1963). Introduction to the formal analysis of natural languages. In R. D. Luce, R. R. Bush, and E. Galanter (eds.), *Handbook of Mathematical Psychology*, Vol. 2, pp. 269–321. New York: John Wiley and Sons.

——and M. P. Schutzenberger (1963). The algebraic theory of context-free languages. In P. Braffort and D. Hirshberg (eds.), *Computer Programming and Formal Systems: Studies in Logic*, pp. 118–61. Amsterdam: North Holland.

Christiansen, M. H. and N. Chater (1999). Toward a connectionist model of recursion in human linguistic performance. *Cognitive Science* 23(2), 157–205.

——and N. Chater (2008). Language as shaped by the brain. *Behavioral and Brain Sciences* 31(5), 489–558.

Christianson, K., A. Hollingworth, J. Halliwell, and F. Ferreira (2001). Thematic roles assigned along the garden path linger. *Memory and Cognition* 21, 477–87.

Chung, K. S. (1994). Verb+noun function-describing compounds. *Bulletin of the College of Liberal Arts, Taiwan National University* 41, 181–221. (Revised version online at http://homepage.ntu.edu.tw/~karchung/pubs/vncomp_rev.pdf.)

Chung, S. and J. McCloskey (1983). On the interpretation of certain island facts in GPSG. *Linguistic Inquiry* 14(4), 704–13.

Churchward, C. M. (1953). *Tongan Grammar*. Oxford: Oxford University Press.

Churchward, S. (1951). *A Samoan Grammar*. Melbourne: Spectator Publishing Co. Pty. Ltd. (2nd edition, revised and enlarged).

Citko, B. (2008). Missing labels. *Lingua* 118(7), 907–44.

Clark, A. (1998). Magic words: How language augments human cognition. In P. Carruthers and J. Boucher (eds.), *Language and Thought: Interdisciplinary Themes*, pp. 162–83. Cambridge: Cambridge University Press.

——and C. Thornton (1997). Trading spaces: Computation, representation, and the limits of uninformed learning. *Behavioral and Brain Sciences* 20(1), 57–92.

Clark, E. V. (1988). On the logic of contrast. *Journal of Child Language* 15, 317–35.

——(1990). On the pragmatics of contrast. *Journal of Child Language* 17, 417–31.

——(2004). How language acquisition builds on cognitive development. *Trends in Cognitive Sciences* 8(10), 472–8.

Clark, E. V. and B. F. Kelly (eds.) (2006). *Constructions in Acquisition*. Stanford, CA: Center for the Study of Language and Information.

Clay, Z. and K. Zuberbühler (2009). Food-associated calling sequences in bonobos. *Animal Behaviour* 77, 1387–96.

Cleland, A. A. and M. J. Pickering (2006). Do writing and speaking employ the same syntactic representations? *Journal of Memory and Language* 54, 185–98.

Cochran, G. and H. Harpending (2009). *The 10,000 Year Explosion: How Civilization Accelerated Human Evolution*. Philadelphia, PA: Basic Books.

Codrington, R. (1885). *The Melanesian Languages*. Oxford: Clarendon Press.

Collins, C. (2002). Eliminating labels. In S. Epstein and D. T. Seely (eds.), *Derivation and Explanation in the Minimalist Program*, pp. 42–64. Oxford: Blackwell Publishing.

Comrie, B. (1985). Derivation, inflection, and semantic change in the development of the Chukchi verb paradigm. In J. Fisiak (ed.), *Historical Semantics, Historical Word Formation*, pp. 85–96. Berlin: Mouton (Walter de Gruyter).

——(1992). Before complexity. In J. A. Hawkins and M. Gell-Mann (eds.), *The Evolution of Human Languages*, pp. 193–211. Redwood City, CA: Addison-Wesley Publishing Company.

——(1997). On the origin of the Basic Variety. *Second Language Research* 13(4), 367–73.

Conant, L. L. (1923). *The Number Concept: Its Origin and Development*. New York: Macmillan and Co.

Connolly, K. J. and M. Dalgliesh (1989). The emergence of a tool-using skill in infancy. *Developmental Psychology* 25(6), 894–912.

Coolidge, F. L. and T. Wynn (2005). Working memory, its executive functions, and the emergence of modern thinking. *Cambridge Archaeological Journal* 15(1), 5–26.

——and ——(2009). *The Rise of Homo Sapiens: The Evolution of Modern Thinking*. Chichester, UK: Wiley-Blackwell.

Cooper, D. N. (1999). *Human Gene Evolution*. Oxford: Bios Scientific Publishers.

Cooper, T. (1997). Assessing vocabulary size: So, what's the problem? *Language Matters* 26(1), 96–117.

Coppock, E. (2001). Gapping: In defense of deletion. In M. Andronis, C. Ball, H. Elston, and S. Neuvel (eds.), *Proceedings of the Chicago Linguistics Society* 37, pp. 133–48. Chicago: University of Chicago.

Coqueugniot, H., J.-J. Hublin, F. Houët, and T. Jacob (2004). Early brain growth in *Homo erectus* and implications for cognitive ability. *Nature* 431, 299–302.

Corballis, M. C. (1991). *The Lopsided Ape*. Oxford: Oxford University Press.

——(2002). *From Hand to Mouth: the Origins of Language*. Princeton: Princeton University Press.

——(2003). From mouth to hand: Gesture, speech, and the evolution of right-handedness. *Behavioral and Brain Sciences* 26, 199–260.

——and I. L. Beale (1983). *The Ambivalent Mind the Neuropsychology of Left and Right*. Chicago: Nelson-Hall.

Corder, S. P. (1967). The significance of learners' errors. *International Review of Applied Linguistics* 5, 161–70.

——(1971). Idiosyncratic dialects and error analysis. *International Review of Applied Linguistics* 9, 147–59.

Corkum, V. L. and C. Moore (1992). Cues for joint visual attention in infants. (Poster presented at the meeting of the International Conference on Infant Studies, Miami.)

——and——(1995). Attention in infants. In C. Moore and P. J. Dunham (eds.), *Joint Attention: Its Origins and Role in Development*, pp. 61–83. Hillsdale, NJ: Lawrence Erlbaum Associates.

Corley, M. M. B. and C. Scheepers (2002). Syntactic priming in English sentence production: Categorical and latency evidence from an internet-based study. *Psychonomic Bulletin and Review* 9, 126–31.

Cornips, L. (2006). Intermediate syntactic variants in a dialect-standard speech repertoire and relative acceptability. In G. Fanselow, C. Féry, R. Vogel, and M. Schlesewsky (eds.), *Gradience in Grammar: Generative Perspectives*, pp. 85–105. Oxford: Oxford University Press.

Coudé, G., P. F. Ferrara, F. Roda, M. Maranesi, V. Veroni, F. Monti, G. Rizzolatti, and L. Fogassi (2007). Neuronal responses during vocalization in the ventral premotor cortex of macaque monkeys. *Society for Neuroscience Annual Meeting (San Diego California)* Abstract 636.3.

Cowart, W. (1997). *Experimental Syntax: Applying Objective Methods to Sentence Judgments*. Thousand Oaks, CA: Sage Publications.

Creider, C. A. (1979). On the explanation of transformations. In T. Givón (ed.), *Syntax and Semantics, Volume 12; Discourse and Syntax*, pp. 3–21. New York: Academic Press.

Critchley, M. (1970). *Aphasiology and other Aspects of Language*. London: Edward Arnold, Ltd.

Crockford, C. and C. Boesch (2003). Context-specific calls in wild chimpanzees, *Pan troglodytes verus*: Analysis of barks. *Animal Behaviour* 66, 115–25.

Croft, W. (2001). *Radical Construction Grammar: Syntactic Theory in Typological Perspective*. Oxford: Oxford University Press.

Cross, I. and G. E. Woodruff (2009). Music as a communicative medium. In R. Botha and C. Knight (eds.), *The Prehistory of Language*, pp. 77–98. Oxford: Oxford University Press.

Crowley, T. (2002). *Serial Verbs in Oceanic: A Descriptive Typology*. Oxford: Oxford University Press.

——(2003). The emergence of transitive verbal morphology in Bislama. *Te Reo: Journal of the Linguistic Society of New Zealand* 46, 19–30.

Culicover, P. W. (1999). *Syntactic Nuts: Hard Cases in Syntax*. Oxford: Oxford University Press.

——and R. S. Jackendoff (2005). *Simpler Syntax*. Oxford: Oxford University Press.

——and A. Nowak (2003). *Dynamical Grammar*. Oxford: Oxford University Press.

Cummins, D. D. (1998). Can humans form hierarchically embedded mental representations? *Behavioral and Brain Sciences* 21, 687–8.

Curtiss, S. (1977). *Genie: A Psycholinguistic Study of a Modern-Day 'Wild Child'*. New York: Academic Press.

Cuskley, C., J. Simner, and S. Kirby (2009). Cross-modally bootstrapping protolanguage: Reconsidering the evidence. (Poster given at European Human Behaviour and Evolution Conference, St Andrews, UK.)

Cutler, A. (1994). The perception of rhythm in language. *Cognition* 50, 79–81.

——, J. McQueen, and K. Robinson (1990). Elizabeth and John: Sound patterns of men's and women's names. *Journal of Linguistics* 26, 471–82.

Cutting, J. C. and K. Bock (1997). That's the way the cookie bounces: Syntactic and semantic components of experimentally elicited idiom blends. *Memory and Cognition* 25(1), 57–71.

Cynx, J. (1990). Experimental determination of a unit of song production in the zebra finch (*Taeniopygia guttata*). *Journal of Comparative Psychology* 104, 3–10.

Czaykowska-Higgins, E. and M. D. Kinkade (1998). Salish languages and linguistics. In E. Czaykowska-Higgins and M. D. Kinkade (eds.), *Salish Languages and Linguistics: Theoretical and Descriptive Perspectives*, pp. 1–68. Berlin: Mouton de Gruyter.

Dąbrowska, E. (1997). The LAD goes to school: A cautionary tale for nativists. *Linguistics* 35(4), 735–66.

da Costa, R. G., A. Braun, M. Lopes, M. D. Hauser, R. E. Carson, P. Herscovitch, and A. Martin (2004). Toward an evolutionary perspective on conceptual representation: Species-specific calls activate visual and affective processing systems in the macaque. *Proceedings of the National Academy of Sciences of the U.S.A.* 101(50), 17516–21.

Daelemans, W., K. De Smedt, and G. Gazdar (1992). Inheritance in natural language processing. *Computational Linguistics* 18(2), 205–18.

Dahl, Ö. (2001). Complexification, erosion, and baroqueness. *Linguistic Typology* 5, 374–7.

——(2004). *The Growth and Maintenance of Linguistic Complexity*. Amsterdam: John Benjamins.

——(2009). Testing the assumption of complexity invariance: The case of Elfdalian and Swedish. In G. Sampson, D. Gil, and P. Trudgill (eds.), *Language Complexity as an Evolving Variable*, pp. 50–63. Oxford: Oxford University Press.

Dale, P. S., G. Dionne, T. C. Eley, and R. Plomin (2000). Lexical and grammatical development: A behavioral genetic perspective. *Journal of Child Language* 27, 619–42.

Damasio, A. R. and D. Tranel (1993). Nouns and verbs are retrieved with differently distributed neural systems. *Proceedings of the National Academy of Sciences of the U.S.A.* 90, 4957–60.

Damasio, H., T. J. Grabowski, D. Tranel, R. D. Hichwa, and A. R. Damasio (1996). A neural basis for lexical retrieval. *Nature* 380, 499–505.

Daniele, A., L. Giustolisi, M. C. Silveri, C. Colosimo, and G. Gainotti (1994). Evidence for a possible neuroanatomical basis for lexical processing of nouns and verbs. *Neuropsychologia* 32(11), 1325–41.

Darwin, C. (1871). *The Descent of Man, and Selection in Relation to Sex*. London: John Murray. (Reprinted in 1981 by Princeton University Press).

——(1877). A biographical sketch of an infant. *Mind* 2, 285–94.

de Boer, B. (2001). *The Origins of Vowel Systems*. Oxford: Oxford University Press.

De Cecco, J. P. (ed.) (1967). *The Psychology of Thought, Language and Instruction*. New York: Holt, Reinhart and Winston.

de Groot, A. (1984). *Tweedelig woordregister: Auka-Nederlands/Nederlands-Auka*. Paramaribo, Surinam: Artex.

De Marco, R. and R. Menzel (2005). Encoding spatial information in the waggle dance. *Journal of Experimental Biology* 208, 3885–94.

de Quervain, D. J., U. Fischbacher, V. Treyer, M. Schellhammer, U. Schnyder, A. Buck, and E. Fehr (2004). The neural basis of altruistic punishment. *Science* 305, 1254–8.

de Reuse, W. J. (1986). The lexicalization of sound symbolism in Santiago del Estro Quechua. *International Journal of American Linguistics* 52, 54–65.

De Smet, H. J., H. Baillieux, P. P. De Deyn, P. Mariën, and P. Paquie (2007). The cerebellum and language: The story so far. *Folia Phoniatrica et Logopaedica* 59(4), 165–70.

de Villiers, J. G. (1995). Empty categories and complex sentences: The case of wh-questions. In P. Fletcher and B. MacWhinney (eds.), *The Handbook of Child Language*, pp. 508–40. Oxford: Blackwell.

——and P. A. de Villiers (1978). *Language Acquisition*. Cambridge, MA: Harvard University Press.

de Waal, F. B. M. (1996). *Good Natured: The Origins of Right and Wrong in Humans and Other Animals*. Cambridge, MA: Harvard University Press.

Deacon, T. W. (1984). *Connections of the Inferior Periarcuate Area in the Brain of Macaca fascicularis: An Experimental and Comparative Investigation of Language Circuitry and its Evolution*. Ph.D. thesis, Harvard University.

——(1988). Human brain evolution II: Embryology and brain allometry. In H. Jerison and I. Jerison (eds.), *Intelligence and Evolutionary Biology*, pp. 383–415. Berlin: Springer Verlag.

——(1992). Brain-language coevolution. In J. A. Hawkins and M. Gell-Mann (eds.), *The Evolution of Human Languages*, pp. 49–83. Redwood City, CA: Addison-Wesley Publishing Company.

——(1996). Prefrontal cortex and symbol learning: Why a brain capable of language evolved only once. In B. M. Velichkovskiĭ and D. M. Rumbaugh (eds.), *Communicating Meaning: the Evolution and Development of Language*, pp. 103–38. Mahwah, NJ: Lawrence Erlbaum.

——(1997). *The Symbolic Species*. London: Penguin.

——(2010). On the human: Rethinking the natural selection of human language. *On the Human*. (Online forum provided by the National Humanities Center, North Carolina. This paper is at http://onthehuman.org/2010/02/on-the-human-rethinking-the-natural-selection-of-human-language/).

Deane, P. D. (1991). Limits to attention: A cognitive theory of island phenomena. *Cognitive Linguistics* 2, 1–63.

Deane, P. D. (1992). *Grammar in Mind and Brain: Explorations in Cognitive Syntax*. Berlin: Mouton de Gruyter.

——(1995). Neurological evidence for a cognitive theory of syntax: Agrammatic aphasia and the spatialization of form hypothesis. In E. H. Casad (ed.), *Cognitive Linguistics in the Redwoods: The Expansion of a New Paradigm in Linguistics*, pp. 55–115. Berlin: Mouton de Gruyter.

Decety, J., D. Perani, M. Jeannerod, V. Bettinardi, B. Tadary, R. Woods, J. C. Mazziotta, and F. Fazio (1994). Mapping motor representations with positron emission tomography. *Nature* 371, 600–2.

——, J. Grèzes, N.Costes, D. Perani, M.Jeannerod, E. Procyk, F. Grassi, and F. Fazio (1997). Brain activity during observation of actions: Influence of action content and subject's strategy. *Brain* 120, 1763–77.

Dediu, D. and D. R. Ladd (2007). Linguistic tone is related to the population frequency of the adaptive haplogroups of two brain size genes, ASPM and Microcephalin. *Proceedings of the National Academy of Sciences of the U.S.A.* 104(26), 10944–9.

DeGraff, M. (2001a). Morphology in creole genesis: Linguistics and ideology. In M. Kenstowicz (ed.), *Ken Hale: A Life in Language*, pp. 53–121. Cambridge, MA: MIT Press.

——(2001b). On the origin of creoles: A Cartesian critique of Neo-Darwinian linguistics. *Linguistic Typology* 5, 213–310.

Dehaene, S. (1997). *The Number Sense*. New York: Oxford University Press.

Delafosse, M. (1929). *La Langue Mandingue et ses Dialectes (Malinké, Bambara, Dioula)*. Paris: Paul Geuthner.

Dell, G. S., L. K. Burger, and W. R. Svec (1997). Language production and serial order: A functional analysis and a model. *Psychological Review* 104, 123–47.

Della Croce, F. and V. T. Paschos (2008). Exploiting dominance conditions for computing non trivial worst-case complexity for bounded combinatorial optimization problems. *Operational Research* 8(3), 235–56.

Delplanque, A. (1998). Le mythe des 'séries verbales'. *Faits de Langues* 11/12, 231–50.

Demers, R. A. and E. Jelinek (1982). The syntactic functions of person marking in Lummi. Paper presented at the 17th ICNSL, Portland, Oregon.

——and ——(1984). Word-building rules and grammatical categories in Lummi. Paper presented at the 19th ICNSL, Victoria, BC.

Denny, J. P. (1991). Rational thought in oral culture and literate decontextualization. In D. R. Olson and N. Torrance (eds.), *Literacy and Orality*, pp. 66–89. Cambridge: Cambridge University Press.

Derbyshire, D. C. (1976). *Khoryenkom Karyehtanà: O Novo Testamento na Língua Hixkaryána*. Brasilia: Livraria Cristã Unida. (The New Testament, translated into Hixkaryana by Desmond C. Derbyshire).

——(1977). Word order universals and the existence of OVS languages. *Linguistic Inquiry* 8(3), 590–9.

——(1979a). *Hixkaryana*. Amsterdam: North Holland Publishing Company. (Lingua Descriptive Studies, Volume 1.)

Derbyshire, D. C. (1979b). *Hixkaryana Syntax*. Ph.D. thesis, University of London.

Descartes, R. (1637). *Discours de la Méthode, Pour bien conduire sa raison, et chercher la vérité dans les sciences*. Leyden: Ian Maire.

Deutscher, G. (2000). *Syntactic Change in Akkadian: The Evolution of Sentential Complementation*. Oxford: Oxford University Press.

——(2005). *The Unfolding of Language*. London: William Heinemann.

DeVoogd, T. J. (2004). Where is the bird? *Annals of the New York Academy of Sciences* 1016, 778–86.

Di Sciullo, A. M. and E. Williams (1987). *On the Definition of Word*. Cambridge, MA: MIT Press.

Dibble, H. L. (1989). The implications of stone tool types for the presence of language during the Lower and Middle Palaeolithic. In P. Mellars and C. B. Stringer (eds.), *The Human Revolution: Behavioural and Biological Perspectives on the Origins of Modern Humans*, pp. 415–32. Edinburgh: Edinburgh University Press.

Dickinson, J. A. and F. C. Dyer (1996). How insects learn about the sun's course: Alternative modeling approaches. In P. Maes, M. J. Mataric, J.-A. Meyer, J. Pollack, and S. W. Wilson (eds.), *From Animals to Animats 4*, pp. 193–203. Cambridge, MA: MIT Press.

Diessel, H. (1999). *Demonstratives: Form, Function and Grammaticalization*. Amsterdam: John Benjamins.

Dietl, T., P. Trautner, M. Staedtgen, M. Vannuchi, A. Mecklinger, T. Grunwald, H. Clusmann, C. E. Elger, and M. Kurthen (2005). Processing of famous faces and medial temporal lobe event-related potentials: A depth electrode study. *Neuroimage* 25(2), 401–7.

Diffloth, G. (1994). i: *big*, a: *small*. In L. Hinton, J. Nichols, and J. Ohala (eds.), *Sound Symbolism*, pp. 107–14. Cambridge: Cambridge University Press.

Dikovsky, A. (2004). Dependencies as categories. COLING: 20th International Conference on Computational Linguistics, 28 August 2004. (Online at http://acl.ldc.upenn.edu/coling2004/W4/pdf/12.pdf.)

Diller, K. C. (1978). *The Language Teaching Controversy*. Rowley, MA: Newbury House.

Dinneen, M. J. (1995). *Bounded Combinatorial Width and Forbidden Substructures*. Ph.D. thesis, University of Victoria, New Zealand.

Ditzinger, T. and H. Haken (1989). Oscillations in the perception of ambiguous patterns. A model based on synergetics. *Biological Cybernetics* 61, 279–87.

Diver, W. (1995). Theory. In E. Contini-Morava and B. S. Goldberg (eds.), *Meaning as Explanation: Advances in Linguistic Sign Theory*, pp. 43–114. Berlin: De Gruyter.

Dixon, R. M. W. (1980). *The Languages of Australia*. Cambridge: Cambridge University Press.

——(1982). *Where have all the Adjectives Gone? And other Essays in Semantics and Syntax*. Berlin: Mouton.

——(2002). Copula clauses in Australian languages: A typological perspective. *Anthropological Linguistics* 44(1), 1–36.

Dobel, D. M., J. Poole, M. Fisher, and S. Vinogradov (2003). An examination of cross-racial differences in cognitive and psychosocial variables across two patient groups with schizophrenia. *Schizophrenia Research* 60(1), 132–3.

Doke, C. (1931a). *The Problem of Word-Division in Bantu.* (Occasional paper No. 2, Department of Native Development, Salisbury, Rhodesia (now Harare, Zimbabwe).)

——(1931b). *Southern Rhodesia; Report on the Unification of the Shona Dialects. Carried out under the auspices of the Government of Southern Rhodesia and the Carnegie Corporation.* Salisbury (now Harare): Government of Southern Rhodesia (Now Zimbabwe). (Printed by Stephen Austin & Sons, Hertford, England.)

Dominey, P. and M. Hoen (2006). Structure mapping and semantic integration in a construction-based model of sentence processing. *Cortex* 42(4), 476–9.

Dor, D. and E. Jablonka (2000). From cultural selection to genetic selection: A framework for the evolution of language. *Selection* 1(1-3), 33–55. (*Selection* was a short-lived journal. This paper is online at http://www3.isrl.illinois.edu/~junwang4/langev/localcopy/pdf/dor01selection.pdf.)

Dorus, S., E. J. Vallender, J. R. A. Patrick D. Evans, S. L. Gilbert, M. Mahowald, G. J. Wyckoff, C. M. Malcom, and B. T. Lahn (2004). Accelerated evolution of nervous system genes in the origin of *Homo sapiens. Cell* 119(7), 1027–40.

Doupe, A. J. and P. K. Kuhl (1999). Birdsong and human speech: Common themes and mechanisms. *Annual Review of Neuroscience* 22, 567–631.

Dowman, M. (2008). The nature of words in human protolanguages: It's not a holophrastic-atomic meanings dichotomy. *Artificial Life* 14, 445–65.

Dronkers, N. F. (2000). The gratuitous relationship between Broca's aphasia and Broca's area. *Behavioral and Brain Sciences* 23, 30–1.

Dryer, M. S. (1992). The Greenbergian word order correlations. *Language* 68, 81–138.

——(1996). Word order typology. In J. Jacobs (ed.), *Handbook on Syntax, Vol. 2,* pp. 1050–65. Berlin: Walter de Gruyter.

——(2008). Indefinite articles. In M. Haspelmath, M. S. Dryer, D. Gil, and B. Comrie (eds.), *The World Atlas of Language Structures Online,* Ch. 38. Munich: Max Planck Digital Library. (Available online at http://wals.info/feature/38.)

Dunbar, R. I. M. (1996a). Determinants of group size in primates: A general model. In W. G. Runciman, J. M. Smith, and R. I. M. Dunbar (eds.), *Evolution of Social Behaviour Patterns in Primates and Man,* pp. 33–57. Oxford: Oxford University Press.

——(1996b). *Grooming, Gossip and the Evolution of Language.* London: Faber and Faber.

Duncker, K. (1945). On problem solving. *Psychological Monographs* 58(5). (Translated by L. S. Lees from Duncker's *Zur Psychologie des Produktiven Denkens,* Berlin: Springer (1935).)

Dunsworth, H. M. (2007). *Human Origins 101.* Santa Barbara, CA: Greenwood Publishing Group.

Durand, M. (1961). Les impressifs en vietnamien, étude préliminaire, *Bulletin de la Société des Etudes Indo Chinoises,* 36(1), 5–51.

Durham, W. H. (1991). *Coevolution: Genes, Culture and Human Diversity*. Stanford, CA: Stanford University Press.

Durie, M. (1985). *A Grammar of Acehnese on the Basis of a Dialect of North Aceh*. Dordrecht, Netherlands: Foris Publications.

——(1988). Verb serialization and 'verbal-prepositions' in Oceanic languages. *Oceanic Linguistics* XXVII(1/2), 1–23.

——(1997). Grammatical structures in verb serialization. In A. Alsina, J. Bresnan, and P. Sells (eds.), *Complex Predicates*, pp. 289–354. Stanford, CA: Center for the Study of Language and Information.

Dwyer, D. (1986). What are the chimpanzees telling us about language? *Lingua* 69(3), 219–44.

Dyer, F. C. (1991). Bees acquire route-based memories but not cognitive maps in a familiar landscape. *Animal Behaviour* 41(2), 239–46.

——and J. A. Dickinson (1994). Development of sun compensation by honeybees: How partially experienced bees estimate the sun's course. *Proceedings of the National Academy of Sciences of the U.S.A.* 91, 4471–4.

——and J. A. Dickinson (1996). Sun-compass learning in insects: Representation in a simple mind. *Current Directions in Psychological Science* 5(3), 67–72.

Eberhardt, M. (1940). A study of phonetic symbolism of deaf children. *Psychological Monographs* 52, 23–41.

Ehret, G. (1987). Left hemisphere advantage in the mouse brain for recognising ultrasonic communication calls. *Nature* 325, 249–51.

Elliott, D., W. F. Helsen, and R. Chua (2001). A century later: Woodworth's (1899) two component model of goal-directed aiming. *Psychological Bulletin* 127, 342–57.

Elman, J. (1993). Learning and development in neural networks: The importance of starting small. *Cognition* 48, 71–99.

Enard, W., M. Przeworski, S. E. Fisher, C. S. Lal, V. Wlebe, T. Kitano, A. Monaco, and S. Pääbo (2002). Molecular evolution of *FOXP2*, a gene involved in speech and language. *Nature* 418, 869–72.

Enfield, N. J. and S. C. Levinson (eds.) (2006). *Roots of Human Sociality: Culture, Cognition and Interaction*. Oxford: Berg.

Epstein, R., C. E. Kirshnit, R. P. Lanza, and L. C. Rubin (1984). 'Insight' in the pigeon: antecedents and determinants of an intelligent performance. *Nature* 308, 61–2.

Erickson, T. A. and M. E. Mattson (1981). From words to meanings: A semantic illusion. *Journal of Verbal Learning and Verbal Behavior* 20, 540–52.

Ertel, S. (1969). *Psychophonetik, Untersuchungen über Lautsymbolik und Motivation*. Göttingen: Verlag für Psychologie.

Erteschik-Shir, N. (1973). *On the Nature of Island Constraints*. Ph.D. thesis, MIT.

——(1981). More on extractability from quasi-NPs. *Linguistic Inquiry* 12(4), 665–70.

——(2007). *Information Structure: The Syntax-Discourse Interface*. Oxford: Oxford University Press.

——and S. Lappin (1979). Dominance and the functional explanation of island phenomena. *Theoretical Linguistics* 6, 41–86.

Etienne, A. S., R. Maurer, J. Berlie, B. Reverdin, T. Rowe, J. Georgakopoulos, and V. Séguinot (1998). Navigation through vector addition. *Nature* 396, 161–4.

Evans, N. and S. C. Levinson (2009). The myth of language universals: Language diversity and its importance for cognitive science. *Behavioral and Brain Sciences* 32(5), 429–92.

Evans, P. D., S. Gilbert, N. Mekel-Bobrov, E. Vallender, J. Anderson, L. Vaez-Azizi, S. Tishkoff, R. Hudson, and B. Lahn (2005). Microcephalin, a gene regulating brain size, continues to evolve adaptively in humans. *Science* 309, 1717–20.

——, J. R. Anderson, E. J. Vallender, S. L. Gilbert, C. M. Malcom, S. Dorus, and B. T. Lahn (2004). Adaptive evolution of *ASPM*, a major determinant of cerebral cortical size in humans. *Human Molecular Genetics* 13, 489–94.

Evans, S. E. (2000). General discussion II: Amniote evolution. In G. R. Bock and C. G. Chichester (eds.), *Evolutionary Developmental Biology of the Cerebral Cortex*, pp. 109–13. New York: Wiley.

Everett, D. L. (1986). Pirahã. In D. C. Derbyshire and G. K. Pullum (eds.), *Handbook of Amazonian Languages*, pp. 200–325. Berlin: Mouton de Gruyter.

——(1987). *A língua Pirahã e a teoria da sintaxe: Descrição, perspectivas e teoria*. Campinas, Brazil: Editora da Unicamp.

——(2005). Cultural constraints on grammar and cognition in Pirahã: Another look at the design features of human language. *Current Anthropology* 46(4), 621–46.

——(2008). *Don't Sleep, there are Snakes: Life and Language in the Amazonian Jungle*. New York: Knopf Publishing.

——(2009). Pirahã culture and grammar: A response to some criticisms. *Language* 85(2), 405–42.

Fabrega, H. (2004). Culture and the origins of psychopathology. In U. P. Gielen, J. M. Fish, and J. G. Draguns (eds.), *Handbook of Culture, Therapy, and Healing*, pp. 15–35. London: Routledge.

Falk, Y. N. (2006). *Subjects and Universal Grammar: An Explanatory Theory*. Cambridge: Cambridge University Press.

Fallesen, J. J. and S. A. Halpin (2004). Representing cognition as an intent-driven process. In J. W. Ness, V. Tepe, and D. Ritzer (eds.), *The Science and Simulation of Human Performance*, pp. 195–266. Oxford: Elsevier, Ltd.

Fandiño-Mariño, H. and J. M. Vielliard (2004). Complex communication signals: the case of the Blue-black Grassquit *Volatinia jacarina* (Aves, Emberizidae) song. Part I—A structural analysis. *Anais da Academia Brasileira de Ciências (Annals of the Brazilian Academy of Sciences)* 76(2), 325–34.

Fanselow, G., C. Féry, R. Vogel, and M. Schlesewsky (eds.) (2006). *Gradience in Grammar: Generative Perspectives*. Oxford: Oxford University Press.

Faraclas, N. (1989). Rumours of the demise of Descartes are premature. *Journal of Pidgin and Creole Languages* 3, 119–35.

——, Y. Rivera-Castilla, and D. E. Walicek (2007). No exception to the rule: The tense-modality-aspect system of Papiamentu reconsidered. In M. Huber and V. Velupillai (eds.), *Synchronic and Diachronic Perspectives on Contact Languages*, pp. 257–78. Amsterdam: John Benjamins.

Fauconnier, G. and M. Turner (2008). The origin of language as a product of the evolution of modern cognition. In B. Laks (ed.), *Origin and Evolution of Languages: Approaches, Models, Paradigms*, pp. 133–56. London: Equinox Publishing.

Fay, N., S. Garrod, L. Roberts, and N. Swoboda (2010). The interactive evolution of human communication systems. *Cognitive Science* 34(3), 351–86.

Fecteau, S., J. L. Armony, Y. Joanette, and P. Belin (2005). Sensitivity to voice in human prefrontal cortex. *Journal of Neurophysiology* 94, 2251–4.

——P. Belin, Y. Joanette, and J. L. Armony (2007). Amygdala responses to nonlinguistic emotional vocalizations. *Neuroimage* 36, 480–7.

Fee, M. S., A. A. Kozhevnikov, and R. H. R. Hahnloser (2004). Neural mechanisms of vocal sequence generation in the songbird. *Annals of the New York Academy of Sciences* 1060, 153–70.

Fehér, O., H. Wang, S. Saar, P. P. Mitra, and O. Tchernichovski (2009). *De novo* establishment of wild-type song culture in the zebra finch. *Nature* 459, 564–8.

Feldhütter, I., M. Schleidt, and I. Eibl-Eibesfeld (1990). Moving in the beat of seconds: Analysis of the time structure of human action. *Ethology and Sociobiology* 11, 1–10.

Feng, A. S., J. C. Hall, and D. M. Gooler (1990). Neural basis of sound pattern recognition in anurans. *Progress in Neurobiology* 34, 313–29.

Fenk-Oczlon, G. and A. Fenk (2002). The clausal structure of linguistic and prelinguistic behavior. In T. Givón and B. F. Malle (eds.), *The Evolution of Language out of Pre-Language*, pp. 215–29. Amsterdam: John Benjamins.

Fennell, B. A. (2001). *A History of English: A Sociolinguistic Approach*. Oxford: Blackwell.

Fentress, J. C. (1992). Emergence of pattern in the development of mammalian movement sequences. *Journal of Neurobiology* 23(10), 1529–56.

——and F. P. Stillwell (1973). Grammar of a movement sequence in inbred mice. *Nature* 244, 52–3.

Ferguson, C. A. (1971). Absence of copula and the notion of simplicity: A study of normal speech, baby talk, foreigner talk, and pidgins. In D. Hymes (ed.), *Pidginization and Creolization of Languages*, pp. 141–50. Cambridge: Cambridge University Press.

Ferland, R. J., W. Eyaid, R. V. Collura, L. D. Tully, R. S. Hill, D. Al-Nouri, A. Al-Rumayyan, M. Topcu, G. Gascon, A. Bodell, Y. Y. Shugart, M. Ruvolo, and C. A. Walsh (2004). Abnormal cerebellar development and axonal decussation due to mutations in *AHI1* in Joubert syndrome. *Nature Genetics* 36(9), 1008–13.

Ferrari, P. F., V. Gallese, G. Rizzolatti, and L. Fogassi (2003). Mirror neurons responding to the observation of ingestive and communicative mouth actions in the monkey ventral premotor cortex. *European Journal of Neuroscience* 17, 1703–14.

Ferraz, L. and A. Traill (1981). The interpretation of tone in Principense Creole. *Studies in African Linguistics* 12(2), 205–15.

Ferreira, F. and F. J. Morrison (1994). Children's metalinguistic knowledge of syntactic constituents: Effects of age and schooling. *Developmental Psychology* 30(5), 663–78.

Ferreira, F. and N. D. Patson (2007). The 'good enough' approach to language comprehension. *Language and Linguistics Compass* 1(1–2).

——, K. G. Bailey, and V. Ferraro (2002). Good-enough representations in language comprehension. *Current Directions in Psychological Science* 11(1), 11–15.

Ficken, M. S., K. M. Rusch, S. J. Taylor, and D. R. Powers (2000). Blue-throated hummingbird song: A pinnacle of nonoscine vocalizations. *The Auk* 117, 120–8.

Fiete, I. R. and H. S. Seung (2009). Birdsong learning. In L. R. Squire (ed.), *Encyclopedia of Neuroscience*, pp. 227–39. Amsterdam: Elsevier.

Fiez, J. A. and D. Tranel (1996). Action recognition and naming impairments in subjects with left frontal lesions. *Society for Neuroscience* 22, 724.

Fillmore, C. and P. Kay (1993). *Construction Grammar Coursebook*. Berkeley, CA: Department of Linguistics, University of California, Berkeley.

——, ——, L. A. Michaelis, and I. Sag (2003). *Construction Grammar*. Chicago: University of Chicago Press.

Finkel, R. and G. Stump (2007). A default inheritance hierarchy for computing Hebrew verb morphology. *Literary and Linguistic Computing* 22(2), 117–36.

Fischer, S. (1975). Influences on word order change in American Sign Language. In C. Li (ed.), *Word Order and Word Order Change*, pp. 1–25. Austin, TX: University of Texas Press.

Fischer-Jorgensen, E. (1978). On the universal character of phonetic symbolism with special reference to vowels. *Studia Linguistica* 32(1-2), 80–90. (Special issue, *Sign and Sound, Studies Presented to Bertil Malmberg on the Occasion of his Sixty-fifth Birthday*.)

Fish, J. L. and C. A. Lockwood (2003). Dietary constraints on encephalization in primates. *American Journal of Physical Anthropology* 120, 171–81.

Fisher, K. L. (1988). Agreement and the distribution of anaphora. In M. Hammond, E. A. Moravcsik, and J. R. Wirth (eds.), *Studies in Syntactic Typology*, pp. 25–36. Amsterdam: John Benjamins.

Fisher, S. E. and G. F. Marcus (2005). The eloquent ape: Genes, brains and the evolution of language. *Nature Reviews: Genetics* 7, 9–20.

Fitch, R. H., C. P. Brown, K. O'Connor, and P. Tallal (1993). Functional lateralization for auditory temporal processing in male and female rats. *Behavioral Neuroscience* 107(5), 844–50.

Fitch, W. T. (2004). Imitation, quoting and theory of mind. *Interdisciplines*. (Moderated online discussion at http://www.interdisciplines.org/coevolution/papers/4/language/fr.)

——(2005). The evolution of music in comparative perspective. *Annals of the New York Academy of Sciences* 1060, 1–21.

——(2008). Co-evolution of phylogeny and glossogeny: There is no 'logical problem of language evolution'. *Behavioral and Brain Sciences* 31(5), 521–2.

——(2010). *The Evolution of Language*. Cambridge: Cambridge University Press.

——and M. D. Hauser (2004). Computational constraints on syntactic processing in a nonhuman primate. *Science* 303, 377–80.

Fitch, W. T., M. D. Hauser, and N. Chomsky (2005). The evolution of the language faculty: Clarifications and implications. *Cognition* 97, 179–210.

Fodor, J. A. (1975). *The Language of Thought*. Sussex: Harvester Press.

——and M. Garrett (1966). Some reflections on competence and performance. In J. Lyons and R. Wales (eds.), *Psycholinguistics Papers*, pp. 135–54. Edinburgh: Edinburgh University Press.

——and——(1967). Some syntactic determinants of sentential complexity. *Perception and Psychophysics* 2, 289–96.

Fogassi, L. and P. F. Ferrari (2007). Mirror neurons and the evolution of embodied language. *Current Directions in Psychological Science* 16(3), 136–41.

Fogle, T. (2000). The dissolution of protein coding genes in molecular biology. In P. J. Beurton, R. Falk, and H. Rheinberger (eds.), *The Concept of the Gene in Development and Evolution: Historical and Epistemological Perspectives*, pp. 3–25. Cambridge: Cambridge University Press.

Foley, W. A. (1986). *The Papuan Languages of New Guinea*. Cambridge: Cambridge University Press.

——(2005). Do humans have innate mental structures? Some arguments from linguistics. In S. McKinnon and S. Silverman (eds.), *Complexities: Beyond Nature and Nurture*, pp. 43–63. Chicago: University of Chicago Press.

Fónagy, I. (1963). *Die Metaphern in der Phonetik*. The Hague: Mouton.

Ford, C. E. and S. Thompson (1996). Interactional units in conversation: Syntactic, intonational, and pragmatic resources for the management of turns. In E. Ochs, E. Schegloff, and S. Thompson (eds.), *Interaction and Grammar*, pp. 134–84. Cambridge: Cambridge University Press.

Ford, M. and V. M. Holmes (1978). Planning units in sentence production. *Cognition* 6, 35–53.

Fornander, A. (1878). *An Account of the Polynesian Race*. English and Foreign Philosophical Library. London. (Extra Series, Vols. 3, 6, 7.)

Fortescue, M. (1984). *West Greenlandic*. London: Croom Helm.

Fortune, G. (1969). 75 years of writing in Shona. *Zambezia* 1(1), 55–68.

Fox, B. and R. Jasperson (1996). A syntactic exploration of repair in English conversation. In P. W. Davis (ed.), *Alternative Linguistics: Descriptive and Theoretical Modes*, pp. 77–134. Amsterdam: John Benjamins.

Francis, N. and H. Kučera (1982). *Frequency Analysis of English Usage: Lexicon and Grammar*. Boston: Houghton Mifflin.

Frank, M. C., D. L. Everett, E. Fedorenko, and E. Gibson (2008). Number as a cognitive technology: Evidence from Pirahã language and cognition. *Cognition* 108(3), 819–24.

——, N. D. Goodman, and J. B. Tenenbaum (2009). Using speakers' referential intentions to model early cross-situational word learning. *Psychological Science* 20, 578–85.

Franz, M. and F. Goller (2002). Respiratory units of motor production and song imitation in the zebra finch. *Journal of Neurobiology* 51(2), 129–41.

Fraser, B. (1970). Some remarks on the action nominalization in English. In R. A. Jacobs and P. S. Rosenbaum (eds.), *Readings in English Transformational Grammar*, pp. 83–98. Waltham, MA: Ginn and Company.

Fraser, N. M. and R. A. Hudson (1992). Inheritance in word grammar. *Computational Linguistics* 18(2), 133–58.

Frege, G. (1892). Über Sinn und Bedeutung. *Zeitschrift für Philosophie und philosophische Kritik* 100, 25–50. (Page references here are to *Translations from the Philosophical Writings of Gottlob Frege*, edited by Peter Geach and Max Black, published by Basil Blackwell, Oxford, 1970.)

Frey, S. H. (2008). Tool use, communicative gesture and cerebral asymmetries in the modern human brain. *Philosophical Transactions of the Royal Society* B 363, 1951–1957. (Scott H. Frey is the same person as Scott H. Johnson-Frey.)

Friederici, A. D. (1982). Syntactic and semantic processes in aphasic deficits: The availability of prepositions. *Brain and Language* 15(2), 249–58.

——(1985). Levels of processing and vocabulary types: Evidence from online comprehension in normals and agrammatics. *Cognition* 19(2), 133–66.

——, K. Steinhauer, and S. Frisch (1999). Lexical integration: Sequential effects of syntactic and semantic information. *Memory and Cognition* 27(3), 438–53.

——, J. Bahlmann, S. Heim, R. I. Schubotz, and A. Anwander (2006a). The brain differentiates human and non-human grammars: Functional localization and structural connectivity. *Proceedings of the National Academy of Sciences of the U.S.A.* 103(7), 2458–63.

——, C. J. Fiebach, M. Schlesewsky, I. D. Bornkessel, and D. Y. von Cramon (2006b). Processing linguistic complexity and grammaticality in the left frontal cortex. *Cerebral Cortex* 16(12), 1709–17.

Fromkin, V. A. (1995). Introduction. *Brain and Language* 50(1), 1–9.

——, S. Curtiss, B. P. Hayes, N. Hyams, P. A. Keating, H. Koopman, P. Munro, D. Sportiche, E. P. Stabler, D. Steriade, T. Stowell, and A. Szabolcsi (2000). *Linguistics: An Introduction to Linguistic Theory*. Hoboken, NJ: Wiley.

Galantucci, B. (2005). An experimental study of the emergence of human communication systems. *Cognitive Science* 29, 737–67.

——(2006). Rapidity of fading and the emergence of duality of patterning. In A. Cangelosi, A. D. M. Smith, and K. Smith (eds.), *The Evolution of Language*, pp. 413–14. Singapore: World Scientific.

——(2009). Experimental semiotics: A new approach for studying communication as a form of joint action. *Topics in Cognitive Science* 1, 393–410.

Gallese, V. (2003a). A neuroscientific grasp of concepts: From control to representation. *Philosophical Transactions of the Royal Society of London* B 358, 1231–40.

——(2003b). The roots of empathy: The shared manifold hypothesis and the neural basis of intersubjectivity. *Psychopathology* 36(4), 171–80.

——(2003c). The 'Shared Manifold' Hypothesis: From mirror neurons to empathy. *Journal of Consciousness Studies* 8(5–7), 33–50.

Gallese, V. (2004). 'Being like me': Self-other identity, mirror neurons and empathy. In S. Hurley and N. Chater (eds.), *Perspectives on Imitation: From Cognitive Neuroscience to Social Science*, pp. 101–18. Boston, MA: MIT Press.

——, L. Fadiga, L. Fogassi, and G. Rizzolatti (1996). Action recognition in the premotor cortex. *Brain* 119, 593–609.

Galtier, N. and L. Duret (2007). Adaptation or biased gene conversion? Extending the null hypothesis of molecular evolution. *Trends in Genetics* 3(6), 273–77.

García, E. (1979). Discourse without syntax. In T. Givón (ed.), *Discourse and Syntax*, pp. 23–49. New York: Academic Press. (Syntax and Semantics 12.)

Gärdenfors, P. (2003). *How Homo Became Sapiens: On the Evolution of Thinking*. Oxford: Oxford University Press.

Gardner, R. A. and B. T. Gardner (1969). Teaching sign language to a chimpanzee. *Science* 165, 664–72.

—— and —— (1974). Comparing the early utterances of child and chimpanzee. *Minnesota Symposium on Child Psychology* 8, 3–23.

Garman, M. (1979). Early grammatical development. In P. Fletcher and M. Garman (eds.), *Language Development*, pp. 177–208. Cambridge: Cambridge University Press.

Garrett, M. (1975). The analysis of sentence production. In G. Bower (ed.), *Psychology of Learning and Motivation*, 9, pp. 505–29. New York: Academic Press.

—— (1982). Production of speech: Observations from normal and pathological language use. In A. W. Ellis (ed.), *Normality and Pathology in Cognitive Functions*, pp. 19–76. London: Academic Press.

Garver, N. (1996). Philosophy as grammar. In H. Sluga and D. G. Stern (eds.), *The Cambridge Companion to Wittgenstein*, pp. 139–70. Cambridge: Cambridge University Press.

Gasser, M. (2004). The origins of arbitrariness in language. In *Proceedings of the Cognitive Science Society Conference*, 26, pp. 434–39. Hillsdale, NJ: Lawrence Erlbaum Associates.

Gathercole, V. C. (1989). Contrast: A semantic constraint? *Journal of Child Language* 16(3), 685–702.

Gazdar, G., E. Klein, G. K. Pullum, and I. A. Sag (1985). *Generalized Phrase Structure Grammar*. Oxford: Blackwell.

Gell-Mann, M. (2005). Language and complexity. In J. W. Minett and W. S. Wang (eds.), *Language Acquisition, Change and Emergence: Essays in Evolutionary Linguistics*, pp. 389–409. Hong Kong: City University of Hong Kong Press.

Gemba, H., N. Miki, and K. Sasaki (1997). Cortical field potentials preceding vocalization in monkeys. *Acta Oto-Laryngologica* 117, 96–8.

——, S. Kyuhou, R. Matsuzaki, and Y. Amino (1999). Cortical field potentials associated with audio-initiated vocalization in monkeys. *Neuroscience Letters* 272, 49–52.

——, ——, ——, and —— (2002). Monkey vocalization and cortical field potential. *International Congress Series* 1232, 29–33.

Gentilucci, M. (2003). Grasp observation influences speech production. *European Journal of Neuroscience* 17(1), 179–84.

Gentner, D. (1981). Some interesting differences between verbs and nouns. *Cognition and Brain Theory* 4(2), 161–78.

——and L. Boroditsky (2001). Individuation, relational relativity and early word learning. In M. Bowerman and S. C. Levinson (eds.), *Language Acquisition and Conceptual Development*, pp. 215–56. Cambridge: Cambridge University Press.

Gentner, T. Q., K. M. Fenn, D. Margoliash, and H. C. Nusbaum (2006). Recursive syntactic pattern learning by songbirds. *Nature* 440, 1204–7.

George, I. (1985). Complex verbs in Nupe and Yoruba. *Studies in African Linguistics* 16, 295–321.

Geschwind, N. (1964). The development of the brain and the evolution of language. *Monograph Series in Language and Linguistics* 17, 155–69. (Page references are to the republished version in *Selected Papers on Language and the Brain*, edited by Norman Geschwind, pp. 89–104, D. Reidel, Dordrecht, Holland, 1974.)

Ghazanfar, A. A. (2008). Language evolution: Neural differences that make a difference. *Nature Neuroscience* 11(4), 382–4.

——and M. D. Hauser (2001). The auditory behaviour of primates: A neuroethological perspective. *Current Opinion in Neurobiology* 11, 712–20.

——, D. Smith-Rohrberg, and M. D. Hauser (2001). The role of temporal cues in rhesus monkey vocal recognition: Orienting asymmetries to reversed calls. *Brain, Behavior and Evolution* 58, 163–72.

Gibson, E. (1998). Linguistic complexity: Locality of syntactic dependencies. *Cognition* 68(1), 1–76.

——, M. C. Frank, D. L. Everett, E. Stapert, J. Sakel, and E. Sakel. New experimental results. (Talk given at various universities and research centres; work in progress.)

Gibson, K. R. (1996). The ontogeny and evolution of the brain, cognition, and language. In A. Lock and C. R. Peters (eds.), *Handbook of Human Symbolic Evolution*, pp. 407–31. Oxford: Oxford University Press.

Gignac, G., P. A. Vernon, and J. C. Wickett (2003). Factors influencing the relationship between brain size and intelligence. In H. Nyborg (ed.), *The Scientific Study of General Intelligence: Tribute to Arthur R Jensen*, pp. 93–106. London: Elsevier.

Gil, D. (1994a). Expressive power. In R. E. Asher and J. M. Y. Simpson (eds.), *The Encyclopedia of Language and Linguistics*, pp. 1195–8. Oxford: Pergamon Press.

——(1994b). The structure of Riau Indonesian. *Nordic Journal of Linguistics* 17, 179–200.

——(2000). Riau Indonesian: A VO language with internally-headed relative clauses. *Snippets* 1, 6–7. (online journal at http://www.ledonline.it/snippets).

——(2001). Creoles, complexity, and Riau Indonesian. *Linguistic Typology* 5, 325–71.

——(2004). Riau Indonesian *Sama*: Explorations in macrofunctionality. In M. Haspelmath (ed.), *Coordinating Constructions*, pp. 371–424. Amsterdam: John Benjamins.

——(2005). Word order without syntactic categories: How Riau Indonesian does it. In A. Carnie, H. Harley, and S. A. Dooley (eds.), *Verb First: On the Syntax of Verb-initial Languages*, pp. 243–64. Amsterdam: John Benjamins.

Gil, D. (2006). Early human language was isolating-monocategorial-associational. In A. Cangelosi, A. D. M. Smith, and K. Smith (eds.), *The Evolution of Language*, pp. 91–8. Singapore: World Scientific.

——(2008). How complex are isolating languages? In F. Karlsson, M. Miestamo, and K. Sinnemäki (eds.), *Language Complexity: Typology, Contact, Change*, pp. 109–31. Amsterdam: John Benjamins.

——(2009). How much grammar does it take to sail a boat? In G. Sampson, D. Gil, and P. Trudgill (eds.), *Language Complexity as an Evolving Variable*, pp. 19–33. Oxford: Oxford University Press.

——and P. J. Slater (2000). Multiple song repertoire characteristics in the willow warbler (*Phylloscopus trochilus*): Correlations with female choice and offspring viability. *Behavioral Ecology and Sociobiology* 47, 319–26.

Gilbert, A. L., T. Regier, P. Kay, and R. B. Ivry (2006). Whorf hypothesis is supported in the right visual field but not the left. *Proceedings of the National Academy of Sciences of the U.S.A.* 103(2), 489–94.

Gillan, D. J. (1981). Reasoning in the chimpanzee: II, transitive inference. *Journal of Experimental Psychology: Animal Behavior Processes* 7(2), 150–64.

——, D. Premack, and G. Woodruff (1981). Reasoning in the chimpanzee: I., analogical reasoning. *Journal of Experimental Psychology: Animal Behavior Processes* 7(1), 1–17.

Gillett, G. (2003). Cognitive structure, logic and language. *Behavioral and Brain Sciences* 26, 292–3.

Givón, T. (1971). Historical syntax and synchronic morphology: An archaeologist's field trip. *Papers from the Regional Meetings of the Chicago Linguistic Society* 7, 394–415.

——(1976). Topic, pronoun and grammatical agreement. In C. N. Li (ed.), *Subject and Topic*, pp. 149–88. New York: Academic Press.

——(1979a). *On Understanding Grammar*. New York: Academic Press.

——(1979b). Prolegomena to any sane creology. In I. F. Hancock (ed.), *Readings in Creole Studies*, pp. 3–35. Ghent: Story-Scientia.

——(1990). *Syntax: A Functional-Typological Introduction*. Amsterdam: John Benjamins.

——(1991). Some substantive issues concerning verb serialization: grammatical vs. cognitive packaging. In C. Lefebvre (ed.), *Serial Verbs: Grammatical, Comparative, and Cognitive Approaches*, pp. 137–84. Amsterdam: John Benjamins.

——(2001). *Syntax: An Introduction, Volume 1*. Amsterdam: John Benjamins.

——(2002). *Bio-Linguistics: The Santa Barbara Lectures*. Amsterdam: John Benjamins.

——(2009). *The Genesis of Syntactic Complexity*. Amsterdam: John Benjamins.

Glastonbury, M. (1996). Incommunicado: On trying to understand autistic lives. *Changing English* 3(2), 119–30.

Glaze, C. M. and T. W. Troyer (2006). Temporal structure in zebra finch song: Implications for motor coding. *The Journal of Neuroscience* 26(3), 991–1005.

Glover, S. (2004). Separate visual representations in the planning and control of action. *Behavioral and Brain Sciences* 27(1), 3–78.

Glucksberg, S. and R. W. Weisberg (1966). Verbal behavior and problem-solving: Some effects of labelling on a functional fixedness problem. *Journal of Experimental Psychology* 71(5), 659–64.

Goldberg, A. E. (1995). *Constructions: A Construction Grammar Approach to Argument Structure*. Chicago: University of Chicago Press.

—— (2006). *Constructions at Work: The Nature of Generalization in Language*. Oxford: Oxford University Press.

Goldberg, E. (2009). *The New Executive Brain: Frontal Lobes in a Complex World*. Oxford: Oxford University Press.

Goldberg, R. F., C. A. Perfetti, J. A. Fiez, and W. Schneider (2007). Selective retrieval of abstract semantic knowledge in left prefrontal cortex. *The Journal of Neuroscience* 27(14), 3790–8.

Goldfield, B. A. (1986). Referential and expressive language: A study of two mother-child dyads. *First Language* 6(17), 119–31.

—— and C. Snow (1985). Individual differences in language acquisition. In J. Gleason (ed.), *Language Development*, pp. 307–30. Columbus, OH: Merrill Publishing Company.

Goldin-Meadow, S. (2003). *Hearing Gesture: How Our Hands Help Us Think*. Cambridge, MA: Harvard University Press.

—— (2005). *The Resilience of Language: What Gesture Creation in Deaf Children can Tell us about how All Children Learn Language*. New York: Psychology Press, Taylor& Francis Group.

—— and C. Butcher (2003). Pointing toward two-word speech in young children. In S. Kita (ed.), *Pointing: Where Language, Culture, and Cognition Meet*, pp. 85–107. Mahwah, NJ: Lawrence Erlbaum Associates.

—— and C. Mylander (1998). Spontaneous sign systems created by deaf children in two cultures. *Nature* 391, 279–81.

Goldowsky, B. N. and E. J. Newport (1993). Modeling the effects of processing limitations on the acquisition of morphology: The less is more hypothesis. In E. Clark (ed.), *Proceedings of the 24th Annual Child Language Research Forum*, pp. 124–38. Stanford, CA: Center for the Study of Language and Information.

Goldsmith, J. (2001). Unsupervised learning of the morphology of a natural language. *Computational Linguistics* 27(2), 153–98.

Goldstone, R. L. (1994). Influences of categorization on perceptual discrimination. *Journal of Experimental Psychology: General* 123, 178–200.

—— (1998). Perceptual learning. *Annual Review of Psychology* 49, 585–612.

——, Y. Lippa, and R. M. Shiffrin (2001). Altering object representations through category learning. *Cognition* 78, 27–43.

Goodman, M. (1985a). Rates of molecular evolution : The hominoid slowdown. *BioEssays* 3(1), 9–14.

Goodman, M. F. (1985b). Review of Bickerton (1981). *International Journal of American Linguistics* 51(1), 109–37.

Gopnik, M. (1990). Feature-blind grammar and dysphasia. *Nature* 344, 715.

——and M. B. Crago (1991). Familial aggregation of a developmental language disorder. *Cognition* 39, 1–50.

Gordon, P. C., R. Hendrick, and M. Johnson (2001). Memory interference during language processing. *Journal of Experimental Psychology: Learning, Memory, and Cognition* 27(6), 1411–23.

Gould, J. L. (1986). The locale map of honey bees: Do insects have cognitive maps? *Science* 232, 861–3.

Gould, S. J. and E. A. Lloyd (1999). Individuality and adaptation across levels of selection: How shall we name and generalize the unit of Darwinism? *Proceedings of the National Academy of Sciences of the U.S.A.* 96, 11904–9.

Goulden, R., P. Nation, and J. Read (1990). How large can a receptive vocabulary be? *Applied Linguistics* 11(4), 341–63.

Gowlett, J. A. J., J. W. K. Harris, D. Walton, and B. A. Wood (1981). Early archaeological sites, hominid remains and traces of fire from Chesowanja, Kenya. *Nature* 294, 125–9.

——, ——, and B. A. Wood (1982). Early hominids and fire at Chesowanja, Kenya (reply). *Nature* 296, 870.

Grace, G. W. (1987). *The Linguistic Construction of Reality*. London: Routledge.

Grafton, S. T., M. A. Arbib, L. Fadiga, and G. Rizzolatti (1996). Localization of grasp representations in humans by positron emission tomography, II: Observation compared with imagination. *Experimental Brain Research* 112, 103–11.

Grandjean, D., D. Sander, G. Pourtois, S. Schwartz, M. L. Seghier, K. R. Scherer, and P. Vuilleumier (2005). The voices of wrath: Brain responses to angry prosody in meaningless speech. *Nature Neuroscience* 8, 145–6.

Green, R. E., J. Krause, A. W. Briggs, T. Maricic, U. Stenzel, M. Kircher, N. Patterson, H. Li, W. Zhai, M. H.-Y. Fritz, N. F. Hansen, E. Y. Durand, A.-S. Malaspinas, J. D. Jensen, T. Marques-Bonet, C. Alkan, K. Prüfer, M. Meyer, H. A. Burbano, J. M. Good, R. Schultz, A. Aximu-Petri, A. Butthof, B. Höber, B. Höffner, M. Siegemund, A. Weihmann, C. Nusbaum, E. S. Lander, C. Russ, N. Novod, J. Affourtit, M. Egholm, C. Verna, P. Rudan, D. Brajkovic, Željko Kucan, I. Gušic, V. B. Doronichev, L. V. Golovanova, C. Lalueza-Fox, M. de la Rasilla, J. Fortea, A. Rosas, R. W. Schmitz, P. L. F. Johnson, E. E. Eichler, D. Falush, E. Birney, J. C. Mullikin, M. Slatkin, R. Nielsen, J. Kelso, M. Lachmann, D. Reich, and S. Pääbo (2010). A draft sequence of the Neandertal genome. *Science* 328, 710–22.

Greenberg, J. H. (1963). Some universals of grammar with particular reference to the order of meaningful elements. In *Universals of Language*, pp. 73–113. MIT Press.

——(1987). *Language in the Americas*. Stanford, CA: Stanford University Press.

Greenfield, P. M. (1979). Informativeness, presupposition, and semantic choice in single-word utterances. In E. Ochs and B. B. Schieffelin (eds.), *Developmental Pragmatics*, pp. 159–66. New York: Academic Press.

Greenfield, P. M. (1991). Language, tools, and brain—the ontogeny and phylogeny of hierarchically organized sequential behavior. *Behavioral and Brain Sciences* 14(4), 531–50.

——and E. S. Savage-Rumbaugh (1990). Grammatical combination in *Pan paniscus*: processes of learning and invention in the evolution and development of language. In S. T. Parker and K. R. Gibson (eds.), *'Language' and Intelligence in Monkeys and Apes: Comparative Developmental Perspectives*, pp. 540–78. Cambridge: Cambridge University Press.

——and J. H. Smith (1976). *The Structure of Communication in Early Language Development*. New York: Academic Press.

——, J. Reilly, C. Leaper, and N. Baker (1985). The structural and functional status of single-word utterances and their relationship to early multi-word speech. In M. D. Barrett (ed.), *Children's Single-Word Speech*, pp. 233–67. New York: John Wiley and Sons.

——, H. Lyn, and E. S. Savage-Rumbaugh (2008). Protolanguage in ontogeny and phylogeny. *Interaction Studies* 9(1), 34–50. (Special issue, edited by Derek Bickerton and Michael Arbib, entitled *Holophrasis, Compositionality and Protolanguage*.)

Grèzes, J., N. Costes, and J. Decety (1998). Top-down effects of strategy on the perception of human biological motion: A PET investigation. *Cognitive Neuropsychology* 15(6/7/8), 553–82.

Griffiths, P. (2003). Beyond the Baldwin Effect: James Mark Baldwin's 'social heredity', epigenetic inheritance and niche-construction. In B. Weber and D. Depew (eds.), *Learning, Meaning and Emergence: Possible Baldwinian Mechanisms in the Co-Evolution of Mind and Language*, pp. 193–215. Cambridge, MA: MIT Press.

Grinder, J. (1972). On the cycle in syntax. In J. P. Kimball (ed.), *Syntax and Semantics, Volume 1*, pp. 81–111. New York: Seminar Press.

Grodzinsky, Y. (1989a). Agrammatic comprehension of relative clauses. *Brain and Language* 31, 480–99.

——(1989b). The language learner: A trigger-happy kid? *Behavioral and Brain Sciences* 12(2), 342–3.

——(2006). The language faculty, Broca's region, and the Mirror System. *Cortex* 42(4), 464–8.

Gross, M. (1979). On the failure of generative grammar. *Language* 55, 859–85.

Grossman, M. and S. Haberman (1982). Aphasics' selective deficits in appreciating grammatical agreements. *Brain and Language* 16(1), 109–20.

Gruber, J. (1967). Topicalization in child language. *Foundations of Language* 3, 37–65.

Guillem, F., B. N'Kaoua, A. Rougier, and B. Claverie (1995). Intracranial topography of event-related potentials (N400/P600) elicited during a continuous recognition memory task. *Psychophysiology* 32(4), 382–92.

Guimarães, M. (2008). A note on the strong generative capacity of standard Antisymmetry. *Snippets* 18, 5–7. (online journal at http://www.ledonline.it/snippets.)

Gumperz, J. J. (1969). Communication in multilingual communities. In S. Tyler (ed.), *Cognitive Anthropology*, pp. 335–449. New York: Holt, Rinehart and Winston.

Gumperz, J. J. and S. C. Levinson (1996). *Rethinking Linguistic Relativity*. Cambridge: Cambridge University Press.

——and R. Wilson (1971). Convergence and creolization: A case from the Indo-Aryan/Dravidian border. In D. Hymes (ed.), *Pidginization and Creolization of Languages*, pp. 151–68. Cambridge: Cambridge University Press.

Günther, W. (1973). *Das portugiesische Kreolisch der Ilha do Principe*. Marburg, Germany: Marburger Studien zur Afrika- und Asienkunde.

Haas, M. (1966). Wiyot-Yurok-Algonkian and problems of comparative Algonkian. *International Journal of American Linguistics* 32, 101–7.

——(1978). Consonant symbolism in Northwestern California: A problem in diffusion. In A. S. Dil (ed.), *Language, Culture and History*, pp. 339–53. Stanford, CA: Stanford University Press.

Haeckel, E. (1866). *Generelle Morphologie der Organismen*. Berlin: Reimer.

Hagège, C. (1976). Relative clause center-embedding and comprehensibility. *Linguistic Inquiry* 7, 198–201.

Hagoort, P. (2009). Reflections on the neurobiology of syntax. In D. Bickerton and E. Szathmáry (eds.), *Biological Foundations and Origin of Syntax*, pp. 279–96. Cambridge, MA: MIT Press.

Hahnloser, R. H. R., A. A. Kozhevnikov, and M. S. Fee (2002). An ultra-sparse code underlies the generation of neural sequences in a songbird. *Nature* 419, 65–70.

Haider, H. (1989). Language acquisition: What triggers what? *Behavioral and Brain Sciences* 12(2), 343–4.

Hailman, J. P., M. S. Ficken, and R. W. Ficken (1985). The 'chick-a-dee' calls of *Parus atricapillus*: A recombinant system of animal communication compared with written English. *Semiotica* 56(3/4), 191–224.

Hakes, B., J. Evans, and L. Brannon (1976). Understanding sentences with relative clauses. *Memory and Cognition* 4, 283–96.

Hale, K. (1976). The adjoined relative clause in Australia. In R. M. W. Dixon (ed.), *Grammatical Categories in Australian Languages*, pp. 78–105. Canberra: AIAS.

——(1983). Warlpiri and the grammar of non-configurational languages. *Natural Language & Linguistic Theory* 1(1), 5–47.

Hall, R. A. (1962). The life cycle of pidgins. *Lingua* 11, 151–6.

Halle, M. (1962). Phonology in a generative grammar. *Word* 18, 54–72. (Reprinted in *The Structure of Language*, edited by Jerry A. Fodor and Jerrold J. Katz, 1964, Prentice Hall, Englewood Cliffs, NJ. pp. 334–54.)

Halliday, M. A. K. (1975). *Learning how to Mean: Explorations in the Development of Language*. London: Edward Arnold.

Hamilton, J. A. (1935). *The Association between Brain Size and Maze Ability in the White Rat*. Ph.D. thesis, University of California, Berkeley.

Hammer, A., B. M. Jansma, M. Lamers, and T. F. Münte (2008). Interplay of meaning, syntax and working memory during pronoun resolution investigated by ERPs. *Brain Research* 1230, 177–91.

Hamzei, F., M. Rijntjes, C. Dettmers, V. Glauche, C. Weiller, and C. Buchel (2003). The human action recognition system and its relationship to Broca's area: An fMRI study. *NeuroImage* 19, 637–44.

Hancock, A. M. and A. Di Rienzo (2008). Detecting the genetic signature of natural selection in human populations: Models, methods, and data. *Annual Review of Anthropology* 37, 197–217.

Harada, S. I. (1976). Honorifics. In M. Shibatani (ed.), *Syntax and Semantics, Volume 5*, pp. 499–561. New York: Academic Press.

Harbour, D. (2008). *Klivaj predika*, or predicate clefts in Haitian. *Lingua* 118(7), 853–71.

Hare, B., J. Call, and M. Tomasello (2001). Do chimpanzees know what conspecifics know? *Animal Behaviour* 61(1), 139–51.

Harms, W. F. (2004). Primitive content, translation, and the emergence of meaning in animal communication. In D. K. Oller and U. Griebel (eds.), *Evolution of Communication Systems: A Comparative Approach*, pp. 31–48. Cambridge, MA: MIT Press.

Harris, M. (1978). *The Evolution of French Syntax: A Comparative Approach*. London: Longman.

Harris, Z. S. (1946). From morpheme to utterance. *Language* 22, 161–83.

——(1951). *Methods in Structural Linguistics*. Chicago, IL: University of Chicago Press.

——(1957). Co-occurrence and transformations in linguistic structure. *Language* 33(3), 283–340.

Hartley, R. S. and R. A. Suthers (1989). Air-flow and pressure during canary song—direct evidence for mini-breaths. *Journal of Comparative Physiology A–Sensory Neural and Behavioral Physiology* 165(1), 15–26.

Hashiya, K. and S. Kojima (2001). Hearing and auditory-visual intermodal recognition in the chimpanzee. In T. Matsuzawa (ed.), *Primate Origins of Human Cognition and Behavior*, pp. 155–89. Tokyo: Springer Verlag.

Haspelmath, M. (1999). Why is grammaticalization irreversible? *Linguistics* 37(6), 1043–68.

Hasselquist, D., S. Bensch, and T. von Schantz (1996). Correlation between male song repertoire, extra-pair paternity and offspring survival in the great reed warbler. *Nature* 381, 229–32.

Hast, M. H., J. M. Fischer, A. B. Wetzel, and V. E. Thompson (1974). Cortical motor representation of the laryngeal muscles in *Macaca mulatta*. *Brain Research* 73, 229–40.

Hauser, M. D. and K. Andersson (1994). Left hemisphere dominance for processing vocalizations in adult, but not infant, rhesus monkeys: Field experiments. *Proceedings of the National Academy of Sciences of the U.S.A.* 91, 3946–8.

——and W. T. Fitch (2003). What are the uniquely human components of the language faculty? In M. H. Christiansen and S. Kirby (eds.), *Language Evolution*, pp. 158–81. Oxford: Oxford University Press.

Hauser, M. D., N. Chomsky, and W. T. Fitch (2002). The faculty of language: What is it, who has it, and how did it evolve? *Science* 298, 1569–79.

Haviland, J. (1979). Guugu Yimidhirr. In R. M. W. Dixon and B. Blake (eds.), *Handbook of Australian Languages*, pp. 27–180. Amsterdam: John Benjamins.

Hawkins, J. A. (1994). *A Performance Theory of Order and Constituency*. Cambridge: Cambridge University Press.

——(2009). Language universals and the performance-grammar correspondence hypothesis. In M. H. Christiansen, C. Collins, and S. Edelman (eds.), *Language Universals*, pp. 54–78. Oxford: Oxford University Press.

Hayek, F. A. (1944). *The Road to Serfdom*. London: Routledge.

——(1988). *The Fatal Conceit: The Errors of Socialism*. Chicago: University of Chicago Press.

Heaney, R. R. (1997). The roles of calcium and vitamin D in skeletal health: An evolutionary perspective. *Food, Nutrition and Agriculture* 20, 4–12.

Heffner, H. E. and R. S. Heffner (1984). Temporal lobe lesions and perception of species-specific vocalizations by macaques. *Science* 4670, 75–6.

——and ——(1986). Effect of unilateral and bilateral auditory cortex lesions on the discrimination of vocalizations by Japanese macaques. *Journal of Neurophysiology* 56, 683–701.

Heine, B. (1989). Adpositions in African languages. *Linguistique Africaine* 2, 77–127.

——and T. Kuteva (2007). *The Genesis of Grammar*. Oxford: Oxford University Press.

——, U. Claudi, and F. Hünnemeyer (1991). *Grammaticalization: A Conceptual Framework*. Chicago: University of Chicago Press.

Helekar, S. A., G. G. Espino, A. Botas, and D. B. Rosenfield (2003). Development and adult phase plasticity of syllable repetitions in the birdsong of captive zebra finches (*Taeniopygia guttata*). *Behavioral Neuroscience* 117(5), 939–51.

Helms-Park, R. (2003). Transfer in SLA and creoles: The implications of causal serial verbs in the interlanguage of Vietnamese ESL learners. *Studies in Second Language Acquisition* 25(2), 211–44.

Henrich, J. and R. McElreath (2003). The evolution of cultural evolution. *Evolutionary Anthropology* 12, 123–35.

Henshilwood, C. S. and B. Dubreuil (2009). Reading the artifacts: Gleaning language skills from the Middle Stone Age in southern Africa. In R. Botha and C. Knight (eds.), *The Cradle of Language*, pp. 41–61. Oxford: Oxford University Press.

Hermann, E. (1895). Gab es im Indogermanischen Nebensätze? *Zeitschrift für vergleichende Sprachforschung* 33, 481–535.

Hermer-Vazquez, L., A. Moffet, and P. Munkholm (2001). Language, space, and the development of cognitive flexibility in humans: The case of two spatial memory tasks. *Cognition* 79(3), 263–99.

Hernández, M., A. Caño, A. Costa, N. Sebastián-Gallés, M. Juncadella, and J. Gascón-Bayarri (2008). Grammatical category-specific deficits in bilingual aphasia. *Brain and Language* 107(1), 68–80.

Hewes, G. (1973). Primate communication and the gestural origin of language. *Current Anthropology* 14(1–2), 5–24.

Hickok, G., E. Zurif, and E. Canseco-Gonzales (1993). Structural description of agrammatic comprehension. *Brain and Language* 45, 371–95.

Hihara, S., H. Yamada, A. Iriki, and K. Okanoya (2003). Spontaneous vocal differentiation of coo-calls for tools and food in Japanese monkeys. *Neuroscience Research* 45, 383–9.

Hillert, D. and D. Swinney (2001). The processing of fixed expressions during sentence comprehension. In A. Cienki, B. J. Luka, and M. B. Smith (eds.), *Conceptual and Discourse Factors in Linguistic Structure*, pp. 107–122. Stanford, CA: CSLI Publications.

Himmelmann, N. (1991). *The Philippine Challenge to Universal Grammar*. Cologne: Institut für Sprachwissenschaft, Universität zu Köln. (Arbeitspapier Nr. 15; Neue Folge.)

Hinton, G. and S. Nowlan (1987). How learning can guide evolution. *Complex Systems* 1, 495–502.

Hinton, L., J. Nichols, and J. Ohala (1994). Introduction: Sound-symbolic processes. In L. Hinton, J. Nichols, and J. Ohala (eds.), *Sound Symbolism*, pp. 1–12. Cambridge: Cambridge University Press.

——, ——, and —— (eds.) (1995). *Sound Symbolism*. Cambridge: Cambridge University Press.

Hockett, C. F. (1958). *A Course in Modern Linguistics*. New York: Macmillan.

Hoffmann, J. (1903). *Mundari Grammar*. Calcutta: The Secretariat Press.

Holm, J. (2000). *An Introduction to Pidgins and Creoles*. Cambridge: Cambridge University Press.

Holmes, V. M. (1973). Order of main and subordinate clauses in sentence perception. *Journal of Verbal Learning and Verbal Behavior* 12, 285–93.

Hombert, J.-M. (2008). Continuity between non-human primates and modern humans? In A. D. M. Smith, K. Smith, and R. Ferrer i Cancho (eds.), *The Evolution of Language*, pp. 441–2. Singapore: World Scientific. Proceedings of the 7th International Conference on the Evolution of Language (EVOLANG7).

Honda, E. and K. Okanoya (1999). Acoustical and syntactical comparisons between songs of the white-backed munia *Lonchura striata* and its domesticate strain, the Bengalese finch *Lonchura striata* var. *domestica*. *Zoological Science* 16(2), 319–26.

Hook-Costigan, M. A. and L. J. Rogers (1998). Lateralized use of the mouth in production of vocalizations by marmosets. *Neuropsychologia* 36(12), 1265–73.

Hopkins, W. D. and C. Cantalupo (2004). Handedness in chimpanzees (*Pan troglodytes*) is associated with asymmetries of the primary motor cortex but not with homologous language areas. *Behavioral Neuroscience* 118(6), 1176–83.

—— and —— (2005). Individual and setting differences in the hand preferences of chimpanzees (*Pan troglodytes*): A critical analysis and some alternative explanations. *Laterality: Asymmetries of Body, Brain, and Cognition* 10(1), 65–80.

—— and D. A. Leavens (1998). Hand use and gestural communication in chimpanzees (*Pan troglodytes*). *Journal of Comparative Psychology* 112(1), 95–9.

Hopkins, W. D., R. D. Morris, E. S. Savage-Rumbaugh, and D. M. Rumbaugh (1992). Hemispheric priming by meaningful and non-meaningful symbols in language-trained chimpanzees *Pan troglodytes*: Further evidence of a left hemisphere advantage. *Behavioral Neuroscience* 106(3), 575–82.

Hopp, H. C. (2004). Syntax and its interfaces in L2 grammars—situating L1 effects. In J. van Kampen and S. Bauw (eds.), *Proceedings of GALA 2003, Volume 1*, Utrecht, pp. 211–22. Landelijke Onderzoekschool Taalwetenschap.

Hopper, P. J. (1985). Causes and effects. In W. Eilfort, P. Kroeber, and K. Peterson (eds.), *CLS, part 2: Papers from the Parasession on Causatives and Agentivity at the Twenty-First Annual Meeting of the Chicago Linguistic Society*, pp. 67–88. Chicago: Chicago Linguistic Society, University of Chicago.

——(1987). Emergent grammar. *Berkeley Linguistics Conference (BLS)* 13, 139–57. (Online at http://www.isrl.uiuc.edu/amag/langev/paper/hopper87emergentGrammar.html.)

——(1991). On some principles of grammaticalization. In E. C. Traugott and B. Heine (eds.), *Approaches to Grammaticalization*, pp. 17–35. Amsterdam: John Benjamins.

——and E. C. Traugott (1993). *Grammaticalization*. Cambridge Textbooks in Linguistics. Cambridge: Cambridge University Press.

Hudson, R. A. (1984). *Word Grammar*. Oxford: Blackwell.

——(1990). *English Word Grammar*. Oxford: Blackwell.

——(2000). Language as a cognitive network. In H. G. Simonsen and R. T. Endresen (eds.), *A Cognitive Approach to the Verb: Morphological and Constructional Perspectives*, pp. 49–70. Berlin: Walter de Gruyter.

——(2002). Mismatches in default inheritance. In E. Francis and L. Michaelis (eds.), *Mismatch: Form–Function Incongruity and the Architecture of Grammar*, pp. 355–402. Stanford, CA: Center for the Study of Language and Information.

——(2007). *Language Networks: The New Word Grammar*. Oxford: Oxford University Press.

Hudson, R. R., M. Kreitman, and M. A. Aguade (1987). Test of neutral molecular evolution based on nucleotide data. *Genetics* 116, 153–9.

Hudson Kam, C. L. and E. L. Newport (2005). Regularizing unpredictable variation: The roles of adult and child learners in language formation and change. *Language Learning and Development* 1(2), 151–95.

Hughes, D. J. D. (2006). Towards Hilbert's 24th problem: Combinatorial proof invariants: (preliminary version). *Electronic Notes in Theoretical Computer Science* 165, 37–63.

Hultsch, H. and D. Todt (1989). Memorization and reproduction of songs in nightingales *(Luscinia megarhynchos)*: Evidence for package formation. *Journal of Comparative Physiology* A 165, 197–203.

——, R. Mundry, and D. Todt (1999). Learning, representation and retrieval of rule-related knowledge in the song system of birds. In A. D. Friederici and R. Menzel (eds.), *Learning: Rule Extraction and Representation*, pp. 89–116. Berlin: Walter de Gruyter.

Humboldt, W. v. (1832–9). *Über die Kawi-Sprache auf der Insel Java*. Abhandlungen der Königlichen Akademie der Wissenschaften zu Berlin. Berlin.

Hunt, E. and F. Agnoli (1991). The Whorfian Hypothesis: A cognitive psychology perspective. *Psychological Review* 98, 377–89.

Hurford, J. R. (1967). *The Speech of One Family: A phonetic comparison of the speech of three generations in a family of East Londoners*. Ph.D. thesis, University of London.

—— (1975). *The Linguistic Theory of Numerals*. Cambridge: Cambridge University Press.

—— (1987). *Language and Number: The Emergence of a Cognitive System*. Oxford: Basil Blackwell.

—— (1989). Biological evolution of the Saussurean sign as a component of the language acquisition device. *Lingua* 77, 187–222.

—— (1991a). The evolution of critical period for language acquisition. *Cognition* 40, 159–201.

—— (1991b). Nativist and functional explanations in language acquisition. In I. Roca (ed.), *Logical Issues in Language Acquisition*, pp. 85–136. Dordrecht, Holland: Foris Publications.

—— (1998). Review of Terrence Deacon's *The Symbolic Species*. *The Times Literary Supplement* 23 October 1998, 34.

—— (1999). Language learning from fragmentary input. In K. Dautenhahn and C. Nehaniv (eds.), *Proceedings of the AISB '99 Symposium on Imitation in Animals and Artifacts*, pp. 121–9. Society for the Study of Artificial Intelligence and the Simulation of Behaviour.

—— (2000a). Introduction: The emergence of syntax. In C. Knight, M. Studdert-Kennedy, and J. Hurford (eds.), *The Evolutionary Emergence of Language: Social Function and the Origins of Linguistic Form*, pp. 219–30. Cambridge: Cambridge University Press.

—— (2000b). Social transmission favours linguistic generalization. In C. Knight, M. Studdert-Kennedy, and J. Hurford (eds.), *The Evolutionary Emergence of Language: Social Function and the Origins of Linguistic Form*, pp. 324–52. Cambridge: Cambridge University Press.

—— (2001a). Languages treat 1–4 specially. *Mind and Language* 16(1), 69–75.

—— (2001b). Protothought had no logical names. In J. Trabant and S. Ward (eds.), *New Essays on the Origin of Language*, pp. 117–30. Berlin: de Gruyter.

—— (2003). The neural basis of predicate-argument structure. *Behavioral and Brain Sciences* 26(3), 261–83.

—— (2004). Language beyond our grasp: What mirror neurons can, and cannot, do for language evolution. In D. K. Oller and U. Griebel (eds.), *Evolution of Communication Systems: A Comparative Approach*, pp. 297–313. Cambridge, MA: MIT Press.

—— (2007). *The Origins of Meaning: Language in the Light of Evolution*. Oxford: Oxford University Press.

Hurford, J. R. (2009). Universals and the diachronic life cycle of languages. In M. Christiansen, C. Collins, and S. Edelman (eds.), *Language Universals*, pp. 40–53. Oxford: Oxford University Press.

——and D. Dediu (2009). Diversity in language, genes and the language faculty. In R. Botha and C. Knight (eds.), *The Cradle of Language*, pp. 163–84. Oxford: Oxford University Press.

——and B. Heasley (1983). *Semantics: A Coursebook*. Cambridge: Cambridge University Press.

——and S. Kirby (1999). Co-evolution of language-size and the critical period. In D. Birdsong (ed.), *New Perspectives on the Critical Period Hypothesis and Second Language Acquisition*, pp. 39–63. Mahwah, NJ: Lawrence Erlbaum.

Hurst, J. A., M. Baraitser, E. Auger, F. Graham, and S. Norell (1990). An extended family with a dominantly inherited speech disorder. *Developmental Medicine and Child Neurology* 32(4), 352–5.

Huttar, M. L. and G. L. Huttar (1997). Reduplication in Ndyuka. In A. K. Spears and D. Winford (eds.), *The Structure and Status of Pidgins and Creoles*, pp. 395–414. Amsterdam: John Benjamins.

Hutton, J. (1788). Theory of the earth. *Transactions of the Royal Society of Edinburgh* 1(2), 209–304. (From a paper presented in 1785.)

Huxley, R. (1970). The development of the correct use of subject personal pronouns in two children. In G. B. Flores d'Arcais and W. J. M. Levelt (eds.), *Advances in Psycholinguistics: Research Papers Presented at the Bressanone Conference on Psycholinguistics, Summer Courses of the University of Padova*. Amsterdam: North Holland.

Hymes, D. (1971). Introduction [to Part III]. In D. Hymes (ed.), *Pidginization and Creolization of Languages*, pp. 65–90. Cambridge: Cambridge University Press.

Iacoboni, M., J. Kaplan, and S. Wilson (2007). A neural architecture for imitation and intentional relations. In B. C. L. Nehaniv and K. Dautenhahn (eds.), *Imitation and Social Learning in Robots, Humans and Animals: Behavioural, Social and Communication Dimensions*, pp. 71–88. Cambridge: Cambridge University Press.

——, R. P. Woods, M. Brass, H. Bekkering, J. C. Mazziotta, and G. Rizzolatti (1999). Cortical mechanisms of human imitation. *Science* 286, 2526–8.

Immelmann, K. (1969). Song development in the zebra finch and other estrildid finches. In R. A. Hinde (ed.), *Bird Vocalizations*, pp. 61–74. Cambridge: Cambridge University Press.

Ince, S. A., P. J. B. Slater, and C. Weismann (1980). Changes with time in the songs of a population of chaffinches. *Condor* 82(3), 285–90.

Inoue, S. and T. Matsuzawa (2007). Working memory of numerals in chimpanzees. *Current Biology* 17(23), R1004–R1005.

Isaac, G. (1982). Early hominids and fire at Chesowanja, Kenya. *Nature* 296, 870.

Isbell, L. A. (1991). Contest and scramble competition: Patterns of female aggression and ranging behavior among primates. *Behavioral Ecology* 2, 143–55.

Iverson, J. M. and S. Goldin-Meadow (2005). Gesture paves the way for language development. *Psychological Science* 16(5), 367–71.

Jablonski, N. G. and G. Chaplin (2000). The evolution of human skin coloration. *Journal of Human Evolution* 39(1), 57–106.

Jackendoff, R. S. (2002). *Foundations of Language: Brain, Meaning, Grammar, Evolution*. Oxford: Oxford University Press.

——(2007). *Language, Consciousness, Culture: Essays on Mental Structure*. Cambridge, MA: MIT Press.

——, M. Y. Liberman, G. K. Pullum, and B. C. Scholz (2006). Disc: Starling Study: Recursion. (The points made by these authors are included in an online posting to The Linguist List by Geoff Pullum at http://linguistlist.org/issues/17/17-1528.html. These points were originally made in a letter to *Nature*, but not published there.)

Jacobs, R. A. and P. S. Rosenbaum (1968). *English Transformational Grammar*. Waltham, MA: Blaisdell Publishing Company.

Jacobsen, W. H. (1976). Noun and verb in Nootkan. In B. S. Efrat (ed.), *The Victoria Conference on Northwestern Languages (British Columbia Provincial Museum Heritage Record, No. 4)*, pp. 83–155. Victoria, BC: British Columbia Provincial Museum.

Jacques, G. (2007). A shared suppletive pattern in the pronominal systems of Chang Naga and Southern Qiang. *Cahiers de Linguistique Asie Orientale* 36(1), 61–78.

Jahr, E. H. (1996). On the pidgin status of Russenorsk. In E. H. Jahr and I. Broch (eds.), *Language Contact in the Arctic: Northern Pidgins and Contact Languages*, pp. 107–22. Berlin: Mouton de Gruyter.

Jakobovits, L. A. and M. S. Miron (eds.) (1967). *Readings in the Psychology of Language*. Englewood Cliffs, NJ: Prentice-Hall.

Jakobson, R. (1941). *Kindersprache, Aphasie und allgemeine Lautgesetze*. Uppsala: Almqvist and Wiksell. (Page references are to the translation as *Child Language, Aphasia and Phonological Universals* by A. R. Keiler, 1968. The Hague: Mouton.)

——(1960). Why 'Mama' and 'Papa'? In B. Kaplan and S. Wapner (eds.), *Perspectives in Psychological Theory, Essays in Honor of Heinz Werner*, pp. 21–9. New York: International Universities Press. (Reprinted in *Child Language: A Book of Readings* edited by Aaron Bar-Adon and Werner F. Leopold, Prentice-Hall, Englewood Cliffs, NJ, 1971, pp. 212–17.)

——(1978). *Six Lectures on Sound and Meaning*. Brighton: Harvester.

——and L. Waugh (1979). *The Sound Shape of Language*. Brighton: Harvester.

James, S. R. (1989). Hominid use of fire in the Lower and Middle Pleistocene: A review of the evidence. *Current Anthropology* 30(1), 1–26.

James, W. (1890). *The Principles of Psychology*. London: Macmillan.

Jarvis, E. D. (2004a). Brains and birdsong. In P. Marler and H. Slabbekoorn (eds.), *Nature's Music: The Science of Bird Song*, pp. 226–71. San Diego, CA: Elsevier/Academic Press.

——(2004b). Learned birdsong and the neurobiology of human language. *Annals of the New York Academy of Sciences* 1016, 749–77.

Jarvis, E. D. (2007). Neural systems for vocal learning in birds and humans: a synopsis. *Journal of Ornithology* 148 (Supplement), S35–S44.

Jelinek, E. (1993). Prepositions in Straits Salish and the noun/verb question. (Paper presented at the 28th ICNSL, Seattle, Washington.)

——(1998). Prepositions in Northern Straits Salish. In E. Czaykowska-Higgins and M. D. Kinkade (eds.), *Salish Languages and Linguistics: Theoretical and Descriptive Perspectives*, pp. 325–46. Berlin: Mouton de Gruyter.

——and R. A. Demers (1994). Predicates and pronominal arguments in Straits Salish. *Language* 70, 697–736.

Jespersen, O. (1922). *Language: its Nature, Development and Origin.* London: G. Allen and Unwin Ltd. (Reprinted by W.W. Norton & Co, New York, 1964.)

Johnson, A. (2003). *Families of the Forest: The Matsigenka Indians of the Peruvian Amazon.* Berkeley, CA: University of California Press.

Johnson, K. (2000). Few dogs eat Whiskas or cats Alpo. In K. Kusumoto and E. Villalta (eds.), *University of Massachusetts Occasional Papers 23: Issues in Semantics*, pp. 59–82. Amherst, MA: Graduate Linguistics Student Association, University of Massachusetts.

Johnson-Frey, S. H. (2004). The neural bases of complex tool use in humans. *Trends in Cognitive Sciences* 8(2), 71–8. (Scott H. Johnson-Frey is the same person as Scott H. Frey.)

——, F. R. Maloof, R. Newman-Norlund, C. Farrer, S. Inati, and S. T. Grafton (2003). Actions or hand-object interactions? Human inferior frontal cortex and action observation. *Neuron* 39, 1053–8. (Scott H. Johnson-Frey is the same person as Scott H. Frey.)

Johnson-Laird, P. (1983). *Mental Models: Towards a Cognitive Science of Language, Inference and Consciousness.* Cambridge: Cambridge University Press.

Joshi, A. (1987). An introduction to Tree Adjoining Grammars. In A. Manaster-Ramer (ed.), *The Mathematics of Language*, pp. 87ff. Amsterdam: John Benjamins.

——, L. Levy, and M. Takahashi (1975). Tree adjunct grammars. *Journal of Computer and System Sciences* 10, 136–63.

——, T. Becker, and O. Rambow (2000). Complexity of scrambling: A new twist to the competence-performance distinction. In A. Abeillé and O. Rambow (eds.), *Tree Adjoining Grammars: Formalisms, Linguistic Analysis and Processing*, pp. 167–81. Stanford, CA: CSLI Publications. (Distributed by the University of Chicago Press.)

Joyce, R. (2006). *The Evolution of Morality.* Cambridge, MA: MIT Press.

Judd, H. P., M. K. Pukui, and J. F. G. Stokes (1945). *Introduction to the Hawaiian Language.* Honolulu: Tongg Publishing Co.

Jürgens, U. (2002). Neural pathways underlying vocal control. *Neuroscience and Biobehavioural Reviews* 26, 235–58.

Just, M. A., P. A. Carpenter, and T. A. Keller (1996). The capacity theory of comprehension: new frontiers of evidence and arguments. *Psychological Review* 103, 773–80.

Just, M. A., P. A. Carpenter, T. A. Keller, W. F. Eddy, and K. R. Thulborn (1996). Brain activation modulated by sentence comprehension. *Science* 274, 114–16.

Kagan, J. (1981). *The Second Year*. Cambridge: Cambridge University Press.

Kalmár, I. (1979). *Case and Context in Inuktitut (Eskimo)*. Ottawa: National Museums of Canada. (National Museums of Man Mercury Series 49.)

——(1985). Are there really no primitive languages? In D. R. Olson, N. Torrance, and A. Hildyard (eds.), *Literacy, Language, and Learning: the Nature and Consequences of Reading and Writing*, pp. 148–66. Cambridge: Cambridge University Press.

Kalmus, H. (1956). Sun navigation in *Apis mellifica L.* in the southern hemisphere. *Journal of Experimental Biology* 33, 554–65.

Kaminski, J., J. Call, and J. Fischer (2004). Word learning in a domestic dog: Evidence for 'fast mapping'. *Science* 304, 1682–3.

Kant, I. (1781). *Kritik der Reinen Vernunft*. Riga: Johann Friedrich Hartknoch. (See *Immanuel Kant's Critique of Pure Reason. In Commemoration of the Centenary of its First Publication*, translated into English by F. Max Müller (2nd revised edn.), New York: Macmillan, 1922. Any page reference is to this translated edition.)

Karlsson, F. (1983). *Finnish Grammar*. Helsinki: Werner Söderström Osakeyhtiö.

——(2007). Constraints on multiple center-embedding of clauses. *Journal of Linguistics* 43(2), 365–92.

Kastenholz, R. (1979). Essai de classification des dialectes mandékan. *Sprache und Geschichte in Afrika* 1, 205–23.

Katahira, K., K. Okanoya, and M. Okada (2007). A neural network model for generating complex birdsong syntax. *Biological Cybernetics* 97, 441–8.

Katz, P. A. (1963). Effects of labels on children's perception and discrimination learning. *Journal of Experimental Psychology* 66, 423–8.

Kay, P. (1977). Language evolution and speech style. In B. Blount and M. Sanches (eds.), *Sociocultural Dimensions of Language Change*, pp. 21–33. New York: Academic Press.

——(2004). Pragmatic aspects of grammatical constructions. In L. R. Horn and G. Ward (eds.), *Handbook of Pragmatics*, pp. 675–700. Malden, MA: Blackwells.

——(2005). Commentary on Everett (2005). *Current Anthropology* 46(4), 636–7.

——and G. Sankoff (1974). A language-universals approach to pidgins and creoles. In D. DeCamp and I. Hancock (eds.), *Pidgins and Creoles: Current Trends and Prospects,*, pp. 61–72. Washington, DC: Georgetown University Press.

Kayne, R. (1994). *The Antisymmetry of Syntax*. Cambridge, MA: MIT Press. (*Linguistic Inquiry* Monographs, No. 25.)

——(2005). *Movement and Silence*. Oxford: Oxford University Press.

Keenan, E. L. (1976). Towards a universal definition of 'Subject'. In C. N. Li (ed.), *Subject and Topic*, pp. 303–33. New York: Academic Press.

——and B. Comrie (1977). Noun phrase accessibility and universal grammar. *Linguistic Inquiry* 8(1), 63–100.

Keesing, R. M. (1988). *Melanesian Pidgin and the Oceanic Substrate*. Stanford, CA: Stanford University Press.

Kegl, J. (2002). Language emergence in a language-ready brain: Acquisition issues. In C. Morgan and B. Woll (eds.), *Language Acquisition in Signed Languages*, pp. 207–54. Cambridge: Cambridge University Press.

——and G. A. Iwata (1989). Lenguaje de Signos Nicaraguense: A pidgin sheds light on the 'creole?' ASL. In R. Carlson, S. DeLancey, S. Gildea, D. Payne, and A. Saxena (eds.), *Proceedings of the Fourth Meeting of the Pacific Linguistics Conference*, pp. 266–94. Eugene, OR: University of Oregon.

——, A. Senghas, and M. Coppola (1999). Creation through contact: Sign language emergence and sign language change in Nicaragua. In M. DeGraff (ed.), *Language Creation and Language Change: Creolization, Diachrony, and Development*, pp. 179–237. Cambridge, MA: MIT Press.

Keightley, P. D., M. J. Lercher, and A. Eyre-Walker (2005). Evidence for widespread degradation of gene control regions in hominid genomes. *PLoS Biology* 3(2), e42. (Public Library of Science, online journal.)

Keller, H., J. A. Macy, A. Sullivan, and A. M. Sullivan (1903). *The Story of my Life*. New York: Doubleday, Page & Co.

Keller, M. C. and G. Miller (2006). Resolving the paradox of common, harmful, heritable mental disorders: Which evolutionary genetic models work best? *Behavioral and Brain Sciences* 29(4), 385–404.

Keller, R. (1989). Invisible-hand theory and language evolution. *Lingua* 77, 113–27.

——(1994). *On Language Change: the Invisible Hand in Language*. London: Routledge. (Translation and expansion of *Sprachwandel: Von der unsichtbaren Hand in der Sprache*. Tübingen: Francke.)

Kelley, J. L. and W. J. Swanson (2008). Positive selection in the human genome: From genome scans to biological significance. *Annual Review of Genomics and Human Genetics* 9, 143–60.

Kelly, M. H. (1988). Phonological biases in grammatical category shifts. *Journal of Memory and Language* 27, 343–58.

——(1992). Using sound to solve syntactic problems: The role of phonology in grammatical category assignments. *Psychological Review* 99, 349–64.

——(1996). The role of phonology in grammatical category assignment. In J. L. Morgan and K. Demuth (eds.), *Signal to Syntax: Bootstrapping from Speech to Grammar in Early Acquisition*, pp. 249–62. Mahwah, NJ: Lawrence Erlbaum Associates.

Kempson, R. M., W. Meyer-Viol, and D. M. Gabbay (2001). *Dynamic Syntax: The Flow of Language Understanding*. Oxford: Blackwell Publishing.

Kidwai, A. (1999). Word order and focus positions in universal grammar. In G. Rebuschi and L. Tuller (eds.), *The Grammar of Focus*, pp. 213–44. Amsterdam: John Benjamins.

Kien, J., M. Schleidt, and B. Schöttner (1991). Temporal segmentation in hand movements of chimpanzees (*Pan troglodytes*) and comparisons with humans. *Ethology* 89, 297–304.

Kierkegaard, S. (1985). *Philosophical Fragments*. Princeton, NJ: Princeton University Press.

Kimenyí, A. (1980). *A Relational Grammar of Kinyarwanda*. Berkeley, CA: University of California Press.

Kimura, M. (1961). Natural selection as a process of accumulating genetic information in adaptive evolution. *Genetical Research, Cambridge* 2, 127–40.

King, J. and M. A. Just (1991). Individual differences in syntactic processing: the role of working memory. *Journal of Memory and Language* 30, 580–602.

King, M.-C. and A. C. Wilson (1975). Evolution at two levels in humans and chimpanzees. *Science* 188, 107–16.

King-Casas, B., D. Tomlin, C. Anen, C. F. Camerer, S. R. Quartz, and P. Montague (2005). Getting to know you: reputation and trust in a two-person economic exchange. *Science* 308, 78–83.

Kinkade, M. D. (1976). Columbian parallels to Thompson //-xi// and Spokane //s&i//. In *Proceedings of the International Conference on Salishan Languages*. Seattle: University of Washington.

——(1983). Salish evidence against the universality of 'noun' and 'verb'. *Lingua* 60, 25–40.

Kinsella, A. R. (2009). *Language Evolution and Syntactic Theory*. Cambridge: Cambridge University Press. (Anna Parker and Anna Kinsella are the same person.)

Kiparsky, P. (1968). Linguistic universals and linguistic change. In E. Bach and R. T. Harms (eds.), *Universals in Linguistc Theory*, pp. 171–202. New York: Holt, Rinehart & Winston.

——(in press). Grammaticalization as optimization. In D. Jonas, J. Whitman, and A. Garrett (eds.), *Grammatical Change: Origins, Nature, Outcomes*. Oxford: Oxford University Press.

Kirby, S. (1999a). *Function, Selection and Innateness: The Emergence of Language Universals*. Oxford: Oxford University Press.

——(1999b). Syntax out of learning: the cultural evolution of structured communication in a population of induction algorithms. In D. Floreano, J. D. Nicoud, and F. Mondada (eds.), *Advances in Artificial Life*, Number 1674 in Lecture notes in computer science. Springer.

——(2000). Syntax without natural selection: how compositionality emerges from vocabulary in a population of learners. In C. Knight, M. Studdert-Kennedy, and J. R. Hurford (eds.), *The Evolutionary Emergence of Language: Social Function and the Origins of Linguistic Form*, pp. 303–23. Cambridge: Cambridge University Press.

——(2001). Spontaneous evolution of linguistic structure: an iterated learning model of the emergence of regularity and irregularity. *IEEE Journal of Evolutionary Computation* 5(2), 102–10.

——and J. R. Hurford (2002). The emergence of linguistic structure: An overview of the iterated learning model. In A. Cangelosi and D. Parisi (eds.), *Simulating the Evolution of Language*. Springer Verlag.

——, M. Dowman, and T. Griffiths (2007). Innateness and culture in the evolution of language. *Proceedings of the National Academy of Sciences of the U.S.A.* 104, 5241–5.

Kirzinger, A. and U. Jürgens (1982). Cortical lesion effects and vocalization in the squirrel monkey. *Brain Research* 233, 299–315.

Kita, S. (2008). World-view of protolanguage speakers as inferred from semantics of sound-symbolic words: A case of Japanese mimetics. In N. Masataka (ed.), *The Origins of Language: Unraveling Evolutionary Forces*, pp. 25–38. Berlin: Springer.

Klein, R. G. (1995). Anatomy, behaviour and modern human origins. *Journal of World Prehistory* 9, 167–98.

——(1999). *The Human Career: Human Biological and Cultural Origins*. Chicago, IL: University of Chicago Press.

Klein, W. and C. Perdue (1997). The Basic Variety (or: couldn't natural languages be much simpler?). *Second Language Research* 13, 301–47.

Kluender, R. (1992). Deriving island constraints from principles of predication. In H. Goodluck and M. S. Rochemont (eds.), *Island constraints: theory, acquisition, and processing*, pp. 223–58. Dordrecht, Holland: Kluwer.

Koebnick, C., C. Strassner, I. Hoffmann, and C. Leitzmann (1999). Consequences of a long-term raw food diet on body weight and menstruation: Results of a questionnaire survey. *Annals of Nutrition & Metabolism* 43, 69–79.

Koechlin, E. and T. Jubault (2006). Broca's Area and the hierarchical organization of human behavior. *Neuron* 50(6), 963–74.

Koffka, K. (1935). *Principles of Gestalt Psychology*. New York: Harcourt, Brace & World.

Köhler, W. (1925). *The Mentality of Apes*. London: Routledge and Kegan Paul.

——(1929). *Gestalt Psychology*. New York: Liveright.

——(1947). *Gestalt Psychology*. New York: Liveright. (2nd edition).

Kojima, S. and S. Kiritani (1989). Vocal-auditory functions in the chimpanzee: Vowel perception. *International Journal of Primatology* 10(3), 199–213.

——, I. F. Tatsumi, S. Kiritani, and H. Hirose (1989). Vocal-auditory functions of the chimpanzee: consonant perception. *Human Evolution* 4(5), 403–16.

Kolk, H. and L. Blomert (1985). On the Bradley hypothesis concerning agrammatism: The nonword-interference effect. *Brain and Language* 26, 94–105.

Konishi, M. (1965). The role of auditory feedback in the control of vocalization in the white-crowned sparrow. *Zeitschrift für Tierpsychologie* 22, 770–83.

Konopka, G., J. M. Bomar, K. Winden, G. Coppola, Z. O. Jonsson, F. Gao, S. Peng, T. M. Preuss, J. A. Wohlschlegel, and D. H. Geschwind (2009). Human-specific transcriptional regulation of CNS development genes by FOXP2. *Nature* 462, 213–18.

Kouprina, N., A. Pavlicek, G. H. Mochida, G. Solomon, W. Gersch, Y. H. Yoon, R. Collura, M. Ruvolo, J. C. Barrett, C. G. Woods, C. A. Walsh, J. Jurka, and V. Larionov (2004). Accelerated evolution of the ASPM gene controlling brain size begins prior to human brain expansion. *PLoS Biology* 2(5), E126. (Public Library of Science, online journal.)

Kouwenberg, S. (1994). *A Grammar of Berbice Dutch Creole*. Berlin: Mouton de Gruyter.

Kouwenberg, S. and P. L. Patrick (2003). Introduction. *Studies in Second Language Acquisition* 25(2), 175–84.

Kovas, Y. and R. Plomin (2006). Generalist genes: implications for the cognitive sciences. *Trends in Cognitive Sciences* 10(5), 198–203.

Kozulin, A. (1986). Vygotsky in context. MIT Press. (Translator's introduction to *Thought and Language* by L. S. Vygotsky.)

Krause, J., C. Lalueza-Fox, L. Orlando, W. Enard, R. E. Green, H. Burbano, J. J. Hublin, C. Hänni, J. Fortea, M. de la Rasilla, J. Bertranpetit, A. Rosas, and S. Pääbo (2007). The derived FOXP2 variant of modern humans was shared with Neandertals. *Current Biology* 17(21), 1908–12.

Krifka, M. (2006). A note on the pronoun system and the predicate marker in Tok Pisin. In P. Brandt and E. Fuss (eds.), *Form, Structure and Grammar: A Festschrift Presented to Günther Grewendorf on the Occasion of his 60th Birthday*, pp. 79–92. Berlin: Akademie Verlag.

Kristeva, J. (1986). Word, dialogue and novel. In T. Moi (ed.), *The Kristeva Reader*, pp. 34–61. New York: Columbia University Press. (Originally written in 1966.)

Kroodsma, D. E. and L. D. Parker (1977). Vocal virtuosity in the brown thrasher. *Auk* 94, 783–5.

Kuhl, P. K. and J. D. Miller (1978). Speech perception by the chinchilla: Identification functions for synthetic VOT stimuli. *Journal of the Acoustical Society of America* 63, 905–17.

Kuipers, A. (1968). The categories verb-noun and transitive-intransitive in English and Squamish. *Lingua* 21, 610–26.

Kuno, S. (1987). *Functional Syntax: Anaphora, Discourse and Empathy*. Chicago: University of Chicago Press.

——and K. Takami (1993). *Grammar and Discourse Principles: Functional Syntax and GB Theory*. Chicago: University of Chicago Press.

Kusters, W. (2003). *Linguistic Complexity: The Influence of Social Change on Verbal Inflection*. Utrecht, Netherlands: LOT (Landelijke Onderzoekschool Taalwetenschap). (Online at http://www.lotpublications.nl/publish/issues/Kusters/index.html.)

Kutas, M. and S. A. Hillyard (1984). Brain potentials during reading reflect word expectancy and semantic association. *Nature* 307, 161–3.

Kyllonen, P. C. and E. C. Alluisi (1987). Learning and forgetting facts and skills. In G. Salvendy (ed.), *Handbook of Human Factors*, pp. 124–53. New York: Wiley.

Laakso, A. (1993). Language equals mimesis plus speech. *Behavioral and Brain Sciences* 16(4), 765–6.

Labelle, M. (2005). The acquisition of grammatical categories: The state of the art. In H. Cohen and C. Lefebvre (eds.), *Handbook of Categorization in Cognitive Science*, pp. 433–57. Oxford: Elsevier.

Lachlan, R. F. and M. W. Feldman (2003). Evolution of cultural communication systems: the coevolution of cultural signals and genes encoding learning preferences. *Journal of Evolutionary Biology* 16(6), 1084–95.

Lahiri, A. (2000). Hierarchical restructuring in the creation of verbal morphology in Bengali and Germanic: Evidence from phonology. In A. Lahiri (ed.), *Analogy, Levelling, Markedness: Principles of Change in Phonology and Morphology*, pp. 71–123. Berlin: Mouton de Gruyter.

Lai, C., S. Fisher, J. Hurst, F. Vargha-Khadem, and P. Monaco (2001). A forkhead-domain gene is mutated in a severe speech and language disorder. *Nature* 413, 519–23.

——, D. Gerrelli, A. P. Monaco, S. E. Fisher, and A. J. Copp (2003). FOXP2 expression during brain development coincides with adult sites of pathology in a severe speech and language disorder. *Brain* 126, 2455–62.

Lakoff, G. (1987). *Women, Fire and Dangerous Things*. Chicago: Chicago University Press.

Laland, K., J. Odling-Smee, and M. W. Feldman (2000). Niche construction, biological evolution, and cultural change. *Behavioral and Brain Sciences* 23(1), 131–75.

Lambrecht, K. (1981). *Topic, Antitopic and Verb Agreement in Non-Standard French*. Amsterdam: John Benjamins.

Lampe, H. M. and G.-P. Saetre (1995). Female pied flycatchers prefer males with larger song repertoires. *Behavioral Ecology and Sociobiology* 262, 163–7.

Landau, W. and F. Kleffner (1957). Syndrome of acquired aphasia with convulsive disorder in children. *Neurology* 7, 523–530.

Lane, H. (1980). A chronology of the oppression of sign language in France and the United States. In H. Lane and F. Grosjean (eds.), *Recent Perspectives on American Sign Language*, pp. 119–61. Hillsdale, NJ: Erlbaum.

Langacker, R. W. (1987). *Foundations of Cognitive Grammar: Vol. 1, Theoretical Prerequisites*. Stanford, CA: Stanford University Press.

Langdon, M. (1970). *A Grammar of Diegueño, the Mesa Grande Dialect*. Berkeley, CA: University of California Press.

Langendoen, D. T. (1998). Limitations on embedding in coordinate structures. *Journal of Psycholinguistic Research* 27, 235–59.

LaPolla, R. J. (1992). On the dating and nature of verb agreement in Tibeto-Burman. *Bulletin of the School of Oriental and African Studies, University of London* 55(2), 298–315.

Lappin, S., R. D. Levine, and D. E. Johnson (2000). The structure of unscientific revolutions. *Natural Language & Linguistic Theory* 18(3), 665–71.

Lascarides, A. and A. Copestake (1999). Default representation in constraint-based frameworks. *Computational Linguistics* 25, 55–105.

Lashley, K. S. (1951). The problem of serial order in behavior. In L. A. Jeffress (ed.), *Cerebral Mechanisms in Behavior*, pp. 112–31. New York: John Wiley and Sons. (Reprinted in F. A. Beach, D. O. Hebb, C. T. Morgan and H. W. Nissen (eds), *The Neuropsychology of Lashley*, McGraw Hill, New York, 1960.)

Le Doux, J. E. (1983). Cerebral symmetry and the integrated function of the brain. In A. W. Young (ed.), *Functions of the Right Cerebral Hemisphere*, pp. 203–16. London: Academic Press.

Le Doux, J. E., D. H. Wilson, and M. S. Gazzaniga (1977). Manipulo-spatial aspects of cerebral lateralization: clues to the origin of lateralization. *Neuropsychologia* 15, 743–50.

Le Prell, C. G., M. D. Hauser, and D. B. Moody (2002). Discrete or graded variation within rhesus monkey screams? Psychophysical experiments on classification. *Animal Behaviour* 63(1), 47–62.

Leavens, D. A. and W. D. Hopkins (2005). Multimodal concomitants of manual gesture by chimpanzees (*Pan troglodytes*): Influence of food size and distance. *Gesture* 5(1/2), 75–90.

Lee, N., L. Mikesell, A. D. L. Joaquin, A. W. Mates, and J. H. Schumann (2009). *The Interactional Instinct: The Evolution and Acquisition of Language*. New York: Oxford University Press.

Lefebvre, C. (1998). *Creole Genesis and the Acquisition of Grammar: The Case of Haitian Creole*. Cambridge: Cambridge University Press.

——(2001a). Relexification in creole genesis and its effects on the development of the creole. In N. Smith and T. Veenstra (eds.), *Creolization and Contact*, pp. 9–42. Amsterdam: Benjamins.

——(2001b). What you see is not always what you get: Apparent simplicity and hidden complexity in creole languages. *Linguistic Typology* 5, 186–213.

——(2004). *Issues in the Study of Pidgin and Creole Languages*. Amsterdam: John Benjamins.

——(2009). The contribution of relexification, grammaticalisation, and reanalysis to creole genesis and development. In J. C. Clements and S. Gooden (eds.), *Language Change in Contact Languages*, pp. 277–311. Amsterdam: Benjamins.

Legendre, G., J. Grimshaw, and S. Vikner (eds.) (2001). *Optimality-Theoretic Syntax*. Cambridge, MA: MIT Press.

Lehmann, C. (1982). *Thoughts on Grammaticalization*. Munich: LINCOM Europa.

——(1985). Grammaticalization: Synchronic variation and diachronic change. *Lingua e Stile* 20(3), 308–18. (Page references are to the reprinting in *Morphology: Its Place in the Wider Context*, edited by Francis Katamba, Routledge, London (2004) pp. 444–58.)

Leitão, A. and K. Riebel (2003). Are good ornaments bad armaments? Male chaffinch perception of songs with varying flourish length. *Animal Behaviour* 66, 161–7.

Leonard, L. B. (1982). Is specific language impairment a useful construct? In S. Rosenberg (ed.), *Advances in Applied Psycholinguistics, Volumes 1–2*, pp. 1–39. Cambridge: Cambridge University Press.

Leonard, W. R. and M. L. Robertson (1994). Evolutionary perspectives on human nutrition: The influence of brain and body size on diet and metabolism. *American Journal of Human Biology* 6, 77–88.

——, ——, J. J. Snodgrass, and C. W. Kuzawa (2003). Metabolic correlates of hominid brain evolution. *Comparative Biochemistry and Physiology Part A: Molecular & Integrative Physiology* 136(1), 5–15.

Leonardo, A. (2002). *Neural Dynamics Underlying Complex Behavior in a Songbird*. Ph.D. thesis, California Institute of Technology.

Levelt, W. J. M. (1989). *Speaking: From Intention to Articulation.* Cambridge, MA: MIT Press.

——(1992). Accessing words in speech production: Stages, processes and representations. *Cognition* 42, 1–22.

Levin, B. (1993). *English Verb Classes and Alternations: A Preliminary Investigation.* Chicago, IL: University of Chicago Press.

Levine, R. D. and W. D. Meurers (2006). Head-Driven Phrase Structure Grammar. In E. K. Brown (ed.), *Encyclopedia of Language and Linguistics*, pp. 237–52. Oxford: Elsevier, 2nd edition.

Levinson, S. C. (1996). Frames of reference and Molyneux's question: Crosslinguistic evidence. In P. Bloom and M. Peterson (eds.), *Language and Space*, pp. 109–69. Cambridge, MA: MIT Press.

——(2003). Deixis and pragmatics. In L. R. Horn and G. Ward (eds.), *The Handbook of Pragmatics*, pp. 97–121. Malden, MA: Blackwells.

Lewin, D. (2007). *Generalized Musical Intervals and Transformations.* New York: Oxford University Press.

Lewis, D. (1969). *Convention: A Philosophical Study.* Cambridge, MA: Harvard University Press.

Li, C. N. and S. Thompson (1976). Subject and topic: A new typology of language. In C. N. Li (ed.), *Subject and Topic*, pp. 457–89. New York: Academic Press.

Li, P. and L. Gleitman (2002). Turning the tables: Language and spatial reasoning. *Cognition* 83, 265–94.

Li, W.-H. and M. Tanimura (1987). The molecular clock runs more slowly in man than in apes and monkeys. *Nature* 326, 93–6.

Liberman, M. Y. and A. Prince (1977). On stress and linguistic rhythm. *Linguistic Inquiry* 8(2), 249–336.

——and G. K. Pullum (2006). *Far from the Madding Gerund, and other Dispatches from the Language Log.* Wilsonville, OR: William James & Co.

Liddell, S. K. (1980). *American Sign Language.* The Hague: Mouton.

Lieberman, P. (1984). *The Biology and Evolution of Language.* Cambridge, MA: Harvard University Press.

——(1991). *Uniquely Human: Speech, Thought, and Selfless Behavior.* Cambridge, MA: Harvard University Press.

——(2007). The evolution of human speech: its anatomical and neural bases. *Current Anthropology* 48, 39–66.

Lieven, E. V. M., J. M. Pine, and H. D. Barnes (1992). Individual differences in early vocabulary development: Redefining the referential-expressive distinction. *Journal of Child Language* 19, 287–310.

Lightfoot, D. (1979). *Principles of Diachronic Syntax.* Cambridge: Cambridge University Press.

——(1989). The child's trigger experience: Degree-0 learnability. *Behavioral and Brain Sciences* 12, 321–3.

Lightfoot, D. (1991a). *How to Set Parameters: Arguments from Language Change.* Cambridge, MA: MIT Press.

—— (1991b). Subjacency and sex. *Language and Communication* 11(1/2), 67–9.

—— (1999). *The Development of Language: Acquisition, Change, and Evolution.* Oxford: Blackwell.

—— (2006). *How New Languages Emerge.* Cambridge: Cambridge University Press.

Linardopoulou, E. V., E. M. Williams, Y. Fan, C. Friedman, J. M. Young, and B. J. Trask (2005). Human subtelomeres are hot spots of interchromosomal recombination and segmental duplication. *Nature* 437, 94–100.

Lindauer, M. (1961). *Communication among Social Bees.* Cambridge, MA: Harvard University Press.

Linebarger, M. C. (1989). Neuropsychological evidence for linguistic modularity. In G. N. Carlson and M. K. Tanenhaus (eds.), *Linguistic Structure in Language Processing,* pp. 197–238. Dordrecht, Holland: Kluwer.

—— (1990). Neuropsychology of sentence parsing. In A. Caramazza (ed.), *Cognitive Neuropsychology and Neurolinguistics,* pp. 55–122. Hillsdale, NJ: Lawrence Erlbaum.

——, M. F. Schwartz, and E. M. Saffran (1983). Sensitivity to grammatical structure in so-called agrammatic aphasics. *Cognition* 13, 361–92.

Lock, A. and M. Colombo (1996). Cognitive abilities in a comparative perspective. In A. Lock and C. R. Peters (eds.), *Handbook of Symbolic Evolution,* pp. 596–643. Oxford: Clarendon Press.

—— and C. R. Peters (1996). Editorial introduction to Part III. In A. Lock and C. R. Peters (eds.), *Handbook of Symbolic Evolution,* pp. 371–99. Oxford: Clarendon Press.

Loewenstein, J. and D. Gentner (2005). Relational language and the development of relational mapping. *Cognitive Psychology* 50, 315–53.

Longacre, R. (1979). The paragraph as a grammatical unit. In T. Givón (ed.), *Syntax and Semantics, Volume 12, Discourse and Syntax,* pp. 115–34. New York: Academic Press.

Loomis, J. M., R. L. Klatzky, R. G. Golledge, J. G. Cicinelli, J. W. Pellegrino, and P. A. Fry (1993). Nonvisual navigation by blind and sighted: Assessment of path integration ability. *Journal of Experimental Psychology: General* 122(1), 73–91.

Lord, C. (1993). *Historical Change in Serial Verb Constructions.* Amsterdam: John Benjamins.

Lucy, J. (1992). *Grammatical Categories and Cognition: A Case Study of the Linguistic Relativity Hypothesis.* Cambridge: Cambridge University Press.

Lukatela, K., S. Crain, and D. Shankweiler (1988). Sensitivity to inflectional morphology in agrammatism: Investigation of a highly inflected language. *Brain and Language* 33(1), 1–15.

Lumsden, C. J. and E. O. Wilson (1981). *Genes, Mind and Culture: The Coevolutionary Process.* Cambridge, MA: Harvard University Press.

Lúpke, F. (2005). *A Grammar of Jalonke Argument Structure*. Ph.D. thesis, Katholieke Universiteit Nijmegen, Nijmegen.

Lupyan, G. (2005). Carving nature at its joints and carving joints into nature: How labels augment category representations. In A. Cangelosi, G. Bugmann, and R. Borisyuk (eds.), *Modelling Language, Cognition and Action: Proceedings of the 9th Neural Computation and Psychology Workshop*, pp. 87–96. Singapore: World Scientific.

——and R. Dale (2010). Language structure is partly determined by social structure. *PLoS ONE* 5(1), e8559. (Public Library of Science, online journal.)

Luria, A. R. (1968). *The Mind of a Mnemonist: A Little Book about a Vast Memory*. New York: Basic Books. (Translated from the Russian version of 1902 by Lynn Solotaroff.)

Lyn, H. and E. S. Savage-Rumbaugh (2000). Observational word learning in two bonobos (*Pan paniscus*): Ostensive and non-ostensive contexts. *Language and Communication* 20(3), 255–73.

Lyons, J. (1977). Semantics (2 vols.). Cambridge: Cambridge University Press.

McBrearty, S. and A. S. Brooks (2000). The revolution that wasn't: a new interpretation of the origin of modern human behavior. *Journal of Human Evolution* 39(5), 453–563.

McCawley, J. D.(1982). *Thirty Million Theories of Grammar*. Chicago, IL: University of Chicago Press.

——(1993). Gapping with shared operators. In J. Guenter, B. Kaiser, and C. Zoll (eds.), *Proceedings of the 19th Annual Meeting of the Berkeley Linguistics Society*, pp. 245–53. Berkeley, CA: Berkeley Linguistics Society.

MacColl, H. (1909). *Man's Origin, Destiny and Duty*. London: Williams and Norgate.

McDaniel, M. A. (2005). Big-brained people are smarter: A meta-analysis of the relationship between in vivo brain volume and intelligence. *Intelligence* 3(4), 337–46.

McDonough, L., S. Choi, and J. M. Mandler (2003). Understanding spatial relations: Flexible infants, lexical adults. *Cognitive Psychology* 46(3), 229–59.

McGrew, W. C. and L. F. Marchant (1997). On the other hand: Current issues in and meta-analysis of the behavioral laterality of hand function in nonhuman primates. *Yearbook of Physical Anthropology* 40, 201–32.

McMahon, A. (1994). *Understanding Language Change*. Cambridge: Cambridge University Press.

Macnamara, J. (1982). *Names for Things: A Study of Human Learning*. Cambridge, MA: MIT Press.

McNamara, P. and R. Durso (2000). Language functions in Parkinson's Disease: Evidence for a neurochemistry of language. In M. L. Albert, L. T. Connor, and L. K. Obler (eds.), *Neurobehavior of Language and Cognition: Studies of Normal Aging and Brain Damage: Honoring Martin L. Albert*, pp. 201–40. Dordrecht, Netherlands: Kluwer.

MacNeilage, P. F. (2008). *The Origin of Speech*. Oxford: Oxford University Press.

McNeill, D., S. B. Duncan, J. Cole, S. Gallagher, and B. Bertenthal (2008). Growth points from the very beginning. *Interaction Studies* 9(1), 117–32. (Special issue, edited by Derek Bickerton and Michael Arbib, entitled *Holophrasis, Compositionality and Protolanguage.*)

MacPhail, R. M. (1953). *An Introduction to Santali*. Benagaria, Santal Parganas, India: The Benagaria Mission Press, 2nd edition.

MacSwan, J. and K. Rolstad (2005). Modularity and the facilitation effect: Psychological mechanisms of transfer. *Hispanic Journal of Behavioral Science* 27(2), 224–243.

McWhorter, J. H. (1997). *Towards a New Model of Creole Genesis*. New York: Peter Lang.

——(1998). Identifying the Creole prototype: Vindicating a typological class. *Language* 74(4), 788–818.

——(2001a). What people ask David Gil and why: Rejoinder to the replies. *Linguistic Typology* 5, 388–412.

——(2001b). The world's simplest grammars are creole grammars. *Linguistic Typology* 5, 125–66.

Maddieson, I. (2008). Tone. In M. Haspelmath, M. S. Dryer, D. Gil, and B. Comrie (eds.), *The World Atlas of Language Structures Online*, Chapter 13. Munich: Max Planck Digital Library. (Online at http://wals.info/feature/description/13.)

Maeda, H., S. Kato, K. Kogure, and H. Iida (1988). Parsing Japanese honorifics in unification-based grammar. In *26th Annual Meeting, Proceedings*. Association for Computational Linguistics. (Online at http://www.aclweb.org/anthology/P/P88/P88-1017.pdf.)

Malkiel, Y. (1987). Integration of phonosymbolism with other categories of language change. In A. G. Ramat et al. (ed.), *Papers from the 7th International Conference on Historical Linguistics*, pp. 373–406. Amsterdam: Benjamins.

Mallery, G. (1881). *Sign Language among North American Indians Compared with that among Other Peoples and Deaf Mutes*. Washington, DC: Smithsonian Institution, Bureau of Ethnology.

Mandler, J. M. (2004). Thought before language. *Trends in Cognitive Sciences* 8(11), 509–13.

Manessy, G. (1962). Nom et verbe dans les langues mandé. *Journal of African Languages* 1(1), 57–68.

Manly, J. J., S. W. Miller, R. K. Heaton, D. Byrd, R. J. Velasquez, D. P. Saccuzzo, I. Grant, and The HIV Neurobehavioral Research Center (HNRC) Group (1998). The effect of African-American acculturation on neuropsychological test performance in normal and HIV-positive individuals. *Journal of the International Neuropsychological Society* 4, 291–302.

Manning, C. D. (2003). Probabilistic syntax. In R. Bod, J. Hay, and S. Jannedy (eds.), *Probabilistic Linguistics*, pp. 289–342. Cambridge, MA: MIT Press.

Mantel, N. (1967). The detection of disease clustering and a generalized regression approach. *Cancer Research* 27, 209–20.

Marantz, A. (1991). Case and licensing. In *ESCOL '91: Proceedings of the eighth Eastern States Conference on Linguistics*, Columbus, OH, pp. 234–53. Ohio State

University. (Reprinted in *Arguments and Case: Explaining Burzio's Generalization*, edited by E. Reuland, pp. 11–30, John Benjamins, Amsterdam, 2000.)

Marantz, A. (1995). The minimalist program. In G. Webelhuth (ed.), *Government and Binding Theory and the Minimalist Program: Principles and Parameters in Syntactic Theory*, pp. 351–81. Hoboken, NJ: Wiley.

Margoliash, D. (1997). Functional organization of forebrain pathways for song production and perception. *Journal of Neurobiology* 33(5), 671–93.

Markman, E. M. (1990). Constraints children place on word meanings. *Cognitive Science* 14(1), 57–77.

——(1992). Constraints on word learning: Speculations about their nature, origins, and domain specificity. In M. Gunnar and M. Maratsos (eds.), *Modularity and Constraints in Language and Cognition: the Minnesota Symposium on Child Psychology*, Volume 25, pp. 59–101. Erlbaum.

——and J. E. Hutchinson (1984). Children's sensitivity to constraints on word meaning: Taxonomic vs. thematic relations. *Cognitive Psychology* 16, 1–27.

——and G. F. Wachtel (1988). Children's use of mutual exclusivity to constrain the meaning of words. *Cognitive Psychology* 20, 121–57.

Marks, L. E. (1978). *The Unity of the Senses: Interrelations among the Modalities*. New York: Academic Press.

Marler, P. (1998). Animal communication and human language. In N. G. Jablonski and L. C. Aiello (eds.), *The Origin and Diversification of Language*, pp. 1–19. San Francisco, CA: California Academy of Sciences.

——(2004). Bird calls: their potential for behavioral neurobiology. *Annals of the New York Academy of Sciences* 1016, 31–44.

——and L. Hobbett (1975). Individuality in a long-range vocalisation of wild chimpanzees. *Zeitschrift für Tierpsychologie* 38, 97–109.

——and S. Peters (1981). Sparrows learn adult song and more from memory. *Science* 213, 780–2.

Marsh, R. (1967). *Comparative Sociology*. New York: Harcourt, Brace, and World.

Martin, A. (1998). Organization of semantic knowledge and the origin of words in the brain. In N. G. Jablonski and L. C. Aiello (eds.), *The Origin and Diversification of Language*, pp. 69–88. San Francisco, CA: California Academy of Sciences.

——, C. L. Wiggs, L. G. Ungerleider, and J. V. Haxby (1996). Neural correlates of category-specific knowledge. *Nature* 379, 649–52.

Marx, K. (1867). *Das Kapital: Kritik der politischen Oekonomie*. Hamburg: Verlag von Otto Meissner. (Page reference is to the Penguin Classics edition, London, 1990, *Capital: A Critique of Political Economy*.)

Matsumoto, Y. (1999). On the extension of body-part nouns to object-part nouns and spatial adpositions. In B. A. Fox, D. Jurafsky, and L. A. Michaelis (eds.), *Cognition and Function in Language*, pp. 15–28. Stanford, CA: CSLI Publications.

Matthei, E. H. and M.-L. Kean (1989). Postaccess processes in the open vs. closed class distinction. *Brain and Language* 36, 163–80.

Matthews, R. J. (2006). Knowledge of language and linguistic competence. *Philosophical Issues* 16, 200–20.

Matthey de l'Etang, A. and P. J. Bancel (2002). Tracing the ancestral kinship system: The global etymon KAKA. Part II: An anthropological study. *Mother Tongue* VII, 245–58.

——and P. J. Bancel (2005). The global distribution of (P)APA and (T)ATA and their original meaning. *Mother Tongue* IX, 133–69.

——and ——(2008). The age of Mama and Papa. In J. D. Bengtson (ed.), *In Hot Pursuit of Language in Prehistory: Essays in the Four Fields of Anthropology—in Honor of Harold Crane Fleming*, pp. 417–38. Amsterdam: John Benjamins.

Mattick, J. S. (2003). Challenging the dogma: the hidden layer of non-protein-coding RNAs in complex organisms. *BioEssays* 25, 930–9.

Maturana, H. R. and F. J. Varela (1980). *Autopoiesis and Cognition: The Realization of the Living*. Dordrecht, Holland: D. Reidel.

Maurer, D. (1993). Neonatal synesthesia: implications for the processing of speech and faces. In B. de Boysson-Bardies, S. de Schonen, P. Jusczyk, P. McNeilage, and J. Morton (eds.), *Developmental Neurocognition: Speech and Face Processing in the First Year of Life*, pp. 109–24. Dordrecht, Holland: Kluwer.

——and C. J. Mondlach (2005). Neonatal synaesthesia: A reevaluation. In L. C. Robertson and S. Sagiv (eds.), *Synaesthesia: Perspectives from Cognitive Neuroscience*, pp. 193–213. New York: Oxford University Press.

Mayberry, R. I. and E. Nicoladis (2000). Gesture reflects language development: Evidence from bilingual children. *Current Directions in Psychological Science* 9(6), 192–6.

Mayley, G. (1996). Landscapes, learning costs, and genetic assimilation. *Evolutionary Computation* 4(3), 213–234. (Special issue: *Evolutionary Competition, Evolution, Learning and Instinct: 100 Years of the Baldwin Effect*, edited by P. Turner, D. Whitely and R. Anderson.)

Maynard Smith, J. (2000). The concept of information in biology. *Philosophy of Science* 67(2), 177–94.

Mayr, E. (1976). *Evolution and the Diversity of Life: Selected Essays*. Cambridge, MA: Harvard University Press.

Mayrose, I., T. Shlomi, N. D. Rubinstein, J. M. Gershoni, E. Ruppin, R. Sharan, and T. Pupko (2007). Epitope mapping using combinatorial phage-display libraries: A graph-based algorithm. *Nucleic Acids Research* 35(1), 69–78.

Mazuka, R. (1998). *The Development of Language Processing Strategies: A Cross-Linguistic Study between Japanese and English*. Mahwah, NJ: Lawrence Erlbaum Associates.

Meillet, A. (1912). L'évolution des formes grammaticales. *Scientia (Rivista di scienza)* XII/XXVI. (Reprinted in the author's *Linguistique Historique et Linguistique Générale*, Champion, Paris, pp. 131–48, 1921).

——(1921). *Linguistique Historique et Linguistique Générale*. Paris: Champion.

——and M. Cohen (eds.) (1952). *Les Langues du Monde*. Paris: Centre International de la Recherche Scientifique.

Meir, I., C. A. Padden, M. Aronoff, and W. Sandler (2007). Body as subject. *Journal of Linguistics* 43, 531–63.

——, W. Sandler, C. A. Padden, and M. Aronoff (2010). Emerging sign languages. In M. Marschark and P. E. Spencer (eds.), *Oxford Handbook of Deaf Studies, Language, and Education*, Volume 2. Oxford: Oxford University Press.

Meisel, J. M. (1995). Parameters in acquisition. In P. Fletcher and B. MacWhinney (eds.), *The Handbook of Child Language*, pp. 10–35. Oxford: Blackwell.

Mekel-Bobrov, N., S. Gilbert, P. Evans, E. Vallender, J. Anderson, R. Hudson, S. Tishkoff, and B. Lahn (2005). Ongoing adaptive evolution of ASPM, a brain size determinant in *Homo sapiens*. *Science* 309, 1720–2.

Mel'chuk, I. A. (1979). *Studies in Dependency Syntax*. Ann Arbor, MI: Karoma.

——(1988). *Dependency Syntax: Theory and Practice*. Albany, NY: State University of New York Press.

Menn, L. (1990). Agrammatism in English: Two case studies. In L. Menn and L. K. Obler (eds.), *Agrammatic Aphasia: A Cross-Language Narrative Source Book* (3 vols), pp. 117–78. Amsterdam: John Benjamins.

Menzel, C. (2005). Progress in the study of chimpanzee recall and episodic memory. In H. S. Terrace and J. Metcalfe (eds.), *The Missing Link in Cognition: Origins of Self-Reflective Consciousness*, pp. 188–224. Oxford: Oxford University Press.

Menzel, E. W. (1972). Spontaneous invention of ladders in a group of young chimpanzees. *Folia Primatologica* 17, 87–106.

Menzel, R., U. Greggers, A. Smith, S. Berger, R. Brandt, S. Brunke, G. Bundrock, S. Hülse, T. Plümpe, F. Schaupp, E. Schüttler, S. Stach, J. Stindt, N. Stollhoff, and S. Watzl (2005). Honey bees navigate according to a map-like spatial memory. *Proceedings of the National Academy of Sciences of the U.S.A.* 102(8), 3040–5.

Merchant, J. (2004). Fragments and ellipsis. *Linguistics and Philosophy* 27, 661–738.

Meyer, A. S. (1996). Lexical access in phrase and sentence production: Results from picture-word interference experiments. *Journal of Memory and Language* 35, 477–96.

Meyer, G., A. M. Goffinet, and A. Fairén (1999). What is a Cajal-Retzius cell? A reassessment of a classical cell type based on recent observations in the developing neocortex. *Cerebral Cortex* 9(8), 765–75.

Meyerhoff, M. (2000). The emergence of creole subject–verb agreement and the licensing of null subjects. *Language Variation and Change* 12, 203–30.

——(2001). Another look at the typology of serial verb constructions: The grammaticalization of temporal relations in Bislama (Vanuatu). *Oceanic Linguistics* 40(2), 247–68.

Michaelis, L. (in press). Sign-based construction grammar. In B. Heine and H. Narrog (eds.), *The Oxford Handbook of Linguistic Analysis*, pp. 139–58. Oxford: Oxford University Press.

Miller, E. K. and J. D. Cohen (2001). An integrative theory of prefrontal cortex function. *Annual Review of Neuroscience* 24, 167–202.

Miller, G. A. (1962). Some psychological studies of grammar. *American Psychologist* 1, 748–62. (Also in Jakobovits and Miron (eds.) 1967, and De Cecco (ed.) 1967.)

——and N. Chomsky (1963). Finitary models of language users. In R. D. Luce, R. R. Bush, and E. Galanter (eds.), *Handbook of Mathematical Psychology. Volume II*, pp. 419–91. New York: John Wiley and Sons.

——and K. McKean (1964). A chronometric study of some relations between sentences. *Quarterly Journal of Experimental Psychology* 16, 297–308. (Also in Oldfield and Marshall, 1968).

——and J. A. Selfridge (1950). Verbal context and the recall of meaningful material. *The American Journal of Psychology* 63(2), 176–185. (Reprinted in Saporta (ed.) 1961.)

Miller, J. E. (2005a). Relative clauses in spoken discourse. In E. K. Brown (ed.), *Elsevier Encyclopedia of Language and Linguistics*, pp. 508–11. Oxford: Elsevier, 2nd edition, vol. 10

——(2005b). Subordination in spoken discourse. In E. K. Brown (ed.), *Elsevier Encyclopedia of Language and Linguistics*, 2nd edition, vol. 12. 255–7.

——and R. Weinert (1998). *Spontaneous Spoken Language: Syntax and Discourse*. Oxford: Oxford University Press.

Millikan, R. G. (2005). *Language: A Biological Model*. Oxford: Oxford University Press.

Milroy, L. (1980). *Language and Social Networks*. Oxford: Basil Blackwell.

Mishmar, D., E. Ruiz-Pesini, P. Golik, V. Macaulay, A. G. Clark, S. Hosseini, M. Brandon, K. Easley, E. Chen, M. D. Brown, R. I. Sukernik, A. Olckers, and D. C. Wallace (2003). Natural selection shaped regional mtDNA variation in humans. *Proceedings of the National Academy of Sciences of the U.S.A.* 100(1), 171–6.

Mitani, J. C. (1994). Social factors influencing the acoustic variability in long-distance calls of male chimpanzees. *Ethology* 96, 233–52.

——T. Hasegawa, J. Gros-Louis, P. Marler, and R. Byrne (1992). Dialects in wild chimpanzees? *American Journal of Primatology* 27, 233–43.

Mithen, S. (2005). *The Singing Neanderthals: The Origins of Music, Language, Mind, and Body*. London: Weidenfeld and Nicolson.

——(2009). Holistic communication and the co-evolution of language and music: Resurrecting an old idea. In R. Botha and C. Knight (eds.), *The Prehistory of Language*, pp. 58–76. Oxford: Oxford University Press.

Mithun, M. (1984). The evolution of noun incorporation. *Language* 60(4), 847–94.

——(1999). *The Languages of Native North America*. Cambridge: Cambridge University Press.

Molnar-Szakacs, I. and K. Overy (2006). Music and mirror neurons: from motion to 'e'motion. *Social Cognitive and Affective Neuroscience* 1(3), 235–41.

Monaghan, P. and M. H. Christiansen (2006). Iconic versus arbitrary mappings and the cultural transmission of language. In A. Cangelosi, A. D. M. Smith, and K. Smith (eds.), *The Evolution of Language*, pp. 430–1. Singapore: World Scientific.

Monaghan, P., N. Chater, and M. H. Christiansen (2005). The differential role of phonological and distributional cues in grammatical categorisation. *Cognition* 96, 143–82.

Monti, M. M., L. M. Parsons, and D. N. Osherson (2009). The boundaries of language and thought in deductive inference. *Proceedings of the National Academy of Sciences of the U.S.A.* 106(30), 12554–9.

Mooney, R. (2000). Different subthreshold mechanisms underlie song selectivity in identified HVc neurons of the zebra finch. *Journal of Neuroscience* 20, 5420–36.

——(2004). Synaptic mechanisms for auditory-vocal integration and the correction of vocal errors. *Annals of the New York Academy of Sciences* 1016, 476–94.

——, W. Hoese, and S. Nowicki (2001). Auditory representation of the vocal repertoire in a songbird with multiple song types. *Proceedings of the National Academy of Sciences of the U.S.A.* 98(22), 12778–83.

Morgan, J. L. (1975). Some interactions of syntax and pragmatics. In P. Cole and J. L. Morgan (eds.), *Syntax and Semantics, Vol. 3: Speech Acts*, pp. 289–304. New York: Academic Press.

Morrison, F., L. Smith, and M. Dow-Ehrensberger (1995). Education and cognitive development: A natural experiment. *Developmental Psychology* 31, 789–99.

Mosel, U. (1980). *Tolai and Tok Pisin: the Influence of the Substratum on the Development of New Guinea Pidgin.* Canberra: Australian National University.

——and E. Hovdhaugen (1992). *Samoan Reference Grammar.* Oslo: Universitetsforlaget AS.

Mufwene, S. S. (1986). The universalist and substrate hypotheses complement one another. In P. C. Muysken and N. Smith (eds.), *Substrata versus Universals in Creole Genesis*, pp. 129–62. Amsterdam: Benjamins.

——(1999). On the language bioprogram hypothesis: Hints from Tazie. In M. DeGraff (ed.), *Language Creation and Language Change*, pp. 95–127. Cambridge, MA: MIT Press.

——(2008). What do creoles and pidgins tell us about the evolution of language? In B. Laks, S. Cleuziou, J.-P. Demoule, and P. Encrevé (eds.), *The Origin and Evolution of Languages: Approaches, Models, Paradigms*, pp. 272–97. London: Equinox.

Mühlhäusler, P. (1986). *Pidgin and Creole Linguistics.* Oxford: Blackwell.

——(1997). *Pidgin and Creole Linguistics.* London: University of Westminster Press. (This is an enlarged and updated version of Mühlhäusler (1986).)

Müller, M. (1864). *Lectures on the Science of Language.* London: Longmans, Green. Lectures delivered at the Royal Institution of Great Britain in April, May, & June, 1861.

Murdock, G. P. (1959). Cross-language parallels in parental kin terms. *Anthropological Linguistics* 1(9), 1–5.

Murphy, C. M. and D. J. Messer (1977). Mothers, infants, and pointing: A study of gesture. In H. R. Schaffer (ed.), *Studies in Mother–Infant Interaction*, pp. 325–54. London: Academic Press.

Musso, M., A. Moro, V. Glauche, M. Rijntjes, J. Reichenbach, C. Büchel, and C. Weiller (2003). Broca's area and the language instinct. *Nature Neuroscience* 6(7), 774–81.

Muysken, P. C. (1981). Creole Tense/Mood/Aspect systems: The unmarked case? In P. Muysken (ed.), *Generative Studies on Creole Languages*, pp. 181–99. Dordrecht, Holland: Foris.

——(1988a). Are creoles a special type of language? In F. J. Newmeyer (ed.), *Linguistics: The Cambridge Survey, Vol. 2, Linguistic Theory: Extensions and Implications*, pp. 285–301. Cambridge: Cambridge University Press.

——(1988b). Parameters for serial verbs. In K. A. Demuth and V. Manfredi (eds.), *Niger-Congo Syntax and Semantics 1*, pp. 65–75. Boston, MA: Boston University.

——(2008). *Functional Categories*. Cambridge: Cambridge University Press.

Myers-Scotton, C. (2001). Implications of abstract grammatical structure: two targets in creole formation. *Journal of Pidgin and Creole Languages* 16(2), 217–73.

Narins, P. M. and R. R. Capranica (1976). Sexual differences in the auditory system of the tree frog *Eleutherodactylus coqui*. *Science* 192, 378–80.

Nater, H. F. (1984). *The Bella Coola Language*. Ottawa: National Museums of Canada. (National Museum of Man, Mercury Series, Canadian Ethnology Service, paper no. 92.)

Nelson, K. (1981). Individual differences in language development: Implications for development and language. *Developmental Psychology* 17(2), 170–87.

Nevins, A., D. M. Pesetsky, and C. Rodrigues (2009a). Evidence and argumentation: A reply to Everett (2009). *Language* 85(3), 671–81.

——, ——, and ——(2009b). Pirahã exceptionality: A reassessment. *Language* 85(2), 355–404.

Newman, S. S. (1933). Further experiments in phonetic symbolism. *American Journal of Psychology* 45, 53–75.

Newmeyer, F. J. (1998). *Language Form and Language Function*. Cambridge, MA: MIT Press.

——(2000). On the reconstructing 'Proto-World' word order. In C. Knight, M. Studdert-Kennedy, and J. R. Hurford (eds.), *The Evolutionary Emergence of Language: Social Function and the Origins of Linguistic Form*, pp. 372–88. Cambridge: Cambridge University Press.

——(2004). Some thoughts on the serial verb construction. (Paper presented at *Atelier du 9 décembre 2004, EHESS, Paris. La notion de "construction verbale en série" est-elle opératoire? Fédération TUL.* Online version at http://www.typologie.cnrs.fr/IMG/pdf/TULNewmeyer.pdf.)

——(2005). *Possible and Probable Languages*. Oxford: Oxford University Press.

Nichols, J. (1986). Head-marking and dependent-marking grammar. *Language* 62(1), 56–119.

——(1992). *Linguistic Diversity in Space and Time*. Chicago: University of Chicago Press.

——(2009). Linguistic complexity: A comprehensive definition and survey. In G. R. Sampson, D. Gil, and P. Trudgill (eds.), *Language Complexity as an Evolving Variable*, pp. 110–25. Oxford: Oxford University Press.

Nichols, J. and D. A. Peterson (2008a). M-t pronouns. In M. Haspelmath, M. S. Dryer, D. Gil, and B. Comrie (eds.), *The World Atlas of Language Structures Online*, ch. 136. Munich: Max Planck Digital Library. (Available online at http://wals.info/feature/136.)

——and D. A. Peterson (2008b). N-m pronouns. In M. Haspelmath, M. S. Dryer, D. Gil, and B. Comrie (eds.), *The World Atlas of Language Structures Online*, ch. 136. Munich: Max Planck Digital Library. (Available online at http://wals.info/feature/137.)

Nicoladis, E., R. Mayberry, and F. Genesee (1999). Gesture and early bilingual development. *Developmental Psychology* 35(2), 514–26.

Nicolis, M. (2008). The null subject parameter and correlating properties: the case of Creole languages. In T. Biberauer (ed.), *The Limits of Syntactic Variation*, pp. 271–94. Amsterdam: John Benjamins.

Nielsen, R., I. Hellmann, M. Hubisz, C. Bustamante, and A. G. Clark (2007). Recent and ongoing selection in the human genome. *Nature Reviews, Genetics* 8, 857–68.

Nietzsche, F. W. (1873). *Über Wahrheit und Lüge im aussermoralischem Sinne (On Truth and Lies in a Nonmoral Sense)*. (In *Friedrich Nietzsche: Kritische Studienausgabe*, 15 volumes, edited by Mazzino Montinari and Giorgio Colli. 1967. Walter de Gruyter, Berlin.)

——(1887). *Zur Genealogie der Moral*. (English translation by Ian C. Johnston as *On the Genealogy of Morals: A Polemical Tract*, online at http://records.viu.ca/~johnstoi/Nietzsche/genealogytofc.htm.)

Nikolaeva, I. (2007). Constructional economy and nonfinite independent clauses. In I. Nikolaeva (ed.), *Finiteness: Theoretical and Empirical Foundations*, pp. 138–80. Oxford: Oxford University Press.

Ninio, A. (2006). *Language and the Learning Curve: A New Theory of Syntactic Development*. Oxford: Oxford University Press.

Noble, W. and I. Davidson (1996). *Human Evolution, Language and Mind: a Psychological and Archaeological Inquiry*. Cambridge: Cambridge University Press.

Noonan, M. (2008). Contact-induced change: The case of the Tamangic languages. In P. Siemund and N. Kintana (eds.), *Language Contact and Contact Languages*, pp. 81–106. Amsterdam: John Benjamins.

Nordeen, K. W. and E. J. Nordeen (1992). Auditory feedback is necessary for the maintenance of stereotyped song in adult zebra finches. *Behavioral and Neural Biology* 57, 58–66.

Nordlinger, R. (2006). Spearing the emu drinking: Subordination and the adjoined relative clause in Wambaya. *Australian Journal of Linguistics* 26(1), 5–29.

Norton, H. L., R. A. Kittles, E. Parra, P. McKeigue, X. Mao, K. Cheng, V. A. Canfield, D. G. Bradley, B. McEvoy, and M. D. Shriver (2007). Genetic evidence for the convergent evolution of light skin in Europeans and East Asians. *Molecular Biology and Evolution* 24(3), 710–22.

Nottebohm, F. (1977). Asymmetries for neural control of vocalization in the canary. In S. Harnad, R. W. Doty, L. Goldstein, J. Jaynes, and G. Krauthamer. (eds.), *Lateralization in the Nervous System*, pp. 23–44. New York: Academic Press.

Nottebohm, F. and A. P. Arnold (1976). Sexual dimorphism in vocal control areas of the songbird brain. *Science* 194, 211–13.

Novoa, O. P. and A. Ardila (1987). Linguistic abilities in patients with prefrontal damage. *Brain and Language* 30(2), 206–25.

Nucifora, P. G. P., R. Verma, E. R. Melham, R. Gur, and R. C. Gur (2005). Leftward asymmetry in relative fiber density of arcuate fasciculus. *Neuroreport* 16, 791–4.

Nuckolls, J. B. (1999). The case for sound symbolism. *Annual Review of Anthropology* 28, 225–52.

Nunberg, G., I. A. Sag, and T. Wasow (1994). Idioms. *Language* 70, 491–538.

Odling-Smee, F. J., K. N. Laland, and M. W. Feldman (1996). Niche construction. *The American Naturalist* 147(4), 641–8.

——, ——, and —— (2003). *Niche Construction: The Neglected Process in Evolution.* Princeton, NJ: Princeton University Press.

Okanoya, K. (2004). The Bengalese finch: A window on the behavioral neurobiology of birdsong syntax. *Annals of the New York Academy of Sciences* 1016, 724–35.

Oldfield, R. C. and J. C. Marshall (eds.) (1968). *Language: Selected Readings.* Harmondsworth, UK: Penguin Books.

Oliphant, M. (1999). The learning barrier: Moving from innate to learned systems of communication. *Adaptive Behavior* 7(3/4), 371–84.

Orr, J. (1944). On some sound values in English. *British Journal of Psychology* 35, 1–8.

Osborne, T. (2005). Beyond the constituent: A dependency grammar analysis of chains. *Folia Linguistica* 35(3–4), 251–97.

Osterhout, L. and P. J. Holcomb (1992). Event-related brain potentials elicited by syntactic anomaly. *Journal of Memory and Language* 31, 785–806.

—— and —— (1993). Event-related potentials and syntactic anomaly: Evidence of anomaly detection during the perception of continuous speech. *Language and Cognitive Processes* 8, 413–39.

——, M. Allen, and J. McLaughlin (2002). Words in the brain: Lexical determinants of word-induced brain activity. *Journal of Neurolinguistics* 15(1–3), 171–87.

Osvath, M. (2009). Spontaneous planning for future stone throwing by a male chimpanzee. *Current Biology* 19(5), R190–R191.

—— and H. Osvath (2008). Chimpanzee (*Pan troglodytes*) and orangutan (*Pongo abelii*) forethought: Self-control and pre-experience in the face of future tool use. *Animal Cognition* 11(4), 661–74.

Ott, I., M. Schleidt, and J. Kien (1994). Temporal organisation of action in baboons: Comparisons with temporal segmentation in chimpanzee and human behaviour. *Brain Behavior and Evolution* 44(2), 101–7.

Ouattara, K., A. Lemasson, and K. Zuberbühler (2009). Campbell's monkeys concatenate vocalizations into context-specific call sequences. *Proceedings of the National Academy of Sciences of the U.S.A.* 106(51), 22026–31.

Oudeyer, P.-Y. (2006). *Self-Organization in the Evolution of Speech.* Oxford: Oxford University Press. (Translated from French *L'auto-organisation de la parole* by James R. Hurford.)

Padden, C. A., I. Meir, W. Sandler, and M. Aronoff (2010). Against all expectations: Encoding subjects and objects in a new language. In D. B. Gerdts, J. C. Moore, and M. Polinsky (eds.), *Hypothesis A/Hypothesis B: Linguistic Explorations in Honor of David M. Perlmutter*, pp. 383–400. Cambridge, MA: MIT Press.

Pagel, M. (2000a). The history, rate and pattern of world linguistic evolution. In C. Knight, M. Studdert-Kennedy, and J. R. Hurford (eds.), *The Evolutionary Emergence of Language*, pp. 391–416. Cambridge: Cambridge University Press.

——(2000b). Maximum likelihood models for glottochronology and for reconstructing linguistic phylogenies. In C. Renfrew, A. MacMahon, and L. Trask (eds.), *Time-Depth in Historical Linguistics*, pp. 189–207. Cambridge: The McDonald Institute of Archaeology.

Paivio, A. (2007). *Mind and its Evolution: A Dual Coding Theoretical Approach.* Mahwah, NJ: Lawrence Erlbaum.

Pallier, C., N. Sebastien-Gallés, E. Dupoux, A. Christophe, and J. Mehler (1998). Perceptual adjustment to time-compressed speech: A cross-linguistic study. *Memory and Cognition* 26(4), 844–51.

Papineau, D. (2005). Social learning and the Baldwin effect. In A. Zilhao (ed.), *Rationality and Evolution.* London: Routledge.

Pappert, S., J. Schliesser, D. P. Janssen, and T. Pechmann (2007). Corpus and psycholinguistic investigations of linguistic constraints on German object order. In A. Späth (ed.), *Language Context and Cognition*, pp. 299–328. Berlin: Walter de Gruyter.

Parker, A. R. (2006). *Evolution as a Constraint on Theories of Syntax: The case against Minimalism.* Ph.D. thesis, The University of Edinburgh. (Anna Parker and Anna Kinsella are the same person.)

Patterson, F. G. (1979). *Linguistic Capabilities of a Lowland Gorilla.* Ph.D. thesis, Stanford University.

Paul, H. (1920). *Prinzipien der Sprachgeschichte.* Halle an der Saale: Max Niemeyer, 5th edition.

Pawley, A. (1987). Encoding events in Kalam and English: Different logics for reporting experience. In R. S. Tomlin (ed.), *Coherence and Grounding in Discourse*, pp. 329–60. Amsterdam: John Benjamins.

——and F. H. Syder (1975). On sentence formulation in spontaneous speech. *New Zealand Speech Therapists' Journal* 30(2), 2–11.

——and ——(1976). The one-clause-at-a-time hypothesis. (Paper read at 1st Congress of New Zealand Linguistic Society, Auckland, Aug. 1976.)

——and ——(1983). Two puzzles for linguistic theory: Nativelike selection and nativelike fluency. In J. C. Richards and R. W. Schmidt (eds.), *Language and Communication*, pp. 317–31. London: Longman.

——and ——(2000). The one clause at a time hypothesis. In H. Riggenbach (ed.), *Perspectives on Fluency*, pp. 163–91. Ann Arbor, MI: University of Michigan Press.

Payne, K., P. Tyack, and R. Payne (1983). Progressive changes in the songs of *Megaptera novaeanglia*: A detailed analysis of two seasons in Hawaii. In R. Payne (ed.),

Communication and Behavior of Whales, pp. 9–57. Boulder, CO: Westview. (AAAS Selected Symposium 76.)

Payne, R. S. and S. McVay (1971). Songs of humpback whales. *Science* 173, 587–97.

Payne, T. E. (1997). *Describing Morphosyntax: A Guide for Field Linguists*. Cambridge: Cambridge University Press.

Pederson, E., E. Danziger, D. Wilkins, S. Levinson, S. Kita, and G. Senft (1998). Semantic typology and spatial conceptualization. *Language* 74, 557–88.

Peña Casanova, J., I. Bertran-Serra, A. Serra, and T. Bori (2002). Uncommonly long sequence of speech automatisms in a young woman with traumatic brain injury. *Journal of Neurolinguistics* 15, 109–28.

Penttilä, E., M. Nenonen, and J. Niemi (1998). Cultural and biological bases of idioms: A crosslinguistic study. In J. Niemi, T. Odlin, and J. Heikkinen (eds.), *Language Contact, Variation, and Change*, pp. 234–45. Joensuu, Finland: University of Joensuu.

Pepperberg, I. M. (2000). *The Alex Studies: Cognitive and Communicative Abilities of Grey Parrots*. Cambridge, MA: Harvard University Press.

—— and S. E. Wilcox (2000). Evidence for a form of mutual exclusivity during labelling by grey parrots (*Psittacus erithacus*). *Journal of Comparative Psychology* 110, 286–97.

Perkins, R. D. (1980). *The Evolution of Culture and Grammar*. Ph.D. thesis, State University of New York, Buffalo.

—— (1992). *Deixis, Grammar and Culture*. Amsterdam: John Benjamins.

Perruchet, P. and A. Rey (2005). Does the mastery of center-embedded linguistic structures distinguish humans from nonhuman primates? *Psychonomic Bulletin and Review* 12(2), 307–13.

Perry, G. H., N. J. Dominy, K. G. Claw, A. S. Lee, H. Fiegler, R. Redon, J. Werner, F. A. Villanea, J. L. Mountain, R. Misra, N. P. Carter, C. Lee, and A. C. Stone (2007). Diet and the evolution of human amylase gene copy number variation. *Nature Genetics* 39(1), 1256–60.

Pesetsky, D. (2005). *Zero Syntax*. Cambridge, MA: MIT Press.

Peters, A. M. (1977). Language learning strategies: Does the whole equal the sum of the parts? *Language* 53(3), 560–73.

—— (1983). *Units of Language Acquisition*. Cambridge: Cambridge University Press.

Peters, S. and R. Ritchie (1973). On the generative power of transformational grammars. *Information Sciences* 6, 49–83.

——, W. A. Searcy, M. D. Beecher, and S. Nowicki (2000). Geographic variation in the organization of Song Sparrow repertoires. *The Auk* 117(4), 936–42.

Petersen, M. R., M. D. Beecher, S. R. Zoloth, D. B. Moody, and W. C. Stebbins (1978). Neural lateralization of species-specific vocalizations by Japanese macaques (*Macaca fuscata*). *Science* 202, 324–7.

Petkov, C. I., C. Kayser, T. Steudel, K. Whittingstall, M. Augath, , and N. K. Logothet (2008). A voice region in the monkey brain. *Nature Neuroscience* 11(3), 367–74.

Pfaff, J. A., L. Zanette, S. A. MacDougall-Shackleton, and E. A. MacDougall-Shackleton (2007). Song repertoire size varies with HVC volume and is indicative of male quality in song sparrows (*Melospiza melodia*). *Proceedings of the Royal Society, B* (published online).

Phillips, C. and M. Wagers (2006). Constituent structure and the binding problem. *Behavioral and Brain Sciences* 29(1), 81–2.

Piaget, J. (1973). *The Child's Conception of the World*. St Albans, UK: Granada Publishing Ltd. (Paladin Imprint).

Pickering, M. J. and H. P. Branigan (1998). The representation of verbs: Evidence from syntactic priming in language production. *Journal of Memory and Language* 39, 633–51.

Pienemann, M. (2005). An introduction to processability theory. In M. Pienemann (ed.), *Cross-linguistic Aspects of Processability Theory*, pp. 1–60. Amsterdam: John Benjamins.

Pigliucci, M. and C. J. Murren (2003). Perspective: Genetic assimilation and a possible evolutionary paradox: Can macroevolution be so fast as to pass us by? *Evolution* 57(7), 1455–64.

Pika, S., K. Liebal, J. Call, and M. Tomasello (2005). The gestural communication of apes. *Gesture* 5(1/2), 41–56.

Pinker, S. and R. S. Jackendoff (2005). The faculty of language: What's special about it? *Cognition* 95(2), 201–36.

Pizzuto, E. and M. Capobianco (2005). The link (and differences) between deixis and symbols in children's early gestural-vocal system. *Gesture* 5, 175–99.

Plomin, R. and J. C. DeFries (1998). The genetics of cognitive abilities and disabilities. *Scientific American* 278(5), 62–9. (Reprinted in *The Nature–nurture Debate: The Essential Readings* edited by Stephen J. Ceci and Wendy Melissa Williams. Oxford: Blackwells, (1999) pp.178–96. Page reference is to the reprinted version.)

Ploog, D. (1981). Neurobiology of primate audio-vocal behavior. *Brain Research Reviews* 3, 35–61.

Podos, J., S. Peters, T. Rudnicky, P. Marler, and S. Nowicki (1992). The organization of song repertoires in song sparrows: Themes and variations. *Ethology* 90, 89–106.

Poizner, H. and P. Tallal (1987). Temporal processing in deaf signers. *Brain and Language* 30, 52–62.

Pollard, C. J. and I. A. Sag (1987). *Information-Based Syntax and Semantics, Volume 1, Fundamentals*. Stanford, CA: Center for the Study of Language and Information (CSLI).

——and —— (1994). *Head-Driven Phrase Structure Grammar*. Chicago: University of Chicago Press.

Pollard, K. S. (2009). What makes us human? *Scientific American* 300(5), 44–9.

——, S. R. Salama, B. King, A. D. Kern, T. Dreszer, S. Katzman, A. Siepel, J. S. Pedersen, G. Bejerano, R. Baertsch, K. R. Rosenbloom, J. Kent, and D. Haussler (2006a). Forces shaping the fastest evolving regions in the human genome. *PLoS Genetics* 2(10), e168. (Public Library of Science, online journal.)

Pollard, K. S., S. R. Salama, N. Lambert, M. A. Lambot, S. Coppens, J. S. Pedersen, S. Katzman, B. King, C. Onodera, A. Siepel, A. D. Kern, C. Dehay, H. Igel, M. J. Ares, P. Vanderhaeghen, and D. Haussler (2006b). An RNA gene expressed during cortical development evolved rapidly in humans. *Nature* 443, 167–72.

Pollick, A. S. and F. B. M. de Waal (2007). Ape gestures and language evolution. *Proceedings of the National Academy of Sciences of the U.S.A.* 104, 8184–9.

Pöppel, E. (1978). Time perception. In R. Held, H. Leibowitz, and H.-L. Teuber (eds.), *Handbook of Sensory Physiology*, vol. VIII, pp. 713–29. Heidelberg: Springer.

——(1997). A hierarchical model of temporal perception. *Trends in Cognitive Sciences* 1(2), 56–61.

——and M. Wittmann (1999). Time in the mind. In R. A. Wilson and F. Keil (eds.), *The MIT Encyclopedia of the Cognitive Sciences*, pp. 841–3. Cambridge, MA: MIT Press.

Poremba, A., M. Malloy, R. C. Saunders, R. E. Carson, P. Herscovitch, and M. Mishkin (2004). Species-specific calls evoke asymmetric activity in the monkey's temporal poles. *Nature* 427, 448–51.

Post, E. (1943). Formal reductions of the general combinatorial decision problem. *American Journal of Mathematics* 65, 197–215.

Postal, P. M. (1966). On so-called 'pronouns' in English. In F. Dinneen (ed.), *Report on the Seventeenth Annual Round Table Meeting on Linguistics and Language Studies*, pp. 177–206. Washington, DC: Georgetown University Press.

——(1974). *On Raising*. Cambridge, MA: MIT Press.

Posthuma, D., E. J. C. De Geus, W. F. C. Baaré, H. E. Hulshoff Pol, R. S. Kahn, and D. I. Boomsma (2002). The association between brain volume and intelligence is of genetic origin. *Nature Neuroscience* (2), 83–4.

Postma, A. and H. Kolk (1993). The covert repair hypothesis: Prearticulatory repair processes in normal and stuttered disfluencies. *Journal of Speech and Hearing Research* 36, 472–87.

Powers, S. (1995). The acquisition of case in Dutch. In M. Verrips and F. Wijnen (eds.), *Proceedings From the Dutch-German Colloquium on Language Acquisition, Amsterdam Series in Child Language Development*. Amsterdam: Institute for General Linguistics, University of Amsterdam.

Prabhakar, S., A. Visel, J. A. Akiyama, M. Shoukry, K. D. Lewis, A. Holt, I. Plajzer-Frick, H. Morrison, D. R. FitzPatrick, V. Afzal, L. A. Pennacchio, E. M. Rubin, and J. P. Noonan (2008). Human-specific gain of function in a developmental enhancer. *Science* 321, 1346–50.

Prather, J. F., S. Peters, S. Nowicki, and R. Mooney (2008). Precise auditory-vocal mirroring in neurons for learned vocal communication. *Nature* 451, 305–10.

Preissl, H., F. Pulvermüller, W. Lutzenberger, and N. Birbaumer (1995). Evoked potentials distinguish between nouns and verbs. *Neuroscience Letters* 198(1), 81–3.

Premack, A. J. and D. Premack (1972). Teaching language to an ape. *Scientific American* 227(4), 92–9.

Premack, D. (1976). *Intelligence in Ape and Man*. Hillsdale, NJ: Erlbaum.

Prince, A. and P. Smolensky (2004). *Optimality Theory: Constraint Interaction in Generative Grammar*. Oxford: Blackwell Publishers.

Progovac, L. (2009). Layering of grammar: Vestiges of protosyntax in present-day languages. In G. Sampson, D. Gil, and P. Trudgill (eds.), *Language Complexity as an Evolving Variable*, pp. 203–12. Oxford: Oxford University Press.

Pullum, G. K. (1989). The great Eskimo vocabulary hoax. *Natural Language and Linguistic Theory* 7, 275–281. (Reprinted in Pullum, 1991, pp. 159–71.)

——(1991). *The Great Eskimo Vocabulary Hoax, and other Irreverent Essays on the Study of Language*. Chicago: Chicago University Press.

——and B. C. Scholz (2010a). For universals (but not for finite-state learning) visit the zoo. *Behavioral and Brain Sciences* 32(5), 466–7.

——and ——(2010b). Recursion and the infinitude claim. In H. van der Hulst (ed.), *Recursion in Human Language*, pp. 113–38. Berlin: Mouton de Gruyter.

Pulman, S. G. (1985). A parser that doesn't. In *Proceedings of the 2nd European Meeting of the Association for Computational Linguistics, Geneva, ACL*, pp. 128–35. (Available online at http://www.clg.ox.ac.uk/pulman/ pdfpapers/acl85.pdf.)

Pulvermüller, F. (2002). *The Neuroscience of Language*. Cambridge: Cambridge University Press.

——and Y. Shtyrov (2009). Spatiotemporal signatures of large-scale synfire chains for speech processing as revealed by MEG. *Cerebral Cortex* 19(1), 79–88.

——, B. Mohr, and H. Schleichert (1999). Semantic or lexico-syntactic factors: what determines word-class specific activity in the human brain? *Neuroscience Letters* 275(2), 81–4.

Pustet, R. (2008). Discourse frequency and the collapse of the adposition vs. affix distinction in Lakota. In E. Seoane and M. J. López-Couso (eds.), *Theoretical and Empirical Issues in Grammaticalization*, pp. 269–92. Amsterdam: John Benjamins.

Putnam, H. (1975). The meaning of "Meaning". In K. Gunderson (ed.), *Language, Mind and Knowledge*, pp. 131–93. University of Minnesota Press.

Pylyshyn, Z. W. (2000). Situating vision in the world. *Trends in Cognitive Sciences* 4(5), 197–207.

Quine, W. V. O. (1960). *Word and Object*. Cambridge, MA: MIT Press.

Quinn, M. (2001). Evolving communication without dedicated communication channels. In J. Kelemen and P. Sosík (eds.), *Advances in Artificial Life: Proceedings of the 6th European Conference on Artifical Life, Prague, September 2001*, pp. 357–66. Berlin: Springer-Verlag.

Radford, A. (1995). Phrase structure and functional categories. In P. Fletcher and B. MacWhinney (eds.), *The Handbook of Child Language*, pp. 483–507. Oxford: Blackwell.

——(1997). *Syntactic Theory and the Structure of English: A Minimalist Approach*. Cambridge: Cambridge University Press.

——(2004). *Minimalist Syntax: Exploring the Structure of English*. Cambridge: Cambridge University Press.

Radnikow, G., D. Feldmeyer, and J. Lüke (2002). Axonal projection, input and out-put synapses, and synaptic physiology of Cajal-Retzius cells in the developing rat neocortex. *The Journal of Neuroscience* 22(16), 6908–19.

Ragir, S. (2002). Constraints on communities with indigenous sign languages: Clues to the dynamics of language origins. In A. Wray (ed.), *The Transition to Language*, pp. 272–94. Oxford: Oxford University Press.

Raible, W. (2001). Language universals and language typology. In M. Haspelmath (ed.), *Language Typology and Language Universals, An International Handbook, Volume 1. Sprachtypologie und Sprachliche Universalien, Ein Internationales Handbuch, 1 Halbband. Typologie des Langues et Universaux Linguistiques, Manuel International, Tome 1*, pp. 1–24. Berlin: de Gruyter.

Ramachandran, V. S. and E. M. Hubbard (2001). Synaesthesia—a window into per-ception, thought and language. *Journal of Consciousness Studies* 8(12), 3–34.

Rapp, B. and A. Caramazza (1998). A case of selective difficulty in writing verbs. *Neurocase* 4, 127–40.

——and ——(2002). Selective difficulties with spoken nouns and written verbs: A single case study. *Journal of Neurolinguistics* 15(3–5), 373–402.

Raup, D. M. (1991). *Extinction: Bad Genes or Bad Luck?* Oxford: Oxford University Press.

Raz, N., I. J. Torres, W. D. Spencer, D. Millman, J. C. Baertschi, and G. Sarpel (1993). Neuroanatomical correlates of age-sensitive and age-invariant cognitive abilities: An in vivo MRI investigation. *Intelligence* 17(3), 407–22.

Reader, S. M. and K. N. Laland (2002). Social intelligence, innovation, and enhanced brain size in primates. *Proceedings of the National Academy of Sciences of the U.S.A.* 99(7), 4436–41.

Reali, F. and T. L. Griffiths (2009). The evolution of frequency distributions: Relating regularization to inductive biases through iterated learning. *Cognition* 111, 317–28.

Rendell, L. and H. Whitehead (2004). Do sperm whales share coda vocalizations? Insights into coda usage from acoustic size measurement. *Animal Behaviour* 67, 865–74.

Ressel, V., M. Wilke, K. Lidzba, W. Lutzenberger, and I. Krägeloh-Mann (2008). Increases in language lateralization in normal children as observed using magne-toencephalography. *Brain and Language* 106(3), 167–76.

Reznikova, Z. (2007). Dialog with black box: Using Information Theory to study animal language behaviour. *Acta Ethologica* 10(1), 1–12.

——and B. Y. Ryabko (1986). Analysis of the language of ants by information-theoretical methods. *Problems of Information Transmission* 22(3), 245–9.

Rice, M. L., K. Wexler, and P. L. Cleave (1995). Specific language impairment as a period of extended optional infinitive. *Journal of Speech, Language, and Hearing Research* 38(4), 850–63.

——, J. B. Tomblin, L. Hoffman, W. A. Richman, and J. Marquis (2004). Grammatical tense deficits in children with SLI and nonspecific language impairment: Relation-ships with nonverbal IQ over time. *Journal of Speech, Language, and Hearing Research* 47, 816–34.

——, L. Hoffman, and K. Wexler (2009a). Judgments of omitted BE and DO in questions as extended finiteness clinical markers of specific language impairment (SLI) to 15 years: A study of growth and asymptote. *Journal of Speech, Language, and Hearing Research* 52, 1417–33.

——, S. D. Smith, and J. Gayán (2009b). Convergent genetic linkage and associations to language, speech and reading measures in families of probands with Specific Language Impairment. *Journal of Neurodevelopmental Disorders*. (Online publication, August 2009.)

Richerson, P. J. and R. Boyd (2005). *Not by Genes Alone: How Culture Transformed Human Evolution*. Chicago: University of Chicago Press.

Riebel, K. and P. J. B. Slater (1998). Testing female chaffinch song preferences by operant conditioning. *Animal Behaviour* 56, 1443–53.

—— and —— (2003). Temporal variation in male chaffinch song depends on the singer and the song type. *Behaviour* 140(2), 269–88.

Rijkhoff, J. (2003). When can a language have nouns and verbs? *Acta Linguistica Hafniensa* 35, 7–38.

Riley, J. R., U. Greggers, A. D. Smith, D. R. Reynolds, and R. Menzel (2005). The flight paths of honeybees recruited by the waggle dance. *Nature* 435, 205–7.

Rilling, J. K. and R. A. Seligman (2002). A quantitative morphometric comparative analysis of the primate temporal lobe. *Journal of Human Evolution* 42(5), 505–33.

——, M. F. Glasser, T. M. Preuss, X. Ma, T. Zhao, X. Hu, and T. E. J. Behrens (2008). The evolution of the arcuate fasciculus revealed with comparative DTI. *Nature Neuroscience* 11(4), 426–8.

Rispoli, M. (1994). Pronoun case overextensions and paradigm building. *Journal of Child Language* 21, 157–72.

Rissanen, J. (1978). Modeling by shortest data description. *Automatica* 14, 465–71.

—— (1989). *Stochastic Complexity in Statistical Enquiry*. Singapore: World Scientific Publishing.

Rizzi, L. (2009). Some elements of syntactic computation. In D. Bickerton and E. Szathmáry (eds.), *Biological Foundations and Origin of Syntax*, pp. 63–87. Cambridge, MA: MIT Press.

Rizzolatti, G. and M. A. Arbib (1998). Language within our grasp. *Trends in Neuroscience* 21, 188–94.

——, L. Fadiga, V. Gallese, and L. Fogassi (1996a). Premotor cortex and the recognition of motor actions. *Cognitive Brain Research* 3(2), 131–41.

——, L. Fadiga, M. Matelli, E. Bettinardi, V. Paulesu, D. Perani, and F. Fazio (1996b). Localization of grasp representations in humans by PET, I: Observation versus execution. *Experimental Brain Research* 111, 246–52.

——, L. Fogassi, and V. Gallese (2001). Neurophysiological mechanisms underlying the understanding and imitation of action. *Nature Reviews Neuroscience* 2, 661–70.

Roberts, S. J. (2000). Nativization and the genesis of Hawaiian Creole. In J. McWhorter (ed.), *Language Change and Language Contact in Pidgins and Creoles*, pp. 257–300. Amsterdam: John Benjamins.

Robinson, B. W. (1967). Vocalization evoked from forebrain in *Macaca mulatta*. *Physiology and Behavior* 2, 345–54.

Röder, B., O. Stock, H. Neville, S. Bien, and F. Rösler (2002). Brain activation modulated by the comprehension of normal and pseudo-word sentences of different processing demands: A functional magnetic resonance imaging study. *NeuroImage* 15, 1003–14.

Rogers, J. and G. K. Pullum (2007). Aural pattern recognition experiments and the subregular hierarchy. (This paper apparently fell through a crack while *UCLA Working Papers in Linguistics* was being reorganized. It is available online at http://www.cs.earlham.edu/⌐jrogers/mol10.pdf.)

Rogers, L. J. and R. Andrew (2002). *Comparative Vertebrate Lateralization*. Oxford: Oxford University Press.

Romaine, S. (1992). *Language, Education, and Development: Urban and Rural Tok Pisin in Papua New Guinea*. Oxford: Oxford University Press.

Rose, G. J., F. Goller, H. J. Gritton, S. L. Plamondon, A. T. Baugh, and B. G. Cooper (2004). Species-typical songs in white-crowned sparrows tutored with only phrase pairs. *Nature* 432, 753–8.

Rosen, S. T. (1989). Two types of noun incorporation: A lexical analysis. *Language* 65(2), 294–317.

Ross, J. R. (1967). *Constraints on Variables in Syntax*. Ph.D. thesis, MIT. (Published as Ross, 1986.)

——(1970a). Gapping and the order of constituents. In M. Bierwisch and K. E. Heidolph (eds.), *Progress in Linguistics*, pp. 249–59. The Hague: Mouton.

——(1970b). On declarative sentences. In R. A. Jacobs and P. S. Rosenbaum (eds.), *Readings in English Transformational Grammar*, pp. 222–72. Waltham, MA: Ginn.

——(1975). Where to do things with words. In P. Cole and J. L. Morgan (eds.), *Syntax and Semantics, Volume 3: Speech Acts*, pp. 233–56. New York: Academic Press.

——(1986). *Infinite Syntax!* Norwood, NJ: ABLEX.

Ross, M. (2007). Calquing and metatypy. *Journal of Language Contact THEMA* 1, 116–43.

Rubba, J. (1994). Grammaticalization as semantic change. In W. Pagliuca (ed.), *Perspectives on Grammaticalization*, pp. 81–101. Amsterdam: John Benjamins.

Ruff, C. B., E. Trinkaus, and T. W. Holliday (1997). Body mass and encephalization in Pleistocene *Homo*. *Nature* 387, 173–6.

Ruhlen, M. (1994). *The Origin of Language: Tracing the Evolution of the Mother Tongue*. New York: John Wiley & Sons.

——(2005). Taxonomy, typology and historical linguistics. In J. W. Minett and W. S. Wang (eds.), *Language Acquisition, Change and Emergence: Essays in Evolutionary Linguistics*, pp. 341–68. Hong Kong: City University of Hong Kong.

Ruiz-Pesini, E., D. Mishmar, M. Brandon, V. Procaccio, and D. C. Wallace (2004). Effects of purifying and adaptive selection on regional variation in human mtDNA. *Science* 303, 223–6.

Rumbaugh, D. M. and T. Gill (1977). Language and language-type communication: Studies with a chimpanzee. In M. Lewis and L. Rosenblum (eds.), *Interaction, Conversation and the Development of Language*, pp. 115–31. New York: John Wiley and Son.

Russell, G., J. Carroll, and S. Warwick-Armstrong (1991). Multiple default inheritance in a unification-based lexicon. In *Proceedings of the 29th Annual Meeting of the Association for Computational Linguistics*, Berkeley, California, USA, pp. 215–21. Association for Computational Linguistics.

Sabeti, P. C., S. F. Schaffner, B. Fry, J. Lohmueller, P. Varilly, O. Shamovsky, A. Palma, T. S. Mikkelsen, D. Altshuler, and E. S. Lander (2006). Positive natural selection in the human lineage. *Science* 312, 1614–20.

——, P. Varilly, B. Fry, J. Lohmueller, E. Hostetter, C. Cotsapas, X. Xie, E. H. Byrne, S. A. McCarroll, R. Gaudet, S. F. Schaffner, E. S. Lander, and The International HapMap Consortium (2007). Genome-wide detection and characterization of positive selection in human populations. *Nature* 449, 913–18.

Sachs, J. S. (1967). Recognition memory for syntactic and semantic aspects of connected discourse. *Perception and Psychophysics* 2, 437–42.

Sacks, H., E. Schegloff, and G. Jefferson (1974). A simplest systematics for the organization of turn-taking for conversation. *Language* 50, 696–735.

Saffran, E. M. and M. F. Schwartz (1994). Of cabbages and things: Semantic memory from a neuropsychological perspective—a tutorial review. In C. Umiltà and M. Moscovitch (eds.), *Attention and Performance XV: Conscious and Unconscious Processes*, pp. 507–35. Cambridge, MA: MIT Press.

Sag, I. A. (2007). Sign-based construction grammar: An informal synopsis. (Unpublished paper from Stanford University, available online at http://lingo.stanford.edu/sag/papers/theo-syno.pdf.)

——, T. Wasow, and E. M. Bender (2003). *Syntactic Theory: A Formal Introduction*. Stanford, CA: CSLI Publications. 2nd edition.

Sakel, J. (in preparation). *Dictionary Pirahã–English–Portuguese*.

Sampson, G. R. (1995). *English for the Computer: The SUSANNE Corpus and Analytic Scheme*. Oxford: Clarendon Press.

——(2005). *The Language Instinct Debate*. London: Continuum. (Revised edition of *Educating Eve: The 'Language Instinct' Debate*, by G. R. Sampson, (1997), Cassell, London.)

Sampson, R. J., P. Sharkey, and S. W. Raudenbush (2008). Durable effects of concentrated disadvantage on verbal ability among African-American children. *Proceedings of the National Academy of Sciences of the U.S.A.* 105(3), 845–52.

Samson, D. and A. Pillon (2003). A case of impaired knowledge for fruit and vegetables. *Cognitive Neuropsychology* 20(3–6), 373–400.

Sander, K. and H. Scheich (2001). Auditory perception of laughing and crying activates human amygdala regardless of attentional state. *Cognitive Brain Research* 12(2), 181–98.

Sandler, W., I. Meir, C. A. Padden, and M. Aronoff (2005). The emergence of grammar: Systematic structure in a new language. *Proceedings of the National Academy of Sciences of the U.S.A.* 102(7), 2661–5.

Sankoff, G. (1994). An historical and evolutionary approach to variation in the Tok Pisin verb phrase. In K. Beals, J. Denton, R. Knippen, L. Melnar, H. Suzuki, and E. Zeinfeld (eds.), *CLS 30 Papers from the 30th regional meeting of the Chicago Linguistic Society. 1994. Volume 2: The parasession on variation in linguistic theory*, pp. 293–320. Chicago: Chicago Linguistic Society.

Sapir, E. (1911). Diminutive and augmentative consonantism in Wishram. In *Handbook of American Indian Languages*, pp. 638–46. Washington, DC: BAE Bulletin 40, Part 1.

——(1921). *Language: An Introduction to the Study of Speech*. New York: Harcourt, Brace & Co.

——(1929). A study in phonetic symbolism. *Journal of Experimental Psychology* 12, 225–39.

——(1949). A study in phonetic symbolism. In D. G. Mandelbaum (ed.), *Selected Writings of Edward Sapir*, pp. 61–72. Berkeley, CA: University of California Press.

Saporta, S. (ed.) (1961). *Psycholinguistics: A Book of Readings*. New York: Holt, Rinehart and Winston.

Sasse, H.-J. (1993). Syntactic categories and subcategories. In J. Jacobs, A. von Stechow, W. Sternefeld, and T. Vennemann (eds.), *Syntax: An International Handbook of Contemporary Research*, pp. 646–86. Berlin: Walter de Gruyter.

Saussure, F. d. (1959). *Course in General Linguistics*. New York: The Philosophical Library. (Translated by Wade Baskin from Saussure's *Cours de Linguistique Générale*, 1916, Paris: Payot.)

Savage, C., E. Lieven, A. Theakston, and M. Tomasello (2003). Testing the abstractness of young children's linguistic representations: Lexical and structural priming of syntactic constructions? *Developmental Science* 6(5), 557–67.

Savage-Rumbaugh, E. S. (1986). *Ape Language: From Conditioned Response to Symbol*. New York: Columbia University Press.

——(1990). Language acquisition in a nonhuman species: Implications for the innateness debate. *Developmental Psychobiology* 23(7), 599–620.

——(1999). Ape language: Between a rock and a hard place. In B. J. King (ed.), *The Origins of Language: What Nonhuman Primates can Tell us*, pp. 115–88. Santa Fe, NM: School of American Research Press.

——and K. E. Brakke (1996). Animal language: Methodological and interpretive issues. In M. Bekoff and D. Jamieson (eds.), *Readings in Animal Cognition*, pp. 269–88. Cambridge, MA: MIT Press.

——, D. M. Rumbaugh, and S. Boysen (1978). Symbolization, language and chimpanzees: A theoretical reevaluation based on initial language acquisition processes in four young *Pan troglodytes*. *Brain and Language* 6(3), 265–300.

——, D. M. Rumbaugh, S. T. Smith, and J. Lawson (1980). Reference: The linguistic essential. *Science* 210, 922–5.

Savage-Rumbaugh, E. S., J. Murphy, R. A. Sevcik, K. E. Brakke, S. L. Williams, D. M. Rumbaugh, and E. Bates (1993). *Language Comprehension in Ape and Child.* Society for Research in Child Development. (*Monographs of the Society for Research in Child Development*, vol. 58, No. 3/4.)

Savin, H. and E. Perchonock (1965). Grammatical structure and the immediate recall of English sentences. *Journal of Verbal Learning and Verbal Behavior* 4, 348–53.

Scaife, M. and J. S. Bruner (1975). The capacity for joint visual attention in the infant. *Nature* 253, 265–6.

Scarnà, A. and A. W. Ellis (2002). On the assessment of grammatical gender knowledge in aphasia: The danger of relying on explicit, metalinguistic tasks. *Language and Cognitive Processes* 17(2), 185–201.

Schachter, P. (1985). Part of speech systems. In T. Shopen (ed.), *Language Typology and Syntactic Description, Vol. 1: Clause Structure*, pp. 3–61. Cambridge: Cambridge University Press.

Schaller, S. (1995). *A Man without Words.* Berkeley, CA: University of California Press.

Scharff, C. and F. Nottebohm (1991). A comparative study of behavioral deficits following lesions of various parts of the zebra finch song system: Implications for vocal learning. *Journal of Neuroscience* 11, 2896–913.

Schegloff, E. (1996). Turn organization: One intersection of grammar and interaction. In E. Ochs, E. Schegloff, and S. Thompson (eds.), *Interaction and Grammar*, pp. 52–133. Cambridge: Cambridge University Press.

Schenker, N. M., A.-M. Desgouttes, and K. Semendeferi (2005). Neural connectivity and cortical substrates of cognition in hominoids. *Journal of Human Evolution* 49(5), 547–69.

Schirmer, A. and S. Kotz (2006). Beyond the right hemisphere: Brain mechanisms mediating vocal emotional processing. *Trends in Cognitive Science* 10, 24–30.

Schleicher, A. (1850). *Die Sprachen Europas in systematischer Übersicht: Linguistische Untersuchungen.* Bonn: H. B. König. (Facsimile edition edited and with an introduction by E. F. K. Koerner, published by John Benjamins, Amsterdam (1983).)

——(1863). *Die Darwinsche Theorie und die Sprachwissenschaft. Offenes Sendschreiben an Herrn Dr. Ernst Häckel, a.o. Professor der Zoologie.* Weimar: Hermann Böhlau. (Page references are to the reprint of the English translation (*Darwinism Tested by the Science of Language*, translated by Alex V. W. Bikkers, published by John Camden Hotten, London, 1869); reprinted in *Linguistics and Evolutionary Theory: Three Essays by August Schleicher, Ernst Haeckel, and Wilhelm Bleek*, edited by Konrad Koerner, John Benjamins, Amsterdam (1983).).

Schleidt, M. and J. Kien (1997). Segmentation and what it can tell us about brain function. *Human Nature* 8(1), 77–111.

Schlichter, A. (1981). *Wintu Dictionary. Survey of California and Other Indian Languages.* Berkeley, CA: University of California Press.

Schmidt, J. (1872). *Die Verwandtschaftsverhältnisse der Indogermanischen Sprachen.* Weimar: Böhlau.

Schmidtke-Bode, K. (in press). The performance basis of grammatical constraints on complex sentences: A preliminary survey. In V. Gast and H. Diessel (eds.), *Clause Combining in Cross-Linguistic Perspective*. Berlin: Mouton de Gruyter.

Schoenemann, P. T. (2005). Conceptual complexity and the brain: Understanding language origins. In J. W. Minett and W. S. Wang (eds.), *Language Acquisition, Change and Emergence: Essays in Evolutionary Linguistics*, pp. 47–94. Hong Kong: City University of Hong Kong Press.

——(2006). Evolution of the size and functional areas of the human brain. *Annual Review of Anthropology* 35, 379–406.

——, M. J. Sheehan, and L. D. Glotzer (2005). Prefrontal white matter volume is disproportionately larger in humans than in other primates. *Nature Neuroscience* 8, 242–52.

Scholz, B. C. and G. K. Pullum (2007). Review of *Tracking the Origins of Transformational Generative Grammar* by Marcus Tomalin, Cambridge University Press, Cambridge, 2006. *Journal of Linguistics* 43, 701–23.

Schourup, L. (1985). *Common Discourse Particles*. New York: Garland.

Schuchardt, H. (1868). *Vokalismus*, Vol.3. Leipzig: Teubner.

Schulz, G. M., M. Varga, K. Jeffires, C. L. Ludlow, and A. R. Braun (2005). Functional neuroanatomy of human vocalization: An $H_2^{15}O$ PET study. *Cerebral Cortex* 15(12), 1835–47.

Schumann, J. H. (1978). *The Pidginization Process: a Model for Second Language Acquisition*. Rowley, MA: Newbury House.

——(2007). A linguistics for the evolution and neurobiology of language. *Journal of English Linguistics* 35(3), 278–87.

Schütze, C. T. (1996). *The Empirical Base of Linguistics: Grammaticality Judgments and Linguistic Methodology*. Chicago: University of Chicago Press.

——(2001). On the nature of default case. *Syntax* 4(3), 205–38.

Schwartz, M. F. (1995). Re-examining the role of executive functions in routine action production. *Annals of the New York Academy of Sciences* 769, 321–35.

Scott-Phillips, T. (2010). The evolution of communication: Humans may be exceptional. *Interaction Studies* 11(1), 119–40.

——, S. Kirby, and G. R. S. Ritchie (2009). Signalling signalhood and the emergence of communication. *Cognition* 113(2), 226–33.

——, J. R. Hurford, G. Roberts, and S. Roberts (2010). Pragmatics not semantics as the basis for clause structure. In A. D. M. Smith, B. de Boer, M. Schouwstra, and K. Smith (eds.), *The Evolution of Language (EVOLANG 8)*. Singapore: World Scientific.

Searcy, W. A. and P. Marler (1981). A test for responsiveness to song structure and programming in song sparrows. *Science* 213, 926–8.

——, J. Podos, S. Peters, and S. Nowicki (1995). Discrimination of song types and variants in song sparrows. *Animal Behaviour* 49(5), 1219–26.

Searle, J. R. (1979). *Expression and Meaning: Studies in the Theory of Speech Acts*. Cambridge: Cambridge University Press.

Sebba, M. (1987). *The Syntax of Serial Verbs*. Amsterdam: John Benjamins.

——(1997). *Contact Languages: Pidgins and Creoles*. Basingstoke, UK: Palgrave Macmillan.

Selinker, L. (1972). Interlanguage. *International Review of Applied Linguistics* 10, 209–31.

Sellen, A. J. and D. A. Norman (1992). The psychology of slips. In B. Baars (ed.), *Experimental Slips and Human Error: Exploring the Architecture of Volition*, pp. 317–39. New York: Plenum Press.

Sells, P. (ed.) (2001). *Formal and Empirical Issues in Optimality Theoretic Syntax*. Stanford, CA: CSLI Publications.

Senghas, A. (1995a). *Children's Contribution to the Birth of Nicaraguan Sign Language*. Ph.D. thesis, MIT.

——(1995b). The development of Nicaraguan Sign Language via the language acquisition process. In D. MacLaughlin and S. McEwen (eds.), *Proceedings of the Boston Conference on Language Development*, 19, pp. 534–52. Boston: Cascadilla Press.

——(2000). The development of early spatial morphology in Nicaraguan Sign Language. In S. C. Howell, S. A. Fish, and T. Keith-Lucas (eds.), *Proceedings of the Boston University Conference on Language Development*, 24, pp. 696–707. Boston: Cascadilla Press.

——(2001). Children creating language: How Nicaraguan Sign Language acquired a spatial grammar. *Psychological Science* 12(4), 323–8.

——(2003). Intergenerational influence and ontogenetic development in the emergence of spatial grammar in Nicaraguan Sign Language. *Cognitive Development* 18, 511–31.

——and S. Littman (2004). Segmentation in the expression of motion events in co-speech gesture, Nicaraguan Sign Language (NSL) and Spanish Sign Language (LSE). pp. 160–1. 8th International Conference on Theoretical Issues in Sign Language Research, Barcelona. (online at http://www.ub.edu/ling/tislr8/Senghas-Littman.doc).

——, M. E. V. Coppola, E. L. Newport, and T. Supalla (1997). Argument structure in Nicaraguan Sign Language: The emergence of grammatical devices. In E. Hughes, M. Hughes, and A. Greenhill (eds.), *Proceedings of the Boston University Conference on Language Development*, 21, pp. 550–61. Boston: Cascadilla Press.

Sereno, J. A. (1994). Phonosyntactics. In L. Hinton, J. Nichols, and J. Ohala (eds.), *Sound Symbolism*, pp. 263–75. Cambridge: Cambridge University Press.

Seuren, P. A. M. (1983). Review article on James D. McCawley's *Thirty Million Theories of Grammar* (1982). *Journal of Semantics* 2(3/4), 325–41.

——(1990). Still no serials in Seselwa: A reply to 'Seselwa serialization and its significance'. *Journal of Pidgin and Creole Languages* 5(2), 271–92.

——(2004). *Chomsky's Minimalism*. Oxford: Oxford University Press.

——and H. Wekker (1986). Semantic transparency as a factor in creole genesis. In P. C. Muysken and N. J. Smith (eds.), *Substrata versus Universals in Creole Genesis*, pp. 57–70. Amsterdam: John Benjamins.

Seyfarth, R. M. and D. L. Cheney (1982). How monkeys see the world: A review of recent research on East African vervet monkeys. In C. T. Snowdon, C. H. Brown, and M. R. Petersen (eds.), *Primate Communication*, pp. 239–52. Cambridge: Cambridge University Press.

Shankweiler, D., S. Crain, P. Gorell, and B. Tuller (1989). Reception of language in Broca's aphasia. *Language and Cognitive Processes* 4, 1–33.

Shannon, C. E. and W. Weaver (1963). *The Mathematical Theory of Communication.* Champaign, IL: University of Illinois Press.

Shaw, P., N. J. Kabani, J. P. Lerch, K. Eckstrand, R. Lenroot, N. Gogtay, D. Greenstein, L. Clasen, A. Evans, J. L. Rapoport, J. N. Giedd, and S. P. Wise (2008). Neurodevelopmental trajectories of the human cerebral cortex. *The Journal of Neuroscience* 28(14), 3586–94.

Sherwood, C. C., R. L. Holloway, J. M. Erwin, A. Schleicher, K. Zilles, and P. R. Hof (2004). Cortical orofacial motor representation in old world monkeys, great apes, and humans. *Brain, Behavior and Evolution* 63, 61–81.

Shi, R. (1996). *Perceptual Correlates of Content Words and Function Words in Early Language Input.* Ph.D. thesis, Brown University.

—— (2005). Early syntactic categories in infants' language. In H. Cohen and C. Lefebvre (eds.), *Handbook of Categorization in Cognitive Science*, pp. 481–95. Oxford: Elsevier.

——, J. Morgan, and P. Allopenna (1998). Phonological and acoustic bases for earliest grammatical category assignment: A crosslinguistic perspective. *Journal of Child Language* 25, 169–201.

Shillcock, R. C. and E. G. Bard (1993). Modularity and the processing of closed-class words. In G. T. M. Altmann and R. C. Shillcock (eds.), *Cognitive Models of Speech Processing: the Second Sperlonga Meeting*, pp. 163–85. London: Psychology Press.

Shu, W., H. Yang, L. Zhang, M. M. Lu, and E. E. Morrisey (2001). Characterization of a new subfamily of winged-helix/forkhead (Fox) genes that are expressed in the lung and act as transcriptional repressors. *Journal of Biological Chemistry* 276(29), 27488–97.

Sidow, A. (1996). Gen(om)e duplications in the evolution of early vertebrates. *Current Opinion in Genetics & Development* 6(6), 715–22.

Siegel, J. (1998). Substrate reinforcement and dialectal differences in Melanesian Pidgin. *Journal of Sociolinguistics* 2/3, 347–73.

—— (2003). Substrate influence in creoles and the role of transfer in second language acquisition. *Studies in Second Language Acquisition* 25(2), 185–209.

—— (2008). *The Emergence of Pidgin and Creole Languages.* Oxford: Oxford University Press.

Siegel, M. (1984). Gapping and interpretation. *Linguistic Inquiry* 15, 523–30.

—— (2002). *Like*: the discourse particle and semantics. *Journal of Semantics* 19(1), 35–71.

Silva, I. S. (1985). *Variation and Change in the Verbal System of Cape Verdean Crioulo.* Ph.D. thesis, Georgetown University.

Silva, I. S. (1990). Tense and aspect in Capeverdean Crioulo. In J. V. Singler (ed.), *Pidgin and Creole Tense/Mood/Aspect Systems*, pp. 143–68. Amsterdam: John Benjamins.

Silverman, S. W. and N. B. Ratner (1997). Syntactic complexity, fluency, and accuracy of sentence imitation in adolescents. *Journal of Speech, Language, and Hearing Research* 40, 95–106.

Simon, H. A. (1997). *Models of Bounded Rationality*. Cambridge, MA: MIT Press.

Simpson, G. G. (1953). The Baldwin Effect. *Evolution* 7, 110–17.

Sinclair, J. (ed.) (1987). *Collins COBUILD English Language Dictionary*. London: Collins ELT. (John Sinclair was Editor in Chief of this work.).

Singler, J. V. (1992). Nativization and pidgin/creole genesis: A reply to Bickerton. *Journal of Pidgin and Creole Languages* 7, 319–33.

Sinha, N. K. (1975). *Mundari Grammar*. Mysore, India: Central Institute of Indian Languages.

Sinnemäki, K. (2008). Complexity tradeoffs in core argument marking. In M. Miestamo, K. Sinnemäki, and F. Karlsson (eds.), *Language Complexity: Typology, Contact, Change*, pp. 67–88. Amsterdam: John Benjamins.

Siskind, J. (1996). A computational study of cross-situational techniques for learning word-to-meaning mappings. *Cognition* 61(1–2), 39–91. (Also in *Computational Approaches to Language Acquisition*, edited by Michael R. Brent, MIT Press, Cambridge, MA, 1996, pp. 39–91.)

Skyrms, B. (2004). *The Stag Hunt and the Evolution of Social Structure*. Cambridge: Cambridge University Press.

Slater, A. S. and S. Feinman (1985). Gender and the phonology of North American first names. *Sex Roles* 13, 429–40.

Slater, P. J. B. and S. A. Ince (1982). Song development in chaffinches: What is learnt and when? *Ibis* 124, 21–6.

Slobin, D. I. (ed.) (1985–1997). *The Cross-Linguistic Study of Language Acquisition, Volumes 1–4*. Mahwah, NJ: Lawrence Erlbaum Associates.

——(1996). From 'Thought and Language' to 'Thinking for Speaking'. In J. J. Gumperz and S. C. Levinson (eds.), *Rethinking Linguistic Relativity*, pp. 70–96. Cambridge: Cambridge University Press.

——(2001). Form–function relations: How do children find out what they are? In *Language Acquisition and Conceptual Development*, pp. 406–99.

——(2002). Language evolution, acquisition, diachrony: Probing the parallels. In T. Givón and B. F. Malle (eds.), *The Evolution of Language out of Pre-Language*, pp. 375–392. Amsterdam: John Benjamins.

Slocombe, K. E. and K. Zuberbühler (2005a). Agonistic screams in wild chimpanzees (*Pan troglodytes schweinfurthii*) vary as a function of social role. *Journal of Comparative Psychology* 119(1), 67–77.

——and K. Zuberbühler (2005b). Functionally referential communication in a chimpanzee. *Current Biology* 15, 1779–84.

——and K. Zuberbühler (2006). Food-associated calls in chimpanzees: Responses to food types or food preferences? *Animal Behaviour* 72, 989–99.

Slocombe, K. E. and K. Zuberbühler (2008a). Chimpanzees modify recruitment screams as a function of audience composition. *Proceedings of the National Academy of Sciences of the U.S.A.* 104(43), 17228–33.

—— and —— (2008b). Wild chimpanzees modify the structure of victim screams according to audience composition. In A. D. M. Smith, K. Smith, and R. Ferrer i Cancho (eds.), *The Evolution of Language*, pp. 499–500. Singapore: World Scientific.

Smania, D. (2001). Complex bounds for multimodal maps: Bounded combinatorics. *Nonlinearity* 14(5), 1311–30.

Smith, A. (1786). *An Inquiry into the Nature and Causes of the Wealth of Nations: in three volumes*. London: A. Strahan, and T. Cadell, 5th edition.

Smith, A. D. M. (2005a). The inferential transmission of language. *Adaptive Behavior* 13(4), 311–24.

—— (2005b). Mutual exclusivity: Communicative success despite conceptual divergence. In M. Tallerman (ed.), *Language Origins: Perspectives on Evolution*, pp. 372–88. Oxford: Oxford University Press.

—— (2006). Semantic reconstructibility and the complexification of language. In A. Cangelosi, A. D. M. Smith, and K. Smith (eds.), *The Evolution of Language*, pp. 307–14. Singapore: World Scientific.

—— (2008a). Protolanguage reconstructed. *Interaction Studies* 9(1), 100–16. (Special issue, edited by Derek Bickerton and Michael Arbib, entitled *Holophrasis, Compositionality and Protolanguage*).

Smith, H. F., R. E. Fisher, M. L. Everett, A. D. Thomas, R. R. Bollinger, and W. Parker (2009). Comparative anatomy and phylogenetic distribution of the mammalian cecal appendix. *Journal of Evolutionary Biology* 22(10), 1984–99.

Smith, K. (2004). The evolution of vocabulary. *Journal of Theoretical Biology* 228, 127–42.

—— (2008b). Is a holistic protolanguage a plausible precursor to language? A test case for modern evolutionary linguistics. *Interaction Studies* 9(1), 1–17. (Special issue, edited by Derek Bickerton and Michael Arbib, entitled *Holophrasis, Compositionality and Protolanguage*).

Smith, M. and L. Wheeldon (1999). High level processing scope in spoken sentence production. *Cognition* 17(3), 205–46.

—— and —— (2001). Syntactic priming in spoken sentence production: An online study. *Cognition* 78, 123–64.

Smith, S. T. (1972). *Communication and other Social Behavior in Parus carolinensis*. Cambridge, MA: The Nuttall Ornithological Club. Publications of the Nuttall Ornithological Club, No. 11.

Snell, W. (1964). Kinship Relations in Machiguenga. Master's thesis, Hartford Seminary, Hartford, Connecticut.

Snow, C. E., W. S. Barnes, J. Chandler, L. Hemphill, and I. F. Goodman (1991). *Unfulfilled Expectations: Home and School Influences on Literacy*. Cambridge, MA: Harvard University Press.

Soha, J. A. and P. Marler (2001). Vocal syntax development in the white-crowned sparrow (*Zonotrichia leucophrys*). *Journal of Comparative Psychology* 115(2), 172–80.

Sokal, R. R. and F. J. Rohlf (1995). *Biometry: The Principles and Practices of Statistics in Biological Research*, 3rd edition. New York: Freeman.

Sorace, A. and F. Keller (2005). Gradience in linguistic data. *Lingua* 115(11), 1497–524.

Sowa, J. F. (2006). Language games, natural and artificial. In *FLAIRS Conference, 2006: Proceedings of the Nineteenth International Florida Artificial Intelligence Research Society Conference*, pp. 688–93. (Online at http://www.aaai.org/Papers/FLAIRS/2006/Flairs06-135.pdf.)

Spencer, H. (1861). *Education: Intellectual, Moral and Physical*. London: G. Manwaring.

Sperber, D. (2000). Metarepresentations in an evolutionary perspective. In D. Sperber (ed.), *Metarepresentations: A Multidisciplinary Perspective*, pp. 117–37. Oxford: Oxford University Press.

——and D. Wilson (1986). *Relevance: Communication and Cognition*. Oxford: Blackwell.

Sprenger, S. A., W. J. Levelt, and G. Kempen (2006). Lexical access during the production of idiomatic phrases. *Journal of Memory and Language* 54, 161–84.

Sreedhar, M. V. (1974). *Naga Pidgin: A Sociolinguistic Study of Inter-lingual Communication Pattern in Nagaland*. Mysore, India: Central Institute of Indian Languages.

——(1976). Standardization of Naga pidgin. *Anthropological Linguistics* 18, 371–9.

——(1977). Standardization of Naga pidgin. *Journal of Creole Studies* 1, 157–70.

Srinivasan, M. V., S. Zhang, M. Altwein, and J. Tautz (2000). Honeybee navigation: Nature and calibration of the 'odometer'. *Science* 287, 851–3.

Stäbler, C. K. (1975a). *Entwicklung mündlicher romanischer Syntax. Das 'français cadien' in Louisiana*. Tübingen: Narr.

——(1975b). *La Vie dans le Temps et Asteur. Ein Korpus von Gesprächen mit Cadiens in Louisiana*. Tübingen: Narr.

Stabler, E. (1991). Avoid the pedestrian's paradox. In R. C. Berwick, S. P. Abney, and C. Tenny (eds.), *Principle-Based Parsing: Computation and Psycholinguistics*, pp. 199–237. Dordrecht, Holland: Kluwer.

Stapert, E. (2009). Universals in language or cognition? Evidence from English language acquisition and Pirahã. In G. Sampson, D. Gil, and P. Trudgill (eds.), *Language Complexity as an Evolving Variable*, pp. 230–42. Oxford: Oxford University Press.

Steedman, M. (1993). Categorial grammar. *Lingua* 90, 221–58.

——(2000). *The Syntactic Process*. Language, Speech and Communication. Cambridge, MA: MIT Press.

——(2002). Plans, affordances, and combinatory grammar. *Linguistics and Philosophy* 25(5–6), 723–53.

——and J. Baldridge (in press). Combinatory categorial grammar. In R. D. Borsley and K. Börjars (eds.), *Non-Transformational Theories of Syntax*. Oxford: Blackwell. (Online at ftp://ftp.cogsci.ed.ac.uk/pub/steedman/ccg/manifesto.pdf.)

Steels, L. (1999). *The Talking Heads Experiment*, Volume I. Words and Meanings. Antwerpen: Laboratorium. Special pre-edition.

Stevens, S. S. (1975). *Psychophysics: Introduction to its Perceptual, Neural, and Social Prospects*. New York: John Wiley.

Stoddard, P. K., M. D. Beecher, P. Loesche, and S. E. Campbell (1992). Memory does not constrain individual recognition in a bird with song repertoires. *Behaviour* 122(3–4), 274–87.

Stoke, W. T. and S. Holden (1980). Individual patterns in early language development: Is there a one-word period? (Paper presented at the 5th annual Boston University Conference on Language Development).

Stromswold, K. (2001). The heritability of language: A review and metaanalysis of twin, adoption, and linkage studies. *Language* 77(4), 647–723.

——, D. Caplan, N. Alpert, and S. Rauch (1996). Localization of syntactic comprehension by positron emission tomography. *Brain and Language* 52, 452–73.

Sturdy, C. B., L. S. Phillmore, and R. G. Weisman (1999). Note types, harmonic structure, and note order in the songs of zebra finches (*Taeniopygia guttata*). *Journal of Comparative Psychology* 113(2), 194–203.

Suthers, R. A. and D. Margoliash (2002). Motor control of birdsong. *Current Opinion in Neurobiology* 12(6), 684–90.

Sutton, D., C. Larson, and R. C. Lindeman (1974). Neocortical and limbic lesion effects on primate phonation. *Brain Research* 71(1), 61–75.

Suzuki, R., J. R. Buck, and P. L. Tyack (2006). Information entropy of humpback whale songs. *Journal of the Acoustical Society of America* 119(3), 1849–66.

Swadesh, M. (1938). Nootka internal syntax. *International Journal of American Linguistics* 9(2/4), 77–102.

——(1971). *The Origin and Diversification of Language*. Chicago: Aldine-Atherton. (Edited after the author's death by Joel F. Sherzer, with a foreword by Dell Hymes. Page references are to the 2006 reprint published by Transaction Publishers, New Brunswick, NJ.)

Swinney, D. (1979). Lexical access during sentence comprehension: (Re)consideration of context effects. *Journal of Verbal Learning and Verbal Behavior* 15, 545–69.

Tager-Flusberg, H. (2005). Putting words together: Morphology and syntax in the preschool years. In J. B. Gleason (ed.), *The Development of Language*. pp. 148–90. Boston: Pearson Education Inc. 6th edition.

Tallal, P., S. Miller, and R. H. Fitch (1993). Neurobiological basis of speech: A case for the preeminence of temporal processing. *Annals of the New York Academy of Sciences* 682, 27–47.

Tallerman, M. (2005). *Understanding Syntax*. London and New York: Hodder Arnold and Oxford University Press.

——(2007). Did our ancestors speak a holistic protolanguage? *Lingua* 117, 579–604.

——(2009a). The origins of the lexicon: How a word-store evolved. In R. Botha and C. Knight (eds.), *The Prehistory of Language*, pp. 181–200. Oxford: Oxford University Press.

Tallerman, M. (2009b). Phrase structure vs. dependency: the analysis of Welsh syntactic soft mutation. *Journal of Linguistics* 45, 167–201.

Talmy, L. (1983). How language structures space. In H. Pick and L. Acredolo (eds.), *Spatial Orientation: Theory, Research and Application*, pp. 225–82. New York: Plenum.

Tamariz, M. (2004). *Exploring the Adaptive Structure of the Mental Lexicon*. Ph.D. thesis, The University of Edinburgh. (Author's full name on thesis: Mónica Tamariz-Martel Mirêlis.)

Tanz, C. (1974). Cognitive principles underlying children's errors in pronominal case-marking. *Journal of Child Language* 1, 271–6.

Tao, H. and C. F. Meyer (2006). Gapped coordinations in English: Form, usage, and implications for linguistic theory. *Corpus Linguistics and Linguistic Theory* 2(2), 129–63.

Tchekhoff, C. (1984). Une langue sans opposition verbo-nominale. *Modèles Linguistiques* 6, 125–32.

Tchernichovski, O. and J. Wallman (2008). Neurons of imitation. *Nature* 451, 249–50.

Temme, F. P. (1993). $S_{28} - S_{28} \downarrow T_d$ subduction within $SU2 \times S_{28}$ spin algebras. Semi-combinatorial aspects of NMR spin clusters of $[^{13}C]_{28}$ and $[^{13}C]_{28}[H]_4$ fullerenes. *Chemical Physics Letters* 207(2–3), 236–44.

Terrace, H. S. (1979). How Nim Chimpsky changed my mind. *Psychology Today* 13(6), 65–76.

——, L. A. Petitto, R. J. Sanders, and T. G. Bever (1979). Can an ape create a sentence? *Science* 206, 891–902.

Tervoort, B. T. (1968). You me downtown movie fun? *Lingua* 21, 455–65. (Page references are to a reprinted version in *Syntactic Theory 1: Structuralist*, edited by Fred W. Householder, 1972, Harmondsworth: Penguin Books, pp. 308–16.)

Tesnière, L. (1959). *Eléments de Syntaxe Structurale*. Paris: Klincksieck.

Tettamanti, M. and D. Weniger (2006). Broca's area: A supramodal hierarchical processor? *Cortex* 42(4), 491–4.

Theunissen, F. E. and A. J. Doupe (1998). Temporal and spectral sensitivity of complex auditory neurons in the nucleus HVc of male zebra finches. *The Journal of Neuroscience* 18(10), 3786–802.

Thomason, S. G. (2001). *Language Contact: An Introduction*. Edinburgh: Edinburgh University Press.

—— and A. Elgibali (1986). Before the Lingua Franca: Pidginized Arabic in the eleventh century A.D. *Lingua* 68(4), 317–49.

—— and T. Kaufman (1988). *Language Contact, Creolization, and Genetic Linguistics*. Berkeley, CA: University of California Press.

Thompson, H. (1977). The lack of subordination in American Sign Language. In L. A. Friedman (ed.), *On the Other Hand: New Perspectives on American Sign Language*, pp. 181–95. New York: Academic Press.

Thompson, L. C. and M. T. Thompson (1980). Thompson Salish //-xi//. *International Journal of American Linguistics* 46, 27–32.

Thompson, R., D. Oden, and S. Boysen (1997). Language-naive chimpanzees (*Pan troglodytes*) judge relations between relations in a conceptual matching-to-sample task. *Journal of Experimental Psychology: Animal Behavior Processes* 23(1), 31–43.

Thompson, R. K. R. and D. L. Oden (1998). Why monkeys and pigeons, unlike certain apes, cannot reason analogically. In *Advances in Analogy Research: Integration of Theory and Data from the Cognitive, Computational, and Neural Sciences*, pp. 269–73. Sofia: New Bulgarian University.

Thorpe, W. H. and J. Hall-Craggs (1976). Sound production and perception in birds as related to the general principles of pattern perception. In P. P. G. Bateson and R. A. Hinde (eds.), *Growing Points in Ethology*, pp. 171–89. Cambridge: Cambridge University Press.

Thurman, R. C. (1975). Chuave medial verbs. *Anthropological Linguistics* 17(7), 342–53.

——(1978). Clause chains in Chuave. Master's thesis, UCLA.

Tincoff, R., M. D. Hauser, F. Tsao, G. Spaepen, F. Ramus, and J. Mehler (2005). The role of speech rhythm in language discrimination: Further tests with a non-human primate. *Developmental Science* 8(1), 26–35.

Tishkoff, S. A., F. A. Reed, A. Ranciaro, B. F. Voight, C. C. Babbitt, J. S. Silverman, K. Powell, H. M. Mortensen, J. B. Hirbo, M. Osman, M. Ibrahim, S. A. Omar, G. Lema, T. B. Nyambo, J. Ghori, S. Bumpstead, J. K. Pritchard, G. A. Wray, and P. Deloukas (2007). Convergent adaptation of human lactase persistence in Africa and Europe. *Nature Genetics* 39(1), 7–8.

Todt, D. (2004). From birdsong to speech: A plea for comparative approaches. *Anais da Academia Brasileira de Ciências (Annals of the Brazilian Academy of Sciences)* 76(2), 201–8.

——and H. Hultsch (1996). Acquisition and performance of song repertoires: Ways of coping with diversity and versatility. In D. E. Kroodsma and E. H. Miller (eds.), *Ecology and Evolution of Acoustic Communication in Birds*, pp. 79–96. Ithaca, NY: Comstock Publishing Associates, a division of Cornell University Press.

——and——(1998). How songbirds deal with large amounts of serial information: Retrieval rules suggest a hierarchical song memory. *Biological Cybernetics* 79, 487–500.

Tollefson, J. W. (1980). Types of language contact and the acquisition of language. *Language Sciences* 2(2), 231–44.

Tomasello, M. (2003). Introduction: Some surprises for psychologists. In M. Tomasello (ed.), *The New Psychology of Language: Cognitive and Functional Approaches to Language Structure*, pp. 1–14. Mahwah, NJ: Lawrence Erlbaum Associates.

——(2006). Acquiring linguistic constructions. In D. Kuhn and R. Siegler (eds.), *Handbook of Child Psychology*, pp. 255–98. New York: Wiley.

——and M. J. Farrar (1986). Joint attention and early language. *Child Development* 57, 1454–63.

——and J. Todd (1983). Joint attention and lexical acquisition style. *First Language* 4(12), 197–211.

Tomasello, M., J. Call, K. Nagell, R. Olguin, and M. Carpenter (1994). The learning and use of gestural signals by young chimpanzees: A trans-generational study. *Primates* 35(2), 137–54.

——, M. Carpenter, J. Call, T. Behne, and H. Moll (2005). Understanding and sharing intentions: The origins of cultural cognition. *Behavioral and Brain Sciences* 28, 675–735.

Tops, G. A. J. (1974). *The Origin of the Germanic Dental Preterit*. Leiden: E. J. Brill.

Townsend, D. J. and T. G. Bever (2001). *Sentence Comprehension: The Integration of Habits and Rules*. Cambridge, MA: MIT Press.

Tranel, D., H. Damasio, and A. R. Damasio (1997). On the neurology of naming. In H. Goodglass and A. Wingfield (eds.), *Anomia: Neuroanatomical and Cognitive Correlates*, pp. 65–90. New York: Academic Press.

——, ——, and —— (1998). The neural basis of lexical retrieval. In R. Parks, D. S. Levine, and D. L. Long (eds.), *Fundamentals of Neural Network Modeling: Neuropsychology and Cognitive Neuroscience*, pp. 65–90. Cambridge, MA: MIT Press.

Traugott, E. C. and B. Heine (1991). Introduction. In E. C. Traugott and B. Heine (eds.), *Approaches to Grammaticalization*, vol. I, pp. 1–14. Amsterdam: John Benjamins.

Traunmüller, H. (2000). Sound symbolism in deictic words. In H. Aili and P. af Trampe (eds.), *Tongues and Texts Unlimited: Studies in Honour of Tore Janson*, pp. 213–34. Stockholm: Stockholms Universitet.

Traxler, M., R. Morris, and R. Seely (2002). Processing subject and object relative clauses: Evidence from eye movements. *Journal of Memory and Language* 53, 204–24.

Treisman, A. and G. Gelade (1980). A feature integration theory of attention. *Cognitive Psychology* 12, 97–136.

Trombetti, A. (1905). *L'Unità d'origine del linguaggio*. Bologna: Luigi Beltrami.

Trudgill, P. (1992). Dialect typology and social structure. In E. H. Jahr (ed.), *Language Contact: Theoretical and Empirical Studies*, pp. 195–211. Berlin: Mouton De Gruyter.

—— (2002). Linguistic and social typology. In J. K. Chambers, P. Trudgill, and N. Schilling-Estes (eds.), *The Handbook of Language Variation and Change*, pp. 707–28. Oxford: Blackwell.

—— (2003). The impact of language contact and social structure on linguistic structure: Focus on the dialects of Modern Greek. In B. Kortmann (ed.), *Dialectology meets Typology: Dialect Grammar from a Cross-Linguistic Perspective*, pp. 435–52. Berlin: Mouton de Gruyter.

Truswell, R. (2009). Constituency and Bonobo Comprehension. Unpublished paper. University of Edinburgh Linguistics Department.

Tryon, D. T. and J.-M. Charpentier (2004). *Pacific Pidgins and Creoles: Origins, Growth and Development*. Berlin: Mouton de Gruyter.

Turkel, W. J. (2002). The learning guided evolution of natural language. In E. Briscoe (ed.), *Linguistic Evolution through Language Acquisition: Formal and Computational Models*, pp. 235–54. Cambridge: Cambridge University Press.

Tyler, L. K., R. Russell, J. Fadili, and H. E. Moss (2001). The neural representation of nouns and verbs: PET studies. *Brain* 124, 1619–34.

Uchuimi, T. (2006). The nominative island condition is a false generalization. In *Proceedings of the 2006 annual conference of the Canadian Linguistic Association.* (Available online at http://ling.uwo.ca/publications/CLA2006/Uchiumi.pdf.)

Uhlenbroek, C. (1996). *Structure and Function of the Long-distance Calls Given by Male Chimpanzees in Gombe National Park.* Ph.D. thesis, University of Bristol.

Ultan, R. (1984). Size-sound symbolism. In J. Greenberg (ed.), *Universals of Human Language*, vol. 4, pp. 525–68. Stanford: Stanford University Press.

Ungerleider, L. G. and M. Mishkin (1982). Two cortical visual systems. In D. J. Ingle, M. A. Goodale, and R. J. W. Mansfield (eds.), *Analysis of Visual Behavior*, pp. 549–86. Cambridge, MA: MIT Press.

Urban, G. (2002). Metasignaling and language origins. *American Anthropologist* 104(1), 233–46.

Vainikka, A. (1993/1994). Case in the development of syntax. *Language Acquisition* 3(3), 257–325.

——and M. Young-Scholten (2006). The roots of syntax and how they grow: Organic Grammar, the Basic Variety, and Processability Theory. In S. Unsworth, T. Parodi, A. Sorace, M. Young-Scholten, and B. D. Schwartz (eds.), *Paths of development in L1 and L2 acquisition: In Honor of Bonnie D. Schwartz (Language Acquisition and Language Disorders)*, pp. 77–106. Amsterdam: John Benjamins.

Vallender, E. J. and B. T. Lahn (2004). Positive selection on the human genome. *Human Molecular Genetics* 13, Review issue 2, R245–R254.

Van Bergen, G. and H. de Hoop (2009). Topics cross-linguistically. *The Linguistic Review* 26, 173–6.

van der Lely, H. K. J. (2005). Domain-specific cognitive systems: insight from grammatical-SLI. *Trends in Cognitive Sciences* 9(2), 53–9.

——and J. Battell (2003). Wh-movement in children with grammatical SLI: A test of the RDDR hypothesis. *Language* 79(1), 153–81.

van der Velde, F. and M. de Kamps (2006). Neural blackboard architectures of combinatorial structures in cognition. *Behavioral and Brain Sciences* 29(1), 37–70.

Van Lancker, D. (1980). Cerebral lateralization of pitch cues in the linguistic signal. *International Journal of Human Communication* 13, 227–77.

——(1988). Nonpropositional speech: Neurolinguistic studies. In A. E. Ellis (ed.), *Progress in the Psychology of Language. (Vol. III)*, pp. 49–118. Hove, UK: Lawrence Erlbaum Associates Ltd.

Van Lancker Sidtis, D. (2001). Preserved formulaic expressions in a case of transcortical sensory aphasia compared to incidence in normal everyday speech. *Brain and Language* 79(1), 38–41.

——and W. A. Postman (2006). Formulaic expressions in spontaneous speech of left- and right-hemisphere-damaged subjects. *Aphasiology* 20(5), 411–26.

Van Valin, R. D. (2001). *An Introduction to Syntax*. Cambridge: Cambridge University Press.

Vanderveken, D. (1990). *Meaning and Speech Acts (Vol. I, Principles of Language Use)*. Cambridge: Cambridge University Press.

Vargha-Khadem, F. and R. E. Passingham (1990). Speech and langage defects. *Nature* 346, 226.

——, K. E. Watkins, K. Alcock, P. Fletcher, and R. E. Passingham (1995). Praxic and nonverbal cognitive deficits in a large family with a genetically transmitted speech and language disorder. *Proceedings of the National Academy of Sciences of the U.S.A.* 92(3), 930–3.

Varki, A., D. H. Geschwind, and E. E. Eichler (2008). Explaining human uniqueness: genome interactions with environment, behaviour and culture. *Nature Reviews, Genetics* 9, 749–63.

Versteegh, K. (1984). *Pidginization and Creolization: The Case of Arabic*. Amsterdam: Benjamins.

Vigner, E. (1960). The unreasonable effectiveness of mathematics in the natural sciences. *Communications in Pure and Applied Mathematics*, 13(1), 1–14.

Vijay-Shanker, K., D. Weir, and A. Joshi (1987). On the progression from context-free to tree adjoining languages. In A. Manaster-Ramer (ed.), *Mathematics of Language*, pp. 389–401. Amsterdam: John Benjamins.

Vogt, P. and A. D. M. Smith (2005). Learning colour words is slow: A cross-situational learning account. *Behavioral and Brain Sciences* 28(4), 509–10.

Voight, B. F., S. Kudaravalli, X. Wen, and J. K. Pritchard (2006). A map of recent positive selection in the human genome. *PLoS Biology* 4(3), e72. (Public Library of Science, online journal.)

Volman, S. E. and H. Khanna (1995). Convergence of untutored song in group-reared zebra finches (*Taeniopygia guttata*). *Journal of Comparative Psychology* 103, 366–80.

von Chamisso, A. (1837). *Über die Hawaiische Sprache*. (Original publication, Leipzig. Facsimile with a critical introduction and an annotated bibliography of literature relating to the Hawaiian language; Samuel H. Elbert; Philo Press, Amsterdam, 1969.)

von Frisch, K. (1923a). Über die 'Sprache' der Bienen. *Naturwissenschaften* 11(28), 633–5.

——(1923b). Über die 'Sprache' der Bienen. Eine tierpsychologische Untersuchung. *Zoologischer Jahrbücher (Physiologie)* 40, 1–186.

——(1967). *The Dance Language and Orientation of Bees*. Cambridge, MA: Harvard University Press.

——(1974). Decoding the language of the bee. *Science* 185, 663–8.

von Weizsäcker, E. U. and C. von Weizsäcker (1998). Information, evolution and 'error-friendliness'. *Biological Cybernetics* 79, 501–6.

Vosse, T. and G. Kempen (2000). Syntactic structure assembly in human parsing: A computational model based on competitive inhibition and a lexicalist grammar. *Cognition* 75(2), 105–43.

Vu, E. T., M. E. Mazurek, and Y.-C. Kuo (1994). Identification of a forebrain motor programming network for the learned song of zebra finches. *The Journal of Neuroscience* 14(11), 6924–34.

Vygotsky, L. S. (1986). *Thought and Language*. Cambridge, MA: MIT Press (translation newly revised and edited by Alex Kozulin).

Waddington, C. H. (1953). Genetic assimilation of an acquired character. *Evolution* 7, 118–26.

Wagers, M. W. and C. Phillips (2009). Multiple dependencies and the role of the grammar in real-time comprehension. *Journal of Linguistics* 45(2), 395–433.

Wagner, M. (2005). *Prosody and Recursion*. Ph.D. thesis, Massachusetts Institute of Technology.

Wang, E. T., G. Kodama, P. Baldi, and R. K. Moyzis (2006). Global landscape of recent inferred Darwinian selection for *Homo sapiens*. *Proceedings of the National Academy of Sciences of the U.S.A.* 103, 135–40.

Wanner, E. and M. Maratsos (1978). An ATN approach in comprehension. In M. Halle, J. Bresnan, and G. Miller (eds.), *Linguistic Theory and Psychological Reality*, pp. 119–61. Cambridge, MA: MIT Press.

Ward, J. and J. Simner (2003). Lexical-gustatory synaesthesia: Linguistic and conceptual factors. *Cognition* 89, 237–61.

Ward, J. P. and W. D. Hopkins (1993). *Primate Laterality: Current Behavioral Evidence of Primate Asymmetries*. New York: Springer Verlag.

Wardhaugh, R. (2005). *An Introduction to Sociolinguistics*, 5th edition. Hoboken, NJ: Wiley.

Warneken, F., B. Hare, A. P. Melis, D. Hanus, and M. Tomasello (2007). Spontaneous altruism by chimpanzees and young children. *PLoS Biology* 5(7), e184. (Public Library of Science, online journal.)

Wason, P. C. and S. S. Reich (1979). A verbal illusion. *Quarterly Journal of Experimental Psychology* 31(4), 591–7.

Watkins, K. E., F. Vargha-Khadem, J. Ashburner, R. E. Passingham, A. Connelly, K. Friston, R. S. J. Frackowiak, M. Mishkin, and D. G. Gadian (2002). MRI analysis of an inherited speech and language disorder: Structural brain abnormalities. *Brain* 125, 465–78.

Weber, A. and K. Müller (2004). Word order variation in German main clauses: A corpus analysis. In *Proceedings of the 20th International Conference on Computational Linguistics, COLING 2004*, Geneva, pp. 71–7.

Wedgwood, D. J. (2003). *Predication and Information Structure: A Dynamic Account of Hungarian Pre-verbal Syntax*. Ph. D. thesis, The University of Edinburgh.

——(2005). *Shifting the Focus: From Static Structures to the Dynamics of Interpretation*. Amsterdam: Elsevier Science.

Weir, A. A. S., J. Chappell, and A. Kacelnik (2002). Shaping of hooks in New Caledonian crows. *Science* 297, 981.

Wells, G. (1986). Variation in child language. In P. Fletcher and M. Garman (eds.), *Language Acquisition: Studies in First Language Development*, pp. 109–39. Cambridge: Cambridge University Press.

Werner, H. (1934). L'unité des sens. *Journal de Psychologie Normale et Pathologique* 31, 190–205.

——(1957). *Comparative Psychology of Mental Development*. New York: International Universities Press (revised edition).

——and S. Wapner (1952). Toward a general theory of perception. *Psychological Review* 59, 324–38.

Wertheimer, M. (1950). Laws of organization in perceptual forms. In W. D. Ellis (ed.), *A Source Book of Gestalt Psychology*, pp. 71–88. New York: Humanities.

Wescott, R. (1980). *Sound and Sense*. Lake Bluff, IL: Jupiter.

Whitaker, H. A. (1976). A case of isolation of the speech functions. In H. Whitaker and H. A. Whitaker (eds.), *Studies in Neurolinguistics*, pp. 1–58. London: Academic Press.

Whiten, A. (2000a). Chimpanzee cognition and the question of mental re-representation. In D. Sperber (ed.), *Metarepresentations: A Multidisciplinary Perspective*, pp. 139–67. Oxford: Oxford University Press.

——(2000b). Primate culture and social learning. *Cognitive Science* 24(3), 477–508.

——, J. Goodall, W. McGrew, T. Nishida, V. Reynolds, Y. Sugiyama, C. E. G. Tutin, R. W. Wrangham, and C. Boesch (1999). Cultures in chimpanzees. *Nature* 399, 682–5.

——, V. Horner, and F. B. de Waal (2005). Conformity to cultural norms of tool use in chimpanzees. *Nature* 437, 737–40.

Whorf, B. L. (1956). *Language, Thought and Reality*. Cambridge, MA: MIT Press.

Wickett, J. C., P. A. Vernon, and D. H. Lee (1994). In vivo brain size, head perimeter, and intelligence in a sample of healthy adult females. *Personality and Individual Differences* 16(6), 831–8.

Wierzbicka, A. (1982). Why can you *have a drink* when you can't *have an eat*? *Language* 58(4), 753–99.

Wild, J. M. (2004). Functional neuroanatomy of the sensorimotor control of singing. *Annals of the New York Academy of Sciences* 1016, 438–62.

Wilkins, J. (1668). *An Essay towards a Real Character and a Philosophical Language*. London: S. A. Gellibrand and John Martin, printer to the Royal Society.

Willerman, L., R. Schultz, J. N. Rutledge, and E. D. Bigler (1991). In vivo brain size and intelligence. *Intelligence* 15, 223–8.

Williams, B. (1978). *Descartes, The Project of Pure Enquiry*. London: Penguin.

Williams, G. C. (1966). *Adaptation and Natural Selection: A Critique of some Current Evolutionary Thought*. Princeton: Princeton University Press.

Williams, H. (2004). Birdsong and singing behavior. *Annals of the New York Academy of Sciences* 1016, 1–30.

——and K. Staples (1992). Syllable chunking in zebra finch (*Taeniopygia guttata*) song. *Journal of Comparative Psychology* 106(3), 278–86.

Wilson, E. O. (1975). *Sociobiology: The New Synthesis*. Cambridge, MA: Harvard University Press.

Wilson, S. J., M. A. Sayette, M. R. Delgado, and J. Fiez (2008). Effect of smoking opportunity on responses to monetary gain and loss in the caudate nucleus. *Journal of Abnormal Psychology* 117(2), 428–34.

Winford, D. (1993). *Predication in Caribbean English Creoles*. Amsterdam: John Benjamins.

——(2003). *An Introduction to Contact Linguistics*. Oxford: Blackwell Publishing.

——(2006). The restructuring of tense/aspect systems in creole formation. In A. Deumert and S. Durrieman-Tame (eds.), *Structure and Variation in Language Contact*, pp. 85–110. Amsterdam: John Benjamins.

Wingfield, A. (1975). Acoustic redundancy and the perception of time-compressed speech. *Journal of Speech and Hearing Research* 18, 96–104.

Winn, H. E. and L. K. Winn (1978). The song of the humpback whale (*Megaptera novaeangliae*) in the West Indies. *Marine Biology* 47, 97–114.

Wistel-Wozniak, A. and H. Hultsch (1992). Song performance in nightingales (*Luscinia megarhynchos*) which had been raised without exposure to acoustic learning programs. *Verhaltungen der Deutschen Zoologischen Gesellschaft* 85, 246.

Witelson, S. F., H. Beresh, and D. L. Kigar (2006). Intelligence and brain size in 100 postmortem brains: sex, lateralization and age factors. *Brain* 129(2), 386–98.

Wittgenstein, L. (1922). *Tractatus Logico-Philosophicus*. London: Routledge. (Translated by C. K. Ogden from the original German 'Logisch-Philosophische Abhandlung' in *Annalen der Naturphilosophie* 14 (1921), 185–262.)

——(1953). *Philosophical Investigations*. Oxford: Basil Blackwell. (Translated by G. E. M. Anscombe from the author's *Philosophische Untersuchungen*, unpublished in his lifetime.)

Woodrow, H. (1951). Time perception. In S. S. Stevens (ed.), *Handbook of Experimental Pychology*, pp. 1224–36. New York: John Wiley.

Woods, W. A. (1970). Transition network grammars of natural language analysis. *Communications of the ACM* 13, 591–606. (Reprinted in Barbara J. Grosz, Karen Spark Jones, and Bonnie Lynn Webber (eds), *Readings in Natural Language Processing*. Los Altos, USA: Morgan Kaufmann, 1986, pp. 71–87.)

Woodworth, N. L. (1991). Sound symbolism in proximal and distal forms. *Linguistics* 29, 273–99.

Woodworth, R. S. (1899). The accuracy of voluntary movements. *Psychological Review Monograph 3 Supplement* 3, No.13, 1–119.

Worden, R. (1992). Navigation by fragment fitting: A theory of hippocampal function. *Hippocampus* 2(2), 165–87.

——(1995). A speed limit for evolution. *Journal of Theoretical Biology* 176(1), 137–52.

——(1998). The evolution of language from social intelligence. In J. R. Hurford, M. Studdert-Kennedy, and C. Knight (eds.), *Approaches to the Evolution of Language: Social and Cognitive Bases*, pp. 148–66. Cambridge: Cambridge University Press.

Wrangham, R. and N. Conklin-Brittain (2003). Cooking as a biological trait. *Comparative Biochemistry and Physiology Part A: Molecular & Integrative Physiology* 136(1), 35–46.

Wray, A. (1998). Protolanguage as a holistic system for social interaction. *Language and Communication* 18, 47–67.

——(2000). Holistic utterances in protolanguage. In C. Knight, M. Studdert-Kennedy, and J. R. Hurford (eds.), *The Evolutionary Emergence of Language: Social Function and the Origins of Linguistic Form*, pp. 285–302. Cambridge: Cambridge University Press.

——(2002a). Dual processing in protolanguage: performance without competence. In A. Wray (ed.), *The Transition to Language*, pp. 112–37. Oxford: Oxford University Press.

——(2002b). *Formulaic Language and the Lexicon*. Cambridge: Cambridge University Press.

——and G. W. Grace (2007). The consequences of talking to strangers: Evolutionary corollaries of socio-cultural influences on linguistic form. *Lingua* 117, 543–78.

Wright, B. A., L. J. Lombardino, W. M. King, C. S. Puranik, C. M. Leonard, and M. M. Merzenich (1997). Deficits in auditory temporal and spectral resolution in language-impaired children. *Nature* 387, 176–9.

Wright, S., J. Hay, and T. Bent (2005). Ladies first? Phonology, frequency, and the naming conspiracy. *Linguistics* 44(3), 531–61.

Wynne, C. D. L. (2004). *Do Animals Think?* Princeton, NJ: Princeton University Press.

Xu, F. (2002). The role of language in acquiring object kind concepts in infancy. *Cognition* 85, 223–50.

Xu, J., P. J. Gannon, K. Emmorey, J. F. Smith, and A. R. Braun (2009). Symbolic gestures and spoken language are processed by a common neural system. *Proceedings of the National Academy of Sciences of the U.S.A.* 106(49), 20664–9.

Yamauchi, H. (2001). The difficulty of the Baldwinian account of linguistic innateness. In J. Kelemen and P. Sosik (eds.), *Advances in Artificial Life (Proceedings of the 6th European Conference on Artificial Life)*. Heidelberg: Springer-Verlag.

——(2004). *Baldwinian Accounts of Language Evolution*. Ph.D. thesis, The University of Edinburgh.

Young, A. W. and G. Ratcliff (1983). Visuospatial abilities of the right hemisphere. In A. W. Young (ed.), *Functions of the Right Cerebral Hemisphere*, pp. 1–32. London: Academic Press.

Yu, A. C. and D. Margoliash (1996). Temporal hierarchical control of singing in birds. *Science* 273, 1871–5.

Yu, C., D. H. Ballard, and R. N. Aslin (2005). The role of embodied intention in early lexical acquisition. *Cognitive Science* 29, 961–1005.

Zann, R. (1993). Structure, sequence and evolution of song elements in wild Australian zebra finches. *The Auk* 110, 702–15.

Zegura, S. L. (2008). Current topics in human evolutionary genetics. In J. D. Bengt-
son (ed.), *In Hot Pursuit of Language in Prehistory: Essays in the Four Fields of
Anthropology—in Honor of Harold Crane Fleming*, pp. 343–58. Amsterdam: John
Benjamins.

Zeshan, U. (2008). Question particles in sign languages. In M. Haspelmath, M. S.
Dryer, D. Gil, and B. Comrie (eds.), *The World Atlas of Language Structures Online, Chapter 140*. Munich: Max Planck Digital Library. (Online at
http://wals.info/feature/140.)

Zhang, J. (2003). Evolution of the human *ASPM* gene, a major determinant of brain
size. *Genetics* 165, 2063–70.

——, D. M. Webb, and O. Podlaha (2002). Accelerated protein evolution and origins
of human-specific features: Foxp2 as an example. *Genetics* 162, 1825–35.

Zoloth, S. R., R. Petersen, M, M. D. Beecher, S. Green, P. Marler, D. B. Moody,
and W. Stebbins (1979). Species-specific perceptual processing of vocal sounds by
monkeys. *Science* 204, 870–3.

Zuberbühler, K. (2002). A syntactic rule in forest monkey communication. *Animal
Behaviour* 63, 293–9.

Index

The section and subsection headings in the Detailed Table of Contents are complementary to this index.

OXFORD STUDIES IN THE EVOLUTION OF LANGUAGE

General Editors

Kathleen R. Gibson,*University of Texas at Houston*, and James R. Hurford, *University of Edinburgh*

PUBLISHED

1

The Origins of Vowel Systems
Bart de Boer

2

The Transition to Language
Edited by Alison Wray

3

Language Evolution
Edited by Morten H. Christiansen and Simon Kirby

4

Language Origins
Perspectives on Evolution
Edited by Maggie Tallerman

5

The Talking Ape
How Language Evolved
Robbins Burling

6

Self-Organization in the Evolution of Speech
Pierre-Yves Oudeyer
Translated by James R. Hurford

7

Why we Talk
The Evolutionary Origins of Human Communication
Jean-Louis Dessalles
Translated by James Grieve

8

The Origins of Meaning
Language in the Light of Evolution 1
James R. Hurford

9

The Genesis of Grammar
Bernd Heine and Tania Kuteva

10

The Origin of Speech
Peter F. MacNeilage

11

The Prehistory of Language
Edited by Rudolf Botha and Chris Knight

12

The Cradle of Language
Edited by Rudolf Botha and Chris Knight

13

Language Complexity as an Evolving Variable
Edited by Geoffrey Sampson, David Gil, and Peter Trudgill

14

The Evolution of Morphology
Andrew Carstairs McCarthy

15

The Origins of Grammar
Language in the Light of Evolution 2
James R. Hurford

Oxford Studies in the Evolution of Language

General Editors
Kathleen R. Gibson, *University of Texas at Houston*, and James R. Hurford, *University of Edinburgh*

In Preparation

Darwinian Linguistics
Evolution and the Logic of Linguistic Theory
Stephen R. Anderson

Published in Association with the Series

The Oxford Handbook of Language Evolution
edited by Maggie Tallerman and Kathleen R. Gibson

Language Diversity
Daniel Nettle

Function, Selection, and Innateness
The Emergence of Language Universals
Simon Kirby

The Origins of Complex Language
An Inquiry into the Evolutionary Beginnings of Sentences, Syllables, and Truth
Andrew Carstairs McCarthy